DATE DUE

DEMCO 38-296

ENCYCLOPEDIA OF
HUMAN INTELLIGENCE

ENCYCLOPEDIA OF HUMAN INTELLIGENCE

Robert J. Sternberg

Editor in Chief

Volume 2

MACMILLAN PUBLISHING COMPANY
NEW YORK

Maxwell Macmillan Canada
TORONTO

Maxwell Macmillan International
NEW YORK   OXFORD   SINGAPORE   SYDNEY

Copyright © 1994 by Macmillan Publishing Company
A Division of Macmillan, Inc.

All rights reserved. No part of this book may be reproduced
or transmitted in any form or by any means, electronic or
mechanical, including photocopying, recording, or by any
information storage and retrieval system, without permission
in writing from the Publisher.

Macmillan Publishing Company
866 Third Avenue, New York, NY 10022

Maxwell Macmillan Canada, Inc.
1200 Eglinton Avenue East, Suite 200, Don Mills, Ontario M3C 3N1

Macmillan, Inc., is part of the Maxwell Communication Group
of Companies.

PRINTED IN THE UNITED STATES OF AMERICA

printing number
   3 4 5 6 7 8 9 10

Library of Congress Cataloging-in-Publication Data

Encyclopedia of human intelligence / Robert J. Sternberg, editor in
  chief.
       p.   cm.
    Includes bibliographical references and index.
    ISBN 0-02-897407-7 (set : alk. paper) :
      1. Intellect—Encyclopedias.   2. Intelligence levels—
  Encyclopedias.   I. Sternberg, Robert J.
    BF431.E59   1994
    153.9′03—dc20   93-46975
                                               CIP

The paper used in this publication meets the minimum
requirements of American National Standard for Information
Sciences—Permanence of Paper for Printed Library Materials.
ANSI Z39.48-1984.

J

JAPANESE Examination of the average score on tests of intelligence for the Japanese living in Japan has yielded inconsistent findings. As R. Lynn and S. Hampson (1986) report in their review of the literature, the estimated average full scale intelligent quotient (IQ) of the Japanese has ranged from 106 to 138, depending upon the test used to measure intelligence. Subscale IQs such as verbal and performance IQs have demonstrated a slightly greater range. Average IQs for Americans generally fall at approximately 100 for most measures. The purpose of this entry is to highlight briefly some of the issues pertaining to the intellectual abilities of the Japanese as indicated in the literature, and biological, cultural, and environmental factors as they impact scores on tests of intelligence. The areas to be covered include differences in intelligence between Japanese and Americans and cultural and biological factors noted with respect to intellectual abilities.

DIFFERENCES IN INTELLIGENCE BETWEEN JAPANESE AND AMERICANS

In the 1950s and 1960s, Japanese psychologists examined the construct of intelligence based upon tests developed and standardized in Japan (Iwakaki & Vernon, 1988). In the 1970s, Iwakaki and Vernon noted that the measurement of intelligence in Japan focused on differences in abilities and was believed to promote the spread of inequality in the schools. Tests of IQ were viewed as "imperfect instruments of measurement by both professionals and nonpsychologists" (p. 368).

Despite these unfavorable attitudes, American tests measuring cognitive abilities have been translated and restandardized in Japan (Lynn, 1987). For example, all of the Wechsler Intelligence Scales have been adapted for use in Japan. The Wechsler scales represent the most frequently used individual IQ tests in the United States. Comparisons of scores obtained on the Wechsler scales for Japanese and Americans have been questioned, however, given the changes made on items translated from English to Japanese to maintain cultural relevance, differences in time allotments for particular tasks, and the sampling characteristics of the Japanese standardization sample. For example, to ask a Japanese child the distance between two cities in America, as is done in some American IQ tests, would not be relevant. Rather, the item would be changed to reflect two cities in Japan.

H. W. Stevenson and colleagues (1985) examined the performance of Chinese, Japanese, and American children on ten cognitive and achievement tests. These researchers found similarities among the three groups in the structure of their cognitive abilities. However, the Chinese and Japanese children obtained higher average scores in mathematics.

Research has indicated that the Japanese have higher average IQs than other ethnic groups. According to Iwakaki and Vernon (1988), overall findings reveal that the Japanese have a mean IQ of 110 on nonverbal and spatial tests and 100 on verbal tests. Although they do not specify a full scale IQ, Iwakaki and Vernon cited research indicating that the overall intelligence of the Japanese is higher than that of adults and children in the United States.

In 1982, R. Lynn published an article addressing the growing disparity in IQ on the Japanese Wechsler Intelligence Scale for Children–Revised (J–WISC–R) in comparison with the American Wechsler Intelligence Scale for Children–Revised (WISC–R). Given the changes made in translating the test, Lynn utilized only five of the nonverbal performance subtests (Block Design, Mazes, Picture Arrangement, Object Assembly, and Coding) and one of the verbal subtests, Digit Span. These subtests remained virtually unchanged in the translation from the American to the Japanese version of this test. Lynn then took the average raw scores reported in the Japanese manual for these subtests and converted them to IQs based on the norms contained in the American WISC–R manual. Based on this analysis, he concluded that the Japanese "superiority is most pronounced on the tests of Block Design, Mazes, Picture Arrangement, and Object Assembly" (p. 297). These subtests involve visual-motor abilities and visual-spatial reasoning. The Japanese children were found to do less well on the digit span and coding subtests. These subtests both involve short-term memory. Parallel findings were noted in conducting a similar analysis of the Japanese Wechsler Adult Intelligence Scale and the American Wechsler Adult Intelligence Scale (Lynn, 1982).

Japanese children typically obtain higher full scale IQs (Lynn, 1987). This difference in the full scale IQ reflects superior performance on the visual-spatial subtests, although the Japanese score lower than Americans on verbal subtests.

The superiority of the Japanese on visual-spatial abilities varies depending upon age. The developmental trend noted in Lynn's (1987) review indicates that all abilities show gains over the years. With increasing age, both verbal memory and numerical abilities improve. In particular, Lynn suggests that school exposure may influence this developmental trend. Specifically, "compulsory schooling in Japan begins at the age of 6 years, and it is from about this age that Japanese children show a strong increase in their number and memory span abilities" (p. 817).

Lynn's (1982) work also revealed a growing disparity between the averages obtained on tests of IQ in Japan and the United States. Based on his examination of studies comparing IQ data on the Japanese with American norms for over seven decades, Lynn concluded that Japanese children born between 1910 and 1945 had an average IQ of approximately 102–105. Japanese children born from 1946 to 1969 have a mean of 108–115. "This suggests that the mean Japanese IQ has been rising relative to the American (IQ) during the 20th century" (p. 222).

Differences in information processing may also distinguish between American and Japanese abilities. Japanese children demonstrate a preference for tasks requiring simultaneous processing in comparison with sequential processing. The test used to assess these forms of processing for children aged 6 to 16 is the KAUFMAN ASSESSMENT BATTERY FOR CHILDREN (K–ABC; Kaufman et al., 1989). *Simultaneous processing* refers to making decisions and solving problems based upon an integrated and simultaneous approach to tasks often presented in spatial form. Successive or sequential processing on the other hand involves processing in a step-by-step, sequential manner. Sequential processing tasks include short-term memory tasks and word reading (Sattler, 1992).

A. S. Kaufman and associates (1989) suggest that these findings regarding processing differences are consistent with the noted strengths in spatial reasoning and auditory memory, and the relative weaknesses in serial memory and verbal memory for Japanese children. Results of a study by Stevenson and colleagues (1985) supported this pattern of abilities for Japanese children in grades one and five in comparison to American children.

EVOLUTIONARY, NEUROLOGICAL, LANGUAGE, AND CULTURAL HYPOTHESES

Researchers have advanced numerous hypotheses to account for the differences observed in IQ for the Japanese (e.g., visual-spatial versus verbal abilities).

These include evolutionary, neurological, language, cultural, and educational explanations. The following discussion highlights some of these issues.

Evolutionary, Neurological, and Language Hypotheses. Lynn's (1987) evolutionary and neurological theory suggests that during the Ice Age the extreme cold created "a selection pressure for increases in 'g' and visuospatial abilities" (p. 813). During this time Asians became dependent upon hunting for their food, and "visuospatial skills underlie good hunting skills" (p. 833). The "enhancement" of visuospatial skills "took place at the expense of verbal abilities [and] verbal abilities were sacrificed to permit an increase in visuospatial abilities" (p. 833).

Given this suggested evolution of abilities, Lynn hypothesized that distinctive features of the neurology of the brain developed. He cites literature indicating that verbal abilities are located in the left hemisphere and visuospatial abilities are located in the right hemisphere. Lynn suggests that the pattern of Japanese abilities and the resulting neurology must have some "genetic basis which may possibly be enhanced by environmental processes" (p. 837).

Tsunoda (cited in Vernon, 1982) also supports the notion, admittedly supported only weakly by biomedical research, that Japanese performance on IQ tests correlate with neurological processes. He uses the example of the Japanese language to support the linkage between neurology and intellectual abilities. In particular, he believes that the Japanese language determines to some extent the neurological pathways of auditory processing. The few researchers who accept this relationship hypothesize that the Japanese may make more use of the right hemisphere of the brain, and Americans generally make more use of the left hemisphere (Iwakaki & Vernon, 1988).

P. E. VERNON (1982) cites differences, again supported only weakly by biomedical investigators, between the Japanese and Western (American and European) brain hemispheres in terms of the processing of auditory information. Generally in the Western brain, the left hemisphere processes analytical and verbal information. The right hemisphere processes spatial, musical, and creative information. The Japanese brain, on the other hand, processes emotional stimuli, music, as well as analytical calculations and language in the left hemisphere. The right hemisphere processes primarily mechanical sounds, pure tones, and Western music.

Further support is possible for the hemispheric differences between the Japanese and Americans with respect to the processing differences. Again, the Japanese reportedly demonstrate a preference for tasks involving simultaneous processing in comparison with sequential processing. Research on cerebral functioning of the brain indicates that sequential processing correlates with the left hemisphere and simultaneous processing with the right hemisphere. Thus, the Japanese may have a differential preference for processing and utilization of the abilities located in the right hemisphere.

Differences in hemispheric processing are also apparent from examination of writing systems. The Japanese language is notably different from European languages. There are four systems of writing in the Japanese language—Katakana and Hiragana, the phonetic writing systems; Kanji, which is the ideographic system adapted from the Chinese characters; and Romaji, which uses the Latin alphabet (Vernon, 1982). The Japanese use some 2,400 characters in day-to-day life. In addition, children learn approximately 100 Kanji characters by second grade and nearly 1,000 by the sixth grade. Children learn many of the Kanji characters by rote, though phonetic components are included. Hatta (cited in Iwakaki & Vernon, 1988) indicates that the processing of Japanese Kanji is located in the right hemisphere, whereas language processing occurs primarily in the left hemisphere for American groups. Thus, language processing differences may exist between the Japanese and American based upon hemispheric differences.

Cultural and Educational Hypotheses. An alternative to the evolutionary, biological, and language hypotheses are cultural and educational explanations for the slightly higher average Japanese IQ patterns. M. Kornhaber, M. Krechevsky, and H. Gardner (1990) suggest that in Japan "the development of intelligence is fostered by widely shared values which in turn are supported by the institutions of the society" (p. 184).

Children socialize early to abide by the norms and mores of the Japanese culture. Vernon (1982) notes that the average scores earned by Japanese on performance subtests reflect the Japanese family traditions, which emphasize nonverbal rather than verbal abilities. The Japanese demonstrate a preference for nonverbal signals to communicate feelings and status (Vernon, 1982). Hsu and colleagues (1986) offer the following opinion:

> As clear statements of individual feelings and thoughts may risk disagreement, it is culturally adaptive for one to be more indirect and ambiguous. The Japanese also value implicit, nonverbal, intuitive communication over explicit, verbal, and rational exchange of information. Family and in-group members rely more on nonverbal cues and physical contact for real communications. One should, they believe, be sensitive to what is implied rather than what is expressed [p. 320].

H. Morsbach (1980) cites historical factors that promote the nonverbal "style" of Japanese culture. In particular, he points to the influence of Zen Buddhism and the development of a highly prescribed social structure as considerations in understanding the nonverbal emphasis of the Japanese. For example, in Zen, the means to enlightenment is through mediation rather than action or performance.

The emphasis placed upon high achievement in Japanese society has been identified through history. Children perhaps attain high scholastic goals through hard work and commitment rather than through innate intelligence. Strengths in numerical reasoning for the Japanese also appear in the research literature. Vernon (1982) indicates that the mathematics curriculum in Japan is clearly more advanced than in the United States. A study by Stevenson and associates (1986) reveals that in comparing the educational curriculum of American schools, such as in Minneapolis, and Japanese schools, such as in Sendai, American first-grade teachers spent approximately half as much time on mathematics as did first-grade teachers in Japan. On the other hand, reading, spelling, and writing received much more focus in American classrooms in comparison with Japanese classrooms. The study also concluded that differences in mathematics achievement were evident before the children had finished their first year in school. The authors suggest that parental factors also may play a role to account for this finding. Japanese children appear to spend more time in school (240 days of instruction, 5 ½ days per week) in comparison with American children (178 days of instruc-

tion, 5 days per week). American children appear to be less attentive to teacher instruction during school and to complete less homework than their Japanese counterparts.

CONCLUSIONS

Although much research continues in the area of the slightly higher-than-average scores on IQ tests of the Japanese, direct comparison of Japanese and Americans is difficult, given differences in cultural, environmental, language, education, and other related factors. Findings are a bit more consistent, however, regarding the relatively higher visual-spatial and numerical reasoning abilities of the Japanese in comparison with verbal abilities and preferences for simultaneous rather than sequential processing.

(*See also:* ASIAN AMERICANS.)

BIBLIOGRAPHY

HSU, J., TSENG, W., ASHTON, G., McDERMOTT, J. F., & CHAR, W. (1986). Family interaction patterns among Japanese–American and Caucasian families in Hawaii. In S. Chess & A. Thomas (Eds.), *Annual progress in child psychiatry and child development 1986* (pp. 314–350). New York: Brunner/Mazel.

IWAKAKI, S., & VERNON, P. E. (1988). Japanese abilities and achievements. In S. H. Irvine & J. W. Berry (Eds.), *Human abilities in cultural context* (pp. 358–382). New York: Cambridge University Press.

KAUFMAN, A. S., McLEAN, J. E., ISHIKUMA, T., & MOON, S. (1989). Integration of the literature on the intelligence of Japanese children and analysis of the data from a sequential–simultaneous perspective. *School Psychology International, 10,* 173–183.

KORNHABER, M., KREĆHEVSKY, M., & GARDNER, H. (1990). Engaging intelligence. *Educational Psychologist, 25,* (3–4), 177–199.

LYNN, R. (1982). IQ in Japan and the United States. *Nature, 306,* 292.

LYNN, R. (1987). The intelligence of the Mongoloids: A psychometric, evolutionary and neurological theory. *Personality and Individual Differences, 8*(6), 813–844.

LYNN, R., & HAMPSON, S. (1985–1986). The structure of Japanese abilities: An analysis in terms of the hierarchical model of intelligence. *Current Psychological Research and Reviews, 4*(4), 308–322.

LYNN, R., & HAMPSON, S. (1986). Intellectual abilities of Japanese children: An assessment of 2 1/2–8 1/2-year-olds derived from the McCarthy Scales of Children's Abilities. *Intelligence, 10,* 41–58.

LYNN, R., & HAMPSON, S. (1987). Further evidence on the cognitive abilities of the Japanese: Data from the WPPSI. *International Journal of Behavioral Development, 10*(1), 23–36.

MORSBACH, H. (1980). Major psychological factors influencing Japanese interpersonal relations. In N. Warren (Ed.), *Studies in cross-cultural psychology* (Vol. 2, pp. 317–342). New York: Academic Press.

SATTLER, J. M. (1992). *Assessment of children* (3rd ed.). San Diego, CA: Jerome M. Sattler.

STEVENSON, H. W., STIGLER, J. W., LEE, S., LUCKER, G. W., KITAMURA, S., AND HSU, C. (1985). Cognitive performance and academic achievement of Japanese, Chinese and American children. *Child Development, 56,* 718–734.

STEVENSON, H. W., STIGLER, J. W., LEE, S. Y., KITAMURA, S., KIMURA, S., & KATO, T. (1986). Achievement in mathematics. In H. Stevenson, H. Azuma, & K. Hakuta (Eds.), *Child development and education in Japan* (pp. 201–216). New York: W. H. Freeman.

VERNON, P. E. (1982). *The abilities and achievements of Orientals in North America.* San Diego, CA: Academic Press.

LISA A. SUZUKI
TERRY B. GUTKIN

JENSEN, ARTHUR R. (1923–)

One of the highly visible educational psychologists and research methodologists currently working, Arthur Jensen was born in San Diego in 1923, where he obtained his primary and secondary education, graduating from Herbert Hoover High in 1941. Jensen played clarinet in his high school band and orchestra, an activity he currently enjoys as a leisure activity. In 1945, he earned a B.A. degree in psychology from the University of California at Berkeley followed by an M.A. in psychology from San Diego State University (1952), and the Ph.D. in psychology from Teachers College of Columbia University in 1956. From 1956 through 1958, Jensen was a United States Public Health Service (USPHS) Postdoctoral Research Fellow working under Hans J. EYSENCK, then head of the psychology department of the University of London's renowned Institute of Psychiatry. According to Jensen, nearly all of his subsequent research in psychology was stimulated directly or indirectly by his stint under Eysenck, with whom he has maintained a friendship. Jensen, originally trained as a clinical psychologist, views himself principally as a differential psychologist, that is, a psychologist who studies the presentation, nature, and nurture of individual differences.

Following his USPHS Postdoctoral Research Fellowship, Jensen returned to the University of California at Berkeley as an assistant professor of education. He earned the rank of professor of educational psychology in 1966 and has remained at Berkeley throughout his academic career.

Widely known among researchers in educational psychology by the early 1960s due to his book with the distinguished psychologist (and Jensen's first mentor) Percival Symonds (Symonds & Jensen, 1961) and his research in learning, Jensen was catapulted into the light of a broad, national controversy by his most famous paper, "How much can we boost I.Q. and scholastic achievement?" (Jensen, 1969), the 123-page paper being the longest ever published in the prestigious *Harvard Educational Review.*

In that paper, hailed in the *New York Post* (April 4, 1969) as the most discussed professional article of the year, Jensen argued that genetic as well as environmental and cultural factors should be considered in developing an understanding of individual differences in IQ, including social class and racial differences (Fletcher-Janzen, 1987). Many saw his position—that genetic contributions to race differences in intelligence were significant and substantial—as deeply disturbing and racist. Jensen reports (personal communication) that he was subsequently harassed, had his personal safety threatened in person and via telephone, and was threatened with the loss of his academic position at Berkeley.

Subsequently, the term *Jensenism* was coined to refer to the position that race differences in intelligence were primarily due to genetic causes. The hypothesis of Jensenism remains much contested and debated today. Jensen continues to receive threats to his life on an infrequent basis and continues to be viewed as controversial. In the mid-1980s, when I introduced Jensen at his invited address to the annual convention of the American Psychological Association, held in Anaheim, two weeks prior to the meeting, participants were notified by the Anaheim police that they had received a serious threat against Jensen's life, should he be allowed to speak. With police and special security guards, Jensen subsequently addressed a standing-room-only crowd in one of the largest meeting rooms available at the convention.

Jensen has continued his work and is a prolific scholar. The Social Science Citation Index lists four of his works as "Citation Classics," including the aforementioned *Harvard Educational Review* article and two of his six books: *Educability and Group Differences* (Jensen, 1973) and *Bias in Mental Testing* (Jensen, 1980).

In the mid-1960s, Jensen's work led him to propose a theory of intelligence that hypothesizes two types of learning ability. He referred to these as Level I and Level II abilities. Level I abilities are simple associative activities requiring little more than memory functions. Level II abilities require abstract, conceptual thought and are most strongly related to general intelligence tests, such as the Wechsler scales. Jensen's theory prompted a significant amount of research and is one of many models often used in the interpretation of intelligence test performance (e.g., Kaufman, 1979).

Jensen currently views the general factor of intelligence, or g, as (1) reflecting some property or processes of the human brain manifest in many forms of adaptive behavior in which individuals (and probably populations) differ; (2) increasing from birth to maturity and declining in old age; (3) showing physiological as well as behavioral correlates; (4) having a hereditary component; (5) being subject to natural selection in the course of human evolution; and (6) having important educational, occupational, economic, and social correlates in all industrialized societies (Fletcher-Janzen, 1987).

Beginning in the late 1970s, Jensen became the primary catalyst in a revival of the Galtonian (see Francis GALTON) approach to research on mental ability, particularly as it concerns the relationship between reaction time and intelligence, which Jensen refers to as the chronometric study of intelligence (e.g., Jensen, 1985). Jensen's reaction time paradigm and methods are perhaps best explicated in his 1985 methodological treatise. At the same time, Jensen fostered a revival of

research interest in the concept of g, or GENERAL INTELLIGENCE, as represented in Charles SPEARMAN's early work (e.g., Jensen, 1979). Much of his work is linked in various ways to the Spearman Hypothesis, which specifies that group differences in aptitude or abilities are essentially manifestations of differences in g.

Jensen is author or coauthor of more than 300 articles in scholarly journals and six books. Two books have been written about Jensen and his work: Flynn (1980) and Modgil and Modgil (1986). During his career, Jensen held appointments as a Guggenheim Fellow (1964–65), a Fellow of the Center for Advanced Studies in the Behavioral Sciences (1966–67), and a Research Fellow at the National Institutes of Mental Health. He is a Fellow of the American Psychological Association, the American Association for the Advancement of Science, and the Eugenics Society of London, and is a member of most of the major professional societies of his discipline.

(*See also:* RACE AND IQ SCORES.)

BIBLIOGRAPHY

FLETCHER-JANZEN, E. (1987). Jensen, Arthur R. In C. R. Reynolds & L. Mann (Eds.), *Encyclopedia of Special Education.* New York: Wiley, 873–874.

FLYNN, J. R. (1980). *Race, IQ and Jensen.* London: Routledge & Kegan Paul.

JENSEN, A. R. (1969). How much can we boost I.Q. and scholastic achievement? *Harvard Educational Review, 39,* 1–123.

JENSEN, A. R. (1973). *Educability and group differences.* New York: Harper and Row.

JENSEN, A. R. (1979). g: Outmoded theory or unconquered frontier? *Creative Science and Technology, 2,* 16–29.

JENSEN, A. R. (1980). *Bias in mental testing.* New York: Free Press.

JENSEN, A. R. (1985). Methodological and statistical techniques for the chronometric study of mental abilities. In C. R. Reynolds & V. L. Willson (Eds.), *Methodological and statistical advances in the study of individual differences.* New York: Plenum.

KAUFMAN, A. S. (1979). *Intelligent testing with the WISC-R.* New York: Wiley.

MODGIL, S., & MODGIL, C. (Eds.). (1986). *Arthur Jensen: Consensus and controversy.* Philadelphia: Falmer Press.

SYMONDS, P., & JENSEN, A. R. (1961). *From adolescent to adult.* New York: Teachers College Press.

CECIL R. REYNOLDS

JOB PERFORMANCE   One of the important tasks of a test is to predict meaningful and important criteria. Although intelligence tests have been used to make statistical prediction of many criteria such as educational attainment or of life adjustment, among the most important of these criteria is job performance (see also OCCUPATIONS). Like many other issues concerning intelligence, its relationship to job performance has been the subject of argument and controversy for nearly a century. The most extreme forms of the argument state that intelligence has no relationship to job performance, or conversely, that job performance is solely dependent on intelligence. Both extreme positions seem untenable. For example, the idea that intelligence has no relationship to job performance ignores a large body of published literature demonstrating otherwise. The idea that nothing other than intelligence determines job performance ignores the literature that shows the effects of interests, training, or experience.

C. Brand (1987) points out that one reason for the argument is that intelligence shows correlations with so many other variables, including socioeconomic status, educational achievement, and job status, just to name a few. Insofar as the variables of intelligence, socioeconomic status, educational achievement, and job status are correlated, they can all be expected to predict job performance.

Job performance has several components, including job knowledge, job skills, willingness to apply skills, and knowledge and behavior on the job. Job knowledge is the specific knowledge used on the job, such as the rules for using a block plane, double-entry cost accounting, or positioning a patient in a medical imaging machine. Job skills are the behavioral manifestation of knowledge such as leveling wood, entering credits and debits, and spatially aligning a patient. Additionally, there are behaviors that are not, strictly speaking, job performance but that are related to employee performance. For example, personal honesty is expected in all jobs but is frequently not specifically mentioned in job descriptions. Some have argued that to evaluate job performance, all components of job performance must be measured, and that the validity of measures must be evaluated for each separate component of job performance.

The first part of job performance is the acquisition of the knowledge and skills required of the job. There is an accumulation of evidence by Hunter and Hunter (1984) showing that intelligence predicts the acquisition of all kinds of knowledge—both academic, as needed in highly abstract jobs, and practical, as needed in jobs of a less abstract nature. Job-related skills ranging from baking jelly rolls to flying aileron rolls can be predicted from intelligence.

The American military has been a good source of research on the relationship of intelligence to job performance. During World War I, the Army Alpha was used to assign men to jobs on the basis of measured intelligence. The paper-and-pencil Army Alpha test was built to mimic individually administered intelligence tests. Toward the end of World War II, N. Stewart (1947) computed the average intelligence of draftees by occupation. In general, the average intelligence required for jobs increased as jobs went from those demanding low skills to those demanding high skills. Validation of intelligence measures for the prediction of technical training has been frequent. Army's Project A and the Air Force Job Performance Measurement Project extended the investigation of intelligence to its relationship with hands-on-work sample criteria, technical interviews, and some noncore job criteria, such as discipline and military bearing. Across the many jobs, intelligence was found to statistically predict all criteria.

John Hunter and his colleagues have done numerous studies of many predictors of job performance in the civilian sector. They have examined the validity of intelligence for many jobs and concluded that intelligence was predictive in all cases. In addition, they and others have found other personal attributes predictive of job performance.

Among the personal attributes frequently found to be predictive of job performance are job knowledge, interest, personality, and psychomotor skills.

Job knowledge is frequently found to be predictive, especially as a function of job tenure. As people gain experience, their job knowledge usually increases. Schmidt, Hunter, and Outerbridge (1986) have argued that intelligence enables employees to garner job knowledge, solve novel problems, and make appropriate judgments when routine procedures do not apply. Job knowledge is almost always predictive of job performance.

Interest, whether measured directly from specially prepared inventories or inferred from scores on specialized knowledge tests (such as tests of aviation information, cockpit instrument comprehension, automotive information, or electronics knowledge) is a good predictor of job performance. This would be especially true where the special knowledge was not available in common educational curricula. An example is flying information, which might be sought out in special publications. The United States Air Force uses such measures (Aviation Information and Instrument Comprehension) to select pilots.

Through meta-analyses, personality measures have been found to be predictive of job performance. The most frequently valid variable is a measure of conscientiousness, the trait of sticking with a task until it is completed. Another characteristic found to be predictive of job performance is the level of psychomotor skills, especially for jobs requiring low abstract reasoning. It has been found that as job complexity decreases, the salience of intelligence as a predictor decreases and that of psychomotor ability tends to increase.

Clearly, the role of intelligence in predicting job performance is substantial, but other determinants exist as well, and all should be considered in personnel selection.

(*See also:* ARMY ALPHA AND BETA TESTS OF INTELLIGENCE.)

BIBLIOGRAPHY

BRAND, C. (1987). The importance of general intelligence. In S. Modgil & C. Modgil (Eds.), *Arthur Jensen: Consensus and controversy*. New York: Falmer Press. Includes a list showing correlates of intelligence and providing information on the many human attributes which correlate with intelligence.

CAMPBELL, J. P. (1990). An overview of the Army selection and classification project (Project A). *Personnel Psychology, 43,* 231–239.

CARRETTA, T. R. (1990). Cross-validation of experimental USAF pilot training performance models. *Military Psychology, 2,* 257–264. An explanation of the role of psychomotor ability in the selection of pilots. (See also Hunter & Hunter, below.)

HEDGE, J. W., & TEACHOUT, M. S. (1992). An interview approach to work sample criterion development. *Journal of Applied Psychology, 77,* 453–461.

HUNTER, J., & HUNTER, R. (1984). The validity and utility of alternative predictors of job performance. *Psychological Bulletin, 96,* 72–98.

SCHMIDT, F. L., & HUNTER, J. E. (1977). A general solution to the problem of validity generalization. *Journal of Applied Psychology, 62,* 529–540.

SCHMIDT, F. L., HUNTER, J. E., & OUTERBRIDGE, A. N. (1986). Impact of job experience and ability on job knowledge, work sample performance, and supervisory ratings of job performance. *Journal of Applied Psychology, 71,* 432–439.

STEWART, N. (1947). A.G.C.T. scores of Army personnel grouped by occupation. *Occupations, 26,* 1–37. Provides average intelligence scores for numerous occupational groups tested in the 1940s.

TETT, R. P., JACKSON, D., & ROTHSTEIN, M. (1991). Personality measures as predictors of job performance: A meta-analytic review. *Personnel Psychology, 44,* 703–742. See also Barrick, M. R., & Mount, M. K. (1991). The Big Five personality dimensions and job performance: A meta-analysis. *Personnel Psychology, 44,* 1–26. The two best explanations of the role of personality in predicting job performance.

MALCOLM REE

K

KAUFMAN ASSESSMENT BATTERY FOR CHILDREN (K-ABC)

The Kaufman Assessment Battery for Children (K-ABC) was published in 1983 (Kaufman & Kaufman, 1983) by the American Guidance Service, under the authorship of Alan S. Kaufman and Nadeen L. Kaufman, after five years of research and development. An individually administered test of intelligence and achievement, the K-ABC was the first major challenge to the Binet and the Wechsler monopoly over the individual intelligence testing market. The K-ABC is also one of the few tests of intelligence to be devised on the basis of an a priori theory of intelligence, because Kaufman and Kaufman (a husband-and-wife research-and-development team) based the structural development of the scales on their reinterpretation of Luria's neuropsychological theory of intelligence (e.g., Luria, 1966).

The K-ABC consists of ten mental processing subtests divided into a sequential (three subtests) and a simultaneous (seven subtests) processing scale, each yielding a composite normalized standard score scaled to a mean of 100 and a standard deviation of 15. A summary score, the mental processing composite (MPC), a composite of the sequential scale (SEQ) and the simultaneous scale (SIM) are also available. For children with language-related problems or for whom English is a secondary language, as well as for non-English speakers, the K-ABC includes a nonverbal intelligence scale, which may be administered using standard instructions or via a pantomime procedure. The K-ABC subtests and scales are described in more detail at the end of this article.

An achievement scale is also present on the K-ABC and consists of seven subtests covering vocabulary, language development, general factual knowledge, mental arithmetic, and reading (using separate subtests for decoding and for comprehension). Many of the K-ABC achievement scale subtests are commonly viewed on other tests as measures of verbal intelligence, and some researchers (e.g., Keith & Dunbar, 1984) have suggested that the K-ABC achievement scale may be a better measure of g (general intelligence) than the MPC. This controversy has yet to be resolved and reflects a philosophical difference of opinion regarding the nature of intelligence that is unlikely to be resolved on research or a data-based basis (e.g., Kamphaus & Reynolds, 1987, chaps. 3 and 5).

In response to these arguments and other analyses, Kamphaus and Reynolds (1987) developed and provided normative data for the K-ABC standardization sample for three additional composite scores: verbal intelligence, global intelligence composite, and a reading composite. The verbal intelligence scale is composed of all K-ABC achievement subtests with the exception of Reading/Decoding and Reading/Understanding, which form the reading composite. The global intelligence composite is determined through rescaling the sum of the SEQ, SIM, and verbal intelligence scores. Each of the Kamphaus-Reynolds K-ABC composites is scaled to the familiar metric of a mean of 100 and a standard deviation of 15.

The K-ABC was standardized on 2,000 children between the ages of 2½ years and 12 ½ years by means of a population-proportionate stratified-random-sampling plan. The sample was stratified on the basis of age (at one-year intervals), gender (equal numbers of boys and girls), ethnicity (African-American, white, Hispanic, Asian-American, and Native American), parental socioeconomic status as represented by parental educational level, geographical region of residence (Northeast, Northcentral, South, or West), and community size. The test developers were quite successful in approximating the target U.S. population statistics in the obtained sample. African Americans were oversampled for the purpose of generating a set of sociocultural norms that could be used with either black or white children in an attempt to correct for any sociocultural biases that might occur. These latter norms have proven neither useful nor popular (e.g., Kamphaus & Reynolds, 1987).

The K-ABC manuals provide extensive data on reliability and validity, an amount of data that was extraordinary when published in 1983 and that set a new standard for the comprehensiveness of test manuals for individually administered tests of intelligence. The K-ABC subtests and composites have good internal consistency reliability, with most subtest reliability estimates between .60 and .90, and the composites consistently exceeding .90 reliability at most ages. Extensive factor-analytic data are also recounted that support the groupings of the subtests into their respective scales although, as noted above, the designation of the constructs assessed remains controversial. The various composites of the K-ABC are also related to academic achievement, with validity coefficients ranging from about .50 to .70 between the K-ABC composites and various measures of academic skill. The K-ABC also correlates appropriately with other individually administered intelligence scales; the correlation, for example, between the K-ABC MPC and the WISC-R full-scale IQ hovers around .70.

Kaufman and Kaufman's (1983) development plan for the K-ABC included six broad goals for the new scale:

1. to measure intelligence from a strong theoretical and research base;
2. to separate acquired factual knowledge from the ability to solve unfamiliar problems;
3. to yield scores that can be used to plan educational intervention;
4. to include novel tasks;
5. to be easy to administer and objective to score;
6. to be sensitive to the diverse needs of preschool, minority group, and exceptional children.

The extent to which these goals have been met continues to be the fodder of academic debate. However, the Kaufmans did break with tradition in a number of ways: The test was developed in light of an a priori theory; factual knowledge and vocabulary, mainstays of intelligence tests since the late 1800s, were deemed important but as measures of achievement; the test was designed so that specific educational interventions could be prescribed on the basis of specific score patterns (also see Kaufman, Kaufman, & Goldsmith, 1984); new tasks were devised, and standard laboratory procedures were made clinically practicable; practice and teaching items were made available to ensure that children understood what was expected of them on the intellectual portions of the test; and, the publisher undertook an extensive training effort to prepare practitioners to use the K-ABC.

The K-ABC is widely known among school psychologists and other practitioners in the broad field of child psychology. Although it has made inroads in assessment practice, it remains secondary to the Wechsler scales and the Stanford-Binet for frequency of use. It has achieved popularity among neuropsychologists, many of whom have incorporated the K-ABC into the standard neuropsychological evaluation of the young child. Few good standardized neuropsychological instruments are available at this age level (2½ years to 12½ years), and the strong psychometric properties and theoretical links to brain-behavior relationships make the K-ABC attractive to the child-clinical neuropsychologist (e.g., see Kamphaus & Reynolds, 1987, chap. 7).

The K-ABC seems particularly useful with language-disordered children but is not a good choice for the visually impaired child because of its heavy reliance on visual stimuli. The K-ABC has been touted as a good choice of instrument for minority children (both gifted ones and those referred for suspected mental retardation), because the black–white score difference on the K-ABC is half the traditionally occurring standard deviation of 1. For gifted children, the K-ABC lacks sufficient ceiling after about age 10, and insufficient floor is evident for low-functioning children below age 4. Very little is known about the use of the K-ABC as an intellectual assessment device for children with serious emotional disturbance.

The K-ABC is one of the most reviewed of intelligence tests, and a plethora of information and opinion exists regarding it. A special issue of the *Journal of Special Education* was devoted to the K-ABC (Reynolds, 1984), and a book-length treatment of its strengths, weaknesses, and clinical and research applications is available (Kamphaus & Reynolds, 1987). Extensive reviews of the K-ABC have also been completed by Coffman (1985), Narrett (1984), Page (1985), and Vance and Kutsick (1983).

Specific criticisms of the construct validity of the K-ABC have been proffered by Keith and Dunbar (1984) and by Sternberg (1984), who view the K-ABC as largely inadequate in achievement of its stated goals. Jensen (1984) explores psychometric limitations of the K-ABC that he believes are responsible for the significant reduction of black–white score differences on the K-ABC relative to other traditional intelligence tests (e.g., Wechsler scales, Binet scales, RAVEN PROGRESSIVE MATRICES). He argues that the K-ABC is not as strong a measure of g, or general intelligence. The K-ABC continues to be controversial, and a thorough understanding of its strengths and its limitations should be acquired prior to using the K-ABC in clinical practice. Much research remains to be done, since the K-ABC has been in use a much shorter time than have other popular tests of intelligence.

DESCRIPTION OF THE K-ABC SUBTESTS BY SCALE

Sequential Processing Scale. This scale measures skills involved in linear, step-by-step, sequential problem-solving tasks and emphasizes memory as serial recall. Subtest 1 is also part of the nonverbal scale.

Subtest 1. Hand Movements. The child imitates a sequenced presentation of hand positions.

Subtest 2. Number Recall. The child recalls in order a series of digits presented orally.

Subtest 3. Word Order. The child recalls in order a series of pictures named by the examiner. At upper ages an interference task is introduced between stimulus presentation and recall.

Simultaneous Processing Scale. This scale measures problem-solving skills by means of primarily spatial stimuli requiring the synthesis of information. Subtests 2 and 4–7 are also part of the nonverbal scale.

Subtest 1. Magic Window. The child names objects after seeing a picture presented gradually through a cutout on a cardboard wheel, never seeing the entire picture at once.

Subtest 2. Face Recognition. The child picks out of a group of pictures, photo(s) of faces exposed previously for 5 seconds each.

Subtest 3. Gestalt Closure. The child names partially pictured objects drawn in black "silhouette" form.

Subtest 4. Triangles. The child constructs geometric designs to match a pictured standard using blue and yellow triangles.

Subtest 5. Matrix Analogies. The child solves standard nonverbal analogy problems that gradually become more abstract.

Subtest 6. Spatial Memory. The child recalls the location of pictured objects on a 3 × 3 or 3 × 4 grid.

Subtest 7. Photo Series. The child arranges a series of photographs in order to depict the occurrence of a specific event (e.g., an egg's being broken and cooked).

Achievement Scale. This scale measures acquired knowledge, including vocabulary, mental arithmetic, and reading.

Subtest 1. Expressive Vocabulary. The child names pictures of everyday objects.

Subtest 2. Faces and Places. The child names pictures of famous places (e.g., Grand Canyon) and famous faces (e.g., George Washington, Santa Claus).

Subtest 3. Arithmetic. The child performs mental arithmetic beginning with simple counting through two-step calculations based on a story read by the examiner and on accompanying pictures.

Subtest 4. Riddles. The child "guesses" words based on two or three clues provided by the examiner on a task highly correlated with language development.

Subtest 5. Reading/Decoding. A traditional letter and word recognition task.

Subtest 6. Reading/Understanding. A measure of reading comprehension requiring the child to carry out written instructions.

BIBLIOGRAPHY

COFFMAN, W. E. (1985). Review of the Kaufman Assessment Battery for Children. In J. Mitchell (Ed.), *Ninth Mental Measurements Yearbook.* Lincoln, NE: Buros Institute.

JENSEN, A. R. (1984). The black-white difference on the K-ABC: Implications for future tests. *Journal of Special Education, 18*(3), 377–408.

KAMPHAUS, R. W., & REYNOLDS, C. R. (1987). *Clinical and research applications of the K-ABC.* Circle Pines, MN: American Guidance Service.

KAUFMAN, A. S., & KAUFMAN, N. L. (1983). *Kaufman Assessment Battery for Children.* Circle Pines, MN: American Guidance Service.

KAUFMAN, A. S., KAUFMAN, N. L., & GOLDSMITH, B. Z. (1984). *K-SOS: Kaufman sequential or simultaneous.* Circle Pines, MN: American Guidance Service.

KEITH, T. Z., & DUNBAR, S. B. (1984). Hierarchical factor analysis of the K-ABC: Testing alternate models. *Journal of Special Education, 18*(3).

LURIA, A. R. (1966). *The human brain and psychological processes.* New York: Harper & Row.

NARRETT, C. M. (1984). Test review: Kaufman Assessment Battery for Children (K-ABC). *Reading Teacher, 37,* 636–637.

PAGE, E. B. (1985). Review of the Kaufman Assessment Battery for Children. In J. Mitchell (Ed.), *Ninth Mental Measurements Yearbook.* Lincoln, NE: Buros Institute.

REYNOLDS, C. R. (ED.). (1984). The K-ABC [Special issue]. *Journal of Special Education, 18*(3).

STERNBERG, R. J. (1984). The Kaufman Assessment Battery for Children: An information processing analysis and critique. *Journal of Special Education, 18*(3), 269–279.

VANCE, H. B., & KUTSICK, K. (1983). Diagnosing learning disabilities with the K-ABC. *Academic Therapy, 19,* 102–112.

CECIL R. REYNOLDS

KNOWLEDGE A popular assumption about more intelligent people is that they acquire new knowledge faster and then retain and recall that knowledge more effectively than those who are less intelligent. Likewise, someone who rapidly acquires, retains, and recalls considerable volumes of knowledge is supposedly intelligent. A certain circularity exists in everyday thinking that sees being knowledgeable as a sign of intelligence and intelligence as a predictor of being knowledgeable. The possible connections between intelligence and knowledge are the subject of this entry.

KNOWLEDGE AND INTELLIGENCE

"Knowledge" may be defined as acquired information. Clearly the knowledge that a person brings to any task must be a major determinant of performance. Thus, performance on tasks that make up an intelligence test will reflect the relevant knowledge that the person tested remembers and uses in response to the test items. For example, vocabulary items, which play a role in many tests, will reflect ability to retrieve word meanings; such a knowledge-based ability is often called a form of *crystallized intelligence.* Other verbal items may require novel relationships among word meanings to be detected and may reflect *fluid intelligence* in addition to the crystallized knowledge of meanings (see FLUID AND CRYSTALLIZED INTELLIGENCE, THEORY OF). Culture-fair tests attempt to minimize the role of acquired knowledge and involve, for instance, abstract patterns among which relationships can be detected and extrapolated, as is the case in RAVEN PROGRESSIVE MATRICES. However, even such abstract materials require prior knowledge to understand the instruction. The subject must also extract information (knowledge) from the items themselves. In practice, knowledge and intelligence are inextricably intertwined, although theorists have taken different views. On the one hand, some reduce intelligence to accumulated knowledge. On the other hand, some reduce knowledge acquisition to basic processes presumed to underlie intelligence.

In discussing knowledge, certain distinctions generally recur, such as knowing that versus knowing how, declarative versus procedural knowledge, explicit versus implicit knowledge, and semantic versus episodic knowledge. The first three distinctions are virtually synonymous. "Knowing that"—declarative, explicit knowledge—is consciously known and can be expressed in a publicly understood code, such as spoken or written language or in some specialized code, such as notation in music or dance movement. "Knowing how"—procedural, or implicit, knowledge—is not accessible consciously. Although it is demonstrable in behavior, it is not explicitly communicable. Typical examples of such knowledge are sensorimotor skills such as bicycle riding or swinging a golf club to good effect. Procedural knowledge is often spared in amnesic memory disorders brought on by brain damage when declarative knowledge is lost. In a sense, procedural knowledge is more basic than declarative knowledge and is present in nonhuman species as well as in humans. In contrast, declarative knowledge, being dependent on shared flexible codes—notably natural language—seems limited to humans. Our ability to use communication codes, however, depends on implicit processes that are not themselves accessible to consciousness. Therefore, although a person may be able to retrieve the explicit information that a word, for example, *maelstrom,* means "a whirlpool or a confused and disordered state of affairs," that person will not be able to report explicitly the recognition of the word or the retrieval of the semantic knowledge of its meaning. Only through the indirect methods of experiment and theory in cognitive research do scientists acquire knowledge of implicit processes.

Researchers often make a further distinction between semantic and episodic knowledge. Semantic knowledge is knowledge of general concepts, principles, and word meanings, while episodic knowledge is autobiographical knowledge of specific experiences. Both types of knowledge can be useful in everyday problem solving. Recalling a previous occasion when some present problem was encountered and solved may provide a quick route to a solution. Even if the current problem is not identical to the earlier one, retrieval of a sufficiently similar past problem-solving experience may yield a solution. Intelligence test items typically draw on semantic knowledge or word meanings, properties of numbers, and so on. Semantic knowledge is, of course, often vital in real-life tasks. General principles of physics, for example, which have been formulated culturally, permit solution of new problems in engineering and architecture where simple past experience is insufficient for effective solutions. General principles enshrined in semantic knowledge economically convey a great deal of information, and their acquisition through formal education permits more effective problem solving than does reliance on personal experience alone.

In terms of knowledge *structure,* a striking fact is that formal human knowledge seeks cognitive economy in terms of rules or principles with the widest range and the maximum simplicity. This preference is due to the limited capacity of working memory within which current information is processed. The risk of this preference is that oversimplifications will occur to minimize cognitive effort—at the cost of inaccuracies. Further, knowledge tends to be organized into hierarchical structures of areas and subareas (Simon, 1981). For example, psychology may be divided into several areas: cognitive, social, developmental, individual differential, and biological. Cognitive psychology in turn can be divided into learning, memory, perception, attention, language, and problem solving. Each of these areas has further subdivisions. Because people can actively process in focal attention at any one time only a limited amount of their vast store of information, the hierarchical organization of knowledge helps ensure that associations to related information are strongest. While this focusing mechanism is generally useful, it is also one reason why creative combinations of unrelated items are difficult and why use of unusual analogies are rare in problem solving (Perkins, 1981).

Although it is clear that all the types of knowledge outlined above are extremely important for individuals, explicit declarative knowledge has the key role at the social or cultural level because of its unique advantage of being readily transmittable from person to person. This transmission can now take place not just face to face but over vast gaps in time and space, by means of print and telecommunications. The cultural accumulation and transmission of knowledge has led to tremendous increases in the effectiveness of human behavior over the millennia and gives the species its dominance over other species that are limited to instinct, direct learning from experience, and possibly learning from imitation. If intelligence is equated with problem-solving performance, then successive generations have increased in intelligence thus measured because they benefit from the problem-solving discoveries of their ancestors (although without increase in intelligence as inborn potential to learn). To take advantage of the culturally accumulated stock of knowledge, the individual must acquire the basic knowledge-gathering skills of language comprehension and production, literacy, and numeracy, and must also be able to retrieve and apply acquired information when required. Suitable environments and encouragements are necessary to ensure these outcomes.

What are the possible relationships between intelligence and knowledge? The speed and efficiency of basic neural processes may underlie the different rates of information acquisition among individuals in a similar environment. If differences in basic neural processes ultimately result in measured differences in intelligence, and if such processes are indeed the biological bases of intelligence (Eysenck, 1986), then biologically-defined intelligence could be said to determine knowledge, in a given environment. On the other hand, because measured intelligence does not correlate well with performance in knowledge-intensive domains of expertise (Ericsson & Smith, 1991), therefore domain-specific practice and training are much more important than any likely differences in basic neural processes for knowledge acquisition. The cases of idiot savants who perform very poorly on general intelligence tests yet have exceptional levels of knowledge-based performance in limited areas (giving days of the week for any date from C.E. to 200 C.E.) show the effectiveness of practice. Also, world-class performances in knowledge-rich domains such as chess and music seem to depend on regular, frequent, and systematic practice and training over at least a decade. Amount and quality of practice rather than measured intelligence seem to be crucial in determining level of performance in real-life areas of expertise. Indeed, some have argued that intelligence tests tap acquired skills developed through experience and thus that knowledge differences underlie differences in intelligence test performance (Howe, 1990). The knowledge-based approach has the testable and optimistic consequence that intelligence scores can be boosted by training, and some research has supported this prediction (e.g., Feuerstein, 1980). Less supportive of the pure-knowledge explanation are the results on genetically related similarities in intelligence test scores that seem to hold up in cases of separated twins and separated biological parents and offspring (Plomin & Daniels, 1987). Such results point to some biological component as a factor in measured differences in intelligence, even if this component is by no means the sole determinant. Overall, the "middle view" seems likely to remain most plausible and fruitful for a considerable time: Some biological contribution exists in measured intelligence, but a large contribution from knowledge acquisition is also present.

BIBLIOGRAPHY

Ericsson, K. A., & Smith, J. (1991). Prospects and limits of the empirical study of expertise: An introduction. In K. A. Ericsson & J. Smith (Eds.), *Toward a general theory of expertise: Prospects and limits* (pp. 1–38). Cambridge: Cambridge University Press.

Eysenck, H. J. (1986). The theory of intelligence and the psychophysiology of cognition. In R. J. Sternberg (Ed.), *Advances in the psychology of human intelligence* (Vol. 3, pp. 1–34). Hillsdale, NJ: Erlbaum.

Feuerstein, R. (1980). *Instrumental enrichment: an intervention program for cognitive modifiability.* Baltimore: University Park Press.

Howe, M. J. A. (1990). *The origins of exceptional abilities.* Oxford: Basil Blackwell.

Perkins, D. N. (1981). *The mind's best work.* Cambridge, MA: Harvard University Press.

Plomin, R., & Daniels, D. (1987). Why are children in the same family so different from one another? *Behavioral and Brain Sciences, 10,* 1–60.

Simon, H. A. (1981). *The sciences of the artificial.* Cambridge, MA: MIT Press.

Kenneth J. Gilhooly

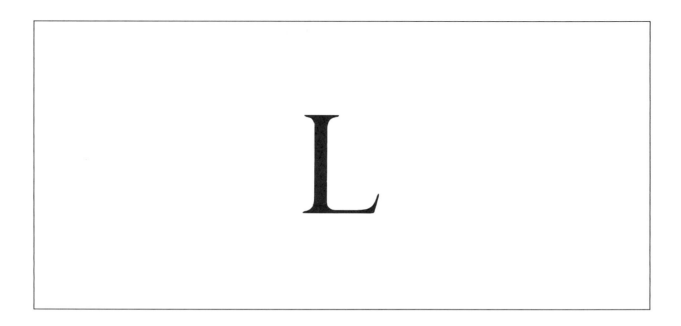

L

LANGUAGE AND INTELLIGENCE Language has traditionally played an important role in the definition and measurement of intelligent behavior. Verbal ability not only determines roughly half of an individual's intelligence quotient (IQ) but is also a strong predictor of nonverbal intelligence. The importance of verbal ability has been recognized both in formal theories of intelligence and in the implicit theories of intelligence held by everyday people (Sternberg et al., 1981). As discussed below, however, there are at least as many views on the relationship between language and intelligence as there are theories of intelligence.

DEFINING LANGUAGE AND INTELLIGENCE

To discuss the relationship between language and intelligence, one must first provide a working definition for these two constructs. In popular usage and among many theorists, the term *intelligence* has become virtually synonymous with *intelligence quotient*. Although the equation of the two has been increasingly disputed in recent years, almost no one would deny that IQ provides at least a partial measure of the attributes that constitute intelligence. Standardized tests of intelligence, such as the Wechsler Intelligence Scales and the Stanford-Binet, are designed to tap a set of primary factors or mental abilities, which typically in-

clude both verbal and nonverbal abilities (e.g., vocabulary, verbal comprehension, fluency, verbal and nonverbal memory, visual-spatial skills, and mathematical skills). Very often, an individual's performance on verbal and nonverbal IQ subtests is highly correlated. This finding has been interpreted by some researchers to support the existence of a "common underlying intellect" responsible for mediating all aspects of mental behavior, verbal and otherwise (Hunt, 1985; Jensen, 1981; Spearman, 1927; Sternberg, 1985). In other words, the reason that tasks as diverse as these are correlated is because they share a common ingredient known as GENERAL INTELLIGENCE, designated *g*.

Like intelligence, language is a multifaceted construct and can be defined in terms of its many subcomponents. Language subcomponents range from low-level, or rudimentary, processes, such as the ability to discriminate between speech and nonspeech sounds, to highly abstract rules of grammar. For the most part, linguists define language according to the following subcomponents: phonology, the sounds of speech; syntax, the grammar of a language; semantics, the meaning of individual words and sentences; and pragmatics, the social use of language (inferences, gestures, etc.). Each of these subcomponents measures a relatively discrete aspect of language knowledge. Together, they represent what it means to know a language.

THEORIES OF LANGUAGE
AND INTELLIGENCE

Because language and intelligence are both multi-faceted, theories on the relationship between the two depend largely on which particular subcomponents of each are being compared. Different theories of intelligence emphasize slightly different aspects of language performance.

Psychometric, or "factor theories," of intelligence are best represented by current IQ tests and place a great deal of emphasis on the role of "crystallized" verbal abilities (Spearman, 1927; Thurstone, 1938). Crystallized abilities represent a static type of knowledge, a knowledge of facts, heavily influenced by schooling and acculturation (Cattell, 1963). For example, an individual's vocabulary level and general world knowledge of the kind assessed on traditional IQ tests fall under the heading of crystallized abilities. Proponents of the psychometric approach justify their reliance on crystallized abilities by noting that performance on such tasks (e.g., vocabulary) is a strong predictor of overall IQ performance.

Critics of psychometric theories contend that the strong association between vocabulary and IQ is not surprising, given that both these measures are highly dependent on a third variable, namely academic training (Ceci, 1990). The strong association between academic success and IQ has led some researchers to challenge the validity of IQ tests and their ability to measure anything more than academic success (Ceci, 1990; Flynn, 1988). Ceci's (1990) BIOECOLOGICAL THEORY OF INTELLIGENCE and other contextualist theories contend that intelligence is context-dependent and can and should be defined in many different ways. For Ceci, the strong association between IQ, verbal ability, and academic training is epiphenomenal: Individuals with low verbal skills may possess the cognitive aptitude for advanced verbal abilities but lack the appropriate educational experience.

Some information-processing theories of intelligence attribute individual differences in intelligence to individual differences in neural functioning. These neural differences determine the speed and efficiency with which an individual can process sensory information, which in turn determine an individual's intellectual power, or g. In support of this theory,

information-processing studies of language frequently report that individuals with high verbal abilities respond faster to linguistic stimuli than do individuals with low verbal abilities. For example, R. A. Goldberg, S. Schwartz, and M. Stewart (1977) reported that "high verbal" individuals were faster than "low verbal" individuals in their ability to make same–different judgments about physical (*dear-dear*), homophonic (*dear-deer*), and semantic (*deer-elk*) properties of individual word pairs. High-verbal individuals were also better than low-verbal individuals in remembering the sequence of auditory speech sounds (e.g., *dae, bae*). For information-processing psychologists, these results support the notion that verbal ability is dependent on the speed with which an individual can access verbal information, but they are also consistent with an alternative explanation, namely, that individuals with good verbal skills simply require less time to process linguistic information.

R. J. Sternberg's (1985) TRIARCHIC THEORY OF INTELLIGENCE is one that places a great deal of emphasis on verbal behavior, and in particular, verbal behavior's strong dependence on novel problem-solving skills. The theory consists of three components: metacomponents, which represent the executive processes used in planning and developing strategies for how to go about solving a problem (recognizing what the problem is, allocating resources, interpreting feedback, etc.); performance components, skills used to carry out the task (encoding and decoding skills, memory, etc.); and knowledge-acquisition components, skills used in acquiring new information (deciding what information is meaningful and worth learning, selective encoding, etc.). For Sternberg, the interpretation of verbal analogies, metaphors, and inferences requires the capacity to solve problems in novel situations. For example, analogies (e.g., *lawyer:client::doctor:patient*) and inferences (e.g., *Bill is bigger than John; John is bigger than Tom; therefore, Bill is bigger/smaller than Tom?*) require the ability to derive structure or meaning from a given context and to apply this structure in a new setting. On a microlevel, this type of reasoning resembles the novel problem-solving behavior viewed by Sternberg as a hallmark of intelligent behavior. Likewise, Sternberg views vocabulary, a crystallized form of intelligence, as a good predictor of intelligence because vocabulary acquisition requires the ability to exploit contextual cues that facilitate learning (Sternberg & Powell, 1983; see also Keil, 1989; Werner & Kaplan, 1950). Consider the following sentence taken from a study by Sternberg in which high school students were asked to decipher the meaning of unknown words embedded within short paragraphs: "The mother, Tanith, peered at her son through the *oam* of the bubbling stew" (Sternberg & Powell, 1983).

Sternberg's research has shown that successful comprehension of verbal analogies, metaphors, novel vocabulary items, and the like depends in part on an individual's preexisting knowledge base. That is, the greater your vocabulary, the more successful your attempts to decipher the meanings of novel words. The notion that knowing more helps you learn more is the basic tenet of knowledge-based theories of intelligence (Chi, Glaser, & Rees, 1982). Having a preexisting knowledge base provides you with a context, a structure, in which to integrate new information. This in turn facilitates the encoding, storage, and retrieval of new information. For example, a stockbroker would be much more likely to remember a list of stock statistics than would someone who knows nothing about the stock market. On this view, knowledge or intelligence is considered domain-specific, in that you may know a lot about one topic but very little about another.

THE MODULARITY HYPOTHESIS

Each of the theories of intelligence discussed above places language within the context of general intelligence. Language is considered a by-product of general intelligence, and consequently, performance on any and all language tasks should be predicted on the basis of *g*. A very different view of intelligence and, consequently, the relationship between language and intelligence is taken by theories of "modularity." These theories claim the existence of multiple subcomponents of cognition, each neuroanatomically defined and capable of functioning relatively independently of each other (e.g., language versus spatial skills). For example, in the case of language, an individual's knowledge of language, the mechanisms used to process language, and the neural structures mediating language would represent a self-contained, functionally autonomous module.

This notion of modularity is reflected in Howard Gardner's theory of MUTLIPLE INTELLIGENCES (Gardner, 1983), which claims the existence of seven different components of intelligent behavior: linguistic, musical, logical-mathematical, spatial, bodily-kinesthetic, interpersonal, and intrapersonal forms of intelligence. On this view, an individual can be highly intelligent in one domain but not so intelligent in another domain.

Support for the independence of cognitive subcomponents comes from the study of brain damage and its ability to impair certain cognitive functions selectively, leaving other intact. Such dissociations are perhaps most obvious in instances of aphasia. *Aphasia* refers to a loss of speech and/or language functions resulting from damage to the left hemisphere of the brain. Studies of aphasic patients frequently reveal normal levels of nonverbal intelligence and a tendency for aphasic symptoms to be associated with damage to particular regions of the left hemisphere. Damage to regions of the brain located within the right hemisphere can selectively impair spatial aspects of cognition (e.g., block design, matrices), leaving language abilities intact (Young, 1983). Dissociations in verbal and nonverbal abilities such as these have provided perhaps the strongest evidence in favor of modularity and the strongest evidence against a theory of *g*.

MODULAR AND NONMODULAR THEORIES OF LANGUAGE DEVELOPMENT

A modular theory of language that has received considerable attention within the field of first-language acquisition is the theory of universal grammar put forth by the linguist Noam Chomsky (1986). According to Chomsky's theory, the mental representation of all languages can be defined in terms of an innate set of linguistic principles and parameters along which individual languages can vary. Because these principles and parameters are innate, the child brings to the language-learning task a means by which to parse incoming language information and eventually break the grammatical code of his or her language. For Chomsky, the acquisition of language is not viewed as dependent on general intelligence but is considered a predetermined biological event, a maturation of language abilities. Support for a biological unfolding of language is reflected in the high degree of regularity and predictability with which children of all cultures acquire language, despite vast differences in the language being acquired.

In contrast to Chomsky's claims for an innate set of language-learning principles is the notion that language develops within the larger context of general cognition (Bates, Bretherton, & Snyder, 1988; Piaget, 1962; see also the Piaget–Chomsky debate in Piattelli-Palmarini, 1980). This view is perhaps best represented by the developmental psychologist Jean PIAGET and his theory of intellectual development. According to Piaget, language is considered an outgrowth of more rudimentary forms of mental representation, as in the child's ability to conjure up mental images of objects and events. The emergence of certain language milestones is viewed as contingent on a prior mastery of "cognitive precursors."

In support of Piaget's theory of language development, several studies have noted parallels in the emergence of certain linguistic and cognitive milestones (Bates, Bretherton, & Snyder, 1988; Corrigan, 1979; Johnston, 1985). For example, conceptual development and the use of gesture have both been associated with the child's production of first words.

Other studies have failed to document the existence of "cognitive precursors" (Bates, Bretherton, & Snyder, 1988; Corrigan, 1979; Miller et al., 1980), and critics argue that a parallel emergence of language and cognition in no way justifies a causal relationship between the two (Piattelli-Palmarini, 1980).

Theories of language development operating within the knowledge-base tradition lie somewhere in between the claims of modular and antimodular theories. For example, theories of semantic development put forth by F. Keil (1989) and by E. Markman (1987) recognize the role of innate constraints on language learning but also emphasize the role that preexisting knowledge of semantic concepts and categories plays in determining verbal intelligence.

DISORDERED LANGUAGE DEVELOPMENT AND INTELLIGENCE

The debate over the modularity of language has also characterized the study of children who fail to develop language normally. Children with specific language impairment (SLI) are children who, by definition, are impaired in their language development, despite age-appropriate levels of social, intellectual, and sensory development (Rice, 1983).

In support of a modular explanation of SLI, several studies have documented selective deficits in the knowledge, representation, and processing of linguistic stimuli by SLI children. Other researchers have attributed the inferior language skills of SLI children to more global deficits in cognitive and perceptual abilities, including deficits in symbolic representation and other nonverbal aspects of cognition (see Rice, 1983, and references cited therein).

The study of children with early hemisphere damage has also been brought to bear on the modularity debate. If the development of language is dependent on general intelligence, then we would predict delays in language following early brain injury to mirror delays in intellectual development. Contrary to this expectation, several studies of children with left- or right-hemisphere damage have revealed more selective deficits in language and nonlinguistic abilities (Aram, 1991; Aram & Eisele, 1992, for a review). In many cases, children with focal brain injury go on to achieve normal and even above-normal levels of intellectual performance, despite subtle deficits in vocabulary, naming, comprehending and producing complex syntax, and judging inferences of truth.

A final argument in support of the modularity of language comes from a group of children with the genetic disorder known as Williams' syndrome. Language abilities in children with Williams' syndrome are uniquely spared, despite the fact that these children typically possess IQs of 40–60 points and present with significant visual-spatial deficits (Bellugi et al., 1988).

In summary, modular and nonmodular theories of intelligence posit two very different views on the relationship between language and intelligence. In support of theories of intelligence that posit the existence of g, most literate individuals do exhibit a great deal of overlap in their verbal and nonverbal abilities. Where theories of general intelligence fail is in their ability to account for the dissociations of language and intelligence frequently observed in neurologically, developmentally, and genetically impaired populations. Knowledge-based theories can account for disparities between language and other cognitive skills in neurologically intact individuals by positing the domain-specificity of knowledge and intelligence.

As shown, attempts to define the relationship between language and intelligence depend largely on how these two constructs are measured. Language and intelligence are both highly complex, multifaceted constructs that can be measured and compared in an infinite number of ways. Standardized IQ and verbal tests succeed in capturing only a fraction of this complexity.

BIBLIOGRAPHY

ARAM, D. (1991). Acquired aphasia in children. In M. Sarno (Ed.), *Acquired aphasia* (2nd ed.). San Diego: Academic Press.

ARAM, D., & EISELE, J. (1992). Plasticity and recovery of higher cortical functions following early brain injury. In I. Rapin & S. J. Segalowitz (Eds.), *Handbook of neuropsychology: Vol. 6. Child neuropsychology* (pp. 73–92). New York: Elsevier.

BATES, E.; BRETHERTON, I.; & SNYDER, L. (1988). *From First Words to Grammar*. Melbourne, Australia: Press Syndicate of the University of Cambridge.

BELLUGI, U.; MARKS, S.; BIHRLE, A. M.; & SABO, H. (1988). Dissociation between language and cognitive functions in Williams Syndrome. In D. Bishop & K. Mogford (Eds.), *Language development in exceptional circumstances* (pp. 177–189). London: Churchill.

CATTELL, R. B. (1963). Theory of fluid and crystallized intelligence: A critical experiment. *Journal of Educational Psychology, 54,* 1–22.

CECI, S. J. (1990). *On intelligence . . . more or less. A bioecological treatise on intellectual development.* Englewood Cliffs, NJ: Prentice-Hall.

CHI, M.; GLASER, R.; & REES, E. (1982). Expertise in problem solving. In R. Sternberg (Ed.), *Advances in the Psychology of Human Intelligence* (Vol. 1). Hillsdale, NJ: Erlbaum.

CHOMSKY, N. (1986). *Knowledge of language: Its origin, nature, and use.* New York: Praeger.

CORRIGAN, R. (1979). Cognitive correlates of language: Differential criteria yield differential results. *Child Development, 50,* 617–631.

FLYNN, J. R. (1988). The ontology of intelligence. In J. Forge (Ed.), *Measurement, realism, and objectivity* (pp. 1–40). Dordrecht, Netherlands: D. Reidel.

GARDNER, H. (1983). *Frames of mind: The theory of multiple intelligences.* New York: Basic Books.

GOLDBERG, R. A.; SCHWARTZ, S.; & STEWART, M. (1977). Individual differences in cognitive processes. *Journal of Educational Psychology, 69,* 9–14.

GUILFORD, J. P. (1967). *The nature of human intelligence.* New York: McGraw-Hill.

HUNT, E. (1985). Verbal Ability. In R. J. Sternberg (Ed.), *Human abilities: An information-processing approach.* San Francisco: W. H. Freeman.

HUNT, E.; LUNNEBORG, C.; & LEWIS, J. (1975). What does it mean to be high verbal? *Cognitive Psychology, 7,* 449–474.

JENSEN, A. R. (1981). *Straight talk about mental tests.* New York: Free Press.

JOHNSTON, J. R. (1985). Cognitive prerequisites: The evidence from children acquiring English. In D. I. Slobin (Ed.), *The cross-linguistic study of language acquisition.* Hillsdale, NJ: Erlbaum.

KEIL, F. (1989). *Concepts, kinds, and cognitive development.* Cambridge, MA: MIT Press.

MARKMAN, E. (1987). How children constrain the possible meanings of words. In U. Neisser (Ed.), *Concepts and Conceptual Development.* Cambridge: Cambridge University Press.

MILLER, J. F.; CHAPMAN, R. S.; BRANSTON, M. B.; & REICHLE, J. (1980). Language comprehension in sensorimotor stages V and VI. *Journal of Speech and Hearing Research, 23,* 284–311.

PIAGET, J. (1962). *Play, dreams, and imitation in childhood.* New York: Norton.

PIATTELLI-PALMARINI, M. (ED.). (1980). *Language and learning: The debate between Jean Piaget and Noam Chomsky.* Cambridge, MA: Harvard University Press.

RICE, M. L. (1983). Contemporary accounts of the cognition/language relationship: Implications for speech-language clinicians. *Journal of Speech and Hearing Disorders, 48,* 347–359.

SPEARMAN, C. (1927). *The abilities of man.* New York: Macmillan.

STERNBERG, R. J. (1985). *Beyond IQ: A triarchic framework for intelligence.* New York: Springer-Verlag.

STERNBERG, R. J.; CONWAY, B.; KETRON, J.; & BERNSTEIN, M. (1981). People's conceptions about intelligence. *Journal of Personality and Social Psychology, 41,* 37–55.

STERNBERG, R. J., & POWELL, J. S. (1983). Comprehending verbal comprehension. *American Psychologist, 38,* 878–893.

THURSTONE, L. L. (1938). *Primary mental abilities.* Chicago: University of Chicago Press.

WERNER, H., & KAPLAN, E. (1950). Development of word

meaning through verbal context: An experimental study. *Journal of Psychology, 29,* 251–257.

YOUNG, A. W. (ED.). (1983). *Functions of the right cerebral hemisphere.* London: Academic Press.

JULIE A. EISELE
DOROTHY M. ARAM

LATENT TRAIT THEORY

LATENT TRAIT THEORY   Latent trait theory, better known as item response theory (IRT), provides a psychometric basis for measuring individuals. The number of correct responses has no direct meaning without a psychometric model for several reasons. First, the specific items on a test are not a criterion for ability. Ability is a latent quality that is manifested in many different items or tasks, which vary in both difficulty level and quality. Second, the optimal combination of responses to estimate a person's ability may not be the simple sum. Third, the distances between total scores may not have the same meaning at different levels. A psychometric model specifies how performance on a specific set of items is related to ability.

Latent trait theory is a replacement for what is referred to as "classical" test theory (Gulliksen, 1950). IRT provides solutions to problems that arise in classical test theory. Furthermore, IRT permits a greater link than classical test theory between substantive theory and a measurement model.

Latent trait theory is often traced to F. M. Lord's 1952 monograph on item regressions and G. Rasch's 1960 book on the means by which the application of his model leads to some optimal measurement properties. Latent trait theory became influential internationally with the publication of books by Lord and M. R. Novick (1968) and G. H. Fischer (1974). IRT has been applied to many types of tests, especially aptitude and achievement tests, and is becoming increasingly commonplace in test development.

THE ADVANTAGES OF IRT OVER CLASSICAL TEST THEORY

A psychometric rationale provides several indices, including estimates of ability, item-difficulty level, and item quality. In classical test theory, the person indices are based on the number of correct responses. The total scores are linearly transformed to a standard score, which indicates position in relevant population of persons. The index for item difficulty is the p-value, which is the proportion correct. The index for item quality is item discrimination, which is the correlation between solving the item and total score on the test.

Unlike IRT, classical test theory is limited in achieving three important psychometric properties: (1) the indices for persons and items (i.e., parameters) are invariable; (2) ability is measured on an interval scale; and (3) persons and items are located on a common scale. In contrast, if the assumptions are met, IRT models do achieve these properties. The meaning of these properties and the limitations of classical test theory for obtaining them will now be considered.

The first property, invariable person and item indices, is fundamental to objective measurement. It means that the ability index for the person will not be biased by the specific items that happen to appear on the test. Further, the indices for the level and quality of an item for estimating ability will not be biased by the specific people who take the test.

Unfortunately, the classical-person index, total test score, depends on the items that appear on the test. Item level and quality influences total score levels. This bias is adjusted in classical test theory, however, by standardizing total scores to represent location on a normal distribution. A worse problem is that item difficulties and discriminations also influence the distances between persons, which determine the accuracy with which differences between them can be detected. For example, the score distances between high-ability persons is greater when the test has more difficult items. Conversely, the distances between low-ability persons is greater when the test has easy items.

Classical test theory does not resolve the distance problem adequately. Requiring parallel forms (equated for item level and quality) to compare scores across tests assures that the two tests scale distances between persons in the same way. What is not assured is that ability distances are comparable to the various levels within the test. That assurance requires an adaptive test such that items of optimal difficulty are selected for each person. Classical test theory has no way of equating tests, however, with different difficulty levels. Ruling out adaptive testing is also a disadvantage for intelligence research, especially if many tests are administered. Adaptive testing permits reliable measurements to be obtained from shorter testing sessions.

Classical test theory item indices are also biased. R. K. Hambleton and colleagues (1991) demonstrate clearly how both the level and distribution of item difficulty (p-values), as well as item discriminations, depend on ability levels in the population that is tested. Population-dependent item indices not only create many practical problems in test development but also confound results from cognitive studies that model item difficulty from task features. That is, the relationships between task features and item difficulty will be biased by the distances between the p-values in the particular population that is studied.

The second property, measuring ability on an interval level, also is not achieved in analyses based on classical test theory. An interval scale is obtained when the score distances between persons have equal meaning for ability differences. Because classical test theory does not provide person indices that are invariant across tests, the scores may provide only information about rank order. In turn, the ordinal nature of the classical test scores biases comparisons of differences between both persons and groups. For example, studies on cognitive growth can be misleading if intelligence is not measured on an interval scale. The difference in cognitive ability between say, six- and seven-year-olds can appear larger, equal to, or smaller than the difference between nine- and ten-year-olds, depending on the difficulty level of the items in the test.

The third property, placing items and persons on a common scale, also is not achieved in classical test theory. The classic model of a test score, as the sum of true score and error, does not include item parameters. Therefore, item p-values are not linked numerically to ability. This is a disadvantage for intelligence research, particularly developmental studies. For example, although ability levels can be compared between various ages or between different groups, theoretical interpretations about changes in the tasks or problems that can be solved cannot be made directly.

In contrast, IRT models do place items and persons on a common scale. Substantive theories of intelligence

or development are more readily incorporated into the IRT measurement model in several ways. First, abilities and ability changes may be linked to changes in item performance because the items that correspond to a particular ability level may be identified. Developmental or lifespan changes in ability levels, for example, could be referenced to the different tasks that correspond to the means on the two measurement occasions. Second, substantive theories of the ability test (e.g., as concerns the processes, strategies, knowledge structures that are used to solve items) can be incorporated directly into several more specialized IRT models (see Embretson, 1985) if the item features that influence processing difficulty can be discerned. Then, the cognitive demands of items can be estimated in the context of the IRT model, which in turn, also can provide a systematic basis for item and test design (Embretson, 1985).

MEASUREMENT THEORY: CLASSICAL TEST THEORY VERSUS IRT

Giving meaning to a test score involves specifying a comparison. For any comparison to be made, two specifications are necessary: the standard to which the score is to be compared, and the numerical basis of the comparison (order, difference, ratio). When the evidence indicates that the properties of common-scale, interval-level measurement and invariant properties obtain, the advantages of IRT over the classical approach stem from these two specifications.

First, unlike IRT, classical test theory specifies comparisons with other scores as the standard for score meaning (i.e., other persons, other occasions, other tests). Most often, a comparison with other persons provides the meaning for a classical test score. Nonetheless, how well a person does in comparison with others (or with other occasions or other tests) does not indicate how well the person masters the tasks of a test. Specifying the changes in percentage of items passed, as in criterion-referenced scores, offers little improvement because item-difficulty level is arbitrary in an ability test; the specific test items are a subset of the many tasks that could measure ability. Rather, interpretability requires an internal structure of the tasks by difficulty; therefore, scores may be understood by the type of items that are mastered.

In contrast, IRT scaling provides a basis for ordering persons in accordance with level of ability because persons are compared to items. The difference between a person's ability and the difficulty of an item determines the probability of success the person has on the item. For example, with a simple IRT model (i.e., the Rasch model), when the scale value of a person exceeds the scale value of an item, the corresponding probability of success is higher than .5. When the scale value of the person is lower, then the probability of success is lower than .5. When the two scale values are equal, the probability of success equals .5. In the latter case, the item corresponds to the ability level, analogous to a psychophysical scale in which a stimulus is at the threshold value. Because persons and items are located on the same scale, persons can still be compared with each other also, as in the classical approach.

Second, unlike IRT, the decision on the numerical basis of score comparisons is arbitrary in the classical approach. No clear rationale exists for which numerical aspects of a test score generalize to the underlying dimension that is measured. That is, no way exists to derive empirically or evaluate the form of the function(s) connecting the latent variable (ability) with the manifest variable (the test score). One approach is to assume only that the functions are monotonically increasing (or decreasing), meaning that scores merely order people by ability level. However, if the scores are to be compared for differences or statistics are to be computed that require meaningful score differences (such as the mean and standard deviation), then a strong assumption is required. Typically, a linear function is assumed arbitrarily, implying that one can also trust the order and the differences between scores.

The IRT solution to the numerical basis of scores uses the principle of additive decomposition, a major aspect of fundamental measurement. For test data, an index of accuracy level is decomposed; the choice of the accuracy index depends on the score comparisons that are desired (e.g., differences) and certain practical considerations. In the most simple model, the Rasch model, the natural logarithm of the odds for solving each item is decomposed. The odds are that the probability of success is divided by the probability of failure; therefore $\text{Log Odds}_{\text{item 1}} = \text{Ln}(\text{Prob}_{\text{success}}/$

$\text{Prob}_{\text{failure}})$. The log odds is postulated to equal the difference between ability and item difficult; therefore, $\text{Log Odds}_{\text{item 1}} = \text{Ability–Item Difficulty}$. This term is called the *logit*. Successful scaling of ability and item difficulty has been obtained when item responses for a test are well predicted by the model. This evidence thus supports the hypothesis of additive decomposition.

Thus, the logit is useful for additive decomposition because it fulfills the condition of increasing and decreasing directly with ability. The logit provides the common scale for items and abilities. In this model, when ability equals item difficulty, the logit, of course, is zero. This situation results when the odds equal 1.0, which in turn happens only when the probability of success is .50, analogous to a psychophysical threshold value. Positive and negative logits mean that probabilities of success that are higher and lower than .5 respectively. This simple difference scale has the desirable property of defining equal distances with an absolute meaning for the accuracy level index. No transformation of either ability or item difficulty is permitted that would change the difference scale because the associated log odds and probabilities would change. Thus, the empirical fit of the test data to the model would change.

The three desirable features of measurement—common-scale measurement of persons and items, interval scale for abilities and invariant indices—follow from the difference model. Ability and item difficulty are measured on a common scale because changing either by the same amount has the same effect on the log odds. That is, increasing ability or decreasing item difficulty by the same amount has the same impact on log odds. The interval scale properties also follow from the model. Equal differences between pairs of abilities have the same meaning for accuracy level. For any two abilities that differ by some value, the log odds for solving an item also differ by that same value. Lastly, the invariance of the item and person parameters can also be shown as a consequence of the model in a similar way. For example, that abilities do not depend on item difficulty can be shown. The same difference log odds will be given regardless of the difficulty of the item. Conversely, the same difference in log odds between two different items will be given regardless of the person on which they are compared.

The additive decomposition idea can also be further employed to analyze the abilities into parts, each referring to a different underlying dimension, and to analyze the item difficulties into parts, each referring to the contribution from a different item stimulus feature. This further extension of additive decomposition permits both multidimensional models of the traits to be formulated and mathematical models of item difficulty to be incorporated into the model. The former property is crucial for change measurement, and the latter is crucial for incorporating substantive aspects of items and tasks into test interpretations and test design (see Embretson, 1985, 1991).

CONCLUSION

IRT models offer many desirable properties for intelligence research. Nonetheless, caveats should be given. First, the models must fit the data. If the Rasch model does not fit, then a more complex IRT model such as the two-parameter or three-parameter logistic model may prove suitable. If these do not fit, then yet more complex models, such as multidimensional IRT models, may be applied. Second, the more complex the IRT model, the larger is the required sample size to obtain useful item calibrations. The three-parameter logistic model, which contains item discrimination and guessing parameters, may require as many as 1,000 persons to obtain stable results. In contrast, useful results may be obtained from the simple Rasch model with as few as 150 persons. Although special item selection may be required for test data to fit the Rasch model, the classical test theory has operated as if the Rasch model were true. Classical test scores, like the Rasch model, weight items equally. In the more complex models, such as the three-parameter logistic, items are weighted by a discrimination index, which indicates item quality. Thus, fitting the Rasch model may require some extra effort, but the model is consistent with implicit classical beliefs about item equality and further affords the many advantages of IRT without prohibitively large sample sizes.

BIBLIOGRAPHY

EMBRETSON, S. E. (1985). *Test design: Developments in psychology and psychometrics.* New York, NY: Academic Press.

EMBRETSON, S. E. (1991). A multidimensional latent trait model for measuring learning and change. *Psychometrika, 56,* 495–516.

FISCHER, G. H. (1974). Einführung in die Theorie psychologischer Tests. Bern: Hans Huber.

GULLIKSEN, H. (1950). *Theory of mental tests.* New York: Wiley.

HAMBLETON, R. K., SWAMINATHAN, H., & ROGERS, H. J. (1991). *Fundamentals of item response theory.* Newbury Park, CA: Sage.

LORD, F. M. (1952). *A theory of test scores.* (Psychometric Monograph No. 7). Iowa City, IA: The Psychometric Society.

LORD, F. M., & NOVICK, M. R. (1968). Statistical theories of mental test scores. Reading, MA: Addison-Wesley.

RASCH, G. (1960). *Probabilistic models for some intelligence and attainment tests.* Copenhagen: Danish Institute for Educational Research.

SUSAN EMBRETSON
PAUL DEBOECK

LATERALIZATION   *See* BRAIN; LOCALIZATION OF BRAIN FUNCTION.

LEARNING DISABILITY   Learning disability refers to a subset of instances in which individuals cannot master skills important in school success, such as reading, spelling, mathematics, communication, or social skills. The term *learning disability* cannot be equated with poor academic performance, or with the broader term, *learning disorder.* Many children perform poorly in school but do not have either a learning disorder or a learning disability; for example, depending on age and grade of entry, children whose native language is not English may not perform well in U.S. schools, although their ability to learn is not impaired. Many children who have academic difficulty do, however, have a learning disorder—such as mental retardation, autism, brain injury, or a specific learning disability. The term learning disorder includes any condition in which the individual's ability to learn is impaired, whether that condition occurred before or after birth.

Within the broad range of learning disorders, learning disability specifies a subset of situations in which individuals have poor academic skills—in spite of substantially higher intellectual ability—when the academic difficulty is not due to visual, hearing, or motor handicaps; mental retardation; emotional disturbance; or environmental, cultural, or economic disadvantage. This definition comes, not primarily from psychological, educational, and medical knowledge, but from the definition of the concept in federal law (Public Law 94–142 and its update, PL 101–476). This legal definition of learning disability has been criticized as vague and hard to implement; no generally accepted scientific definition exists that might replace it, however. Scientific controversy rages over most elements of the federal definition, including whether a discrepancy between intellectual ability and academic achievement is necessary to consider an individual learning disabled (Pennington, 1991).

Federal law charges school districts with interpreting the definition; as a result, from state to state, there are large differences in the way children are identified as learning disabled. Some states identify nearly five times as many students as learning disabled as do other states (Reynolds, 1990). Estimates of what percentage of the population has a learning disability (prevalence) depend, therefore, on how one defines learning disability (Barkley, 1990); estimates of prevalence are as low as 5 percent and as high as 20 to 30 percent. Estimates of prevalence in special populations, such as children with ATTENTION DEFICIT HYPERACTIVITY DISORDER (Barkley, 1990) or diagnosed emotional disturbance (Greenblatt, Mattis, & Trad, 1990), are higher than estimates of prevalence in normal populations. The technical problems in identifying individuals as learning disabled center on defining what a "severe discrepancy" between intellectual ability and academic achievement is and how to measure this (Reynolds, 1990).

Experts have urged that learning disabilities in children be identified as early as possible, technical problems notwithstanding, to reduce their immediate and long-term effects (Satz & Fletcher, 1988). In addition to academic problems, many children develop secondary emotional and behavioral problems. Reading and learning disabilities are the major single cause of school dropouts in our educational system. Learning disabilities afflict many children who are referred to clinics and juvenile courts. The federal definition of learning disability is a stumbling block to early identification, however, in that students must fall behind in their academic skills before they can be identified. Some experts have argued for the development of early screening batteries, to be used with every child in kindergarten or earlier, so that children at risk for academic failure could receive full assessment and early intervention (Satz & Fletcher, 1988).

TYPES OF LEARNING DISABILITY

A number of typologies of learning disability have been proposed, based on empirical studies, theoretical understanding of brain function, clinical experience, or all three (Feagans, Short, & Meltzer, 1991; Rourke, 1985). Many theoretical and methodological problems stand in the way of developing a definitive typology; for example, definitions differ across studies, as do methods of measuring intellectual ability, academic success, and the discrepancy between the two. A major reason that we should understand what subtypes may exist is that individuals with different types of learning disability may benefit from different methods of instruction.

Experts agree that those whose primary problem is learning to read and to spell have a different kind of learning disability than do those whose primary problem is learning arithmetic or mastering handwriting. Technical terms for reading and spelling problems are *reading disability, verbal learning disability,* or *dyslexia.* There is less agreement, however, on subtypes that may exist within this large group of learning-disabled individuals. The terms often used for problems with arithmetic and handwriting are *nonverbal learning disability* and *right hemisphere learning disability.*

Dyslexia or Verbal Learning Disability. The primary characteristics of dyslexia are unexpected difficulty in learning to read or spell. The best-supported explanation of dyslexia holds that underlying these characteristics is difficulty with language-processing skills that enable children to learn and to use the rules of phonics (recognizing and using sound values of letters, letter groups, and syllables to pronounce words). Children must be able to engage in *phonological coding,* as well, to decode printed letters into blended sounds.

For efficient reading, phonological coding must be effortless; even good readers rely on this strategy—and not primarily on recognizing words by sight—to decode written language.

Dyslexic children are deficient in phonological coding and thus have difficulty in learning to read. Slow, halting, labored oral reading exposes this condition. Some may also have had disorders of articulation as younger children (in which speech sounds are mispronounced), because of difficulty with phonological coding. Underlying this difficulty, we have found, is a deficit in *phoneme segmentation skills* (the ability to recognize phonemes, or individual sounds, in spoken words) (Pennington, 1991).

Several lines of evidence bear on the causes of dyslexia. Phonological coding and phoneme segmentation are now known to be heritable skills (Pennington, 1991). Electroencephalograph (EEG), evoked potentials, and positron emission tomography (PET) brain scans show that the way the left hemisphere of the brain functions is different in dyslexics than in normal individuals. Autopsy and magnetic resonance imaging (MRI) studies have revealed that in normal readers, the planum temporale (a portion of the surface area of the brain's temporal lobe) is larger in the left hemisphere than in the right hemisphere; in dyslexics, however, these two areas are the same size. The left-hemisphere planum temporale subserves processing abilities such as phonological coding and phoneme segmentation.

Dyslexia is three or four times as common in boys as it is in girls. Recent research suggests the reasons for this difference are biological.

Identification and Treatment of Dyslexia. According to federal law (PL 94–142), children must be identified as learning disabled by a multidisciplinary team to receive special education services in the public school system. Assessment by a psychologist as a member of the team is necessary to make the diagnosis; tests used must include a measure of intellectual ability, such as the Wechsler Intelligence Scale for Children-Third Edition (WISC-III) and a battery of individual achievement tests that help assess word identification, reading comprehension, spelling and phonetic skills, as well as mathematics and written language. Most psychological assessment approaches to identifying dyslexic children look for a significant discrepancy between general intellectual ability and ability in reading and spelling skills. Often, but not always, dyslexic children perform better on nonlanguage tasks than on language tasks when tests measure intellectual ability. Such children display poor reading skills, including an inadequate understanding of phonics, as compared with their performances in other achievement areas.

Many treatment programs for dyslexia have been advocated, but few have demonstrated any effectiveness. Some experts now agree that dyslexic children must be taught to read using a phonics-based approach (learning to read words by sounding them out). Individual tutoring is advisable, but not by parents. Pennington (1991) discusses this in detail.

In addition to treating the specific, school-related deficits that define learning disability, it often is important to treat the dyslexic child's emotional or behavioral problems, whether caused by or a cause of the disability.

Right Hemisphere or Nonverbal Learning Disability. Individuals who manifest this type of learning disability show poor skills in mathematics, handwriting, or social cognition (understanding). Individuals with difficulties in all three areas have been described by Rourke (1989) as having a nonverbal learning disability. Other researchers see these three types of difficulties as separable, though related, because of their likely origin in right-brain-hemisphere dysfunction (Pennington, 1991).

The prevalence of nonverbal learning disabilities has been estimated to be from 1 percent to 10 percent of learning-disabled individuals, or from 0.1 percent to 1.0 percent of the total population, and is thus much lower than the prevalence of dyslexia. Unlike dyslexia, the sex ratio of individuals with nonverbal learning disabilities has been estimated to be even, 1:1. There is some evidence that a nonverbal learning disability characterizes females with either the Turner syndrome or the fragile X types of genetic disorder; but little else is known about possible genetic or environmental causes. Nonverbal learning disabilities have been reported to occur as a result of complications at birth, seizure disorders, closed head injury early in development, cranial radiation, unsuccessfully treated hydrocephalus, and congenital absence of the corpus callosum.

The main learning problem that individuals with nonverbal learning disabilities have is with mathematics. This is because of their poor concept-formation skills, thought to be related to a deficit in spatial cognition (a right hemisphere ability). Visuospatial deficits in the brain have also been linked to poor handwriting. Dyslexic children (who presumably have left-brain-hemisphere dysfunction) may perform poorly in mathematics because of their inability to memorize basic math facts or to read and understand word problems; reading and memorizing written material are strengths for children with a nonverbal learning disability, however. Instead, these children make reasoning errors in math problems, often by failing to see how to "set up" the problem in their minds. In arithmetic, they do not understand "place value" (i.e., the place of a numeral determines whether its value is in ones, tens, hundreds, etc.); their poor handwriting and poor spatial organization also produce messy, illegible written work, which in turn makes correct computations difficult.

Because the reading level is normal, children with nonverbal learning disabilities may be identified as learning disabled later than is the dyslexic child. Nevertheless, they may display some problems early in development, such as poor coordination; dislike of puzzles, art, and building things; and slow, effortful, disjointed handwriting. Because children with these problems may do adequately in school until written work becomes important, they may be perceived as merely uncooperative (rather than as learning disabled) when they first begin to have great difficulty completing written work.

Identification and Treatment of Nonverbal Learning Disability. A psychological assessment approach using a test battery similar to that described for dyslexia is needed to identify nonverbal learning disabilities. Children with nonverbal learning disabilities show different patterns of performance on standard intelligence and achievement tests than do dyslexic children. Usually, on tests of intellectual functioning, children with nonverbal learning disabilities display better language skills than visuospatial skills or visuomotor skills, along with selective difficulty on mathematics achievement tests or samples of handwriting. The preferred treatment of a specific handwriting disability is to teach the child to type and to allow more time to complete written work. The treatment of a specific math disability depends on whether the source of the child's difficulty is spatial reasoning (in which case, teach place value; use graph paper to align problems; estimate and check answers), or executive (integrative) functioning (in which case, teach planning and organization skills; step-by-step reasoning and learning strategies). Children with difficulty in executive functioning that impairs their math performance will likely need help with other tasks that require organization as well (such as writing down homework assignments; getting homework turned in).

In addition to treating the school-related deficits that define learning disability, it is important to treat the emotional or behavioral problems that learning-disabled children may have.

SECONDARY SYMPTOMS: EMOTIONAL AND BEHAVIORAL PROBLEMS

Learning-disabled children are more likely than other children to have emotional or behavioral problems. In fact, the rate of socioemotional or behavioral disturbances reported in some samples of learning-disabled children is 50 percent (Rourke, 1988a) or even higher (Spreen, 1989). The *Diagnostic and Statistical Manual of Mental Disorders, Third Edition, Revised* (DSM-III-R), used by psychologists and others, states that a common complication of a learning disability is *conduct disorder* (severe antisocial behavior disturbance). Also, children with conduct disorders, attention deficit disorders, or involvement with the juvenile justice system are more likely to be learning disabled than are normal children. Children with learning disabilities are apt to have emotional or behavioral problems because the deficits they have in processing information make social adjustment more difficult; the experience of academic failure places children at risk for subsequent poor motivation, for peer rejection, and for behavioral problems. By no means do all learning-disabled children have behavioral or emotional problems (Rourke, 1988a), and not all children with a conduct disorder have a learning disability, although many fail in school. School failure may result from noncompliance, a negative attitude, and poor social skills, as well as from a learning disability (Patterson, Reid, & Dishion, 1992).

It may seem obvious that learning-disabled children should and do have high rates of behavioral and emotional disturbance, but the reasons are not well understood. One theory is that the experience of having a learning disability causes emotional and behavioral problems because of school failure and frustration, but this does not explain why some studies indicate behavior problems may develop before school age (Spreen, 1989). Another theory is that emotional and behavioral problems cause learning disability, but this does not explain why approximately 50 percent of all children with a learning disability do not have emotional or behavioral problems. A third theory suggests that both learning disabilities and behavioral and emotional disturbances are caused by a third factor— namely, some type of dysfunction in the brain itself. Spreen (1989) has concluded that this third theory is attractive but oversimplified.

Many studies have grouped all learning-disabled children together, instead of separating them by subtype; this strategy obscures emotional and behavioral problems that may be specific to the different subtypes (Rourke, 1988a). Yet the lack of agreement about learning disability subtypes, and the many methods of identifying them, prevent researchers from reaching precise conclusions (Spreen, 1989).

Rourke (1988b, 1989) has described the Nonverbal Learning Disability syndrome as including a particular set of psychological problems. Young children with this syndrome may have behavior disorders, but later are more likely to have psychological problems that may "internalize" (express inwardly), such as by depression, anxiety, and social withdrawal. According to Rourke, these problems are related to the social and adaptive deficits that characterize the disorder, including difficulty adapting to new or complex situations, deficits in understanding and evaluating social situations, and poor ability to interact with others. Other experts question whether these deficits in social cognition and social functioning always accompany the nonverbal learning disability (Pennington, 1991). Spreen (1989) reported a slight tendency for dyslexic children to show more depression, whereas children with math disability showed more behavior problems. Except for the small group described by Rourke, relationships between type of learning disability and the type of emotional or behavioral disturbance remain unclear.

Evidence suggests that when a conduct disorder has developed, treatment of academic problems alone is not sufficient to correct the conduct disorder (Patterson, Reid, & Dishion, 1992). Some comprehensive early interventions, however, with family and academic components designed to prevent academic problems (in children at risk for school failure, but who may not have had learning disabilities) have had the unexpected benefit of reducing the rate at which conduct disorders develop (Zigler, Taussig, & Black, 1992). Children with learning disabilities who also have behavioral or emotional problems need appropriate psychological counseling or therapy accompanying any educational intervention.

(See also: MENTAL RETARDATION, CULTURAL-FAMILIAL; MENTAL RETARDATION, ORGANIC.)

BIBLIOGRAPHY

AMERICAN PSYCHIATRIC ASSOCIATION. (1987). *Diagnostic and statistical manual of mental disorders* (3rd ed., rev.). Washington, DC: APA.

BARKLEY, RUSSELL A. (1990). *Attention-deficit hyperactivity disorder: A handbook for diagnosis and treatment.* New York: Guilford Press.

FEAGANS, L. V., SHORT, E. J., & MELTZER, L. (Eds.). (1991). *Subtypes of learning disabilities: Theoretical perspectives and research.* Hillsdale, NJ: Erlbaum.

GREENBLATT, E., MATTIS, S., & TRAD, P. V. (1990). Nature and prevalence of learning disabilities in a child psychiatric population. *Developmental Neuropsychology, 6*(2), 71–83.

PATTERSON, G. R., REID, J. B., & DISHION, T. J. (1992). *Antisocial boys.* Eugene, OR: Castalia Press.

PENNINGTON, B. F. (1991). *Diagnosing learning disorders: A neuropsychological framework.* New York: Guilford Press.

REYNOLDS, C. R. (1990). Conceptual and technical problems in learning disability diagnosis. In Reynolds, C. R., & Kamphaus, R. W. (Eds.), *Handbook of psychological and educational assessment of children: Intelligence and achievement.* New York: Guilford Press.

ROURKE, B. P. (Ed.). (1985). *Neuropsychology of learning disabilities: Essentials of subtype analysis.* New York: Guilford Press.

Rourke, B. P. (1988a). Socioemotional disturbances of learning disabled children. *Journal of Consulting and Clinical Psychology, 56*(6), 801–810.

Rourke, B. P. (1988b). The syndrome of nonverbal learning disabilities: Developmental manifestations in neurological disease, disorder, and dysfunction. *The Clinical Neuropsychologist, 2*(4), 293–330.

Rourke, B. P. (1989). *Nonverbal learning disabilities: The syndrome and the model.* New York: Guilford Press.

Satz, P., & Fletcher, J. M. (1988). Early identification of learning disabled children: An old problem revisited. *Journal of Consulting and Clinical Psychology, 56,* 824–829.

Spreen, O. (1989). The relationship between learning disability, emotional disorders, and neuropsychology: Some results and observations. *Journal of Clinical and Experimental Neuropsychology, 11*(1), 117–140.

Zigler, E., Taussig, C., & Black, K. (1992). Early childhood intervention: A promising preventative for juvenile delinquency. *American Psychologist, 47*(8), 997–1006.

ANTONIA A. FORSTER

LEARNING AND INTELLIGENCE People say they have learned when as a result of study or experience they know things they did not know before or can do things they could not do before.

As R. J. Sternberg (1990) observed, the idea that learning relates to intelligence appeared in the writings of ancient philosophers. To elaborate his views of intelligence, Plato drew the metaphor of a block of wax in the mind on which learning is etched. According to Plato's metaphor, different men's blocks have different sizes, hardness, moistness, and purity, and a mind learns and remembers easily only when its wax is pure, clear, and deep.

In modern times, the question of how learning relates to intelligence has been taken up by psychologists, who have offered three hypotheses. One hypothesis, embraced avidly during the early 1900s, was that intelligence *is* learning. This hypothesis is seldom heard today, in part because many laboratory studies failed to find a relationship between learning and intelligence, which they must if the two are the same, unless the studies should have been done differently. J. C. Campione, A. L. Brown, and R. A. Ferrara (1982) noted that researchers who studied learning and intelligence had students practice (but did not teach or reward them) trivial tasks requiring no new skill or knowledge; the students' performance did not improve, as it would have if they had learned. In other words, research relating intelligence to learning had nothing to do with learning.

Campione, Brown, and Ferrara argued that different kinds of experiments are needed to see whether intelligence relates to learning. They hypothesized that people with greater intelligence would learn more and faster in experiments and schools that directly teach new knowledge and procedures required by cognitively demanding activities. Their argument was convincingly affirmed only in the 1990s (Ferretti & Butterfield, 1992).

A second hypothesis of modern psychologists is that intelligence depends on many ways of thinking and processing information, and those ways of thinking and processing are learned (Brown & French, 1979; Butterfield, 1986; Butterfield & Ferretti, 1987; Sternberg, Ketron, & Powell, 1980). Intelligence is broader than learning, but tools of intelligence are learned.

A third hypothesis is that quick learning is one reflection of intelligence. Said more precisely, intelligent people are hypothesized to learn from less-complete instruction than unintelligent people, because they possess knowledge and ways of thinking that fill instructional gaps (Brown & Campione, 1981).

TOOLS OF INTELLIGENT ACTION

Five tools of intelligence are cognitive knowledge, cognitive strategies, metacognitive monitoring, metacognitive control, and metacognitive understanding. This article will rely on inclined planes to illustrate these tools. (See also METACOGNITION.)

As psychologists have used them, inclined planes are like ski jumps down which balls roll and then fly and land in a long box compartmentalized lengthwise to show distance traveled from the end of a plane (see Figure 1 and Ferretti & Butterfield, 1986, p. 1422). Before balls are allowed to roll, each of two planes is set at an angle above horizontal with one or more props. The more props, the greater the angle of a plane, and props are readily counted. The ball on each plane is held stationary by one of several stops located

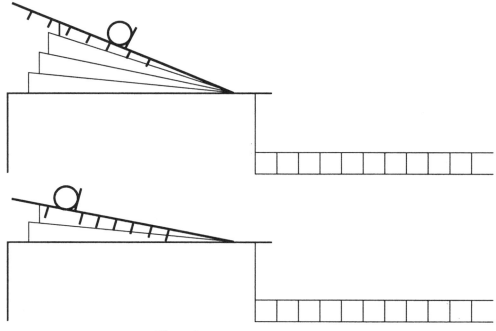

Figure 1
When released, which ball will fly farther?

at different distances from where the angle meets a short flat surface. The number of stops between a ball and the end of a plane is also readily counted. Having shown a student two propped planes, each with a stopped ball, psychologists ask the student to predict which of three things will happen when the balls are unstopped (Ferretti & Butterfield, 1986; Siegler, 1976, 1981). A student's choices are whether one ball, the other, or neither will go farther.

One tool for making such choices is knowledge. In this case, it is knowing an inclined plane's relevant dimensions and how they influence distance flown. A plane's relevant dimensions are its angle of incline and its ball's distance from where the plane meets its horizontal extension. Greater angle and greater distance both work for longer flight of a ball once it leaves a plane. Learning the relevant dimensions of a problem such as an inclined plane is not trivial, because many dimensions can be used to describe a plane and its balls and because the relevant dimensions of many planes influence problem outcome in complex ways.

Like balance scales, inclined planes come in several subtypes that require different strategies for their so-

lution (Butterfield & Nelson, 1991; Ferretti & Butterfield, 1986; Siegler, 1976, 1981). The strategies vary in their complexity, with more-complex strategies learned at later ages. Young children approach all problems as if they were solvable by the simplest strategy, whereas mature problem solvers use more-complex strategies when they are required by the problem they face. Here only the simplest and the most-complex of the five strategies applicable to inclined-plane problems will be described. For descriptions of intermediate strategies, see R. S. Siegler (1976) or E. C. Butterfield and G. D. Nelson (1991).

Students using the simplest dimensional comparison strategy predict on the basis of one relevant dimension. For example, if comparison of two inclined planes reveals that they have unequal angles, a student who relies only on angle predicts that the ball on the plane with a greater angle will go farther, regardless of the distances of the two balls up their inclines. Despite its seeming naïveté, dimensional comparison allows correct prediction for problems whose uncompared distance dimension has equal values on both planes or a larger value on the same plane with the larger angle.

The most complex strategy for solving inclined planes is required by problems having unequal and conflicting values for both of a planes' relevant dimensions. Consider one plane with 4 angle props and a ball on stop 6 and another plane with 7 angle props and a ball on stop 3. Comparing only number of props (angle) says one plane's ball will go farther; comparing only distance says the ball on the other plane will go farther. Resolving such conflicting predictions requires multiplying angle and distance separately for the two planes ($4 \times 6 = 24$ and $7 \times 3 = 21$); the ball on the plane with the greater product flies farther.

Both dimensional comparison and integration by multiplication require that a student quantify relevant dimensions and either compare the quantities or integrate them arithmetically and compare the integrated values. Knowledge of relevant dimensions allows problem solution only if a person also uses appropriate tactics for quantifying the dimensions and integrating the quantities. It is true in general, not only for inclined planes, that knowledge and strategies are both necessary for intelligent action, and other tools are needed too.

In contemporary theory, knowledge and strategies are referred to as "cognition," and monitoring and controlling cognition makes it effective. Monitoring and controlling knowledge and strategies is called "metacognition," which means cognition about cognition. Effective metacognitive control depends on accurate metacognitive monitoring. A student must monitor what he knows about the implications of inclined planes' features in order to select an appropriate strategy, such as dimensional comparison or dimensional integration by multiplication. Strategy selection is a form of control of cognition, and like other forms of control, it requires monitoring what one knows about encountered problems. Monitoring and control are also required when using knowledge and strategies to solve problems. Thus, when using either dimensional comparison or integration, a student should monitor the accuracy of his assessments of dimensional values and correct his counts or estimates as needed, again basing his control of cognition (correcting his assessments) on monitoring it. Especially when using dimensional integration, students must keep track of (monitor) where they stand in the sequences of tactics that make up their strategies. Without such monitor-

ing, students cannot know what to do next. Following his or her prediction for a pair of stopped planes, a student must monitor the two balls' actions after they are unstopped in order to decide whether a different strategy should be used on future problems. An important feature of this sort of monitoring and control is that they can result in learning how to solve future problems (Butterfield, 1986).

Effective control of ongoing cognition depends on knowing what to monitor and on metacognitive understanding of the implications of what the monitoring reveals. The following are some of the metacognitive understandings needed to control effectively one's solution of such simple physics problems as inclined planes, balance scales, and shadow projectors: (1) There are many different kinds of simple physics problems. (2) Only a few of any problem's many dimensions are relevant to its solution. (3) Different strategies solve different subsets of problems, and the strategies form a hierarchy. (4) Dimensional comparison strategies are lower in the hierarchy than dimensional integration strategies. (5) It is easier and more efficient to use dimensional comparison than integration whenever possible. (6) Trying to solve a problem by comparison tells when integration is required by revealing conflicting predictions from different compared dimensions.

UNITS OF LEARNING

Several theories of learning (Bower & Hilgard, 1981) exist, and all of them justify the same methods of teaching knowledge, strategies, monitoring, and control techniques, and metacognitive understandings. Certainly behavior-analytic theory (Catania, 1984; Michael, 1982, 1989; Skinner, 1957, 1968) and cognitive production-system theory (Anderson, 1983; Butterfield & Nelson, 1989; Klahr & Carver, 1988) justify the same teaching techniques (Bransford, Franks, Vye, & Sherwood, 1989; Butterfield, Slocum, & Nelson, 1992; Engelmann & Carnine, 1982; Gick & Holyoak, 1987), even though they are widely regarded as highly different theories (Catania & Harnad, 1988). To appreciate the techniques recommended by all, it helps to consider some details of what is learned. Because of the similarities among different theories of what is learned, this article will only describe particulars of productions, a concept of contemporary cognitive psychologists (Anderson, 1983; Gagné, 1985).

Productions as the Units of Learning. A *production* is a condition–action rule written as IF and THEN statements. When its conditions (IFs) are satisfied, its action (THEN) happens. A production's IF terms are goals and context descriptions. A production's THEN terms are physical or mental procedures, including the setting of goals. Productions are linked into systems in two ways: An earlier production sets goal conditions for later productions, or earlier productions create context descriptions for later productions.

Imagine that a child's teacher asks for a prediction about which of two balls on inclined planes will go farther when the balls are unstopped. Each ball is stopped a different distance from the end of its plane, and the two planes are inclined at different angles. Suppose that before the teacher's request the student has learned more than a child who uses the simplest strategy described above; a child using the simplest strategy believes that only angle is relevant to how far a ball goes, whereas your imaginary student knows that distance is relevant too. Nevertheless, your imaginary student has not learned to integrate dimensions by multiplying; instead, when angle and distance dimensions give different predictions your imaginary student predicts from one preferred dimension. Such a child's thinking as she tries to predict which of two balls will go farther is described in Table 1 as a system of seven related productions. Table 1 also describes environmental events that are represented in the IF statements of the seven productions.

In Table 1, the IF term of P1 depicts your student as having a goal to follow teacher's instructions (not all children have this goal). When the teacher asks for a prediction (the context portion of the IF term), the child's THEN action of P1 sets a goal to predict. This goal carries over to P2, whose context statement describes a pair of inclined planes differing in both angle and distance (mentioned in Table 1 under *Environmental Events*). The THEN term of P2 specifies counting and comparing props (angles of incline). Because P2 did not set a new goal or change the planes, the IF term of P3 differs from the IF term of P2 only by noting prior counting and comparing of props. Like goal setting, this is a production-system way of showing that

what happens next is determined often by prior mental actions that have no environmental effects. In fact, there are no environmental changes from P2 through P7.

The THEN term of P3 shows counting and comparing stops (distances of balls) on the two planes. The IF term of P4 represents the situation in which prior counting and comparing said that one plane had both a larger angle and a larger distance (relevant dimensions) than the other plane. The THEN term of P4 predicts that the ball on the plane with the larger angle and distance will go farther than the ball on the other plane. As a group, P1 through P4 constitute a strategy fully within the grasp of your imaginary child.

If the conditions of P4 were not met, those of P5 could be. Prior counts and comparisons could have shown that only one dimension distinguishes the two planes. If so, the THEN term of P5 predicts that the ball on the plane with the larger single dimension will go farther. As a group, P1, P2, P3, and P5 form another strategy within the grasp of your imaginary child.

P6 has a context description for which your imaginary child has not yet learned enough always to predict accurately: one plane has a greater angle; the other has greater distance. Because the child does not know about multiplying dimensions, he or she selects one preferred dimension and predicts that the ball on the plane with a larger value for angle or distance will go farther. By accident, the prediction of the strategy composed of P1, P2, P3, and P6 will be correct part of the time, even though it results from your imaginary child not knowing enough.

The context description in P7 stems from inadequate knowledge of your imaginary child and contradicts environmental facts. Even though the two planes differ in both angle and distance, counting or comparing incorrectly could say that the planes have equal angles and distances. Such a strategic error would yield the prediction that the two balls will go the same distance. This possibility shows that it is mental representations of events, not events themselves, that determine whether the conditions of a production are met.

How Tools Are Represented in Productions. Knowledge is expressed in context statements of production's IF terms. Recall that context statements are

TABLE 1

An analysis of seven productions (P1–P7) of a child's thinking while predicting which of two balls on inclined planes will fly farther

Environmental Events	Productions (P)
Teacher instructs child to predict which ball, each stopped on its own inclined plane, will go farther when the balls are unstopped.	**P1** IF a goal is to follow instructions and teacher says to predict which of two balls on inclined planes will go farther, THEN set a goal to predict.
Two planes inclined at different angles with balls stopped at different distances.	**P2** IF a goal is to predict and two planes are present, THEN count props that set angles of the planes, and compare counts to see which angle is steeper.
Two planes inclined at different angles with balls stopped at different distances.	**P3** IF a goal is to predict, two planes are present, and their props have been counted and compared, THEN count stops up to the ones holding the balls, and compare counts to see which ball is farther from end of the plane.
Two planes inclined at different angles with balls stopped at different distances.	**P4** IF a goal is to predict and both angle and distance are larger on one of the planes, THEN predict that plane's ball will go farther.
Two planes inclined at different angles with balls stopped at different distances.	**P5** IF a goal is to predict, and angles or distance are the same on the two planes, but the other relevant dimension differs, THEN predict that the ball on the plane with one larger dimension will go farther.
Two planes inclined at different angles with balls stopped at different distances.	**P6** IF a goal is to predict, and angle is larger on one plane and distance is larger on the other plane, THEN predict that the ball on the plane with the larger angle (or distance) will go farther.
Two planes inclined at different angles with balls stopped at different distances.	**P7** IF a goal is to predict and counts have been compared, and angles and distances are the same on the two planes, THEN predict that the two balls will go the same distance.

representations of environmental events, not environmental events themselves. People draw representations from their knowledge bases. Thus, young children represent inclined planes as machines with only one relevant dimension, whereas many adults represent them as machines with two relevant dimensions that can be integrated by multiplying their values. The values themselves are representations of results of production-guided computations. Such differences in representation (context statements) flow from differences in knowledge.

Strategies are the active ingredients of intelligence, and they are based in action statements of THEN terms of productions. Recall, however, that without knowledge and goals, strategies do nothing. The discussion of Table 1 mentioned several strategies composed of a number of productions. This reflects the fact that the productions in Table 1 were written more simply and less redundantly than they could have been, to make them easier to explain. It is always possible to write a strategy as one production (Butterfield, Slocum, & Nelson, 1992; Klahr & Carver, 1988), and the strategy always resides in the action statement of the production's THEN term.

As explained above, representations of environmental events and the outcomes of productions (knowledge) enter context statements of productions that are parts of a strategy or larger cognitive routine and allow their control. Metacognitive monitoring represents the actions of such productions so that they can be controlled:

> IF a goal is to predict with perfect accuracy which of two balls will fly farther when they leave their inclined planes, and the angles of the two planes have been calculated,
> THEN calculate the angles again
> and compare the two calculations,
> and if they are not the same, calculate and compare again.

In this production, metacognitive monitoring is the source of the context statement "and the angles of the two planes have been calculated." Notice that the IF terms of productions like this one, which monitor and control cognition, do not refer to environmental events; they refer only to the actions of other productions. The entire THEN term of this production exerts metacognitive control. The THEN terms of such productions always act on other productions, never on the world. Such productions are metacognitive, not cognitive.

Metacognitive Understanding. Metacognitive understandings are highly general productions that can be translated into productions like the one immediately above. Thus, a general production from which the one above could have been derived is as follows:

> IF a goal is to solve problems accurately,
> and you are solving a problem,
> THEN check each of your intermediate calculations
> and correct them if necessary before continuing your solution.

Notice that such an understanding can guide the creation of checking routines for any calculation made in the course of solving any problem. The reason it is so general is that the checking operations come either from known productions used to solve the problem at hand or from the production guiding the checking. Both kinds of production are immediately available to a problem solver. Also, notice that the IF-term goal of such productions also expresses a metacognitive understanding—in this case, the understanding that calculations can be inaccurate, and if they are, the solution will be wrong, but they can be corrected by checking.

HOW NEW TOOLS ARE LEARNED

New knowledge, strategies, metacognitive monitoring, control, and understanding are learned from others and by oneself.

Learning from Others. Learning from others is either informal, by observation and imitation, or formal, by teaching. Whether formal or informal, learning from others results from exemplification, explanation, and feedback, which are recommended by all learning theorists as teaching tools. More or less systematic illustration (exemplification) of environmental events and distinctions among them promotes context-statement or knowledge learning. Exemplification of ways of acting promotes learning of strategies and metacognitive control (action). Exemplification of ways of thinking promotes learning of metacognitive monitoring and control. Explanation conveys rules about the conditions under which (knowledge) to think or act in particular ways (strategies), and it conveys goals and metacognitive understandings. Feedback that is rewarding promotes learning of all tools of intelligence.

Recall the child imagined earlier: the child who knows that angle and distance are relevant dimensions of inclined planes but does not know when or how to integrate the dimensions by multiplication. Now imagine that a teacher wishes the child to learn when and how to integrate angle and distance. The teacher could begin by showing the child how to distinguish between problems that do and do not require integration. That is, the teacher could exemplify problems for which one plane has greater angle and distance than the other plane, explaining that such problems can be solved by dimensional comparison, without integration by multiplication. Similarly, the teacher would exemplify and explain about problems that are equal on one of the relevant dimensions, but not the other; again, integration is not required. Finally, the teacher could exemplify and explain problems with one plane having a larger angle and the other a larger distance. Such problems do require integration. Before teaching how to integrate, the teacher would ask the child to classify a series of problems as requiring integration or not, praising the child as feedback for correct classifications until the child is always correct. Such teaching would promote learning of the productions represented in Table 1. (Butterfield & Nelson, 1989, and Butterfield, Slocum, & Nelson, 1992, give other illustrations of exemplification, explanation, and feedback.)

Teaching Oneself. An opportunity to learn on one's own exists whenever a person faces a problem for which he or she does not already have an effective strategy. The opportunity might be as simple as the chance to learn that a strategy already learned for the solution of another problem (inclined planes) works for the new problem (balance scale). The learning would be that a strategy (multiplying dimensions) that works for inclined planes also works for balance scales. Such learning results when a person uses a metacognitive understanding to recognize that a novel problem is similar to other problems that the person can solve, calls up from memory knowledge and a strategy that work for similar problems, applies the called-up knowledge and strategy to the novel problem, and monitors feedback and sees that the strategy works.

Except when feedback must come from another person, such learning is fairly viewed as teaching oneself. It requires that the person have metacognitive understandings and productions for trying and evaluating known knowledge and strategies in unfamiliar situations. In effect, metacognitive understandings and production for trying and evaluating serve as internalized teachers.

Much intellectual development may result from teaching oneself. The stage is set for such learning when a problem is presented for which one does not know a solution and the solution involves knowledge and strategies that are typically learned at a later age. The situation described in the preceding section, on learning from others, would fit these criteria if no teacher were there. At first, the imaginary child in that situation does not know how to integrate inclined-plane dimensions by multiplying, because integration is typically learned much later than learning that two dimensions are relevant (Siegler, 1976).

Imagine that situation again, but this time without a teacher. To learn on his own, your imaginary child could arrange inclined-plane problems for himself. He could exemplify for himself various kinds of problems, and doing so would require a metacognitive understanding of experimenting with novel problems that provide their own feedback, as inclined planes do. He could exemplify problems by changing values of planes' variable dimensions, thereby allowing discovery problem types for which regularly accurate prediction is impossible (without integration). Then, concentrating on such problems, he could see that there must be another relevant dimension on which to rely or some other solution requirement. Finding no other dimension to vary, he could explore different ways of treating the planes' two dimensions, such as adding them. Adding dimensions solves many, but not all, inclined planes, and addition is a form of arithmetic integration. The only additional step required would be to explore other arithmetic operations until evaluating feedback revealed that multiplying angle and distance invariably allows correct prediction for inclined-plane problems. Further experimentation with other problems, such as balance scales, shadow projectors, and volume estimation, could allow additional learning of the type called *intellectual development*. Such other problems are solvable by the same strategy as inclined planes; only their relevant dimensions differ.

A child need not be alone to instruct himself. Indeed, it is possible that the reason more-intelligent children learn more and faster from instruction is that they more actively "assist" their teachers in their instruction. More often than less-intelligent children, they may fill in larger gaps left by their instructors.

WHY THE INTELLIGENT LEARN MORE RAPIDLY

That intelligent people learn more knowledge and procedures than unintelligent people has been known since Plato's time at least. During the 1920s and 1930s, much research was directed at establishing this fact scientifically. It could be that intelligent people learn at the same rate as unintelligent ones, but spend more time learning. That could still be part of the story, but more recent research has established that more intelligent people do learn more in the same time with identical instruction than less intelligent people (Ferretti & Butterfield, 1992).

Why intelligent people learn more rapidly is still a matter of conjecture. Perhaps the most reasonable conjecture is that they instruct themselves more fully, effectively, or often. If so, the central source of their greater rate of learning would be metacognitive monitoring, control, and understanding. This would be consistent with hypotheses advanced by many current theorists (Butterfield, 1986; Campione, Brown, & Ferrara, 1982; Sternberg, 1985).

(*See also*: LEARNING, SKILL, AND TRANSFER; MEMORY.)

BIBLIOGRAPHY

ANDERSON, J. R. (1983). *The architecture of cognition.* Cambridge, MA: Harvard University Press.

BOWER, G. F., & HILGARD, E. R. (1981). *Theories of learning.* Englewood Cliffs, NJ: Prentice-Hall.

BRANSFORD, J. D., FRANKS, J. J., VYE, N. J., & SHERWOOD, R. D. (1989). New approaches to instruction: Because wisdom can't be told. In S. Vosniadou & A. Ortony (Eds.), *Similarity and analogical reasoning* (pp. 470–497). New York: Cambridge University Press.

BROWN, A. L., & CAMPIONE, J. C. (1981). Inducing flexible thinking: A problem of access. In M. Friedman, J. P. Das, & N. O'Connor (Eds.), *Intelligence and learning* (pp. 515–529). New York: Plenum.

BROWN, A. L., & FRENCH, L. A. (1979). The zone of potential development: Implications for intelligence testing in the year 2000. *Intelligence, 3,* 255–273.

BUTTERFIELD, E. C. (1986). Intelligent action, learning, and cognitive development might all be explained by the same theory. In R. J. Sternberg & D. K. Detterman (Eds.), *What is intelligence: Contemporary viewpoints on its nature and definition* (pp. 45–50). Norwood, NJ: Ablex.

BUTTERFIELD, E. C., & FERRETTI, R. P. (1987). Toward a theoretical integration hypothesis about intellectual differences among children. In J. G. Borkowski & J. D. Day (Eds.), *Cognition in special children* (pp. 195–233). Norwood, NJ: Ablex.

BUTTERFIELD, E. C., & NELSON, G. D. (1989). Theory and practice of teaching for transfer., *Educational Technology Research and Development, 37,* 5–38.

BUTTERFIELD, E. C., & NELSON, G. D. (1991). Promoting positive transfer of different types. *Cognition and Instruction, 8,* 69–102.

BUTTERFIELD, E. C., SLOCUM, T. A., & NELSON, G. D. (1992). Cognitive and behavioral analyses of learning and transfer: Are they different? In D. K. Detterman & R. J. Sternberg (Eds.), *Transfer on trial* (pp. 192–257). Norwood, NJ: Ablex.

CAMPIONE, J. C., BROWN, A. L., & FERRARA, R. A. (1982). Mental retardation and intelligence. In R. J. Sternberg (Ed.), *Handbook of human intelligence* (pp. 392–490). New York: Cambridge University Press.

CATANIA, A. C. (1984). *Learning* (2nd ed.). Englewood Cliffs, NJ: Prentice-Hall.

CATANIA, A. C., & HARNAD, S. (ED.). (1988). *The selection of behavior.* New York: Cambridge University Press.

EDITORS (1921). Intelligence and its measurement: A symposium (special issue). *Journal of Educational Psychology, 12,* 123–147, 195–216.

ENGELMANN, S., & CARNINE, D. (1982). *Theory of instruction: Principles and applications.* New York: Irvington.

FERRETTI, R. P., & BUTTERFIELD, E. C. (1986). Are children's rule assessment classifications invariant across instances of problem types? *Child Development, 57,* 1419–1428.

FERRETTI, R. P., & BUTTERFIELD, E. C. (1992). Intelligence-related differences in the learning, maintenance, and transfer of problem-solving strategies. *Intelligence, 16,* 207–224.

GAGNÉ, E. D. (1985). *The cognitive psychology of school learning.* Boston: Little, Brown.

GICK, M. L., & HOLYOAK, K. J. (1987). The cognitive basis of knowledge transfer. In S. M. Cormier & J. D. Hagman (Eds.), *Transfer of learning: Contemporary research and applications* (pp. 9–47). San Diego, CA: Academic Press.

KLAHR, D., & CARVER, S. M. (1988). Cognitive objectives in a LOGO debugging curriculum: Instruction, learning, and transfer. *Cognitive Psychology, 20,* 362–404.

MICHAEL, J. (1982). Distinguishing between discriminative and motivational functions of stimuli. *Journal of the Experimental Analysis of Behavior, 37,* 149–155.

MICHAEL, J. (1989). *Verbal and nonverbal behavior: Concepts and principles.* Unpublished manuscript, Western Michigan University, Kalamazoo.

SIEGLER, R. S. (1976). Three aspects of cognitive development. *Cognitive Psychology, 8,* 481–520.

SIEGLER, R. S. (1981). Developmental sequences within and between concepts. *Monographs of the Society for Research in Child Development, 46* (Serial No. 189).

SKINNER, B. F. (1957). *Verbal behavior.* New York: Appleton.

SKINNER, B. F. (1968). *The technology of teaching.* Englewood Cliffs, NJ: Prentice-Hall.

STERNBERG, R. J. (1985). *Beyond IQ: A triarchic theory of human intelligence.* New York: Cambridge University Press.

STERNBERG, R. J. (1990). *Metaphors of mind.* New York: Cambridge University Press.

STERNBERG, R. J., KETRON, J. L., & POWELL, J. S. (1980). *Componential approaches to the training of intelligent performance* (Tech. Rep. No. 22). New Haven, CT: Yale University, Department of Psychology.

EARL C. BUTTERFIELD

LEARNING POTENTIAL ASSESSMENT DEVICE

The Learning Potential Assessment Device (LPAD) is one of the applied systems, mainly the DYNAMIC ASSESSMENT OF MENTAL ABILITIES, which together with Cognitive Intervention (known as Instrumental Enrichment) and Shaping Modifying Environments, derive from the theory of structural cognitive modifiability. The theory defines intelligence as the propensity of an individual to adapt to new situations through modifications of the cognitive system. The theory postulates that human beings are modifiable structurally in their cognitive, affective, and behavioral systems. The theoretical point of departure of the LPAD is that assessment and evaluation of the individual should not focus on the currently manifest level of functioning and present cognitive, behavioral, and emotional structures. Instead, they should evaluate the propensity for modification of these structures and should study the effects of the observed changes on the individual's behavior and adaptability.

The evaluator should attempt to answer the following questions:

1. To what extent is the individual's functioning accessible to structural changes, regardless of how low, how deviant, or how diverse from the norm it currently is?
2. What is the significance of the changes that are produced for the individual's future adaptation to more complex tasks?
3. How permanent and how generalized will such observed changes be?
4. What modes of intervention are preferable to produce the desired changes in the individual's cognitive, emotional, and behavioral structure?

TEST–MEDIATE–TEST APPROACH

The LPAD is focused, although not exclusively, on assessment of the individual's cognitive functioning. A Test–Mediate–Test (TMT) approach produces a *sample* of changes in the structure of the individual's functioning. The test phase is meant to establish the baseline of the individual's functioning in selected dimensions that are critical to the individual's needs and require meaningful change. The chosen dimensions are related to developmental stages or to specific functions. The phase of mediational interaction creates a sample of changes in these critical baseline areas. The retesting phase reveals the extent to which the mediated changes have modified the individual's functioning in a series of tasks that are progressively more complex and remote from the task used for the mediational process.

The dynamic use of TMT in the evaluation of the individual's functioning is meant to substitute for the usual static measurements that result in an IQ score or mental age. These static techniques measure current functioning as if it were fixed and immutable. This shift from a static to a dynamic approach requires change in four dimensions of the measurement of intelligence: test instruments, test situation, process instead of product orientation, and interpretation of results and the changes produced in the examinee's functioning. Each of these four dimensions needs to be changed as specified in the following sections.

Test Instruments. To produce a sample of change in an individual's cognitive functioning that will reflect a difference in cognitive structure, the assessment instruments should incorporate the following three basic elements:

1. Accessibility to a learning process. Mediation of the tasks has as its goals the production of a structural change that is generalizable, transferable, and able to generate prerequisites of further learning.
2. Utilization of generic mental processes that are present in as many cognitive functions as possible.
3. Detection of the smallest change in the individual's functioning.

An illustration of the model construction for such test instruments appears in Figure 1.

Test Situation. In conventional, static measurement models, the test situation is kept as isolated and sterile as possible from factors other than the individual's supposed "fixed capacity." The nature of the task and the conditions under which it is presented are kept stable. All variations in the observed responses have to be attributable to the fixed and immutable intelligence of the person who is being assessed. A uniform, constant presentation assures accurate comparability of the results to those obtained by the normative group.

In dynamic assessment, the standardized and uniform mode of interaction is substituted by a flexible, individualized mediational interaction. Tasks, instructions, and the modality of interaction are adaptable to the needs of the particular individual. Feedback is constantly offered, not only to help the examinee correct responses but also to learn from these responses. The major determinant of the nature of interaction between the examiner and the examinee is mediated learning experience, which guides the intervention

that induces changes in the examinee's functioning. Instead of rigid restrictions on interaction between the examiner and the examinee, the examiner does everything possible to enhance the individual's functioning and performance by correcting the deficient functions producing insight, propensity to generalize, and ability to transfer and apply newly acquired prerequisites for further learning and thinking. The sample of "change" in performance of the tasks is interpreted as representing the examinee's propensity of modifiability. The altered test situation is, therefore, the pivotal element of dynamic assessment creating the sample of changes that serve as a profile of the examinee's modifiability.

Process Orientation. The usual measurement of intelligence occurs through registration of the products of behavior elicited through a particular instruction or through observation of spontaneous behavior. The product is then measured, compared, and interpreted as representative of a universe of behaviors that reflect the norm. The results are then placed on the scale of the normative behavior of the reference group. The major concern, however, is the product.

Although the LPAD dynamic assessment approach uses the product only as a baseline, it is the process that has engendered the product that is the major focus of the assessment. Everything possible is done to capture this process, understand it, and attribute to it adequate weight in assessing the individual's cognitive structure. The ultimate goal of using the LPAD is to develop an intervention program for the examinee. The examiner is able to consider and choose the preferential modalities of intervention only through understanding the process related to the person's basic functioning and the change in the process that is produced during administration of the LPAD.

Such understanding of the individual's basic functioning and access to change is assisted by two conceptual frameworks. The first is a list of deficient functions (Table 1) that are potentially responsible for the individual's failure to solve problems, to benefit from learning, and to adapt to tasks. These functions, whether absent, deficient, or fragile, describe the cognitive characteristics of the individual. Deficient functions are defined for the three stages of mental activity—input, elaboration, and output—and help describe why the individual exhibits certain difficulties and is more or less resistant to learning. The list of

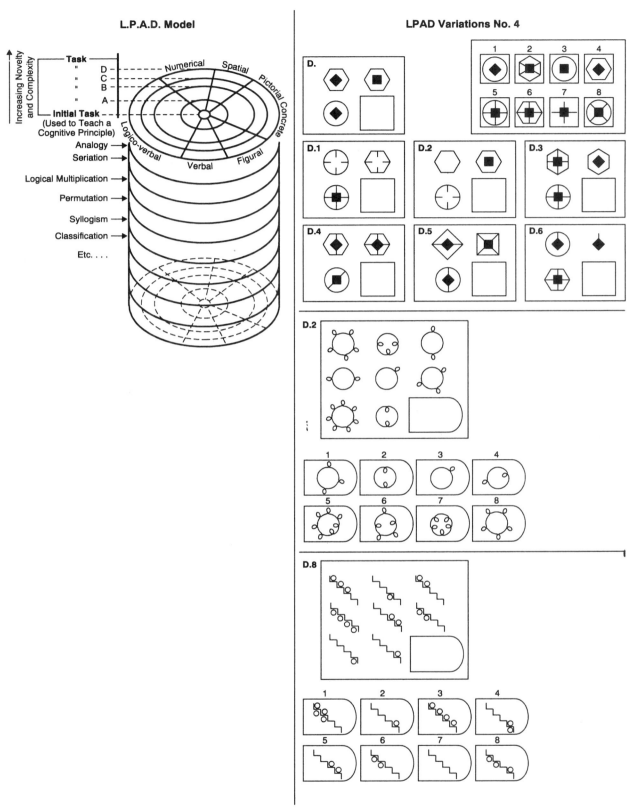

Figure 1
The LPAD model with sample from an LPAD test

TABLE 1
Deficient cognitive functions

The locus of the deficiencies resulting from the lack of mediated learning experience is peripheral rather than central. It reflects attitudinal and motivational deficiencies, lack of working habits and learning sets *rather than* structural and elaborational incapacities. Evidence of the reversibility of the phenomena has been provided by clinical and experimental work—especially through dynamic assessment (Learning Potential Assessment Device [LPAD]). The LPAD has also enabled the establishment of an inventory of cognitive functions that are undeveloped, poorly developed, arrested and/or impaired. These cognitive functions are categorized into the input, elaborational, and output levels.

Impaired cognitive functions affecting the input level include those impairments concerning the quantity and quality of data gathered by the individual when confronted by a given problem, object, or experience. They include the following factors:

1. Blurred and sweeping perception.
2. Unplanned, impulsive, and unsystematic exploratory behavior.
3. Lack of or impaired receptive verbal tools, which affect discrimination (e.g., objects, events, and relationships do not have appropriate labels).
4. Lack of or impaired spatial orientation; the lack of stable systems of references impairs the establishment of topological and Euclidian organization of space.
5. Lack of or impaired temporal concepts.
6. Lack of or impaired conservation of constancies (size, shape, quantity, orientation) across variation in these factors.
7. Lack of or deficient need for precision and accuracy in data gathering.
8. Lack of capacity for considering two or more sources of information at once. This is reflected in dealing with data in a piecemeal fashion, rather than as a unit of organized facts.

The severity of impairment at the input level may also, but not necessarily, affect ability to function at levels of elaboration and output.

Impaired cognitive function affecting the elaborational level include those factors that impede the efficient use of available data and existing cues such as the following factors:

1. Inadequacy in the perception of the existence and definition of an actual problem.
2. Inability to select relevant versus nonrelevant cues in defining a problem.
3. Lack of spontaneous comparative behavior or limitation of its application by a restricted need system.
4. Narrowness of the psychic field.
5. Episodic grasp of reality.
6. Lack of or impaired need for pursuing logical evidence.
7. Lack of or impaired interiorization.
8. Lack of or impaired inferential-hypothetical "iffy" thinking.
9. Lack of or impaired strategies for hypothesis testing.
10. Lack of or impaired ability to define the framework necessary for problem-solving behavior.
11. Lack of or impaired planning behavior.
12. Nonelaboration of certain cognitive categories because the verbal concepts are not part of the individual's verbal inventory on a receptive level or they are not mobilized at the expressive level.

"Thinking" usually refers to the elaboration of cues. Highly original, creative, and correct elaboration may well exist that yields wrong responses because it is based on inappropriate or inadequate data on the input level.

Impaired cognitive functions on the output level include those factors that lead to an inadequate communication of final solutions. Even adequately perceived data and appropriate elaboration can be expressed as an incorrect or haphazard solution if difficulties exist at this level. Examples are the following situations:

1. Egocentric communicational modalities.
2. Difficulties in projecting virtual relationships.
3. Blocking.
4. Trial and error responses.
5. Lack of or impaired tools for communicating adequately elaborated responses.
6. Lack of or impaired need for precision in communicating the individual's responses.
7. Deficiency of visual transport.
8. Impulsive, acting-out behavior.

The three disparate levels were conceived to bring some order to the array of impaired cognitive functions seen in culturally deprived persons. Interaction exists, however, between and among the levels that is of vital significance in understanding the extent and pervasiveness of cognitive impairment.

deficient functions permits localization of the site of deficiency responsible for the dysfunctioning of the individual.

The second conceptual apparatus, the cognitive map (Figure 2), helps in understanding the nature of the task as a determinant of success or failure in the individual's adaptation. The following seven parameters explain why the individual is failing or succeeding in a particular task: (1) content; (2) modality; (3) phase of the cognitive function; (4) mental operation; (5) level of abstraction; (6) degree of complexity; and (7) level of efficiency. Using the cognitive map and list of deficient functions opens the way to understanding the process that underlies the individual's failure. The sample of change produced during the LPAD relates to correction of deficient functions as well as to manipulation of the tasks and their meaning. It holds predictive value for the materialization of learning potential and the propensity to become modified.

Interpretation of Results. In the conventional static test approach, interpretation of the results is a function of comparison of the individual's results with those of the supposed referential group. Interpretation is usually comprehensive; the results are reduced to an index, such as the IQ, which does not allow for distinction between the different level of responses that are the basis for the results. In a dynamic approach, on the other hand, interpretation of the results takes into consideration first and foremost the nature of the

tasks that the individual has mastered. The presence of peaks in the person's functioning is interpreted as indicative of the true propensity of that individual to learn, rather than of the lower global result. Interpretation results from using the cognitive map that enables analysis of the task, assignment of a specific weight of a particular parameter for the individual's adaptive capacities, and evaluation of the changes produced. Interpretation of the process enables an evaluation of the propensity for change, of the conditions under which such changes have been produced, and of the modalities by which such modes of functioning can become accessible in a more pervasive way to the individual.

CONCLUSION

Researchers have applied the LPAD to a large variety of populations whose manifest level of functioning suffers from cultural differences, cultural deprivation, and/or deficient organic and emotional conditions of the individuals involved. The resulting profiles of modifiability have led to mainstreaming tens of thousands of low-functioning and otherwise affected individuals. The LPAD has generated instructional and enrichment programs that have enhanced the modifiability of individuals by helping them become sensitive, efficient learners. Last but not least, the use of the LPAD with individuals in both clinical

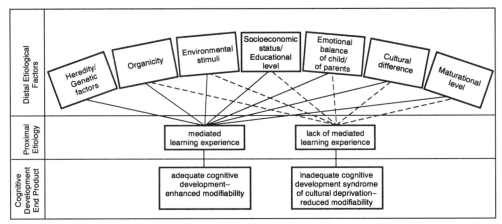

Figure 2
The cognitive map: Distal and proximal determinants of differential cognitive development

settings and experimental group testing situations has led to the formulation of the construct of intelligence as the propensity to change and adapt.

(*See also:* MEASUREMENT AND PREDICTION OF INTELLIGENCE.)

BIBLIOGRAPHY

FEUERSTEIN, R., KLEIN, P., & TANNENBAUM, A. (EDS.). (1990). *Mediated learning experience: Theoretical, psychosocial and educational implications.* Proceedings of the First International Conference on Mediated Learning Experience. London and Tel Aviv: Freund.

FEUERSTEIN, R., MILLER, R., & JENSEN, M. (1981). Can evolving techniques better measure cognitive change? *Outlooks: Journal of Special Education, 15*(2), 201–219.

FEUERSTEIN, R., RAND, Y., & HOFFMAN, M. (1979). *The dynamic assessment of retarded performers: Learning potential assessment device, theory, instruments and techniques.* Baltimore, MD: University Park Press.

FEUERSTEIN, R., RAND, Y., HOFFMAN, M., & MILLER, R. (1980). *Instrumental enrichment: An intervention program for cognitive modifiability.* Baltimore, MD: University Park Press.

FEUERSTEIN, R., RAND, Y., JENSEN, M., KANIEL, S., & TZURIEL, D. (1987). The dynamic assessment of structural cognitive modifiability: The Learning Potential Assessment Device—a paradigm, a theory and an applied system. In C. Lidz (Ed.), *Dynamic assessment: An interactional approach to evaluating learning potential.* New York: Guilford Press.

FEUERSTEIN, R., RAND, Y., JENSEN, M., KANIEL, S., TZURIEL, D., & BEN-SHACHAR, N. (1986). Learning potential assessment: Emerging perspectives on assessment of exceptional children. *Special Services in the Schools, 2*(2/3), 85–106.

REUVEN FEUERSTEIN

LEARNING, SKILL, AND TRANSFER

Since the beginning of twentieth-century attempts to measure human intelligence, the relationship between intelligence and learning has been certain yet elusive. On the one hand, all psychological tests of intelligence assess the cumulative degree of learning that an individual has acquired up to the point of the test—or even the degree of learning *within* the testing situation. As such, intelligence tests measure what the individual has learned from the environment (e.g., see Humphreys, 1979). This type of linkage between intelligence and learning is an integral part of the theory and practice of intelligence testing, and it is central to the use of intelligence tests for academic placement (Binet & Simon, 1906; Stern, 1914). By assessing how much an individual has learned, predictions can be made regarding how much an individual may learn in the future. Correlations between intelligence test scores and school grades, or advancement/failure, provide the primary source of validation of nearly all intelligence tests for children and adolescents. On the other hand, the history of psychological inquiry shows that it has been exceedingly difficult to assess the relations between intelligence and *specific* learning situations (Woodrow, 1946). The problems in establishing a specific linkage between intelligence and learning are in part statistical and in part conceptual. Satisfactory resolution of these problems has demonstrated that intelligence and specific learning are indeed related, but only in some circumstances and under specific conditions.

The school environment is best defined as consisting of open-ended tasks. Tasks are open ended to the degree that when individuals master one set of concepts or skills, they are moved on to another set—based on the preceding set or a more difficult task to master. This kind of process is illustrated by the mathematics curriculum—once learners master addition and subtraction, the next step is to master multiplication and division, then algebra and geometry, and so on. Intelligence tests well predict who succeeds and fails in such situations.

Outside the school (e.g., in on-the-job situations), many tasks are closed ended. There, a task, once mastered, represents a terminal skill. Learning how to drive a car is one such situation; learning typing skills or the technical skills needed to master a musical instrument are other such situations. The relationship between intelligence and the learning of such closed-ended skills is far more complex than the learning of open-ended skills.

Deriving a framework for explaining these different situations is the goal of psychologists who are interested in mapping out the relations between intelligence, learning, and transfer.

TYPES OF INFORMATION PROCESSING

Many ways exist to categorize types of human information processing. For a discussion of human skill acquisition, two categories of information processing are needed to understand and predict the relationship between intellectual abilities and learning. These categories are called *controlled information processing* and *automatic information processing* (Schneider & Shiffrin, 1977; Shiffrin & Schneider, 1977). Controlled information processing is the way people handle novel or inconsistent information—as when someone confronts a new task to be learned. Controlled processing is used for gaining an understanding of how to do a task, and it is involved in strategy development and initial implementation. Controlled information processing is typically slow and requires a great deal of mental effort or attention. Automatic information processing develops after someone has performed a task many times. When the performance of a task becomes highly speeded and accurate, an individual typically is using automatic information processing. When automatic processing has been developed, tasks can be performed with little mental effort. Many aspects of touch-typing, or driving a car, or the mechanics of reading can become automatic with practice.

STAGES OF SKILL ACQUISITION

When people acquire a task skill, they typically go through a transitional process—starting with controlled information processing and ending up with automatic information processing. For example, if you have learned to touch-type, you probably can remember how difficult and error prone your typing was when you began to learn the skill and how you had to rehearse mentally where each of the keys was in relation to others. After a great deal of practice, you probably found that you could type the letters you wanted almost automatically, without devoting very much attention to the task of typing at all.

Researchers have suggested that there are three loosely defined stages of skill acquisition—a cognitive (or controlled processing stage); an associative (or intermediate stage); and an autonomous (or automatic processing stage) (Fitts & Posner, 1967). The ways intelligence is related to skilled performance depend primarily on what stage of skill acquisition is being considered (Ackerman, 1988, 1990).

INTELLIGENCE AND
SKILL ACQUISITION

During the first, cognitive, stage of skill acquisition (and, generally, when tasks require controlled information processing), general intelligence and broad content abilities (i.e., spatial, verbal, numerical) are most highly associated with individual differences in performance. That is, an individual's level of general intelligence determines how well that person can understand task instructions, memorize new information, and develop efficient strategies for task performance (Ackerman & Woltz, 1993; Kyllonen & Christal, 1990; Woltz, 1988).

During the second, associative, stage of skill acquisition, individuals typically are engaged in refinement of their strategies for performing a task, and are strengthening their associations between the inputs of the task (stimuli) and the responses that are required. In this stage of skill acquisition, general intelligence plays a less dominant role, and individual differences in perceptual speed abilities are typically most highly associated with individual differences in performance.

During the third, autonomous, stage of skill acquisition, when automatic information processing is used to perform a task, general intellectual abilities and perceptual speed abilities have a greatly diminished association with individual differences in task performance. Instead, when task performance is dependent on the speed and accuracy of motor processes, the only abilities that regularly predict individual differences in performance are psychomotor abilities (such as reaction time, rate of arm movement, and dexterity; Ackerman, 1988).

There are two especially important points to be derived from these findings. First, intelligence is most highly associated with the *early* stages of skill acquisition, when controlled processing is used, and intelligence is least associated with *late* stages of skill acquisition, after nearly all individuals have successfully developed efficient strategies for performance. These situations are common when someone is confronting a closed-ended task—that is, one that allows for the development of some terminal, automatic skill (Ackerman, 1990).

Second, when tasks require controlled information processing *and* do not allow for development of automatic information processing, performance is nearly always highly associated with individual differences in intelligence. Such situations are common when the task continues to involve a great deal of information to be memorized, or when tasks are highly complex. Under such circumstances, learners with lower levels of general intelligence may be incapable of developing

automatic processing, and thus are required to continue to use their controlled information-processing resources. This has been found in students who have difficulty acquiring reading skills (Frederiksen, Warren, & Rosebery, 1985), and also for the complex tasks in which air traffic controllers engage, where each day provides a unique set of information that must be memorized and processed (Ackerman, 1992).

INTELLIGENCE AND TRANSFER

As Ferguson (1954, 1956) pointed out, except for the newborn child, learning is properly considered to be transfer (of knowledge or skills previously developed). No consideration of child or adult learning, then, is complete without attention to the role of intelligence in transfer of training. Sullivan (1964), for example, has suggested that the essence of intellectual ability is a repertoire for distant transfer of training. High-ability learners are expected to benefit more than low-ability learners under *far-transfer* conditions (that is, when the initial task is remotely related to transfer task), whereas low-ability learners benefit to a relatively greater degree under *near-transfer* conditions (when the initial task is highly related to the transfer task). To put this framework into the current skill acquisition perspective, the expectation from Sullivan's hypothesis, practice on far transfer tasks will lead to a *greater* dependence of transfer task performance on general intelligence, while practice on near transfer tasks will lead to a *diminished* dependence of the transfer task performance on general intelligence. These arguments are entirely consonant with an aptitude-treatment interaction approach to transfer of training (for a discussion of aptitude-treatment interactions, see Cronbach & Snow, 1977). In a series of studies with school children, Sullivan and his colleagues (Skanes, Sullivan, Rowe, & Shannon, 1974; Sullivan & Skanes, 1971) have found evidence in support of this hypothesis. That is, when children were given a remote-transfer task (e.g., number series practice and letter-series transfer test) those children with higher levels of intelligence performed much better than those with lower levels of intelligence. However, when children were given a near-transfer task (e.g., letter series practice and letter series transfer test), the children with higher levels of intelligence benefited relatively less than the children with lower levels of intelligence.

These results fit reasonably well with the stages of skill acquisition discussed earlier. That is, when transfer of training requires application of controlled processing strategies (far transfer), learners of higher intellectual ability benefit the most from instruction. When training focuses on development of associative or automatic information processing skills, however, and the intellectual demands during transfer of training are diminished (near transfer), learners with lower intelligence benefit the most, as they have proceeded past the cognitive, or controlled information-processing stage of skill acquisition into a stage of skill acquisition that is less dependent on general intelligence.

CONCLUSIONS

As stated at the beginning, learning and intelligence have a relationship that is at once both certain and elusive. At a broad level of learning, such as grades earned in school, intelligence and learning are tightly linked. Intelligence is most closely related to learning over long periods of time, for broad transfer of training, and especially for open-ended tasks—those that repeatedly challenge the learner to memorize new information or acquire new task strategies. To take the analogy to the tortoise and the hare—only the hare is capable of succeeding in long-term confrontation with open-ended tasks. The tortoise gets left behind. When closed-ended tasks are considered, though, and when it is possible to acquire an automatic information-processing method of performing a task, intellectual abilities are most highly associated with individual differences in performance *only* during the early stages of skill acquisition. As individuals develop automatic procedures for performing such tasks, other types of abilities (such as perceptual and psychomotor) more often determine who performs the best, or the fastest. For the tortoise and the hare analogy, skilled performance can be acquired by either the tortoise or the hare—one fundamental determinant of final skill level is amount of practice. Eventually, the tortoise approaches the performance level of the hare, and if the tortoise continues to practice the task after the hare moves on to some other activity, the tortoise may be

the one with the higher level of skilled performance (Ackerman, 1987).

(*See also:* LEARNING AND INTELLIGENCE.)

BIBLIOGRAPHY

ACKERMAN, P. L. (1987). Individual differences in skill learning: An integration of psychometric and information processing perspectives. *Psychological Bulletin, 102,* 3–27.

ACKERMAN, P. L. (1988). Determinants of individual differences during skill acquisition: Cognitive abilities and information processing. *Journal of Experimental Psychology: General, 117,* 288–318.

ACKERMAN, P. L. (1990). A correlational analysis of skill specificity: Learning, abilities, and individual differences. *Journal of Experimental Psychology: Learning, Memory, and Cognition, 16,* 883–901.

ACKERMAN, P. L. (1992). Predicting individual differences in complex skill acquisition: Dynamics of ability determinants. *Journal of Applied Psychology, 77,* 598–614.

BINET, A., & SIMON, T. (orig., 1906, repr., 1961). The development of intelligence in children. New methods for the diagnosis of the intellectual level of subnormals. The development of intelligence in the child. Translated and reprinted in J. J. Jenkins & D. G. Paterson (Eds.), *Studies of individual differences: The search for intelligence.* New York: Appleton-Century-Crofts.

CRONBACH, L. J., & SNOW, R. E. (1977). *Aptitudes and instructional methods: A handbook for research on interactions.* New York: Irvington.

FERGUSON, G. A. (1954). On learning and human ability. *Canadian Journal of Psychology, 8,* 95–112.

FERGUSON, G. A. (1956). On transfer and the abilities of man. *Canadian Journal of Psychology, 10,* 121–131.

FITTS, P., & POSNER, M. I. (1967). *Human performance.* Belmont, CA: Brooks/Cole.

FREDERIKSEN, J. R., WARREN, B. M., & ROSEBERY, A. S. (1985). A componential approach to training reading skills: Part 1. Perceptual units training. *Cognition and Instruction, 2,* 91–130.

HUMPHREYS, L. G. (1979). The construct of general intelligence. *Intelligence, 3,* 105–120.

KYLLONEN, P. C., & CHRISTAL, R. E. (1990). Reasoning ability is (little more than) working memory capacity?! *Intelligence, 14,* 389–433.

SCHNEIDER, W., & SHIFFRIN, R. M. (1977). Controlled and automatic human information processing: I. Detection, search, and attention. *Psychological Review, 84,* 1–66.

SHIFFRIN, R. M., & SCHNEIDER, W. (1977). Controlled and automatic human information processing: II. Perceptual learning, automatic attending, and a general theory. *Psychological Review, 84,* 127–190.

SKANES, G. R., SULLIVAN, A. M., ROWE, E. J., & SHANNON, E. (1974). Intelligence and transfer: Aptitude by treatment interactions. *Journal of Educational Psychology, 66,* 563–568.

STERN, W. (1914). *The psychological methods of testing intelligence.* (Guy Montrose Whipple, Trans.). Baltimore: Warwick & York.

SULLIVAN, A. M. (1964). *The relation between intelligence and transfer.* Unpublished doctoral dissertation, McGill University, Montreal.

SULLIVAN, A. M., & SKANES, G. R. (1971). Differential transfer of training in bright and dull subjects of the same mental age. *British Journal of Educational Psychology, 41,* 287–293.

WOLTZ, D. J. (1988). An investigation of the role of working memory in procedural skill acquisition. *Journal of Experimental Psychology: General, 117,* 319–331.

WOODROW, H. (1946). The ability to learn. *Psychological Review, 53,* 147–158.

PHILLIP L. ACKERMAN

LEGAL ISSUES IN INTELLIGENCE

Because the modern concept of intelligence carries implications of individual differences in ability and merit, the measurement of intelligence has aroused extensive controversy. Social critics, legal experts, and legislators have scrutinized individual intelligence tests and group aptitude tests, especially their use in allocating highly valued educational and employment opportunities. The sharp and even litigious debate over aptitude testing is not surprising.

Many persons believe that intelligence tests are a major and unfair obstacle to the advancement of people of African or Hispanic heritage. Some critics have even called intelligence testing inherently racist, particularly when intelligence is conceived as a unidimensional ranking and when test items appear to reflect white culture or middle-class experience and values. Testing has been stoutly defended, however, by educators, by employers, and by the testing industry, who claim that it can identify "diamonds in the rough" and open doors of opportunity for deserving individuals who might otherwise be overlooked. Employers say they need tests to select the most qualified applicants for the job.

The legal evidence has shown that intelligence and aptitude tests have sometimes been improperly used, with unfair impact on minorities. Although courts have occasionally banned the use of intelligence tests altogether, for the most part the law has no absolute prohibition against intelligence testing. Slowly, American courts, government agencies, and professional organizations have developed a legal and ethical framework to regulate intelligence testing to prevent uses that are clearly unfair to certain groups.

The general guidelines for the use of tests as employment selection criteria were laid down in a series of crucial Supreme Court opinions in the early 1970s and have been refined continually through federal regulations and congressional action. These criteria for analyzing claims of employment discrimination, often called disparate impact analysis, comprise one of the leading achievements of American civil rights law.

INTELLIGENCE IS A MORALLY AMBIGUOUS CONCEPT

Fundamentally the law is a moral enterprise, that is, lawmaking and litigation necessarily involve ideas of fairness and justice. Underlying a claim about the unfairness of a test is an implicit theory about what a fair test or selection procedure would be. Neither lawyers nor psychometricians have yet reached a consensus, however, on what constitutes a fair test and a fair selection procedure.

Because intelligence is a morally ambiguous concept, legal consensus is difficult to attain. A common mistake is the viewing of intelligence rankings as equivalent to moral merit ranking. The higher a test taker's score, the more opportunities are deserved. Under utilitarian moral theories, this approach has some appeal. Utilitarian theories seek to maximize human happiness, which is often conceived in this context as economic productivity. Employers argue that the applicants who deserve jobs are those with the greatest potential as successful workers. *General intel-*

ligence tests correlate with success in a wide variety of jobs, that is, the tests have predictive validity. The lower the score, the greater the chance that a person will fail on the job. As scores increase, so does the likelihood of excellence. A test with predictive validity may be used as the selection criterion, and applicants are chosen from the top scores down until all the positions are filled.

The problem with this rationale is that utilitarian theories do not completely satisfy our sense of justice. A person's future productivity is not the only aspect we examine when determining fair treatment. We also look to the past efforts made by and past opportunities received by the person. If a child of wealthy parents is lazy but has an intelligence quotient (IQ) of 110, does that child deserve preference to a child of poor parents, who is hard-working but has an IQ of 100? Many critics would argue that if a person's current functioning—as reflected in a test score—is partly the result of a disadvantaged background, the denial of a job or entrance to a competitive university would be an unfair further penalty. This argument is especially true if the individual's future performance will be at least adequate, if not excellent, or if new opportunities have some chance of correcting the deprivations of the past. Because intelligence test scores reflect the influence of many biological and environmental factors, most of which are beyond the person's control, intelligence rankings are not reliable measures of who deserves what. Intelligence can be viewed as a gift, not as a moral or legal entitlement to admission to a university or a high-paying job.

This point is part of the lesson of one of the most famous cases involving educational testing, *Bakke v. Regents of the University of California,* 438 U.S. 265 (1978). Allan Bakke had argued that the university violated the equal protection clause of the Fourteenth Amendment to the U.S. Constitution by rejecting him for admission to medical school but accepting minority applicants who had lower scores on the Medical College Admissions Test. The Supreme Court agreed that rigid quotas based solely on race could constitute unconstitutional reverse discrimination. The court's decision also makes clear, however, that high test scores alone do not create a legal right to admission over those with lower scores. University admissions officers can look to other goals, including undoing the effects of past

discrimination and creating an ethnically diverse student body.

RACE-CONSCIOUS ANALYSIS

One of the unfortunate facts about the legal scrutiny of intelligence testing is that it is bound up with hotly contested claims about racial discrimination. Although many of the moral arguments about test fairness could be raised by a poor white against a wealthy one, courts have examined intelligence testing through the lens of civil rights law. This view focuses attention on race and forces the issues to be analyzed in terms of group rather than individual differences. When lawyers file a brief challenging a selection procedure, they must make a claim within the recognized legal causes of action, and these causes involve claims of racial or gender discrimination. No other way to get into court exists.

As a result, most legal assaults on intelligence testing start with a comparison of the average scores attained by blacks, whites, or other legally recognizable groups. (Civil rights laws generally contain a list of groups who are recognized as historic victims of discrimination and who are thus entitled to special legal protection.) On general intelligence measures, African Americans, as a group, typically have an average or mean score one standard deviation (about 15 IQ points) below the average for whites. This fact is cited as proof that the test is unfair and that any decision based on the test is discriminatory.

A similar argument was made in the case of *Larry P. v. Wilson Riles,* one of longest running battles involving individual IQ testing. Black schoolchildren in California who were placed in classes for the educable mentally retarded (EMR) brought suit under Title VI of the Civil Rights Act and federal and state constitutions. The crucial evidence was the disproportionate number of black children placed in these classes. Although only 9 percent of California schoolchildren were black, they comprised 27 percent of students in the EMR classes.

The judge heard extensive testimony from experts on both sides of the case and reviewed carefully the history of the development of IQ tests and the decision by the California Department of Education to use them in EMR placement decisions. The court found that individual IQ tests, such as the Stanford-Binet and the Wechsler Intelligence Scale for Children–Revised (WISC–R), played a substantial role in placing students in the EMR classes, and that blacks scored significantly lower on average than did whites. Further, the state had made use of these tests mandatory, knowing that considerable controversy surrounded them, including allegations that the tests were culturally biased.

Cultural Bias. The court examined several possible explanations for the differences in average scores for blacks and whites. The genetic explanation was rejected because studies of genetic differences in intelligence themselves used test scores; therefore, the court reasoned that these studies cannot disprove cultural bias in the test. Socioeconomic factors were discounted because some differences in test scores remain among blacks and whites of the same socioeconomic level.

The most plausible explanation for the score differences, the court concluded, was bias in the test. The judge in the *Larry P. v. Wilson Riles* case was struck by the racist assumptions and eugenic goals of early American test developers. The tests were first standardized and validated on whites but not on blacks. Items were discarded if boys and girls scored differently on them. No effort was made to ensure that blacks and whites attained the same scores, however, apparently because racial differences in intelligence were assumed. In addition, testing experts conceded at the trial that because of cultural differences, black children may not do as well as middle class whites on particular items—such as the "fight item," which asked what one should do if struck by a smaller child of the same sex. (According to the "correct" answer, one should not strike back.)

The court concluded that the tests had not been properly validated for placing black children in EMR classes. It ordered that the schools stop using these or any test not validated properly, that all students currently in EMR classes be reevaluated without the tests, and that each school district report back to the court in three years if any disproportionate representation of black students in EMR classes remained.

The use of IQ tests to make EMR placement decisions has been examined by other courts that have not found fatal cultural bias. The judge in *PASE v. Hannon*, 506 F. Supp. 831 (1980) painstakingly reviewed each item of the WISC, WISC–R, and Stanford-Binet tests, searching for signs of cultural bias. Nine items on the three tests appeared biased to the judge (for example, "What is the color of rubies?" and "What does C.O.D. mean?," both from the now little-used WISC.) The judge also noted, however, that most of the students in the EMR class were from poor neighborhoods, and he concluded that their economic background, not genetics or cultural bias in the test, was the most likely explanation of the disproportionate numbers.

Test developers cringe at the crude assessment of face validity that some courts have employed to assess cultural bias. Test developers have learned to be more sensitive, however, to the appearance of bias. Most tests are now carefully screened to ensure a fair representation of content familiar to minorities and to avoid language or knowledge that is familiar primarily to whites. More sophisticated item analyses, for example, a statistical search for item by race-interaction effects, are also performed. These have rarely uncovered test items that are uniquely difficult for minorities or women.

SPECIFIC VALIDATION

Despite the increased sensitivity of test developers and the elimination of biased items, group differences in test score distributions remain. Could it be that not only particular items but every item, indeed the entire definition of intelligence, is biased against blacks and Hispanics? The best answer to this charge is predictive validation of the test. Standard intelligence tests measure abstract reasoning more than interpersonal, athletic, or ethical skills. However, if test scores correlate with, and are able to predict, school grades, job success, and performance on a wide variety of tasks that demand abstract reasoning, then the tests must be measuring something useful. They can provide valuable information for admissions or personnel officers who must select from a large pool of applicants.

The definition of intelligence as a broad common factor (see FACTOR ANALYSIS) tells us that persons of high intelligence tend to do well on a wide variety of intellectual tasks. Nonetheless, researchers have long recognized that there are more specific subsets of skills. The more specific the test, the better the prediction of performance in a job that demands the specific measured skills. The verbal scale of the Scholastic Aptitude Test for example, could be a good tool for choosing members of the debate team, less useful for organizing members of the math team, and perhaps of no use at all for selecting the football team.

For these reasons, the law has a preference for tests that are specifically validated for the purpose they are being used. The best possible validation evidence is a predictive validity study that demonstrates a high correlation between test scores and some independent measure of performance on the job, such as supervisor ratings or grade-point average. In some cases, the courts are willing to accept other evidence of validity, such as a content analysis of the test and the job. Or the validity of a test may be generalized from one job to other similar jobs. The safest bet always is to validate a test specifically for its purpose.

DISPARATE IMPACT ANALYSIS

The laws concerning employee selection tests spell out exactly what each party in an employment discrimination lawsuit must prove, including the kinds of validation that an employer needs to defend against charges of discrimination. First developed in a series of Supreme Court cases beginning with *Griggs v. Duke Power Company,* 401 U.S. 424 (1971), the principles of disparate impact analysis were put into federal statutes through the Civil Rights Act of 1991. In addition, further technical guidance is found in the *Uniform Guidelines on Employee Selection Procedures* developed by the Equal Employment Opportunity Commission (EEOC) and other federal agencies. Federal law prohibits intentional discrimination, but by applying disparate impact analysis the courts can prohibit the use of certain tests and award damages to rejected applicants even without evidence of intentional discrimination.

Disparate impact analysis begins with the kind of group comparisons that were shown in the *Larry P.* case. *Disparate* or *adverse impact* is the legal term for a disproportionate representation of a protected group, such as blacks, among persons who are rejected for a job. The EEOC guidelines use the "four-fifths" rule. If the proportion of minority applicants accepted for a job is less than four-fifths of the proportion of whites, then an initial presumption is raised that the selection criteria used were discriminatory. Complainants must

try to identify which particular selection practices cause the adverse impact. For example, to challenge the use of an intelligence test to screen applicants, the complainant must demonstrate that minorities fall in disproportionate numbers below the cut-off score used to select employees.

To rebut the presumption of unlawful discrimination, the employer must show that the test is related to the position being filled and is "consistent with business necessity." Just what this means will be determined by courts interpreting the statute in the years ahead, but the EEOC guidelines provide some help. They contain technical advice on how to design validation studies and the kinds of findings needed to support use of a test. The relationship between the test and a measure of job performance should be statistically significant at normal levels of confidence. Where adverse impact is severe, employers must be sure that differences in test scores reflect real differences in job performance and that the test predicts fairly for all groups. Finally, if several selection procedures are equally related to the job, employers must use the one with the least disparate impact.

Thus the law of employment discrimination clearly permits a utilitarian approach; employers can hire the most intelligent employees they can find, regardless of race, as long as they can prove that intelligence is significantly related to performance on the job. Nonetheless, the law does not require this approach. Employers may hire randomly or give preference to applicants from disadvantaged backgrounds or use whatever system they like as long as it does not result in an adverse impact on a protected group.

INTELLIGENCE AND RESPONSIBILITY

Just as courts have held that superior intelligence does not entitle a person to special rights, they have maintained also that inferior intelligence does not necessarily relieve a person of rights or responsibilities. Intelligence is one of the factors that courts consider when assessing a person's legal competence, for example, to stand trial, or refuse medical treatment, or make other decisions that require informed and rational decision making. Intelligence may be considered in decisions about acquittal under the so-called insanity defense. In severe cases, mental retardation can be the major or even determining factor, but in milder cases it is only one factor among many that judges and juries consider. Courts have rarely held that intelligence as measured by intelligence tests is sufficient to make categorical judgments about a person's rights or responsibilities.

This fact was vividly illustrated in the Supreme Court case of *Penry v. Lynaugh,* 492 U.S. 302 (1989). Penry was a 22-year-old man with an IQ of 50–63. He was convicted of brutally beating, raping, and killing a Texas woman. At sentencing, the jury was not told that Penry's retardation could mitigate his sentence. Because they found that he had acted deliberately and was a continued threat to society, Texas law mandated the death penalty.

Penry's lawyer argued that his retardation made the death sentence cruel and unusual punishment. The Supreme Court agreed that the jury should be told to consider that evidence. The Supreme Court did not agree, however, that mental retardation, per se, made the death penalty inappropriate (although some state courts and legislatures have decided otherwise). The court concluded that persons of similar intelligence can vary greatly in their cognitive and moral capacities and in their life experiences and that a person's total character, not intelligence alone, must be considered.

Legal issues in the use of intelligence tests are closely tied to questions about the measurement of intelligence, mental disabilities, nature/nurture debate, retardation and validity.

(*See also:* AFRICAN AMERICANS; HISPANICS; RACE AND IQ SCORES.)

BIBLIOGRAPHY

ARVEY, R. D. (1979). *Fairness in selecting employees.* Reading, MA: Addison-Wesley.

BERSOFF, D. N. (1982). Larry P. and PASE: Judicial report cards on the validity of individual intelligence tests. In T. Kratochwill (Ed.), *Advances in school psychology, Vol. 2,* (pp. 61–95). Hillsdale, NJ: Erlbaum.

BLOCK, N. J., & DWORKIN, G. (1976). *The IQ controversy.* New York: Pantheon.

DREYFUSS, J. (1979). *The Bakke case: The politics of inequality.* New York: Harcourt Brace Jovanovich.

JENSEN, A. (1980). *Bias in mental testing.* New York: Free Press.

KAMIN, L. J. (1974). *The science and politics of IQ.* Hillsdale, NJ: Erlbaum.

PAUL J. HOFER

LOCALIZATION OF BRAIN FUNCTION

Localization refers to the theory that specific cognitive functions (e.g., linguistic ability, memory) are associated with distinct regions of the brain. Paul Broca's identification of an area associated with expressive language function in 1861 initiated the careful study of brain-behavior relationships. Since that time, numerous theories about the nature and extent of localization have been proposed. Although some scientists have argued against the notion of specialized functional areas within the brain, more contemporary studies assume some type or degree of localization. The current view of the localization of cognitive functions holds that overt or covert complex psychological activity and its resulting behavior result from the interaction of different brain regions, each of which primarily controls a particular cognitive function. This does not imply that a specific function is mediated exclusively by one brain area but suggests that most functions require the integrated action of neural systems in different specialized regions. The development of localized systems in the brain is not unique to humans and is believed to have evolutionary advantages. Studies have shown that evolutionary development is associated with a greater degree of functional localization and hence greater adaptability of the organism to its environment.

This article will examine the evidence that certain functional systems are localized in specific areas of the brain. It will first discuss what is called *laterality,* or *hemispheric specialization,* the division of cognitive function between the two hemispheres of the brain, with the left hemisphere primarily controlling certain broad groups of functions and the right hemisphere primarily controlling other broad groups. Next it will discuss the localization of specific cognitive functions in the frontal, parietal, occipital, and temporal lobes (see figure 1). In general, the majority of this evidence is gained from the careful behavioral study of "accidents of na-

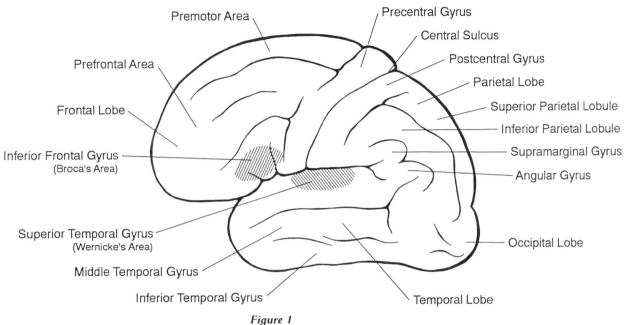

Figure 1
Localization of brain function

ture," such as strokes or brain tumors, which may damage specific brain regions. Data on hemispheric lateralization in the vast majority of right-handed individuals is highly suggestive of a verbal (left hemisphere) versus visuospatial (right hemisphere) dichotomy. The evidence of lateralization of function in left-handed individuals is less clear in light of the fact that approximately 30 percent have language in either the right hemisphere or in both hemispheres. Evidence that the left and right cerebral hemispheres are critical in mediating language and visuospatial ability, respectively, has been repeatedly demonstrated in studies of brain-injured patients. Intellectual assessment of brain-injured patients has shown that patients with right hemisphere damage perform more poorly on visuospatial tasks (such as a three-dimensional construction task) than on verbal tasks. The pattern of performance is less clear with left-hemisphere–damaged patients.

However, the verbal-visuospatial dichotomy has been criticized as failing to account for the right hemisphere role in language as well as the left hemisphere role in understanding music. Some have offered an analytic versus holistic dichotomy. Others have suggested that the left hemisphere processes information sequentially, whereas the right hemisphere processes information simultaneously. In light of these findings, many clinicians and researchers now view the left–right hemisphere dichotomy in terms of a verbal and analytic ability versus spatial and holistic ability dichotomy.

In many ways, the importance of the frontal lobes to human behavior cannot be understated. There is perhaps no other structure in the brain that, when damaged, is associated, as are the frontal lobes, with a wider range of behavioral deficits. Among the myriad functions, the frontal lobes appear to subserve superordinate or "executive" functions, such as intellectual synthesis and the control of ethical behavior. Comparative neuroanatomic studies demonstrate a progressive increase in the size of the frontal lobes among mammals culminating with the human species (24 to 33 percent of the cortex, or outer covering of the brain). One area of the frontal lobe which has shown the greatest comparative development in the human is the prefrontal cortex. In addition, studies of the evolution of organisms show that it is the last area of the brain to develop, suggesting a unique evolutionary status. With the exception of the precentral gyrus, function is not easily localized in the frontal lobes. Nevertheless, the behavioral effects of lesions in the frontal lobe are relatively consistent. The following discussion will focus on the effects of lesions to the precentral gyrus, lateral premotor, and supplementary motor areas, Broca's area, and the prefrontal area. The *precentral gyrus* is primarily concerned with controlling movement of body parts on the opposite side of the body. It is organized in such way that differential space is allocated to functionally important body parts. Direct electrical stimulation of this "motor strip" produces simple motor movements. Destructive lesions in the precentral gyrus produce weakness or paralysis.

The *lateral premotor* and *supplementary motor* areas are concerned with the planning, integration, and refinement of complex motor acts. Direct electrical stimulation produces complex motor movements. Destructive lesions to the supplementary motor and lateral premotor area impair the ability to develop an appropriate strategy for movement and impair the smooth integration of complex acts, respectively. As a result, patients with destructive lesions exhibit *apraxia,* a disorder characterized by an inability to accurately perform complex motor movements, although they may be able to perform simple motor movements and show no lack of strength or sensory loss.

The *posterior inferior* (or lower back) surface of the left frontal lobe (*Broca's area*) is specialized for producing the motor programs for speech. Patients with damage to this area speak with long pauses between words and exhibit grammatical processing deficits in speech. These patients typically omit conjunctions and pronouns. Some researchers have also proposed that Broca's area may be critical in usage and retrieval of verbs. There is also some evidence that patients with corresponding right frontal lobe lesions display speech that is lacking in emotional tone (*motor aprosodia*).

The *prefrontal* area has extensive connections to other areas of the brain. Because these connections exist, this area is believed to function as an executive control center, which regulates activity and corrects mistakes by means of an elaborate system of feedback circuits. A disruption in this system produces an array of behavioral disturbances related to the organization and regulation of complex behavioral sequences. In general, prefrontal lesions tend to result in difficulty in directing attention, developing alternative problem-solving strategies, and using information to regulate behavior. Such patients demonstrate an inability to inhibit behavioral responses or exhibit a tendency to exhibit repeatedly the same response to varied stimuli

(*perseveration*). In addition, prefrontal lesions are associated with deficits in retaining and manipulating information in memory (working memory). Although patients with prefrontal lesions do not typically exhibit decline on intellectual measures, lesions to the prefrontal area are associated with a consistent pattern of deficit based on the general asymmetrical organization of the brain. Patients with lesions in the left prefrontal area show deficits in planning and organizing verbal responses. Patients with lesions to the right prefrontal area show deficits in planning and organizing nonverbal or spatial responses. Left–right differences have also been reported in regard to the regulation of various emotional reactions. Left prefrontal lesions are associated with depression, whereas right prefrontal lesions are associated with mild euphoria. Other personality changes related to the control of certain motor functions have also been observed. Patients with bilateral medial frontal lesions (refers to areas in the middle of both frontal lobes) may be slow and lethargic, and exhibit a lack of initiative and spontaneity. Patients with orbital (above the eyes) or lateral (the side area) convexity pathology tend to be restless, hyperkinetic, explosive, and impulsive. Finally, patients with bilateral mesial (or middle) orbital area damage frequently exhibit false or bizarre responses to routine questions (*confabulation*).

Before discussing the behavioral effects of lesions to the parietal, temporal, and occipital lobes, an understanding of the primary, secondary, and tertiary zones found within these regions is required. Primary association areas or zones receive high modality-specific (e.g., visual, auditory, and somatosensory or touch) information and are topographically arranged on the cortex. Secondary association zones, which are adjacent to the primary association areas, are where modality-specific information becomes integrated into meaningful wholes. Therefore, primary association areas are concerned with sensation, while secondary zones are concerned with perception. Tertiary association areas or zones are not modality-specific but serve to integrate information across sense modalities. These zones typically lie at the borders of the parietal, temporal, and occipital lobes.

The parietal lobe is a functionally complex area of brain associated with somatosensory perception or touch, body awareness, spatial localization, verbal comprehension, and information processing. The postcentral gyrus is composed of regions specialized for primary tactile sensation such as light touch, deep pressure, joint movement, and temperature. Somatotopic maps (maps of touch sensitivity developed via direct electrical stimulation of the brain) show that the subjective experience of sensitivity in different parts of the body is disproportionate to the body surface. For example, the lips, tongue, and hands, which are the most sensitive parts of the body, occupy more cortical area within the postcentral gyrus than the rest of the body. Lesions to the postcentral gyrus result in an immediate loss of all sensory modalities on the opposite side of the body. Lesions to the secondary somatosensory cortex, located in the upper part of the parietal lobe (superior parietal lobule), result in an inability to identify objects by feel as well as a loss of weight, texture, and form discrimination.

Lesions to the tertiary association areas of the parietal lobes result in a consistent pattern of deficit based on the general asymmetrical organization of the brain. Lesions to the right parietal tertiary association area often result in impairments of visuospatial and constructional ability. Such deficits result in an inability to construct or assemble objects from their constituent parts (*constructional apraxia*). One common finding is an inability to dress oneself (*dressing apraxia*). In addition, right parietal lobe lesions often result in disturbances of body image. Such patients often neglect visual, auditory, and somatosensory stimulation on the left side of their body and of space (*contralateral neglect*), deny paralysis of the left side of their body (*anosagnosia*), or appear mildly unconcerned about it (*anosodiaphoria*). Damage to the parietal-occipital area may result in an inability to recognize faces (*propsagnosia*) or an inability to form or recognize spatial relationships. Lesions to the right parietal-temporal areas have been associated with an inability to appreciate or recognize familiar musical tunes (*amusia*).

In contrast, lesions to the left parietal lobe typically are associated with a variety of impairments in understanding language. For example, lesions to the parietal-occipital area are associated with difficulties or an inability in comprehending written information (*dyslexia* and *alexia*, respectively). In addition, an inability to comprehend spoken language has been associated with lesions to the parietal-temporal zone. Patients with left parietal lobe lesions also exhibit an inability to execute or recall a purposeful activity upon command, but may do so spontaneously in the course of normal activity (*ideomotor apraxia*). In addition, these patients are usually unable to imitate specific actions. Some have theorized that the memories for skilled actions are stored in the left parietal lobe. Left parietal lobe lesions may also produce writing disabilities (*agraphia*), calculation difficulties (*acalculia*), left–right confusion, an inability to discriminate fingers without visual cues (*finger agnosia*), and an inability to localize and name parts of one's own body (*autotopagnosia*).

The occipital lobes are specialized for the processing of visual information. The primary visual cortex resides at the back or most posterior part of the occipital lobe and borders the calcarine fissure. The central portion of the visual field is disproportionately represented relative to the surface area of the retina and accounts for one-third of the visual cortex. Destructive lesions to the visual cortex produce areas of visual loss commensurate with the size and location of the lesion. The secondary visual association area is primarily concerned with visual perception. Bilateral lesions below the calcarine fissure produce a loss of color perception (*achromatopsia*) and the inability to imagine color.

The tertiary association area has extensive connections with the other regions of the cerebral hemispheres. The role of the tertiary association cortex includes the relating of present and past visual experience, with recognition of what is seen and the appreciation of its significance. A destructive lesion results in the inability to recognize the significance of sensory stimuli (*visual agnosia*). Bilateral lesions of the upper or superior region of the tertiary association cortex result in visual disorientation, loss of coordination of eye movements, and an inability to carry out visually guided movements of the hands. Bilateral lesions of the lower or inferior region of the temporal and occipital lobes produce impaired recognition of familiar faces (*prosopagnosia*). Direct electrical stimulation of this area of the brain produces vivid hallucinations of scenes from the past, which suggests a role in the storage and retrieval of visual memories.

Lesions to occipital lobes are associated with a consistent pattern of deficit based on the general left–right asymmetrical organization of the brain. As mentioned earlier, right parietal-occipital lobe damage is associated with a disruption of spatial–perceptual orientation of visual stimuli and spatial neglect or inattention to the side of the body opposite (or contralateral) to the location of the lesion in the brain. Left occipital-temporal lesions produce deficits such as dyslexia which are related to the visual processing of symbolic information. Finally, bilateral parieto-occipital lobe lesions are associated with *Balint's syndrome,* which involves difficulty voluntarily shifting visual attention, peripheral visual inattention, and an inability to localize objects in space by visual guidance. A patient with Balint's syndrome may pour water from a pitcher next to a glass instead of into it.

The temporal lobes, which contain the primary association cortex for both hearing and smell, play a significant role in language function, memory, and visual perception, and form part of the anatomical substrate (with the limbic system) for the integration of the emotional and motivational aspects of human experience as well as consciousness. The primary auditory cortex is located at the junction of the frontal, parietal, and temporal lobes. There is a direct point-to-point projection of sound from the receptor (the cochlea of the ear) to the auditory cortex. Irritative lesions produce auditory hallucinations, such as ringing or buzzing sounds. The primary olfactory cortex is located in a region known as the *uncus* and adjoining parts of another area known as the *parahippocampal gyrus.* Irritative lesions produce olfactory hallucinations. Damage to the olfactory cortex results in a loss of the sense of smell (*anosmia*).

The left superior temporal gyrus (*Wernicke's area*) is associated with the comprehension of speech. Patients with lesions to Wernicke's area are unable to comprehend and repeat speech due to damage to the superior temporal gyrus. Their speech is fluent although incoherent because the intact Broca's area is receiving inadequate feedback from Wernicke's area. Left–right differences have been observed with lesions to the left superior temporal lobe. Just as left superior temporal lobe lesions are associated with verbal comprehension difficulties, right superior temporal lobe lesions are associated with difficulties interpreting the affective components of language (*sensory aprosodia*). This model of language function was later modified to include a role for the left angular gyrus, which is involved in the

activation of visual letter or word patterns when one is spelling or reading words. However, this model has been criticized for failing to account for the role of subcortical structures in language and the fact that surgical destruction of the language zones rarely results in permanent language loss. Recent research has proposed that the superior portion of the left temporal lobe, structures located below the cortex known as the *basal ganglia,* and the inferior portion of the left frontal lobe are associated with the implementation of word forms and sentence structure. In addition, the parietal-temporal-occipital association area and the inferior temporal lobe is associated with the retrieval and usage of nouns. In addition, right temporal lobe lesions have been associated with visual perceptual deficits in the discrimination of complex patterns, deficits in facial perception and recognition, and the failure to appreciate the significance of the visual stimuli.

The role of the temporal lobes in memory was not discovered until the early 1950s, after several patients with epilepsy underwent bilateral removal of the medial temporal lobes. Subsequent to surgery, these patients showed an inability to form new long-term memories, but exhibited no immediate and remote memory problems. It has since been hypothesized that a region of these lobes (*hippocampus*) is the neurologic substrate for the laying down of information into long-term memory. Left temporal lobe lesions are associated with greater verbal memory impairment, whereas right temporal lobe lesions are associated with greater nonverbal memory impairment. Although memory and learning are not localized within the brain, a number of subcortical areas have been implicated in acquisition and retention of knowledge. For example, lesions to the regions of the brain called the *diencephalon, basal forebrain, prefrontal cortex,* and *basal ganglia,* specifically, the *caudate nucleus* and *substantia nigra,* have also been associated with memory or learning deficits. In all cases, impairment is found on measures of explicit memory (i.e., memory for facts and events) with little or no impairment on measures of implicit memory (i.e., forms of learning that do not utilize conscious participation but do require the association of simultaneous stimuli).

The role of the temporal lobes in emotion, perception, and consciousness has been obtained through studies of patients with temporal lobe epilepsy, specifically, complex partial seizure disorder. Such patients will frequently experience a disorientation of time and space, an altered perception of themselves and/or their environment, and abnormal emotional states. Finally, bilateral destruction of the temporal lobes produces *Kluver-Bucy syndrome,* which is characterized by an inability to form new memories, heightened sexual interest and behavior, emotional instability, and a tendency to put all manner of objects into one's mouth.

As indicated earlier, most functions require the integrated action of the neural systems in different specialized regions. An example of such an interaction between systems is a patient with lesions (usually due to a stroke) to the left occipital lobe and the fibers that connect the cerebral hemispheres (splenium of the corpus callosum). Such a patient is unable to read but retains the ability to write (alexia without agraphia). The patient's inability to read is not entirely understood but is proposed to occur because the left posterior language area (angular gyrus) is disconnected from the left and right visual association corticies. However, the patient retains the ability to write because of the intact left posterior language area.

Finally, an important caveat is necessary for a truer understanding of localization of function in the human brain. The functions and deficits described above are generalizations of brain-behavior relationships based largely on a study of patients with cerebral dysfunction. As a result, such generalizations should not be taken as absolute truths. The fact that a specific deficit is associated with damage to a particular area of the brain does not imply that that area regulates the disrupted function. Many variables besides neuroanatomical site of lesion are important in determining the final expression of cognitive and behavioral deficits. Finally, confirmation is required from the study of normal brain function before definitive conclusions are made regarding the functional localization of behavior.

(*See also:* AGNOSIA; BRAIN; BRAIN, PATHOLOGIES OF THE.)

BIBLIOGRAPHY

BRADSHAW, J. L., & NETTLETON, N. C. (1981). The nature of hemispheric specialization in man. *Behavioral and Brain Scien̨ces, 4,* 51–91.

DAMASIO, A. R., & DAMASIO, H. (1992). Brain and language. *Scientific American, 267,* 88–109.

FILSKOV, S. B., & BOLL, T. J. (EDS.). (1981) *Handbook of clinical neuropsychology.* New York: Wiley.

GOLDMAN-RAKIC, P. S. (1992). Working memory and mind. *Scientific American, 267,* 110–117.

GESCHWIND, N., & GALABURDA, A. M. (1984). *Cerebral dominance: The biological foundations.* Cambridge, MA: Harvard University Press.

KANDEL, E. R., & HAWKINS, R. D. (1992). The biological basis of learning and individuality. *Scientific American, 267,* 78–87.

KANDEL, E. R., SCHWARTZ, J. H., & JESSELL, T. M. (1991). *Principles of neural science* (3rd ed.). New York: Elsevier.

KERTESZ, A. (ED.). (1983). *Localization in neuropsychology.* New York: Academic Press.

KOLB, B., & WHISHAW, I. Q. (1990). *Fundamentals of human neuropsychology* (2nd ed.). New York: W. H. Freeman.

MATARAZZO, J. D. (1980). *Wechsler's measurement and appraisal of adult intelligence.* New York: Oxford University Press.

PHILLIPS, C. G., ZEKI, S., & BARLOW, H. B. (1984). Localization of function in the cerebral cortex. *Brain, 107,* 327–361.

SEGALOWITZ, S. J. (1983). *Two sides of the brain: Brain lateralization explored.* Englewood Cliffs, NJ: Prentice-Hall.

WALSH, K. (1987). *Neuropsychology: A clinical approach.* New York: Churchill Livingstone.

ZEKI, S. (1992). The visual image in mind and brain. *Scientific American, 267,* 68–77.

ANTHONY M. PODRAZA
ROBERT A. BORNSTEIN

LURIA, A. R. (1902–1977) Aleksandr Romanovich Luria, who is regarded as one of the founders of neuropsychology, attempted to relate mind, brain, and behavior. Although Luria admitted that the brain—the highest human organ—works as a whole, he showed in his clinical research that it has differentiated functions. Because Luria identified the separate functional organizations of the cortex with major cognitive functions, his view of intelligence can be labeled *multiple, but interdependent cognitive activities.* For him, there was no duality between mental functions and their structural base.

Luria was born in Kazan, Russia, on July 16, 1902, and died in Moscow on August 14, 1977. Both his mother and his father were physicians. Having been denied hospital and faculty privileges because of his Jewish extraction, Luria's father practiced medicine in Kazan but was given the recognition he deserved soon after the Russian revolution. He became a deputy director of the Institute for Advanced Medical Studies in Moscow. A. R. Luria learned German as a child at home and was familiar with nineteenth-century German writings in philosophy, history, and literature. His school and university education began in Kazan. He studied at the university both in the faculty of history and philosophy and in the medical school. He earned a doctorate in psychological sciences and, later, a doctorate in medicine at Moscow's Institute of Medicine. His knowledge and interest in medicine must have given him an unusual advantage to study neurological impairment and, later, to continue his research in neuropsychology at the Bourdenko Neurosurgical Institute in Moscow.

ASSOCIATION WITH VYGOTSKY

Higher mental activities not only include language ability but are essentially defined by it. The ability to use language with meaning is essential for intellectual development. The loss of this ability is seen in APHASIA. A study of language ability became one of Luria's major preoccupations as he and his friend Alexie Leontiev started associating with Lev VYGOTSKY. Luria was 22 when he met Vygotsky. Although Vygotsky was only six years older than Luria, he was readily acknowledged as the leader, and the three, the "troika," shaped the course of Soviet psychology. Luria, Vygotsky, and Leontiev were developmentalists concerned with children's learning and development. In his first well-known book, *The nature of human conflicts,* Luria (1932) set out to study the role of speech in "the organization, regulation and control of man's voluntary movements and affective experiences," an endeavor that continued for many years and appeared in a later publication (Luria, 1959). Vygotsky's initial research and writings on thought and language provided Luria and Leontiev with an orientation for studying internalization of speech, and the mediation of peers and adults that was necessary in the intellectual development of children.

Children's actions and speech are at first separate. Speech provides an energizing role. The experimenter saying "Press!" initiates child's key-pressing activity simply because of its energy; a loud "Press!" brings about a harder and faster key-pressing response. Then external speech initiates an activity but is unable to stop it. The child at this stage often repeats the external instruction, "Don't Press!" while engaged in key-pressing. The next stage occurs when speech can initiate as well as inhibit action. By this stage children have begun to internalize the external instruction of the experimenter. Sometimes they remind themselves of the instruction, talking to themselves. Children acquire language or the meaning of signs through work and experience. Like all higher cognitive activities, language has sociocultural roots.

Although Luria's views on language and internal speech are the same as Vygotsky's, he advanced and elaborated the role of speech much more. An example of his progress is his research on aphasia. Referring to Luria's 1947 book on traumatic aphasia (in Russian), R. Jakobson (1971), himself a renowned aphasiologist, accepts the six different types of aphasia identified by Luria and credits him with helping to remove the chaos in the field. Dissolution of the regulatory function of speech, inability to understand logical–grammatical relationships such as father's brother and brother's father, and aphasia related to either simultaneous or successive linguistic forms that Luria discovered in clinical practice, have their roots in the development of speech. Luria's approach to studying the role of speech nevertheless retained Vygotsky's influence—higher cognitive functions are to be analyzed first in terms of their development in a sociohistorical context and subsequently their dissolution because of neurological impairment.

FUNCTIONAL ORGANIZATION OF THE BRAIN AND ASSOCIATED COGNITIVE FUNCTIONS

Luria's work on brain-damaged patients became important for the Soviet government during World War II, both for diagnosis of the abilities and disabilities of the injured persons as well as for their rehabilitation. Never shy of putting his medical training and psychological knowledge to use, especially relating to speech and other cognitive abilities, Luria devoted himself to relating behavior to brain damage. Systematic clinical observations enabled him to do "syndrome analysis," to identify a cluster of cognitive dysfunctions broadly located in the occipital-parietal (simultaneous processing), fronto-temporal (successive processing), and frontal (planning and decision-making) areas of the cortex as well as the arousal disorders resulting from damage to the brain stem (Luria, 1970). Developmentally, simultaneous and successive processing can be observed in young children, in their figure drawings, design constructions, and categorization of objects (simultaneous), and in repetition of sequential movements or words, and appreciation of syntax (successive). Children's language reveals that successive processes develop earlier than simultaneous ones; syntagmatic associations (the moon shines, the dog barks) appear earlier than paradigmatic associations (moon–sun, dog–cat). Reflecting on his early work, Luria wrote (1974):

> Now, after 40 years I understand my early findings that in children of 6–7 years, syntagmatic connections (such as *the moon*–shines, *the spade*–works) are much more common than paradigmatic (or associative) connections (such as *the moon*–the sun; *the dog*–the cat, etc.), and that associations (by similarity or common features) are not at all basic speech processes, but rather a product of further development of the simultaneous schemes.

Apart from the two coding processes, simultaneous and successive, are two others: arousal-attention and planning. Present at birth in orienting responses, arousal is soon inseparable from attention. Planning and decision making seem to develop later, with the development of speech and the ability to regulate actions through internal speech. Whether this view is acceptable to developmental psychologists does not detract from associating planning with the development of frontal lobe functions. The acronym CNS, which usually denotes the central nervous system, was seriously considered by Luria to indicate the conceptual nervous system. A dynamic rather than a static anatomical view of brain functions led him to provide a new epistemology. His ultimate aim was to study consciousness through discovering the functions of the frontal lobes, which incidentally seems to be one of the preoccupations of current neuropsychology. In 1969 he wrote: "The Human Brain not only recodes the sensory information, turning it into a system of concepts, but establishes human plans and programs and forms a conscious control of human actions. It is really an organ of freedom. . . . How can we come to a scientific solution of the riddle of man's free activity and conscious behavior?" (p. 3). In searching for a solution, Luria comes back to the role of speech and language and its relationship to social and historical factors. "We likewise know that the origin of the highest form of self-regulating behavior doesn't lie in the depths of the organism. . . . We have to turn to the complex forms of a child's relations with its social environment and to its acquisition of language" (p. 19). Luria was envious of the young researchers who would make new discoveries about human consciousness as technology and knowledge progressed.

Luria's influence in conceptualizing intelligence can be seen in contemporary psychology (Das, 1992; Das, Naglieri, & Kirby, 1994). Based on both neuropsychology and cognitive psychology, the major cognitive functions he identified can be recognized in factor analysis of test performance of normal individuals; the factor-analytic results support his syndrome analysis. Luria's comments in response to the paper by Das and colleagues (1975) are instructive: "Up to now the approach from this point of view [simultaneous and successive synthesis] showed its reliability and validity in the studies of neuropsychological syndromes; now it was shown that in a direct approach with factor analysis these ideas are of a certain value" [Luria, 1975].

Luria's ideas have been helpful in understanding cognitive deficits of mentally retarded children (O'Connor & Hermelin, 1963) and the core deficit in dyslexic children that seems to link phonological coding to successive processing (Das, 1992). An attempt at constructing a psychometric test of simultaneous and successive processing (Kaufman & Kaufman, 1983) has received mixed reviews. The extension of Luria's neuropsychological findings to the area of intelligence can be questioned, as is the case with other contemporary theories. The findings themselves, however, have been useful in understanding neurological disorders and have guided rehabilitation after brain injury (Luria, 1963). His neuropsychological caseworks, spanning fifty years of his life, led him to develop a unique view of mental functions that is relevant for viewing mind–brain relationships: Even the elementary functions of the brain are not only biological but are also shaped by an individual's social and cultural experience.

Beyond doubt, Luria is the best known and most frequently cited Russian psychologist in Western psychology. His influence in Europe and in the United States has spread not only through his insightful and extensive publications but also through his many international friends and students. He remained productive under Josef Stalin, did not slow down when removed for a few years from the Neurosurgical Institute to the Institute of Defectology in 1950, retained his optimism, and worked very hard until his death following a heart attack.

(*See also:* NEUROPSYCHOLOGY, CLINICAL.)

BIBLIOGRAPHY

COLE, M., & COLE, S. (EDS.). (1979). *The making of mind.* Cambridge, MA: Harvard University Press.

DAS, J. P. (1992). Beyond a unidimensional scale of merit. *Intelligence, 16,* 137–149.

DAS, J. P., KIRBY, J. R., & JARMAN, R. F. (1975). Simultaneous and successive synthesis: An alternative model for cognitive abilities. *Psychological Bulletin, 82,* 87–103.

DAS, J. P., NAGLIERI, J. A., & KIRBY, J. R. (1994). *Assessment of cognitive processes.* Needham Heights, MA: Allyn & Bacon.

HOMSKAYA, E. D., TSETKOVA, L. S., & ZEIGNARIK, B. W. (EDS.). (1982). *A. R. Luria and contemporary psychology* [In Russian]. Moscow: University Publishing House.

JAKOBSON, R. (1971). *Studies on child language and aphasia.* The Hague: Mouton.

KAUFMAN, A., & KAUFMAN, N. (1983). *The Kaufman assessment battery for children: Interpretive manual.* Circle Pines, MN: American Guidance Service.

LURIA, A. R. (1932). *The nature of human conflicts.* New York: Liveright.

LURIA, A. R. (1959). *The role of speech in the regulation of normal and abnormal behavior.* Oxford: Pergamon Press.

LURIA, A. R. (1963). *Restoration of functions after brain injury.* New York: Macmillan.

LURIA, A. R. (1966a). *Higher cortical functions in man.* New York: Basic Books. This book and the next are Luria's often cited works on neuropsychology.

LURIA, A. R. (1966b). *Human brain and psychological processes.* New York: Harper & Row.

LURIA, A. R. (1969). The origin and cerebral organization of man's conscious action. *Paper presented at the 19th International Congress of Psychology, London.* Moscow: University Publications (pp. 1–23).

LURIA, A. R. (1970). The functional organization of the brain. *Scientific American, 2,* 66–78.

LURIA, A. R. (1973a). The long road of a Soviet psychologist. *International Social Science Journal, 15,* 71–87.

LURIA, A. R. (1973b). *The working brain.* London: Penguin. This book is a summary of Luria's research on cognitive and neuropsychological topics. It contains extensive references to Western literature, with which Luria was familiar.

LURIA, A. R. (1974). Letter to J. P. Das. August 26.

LURIA, A. R. (1975). Letter to J. P. Das. February 20.

O'CONNOR, N., & HERMELIN, B. (1963). *Speech and thought in severe subnormality.* New York: Macmillan.

J. P. DAS

M

MAINSTREAMING Intelligence tests were designed originally to segregate students rather than to integrate them. At the turn of the twentieth century, public school education was burgeoning in France. Increasing as well was the poor performance of many students. The Minister of Public Education commissioned Alfred BINET to devise a system to differentiate between capable and incapable learners. Students in the second category required a "special-education" approach. Working with colleagues, Binet developed a lengthy series of short, everyday tasks to test an individual's basic processes of reasoning. The ascending difficulty level of the tasks caused some children to fail and to terminate the test. Students who did not perform as well were segregated, and the development of a two-track system of education, regular and special, with close ties to psychometric assessment, began.

The use of tests for intelligence quotient (IQ) to determine both different learning abilities and the appropriate educational placement for students continues. Tests for IQ have become controversial, however, particularly in the following two major areas: (1) the assessment and differentiation of students according to intellectual ability, and (2) the assessment of students in terms of *degree* of intellectual ability. Sociodemographic factors such as race, ethnicity, language, and sex complicate the determination of intellectual ability.

These considerations have brought IQ tests into the courtroom. For many students, whether they remain in the mainstream of education or are segregated for special education depends on the assessment of IQ tests.

CONFUSION OF TERMINOLOGY

J. Rogers (1993) points out that part of the controversy results from the use of different terms. Three designations have gained popularity. The term *mainstreaming* often refers to placement of an academically challenged student in a regular classroom for part of a school day or for selected subjects. *Integration* also carries this meaning. In addition, both terms may indicate full-time placement in a regular classroom. Mainstreaming or integration most often occurs in a centrally designated school with segregated special classes and specially trained teachers. Two more recent terms are *inclusion* or *full inclusion,* indicating full-time regular class placement with age-appropriate peers in the individual's neighborhood school regardless of learning ability. The term *regular education initiative* (REI) refers in the United States to the movement toward full inclusion of mildly challenged students (Ysseldyke, Algozzine, & Thurlow, 1992). Because these various terms have not been defined in relation to education laws such as PL 94–142 in the United States or Bill

82 in Ontario, Canada, no common definitive terminology exists.

DESIRABLE CHARACTERISTICS OF IQ TESTS

Since Binet's research, IQ tests have proliferated and taken a variety of forms though continuing for the most part to pose a series of short, diverse tasks that probe basic reasoning processes. In 1976 N. Robinson and H. Robinson stated the prevailing view of educational psychologists and educators: "When properly understood and carefully used, an IQ test can be valuable in assessing a child's rate of progress" (p. 343). This opinion derives from the belief that a well-constructed test of intelligence results in an objective, accurate reading of intellectual ability. Characteristic of such a test are the following factors:

1. Validity. The test measures only what it is supposed to test with sufficient breadth and depth.
2. Reliability. Repeated testings with the same or similar instruments will obtain nearly uniform results.
3. A single score. It provides a simple, relatively fixed index of intellectual ability.
4. Questions formulated to elicit interpretable responses. These replies reveal patterns of reasoning that indicate the level of ability and lead to suggestions for incisive teaching strategies.

IQ TESTS AND LABELING

As noted by educators such as J. Andrews and J. Lupart (1993) and W. L. Heward and M. D. Orlansky (1992), IQ tests generally provide fairly accurate predictions of school failure by students with apparent intellectual challenges. An IQ index indicates the severity of challenge and the terminology that describes the condition of the challenge. The terminology-and-severity combination contributes to an educational decision to "mainstream" or segregate a particular student. Table 1 illustrates the condition of mental retardation with traditional terminology.

Conversely, IQ testing identifies intellectually advantaged students. The label *gifted* applies to some of these students, who are placed in segregated "gifted" classes. No uniform criteria for the distinction "gifted" exist. In general, a score in the 135 range is necessary, and although other criteria (grades, interviews, and achievement tests) have a place in most identification schemata, the IQ score prevails. Few students are labeled "gifted" without an intellectual assessment.

That IQ tests can differentiate students accurately has been the dominant perception of society from the turn of the twentieth century. Tests have contributed strongly to educational placement and teaching decisions. The IQ test has become a fundamental tool for understanding the learning capacities and abilities of students who did not fit well into what was considered

TABLE 1
Relationship among IQ level, descriptive terminology, and educational placement

IQ Range	Severity of Mental Retardation	Educational Terminology	Educational Placement
50 to 75	mild	educable	public school special class with part-time mainstreaming
40 to 55	moderate	trainable	public school full-time special class or special school
25 to 40	severe	custodial	at home or in an institution
below 25	profound	custodial	at home or in an institution

"average." The tests routinely separate nonaverage from other learners in accordance with the prevailing educational view that segregation into special classes leads to more efficient and effective education.

CONCERNS REGARDING THE RELATIONSHIP OF IQ TESTS AND INTEGRATION

Not all educators agree that tests of intelligence, even when well constructed, possess the strengths attributed to them by their designers and advocates. Their contribution to decisions for educational placement is one controversial area. The debate over IQ tests covers four primary issues. All relate to the segregation of students from the mainstream of regular education. These issues are race, mental retardation, learning disability, and inclusive education.

Race. The issue of race arose because of the disproportionate number of black students in the United States in classes for children labeled *mentally retarded.* Rogers Elliott (1987) noted the heavy overrepresentation of black students in classes for students labeled *educationally mentally retarded* (EMR) relative to the overall number of blacks in the American population. Some critics of the disproportionate representation attributed it to the use of IQ tests that were culturally biased against blacks. Elliott reviewed two celebrated legal cases. In the 1972 case, *Larry P. v. Riles,* Judge R. F. Peckham (1972, 1979) ruled in a preliminary injunction that "intelligence tests are discriminatory towards blacks and can no longer be used for educational placement in California." A permanent injunction was issued in 1979 and reaffirmed in 1984.

> Elliott (1987) summarized Judge Peckham's reasoning as follows: Black children would score higher if they had better opportunities to learn, but they don't have such opportunities. Their low scores are wrongly interpreted to say something about their innate ability. A *culturally fair test* would show their ability to learn to be as high as that of whites [p. 14].

The second influential case had the opposite verdict. In *PASE (Parents in Action on Special Education) v. Hannon* (Grady, 1980), Judge J. Grady rejected the claims of nonvalidity and nonreliability of IQ tests in reference to black students. He agreed that blacks were overrepresented in EMR classes but not that IQ tests were responsible. Other factors, such as teachers' ratings of students, should be taken into consideration. Indeed, expert witnesses argued that IQ tests prevented some students from being placed incorrectly in EMR classes.

In part because of these conflicting legal findings, educators and psychologists use information from IQ tests with caution and in conjunction with other forms of intellectual assessment, such as parent and teacher nomination. Some psychologists, such as those belonging to the Association of Black Psychologists, however, support parents who "have chosen to defend their rights by refusing to allow their children and themselves to be subjected to achievement, intelligence, aptitude, and performance tests" that they believe to be inimicable to their interests specifically because they "place Black children in 'special' classes and schools" (Williams cited in Elliott, 1987).

Mental Retardation. Perhaps the persons most directly affected by IQ tests are those designated as *mentally retarded, developmentally delayed,* or *intellectually challenged.* As Robinson and Robinson wrote in 1976:

> "Nowhere has the IQ proved to be a more mixed blessing than in matters concerning the welfare of mentally retarded children.... The apparent simplicity of the IQ led to an enthusiastic but largely misguided movement to label or classify children primarily on the basis of their scores on the intelligence tests" [p. 343].

Scores and classification led many to segregated educational or institutional placement (see Table 1).

J. Sattler (1988) and others have warned against the use of a single score as a determination of functional ability. In the 1970s, because of recognized limitations in focusing on the intellectual component, the American Association on Mental Deficiency altered its definition of mental retardation to include deficits in adaptive behavior concurrent with subaverage general intellectual functioning (Grossman, 1973). This change was a strong indication that scores on IQ tests alone were insufficient criteria for placement of students in different classes. I. M. Evans (1991) notes that "Today ... the legal, medical, and educational criteria for designating an individual as mentally retarded are almost exclusively contained in obtaining a score of a certain level on an individual test of 'general intelligence'."

Those who consider the IQ test to be objective, valid, and reliable, and clinicians to be capable of undertaking appropriate interpretation of test performance, judge IQ tests to be beneficial. Such a view is consonant with the historical perception of tests of intelligence. Practical and moral criticism of the use of IQ tests in educational placement decisions derives from the nature of tests of intelligence, inadequately trained clinicians, and the widespread aversion to any dynamic that contributes to the labeling and separation of individuals.

Concern for the misuse of IQ tests is not new. Stephen J. Gould cites Binet's fear about educators who regard "special education classes as 'an excellent opportunity for getting rid of all the children who trouble us,' and without the true critical spirit . . . designate all who are unruly, or disinterested in the school" (Gould, 1981). Many parents, educators, psychologists, and others consider the fear of Binet well founded in today's practices.

Learning Disability. The students labeled *learning disabled* comprise the largest group of persons assigned to special education since the 1960s. *Learning disability* is a new, umbrella term for a variety of conditions. In education, more than in psychology or medicine, it has superseded terms such as DYSLEXIA (difficulty with reading), DYSCALCULIA (difficulty with mathematics, and APHASIA (difficulty with language), and other designations for specific conditions.

The all-encompassing nature of the category "learning disability" has created difficulty in determining its characteristics. For many, however, the finding of a "severe discrepancy between achievement and intellectual ability" in one or more academic areas has been a tell-tale sign of learning disability (Gearhart, Mullen, & Gearhart, 1993). A major result of this belief has been the widespread use of IQ tests in determining educational placement. Clinicians watch for a diagnostic signpost in discrepancies among various tasks. For instance, on the Wechsler Intelligence Scale for Children (WISC) and its revisions, the most commonly used instrument in North America, a discrepancy between verbally loaded subtests and performance subtests indicates a possible learning disability. In association with findings from other sources such as achievement tests, the degree of discrepancy leads to

a recommendation to mainstream completely or partially, or to segregate. According to Sattler (1988), research has not supported the contention that patterns on the WISC, verbal-performance discrepancy, subtest-score pattern, and range of scatter of scores can distinguish the different learning abilities of children. Nonetheless, the inclusion of an IQ test as a primary instrument in a battery of diagnostic tests in instances of suspected learning disability is the general rule.

Although many clinicians and educators trust IQ tests, others remain concerned about their validity, reliability, cultural bias, diagnostic strength, and the expertise of the clinician. Not all psychologists are closely familiar with the educational process. In some educational jurisdictions IQ tests are administered by psychometrists who lack training in interpretation.

Inclusive Education. The terms *inclusion* and *full inclusion* refer to the belief in mainstream education for all students. Advocates for inclusion argue that special education has not lived up to its promise of increased efficiency and effectiveness of learning for students with various learning challenges. They call for the merger of mainstream and special education (Stainback, Stainback, & Bunch, 1989), the redefinition of criteria for attendance in regular classes, and the roles of regular and special-education teachers (Bunch, 1992). They point to the vigorous movement toward fuller integration into community life of people with various other challenges and wish it extended to the educational system. In the United States the tendency toward inclusive education is apparent in the regular-education initiative (Will, 1986), which extends past the concept of mainstreaming to routine inclusion of students with mild to moderate degrees of challenge. As noted extensively by T. M. Skrtic (1991) and others, the concept of inclusion is complex and contentious.

Advocates of inclusion question the technical merits of intelligence tests. They believe that intellectual assessment derives too much from a student's performance on a test and not enough from abilities in the classroom or the home. Supporters of inclusive education urge at least a turn away from classification and educational placement rising from the human-pathology theoretical framework common to psychology and medicine. They prefer emphasis on functional evaluation by teachers, parents, and others in frequent contact with a child. More radical proponents of inclusive education deny any role for intelligence tests in educational placement. They do not believe that current clinical practices contribute significantly to the determination of educational needs and strategies.

CONCLUSION

The value of tests of intelligence to integrate or to segregate students with various learning abilities is a contentious issue. According to the traditional view, IQ tests are valid if administered proficiently and are significant to the decision-making process. A well-constructed test is objective in assessment, and reliable in obtaining closely similar scores in repeated applications. IQ tests yield accurate individual assessments, which lead to powerful teaching strategies. Advocates of IQ tests support their routine use in educational placement.

An increasing number of psychologists, educators, parents, legal experts, and students in special-education classes dispute these opinions. The court system has queried the objectivity, validity, and reliability of IQ tests and their use in decisions to integrate or segregate. The single score does not reveal the many facets of intelligence. Clinicians have no experience of the classroom; their contributions to integration–segregation decisions and teaching strategies are questionable. Research indicates that IQ tests cannot differentiate conditions of challenge. This finding has implications for the educational classification strategy. Advocates of inclusive education see no need for instruments whose original and, to a significant extent, continuing purpose is to separate students with below-average academic progress.

Although the majority of educational authorities in North America continue to use IQ tests, they have other means of assessment. IQ tests are thus no longer the dominant factor in decision making. The courts have required some educational authorities to discontinue the use of IQ tests for placement decisions. Other educational jurisdictions have banned or limited the use of IQ tests. The general societal movement toward integration of persons previously segregated has also contributed to the questions about the validity of IQ tests. No longer are tests of intelligence the

norm. Today their perceived value in contributing to educational-placement decisions is diminishing.

(*See also:* SCHOOLING.)

BIBLIOGRAPHY

ANDREWS, J., & LUPART, J. (1993). *The inclusive classroom: Educating exceptional children.* Scarborough, Ontario: Nelson Canada.

BUNCH, G. O. (1992). The need for redefinition. In J. Pearpoint, M. Forest, & J. Snow (Eds.), *The inclusion papers: Strategies to make inclusion work* (pp. 111–113). Toronto: Inclusion Press.

ELLIOTT, R. (1987). *Litigating intelligence: IQ tests, special education, and social science in the courtroom.* Dover, MA: Auburn House.

EVANS, I. M. (1991). Testing and diagnosis: A review and evaluation. In L. H. Meyer, C. A. Peck, & L. Brown (Eds.), *Critical issues in the lives of people with severe disabilities* (pp. 24–44). Baltimore: Paul H. Brookes.

GEARHART, B., MULLEN, R. C., & GEARHART, C. J. (1993). *Exceptional individuals: An introduction.* Pacific Grove, CA: Brooks/Cole.

GOULD, S. J. (1981). *The mismeasure of man.* New York: W. W. Norton.

GRADY, J. (1980). Opinion. PASE v. Hannon. *Federal Supplement, 506,* 831–883.

GROSSMAN, H. (1973). *Manual on terminology and classification in mental retardation.* Baltimore: Garamond/Pridemark.

HEWARD, W. L., & ORLANSKY, M. D. (1992). *Exceptional children: An introductory survey of special education.* New York: Merrill.

PECKHAM, R. F. (1972). Opinion. Larry P. v. Riles. *Federal Supplement, 343,* 1306–1315.

PECKHAM, R. F. (1979). Opinion. Larry P. v. Riles. *Federal Supplement 495,* 926–992.

ROBINSON, N., & ROBINSON, H. (1976). *The mentally retarded child.* New York: McGraw-Hill.

ROGERS, J. (1993, May). *The inclusion revolution.* Research Bulletin. Bloomington, IN: Center for Evaluation, Development, and Research, Phi Delta Kappa.

SATTLER, J. (1988). *Assessment of children.* San Diego, CA: Jerome M. Sattler.

SKRTIC, T. M. (1991). *Behind special education: A critical analysis of professional culture and school organization.* Denver, CO: Love.

STAINBACK, W., STAINBACK, S., & BUNCH, G. (1989). A rationale for the merger of regular and special education. In S. Stainback, W. Stainback, & M. Forest (Eds.), *Educating all students in the mainstream of regular education* (pp. 15–26). Baltimore: Paul H. Brookes.

YSSELDYKE, J., ALGOZZINE, B., & THURLOW, M. L. (1992). *Critical issues in special education.* Boston: Houghton-Mifflin.

WILL, M. (1986). *Educating children with learning problems: A shared responsibility.* Washington, DC: U. S. Department of Education, Office of Education.

GARY BUNCH

MATHEMATICAL ABILITY Mathematical ability has been recognized repeatedly as a major category of human intelligence. For example, the original intelligence tests devised by Alfred BINET and his colleagues in the early 1900s included mathematical problems, as have many of the subsequent intelligence tests (Wolf, 1973). L. L. THURSTONE's statistical analysis of human intelligence revealed "number," the ability to solve computation and word problems, as one of seven primary mental abilities. Howard Gardner's (1983) theory of MULTIPLE INTELLIGENCES lists logical-mathematical intelligence as one of seven proposed types of intelligence. Widely used standardized tests of human intellectual ability and achievement such as the Scholastic Aptitude Test (SAT) include quantitative performance as a major scale.

Two ways of defining mathematical ability come, respectively, from the psychometric and the information-processing approaches to ability (Mayer, 1985, 1992). In the psychometric perspective, mathematical ability is the ability to solve the problems on a mathematics test. For example, these problems may involve counting objects such as 13 coins, adding single digit numbers such as $6 + 7 = \_\_$, solving simple word problems such as "How much do three cookies cost if they sell for 5 cents each?" or solving equations such as $2X = X + 2$. This definition is circular because it describes mathematical ability simply by listing the specific problems on a test.

In the cognitive perspective, mathematical ability refers to the cognitive processes or pieces of knowledge that are needed to solve mathematical problems. In componential analysis, a mathematical problem is broken down into information-processing components, which are basic cognitive processes or pieces of knowledge that are required for solution (Resnick & Ford, 1981; Sternberg, 1985). Thus, by asking what a person needs to know in order to solve mathematics problems, the information-processing approach overcomes the limitations of the psychometric definition of mathematical ability.

COGNITIVE ANALYSIS OF MATHEMATICAL ABILITY

Mathematical problem solving can be analyzed into four component processes: translating, integrating, planning/monitoring/reviewing, and executing (Mayer, 1985, 1992). For example, each of these component processes is required to solve a simple word problem, such as "Mary has 1 marble. Sue has a dozen more marbles than Mary. How many marbles does Sue have?"

In the first two processes, the problem solver represents the problem. *Translating* refers to converting each sentence or major clause of the problem into an internal mental representation, such as converting "Mary has 1 marble" into another form such as $M = 1$. This process requires linguistic knowledge (such as knowing that *marbles* is the plural form of *marble*) and declarative knowledge (such as knowing that there are 12 marbles in a dozen). Students have particular difficulty in translating relational sentences into equations, such as translating "There are 6 times as many students as professors at this university" into $6S = P$ (Clement, Lochhead, & Monk, 1980), but they can be taught to improve their problem-translation skills (Lewis, 1989; Lewis & Mayer, 1987).

Integrating refers to selecting relevant information and building a coherent mental representation of the situation being described. In the marble problem, the situation is that one person (Sue) has more marbles than another person (Mary), so that the set of Sue's marbles is equal to the set of Mary's marbles plus the difference set. This process requires schematic knowledge (knowledge of problem types), such as recognizing that the marble problem is an example of a comparison problem consisting of one superset and two subsets. Students have difficulty in determining which information is relevant and which is irrelevant in word problems, but can be taught to improve their problem-integration skills (Low & Over, 1990).

In the last two processes, the problem solver solves the problem. *Planning/monitoring/reviewing* refers to devising and, when necessary, revising a method for solving the problem. In the marble problem, the plan is straightforward: add 1 to 12. In more complex problems, such as two- or three-step problems, the problem solver must break the problem into parts, which are then solved successively. This requires strategic knowledge (heuristics for how to solve problems), such as breaking a large problem into parts or remembering a related problem. Problem-solving heuristics in mathematics can be assessed by asking students which arithmetic operations are necessary to solve a word problem, and can be taught by providing worked-out examples (Reed, 1987; Schoenfeld, 1985).

Executing refers to carrying out an arithmetic, algebraic, or other mathematical operation. In the marble problem, executing involves determining that the sum of 1 and 12 is 13. This process requires procedural knowledge (a specific step-by-step algorithm for accomplishing some task), such as the counting-on procedure for simple addition. In the counting-on procedure, which sometimes is used by beginning arithmetic students (Fuson, 1992), a student begins with one number (such as 12) and increments it by the second number (such as 1) to yield the total (13). The ability to use complex procedures is restricted by limits on the capacity of short-term memory (Sweller, 1989); when students automate their mathematical procedures, this reduces the load on short-term memory and allows cognitive capacity to be allocated to high-level processing.

Although this cognitive task analysis of mathematical problem solving produces four distinct component processes, they do not necessarily occur in a systematic order within a problem-solving session. For example, M. Hegarty, R. E. Mayer, and C. Green (1992) have shown that successful problem solvers continually move between qualitative understanding of the situation described in the problem and quantitative reasoning about how to manipulate the numbers in the problem. A. H. Schoenfeld (1985) has provided case studies demonstrating the importance of metacognitive skills such as monitoring and reviewing one's chain of cognitive processing.

SEX DIFFERENCES IN MATHEMATICAL ABILITY

A recurring issue concerns whether males and females differ in mathematical ability and, if so, why they differ. A review of the research reveals that average scores on mathematics tests are higher for males than females in secondary school but not in elementary school (Halpern, 1986; Maccoby & Jacklin, 1974). In addition, the size of the difference is often very small; in one review, for example, 1 percent of the variance among test scores was attributable to the sex of the students (Hyde, 1981). In contrast, other factors, such as the number of mathematics courses taken or the educational level of the parents, have been shown to account for much larger percentages of the variance among scores (Halpern, 1986; Maccoby & Jacklin, 1974). In short, sex differences in mathematical ability favoring males emerge after approximately age 12 and tend to be relatively small.

Why do sex differences occur? According to the different-experience argument, the pattern of sex differences in mathematical performance is caused by differences in the math-related experiences of boys and girls. For example, on the average, boys take more math courses than do girls in secondary school (Fennema & Sherman, 1977). According to the socialization argument, boys are more likely to be encouraged and expected to do well in math, whereas girls are less likely to be encouraged to develop confidence and positive attitudes toward math. Although children entering elementary school do not view math as a male domain, they tend to adopt this view by the time they move on to secondary school (Fennema & Sherman, 1977). Finally, the biological argument is based on the idea that genetic factors contribute to the observed sex differences in mathematical ability (Benbow & Stanley, 1980, 1983). Continuing research is needed to determine the relative contributions of experiential, socialization, and genetic factors to differences in mathematics performance.

GIFTEDNESS IN MATHEMATICAL ABILITY

Another issue concerns the nature of giftedness in mathematics. Mathematical giftedness is manifested by extremely high levels of performance in mathematics. For example, in order to identify mathematically talented students, J. C. Stanley and his colleagues (Benbow & Stanley, 1980, 1983; Stanley, 1986) administered the Scholastic Aptitude Test–Mathematical (SAT–M) to seventh- and eighth-graders who had been identified as excellent mathematicians. Over the course of several years, approximately 5 percent of the students scored above 600, with some students scoring at, or near, the maximum score of 800.

What are the characteristics of students who can reason extremely well in mathematics? Compared to average-ability students, mathematically gifted students were more likely to be boys, have highly educated parents, be accelerated in school grade placement, and score well in verbal ability (Stanley, 1986). In a more detailed analysis, V. J. Dark and C. P. Benbow (1990) found that mathematically gifted students were better able to translate a word problem into an equation and manipulate mathematical information in short-term memory than average-ability students. Additional research is needed to specify differences in the cognitive processing and knowledge of gifted, average, and learning-disabled students.

(*See also:* GENDER DIFFERENCES IN INTELLECTUAL ABILITIES; GIFTEDNESS.)

BIBLIOGRAPHY

BENBOW, C. P., & STANLEY, J. C. (1980). Sex differences in mathematical ability: Fact or artifact? *Science, 210,* 1262–1264.

BENBOW, C. P., & STANLEY, J. C. (1983). Sex differences in mathematical reasoning ability: More facts. *Science, 222,* 1029–1031.

CLEMENT, J., LOCHHEAD, J., & MONK, G. S. (1980). Translation difficulties in learning mathematics. *American Mathematical Monthly, 88,* 286–290.

DARK, V. J., & BENBOW, C. P. (1990). Enhanced problem translation and short-term memory: Components of mathematical talent. *Journal of Educational Psychology, 82,* 420–429.

FENNEMA, E. L., & SHERMAN, J. A. (1977). Sex-related differences in mathematics achievement, spatial visualization, and affective factors. *American Educational Research Journal, 14,* 51–71.

FUSON, K. C. (1992). Research on learning and teaching addition and subtraction of whole numbers. In G. Leinhardt, R. Putman, & R. A. Hattrup (Eds.), *Analysis of arithmetic for mathematics teaching* (pp. 53–187). Hillsdale, NJ: Erlbaum.

GARDNER, H. (1983). *Frames of mind: The theory of multiple intelligences.* New York: Basic Books.

HALPERN, D. F. (1986). *Sex differences in cognitive abilities.* Hillsdale, NJ: Erlbaum.

HEGARTY, M., MAYER, R. E., & GREEN, C. (1992). Comprehension of arithmetic word problems: Evidence from students' eye fixations. *Journal of Educational Psychology, 84,* 76–84.

HYDE, J. S. (1981). How large are cognitive gender differences? *American Psychologist, 36,* 892–901.

LEWIS, A. B. (1989). Training students to represent arithmetic word problems. *Journal of Educational Psychology, 81,* 521–531.

LEWIS, A. B., & MAYER, R. E. (1987). Students' misconceptions of relational statements in arithmetic word problems. *Journal of Educational Psychology, 79,* 363–371.

LOW, R., & OVER, R. (1990). Text editing of algebraic word problems. *Australian Journal of Psychology, 43,* 63–70.

MACCOBY, E. E., & JACKLIN, C. N. (1974). *The psychology of sex differences.* Stanford, CA: Stanford University Press.

MAYER, R. E. (1985). Mathematical ability. In R. J. Sternberg (Ed.), *Human abilities: An information-processing approach* (pp. 127–150). New York: W. H. Freeman.

MAYER, R. E. (1992). *Thinking, problem solving, cognition* (2nd ed.). New York: W. H. Freeman.

REED, S. K. (1987). A structure-mapping model for word problems. *Journal of Experimental Psychology: Learning, Memory, and Cognition, 13,* 124–139.

RESNICK, L. B., & FORD, W. W. (1981). *The psychology of mathematics for instruction.* Hillsdale, NJ: Erlbaum.

SCHOENFELD, A. H. (1985). *Mathematical problem solving.* Orlando, FL: Academic Press.

STANLEY, J. C. (1988). Some characteristics of SMPY's "700–800 on SAT–M before age 13 group": Youths who reason extremely well mathematically. *Gifted Child Quarterly, 32,* 205–209.

STERNBERG, R. J. (1985). *Beyond IQ: A triarchic theory of human intelligence.* Cambridge: Cambridge University Press.

SWELLER, J. (1989). Cognitive technology: Some procedures for facilitating learning and problem solving in mathematics and science. *Journal of Educational Psychology, 81,* 457–466.

THURSTONE, L. L. (1938). *Primary mental abilities.* Chicago: University of Chicago Press.

THURSTONE, L. L., & THURSTONE, T. G. (1941). *Factorial studies of intelligence.* Chicago: University of Chicago Press.

WOLF, T. H. (1973). *Alfred Binet.* Chicago: University of Chicago Press.

RICHARD E. MAYER

MCCARTHY SCALES OF CHILDREN'S ABILITIES

The McCarthy Scales of Children's Abilities (MSCA), developed by Dorothea McCarthy (1972), were designed to enable psychologists to determine the overall intellectual level and the particular strengths and weaknesses of young children. Intended for use with children aged 2 years, 4 months, 16 days (2½) to 8 years, 7 months, and 15 days (8½ years), the MSCA has been described as child-friendly and accommodating of many unique situations that arise in preschool assessment (Bracken, 1991; Kaufman & Kaufman, 1977). Since its publication, the MSCA has been used in a wide variety of research projects, including the assessment of children diagnosed as mentally retarded (Bickett, Reuter, & Stancin, 1984), the assessment of school readiness (Massoth & Levenson, 1982), and the prediction of later academic achievement (Massoth, 1985).

Advantages and Disadvantages. The MSCA offers many advantages over other measures of children's intelligence. Perhaps its most important advantage is that it is designed to be interesting to young children. By offering bright stimulus materials and multiple practice items, and requiring little initial verbal output by the child, the MSCA recognizes the importance of building and maintaining rapport with a youngster. In addition to being child-friendly, the MSCA provides tasks that are developmentally appropriate for young children.

The disadvantages of the MSCA primarily concern the less-than-desirable reliability of the individual subtests, making interpretation beyond the composite scale level inadvisable. A second shortcoming is that the scoring can be cumbersome for the inexperienced examiner. The presence of multiple conversions, weighting, and subtests scored on more than one scale all contribute to difficulty in scoring. Overall, the advantages of the MSCA are numerous and outweigh the few disadvantages; thus, the MSCA is a widely used and respected research and clinical instrument.

DESCRIPTION OF THE SCALE

The MSCA contains eighteen separate tasks (subtests) that are grouped in six clinically useful scales (see Table 1).

1. Verbal Scale: This scale consists of five subtests that measure a child's verbal expression and mastery of verbal concepts. Included in this scale are tasks that measure the child's short- and long-term memory, divergent thinking, and deductive reasoning. Examples of some tasks in this scale include recalling names of pictured objects, defining words, naming objects, and repeating parts of sentences.

2. Perceptual-Performance Scale: This scale consists of seven subtests that assess a child's imitation of designs, classification of objects into logical groups, and visual-spatial ability. For example, the child may be asked to construct a puzzle depicting a common animal, copy a design made of blocks, or classify objects according to shared characteristics (e.g., color, size, shape, etc.).

3. Quantitative Scale: This scale consists of three subtests that measure a child's facility with numbers and quantitative concepts. Subtests in this scale examine such abilities as digit repetition (repeating lists of numbers of varying length), counting, and sorting, which are felt to be less school-related but more related to developmental computational skills.

4. General Cognitive Scale: This scale is composed of the Verbal, Perceptual-Performance, and Quantitative scales. Its summary score is felt to represent a child's general level of cognitive functioning, because each of the subtests measures an ability that is cognitive in nature. This scale is not considered an intelligence quotient (IQ) scale but one reflecting a child's

TABLE 1
The McCarthy's six scales and eighteen subtests

Test	Verbal	Perceptual Performance	Quantitative	General Cognitive	Memory	Motor
1. Block Building		P		GC		
2. Puzzle Solving		P		GC		
3. Pictorial Memory	V			GC	Mem	
4. Word Knowledge	V			GC		
5. Number Questions			Q	GC		
6. Tapping Sequence		P		GC	Mem	
7. Verbal Memory	V			GC	Mem	
8. Right-Left Orientation		P		GC		
9. Leg Coordination						Mot
10. Arm Coordination						Mot
11. Imitative Action						Mot
12. Draw-A-Design		P		GC		Mot
13. Draw-A-Child		P		GC		Mot
14. Numerical Memory			Q	GC	Mem	
15. Verbal Fluency	V			GC		
16. Counting and Sorting			Q	GC		
17. Opposite Analogies	V			GC		
18. Conceptual Grouping		P		GC		

ability to integrate accumulated learnings and apply them to the specific tasks of the MSCA.

5. Memory Scale: This scale consists of four subtests that specifically assess a child's short-term memory ability. Memory is assessed in both the auditory and visual modalities. For example, a child might be asked to recall a recently presented picture of a common object or to recall a sequence of tones produced from a xylophone. The subtests on this scale have also been included as part of the Verbal and Quantitative scales, because the abilities measured are thought to be highly related to a child's verbal and numerical skills.

6. Motor Scale: This scale consists of five subtests that measure a variety of fine and gross motor activities. Three of the subtests from this scale—Leg Coordination, Arm Coordination, and Imitative Action—are not part of any other scale and thus do not contribute to the Composite.

DEVELOPMENT AND STANDARDIZATION OF THE SCALE

The content for the MSCA and the grouping of subtests into the six scales was based primarily on the author's extensive teaching and clinical experience. The final item set was selected from a large number of items measuring the relevant domain(s). Several tryout tests were performed both with children who were normal and with those who were mentally retarded. The results of factor analyses on the standardization sample were also used in determining the groupings of subtests into scales.

The MSCA was standardized on a national sample of 1,032 children aged 2½ years to 8½ years. This sample was stratified by age, gender, color, geographic region, urban/rural residence, and father's occupation. Color was used to represent white versus nonwhite categorization. The percentages of children obtained for each of these stratification variables were established based on the 1970 U.S. Census (U.S. Bureau of Census, 1972) and a review of the sample suggests that the sample was a reasonable representation of the U.S. population at that time.

Administration of the MSCA. The MSCA is administered to a child in a standard format. Subtests should be presented in the sequence in which they appear on the protocol. To facilitate the flow of administration, subtests 9–13 (the Motor Scale) have been placed in the middle of the battery in order to provide the child with a natural break from the more sedentary items of the other scales. The scale is designed to be administered in its entirety in 50 to 75 minutes.

Item directions are explicit as to what can be said to a child, and the specific actions that can be performed by the examiner in order to elicit the child's performance; however, to prevent a stilted presentation, good rapport with the child is essential. Further, so as not to frustrate the child unnecessarily, starting (basal) and stopping (ceiling) points for each subtest are provided.

Scoring of the MSCA. The MSCA is scored at two levels. First, the General Cognitive Index (GCI) is expressed as a scaled score with a mean of 100 and a standard deviation of 16. The GCI scaled score is computed by summing the weighted raw scores from the Verbal, Perceptual-Performance, and Quantitative scales and then converting this weighted sum by use of the normative tables provided in the manual.

To score the MSCA at the index level, one must first sum the weighted raw scores from each of the component subtests. This sum of weighted raw scores is converted to a scaled score with a mean of 50 and a standard deviation of 10 by using the normative tables in the manual.

Concurrent Validity. The McCarthy has been demonstrated to correlate with several other measures of children's intelligence. For example, in a study examining the relationship between the WPPSI–R and the McCarthy, correlations range from .71 to .81 at the scale level, with the highest correlation being the GCI with the WPPSI–R Full Scale IQ (r = .81).

In a study with the K-ABC Achievement Scale, the MSCA correlated in the moderate-to-high range (.59 to .79). Similarly, the MSCA was found to correlate in the moderate range (r = .59) with the Metropolitan Achievement Test.

The studies suggest that the McCarthy measures global intelligence much as other children's intelligence tests do, and that the McCarthy is a good predictor of later achievement.

Interpretation of MSCA Scores. Any interpretation of a child's performance on the MSCA should start at the GCI level, since this is the most reliable of all MSCA scores. When interpreting this score for clinicians, a child's performance is best described in quantitative terms such as how far the score deviates from the average or the percentile rank of the score. Alternatively, when interpreting the child's performance to a parent or other nonclinician, a more descriptive approach, such as the range of functioning (e.g., average, above average, etc.) is more likely to be helpful.

A second level of interpretation is the index level. Because of the questionable reliability and construct validity of the Quantitative, Memory, and Motor Indexes, interpretation at this level should be undertaken with a great deal of caution. Interpretation below this level, at the subtest level, should not be done, as the individual subtests are even more unreliable than the indices (Bracken, 1991).

CONCLUSION

The MSCA is a child-friendly method of assessment of intellectual functioning in children aged 2½ to 8½ years. The scale consists of eighteen subtests that form six overlapping indices. Three of the indices form the General Cognitive Index. The scale is administered in a standard format and yields standard scores for both the GCI and the six separate indices.

BIBLIOGRAPHY

BICKETT, L., REUTER, J., & STANCIN, T. (1984). The use of the McCarthy Scales of Children's Abilities to assess moderately retarded children. *Psychology in the Schools, 21,* 305–312.

BRACKEN, B. (1991). The assessment of preschool children with the McCarthy Scales of Children's Abilities. In B. Bracken (Ed.), *The Psychoeducational Evaluation of Preschool Children: Second Edition.* Boston: Allyn & Bacon.

KAUFMAN, A., & KAUFMAN, N. (1977). *Clinical evaluation of young children with the McCarthy Scales.* San Antonio, TX: The Psychological Corporation.

MASSOTH, N. (1985). The McCarthy Scales of Children's Abilities as a predictor of achievement: A five-year follow-up. *Psychology in the Schools, 22,* 10–13.

MASSOTH, N., & LEVENSON, R. (1982). The McCarthy Scales of Children's Abilities as a predictor of reading readiness and reading achievement. *Psychology in the Schools, 19,* 293–296.

McCARTHY, D. (1972). *Manual for the McCarthy Scales of Children's Abilities.* San Antonio, TX: The Psychological Corporation.

U.S. BUREAU OF THE CENSUS. (1972). *Census of Population: 1970.* (Final Report PC (1)-B1 United States Summary). Washington, DC: U.S. Government Printing Office.

JAMES S. GYURKE

MEASUREMENT AND PREDICTION OF INTELLIGENCE

The measurement of intelligence has two prerequisites. First, a definition of intelligence is necessary. Second, intelligence must be measurable in terms of the definition. Common definitions of intelligence derived from philosophical or popular usage of the word do not meet these requirements.

A BASIS FOR MEASUREMENT

Nonetheless one definition of intelligence does lead directly to measurements that are valid according to that definition. This definition and the resulting measurements also produce test scores that have many sizable correlations with individual differences in important roles in our society.

The Positive Manifold. This definition of intelligence is based on the observation of positive correlations among a broad spectrum of tests that measure narrow cognitive behaviors. This phenomenon is known as the *positive manifold* and is seen most clearly in wide ranges of intellectual talent.

Correlations are smaller for those tests that measure relatively simple behaviors (accuracy in checking lists of names or numbers) than for those that measure more complex behaviors (various forms of reasoning). As long as there are no zero correlations in the matrix, all tests measure something in common, but those with the higher levels of correlations are more accurate measures of that common function or factor.

When intelligence is identified with this common factor, the methodological problems of constructing an intelligence test are solved by analyses of the intercorrelations. No one test or type of test stands out as a possible sole measure of the common factor in terms of the average size of its correlations with other tests. For example, RAVEN PROGRESSIVE MATRICES are not the measure of choice because scores are determined partially by content and operations that are independent of the common factor. Other kinds of tests have equally high correlations with other tests in the positive manifold, but scores on each are also mixtures of common content and other factors. All positively intercorrelated tests qualify for representation, but each carries its own excess baggage.

Identifying the Common Factor. Each type represented by a narrow ability test is evaluated for its importance in selecting items for an intelligence test by the size of its correlations with other, clearly different item types. The correlations of these narrow tests with a general factor with which all tests have nonzero, positive loadings can serve as a guide to the selection of items. Correlations between items and total score based on a preliminary total score provide similar information.

A general factor described in one set of tests can also be replicated in a different selection of tests when an appropriate methodology is used. Replicability allows discussion of *the* general factor. Large samples of test takers, large heterogeneous sets of tests, and factor analyses in one or more orders of factoring beyond the first are required (see FACTOR ANALYSIS). Hierarchical factor analysis allows replicability in spite of highly disproportionate representations of different types of tests in various sets.

Heterogeneity of Items. Because no types or tasks exist as pure measures of the general factor, a valid test requires a wide array of items that meet two distinct criteria. Each item must assess the general factor to some degree, and the attributes independent of the general factor that it also assesses must be as varied as possible. Meeting the variability criterion for item selection requires more than using items representing narrow group factors. Items in the pool should represent as well the means by which the group factors are measured. As the test designer increases the number of items meeting the two criteria, the correlation between the total score and the general factor approaches unity, and the total of the "noise" that was inextricably present in individual items shrinks toward zero.

A test of intelligence with high construct validity (see VALIDITY) in this definition is not strictly unidimensional, but it does measure one dominant dimension. Behavioral measurement inevitably introduces unwanted variance because items must have content, operations, and products, but the effects of unwelcome "noise" are reduced to insignificance by maximizing the heterogeneity of the "noise." Behavioral measurement estimates only the hypothetical score on the general factor, but the estimate can be made with little error.

Existing Intelligence Tests. When viewed in terms of this definition, the existing measures of general intelligence, such as the various Wechsler tests and the Stanford-Binet tests have come close to meeting these specifications over a period of many years. The correlates of these tests, as well as of others that contain heterogeneous items substantially correlated with the general factor, can be treated readily as correlates of intelligence under the current definition.

PREDICTING LATE INTELLIGENCE FROM EARLY INTELLIGENCE

Predicting adult intelligence from tests administered earlier in a person's development may involve nothing more than a single correlation and a regression equation linking the early predictor to the adult test score. If the same definition of intelligence applies to tests in both early and adult development, however, the stability of individual differences in intelligence quotients (IQ, which measures relative intelligence) over spans of development has theoretical interest. To assess stability, valid and appropriate tests are required.

Selecting Items for Any Age. To select an adequate number of items for measurement purposes, an appropriate selection of cognitive items should exist at each developmental level. The array of possibilities is seemingly limited in infancy, but developmental psychologists are expanding it. By 2 years of age many cognitive tasks are available. The objective is to use the data at each age level to select appropriate items by applying the criteria described previously. That is, phenotypic (observed, measurable) intelligence is measured as defined at each level of development just as phenotypic height or weight is measured. The stability of individual differences in relative intelligence, height, or weight over any given developmental period is then an empirical matter.

Longitudinal Data Available. Longitudinal studies of stability of individual differences in relative intelligence include those of N. Bayley (1949), R. G. McCall and colleagues (1972), T. L. Hilton and others (1971), and R. S. Wilson (1983). In addition, L. G. Humphreys and colleagues (1985) obtained intercorrelations for both height and intelligence from the scores published by Dearborn and others (1938). Scores from infant tests of development are included tentatively in the discussion of general intelligence. Such measures may have higher loadings on the general factor of intelligence early in life than similar measures have later.

Sample sizes and tests vary widely, but the intercorrelations over a wide range of ages approximate the pattern of Louis GUTTMAN's simplex or RADEX THEORY (1954). The largest correlation in every column of a given matrix tends to be adjacent to the principal diagonal. The remaining correlations, all positive, tend to decrease monotonically from the diagonal to the periphery of the matrix. In addition, holding time between occasions constant, scores become progressively more stable during development. An important conclusion follows: The earlier the initial measure and the longer the interval between occasions, the less accurate the prediction.

Contrasting Interpretations of the Stabilities. Because of the small size of early correlations, conventional explanations claim that early tests lack proper content to measure intelligence. Intelligence quotients do not stabilize completely, however, even when content becomes stable from year to year. A hypothesis that cannot be rejected using current data holds that the same general factor is measured from the ages of 12 months to 17 years and older (Humphreys & Davey, 1988).

Less stability early in development when growth is most rapid should not be surprising. Acceptable fits of a simplex model (Humphreys & Parsons, 1979; Humphreys, Park, & Parsons, 1979; Humphreys & Davey, 1988) are congruent with continuity in development on an underlying dimension. Near zero correlations between growth increments and initial bases can account for the changing sizes of correlations over time.

In addition to explaining present data, the hypothesis has an important additional merit. It can be dis-

confirmed. If an investigator were to find a task at age 12 months that is significantly correlated more highly with IQ at age 3 or later than at age 2, the hypothesis would fail.

(*See also:* BIOLOGICAL MEASURES OF INTELLIGENCE; STATISTICAL CONCEPTS.)

BIBLIOGRAPHY

BAYLEY, N. (1949). Consistency and variability in the growth of intelligence from birth to eighteen years. *Journal of Genetic Psychology, 25,* 165–196.

DEARBORN, W. F., ROTHNEY, J. W., & SHUTTLEWORTH, F. K. (1938). Data on the growth of public school children. *Monographs of the Society for Research on Child Development, 3* (1, Serial No. 14).

FRIEDMAN, M. P., DAS, J. P., & O'CONNOR, N. (1981). *Intelligence and learning.* New York: Plenum.

GUTTMAN, L. (1954). A new approach to factor analysis: the radex. In P. Lazarsfeld (Ed.), *Mathematical thinking in the social sciences.* New York: Free Press.

HILTON, T. L., BEATON, A. E., & BOWER, C. P. (1971). *Stability and instability in academic growth: A compilation of longitudinal data.* Princeton, NJ: Educational Testing Service.

HUMPHREYS, L. G. (1985). General intelligence: An integration of factor, test, and simplex theory. In B. Wolman (Ed.), *Handbook of intelligence: Theories, measurement, and applications* (pp. 201–224). New York: Wiley.

HUMPHREYS, L. G., & DAVEY, T. C. (1988). Continuity in intellectual growth from 12 months to 9 years. *Intelligence, 12,* 183–197.

HUMPHREYS, L. G., DAVEY, C. T., & PARK, R. K. (1985). Longitudinal correlation analysis of standing height and intelligence. *Child Development, 56,* 1465–1478.

HUMPHREYS, L. G., PARK, R. K., & PARSONS, C. K. (1979). Application of a simplex process model to six years of cognitive development in four demographic groups. *Applied Psychological Measurement, 3,* 51–64.

HUMPHREYS, L. G., & PARSONS, C. K. (1979). A simplex process model for describing differences between cross-lagged correlations. *Psychological Bulletin, 86,* 325–334.

MCCALL, R. G., HOGARTY, P. S., & HURLBURT, N. (1972). Transitions in infant sensori-motor development and the prediction of childhood IQ. *American Psychologist, 27,* 228 (Abstract).

Wilson, R. S. (1983). The Louisville twin study: Developmental synchronies in behavior. *Child Development, 54,* 198–216.

Lloyd G. Humphreys

MECHANICAL ABILITY   In psychological testing, mechanical ability has nothing to do with skilled proficiency or manual dexterity with tools. Rather, mechanical ability reflects knowledge of the workings of pulleys, levers, inclined planes, gears, springs, gravity, force and motion, and simple electrical circuits. Mechanical knowledge can be formal and mathematical (e.g., in physics, when calculating the mechanical advantage of pulley systems) or it may be intuitive (e.g., knowing that a heavy person will lift a lighter one seated on the opposite end of a teeter-totter). Mechanical ability predicts success in many technical courses, such as geometry, drafting, and shop. It is important to success in many jobs in industry (e.g., for machinists, architects, and engineers) and in the military (e.g., for structural mechanics, machinery repairers, and pilots). For these reasons, mechanical ability tests are used for vocational guidance and as qualification tests for industrial and military jobs throughout the industrialized world.

TESTS OF MECHANICAL ABILITY

Because many job applicants, or individuals pondering a vocation, do not have formal training in mechanics and physics, most mechanical ability tests use pictures of simple, frequently encountered mechanisms (such as teeter-totters) that do not require special knowledge or mathematical computations. Three typical mechanical test items are displayed in Figure 1. The first item (left) shows two pulley systems. With additional information, the exact mechanical advantage of B over A could be calculated, but this is unnecessary; knowing that one downward unit of pull in B exerts two upward units on the weight (versus one upward unit in A) is sufficient to select the correct answer. The second item (center) shows a graded heap of sand submerged in water. As with the pulley question, more information could be provided that would allow accurate estimates of the downward pressure at points A and B. A person could select point A, however, simply by realizing that weight exerts pressure and that there is more weight (water) above A than above B. The third item (right) concerns fulcrums and balance points. Physical rules can be applied to determine where a fulcrum should be placed to achieve equilibrium (balance). For this item, the only information required to reject A (and select B) is that with unequal weights on a centered fulcrum, the heavier side will drop.

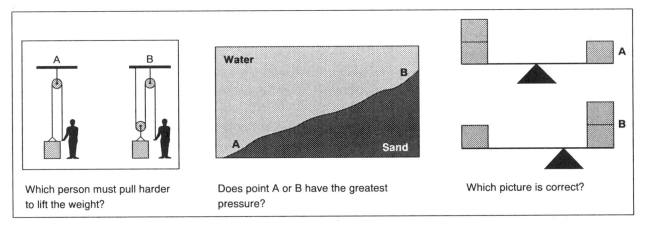

Figure 1

Typical items on a mechanical ability test

History of Mechanical Ability Tests. Mechanical ability tests were used in the late 1800s as qualification tests for vocational schools and apprenticeships in various trades (Smith, 1964). Early tests were true performance tests, where individuals had to screw nuts onto bolts, assemble wooden puzzles, construct wheelbarrows, and so forth. Today they would be called job sample tests. These tests were difficult to administer, score, and transport between locations; they were also expensive to manufacture and reproduce. These problems, together with advances in psychometrics, led to the development of printed mechanical ability tests in the 1920s. The Stenquist Mechanical Aptitude Tests (Stenquist, 1922) and the Cox Mechanical Aptitude Tests (Cox, 1928) were the earliest printed tests; today's tests are direct descendants of these two mechanical ability batteries. Both batteries included mechanical comprehension items, similar to those described earlier, and information items that required specific factual knowledge, such as the names of tools and machines. Cox (1928) particularly influenced the character of modern mechanical ability tests by arguing against using test items that would be overly influenced by prior training and experience. The Cox and Stenquist tests, and their variants, were used successfully but almost exclusively in industrial settings until World War II, when mechanical ability tests were adapted for military use and administered to millions of individuals. The tests were very effective in assigning personnel, particularly for vehicle operators, mechanical repairers, bombardiers, and pilots (e.g., Guilford & Lacey, 1947; Smith, 1964).

Modern Mechanical Ability Tests. Many tests of mechanical ability are used today, and most include items similar to those discussed earlier. The Bennett Mechanical Comprehension Test (MCT) (Bennett, 1969) is internationally used by industries for employee selection in mechanical, assembly, and engineering jobs. MCT is appropriate for all ages above 15, covering novices through engineering students. There are sixty-eight test items, administered with a 30-minute time limit. Over seventeen different aspects of machines are represented in the test, but reasoning about physical forces in common settings is emphasized. The Mechanical Reasoning (MR) test of the Differential Aptitude Test battery (Bennett, Seashore, &

Wesman, 1974) is quite similar to the MCT. MR, however, is primarily a vocational guidance tool for students in grades 9–12. Therefore, test items are easier and less dependent on specific technical information. MR has seventy items and a 30-minute time limit. Another widely used mechanical test is the Mechanical Comprehension (MC) test of the ARMED SERVICES VOCATIONAL APTITUDE BATTERY (ASVAB). This test is used by all of the U.S. armed forces to qualify and classify applicants for enlisted ranks. The ASVAB is also widely used in high schools for vocational counseling. MC is similar in content and format to MR and MCT but contains more items employing gears, cams, and drive shafts. This test has twenty-five items and is administered with a 19-minute time limit. In the United States alone, these three mechanical ability tests are administered more than 4 million times a year.

USEFULNESS OF MECHANICAL ABILITY TESTS

The usefulness of psychological tests is typically measured in terms of validity. Validity refers to how well a test predicts success in relevant activities. For mechanical ability tests, relevant activities include mechanical and technical coursework or training as well as mechanical and technical job performance. The accuracy of a test is measured by its validity coefficient. A coefficient of 1 indicates perfect accuracy and zero indicates no accuracy at all. For a nonstatistical interpretation, remember that the validity of an adult's height as a predictor of weight is about .5.

Technical Training/Coursework. The validities of mechanical ability tests for predicting the outcome of technical training have ranged from zero to as high as .8. Ghiselli (1966) reported validities for training success as high as .54 for packers, .49 for electrical workers, .39 for mechanical repairers, and .36 for vehicle operators; he estimated that the training success validity is .41 across all trades and crafts. Guilford and Lacey (1947) reported validities of .31 for combat crew members, .25 for navigators, .33 for air mechanics, and .35 for pilot training. The ASVAB MC test has a proven record for predicting success in a number of military technical training courses. In the Navy, for example, the majority of jobs for which MC is valid are in the construction and mechanical areas, including those of builders, carpenters, equipment operators, structural mechanics, steelworkers, machinists, repairers, and welders. Because of the nature of work aboard submarines, all enlisted personnel must have at least average mechanical ability for assignment to a submarine, no matter what their job (e.g., sonar operator or cook).

The MR test manual reports dozens of validity coefficients for academic and vocational coursework. Among science classes, MR had a median validity of .30. The test performed better in general and physical sciences (especially physics, with a median validity of .55) than in biology and chemistry. Across high school mathematics courses, MR had a median validity of .27. The highest values were for geometry coursework (.63), with the next best predictions in general mathematics. Prediction of success in English, literature, history, and social studies was generally lower than in science and mathematics. In vocational schools, MR produced the largest validities for drafting, machine shop, and welding courses, with substantially lower validities for academic portions of the curriculum.

Job Performance/Proficiency. Ghiselli (1966) reported that mechanical ability is particularly important for the job performance of complex machine operators (.40), machining workers (.44), structural workers (.24), and mechanical repairers (.24). Across all trades and crafts, Ghiselli estimated the average job performance validity as .26. Guilford and Lacey (1947) found that the single best predictor of pilot performance was mechanical ability (.37). For navigators' in-flight performance, mechanical ability tests showed validities of .29 for celestial navigation and .22 for dead-reckoning navigation. Mechanical ability has proven valid against performance on job-sample tests among Navy machinist mates and Marine Corps automotive and helicopter mechanics. In factory settings, mechanical ability has proven valid in determining the performance of sewing machine operators, assembly-line workers, wire benders, strippers, and painters. In a study cited in Cronbach (1984, pp. 365–366), there was evidence that as the criteria (engine room operations) became more performance based and less academically based, the validities of mechanical ability tests improved.

PSYCHOLOGICAL NATURE OF MECHANICAL ABILITY

A psychological description of mechanical ability must go beyond a list of item types, uses, and validity. Statistically, mechanical ability tests are quite reliable with retest reliability coefficients between .75 and .90 and single-administration reliabilities in the .75–.95 range. Although these stability measures might suggest that mechanical ability tests are measuring a single trait or inherent ability, certain evidence makes this unlikely.

Socialization practices, exposure, and education improve performance on mechanical ability tests. Males consistently outscore females, by as much as 1 standard deviation. Average scores for males and females improve between grades eight and twelve, but the male advantage actually increases (Bennett, Seashore, & Wesman, 1974). The magnitude of improvement in mechanical ability has been related to the technical nature of a person's education and training (Balke-Aurell, 1982). Furthermore, formal training in physics actually improves performance on mechanical tests (Bennett, Seashore, & Wesman, 1974). These results suggest that mechanical ability tests are partially technical knowledge tests.

Factor analyses suggest that performance on mechanical ability tests is a function of general reasoning (intelligence), spatial ability, and mechanical knowledge and experience. Guilford and Lacey's (1947) statistical analysis indicated that on average nearly 30 percent of a person's mechanical ability test score was attributable to spatial ability among their subjects. Ekvall (1969) summarizes his comprehensive study of the intellectual components of mechanical ability tests in this way: "[They are] more of an intelligence test than a mechanical knowledge test. Of the different intelligence factors the spatial seems to be the one that carries the greatest weight.... The variance due to differences in manual dexterity seems small" (p. 78). Across different tests and nine groups with very different backgrounds and training, he found that general reasoning (including verbal ability) accounted for between 30 percent and 37 percent of performance on mechanical ability tests, while spatial ability accounted for between 27 percent and 52 percent of performance. Mechanical knowledge and experience accounted for between 1 percent and 31 percent of performance; however, the majority of values were between 12 percent and 19 percent. These results indicate that mechanical knowledge is not even the dominant determinant of performance on these tests.

Hegarty, Just, and Morrison (1988) conducted a cognitive analysis of performance on mechanical ability tests, including verbal protocol analyses of how items were actually solved. The authors found that all except one of their best subjects had advanced, college-level training in physics. Apart from coursework, they found that three aspects of problem solving distinguished good from bad performers. One was the ability to identify which attributes of an object were relevant to its mechanical function (such as the number of pulleys in the first item shown in Figure 1). A second factor was the ability to use rules consistently across problems (e.g., always counting the number of pulleys in a pulley problem). The final factor was the ability to combine information about two or more relevant attributes in a problem (such as combining the unequal weights and the location of the fulcrum in the last item shown in Figure 1). Siegler (1981) found similar factors to explain problem-solving differences among children of different ages. These results suggest that mechanical ability is an example of general, systematic problem solving with acquired mechanical knowledge.

CONCLUSION

Mechanical ability tests appear to measure general reasoning and spatial ability as applied to special, pictorially presented, simple mechanical scenarios. A significant portion of test performance is a function of specific knowledge about mechanical devices, or simple physical machines. Thus, test scores can be improved through study and practical experience, which is why scores improve with age and specialized education. Performance on such tests is predictive of coursework, training success, and job performance in a very broad range of activities related to the utilization of mechanical devices and knowledge.

BIBLIOGRAPHY

BALKE-AURELL, G. (1982). Changes in ability as related to educational and occupational experience. Gothenburg, Sweden: Acta Universitatis Gothoburgensis.

BENNETT, G. K. (1969). Bennett Mechanical Comprehension Test. New York: The Psychological Corporation.

BENNETT, G. K., SEASHORE, H. G., & WESMAN, A. G. (1974). Manual for the Differential Aptitude Test (5th ed.). New York: The Psychological Corporation.

COX, J. W. (1928). Mechanical aptitude: Its existence, nature, and measurement. London: Methuen.

CRONBACH, L. J. (1984). Essentials of psychological testing (4th ed.). New York: Harper & Row.

EKVALL, G. (1969). The construct validity of mechanical aptitude tests (Report No. 58). Stockholm: The Swedish Council for Personnel Administration.

GHISELLI, E. E. (1966). The validity of occupational aptitude tests. New York: Wiley.

GUILFORD, J. P., & LACEY, J. I. (EDS.). (1947). Printed classification tests. (Army Air Forces aviation psychology research program reports, No. 5). Washington, DC: U.S. Government Printing Office.

HEGARTY, M., JUST, M. A., & MORRISON, I. R. (1988). Mental models of mechanical systems: Individual differences in qualitative and quantitative reasoning. Cognitive Psychology, 20, 191–236.

SIEGLER, R. S. (1981). Developmental sequences within and between concepts. Monographs of the Society for Research in Child Development, 46, 1–149.

SMITH, I. M. (1964). Spatial ability: Its educational and social significance. London: University of London Press.

STENQUIST, J. L. (1922). Mechanical aptitude tests. Yonkers, NY: World Book.

DAVID L. ALDERTON

MEMORY   You frequently will hear people say "I have a terrible memory," or "I can remember faces but not names." Such statements imply that human memory is a single organ, like a heart or spleen, and that some people have a large memory while others may come equipped with a small one or a defective one. In fact, the term *memory* reflects a rather complex assortment of systems for knowing. Human memories include a vast amount of knowledge about ourselves and our world plus an extensive set of strategies for learning, retrieving, and using that knowledge. We are aware of some of these strategies, which are under conscious control. Many other procedures for processing information may occur without our awareness, however. They occur automatically, with little or no effort.

This vast store of what we know and the strategies for knowing are the *long-term memory*. We can only think about or attend to a small part of this long-term memory at one time. This active part of long-term memory is called *working memory*. The capacity of working memory corresponds to the amount of our memory and our environment that each of us can attend to at any given time.

Individual differences in memory that are important to learning appear to be confined to three areas: (1) limits on working-memory capacity, (2) strategies for learning, using, and retrieving information, and (3) domain-specific knowledge—relevant knowledge the learner already possesses. Working memory will be discussed in more detail than the other two. Then I will discuss the relative importance of all three areas to learning.

A MODEL OF WORKING MEMORY

Alan Baddeley has envisioned a multicomponent working memory with a limited amount of attentional resources to do mental work. This component, called the central executive, is an important source of individual differences in memory. Several methods can be used to code and maintain information in working memory. One method is to translate concepts to a verbal (phonological) form. Another is to convert the concepts to a visual/spatial form. For example, if I tell you to think of a dog and a cat, you might think of the words "dog" and "cat" and rehearse them repeatedly. You might, instead, make a mental picture of a dog and cat playing together. Probably other coding methods exist, but the majority of research studies concern the phonological and visual/spatial codes.

Individual differences exist in the extent to which people use these two codes, and those differences are important to learning. Children who do not use the phonological code are slower to learn to read and

slower at acquiring vocabulary than children who do use this code (Baddeley, 1990). The visual/spatial code is important for tasks in which we must mentally move or transform one or more objects (Salthouse et al., 1990). For example, if you try to pack a large number of suitcases into a small car trunk, you are more likely to succeed if you use a spatial code to solve the problem.

Individual differences in the working-memory capacity of the central executive appear to be an important factor in learning and retrieval of information. Some have even argued that this aspect of working memory is the important mechanism responsible for general intelligence (Larson & Alderton, 1990).

Measurement of Working-Memory Capacity. Digit- and word-span tasks have been used since the 1800s as tests of individual differences in memory. Such tests distinguish the extremes of intelligence, for example, between retarded and normal individuals. Even a simple test like the digit span reflects, not just fixed capacities, but strategies of information processing that are the result of prior learning (Estes, 1982).

Over the range of normal intelligence, digit- and word-span tasks do not seem to tap that aspect of working-memory capacity important to most complex cognitive tasks. To measure working-memory capacity, we must measure the number of words or digits an individual can retain while being forced to attend to some other part of memory or the environment. Turner and Engle (1989) had subjects perform a variety of such tasks: In one task, subjects saw a set of simple arithmetic problems each of which was followed by a word or digit, for example, "Is $(3 \times 5) - 6 = 7$?" TABLE. Subjects saw sets of two to six problems, solved each one, and then tried to recall the words that followed the problems. Another task required subjects to read a set of sentences aloud and to recall the last word of each sentence. The number of words recalled was assumed to reflect the amount of information the subjects could keep active in memory while periodically shifting their attention to the problems in one task or the reading of the sentences in the other task. These measures of working-memory capacity consistently predict performance on important real-world cognitive tasks, such as those that are described below.

Role of Working-Memory Capacity in Educationally Relevant Cognitive Tasks.

Reading. When we read for comprehension, it is frequently necessary to keep facts or phrases in working memory for a period of time so that we can integrate them with new information. Individuals with high working-memory capacity are much better at retaining earlier information in working memory and integrating that information to aid comprehension. Measures of working-memory capacity reliably predict performance on reading comprehension tests (Daneman & Carpenter, 1983).

Following Directions. Being able to do something we have been shown or told how to do is an important aspect of everyday cognition. Most teachers assume that all children can easily follow such directions as "Take out your math book, turn to page 73, and do the even-numbered problems, except number 6." Some children may not be able to complete this assignment even if they were paying attention to the teacher. Individuals of all ages with high working-memory capacity are able to follow more complex directions because they can keep more information in working memory (Engle, Carullo, & Collins, 1991).

Spelling. Spelling, at least in the early stages of learning, is an activity that depends on the amount of information we can keep in working memory at one time. Individual differences in working-memory capacity are an important factor in some children's difficulty in learning to spell. This is true even when reading ability is controlled (Ormrod & Cochran, 1988).

Arithmetic. Working memory has been shown to be important in the solution of arithmetic problems (Hitch, 1978). While this suggests that arithmetic learning probably varies with individual differences in working-memory capacity, no studies on such a relationship have been reported.

Vocabulary Learning. We commonly learn a new word by encountering that word in a context defining its meaning. For example, suppose I am talking to a woman and I know that she just won the lottery. I can see a broad smile on her face, and she says "I feel euphoric!" If I have sufficient information about the events in working memory at the time the word *euphoric* occurs, I can deduce the meaning. If I do not have adequate information about the events active in

memory when the word occurs, I may not be able to deduce the meaning. Just such a relationship has been found. Subjects with high working-memory capacity are better able than those with low capacity to deduce the meaning of very unusual words from a context (Daneman & Green, 1986).

Notetaking. Working-memory capacity is an important factor in whether students are good notetakers. Working-memory span predicts the number of words, complex propositions, and main ideas recorded in notes. In fact, working-memory capacity is a better predictor of notetaking ability than grade point average or scores on the American College Test (ACT), a standardized aptitude test (Kiewra & Benton, 1988).

Writing. Good writers hold more information in working memory and simultaneously manipulate that information more effectively and more rapidly than do poor writers. Thus, working-memory capacity is an essential distinction between good and poor writers (Benton et al., 1984).

Problem Solving. The overloading of working memory is the principal source of errors in many different types of problem solving. For example, the demands of working memory exert a strong influence on performance on problems involving number-series-completion, such as 2, 6, 10, _____ . This has also been found for number analogy problems, letter series completions, and geometric analogies (Holzman, Pellegrino, & Glaser, 1983). One reason that working-memory capacity is so important to complex problem solving is because we can keep only a limited number of alternative solutions in working memory at one time.

Complex Learning. Perhaps the most impressive demonstration of the role of individual differences in working-memory capacity on learning comes from studies of computer programming. Shute (1991) gave subjects an extensive battery of tests for both general abilities and specific information-processing abilities, such as working-memory capacity. Her 260 subjects then received a forty-hour computer-aided course on Pascal programming. The most important factor predicting who learned the most from the course was a set of tests measuring working-memory capacity, which was more predictive than general knowledge of how to solve algebra word problems. Similar work showed that working-memory capacity was predictive of how well children would learn the Logo programming language (Lehrer, Guckenberg, & Lee, 1988).

STRATEGIES

One important source of individual differences in memory is simply the strategies we possess to learn, retrieve, and use information. Some individuals are capable of remarkable feats of learning using strategies such as those described in popular books on memory (Lorayne & Lucas, 1974). When retarded children are taught to use the same strategies in a simple memory task that are used by normal children, they will recall information as well as the normal children do (Butterfield, 1981). Such training, however, appears to have limited value because when the task is changed, even slightly, the retarded children again show memory deficits—they do not transfer their training to new situations. Campione, Brown, and Ferrara (1982) have argued that knowing a strategy for performing a given task is not sufficient for intelligent behavior. Individuals must have a capacity for self-awareness, understand the limits of the memory system, know when a strategy would be effective, be able to monitor the effectiveness of that strategy, and change to another strategy if that one is ineffectual.

It is important to understand that strategies can be difficult to learn and to manage. Thus, strategy learning, like other types of learning, is affected by capacity limitations. For example, children with greater working-memory capacity are able to learn and use a strategy for forming images to learn sentences. Children with smaller working-memory capacities do not learn or use such a strategy (Cariglia-Bull & Pressley, 1990). Once a strategy is learned well enough that executing it takes little attention, the role of working-memory capacity is probably less important than the quality of the strategy.

DOMAIN-SPECIFIC KNOWLEDGE

One of the most important individual differences in memory is simply in what has been learned already. It is much easier to learn and remember something if we have a framework in which to embed that new knowledge. For example, Spilich et al. (1979) tested subjects who either knew a great deal or not very much about baseball. The subjects read a description of a half-

inning of a baseball game and were later tested on their memory for the game. Those people who knew the most about baseball also learned the most. They recalled more about what they had read than did subjects who were ignorant about baseball.

An important example of the role of domain-specific knowledge and the use of strategies comes from work done by Ericsson and Staszewski (1989). They worked with a subject who developed the ability to recall perfectly a list of over 100 digits that had been presented at a 1-per-second rate. This incredible feat was possible because the subject used his vast knowledge of times associated with track events. He coded the digit times associated with various events and used a very specific learning strategy for grouping the digits in his memory in a way that could be easily retrieved later. This individual had the same limitations of working-memory capacity as do the rest of us, but he had learned to circumvent those limitations, at least in this specific task, by using his knowledge and strategies for learning and retrieval. When asked to remember a similarly presented list of letters, this subject was just as vulnerable to the limits of working memory as others and could recall only six to eight of the letters.

The relative importance of working-memory capacity and existing knowledge was studied by Kyllonen and Stephens (1990). They had Air Force recruits learn and use a variety of logic rules, such as those used in electronic circuits. A variety of tests were administered to test for individual differences in processing speed, working-memory capacity, general knowledge, and the ability to transform factual knowledge into effective problem-solving skill. The results indicated that the most important determinant of successful learning of a cognitive skill is working-memory capacity. Both initial learning of the rules and translating those rules into effective problem-solving procedures were determined by the working-memory capacity of the subjects.

CONCLUSION

There are three aspects of memory in which individual differences can play an important role in learning new material: (1) working-memory capacity; (2) strategies; and (3) domain-specific knowledge. Working-memory capacity has been shown to be important in many different kinds of complex learning, including much that is done in the classroom. Once we learn strategies for processing information and specific information about a topic, however, the limits of basic abilities, such as working-memory capacity, become less important. If we try to learn in a new domain, in a manner not conducive to the strategies we have learned, we quickly see that the importance of working-memory capacity reemerges.

BIBLIOGRAPHY

BADDELEY, A. (1990). *Human memory: Theory and practice.* Boston: Allyn & Bacon.

BENTON, S. L., KRAFT, R. G., GLOVER, J. A., & PLAKE, B. S. (1984). Cognitive capacity differences among writers. *Journal of Educational Psychology, 76,* 820–834.

BUTTERFIELD, E. C. (1981). Testing process theories of intelligence. In M. Friedman, J. P. Das, & N. O'Connor (Eds.), *Intelligence and learning.* New York: Plenum.

CAMPIONE, J. C., BROWN, A. L., & FERRARA, R. A. (1982). Mental retardation and intelligence. In R. J. Sternberg (Ed.), *Handbook of human intelligence.* New York: Cambridge University Press.

CARIGLIA-BULL, T., & PRESSLEY, M. (1990). Short-term memory differences between children predict imagery effects when sentences are read. *Journal of Experimental Child Psychology, 49,* 384–398.

DANEMAN, M., & CARPENTER, P. A. (1983). Individual differences in integrating information between and within sentences. *Journal of Experimental Psychology: Learning, Memory and Cognition, 9,* 561–583.

DANEMAN, M., & GREEN, I. (1986). Individual differences in comprehending and producing words in context. *Journal of Memory and Language, 25,* 1–18.

ENGLE, R. W., CARULLO, J. J., & COLLINS, K. W. (1991). Individual differences in the role of working memory in comprehension and following directions in children. *Journal of Educational Research, 84,* 253–262.

ERICSSON, K. A., & STASZEWSKI, J. (1989). Skilled memory and expertise: Mechanisms of exceptional performance. In D. Klahr & K. Kotovsky (Eds.), *Complex information processing: The impact of Herbert A. Simon.* Hillsdale, NJ: Erlbaum.

ESTES, W. K. (1982). Learning, memory, and intelligence. In R. J. Sternberg (Ed.), *Handbook of human intelligence.* New York: Cambridge University Press.

HITCH, G. J. (1978). The role of short-term working memory in mental arithmetic. *Cognitive Psychology, 10,* 302–323.

HOLZMAN, T. G., PELLEGRINO, J. W., & GLASER, R. (1983). Cognitive variables in series competition. *Journal of Educational Psychology, 75,* 603–618.

KIEWRA, K. A., & BENTON, S. L. (1988). The relationship between information-processing ability and notetaking. *Contemporary Educational Psychology, 13,* 33–44.

KYLLONEN, P. C., & STEPHENS, D. L. (1990). Cognitive abilities as determinants of success in acquiring logic skill. *Learning and Individual Differences, 2,* 129–160.

LARSON, G. E., & ALDERTON, D. L. (1990). The structure and capacity of thought: Some comments on the cognitive underpinnings of g. In D. K. Detterman (Ed.), *Current topics in human intelligence: Vol 2. Is the mind modular or unitary?* Norwood, NJ: Ablex.

LEHRER, R., GUCKENBERG, T., & LEE, O. (1988). Comparative study of the cognitive consequences of inquiry-based Logo instruction. *Journal of Educational Psychology, 80,* 543–553.

LORAYNE, H., & LUCAS, J. (1974). *The memory book.* New York: Ballantine Books.

ORMROD, J. E., & COCHRAN, K. F. (1988). Relationship of verbal ability and working memory to spelling achievement and learning to spell. *Reading Research and Instruction, 28,* 33–43.

SALTHOUSE, T. A., BABCOCK, R. L., MITCHELL, D. R. D., PALMON, R., & SKOVRONEK, E. (1990). Sources of individual differences in spatial visualization ability. *Intelligence, 14,* 187–230.

SHUTE, V. J. (1991). Who is likely to acquire programming skills? *Journal of Educational Computing Research, 7,* 1–24.

SPILICH, G. J., VESONDER, G. T., CHIESI, H. L., & VOSS, J. F. (1979). Text processing of domain-related information for individuals with high and low domain knowledge. *Journal of Verbal Learning and Verbal Behavior, 18,* 275–290.

TURNER, M. L., & ENGLE, R. W. (1989). Is working-memory capacity task dependent? *Journal of Memory and Language, 28,* 127–154.

RANDALL W. ENGLE

MEMORY, EXCEPTIONAL Everyday experience shows that individuals differ in their memory capacities. Some individuals have a memory ability that is so vastly superior that their exceptional memory performance appears to be mediated by qualitatively different memory processes. For example, Alfred BINET studied a mental calculator who could recall perfectly more than 30 digits read to him, as compared with the ability of normal adults of recalling only between 4 and 10 digits under such conditions. Susukita studied Isihara, a Japanese mnemonist, who memorized over 2,000 digits in around four hours. Aleksandr LURIA examined a subject (S) who could memorize poetry in a foreign language and a 50-digit matrix in a couple of minutes simply by looking at the material. Most interesting is that S was able to recall the matrix by rows or columns as if he had a photographic memory of it. Most chess masters can play blindfold chess, in which they are not allowed to see the chess boards but have to keep the current chess positions in memory. Musical savants can play an unfamiliar musical piece after one or two hearings. A more complete listing of documented instances of exceptional memory performance is available in reviews by Brown and Deffenbacher (1988), Ericsson (1985), and Ericsson and Faivre (1988).

Such feats of memory are clearly outside the range of performance of normal adults. Some of the tasks (e.g., memory for digits) are similar to standardized tests of basic memory ability. The performance of the exceptional individuals is in some instances ten to fifty times greater than that of normal adults on these tests. Such large individual differences in measured performance are rarely, if ever, obtained in tests of other basic abilities, which led psychologists to conclude that these exceptional individuals must have a fundamentally different and superior memory system. However, recent research has generated an alternative account of exceptional memory performance in terms of acquired skill rather than differences in basic capacity. It has shown that exceptional memory is demonstrated only for unfamiliar materials, such as digits, for which normal memory is poor. Normal memory is far better for familiar meaningful activities, such as test comprehension, and similar memory mechanisms appear to mediate this type of memory and exceptional memory performance.

The study of exceptional memory is, by definition, linked to identifying exceptions to the general laws of normal memory. The modern understanding of normal memory began with the pioneering work of Hermann Ebbinghaus in the nineteenth century.

BRIEF HISTORICAL BACKGROUND

At the time of Hermann Ebbinghaus's first laboratory study of memory, it was recognized that memory performance is primarily influenced by an individual's knowledge, experience, and interests. The experience and knowledge that individuals acquired during the decades of their unique lives would make any scientific study of general laws governing memory in adults very difficult, if not almost impossible. To address this problem, Ebbinghaus designed an unfamiliar type of material, nonsense syllables (e.g., DAF, WIQ), for which no relevant knowledge or experience is readily available. When lists of nonsense syllables were presented at a fast rate, memory for the lists was assumed to reflect associations generated by basic memory processes uncontaminated by prior knowledge and experience. In the century following Ebbinghaus's pioneering research, his general findings about memory performance have been consistently replicated as well as extended to a wide range of other types of material, such as lists of unrelated words and digits, and to slower rates of presentation.

Ebbinghaus's approach to studying basic memory processes was designed so that no further information about the cognitive processes mediating storage and retrieval from memory could be obtained. In his research, Ebbinghaus used himself as his only subject and reported simply attending to each nonsense syllable during learning.

The assumption that memorization of lists of unrelated items in the laboratory is mediated only by basic memory processes has been theoretically useful and is maintained by many investigators even today. The same assumption implies that subjects exhibiting vastly superior memory performance on similar memory tasks must differ in their basic memory processes. In the latter part of the nineteenth century, Binet systematically tested the exceptional memory of a mental calculator (Inaudi) and found that this subject had exceptional memory for digits presented auditorily. One of the primary issues at that time was to distinguish auditory memory, such as rote memorization of a song, from visual memory. Binet (1894) designed a test involving memorization of the matrix of digits shown in Figure 1, tested with several different orders for recalling the digits.

If the digits had been memorized auditorily as a long rote sequence, the recall should be rapid only for the memorized order, and the subjects should have great difficulties with other orders of recall. But a visual image of the matrix should allow flexible retrieval according to any order of recall. Binet confirmed that Inaudi's memory seemed to be of an auditory type, whereas other exceptional subjects' memories were of a visual type. In further research, Binet interviewed chess players, asking them to memorize chess positions. Some chess players reported having complete "visual" images of the chess position, claiming that they "saw" visual features of the pieces. Other chess

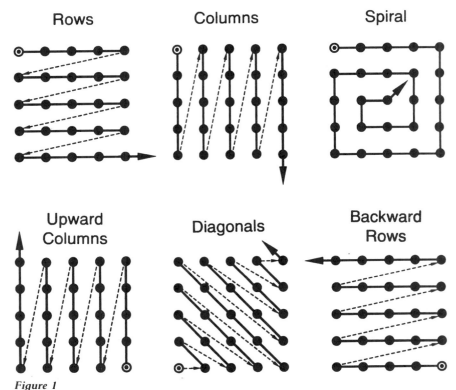

Figure 1

At the top is a twenty-five-digit matrix of the type used by Alfred Binet to test his memory experts. He asked subjects to repeat the whole matrix in the various orders shown, starting with the position marked by the circle and ending with the arrow.

players, however, clearly rejected the idea of "visual" images; instead, they reported experiencing an abstract spatial representation of the chess position, with the relations among the attacking and defending chess pieces directly available. Hence, it appears that some individuals can have an accurate memory of a chess position without reporting a clear visual image of it.

Among many studies of individuals with exceptional memory during the twentieth century, Luria's (1968) study of the mnemonist S is perhaps the most famous. S reported learning unfamiliar material such as Italian poetry by using associations to similar sounding words in Russian (his native language) and memorizing the sequence of Russian words by creating vivid visual images. To memorize long sequences of words, S generated visual images of the words interacting with physical locations on a street in Moscow with which S was very familiar. At the time of recall, he would regenerate an image of the street and retrieve the generated images and then recall the words. In the case of digit memorization, which S claimed was especially easy for him, S simply looked at the matrix of fifty digits and managed to form a clear visual image of it within a few minutes. S could then easily recall information from the matrix according to different orders.

These and other studies of exceptional memory have found that such subjects memorize the information in a different manner than do average adults. These individuals appear to be able to form "photographic" sensory copies of the material, as suggested by their own descriptions as well as by their superior ability to reproduce the information. Research has shown that this is not the case.

SPECIFICITY OF EXCEPTIONAL MEMORY

If individuals had a truly photographic memory, they should be able to memorize any kind of visual information equally well. Systematic tests of individuals with exceptional memory show that their memory performance is exceptional only for a single type of information, such as digits. Their performance can be above average for other materials, but not outside the normal range of other adult subjects. It has also been relatively easy to find types of material on which their

memory performance is average or even below average (Ericsson, 1985). The same pattern of individual differences in memory performance for different types of materials is obtained in "normal" adults, with low correlations between performance on different materials. It is implausible to assume that exceptional memory for a specific type of material, such as digits, could be inherited. Instead, such a specific superiority is likely to be due to an ability acquired through experience.

ROLE OF PRIOR KNOWLEDGE IN MEMORY PERFORMANCE

It is well known that knowledge about a given type of material influences the ability to recall that material. Miller (1956) summarized the research on immediate memory and showed that the amount recalled is typically about seven familiar patterns or "chunks." For example, on average, subjects can recall six or seven unrelated consonants—or words, even though seven words are made up of twenty-five to thirty individual letters. Even when the presented material did not directly match any familiar patterns, such as nonsense syllables (e.g., XAJ, MIB), college students tended to memorize the information by using associations with similar words (e.g., XAJ = exaggerate, MIB = misery). The more easily the subjects could retrieve a similar word, the better they were able to memorize a given nonsense syllable (Montague, 1972). Efficient memorization is not linked to rote memorization of the information as presented, but rather is mediated by a search for associated patterns already stored in memory. Luria's Russian subject S generated similar words to memorize poetry in a foreign language. His method of generating interactive visual images of unrelated words is another effective procedure for memorization. Such procedures are referred to as mnemonics.

Mnemonic methods have a long history; they were originally developed by the Greeks to improve memory and were refined during the Middle Ages. Recent laboratory research has shown that instructing normal subjects to use mnemonic methods improves their memory performance (Bellezza, 1986). Brief instruction in mnemonic methods and a small amount of practice do not allow subjects to attain an exceptional level of performance, however. Exceptional individuals have spent many years practicing and refining their techniques for specific types of materials; this is, of course, consistent with the specificity of their exceptional memory.

EXCEPTIONAL MEMORY IN EXPERTS

The effects of extended experience and practice on superior memory can be studied in the performance of experts. In a classic study, Chase and Simon (1973) followed up earlier research that showed that chess masters have superior memory only for chess positions. They briefly presented regular middle-game chess positions as well as chess boards with a random rearrangement of the same chess pieces to chess players ranging in skill from novice to chess masters. For regular chess positions, subjects' recall was directly proportional to their chess skill, but recall for the random boards did not differ between the two groups of subjects and was uniformly low. This important finding rules out the possibility that general familiarity with chess pieces is crucial; instead the critical factor for superior memory of chess positions is that the pieces must be arranged in familiar meaningful patterns of attacking and defending pieces. Other studies have shown that superior memory performance for representative stimuli in the domain of expertise, but not for random arrangements of the same stimuli, is related to the level of expert performance in many domains, such as bridge, Go, electrical engineering, and sports. Recent studies of chess showed that the superior memory for a briefly presented chess position reflects storage in long-term memory and is found even when chess players are selecting the best move for a position and are unaware of any subsequent request for recall (Charness, 1991).

ACQUISITION OF EXCEPTIONAL PERFORMANCE WITH EXTENDED PRACTICE

Evidence that the memory performance of normal subjects can be improved by practice and instruction in mnemonic techniques supports the hypothesis that exceptional performance is the result of extended practice with such techniques. More conclusive evidence for such a hypothesis would require a demonstration that subjects with initially average memory can attain exceptional levels of memory performance after extended practice. Chase and Ericsson arranged for a college student (SF) to practice on a digit-span task, in which a list of digits is rapidly presented (one digit per second) and then the digits have to be recalled in their presented order without any errors. During the first practice sessions, SF rehearsed the digits to himself and was able to reproduce lists of about seven digits. His performance was typical for untrained college students in this task. After about 200 practice sessions of about one hour each, SF could reproduce lists with over eighty digits, which is more than any other exceptional subject has done with this rapid presentation procedure. In fact, the individuals with exceptional memory who were mentioned earlier typically had digit spans below twenty. Later research has shown that SF was not unique; three other subjects (RE, DD, NB) have attained digit spans over twenty after training and practice. With extended digit-span practice, even exceptional subjects improve—Professor Rückle's (Müller, 1913) and Rajan's (Thompson, Cowan, Frieman, Mahadevan, & Vogl, 1991) performance was more than doubled.

GENERAL PRINCIPLES OF EXCEPTIONAL MEMORY

Based on the evidence from the trained subjects as well as from other individuals with exceptional memory, Chase and Ericsson (1982) proposed a theory of skilled memory. According to this theory, superior and exceptional memory reflect an acquired ability to store information in long-term memory in a retrievable form. Rapid storage of information in memory requires a body of associated knowledge and patterns. To store a list of digits, subjects segment the digits into groups of three or four, as shown in Figure 2. Several of the trained subjects were experienced runners who used their knowledge about running times along with numerical patterns to encode each group of digits. For example, 3521 could be encoded as near world record time for the mile—3 minutes 52.1 seconds. Several exceptional subjects relied on their vast knowledge about numbers. Rückle, a professor of mathematics, reported encoding 451697 as $451 = 41 \times 11$ and $697 = 41 \times 17$. Several mnemonists reported using previously learned concrete words for each number between 00 and 99 and memorizing the sequence of words. With training, the speed of encoding and storage in long-term memory can be dramatically increased.

To make it possible to retrieve all the stored digit groups in their presented order, skilled memory theory claims that during the original encoding each digit group is associated with a unique retrieval cue. Trained subjects encode the digit groups in a hierarchy exemplified in Figure 2.

Before a trial starts, the subject accesses the appropriate hierarchy (retrieval structure) for the given list length. The first group of four digits is encoded and associated with the corresponding location in the hierarchy—the first four-digit group in the first supergroup, and so on. At the time of recall, the subject then generates the location cue and uses it to retrieve the associated digit-group from memory. Some exceptional subjects, such as Professor Rückle, were found to use a similar hierarchical retrieval structure. Mnemonists like S and Isihara used a linear retrieval structure corresponding to a prelearned sequence of physical locations (the method of loci).

The acquired mechanisms proposed by skilled memory theory, that is encoding and retrieval structures, imply that the presented information is stored

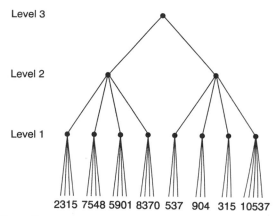

Figure 2

Hierarchical organization of SF's memory encoding of thirty presented digits. The first level contains mnemonic encodings of digit groups and the second level consists of supergroups where the relative location of several digit groups are encoded.

in long-term memory and that the exceptional memory performance is restricted to practiced encoding processes that are specific to a particular type of material. Storage in long-term memory has been demonstrated by the trained subjects' ability to recall nearly all of 200 to 300 digits belonging to different lists at the end of a test session. The specificity of the acquired exceptional memory performance is demonstrated by the lack of transfer to other materials by subjects trained on the digit-span task. For example, when SF's digit-span had increased by over 1,000 percent, his memory span for consonants remained at only six letters. The specificity of exceptional memory performance described earlier is consistent with this account.

FURTHER ISSUES IN EXCEPTIONAL MEMORY

Skilled-memory theory of exceptional memory can account for the subjective experience of photographic memory and also for subject S's memorization of the digit matrix as well as for the superior memory of idiots savants. Chase and Ericsson had their trained subjects memorize and recall the digit matrix used by Luria with S and the digit matrices used by Binet (see Figure 1). The trained subjects were able to match and even surpass the study and recall times of the "exceptional" individuals. The digit matrices were memorized by the trained subjects in terms of an encoded digit group for each row. Retrieval of digits according to the specified orders was achieved by first recalling the relevant row and then extracting the relevant digit or digits. The pattern of times to complete recall according to the special orders in Figure 1 were consistent with this process not only for the trained subjects but also for the exceptional individuals. Rapid and flexible access to spatially organized information can thus be attained without drawing on visual information or on "photographic memory." Perhaps once the relevant information is retrieved, additional features of the stimuli can be visualized and lead to a misattribution of the nature of active memory encoding.

The severe mental retardation of idiots savants has seemed to rule out any complex cognitive mediation of their performance, thus implying that a superior basic memory is the cause of their exceptional performance. Recent research that examined this type of performance in more detail, however, found it to be cognitively mediated (see Howe, 1990, for a review). For example, musical savants, who can reproduce music pieces after one or two presentations, can only reproduce classical music; their memory skill does not transfer to atonal music, ruling out any basic memory similar to a tape recorder. Furthermore, the majority of recall errors by musical savants obey the rules of music, suggesting that these rules must have been internalized. Most musical savants are blind, which means that the only way in which they can learn new music pieces is by memorizing them by listening to them. Many years of practice in memorizing music can account for the exceptional memory performance of musical savants.

CONCLUSION

Unusual and exceptional feats of memory have been documented for experts in their domain of expertise, for individuals with exceptional memory for special types of materials, such as digits, and for idiots savants in particular domains like music. For each demonstration of exceptional memory it is possible to identify a set of preconditions for the acquired skill— a body of relevant knowledge and an extended period of preparation and practice—before the individual can demonstrate exceptional memory performance with a specific type of information. Exceptional memory is mostly displayed for materials such as digits, for which ordinary adults lack the prerequisite knowledge and retrieval structures, and thus exhibit comparatively poor memory performance. When exceptional memory performance for digits is compared to ordinary subjects' memory for sentences and texts in their native language, however, the two types of performance appear to be about the same. Under the assumption that exceptional memory reflects acquired mechanisms similar to those used efficiently in everyday memory, continued study of exceptional memory should yield further insight into the complex processes and representations mediating everyday memory.

(See also: MEMORY; SAVANTS.)

BIBLIOGRAPHY

BELLEZZA, F. S. (1986). Mental cues and verbal reports in learning. *The Psychology of Learning and Motivation, 20,* 237–273.

BINET, A. (1894). *Psychologie des grands calculateurs et joueurs d'echecs* (Psychology of exceptional mental calculators and chess players). Paris: Libraire Hachette.

BROWN, E., & DEFFENBACHER, K. (1988). Superior memory performance and mnemonic encoding. In L. K. Obler and D. Fein (Eds.), *The exceptional brain* (pp. 191–211). New York: Guilford Press.

CHARNESS, N. (1991). Expertise in chess: The balance between knowledge and search. In K. A. Ericsson and J. Smith (Eds.), *Toward a general theory of expertise: Prospects and limits* (pp. 39–63). New York: Cambridge University Press.

CHASE, W. G., & ERICSSON, K. A. (1982). Skill and working memory. In G. H. Bower (Ed.), *The psychology of learning and motivation* (Vol. 16, pp. 1–58). New York: Academic Press.

CHASE, W. G., & SIMON, H. A. (1973). The mind's eye in chess. In W. G. Chase (Ed.), *Visual information processing* (pp. 215–281). New York: Academic Press.

ERICSSON, K. A. (1985). Memory skill. *Canadian Journal of Psychology, 39,* 188–231.

ERICSSON, K. A., & FAIVRE, I. A. (1988). What's exceptional about exceptional abilities? In I. K. Obler, & D. Fein (Eds.), *The exceptional brain: Neuropsychology of talent and special abilities* (pp. 436–473). New York: Guilford Press.

HOWE, M. J. A. (1990). *The origins of exceptional abilities.* Oxford: Basil Blackwell.

LURIA, A. R. (1968). *The mind of a mnemonist.* New York: Avon.

MILLER, G. A. (1956). The magical number seven, plus or minus two. *Psychological Review, 63,* 81–97.

MONTAGUE, W. E. (1972). Elaborative strategies in verbal learning and memory. In G. Bower (Ed.), *The psychology of learning and motivation* (Vol. 6, pp. 225–302). New York: Academic Press.

MÜLLER, G. E. (1913). Neue versuche mit Rückle (New experiments with Rückle). *Zeitschrift für Psychologie und Physiologie der Sinnesorgane, 67,* 193–213.

THOMPSON, C. P., COWAN, T., FRIEMAN, J., MAHADEVAN, R. S., & VOGL. R. J. (1991). Rajan: A study of a memorist. *Journal of Memory and Language, 30,* 702–724.

K. ANDERS ERICSSON

MENTAL AGE Between 1905 and 1911 in Paris, Alfred BINET and Théophile Simon introduced a method to rank the intellectual performance of sub-normal schoolchildren in relation to the average age at which normal children earned the same score on the same test. A sampling of children at each age level (6, 7, 8, 9, 10, 11, 12) was tested with the standardized test they were then developing, and the number of items correctly answered by the majority at each age was obtained. Then the number of items answered correctly by the child being tested was related to the age of the normal children who had answered the same number of items correctly. Thus, the earned test age of a child was matched to a control, and the result termed the *mental age* (MA), regardless of the actual chronological age (CA) of the child. A subnormal 9 year old might have a mental age of 6. The concept of mental age provided teachers and parents with an empirically derived index by which to judge a child's rate of development.

When in 1912 Wilhelm Stern elaborated on this initial testing and measuring index by dividing a child's earned mental age by that child's chronological age, and multiplying by 100, he termed the result the *intelligence quotient* (IQ).

BIBLIOGRAPHY

KAUFMAN, ALAN S. (1990). *Assessing adolescent and adult intelligence.* Boston: Allyn & Bacon.

MATARAZZO, J. D. (1972). *Wechsler's measurement and appraisal of adult intelligence: Fifth and enlarged edition.* New York: Oxford University Press.

JOSEPH D. MATARAZZO

MENTAL DISABILITIES See AGNOSIA; DYSCALCULIA; DYSLEXIA; HYPERACTIVITY; LEARNING DISABILITY.

MENTAL MEASUREMENTS YEARBOOK

In 1938, Oscar K. Buros began publishing a book entitled the *Mental Measurements Yearbook* (*MMY*), which contained critical reviews of the hundreds of psychological tests available. The eleven editions to date and their companion offshoots contain candid evaluations of nearly all commercially available psychological, occupational, and educational tests published in English.

Beginning in 1979, the offices of the *MMY* moved from New Jersey to the newly established Buros Institute of Mental Measurements, located at the University of Nebraska, with Professor James V. Mitchell as editor. He retired as editor in 1988 to be succeeded by coeditors Jane Close Conoley and Jack J. Kramer.

BIBLIOGRAPHY

CONOLEY, J. C., & KRAMER, J. J. (Eds.). (1991). *The Mental Measurements Yearbook: Eleventh edition.* Lincoln, NE: Buros Institute of Mental Measurements.

JOSEPH D. MATARAZZO

MENTAL RETARDATION, CULTURAL-FAMILIAL

Cultural-familial mental retardation, or familial MR, is retardation for which there is no known organic cause. It is defined by intelligence-test scores 2 or more standard deviations below average, that is, intelligence quotient (IQ) scores of 70 or lower. It is believed often to run in families; some argue that only when parents or other family members are themselves retarded is familial MR an appropriate diagnosis.

Familial MR is at the heart of almost every major issue in the field of mental retardation. The problem of test bias arises in that the diagnosis is made disproportionately often among minority children and those of low socioeconomic status (see LEGAL ISSUES IN INTELLIGENCE). In addition, many of these children and adults perform relatively adequately in everyday life, leading to debates about the role of ADAPTIVE BEHAVIOR in the definition of mental retardation (American Association on Mental Retardation, 1992; Jacobson & Mulick, 1992).

But the largest unresolved issue involves etiology. It is simply not known what causes familial MR. Is it the result of natural variation in the population with regard to intelligence, of depriving (or, conversely, of chaotic and overstimulating) environments, or of some unknown genetic or biological factors? Even the names used by different researchers suggest disagreement about its etiology: It has been called "cultural-familial," "sociocultural," and "sociocultural-familial" mental retardation; "retardation due to environmental deprivation"; "nonspecific," "idiopathic," and "nonorganic" mental retardation; and, in earlier ages, "garden variety" mental retardation.

In order for the reader to understand this baffling disorder, this article will first discuss the two-group approach to mental retardation and then detail several of the disorder's hypothesized causes. With these discussions as background, it will then explore the definitional role of adaptive behavior as well as the many service-delivery implications brought about by familial MR.

THE TWO-GROUP APPROACH

Throughout the twentieth century, researchers have identified two types of persons with mental retardation, those who do and those who do not show clear organic impairment. E. Zigler (1969) formalized this two-group approach to mental retardation, and the approach forms the background to all discussions of both organic and familial MR.

The first group comprises persons whose retardation is caused by one or more than 300 known organic causes of mental retardation. These causes can be prenatal, perinatal, or postnatal in origin. Prenatal causes consist of many genetic disorders (such as DOWN SYNDROME, fragile-X syndrome), rubella, and all other accidents in utero. Perinatal causes include prematurity and anoxia at birth. Postnatal causes include viral meningitis, head trauma, and the many debilitating diseases that cause intellectual and adaptive delays during the childhood years. Organic forms of mental retardation together account for 25–50 percent of all cases of mental retardation (Zigler & Hodapp, 1986).

The second group consists of all individuals with retardation for whom no clear organic cause is apparent. In his original formulation, Zigler (1969) noted that in every way other than their lowered levels of intellectual functioning, this familial group seems indistinguishable from nonretarded persons. These individuals appear physically normal, have normal life spans, develop along the same Piagetian sequences as nonretarded children, and show the same cross-domain structures of cognitive and linguistic development. Because such persons are more likely to be born into families in which other members have similar levels of intelligence, Zigler used the term *familial* to describe this type of mental retardation. Persons with familial MR constitute 50–75 percent of all persons with mental retardation.

Zigler also noted that individuals with the two types of retardation clustered at different parts of the distribution of measures of IQ. Persons with organic mental retardation were often at the moderate, severe, and profound levels of retardation, with IQs below 50. In contrast, persons with familial retardation were more often in the mildly retarded range, with IQs from 50 to 70. There thus appeared to be two groups of persons with retardation. Individuals in the organic group suffered from some type of organic insult and were disproportionately found at the lowest IQ levels, whereas persons with familial MR formed the lower end of the normal distribution of intelligence (Figure 1). Because the two-group approach is controversial within the mental retardation field, the next sections describe arguments against and in favor of this approach.

Arguments Against the Two-Group Approach.

1. *All mental retardation is evidence of organic impairment.* Many argue that a diagnosis of mental retardation is itself evidence of an individual's organic impairment. They point out that proponents of the two-group approach do not identify an explicit cause of familial MR, and they reason that even normal variations in intelligence must be due to brain mechanisms of some type. As A. Baumeister and W. MacLean (1979, p. 199) noted, "If we make the assumption that intelligent behavior is mediated through the central nervous system, then one may conclude that, to the extent that behavior is impaired, defects of the central nervous system are inevitably implicated."

A corollary to this view is that much retardation involves organicity not detectable by currently available procedures. Advocates of defect theories note that as diagnostic procedures improve, individuals previously considered to suffer familial MR are being diagnosed with various organic conditions. Fragile-X syndrome (see below) is the most prevalent disorder previously diagnosed as familial MR, but other genetic disorders were similarly misdiagnosed until the 1970s.

2. *Exclusionary diagnosis.* Unlike diagnoses of organic conditions, a diagnosis of familial MR is done by ex-

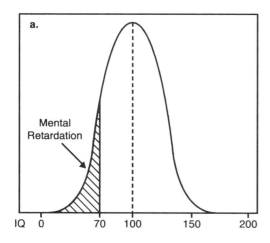

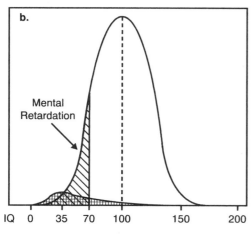

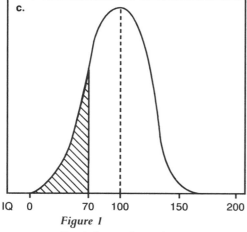

Figure 1

Familial mental retardation

a: conventional representation of the distribution of intelligence

b: distribution of intelligence as represented in the two-group approach

c: actual distribution of intelligence

clusion—that is, if, after careful screening for the many organic forms, there appears to be no organic cause for the person's retardation. Unfortunately, no positive criteria exist to diagnose familial retardation, and little progress has been made toward identifying symptoms or sequelae that, when present, signify that the person has familial MR.

A diagnosis of familial MR is highly dependent on the skill of the diagnostician, who must rule out the presence of several hundred organic causes before arriving at that diagnosis. Differences in diagnosticians' skill undoubtedly affect prevalence rates of many medical and psychiatric conditions, but the differences remain troublesome nonetheless. Indeed, different researchers find different percentages of persons with familial MR, even within similar populations (all rural or all Scandinavian).

Also influencing prevalence rates is the date of the research. Since the early 1970s, advances in genetics and other biomedical areas have notably changed diagnoses. Many persons originally diagnosed with familial MR are now diagnosed with previously unknown genetic and biological disorders. Diagnoses of each disorder decrease the numbers of persons in the familial MR group. Although this issue is discussed below, suffice to say that the date of a particular study plays a role in how many persons one finds to have familial MR. Thus, those opposed to the two-group approach argue that exclusionary diagnoses are too cumbersome and unreliable to be of value.

3. *Unclear definition.* Unlike organic forms of mental retardation, the very definition of familial MR is arguable. As in this article, some maintain that all retarded persons who evidence no clear organic cause for their retardation should be considered to have familial MR. Others underline the familial aspect of this disorder, emphasizing that the term should be reserved for those persons with one or more family members who also have retardation.

4. *Overrepresentation of minority-group members and persons of low socioeconomic status (SES).* Individuals with familial MR disproportionately come from minority and low-SES groups. Many argue that intelligence tests are biased, that minority and low-SES children are penalized by not having been exposed to white middle-class experiences, values, or linguistic codes. Others note that overstimulating or inconsistent environments are more often found in lower-SES homes, leading to a deprived environment for children raised in such environments. In either case, an overabundance of children from poor and minority households scores lower on IQ tests, some even in the retarded range (below IQ 70). This issue remains unresolved (Macmillan, 1988) (see also RACE AND INTELLIGENCE; VALIDITY).

The four issues of hidden organicity, exclusionary diagnosis, unclear definition, and overrepresentation of minority and low-SES individuals do not invalidate the two-group approach. Yet, each hinders examination of familial MR and its acceptance by mental retardation workers.

Arguments in Favor of the Two-Group Approach.

1. *Too many individuals at low IQs.* Since the 1930s, researchers have suspected that there are too many individuals with severe and profound mental retardation and that many of these people are organically retarded. The "too many" refers to the normal distribution, or bell curve (see STATISTICAL CONCEPTS). Measures of intelligence are approximately normally distributed in large samples: The majority of people are about average in intelligence, with lesser numbers at extremely high and low levels. If the measures were perfectly normally distributed, 0.0013 percent of the population would have IQs 3 or more standard deviations below the population mean (i.e., have IQs of 55 or less when the standard deviation for the distribution is 15). The numbers of individuals with IQs below 40 (4 standard deviations) should be less than 1,000 among the current U.S. population of 255 million people.

H. F. Dingman and G. Tarjan (1960) found 87,000, 194,000, and 52,000 more persons than would be expected in a normal distribution at profound (IQ 0–20), severe–moderate (IQ 20–50), and mild (IQ 50–70) levels of mental retardation. One possible explanation for the overabundance of persons at lower IQ levels is that there is a second distribution superimposed over the normal distribution, as illustrated in Figure 1b. This second curve, showing persons with different organic conditions, seemed to start at IQ 0, reach a peak somewhere in the severely retarded range, and extend throughout the retarded (and even nonretarded) range.

2. *Siblings.* Although professionals disagree as to whether the presence of other retarded family members is necessary for a diagnosis of familial MR, it is instructive to examine the siblings of persons with familial MR in considering the utility of the two-group approach. Specifically, if the two-group approach is correct, then siblings of individuals with familial MR should themselves be lower in IQ, demonstrating the familial nature of the condition. Siblings of persons with organic retardation, by contrast, should have IQs close to 100, under the assumption that individuals with retardation have a discrete organic condition that does not run in families.

In an extensive, multisite study of children with retardation and their families, S. Broman and associates (1987) compared the IQs of two sets of siblings, children with severe mental retardation (most of whom showed organicity) and children with mild mental retardation (most of whom were diagnosed with familial MR). As predicted by the two-group approach, siblings of children with severe retardation were generally higher in IQ than were siblings of children with mild mental retardation. Even considering only those children with severe retardation, those who showed clear evidence of damage to the central nervous system (CNS) had siblings with higher IQs than did the siblings of severely retarded children without CNS damage. The distinction between sibling scores were less clearcut for the subsample of African-American children. Broman and associates' findings overall provide support for distinguishing between organic and familial MR.

3. *Surveys of organicity at various IQ levels.* If Figure 1b is accurate, then more persons with the lowest IQs should be organically retarded, and lesser percentages of persons with mild retardation should have one or another organic form. In contrast, greater percentages of persons with mild mental retardation should have familial MR, whereas lesser percentages of those with moderate, severe, or profound retardation should have familial MR. Summarizing the various studies of this issue, Zigler and Hodapp (1986) found this to be true: Among severely retarded persons, 40.2 percent showed familial MR, whereas 59.8 percent showed clear organicity. Among persons with mild retardation, 65.8 percent showed familial retardation, while only 34.2 percent showed organicity.

Looked at another way, consider only those persons who have been diagnosed with either organic or familial MR. According to the two-group approach, more persons with the organic diagnosis should have IQs in the severe, profound, and moderate ranges of mental retardation, and fewer in the mild range. Conversely, most persons diagnosed with familial MR should be in the mild range of IQs, and increasingly fewer of these persons should be at the lowest IQ levels. These predictions were supported: Across four studies, the median percentage of persons with the organic diagnosis whose IQs were below 50 or 55 (depending on the study) was 63.6 percent; mild retardation was noted in only 36.4 percent of these persons. In contrast, only 27.7 percent of persons identified as familial MR were at the severe levels of retardation; 72.3 percent of these individuals had IQs in the mildly retarded range (Zigler & Hodapp, 1986).

CAUSES OF FAMILIAL
MENTAL RETARDATION

Polygenic Factors.   Many continuous human traits (height and skin color) are thought to be the result of many separate genes working together. Geneticists have offered models for the inheritance of intelligence based on the child's receiving multiple genes for high intelligence from each parent (see GENETICS, BEHAVIOR). There might be tens or even hundreds of genes contributing to one's intellectual level.

The word *familial* here refers to the level of intelligence of the mother and father. If there is some degree of polygenic determination in IQ, children from families in which one or more parents have familial retardation are themselves more likely to be retarded. E. W. Reed and S. C. Reed (1965) found that low-IQ parents tend to produce children with low IQs and high-IQ parents tend to produce children with high IQs. Children with only one parent with very high or low IQs were generally less extreme, as might be expected if intelligence is partly determined by numerous genes from each parent. Reed and Reed's data thus are consistent with a polygenic explanation for some cases of familial mental retardation (Zigler & Hodapp, 1986).

Environmental Factors.   Evidence is also consistent with a hypothesis that intelligence is at least partly determined by the environment. Environmental effects may operate in either of two directions. Children adopted into high-SES families show slightly higher IQs than children adopted into low-SES families, regardless of whether the child was born of parents who were either high or low in SES (Capron & Duyme, 1989). More and less affluent environments, with their concomitant levels of intellectual stimulation, thus appear to affect all children to some degree.

The evidence thus suggests that both genetic and environmental factors determine levels of intelligence. Behavioral geneticists (Plomin & Rende, 1991) now conclude that within the normal range of IQ, approximately half of the variance is due to genetics, and the other half to the environment. Little evidence suggests that this is true for persons diagnosed with organic MR.

Undiscovered Organic Factors.   Many retardation researchers (e.g., Baumeister & MacLean, 1979) criticize the idea of familial MR, suggesting instead that many causes of retardation are as yet undiscovered. Although this explanation seems unlikely to account for all individuals with familial MR, it does account for some.

A good example is fragile-X syndrome. Fragile-X syndrome is a sex-linked disorder that is, after Down syndrome, the second most common genetic cause of mental retardation. But unlike Down syndrome and most genetic disorders, fragile-X syndrome is inherited. This disorder also differs from most sex-linked disorders, which usually affect only males, in that fragile-X syndrome can cause retardation in both males and females. Until its genetics were identified in the late 1960s and early 1970s, many persons with fragile-X syndrome were diagnosed as having familial MR. Among individuals previously thought to have no clear organic cause of mental retardation, approximately 10 percent of males were found to have fragile-X syndrome (Dykens, Hodapp, & Leckman, 1994). Although fragile-X syndrome differs from most newly discovered genetic disorders in that it accounts for a sizable percentage of retarded individuals, the syndrome shows how each new discovery serves to decrease the numbers of persons originally thought to have familial MR.

TWO REMAINING ISSUES

Two additional questions challenge researchers and practitioners dealing with the concept of familial MR: the disjunction between low IQ and adaptive behavior, and ways of enabling persons with retardation to live rewarding lives.

IQ and Adaptive Behavior. Mental retardation is defined by the presence of intellectual impairment (IQ scores 2 or more standard deviations below 100), concomitant with deficits in adaptive behavior (Grossman, 1983). Adaptive behavior involves everyday-life activities, such as communicating to others, daily living skills, and socialization. (See ADAPTIVE BEHAVIOR, ASSESSMENT OF.)

It is often the case, however, that one's intellectual and adaptive abilities are not perfectly in synchrony. For individuals with IQs below 50, IQs and adaptive behaviors are highly correlated, but for persons of IQs 50–70 (i.e., the IQs of most persons with familial MR), the two are not so highly correlated. In a forty-year follow-up study of individuals originally in special-education classes, R. T. Ross and associates (1985) found that different individuals with mild retardation had attained widely varied life success during adulthood. Most (64%) functioned independently, but others of the same IQ levels were either partially (24%) or totally (12%) dependent on others. IQ scores did not predict how different individuals would fare later in life.

Such findings call into question the definition of mental retardation, particularly as it relates to the familial form. Some argue that deficits in both IQ and adaptive behavior should determine mental retardation (Grossman, 1983). Others respond that a diagnosis of mental retardation should be based on intelligence alone, either IQ or some other measure when available (Zigler, Balla, & Hodapp, 1984). In the early 1990s the main professional organization in the field, the American Association on Mental Retardation, or AAMR (1992), advanced a definition employing ten proposed domains of adaptive behavior. Criticized by many (e.g., Jacobson & Mulick, 1992), the organization's definition is not likely to be widely used by professionals in mental retardation. The uncertain definition of mental retardation—particularly as concerns adaptive behavior—makes unclear which persons showing no obvious organic impairments and with IQs from 50 to 69 will be considered to have familial MR in the years to come.

Service Delivery. Since the early 1970s, professionals in mental retardation have strongly emphasized the need to enable persons with retardation to lead normal lives. Such a normal life would include schooling within mainstreamed classes and living within group homes, apartments, or other community-living settings. Practices designed to enable such living have emphasized the need to make the delivery of such services as natural and as fully integrated into the society as possible. For the most part, the effects of such efforts have been beneficial, particularly for individuals with familial MR. Many of these persons now go to school in mainstream classes and, as adults, blend into the larger society.

But such blending may at times have adverse effects. For example, consider the service-delivery implications of changing definitions. The AAMR's move to emphasize adaptive, as opposed to intellectual, deficits in its definition of mental retardation has produced a decrease of persons considered to have mild mental retardation. D. L. MacMillan (1988) documented that between the 1970s and late 1980s, the number of schoolchildren in the United States considered to have educable mental retardation (EMR, the educational term for mild mental retardation) decreased approximately 15 percent. Not all of these children have received other diagnoses, leaving many unable to qualify for special services. MacMillan argues that such children are falling into a "demilitarized zone" of mental retardation, unable to receive needed services because they no longer qualify for any classification.

Were these individuals performing adequately in school and later life, such definitional concerns might be unimportant, but many persons with familial MR are not performing well (Ross et al., 1985). These individuals often have difficulties in school, move from job to job as adults, and need supportive services at various points throughout their lives. Their problems appear unrelated to intelligence alone: K. Granat and S. Granat (1978) found that difficulties in persisting at a task, accepting social responsibilities, and complying with social and moral codes are the main factors leading to unsuccessful life histories for adults with mild mental retardation.

Familial MR thus presents difficulties on many levels. Its very existence is debated by those who think that all retardation must involve organic impairment. Experts differ as to its definition and its causes. Higher prevalence rates among minority and low-SES groups make familial MR politically troublesome, as do the many different views as to what constitutes appropriate school and living arrangements for these individuals. Yet, a large group of persons—from half to three-quarters of all persons with retardation—continues to show no organic cause for their mental retardation. This group, while it may get smaller in future years, is unlikely to go away completely, leaving unresolved all of the many issues concerning persons with familial mental retardation.

(*See also:* MENTAL RETARDATION, ORGANIC.)

BIBLIOGRAPHY

AMERICAN ASSOCIATION ON MENTAL RETARDATION (1992). *Definition, classification, and systems of supports* (9th ed.). Washington, DC: Author.

BAUMEISTER, A., & MACLEAN, W. (1979). Brain damage and mental retardation. In N. R. Ellis (Ed.), *Handbook of mental deficiency: Psychological theory and research* (2nd ed.). Hillsdale, NJ: Erlbaum.

BROMAN, S., NICHOLS, P., SHAUGHNESSY, P., & KENNEDY, W. (1987). *Retardation in young children: A developmental study of cognitive deficit*. Hillsdale, NJ: Erlbaum.

CAPRON, C., & DUYME, M. (1989). Assessment of the effects of socio-economic status on IQ in a full cross-fostering study. *Nature, 340,* 552–554.

DINGMAN, H. F., & TARJAN, G. (1960). Mental retardation and the normal distribution curve. *American Journal of Mental Deficiency, 64,* 991–994.

DYKENS, E. M., HODAPP, R. M., & LECKMAN, J. F. (1994). *Behavior and development in fragile X syndrome.* Newbury Park, CA: Sage Publications.

GRANAT, K., & GRANAT, S. (1978). Adjustment of intellectually below-average men not identified as mentally retarded. *Scandinavian Journal of Psychology, 19,* 41–51.

GROSSMAN, H. J. (ED.). (1983). *Manual on terminology and classification in mental retardation* (3rd ed.—rev.). Washington, DC: American Association on Mental Retardation.

JACOBSON, J. W., & MULICK, J. A. (1992). A new definition of mental retardation or a new definition of practice? *Psychology in Mental Retardation and Developmental Disabilities, 18,* 9–14.

MACMILLAN, D. L. (1988). Issues in mild mental retardation. *Education and Training in Mental Retardation, 23,* 273–284.

PLOMIN, R., & RENDE, R. (1991). Human behavioral genetics. *Annual Review of Psychology, 42,* 161–190.

REED, E. W., & REED, S. C. (1965). *Mental retardation: A family study.* Philadelphia: W. B. Saunders.

ROSS, R. T., BEGAB, M. J., DONDIS, E. H., GIAMPICCOLO, J. S., & MEYERS, C. E. (1985). *Lives of the retarded: A forty-year follow-up study.* Stanford, CA: Stanford University Press.

ZIGLER, E. (1967). Familial mental retardation: A continuing dilemma. *Science, 155,* 292–298.

ZIGLER, E. (1969). Developmental versus difference theories of mental retardation and the problem of motivation. *American Journal of Mental Deficiency, 73,* 536–556.

ZIGLER, E., BALLA, D., & HODAPP, R. M. (1984). On the definition and classification of mental retardation. *American Journal of Mental Deficiency, 89,* 215–230.

ZIGLER, E., & HODAPP, R. M. (1986). *Understanding mental retardation.* New York: Cambridge University Press.

ROBERT M. HODAPP

MENTAL RETARDATION, ORGANIC

Mental retardation (MR) is signaled when a child's cognitive, personal, and social skills develop too slowly to meet society's minimum expectations. The severity of MR is formally established by standardized tests of intelligence and ADAPTIVE BEHAVIOR, and by estimates of the special educational, medical, and other services the child will require. The less ready the family or society is to meet the special requirements, and the more severe the cognitive deficits are, the poorer will be the child's prospects for good health and a fulfilling life.

The severity of MR is determined chiefly by its causes or origins (etiology). The child's and the family's medical, psychological, educational, and social histories, taken together, can indicate two broad etiological classes: organic and cultural–familial. As a rule, organic MR is much more severe than cultural–familial MR, placing much greater burdens on the child, the family, and society.

The diagnosis of *organic* MR requires that the affected child have a clearly documented organic-MR condition (that is, a current or past physical condition or disease that is known to cause MR directly or to be regularly accompanied by it). By contrast, *cultural-*

familial MR is signified chiefly by the absence of organic-MR conditions. It is often accompanied by psychosocial risks, such as having a retarded mother or father, a chronically disrupted family, or impoverished learning opportunities.

Organic-MR conditions are traditionally classified according to their physical causes or characteristics, yet etiologic study often reveals contributory socioenvironmental influences. This article focuses on direct and contributory determinants of the occurrence of organic MR and the severity of its associated intellectual impairments.

GENERAL CONSIDERATIONS

There are at least 364 different organic-MR conditions. According to the timing of their appearance in the life of the affected child, these include 225 *prenatal* (existing at conception or arising during the first six months of pregnancy), 49 *perinatal* (arising during the last three months of pregnancy or during childbirth) and 90 *postnatal* (arising in infancy and childhood).

The diversity of organic causes is seen in their medical names (Table 1), which indicate the causative agent, such as a virus, poison, head injury, or genetic defect, or else some associated bodily characteristic, such as a particular defect of the brain or abnormality in physical appearance, body chemistry, or chromosomal endowment.

Organic MR is often linked to indirect, contributory conditions that facilitate its occurrence or increase the severity of its associated cognitive impairments (Table 2). Such contributory conditions may be active (decorating a crib with poisonous paint) or passive (failure to vaccinate a child).

Contributory conditions vary widely across geographic, social, and ethnic boundaries. They tend to affect children most severely who are born and reared under crowded, impoverished, or unsanitary conditions, and they often work by interfering with measures designed to prevent or ameliorate MR. Such measures include administering specific vaccines or prophylactic (preventive) antimicrobials; avoiding childbearing when the couple carries abnormal genes or chromosomes; avoiding harmful substances and maintaining good health and adequate medical care during pregnancy; eliminating hazardous environmental conditions; and giving afflicted children and adults appropriate educational, social, and employment opportunities. These measures are susceptible to inference by the following:

1. misconceived public health or educational policies
2. economic, religious or other cultural constraints
3. deliberate or thoughtless neglect by parents, health-care workers, and society generally

TABLE 1
Direct causes of organic mental retardation

Chromosomal disorder
  Down syndrome; fragile-X syndrome; Klinefelter's syndrome; Turner's syndrome
Metabolic disorder
  Phenylketonuria; galactosemia
Prenatal developmental disorder/malformation
  Spina bifida; hypothyroidism; hydrocephalus; microcephaly
Intoxication (poisoning)
  Fetal alcohol syndrome; cocaine poisoning; lead poisoning
Brain disease
  Toxoplasmosis; syphilis; rubella; cytomegalovirus; herpes; HIV
Trauma (physical injury)/malnutrition
  Birth injury; famine; child abuse; automobile collision
Other conditions at birth
  Prematurity; fetal growth retardation

SOURCE: Grossman, 1983.

TABLE 2
Conditions that contribute indirectly to organic mental retardation or increase its severity

Physical and mental abuse
  Prenatal alcohol abuse; beatings; sensory/social isolation
Nutritional, educational and medical neglect
  Failure to feed; failure to educate; failure to vaccinate
Social prejudice and discrimination
  Ostracism of the handicapped
Industrial/commercial negligence
  Lead poisoning; product-related brain injury

Such contributory conditions must be accounted for when planning prevention or treatment of organic MR, or rehabilitation of affected individuals.

Prevalence and Probable Outcome. The prevalence of organic-MR conditions varies widely across national boundaries, depending upon the country's concentration of carriers of genetic disease; its nutritional, health, and educational standards; its control over industrial pollution and consumption of drugs and alcohol; and its provisions for mass vaccination against disease, mass screening to detect disease, and accessible facilities for genetic counseling and elective abortion.

In the United States, the most and least prevalent organic-MR conditions are found among the 274 that originate in the prenatal and perinatal periods. Separately occurring in 1 in 350 to less than 1 in 100,000 live births, these 274 together affect perhaps 1 in 20 (5%) of live births.

Some organic-MR conditions are low-risk for MR, meaning that most of the affected children will have normal cognitive development. A few others are high-risk for MR, but if the affected child is given timely treatment, cognitive development is only slightly retarded, if not normal. For the remaining (great majority) of conditions, no treatment is available to prevent MR. In some of these, the child's predictable ultimate intellectual status is severely to profoundly subnormal, in others mildly or moderately subnormal, and in still others quite variable depending upon the sex of the child; the parents' genetic constitutions; the duration, timing, or intensity of exposure to harmful substances; or other influences.

Despite the large range of possible outcomes of organic-MR conditions, the following rule applies: Profound, severe, or moderate MR is practically always of organic origin, whereas mild MR is much more likely to result from psychosocial influences.

Prevention, Treatment, and Ethical Considerations. Prevention of organic-MR conditions is a high priority for public health officials and medical researchers worldwide. Three general concerns motivate this effort:

1. the extraordinary emotional, social, and educational costs of rearing, supporting, and protecting the affected child

2. the extraordinary medical costs of sometimes life-threatening physical disabilities that accompany many organic-MR conditions, whether or not intelligence is affected

3. the useful knowledge of diseases in general that comes from studying these particular ones

The responsibility for prevention is widely distributed. Basic researchers seek physical causes and diagnostic signs, and develop specific preventive measures. Public health and educational institutions evaluate the basic discoveries and seek to promulgate by law and public education those measures that are deemed economically and practically feasible. Corporations and educators, clinics, and parents are then responsible for implementation. The complexities of this enterprise (including the imperfections inherent in social organizations) nearly always result in incomplete prevention, regardless of the reliability of the medical findings or the demonstrated effectiveness of the medical approach.

The variety of organic-MR etiologies dictates a variety of preventive approaches. It is useful to distinguish between primary prevention (of the disease, injuries, and other conditions themselves), and secondary prevention (of their adverse effects). Adverse effects include not only the child's retarded personal, social, and cognitive development but also the complex medical problems, physical handicaps, and gross disfigurements that often accompany organic MR.

Primary Prevention. Assisted by genetic counseling and health education, primary *prenatal* and *perinatal* prevention includes avoidance of pregnancy when the offspring would be at unusual risk of acquiring genetic or chromosomal disorders; immunization and prophylactic treatment to prevent infectious diseases from damaging the developing embryo or fetus; proper nutrition; and avoidance of high temperatures (saunas, hot tubs), alcohol, drugs (prescription and recreational), undercooked meat, and cat feces.

Primary *postnatal* prevention focuses on immunization against infectious diseases, elimination of poisonous substances from the environment, provision of appropriate nutrition, and protection from physical injury.

Secondary Prevention. The goal of secondary prevention is to avert or ameliorate an existing condition's associated cognitive and physical abnormalities. If detected early enough, the following prenatal and perinatal conditions can be treated to prevent MR: Rh-incompatibility disease, by fetal blood transfusions; syphilis (and perhaps toxoplasmosis), by giving antimicrobials to the mother; and hypothyroidism, by injecting thyroxine into the fluid surrounding the fetus (amniotic fluid).

Secondary prevention in infancy and childhood begins in all developed nations by requiring newborns' blood to be tested for rare congenital diseases that can be treated to prevent MR. These diseases include hypothyroidism, phenylketonuria (PKU), and galactosemia. MR caused by hypothyroidism is prevented by administering thyroxine throughout childhood. PKU and galactosemia are treated by instituting specially restricted diets immediately after birth.

Hydrocephalus (a potentially damaging accumulation of fluid in the brain) occurs in at least forty-seven prenatal and postnatal conditions, many of which have other associated brain anomalies. When hydrocephalus itself is the principal threat to cognitive development, the risk can be minimized or eliminated by relieving the intracranial fluid pressure with repeated surgical interventions beginning before or soon after birth.

Infections are treated aggressively with antimicrobials to prevent brain disease (meningitis, encephalitis). Severe head injury is treated surgically and medically to prevent permanent neurological impairment, including MR and related learning disorders that result from hemorrhage and other physical effects and rarely from secondary bacterial infections. Food deprivation is treated with supplemental feeding starting as early as possible in infancy.

Prenatal Testing and Elective Abortion. Several hundred chromosomal and genetic diseases (many MR-related) have been discovered since the 1970s, stimulating widespread use and continuing development of prenatal diagnostic tests. The aim is to give the earliest possible warning of an affected fetus. The tests involve either examination of the fetus using ultrasonic or magnetic resonance imaging or analysis of maternal blood, fetal blood cells found in maternal blood, fetal blood from the umbilical cord, or fetal tissue from the embryonic sac (chorionic villus sampling) or the amniotic fluid. For many conditions, the test is conclu-

sive; for others, it provides an estimate of fetal risk, which may vary widely.

As of 1993, at least 116 (including all of the most important) MR-related chromosomal, genetic, infectious, and malformation diseases could be detected between the ninth and twentieth weeks of pregnancy. As noted, a few of these are treated successfully before birth and others in early infancy. The great majority cannot be treated at any time, however, and they permit no intervention other than elective abortion, which is controversial in some locales.

The decision about abortion ultimately rests with the mother, who is more likely to choose it under the following conditions:

1. when the condition is detected fairly early in pregnancy
2. when there is a high risk of severe handicap
3. when society and government encourage it

The largest U.S. experience with prenatal screening is in California. Since 1986 physicians there have had to offer all pregnant women free tests to detect abnormal levels of alpha-fetoprotein (AFP) in their blood. High AFP suggests fetal neural tube defects (e.g., spina bifida); low AFP suggests chromosomal disorders (e.g., DOWN SYNDROME). About half the eligible women participate, and the first 176,000 tests led to diagnoses of over 150 cases of neural tube defects, Down syndrome, and other chromosomal disorders. In these, abortion was elected in 91, 78, and 63 percent of the pregnancies, respectively, for an overall rate of 84 percent.

An ethical problem in the use of abortion to prevent the birth of affected children arises out of the following five general considerations:

1. The mother is entitled to know if her fetus is abnormal.
2. Because nearly all prenatal tests are done to detect relatively rare conditions, more than 97 percent reveal no abnormality. At-risk fetuses that are shown to be unafflicted can be brought confidently to term. In earlier times those same fetuses might have been aborted because of unrelieved fear of abnormality.
3. The clinic's description of a condition and what the mother learns elsewhere determine the accuracy of

her understanding of its probable severity and its practical implications. Decisions regarding abortion, however, often cannot be delayed for long and are therefore based on new learning that is rapid and usually incomplete.

4. For some conditions the prenatal test can reveal only the degree of risk. The decision is especially burdensome in such cases because objective "risk" is often misunderstood, especially when it is close to 50 percent.

5. The mother may be opposed to abortion in principle but may also recognize that in her particular case the medical costs or long-term care would be personally ruinous.

The ethics of prenatal testing thus seek a satisfactory balance among potentially conflicting sociocultural influences in view of the desire to produce healthy children and to avert perceived calamity, and the need to resolve uncertainty about an affected child's future in the family and in society. Similar ethical considerations apply to postnatal decisions to treat or withhold treatment in life-threatening conditions that carry a high risk of MR.

COMMON CONDITIONS

Genetic disorders are by far the most diverse class of organic-MR conditions. There are over 140 related to MR, and some are among its most common causes. Prevention often presents technical and ethical difficulties. Only a few are treatable, and many are fatal before or soon after birth. If not fatal, they can present a daunting array of physical problems that seriously complicate the lives of the affected children, their caretakers, and teachers.

The genetic disorders fall into three large subclasses: chromosomal disorders, metabolic disorders, and developmental/malformation diseases.

Chromosomal Disorders. Every normal human cell contains forty-six chromosomes, including twenty-two matched pairs plus two sex chromosomes. Each parent donates one chromosome to each pair. To diagnose most chromosomal disorders, a photomicrograph of the chromosomes is cut up and arranged in pairs in a standard format from largest to smallest (the

karyotype). Abnormal karyotypes may show extra whole or partial chromosomes, or partial or total deletions. Such abnormalities generally affect every cell in the body and are always accompanied by physical abnormalities in addition to cognitive deficits. The older the mother past age 30, the greater the risk of a chromosomal disorder in her fetus.

The first MR-related karyotype was reported in 1959. More than thirty have since been identified, and research continues. The 1959 discovery was from a child with Down syndrome (DS), and it showed three chromosomes rather than two in the twenty-first pair (trisomy 21). The extra chromosome in DS is associated with about thirty different symptoms, though DS children seldom show more than a few of them. Symptoms include about twenty unusual physical features plus elevated risks of heart and intestinal disease and loss of hearing and vision. The associated MR usually ranges from moderate to severe. Occurring in about 1 in 750 live births, DS affects males and females equally, and it is one of the two most common chromosomal disorders. The other, fragile-X syndrome, occurs in 1 in 1,500 live male births. It is primarily a disease of males, and the MR associated with it is more severe in the male. Unlike DS, most females and some males who carry the fragile-X chromosome are not mentally retarded.

Metabolic Disorders. Each chromosome contains a long sequence of amino acids (genes). In the aggregate, the genes determine the patterns of physical development and the series of chemical reactions (metabolism) by which nutrients (sugars, proteins, and other substances) are converted into body structure and energy.

Each metabolic reaction is enabled, in turn, by its own specific gene (enzyme). If an enzyme is missing or is present in insufficient quantity, the metabolic sequence is interrupted at that point. As a result, the substance that would be converted (precursor) builds up, and the normal conversion product does not materialize. High concentrations of precursors in blood or tissue or the absence of normal conversion products can cause brain damage or brain maldevelopment.

There are over eighty such enzyme deficiencies associated with MR, but most are extremely rare (less than 1 in 50,000 live births). Primary prevention focuses on genetic counseling and prenatal detection with subsequent abortion. Secondary prevention of MR (possible only in PKU and galactosemia) involves eliminating the nonconvertible precursor from the child's diet, ideally starting at birth and continuing throughout childhood. The diet for galactosemia aims to eliminate galactose-containing foods. It is often unsuccessful. The diet for PKU, which restricts phenylalanine, is effective but severe, and it must be closely followed throughout childhood. It must also be reinstated before and during the pregnancy of a PKU-affected mother; otherwise the phenylalanine excess and the tyrosine deficiency in her blood will cause catastrophic damage to her fetus. This risk is eliminated if a non-PKU surrogate mother is employed to carry the fertilized egg through pregnancy.

Developmental/Malformation Diseases. The fetal developmental/malformation syndromes, of which over seventy distinct MR-related types exist, are usually rare. Most have clear genetic bases. The newborn infant tends to have gross deformations of the brain and head (such as in hydrocephalus and microcephaly) and face. Limbs and internal organs are also commonly affected.

An important exception is the comparatively common neural-tube defect known as *spina bifida,* which arises very early in pregnancy as the result of improper closure of the embryonic spinal column. Associated hydrocephalus is the principal threat to cognitive development, and this disorder can often be treated successfully by surgery. Although spina bifida has a genetic component, the risk is increased by maternal exposure to certain drugs and to high temperatures and possibly by a dietary folic acid deficiency (correctable by supplemental vitamins taken before and after conception). Spina bifida paralyzes the affected child to varying degrees, often making for an extremely difficult personal–social adjustment in childhood and especially adolescence.

Damaging Prenatal Agents. Agents that damage the fetus are called *teratogens.* Alcohol and drugs are among the most frequent MR-related teratogens. In addition, prenatal irradiation used for medical diagnosis and for treatment of cancer can cause permanent fetal brain damage. Excessive heat (hyperther-

mia), as from use of hot tubs or saunas early in pregnancy, substantially elevates the risk of neural-tube defects (spina bifida, anencephaly). Electric blankets and water beds do not seem to pose similar risks.

Fetal Alcohol Syndrome. The direct cause of FETAL ALCOHOL SYNDROME (FAS) is alcohol in the mother's blood. High blood alcohol interferes with fetal development throughout pregnancy, but it may be particularly damaging during the first three months. Symptoms include retarded fetal and postnatal growth, distinctive facial and other physical features, defects in various organs, and behavioral disturbances. MR is a frequent concomitant of FAS, which is one of the most prevalent organic-MR conditions.

As FAS is the direct consequence of elective human activity (the mother's abusive drinking), the contributory conditions are the most important preventive concerns. The drinking is seldom simply a matter of personal choice, for family circumstances often contribute to it. Moreover, the socioeconomic circumstances that determine or support maternal drinking may independently compromise the FAS child's prospects for postnatal physical, social, and intellectual growth. Thus, although the primary cause—alcohol—is a clearly identifiable teratogen, FAS-related MR is an extremely complex socioenvironmental problem.

Drugs. Medications taken to control maternal seizures during pregnancy can cause fetal brain malformation. Protecting fetal development by withholding these drugs, however, can seriously compromise the seizure-prone mother's own physical and personal integrity. As with PKU mothers, using a surrogate for the pregnancy eliminates the risk.

Narcotics (cocaine in particular) can cause fetal addiction and cognitive and emotional effects of variable severity in childhood. Prevention focuses on abstention during pregnancy. Socioenvironmental factors in abuse of narcotics are similar to those in FAS.

Infectious Diseases. The important MR-related *prenatal* infections are viral (cytomegalovirus, HIV, rubella) or parasitic (toxoplasmosis). They are transmitted to the fetus when the mother is infected during pregnancy. Maternal toxoplasmosis occurs from eating undercooked contaminated meat or by handling infected cat feces. It is treated immediately with antimicrobials, the dosage being increased if the fetus is also infected.

Some viruses that cause devastating brain damage in fetuses, such as rubella (German measles) and cytomegalovirus, produce practically harmless diseases in children and adults. In such cases, children and women of childbearing age are vaccinated (rubella) or directly exposed. The resulting immunity prevents their infection or reinfection, and hence prevents fetal disease during pregnancy. The near eradication of rubella by mass vaccination programs in the 1970s and 1980s is one of the landmark achievements in the medicine of MR. This serious fetal disease still occurs but only through failures to vaccinate.

The important *perinatal* and *postnatal* infections are viral (Herpes simplex) and bacterial (group B Streptococcus, Hemophilus influenzae-Type b; Escherichia coli; Streptococcus pneumoniae; Neisseria meningiditis). Group B Streptococcus infection is sometimes preventable by giving antimicrobials to the mother just prior to birth. By 1992 mass vaccination against the most common MR-related bacterial disease of infancy, Hemophilus influenzae-Type b, had succeeded in eradicating the disease in Finland. Eradication has not been effected in other countries only because of public health policy failures and lax implementation. Development of vaccines against the other common MR-related postnatal bacterial diseases was well under way by 1993.

Traumatic Brain Injury (TBI). Physical abuse, falls, and automobile collisions are the principal causes of cognitive deficiencies and MR from severe TBI. The deficiencies are more severe the younger the child at the time of head injury and the longer the period of unconsciousness (coma).

Infants and Toddlers. Below the age of 1 year, over 90 percent of severe TBI results from physical abuse, and it is often precipitated by infants' inconsolable crying. Beyond 1 year of age, abusive head injury is often precipitated by infants' bowel or bladder mishaps. At this age TBI tends to involve violent shaking, combined in the worst cases with blows to the head. Physical abuse of this sort is usually associated with disrupted family relationships, and MR-related infant TBI therefore has complex contributory conditions. Prevention is not

well understood, and the effectiveness of enjoining new mothers against shaking their infants has yet to be demonstrated. The contrary cultural norm ("I'll shake some sense into you") suggests that the educational goal will be difficult to achieve.

Later Childhood. Severe TBI later in childhood is most often associated with falls (playground accidents being common causes) or automobile collisions (when child restraints and seat belts are not used). These rarely result in MR, but subtle learning disabilities and other thinking disorders are common outcomes. Medical treatment to prevent cognitive disorders (secondary prevention) is often ineffective in severe childhood TBI. Primary prevention is therefore paramount and must emphasize educating parents and children in the use of seat belts and recreational equipment.

Environmental Diseases. The principal MR-related environmental diseases are malnutrition and lead poisoning. Both of these are linked to unfavorable child-rearing conditions (poverty, crowding), making it difficult for researchers to determine the unique effects of the diseases.

Malnutrition. In infancy and early childhood, chronic moderate-to-severe protein-calorie deprivation (likely in combination with associated lacks of micronutrients, such as minerals) causes gross physical wasting and low intelligence. In the early 1990s it was shown that *mild* malnutrition in infancy, long-known to lead to physical stunting, is also associated with weaknesses in specific areas of cognitive functioning. Because infant nutritional status and socioeducational environment are closely linked, prevention of malnutrition-related cognitive deficiencies depends jointly on adequate food supplies and adequate social and educational opportunities—at least in the home. Gross nutritional failures are widespread in impoverished countries. They generally result from governmental ineptness in economics and public-health (contributory conditions).

Lead Poisoning. Metallic lead taken in from contaminated air, soil, water, household dust, utensils, or flaking lead-based paint causes reduced intelligence or MR, and a variety of thinking disorders. Because a direct association exists between the blood lead level and loss of intelligence, no claim for safe levels is justified.

Lead exposure is dangerous at all ages. Fetal exposure via the mother's blood is related to poor early cognitive development, and a peak vulnerability—with very long-term consequences—may occur at around age 2. Medical treatment (chelation therapy) can lower dangerously elevated blood lead levels, but it also reduces beneficial trace elements, and salutory effects on cognitive development are not proven.

Lead poisoning is the most important environmental public health problem for children in industrialized countries. Although it is concentrated in impoverished urban living conditions, it is known to affect children in rural settings and at all socioeconomic levels. The effects of lead on cognitive development are universally appreciated as a worldwide result of automotive, industrial, and commercial pollution; its continuation constitutes contributory negligence by industry and governments. Like prenatal drug abuse and fetal alcohol syndrome, lead poisoning originates strictly from human activity. Prevention is therefore necessarily focused on contributory conditions.

(*See also:* CHROMOSOMAL ABNORMALITIES; MENTAL RETARDATION, CULTURAL-FAMILIAL.)

BIBLIOGRAPHY

BELL, W. E., & MCCORMICK, W. F. (1975). *Neurologic infections in children.* Philadelphia: W. B. Saunders.

BRENTON, D. P. (1989). Maternal phenylketonuria. *European Journal of Clinical Nutrition, 43,* 13–17.

GROSSMAN, H. J. (ED.). (1983). *Classification in mental retardation (rev. ed.).* Washington, DC: American Association on Mental Retardation (formerly, American Association on Mental Deficiency).

MATSON, J. L., & MULICK, J. A. (EDS.). (1983). *Handbook of mental retardation.* New York: Pergamon Press.

NIGHTINGALE, E. O., & GOODMAN, M. (1990). *Before birth: Prenatal testing for genetic disease.* Cambridge, MA: Harvard University Press.

SCHROEDER, S. R. (ED.). (1987). *Toxic substances and mental retardation: Neurobehavioral toxicology and teratology.* (Monographs of the American Association on Mental Deficiency, No. 8.) Washington, DC: American Association on Mental Retardation (formerly, American Association on Mental Deficiency).

SIMEON, D. T., & GRANTHAM-MCGREGOR, S. M. (1990). Nutritional deficiencies and children's behaviour and mental development. *Nutrition Research Reviews, 3,* 1–24.

SWAIMAN, K. F. (ED.). (1989). *Pediatric neurology: Principles and practice* (Vols. 1–2). Baltimore, MD: Mosby.

WEAVER, D. D. (1992). *Catalog of prenatally diagnosed conditions* (2nd ed). Baltimore, MD: Johns Hopkins University Press.

JOHN M. BELMONT

MERCER, JANE R. (1924–) Born on December 5, 1924, in Pittsburgh, Pennsylvania, Jane Mercer received her postgraduate education at the University of Chicago (M.A. in sociology, 1947) and at the University of Southern California (Ph.D. in sociology, 1962). From 1963 through 1965, she worked for the State of California Department of Mental Hygiene as a research specialist under a grant from the National Institute of Mental Health to investigate aspects of mental retardation in community settings. She maintained a position in research with this agency after joining the faculty at the University of California at Riverside in 1965 with the rank of associate professor at this same institution.

Mercer's academic work in intelligence began with several grant projects related to the incidence, prevalence, and other aspects of the epidemiology of mental retardation, with a focus on community settings. Mercer was a proponent of labeling theory (the theory that people will live up to others' positive expectations—and down to negative ones) and a supporter of the hypothesis of the "six-hour retarded child" (the child who acts retarded only in school) (also see Gordon [1984] and Lambert [1987]). Her work in mental retardation eventually led to the development of the SYSTEM OF MULTICULTURAL PLURALISTIC ASSESSMENT (SOMPA) (Mercer & Lewis, 1979). Mercer adopted the view that most children diagnosed as mentally retarded appeared to be so only in a school setting (hence the term *six-hour retarded child*) and that they functioned at normal levels within their indigenous sociocultural settings. SOMPA was supposed to correct what was seen as a problem of bias in the diagnosis of mental retardation.

In developing SOMPA, her best-known and most influential work related to intelligence, Mercer adopted the cultural test bias hypothesis and developed correction factors to remove the cultural bias of tests and thus reflect the true, or innate, intelligence of the child.

SOMPA was designed to provide a comprehensive measure of the cognitive abilities, perceptual and motor abilities, sociocultural background, and adaptive behavior of children aged 5 through 11. It uses three models of assessment and attempts to integrate them into a comprehensive assessment: (1) the medical model, defined as any abnormal organic condition interfering with physiological functioning; (2) the social system model, derived principally from labeling theory and social deviance perspectives from the field of sociology, which attempts to correct the "Anglo conformity" biases of the test developers who have designed IQ tests for the last eighty years; and (3) the pluralistic model, which compares the scores of a child with the scores of children of a similar ethclass (that is, the same demographic, socioeconomic, and cultural background), correcting for any scoring discrepancies between the ethclass and the white middle class. Nevertheless, the main purpose of SOMPA is to remove cultural bias from assessment of intelligence by providing a corrected estimate of intellectual abilities, an estimated learning potential (ELP). While adding a "correction factor" to the obtained IQs of disadvantaged children is not a new idea, SOMPA corrections are unique in their objectivity and in having a clearly articulated, if controversial, basis. The corrections are based on the child's sociocultural characteristics and equate the mean IQs of blacks, whites, and Hispanics with various other cultural characteristics, such as family structure and degree of urban acculturation.

Unfortunately for SOMPA, its underlying assumption that mean differences among sociocultural groups indicate cultural bias in tests has been rejected by almost all psychometricians who have researched the cultural test bias hypothesis. The conceptual basis for SOMPA is thus far more controversial than it appears in the test manuals and, indeed, is open to serious question.

Initially, SOMPA aroused much enthusiasm, but it failed to contribute to the development of better diagnostic and intervention plans. It did stimulate to some extent considerable research in the field of test bias and prompted greater use of the concept of adaptive behavior in the diagnosis of mental retardation. Following her efforts with SOMPA, Mercer turned to work with what she deemed "bicognitive" children (i.e., children reared in bilingual environments), focusing on their unique cognitive development and its challenges to assessment.

BIBLIOGRAPHY

GORDON, R. (1984). Digits backward and the Mercer-Kamin law: An empirical response to Mercer's treatment of internal validity of IQ tests. In C. R. Reynolds & R. T. Brown (Eds.), *Perspectives on bias in mental testing* (pp. 367–506). New York: Plenum.

JACQUES CATTELL PRESS (1973). *American men and women of science: The social and behavioral sciences* (Vol. 2, 12th ed.). New York: Author.

LAMBERT, N. M. (1987). Six-hour retarded child. In C. R. Reynolds & L. Mann (Eds.), *Encyclopedia of special education* (pp. 1440–1441). New York: Wiley-Interscience.

MERCER, J. R., & LEWIS, J. (1979). *System of multicultural pluralistic assessment.* San Antonio: The Psychological Corporation.

CECIL R. REYNOLDS
BETH MURDOCK

METACOGNITION   Metacognition is "cognition about cognition." Whereas cognition involves knowledge of the world and strategies for using that knowledge to solve problems, metacognition concerns monitoring, controlling, and understanding one's knowledge and strategies.

In contemporary theory the human intellectual system is viewed as having many levels, only some of which are directly related to one another. For any two directly related levels, a monitoring and controlling level is called "metacognitive" and a monitored and controlled level is called "cognitive" (Broadbent, 1977; Nelson & Narens, 1990). Knowledge and strategies are located at, and operate from, a cognitive level. They are understood, monitored, and controlled by a directly related metacognitive level. Monitoring and control by any metacognitive level are enabled by a model of its directly related cognitive level (Butterfield & Nelson, 1991; Conant & Ashby, 1970). Such models include representations of what the cognitive level can do (its strategies) with problems and their contexts (its knowledge). They include understandings of what influences operation of the cognitive level and operational plans for directing it (Flavell, 1979). Figure 1 is a sketch of how cognition and metacognition are related.

In what follows, the foregoing definitions and theory are illustrated with physics problems and how they are solved. The definitions could have been illustrated with many memorization tasks, reading comprehension, writing, or arithmetic problems. Following illustration of the theory, inferential, introspective, and instructional experiments are described to illustrate some of what is known about metacognition and how it changes as people mature. For example, novices', children's, and mentally retarded people's failure to use known strategies for solving problems is the result of their lack of metacognitive understanding and their failure to monitor accurately their problem-solution efforts; metacognitive monitoring, control, and understanding increase with age and experience; college students and other effective learners base their study efforts on their monitoring of how well they already know what they are studying and on their monitoring of how easy it will be to learn what they do not know; children and mentally retarded people can be taught to accurately monitor the effectiveness of their strategies; and prompting children to use metacognition leads them to generalize newly learned strategies that they would not generalize without metacognitive prompting.

DISTINGUISHING METACOGNITION FROM COGNITION

Two Illustrative Problems. Balance-scale and shadow-projection problems allow illustration of the distinction between the cognitive matters of knowledge and strategies and the metacognitive matters of understanding, monitoring, and control. A balance scale is like a well-balanced seesaw (see Figure 2). It can be latched to remain level and loaded with a num-

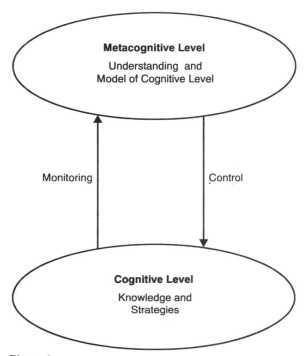

Figure 1

Composition of and relations between directly related cognitive and metacognitive levels of a mental system

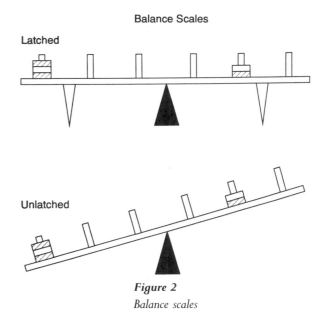

Figure 2

Balance scales

ber of equally heavy weights at different distances from the fulcrum. Having shown a student a static arrangement of either of these or any of many other simple physics problems, psychologists have asked the student to predict which of three things will happen when the static arrangement is allowed to change according to mechanical laws. A student's choices are whether one side, the other, or neither side will go down when the scale is unlatched. For a shadow-projection problem, the choices are for one of two variable-length pegs located variable distances from a screen to cast a taller shadow or for the shadows to be equally tall when fixed projection lights are turned on.

Knowledge as Cognition. One requirement of problems such as a balance scale and pair of shadow projectors is knowledge of relevant dimensions and how they influence problem outcome. Weights placed on both sides of the fulcrum and the distances of those weights from the fulcrum are the relevant dimensions for a balance scale. More weights and greater distance from the fulcrum both work toward downward movement of their side of the fulcrum. Heights of two shadow-casting pegs and their distances from a projection screen are relevant dimensions for a pair of shadow projectors. Greater height and greater distance both work for taller shadows.

Learning even a simple problem's relevant dimensions and how they influence problem outcome is not trivial, because many dimensions can be used to describe balance-scale and shadow-projector problems. Also, depending on what is allowed to vary, more than two dimensions can be relevant. Thus, vertical placement of projection lights relative to tops of the pegs that cast shadows influences shadow height. Such knowledge is considered cognitive rather than metacognitive because it is about the world.

Knowledge is relevant to most cognitive activities. Thus, when reading a text or memorizing a list of names, what one needs to study most is novel or unfamiliar material or names. When one is revising a text, the revision will depend on how the text squares with what one knows or believes about the topic of the text.

Strategies as Cognition. Balance-scale and shadow-projection problems come in several subtypes that require different strategies for their solution. The strategies vary in their complexity, which correlates strongly with the age at which they are first used. Young children approach all problems as if they were solvable by the simplest strategy, and mature problem solvers use the simplest strategy suitable to the problem they face. This entry describes only the simplest and the most complex of the five strategies applicable to balance-scale and other multidimensional problems.

Students using the simplest dimensional-comparison strategy predict on the basis of one of a problem's two relevant dimensions. For example, if comparison reveals unequal weights on the two sides of a balance scale, a student predicts that the side with greater weight will go down, regardless of the distance of the two sides' weights from the fulcrum. This simplest dimensional comparison allows correct prediction for all problems whose uncompared dimension has equal values on both sides or a larger value on the same side as the larger compared dimension.

Integrating the dimensions of weight and distance by calculating torque is required by balance scales having unequal values for weight and distance on opposite sides. Consider a balance scale with four weights placed 6 distance units to the left of its fulcrum and seven weights placed 3 distance units to the right. Comparing only weight says the right side will go down, but comparing only distance says the left side. Such conflicting predictions are resolved by multiplying weights and distances separately for the two sides: $4 \times 6 = 24$ and $7 \times 3 = 21$. The left side has the greater product, or torque, so it goes down.

Both the simplest dimensional comparison and the most complex dimensional integration strategies require quantifying values of two or more dimensions and either comparing the dimensions or integrating them arithmetically. It is this doing of quantification and calculation, as distinct from knowing facts about the world, that justifies calling comparison and integration "strategies" rather than "knowledge." It is doing them to representations of the world that makes strategies cognitive rather than metacognitive.

All intellectually demanding problems can be solved more effectively if appropriate strategies are used. Thus, an effective strategy for learning names of new people met at a party is to call to mind a familiar scene and to visualize each person and his or her name at a different location in the scene. Later, a name can be retrieved by recalling the constructed image and locating the image of the person whose name is desired.

Metacognitive Monitoring and Control of Cognition. The distinction between doing and knowing drawn for cognitive levels of the intellectual system also applies to metacognitive levels, where monitoring and controlling cognition are kinds of doing and where understanding cognition is knowing. Balance-scale problems provide examples.

Effective control of cognition is realized by metacognitive monitoring. Students must monitor what they know about the implications of a balance scale's features in order to select an appropriate dimensional comparison or dimensional integration strategy. Such selection, which depends on monitoring, is a form of control of cognition. When using either dimensional comparison or integration, students must monitor the accuracy of their assessments of dimensional values and correct their counts or estimates as needed, again basing their control of cognition (correcting their assessments) on monitoring it. Especially when using dimensional integration, students must keep track of (monitor) where they stand in the sequence of tactics that make up their strategy so that they will know what to do next. Following their predictions for a latched scale, students must monitor the scale's action after it is unlatched, to decide whether a different strategy should be used on future problems. An important feature of monitoring and control of this sort is that they can result in one's learning about how to solve future problems (Butterfield, 1986).

Studying for a test in school provides other examples of monitoring and control of cognition. While reading an assigned text, college students can write down questions they wish to be able to answer later. Then, some time after finishing the reading, they can try to answer the questions. Those that monitoring says are difficult can be used to guide further study, until monitoring says that all questions can be answered.

Metacognitive Understanding. Effective control of ongoing cognition depends on knowing what to monitor and on understanding the implications of what the monitoring reveals. The following are some

of the metacognitive understandings needed to control effectively one's solution of simple physics problems, such as those involving balance scales and shadow projectors:

1. There are many different kinds of simple physics problems.
2. Only a few of any problem's many dimensions are relevant to its solution.
3. Different strategies solve different subsets of problems, and the strategies form a hierarchy.
4. Dimensional comparison strategies are lower in the hierarchy than dimensional integration strategies.
5. It is easier and more efficient to use dimensional comparison than integration whenever possible.
6. Trying to solve a problem by comparison tells that integration is required when it reveals conflicting predictions from different compared dimensions.

Concerning study for a school test, a useful metacognitive understanding is that one knows information only if he or she can recall it some time after studying it and without help from looking at studied material. Thus, it is more useful to test oneself after putting away a reading than by asking while reading, Do I know what this author is saying?

HOW METACOGNITION IS STUDIED

Cognitive matters are studied directly by task analysis. Thus, the above-cited descriptions of knowledge and strategies used to solve simple physics problems are based on analyses of how people of different ages solve such problems. Such task analyses are tested very strongly by translating them into instructions and determining whether teaching the analyses turns inaccurate into accurate problem solvers. Often it does.

Task-analytic and instructional investigation of knowledge and strategies provide the best view scientists have of the models of cognition hypothesized to guide metacognitive monitoring and control of cognition (see Figure 1). Nevertheless, metacognition is not directly observable. Because metacognition is not directly observable, it has been studied largely by inference from cognition. It has also been studied by indirect observation through introspective reports (Kreutzer, Leonard, & Flavell, 1975) or through observation of what happens to strategies or base knowledge when something is done to influence metacognition (Butterfield & Belmont, 1977). Relying on introspection is useful because, despite its limits (Ericsson & Simon, 1980; Nisbett & Wilson, 1977), it provides data about metacognitive understandings (Schneider, 1985) and metacognitive monitoring (Nelson & Narens, 1990) that can be checked against performance. Observing what happens to strategies and base knowledge is justifiable because they are readily observed and metacognition is believed to control them.

QUESTIONS THAT HAVE BEEN ANSWERED ABOUT METACOGNITION

Questions Answered by Inference. A person who uses a strategy only when told to do so is said to have a production deficiency (Flavell, 1970). Problem-solving novices, children, and mentally retarded people are especially likely to be production-deficient. In other words, they often fail to use a known strategy when it would solve a problem they face (Rohwer, 1973). Lack of metacognitive understandings (Flavell, 1979) is a main inferred reason for production deficiencies.

It has been known for years that particular patterns of practice are needed to learn a list of six or more words (Belmont & Butterfield, 1969, 1977). For example, people who are asked to study a list of nine words so they will be able to recall them in any order they choose immediately after study should study increasingly as they work their way through the first six or seven words but should not study following the last two or three words. Adults recognize after very few lists that the last two or three words can be remembered for a short time without any study but that early items must be studied or they will not be recalled. Children as young as 10 recognize this fact too, but it takes them nearly twice as many lists as it takes adults. The inferred reason is that children are less able to diagnose the strategic requirements of a memory task; they have less adequate metacognitive monitoring or metacognitive understanding of memory.

Mentally retarded adolescents can be taught to use effective learning strategies. For example, they can be taught to combine the repeated saying (i.e., rehearsal) of early words in a list with the simple reading of end-ing words (Butterfield, Wambold, & Belmont, 1973). When normal adults use this strategy, they recall all words studied by circularly reciting a list's read but unrehearsed ending words before its rehearsed beginning words and then its rehearsed middle words. Mentally retarded adolescents who have been taught the study strategy try to recall from the beginning of a studied list instead of circularly from near its end, so their own recitation of rehearsed words interferes with their recall of the ending, unrehearsed words. Simply telling mentally retarded adolescents to use circular recall leads them to do so, indicating that if they understood that reciting rehearsed words prevents later recall of unrehearsed words, they could adopt the required circular strategy without instruction. It is a reasonable inference that they lack the metacognitive understanding that words that are only read will be forgotten if they are not recited before words that were rehearsed.

Questions Answered by Introspective Reports. If inferences like those drawn to answer the foregoing three questions are valid, then children should report more metacognitive understandings as they age. Kreutzer, Leonard, and Flavell (1975) built an interview based on established facts about memory. Thus, among other things, they asked questions to assess 5-, 6-, 8-, and 10-year-old children's appreciation of the effects of a delay between hearing an unknown phone number and trying to dial it, the effects of a story about a group of pictures on how well the pictures can be remembered, and the like. Older children reported significantly greater understanding of how memory works. The older children reported, among other things, greater appreciation of the fragility of unrehearsed memories and more ways of trying to recall forgotten memories that were well learned.

Nelson et al. (1986) related college students' introspective reports about their memory monitoring to their allocation of study time. They were interested in determining whether monitoring memory for knowledge of material to be learned influenced the study of that material. Their experiments are among the most direct of those testing the idea that controlling cognitive activity depends on monitoring it. They asked students to judge how easy it would be for them to learn pairs of nonsense syllables and then timed how long the students studied each of the judged pairs. Those pairs that were judged easiest to learn were studied less. The researchers also asked students to judge the degree to which they believed they could recognize answers to questions that they could not recall. Subsequent study of the answers was less for answers students believed they would recognize. These data show that metacognitive monitoring is used to control such cognitive activity as studying.

Questions Answered by Teaching Metacognition. The fact that young children do not monitor relationships between their strategic behavior and its outcomes has been hypothesized as the reason why they infrequently use the best strategy they know to solve problems. Lodico et al. (1983) tested whether young children who do not monitor the relationship between their strategic behaviors and memory performance could be taught to do so. They taught 7-year-olds two task-specific strategies for each of two memory tasks. While teaching these strategies, they also taught memory monitoring to half of their subjects. Then, they taught two additional memory strategies for a third task. When performing the third task, for which no memory monitoring was taught, each child was asked which strategy he or she should use the next time the child did the third task. Far more of the children who were taught to monitor their memories to see which strategy worked best said they would use the best strategy another time. Memory monitoring can be taught.

Butterfield and Nelson (1991) taught 8-year-olds dimensional-integration strategies for solving two of three problem types—balance-scale, inclined-plane, and shadow-projection tasks. Most college students who have not taken a physics course fail to solve problems like the ones used to assess two types of transfer of the instructed strategies. Positive transfer within tasks was defined as use of dimensional integration on novel problems of a type for which the strategy had been taught (e.g., solving novel balance-scale problems following instruction about dimensional integration on other balance-scale problems). Positive transfer across problems was defined as use of dimensional integration on one task following instruction on a different task (e.g., solving shadow-projection problems following instruction on balance scales and inclined planes, in the absence of instruction on shadow projection). About 80 percent of the third-grade children transferred their instructed dimensional-integration strategies within tasks before any metacognitive manipulation, indicating that they had learned the strategy. Nevertheless, only 32 percent transferred across tasks before metacognitive manipulation, indicating that few children generalized their learning.

To involve metacognition in transfer, children were asked to say why they had failed each of several conflict problems from an uninstructed problem type after they had been instructed to use isomorphic strategies for the two other problem types. It was hoped that children would draw on their recollection of reasons for solving instructed problems when offering reasons for failing uninstructed problems. If they had, more children should have shown transfer across problems following the questioning, which is what happened. Whereas 32 percent transferred across problems before questioning, 65 percent did so after questioning. Metacognition promotes the generalization of new learning.

THE IMPORTANCE OF METACOGNITION

Metacognition, within twenty years of its being named (Flavell, 1979), became profoundly influential. Ideas about metacognition are invoked with great frequency by theorists and practitioners alike. For example, it has been argued that skilled performance of all sorts, including computer programming, reading, writing, and intelligence itself, can be understood only by reference to metacognitive understanding, monitoring, and control. It has been suggested that the central problem of education—namely, its frequent failure to promote generalized learning—might be solved by combining cognitive and metacognitive instruction. Another reason for great enthusiasm about metacognition is the possibility that is can eliminate fragmentation of cognitive theory.

A great strength of modern cognitive science is that it has provided strong accounts of many sorts of task-specific action, but those accounts have not been put together in such a way as even to approximate a general theory of intelligence. In metacognitive theory, task-specific models like those developed by cognitive science are guides to cognitive action. Researchers and theorists assume that people's intercourse with the problems in their lives provides them with metacognitive models of their cognition that are equivalent to those generated by scientists' task analyses of how people solve problems. Only a plausible mechanism for linking metacognitive levels of the intellectual system is required for metacognitive theory to become the glue that sticks presently dissociated cognitive models to a general theory of intelligence.

BIBLIOGRAPHY

BELMONT, J. M., & BUTTERFIELD, E. C. (1969). The relations of short-term memory to development and intelligence. In L. P. Lipsett & H. Reese (Eds.), *Advances in child development and behavior.* New York: Academic Press.

BELMONT, J. M., & BUTTERFIELD, E. C. (1977). The instructional approach to developmental cognitive research. In R. Kail & J. Hagen (Eds.), *Perspectives on the development of memory and cognition.* Hillsdale, NJ: Erlbaum.

BROADBENT, D. E. (1977). Levels, hierarchies, and the locus of control. *Quarterly Journal of Experimental Psychology, 29,* 181–201.

BUTTERFIELD, E. C. (1986). Intelligent action, learning, and cognitive development might all be explained by the same theory. In R. J. Sternberg & D. K. Detterman (Eds.), *What is intelligence: Contemporary viewpoints on its nature and definition.* Norwood, NJ: Ablex.

BUTTERFIELD, E. C., & BELMONT, J. M. (1977). Assessing and improving the executive cognitive functions of mentally retarded people. In I. Bialer & M. Sternlicht (Eds.), *Psychology of mental retardation: Issues and approaches.* New York: Psychological Dimensions.

BUTTERFIELD, E. C., & FERRETTI, R. P. (1984). Some extensions of the instructional approach to cognitive development and a sufficient condition for transfer of training. In P. H. Brooks, C. McCauley, & R. Sperber (Eds.), *Learning and cognition in the mentally retarded.* Hillsdale, NJ: Erlbaum.

BUTTERFIELD, E. C., & FERRETTI, R. P. (1987). Toward a theoretical integration of hypotheses about intellectual differences among children. In J. G. Borkowski & J. D. Day (Eds.), *Cognition in special children.* Norwood, NJ: Ablex.

BUTTERFIELD, E. C., & NELSON, T. O. (1991). Promoting positive transfer of different types. *Cognition and Instruction, 8,* 69–102.

BUTTERFIELD, E. C., SILADI, D., & BELMONT, J. M. (1980). Validating theories of intelligence. In H. Reese & L. P. Lipsitt (Eds.), *Advances in child development and child behavior.* New York: Academic Press.

BUTTERFIELD, E. C., WAMBOLD, C., & BELMONT, J. M. (1973). On the theory and practice of improving short-term memory. *American Journal of Mental Deficiency, 77,* 654–669.

CONANT, R. C., & ASHBY, W. R. (1970). Every good regulator of a system must be a model of that system. *International Journal of Systems Science, 1,* 89–97.

ERICSSON, K. A., & SIMON, H. A. (1980). Verbal reports as data. *Psychological Review, 87,* 215–251.

FERRETTI, R. P., & BUTTERFIELD, E. C. (1986). Are children's rule assessment classifications invariant across instances of problem types? *Child Development, 57,* 1419–1428.

FERRETTI, R. P., & BUTTERFIELD, E. C. (1989). Intelligence as a correlate of children's problem solving. *American Journal of Mental Retardation, 93,* 424–433.

FERRETTI, R. P., & BUTTERFIELD, E. C. (1992). Intelligence-related differences in the learning, maintenance, and transfer of problem-solving strategies. *Intelligence, 16*(2), 207–223.

FERRETTI, R. P., BUTTERFIELD, E. C., CAHN, A., & KERKMAN, D. (1985). The classification of children's knowledge: Development on the balance scale and inclined-plane problems. *Journal of Experimental Child Psychology, 39,* 131–160.

FLAVELL, J. H. (1970). Developmental studies of mediated memory. In H. W. Reese & L. P. Lipsitt (Eds.), *Advances in child development and behavior.* New York: Academic Press.

FLAVELL, J. H. (1979). Metacognition and cognitive monitoring: A new area of cognitive-developmental inquiry. *American Psychologist, 34,* 906–911.

INHELDER, B., & PIAGET, J. (1958). *The growth of logical thinking from childhood to adolescence.* New York: Basic Books.

KREUTZER, M. A., LEONARD, S. A., & FLAVELL, J. H. (1975). An interview study of children's knowledge about memory. *Monographs of the Society for Research in Child Development, 40,* 40–57.

LODICO, M. G., GHATALA, E. S., LEVIN, J. R., PRESSLEY, M., & BELL, J. A. (1983). The effects of strategy-monitoring training on children's selection of effective memory strategies. *Journal of Experimental Child Psychology, 35,* 263–277.

NELSON, T. O., LEONESIO, R. J., LANDWEHR, R. S., & NARENS, L. (1986). A comparison of three predictors of an individual's memory performance: The individual's feeling of knowing versus the normative feeling of knowing versus base-rate item difficulty. *Journal of Experimental Psychology: Learning, Memory, and Cognition, 8,* 279–288.

NELSON, T. O., & NARENS, L. (1990). Metamemory: A theoretical framework and new findings. *The Psychology of Learning and Motivation, 26,* 125–141.

NISBETT, R., & WILSON, T. (1977). Telling more than we can know: Verbal reports on mental processes. *Psychological Review, 84,* 231–259.

ROHWER, W. D., JR. (1973). Elaboration and learning in childhood and adolescence. In H. W. Reese (Ed.), *Advances in child development and behavior.* New York: Academic Press.

SCHNEIDER, W. (1985). Developmental trends in the metamemory-memory behavior relationship: An integrative review. In D. L. Forrest-Pressley, G. E. MacKinnon, & T. G. Waller (Eds.), *Cognition, metacognition, and human performance.* New York: Academic Press.

SIEGLER, R. S. (1976). Three aspects of cognitive development. *Cognitive Psychology, 8,* 481–520.

SIEGLER, R. S. (1978). The origins of scientific reasoning. In R. S. Siegler (Ed.), *Children's thinking: What develops?* Hillsdale, NJ: Erlbaum.

SIEGLER, R. S. (1981). Developmental sequences within and between concepts. *Monographs of the Society for Research in Child Development, 46* (2, Serial No. 189).

WILKENING, F., & ANDERSON, N. H. (1982). Comparison of the two rule-assessment methodologies for studying cognitive development and knowledge structure. *Psychological Bulletin, 92,* 215–237.

EARL C. BUTTERFIELD

MORAL DEVELOPMENT   *See* REASONING, MORAL.

MOTIVATION   Motivation is a key to success at any task, as it impels one to learn the necessary intellectual skills. Motivation also affects the application of skills, and thus helps explain why performance may not approach intellectual competence, or why a person underachieves.

For most people, motivation is simply the desire to do well and achieve some goal. This desire to achieve is perhaps the aspect of motivation most closely associated with human intelligence; however, motivation is a complex concept with many other aspects. These aspects include the desire to be helpful to others without personal gain and the desire to avoid negative emotions or pain.

The concept of motivation has at least three salient dimensions. One dimension derives from four interrelated components: *homeostatic* processes, *physiological* needs or drives, *emotions,* and *cognition.* Each component must be considered for an understanding of the role played by motivation in translating intellectual competence into performance. For example, emotion influences the intensity and durability of motivation, and cognition involves judgments about worthwhile goals and the nature of intelligence. Affective-cognitive processes that reflect the interaction of emotion and cognition help determine the effort devoted to a task and persistence in the face of difficulty.

These four components underlie the second and third dimensions of motivation. The second dimension concerns individual differences in motivation that yield performances that either match intellectual competence or result in underachievement. Individual differences reflect adaptive behavior and thus vary with specific and momentary goals and the demands of specific situations. When pressed by time or energy demands, for example, we all order activities by importance (create priorities), and consequently devote more effort to some activities than to others. Motivation, however, is also a personal characteristic of an individual that is stable over time for any specific activity, and it sometimes reflects a general orientation to all activities. Some adolescents are excellent athletes or social leaders but indifferent students; some are generally enthusiastic about whatever they do. Conversely, some people seem generally unmotivated; they lack spark, initiative, and energy.

The third dimension concerns developmental factors that contribute to individual differences. A critical factor is the quality of the emotional bond between parents and their infant that is the foundation of a child's later feelings of curiosity and self-efficacy.

Other factors include parent socialization practices that influence both the development of intellectual skill and a child's self-perception of competence or incompetence, and the development of social-cognitive skills that enable the child to represent and assess accurately the internal psychological characteristics of people that underlie performance.

COMPONENTS OF MOTIVATION

Intelligent behavior is goal-directed, and thus is motivated, whether the behavior is taking a test or keeping safe while walking through a high-crime district. To the extent that behavior is purposeful, motivation is a *cause* of behavior. Motivation is not a concrete thing, however, but rather a set of processes that impel action and translate ability into performance. In the first half of the twentieth century, psychologists examining motivation focused attention on homeostatic processes and physiological drives as key components. Appreciation of the contributions of emotions and cognitive processes is more recent.

Homeostatic Processes. Homeostatic processes are the continuous, internal, electrochemical changes that regulate body temperature, respiration, heart rate, blood pressure, and numerous other bodily activities that are vital to physical and psychological well-being. Although the normal functioning of homeostatic mechanisms is necessary to our very survival, we rarely become aware of them. Homeostasis, or the steady state of our vital processes, is maintained by unconscious, automatic, and silent electrochemical activity.

People become aware of homeostatic processes only in emergencies or in unusual circumstances. For example, individuals become aware that breathing is automatic and continuous when they have to consciously *inhibit* breathing for a dive into water. If one stays under water too long, the urge to breathe becomes strong. If swimmers think that an undertow might prevent them from getting to the surface, this appraisal is likely to trigger fear. Fear then becomes a powerful motivation to escape.

More chronic influences of homeostatic processes on intellectual performance can result from structural impairments that prevent homeostasis. An example is a thyroid deficiency that lowers body temperature and increases discomfort and irritability, both of which can interfere with intellectual performance. Normally, a homeostatic process becomes important in motivation only when it is interrupted and the resulting bodily change causes pain or triggers a negative appraisal that elicits emotion. Such negative effects could interfere with learning and the application of intellectual ability.

Physiological Drives and Drive-Free Behavior. A great amount of evidence shows that motivation derives from physiological drive states, such as sex, pain, hunger, thirst, fatigue, and the need for sleep. A classic example is that deprived or threatened laboratory animals learn mazes to obtain food or to escape pain, but that sleep deprivation dulls interest in a task.

These physiological drives also play a role in complex behaviors through conditioning processes. Psychologists have shown that associating a neutral stimulus with the original physiological stimulus conditions the neutral stimulus. The result is that the neutral stimulus elicits behavior similar to that elicited by the original stimulus. Because this secondary conditioning process can empower a wide variety of stimuli, conditioning represents an important general aspect of motivation, learning, and performance. For example, conditioning helps explain why many college students will work so diligently for a grade but are reluctant to do work that is not graded. To the extent that behavior varies with external reinforcement or reward, an individual exhibits extrinsic motivation.

These ideas about the importance of physiological drives as primary motivators are consistent with the highly influential work of Sigmund Freud. Freud (1938) claimed that libidinal drives, particularly sex and aggression, strongly influence human behavior. The sublimation and repression of these drives influence unconscious motivation.

Although most psychologists agree that drives and conditioned stimuli affect motivation, research has shown that other components are important as well, in at least three ways. First, human and other animals are genetically predisposed to learn certain responses appropriate to certain stimuli. For these biologically prepared stimuli, the role of conditioning may be minimal in generating a response. For example, humans rapidly learn a fear response to such stimuli as snakes, heights, strangeness, and darkness.

Second, Harry Harlow (1950) showed that monkeys who are satiated and comfortable will still work to solve puzzles. This can be considered as drive-free behavior because the monkeys could not have been motivated by any of the primary drive states or secondary conditioned drives. Findings such as this suggest that emotions are a key to motivation. One way in which an emotion influences learning is that certain objects or events and the information they afford are inherently interesting. Another way is that most mammals show innate curiosity, play behavior, and exploration impulses that are independent of external reward and seem intrinsically rewarding. Individuals who show these behaviors exhibit intrinsic motivation, which may be a manifestation of the emotion of *interest*. These behaviors form the basis of many transactions with the environment and are involved in problem solving and creative activity.

Third, Edward Tolman (1945) showed that many aspects of learning are not explained easily in terms of stimulus-response-reinforcement sequences. Later research showed that people behave according to the way they perceive or interpret a stimulus and its context. Often the interpreted or functional stimulus is different from the physical stimulus, and individuals differ in their interpretations. Thus, interpretative or cognitive processes contribute to motivation and learning.

Emotions. Emotion is the heart of motivation, the dynamic aspect of motivation. Countless authors from Homer and Aristotle to Shakespeare and Faulkner have used emotion to inspire action. William James, one of the founders of psychology, thought that emotions gave focus and direction to cognition and that feelings were the basis of individuality. For example, E. L. Thorndike, another early psychologist, first helped conceptualize the relation between emotion and motivation in the learning process. Thorndike (1913) described several motivational conditions that limit learning, including (1) interest in the work; (2) interest in improvement; (3) the significance of the matter for the individual; (4) attentiveness; and (5) the absence of irrelevant emotion. These conditions center on the emotion of interest and the absence of negative emotions that may divert or dilute interest. As every teacher knows, a child's interest in a task is critical for optimal performance. Conversely, negative mood de-

presses motivation and performance, and a chronically depressed mood inhibits effective action.

More recent research testifies to the importance of emotions in intellectual functioning. Carroll Izard (1991) has shown that positive emotion generally enhances learning, creative thinking, and problem solving, whereas negative emotion inhibits performance. One specific mechanism is that positive and negative emotions increase the selectivity of perception, actually controlling the brain's accessibility to information. Renninger and Wozniak (1985) have shown, for example, that preschool children attend more to photographs of toys of high interest to them than those of low interest, and subsequently have better memory for the more interesting ones. Similarly, Gordon Bower (1987) has shown that emotions influence the selectivity of memory. For example, a person remembers more happy material when in a happy mood than in a sad mood.

Several characteristics of emotions contribute to their effectiveness in motivating behavior. First, emotions are activated by a variety of systems, ranging from naturally occurring neural activity to the higher-order cognitive processes of reasoning and imagination involved in goal-oriented behavior. This diversity of activating systems assures that there is an emotion for all contingencies, including creative thought. Second, theorists have described as many as eleven basic emotions—interest, joy, surprise, sadness, anger, disgust, contempt, fear, shyness, shame, and guilt—and each has a unique motivational capacity to impel action. Third, each emotion can be activated at any time by a virtually limitless variety of stimuli and associated with a virtually limitless variety of responses. The emotion of interest, for example, can be activated by almost anything that moves or changes or is novel, and interest can motivate behavior relevant to any of these activating conditions. In sharp contrast, each of the physiological drive states has a limited set of specific activators and motivates a limited set of specific responses. Furthermore, drive activation and satisfaction are cyclical, as a rule; for example, three to five hours after a meal, the sight and smell of food activate the hunger drive.

Cognitive Processes. Cognition is the process that regulates motivation and directs goal-oriented behavior. Without a cognitive analysis of realistic goals, a student may set goals that are impossible to achieve or trivial. Failure or success in these situations may impede achievement motivation in future situations. Similarly, without an accurate analysis of the causes of failure or success in a task, a student's feelings of self-efficacy and control may be undermined. In these ways, cognitive processes are intimately related to the emotions that accompany a task outcome and influence future motivation. Although emotions (e.g., interest) continually influence cognition, cognition is essential in articulating plans and goals.

The cognitive component of motivation mediates a person's sense of self-efficacy, which is the feeling that actions have the intended effect and that events are controllable. Thus, cognition defines the success of an action for the individual. In this way, self-efficacy underlies the motivational orientation that translates intellectual capacity into actual performance.

According to Albert Bandura (1977, 1991), a leading theorist, self-efficacy reflects emotions, cognized goals, outcome expectancies, and attributions about the causes of task performance. The four principal sources of information that contribute to self-efficacy are physiological states, vicarious experiences, performance accomplishments, and self-instruction or verbal persuasion. These sources of information influence the sense of self-efficacy through the emotions they activate. For example, successful performance on a difficult task generates interest and enjoyment, and an actual or vicarious experience of failure elicits shame or sadness. The positive emotions enhance feelings of self-efficacy and the construction of future goals, whereas the negative emotions have the opposite effect.

Current cognitive representations of future goals and expected outcomes influence behavior through an anticipatory mechanism, in that forethought about how to realize present values (desires) influences goal selection and the choice of behavioral strategies that affect goal achievement. For example, different goals affect behavior by motivating students to seek or avoid particular tasks that might be profitable, or to pursue strategies that maximize personal success on a task as opposed to group accomplishment. Goal differences motivate students to behave in a way that maximizes extrinsic rewards such as grades, as opposed to engaging in mastery processes that lead to skill development

and intrinsic rewards. A student might, for example, choose an easy task because it usually results in an "A" grade, rather than a hard task that fosters skill development. Similarly, outcome expectancies affect the effort devoted to goal achievement. Students who appraise the chance of success as modest or poor may not try hard because they anticipate the shame of failure. Over the long term, these perceptions of self-efficacy impair achievement strivings, irrespective of actual intellectual competence.

Perceptions of self-efficacy also are affected by causal attributions about outcomes, which occur retrospectively. Bernard Weiner (1991) has contributed much to this attribution theory of motivation, showing, for example, that those who credit successes to personal competence and failure to lack of effort or situational factors, are more likely to experience positive emotions and hence to undertake and persist in difficult tasks. Causal attributions involve a set of personal constructs about the involvement of self in a task outcome, including whether the outcome reflected luck or skill, and effort or ability, and the retrospective judgement about the ease or difficulty of the task. Such causal attributions affect students' moods—and moods, in turn, affect students' confidence about future success and motivation to try. The causal attributions and resulting mood affect the anticipatory cognition involving goals and outcome expectancies.

INDIVIDUAL DIFFERENCES

These component processes form the basis of stable motivational differences among individuals in any particular performance domain. They help explain, for example, why children might be underachievers in a specific subject in school, or why adults might have low career aspirations.

Individuals vary greatly in motivational orientation. One important aspect of motivational orientation toward academic tasks concerns a student's theory about intellectual ability and intelligence. Carol Dweck (1991) has isolated two general theories that reflect whether intelligence is considered a fixed ability, an entity that people possess in differing amounts, or a malleable set of skills that grow incrementally and develop. The motivational consequences are that a student who believes ability is fixed may not try to improve, while a belief in change may drive a continuing attempt to expand skills and grow. Dweck argues that the entity theory is associated with extrinsic motivation and a goal orientation of maximizing positive judgments of competence (i.e., getting good grades). In children of moderate ability, the entity theory also may induce a helpless behavior pattern involving low task persistence and avoidance of challenges. In contrast, the incremental theory is associated with intrinsic motivation and a goal orientation of increasing competence, and with mastery-oriented behavior patterns involving high persistence and the seeking of challenges. Dweck has shown that these general theories about ability result in stable differences among individual children in test anxiety and task persistence, and they help predict short-term academic success because of differences in the motivation to try.

A second aspect of motivational orientation concerns self-perceptions of competence and incompetence, which are based on the sense of self-efficacy. Phillips and Zimmerman (1990) have shown that very able children sometimes underestimate their own academic competence. These perceptions reflect a child's causal attributions about the ingredients of task success. The consequence is a helpless behavior pattern that includes avoidance of demanding tasks, a relative lack of persistence, and a lack of independent work habits. Perceptions of incompetence are a recipe for underachievement.

A third aspect concerns Ellen Langer's (1989) distinction between mindlessness and mindfulness. Mindlessness involves a state of mind associated with a routinized and stereotyped approach to events and situations. The approach reflects both affective and cognitive factors that reduce a person's alertness and sensitivity to the complexity and novelty of situations and that often are expressed in rigid behavior. Mindfulness, in contrast, reflects a state of alertness and lively awareness that results in active processing of information, creation of new distinctions, and both context-sensitive and novel approaches to situations. Although mindless behavior is a pervasive aspect of much of our daily behavior and may be economical in executing routines, such as driving a car, mindlessness also can be severely limiting and may differ among individuals. Langer found, for example, that a simple manipulation inducing mindfulness was associated with increases in longevity for elderly residents of a nursing home. Langer also argues that mindfulness is capacity-increasing and mindlessness is capacity-fixing. This idea links the distinction to the other aspects of orientation that enhance or limit performance.

These aspects of motivational orientation center on the interaction of emotional and cognitive processes in conceptualizing self-worth and approaching environmental challenges. Emotion and conditioning also contribute directly to individual differences in task initiative and persistence. Robert Eisenberger (1992) has shown, for example, that the conditioning of positive emotions to high effort explains learned industriousness, a trait that may be related to both optimal performance and the growth of intelligence. Izard (1991) and Eisenberger speculate that the emotions of interest and enjoyment increase as an individual becomes more engaged and effortfully involved in a task. High effort also leads to a sense of greater control over a task and feelings of self-efficacy, with positive motivational effects.

Finally, individual differences in motivational orientation may be related to knowledge of emotion and its uses in regulating interpersonal behavior. Salovey and Mayer (1990), for example, have suggested that the ability to detect and process information related to emotions can be conceived as *emotional intelligence*. Emotional intelligence involves emotion knowledge and emotion regulation. Emotion knowledge consists of the ability to decode verbal and nonverbal signals of emotion, empathy, and an understanding of the causes and consequences of the emotion-feeling states of self and others, cultural rules relating to experiencing and expressing the various emotions, and the effects of emotion expressions on the behavior of others. Emotion regulation includes reactivity and expressiveness. Research has established that people vary widely in both knowledge and regulation of emotion.

Although the evidence that measures of these emotion-related traits are valid indexes of a kind of intelligence is relatively weak, it is reasonable to expect that individuals who rank high on these traits would perform more effectively on tasks such as solving interpersonal problems. Such problem solving is an important aspect of many jobs, particularly those with leadership responsibility. Emotional intelligence might also be positively correlated with subjective well-being or positive emotionality; and this attribute might have favorable effects on intellectual performance by increasing the sense of self-efficacy and the motivation to persist in goal-oriented behavior.

DEVELOPMENT

Getting children or adolescents to perform at levels that approach their intellectual ability requires that they be able to evaluate the self and understand the concept of ability and the factors that determine performance. In early childhood, self-evaluation in achievement situations seems to develop in three stages. According to Stipek, Riccia, and McClintic (1992), before the age of two, children lack the representational skills necessary to assess the contribution of self to a task outcome. After age two, children are initially motivated extrinsically in seeking positive reactions for successes and avoiding negative reactions to failures. Thereafter children gradually internalize these reactions and develop intrinsic motivation in that they react emotionally to success or failure independently of adult reactions.

Similarly, understanding of ability and performance develops over the early elementary grades, as children develop a differentiated and psychological conception of self. Research has shown, for example, that older children are more modest and more accurate than younger ones in judging their own ability, and are more likely to view intellectual capacity as a stable, general, and internal characteristic of individuals. Older children are also more accurate in their appraisals regarding whether a task outcome reflects luck or skill, effort or ability. These developmental changes reflect both increases in cognitive power and increased social opportunities to compare individual performances. The motivational consequences include task orientation.

These cognitive developments occur for all children. As every teacher knows, however, children also differ individually in feelings of self-worth and confidence. Some children seem to lack interest and joy in intellectual accomplishment, are too dependent on the teacher's approval for any activity, or are too inhibited and fearful to try new things. Thus, children differ in the emotional bases of motivation.

Many of these differences arise out of feelings of self-efficacy and control that develop out of parent-

child interactions in childhood. For example, the security of the attachment relation between parent and infant serves as the foundation for the child's sense of self and perceived efficacy. Infants construct self-concepts, and learn about their ability to control their own impulses and external events, through the effects their actions have on the world and through the sense that others understand their actions and goals. Parents who react to a child's initiative in a sensitive and responsive manner foster a child's sense of self-efficacy, and also the child's initiative and joy in trying to master difficult tasks. Parents who are overly intrusive or unresponsive may foster in a child feelings of insecurity and anxiety that inhibit self-assertion and autonomy in exploring the world.

Similarly, parent socialization practices in early and middle childhood affect children's appraisals of their own ability and thus contribute to underachievement. Phillips and Zimmerman (1990) have shown, for example, that able children who perceive themselves as relatively incompetent have parents who set high performance standards yet have a relatively low estimate of their child's ability.

CONCLUSION

Motivation enables performance to approach intellectual capacity. Since motivation is intimately related to emotion, it reflects a set of component processes that develop with age and differ with parenting practices. These components facilitate adaptation to the demands of a situation. They also contribute to stable individual differences in motivational orientation that influence the acquisition of new intellectual skills and mediate the relation between intellectual capacity and actual performance.

(*See also:* PROFILE INTERPRETATION.)

BIBLIOGRAPHY

BANDURA, A. (1977). Self-efficacy: Toward a unifying theory of behavioral change. *Psychological Review, 84,* 191–215.
BANDURA, A. (1991). Self-regulation of motivation through anticipatory and self-reactive mechanisms. In R. A. Dienstbier (Ed.), *Nebraska symposium on motivation, 1990:*

Perspectives on motivation (pp. 69–164). Lincoln: University of Nebraska Press.

BOWER, G. (1987). Commentary on mood and memory. *Behavioral Research and Therapy, 25,* 443–455.

DWECK, C. A. (1991). Self-theories and goals: Their role in motivation, personality, and development. In R. A. Dienstbier (Ed.), *Nebraska symposium on motivation, 1990: Perspectives on motivation* (pp. 199–235). Lincoln: University of Nebraska Press.

EISENBERGER, R. (1992). Learned industriousness. *Psychological Review, 99,* 248–267.

FREUD, S. (1938). *The basic writings of Sigmund Freud* (A. A. Brill, Trans.). New York: Random House.

HARLOW, H. F. (1950). Learning and satiation of response in intrinsically motivated complex-puzzle performance by monkeys. *Journal of Comparative and Physiological Psychology, 43,* 289–294.

IZARD, C. E. (1991). *The psychology of emotions.* NY: Plenum.

LANGER, E. J. (1989). Minding matters: The consequences of mindlessness-mindfulness. In L. Berkowitz (Ed.), *Advances in experimental social psychology* (Vol. 22, pp. 137–173). San Diego, CA: Academic Press.

PHILLIPS, D. A., & ZIMMERMAN, M. (1990). The developmental course of perceived competence and incompetence among competent children. In R. J. Sternberg & J. Kolligan, Jr. (Eds.), *Competence considered* (pp. 41–66). New Haven, CT: Yale University Press.

RENNINGER, K. A., & WOZNIAK, R. H. (1985). Effect of interest on attentional shift, recognition, and recall in young children. *Developmental Psychology, 21,* 624–632.

SALOVEY, P., & MAYER, J. D. (1990). Emotional intelligence. *Imagination, Cognition, and Personality, 9*(3), 185–211.

STIPEK, D., RECCHIA, S., & McCLINTIC, S. (1992). Self-evaluation in young children. *Monographs of the Society for Research in Child Development* (Serial No. 226).

THORNDIKE, E. L. (1913). *The psychology of learning: Educational psychology* (Vol. II). New York: Teachers College Press.

TOLMAN, E. C. (1945). A stimulus-expectancy, need-cathexis psychology. *Science, 101,* 160–166.

WEINER, B. (1991). On perceiving the other as responsible. In R. A. Dienstbier (Ed.), *Nebraska symposium on motivation, 1990: Perspectives on motivation* (pp. 165–198). Lincoln: University of Nebraska Press.

CARROLL E. IZARD
BRIAN P. ACKERMAN

MOTOR ABILITY The relationship of motor abilities in the early years of human life to other aspects of development, particularly intelligence, has been of enduring interest to child psychologists. Physical performances are among the behaviors that parents typically use informally to assess how their children are behaving and maturing and to compare their children with other children of the same age. Casual observations, as well as pediatric inquiry as to how children are faring developmentally, include notations as to the age at which the child turned over from the prone to supine position, stood up and walked, threw a ball, and picked up small objects. The relationship of motor to mental abilities and the predictive value of motoric accomplishments in relation to later physical performances and to intelligence have been of widespread fascination as well as of scientific significance. Extensive studies have been carried out to explore the normative age of, and individual differences in, the attainment of various motor-development milestones.

EARLIEST MANIFESTATIONS OF MOTOR BEHAVIOR

The earliest appearing motor responses of the human are reflexes. They are present in the behavioral repertoire of the normal newborn. Examples are the grasping reflex, stepping reflex, swimming reflex, respiratory occlusion reflex, and startle response. Placing the newborn in water on its abdomen elicits swimminglike movements. Any threat of obstruction to breathing causes the baby to turn its head from side to side and to "fight" occlusion, even with hand–face activity.

These reflexes, gifts of the species originating during fetal life, are stronger in some infants than in others. Moreover, babies born under conditions of risk (e.g., prematurely or with the umbilicus around the neck) may be compromised in the vigor of their reflexes. This fact may in turn affect the rapidity and effectiveness with which the infant's neuromuscular system makes the transition, as described by Myrtle McGraw (1943), from subcortical mediation of responses to greater involvement of cortically mediated, learned behavior.

McGraw described the development of motor behavior in the first year of life as at first involving mostly reflexive behavior, which eventually is supplanted by "deliberate, voluntary" patterns of mature behavior. The transition is marked by a slowly rising, then declining, manifestation of "disorganized behavior," peaking during the period around two to four months of age. Interestingly, this is the age range within which about 90 percent of all crib deaths occur, suggesting that the phenomenon of "sudden infant death syndrome" may derive, in part, from a psychomotor, and possibly learned, deficiency stemming from failure of the infant to safeguard its respiratory passages from occlusion (Lipsitt, 1979).

ACTION SKILLS

Those motoric behaviors requiring physical coordination, including reaching, walking, and catching, are classified as action skills and are distinguished clearly from reflexes by requiring practice. Psychophysiologically, action skills require cortical elaborations and are manifested increasingly with the gradual proliferation of dendrites and the myelinization of neural pathways. Development of motor skills is affected greatly by other growth factors as well, such as the gradual change in distribution of the weight of the child, and the changing length of legs and arms (Thelen, 1989). Perception plays a key role in such physical feats as seeing a baseball hit by a batter far away, noting the trajectory that the ball is taking as well as its speed, and transporting oneself to an optimal position for trapping the ball before it reaches the ground—and then catching it. That such physical skills as these can be assessed without considering the perceptual facets of the task as well is doubtful. Hence, an expansion of study in the area of perceptual-motor skills has taken place. Even the task of the 1-year-old child in standing and walking is clearly understood to involve more than growth and action.

Every motor skill involves a servo-loop in which the execution of a part of the response serves as stimulus for the next. Moreover, feedback as to the success of the earlier part of the response is critical to the appropriate execution of the next. L. Hay (1984) used wedge lenses to shift the apparent location of an object, much as an object below a water surface is "displaced" by the distortion of the intervening medium. Children were required to reach for an object seen through the distorting medium, and their course of correction within and over trials was studied. Hay found, not surprisingly, that children adjust their actions to their perceptions but that children of 5 years require more visual feedback to make correct reaches. Seven-year-old children make more approaches to the object, starting and stopping to assimilate feedback. Children of 11 years of age begin with direct movements, slow their reach as they approach the object, and then make immediate corrections. The 5-year-old children thus pay little attention to visual feedback, the 7-year-olds overcorrect, and the 11-year-olds use feedback skillfully to avoid incorrect responses. This type of reciprocating interaction between the adaptive, goal-oriented learning child, on the one hand, and environmental feedback contingencies, on the other, exemplifies an elaborate form of operant behavior, which is inextricably interwoven with motor skill acquisition and execution.

MOTOR NORMS

Numerous child development investigators have mapped the onset, course, and change in the response repertoire of the child in the first two years of life. Among the foremost researchers describing early motor development, and creating a motor scale from these norms, was Nancy BAYLEY, who was explicit concerning the value and limitations of infant testing for purposes of predicting later motor and mental development: Although observation and testing of children with hazardous perinatal histories can be useful, predictive validity within the first year of life is insufficient to anticipate accurately the eventual intelligence or psychomotor proficiency of essentially normal children. Nonetheless, group norms chart fairly well the normal developmental course of humans in the first months of life.

After the neonatal period, the infant holds its head erect, pushes its chest up by its arms, turns from back to side at four months, sits with support at four months and sits alone at six months. By three months, the infant's hands are no longer fisted, and the grasp reflex has evolved into a slow, deliberative exploration of the object placed in the fist. The 6-month-old infant reaches for a toy with one hand only, the wrists can be rotated, and thumb-finger opposition in picking up small objects begins to appear and becomes salient by eight months, at which time crawling or creeping appears. A month later the baby pulls itself to standing, and within the next two to three months is walking, first with help, then alone, and playing pattycake. In the first half of the second year, the abilities to throw a ball, walk backward, and use stairs with help appear.

CROSS-CULTURAL CONSIDERATIONS

The most extensive norms of children's development have been derived from Western studies and largely from essentially "normal" populations of youngsters in Western societies. Studies both of children born or reared in jeopardy and of children subjected to special developmental encouragements or cultural enrichments suggest that the norms may be to an extent plastic. For example, African infants tend to sit, stand, walk, and climb stairs months earlier than American babies (Super, 1981). The precocity of the African infants seems to be limited to action skills rather than reflexes, and also appears to be related to the parental presumption that such skills must be practiced to be acquired.

BIBLIOGRAPHY

GALLAHUE, D. L. (1989). *Understanding motor development* (2nd ed.). Carmel, IN: Benchmark Press.

HAY, L. (1984). Discontinuity in the development of motor control in children. In W. Prinz & A. F. Sanders (Eds.), *Cognition and motor processes.* Berlin: Springer-Verlag.

LIPSITT, L. P. (1979). Critical conditions of infancy. *American Psychologist, 34,* 973–980.

McGRAW, M. (1943). *The neuromuscular maturation of the human infant.* New York: Columbia University Press.

SUPER, C. M. (1981). Cross-cultural research on infancy. In H. C. Triandis & A. Heron (Eds.), *Handbook of cross-cultural psychology: Vol. 4. Developmental psychology.* Boston: Allyn & Bacon.

THELEN, E. (1989). The (re)discovery of motor development: Learning new things from an old field. *Child Development, 25,* 946–949.

LEWIS P. LIPSITT

MULTIPLE INTELLIGENCES THEORY

The theory of multiple intelligences (MI theory) was developed in the late 1970s and early 1980s by Howard Gardner and his colleagues. The major claim of the theory is that all human beings have the potential to develop a set of seven relatively autonomous intellectual faculties, called the multiple intelligences. All normal human beings develop each of the intelligences to some extent. No two individuals, however, have precisely the same profile of intelligences, and intelligences assume different forms in different cultures. The theory has generated both support and controversy within psychology (Perkins et al., 1987; Scarr, 1985); it has exerted considerable influence on education, especially in the United States.

Theories of intelligence have traditionally differed on whether they posit a single general factor (g) of intelligence (Spearman, 1923), or a number of primary factors (Thurstone, 1938), and whether they are organized in a hierarchical (Thomson, 1948) or heterarchical (Sternberg, 1985) fashion. However, nearly all attempts to enumerate and organize intellectual factors have been based on the results obtained on short-answer psychological tests. MI theory differs from most theories in its point of departure, in the lines of evidence it draws upon, and in the range of intellectual competences that it posits.

IDENTIFYING MULTIPLE INTELLIGENCES

The starting point for MI theory is a desire to account for the vast range of adult roles, or end-states, around the world, ranging from the scholar or surgeon in a complex literate society to the sailors, shamans, and singers of a preliterate culture. It is assumed that *any* set of adult competences that may be valued in a culture merits consideration as a potential intelligence. As a consequence of this starting point, an intelligence is defined as the ability to solve problems or fashion products that are appreciated in at least one culture or community. Except in exceptional individuals or situations, intelligences cannot be observed in pure, isolated form. Rather they are inferred from behaviors. Thus a violinist is assumed to have musical and bodily-kinesthetic intelligences, while a lawyer is assumed to have linguistic, logical, and personal intelligences.

EVIDENCE OF MULTIPLE INTELLIGENCES

Evidence for candidate intelligences were initially sought in a systematic survey of several bodies of research. In such a search, a candidate ability gains credibility as an intelligence to the extent that one can find evidence for its separate developmental pathway; its organization in specific regions or systems in the nervous system; its isolation in special populations, such as prodigies, autistic individuals, or idiots savants; its occurrence across a range of cultures; its evolutionary history within and across species; and its susceptibility to codification within a symbol system. Taken into account are two forms of psychological evidence—the results of factor-analytic studies of test results and findings about the conditions under which transfer of learning occurs.

THE SEVEN INTELLIGENCES

Gardner (1983) posits the existence of seven separable intelligences:

1. *Linguistic intelligence.* The fluency in the production of language found in a poet or lawyer exemplifies this form of intelligence.

2. *Logical-mathematical intelligence.* Logicians, mathematicians, and scientists exhibit this intelligence. Its developmental course was studied in great detail by Piaget (1983).

3. *Musical intelligence.* Analogous to linguistic intelligence, this intelligence characterizes individuals who think fluently in musical terms. Composers, performers, and connoisseurs exemplify musical intelligence.

4. *Spatial intelligence.* Instances of this intelligence are reflected in the capacity to operate on mental representations of large-scale space (sailor, pilot) or more local forms of space (chess player, sculptor, architect). Possession of spatial intelligence does not indicate whether an individual will be an artist or scientist, but it predicts which science or art form will be favored.

5. *Bodily-kinesthetic intelligence.* Individuals possessing this intelligence are able to solve problems or fashion products by using the whole body (dancer, athlete) or parts of the body, such as the hands or mouth (surgeon, artisan).

6. *Interpersonal intelligence.* Salespeople, leaders, clinicians, teachers, and actors are all able to understand other individuals and to use this understanding to work effectively with them.

7. *Intrapersonal intelligence.* This intelligence, of great value in the contemporary world, entails the capacity to form an accurate working model of oneself and to make effective decisions based upon that model.

MI theory holds that as a species, human beings have evolved to carry out these seven content-linked forms of information processing. In other words, it posits that the human brain is organized to respond to spatial content, numerical content, the informational content transmitted by other persons, and the like. Each intelligence contains subcomponents, with their distinctive processes; and the theory does not claim that only seven intelligences exist. The theory does, however, attempt to establish the plurality of human cognitive competences. Moreover, it claims that these intelligences are merely potentials; for them to be expressed in observable form, individuals must grow up in cultural milieus that feature roles that draw upon one or more of the intelligences.

REACTIONS TO THE THEORY

MI theory has been praised for its breadth, as epitomized by its sensitivity to biological and neurological factors, on the one hand, and to cultural triggering and deployment, on the other. The theory has also been criticized for being too broad (extending well beyond the usual scholastic definitions of intelligence, to include social and emotional considerations); for confounding talent and intelligence; for ignoring the so-called positive manifold, which yields correlations even among allegedly distinct faculties; for a lack of attention to underlying processes; and for failing to incorporate executive processes. These criticisms have been addressed in a number of publications (Gardner 1985; 1987; 1993; Walters & Gardner, 1986). It has been pointed out that there is no rational basis for calling language an intelligence, while relegating musical or spatial abilities to the status of talents; that the positive manifold is always based on paper-and-pencil instruments, which may themselves be loaded on linguistic and logical faculties; and that it would be possible to extend the theory so that it accounts for underlying processes and for executive-type operations.

More recent work on the theory has centered on an investigation of the ways in which intelligences unfold in various contexts and the ways in which they can be distributed among human and artifactual resources (Gardner, 1993). This work is part of a broader movement in psychology to construe intelligence as an interactive or emergent entity, rather than as a capacity that resides exclusively in the head of an individual (Salomon, 1993).

EDUCATIONAL APPLICATIONS

Although the theory was not developed with educational aims in mind, it has been embraced enthusiastically by several sectors of the educational community. It has been particularly invoked in a critique of standardized testing, with its emphasis on linguistic and logical-mathematical factors, and in the movement to create instruments that are "intelligent-fair" and that look directly at desirable performances (Gardner, 1992). A number of specific educational programs based on MI theory have been developed at Harvard Project Zero. Included among them is Project Spectrum, an effort to identify distinctive intellectual profiles in young children; Arts PROPEL, a cooperative project designed to assess learning in the artistically oriented intelligences; and Practical-Intelligences-for-School (PIFS), an attempt to equip middle-school children with a better understanding of their own distinctive intellectual profiles and a greater understanding of the demands and opportunities afforded by school (Gardner, 1993). In addition to these formal educational interventions, many schools, museums, and other educational institutions have fashioned programs that, in one way or another, seek to nurture and assess the several human intelligences.

(*See also:* THOMSON'S RANDOM OVERLAP THEORY.)

BIBLIOGRAPHY

GARDNER, H. (1983). *Frames of mind: The theory of multiple intelligences.* New York: Basic Books. Tenth anniversary edition, 1993.

GARDNER, H. (1985). On discerning new ideas in psychology. *New Ideas in Psychology, 3,* 1, 101–104.

GARDNER, H. (1987). Discussion. In D. Perkins, J. Lochhead, J. Bishop (Eds.), *Thinking: The Second International Conference,* (pp. 86–100). Hillsdale, NJ: Erlbaum.

GARDNER, H. (1992). Assessment in context: The alternative to standardized testing. In B. Gifford & M. O'Connor (Eds.), *Alternative views of aptitude, achievement, and instruction.* Boston: Kluwer.

GARDNER, H. (1993). *Multiple intelligences: The theory in practice.* New York: Basic Books.

PERKINS, D., LOCHHEAD, J., & BISHOP, J. (EDS.). (1987). *Thinking: The Second International Conference* (pp. 77–101). Hillsdale, NJ: Erlbaum.

PIAGET, J. (1983). Piaget's theory. In P. Mussen (Ed.), *Manual of child psychology* (Vol. 1). New York: Wiley.

SALOMON, G. (1993). *Distributed cognition.* New York: Cambridge University Press.

SCARR, S. (1985). An author's frame of mind [Review of *Frames of mind.*] *New Ideas in Psychology, 3,* 95–100.

SPEARMAN, C. (1923). *The nature of intelligence and the principles of cognition.* London: Macmillan.

STERNBERG, R. J. (1985). *Beyond IQ: A triarchic theory of human intelligence.* New York: Cambridge University Press.

THOMSON, G. (1948). *The factorial analysis of human ability.* Boston: Houghton Mifflin.

THURSTONE, L. L. (1938). Primary mental ability. *Psychological Monographs,* 1.

WALTERS, J., & GARDNER, H. (1986). The theory of multiple intelligences: Some issues and answers. In R. J. Sternberg & R. K. Wagner (Eds.), *Practical intelligence.* New York: Cambridge University Press.

HOWARD GARDNER

MUSICAL ABILITY   The achievements of extraordinary musicians provide us with rich sources of speculation concerning the nature of intelligence. What enabled Ludwig van Beethoven, after many years of profound deafness, to compose his magnificent Ninth Symphony? And how could the 14-year-old Wolfgang Amadeus Mozart, when denied access to the secret score of Gregorio Allegri's *Miserere*, write the entire 12-minute piece from memory after a single hearing? Are such astonishing feats of intellect simply manifestations of superb general intelligence or do they reflect the operation of specialized neural circuitry?

EVIDENCE FROM EXCEPTIONALLY GIFTED INDIVIDUALS

Many people who achieve eminence in other intellectual fields are also talented musically. Albert Einstein and Galileo Galilei were both highly accomplished musicians, as was Leonardo da Vinci. Striking counterexamples also exist. Charles Darwin recount. some of his musical experiences in the following passage:

> I acquired a strong taste for music, and used very often to time my walks so as to hear on week days the anthem in King's College Chapel. This gave me intense pleasure, so that my backbone would sometimes shiver.... Nevertheless I am so utterly destitute of an ear, that I cannot perceive a discord, or keep time and hum a tune correctly; and it is a mystery how I could possibly have derived pleasure from music.
>
> My musical friends soon perceived my state, and sometimes amused themselves by making me pass an examination, which consisted in ascertaining how many tunes I could recognise, when they were played rather more quickly or slowly than usual. 'God save the King,' when thus played, was a sore puzzle
>
> [Darwin, 1958, pp. 20–21].

It is clear from this account that an extraordinary general intelligence is no guarantee of musical talent, even for people with a keen interest in music.

EVIDENCE FROM PATIENTS WITH NEUROLOGICAL DAMAGE

Further evidence that music can be dissociated from other intellectual capacities comes from patients who have sustained brain damage (due, for example, to a stroke, a tumor, or a wound to the head). Interest has focused on the relationship between impairments in the processing of music and of language. Although most patients with impaired musical functions have associated linguistic deficits, this situation is not universal. Patients can be afflicted with severe deficits in memory for melodies or rhythms or in perception of musical instrument sounds, but their speech and language remain unaffected.

The converse dissociations have also been reported. A sizable minority of patients who have lost their power of speech generally sing quite well. There are also some remarkable cases of profoundly speech-impaired professional musicians whose musical capacities are preserved. A particularly striking example was documented by A. R. LURIA and colleagues (1965). A renowned Russian composer suffered a stroke that resulted in severe losses in his ability to produce and comprehend speech. Despite this handicap, he contin-

ued to compose a large number of musical compositions that won him high acclaim. Taken together, these studies indicate that although certain brain structures are critical for processing both language and music, others are specialized for only one or the other of these functions. Furthermore, deficits in speech are generally associated with damage to the left hemisphere of the brain (particularly in the case of righthanded persons), and losses in musical function can result from injury to either hemisphere (Benton, 1977).

EVIDENCE FROM DEVELOPMENTALLY DISABLED CHILDREN

Most children who show impairments in general intellectual development also have deficits in musical processing (Shuter-Dyson & Gabriel, 1981). Certain remarkable children, however, have profound linguistic disabilities coupled with excellent musical ability. Such children, called idiots savants, often have absolute pitch—the rare capacity to name a musical note upon hearing it. Some of them also have very good memories for musical passages.

The musical memories of idiots savants appear not to be of the tape-recorder type but rather to reflect an ability to encode and organize the material in an efficient way. L. K. Miller (1989) has reported an extensive study of one such child, called Eddie. One experiment employed a paradigm similar to that devised by Diana Deutsch (1980) to study the ability of adult musicians to organize musically structured material. In this study, subjects were presented with strings of twelve pitches, which they recalled in musical notation. Half of the strings consisted of units of three or four notes that were repeatedly presented under transposition. (For example, one such string might be CDE DEF EFG FGA.) The remaining strings consisted of the same notes presented in haphazard order. The subjects recalled the structured strings with a very high degree of accuracy, yet performed much less well on the unstructured strings.

In Miller's experiment, Eddie listened to similar strings of pitches and recalled them by playing them back on the piano. Although his performance on the structured strings was not quite as good as that of the adult musicians, it was still impressive and far better than for the haphazardly ordered strings. This experiment demonstrated that Eddie's unusually good memory for music was based at least in part on his ability to form well-organized mental representations of the musical patterns.

EVIDENCE FROM LARGE-SCALE TESTING

Many studies have attempted to examine correlations between musical ability and general intelligence in the population at large. Unfortunately these studies suffer from problems of interpretation. Many of the musical tests used had not been validated. Others, such as the Seashore measures of musical talents, have generally shown poor correlations with measures such as teachers' ratings and performance on musical examinations. Those tests that correlate well with measures of musical achievement, such as the Wing standardized tests of musical intelligence, also correlate strongly with degree of musical training and do not measure musical aptitude independently of training. Nevertheless, positive correlations have resulted between performance on such tests and on tests of general intelligence, though such correlations have not been high. The development of more convincing measures should enable scientists to arrive at firmer conclusions concerning the way in which musical ability is distributed in the population at large.

(*See also:* SAVANTS.)

BIBLIOGRAPHY

BENTON, A. L. (1977). The amusias. In M. Critchley & R. A. Henson (Eds.), *Music and the brain.* London: Heinemann.

DARWIN, F. (ED.). (1958). *The autobiography of Charles Darwin.* New York: Dover.

DEUTSCH, D. (1980). The processing of structured and unstructured tonal sequences. *Perception and psychophysics, 28,* 381–389.

LURIA, A. R., TSVETKOVA, L. S., & FUTER, D. S. (1965). Aphasia in a composer. *Journal of neurological science, 2,* 288–292.

MILLER, L. K. (1989). *Musical savants: Exceptional skill in the mentally retarded.* Hillsdale, NJ: Erlbaum.

SHUTER-DYSON, R., & GABRIEL, C. (1981). *The psychology of musical ability.* London: Methuen.

DIANA DEUTSCH

MUSICAL INTELLIGENCE

For musicians, innate giftedness or talent revealed during countless hours of instruction and practice is widely assumed to explain musical ability. Psychologists also typically view musical intelligence as a unitary phenomenon ("of a piece"), as the focus on studies of musical perception suggests. Yet, the most developed forms of musical intelligence (as seen in the capacities of, for example, Isaac Stern or Duke Ellington) call into question this simple perspective. It appears to leave out important contributing factors—the activities, discrimination, and thought (expressed in words, symbols, and actions) that constitute musical intelligence (Gardner, 1983). An alternative view better captures the factors that constitute and support musical intelligence.

Musical intelligence is revealed as three integrated ways of knowing. Each captures a necessary and distinctly different set of cognitive skills. "Perception" involves making discriminations when listening to music. "Production" entails the musical thought expressed in composition and performance. "Reflection" encompasses the critical thinking behind reenvisioning, reconceptualizing, and reworking that leads to a coherent musical composition or interpretative performance. This article discusses these in turn.

Inclined to consider perception as the window onto the field of musical intelligence, psychologists have focused on just what it is that people know and perceive when they listen to music. For example, the musically untrained listener is far more likely to grasp the contour of melodies than distinguish among specific intervals or pitches (Dowling & Fujitani, 1971). In contrast, trained musicians process musical information in a far more articulated way, by employing a hierarchy of relations within the diatonic scale (Krumhansl & Shepard, 1967). Studies demonstrate that structural relations extracted from sequences of notes depend to a great extent on one's level of training and skill. Similarly, the aural memory ability known as "perfect pitch," a skill widely viewed as an innate gift, can be fostered in subjects otherwise untrained in music (Brady, 1970). Overall, these studies demonstrate that musical training transforms the processes of musical perception. Excellent reviews of this approach to understanding MUSICAL ABILITY are provided by D. Deutsch (1982) and D. Butler (1992).

Production has been studied far less than perception. As in research on perception, production studies suggest that experience and training exert a considerable influence on musical knowledge. For example, when children are asked to play melodies on unmarked Montessori bells, children without musical training select one bell for each note of the melody, using duplicate bells as needed. Those children who have some musical training construct their melodies in a very different manner. They first line up the bells to form a scale and then play the melody by selecting the appropriate note of the tune on the scale in front of them, using no duplicate bells (Bamberger, 1992). This shift from a reliance on the "figural" shape of the tune to the more formal construction of the scale was further examined by K. Swanwick and J. Tillman (1986). They showed that with training, students' compositions progress through eight distinct phases of development (For additional information on production in music, see Sloboda, 1988).

Reflection is a neglected area in the psychology of music; however, early evidence is consistent with findings in perception and production research that training exerts a powerful influence on cognitive activities in music. One would look for evidence of reflection in the capacity to respond to modeling and metaphor in performance and to make more effective use of language when describing or specifying musical phenomena (Davidson, 1989; Schon, 1985). Without musical training, students demonstrate little reflective capacity. They are less apt to alter their performance in response to modeling or metaphor, and they have relatively little to say about their own performance or practice strategies. As they gain experience, they become increasingly flexible in their performance, able to specify musical dimensions and to suggest ways to improve their performance in musical terms and metaphors (Davidson & Scripp, 1992).

Looking at the data with respect to perception, production, and reflection, one finds that musical intelligence may not be a fixed capacity, as the term *talent* suggests; no single snapshot will capture it. Measurement of musical cognition requires developmental studies with respect to three ways of knowing, including studies of the relations among them. While little is known about these relations at present, early evidence shows that among untrained subjects, per-

ception, production, and reflection are relatively unconnected. For example, untrained adults singing familiar children's songs are able to perceive errors in their singing, yet are unable to use that knowledge to improve their performance. This suggests that, in the absence of musical training, production knowledge is to some extent independent of perceptual knowledge. Since one expects that trained musicians benefit from the ability to improve their performances based on perceptual and reflective knowledge, it appears that training not only entails qualitative shifts in levels of skill in perception, production, and reflection but also works to integrate these ways of knowing.

Musical intelligence is unique in that it is based on operations of pitch, rhythm, and timbre. Citing studies of remarkable savants in music, many psychologists argue that musical intelligence is a separate and autonomous domain of mentation (Gardner, 1983). Yet, musical intelligence is like other intelligences in that it relies on cultural settings for definition and development. It is through culture that we make sense of the world (Bruner, 1990; Davidson and Torff, 1992). Cultural products in the domain of music include social conventions (e.g., theoretical constructs such as scales), physical artifacts (e.g., instruments and scores), and symbol systems (e.g., tuning systems and notational schemes). Without such cultural tools, sound is not organized as music (Blacking, 1977). Placing their stamp on mental representations, cultural products mediate and structure cognitive activity (Bruner, 1990); people become these tools as much as they use them (Polanyi, 1968). Different music cultures provide vastly different arrays of cultural products; thus, musical cognition varies significantly around the world. For example, tuning systems used in Thailand are unlike those of the West and thus sound very different (and have different meanings) to individuals in the two cultures. In essence, intelligent activity in music cannot be understood apart from the cultural context in which it occurs (Davidson & Torff, 1992).

It is not suggested that individual proclivities for music do not exist; clearly, some individuals show greater aptitude for music than others, as studies of prodigies in music attest (e.g., Feldman, 1986). Arguing for an elaborated understanding of these gifts, this article has presented three points about musical intelligence. First, musical intelligence is not "of a piece";

rather, it comprises three separate, qualitatively different ways of knowing—perception, production, and reflection. One must look at levels of skill in (and relations among) these three ways of knowing in order to investigate the full range of intelligent musical activities. Second, understanding musical intelligence requires a developmental perspective; unlike the fixed capacity that the term *talent* suggests, musical cognition is transformed with the introduction of training and experience. Finally, musical intelligence can be understood only in light of cultural forces supporting the development and use of individual knowledge and skill; imparting meaning to musical activities, cultural products work to constitute musical cognition.

It is not surprising that theories of GENERAL INTELLIGENCE appear remote from musical functioning. Models of intelligence that are either unitary (e.g., Spearman, 1923) or multifactorial (e.g., Guilford, 1967) are grounded in neither the musical materials nor the practices on which cognition in music depends. The alternative approach works to connect the understanding of musical intelligence to musical practice. Thinking of production, perception, and reflection as different ways of knowing, as articulated in developmental levels, and supported by cultural products, psychologists can adopt a view of musical intelligence that extends far beyond the notion of talent.

BIBLIOGRAPHY

BAMBERGER, J. (1992). *The mind behind the musical ear.* Cambridge, MA: MIT Press.

BLACKING, J. (1977). *How musical is man?* Seattle: University of Washington Press.

BRADY, P. (1970). Fixed-scale mechanism of absolute pitch. *Journal of the Acoustical Society of America, 48,* 883–887.

BRUNER, J. (1990). *Acts of meaning.* Cambridge, MA: Harvard University Press.

BUTLER, D. (1992). *Musician's guide to perception and cognition.* New York: Schirmer.

DAVIDSON, L. (1989). Observing a yang-ch'in lesson: Learning by modeling and metaphor in China. *Journal for Aesthetic Education, 23, 1,* 85–99.

DAVIDSON, L., & SCRIPP, L. (1992). Surveying the coordinates of cognitive skills in music. In R. Colwell (Ed.), *Handbook of research on music teaching and learning.* New York: Schirmer.

DAVIDSON, L., & TORFF, B. (1992). Situated cognition in music. *World of Music, 34*(3), 120–139.

DEUTSCH, D. (1982). *The psychology of music.* New York: Academic Press.

DOWLING, W., & FUJITANI, D. (1971). Contour, interval, and pitch recognition in memory for melodies. *Journal of the Acoustical Society of America, 49*(2), 524–531.

FELDMAN, D. (1986). *Nature's gambit.* New York: Basic Books.

GARDNER, H. (1983). *Frames of mind.* New York: Basic Books.

GUILFORD, J. (1967). *The nature of human intelligence.* New York: McGraw-Hill.

KRUMHANSL, K., & SHEPARD, R. (1967). Quantification of the hierarchy of tonal functions within a diatonic context. *Journal of Experimental Psychology: Perception and Performance, 5,* 579–594.

POLANYI, M. (1968). *Personal knowledge: Towards a post-critical philosophy.* Chicago: University of Chicago Press.

SCHON, D. (1985). *The reflective practitioner.* San Francisco: Jossey-Bass.

SHWEDER, R. (1991). *Thinking through culture.* Cambridge, MA: Harvard University Press.

SLOBODA, J. (ED.). (1988). *Generative processes in music.* Oxford: Oxford University Press.

SPEARMAN, C. (1923). *The nature of "intelligence" and the principles of cognition.* London: Macmillan.

SWANWICK, K., & TILLMAN, J. (1986). The sequence of musical development. *British Journal of Music Education, 33*(3), 305–339.

LYLE DAVIDSON
BRUCE TORFF

N

NATIVE AMERICANS Over 600 published research and conceptual papers and agency reports have attempted to examine the use and effectiveness of ability tests in relation to Native Americans and Alaska Natives between 1896 and 1993 (Vraniak, 1993).

Of these published articles, studies and reports, 257 concern general issues of ability testing with minorities that have specific relevance for Native Americans, and 380 are directly about Native Americans. Of the 380 "Indian" articles, 284 are empirical studies, and 96 are nonempirical articles and reports.

Most empirical studies involving Native Americans were published between 1965 and 1985. Most of the study sample populations are described only vaguely as "American Indian," although the specific tribal group studied most frequently is Navajo. Most empirical studies studied rural, off-reservation Indian school-age (5–16 years) youth in public schools. More studies took place in Arizona than in any other state, although most studies specified only that they were done in the United States or in its regions. Most sample sizes involved fewer than 200 subjects.

The following material gives a general overview of what we know about mental abilities of American Indians, and more importantly, outlines significant gaps in our knowledge.

OVERVIEW

Since the 1980s, conferences, proceedings, and books in the field of ability testing have been on the rise.

As the testing field has developed, progress has been reviewed periodically and priorities and recommendations have been made. Although vital studies continue in the field of minority ability testing, little work has been done to integrate and synthesize completed research in relation to American Indians (McShane & Berry, 1988).

An example of the limitations of small selective reviews is the review by P. Dauphinais and J. King (1992), in which the authors report:

[This research] summarizes the relatively few studies involving cognitive assessment with American Indian students. These studies represent seven tribal groups in the United States and Canada (there are approximately 550 federally recognized tribes in the United States alone), with Navajo samples representing five of the [21] studies [p. 14].

These 21 studies or reports, involving seven tribal groups upon which the authors of that literature review focus, are a small subset of the nearly 300 empirical (research, data-oriented) and 90 nonempirical studies and reports involving over 100 tribal groups (with 54 studies concerning the Navajo alone), which Vraniak (1993) deals with in a meta-analysis (a form of sophisticated statistical review). Indeed, most of the previous reviews of this literature have failed to describe comprehensively the existing knowledge (cf. Vraniak & Pickett, 1993).

In the 300 empirical reports published between 1896 and 1993 nearly 400 different mental ability tests, forms of tests, parts of tests, or devised tasks were used. These reports measured 275 different intelligence-related variables. Subjects were involved in 30 different kinds of settings. The studies mentioned over 100 different tribal groups. Over 150 different researchers published only one empirical study. Only seven authors in nearly 100 years published more than three studies.

In terms of the locations of these studies, most of them specified only the general region of the world (North America, United States, western/southwestern/ eastern United States, Canada, Canadian provinces). The most frequently mentioned states included Arizona, Alaska, Oklahoma, New Mexico, Minnesota, South Dakota, and Montana.

By far most of the study samples concerned rural populations (148) as compared to urban (21). This distribution is interesting because as many Native Americans now live in urban as in rural settings. Most published studies reported only that subjects were American Indian, without specifying the particular group(s). The single tribal group studied the most was the Navajo, followed by groups also of larger size: Chippewa/Ojibwa and Cree, Sioux, and Cherokee. Some smaller tribal groups were studied more often (Eskimo, Papago, Hopi, Choctaw). Many tribes figured in only one study using subjects from their communities. No published studies discussed mental ability testing in relation to another 300 specific tribes in the United States.

Of the nearly 400 different tests, forms of tests, parts of tests, or devised tasks used in the studies, the tests most commonly studied/used were: the Wechsler Intelligence Scales for Children (WISC) (54), followed by the RAVEN PROGRESSIVE MATRICES (15), KAUFMAN ASSESSMENT BATTERY FOR CHILDREN (11), DRAW-A-FIGURE (9), Form Assembly (9), direct observation (9), a med-

ical exam (7), questionnaire (7), Gesell Infant Scales (7), and Bender-Gestalt Visual–Motor Reproduction Test (5).

Of the 300 empirical studies reviewed, only 124 reported the gender of subjects. Roughly similar numbers of male and female subjects figured in these reports.

STUDIES USING THE WECHSLER INTELLIGENCE SCALES FOR CHILDREN

The only tests used with enough frequency to enable an examination of possible patterns of results were the Wechsler Intelligence Scales for Children. Of the 30 studies that reported verbal, performance, and full-scale intelligence quotients (IQs) of Indian subjects derived from the Wechsler scales, there were 93 different groups or subgroups of individuals for which these global IQ scores were obtained. When these 93 different groups were analyzed as if they were a single group, the average verbal IQ was 83 (with a range from the lowest to the highest for each individual group of 50–106), the average performance IQ was 100 (range: 71–131), and the average full-scale IQ was 90 (range:56–111). For the 93 groups, the average difference between verbal and performance IQ was 16–17 points (range: 1–50); the performance IQ was always higher for each of the 93 groups. The findings of an average verbal IQ of 83 and an average full-scale IQ of 90 across all studies are lower than those of 100 and 100, respectively, which are the comparable respective IQs of individuals in the standardization sample. The average performance score of 100 for Indians is comparable to the performance score of 100 for all individuals in the standardization sample; however, in a majority of studies, Indian individuals scored higher as a group as compared to white individuals on certain performance subtests such as Mazes and Block Design, while scoring lower on Digit Span.

In general, across all studies reviewed, 5 Native Americans performed as well as or significantly better than other groups in terms of tests measuring visual–spatial processing abilities (abilities to manipulate objects in three dimensional space) and conversely, were delayed or scored more poorly than white comparison groups on tests that measure acquisition of verbal information and abilities. Indications existed for some American Indian groups that this verbal–performance discrepancy increased with age.

QUALITY OF AVAILABLE INFORMATION

Methodological Flaws in Research Designs. Contrary to accepted practices in designing research, most of the studies used small numbers of subjects and did not specify important variables that might affect test results. Variables include gender, the setting in which the Indians were recruited, and the characteristics of the examiners (experience, training). Furthermore, the tests did not consider (or gather information about) the validity and reliability of the instruments used in relation to the population tested.

The utilization of measurement tools within the context of a variety of methodologies and research designs has been problematic in relation to investigations on the mental abilities of American Indians. Past research lacked programmatic consistency, tended to be poor in methodology, and lacked adequate and appropriate design. Most age-related data were taken cross-sectionally at widely differing times, but test results usually were interpreted and compared across cultures without regard to the confounding effects of different historical periods. Small sample sizes had shortcomings. Many studies had both a small number of subjects and limited age range. Many studies also had no behavioral data or used only correlational analyses and thus were unable to determine causal relationships. Other studies utilized few or inappropriate comparison groups, failed to include long-term studies, and did not build upon that single investment as one point of programmatic research. In their review, D. A. McShane and J. M. Plas (1984) found that these flaws in the earlier research were still evident in studies with Native Americans, analysis that failed to consider age and sex variability, inter- and intratribal variability, urban–rural residence, English language proficiency, and variations in expectations for participation.

Methodological Flaws Peculiar to Transcultural Studies. Only one or two studies examined other variables that may be expected to affect systematically the testing of mental abilities of Native American subjects. These important variables or factors that may be critical in transcultural situations for which there were little or no data included the following: language variation of sample populations, cultural adaptation of sample populations, educational continuity and experience of subjects, ethnicity and experience of examiner, time of year, time of day, setting of test administration, previous testing experience of subjects, explained purpose of testing/research, and motivation.

Two Different Ways of Studying Members of Another Culture. In approach transcultural research with Native Americans has been primarily "etic" (attempting to examine performance or behavior from an external, pancultural, or universal perspective) rather than "emic" (trying to understand naturally occurring psychological constructs and phenomena within the context of the particular culture of the studied population; Berry, 1980).

Constructing the Measurement Instrument. In this body of research, various strategies to establish "equivalence" of a given measurement instrument for use in transcultural applications have not been explored systematically and adequately. Functional, conceptual, and metric equivalence (Berry, 1980), linguistic equivalence (Brislin, 1980), and scaler equivalence (Hui & Triandis, 1983; Poortinga, 1982) have not been established for use of most instruments with Native Americans. Measurement validity—establishing the validity of a given measure within the culture in which it is used—has not been confirmed.

Cultural Variables that Influence Results. This primary problem of transcultural measurement, instrument construction, and adequacy still leaves the second major difficulty—the use of the measure within a particular transcultural context. Researchers have pointed out that the utility of an instrument depends upon its susceptibility to a number of culture-specific influences that may affect the interpretability of the obtained data. Issues influencing performance include the clarity and interpretation of the instructions, familiarity with the test materials and concepts used, previous experience working under time pressure, and motivational factors. The understandability of test-taking format is important in societies not accustomed to the testing ritual. Finding the correct answer may be no more of a challenge than finding the spot where it should be marked. Necessary for consideration are such factors as social desirability, deviation from accepted norms of ideological and moral beliefs, and the subjects' approval motive (the degree to which a subject responds in accordance with the experimenter's perceived expectation). Other factors for consideration are socioeconomic status, sex roles, urban–rural dweller differences, "extreme response style" (the tendency of certain cultures to endorse extreme items), and the importance of "examiner variables" (sex, ethnic background, testing style, mono- or bilingual ability of the test administrator). The sheer number of overt, covert, controllable, and uncontrollable variables that affect the reliability, validity, and interpretability of a given measure applied in another culture has resulted in a preponderance of poorly controlled and interpreted studies. Dana (1984) states:

> The application of inappropriate instruments remains an ethical issue.... Assessment that is fair and ethical requires instruments constructed on the basis of theory, or especially designed for American Indians and using these persons as the primary reference group with administration conditions, instructions, and tasks that are culturally appropriate [p. 41].

Susan Philips (1983) and Paul Greenbaum and Susan Greenbaum (1983) discussed the difficulties implicit in attempting to communicate transculturally, especially in terms of cultural differences contributing to sociolinguistic interference in verbal and nonverbal communication. They also explored differing expectations for participant structures (securing and conveying attention), mutual antagonism, and diminished motivation in terms of cross-cultural interaction, and stabilized transactions that facilitate misunderstanding. In the implementation of research designs and methodologies within past research, these factors often have not been addressed, especially when non-Indian interviewers, observers, or testers conduct studies. Typically when Native Americans are the researchers, interrater reliabilities have not been obtained nor have the effects of interpersonal relationships in close-knit tribal communities on the interactions between Indian research staff and other Indian community members who are research subjects, come into account. Language variation, competence, and difference have not

been controlled in most studies during the implementation stages. Finally, major political or other community events or situations that may affect research results typically have not been reported. These omissions severely restrict interpretability of results.

THEORETICAL SPECULATION ABOUT AVAILABLE INFORMATION

Although the sociocultural and biological factors described above have not been examined adequately through empirical research, ample theorizing has focused on what may be causing significantly different mental ability test performance by Native Americans as compared with whites and other racial or ethnic groups. The primary "d" models may be possible mechanisms for explaining higher nonverbal and lower verbal performance on mental abilities tests by American Indians (McShane, 1983; McShane & Berry, 1988). These "d" models include deficit, disadvantage/deprivation, disorganization/disruption/discontinuity, difference, and developmental models.

The deficit model has been of two sorts. An early discriminatory model looked at "blood quantum" (amount of Indian ancestry), subtly and inappropriately suggesting genetic inferiority. Later physiological deficit modeling suggested that extremely high rates of otitis media (ear infections and subsequent hearing loss), visual defects, FETAL ALCOHOL SYNDROME, and lead poisoning were high-risk agents in the physiological impairment of cognitive functioning for American Indians.

The disadvantage/deprivation model focuses upon such environmental factors as malnutrition, poor health, crowded living space, high mobility following jobs leading or related to high absenteeism, lack of continuous educational experience (school transfers), and lower quality educational programs.

The disorganization/disruption/discontinuity model emphasizes the negative effects of cultural disorganization, discrimination, and the subsequent breakdown and dysfunction of family life and intergenerational stability and health, often leading to serious emotional, personality and behavioral problems among Indian children (high rates of suicide, substance abuse, mental health problems) that are known to effect the capacity to learn and acquire certain cognitive skills.

Difference models tend to emphasize three kinds of differences between Native Americans and other ethnic groups: sociocultural, linguistic, and neurological. Possibly differing from one cultural group to another, even from one tribe to another, rules for interacting with others, for performance standards related to doing things, and for answering questions. Differences in native language acquisition, English language skill, bilingualism, and dialect variation all may affect performance on mental ability tests. Some researchers have speculated that Native Americans develop skills specialized to one side of the brain or the other (or to both) differently as a group from whites. McShane (1984) found significant neuroanatomical differences in which side of the brain was larger among groups of American Indians, Vietnamese, blacks, and whites, and others have found differences in the strengths of specific abilities lateralized to one side of the brain or the other.

Finally, in a fashion similar to theories concerning the slower development of language abilities among Asian populations, some persons have speculated that different developmental patterns exist for the acquisition of cognitive abilities among Native Americans, as compared with other groups.

None of these various "d" models has been adequately or systematically researched individually. The "d" models have not competed against one another as hypotheses that try to explain differences in test results for Native Americans compared with other populations.

ETHICAL ISSUES: EFFECTS OF STUDIES ON POPULATIONS STUDIED WHEN THE UTILITY OF TESTS IS QUESTIONABLE

Insufficiently detailed information exists about the data collected, sample population characteristics, and the actual variables studied. Consequently, the present knowledge-base about the mental abilities of Native Americans and Alaska Natives is not coherent, interpretable, or particularly useful. Thus, serious ethical issues have been and continue to be raised concerning the use of mental ability tests with Native Americans.

Because the large majority of existing empirical studies have not been part of systematic programs of research, the existing knowledge-base has limited utility for effective professional and community use. Most authors did only one study; most tests were only used once or twice; and most tribal groups were studied only a few times by different researchers using different methods.

For the most part, the factors that are known to lower IQ scores were not investigated systematically in these studies, thereby raising serious questions about how to interpret the results of tests given to an individual Native American or to groups of Native Americans. With two or three notable exceptions, there were no systematic attempts among the published studies to secure empirical data by which substantially to increase the utility of the test instrument or technique used to be one that is adequate for use with samples from Native American populations.

Furthermore, no systematic examination or understanding of even the most obvious and unique patterns of variation in ability test scores among Indian samples exists. One unexamined variation is the higher score for performance IQ than for verbal IQ for almost all Native Americans. Also, the verbal–performance IQ difference increases with age in certain Indian student groups. Other significant differences include those of language, culture, gender, role socialization, and school experience.

These difficulties and the lack of knowing about or understanding this research have led to overrepresentation of Native American students in special education classes in schools and great difficulties in determining how to best meet the educational needs of such children. These problems have also resulted in frequent misdiagnosis and overpathologizing of the characteristics of Native Americans seeking help in the medical, mental health, and social service systems.

FUTURE RESEARCH NEEDS

Negligible results have appeared for the amount of time, effort, and resources that have been expended in research about the performance of Native Americans and Alaska Natives on mental ability tests over the past one hundred years. Given the amount of participation by and the importance of information needed by Indian communities, this lack of knowledge development and utility is difficult to justify. This situation exists primarily because research into the nature of mental abilities of Native American and Alaska Native peoples has not been focused tightly on understanding the following mediating variables and questions:

1. What role does culture play in mental ability test performance?
2. What roles do language, gender, socioeconomic status, rural–urban residence, continuity and nature of school experience play in mental ability test/performance?
3. How can be understand the unique and differential contribution of verbal and visual–spatial abilities among Indian people to mental ability performance?

Mainstream Anglo authors have indicated some comfort with the utility of their research results with Native Americans (Naglieri, 1984; Reschly, 1978; Reschly & Sabers, 1979). Such indications are in stark contrast to the statements of alarm and serious concern published by Native American researchers and authors (cf. Chrisjohn & Lanigan, 1984; McShane, 1986; McShane & Berry, 1988) about the inadequacies of past research and the dire consequences it has had upon the lives of Native Americans as a result of misclassification, misdirected educational planning, and placement into special programs. Therefore, future research into the nature of mental abilities of Native Americans and Alaska Native peoples should take into consideration the following principles and emphases:

1. Research on differences in the mental abilities of different ethnic groups in relation to Native Americans would be more effective if it were conducted as a part of long-term systematic programs of exploration. This scenario has been true for studies of differences in intelligence test scores of females and males, as well as differences in individuals across the whole life span (from shortly after birth to persons in their 80s and 90s).

2. Such a research program would be most helpful if it clearly detailed in what manner the results would contribute to development of an overall knowledge-base and what utility the results would have for the communities being studied.

3. By facilitating good conversation between the investigators and those studied, more reliable results could be obtained, particularly if the communities participating in the research are considered coinvestigators, with all of the responsibilities that such a role implies.

4. As a vehicle for better assessing the diversity of tribal cultures, languages, and communities, a national center could be established to work directly with the four largest tribal groups in North America—the Ojibwa, Navajo, Sioux, and Cherokee nations. That center could be charged with accomplishing research concerning standardized psychological and psychoeducational testing so that these groups, at the end of an appropriately designated period, would have helped develop appropriate types of tests and techniques that have reliability and validity for use with their members. In time such a center (or consortium) may serve as a technical resource for smaller tribes and may be configured to operate through the many tribal colleges that exist in these communities. As a part of this center concept, a definite need exists to establish a library for Native American and Alaska Native assessment results wherein all existing manuscripts may be housed and where data from across the country could be archived as it is collected. A model for creating community-based archival systems for mental ability testing data, if developed and disseminated, would greatly improve the utility of tests and their use in decision making.

5. Future research into the nature of mental abilities of Native American and Alaska Native peoples would be most cost-efficient if it were concerned with generating sufficient knowledge and techniques that would allow psychoeducational decision making to be relevant, appropriate, reliable, and valid for Indian individuals. Ideally, outcomes of decision making processes and procedures would promote the development of human potential rather than just tracking or gatekeeping. This focus is both on developing the capability of using ability tests to predict performance and the capability of ability tests and techniques to provide information informing the education and promotion of Indian talent and potential, that is, to both predict and promote human achievement.

6. A careful consideration of all future mental abilities testing research could be facilitated by asking tribes and school systems and federal agencies to come together and establish jointly guidelines for such research, which relate to the issues raised above. Guidelines would include requiring researchers to provide detailed and systematic data concerning variables often omitted in past reports so that research would contribute to a cumulative knowledge base.

Finally, at least two notable large-scale attempts by Native American psychologists have addressed some of these issues, involving the two largest tribal groups in North America—one for the Navajo and one for the Ojibwa (Chippewa). P. Tempest and B. Skipper (1988) published a study involving 539 Navajo children aged 6 to 15 years that sought to provide local norms for the WISC–R for school psychologists working with Navajo students. Dauphinais and Vraniak (1993) report a local norming project involving a random sample of 267 Northern Ojibwa children aged 6 to 16 years using a variety of tests and for which curriculum-based assessment data were also collected. This study developed local norms and investigated other issues: relationships between scores on the various tests; relationships of scores to environmental factors (ethnicity of examiner, time of day of testing, gender, educational experience); test–retest variation; patterns of relationship between scores of nonreferred, referred but not placed, and referred and placed students; and the reliability of clinical ratings versus standardized test-score thresholds. The study also attempted to develop effective predictive and decision-making models based upon this extensive data-set. Such efforts are models of how with very little funds, but with informed and competent professional and community collaboration, efficacious efforts may result.

(*See also:* ETHNICITY, RACE, AND MEASURED INTELLIGENCE.)

BIBLIOGRAPHY

BERRY, J. (1980). Introduction to methodology. In H. C. Triandis & J. W. Berry (Eds.), *Handbook of cross-cultural psychology* (Vol. 2). Boston: Allyn & Bacon.

BRISLIN, R. W. (1980). Translation and content analysis of oral and written materials. In H. C. Triandis & J. W. Berry (Eds.), *Handbook of cross-cultural psychology* (Vol. 2). Boston: Allyn & Bacon.

CHRISJOHN, R. D., & LANIGAN, C. B. (1984, July). *Research on Indian intelligence testing: Review and prospects.* Paper pre-

sented at the First MOKAKIT Conference, Winnipeg, Manitoba, Canada.

DAUPHINAIS, P., & KING, J. (1992). Psychological assessment with American Indian children. *Applied & Preventive Psychology, 1,* 97–110.

DAUPHINAIS, P., & VRANIAK, D. (1993). Local norming test results for American Indian children. *Journal of American Indian Education.*

DANA, R. H. (1984). Intelligence testing of American Indian children: Sidesteps in quest of ethical practice. *White Cloud Journal, 15,* 14–21.

GREENBAUM, P. E., & GREENBAUM, S. D. (1983). Cultural differences, nonverbal regulation, and classroom interaction: Sociolinguistic interference in American Indian education. *Peabody Journal of Education, 61*(1), 16–33.

HUI, C. H., & TRIANDIS, H. C. (1983). Multistrategy approach to cross-cultural research: The case of locus of control. *Journal of Cross-Cultural Psychology, 14*(1), 65–68.

MCCULLOUGH, C. S., WALKER, J. L., & DRESSNER, R. (1985). The use of the Wechsler scales in the assessment of Native Americans in the Columbia River basin. *Psychology in the Schools, 22,* 23–28.

MCSHANE, D. A. (1980, February). A review of scores of American Indian children on the Wechsler intelligence scales. *Whitecloud Journal, 1*(4), 3–10.

MCSHANE, D. A. (1982). Otitis media and American Indians: Prevalence, etiology, psychoeducational consequences, prevention and intervention. In S. Manson (Ed.), *New directions in prevention among American Indian and Alaskan Native communities* (pp. 265–297). Portland: Oregon Health Sciences University Press.

MCSHANE, D. A. (1983). Neurocranial form: Differentiating four ethnic populations using a simple CT scan measure. *International Journal of Neuroscience, 21,* 137–145.

MCSHANE, D. A. (1984). Cognition, affect and behavior in American Indian children: A developmental perspective of a transcultural situation. *Peabody Journal of Education, 61*(1), 34–48.

MCSHANE, D. A. (1986). Testing, assessment research and increased control by native communities. In H. A. McCue (Ed.), *Selected papers from the first Mokakit conference, July 25–27, 1984.* Vancouver, British Columbia, Canada: Mokakit Research Association.

MCSHANE, D. A. (1989). Mental abilities testing research with American Indians: A reprise. *Canadian Journal of Native Studies, 15*(3), 105–110.

McShane, D. A., & Berry, J. (1988). Native North Americans: Amerindians and Inuit abilities. In S. H. Irvine & J. W. Berry (Eds.), *Cultural context of human abilities.* London: Oxford University Press.

McShane, D. A., & Plas, J. M. (1982a). Otitis media and psychoeducational difficulties and American Indians: A review and a suggestion. *Psychiatric Prevention, 1*(3), 277–291.

McShane, D. A., & Plas, J. M. (1982b). Wechsler scale performance patterns of American Indian children. *Psychology in the Schools, 19,* 8–17.

McShane, D. A., & Plas, J. M. (1984). The cognitive functioning of American Indian children: Moving from the WISC to the WISC–R. *School Psychology Review, 13*(1), 61–73.

McShane, D. A., Risse, G. L., & Rubens, A. B. (1984). Cerebral asymmetries on CT scan for three ethnic groups. *International Journal of Neuroscience, 23,* 69–74.

McShane, D. A., & Willenbring, M. L. (1984). Alcohol use and cerebral asymmetries. *Journal of Nervous and Mental Diseases, 172*(9), 529–532.

Naglieri, J. A. (1984). Concurrent and predictive validity of the Kaufman Assessment Battery for Children with a Navajo sample. *Journal of School Psychology, 22,* 373–380.

National Commission on Testing and Public Policy. (1990). *From gatekeeper to gateway: Transforming testing in America.* Chestnut Hill, MA: Boston College.

Philips, S. (1983). *The invisible culture.* New York: Longman.

Poortinga, Y. H. (1982). Cross-culturele psychologie en minderhedenonderzoek [Cross-cultural psychology and minority research]. *De Psycholoog, 17,* 708–720.

Reschly, D. J. (1978). WISC–R factor structures among Anglos, Blacks, Chicanos, and Native American Papagos. *Journal of Consulting and Clinical Psychology, 46,* 417–422.

Reschly, D. J., & Sabers, D. L. (1979). Analysis of test bias in four groups with the regression definition. *Journal of Educational Measurement, 16,* 1–9.

Tempest, P., & Skipper, B. (1988). Norms for the Wechsler Intelligence Scale for Children–Revised for Navajo Indians. *Diagnostique, 13,* 123–129.

Vraniak, D. A. (1993). *Analysis of 100 years of mental ability testing with American Indians and Alaska Natives: Technical report to the Bureau of Indian Affairs.* Madison, WI: Author.

Vraniak, D. A., & Pickett, S. (1993). Improving interventions with American ethnic minority children: Recurrent and recalcitrant challenges. Chapter in T. R. Krastowill & R. J. Morris (eds.), *Handbook of psychotherapy with children and adolescents.* Boston: Allyn & Bacon, pp. 502–540.

Damian A. Vraniak

NATURE, NURTURE, AND DEVELOPMENT   The relative influence of nature (heredity) and nurture (environment) on the development of individual differences in performance on intelligence tests is one of the oldest research questions in psychology. A year before Gregor Mendel's seminal paper on the laws of heredity, Francis Galton (1865) published a two-article series on high intelligence and other abilities that he expanded into the first book on heredity and intelligence, *Hereditary Genius: An Inquiry into Its Laws and Consequences* (1869). The first twin and adoption studies in the 1920s focused on intelligence (Burks, 1928; Freeman, Holzinger, & Mitchell, 1928; Merriman, 1924; Theis, 1924).

It should be mentioned at the outset that this article employs the psychometric definition of intelligence as general cognitive ability indexed by *g*, an unrotated first principal component derived from diverse tests of cognitive abilities. Because IQ scores from general tests of intelligence are reasonable indices of *g*, the word *intelligence* is also used to refer to performance on IQ tests. Although specific cognitive abilities such as verbal, spatial, and memory abilities are also important aspects of cognitive ability, less is known about the genetics of specific cognitive abilities (Plomin, 1988). For this reason, the article focuses on general intelligence rather than on specific cognitive abilities.

The article begins with the highlights of the scientific history of genetic research on intelligence. Next, genetic research is reviewed that asks the rudimentary nature–nurture question "whether" and "how much" heredity contributes to the development of individual differences in performance on intelligence tests. The rest of the article addresses three directions for genetic research on intelligence that go beyond the basic nature–nurture question. These directions are developmental, multivariate, and environmental research. Background concerning the theory and methods of the field of quantitative genetics is available elsewhere in overview (Plomin, 1990a) and in detail (Plomin, DeFries, & McClearn, 1990).

SCIENTIFIC HISTORY

Highlights in the history of research on genetics and intelligence include A. M. Leahy's (1935) adoption study, which resolved differences between the first adoption studies by Burks (1928) and Freeman and associates (1928) in favor of Burks. M. Skodak and H. M. Skeels's (1949) study was the first longitudinal adoption study and included intelligence-test results for biological mothers of adopted-away children. Begun in the 1960s, the Louisville Twin Study was the first major longitudinal twin study of intelligence that charted the developmental course of genetic and environmental influence (Wilson, 1983). In 1963, L. Erlenmeyer-Kimling and L. F. Jarvik's review of genetics and intelligence in *Science* was influential in showing the convergence of evidence pointing to genetic influence on intelligence. Cyril BURT's 1966 summary of his decades of research on identical twins reared apart added the dramatic evidence that identical twins reared apart are nearly as similar as identical twins reared together. Although Burt's work was discredited posthumously in the 1970s and 1980s (e.g., Hearnshaw, 1979), two books have reopened the case against Burt (Fletcher, 1990; Joynson, 1989). Furthermore, the results of Burt's lifelong studies of genetics and intelligence, including his results for identical twins reared apart, fit within the confidence limits of the world's literature on genetics and intelligence (e.g., Rowe & Plomin, 1978).

During the 1960s, environmentalism, which had been rampant in American psychology, was beginning to wane, and the stage was set for increasing acceptance of genetic influence on intelligence. Then, in 1969, Arthur JENSEN's monograph on the genetics of intelligence almost brought the field to a halt because the monograph included a few pages suggesting that race differences in IQ test scores might involve genetic differences (see RACE AND IQ SCORES). The causes of average differences between groups need not be related to the causes of individual differences within groups. The former question is much more difficult to investigate than the latter, which is the focus of the vast majority of genetic research on intelligence. For

this reason, the question of the origins of race differences in performance on intelligence tests has been and remains unresolved.

The storm raised by Jensen's article led to intense criticism of all behavioral-genetic research, especially in the area of intelligence (e.g., Kamin, 1974). This criticism had the positive effect of generating motivation to conduct bigger and better behavioral genetic studies of twins and adoptees. Some of these projects include the Colorado Adoption Project; the Colorado Twin Study (Fulker, Cherny, & Cardon, 1993); the Hawaii Family Study of Cognition (DeFries et al., 1976, 1979); the MacArthur Longitudinal Twin Study (Emde et al., 1992); the Minnesota adoption studies of S. Scarr and R. A. Weinberg (1977, 1978); the Minnesota Study of Twins Reared Apart (Bouchard et al., 1990); a Norwegian twin study (Sundet et al., 1988); the Swedish Adoption/Twin Study of Aging (Pedersen et al., 1992); the Texas Adoption Project (Loehlin, Horn, & Willerman, 1989); and the Western Reserve Twin Project (Thompson, Detterman, & Plomin, 1991).

These new projects generated much more data on the genetics of intelligence than had been obtained in the previous fifty years combined. These new data contributed in part to a dramatic shift that occurred in the 1980s in the social and behavioral sciences toward acceptance of the conclusion that hereditary differences between individuals are significantly associated with differences in their performance on tests of cognitive ability (Snyderman & Rothman, 1988).

OVERVIEW OF GENETIC RESEARCH

In 1981, Erlenmeyer-Kimling and Jarvik's (1963) review of genetic research on intelligence was updated in *Science* by T. J. Bouchard, Jr., and M. McGue. The review summarized results from more than 100 separate studies with IQ correlations for more than 100,000 pairs of relatives. An overview of the review is presented in Table 1.

Human quantitative genetic research relies on family, adoption, and twin designs. Family studies of human behavior assess the extent to which genetically related individuals living together resemble each other. Such studies cannot disentangle possible environmental sources of resemblance. As indicated in Table 1, first-degree relatives living together share half their

TABLE 1

Average IQ correlations for family, adoption, and twin studies

Design	Correlation	Number of Pairs
Family Study		
First-degree relatives together (= .50G + Es)		
Parent–offspring	.42	8,433[a]
Sibling	.47	26,473[a]
Adoption Study		
First-degree relatives adopted apart (= .50G)		
Parent–offspring	.24	720[a]
Sibling	.24	203[a]
Unrelated adopted together (= Es)		
Adoptive parent–offspring	.19	1,397[a]
Adoptive sibling	.32	714[a]
Adoptive sibling (new)	.02	385[b]
Identical twins adopted apart (= G)	.72	65[a]
Identical twins adopted apart (new)	.78	93[c]
Twin Study		
Identical twins reared together (= G + Es)	.86	4,672[a]
Fraternal twins reared together (= .5G + Es)	.60	5,533[a]

NOTE: *G* refers to degree of genetic relatedness; *Es* to shared environment.

[a]Based on material in Bouchard and McGue (1981) as corrected in Loehlin (1989).

[b]New data from four studies of adoptive siblings after childhood (Plomin, 1988).

[c]New data for identical twins adopted apart from Bouchard et al. (1990) and Pedersen et al. (1992).

heredity (.5G in Table 1) as well as their family environment (*Es* is shared family environment). This was the problem with Galton's interpretation of his 1869 family study of intelligence: Galton interpreted familial resemblance as if it were solely due to heredity.

Separating genetic and environmental sources of familial resemblance is the point of adoption studies. Genetically related individuals adopted apart give evidence of the extent to which familial resemblance is the result of hereditary resemblance (.5G in Table 1). Genetically unrelated individuals adopted together indicate the extent to which familial resemblance is due to shared family environment (*Es* in Table 1).

Twin studies also provide a kind of natural experiment in which the resemblance of identical twins, whose genetic relatedness is 1.0, is compared to the resemblance of fraternal twins, first-degree relatives whose genetic relatedness is .50. Both types of twins share family environment (*Es*). If heredity affects a trait, identical twins should be more similar for the trait than fraternal twins. As in any quasi-experimental design, these methods have possible problems, most notably, the equal-environments assumption for the twin method and selective placement for the adoption method. Yet, these are empirical issues, and research suggests that these are not major problems. Moreover, the assumptions of the twin method are very different from the assumptions of the adoption method, and yet, the two methods generally converge on the conclusion that genetic effects are important.

Family, adoption, and twin studies can be used to estimate the magnitude of genetic effects as well as their statistical significance. This is the descriptive statistic heritability. In this context, HERITABILITY refers to an estimate of effect size given a particular mix of existing genetic and environmental factors in a particular population at a particular time. Heritability estimates the proportion of phenotypic variance (i.e., individual differences in a population, not behavior of a single individual) that can be accounted for by genetic variance.

Consider height. Correlations for first-degree relatives are about .45 on average, whether relatives are reared together or adopted apart. Identical- and fraternal-twin correlations are .90 and .45, respectively, regardless of whether they are reared together or adopted apart. These results indicate significant genetic effects. For these height data, heritability is estimated as 90 percent. This estimate of effect size indicates that about 90 percent of the variance in height among individuals in the populations sampled is due to hereditary rather than environmental differences.

When these same methods are used to investigate genetic effects on intelligence, they yield evidence for less heritability than for height, but heritability that is nonetheless substantial. Correlations for first-degree relatives living together are similar to their correlation for height. As indicated in Table 1, the average IQ correlation for parents and offspring is .42, and for siblings it is .47. Adopted-apart first-degree relatives are only about half as similar for IQ as are first-degree relatives living together, unlike the situation with height. The average IQ correlation for parents and their adopted-away offspring is .24; for pairs of adopted-apart siblings the correlation is also .24.

The fact that the correlation for adopted-apart relatives is less than the correlation for relatives living together suggests that shared rearing environment contributes to the IQ resemblance of first-degree relatives living together. This fits with another finding from the adoption literature: that genetically unrelated parents and offspring and siblings resemble each other for IQ. The average IQ correlation for adoptive parents and adopted children is .19, and the average correlation for genetically unrelated children adopted into the same adoptive families is .32, although, as explained later, newer studies suggest lower correlations.

Thus, in very rough summary, "genetic" relatives adopted apart correlate about .20, "environment" relatives correlate about .20, and "genetic-plus-environmental" relatives correlate about .40. These adoption results are consistent with a heritability estimate of about .40, about half that for height.

The twin method tends to support this conclusion. The average twin correlations are .86 for identical twins and .60 for fraternal twins. Because identical twins are twice as similar genetically as fraternal twins, a rough estimate of heritability doubles the difference between the identical- and fraternal-twin correlations. This estimate of heritability is about .50. It should be noted that the correlation of .60 for fraternal twins exceeds the correlation of .47 for nontwin siblings, which suggests that shared environmental influences contribute more to the resemblance of twins than nontwin siblings.

One of the most dramatic adoption designs, reared-apart identical twins, suggests a higher estimate of heritability than these other designs, although the number of such twin pairs is small, for obvious reasons. For several small studies published before 1981 involving a total of 65 pairs of identical twins reared apart, the average IQ correlation is .72. The correlation for identical twins reared apart provides a direct estimate of heritability. This high heritability estimate has been confirmed in two studies of twins reared apart. In one report of 45 pairs of identical twins reared apart, the correlation was .78 (Bouchard et al., 1990). In a report of 45 pairs of Swedish identical twins reared apart, the correlation was also .78 (Pedersen et al., 1992). The latter study also included 88 pairs of fraternal twins reared apart whose IQ correlation was .32, as well as matched identical and fraternal twins reared together. A model-fitting estimate of heritability that incorporates data from the four groups of twins in this study was .81, and a follow-up study three years later yielded similar results. A possible explanation for this higher heritability estimate for twins reared apart is that, unlike most of the other twin and adoption studies, these studies involve adults rather than children and adolescents. As explained later, heritability appears to be greater later in life.

Model-fitting analyses that simultaneously analyze all of the family, adoption, and twin data summarized in the review by T. J. Bouchard and M. McGue (1981) yield heritability estimates of about .50 (Chipuer, Rovine, & Plomin, 1990; Loehlin, 1989). The error surrounding this estimate may be as high as .20, so we can only say with confidence that the heritability of IQ scores is between .30 and .70. Nonetheless, even if heritability is at the bottom of this range, it is a remarkable achievement to account for 30 percent of the variance of a trait as complex as general cognitive ability.

If half of the variance of IQ scores can be accounted for by heredity, the other half is attributed to environment. In this sense, these same genetic data provide strong evidence for the importance of the environment. These data also suggest how the environment works. Some of this environmental influence appears to be shared by family members, making them similar to one another. For example, as indicated earlier, pairs of genetically unrelated children adopted into the same adoptive homes yield an average correlation of .32. This suggests that about a third of the total variance of IQ scores may be due to shared rearing environment. The average correlation of .19 between adoptive parents and their adopted children suggests less-shared environmental influence, although it seems reasonable that parents and their children share less-similar environments than do siblings. When we consider these data from a developmental perspective, a very different picture emerges, as described in the following section.

Growing acceptance of the conclusion that genetic influence on intelligence is significant and substantial is only the first chapter in the story of genetics and intelligence (Plomin & Neiderhiser, 1991). Much remains to be learned about other basic quantitative genetic issues that go beyond the rudimentary issue of the relative contribution of nature and nurture. Developmental, multivariate, and environmental examples of this point constitute the remainder of this chapter.

DEVELOPMENTAL GENETIC ANALYSIS

When Galton first studied twins in 1876, he investigated the extent to which the twins' initial similarity or dissimilarity changed during development. Other early studies were also developmental (Merriman, 1924; Thorndike, 1905), but this developmental perspective faded from genetic research until recent times.

Two types of developmental questions can be addressed in genetic research (Plomin, 1986). First, does

heritability change with age? It is reasonable to suppose that environmental factors increasingly account for variance in intelligence as experiences accumulate during the course of life. To the contrary, genetic research suggests that genetic influence on intelligence shows a nearly linear increase from infancy through early childhood (Fulker, DeFries, & Plomin, 1988; Wilson, 1983) and perhaps continuing throughout the life span (McCartney, Harris, & Bernieri, 1990; McGue et al., 1993; Plomin & Thompson, 1987). For example, the first genetic study of older adults reported a heritability of 80 percent for cognitive ability using the powerful design of twins reared apart and twins reared together (Pedersen et al., 1992).

Not only does heritability appear to increase during the life span, but the effects of shared environment appear to decrease. Although genetic research suggests substantial influence of shared environment, as discussed in the previous section, some evidence suggests that shared environmental influence that affects IQ scores may be much less after adolescence (Plomin, 1988). The strongest evidence for the importance of shared environment comes from the correlation for adoptive siblings, that is, pairs of genetically unrelated children adopted into the same adoptive families. As indicated in Table 1, the average IQ correlation for such adoptive siblings is .32. These studies, however, happened to study adoptive siblings in childhood. In 1978 the first study of older adoptive siblings yielded a strikingly different result: the IQ correlation was − .03 for 84 pairs of adoptive siblings who were 16–22 years of age (Scarr & Weinberg, 1978). Other studies of older adoptive siblings have also found similarly low IQ correlations (Kent, 1985; Teasdale & Owen, 1984). The most impressive evidence comes from a ten-year longitudinal follow-up study of more than 200 pairs of adoptive siblings. At the average age of 8 years, the IQ correlation was .26. Ten years later, their IQ correlation was near zero (Loehlin, Horn, & Willerman, 1989). These data suggest that shared environment is important for IQ during childhood, when children are living at home, and then fades in importance as extrafamilial influences become more important.

A second type of developmental question concerns genetic contributions to age-to-age change and continuity in longitudinal analyses. It is important to recognize that genetic factors can contribute to change as well as to continuity in development (Plomin, 1986). Although genetic effects on intelligence contribute substantially to stability during childhood, what is more surprising is evidence for genetic involvement in change from age to age in childhood (Fulker, Cherny, & Cardon, 1993) and perhaps even in adulthood (Loehlin, Horn, & Willerman, 1989). Particularly interesting is the suggestion of substantial new genetic variation during the transition from early to middle childhood.

MULTIVARIATE GENETIC ANALYSIS

A second example of research that goes beyond the basic "whether" and "how much" nature–nurture questions is multivariate genetic analysis. Multivariate genetic analysis extends the univariate genetic analysis of the variance of a single trait to multivariate analysis of the covariance between traits (Plomin & DeFries, 1979). In other words, multivariate genetic analysis makes it possible to investigate the extent to which genetic effects on one trait overlap with genetic effects on another trait. An obvious example is that genetic effects on height overlap with genetic effects on weight. Analyses of this type in the realm of intelligence indicate that specific tests and group factors show some genetic effects unique to each test and factor. Nonetheless, much of the genetic effects are shared across diverse tests and factors (Cardon & Fulker, 1993; Cardon et al., 1992).

Another finding makes a related point: The heritabilities of cognitive tests are strongly correlated with their g loadings, that is, their factor loadings on an unrotated first principal component (Jensen, 1987). In other words, the more a test is related to g, the more heritable it is. For example, in the Swedish study mentioned earlier of twins reared apart and twins reared together, for diverse cognitive ability tests, the correlation between heritabilities and g loadings was .77 after differential reliabilities of the tests were controlled (Pedersen et al., 1992).

Another example of multivariate genetic analysis concerns the genetic relationship between intelligence and school achievement. Academic achievement is in-

teresting from a genetic perspective because it is widely assumed that "achievement" and "ability" are different, almost by definition. Achievement is what a student accomplishes by dint of effort, whereas ability is thought to involve inherent talent. For this reason, achievement-test scores are assumed to be environmental in origin, but a neglected finding is that achievement and ability tests are moderately correlated, which raises the possibility of genetic overlap between the two domains.

Although several twin studies of scholastic achievement in adolescence have been reported, until the 1990s no research was available for middle childhood. In the Western Reserve Twin Project (WRTP), specific cognitive abilities and school achievement were investigated for a sample of 146 pairs of identical twins and 132 pairs of fraternal twins 6–12 years of age (Thompson, Detterman, & Plomin, 1991). School achievement tests yield significant heritability estimates, but these estimates are much lower than heritabilities for cognitive abilities, although evidence from other studies suggests that heritability estimates are greater later in the school years (e.g., Loehlin & Nichols, 1976). Most relevant to the present topic are the results of multivariate genetic analysis: The well-known correlation between cognitive abilities and school achievement tests is due almost entirely to genetic factors in common to the two domains (Thompson et al., 1991). This finding has been replicated in another study as well as in two studies focused on reading achievement (Brooks, Fulker, & DeFries, 1990; Cardon et al., 1990). Conversely, ability–achievement discrepancies are exclusively environmental in origin. In other words, the relationship between intelligence and school achievement involves the same genes but different environments.

GENETIC INFLUENCE ON ENVIRONMENTAL MEASURES

Another new direction for genetic research lies at the interface between nature and nurture. Although it may sound paradoxical at first, widely used measures of the environment show significant genetic influence (Plomin & Bergeman, 1991). Environmental measures relevant to the development of intelligence—for example, parenting measures—are not simply measures of the environment independent of the individual. For example, in some families parents read more often to their child than in other families. Although parental behaviors of this sort are often employed as environmental measures in research on the development of intelligence, the extent to which parents read to their children could reflect genetically influenced characteristics of the parents. For example, more-intelligent parents might especially enjoy this activity or feel that it is especially important. Parental reading to children might also reflect genetically influenced characteristics of the children. For example, brighter children might encourage their parents to read to them.

One of the most widely used measures of the home environment relevant to the development of intelligence is the Home Observation for Measurement of the Environment, or HOME (Caldwell & Bradley, 1978). In the Colorado Adoption Project, the HOME was examined for possible genetic influence in a sibling adoption design that compares the resemblance of genetically related (nonadoptive) siblings and genetically unrelated (adoptive) siblings employing nearly 200 pairs of siblings. Each sibling was assessed in interaction with the child's mother when the child was 12 months of age and again at 24 months of age (Plomin, DeFries, & Fulker, 1988). The HOME scores for each child were correlated across sibling pairs. The sibling correlations for the nonadoptive sibling pairs were .50 at 12 months and again .50 at 24 months. The correlations for adoptive siblings were lower: .36 at 12 months and .32 at 24 months. This suggests that parental behavior as assessed by the HOME in part reflects genetic differences between children. Model-fitting analyses confirmed this conclusion, showing significant genetic influence at both ages (Braungart et al., 1992). Most of the dozens of environmental measures investigated in twin and adoption studies since the early 1980s also show genetic influence.

The HOME was developed as a measure of the home environment in order to predict the development of children's intelligence, but if genetic factors contribute to the HOME as well as to IQ, it is possible that the association between the HOME and IQ is mediated in part by genetic factors. Multivariate genetic analyses were conducted to assess the genetic contribution to covariance between the HOME and IQ, using the sibling adoption design in the Colorado Adoption Project (Braungart et al., 1992). The results indicated no genetic overlap between the HOME and the Bayley Mental Scale at 12 months. At 12 months, the phenotypic correlation between the HOME and the Bayley is only about .20 (Bradley et al., 1989). The correlation between the HOME and the Bayley is twice as great at 24 months. At 24 months, genetic factors account for more than half of the association between the HOME and the Bayley (Braungart et al., 1992). Moreover, the HOME at both 1 and 2 years of age predicts Stanford-Binet IQ at 3 and 4 years, and this prediction is also mediated in part genetically (Plomin, DeFries, & Fulker, 1988).

These findings have been confirmed using a different design that compares the HOME–Bayley correlation in nonadoptive families in which parents share heredity as well as family environment with their children, in contrast to adoptive families in which parents share only family environment with their adopted children (Plomin, Loehlin, & DeFries, 1985). Similar to the multivariate genetic analyses just described, the results of these analyses comparing HOME–Bayley correlations in nonadoptive and adoptive families suggest genetic mediation of the HOME–Bayley relationship at age 2 but not at age 1, when the phenotypic HOME–Bayley relationship is quite weak. At 2 years the correlation between the HOME and Bayley is .42 in nonadoptive families, which is similar to the results of other HOME studies (Bradley et al., 1989), but in this first report of the HOME–Bayley correlation in adoptive families, the correlation is only .27 (Plomin, DeFries, & Fulker, 1988). This suggests that at age 2, genetic factors in part mediate the association between the HOME and the Bayley. This approach, similar to the multivariate genetic results mentioned earlier, also suggests genetic mediation of the longitudinal prediction from the HOME in infancy to IQ in early childhood (Plomin, DeFries, & Fulker, 1988) and even to IQ in middle childhood (Coon et al., 1990).

Which environmental measures are most (and least) affected by genetic factors? What are the processes by which heredity affects measures of environment and their association with intelligence? Answers to questions such as these will surely enrich our understanding of the interface between nature and nurture in the development of intelligence.

CONCLUSION

More is known about the origins of individual differences in intelligence than about the origins of any other behavioral dimension. Research converges on the conclusion that differences between individuals in their performance on tests of intelligence are significantly associated with genetic differences. Few scientists today would dispute this conclusion, which created such a furor in the early 1970s. The magnitude of the genetic effect is not as universally accepted or appreciated, however. Results of model-fitting analyses of the world's literature on the genetics of IQ suggest that about half of the variance in IQ scores can be attributed to genetic differences between individuals. Estimating the magnitude of the genetic effect is more difficult than determining its statistical significance. Regardless of the precise estimate of heritability, the point is that genetic influence on IQ test scores is not only significant but also very substantial.

This is only the beginning of the story, not the end. Three examples were described of current directions in genetic research on intelligence that go beyond the rudimentary question of the relative contributions of nature and nurture. These include developmental, multivariate, and environmental research on genetics and intelligence. Two types of developmental analysis were described. The first involves changes in genetic and environmental components of variance. Two fascinating developmental findings of this type have emerged from genetic research. First, heritability increases linearly throughout the life span. Second, the effects of shared family environmental influence decline to negligible levels during adolescence. The second type of developmental analysis involves longitudinal analyses of age-to-age continuity and change. For intelligence, genetic factors largely contribute to continuity rather than to change during development, but there are interesting examples of developmental changes in genetic effects in childhood.

The second example of new directions for genetic research is multivariate genetic analysis. Recent research indicates the existence of unique genetic effects on specific cognitive abilities that are independent of genetic effects on intelligence. Nonetheless, the more a particular cognitive test relates to general intelligence, the more highly heritable it is. A final multivariate example indicated that measures of intelligence and school achievement involve the same genetic effects but different environmental influences.

The third example involves the incorporation of environmental measures in genetic designs. Research since the early 1980s suggests that genetic factors contribute to measures that are widely used as environmental measures. In addition, associations between environmental measures and developmental measures such as IQ scores can be mediated genetically.

Although space does not permit discussion of additional directions for genetic research on intelligence, three examples should be mentioned briefly. First, genetic research has begun to focus on specific cognitive abilities rather than general cognitive ability (DeFries, Vandenberg, & McClearn, 1976; Plomin, 1988). For example, there is some evidence that verbal and spatial abilities are more heritable than memory abilities. In addition, genetic research has begun to investigate elemental cognitive processes, which are often called information-processing measures (Ho, Baker, & Decker, 1988; McGue & Bouchard, 1989; Vernon, 1989). For example, the Western Reserve Twin Project (Thompson, Detterman, & Plomin, 1991) includes a seven-hour battery of computer-administered, touch-screen tests of elemental cognitive processes that are often called information-processing variables, as well as standard psychometric tests of cognitive abilities and school achievement. Although there are as yet too few studies to draw definitive conclusions, it appears that these measures show a wider range of heritabilities than traditional psychometric tests.

Second, a new analysis makes it possible to broach the fundamental issue of the etiological association between the normal and abnormal, for example, between intelligence and retardation or between cognitive abilities and disabilities (DeFries & Fulker, 1985, 1988). Analyses of this type suggest that mild retardation is etiologically connected with the rest of the IQ distribution (Plomin, 1991). In other words, mild retardation may merely be the low end of the distribution of genetic and environmental factors that affect the rest of the IQ distribution. Severe retardation, on the other, is etiologically distinct from the rest of the IQ distribution. High IQ also appears to be substantially influenced by genetic factors (Saudino et al., 1993; Thompson, Detterman, & Plomin, 1993).

Finally, the most important long-term direction for genetic research on intelligence is just beginning to loom on the horizon. Advances in molecular biology have led to the dawn of a new era for genetic research on intelligence. The "new genetics" of molecular biology provides thousands of genetic markers that will ultimately make it possible to study DNA variation directly in individuals, even for complexly determined characteristics such as intelligence, which are affected by many genes as well as environmental influence (Plomin, 1990b; Plomin & Neiderhiser, 1991).

(*See also:* BIRTH ORDER, SPACING, AND FAMILY SIZE; FAMILY ENVIRONMENTS; PARENTING AND INTELLIGENCE; SOCIOECONOMIC STATUS AND INTELLIGENCE.)

BIBLIOGRAPHY

BOUCHARD, T. J., JR., LYKKEN, D. T., MCGUE, M., SEGAL, N. L., & TELLEGEN, A. (1990). Sources of human psychological differences: The Minnesota Study of Twins Reared Apart. *Science, 250,* 223–228.

BOUCHARD, T. J., JR., & MCGUE, M. (1981). Familial studies of intelligence: A review. *Science, 212,* 1055–1059.

BRADLEY, R., CALDWELL, B., ROCK, S., RAMEY, C., BARNARD, K., GRAY, C., HAMMOND, M., MITCHELL, S., GOTTFRIED, A., SIEGEL, L., & JOHNSON, D. (1989). Home environment and cognitive development in the first three years of life: A collaborative study involving six sites and three ethnic groups in North America. *Developmental Psychology, 25,* 217–235.

BRAUNGART, J. M., PLOMIN, R., FULKER, D. W., & DEFRIES, J. C. (1992). Genetic influence on the home environment during infancy: A sibling adoption study of the HOME. *Developmental Psychology, 28,* 1048–1055.

BROOKS, A., FULKER, D. W., & DEFRIES, J. C. (1990). Reading performance and general cognitive ability: A multivariate genetic analysis of twin data. *Personality and Individual Differences, 11,* 141–146.

BURKS, B. (1928). The relative influence of nature and nurture upon mental development: A comparative study of foster parent–foster child resemblance and true parent–true child resemblance. *Twenty-seventh yearbook of the National Society for the Study of Education,* Pt. 1, 219–316.

BURT, C. (1966). The genetic determination of differences in intelligence: A study of monozygotic twins reared together and apart. *British Journal of Psychology, 57,* 137–153.

CALDWELL, B. M., & BRADLEY, R. H. (1978). *Home observation for measurement of the environment.* Little Rock: University of Arkansas.

CARDON, L. R., DILALLA, L. F., PLOMIN, R., DEFRIES, J. C., & FULKER, D. W. (1990). Genetic correlations between reading performance and IQ in the Colorado Adoption Project. *Intelligence, 14,* 245–257.

CARDON, L. R., & FULKER, D. W. (1993). Genetics of specific cognitive abilities. In R. Plomin & G. E. McClearn (Eds.), *Nature, nurture, and psychology* (pp. 99–120). Washington, DC: American Psychological Association.

CARDON, L. R., FULKER, D. W., DEFRIES, J. C., & PLOMIN, R. (1992). Multivariate genetic analysis of specific cognitive abilities in the Colorado Adoption Project at age 7. *Intelligence, 16,* 383–400.

CHIPUER, H. M., ROVINE, M., & PLOMIN, R. (1990). LISREL modelling: Genetic and environmental influences on IQ revisited. *Intelligence, 14,* 11–29.

COON, H., FULKER, D. W., DEFRIES, J. C., & PLOMIN, R. (1990). Home environment and cognitive ability of 7-year-old children in the Colorado Adoption Project: Genetic and environmental etiologies. *Developmental Psychology, 26,* 459–468.

DEFRIES, J. C., ASHTON, G. C., JOHNSON, R. C., KUSE, A. R., MCCLEARN, G. E., RASHAD, M. N., VANDENBERG, S. G., & WILSON, J. R. (1976). Parent–offspring resemblance for specific cognitive abilities in two ethnic groups. *Nature, 261,* 131–133.

DEFRIES, J. C., & FULKER, D. W. (1985). Multiple regression analysis of twin data. *Behavior Genetics, 15,* 467–473.

DEFRIES, J. C., & FULKER, D. W. (1988). Multiple regression analysis of twin data: Etiology of deviant scores versus individual differences. *Acta Geneticae Medicae et Gemellologiae, 37,* 205–216.

DEFRIES, J. C., JOHNSON, R. C., KUSE, A. R., MCCLEARN, G. E., PLOVINA, J., VANDENBERG, S. G., & WILSON, J. R. (1979). Familial resemblance for specific cognitive abilities. *Behavior Genetics, 9,* 23–43.

DeFries, J. C., Vandenberg, S. G., & McClearn, G. E. (1976). The genetics of specific cognitive abilities. *Annual Review of Genetics, 10,* 179–207.

Emde, R. N., Plomin, R., Robinson, J., Reznick, J. S., Campos, J., Corley, R., DeFries, J. C., Fulker, D. W., Kagan, J., & Zahn-Waxler, C. (1992). Temperament, emotion, and cognition at 14 months: The MacArthur Longitudinal Twin Study. *Child Development, 63,* 1437–1455.

Erlenmeyer-Kimling, L., & Jarvik, L. F. (1963). Genetics and intelligence: A review. *Science, 142,* 1477–1479.

Fletcher, R. (1990). *The Cyril Burt scandal: Case for the defence.* New York: Macmillan.

Freeman, F. N., Holzinger, K. J., & Mitchell, B. C. (1928). The influence of environment on the intelligence, school achievement, and conduct of foster children. *Twenty-seventh yearbook of the National Society for the Study of Education,* Pt. 1, 103–217.

Fulker, D. W., Cherny, S. S., & Cardon, L. R. (1993). Continuity and change in cognitive development. In R. Plomin & G. E. McClearn (Eds.), *Nature, nurture, and psychology* (pp. 77–97). Washington, D.C.: American Psychological Association.

Fulker, D. W., DeFries, J. C., & Plomin, R. (1988). Genetic influence on general mental ability increases between infancy and middle childhood. *Nature, 336,* 767–769.

Galton, F. (1865). Hereditary talent and character. *Macmillan's Magazine, 12,* 157–166, 318–327.

Galton, F. (1869). *Hereditary genius: An inquiry into its laws and consequences.* London: Macmillan.

Galton, F. (1876). The history of twins as a criterion of the relative powers of nature and nurture. *Royal Anthropological Institute of Great Britain and Ireland Journal, 6,* 391–406.

Hearnshaw, L. S. (1979). *Cyril Burt, psychologist.* Ithaca, NY: Cornell University Press.

Ho, H.-Z., Baker, L. A., & Decker, S. N. (1988). Covariation between intelligence and speed of cognitive processing: Genetic and environmental influences. *Behavior Genetics, 18,* 247–261.

Jensen, A. R. (1969). How much can we boost IQ and scholastic achievement? *Harvard Educational Review, 39,* 1–123.

Jensen, A. R. (1987). The *g* beyond factor analysis. In R. R. Ronning, J. A. Glover, J. C. Conoley, & J. C. Witt (Eds.), *The influence of cognitive psychology on testing* (pp. 87–142). Hillsdale, NJ: Erlbaum.

Joynson, R. B. (1989). *The Burt affair.* London: Routledge.

Kamin, L. J. (1974). *The science and politics of IQ.* Potomac, MD: Erlbaum.

Kent, J. (1985). *Genetic and environmental contributions to cognitive abilities as assessed by a telephone test battery.* Unpublished doctoral dissertation, University of Colorado, Boulder.

Leahy, A. M. (1935). Nature–nurture and intelligence. *Genetic Psychology Monographs, 17,* 236–308.

Loehlin, J. C. (1989). Partitioning environmental and genetic contributions to behavioral development. *American Psychologist, 44,* 1285–1292.

Loehlin, J. C., Horn, J. M., & Willerman, L. (1989). Modeling IQ change: Evidence from the Texas Adoption Project. *Child Development, 60,* 993–1004.

Loehlin, J. C., Lindzey, G., & Spuhler, J. N. (1975). *Race differences in intelligence.* San Francisco: W. H. Freeman.

Loehlin, J. C., & Nichols, R. C. (1976). *Heredity, environment and personality.* Austin: University of Texas Press.

McCartney, K., Harris, M. J., & Bernieri, F. (1990). Growing up and growing apart: A developmental meta-analysis of twin studies. *Psychological Bulletin, 107,* 226–237.

McGue, M., & Bouchard, T. J., Jr. (1989). Genetic and environmental determinants of information processing and special mental abilities: A twin analysis. In R. J. Sternberg (Ed.), *Advances in the psychology of human intelligence* (pp. 7–45). Hillsdale, NJ: Erlbaum.

McGue, M., Bouchard, T. J., Jr., Iacono, W. G., & Lykken, D. T. (1993). Behavioral genetics of cognitive ability: A life-span perspective. In R. Plomin & G. E. McClearn (Eds.), *Nature, nurture, and psychology* (pp. 59–76). Washington, DC: American Psychological Association.

Merriman, C. (1924). The intellectual resemblance of twins. *Psychological Monographs, 33* (Whole No. 152).

Pedersen, N. L., Plomin, R., Nesselroade, J. R., & McClearn, G. E. (1992). A quantitative genetic analysis of cognitive abilities during the second half of the life span. *Psychological Science, 3,* 346–353.

Plomin, R. (1986). *Development, genetics, and psychology.* Hillsdale, NJ: Erlbaum.

Plomin, R. (1988). The nature and nurture of cognitive abilities. In R. Sternberg (Ed.), *Advances in the psychology of human intelligence* (pp. 1–33). Hillsdale, NJ: Erlbaum.

Plomin, R. (1990a). *Nature and nurture: An introduction to human behavioral genetics.* Pacific Grove, CA: Brooks/Cole.

PLOMIN, R. (1990b). The role of inheritance in behavior. *Science, 248,* 183–188.

PLOMIN, R. (1991). Genetic risk and psychosocial disorders: Links between the normal and abnormal. In M. Rutter & P. Casaer (Eds.),*Biological risk factors for psychosocial disorders* (pp. 101–138). Cambridge: Cambridge University Press.

PLOMIN, R., & BERGEMAN, C. S. (1991). The nature of nurture: Genetic influence on "environmental" measures. *Behavior and Brain Sciences, 14,* 373–427.

PLOMIN, R., & DEFRIES, J. C. (1979). Multivariate behavioral genetic analysis of twin data on scholastic abilities. *Behavior Genetics, 9,* 505–517.

PLOMIN, R., DEFRIES, J. C., & FULKER, D. W. (1988). *Nature and nurture during infancy and early childhood.* New York: Cambridge University Press.

PLOMIN, R., DEFRIES, J. C., & MCCLEARN (1990). *Behavioral genetics: A primer* (2nd ed.). New York: W. H. Freeman.

PLOMIN, R., LOEHLIN, J. C., & DEFRIES, J. C. (1985). Genetic and environmental components of "environmental" influences. *Developmental Psychology, 21,* 391–402.

PLOMIN, R., & NEIDERHISER, J. M. (1991). Quantitative genetics, molecular genetics, and intelligence. *Intelligence, 15,* 369–387.

PLOMIN, R., & THOMPSON, L. A. (1987). Life-span developmental behavioral genetics. In P. B. Baltes, D. L. Featherman, R. M. Lerner (Eds.), *Life-span development and behavior* (Vol. 8, pp. 1–31). Hillsdale, NJ: Erlbaum.

ROWE, D. C., & PLOMIN, R. (1978). The Burt controversy: A comparison of Burt's data on IQ with data from other studies. *Behavior Genetics, 8,* 81–84.

SAUDINO, K. J., PLOMIN, R., PEDERSEN, N. L., & MCCLEARN, G. E. (1993). *The etiology of high and low cognitive ability during the second half of the life span.* Manuscript submitted for publication.

SCARR, S., & WEINBERG, R. A. (1977). Intellectual similarities within families of both adopted and biological children. *Intelligence, 1,* 170–191.

SCARR, S., & WEINBERG, R. A. (1978). The influence of "family background" on intellectual attainment. *American Sociological Review, 43,* 674–692.

SKODAK, M., & SKEELS, H. M. (1949). A final follow-up on one hundred adopted children. *Journal of Genetic Psychology, 75,* 84–125.

SNYDERMAN, M., & ROTHMAN, S. (1988). *The IQ controversy, the media and public policy.* New Brunswick, NJ: Transaction Press.

SUNDET, J. M., TAMBS, K., MAGNUS, P., & BERG, K. (1988). On the question of secular trends in the heritability of intelligence test scores: A study of Norwegian twins. *Intelligence, 12,* 47–59.

TEASDALE, T. W., & OWEN, D. R. (1984). Heredity and familial environment in intelligence and educational level: A sibling study. *Nature, 309,* 620–622.

THEIS, S. V. S. (1924). *How foster children turn out* (Publicatioin No. 165). New York: State Charities Aid Association.

THOMPSON, L. A., DETTERMAN, D. K., & PLOMIN, R. (1991). Associations between cognitive abilities and scholastic achievement: Genetic overlap but environmental differences. *Psychological Science, 2,* 158–165.

THOMPSON, L. A., DETTERMAN, D. K., & PLOMIN, R. (1993). *Genetic influence on low and high cognitive ability.* Manuscript submitted for publication.

THORNDIKE, E. L. (1905). Measurement of twins. *Archives of Philosophy, Psychology, and Scientific Methods, 1,* 1–64.

VERNON, P. A. (1989). The heritability of measures of speed of information-processing. *Personality and Individual Differences, 10,* 573–576.

WILSON, R. S. (1983). The Louisville Twin Study: Developmental synchronies in behavior. *Child Development, 54,* 298–316.

ROBERT PLOMIN

NEUROPSYCHOLOGY, CLINICAL

Neuropsychology may be defined as the experimental and clinical study of brain-behavior relationships in animals and human beings. Human neuropsychology can be divided into two related areas: (1) experimental study of behavioral correlates of brain functions and (2) clinical neuropsychology, which includes the assessment and treatment of individual persons. The focus of this article will be on clinical neuropsychology.

In general terms, clinical neuropsychology is concerned with the identification of deficits demonstrated by persons with brain damage or dysfunction, retraining of impaired abilities in persons who have sustained brain damage and consequent impairment, and counseling and psychotherapy (in its broad sense) to assist brain-impaired persons in dealing as effectively as possible with the requirements of everyday living.

A major emphasis in clinical neuropsychology is diagnostic evaluation. Such evaluations almost invariably include neuropsychological testing by means of instruments that have been validated as reliable indicators of the biological condition of the brain. The results of neuropsychological testing are related to the history information, the clinical interview, and the findings derived from such neurological examinations as computed tomography (CT) and magnetic resonance imaging (MRI). Some clinical neuropsychologists feel that it is important to conduct the clinical interview personally; others prefer to use the reports done by different psychologists or physicians. To avoid any bias in the clinical interpretation of the test results, some clinical neuropsychologists elect to administer (or have administered) the tests before making themselves aware of the results of diagnostic procedures and the conclusions drawn by other professionals. Other clinical neuropsychologists prefer to be apprised of all available information about the client before interpreting the results of their own testing.

Although clinical neuropsychology is a relatively new discipline, it is growing rapidly, particularly because of the clear evidence that the field can make a unique contribution in the evaluation of individual subjects (Matarazzo, 1990). In some instances, the contribution may involve diagnosis of brain injury or disease that had not been identified with purely neurological methods. More often, however, clinical neuropsychology makes its unique contribution through detailed assessment of brain-based aspects of behavior (as contrasted with diagnostic tests in the field of neurology, which are usually measures of motor and sensory functions, supplemented by tracings of electrical responses or by images).

Neuropsychological assessment is assuming increasing importance in a clinical sense because of the relevance of the results in (1) determining the therapeutic approach most appropriate for the individual; (2) assisting the client to achieve a realistic postinjury adjustment; (3) providing evaluations of loss in cases involving litigation; (4) evaluating the effects of various forms of treatment of brain disease or injury; and (5)

training (in the case of children) or retraining (in the case of adults) higher-level brain functions in order to attain an optimal outcome for the individual.

CLINICAL ASSESSMENT

Determining the Therapeutic Approach. Understanding the brain-related abilities of the individual subject has many implications for therapy. Maladjusted behavior, in the individual case, may result from a wide variety of influences, ranging from brain damage to emotional and environmental stresses. Clinical neuropsychological evaluation aids in the identification of behaviors arising from biological impairment of the brain that are associated with emotional and psychiatric problems. In a child, a reading disability may be the consequence of some type of subtle brain disorder that can be detected by clinical neuropsychological examination, or the disability may result from factors that have no relationship to impaired brain functions. To adopt appropriate therapeutic procedures or training methods, it is imperative to understand the basis of the client's difficulties.

Assisting the Client's Postinjury Adjustment. Clinical neuropsychological evaluation frequently identifies areas of brain-related deficit that have not been recognized in the course of other evaluations. A person with a closed head injury sustained in an automobile accident or a fall, for example, may have significant and even disabling areas of intellectual and cognitive deficit that are not identified by conventional intelligence testing or by medical evaluation (Reitan & Wolfson, 1986, 1988). In such cases, the client is often told that he or she is fortunate that the head injury caused no impairment, and that it should be possible to return to the full range of preinjury activities. It can be extremely traumatic emotionally for such a person to discover later the presence of disabling deficits through on-the-job and other real-life experiences, principally because the individual does not have the knowledge to realistically describe or document the types, severity, or extent of the deficits that he or she knows are present. However, when a brain-impaired individual is assessed with a comprehensive battery of neuropsychological tests, a much more realistic approach, with supportive counseling, can be adopted prior to undertaking challenging or demanding activities.

Evaluations of Loss in Cases Involving Litigation. Clinical neuropsychological assessment is rapidly assuming increased importance in cases involving litigation because of the significance of higher-level brain functions and the fact that an objective, detailed evaluation can be performed. This is not to imply that two clinical neuropsychologists who each examine the same individual routinely reach the same conclusions, but only that in every case the conclusions, even when conflicting, are based upon each clinician's interpretation of the standard and objective examining procedures utilized.

Evaluations of the Effects of Treatment. A great number of treatment procedures have been and continue to be developed that may improve impaired brain functions. These procedures range from surgical interventions to cognitive retraining performed by clinical neuropsychologists. Objective neuropsychological testing has great value in evaluating the possible beneficial effects of various forms of treatment (Reitan & Wolfson, 1992b).

Retraining of Higher-Level Brain Functions. Clinical neuropsychological evaluation allows the identification of an individual's higher-level strengths and limitations in accordance with the biological condition of the brain. Once the cognitive abilities requiring remediation have been identified by a comprehensive neuropsychological assessment, the next step is retraining the areas of impairment. Deficits caused by brain damage include impairment of (1) attention and concentration; (2) memory; (3) language and related symbolic abilities; (4) spatial and temporal relationships; and (5) abstraction, reasoning, logical analysis, and planning abilities. Some progress has been made in clinical neuropsychology in retraining these various abilities in accordance with the needs of the individual subject (Reitan & Sena, 1983; Sena, 1985, 1986; Sena & Sena, 1986).

GENERAL METHODOLOGY

The basic methodology of clinical neuropsychology has been oriented toward establishing relationships between objectively demonstrable instances of cerebral pathology and particular intellectual and cognitive measurements. Implementation of this approach has required evaluation and comparison of persons with specified brain lesions (or diseases) as compared with individuals having biologically normal brains. Obviously, this approach has required close collaboration with neurologists, neurological surgeons, and neuropathologists, particularly in the initial validation of brain-behavior correlates represented by various individual tests.

Although great progress has been made, there has been a tendency among researchers to study single or limited numbers of tests and to relate the findings to neurological criteria, rather than studying an extensive number of tests, which presumably would evaluate the full range of human brain-based abilities, in individual subjects. The resulting focus on tests, rather than persons, has had a restricting influence on the development of neuropsychological assessment because, quite obviously, clinical evaluation must focus on the comparative strengths and weaknesses of the brain of the individual being examined.

As the field of clinical neuropsychology has grown, there has also been an increasing desire to explore a broadened range of neuropsychological functions, even though the tests used for such additional measurements sometimes have not been thoroughly evaluated and validated in terms of their relationships to known information about cerebral disease or damage. This particular problem has a tendency to undercut the validity of the field itself, because the hybrid word *neuropsychology* requires a relationship between behavioral manifestations and the biological condition of the brain.

The emphasis on tests rather than individual human beings has also stemmed from a failure to realize fully the differences between experimental and clinical human neuropsychology. Experimental neuropsychology focuses on establishing generalizations based on comparisons of groups (e.g., how a group of patients who have suffered a stroke in the left hemisphere of the brain differs behaviorally from a group of patients who have suffered a stroke in the right hemisphere), whereas clinical neuropsychology focuses on evaluation of the individual. It is not sufficient to take results based on group comparisons and, uncritically and without verification, use the research results as a basis for definitive conclusions about the individual. Clinical neuropsychological evaluation requires repeated determination of the validity of the test results as a basis for drawing conclusions about a person, as compared to reference to statistically significant differences in comparisons of groups (Reitan & Wolfson, 1986, 1993).

NEUROPSYCHOLOGICAL TESTS

In addition to being statistically standardized, neuropsychological tests must be demonstrated to be related to the condition of the brain. In this sense, they differ from psychological tests used in many other areas of psychology.

A great number of neuropsychological tests have been identified. Lezak (1983) and Spreen and Strauss (1991) describe many hundreds of tests that are used in the field. These tests vary greatly with respect to the evidence that relates them to either general or more specific aspects of brain function.

In an attempt to provide a comprehensive evaluation of neuropsychological functions, batteries of tests have been developed. Batteries intended to cover the full range of neuropsychological functions are represented by the Halstead-Reitan Neuropsychological Test Battery and the Luria-Nebraska Neuropsychological Battery. Other batteries, such as the Wechsler Memory Scale–Revised, have been developed to evaluate specific areas of neuropsychological function. Although psychologists differ greatly in their choice of tests used for neuropsychological evaluation, there is general agreement that higher-level aspects of brain function are sufficiently diversified and complex to require a number of tests for a comprehensive clinical evaluation rather than only a single test. There is no "standard neuropsychological examination," and the tests used in a battery by one neuropsychologist may differ almost entirely from those used by another neuropsychologist. Obviously, this is one of the factors that gives rise to inconsistencies and conflicts in the conclusions reached by different neuropsychologists. Most neuropsychologists, however, regardless of their choice of tests, attempt to evaluate the same neurocognitive functions: memory and learning, attention and concentration, verbal and other communication skills, visual-spatial and temporal-sequential abilities, and abstraction and flexibility in thought processes.

RELATION BETWEEN NEUROPSYCHOLOGICAL TESTS AND TRADITIONAL INTELLIGENCE TESTS

Theoretical and Methodological Considerations. Theories relating intellectual and cognitive functions to the brain have been proposed for more than a century (Reitan & Wolfson, 1992a). There has been relatively little of this type of theorizing in recent years; the best-known theories have been proposed by Halstead (1947), Hebb (1949), and Luria (1966, 1973). Halstead's theory of biological intelligence was the only one of these theories supported by psychological tests that, like traditional intelligence tests, were standardized in their administration and scoring.

Prior to the work of Halstead and Hebb, relatively few neuropsychological functions, except for speech and language skills, had been related to the brain (Weisenberg & McBride, 1935). In 1929, Lashley stated, "The whole theory of learning and intelligence is in confusion. We know at present nothing of the organic basis of these functions and little enough of either the variety or uniformities of their expression in behavior."

Halstead's approach was initially based upon naturalistic observations of persons with cerebral lesions whose locations in the brain were known. When he observed impaired behavior, he returned to his laboratory and attempted to devise a standardized testing procedure that would be appropriate for measuring the impairment. After having developed a number of tests in this manner, his battery was administered to persons with known brain lesions and compared with results obtained by persons having neurologically normal brain functions. He submitted results on thirteen of these tests to a statistical technique called factor analysis and derived four factors that he felt represented (1) the general background and knowledge developed by the individual during the course of his or her life (which he related to traditional measurements of intelligence); (2) an abstraction, or reasoning, factor that he felt represented the basic intellectual function of the brain; (3) a factor representing the intellectual power of the individual, or the ability to mobilize and apply the functions necessary for productive intelligent behavior; and (4) a factor representing input of information to the brain and expression of responses directed by the brain.

Although Hebb (1949) developed a theoretical description of brain functions as related to behavior, he postulated that in practice there were two types of intelligence. He described Type A as "the innate potential, the capacity for development, a fully innate property that amounts to the possession of a good brain and a good neurometabolism." Hebb felt that this type of intelligence was particularly susceptible to impairment caused by brain lesions occurring early in life. Type B intelligence represented "the functioning of a brain in which development has gone on, determining an average level of performance or comprehension by the partly grown or mature person." Hebb felt that this type of intelligence, which he tended to equate with traditional measures of intelligence, was resistant to impairment caused by cerebral lesions unless the damage compromised areas of the cortex devoted to speech and language abilities. His conclusions, as related to traditional tests, were based mainly on his observation that adult subjects, who had developed normally, sometimes had remarkably high IQ values as produced by the Stanford-Binet Intelligence Scale, even after extensive removals of cerebral tissue. Halstead's position was that the Stanford-Binet Intelligence Test did not represent measurement of the full range of intellectual functions dependent upon the brain, and that this was the reason that high IQ values could emerge even in persons in whom significant portions of their brains had been surgically removed.

Luria, like Hebb, broadened the concept of intelligence and placed it in a context of brain-behavior relationships (Luria, 1973). He proposed that the brain had an arousal system that permitted alertness to incoming information, initial receptor areas for registration of incoming information, additional areas for integration and analysis of incoming information, and a mechanism for organization and expression of responses.

It should be noted explicitly that neuropsychological conceptions, rather than excluding conventional views of intelligence, have broadened the behavioral model of intelligence. Factor analyses of the eleven subtests that comprise the Wechsler Scale, for example, have customarily shown that these eleven subtests measure primarily a verbal factor and a performance factor, along with a third factor believed to represent alertness and efficiency in performance. In terms of content, however, the Wechsler Scales appear principally to measure the specialized (left brain and right brain) functions of the cerebrum. Many research results (see Matarazzo [1972] for further discussion) as well as extensive clinical experience have shown that subtests of the Wechsler Adult Intelligence Scale (WAIS) supplement and complement neuropsychological tests in providing a comprehensive assessment of intellectual and cognitive abilities dependent upon the brain.

Empirical Findings. It has been known for many years that there is a statistically significant relationship between the tests included in the Wechsler-Bellevue Scale and its later revisions (traditional intelligence) and tests in the Halstead-Reitan Battery (neuropsychological measures). Reitan (1956) computed intercorrelations between scores on subtests of the Wechsler-Bellevue and those on the Halstead-Reitan Neuropsychological Test Battery for both normal and brain-damaged groups and found a strong overlap between the two sets of measures. Leckliter and Matarazzo (1989) have recently reviewed evidence that relates neuropsychological measurements to age, education, gender (in certain respects), IQ, and even personal behavioral characteristics, such as alcohol abuse. The complementary aspects of traditional and neuropsychological evaluations of intelligence are so pronounced that in clinical evaluation of the individual subject both procedures are nearly always used.

Reitan and Wolfson (1992b) recently reported results that further explicate relationships between Wechsler Scale results and selected variables from the Halstead-Reitan Neuropsychological Test Battery. This study was specifically designed to determine whether traditional intelligence measures were more sensitive to academic achievement and whether biological measures of cognition were more closely correlated to the organic status of the brain. The dependent variables were the Wechsler Verbal IQ, Performance IQ, and

Full Scale IQ and the Halstead-Reitan Impairment Index and Category Test score. For determining the comparative sensitivity to educational achievement (number of grades completed in school) or cerebral damage (as determined by a complete and independent neurological evaluation), the same method that had been employed by Reitan (1959) was used (a method based on the degree of quantitative separation of matched pairs of brain-damaged and control subjects).

The results of that study supported the following conclusions. (1) The Impairment Index was more sensitive to cerebral damage than any of the three Wechsler IQ measures at highly significant levels ($p < .001$ in each comparison). (2) The Category Test error score was significantly more sensitive to cerebral damage than any of the three Wechsler Scale measures ($p < .001$ for Verbal IQ, and $p < .05$ for Performance IQ and for Full Scale IQ). (3) The Impairment Index was somewhat more sensitive to cerebral damage than the Category Test in absolute terms, effecting a greater quantitative degree of separation between brain-damaged and control pairs in 60 percent of the cases but this difference was not statistically significant.

The results suggest that if biological adequacy of brain functions is the preferred criterion for intelligence, the Impairment Index and the Category Test provide better measures. This finding is hardly surprising, considering that these tests were deliberately designed to evaluate brain damage, whereas the IQ measures were devised to reflect intelligence in a normal population.

Evaluation of the sensitivity of the dependent measures to educational achievement was based upon Pearson product-moment coefficients of correlation between test scores and the number of school grades completed. Both the brain-damaged and control subjects showed approximately equivalent relationships among the conventional intelligence measures (Verbal IQ, Performance IQ, and Full Scale IQ) and the neuropsychological tests (the Impairment Index and the Category Test score), a finding also reported earlier by Reitan (1956). The correlation coefficients were consistently significant statistically. Correlations of the IQ measures with educational achievement were also significant and comparable for the two groups, except for low and nonsignificant correlations in the brain-dam-

aged group between the Impairment Index and the number of grades completed and between the Category Test score and the number of school grades completed.

In this latter instance, it appeared that brain damage was such an overriding factor in determining both the Impairment Index and the Category Test score that educational level had little influence on the variance. Among the controls, the magnitude of the coefficients between the Impairment Index and educational level and between the Category Test score and educational level was not statistically different from the comparable coefficients representing the IQ values, even though the absolute magnitude of coefficients was somewhat higher for the IQ variables than the educational level. These results suggest that educational achievement (number of years of school completed) loses its significance nearly entirely in affecting the brain-sensitive measures among persons who have sustained brain damage. Among non-brain-damaged control subjects, however, there was no significant difference among either correlations of educational achievement with Verbal, Performance, and Full Scale IQ or correlations of educational achievement with the brain-sensitive measures (the Impairment Index and Category Test score).

These results identify the special sensitivity to cerebral damage of neuropsychological measures compared with IQ measures and an equivalent level of sensitivity of the two sets of measures to academic achievement. A more general interpretation of the findings would note that although there is a great deal of overlap between traditional intelligence tests and neuropsychological measures, the conventional approach pioneered by Binet and later Wechsler toward evaluation of intellectual and cognitive functions is considerably broadened by using methods, such as the Halstead-Reitan Neuropsychological Test Battery, that were originally designed to measure brain-behavior relationships.

BIBLIOGRAPHY

HALSTEAD, W. C. (1947). *Brain and intelligence: A quantitative study of the frontal lobes.* Chicago: University of Chicago Press.

HEBB, D. O. (1949). *The organization of behavior: A neuropsychological theory.* New York: Wiley.

LASHLEY, K. S. (1929). *Brain mechanisms and intelligence.* Chicago: University of Chicago Press.

LECKLITER, I. N., & MATARAZZO, J. D. (1989). The influence of age, education, IQ, gender, and alcohol abuse on Halstead-Reitan Neuropsychological Test Battery performance. *Journal of Clinical Psychology, 45,* 484–512.

LEZAK, M. D. (1983). *Neuropsychological assessment* (2nd ed.). New York: Oxford University Press.

LURIA, A. R. (1966). *Higher cortical functions in man.* New York: Basic Books.

LURIA, A. R. (1973). The frontal lobes and the regulation of behavior. In K. H. Pribram & A. R. Luria (Eds.), *Psychophysiology of the frontal lobes.* New York: Academic Press.

MATARAZZO, J. D. (1972). *Wechsler's measurement and appraisal of adult intelligence.* Baltimore: Williams & Wilkins.

MATARAZZO, J. D. (1990). Psychological assessment versus psychological testing. Validation from Binet to the school, clinic, and courtroom. *American Psychologist, 45,* 999–1017.

REITAN, R. M. (1956). Investigation of relationships between "psychometric" and "biological" intelligence. *Journal of Nervous and Mental Disease, 123,* 536–541.

REITAN, R. M. (1959). The comparative effects of brain damage on the Halstead Impairment Index and the Wechsler-Bellevue Scale. *Journal of Clinical Psychology, 15,* 281–285.

REITAN, R. M., & SENA, D. A. (1983, August). *The efficacy of the REHABIT technique in remediation of brain-injured people.* Paper presented at the meeting of the American Psychological Association, Anaheim, CA.

REITAN, R. M., & WOLFSON, D. (1986). *Traumatic brain injury: Vol. 1. Pathophysiology and neuropsychological evaluation.* Tucson, AZ: Neuropsychology Press.

REITAN, R. M., & WOLFSON, D. (1988). *Traumatic brain injury: Vol. 2. Recovery and rehabilitation.* Tucson, AZ: Neuropsychology Press.

REITAN, R. M., & WOLFSON, D. (1992a). *Neuroanatomy and neuropathology: A clinical guide for neuropsychologists* (2nd ed.). Tucson, AZ: Neuropsychology Press.

REITAN, R. M., & WOLFSON, D. (1992b). Conventional intelligence measurements and neuropsychological concepts of adaptive abilities. *Journal of Clinical Psychology, 48,* 521–529.

REITAN, R. M., & WOLFSON, D. (1993). *The Halstead-Reitan Neuropsychological Test Battery: Theory and clinical interpretation* (2nd ed.). Tucson, AZ: Neuropsychology Press.

SENA, D. A. (1985). The effectiveness of cognitive retraining for brain-impaired individuals. *International Journal of Clinical Neuropsychology, 7,* 62.

SENA, D. A. (1986). The effectiveness of cognitive rehabilitation for brain-impaired patients. *Journal of Clinical and Experimental Neuropsychology, 8,* 142.

SENA, H. M., & SENA, D. A. (1986). A comparison of subject characteristics between treatment and nontreatment patients. *Archives of Clinical Neuropsychology, 1,* 74.

SPREEN, O., & STRAUSS, E. (1991). *A compendium of neuropsychological tests.* New York: Oxford University Press.

WEISENBURG, T. H., & MCBRIDE, K. E. (1935). *Aphasia.* New York: Commonwealth Fund.

RALPH M. REITAN
DEBORAH WOLFSON

NORMAL DISTRIBUTION *See* STATISTICAL CONCEPTS.

NORMS The term *raw score* for a test usually refers to the number of questions answered correctly. *Norm tables* provide the examiner with information to convert the raw score into one or more *derived scores* that provide a more meaningful basis for describing performance on a test. Those derived scores used most commonly with intelligence tests are the mental age, percentile rank, and standard score (one form of which is the intelligence quotient or IQ).

Important decisions about individuals often derive from normed scores from intelligence tests; consequently, test developers are expected to carefully gather the data from which norms are computed. Typically, these data come from a sample of people representative of a population and the age group(s) that the test serves. The professional user of an intelligence test should be familiar with both the quality of the norming procedure underlying the chosen test's derived scores and the interpretation of those scores.

PURPOSE OF NORMS

Norms are critical for most applications of intelligence tests, especially when used by professionals to evaluate clients. Without norms, the user would not know whether a particular raw score represents a good or a poor level of performance. With norms, the user has information about other people's performance. An exception to the need for norms is the use of intelligence tests in some research studies. For this application, raw scores or some mathematical transformation of them, such as Rasch ability measures (see LATENT TRAIT THEORY) are most useful.

Norming is one aspect of a broader test development process called STANDARDIZATION. Two other important aspects of standardization include specifying both exact instructions for administering the test and criteria for scoring the responses. Standardization promotes constancy from one test administration to another by either the same or different examiners.

Equating also can be done to improve the basis for the interpretation of test scores. Equating is the process by which scores from one test are put on the metric of another, frequently for the purpose of maintaining continuity of score meaning year after year. There are two traditional methods. The first is applicable if the shapes of the two distributions are identical. It is called linear equating as the z-score equivalents are set equal in each distribution and the raw scores equal to the z-scores are thus equated. The second method is used when the distributional shapes vary and the area transform of percentiles is applied to each distribution. Raw scores with identical percentile ranks are thus set equal. Angoff (1971) has provided a complete and lucid description of traditional equating. With the advent of methods based on latent trait theory, many test developers now calibrate collections of items called *banks*. Different subsets of items are selected from a bank to provide equivalent forms of the same test.

TYPES OF DERIVED SCORES

Derived scores are computed from data gathered during the norming phase of standardization. At the option of the test developer, three classes of derived scores are available for inclusion into a test's interpretation plan:

1. Scores that indicate level of development. Examples include the age equivalent (AE), sometimes called *mental age* (MA), and the *grade equivalent* (GE). These scores indicate the age or grade at which a given raw score (or some transformation) was the average score obtained in the norming sample. For example, if the norm tables for a test indicate that a raw score of 14 has an MA of 6–3 (the convention for designating 6 years, 3 months of age), the user knows that 14 was the average raw score for the subjects with an age of 6 years and 3 months in the norming sample. Similarly, if the norm tables indicate that the GE is 9.2 (the convention for writing ninth grade, second month) for a raw score of 40, this indicates that 40 was the average score for the norming sample subjects who were in the second month of the ninth grade.

2. Scores that indicate level of proficiency. Examples include the ratio IQ and the relative proficiency index (RPI). These scores derive from the percent of success demonstrated by the subject on the set of calibrated items comprising the intelligence test. The ratio IQ results from dividing the examinee's MA by the chronological age (CA) and multiplying that quotient by 100 (i.e., $IQ = MA/CA \times 100$). If an examinee has a ratio IQ of 120, this score implies that the person's MA has developed to 120 percent of the CA. The ratio IQ is a score provided by certain older intelligence tests, including early editions of the Stanford-Binet. The ratio IQ has fallen out of general use in the United States and has been replaced by the deviation IQ (described in the next class of scores).

RPI scores provide two bits of information. For example, an RPI of 48/90 indicates that the person can perform with 48 percent success mental tasks that are performed with 90 percent success by average persons of the same age or grade in the norming sample. The RPI and its variants are used in at least one battery of intelligence tests (Woodcock & Johnson, 1989).

3. Scores that indicate standing among peers. Examples include the percentile rank (PR) and the standard score (or deviation IQ). A PR indicates the percent in the norming sample, at the examinee's age or grade level, who received the same or a lower raw score. For example, a PR of 30 means that 30 percent of the norming sample at the examinee's age or grade level received the same raw score or lower.

All intelligence batteries provide standard scores (SS), but referring to these scores as IQs has fallen into disfavor among some professionals: Today many intelligence batteries use some different label for these scores. Standard scores are not straightforward in their interpretation and are usually explained in terms of their corresponding PRs to laypersons. Table 1 presents several examples of standard scores with their corresponding PRs. Most standard score scales set the mean or median (indexes of average score) at 100 and the standard deviation (an index of score spread) at 15 or 16.

Notice that the scores from each of the three classes of norms described above provide a different kind of information about the examinee's test performance and are not interchangeable (e.g., AE and PR). Scores from within each class report the same kind of information, though on a different metric, and can be interchanged (e.g., AE and GE).

PREPARATION OF NORMS

The major steps in the preparation of norms include developing the sampling plan, gathering the norming data, and preparing tables of derived scores from the norming data. In developing the sampling plan, decisions are made regarding the size of the sample and its composition. The larger the sample, the smaller will be the sampling error associated with the computed scores. Typical norming samples for individually administered intelligence batteries range in size from about 2,000 to 6,000 subjects across the age range of intended use.

TABLE 1
Example standard scores (Mean = 100, SD = 15) and corresponding percentile ranks

Standard Score	Percentile Rank
133 and above	99
119	90
110	75
100	50
90	25
81	10
67 and below	1

An even more important consideration than size in the sampling plan is the composition of the sample. The goal of the sampling plan for most intelligence tests is to obtain, in miniature, a replication of the general population. That population can be defined, for example, as all English-speaking persons living in the United States and distributed according to the 1990 census data. Once such a general population is identified, the next task, often complex and difficult, is to sample the population representatively. The aim in obtaining a national norm sample is to select a subsample at each age or grade level that is representative of the population on such variables as sex, race, Hispanic origin, geographic location, size of community, occupation, family socioeconomic characteristics, and community socioeconomic characteristics.

The computation of derived scores from the norming data may proceed in various ways depending in part on the particular computer programs used by a test developer. The following description presents a simplified version of the process, as if it were largely being completed by hand. The first step is the computation of developmental level derived scores (AEs and GEs). The second step describes computation of proficiency level scores (RPIs), and the third step describes computing peer standing scores (PRs and SSs).

Figure 1 illustrates the process of computing age (or grade) equivalent scores. The norming data are ordered by age, and averages (usually medians) are computed for successive subsets of the data. The obtained medians are plotted as coordinates on the age and raw score scales of Figure 1. The next step is to draw a smoothed curve through the plotted medians as shown in Figure 1. The broken lines in Figure 1 illustrate how an age equivalent, corresponding to each raw score, can be read from the curve. The broken line proceeding from a raw score of 14 to the smoothed curve and then down to 6–3 (6 years and 3 months) on the age scale illustrates this process. This process is repeated until the corresponding AE is found for each possible raw score.

Figure 2 illustrates the further steps required to compute the other types of derived scores. The short hatched vertical lines above ages 7, 8, and 9 represent the distribution of scores at each of three ages in the norming sample. Notice how the distributions of scores from one age to another overlap. If the ability

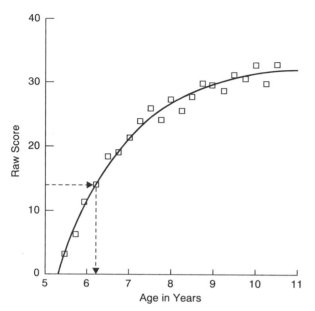

Figure 1

First steps in the computation of norms. Averages for data at several age levels are plotted and a smoothed curve drawn through the points. An example age equivalent of 6–3 is obtained for a raw score of 14.

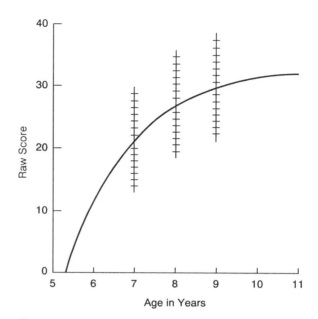

Figure 2

Further steps in the computation of norms. The hatched vertical lines illustrate the distribution of scores at each of three ages in the norming sample.

scale is represented by a set of calibrated measures, perhaps generated by a Rasch program, then distances along the vertical scale have probability of success interpretations relative to the average person at a given age. It is this information that is used to generate scores such as the RPI.

If a proportional frequency distribution (PR) is calculated at each age, then the distributions of scores represented above each age in Figure 2 represent percentiles. Standard scores are determined in two general ways—by linear transformation or by area (nonlinear) transformation. The linear transformation procedure produces standard scores based on the number of standard deviation units that a score is away from the mean score for the distribution. Users of this method sometimes assume that the underlying distribution of ability is at least symmetrical, if not normal. In any case, the distribution of standard scores will have the same shape as the distribution of original raw scores.

The area or nonlinear transformation approach, sometimes called *normalizing,* assigns equivalent standard scores to computed percentile positions in the

distribution of raw scores. The standard score paired with any given percentile is based on the distance, in standard deviation units from the mean, that a given percent of the area under a normal curve falls. This procedure makes no assumptions about the underlying distribution of ability (such as normality), but the result is a normal distribution of standard scores. The area transformation procedure is the most commonly used approach to the calculation of standard scores today.

SOURCES OF BIAS IN NORMS

An important assumption underlying the selection of the norming sample is that it is a miniature replication of the desired reference population. Any bias in the norming data will exert its influence in the opposite direction when the calculated norms are later used in the field. Two examples follow:

1. If the average ability in the norming sample is higher than it is in the population (e.g., by gathering data with too many subjects drawn from high socioeconomic communities), when the calculated

norms are used in practice, all types of derived scores will be too low.

2. If the spread of ability in the norming sample is less than in the population (e.g., by failing to include low- and high-ability subjects proportional to their presence in the population), when the calculated norms are used in practice, high-ability subjects will receive PRs or SSs that are inordinately high and low-ability subjects will receive PRs and SSs that are inordinately low.

CONSIDERATIONS IN THE USE OF NORMS

The norms for an intelligence test are relevant to the extent that they are based on a sample of subjects to which the examinee's performance can be compared meaningfully. Generally, intelligence test results are interpreted using national norms based on a cross-section of the general U.S. population. In some cases, local norms based on data from a particular community or special norms for some subgroup of the population (e.g., southwest American Indians or entering college freshmen) are desirable. Norms with limited application are generally not available because the same requirements exist for the quality of a limited-use norming sample as are required for general population samples. Thus, the expense may be prohibitive. Another reason that most users of intelligence tests prefer general norms rather than limited norms is that the changing nature and mobility of population segments make local and special group norms less useful over time. On the whole, general population characteristics are more stable and change slowly.

With some tests, the user must decide whether to use age-based or grade-based norms, if both come with a test. Age-based norms provide derived scores that are based on subjects in the norming sample at the same age as the examinee. Grade-based norms provide derived scores that are based on subjects in the norming sample who are at the same grade level as the examinee.

Examiners often wish to compare derived scores between tests. Scores from different tests can be compared directly if the tests have been conormed or properly equated. Sometimes, two tests have been conormed, that is, administered at the same time to the same subjects in the norming sample. In this case, no problem exists in comparing scores from the two tests for the same examinee. Another procedure is to conduct an equating study in which both tests are administered to a sample of subjects. The scale of scores for one test can then be adjusted to match the scale of scores on the second test. If different tests have not been conormed or equated, hidden but significant differences in the two sets of derived scores may be present. An incorrect assumption is that because two different tests have yielded the same derived score (say an IQ of 117), the two scores have the same meaning.

A similar problem exists in comparing scores from an earlier version of a test with scores from a revision. Even if the norms were gathered in a similar way for both versions, the derived scores from the newer tests will tend to be lower than those from the earlier test (see IQ GAINS OVER TIME). This effect seems to be on the order of about one-third standard score point increase in population ability each year. Because the ability of the population is higher at the time of the later test, an examinee's performance on the later test will produce lower derived scores than the same level of performance would produce on the older test.

Another consideration in the use of norms relates to the appropriateness of using a particular test with an examinee. This consideration is particularly crucial if an examinee whose native language is not English takes an English language intelligence test. The subject may receive lower scores because of language problems. Users of intelligence tests must be sensitive to such conditions in the evaluation of the examinee's performance on the test.

CONCLUSIONS

The norms of an intelligence test inform the examiner about the meaning of an examinee's performance on the test. This process is accomplished, through norming, by providing derived scores, which may be used instead of the raw scores. Three classes of derived scores report different aspects about the test performance. Developmental level scores indicate the level of development reached by the examinee compared with subjects of different ages or grades in the norming sample. Proficiency level scores indicate the percent of success demonstrated by the subject compared with subjects of the same age or grade in the norming sample. Peer-standing scores report the examinee's relative standing among the subjects in the norming sample who are at the same age or grade.

The quality of the norms provided with a test is a function of the norming sample. Test developers carefully select a sample of subjects, usually representing a cross-section of the U.S. general population, according to several criteria comprising the sampling plan. If the sampling plan or its realization is biased, then the scores used in practice will be in error opposite to the direction of bias. The norms for a test are but a tool for the professional user. The examiner should know about the quality of that tool and about its appropriate use.

(*See also:* PSYCHOMETRIC THEORIES OF INTELLIGENCE.)

BIBLIOGRAPHY

ANASTASI, A. (1987). *Psychological testing* (6th ed.). New York: Macmillan.

ANGOFF, W. H. (1984). *Scales, norms, and equivalent scores.* Princeton, NJ: Educational Testing Service. (Reprint of chapter in R. L. Thorndike (Ed.), *Educational measurement* (2nd ed.). Washington, DC: American Council on Education, 1971.)

CRONBACH, L. J. (1984). *Essentials of psychological testing.* New York: Harper & Row.

PETERSEN, N. S., KOLEN, M. J., & HOOVER, H. D. (1989). Scaling, norming, and equating. In R. L. Lynn (Ed.), *Educational measurement* (3rd ed.). New York: Macmillan.

WOODCOCK, R. W., & JOHNSON, M. B. (1989). *Woodcock–Johnson Tests of Cognitive Ability, Revised.* Chicago: Riverside.

RICHARD W. WOODCOCK

NUTRITION It is well known that children growing up in poverty anywhere in the world face a variety of adverse socioeconomic and environmental conditions that may have a negative effect on their health and physical growth, as well as their mental development and school performance. These conditions may include limited food availability; poor health care, housing, and sanitation; malnutrition and disease; inadequate child care; limited educational and learning opportunities; and family stress. It has been recognized for a long time that children growing up under such environmental circumstances tend to score lower on tests of intellectual competence, and to do less well in school, than children from more favorable socioeconomic backgrounds (Pollitt, 1989).

Beginning in the 1960s, investigators from a variety of disciplines began to ask whether the condition of malnutrition itself, which could have a significant limiting effect on physical growth and brain size, might be a direct cause of delayed intellectual development, and possibly of permanent mental retardation as well. Another topic of growing research interest is whether iron deficiency, a fairly widespread specific nutritional deficiency in children, has a negative effect on brain function and intellectual competence. Finally, there is the question of whether the intelligence quotient (IQ) levels of adequately nourished children can be raised by administration of vitamin and mineral supplements above minimum daily requirements (MDRs), the normally recommended levels.

PROTEIN-ENERGY MALNUTRITION

The most common nutritional problem in poor populations worldwide is protein-calorie, or protein-energy, malnutrition (PEM), involving reduced intake of both protein and calories. The majority of such children are characterized as having "mild-to-moderate" undernutrition, as indicated by their height, weight, and/or head circumference being below average for their age. Less common is severe, or "clinical," malnutrition, which may take the form of "marasmus" (early, chronic, and severe deficiency in protein and calories) or "kwashiorkor" (acute protein deficiency usually appearing in the second year of life). Children with clinical malnutrition are typically quite ill and require hospitalization for treatment and remediation (McLaren, 1984).

Since the late 1960s, there have been many studies reporting an association between PEM and delayed intellectual development in children. These included reports of significantly reduced IQ levels and school performance in poor children with a history of early clinical malnutrition, as well as children assumed to have experienced chronic, mild-to-moderate undernutrition as judged by their relatively short stature. There have also been reports of reduced brain size and number of brain cells, as well as impaired learning in animals who had been experimentally malnourished early in life.

Based on these findings, beginning in the 1970s many scientists as well as policymakers concluded, rather prematurely, that early malnutrition was a direct cause of impaired intellectual development in children, including permanent mental retardation, because of its adverse effect on brain growth. The complementary view was that simply improving the dietary intake of low-income children at risk of chronic malnutrition should produce a significant enhancement of their cognitive development (see Pollitt [1988] and Ricciuti [1991] for overall critical reviews).

These conclusions have been seriously challenged because of a number of significant methodological problems (Martorell, 1984), as well as inconsistent substantive findings. The main problem is that PEM usually occurs in environments characterized by a variety of adverse social, family, and economic conditions—any or all of which can have a negative effect on mental development. This makes it very difficult to separate out the independent effect of PEM, apart from these social and environmental factors. Moreover, the problem is not solved by simply comparing, for example, the intellectual development of malnourished and adequately nourished children from the same low-income neighborhoods. Growing evidence indicates that even among such poor families, substantial between-family differences exist in specific features of the home and family environments, which may influence the children's intellectual development and also put some children at greater health and nutritional risk than others (e.g., maternal attitudes and knowledge, utilization of available resources, quality of early child care provided, family stresses and supports, etc.) (Galler et al., 1983; Ricciuti, 1991). Considerable research effort is therefore being directed at more systematic analysis of the so-called microenvironment of the home, as it may influence both nutritional status and mental development.

With regard to the issue of permanent negative effects on intellectual development, including mental retardation, early conclusions were based on low IQ levels observed in school-age children who had severe PEM early in life. Following hospitalization, however, these children had returned to the same poor home environments that produced clinical PEM in the first place. Other studies, both animal and human, have shown that the effects of early and even severe PEM can be greatly reduced or eliminated by a favorable, developmentally supportive environment (Levitsky & Barnes, 1972; Winick, Meyer, & Harris, 1975).

Can the intellectual development of children at risk of PEM be significantly improved by supplementing their diets so as to improve their nutritional status? The research on this question as of the early 1990s is rather inconsistent and not very promising. Overall results of a number of major nutritional supplementation studies carried out primarily in Third World settings suggest that simply increasing protein and calorie intake in mildly to moderately malnourished children has relatively little meaningful impact on their cognitive development, although physical growth may be significantly enhanced (Joos & Pollitt, 1984; Ricciuti, 1991). Somewhat more promising effects have been reported in a study of low-income Jamaican toddlers receiving twenty-four months of nutritional supplementation, particularly when supplementation was combined with efforts to help mothers provide a more stimulating learning environment for their young children (Grantham-McGregor et al., 1991).

Another promising follow-up investigation reports findings suggestive of modest long-term intellectual benefits of early protein/calorie supplementation, particularly on reading, vocabulary, and general knowledge (Pollitt et al., 1993). The subjects of the study were rural Guatemalan adolescents and young adults who had been participants in a nutritional supplementation program prenatally and during the first few years of life. In summary, while some encouraging findings have been reported, the intellectual benefits of nutritional supplementation alone appear to be quite modest, particularly considering the scope and duration of the nutritional interventions employed.

Despite the various uncertainties just outlined, it is recognized that a fuller understanding of the role of PEM and its potential influence on mental development is a matter of significant scientific as well as public-health concern. Thus, considerable research attention is being addressed at the identification of possible mechanisms through which PEM, in association with various health and socioenvironmental factors, might adversely influence intellectual development, perhaps indirectly rather than directly. For example, there is some evidence indicating that young malnourished children, who tend to be less active and may be delayed in their gross motor development, may be responded to and cared for differently by their mothers or other caregivers; their early experiences may therefore be less developmentally stimulating than those of adequately nourished children, thus leading to lower levels of intellectual functioning (Ricciuti, 1991; Sigman et al., 1989; Wachs et al., 1992).

One of the more promising hypotheses about the potential role of PEM is that it may lower the child's curiosity, responsiveness to the environment, and motivation for learning (as might be true in the case of chronic illness as well). This view is based on observations of malnourished children, as well as studies suggesting that malnourished rats do not respond to or make maximum use of information available to them (Levitsky & Barnes, 1972). If this is the case, it helps explain why providing a developmentally stimulating environment for previously malnourished children (or rats) greatly reduces or eliminates the potential negative effects of malnutrition on cognitive development.

A closely related hypothesis is that PEM leads to a reduction in the metabolic energy required to sustain both physical growth and appropriate levels of activity in the growing child, thus limiting opportunities for learning and mental development (Schurch & Scrimshaw, 1990). This is a topic receiving a good bit of increased research attention in the late twentieth century, which should be quite fruitful, particularly if activity and energy expenditure can be shown to be related to the child's exploratory behavior, attention, and information processing, processes that support the development of intelligence. It would also be important to determine whether chronic illness or health problems, in the absence of significant PEM, also produce equivalent effects.

Finally, there is some evidence suggesting that within low-income populations, the potential negative effect of PEM on mental development may be centered primarily on those children growing up under the most unfavorable environmental circumstances, who may be particularly vulnerable (Ricciuti, 1981, 1991). This is also an issue being examined further by researchers, since such families may be in particular need of preventive intervention.

IRON DEFICIENCY

Children with PEM are also likely to have a deficiency in iron, one of the important specific nutrients required particularly by growing children. At the same time, iron deficiency may be fairly common among poor children without clear signs of PEM. Many studies have reported that iron-deficiency anemia (involving breathlessness, fatigue, and poor concentration) was associated with lower levels of intellectual functioning and school performance in young children (Evans, 1985). For the most part, these studies tended to involve the same methodological and interpretive problems discussed earlier in regard to PEM, so that it has been difficult to demonstrate clearly a direct and independent causal relationship between iron deficiency and impaired intellectual development.

Research on this topic has become considerably more sophisticated methodologically and more promising scientifically, however. It is now possible to measure children's iron status much more precisely, not only in terms of iron-deficiency anemia but also in regard to the status of iron stores at the cellular level in both anemic and nonanemic children. This is important because animal research suggests that low iron stores in brain cells may reduce the kind of neurotransmitter activity relevant for normal information processing and learning. One of the interesting questions to be addressed, therefore, is whether the apparent cognitive effects of iron deficiency in children are due mainly to anemia or to altered brain metabolism and neurotransmitter activity. Iron-deficiency research in the early 1990s has also been strengthened by the increasing use of randomized, double-blind experimental designs, involving measures of both iron status and various cognitive functions before and after the administration of systematic iron supplements.

Despite these significant methodological advances, the causal role of iron deficiency in producing impaired cognitive functioning is not yet fully understood. A number of studies of preschool and school-age children have reported some improvement in cognitive performance following iron treatment. Nevertheless, there is still a good bit of inconsistency in the findings concerning positive cognitive effects, even after iron status has been significantly improved by experimental supplementation. Also, there is little or no evidence thus far that iron deficiency without anemia is associated with lowered intellectual functioning. Thus, while there is considerable suggestive evidence that iron deficiency may directly influence cognitive functioning, this hypothesis requires further confirmation through replicated studies (see Lozoff [1988] or Pollitt & Metallinos-Kataras [1990] for overall review).

MINERAL-VITAMIN SUPPLEMENTS

In the late 1980s and early 1990s there was renewed interest, particularly in Great Britain, in the recurring controversial question of whether supplements of minerals and vitamins in amounts above those typically recommended can enhance brain functioning and raise intelligence levels in populations of schoolchildren not identified as undernourished.

Periodic critical reviews of the empirical research on this issue have generally raised serious doubts about the validity of this hypothesis (Kleijnen & Knipschild, 1991; Pruess, Fewell, & Bennet, 1989). A highly publicized report of raised nonverbal IQ levels in British schoolchildren through vitamin/mineral supplementation triggered a number of renewed studies of this issue, with quite inconsistent findings. One of these, an American study intended to clarify the issue (Schoenthaler et al., 1991), reported that schoolchildren supplemented for twelve weeks with 100 percent of recommended vitamin/mineral levels showed a 3.7 point advantage in nonverbal IQ gain in comparison with a placebo group. (No such advantage was shown by children receiving supplements representing 50% or 200% of recommended levels.) While this very small differential gain is unlikely to be functionally meaningful, the authors point out that some children showed a considerably larger gain, presumably because they were probably vitamin/mineral deficient to start with. This is simply an assumption, however, and the

role of other factors that might account for children's differential gains or losses (such as socioeconomic status) appears not to have been considered.

Advocates of the view that vitamin/mineral supplements above recommended levels will significantly improve intellectual competence in adequately nourished children appear to have paid little attention to the extensive literature on malnutrition and mental development relevant to this issue, particularly that on iron deficiency. This body of literature does not provide much support for the hypothesis. In the final analysis, however, the issue can only be settled empirically through replication of positive findings by neutral, independent investigators employing theories, research designs, and methodologies that take into account the substantial previous literature dealing with malnutrition and mental development.

In conclusion, the role of malnutrition can probably best be understood if it is viewed as one of several important health and environmental risk conditions capable of adversely influencing the physical growth, mental development, and school performance of children growing up in poor populations. Thus far there is little evidence that malnutrition as such has a significant direct, brain-mediated effect on intellectual development, apart from the influence of related social, environmental, and health conditions. Since malnutrition may reduce the child's responsiveness to the environment and opportunities to learn from it, however, it may be involved indirectly as a potentially negative influence on mental development. This is one of the issues being addressed by research in the 1990s, along with the further study of specific features of the home and child-care environments of low-income families, which may either reduce or heighten the risk of malnutrition, as well as the risk of suboptimal mental development in young children.

With regard to preventive programs, available research suggests that these should be directed toward improvement of the overall health, nutrition, and developmental environments of poor children, whether in their own homes, day-care centers, or schools. Preventive efforts of this sort are more likely to be effective in enhancing children's intellectual development than those that are narrowly focused primarily on nutritional or dietary supplementation.

BIBLIOGRAPHY

EVANS, D. I. (1985). Cerebral function in iron deficiency: A review. *Child care, health, and development, 11,* 105–112.

GALLER, J. R., RICCIUTI, H. N., CRAWFORD, M. A., & KUCHARSKI, L. T. (1983). The role of mother–infant interaction in nutritional disorders. In J. R. Galler (Ed.), *Human nutrition: A comprehensive treatise: Vol. 5. Nutrition and behavior* (pp. 269–304). New York: Plenum.

GRANTHAM-MCGREGOR, S. M., ET AL. (1991). Nutritional supplementation, psychosocial stimulation, and mental development of stunted children: The Jamaica study. *Lancet, 338,* 1–5.

JOOS, S. K., & POLLITT, E. (1984). Effects of supplementation on behavioral development in children up to 2 years: A comparison of four studies. In J. Brozek (Ed.), *Malnutrition and behavior: Critical assessment of key issues* (pp. 507–519). Lausanne: Nestlé Foundation.

KLEIJNEN, J., & KNIPSCHILD, P. (1991). Niacin and vitamin B6 in mental functioning: A review of controlled trials in humans. *Biological Psychiatry, 29,* 931–941.

LEVITSKY, D. A., & BARNES, R. H. (1972). Nutritional and environmental interactions in behavioral development of the rat: Long term effects. *Science, 176,* 68–71.

LOZOFF, B. (1988). Behavioral alterations in iron deficiency. *Advances in pediatrics, 35,* 331–360.

MARTORELL, R. (1984). Issues in design and data analysis. In J. Brozek (Ed.), *Malnutrition and behavior: Critical assessment of key issues* (pp. 556–575). Lausanne: Nestlé Foundation.

MCLAREN, D. S. (1984). Forms and degrees of energy-protein deficits. In J. Brozek (Ed.), *Malnutrition and behavior: Critical assessment of key issues.* (pp. 42–50). Lausanne: Nestlé Foundation.

POLLITT, E. (1988). A critical view of three decades of research on the effects of chronic energy malnutrition on behavioral development. In B. Schurch & N. Scrimshaw (Eds.), *Chronic energy deficiency: Consequences and related issues* (pp. 77–92). Lausanne: Nestlé Foundation.

POLLITT, E. (1989). *The impact of poor nutrition and disease on educational outcomes.* Geneva: UNESCO.

POLLITT, E., & METALLINOS-KATARAS, E. (1990). Iron deficiency and behavior: Constructs, methods, and validity of findings. In R. J. Wurtman & J. J. Wurtman (Eds.), *Nutrition and the Brain* (Vol. 8, pp. 101–146). New York: Raven Press.

POLLITT, E., GORMAN, K. S., ENGLE, P. L., MARTORELL, R., & RIVERA, J. (1993). Early supplementary feeding and cognition: Effect over two decades. *Monographs of the Society for Research in Child Development, 58,* 7.

PRUESS, J. B., FEWELL, R. R., & BENNET, F. C. (1989). Vitamin therapy and children with Down syndrome: A review of research. *Exceptional Children, 55,* 336–341.

RICCIUTI, H. N. (1981). Adverse environmental and nutritional influences on mental development: A perspective. *Journal of the American Dietetic Association, 79,* 115–120.

RICCIUTI, H. N. (1991). Malnutrition and cognitive development: Research-policy linkages and current research directions. In L. Okagaki & R. J. Sternberg (Eds.), *Directors of development: Influences on the development of children's thinking* (pp. 59–80). Hillsdale, NJ: Erlbaum.

SCHOENTHALER, S. J., AMOS, S. P., EYSENCK, H. J., PERITZ, E., & YUDKIN, J. (1991). Controlled trial of vitamin-mineral supplementation: Effects on intelligence and performance. *Personality and Individual Differences, 12,* 351–362.

SCHURCH, B., & SCRIMSHAW, N. S. (EDS.). (1990). *Activity, energy expenditure and energy requirements of infants and children.* Lausanne: Nestlé Foundation.

SIGMAN, M., NEUMANN, C., BAKSH, M., BWIBO, N., & MCDONALD, M. A. (1989). Relations between nutrition and development in Kenyan toddlers. *Journal of Pediatrics, 115,* 357–364.

WACHS, T. D., SIGMAN, M., BISHRY, Z., MOUSSA, W., JEROME, N., NEWMANN, C., BWIBO, N., & MCDONALD, M. A. (1992). Caregiver child interaction patterns in two cultures in relation to nutritional intake. *International Journal of Behavioral Development, 15,* 1–18.

WINICK, M., MEYER, K., & HARRIS, R. C. (1975). Malnutrition and environmental enrichment by adoption. *Science, 190,* 1173–1175.

HENRY N. RICCIUTI

OBJECT ASSEMBLY   *See* WAIS-R SUBSCALES.

OCCUPATIONS   Is intelligence related to occupation? Do people in various occupations differ in intelligence? Does intelligence matter in job performance? Is intelligence related to job satisfaction? What role does intelligence play in the choice of careers? What role should it play? (In what follows, "intelligence" is defined, narrowly, as the concept reflected in scores on psychological tests typically called measures of IQ, g, GENERAL INTELLIGENCE, or general mental ability.)

OCCUPATIONAL DIFFERENCES IN INTELLIGENCE

Research on the relation of intelligence to occupation dates back to World War I, when the "group" test of intelligence was invented. The first group intelligence test, the Army Alpha, was developed for the U.S. Army for use in screening and classifying World War I draftees. The Army Alpha data showed that if you grouped draftees according to their (self-reported) civilian occupations, the groups would form a rank order, or hierarchy, according to average intelligence-test scores for the groups. Professional groups always ranked at the top, white-collar and skilled-trades groups in the middle, and unskilled groups at the bottom (see ARMY ALPHA AND BETA TESTS OF INTELLIGENCE). The same finding was observed again in the data for World War II draftees, this time with the use of the Army General Classification Test (AGCT), an improved version of the Alpha. Table 1 illustrates this finding, using ten selected occupations. More recent data for the same occupations are also given in Table 1. These data come from the U.S. Employment Service and were obtained with the General Aptitude Test Battery (GATB, U.S. Department of Labor, 1970).

Table 1 shows that occupations do differ in the average intelligence score of their members, and that the rank order of occupations according to average score has remained essentially the same since the 1920s, with the professional groups at the top and the unskilled groups at the bottom. This finding of an occupational hierarchy in average intelligence score has been confirmed in several studies. One should note, however, that the differences in average score for many occupations is so small as to be of little practical significance. Only broad group differences (top group vs. middle group vs. bottom group) are meaningful.

Table 1 reveals another finding: the range of intelligence scores within any occupation is quite large. Also, the lower the occupation's average (mean) score, the larger the dispersion (standard deviation) of scores within the occupation, generally speaking. Furthermore, as Table 1 shows, there are persons with high intelligence scores in every occupation, including the

TABLE 1

Means and dispersions of intelligence test scores for ten selected occupational groups, by time period

Occupation[a]	World War I (1922)		World War II (1945)			Postwar (1970)	
	Mean	Range	Mean	Range	SD	Mean	SD
Engineer	161	110–183	127	100–151	11.7	130	12
Accountant	137	105–155	128	94–157	11.7	118	12
Teacher	122	97–148	123	76–155	12.8	114	13
Stenographer	103	73–124	121	66–151	12.5	106	12
Bookkeeper	101	77–127	120	70–157	13.1	110	16
Photographer	86	59–107	118	66–147	13.9	108	12
Stock Clerk	80	56–105	112	54–151	16.3	84	12
Machinist	63	40– 89	110	38–153	16.1	104	15
Carpenter	60	40– 84	102	42–147	19.5	99	15
Laborer	21	13– 47	96	26–145	20.1	92	18

NOTE: The test scores are standard scores, NOT IQs. Tests used: Army Alpha (World War I), Army General Classification Test (World War II), and General Aptitude Test Battery (Post–WWII).

[a]Reported civilian occupation.

SOURCE: Fryer (1922); Harrell & Harrell (1945); U.S. Department of Labor (1970).

lowest-ranked and least-skilled (see especially the 1945 data).

What better differentiates occupations than average scores is the minimum intelligence score needed to enter the occupation. Lower-ranked occupations require lower intelligence-score minimums than higher-ranked occupations. Lower-ranked occupations also require less training. We know that as training increases in complexity and length, higher levels of more kinds of ability are required, principally verbal and numerical abilities (which happen to be important components of general intelligence or general mental ability). Higher levels and more kinds of ability are needed, both to enter the training programs and to complete them. Such requirements create a "floor" for the intelligence scores of the people who eventually become members of the occupation. This explains why the rank order of occupations according to intelligence score corresponds closely to the rank order of occupations according to the amount of education or training required.

Occupations also differ in the kinds of specific abilities they require. Table 2 shows that the ranking of occupations according to specific ability can differ from the ranking according to general ability or intelligence. The data shown here are for the GATB's general ability (G), spatial ability (S), and hand–eye coordination ability (K). Table 2 shows how occupational groups are different, not only in general mental ability but in specific abilities as well. Based on findings such as these for a large number of occupations, the U.S. Department of Labor developed Occupational Aptitude Patterns (OAPs) for more than 2,500 occupations, applicable to almost 11,000 occupations (U.S. Department of Labor, 1979). These OAPs give the kinds of ability and the minimum level ("cutting score") for each ability that characterize satisfactory workers in each occupation. As an example, for engineer, the OAP is G115, N105, S110, meaning that general ability (G), numerical ability (N), and spatial ability (S) are the most characteristic abilities of engineers, with minimum scores required of 115, 105, and 110, respectively. By contrast, for accountant, the OAP is G110, V95, N105, Q100; for photographer, it is G100, S100, P85; and for laborer, K85, F80, M80 (where V is verbal ability, Q is clerical ability, P is perceptual ability, K is eye-hand coordination, F is finger dexterity, and M is manual dexterity).

TABLE 2
Rank order of ten selected occupational groups according to mean GATB score on general mental ability (G), spatial ability (S), and hand–eye coordination ability (K)

Rank	Occupation	M(G)	Occupation	M(S)	Occupation	M(K)
1	Engineer	130	Engineer	130	Teacher	114
2	Accountant	118	Photographer	114	Engineer	113
3	Teacher	114	Machinist	111	Stenographer	113
4	Bookkeeper	110	Teacher	109	Accountant	112
5	Photographer	108	Carpenter	109	Laborer	112
6	Stenographer	106	Stenographer	106	Bookkeeper	103
7	Machinist	104	Accountant	103	Photographer	102
8	Carpenter	99	Bookkeeper	103	Carpenter	95
9	Laborer	92	Laborer	94	Machinist	91
10	Stock Clerk	84	Stock Clerk	86	Stock Clerk	91

SOURCE: U.S. Department of Labor (1970).

INTELLIGENCE AND JOB PERFORMANCE

Are workers with higher intelligence scores better workers; do they perform their jobs better? This question has been the object of numerous studies known as VALIDITY studies. "Validity" is the ability of a test to predict a criterion such as job performance. Edwin Ghiselli compiled the validity data from studies published between 1919 and 1973 (Ghiselli, 1966, 1973). His conclusion was that, generally speaking, the workers with the higher intelligence scores were the better workers, on the basis of both supervisors' evaluations and measurements of the workers' productivity. Furthermore, the higher-scoring workers were easier to train and, when given the same training, were the better trained. And the better trained the workers, the better the job performance, as Hunter (1986) has noted—which explains why the workers with the higher intelligence scores tended to have better job-performance records.

Ghiselli also found that specific abilities did not contribute as much to predicting job performance as general mental ability. This finding has been reported by other investigators as well (see Gottfredson, 1986, for research summaries). Hunter (1986), in particular, reports data showing that specific abilities did not add much to general mental ability in the prediction of job performance. This finding, however, might be more a matter of method than of substance. Lubinski and Dawis (1992) show how, with the statistical methods currently used, a composite sum can be superior to the sum of composites, thereby explaining why a test of general mental ability (a composite sum) does "better" than combinations of tests of specific abilities (the sum of separate composites).

Research does show that at least three composites are useful for predicting job performance in a variety of occupations: a cognitive composite (what we have been calling intelligence or general mental ability), a spatial-perceptual composite, and a psychomotor composite. For more cognitively complex jobs (e.g., professional jobs such as accounting and teaching), the cognitive composite is best for predicting job performance. For the less cognitively complex and more physical jobs (e.g., factory work, such as assembling and machine tending), the psychomotor composite predicts job performance best. Finally, performance in certain jobs (e.g., crafts and trades, such as machinist and cabinetmaker) is best predicted by the cognitive composite and the spatial-perceptual composite used together. In other words, different *kinds* of ability are associated with the performance of different kinds of jobs.

Research in the U.S. Army (Project A, Campbell, 1990) shows an even more striking finding: Different kinds of ability are associated with the performance of different *aspects* of the same job. Job performance in

TABLE 3
Pattern of selected abilities used to predict different aspects of military job performance

Ability	Job Performance Aspect[a]				
	GSP	CTP	E&L	P D	PF/MB
Verbal	X	X	X	—	X
Quantitative	X	X	—	X	—
Numerical Speed/					
Accuracy	X	X	X	—	—
Spatial	X	X	X	—	—
Complex Perceptual					
Accuracy	X	X	—	—	—
Psychomotor	X	—	X	—	—
Simple Reaction					
Accuracy	—	—	—	—	X
Reaction Speed	—	—	—	—	X
Speed	—	X	X	—	X

NOTE: The full set of predictors for each job-performance aspect included more than the abilities listed here.
[a]GSP = General Soldiering Proficiency; CTP = Core Technical Proficiency; E&L = Effort and Leadership; PD = Personal Discipline; PF/MB = Physical Fitness/Military Bearing.
SOURCE: Wise, McHenry, & Campbell (1990), Table 4.

the military was found to consist of at least five aspects: general soldiering proficiency, core technical proficiency, effort and leadership, personal discipline, and physical fitness/military bearing. Table 3 shows how different aspects of the soldier's job require different kinds of ability.

INTELLIGENCE AND JOB SATISFACTION

Research shows that job satisfaction (whether reckoned as average level of satisfaction in the group or proportion of the group that is satisfied) is higher for occupations on the higher rungs of the occupational hierarchy, and lower for occupations on the lower rungs (U.S. Department of Labor, 1974). That is, the occupational job satisfaction hierarchy appears to be very similar to the occupational intelligence hierarchy. But the relation of intelligence to job satisfaction turns out to be rather indirect. When intelligence and job satisfaction are correlated *directly,* little or no correlation is generally found. Workers are more satisfied,

however, when their intelligence level is appropriate to the job. And then there are other factors: For instance, workers are more satisfied when their intelligence level is appropriate *and* using their abilities in their jobs is important to them. Generally speaking, workers are more satisfied when they obtain the rewards they seek from their jobs (the rewards that are important to them). If intelligence helps workers do a better job, *and* good job performance brings about the rewards, then one should find that intelligence is related to job satisfaction. If one of these conditions is missing—the rewards they get are not those important to them, job rewards are not tied to job performance, or intelligence does not contribute much to performing the job well—then intelligence will not be found related to job satisfaction (Cranny, Smith, & Stone, 1992).

INTELLIGENCE AND CAREER CHOICE

Intelligence (general mental ability) plays an important role in determining the occupational level that people attain later in adult life. This is the conclusion reached in the few long-term studies that have been conducted. One study (Austin & Hanisch, 1990) followed more than 13,000 of the original 10th-graders of Project TALENT for eleven years after their graduation from high school. General mental ability was found to be the strongest factor in accounting for occupational attainment. Specific abilities (mathematical ability, spatial ability) were the next most important factors. Interest was also a factor but was not even as important as gender and the family's socioeconomic status. These latter factors point to the operation of an *opportunity* factor. Thus, intelligence operates in conjunction with opportunity to influence later occupational attainment. Given opportunity, higher intelligence allows for more progress into higher education, which in turn is what is required for entry into higher-level occupations.

Should intelligence or general mental ability be accorded a role in the choice of careers? In current practice, career counselors accord it only a minor role, if any, preferring instead to focus on interest. The research evidence, however, points the other way: Interest (though important) should not play so dominant a role, and more attention should be accorded intelligence and specific abilities.

A Final Comment. We have seen that the data support an important role for intelligence or general mental ability in the pursuit of occupational success. Intelligence, however, is only the first factor. Specific abilities (such as spatial, mathematical, or psychomotor ability) can also make a difference, and so can interest (motivation) and personality traits (such as persistence). Much depends on what the occupation requires, that is, the occupation "helps" determine what factors are important. And much depends on the individual, as well. This means that with the degree of imprecision that characterizes measurement and prediction in this field, many individuals will be "false negatives"—those who, on the basis of their intelligence-test scores, are not expected to succeed but actually do—as well as "false positives"—those who are expected to succeed but do not. The individual can indeed make a difference.

(*See also:* PRACTICAL INTELLIGENCE; YERKES, ROBERT M.)

BIBLIOGRAPHY

AUSTIN, J. T., & HANISCH, K. A. (1990). Occupational attainment as a function of abilities and interests: A longitudinal analysis using Project TALENT data. *Journal of Applied Psychology, 75,* 77–86.

CAMPBELL, J. P. (1990). An overview of the Army Selection and Classification Project (Project A). *Personal Psychology, 43,* 231–239.

CRANNY, C. J., SMITH, P. C., & STONE, E. F. (1992). *Job satisfaction: How people feel about their jobs and how it affects their performance.* New York: Lexington Books.

FRYER, D. (1922). Occupational-intelligence standards. *School and Society, 16,* 273–277.

GHISELLI, E. E. (1966). *The validity of occupational aptitude tests.* New York: Wiley.

GHISELLI, E. E. (1973). The validity of aptitude tests in personnel selection. *Personnel Psychology, 26,* 461–477.

GOTTFREDSON, L. S. (ED.). (1986). The g factor in employment [Special issue]. *Journal of Vocational Behavior, 29,* 293–450.

HARRELL, T. W., & HARRELL, M. S. (1945). Army General Classification Test scores for civilian occupations. *Educational and Psychological Measurement, 5,* 229–239.

HUNTER, J. E. (1986). Cognitive ability, cognitive aptitudes, job knowledge, and job performance. *Journal of Vocational Behavior, 29,* 340–362.

LUBINSKI, D., & DAWIS, R. V. (1992). Aptitudes, skills, and proficiencies. In M. D. Dunnette & L. M. Hough (Eds.), *Handbook of industrial & organizational psychology* (Vol. 3, 2nd ed.). Palo Alto, CA: Consulting Psychologists Press.

U.S. DEPARTMENT OF LABOR. (1970). *Manual for the USES General Aptitude Test Battery: Section III. Development.* Washington, DC: U.S. Government Printing Office.

U.S. DEPARTMENT OF LABOR. (1974). *Job satisfaction: Is there a trend?* (Manpower Research Monograph No. 30). Washington, DC: U.S. Government Printing Office.

U.S. DEPARTMENT OF LABOR. (1979). *Manual for the USES General Aptitude Test Battery: Section II. Occupational Aptitude Pattern Structure.* Washington, DC: U.S. Government Printing Office.

WISE, L. L., MCHENRY, J., & CAMPBELL, J. P. (1990). Identifying optimal predictor composites and testing for generalizability across jobs and performance factors. *Personnel Psychology, 43,* 355–366.

RENE V. DAWIS

P

PARENTING AND INTELLIGENCE There are as many different perspectives on how to be a good parent as there are parents themselves. Like fashions in clothing, fashions in parenting have come and gone, only to come back again. Children living in colonial days in the United States faced the need to work almost from the moment they could walk; education was a luxury afforded to the fortunate, who had to squeeze book learning and playtime into the farming life-style. Victorian times found children treated like little adults. Discipline and book learning were plentiful, and much of the time parents spent with children went toward reminding them to be seen and not heard.

Since World War II different styles of parenting have developed, all aimed at raising better, smarter children—from the emphasis on discipline and conformity of the 1950s, to the looser, unconstrained, "feelings-first" outlook of the 1970s, with a return to a more controlled approach in the 1990s. Of course, at any given moment different parents are treating their children differently. What all this means is that children have historically managed—and will no doubt continue to manage—to grow up despite the fashions of their times and the opinions of their parents.

Moving beyond the fads and opinions, the key question is, What do we really know about the effects of different parental styles on children's development, particularly in the realm of cognitive abilities? It is this question that this article will consider.

First, what exactly does the term *parental style* mean? Parental style was defined by N. Darling and L. Steinberg (1993, p. 488) as "a constellation of attitudes toward the child that are communicated to the child and that, taken together, create an emotional climate in which the parent's behaviors are expressed." They noted that the parent's behaviors "include both the specific, goal-directed behaviors through which parents perform their parental duties and non-goal-directed parental behaviors, such as gestures, changes in tone of voice, or the spontaneous expression of emotion." In practice, parental style is a totality that is influenced by a parent's intelligence and personality, outlook on child-rearing, childhood experiences, and myriad other factors.

Are there styles of parenting that seem to characterize broad groups of parents? Despite the individuality of parents themselves, the demands of the job appear to give rise to certain basic patterns of behavior, at least within the confines of a given culture. What has arguably been the most influential conceptualization of parenting since the 1960s was developed by D. Baumrind (1991) through extensive research on how parents play their roles. Baumrind saw parental behavior as fitting within three general types or patterns: authoritarian, permissive, and authoritative.

Parents with an authoritarian style try to shape and control their children's behaviors, which they evaluate against a set of rigid standards. Authoritarian parents emphasize obedience, respect for authority, hard work, and traditional values, and discourage real communication in favor of the "listen and obey" mode. Baumrind (1971, 1973) saw authoritarian parents as being high in demandingness and low on responsiveness toward their children. The second parental style, the permissive style, characterizes parents who give their children considerable freedom. Permissive parents have a tolerant and accepting attitude toward their children, rarely punish them, and make few demands and place few restrictions on them. The third style of parenting, the authoritative, sets clear standards and expects children to meet them, treats children maturely, and uses discipline where appropriate to ensure that rules are followed. Authoritative parents encourage their children to develop independence and individuality, and consequently, they practice open communication, giving children's points of view and opinions due consideration. In other words, children's rights as independent human beings are honored within the authoritative family system. (For a review of the complexities underlying the parental style concept, see Darling & Steinberg, 1993.)

Baumrind's program of research explored the interrelationship of parental style and children's cognitive and social competence. She began by studying preschool children to learn what effects parental style had on the children's intelligence and personality. Later, Baumrind and other researchers expanded their investigations to include children in middle and high school, children of different races and ethnic groups, and children of different socioeconomic backgrounds. These studies shared three sets of goals. First, they sought to illuminate the effects of parental style on children's development and performance. Second, they attempted to understand the mechanisms and the processes through which specific parental behaviors and styles influence children. Third, they investigated the roles of cultural background, personal values, racial and ethnic origin, and socioeconomic level in the parent–child relationship. A review of the findings of a few representative studies will give a broad picture of what is known about the effects of parental style on children's cognitive competence.

H. L. Bee and her associates (1982) investigated the mother–child relationship as a predictor of later intelligence quotient (IQ) and language development in the child. This research contrasted the predictive ability of perinatal or infant physical status, early childhood performance, and family ecology (e.g., level of stress, social support, and maternal education) with the predictive ability of measures of mother–infant interaction. The authors found that infant physical status was a poor predictor of 4-year IQ or language, that child performance was a poor predictor before 24 months of age and good thereafter, and that family ecology predicted child IQ and language only within a low-education subsample, but not among mothers with more than high school education. However, the quality of mother–infant interaction was one of the best predictors at every age tested and was as good as actual child performance in predicting IQ and language development.

In another study evaluating the affective quality of the mother–child relationship and its longitudinal consequences for children's cognitive performance, P. Estrada and associates (1987) found that the affective quality of the mother–child relationship when the child was 4 years old was associated with mental ability at age 4, IQ at age 6, and school achievement at age 12. The associations remained significant even after the effects of mother's IQ, her socioeconomic status, and children's mental ability at age 4 were taken into account. The authors suggested that affective relationships influence cognitive development through the parents' willingness to help children solve problems, through the development of children's social competence, and through the encouragement of children's exploratory tendencies.

S. M. Dornbusch and his colleagues (1987) examined the relation of parenting style to adolescent school performance in a sample of 7,836 high school students. The authors found that both authoritarian and permissive styles were associated with lower grades, while authoritative parenting was associated with higher grades. The strongest effect on grades was for authoritarian parenting (in the negative direction). Children of families with a purely authoritative style had the highest average grades, and children of families with mixed or inconsistent styles had the lowest grades.

In a similar study investigating parenting practices and adolescent achievement, L. Steinberg and his colleagues (1992) focused on the impact of authoritative parenting, parental involvement in schooling, and parental encouragement to succeed on adolescent school achievement. The sample was ethnically and socioeconomically heterogeneous, containing 6,400 American high school students. The authors found that authoritative parenting led to better school performance and strong school engagement. Interestingly, they also found that parental involvement with schooling was a positive force in adolescents' lives when the parents had an authoritative style, but less so when the parents had other styles. It is perhaps not surprising that school involvement by demanding, rigid, critical parents does not have the positive impact of school involvement by parents who accept their children's interests and goals and assist them in achieving these goals.

When is the mother's influence on children's school achievement strongest? R. D. Hess and associates (1984) found that maternal measures taken during preschool years predicted school readiness at age 5 and achievement test performance at grade 6. But the prediction was stronger for age 5 than age 12, meaning that the mother's influence on school achievement was stronger during preschool years.

An example of the processes through which parental behavior affects a child's development is provided by the work of B. Rogoff and W. Gardner (1984), who watched 32 middle-class mothers preparing their 6- to 9-year-old children for a memory test. The mothers guided the children in transferring relevant concepts from more familiar settings to the relatively novel laboratory task, thus assisting the children in mastering the task and in developing methods for completing similar future tasks. Formal attempts to measure the processes through which parental style influences child development in the context of more typical parent–child interactions have often focused on the home environment (e.g., Bradley & Caldwell, 1984). Researchers evaluate various features of parenting behavior in the home, such as maternal responsivity, maternal acceptance of the child, maternal involvement, language stimulation, and encouragement of social maturity, through the use of the Home Observation for Measurement of the Environment (HOME) Inventory.

In a study by R. Elardo, R. Bradley, and B. M. Caldwell (1977), various aspects of the early home environment were related to language development at age 3. These aspects were the emotional and verbal responsivity of the mother, the provision of appropriate play materials, and maternal involvement with the child. Bradley and Caldwell (1984) found that HOME scores from age 2 predicted intelligence test scores at ages 3 and 4 1/2, as well as first-grade achievement-test scores. Later, Bradley, Caldwell, and Rock (1988) examined children as infants and at age 10, finding significant correlations between home environments measured at both 2 and 10 and children's achievement test scores and classroom behavior. The HOME Inventory has also been validated as a predictive tool for black children (Bradley & Caldwell, 1981).

Despite the fact that most research has centered on the mother as the primary caregiver, the father is also an integral component of a family system. J. Belsky (1981) discussed the processes of influence of parents on children, more broadly conceived in the context of the mother–father–child triad, and advocated this approach for future research. What about the level of agreement between the two parents regarding how to raise children and its effect on children's cognitive development? In a study of parental agreement during early childhood and adolescent intelligence and personality, B. E. Vaughn, J. H. Block, and J. Block (1988) found that parental agreement regarding child-rearing orientations (evaluated when the children were 3 years old) predicted male children's IQ, aspects of moral judgment, and personality during adolescence. For girls, early parental agreement was associated with adolescent self-esteem. For both genders, parental agreement was associated with personality descriptions provided by outsiders. These findings suggest that parental agreement is in fact important, but differentially important for boys and girls.

Given what has been learned about the significance of parental style, a natural question concerns the extent to which parent's styles can be improved. Can parents be taught to have more effective styles, particularly styles that help children excel? The answer to this question would require several pages; however, two studies suggest a note of caution. J. Madden, J. O'Hara, and P. Levenstein (1984) investigated the impact of a home-based intervention program that modeled verbal interaction between mother and child using selected toys and books. In their low-income population, only small IQ effects were found, and three years later, there were no effects on IQ, achievement, or first-grade teachers' evaluations. Similarly, S. Scarr and K. McCartney (1988), evaluating the same intervention program in Bermuda, found that it had virtually no cognitive, social, or emotional effects. The fact that one training and intervention program does not work does not mean that none could: it simply means that modifying parental style is not a simple matter and that program design must address the needs and characteristics of the population.

When all of the studies have been evaluated, it is apparent that there is a considerable amount of evidence for a strong association between parental style and a child's cognitive competence. The key word here is *association:* Very little evidence exists that can demonstrate clear cause-and-effect relationships between parenting style and a child's intelligence. Scarr (1985, p. 505) argued forcefully that "the implications . . . for improving children's intellectual functioning by intervention in mothers' control and discipline techniques are dismal. Even if we could dramatically improve a mother's positive behaviors toward her child, her improved behavior would have little payoff in the child's IQ score." Scarr noted that mothers with higher IQs tend to have children with higher IQs and that these mothers also tend to have more effective parental styles. Thus, the findings showing a link between parental style and children's cognitive competence are actually due to the effect of shared genetically transmitted intelligence between mother and child. Scarr noted that parents' behaviors are correlated with their children's because of shared genes and that what we observe in the world of parenting and child development is explicable even if parents have no effects on their children or vice versa.

Scarr's view is controversial, but whether one agrees with her or not, her points deserve consideration. As with any argument centered on the nature–nurture issue, the two sides are highly polarized. Undoubtedly, the truth resides somewhere in the middle, perhaps more to one side, perhaps less. We must await future data and empirical research to decide these questions, but for the present, and given the breadth of correlational data indicating a positive link between parental style and children's cognitive competence, it is wise to recall the words of Virgil, "As the twig is bent the tree inclines."

BIBLIOGRAPHY

BAUMRIND, D. (1971). Current patterns of parental authority. *Developmental Psychology Monograph, 4,* 1–103.

BAUMRIND, D. (1973). The development of instrumental competence through socialization. In A. D. Pick (Ed.), *Minnesota symposium on child psychology* (Vol. 7, pp. 3–46). Minneapolis: University of Minnesota Press.

BAUMRIND, D. (1991). Parenting styles and adolescent development. In J. Brooks-Gunn, R. Lerner, & A. C. Peterson (Eds.), *The encyclopedia on adolescence* (pp. 746–758). New York: Garland.

BEE, H. L., BARNARD, K. E., EYRES, S. J., GRAY, C. A., HAMMOND, M. A., SPEITZ, A. L., SNYDER, C., & CLARK, B. (1982). Prediction of IQ and language skill from perinatal status, child performance, family characteristics, and mother–infant interaction. *Child Development, 53,* 1134–1156.

BELSKY, J. (1981). Early human experience: A family perspective. *Developmental Psychology, 17*(1), 3–23.

BRADLEY, R. H., & CALDWELL, B. M. (1981). The HOME Inventory: A validation of the preschool scale for black children. *Child Development, 52,* 708–710.

BRADLEY, R. H., & CALDWELL, B. M. (1984). The relation of infants' home environments to achievement test performance in first grade: A follow-up study. *Child Development, 55,* 803–809.

BRADLEY, R. H., CALDWELL, B. M., & ROCK, S. L. (1988). Home environment and school performance: A ten-year follow-up and examination of three models of environmental action. *Child Development, 59,* 852–867.

DARLING, N., & STEINBERG, L. (1993). Parenting style as context: An integrative model. *Psychological Bulletin, 113*(3), 487–496.

DORNBUSCH, S. M., RITTER, P. L., LEIDERMAN, P. H., ROBERTS, D. F., & FRALEIGH, M. J. (1987). The relation of parenting style to adolescent school performance. *Child Development, 58,* 1244–1257.

ELARDO, R., BRADLEY, R., & CALDWELL, B. M. (1977). A longitudinal study of the relation of infants' home environments to language development at age three. *Child Development, 48,* 595–603.

ESTRADA, P., ARSENIO, W. F., HESS, R. D., & HOLLOWAY, S.

D. (1987). Affective quality of the mother–child relationship: Longitudinal consequences for children's school-relevant cognitive functioning. *Developmental Psychology, 23*(2), 210–215.

HESS, R. D., HOLLOWAY, S. D., DICKSON, W. P., & PRICE, G. G. (1984). Maternal variables as predictors of children's school readiness and later achievement in vocabulary and mathematics in sixth grade. *Child Development, 55,* 1902–1912.

MADDEN, J., O'HARA, J., & LEVENSTEIN, P. (1984). Home again: Effects of the mother–child home program on mother and child. *Child Development, 55,* 636–647.

ROGOFF, B., & GARDNER, W. (1984). Adult guidance of cognitive development. In B. Rogoff & J. Lave (Eds.), *Everyday cognition: Its development in social context* (pp. 95–116). Cambridge, MA: Harvard University Press.

SCARR, S. (1985). Constructing psychology: Making facts and fables for our times. *American Psychologist, 40*(5), 499–512.

SCARR, S., & McCARTNEY, K. (1988). Far from home: An experimental evaluation of the mother–child home program in Bermuda. *Child Development, 59,* 531–543.

STEINBERG, L., LAMBORN, S. D., DORNBUSCH, S. M., & DARLING, N. (1992). Impact of parenting practices on adolescent achievement: Authoritative parenting, school involvement, and encouragement to succeed. *Child Development, 63,* 1266–1281.

VAUGHN, B. E., BLOCK, J. H., & BLOCK, J. (1988). Parental agreement on child rearing during early childhood and the psychological characteristics of adolescents. *Child Development, 59,* 1020–1033.

WENDY M. WILLIAMS

PERCEPTION Before the relationship between individual differences in perception and measures of mental ability can be examined, some appreciation of the nature of perception and how it is studied is necessary. The term *perception* refers to our awareness of objects and events in the external world. The study of perception seeks to specify just how this awareness is accomplished. That is, what is the nature of the processes by which environmental energy is encoded by our sensory systems and transformed into our experience of an organized world?

Some difficulties are encountered at once in defining and in studying the nature of human perception.

The first is that different theoretical approaches to perception place different emphases on particular aspects of the perceptual process. Some approaches (e.g., the ecological approach of Gibson, 1979/1986) place exclusive emphasis on the structure of environmental information, whereas other more cognitively oriented approaches emphasize the active role of processes internal to the perceiver in constructing a representation of the external world (e.g., Hochberg, 1978; Rock, 1983). The approach adopted here views perception as an interaction among external information available to the perceiver, internal processes that actively transform that information, and mental representations of the world that are both constructed from and guide the search for additional sensory information. Under this account, certain forms of high-level cognitive knowledge about the world, as well as information stored in memory, can influence lower-level perceptual processes in significant ways.

A second problem in defining and studying perception is that the relevant processes are quite difficult to observe at a behavioral level. Perception occurs rapidly, automatically, and with such apparent ease, that it is often hard to appreciate that there *is* a problem of perception, let alone analyze its nature. One technique that psychologists use to study perception involves causing this rapid and efficient process to break down by degrading it in some way. (Typical ways of making perceptual processes falter include presenting external information for very brief periods of time, or otherwise reducing the detectability of the information.) By noting the conditions under which disruption of normal perception occurs, some insight can be gained into the operation of the underlying processes.

A related difficulty in studying perceptual activity is that it rarely occurs in isolation. Consider, for example, the processes involved in recognizing a familiar letter presented visually. Presumably, perceptual factors that influence the speed and accuracy of performing this task include registering the sensory information provided in the visual display and encoding the registered information into a useful form (e.g., elementary visual features such as lines, curves, and angles). Higher-level cognitive processes—including comparing the encoded information with representations of letters in memory, and deciding which representation provides the best match to the input—also contribute to performance on this task. The success of these cognitive processes both depends upon and influences the lower-level perceptual processes. For example, if expectations concerning which letter is to be presented are established by displaying the letter as part of a word, then contextual factors might direct the extraction of features from the display or cause certain features to be weighted more strongly than others by the encoding process.

Despite these difficulties, researchers in the area of human intelligence have sought to uncover relationships between individual differences in performance on perceptual tasks, or perceptual components of more complex tasks, and various measures of aptitude or mental ability. Indeed, the idea that overall intellectual prowess might be rooted in important ways in perceptual abilities has been entertained since the early days of intelligence testing (see, e.g., Spearman, 1927; Thurstone, 1938). A very selected discussion of some highlights of the voluminous literature on this topic follows. To anticipate the general conclusion, there is surprisingly little firm evidence for the popular notion that perceptual abilities are significant determinants of intelligence.

PERCEPTUAL CONTRIBUTIONS TO INDIVIDUAL DIFFERENCES IN MENTAL ABILITIES

The following discussion of relationships between perceptual processes and mental abilities examines three different types of tasks with perceptual components for which individual differences in performance have been found. The first section describes some efforts to relate low-level, or sensory, factors to abilities contributing to reading skill. The second section evaluates relationships between individual differences in performance on two information-processing tasks and measures of mental ability. The two tasks used are same–different visual matching and mental rotation. The third section discusses the role of perceptual factors in problem-solving tasks requiring high levels of skill.

Sensory Determinants of Individual Differences in Abilities. Clearly, extreme sensory disabilities place limitations on performance on tasks

measuring mental abilities. Individuals with very poor visual acuity will experience difficulty on any test requiring encoding of detailed visual information; persons with profound hearing impairments will do poorly on tests of listening comprehension. However, within normal limits of sensory functioning, performance is not seriously affected.

The ability to read rapidly with high comprehension is generally thought to be related to intelligence, and it has long been known that faster readers make fewer eye fixations per page of text than do slower readers, even though the two groups devote approximately equal amounts of time to each fixation (Huey, 1908/1968). This observation suggests that fast, effective readers might achieve their level of skill by taking in larger amounts of text per fixation than slower, less effective readers. Jackson and McClelland (1975) assessed this idea directly; they found that faster readers were neither able to extract more information from the periphery of the visual field, nor able to detect single letters better than were slower readers.

Livingstone et al. (1991) reported a provocative, though preliminary, finding concerning perceptual characteristics of developmental dyslexics. (Developmental dyslexia is an impairment specific to reading skill in individuals who are otherwise normal on tests of mental abilities.) These researchers found abnormalities in certain physiological correlates of brain activity (visually evoked potentials) in dyslexics to low-contrast visual stimuli presented rapidly, but normal responses to slower, high-contrast stimuli. Based on limited anatomical evidence, they hypothesized that dyslexia results from defects in a subdivision of the visual pathways (the magnocellular system) that is specialized for processing rapid, transient visual information.

Individual Differences in Perceptual Components of Visual Information-Processing Tasks. Conditions of gross abnormality involving damage to particular areas of the brain can produce marked deterioration in visual processing abilities, including recognition of visual objects and comparison of multiple objects (see Farah, 1990, for a review). One information-processing task that has been studied extensively in normal individuals involves determining whether two visual patterns, presented simultaneously or successively, are the same or different according to some criterion. When the criterion for sameness is strict physical identity of the patterns, perceptual analysis and encoding processes are clearly components of the task that can influence speed and accuracy of performance. Even when familiar patterns like letters are judged for name or categorical identity, perceptual processes are assumed to affect early stages of information extraction and encoding. In this latter case, the nonperceptual processes of memory access and comparison also affect task performance.

Hunt, Lunneborg, and Lewis (1975) reported individual differences, which were related to level of verbal ability, in the speed with which two letters are judged to be the same or different (see Posner, 1978, for a description of the letter-matching task). Specifically, students scoring high on tests of verbal aptitude exhibit a smaller difference in response times than do low-scoring students to pairs of letters that are matching only in name, versus those that are matching in physical identify. Hunt (1978) interprets these performance differences as reflecting different efficiency in accessing familiar information (letter names) in memory, rather than attributing the differences to perceptual extraction, encoding, or matching components of the task. The notion that superior ability is associated with rapid memory access, and not with perceptual processes, is reinforced by Jackson and McClelland's (1979) finding that skilled readers perform more rapidly than average readers on all matching tasks except one involving comparison of unfamiliar dot patterns. However, Tetewsky (1992) recently reported that the speed of matching unfamiliar Hebrew letters is correlated with individual differences in fluid abilities, whereas time for matching familiar letters is not related to the ability measures. Finally, some investigators (e.g., Cooper, 1976; Hock, 1973) have found striking, qualitative patterns of individual differences in performance on same–different visual comparison tasks using novel shapes as stimuli. However, the number of participants in these studies has been too small to determine whether such perceptual-processing differences are related to measures of mental abilities.

Mental Rotation. An information-processing task introduced by Shepard and Metzler (1971) requires comparison of a pair of line drawings of three-dimensional objects, displayed in different orientations, for identity or difference in shape. The general finding is that time to make the comparison increases linearly with the angular difference between the orientations of the portrayed objects (see Shepard & Cooper, 1982, for a review of results obtained with this task and many variants). The linear increase suggests that observers perform the task by "mentally rotating" one object in the pair into congruence with the other, and then comparing the shapes of the transformed and visually displayed objects. The slope of the reaction-time function estimates the rate of the mental-rotation operation; the intercept reflects the time needed for perceptual encoding and comparison.

The mental-rotation task has been used extensively in the search for perceptual factors in intelligence, because of its obvious perceptual character, and because of its similarity to items on standard tests of spatial aptitude and fluid abilities. Many investigators have reported individual differences and group (age, gender) differences in slope and intercept parameters (see Cooper & Mumaw, 1985; Cooper & Regan, 1983; Shepard & Cooper, 1982, for reviews). Nonetheless, it has been difficult to develop a consistent account of whether or how the processes used in the mental-rotation task relate to measures of mental abilities. For example, several investigators (e.g., Just & Carpenter, 1985; Lansman et al., 1982; Lohman, 1988) report that speed of mental rotation is positively correlated with spatial-visualization ability, whereas others (e.g., Salthouse et al., 1990) fail to find this relationship. One reason for the discrepancy may be the use of different rotational strategies by groups of high- and low-spatial-ability individuals. Just and Carpenter (1985) provide an analysis, based in part on observations of eye fixations during mental rotation; they suggest that high-ability individuals select complex but efficient axes for mental rotation.

Perceptual Factors in Complex Skills. Experts and novices in various problem-solving tasks requiring high levels of skill differ in their strategies for coding and operating on perceptual information. Chase and Simon (1973) studied how master and novice chess players perceive and remember board configurations. Master players extract more perceptual information from briefly exposed board positions than do novices; in addition, master players encode board positions into organized perceptual units consisting of meaningful arrangements of pieces. Lesgold et al. (1988) observed residents and expert radiologists making diagnoses from X-ray images. Skilled radiologists differed from students in their ability to shift among various hypotheses about a disease, and they were able to extract relevant perceptual information accordingly. Novices appeared bound to perceptual features of the X ray that were consistent with a single diagnostic category generated early in the problem-solving process. That is, they were unable to extract perceptual information that might lead to an alternative diagnosis. Finally, Cooper (1988) studied engineering students of high and low spatial aptitude as they solved visual problems that required the comprehension of various types of two-dimensional projections of three-dimensional objects. Students high in spatial ability tended to solve problems by using perceptual information to generate a mental model of a three-dimensional structure. Low-ability students were more likely to use local perceptual features of the visual problem displays in their solution process.

CONCLUSIONS

Despite decades of research, little experimental evidence exists as yet to support the idea that individual differences in mental abilities are related to perceptual processes. Exceptions include the clear contribution of perceptual strategies to expertise in specific areas, the probable relationship between spatial ability and speed of mental rotation, and some indications that defects in a particular subdivision of the visual pathways may contribute to reading disabilities. The search for a relationship between perception and intelligence is hindered by the difficulty of isolating and measuring the purely perceptual components of tasks that reflect differences in ability. High-level cognitive components of these tasks—which are affected by and, in turn, influence the extraction and encoding of sensory information—may mask the contribution of perceptual factors.

BIBLIOGRAPHY

CHASE, W. G., & SIMON, H. A. (1973). Perception in chess. *Cognitive Psychology, 4,* 55–81.

COOPER, L. A. (1976). Individual differences in visual comparison processes. *Perception & Psychophysics, 19,* 433–444.

COOPER, L. A. (1988). The role of spatial representations in complex problem solving. In S. Steele & S. Schiffer (Eds.), *Cognition and representation* (pp. 53–86). Boulder, CO: Westview Press.

COOPER, L. A., & MUMAW, R. (1985). Human spatial aptitude. In R. Dillon & R. Schmitt (Eds.), *Individual differences in cognitive processes* (pp. 67–94). New York: Academic Press.

COOPER, L. A., & REGAN, D. T. (1983). Attention, perception, and intelligence. In R. J. Sternberg (Ed.), *The handbook of human intelligence* (pp. 123–169). New York: Cambridge University Press.

FARAH, M. J. (1990). *Visual agnosia: Disorders of object recognition and what they tell us about normal vision.* Cambridge, MA: MIT Press.

GIBSON, J. J. (1979/1986). *The ecological approach to visual perception.* Hillsdale, NJ: Erlbaum.

HOCHBERG, J. E. (1978). *Perception.* Englewood Cliffs, NJ: Prentice-Hall.

HOCK, H. S. (1973). The effects of stimulus structure and familiarity on same-different comparison. *Perception & Psychophysics, 14,* 413–420.

HUEY, F. B. (1908/1968). *The psychology and pedagogy of reading.* Cambridge, MA: MIT Press.

HUNT, E. (1978). Mechanics of verbal ability. *Psychological Review, 85,* 109–130.

HUNT, E., LUNNEBORG, C., & LEWIS, J. (1975). What does it mean to be high verbal? *Cognitive Psychology, 7,* 194–227.

JACKSON, M. D., & MCCLELLAND, J. L. (1975). Sensory and cognitive determinants of reading speed. *Journal of Verbal Learning and Verbal Behavior, 14,* 565–574.

JACKSON, M. D., & MCCLELLAND, J. L. (1979). Processing determinants of reading speed. *Journal of Experimental Psychology: General, 108,* 151–181.

JUST, M. A., & CARPENTER, P. A. (1985). Cognitive coordinate systems: Accounts of mental rotation and individual differences in spatial ability. *Psychological Review, 92,* 137–171.

LANSMAN, M., DONALDSON, G., HUNT, E., & YANTIS, S. (1982). Ability factors and cognitive processes. *Intelligence, 6,* 347–386.

LESGOLD, A., RUBINSON, H., FELTOVICH, P., GLASER, R., KLOPFER, D., & WANG, Y. (1988). Expertise in a complex skill: Diagnosing x-ray pictures. In M. T. H. Chi, R.

Glaser, & M. J. Farr (Eds.), *The nature of expertise* (pp. 311–342). Hillsdale, NJ: Erlbaum.

LIVINGSTONE, M. S., ROSEN, G. D., DRISLANE, F. W., & GALABURDA, A. M. (1991). Physiological and anatomical evidence for a magnocellular defect in developmental dyslexia. *Proceedings of the National Academy of Sciences, 88,* 7943–7949.

LOHMAN, D. F. (1988). Spatial abilities as traits, processes, and knowledge. In R. J. Sternberg (Ed.), *Advances in the psychology of human intelligence* (Vol. 4, pp. 181–248). Hillsdale, NJ: Erlbaum.

POSNER, M. I. (1978). *Chronometric explorations of mind.* Hillsdale, NJ: Erlbaum.

ROCK, I. (1983). *The logic of perception.* Cambridge, MA: MIT Press.

SALTHOUSE, T. A., BABCOCK, R. L., MITCHELL, D. R. D., PALMON, R., & SKOVRONEK, E. (1990). Sources of individual differences in spatial visualization ability. *Intelligence, 14,* 187–230.

SHEPARD, R. N., & COOPER, L. A. (1982). *Mental images and theory transformations.* Cambridge, MA: MIT Press.

SHEPARD, R. N., & METZLER, J. (1971). Mental rotation of three-dimensional objects. *Science, 171,* 701–703.

SPEARMAN, C. (1927). *The abilities of man.* New York: Macmillan.

TETEWSKY, S. (1992). Familiarity effects in visual comparison tasks and their implications for studying human intelligence. *Journal of Experimental Psychology: Learning, Memory, and Cognition, 18,* 577–594.

THURSTONE, L. L. (1938). Primary mental abilities. *Psychological Monographs, 1.*

LYNN A. COOPER

PERSONALITY ASSESSMENT Tests of intelligence were not constructed in order to gather data regarding personality, nor is this the major intent in their use; intelligence tests were developed for the express purpose of assessing people's intellectual functioning. Certain theories in psychology, however, namely, psychoanalytic theory and gestalt theory, are committed to the notion that everything people do (in terms of both behavior and thinking) is a function of the personality. In light of this, the corollary—that personality should be able to be inferred from behavior

and/or thinking—should be true, too. Both these aspects of the thesis that behavior and thinking derive from personality provide the conceptual basis for expecting that personality can be inferred from people's performance on a test of intelligence. This has been believed by the earliest developers of tests of intelligence (e.g., Binet) to the present, and as a consequence, a great deal has been written about this topic. Much of the research and commentary can be found summarized in such resource materials as Allison, Blatt, and Zimet (1967), Blatt and Allison (1968), Frank (1970, 1976, 1983), Glasser and Zimmerman (1967), Matarazzo (1972), Rabin (1965), Rapaport, Gill, and Schafer (1945), and Schafer (1946, 1948).

To understand how tests of intelligence can be used to infer personality attributes, we must examine the structure of the test most used for this purpose—the Wechsler tests of intelligence. Wechsler published his first test (the Wechsler-Bellevue Intelligence Scale, now known as the Wechsler Adult Intelligence Scale, or WAIS) in 1939; he developed a second form of this test in 1946. In 1949 he standardized this second form of his test (which came to be known as the Wechsler Intelligence Scale for Children, or WISC) on school-age children and adolescents, and, in 1963, he standardized the WISC for preschool and primary-grade children. (This became known as the Wechsler Preschool and Primary Scale of Intelligence, or WPSSI.) All these tests have been periodically updated and revised. To understand how and why Wechsler developed his tests the way he did, we must look at what preceded Wechsler's work in the development of intelligence tests.

The first popular test of intelligence was developed by the French psychologist Alfred BINET (1905; Binet & Simon, 1908). Binet put forth the idea that an analysis of the data yielded by tests of intelligence could reveal aspects of personality (Binet & Henri, 1895) and psychopathology (Binet & Simon, 1905). Once this principle and its rationale had been stated, they became dominant themes regarding the use of the test Binet developed.

The first review of the research on the use of the Binet to assess personality and psychopathology (e.g., Harris & Shakow, 1937) did not support its use for this purpose. Nevertheless, the idea that individual differences in intellective functioning could reflect individual differences in personality had such appeal for psychologists that instead of discarding the hypothesis, they blamed the test. The Binet test was criticized for not having the kind of structure that would facilitate an analysis of individual differences in intellective functions (see, e.g., Ayres, 1911; Kuhlmann, 1911, 1912; Stern, 1914; Terman, 1911, 1913; Terman & Childs, 1912).

The test Binet had developed was organized according to mental age level; the individual subtests were grouped by the mental age at which Binet thought a child should be able to give the answers. This item structuring is a function of the history of Binet's work with the testing of intelligence. Because Binet's interest in the study of intelligence was well known, in 1904 he was asked by the minister of public instruction of the city of Paris to join a commission whose task was to develop ways of identifying those children in the Paris public school system who could not keep up with the work at their grade level and determine why they were having difficulty. Binet was asked to assess the children's intellectual functioning at different school levels; therefore, he organized the various test material he was using according to mental age level. In so doing, Binet had not given any thought to equating the tests for length and/or difficulty. Since the individual items in the test were grouped according to mental age level, not function, and the tests for different age levels were not of equivalent difficulty, intertest comparisons were difficult. Because the assessment of personality and psychopathology necessitated comparing performance on tests that represented specific functions, one could see why the Binet test did not lend itself to the kind of analysis of psychological functioning that the assessment of personality and/or psychopathology required.

Another major problem with the Binet test was the kind of material that it used. Much, if not all, of the material was included to assess the intelligence of children. Soon, however, there was a need to assess the intellectual ability of different adults. During the period from the mid-nineteenth century to well into the twentieth century, there was a great influx of émigrés from Europe; most of them were adults who could neither speak nor read English—certainly not well

enough to take a test administered in English. This prompted psychologists to develop intelligence tests that did not require that people express themselves only in words; these new tests called for solving certain problems (such as puzzles). Such tasks were called by Pintner and Patterson (1917) "performance" tests. The need for something different from the Binet test was also highlighted during World War I. To sort out those army recruits who would not be able to comprehend orders and generally take care of themselves during military service, psychologists were again asked to develop a test that could be used to make a relatively quick assessment of the intellectual level of people who did not always have a good education (and hence, might have difficulty on verbal tasks). A whole program of development of so-called performance tests followed.

To address the needs of these adults, a number of performance tests were being developed even before World War I. Healy and Fernald (1911) developed three such tests: Block Design (subjects are asked to use a set of blocks to reproduce a design that is presented to them on a set of cards); Object Assembly (subjects are asked to put together a jigsawlike puzzle that has been presented to them in a way that does not represent whatever the figure is, and they have to rearrange the pieces to make the object represented by the pieces); and Digit Symbol (subjects are asked to perform a codelike task, in which they are presented with a code design for each of the numbers from 1 to 5 and must fill in a blank under each number with its appropriate design). These three tests must be performed within given time limits; the person's score is a function of both a correct performance on the item and extra points for completing it within set time limits—the faster the person completed the task correctly, the higher the score. Healy (1914) developed the Picture Completion test, in which subjects are asked to indicate what parts have been omitted from a set of pictures of common, ordinary objects. Pintner (1919) developed the Picture Arrangement subtest, in which subjects are presented with a series of cards that will depict a story if they are arranged correctly.

Now psychologists had available a number of different verbal and performance tests, each one given individually. This seemed to satisfy the need to have both verbal and nonverbal tasks with which to assess people's intelligence; however, the tests had been developed separately and were given independently of one another, so it was not possible to make meaningful comparisons of a person's performance on each of the different tasks. Moreover, psychologists realized that some people did better with one kind of task as compared to another; therefore, administering a person one of these tasks might not give that individual an opportunity to demonstrate his or her actual intellectual ability. Thus, the next step in the development of intelligence tests was to combine several of the individual tasks (subtests) into one test and standardize these different subtests on a representative sample of persons.

With this objective, Terman and Childs (1912) had taken several of the verbal tasks of the Binet and combined them into one scale, or test. The scale they compiled consisted of Information, Comprehension, Arithmetic, Vocabulary, and Digits subtests. Yerkes, a psychologist working for the military during World War I, used the verbal tests Terman and Childs had put together as a verbal scale and assembled several of the performance tasks (Picture Arrangement, Picture Completion, Object Assembly, Block Design, and Digit Symbol) into a performance scale (Yoakum & Yerkes, 1920). Now psychologists had a set of verbal tasks or a set of performance tasks that individuals could be given as appropriate; a total score was derived from each scale that reflected an individual's general level of intelligence as compiled from the aggregate of the scores on either the verbal or performance tasks.

The verbal and performance scales were given separately, but a psychologist working in England (Alexander, 1935) gave them both at the same time, thereby developing a combination verbal *and* performance scale. Alexander, however, scored these scales separately. A commentary on the appropriate statistical and psychometric properties that such a test should have (Conrad, 1931), outlined the steps Wechsler was to take in the development of his test. Conrad's recommendations were that the test should be a point scale with a definite zero point; provide scores on subtests that could be converted into comparable units across each of the subtests; measure general intelligence as well as specific aspects of intelligence; mea-

sure verbal and nonverbal factors separately, but equally; and be reliable and valid.

Wechsler's test followed each of these prescriptions. Specifically, the test Wechsler developed enabled the calculation of a Verbal IQ (i.e., how people score on subtests that require words to answer and the need to communicate these words to the examiner), a Performance IQ (i.e., how people score on subtests that require hand–eye and other nonverbal responses), and a Full Scale IQ (an assessment of the overall intellectual functioning of the individual when all the verbal and nonverbal tests are combined to yield a single score). The ten subtests Wechsler included in his first 1939 test were those used by Yerkes and Alexander in their tests, as well as the method of developing standard scores that had been presented previously by Yerkes (Yerkes & Bridges, 1914; Yerkes & Foster, 1923). Psychologists could use this instrument to score a person's general intellectual functioning on a battery made up of five verbal and five nonverbal subtests. Wechsler also hoped that the scores on the ten verbal and performance subtests might yield a "profile" of high and low subtest scores (referred to as the "scatter" across subtests) that would help identify specific psychiatric disorders and be used to differentiate patients with one form of psychopathology (e.g., schizophrenia) from those with another form (e.g., bipolar affective disorder). In this way, psychologists hoped, they would be able to discover whether patterns of intellectual functioning (different forms of scatter of high and low subtest scores) were correlated with specific kinds of psychopathology.

At first, Wechsler was quite conservative regarding the use of the profile across the ten subtests to infer personality and/or psychopathology characteristics of the individual. In his first test, Wechsler (1939) gave scant attention to the use of his intelligence test in this manner. Rather, he first embarked on a series of studies (e.g., Balinsky, Israel, & Wechsler, 1939; Wechsler, 1941b; Wechsler, Halpern, & Jaros, 1940; Wechsler, Israel, & Balinsky, 1941) to try to learn if profile, or scatter, analysis could provide such new information about each individual. On the basis of this research, Wechsler produced a second edition of his book (Wechsler, 1941a), in which he discussed the possible use of data from his test in assessing psychopathology.

As research by Wechsler, his associates at Bellevue, and other psychologists around the country using the Wechsler-Bellevue Intelligence Test to assess psychopathology increased (e.g., Rabin, 1945), Wechsler became more positive about the use of the data from his test in this way. Shortly, much more research was done by other investigators using the data from Wechsler's tests for the study of psychopathology; during the next three decades this extensive research was reviewed by a number of individuals (e.g., Frank, 1970, 1976, 1983; Guertin, Frank, & Rabin, 1956; Guertin, Ladd, Frank, Rabin, & Hiester, 1966, 1971; Guertin, Rabin, Frank, & Ladd, 1962; Matarazzo, 1972; Rabin, 1945, 1965; Rabin & Guertin, 1951). These reviews provide the source for the information and discussion that follows.

When Wechsler discussed the use of his tests for assessing personality and psychopathology, he did not explicitly consider the particular personality implications of each subtest. Instead, he wrote about the different profiles that different patterns of high and low subtest scores produced and discussed the implications of the differences between an individual's Verbal IQ and Performance IQ. It was a psychologist named David Rapaport who did the most to introduce the idea that each subtest could have a unique psychological meaning, cognitively as well as with regard to personality traits (Rapaport, Gill, & Schafer, 1945). The research during the next three decades assessing the degree to which each subtest was related to specific personality attributes and traits as postulated by Rapaport, offered no support, however, for his very specific hypotheses relating each subtest score to a different personality characteristic (e.g., Blatt, Allison, & Baker, 1965; Bloom & Entin, 1975; Brower, 1947; Dickstein & Blatt, 1966; Garms, 1970; Holzberg & Belmont, 1952; Krippner, 1964; Lotsof et al., 1958; Spaner, 1950; Turner, Willerman, & Horn, 1976; Winfield, 1953).

Unlike Rapaport who wrote about the potential use of individual tests in personality assessment, Wechsler speculated about the interaction between psychopathology and performance on patterns or profiles made up of all ten subtests as a whole. Pressey (1917) and Wells (1927) had hypothesized that different kinds of psychopathology would produce different patterns

of performance on intelligence tests; Wechsler further pursued this notion of the interaction of intelligence and personality. Much research has been done to test this hypothesis; the bulk of that research has been reviewed in detail by Matarazzo (1972) and by Frank (1983). Taken in entirety, that body of research also did not lend support to the idea that specific kinds of psychopathology produce different patterns of subtest performance on the Wechsler tests.

A third mode of determining psychopathology from tests of intelligence arose from interpreting the "scatter" in the scores on the ten subtests as a unit or profile instead of examining the *magnitude* of the differences among subtest scores. The idea was that the greater the discrepancy among a person's scores on a variety of tests of intellectual ability (such as the subtests), the greater the degree of pathology. Pressey and Cole (1918) had been the first to refer to this as "scatter." The notion seemed reasonable not only to Wechsler, but also to other psychologists who used Wechsler's tests (e.g., Rapaport, Gill, & Schafer, 1945; Reichard & Schafer, 1943; Schafer, 1944; Schafer & Rapaport, 1944). Once again, however, the large body of research that followed failed to lend support to this idea.

Although the research to date does not support the hypothesis that any specific Wechsler subtest score or pattern of subtest scores is associated with any specific type of psychopathology, it does suggest that general cognitive-behavioral style on these tests is related to different kinds of psychopathology. It should be noted, however, that the data on the link to cognitive-behavioral style are neither extensive nor conclusive.

Cognition (i.e., the way people organize and comprehend the data of their experience—in other words, the way they process information) involves such psychological functions as attention, concentration, memory, perception, and thinking. The 1930s and 1940s were filled with research exploring the relationship between cognition and personality, none of which found evidence that any relationship existed. Over the next few decades, however, some research did support the hypothesis of a link between cognition and personality. Shapiro (1965), for example, found a relationship between cognitive style and psychopathological style. Other studies suggested that cognitive performance was influenced by specific kinds of psychopathology, including anxiety, depression, obsessive-compulsive personality, and schizophrenia. Since it has been clinically observed that anxiety can interfere with attention, concentration, and/or immediate memory, it is not surprising that people with relatively high levels of anxiety as measured by various objective tests did relatively poorly on such Wechsler subtests as Digit Span, Arithmetic, and the timed subtests (Picture Arrangement, Block Design, Object Assembly, and Digit Symbol).

(*See also:* WAIS–R SUBTESTS.)

BIBLIOGRAPHY

ALEXANDER, W. P. (1935). Intelligence, concrete and abstract. *British Journal of Psychology,* Monograph Supplement No. 19.

ALLISON, J., BLATT, S. J., & ZIMET, C. M. (1967). *The interpretation of psychological tests.* New York: Harper.

AYRES, L. P. (1911). The Binet-Simon measuring scale for intelligence: Some criticisms and suggestions. *Psychological Clinic, 5,* 187–196.

BALINSKY, B., ISRAEL, H., & WECHSLER, D. (1939). The relative effectiveness of the Stanford-Binet and Bellevue Intelligence Scale in diagnosing mental deficiency. *American Journal of Orthopsychiatry, 9,* 798–801.

BENTON, A. L., WEIDGER, A., & BLAUMVELT, J. (1941). Performance of adult patients on Bellevue and Revised Binet. *Psychiatric Quarterly, 15,* 802–806.

BINET, A. (1905). A propos la mesure de l'intelligence. *L'Année Psychologique, 2,* 411–465.

BINET, A. & HENRI, V. (1895). La psychologie individuelle. *L'Année Psychologique, 2,* 411–465.

BINET, A., & SIMON, T. (1905). Methodes nouvelles pour le diagnostic du niveau intellectual des anormaux. *L'Année Psychologique, 11,* 193–244.

BINET, A., & SIMON, T. (1908). Le development de l'intelligence chez les enfants. *L'Année Psychologique, 14,* 1–94.

BINET, A., & SIMON, T. (1916). *The development of intelligence in children.* Baltimore: Williams & Wilkins.

BLAKE, R. R., & RAMSEY, G. V. (EDS.). (1951). *Perception—An approach to personality.* New York: Ronald Press.

BLATT, S. J., & ALLISON, J. (1968). The intelligence test in personality assessment. In A. I. Rabin (Ed.), *Projective techniques in personality assessment* (pp. 421–460). New York: Springer.

BLATT, S. J., ALLISON, J., & BAKER, B. L. (1965). The Wechsler Object Assembly Subtest and bodily concerns. *Journal of Consulting Psychology, 29,* 223–230.

BLOOM, R. B., & ENTIN, A. D. (1975). Intellectual functioning and psychopathology: A canonical analysis of WAIS and MMPI relationships. *Journal of Clinical Psychology, 31,* 697–698.

BROWER, D. (1947). The relation between intelligence and Minnesota Multiphasic Personality Inventory scores. *Journal of Social Psychology, 52,* 225–230.

BRUNER, J. S., & KRECH, D. (EDS.). (1949). *Perception and personality.* Durham, NC: Duke University Press.

CONRAD, H. S. (1931). The measurement of adult intelligence, and the requisites of a general intelligence test. *Journal of Social Psychology, 2,* 72–85.

DICKSTEIN, L. S., & BLATT, S. J. (1966). Death concern, futurity, and anticipation. *Journal of Consulting Psychology, 30,* 11–17.

FRANK, G. (1970). The measurement of personality from the Wechsler Tests. In B. A. Maher (Ed.), *Progress in experimental personality research* (Vol 5, pp. 169–194). New York: Academic Press.

FRANK, G. (1976). Measures of intelligence and conceptual thinking. In I. B. Weiner (Ed.), *Clinical methods in psychology* (pp. 123–186). New York: Wiley.

FRANK, G. (1983). *The Wechsler enterprise.* Oxford: Pergamon.

GARMS, J. D. (1970). Factor analysis of the WISC and ITPA. *Psychology, 7,* 30–31.

GLASSER, A., & ZIMMERMAN, I. L. (1967). *Clinical interpretation of the WISC.* New York: Grune & Stratton.

GUERTIN, W. H., FRANK, G. H., & RABIN, A. I. (1956). Research with the Wechsler Bellevue Intelligence Scale: 1950–1955. *Psychological Bulletin, 53,* 235–257.

GUERTIN, W. H., LADD, C. E., FRANK, G. H., RABIN, A. I., & HIESTER, D. S. (1966). Research with the Wechsler Intelligence Scale for Adults: 1960–1965. *Psychological Bulletin, 66,* 385–409.

GUERTIN, W. H., LADD, C. E., FRANK, G. H., RABIN, A. I., & HIESTER, D. S. (1971). *Psychological Record, 21,* 289–339.

GUERTIN, W. H., RABIN, A. I., FRANK, G. H., & LADD, C. E. (1962). Research with the Wechsler Intelligence Scale for Adults: 1955–1960. *Psychological Bulletin, 59,* 1–26.

HARRIS, A. J., & SHAKOW, D. (1937). The clinical significance of numerical measures of scatter on the Stanford-Binet. *Psychological Bulletin, 34,* 134–150.

HART, B., & SPEARMAN, C. (1914). Mental tests of dementia. *Journal of Abnormal Psychology, 9,* 217–264.

HEALY, W. (1914). A pictoral completion test. *Psychological Review, 21,* 198–203.

HEALY, W., & FERNALD, G. M. (1911). Tests for practical mental classification. *Psychological Monographs, 13* (No. 54).

HOLZBERG, J. D., & BELMONT, L. (1952). The relationship between factors on the Wechsler-Bellevue and Rorschach having common psychological rationale. *Journal of Consulting Psychology, 16,* 23–29.

KLEIN, G. S. (1970). *Perception, motives, and personality.* New York: Knopf.

KNOX, H. A. (1914). A scale based on the work at Ellis Island for estimating mental defects. *Journal of the American Medical Association, 63,* 742–747.

KRIPPNER, S. (1964). WISC Comprehension and Picture Arrangement subtests as measures of social competence. *Journal of Clinical Psychology, 20,* 366–367.

KUHLMANN, F. (1911). The present status of the Binet and Simon tests of the intelligence of children. *Journal of Psycho-Asthenics, 16,* 113–139.

KUHLMANN, F. (1912). A revision of the Binet-Simon system for measuring the intelligence of children. *Journal of Psycho-Asthenics, 17,* Monograph Supplement.

KUHLMANN, F. (1922). *A handbook of mental tests.* Baltimore: Warwick & York.

LOTSOF, E. J., COMREY, A., BOGARTZ, W., & AINSFIELD, P. (1958). A factor analysis of the WISC and Rorschach. *Journal of Projective Techniques, 22,* 297–301.

MATARAZZO, J. D. (1972). *Wechsler's measurement and appraisal of adult intelligence.* New York: Oxford University Press.

PINTNER, R. (1919). A non-language group intelligence test. *Journal of Applied Psychology, 3,* 199–214.

PINTNER, R., & PATTERSON, D. G. (1917). *A scale of performance testing.* New York: Appleton.

PRESSEY, S. L. (1917). Distinctive features in psychological test measurements made upon dementia praecox and chronic alcoholic patients. *Journal of Abnormal Psychology, 12,* 130–139.

PRESSEY, S. L., & COLE, L. W. (1918). Irregularity in a psychological examination as a measure of mental deterioration. *Journal of Abnormal Psychology, 13,* 285–294.

RABIN, A. I. (1945). The use of the Wechsler-Bellevue Scale with normal and abnormal persons. *Psychological Bulletin, 42,* 410–422.

RABIN, A. I. (1965). Diagnostic use of intelligence tests. In B. B. Wolman (Ed.), *Handbook of clinical psychology.* New York: McGraw-Hill.

RABIN, A. I., & GUERTIN, W. H. (1951). Research with the Wechsler-Bellevue Test: 1945–1950. *Psychological Bulletin, 48,* 211–248.

RAPAPORT, D., GILL, M., & SCHAFER, R. (1945). *Diagnostic psychological testing* (Vol. 1) Chicago: Yearbook Publishers.

REICHARD, S., & SCHAFER, R. (1943). The clinical significance of the scatter on the Bellevue Scale. *Bulletin of the Menninger Clinic, 7,* 93–98.

SCHAFER, R. (1944). The significance of scatter in research and practice of clinical psychology. *Journal of Psychology, 18,* 119–124.

SCHAFER, R. (1946). The expression of personality and maladjustment in intelligence test results. *Annals of the New York Academy of Sciences, 46,* 609–623.

SCHAFER, R. (1948). *The clinical application of psychological tests.* New York: International Universities Press.

SCHAFER, R., & RAPAPORT, D. (1944). The scatter: In diagnostic intelligence testing. *Character and Personality, 12,* 275–284.

SHAPIRO, D. (1965). *Neurotic styles.* New York: Basic Books.

SPANER, F. E. (1950). *An analysis of the relationship between some Rorschach Test determinants and subtest scores on the Wechsler-Bellevue Adult Scale.* Unpublished doctoral dissertation, Purdue University, Lafayette, IN.

SPEARMAN, C. (1923). *The nature of "intelligence" and the principles of cognition.* London: Macmillan.

SPEARMAN, C. (1927). *The ability of man: Their nature and measurement.* New York: Macmillan.

STERN, W. (1914). The psychological methods of testing intelligence. *Educational Psychological Monographs,* No. 13.

STERN, W. (1938). *General psychology from the personalistic standpoint.* New York: Macmillan.

TENDLER, A. D. (1923). The mental status of psychoneurotics. *Archives of Psychology,* No. 60.

TERMAN, L. M. (1911). The Binet-Simon Scale for measuring intelligence. *Psychological Clinic, 5,* 199–206.

TERMAN, L. M. (1913). Suggestions for revising, extending and supplementing the Binet intelligence tests. *Journal of Psycho-Asthenics, 18,* 20–23.

TERMAN, L. M., & CHILDS, H. G. (1912). A tentative revision and extension of the Binet-Simon Scale of intelligence. *Journal of Educational Psychology, 6,* 551–562.

THORNDIKE, E. L., TERMAN, L. M., FREEMAN, F. N., COLVIN, S. S., PINTNER, R., RUML, B., PRESSEY, S. L., HENMON, V. A. C., PETERSON, J., THURSTONE, L. L., WOODROW, H., DEARBORN, W. F., & HAGGERTY, M. E. (1921). Intelligence and its measurement: A symposium. *Journal of Educational Psychology, 12,* 123–147, 195–216.

TURNER, R. G., WILLERMAN, L., & HORN, J. M. (1976). Personality correlates of WAIS performance. *Journal of Clinical Psychology, 32,* 349–354.

WEBB, E. (1915). Character and intelligence. *British Journal of Psychology,* Monograph Supplement No. 3.

WECHSLER D. (1939). *The measurement of adult intelligence.* Baltimore: Williams & Wilkins.

WECHSLER D. (1941a). *The measurement of adult intelligence* (2nd ed.). Baltimore: Williams & Wilkins.

WECHSLER D. (1941b). The effect of alcohol on mental activity, *Quarterly Journal of Studies of Alcoholism, 2,* 479–485.

WECHSLER D. (1944). *The measurement of adult intelligence* (3rd ed.). Baltimore: Williams & Wilkins.

WECHSLER D. (1946). *The Wechsler-Bellevue Intelligence Scale, Form II.* New York: Psychological Corporation.

WECHSLER D. (1949). *Wechsler Intelligence Scale for Children.* New York: Psychological Corporation.

WECHSLER D. (1963). *Manual for the Wechsler Preschool and Primary Scale of Intelligence.* New York: Psychological Corporation.

WECHSLER D., HALPERN, F., & JAROS, E. (1940). Psychometric study of insulin-treated schizophrenics. *Psychiatric Quarterly, 14,* 466–476.

WECHSLER, D., ISRAEL, H., & BALINSKY, B. (1941). A study of the sub-tests of the Bellevue Intelligence Scale in borderline and mental defective cases. *American Journal of Mental Deficiency, 45,* 555–558.

WELLS, F. L. (1927). *Mental tests in clinical practice.* New York: World Book.

WELLS, F. L., & KELLEY, C. M. (1920). Intelligence and psychosis. *American Journal of Insanity, 77,* 17–45.

WINFIELD, D. L. (1953). The relationship between IQ scores and Minnesota Multiphasic Personality Inventory Scores. *Journal of Social Psychology, 38,* 299–300.

WITKIN, H. A. (1977). *Cognitive styles in personal and cultural adaptation.* Worcester, MA: Clark University Press.

WITKIN, H. A., DYK, R. B., FATERSON, H. F., GOUDENOUGH, D. R., & KARP, S. A. (1962). *Psychological differentiation.* New York: Wiley.

WITKIN, H. A., & GOUDENOUGH, D. R. (1981). *Cognitive styles: Essence and origins.* New York: International Universities Press.

WITKIN, H. A., LEWIS, H. B., HERTZMAN, M., MACHOVER, K., MEISSNER, P. B., & WAPNER, S. (1954). *Personality through perception: An experimental and clinical study.* New York: Harper.

YERKES, R. M., & BRIDGES, J. W. (1914). The Point Scale: A new method for measuring mental capacity. *Boston Medical and Surgical Journal, 171,* 857–866.

YERKES, R. M., & FOSTER, J. C. (1923). *A point scale for measuring mental ability.* Baltimore: Warwick & York.

YOAKUM, C. S., & YERKES, R. M. (1920). *Army mental tests.* New York: Holt.

GEORGE FRANK

PHILOSOPHICAL VIEWS OF INTELLIGENCE

Philosophical conceptions of intelligence are difficult to classify owing to the widely varying meanings of the word itself and to the comparably diverse theories of mind in which the concept of intelligence has a place. The contemporary sense of the term, which has been shaped by technical and quantitative approaches, is of relatively recent origin and bears only a slight relationship to more traditional understandings. Then, too, caution must be exercised in attempting to find equivalents of the English *intelligence* in other languages and in remote epochs. Consider only the difference between the *intelligence* of a child earning a high score on the Wechsler Intelligence Scale for Children and the *phronesis* or *sophia* ("wisdom") said to have been possessed by the sages of ancient Greece. Or consider the difference between the Latin *intelligentia* and the Latin *acumen;* where the latter identifies a certain agility and quickness of mind, while the former reaches toward something more akin to erudition. The arbitrariness of what follows is, therefore, unavoidable.

ANCIENT PHILOSOPHICAL CONCEPTIONS OF INTELLIGENCE

In a number of dialogues Plato regards the chief evidence of mental superiority to be of an essentially moral nature. Actions committed in ignorance are taken to be involuntary. Thus, there can be no ethical or moral value assigned to an action unless it proceeds from one who is informed and acting intentionally. According to Plato (*Meno,* 88; *Phaedo,* 69), wisdom *(phronesis)* is the perfection of virtue itself. It is the power of mind at once to control the forces of passion and, at the same time, to conform one's actions to requirements laid down by the good *(kalos);* the requirements of truth, symmetry, and beauty. When possessed by a political leader, this wisdom stands as nothing less than "the mind of the *polis*" (*Republic,* 4.428). Not many ever attain such wisdom, for most lack the capacity itself and others are distracted by the quest for sensuous pleasures.

Wisdom in this view is a knowledge of principles that are universally true and unchanging—a knowledge of what the soul already possesses but can only be recalled through the right sort of philosophical education. But such principles, because they are universal and unchanging, can never be objects of mere perception. Experience, therefore, cannot locate such principles and may well mislead those in search of them. Rather, it is through pure rationality that the abidingly true, the eternally good, and the eternally beautiful are conceived. This is possible only through a lifetime of philosophical reflection and contemplation. Once apprehended, these truths serve as the standards of worth and conduct, the goal toward which those possessed of wisdom dedicate their lives. Wisdom, which expresses itself in a lifetime of devotion to the truth, cannot, however, be *acquired* by practice or schooling, for it is not a mere craft or skill. Instead, it is innate and God-given (*Phaedrus,* 278), though it becomes weak and powerless in those who neglect it.

After twenty years of schooling in Plato's Academy, Aristotle would adopt, modify, and then challenge any number of the central theories of the school. Nevertheless, he preserved the sharp distinction between a factual knowledge of particular things and a rational awareness of general principles. Indeed, in Aristotle's account, rationality is part of the very definition of human life, its exercise being humanity's unique task *(idion ergon).* Every animal has its own proper functions corresponding to certain activities (*Nicomachean Ethics,* 1176A). If human life is to be a flourishing *(eudaimonic)* life, the dominant activity must be that which expresses the essence of humanity, and this Aristotle took to be rationality. Thus, the flourishing human life turns out to be the contemplative life (*Nicomachean Ethics,* 1177A). Aristotle would reserve the term *highly intelligent* for those committed to the contemplation of worthy subjects, quite apart from practical considerations. A scientific knowledge *(episteme)* of technical matters, though not something to neglect or depreciate, is radically different from the contemplation of the good and satisfies a lower order of intelligence.

Although human intelligence for Aristotle culminates in the rational contemplation of the good, his theory of mind at the more practical level is biological in its orientation. Under the usual conditions of daily life, the human mind must deal with the same sorts of problems and possibilities faced by many other animals. Through acute sensory powers, and with the aid of memory and the skills acquired through practice, animals (including human beings) are able to adapt to changing conditions, provide for their offspring, and compete with others for available resources. What is needed here is a kind of functional intelligence *(dianoia),* closely tied to the senses. It is this form of intelligence that varies in proportion to the sensory acuity and memory of the animal. Aristotle reasoned that the sense of touch was of primary importance in this regard, and he judged human beings as having the greatest tactile sensitivity. He concluded that human intelligence of this sort (i.e., functional intelligence) exceeds that found among other animals (*On the Soul,* 421A.15–30). Indeed, even the more elevated forms of intelligence can be affected by sensory processes. Aristotle, noting the dependence of wisdom on discourse, reasoned that people deprived of hearing would possess intellects inferior to those of people deprived of sight (*On Sense and Sensible Objects,* 437A.5–17).

EARLY CHRISTIAN AND MEDIEVAL CONCEPTIONS

The theories of Plato and Aristotle underwent refinements and embellishments as the disciplines and critics of each considered the nature of mental life. In Book II of *The Nature of the Gods,* Cicero is faithful to the Greek philosophical view when he traces the source of human rational intelligence to the gods and takes it as evidence of a rational design and an ordering intelligence behind the cosmos itself. With the incorporation of such theories (derived in large part from the Stoic philosophers) into the evolving doctrines of early Christian theology, something of a cognitive psychology is discernible as early as the second and third centuries A.D. These developments would be brought to greater maturity in the works of St. Augustine (A.D. 354–430), who adopted and modified the ancient distinctions among the functions, or powers *(dunameis),* of the soul. In Augustine's works, the gradations of psychic function move from the merely vegetative to the contemplation of God. Along the way, the powers of the soul come to include discursive, ethical and intellectually abstract operations. As with his classical predecessors and ·models, Augustine regards the ultimate object of intelligence to be entirely beyond the facts and cares of daily life.

With the works of Thomas Aquinas (1225–1274), the later medieval period would host a remarkably developed theory of cognition, much indebted to Aristotle, but with a power and originality of its own. In the new and teeming centers of scholarly research and debate—the medieval universities—the analysis of human mental attributes and the relation between these and the nature of the physical world were topics of central concern. According to the general theory developed in this period, knowledge is not confined to mere things but embraces and recognizes *kinds* of things. Particulars (*this* horse) are understood to be instances of a general or universal class *(horse),* absent which the particular would, as it were, not be an *anything.* But the universal does not exist as an object of sensation. What is its actual standing? So-called Realists in the debate insisted that the universals were real, though obviously nonsensory. The Nominalists, however, argued that universals referred to general, or class, *names,* the category exhausted by the actual, particular instances or things bearing the name in question. But how, then, does the mind apprehend such universal categories, or "find" the universal, when only particulars are reported by the senses? Thomas Aquinas and Duns Scotus, to cite two of the more influential scholars of the period, advanced a two-process theory of intelligence or cognition; a passive intellect acted upon by sensory data *(phantasmata)* and an active intellect (the *intellectus agens*) by which stimulation is able to engage the passive intellect and allow cognitive abstractions (universals) to be discerned in the particulars. Again, and fully consistent with an-

cient views, the Thomistic theory of intelligence regards the capacity for abstraction to be its most defining mark and the one that distinguishes it from the rote memory and sense-based knowledge of non-human animals.

MODERN CONCEPTIONS

In the seventeenth and eighteenth centuries, philosophers became more systematic in separating intellectual and epistemological issues from those germane to ethics and religion. Moreover, the extraordinary achievements in the sciences of astronomy, physics, and optics created great, if perhaps uncritical, confidence in the application of scientific methods to the enduring problems in philosophy of mind. Out of the welter of writings, three more or less distinct perspectives arose regarding the nature of intelligence: (1) a rationalistic perspective, closely identified with the works of René Descartes and Gottfried Wilhelm von Leibnitz; (2) an empiricist perspective, developed chiefly by John Locke and David Hume; and (3) a biological perspective, espoused by any number of commentators and *philosophes,* notably Julien Offray de La Mettrie and "Baron" Holbach.

In the rationalistic view, intelligence refers to the capacity to frame and comprehend abstract principles. Descartes was satisfied that one would always be able to distinguish a human being from a very good mechanical simulation, for the latter would be unable to use language creatively, would not comprehend mathematical abstractions, and would not attain the idea of an omnipotent creator. Accordingly, the criterion of human intellectual prowess is rationality. A device with greater memory or more acute senses, or quicker in solving rudimentary problems would fail to qualify as a rational entity. Thus, its performance could be fully explained on the basis of mechanisms. As for the place of the senses and of factual knowledge, rationalists in the tradition of Descartes and Leibnitz argue that there must be an intellectual power in place prior to experience in order for the endless stream and chaos of sensory stimulation to be reduced to order and intelligibility. The medieval maxim according to which nothing is in the mind except what is first in the senses receives the reply, *Nisi intellectus ipse*—nothing except the intellect itself.

Empiricists have developed retorts to each of the major claims of rationalism. Locke, striving to develop psychology along Newtonian lines, offered something of a corpuscular theory of mind (elementary sensations combining to form simple and then ever more complex ideas), in which the mechanism of association was postulated to do the sort of work that gravity does in the Newtonian system. David Hume developed the principles of association more fully and launched the now quite common line of argument according to which knowledge is reducible either to objects as reported by the senses or to merely verbal conventions yielding no more than definitions.

The biological perspective on intelligence is based on the assumption that an animal's adaptive abilities depend on the overall organization of the body and, especially, the nervous system. *Intelligence,* in this view, is a word referring to the degree and efficiency of this organization and to the problem-solving abilities thereby made possible. When in his controversial *Man: A Machine* (1751), La Mettrie declared the soul to be "an enlightened machine," he recorded no more than the scientific perspective that had already come to dominate the psychological writings of the eighteenth century. The fuller development of this perspective awaited Darwin's theory of evolution, which connected structural development to functions essential to survival.

BIBLIOGRAPHY

AQUINAS. *Basic writings of Thomas Aquinas.* (A. Pegis, Trans.). (1945). New York: Random House.

ARISTOTLE. On the soul. In J. Barnes (Ed.). (1987). *The complete works of Aristotle.* Princeton, NJ: Princeton University Press.

AUGUSTINE. *Basic writings of St. Augustine.* W. Oates (Ed.). (1948). New York: Random House.

DESCARTES, R. *The philosophical works of Descartes.* (E. Haldane & G. Moss, Trans.). (1955). New York: Dover.

HUME, D. *A treatise of human nature.* L. A. Selby-Bigge (Ed.). (1965). New York: Dover.

LA METTRIE, J. O. *L'homme machine* [*Man: A machine*]. (M. W. Calkins, Trans.). (1912). New York: Open Court.

LEIBNIZ, G. W. New essays. In *Leibniz—The monadology and other philosophical writings.* (R. Latta, Trans.). (1898). Oxford: Oxford University Press.

LOCKE, J. *An essay concerning human understanding.* (1956). Chicago: Henry Regnery.

PLATO. *The dialogues,* 2 vols. (B. Jowett, Trans.). (1937). New York: Random House.

DANIEL N. ROBINSON

PHILOSOPHY FOR CHILDREN

Philosophy has not traditionally been an elementary school subject. Its study has been concentrated in colleges and universities, as it is considered a largely conceptual and theoretical discipline. The possibility of reconstructing it so as to make it accessible to elementary school students has seemed remote: To children, its terminology would appear forbidding, its texts austere, its manner of teaching uninviting. Besides, children have been thought to have little interest in philosophical ideas, or in the philosophical version of inquiry.

In recent years, however, a considerable number of educators have begun to show interest in the advantages that might be gained by adding philosophy to the elementary school curriculum, provided that it could be suitably redesigned. These advantages include:

Enriching the curriculum through the addition of a much-needed humanities subject;

Providing a systematic and sequential treatment of reasoning;

Offering children opportunities to engage in logically disciplined discussions of values in which they are intensely interested, such as truth, friendship, and fairness;

Laying out before children a broad range of ideas to which they may respond, in place of the conceptually limited curricula that have been fashionable for the past half century;

Enabling children to understand the criteria, standards, and ideals to which their schoolwork is expected to conform; and

Assisting in the strengthening of children's judgment—their sense of appropriateness, proportion, relevance, and order—through the performance of philosophical exercises.

Those who were attempting to remodel philosophy found an opening wedge in the fact that philosophy is not a completely theoretical discipline: It has a dimension of practice—popularly known as *doing philoso-*

phy—that involves dialogue and deliberation. Perhaps children could be tempted to engage in discussion if they were exposed to unanswerable rather than answerable questions, and perhaps such discussions could be disciplined by logical considerations so that the discussants would move in the direction of greater and greater reasonableness.

So the speculation went, but the first order of business seemed to be the construction of an elementary school philosophy curriculum, and the most immediate challenge was the construction of philosophical texts in the form of children's stories. Subsequently there would be instructional manuals with exercises for the sharpening of thinking and with discussion plans for the improvement of concept-formation.

THE FICTIONAL CURRICULUM

The children's stories that have emerged are actually novels that depict fictional children discovering elements of ethics, logic, aesthetics, metaphysics, and epistemology. Each story becomes, in effect, an experimental probe, portraying how reasonable children might think and act in ordinary life situations. The novels thus become models that depict not only the acquisition of thinking skills, but their appropriate (or inappropriate) uses in specific circumstances. Each novel depicts a classroom community of inquiry in action, and in this fashion provides a schematic model to be fleshed out and emulated by the children *in the* classroom, just as the subsequently formed classroom community of inquiry may later become a microcosm of democratic practice within the larger democratic society.

Since a class session in elementary school philosophy begins with a collaborative reading of a story, in which are depicted the development and orchestration of cognitive skills and dispositions, the children are being given, in effect, an advance opportunity *to learn to learn,* as well as *to learn to think,* and to think in that independent fashion known as "thinking for oneself." Children discover how meanings can be found by tracing out implications and other relationships. For the more thoughtful children are, the more likely they are to discover the connections by which meanings are composed. The experience of stories, with their beginnings, middles, and ends, has important analogies for

the child's efforts to link together his or her past, present, and future. The encounter with stories thus contributes to children's sense of their own growth, rationality, and identity.

Just as the fictional children are represented as engaging in deliberations that constitute conceptual inquiry, so the actual children pick up the unresolved issues and continue to investigate them dialogically. The classroom community, in the process, internalizes the criteria of the fictional children: Their reflections are self-correcting, sensitive to context, reliant upon criteria, and conducted in search of practical applications.

An example of a passage from one of the novels for children is this excerpt from *Pixie,* which is for children of 9 or 10:

> My arm had gone to sleep.
>
> I still can't figure it out. If all of me was awake, how could part of me be asleep?
>
> It was asleep, all right. I couldn't use it. It just sort of hung down off my shoulder. I couldn't even feel it, except maybe a little tingle.
>
> Have *you* ever had *your* arm go to sleep? Isn't it weird? It's like it doesn't even belong to you! How could part of you not belong to you? All of you belongs to you!
>
> But you see, that's what puzzles me. Either my body and I are the same, or they're not the same.
>
> If my body and I are the same, then *it* can't belong to *me.*
>
> And if my body and I are different, then who am I?
>
> It's beginning to sound like *I'm* the one who's some kind of mystery creature!
>
> Afterward, when I talked to Isabel about it, she said, "Pixie, you worry too much. Look, there's really no problem. Your body belongs to you and you belong to your body."
>
> "Sure," I said, "but do I belong to my body *in the same way* that my body belongs to me?"

The children who read and discuss this passage find themselves exploring relationships and meanings that are absent from classrooms in which philosophy is not part of the curriculum. In other courses, they may study historical, geometrical or temporal relationships; in philosophy, they study relationships in their generic, conceptual aspect.

Children seem to be generally delighted to discover in philosophy a form of inquiry that complements scientific inquiry, and one that leaves the questions science investigates more carefully examined, if still unanswered. Philosophy assures them that their persistently interrogative attitude is essential to inquiry, rather than superfluous. Philosophy does not flatly assume that children's "Why?" questions are to be taken as requests for explanation, for it recognizes that the child's "Why?" can just as well be a request that some action or practice or institution by *justified*. If children are ever to develop critical intelligence, the proponents of philosophy contend, it is essential that they learn to see through and criticize practices that are indefensible.

THE PHILOSOPHY CLASSROOM

The upgrading of thinking in the schools is unlikely to take place to any significant extent without the mandating of a class session each day, at every grade level, devoted to the improvement of thinking, in addition to the emphasis upon critical and creative thinking in each of the other subject areas. The optimal format for the newly required class session is likely to be that of a community of philosophical inquiry. Such a format enables students to engage in thinking about their own thinking, in inquiry about their own inquiry, while they are examining such concepts as reasons, relationships, persons, causes, and so on. In effect, they can study the tools of thinking and how to use them, while engaged in deliberations about matters they deem important. For example, in encountering a difference, they are inclined to wonder about the connection between a difference and a distinction, and in encountering a distinction, they are inclined to ask themselves what the criteria are for a *good* distinction.

Whatever is done in a classroom community of inquiry may be considered *exemplary*. To state an opinion is, in effect, to invite everyone to state an opinion. To give a reason or ask a question or disclose an underlying assumption is to open the door to everyone's doing likewise. Each models for the others; each provides an excuse for the others' doing the same. To listen to others results in being listened to; to respect others is followed by being respected, and it is no great distance from there to self-respect.

The ongoing deliberations within the community create a requiredness that invites students to participate, and indeed, draws their participation out of them. Thus, they do not first learn discrete thinking skills and then find themselves puzzled as to when and where to use them. Instead, they respond to the invitations of the inquiry situation when such responses are demanded by the requiredness of that situation. They not only learn by doing, but they learn to identify on which occasions to respond appropriately, along with the modes of skilled conduct. But it must be kept in mind that skills are only as useful as the judgment that dictates how, when, and where they are to be employed. The continued practice of philosophy assures the strengthening of the reasoning and judgment of the participants in the community. It is because each such judgment rests in turn upon countless others that the methodology of judgment comes to be recognized as the central nervous system, as it were, of the reasonable life.

TEACHER PREPARATION

It is assumed by proponents of elementary school philosophy that the single greatest barrier to effective teacher preparation is the fact that teachers generally teach as they have been taught to teach: The lecture method in the school of education produces lecturers in the elementary school. Consequently, those involved in teacher preparation who want to produce teachers adept at forming classroom communities of inquiry should themselves form such communities at the graduate school level. The manner in which teachers are prepared should be symmetrical with the manner in which children are eventually to be taught.

This precept is taken very much to heart in preparing teachers, through in-service or pre-service training, to conduct elementary school philosophy classes. Teachers read the curriculum materials, choose ideas for discussion, and engage in philosophical deliberations in much the same way that the children they eventually teach will perform these activities. Since philosophical ideas are not stratified by age levels (e.g., *friendship* is not a topic of interest to any one age group), teachers do not find such discussions condescending.

The guiding adage of teacher preparation in elementary school philosophy is that teachers should be "pedagogically strong but philosophically self-effacing." Teachers have to be pedagogically strong in that they have to be able to get their students to investigate the ideas they are interested in, rather than merely to chatter about them. The fostering of inquiry is the primary arena in which teachers must be prepared to demonstrate their professional judgment.

On the other hand, it is inappropriate for teachers to take advantage of the youth and vulnerability of students to implant their own philosophical opinions in students' minds. To do so is indoctrination. It is not that teachers are forever forbidden to present their opinions to the classroom community, but that teachers should not do so until children's defenses have been sufficiently strengthened for them to handle such opinions on their own terms rather than uncritically accept them because they think teachers are experts in philosophy.

The formation of pre-service or in-service communities of inquiry has to be collaborative and not merely cooperative. That is, the community of inquiry understands that investigative work is to be done: Mere conversation among the prospective teachers is not enough. The members of the community must find themselves together enmeshed in problematic situations that demand exploration. Otherwise, the individual participants do not become interdependent and mutually helpful.

At the same time, the director of a teacher preparation seminar in elementary school philosophy will make use of the cognitive apprenticeship model where appropriate. Teachers who are being readied to conduct sessions will be given coaching in advance and will subsequently be given debriefing or evaluation sessions. The coaching session is in effect a joint planning session, one purpose of which is to get the prospective teacher to internalize such planning and self-evaluation in preparation for the time when the scaffolding is eventually removed. Among the most important items of business of the coaching session is teaching the expeditious use of appropriate exercises from the instructional manual. Another is the sharpening of the

pedagogical method, to assure that the forward movement of the classroom dialogue continues to retain the interest of the students.

Since philosophy that underscores the use of narrative, fiction, dialogue, community-building, criteria, and value judgment has applications beyond the elementary school classroom, ranging from preschool classes to teacher preparation and university courses, it has been suggested that it be known as *educational philosophy,* rather than as *elementary school philosophy.* Whether or not it takes this new appellation, it seems destined to spread to a wide variety of new and different educational contexts.

IMPLICATIONS FOR IMPACT UPON INTELLIGENCE

More than twenty quantitative studies seeking evidence of the effectiveness of philosophy for children have been performed. Summaries of the reports of most of these studies have appeared in *Thinking: The Journal of Philosophy for Children* (Vol. 6, No. 4, 1986, and Vol. 7, No. 4, 1988). One of the most extensive experiments was conducted by Educational Testing Service and reported by Lipman, Sharp, and Oscanyan (1980, pp. 219–224). When comparing the reading and mathematics gains in terms of average standard scores, using the MAT, experimental students in Newark, New Jersey, registered a 36 percent greater gain over control students in mathematics and a 66 percent greater gain in reading comprehension. The overall impact was at the .0001 level of significance. Highly significant improvement in creative reasoning was noted on most grade levels, and there was significant improvement in formal reasoning in three of the four grade levels in Newark. Teachers' appraisals were also favorable: Students appeared to teachers to be significantly more curious, better oriented toward their tasks, more considerate of one another, and better able to reason. The experiment was supervised by Virginia Shipman, senior research psychologist at ETS.

Longitudinal studies to determine whether students at, say, a secondary school level or college level test higher after an early introduction to the program are not yet available. Nevertheless, the Newark study showed (at .01 significance) that the longer children were in the program, the higher were their scores on the reasoning tests.

The broad spectrum of effects demonstrated by the program, in light of the experimental findings, reflects the complex nature of the intervention. The introduction to humanistic concepts (e.g., truth, friendship, justice) provides enrichment; the continuous appeal to logical criteria, informal as well as formal, encourages enhanced rigor in thinking; the emphasis upon deliberation directs students toward progressive, systematic inquiry, instead of toward reliance upon previously established results; the community-building process of dialogue promotes the acquisition of social skills that include greater self-respect and respect for others, greater civility, increased reflection upon values, and strengthened judgment; and the use of philosophy to attack ill defined but important concepts and problems opens a treasure chest of meanings to many students who had already concluded that schooling was meaningless.

It would consequently be a mistake to assume that a broad-gauge philosophical approach fails to produce significant improvement in specialized cognitive skills. What is debatable is whether it has such a broad-scale educational impact that it actually improves intelligence.

It is likely that philosophical inquiry, employed systematically and sequentially in a community setting, converts uncritical thinking into critical thinking; uncreative thinking into creative, self-expressive thinking; and uncaring, inconsiderate thinking into thinking that fosters the thinking and reasonable conduct of others. In short, there is likely to result a *higher-order thinking* that reveals itself in strengthened judgments of relevance and appropriateness. It is also possible that elementary school philosophy, through its continual insistence upon sharper questioning, its intense, articulate deliberations, and its free-ranging classroom discussions, may be successful in opening up previously blocked pathways of reflection and communication upon which the manifestation of intelligence depends.

BIBLIOGRAPHY

Analytic Teaching. La Crosse, WI: Viterbo College, 1982.

Apprender à Penser. Madrid: Ediciones de la Torre, 1990.

BANDURA, A. (1986). *Social foundations of thought and action: A social cognitive theory* Englewood Cliffs, NJ: Prentice Hall.

BRUNER, J. (1968). *Toward a theory of instruction.* New York: W. W. Norton.

Bulletin of the International Council for Philosophical Inquiry with Children. Madrid: Ediciones de la Torre, 1986.

CARON, A. (ED.). (1990). *Philosophie et pensée chez l'enfant.* Ottawa: Agence d'ARC Inc.

CHANCE, P. (1986). *Thinking in the classroom.* New York: Teachers College Press.

COLES, M. J., & ROBINSON, W. D. (EDS.). (1989). *Teaching thinking: a survey of programs in education.* Bristol: The Bristol Press.

DEWEY, J. (1958). *Experience and nature* (2nd ed.). New York: Dover.

DEWEY, J. (1961). *Democracy and education.* New York: Macmillan.

FISHER, R. (1990). *Teaching children to think.* Oxford: Basil Blackwell.

FREESE, H.-L. (1989). *Kinder sind Philosophen* [Children are philosophers]. Berlin: Quadriga Verlag.

GLATZEL, M., & MARTENS, EKKEHARD. (1982). *Philosophieren im unterricht 5–10.* Munich: Urban und Schwarzenberg.

HORSTER, D. (1991). *Auf den Spuren Sokrates'* [On the trail of Socrates]. Hannover: Frau Schact.

MARCIL-LACOSTE, L. (ED.). (1990). *La philosophie pour enfants: L'Experience Lipman* [Philosophy for children: the Lipman experience]. Sainte-Foy, Quebec: Le griffon d'argile.

LIPMAN, M. (1981). *Pixie.* Upper Montclair, NJ: Institute for the Advancement of Philosophy for Children.

LIPMAN, M. (1991). *Thinking in education.* New York: Cambridge University Press.

LIPMAN, M. (1988). *Philosophy goes to school.* Philadelphia: Temple University Press.

LIPMAN, M., SHARP, A. M., & OSCANYAN, F. S. (1980). *Philosophy in the classroom* (2nd ed.). Philadelphia: Temple University Press.

LIPMAN, M., & SHARP, A. M. (EDS.). (1978). *Growing up with philosophy.* Philadelphia: Temple University Pres.

LIPMAN, M., & BYNUM, T. W. (EDS.). (1976). *Philosophy for children.* Oxford: Basil Blackwell.

MARTENS, E. (1990). *Sich im Denken orientieren: Philosophishe Anfangsschritte mit Kindern* [Orienting yourself in thinking: First philosophical steps with children]. Hannover: Schroedel.

MATTHEWS, G. B. (1980). *Philosophy and the young child.* Cambridge, MA: Harvard University Press.

MATTHEWS, G. B. (1984). *Dialogues with children*. Cambridge, MA: Harvard University Press.

Philosophieren mit Kindern [Philosophizing with children]. (1991). [Special issue]. *Zeitschrift für Didaktik der Philosophie*. Vol. 1/91 Hannover: Schroedel.

PRITCHARD, M. S. (1985). *Philosophical adventures with children*. Lanham, MD: University Press of America.

REED, R. F. (1983). *Talking with children*. Denver, CO: Arden Press.

SEGAL, J. W., CHIPMAN, S. F., & GLASER, R. (EDS.). (1985). *Thinking and learning skills: Vol. 1. Relating instruction to research*. Hillsdale, NJ: Erlbaum.

SHARP, A. M., & REED, R. (EDS.). (1991). *Studies in philosophy for children: Harry Stottlemeier's discovery*. Philadelphia: Temple University Press.

Thinking: The Journal of Philosophy for Children. Upper Montclair, NJ: Institute for the Advancement of Philosophy for Children, 1981.

MATTHEW LIPMAN

PIAGET, JEAN (1896–1980)

Children are asked to drop beads alternately into two glasses. One of the glasses is hidden behind a screen. Even very young children say that there is the same number of beads in each glass even though they cannot see the beads in the hidden glass. But when they are asked what will happen if they keep doing that all day, all night, and keep going and going, very young children will say: "I don't know, I'd have to see." Whereas older children know that there still will be the same number of beads in each pile, because the same process is repeated over and over. Piaget notes that a 5½-year-old expressed this beautifully by saying: "Once you know, you know for ever."

Jean Piaget, a Swiss psychologist, sought to elucidate what constitutes the essence of the human species: our ability to think, to acquire and transmit knowledge, to strive for greater understanding of ourselves and our environment. He was the first to study systematically the development of children's understanding and tried to show that the origins of human knowledge can be found in childhood's grasp of time, space, causality, logic, morality, language, and mathematics. Piaget is best known as a psychologist, but he was also a biologist and a philosopher. However varied his enterprises, a certain unity characterized Piaget's research, the aim of which was to understand how organisms come to know their environment. Though Piaget did not consider himself a child psychologist, he is usually regarded as the most important figure in twentieth-century developmental psychology.

FORMATION AND EARLY WORK

Piaget was born on August 9, 1896, in Neuchâtel, Switzerland. His father, Arthur, was a professor of medieval literature and a historian. His mother, Rebecca-Suzanne Jackson, was "very intelligent, energetic," but also "rather neurotic," according to her son's autobiography (Piaget, 1976). Piaget attributed to his mother's instability the fact that he always disliked any "flight from reality" and found refuge early on in work instead of play.

Zoology was Piaget's first love. At the age of 11, he published his first article, a paragraph in a local natural-history magazine on his observations of an albino sparrow. By the time he was 17, his voluminous publications on mollusks had already brought him to the attention of European zoologists, and he was offered the post of research assistant in a natural-history museum. He had to decline because he was still a high school student. The relation between heredity and environment and the mechanism of evolutionary adaptation, which later occupied much of Piaget's attention, are already discussed in these early works.

Meanwhile, between 16 and 22, Piaget went through a period of religious, philosophical, and political searching. He discovered philosophy, was moved deeply by Henri Bergson, and decided that the biological explanation of knowledge would be his life's aim. His musings of the period are reflected in several publications, among which are *La Mission de l'idée* (1916), a long prose poem, and *Recherche* (1918), a philosophical Bildungsroman. The relations between science and faith, science and morality, the value of science, peace and war, and social salvation were among the young man's preoccupations.

Piaget showed a youthful, idealistic belief in progress and the power of ideas such as justice, equality, and freedom. Disappointed by religion and philosophy, the hero in *Recherche* finds the solution in science. The circle of sciences would give knowledge its own foundation, without need for recourse to anything external to it. The sciences are not organized hierarchically, with mathematics at the top, as others had written. Rather, they are arranged in a circular fashion. Each science makes assumptions that it cannot justify but can rely upon because they are the laws, conclusions, or products of another science adjacent to it in the "circle of the sciences." Thus, the structure of scientific knowledge as a whole stands firm, without any appeal to extrascientific ideas or forces. This idea guides much of Piaget's later work.

Science gives the laws of nature, life, and society; morality can therefore be based on an objective synthesis of scientific knowledge. Morality, like science, like life itself, is in constant evolution. Social salvation is thus seen as "the realization of an ideal equilibrium" between parts and whole, an equilibrium achieved "in oneself, in others, and in society" (Piaget, 1918). Key concepts of Piaget's later work are already sketched here: action as source of knowledge, constructive evolution, the process of equilibration between parts and whole, progress.

Piaget entered the University of Neuchâtel, where he studied zoology and philosophy, receiving his doctorate in zoology in 1918. Because he could not test his hypotheses on knowledge and evolution in zoology, he turned to psychology. He first went to Zurich, where he studied under Eugen Bleuler and Carl Gustav Jung; he was briefly interested in psychoanalysis, but did not find in it the concepts and the methodology that he needed to understand the growth of rational thought. In 1919 he went to Paris, where he spent two years at the Sorbonne.

A WORK IN CONSTANT EVOLUTION

In Paris, Piaget was given free access to the school laboratory of Alfred BINET and was asked by Binet's colleague Théophile Simon to work on the standardization of the Englishman Cyril BURT's tests of reasoning. Piaget soon discovered that trying to understand the causes of children's failures was much more interesting than developing another test of intelligence. He developed his own methodology, the *méthode clinique,*

or clinical interview, a flexible method of assessing children's understanding, and found with amazement that children under 11 years old were unable to perform very simple reasoning tasks that required class inclusion and class relations. He was elated; he had found at last a research method to study "thought in evolution."

In 1921, Piaget returned to Switzerland and settled in Geneva, where he was appointed director of research at the Institut J. J. Rousseau. Four of his books on the child's logic, the child's conception of the world, and the child's ideas about physical causality were published in the 1920s and made Piaget famous. His study of children's moral judgment, published in 1932, completed Piaget's overview of what he saw as the limitations of children's thinking between the ages of 3 and 8. He attributed these limitations to children's egocentrism, something that he would later call an absence of reversibility. From 1926 to 1929, Piaget was professor of philosophy at the University of Neuchâtel. In 1929 he was appointed professor at the University of Geneva, where he stayed until his death.

In 1923, Piaget married Valentine Châtenay, one of his students and early collaborators. Three children were born of this union, Jacqueline in 1925, Lucienne in 1927, and Laurent in 1931, and Piaget found in them a new field of experimentation. In the 1930s two volumes were born out of his daily observations. They gave a detailed description of the evolution of sensorimotor intelligence from birth to the beginning of language and representation. His observations and reflections on the development of his children's representational and symbolic activity (play, dream, imitation, early language) were collected in a third volume, published in the 1940s. In 1936, Harvard University granted him an honorary doctorate, a very early age for this honor and the first of many.

In the 1940s and early 1950s, much of Piaget's research was focused on stages of development and the search for formal models. Having shown in his study on sensorimotor intelligence that action is at the origin of thought, Piaget pursued his work on the development of children's thinking from 4 to 14 with the help of exceptional collaborators, such as Alina Szeminska and Bärbel Inhelder. He chose the terms *operation* and *operational thought,* thus emphasizing the idea that the logico-mathematical aspects of thought find their roots in the child's activity. This work, together with his studies of the different notions and operational domains (number, time, space, speed, causality, and chance), concretized his early idea of the circle of the sciences.

In the 1950s and 1960s, Piaget's formulation of his philosophy of sciences, genetic epistemology, was one of his main interests. In 1955 he established the International Center of Genetic Epistemology in Geneva, with the help of the Rockefeller Foundation. The idea of the circle of the sciences started to materialize within the Center, where psychologists, logicians, mathematicians, physicists, and biologists joined Piaget's regular collaborators in the development of basic epistemological questions. Piaget, however, did not give up psychology. In the 1960s, he published a few major studies on the figurative aspects of thought, perception, memory, and mental imagery, trying to show the reliance of perception and memory on changing operational thought.

In the 1970s, Piaget returned to the study of causality, in particular, the relations between operations and causality. Meanwhile, two of his main collaborators kept working on the relations between language and thought (Sinclair) and learning and thought (Inhelder). Piaget died in Geneva on September 17, 1980, his work still in progress.

PIAGET'S THEORY OF INTELLIGENCE

Piaget's psychology is a psychology of cognitive development, that is, a study of the development of the mental processes through which knowledge is acquired, including perception, memory, and reasoning. Piaget never studied perception, memory, and mental imagery in isolation, but strove to show how these cognitive activities contributed to the development of intelligence and were transformed by it. In that sense, Piaget's psychology is a psychology of intelligence.

While Piaget's theory is very abstract, his experiments were very down-to-earth. For example, in a study of the development of awareness, he asked people to crawl about on all fours and then describe how they did it. Small children were better at this task than were mathematicians.

For Piaget, intelligence is not a repertory of local performances that are added to each other as a subject grows. It is the process of knowing. Intelligence is action or, more precisely, "the most general form in the coordination of actions and operations." He showed empirically how, starting from basic reflexes, actions are progressively coordinated, first forming schemes (physical or mental actions on the environment) and then operations (structured, reversible mental actions).

Children acquire greater numbers of schemes and operations through processes of *assimilation* and *accommodation*. Each action and operation that is repeated may be tested on new objects (assimilation); at the same time, the action or operation is modified to fit the particularities of the new object (accommodation). For example, an infant who has learned to grasp a red ring swinging in front of him may discover that he can also grasp a red block. His grasping scheme is now generalized to include blocks (assimilation), but it is also modified, the grasping of a block necessitating a slightly different movement (accommodation). Adaptation to the environment through the synthesis of assimilation and accommodation is therefore a key factor in a child's development.

Development is not the result of maturation alone but of a constant interaction between the maturing organism and the environment. Organisms have a basic need for equilibrium, but equilibrium can be disturbed by the challenges presented to the organism by the environment. Challenges that cannot be resolved produce a discomfort, or disequilibrium, and a search for a better-organized and better-adapted organization so that contradictions will be resolved and equilibrium restored. Piaget calls this construction of a new organization that restores equilibrium "equilibration." In that sense, intelligence is adaptation.

Different levels in the organization of actions are characteristic of different steps, or "stages of development." The notion of stages of development is not exclusively Piagetian (Freud and others used it before him), but it is a key concept in Piaget's theory, though later in his life Piaget did not consider it as important a concept as his followers did.

Piaget identified four general stages of development in childhood. The age at the beginning of each stage can vary, but the order of succession is constant and each stage integrates the structures of the previous stage. At each stage of development, children strive to create their own model of the world. They ponder at their own level the very basic questions that a scientist would: What are time, matter, space, causality?

First is the sensorimotor stage (birth to 2 years). Piaget called this stage "sensorimotor" to emphasize that infants experience the world via their senses and motor activity. Babies grow from a state of unorganized action, a set of basic reflexes and perceptions, with no awareness of self and the external world, to a state of awareness and recognition.

At the end of the sensorimotor stage, infants not only recognize people and objects in their surroundings but also start having a sense of self and permanence. They know that people and objects do not cease to exist once out of sight; they are able to orient themselves in their space and keep track of time in a primitive way (before/now). Instead of solving problems by trial and error, as younger babies would, they show signs of representational thought.

Piaget not only used detailed observations but developed ingenious procedures to follow babies' early development, such as the search for lost objects. He was the first to describe what is possibly the most memorable revolution in the development of the child, the passage from action to thought.

Second is the preoperational stage (2 years to 7 years). Piaget was ambivalent on the accomplishments of this stage, often emphasizing the lack of logical thinking in children of that age. His early studies on children's thought, symbolic activity (play, imitation, the beginning of language), and moral development broke new ground, but the child's accomplishments were described merely as examples of "egocentric thought." Centered on their own point of view, children are incapable of decentration, that is, they are unable to take another person's point of view. Later on, the word *egocentric* would be dropped and a sanitized version chosen: Younger children are at a preoperational stage. If children at this stage are centered on their own point of view and incapable of decentration, it is because of a lack of reversibility. Prisoners of their immediate perception, they are unable to reverse mentally what they have done. For example, a child at this stage would look at two identical balls of clay, flatten one in a pancake shape, and believe that the one in the pancake shape is actually bigger than the clay ball left untouched.

The revolution in this stage is the progressive mastery of representational thought: language first, but also imitation and symbolic play. It is a time at which, in the mind of the child, fiction and "reality" may be equally true, at which language literally creates the world and the world created can be as real as the real one. It is a world that Piaget, weary of "any flight from reality," could describe well but to which he could not completely render justice. Language for Piaget could only be subjugated to thought, and thought was action, not language.

Third is the concrete operational stage (7 years to 12 years). Conservation is the main acquisition of this stage and the next step in the discovery of object permanency, that is, the conservation of number and physical quantities. Though matter changes, it stays the same. By *conservation,* Piaget meant the logical operations that make children independent of their immediate and possibly distorted perceptions and realize that certain properties remain unchanged when others change.

Two rows of ten matches each still contain the same number of matches, even though the matches in a row are spread out or brought close to each other. At the preoperational stage, a child would be unable to understand that both rows still contain the same number of matches, even though the child could correctly count the number of matches in each row.

Piaget's more famous experiences dealt with the conservation of quantity, weight, and volume. At this stage, children understand, for example, that the water poured from a wide, round container into a tall, narrow cylinder is still the same water, even though it may look as if there is more (or less) water in the tall cylinder. The same can be said for the clay ball flattened into a big pancake.

Children give three types of argument to support their point of view: identity (it is the same; nothing has been added, nothing taken away); reversibility (if you pour the water back into the wide container, you will get the same amount of water as before); and compensation (consideration of two dimensions, width and height: It is taller but it is thinner). Considering the two dimensions of a problem is the more elaborate argument and the only one that resists all counter-suggestions.

Fourth is the formal operational stage (11 years and above). This is the highest stage in Piaget's theory. It involves the ability to reason about hypotheses and probabilities and, to do so, about second-order operations (operations performed on other operations rather than on empirical reality). In other words, it implies the ability to pursue a line of reasoning that begins with an assertion that is purely hypothetical, or even false. Consider this assertion: If mice are bigger than dogs, and dogs are bigger than elephants, then mice are bigger than elephants. The assertion is logically correct, even though it is empirically false. To grasp this point requires an understanding of the term *if* and the *if-then* relationship and an understanding of the idea of transitivity, that is, if $A<B$ and $B<C$, then $A<C$.

Piaget's most important contribution to the field of intellectual development is not his stage theory but his constructivist conception of knowledge acquisition. Knowledge is neither innate nor the result of learning. It is the product of the active mind interacting with its environment. Knowledge is constructed in the interaction of the subject and the object, as the subject knows himself by knowing the object.

PUBLICATIONS

At his death, Piaget had written more than 700 original publications, including more than 80 books. Among Piaget's major works available in English are *The Language and Thought of the Child* (1923, trans. 1926); *The Child's Conception of the World* (1926, trans. 1929); *The Moral Judgment of the Child* (1932); *The Construction of Reality in the Child* (1937, trans. 1954); *Play, Dreams, and Imitation in Childhood* (1945, trans. 1951, though title would be better translated as *The Development of the Symbol*); *The Origins of Intelligence in Children* (1936, trans. 1952); *The Child's Conception of Number*, with Alina Szeminska (1941, trans. 1952); *The Child's Construction of Quantities* (1941, trans. 1974); *The Psychology of the Child*, with Bärbel Inhelder (1966, trans. 1969); *Memory and Intelligence*, with Bärbel Inhelder (1968, trans. 1973); and *Behavior and Evolution* (1974,

1978, though title would be better translated as *Behavior, the Motor of Evolution*).

CONCLUSION

Piaget broke so much new ground in the empirical study of the child that he left almost no sphere of inquiry untouched: action, imitation, play, language, morality, physical causality, logic, space, time, movement and speed, chance, geometry, mathematics. His influence was so strong that for a while Piaget dominated the field of developmental psychology and is still widely respected. His studies, his methodology, his experimental procedures have been replicated, developed, and transformed.

Piaget's views on intelligence and knowledge acquisition caused a reevaluation of earlier ideas on learning and education. Teaching could not be mere transmission of knowledge. Children's active participation in the construction of knowledge and their cognitive limitations as they went through different stages of intellectual development had to be taken into account.

Piaget's insistence on universal stages of development seemed a return to the idea that development is genetically preformed, an idea that Piaget always disputed, insisting on his interactionist position. Much research was done to operationalize Piaget's stages of development, but the results were ambivalent. The general sequence of development posited by Piaget was never disproved, but the idea that each stage relied on a basic structure of mental organization was widely attacked when it was shown that Piaget's age norms were not universal, that preoperational children could function at the operational level on some tasks, and that learning could accelerate development. Interestingly, these criticisms could be used to support Piaget's own point of view on the influence of the environment on a child's growth.

Piaget has also been criticized for neglecting the role of affectivity and for neglecting historical forces and thus giving an overly cognitive, intellectualized view of development. Although these criticisms have some merit, it should be said that Piaget did pay some attention to, and even wrote at some length about, the areas just mentioned. Piaget's limitations, moreover, were the key to his success. By centering on one major question, how knowledge is acquired, he was the first to describe successfully the child's discovery of the world.

(*See also:* PIAGETIAN THEORY OF INTELLECTUAL DEVELOPMENT.)

BIBLIOGRAPHY

GINSBURG, H. P., & OPPER, S. (1988). *Piaget's theory of intellectual development* (3rd ed.). Englewood Cliffs, NJ: Prentice Hall.

GRUBER, H. E., & VONÈCHE, J. J., (EDS.). (1977). *The essential Piaget: An interpretive reference and guide.* New York: Basic Books.

PIAGET, J. (1918). *Recherche.* Lausanne: La Concorde. A chapter-by-chapter summary is in H. E. Gruber & J. J. Vonèche. (Eds.). *The essential Piaget* (1977).

PIAGET, J. (1976). Autobiographie. In *Revue Européenne des Sciences Sociales, 14,* 1–43.

PIAGET, J., & INHELDER, B. (1969). *The psychology of the child.* New York: Basic Books.

CHANTAL BRUCHEZ-HALL
HOWARD E. GRUBER

PIAGETIAN THEORY OF INTELLECTUAL DEVELOPMENT

What distinguishes Jean PIAGET's theory of cognitive development from other such theories and gives it its originality is the fact that it was the result of extensive psychological research. Early in his career, Piaget saw as his main project the elaboration of a theory of knowledge not founded on philosophic speculation but on scientific fact. He replaced Kant's question, "How is knowledge—particularly pure mathematics—possible?" with "How is knowledge constructed and transformed in the course of an individual's development?" The answer, he hoped, would reveal a process of knowledge construction common to the development of thought in the child and to the sociogenesis of scientific thought as evinced in the history of science. Though Piaget's psychological studies might thus be regarded as a mere by-product of his epistemological work—for they constitute, so to speak, only the experimental part of his total endeavor—they certainly were not a minor

product, either in Piaget's view or in terms of their results.

Piaget's epistemological pursuits led him to study the origins and the construction of general and fundamental categories of human knowledge, such as space, time, causality, logical and moral consistency, and the construction of invariants (numerical, physical, and spatial). That is, he studied the development of the various systems that make our adaptation to the world we live in possible. As a trained zoologist who devoted his life to the elaboration of a biological theory of knowledge, Piaget could not conceive of models of analysis of cognitive development in terms of an accumulation of separate units; for him, such models should posit the existence of organized systems. His interest in the construction of invariants (under certain transformations) led to the establishment of structural models, which had already proved fertile in the analysis of human interaction by authors such as Claude Lévi-Strauss. Nonetheless, Piaget warned his readers that he was not an adherent of a structural philosophical theory or dogma.

Developmental psychologists who endeavor to explain mental functions by how they are formed (i.e., by their evolution in the child) have proposed stagelike sequences according to criteria that vary from one author to the next. Piaget concentrated on cognitive development and particularly on the progressive coherence of intelligent behavior; he brought to light a constant order of progression in such behavior, distinguishing three stages. The first is completed by the second half of the second year. The second lasts until 11 or 12 years of age, the first period of the elaboration of mental operations being completed by the age of 6 or 7 and followed by a long period of structuration. The third stage continues into adolescence and beyond. Examples illustrating some of the characteristic attainments and types of progress follow.

LOGIC IN ACTION

During the first year and a half of life, infants make great strides in the intelligent ways they organize their still very limited environment. Using their human hereditary competences, they first bring some stability into their world by the repetition of some simple actions, such as sucking, looking, and grasping. An important concept of Piaget's theory is relevant here: that of an action scheme (i.e., the pattern of what is repeatable in an action). A scheme is an organized structural unit (e.g., stretching a hand, curling the fingers, closing them on an object) but also has a functional aspect, in that it assimilates new objects, since it is continuously applied to new situations (e.g., grasping objects never encountered before). Assimilation brings about accommodation, or modifications of a specific action to a new situation. Action schemes are coordinated into composite activities, such as grasping an object and bringing it to one's mouth (ordering and combining two schemes) or grasping an object, turning it around, and sucking a corner (inserting a scheme as a subscheme). In the second half of a child's first year, such coordinations already constitute intelligent acts in the sense that they serve as a means of obtaining a desired effect, as in shoving away a handkerchief that happened to fall on an object the baby wants to play with or directing the hand of an adult toward a desired toy that is out of reach.

In the first half of the second year, intelligence in action reaches a level where actions of the baby or of somebody with the baby, the objects acted on, and the results of actions have become differentiated; the infant is now capable of apprehending relations between actions and their results, between objects and their properties, and between the self as an agent and others as agents. Among the many small experiments Piaget performed with his own children, some are particularly suited to a demonstration of these attainments and have been repeated innumerable times by different experimenters with many variations. These attainments are known as object-permanence, the spatio-temporal group of displacements, and spatialized objectivized causality.

Object-permanence was described in detail by Piaget (1937/1955). The following developmental sequence emerges: At first infants will not search for an interesting object when it is hidden by the experimenter in front of their eyes and within their reach; by 7 months or so, they will search under a screen if they were already reaching for the object while it was being hidden; by 10 months, they will search and find the object hidden under screen A, but when the object is then immediately hidden under screen B (as always, before their eyes), they will once again try to find it

under A, where previously they were successful; the object is still, as it were, linked to the child's own action of seeking and finding. In the beginning of the second year, by contrast, objects will be found after several displacements; they will by then have acquired an autonomous existence, and the children can coordinate their own movements with those of the object. Difficulties still arise with invisible displacements, as when the experimenter displaces the object from under screen A to B in a closed hand, since this situation demands some kind of mental representation.

The group of displacements is closely linked to object-permanence; moving about the room and encountering various obstacles, the child becomes capable of coordinating a displacement from A to B and one from B to C into a direct move from A to C, of canceling a displacement from A to B by going from B to A, and of constructing various detours to go from one place to another. A coherent system of relations, both temporal and spatial is built up, and the movements are ordered in time and take the position of other objects into account.

The notion of causality undergoes a similar, closely linked development. The causal relations between movements of one object and another are at first totally dependent on the infants' own actions. Having discovered by chance that pulling a blanket toward them will bring a desired toy on it within their reach, they will again pull the blanket when the experimenter puts the toy next to the blanket instead of on it. By the end of the sensorimotor period, they will no longer do so, having come to understand the necessity of spatial contact between the two objects. Similarly, they will have become capable of using a stick to make another object move.

TOWARD THE LOGIC OF THOUGHT

The transition from the logic-in-action of the sensorimotor period to later logic in thinking takes place gradually. Sensorimotor intelligence has the built-in functional property of groping for further development and thus needs some kind of mental representation for its extension into the past and the future, in searching for causes and reasons and for anticipations and plans. Thought operates on symbolic representations of many different kinds. Some are personal and cannot be shared directly, such as mental images; others can have direct communicative value, such as gestures, and can be conventionalized (e.g., waving good-bye). Gestures and drawings usually have some resemblance to whatever they represent. Other symbolic representations do not exhibit such a resemblance and are therefore conventional and collective, such as words, numbers, graphs, and algebraic formulas. In the second year of life, children clearly begin to produce and to understand various symbolic representations and to carry out, without trial and error, certain acts that require mental representation. By contrast, though mental images may be present earlier, infants' intelligent but purely sensorimotor acts do not yet appear to make use of mental representations for the solution of problems. In Piaget's view, thinking means working as actively on symbolic representations as on real objects; it also means constructing symbolic instruments that fit the particular thinking act the individual is performing. The verbal formulation of a series of actions as "First I do this and then that" is useful for certain complicated activities; mental images contribute to the solution of spatial problems. Many logical principles are applied in everyday thinking without the subject having any precise mental representation; thus, if an adult sees that product A is more expensive than product B and that in another store product B is more expensive than product C, he or she knows without paying attention to the exact price that C is the cheapest, using the transitivity principle, usually without knowing the word *transitivity*. Moreover, as Piaget warned, symbols are always closely tied to the thinking subject's knowledge of whatever it is the symbols represent. Words such as *force* and *speed* do not have the same meaning for a young child, a racing driver, and a physicist. The construction and comprehension of the various representative means thus depend both on the level of intellectual development and on the domain of knowledge the subject is engaged in.

Though there has been much less research on the period when thought has just become representative (i.e., between 2 and 4 years of age) than on the period from 4 years onward, a preliminary picture of the main characteristics of younger children's thinking can be constructed. One of the experimental situations reported in Piaget and Szeminska (1941/1951) that was successfully proposed to children as young as 3 was the following: Both the child and the experimenter have in front of them a small equal number of identical chips (only two or three for the youngest subjects). A box full of the same chips is at their disposal. After the child has agreed that each of the participants in the game has the same number of chips, the experimenter announces some tricks and takes away one chip from the child, adding it to his own chips and hiding them. The child is told to take chips from the box and add them to his own collection so that "it is again fair." Younger children (3 and 4 years old) always add one chip to their own collection, and are very surprised that the two collections are not equal when the experimenter's collection is uncovered. Yet, their surprise does not lead them to change their behavior. The experimenter's action results in two changes, but these children take into account only the change in their own collection (one chip less), for which they compensate by adding one chip.

In Piaget's terms, thinking here is unidirectional and irreversible, characteristic of young children when they are faced with situations in which an action results in two related changes (minus one, plus one). The other aspect is quantitative, for 5-year-olds may already take two chips to add to their own collection (when the number is small), but when the initial collections are bigger (ten or twelve chips) or when, instead of one chip, two or more are taken by the experimenter, they can no longer figure how many are needed to reestablish equality. Yet, there is clear progress, for they have now begun to establish a relation between two changes resulting from one action, though an important further development is necessary before the first coherent reasoning systems are constructed. The gradual mastery of various conservation concepts provides good examples of the complex processes at work in the construction of a system of operations. In many of the conservation tasks, the problem concerns two inverse changes resulting from one action but leaving certain properties invariant— as when a ball of clay is rolled into a sausage shape, it becomes longer and thinner, but its weight remains the same.

A series of learning experiments (Inhelder, Sinclair,

& Bovet, 1974) made it possible to follow in more detail the changes in children's reasoning over three or four sessions. In the length problem, children 5–7 years old were presented with the following situations: The experimenter constructed a zigzag road out of five sticks (each 7 centimeters long), and the child was given a collection of shorter sticks (each 5 centimeters long) and asked to construct a straight road directly beneath the zigzag, starting at the left and making it just as long as the model, and to construct a straight road just as long as the model but on another part of the table. Finally, the experimenter put the five sticks in a straight line and asked the child to make a straight road directly underneath the model. In this situation, none of the subjects had any difficulty putting down seven of their sticks so that both the extremities of their road coincided with the model. In the first situation, they used the idea that "not going beyond" means "equal length" and put down four sticks corresponding to the straight distance between the zigzag extremities. When asked to make their road elsewhere on the table, the not-going-beyond principle could not be applied, and many subjects used another idea: They counted the sticks in the model road (five) and made a straight road out of five of their shorter sticks.

In a discussion with the experimenter, the children were led to contemplate the various constructions. Some subjects at first saw no contradiction in their various solutions: Sometimes you have to do it one way, sometimes another. Most interesting were compromise solutions proposed by many subjects, such as breaking one or more of their sticks into bits or doubling them up. About a third of the subjects came to understand the need for two forms of compensation— between length and number of sticks and between zigzags and the extent to which the straight road goes beyond the model—and the heuristic value of the final situation (seven of their sticks for five of the experimenter's). The transitivity principle crowns the new organization. This example illustrates the way in which two separate schemes first direct children's thinking in different ways according to the situation; then children begin to infer from the comparisons that there is a discrepancy and feel the urge to understand it. For some, the compensations remain partial, but for those who succeed the final tests, the counting scheme and

the not-going-beyond scheme are reorganized in a system of operations that integrates both the length of the sticks and the length of the road they compose. Situations where either the counting scheme alone is valid (i.e., when the roads consist of equal-size elements) or the not-going-beyond scheme (i.e., when two straight roads have coinciding extremities) are not understood as special cases that take their place in a larger system. Such progress, observed in various forms in many studies, seems as far removed from the emergence of preprogrammed capacities as from a simple accumulation of empirical data. Further progress will lead to what are called formal operations or hypothetico-deductive operations, in which a sort of reversal takes place; that is, instead of constructing a theory or a notion from observable and representable data and the coordination of mental actions, adolescents start with a hypothetical theory of possible and necessary relations, and verify the hypotheses empirically, and the data provided by reality are inserted into the total set of possible combinations.

OPERATIONS ON OPERATIONS

Many examples of this further progress are given by Inhelder and Piaget (1955/1958). In one of the tasks (pp. 46–47), subjects are asked to investigate the flexibility of various rods of different material (brass or steel), different cross section (round or rectangular), and different length and thickness. The rods can be fixed onto a frame, weights can be attached to their extremities, and their protruding length can be adjusted by clamps. The subject is asked to decide which of the properties (or combination thereof) determines flexibility (that is, how far a rod will bend under the influence of an attached weight). One of the difficulties of this task is that to determine the role of, say, thickness by direct manipulation or by representation, one would need to have rods that have neither length nor cross section, are not made of any material, and have thickness only. One cannot even form a mental image of such objects. Yet, by taking rods that are identical in all respects except thickness, this property is mentally isolated for empirical verification. Subjects 14 or 15 years old were capable of carrying out a complicated series of comparisons in this manner, often after having stated that material, length, thickness, and cross section could all be factors influencing flexibility. Younger subjects, though capable of ordering (e.g., by length), classifying (e.g., by material), and establishing correspondences, did not proceed systemically and often compared rods that differed in more than one characteristic. As expressed by a 9-year-old who wanted to demonstrate the role of length, "It is better to compare a long thin rod to a short thick rod because *they are more different.*"

The older subjects' new kind of reasoning does not, however, lead directly to knowledge about why one metal is more flexible than another. The development of notions of physical causality was the theme of one of Piaget's first published books, and he returned to it forty years later (Piaget & Garcia, 1971/1974). As attested by the many "why" questions of young children, interest in causality starts early. At first, it is totally linked to human action; objects are thought to have humanlike intentions, desires, and fears that account for their behavior, or they behave as they do because humans have arranged matters that way. Later, logical operations—but no longer intentions—of the subject seem to be attributed to the objects. For example, children of 6 or 7 think that greater force is needed to hold a carriage immobile on a slope than to pull it up; when it is immobile, it still tends to roll down, whereas as soon as it starts going up the slope, its downward tendency is canceled. When weight is considered to be invariant during transformations of shape (though this is more difficult than numerical conservation, for example, since the apprehension of differences in muscular force needed to lift various objects intervenes), this is the result of logical reasoning, but does not prevent children at this level from thinking that an object weighs more when it hangs from a string than when it is placed on a scale. In other cases, such as simple movements of an object when pulled or pushed, the object's properties fit the subject's reasoning better. Though the development of coherent reasoning may often bring the subject to see problems that cannot yet be solved, sometimes a problem in causality may reciprocally lead to a reorganization of the subject's logical operations, particularly in the transition toward hypothetico-deductive operations. The behavior of objects often resists the subject's efforts at

understanding, but the challenge may lead to new discoveries.

THEORETICAL ASPECTS

The examples illustrate the theoretical aspects of Piaget's three stages. Each stage is defined by its construction modes and by the form of its final achievements, characterized by a particular structure. The final form of a structure is the threshold of possible transformations and announces the start of a new period. The order of succession of the stages is integrative; that is, the highest forms of a structure at one level become an integral part of the next. Three main stages satisfy these criteria, but the age at which the structures appear, like their duration, varies across individuals and their sociocultural environment.

The first stage can be divided into several substages, as was shown by Piaget (1936/1952, 1937/1955, 1945/1951) in his longitudinal studies of his own children. Its main attainment is the infant's invention of new means to solve new situations—a first Copernican revolution, as Piaget put it. Gradually, a differentiation between infant and environment is achieved and spatiotemporal relations between events and objects (including the infant's own body) are constructed.

The second stage consists of two substages, of which the first (construction of symbolic and representative functions) prepares the second (progressive development of mental operations). Around the age of 6 or 7, with reasoning directed by a focus on the most striking result of a transformation and without reversibility, children may solve a particular problem, often with a kind of sudden insight. At this age, the system of operations becomes reversible (i.e., the inverse of the direct operation annuls a transformation or constitutes a reciprocity of relations). This achievement explains why the 7–11 age period has often been treated as a separate stage. Nonetheless, the generalization or equilibration of such logical insights may take several years and, for certain problems of space, time, and causality, may take until the age of 10 or 11.

The third stage is characterized by the capacity to operate on one's own operations. Not only do subjects make deductions from hypotheses, but they also construct experimental procedures indicative of an exhaustive combinatorial and/or proportional type of thinking.

Piaget elaborated essentially logico-mathematical models in his analysis of the progressive coherence of intelligent behavior. From mathematics he borrowed algebraic structures, order structures, topological structures, morphisms, and categories. An *operation* is defined as an action that can be interiorized and that is reversible; it can mentally take place in two directions. Two forms of reversibility are distinguished, negation and reciprocity. At the first level of a system of operations, these two forms of reversibility apply to different types of problems and cannot yet be combined in a unitary system such as that attained by adolescents (identity, negation, reciprocity, correlative, or the INRC group). When asked why a zoologist by training had become so abstract and what the explanatory value of his structural models might be, Piaget answered, "In my view, to explain means to reconstitute how phenomena are produced," and asserted his belief that abstract models, serving as better means of analysis (i.e., of description) than natural language, are common to psychologists, neurologists, and cyberneticians, and may become explanatory.

In studies on number (Piaget & Szeminska, 1941/1951), physical and spatial quantities (Piaget & Inhelder, 1941/1974; Piaget, Inhelder, & Szeminska, 1948/1960), and the construction of scientific experimental methods (Inhelder & Piaget, 1955/1958), Piaget's collaborators, analyzing their subjects' actions through experimental materials and their verbally expressed reflections, realized the advantage of having at their disposal models of transformatory systems (i.e., structures that express the logical forms underlying the observable behaviors). Piaget's structuralism is instrumental; it is a form of analysis that uses structures as flexible instruments in the study of thought and that introduces an open-ended conception of psychological reality. His abstract structures are dynamic and incorporate content; they provide the means for structuring content, be it concrete or symbolic, and determine the characteristics of newly created structures. Since the various contents to be structured differ in complexity, notions such as the conservation of substance, weight, and mass are not acquired at the same time.

Piaget's continual search for adequate logico-mathematical models led him to reshape his models of the logic of operations in his last work (Piaget & Garcia 1987/1991). Going back to the very roots of logic (i.e., the protologic of the sensorimotor period), Piaget decided to expand and amend his operatory logic in the direction of a logic of meanings. Since an intelligent action always has a meaning for the subject, there are implications between meanings, which lead to inferences, as is clear from infants' anticipatory behavior and expressions of surprise. This reformulation in terms of a logic of meanings allows for a much closer link between the various levels described above, by bringing to light fragments of structures elaborated at the end of the sensorimotor period that prepare not only the system of concrete operations but also its further elaboration. The reformulation also brings the models more in line with Piaget's work on correspondences, contradiction, abstraction, and generalization, aimed at a deeper exploration of the mechanisms that lead to progress (i.e., to the reorganization of an existing system).

MECHANISMS OF PROGRESS

Piaget's biological approach led him to posit as a common source for the evolution of biological and cognitive systems, first, the processes of assimilation and accommodation and, then, that of equilibration; both systems are open systems in continuous interaction with the environment. Consequently, an equilibrium state is always dynamic, fluctuating around some mean, according to the changing situations with which the subject is confronted; at times, the system becomes unstable when certain disturbances can no longer be absorbed, but because of its self-regulatory processes, inherent in the interaction with the environment and characteristic of all living organisms, it can reorganize itself to some degree. In a cognitive system the regulations become constructive, leading to higher levels of knowledge. The most important instrument of such structural reorganizations is that of abstraction, together with its concomitant, generalization. Abstraction is at work as an instrumental process at all levels, but is applied to different contents. Piaget distinguished two types of abstraction. The first is empirical abstraction and bears on observable properties of objects or material aspects of actions, but uses relations constructed previously by the second type of abstraction, called "reflecting abstraction," which bears on the subject's own action schemes, coordinations, and operations. Knowledge of the physical world, understanding the causality of physico-chemical and other effects of objects acting on one another, is obtained by empirical and reflecting abstraction together; the construction of a system of logical operations proceeds essentially by reflecting abstraction, which is at work early in life but leads only gradually to thinking about one's own actions and thoughts, to consciousness and conceptualization. This movement toward ever greater interiorization goes together with that implied by empirical abstraction—a deeper penetration into the properties of objects, their exteriorization and objectivation.

Though Piaget carried out few studies on children's interactions with people, whether peers or adults, he made it clear that such interaction is an essential part of intellectual development, but that it would need extensive research of a different kind than he was mainly interested in; in his less well known theoretical works on social questions (1965), he stated that at every level (sensorimotor, intuitive, and operatory intelligence), the precise form of the child's exchanges with others should be determined. He was convinced that interpersonal and intrapersonal operations are strictly parallel, provided the interactions are cooperative and not based on unilateral submission to authority. Cooperation is literally a coordination of actions or operations between individuals, isomorphous with the coordination of schemes or operations in one individual and constructed by the same mechanisms.

The development of personal interactions, particularly peer interactions, is one of the many domains where Piaget's theories are being worked on at present (cf. Beilin & Pufall, 1992). Piaget's proposed parallelism of such interaction with intrapersonal development of reasoning in interaction with the world of objects leads to questions about how intersubject equilibration is related to subject–object equilibration. In turn, this raises questions of how the self-organizing,

equilibration theory of human intelligence can be worked out in detail. Piaget's view of intelligence as being essentially generative and progressively more coherent led to a great number of observations and experimental studies whose results appear to be as incompatible with nativist as with empiricist theories. In his view, the only other possibility is a theory based on the continuity of biological regulatory processes (i.e., an interactionist constructivist theory of a never-ending cycle of equilibrations). The emphasis on the knowing subject's constructions is no doubt the main difference between Piaget's theory and recent trends that would explain cognitive development by appealing to either neuronal activity in the brain or to the influence of society on the mind.

The concept of equilibration is already present in Piaget's autobiographical novel *Recherche* (1918), but it underwent many reformulations, as did his abstract models. Similarly, his views on biological continuity (i.e., of human intelligence based on deep-seated biological mechanisms inherent in all living beings) led to his view of the human cerebralized nervous system as a new departure that uses earlier ways of adaptive functioning. Piaget's interest in McCulloch and Pitts' model of a network within which neurons function analogously to coherent reasoning systems led him to raise the problems of the relation between abstraction and awareness, which are psychological events, and neuronal organizations, which are not in themselves cognitive mechanisms; it seems hardly possible that we could ever become conscious of their functioning (Piaget, 1967/1971, pp. 222–233). This appears to foreshadow the discussion on symbolic and subsymbolic (connectionist) artificial-intelligence models and the question of meaning and consciousness, which is being much debated in this rapidly expanding field.

Piaget did not intend his theory to be a completed system; each new cycle of research reconstructed his earlier conceptions and raised new questions to be answered experimentally. Many psychologists agree that the theory continues to act in a heuristic manner; new observations and experiments will be carried out on the basic question that underlies Piaget's theory of cognitive development—the continuity of biological mechanisms in the extraordinary creativeness of human intelligence.

BIBLIOGRAPHY

In references in the text with two dates, the first refers to the original, the second to the English edition.

BEILIN, H., & PUFALL, P. B. (EDS.). (1992). *Piaget's theory: Prospects and possibilities.* Hillsdale, NJ: Erlbaum.

INHELDER, B., & PIAGET, J. (1958). *The growth of logical thinking from childhood to adolescence: An essay on the construction of formal operational structures.* New York: Basic Books. (Original work published 1955.)

INHELDER, B., SINCLAIR, H., & BOVET M. (1974). *Learning and the development of cognition.* Cambridge, MA: Harvard University Press.

PIAGET, J. (1918). *Recherche* [The quest]. Lausanne: La Concorde.

PIAGET, J. (1951). *Play, dreams, and imitation in childhood.* New York: W. W. Norton. (Original work published 1945.)

PIAGET, J. (1952). *The origins of intelligence in children.* New York: International University Press. (Original work published 1936.)

PIAGET, J. (1955). *The construction of reality in the child.* London: Routledge. (Original work published 1937.)

PIAGET, J. (1965). *Études sociologiques* [Sociological studies]. Geneva: Droz.

PIAGET, J. (1971). *Biology and knowledge: An essay on the relations between organic regulations and cognitive processes.* Chicago: University of Chicago Press. (Original work published 1967.)

PIAGET, J., & GARCIA, R. (1974). *Understanding causality.* New York: W. W. Norton. (Original work published 1971.)

PIAGET, J., & GARCIA R. (1991). *Towards a logic of meanings.* Hillsdale, NJ: Erlbaum. (Original work published 1987.)

PIAGET, J., GRIZE, J.-B., SZEMINSKA, A., & VINH BANG. (1977). *Epistemology and psychology of function.* Dordrecht and Boston: Reidel. (Original work published 1968.)

PIAGET, J., & INHELDER, B. (1974). *The child's construction of quantities: Conservation and atomism.* London: Routledge.

PIAGET, J., INHELDER, B., & SZEMINSKA, A. (1960). *The child's conception of geometry.* London: Routledge. (Original work published 1941.)

PIAGET, J., & SZEMINSKA, A. (1951). *The child's conception of number.* London: Routledge.

BÄRBEL INHELDER
HERMINA SINCLAIR

PICTURE ARRANGEMENT　　*See* WAIS–R SUBTESTS.

PICTURE COMPLETION　　*See* WAIS–R SUBTESTS.

PRACTICAL INTELLIGENCE　　Practical intelligence refers to the intellectual competencies required by problems and tasks in the everyday world. Although the kinds of intellectual competencies useful in handling worldly affairs have always been included in conceptions of intelligence, they have not been adequately represented on intelligence quotient (IQ) tests, which for the most part assess the subset of intellectual competencies required to succeed in formal schooling. One of the most exciting developments in the field of intelligence in the 1980s and early 1990s has been an emergent interest in practical intelligence. A growing body of evidence suggests that practical intelligence is a second kind of intelligence on equal footing with the largely academic intelligence that is sampled by IQ tests. Due to the relative independence of the two kinds of intelligence, some individuals have a great deal of practical intelligence but relatively little academic intelligence or, conversely, a great deal of academic intelligence but relatively little practical intelligence. Other individuals have a great deal of both kinds of intelligence or very little of either.

Given the recency of interest in practical intelligence, definitional issues have yet to be resolved. These issues are considered first in this entry. Next, relations between practical and academic intelligence will be discussed. Finally, a few comments will be made about the assessment of practical intelligence.

DEFINING PRACTICAL INTELLIGENCE

Precise definitions of practical intelligence, or of any other kind of intelligence for that matter, have been difficult to agree upon. When the editors of the *Journal of Educational Psychology* convened a symposium of seventeen leading researchers in 1921 and asked them to describe what they conceived intelligence to be, they received fourteen different answers and three nonreplies. When Robert J. Sternberg and D. K. Detterman (1986) posed a similar question to contemporary researchers sixty-five years later, their replies included twenty-five different attributes of intelligence (Sternberg & Berg, 1986) and showed no more consensus than the replies of participants in the 1921 symposium.

Although there is considerable variability in definitions of intelligence, there are commonalities as well—for example, most definitions include intellectual competencies required for handling problems found outside the classroom environment. Alfred BINET, who is regarded as the father of the IQ test, considered intelligence to be the collective faculties of "judgment, otherwise called good sense, practical sense, initiative, the faculty of adapting one's self to circumstances" (Binet & Simon, 1916, pp. 42–43). Given the breadth of this definition, the largely academic content of Binet's IQ test is surprising, until one realizes that Binet relied less on his definition of intelligence when assembling tasks than on the empirical criterion of whether a task differentiated older children from younger children (Sattler, 1986). Except for the preschool range of the test, the older children that Binet tested had more years of schooling than did the younger children and thus would be expected to differ considerably in their performance on classroom-type tasks. Wechsler, who developed the competing Wechsler IQ tests, began with a similarly broad definition of intelligence, namely, "The aggregate or global capacity of the individual to act purposefully, to think rationally and to deal effectively with his environment" (Wechsler, 1958, p. 7), and ended up with a similarly uniform academic content on his tests.

Although definitional issues remain largely unresolved, a working definition can at least serve the purpose of guiding inquiry. For the most part, modern investigators have been guided by one of the following four working definitions of practical intelligence.

Definition by Exclusion. This working definition of intelligence is based on exclusion, in other words, by what practical intelligence is not. For example, Norman Frederiksen (1986) considers practical intelligence to be displayed in one's cognitive response to most of what happens outside the classroom. Support for a working definition based on exclusion is provided by apparent differences between the kinds of academic problems found in the classroom and on IQ tests on the one hand and the kinds of practical problems found outside the classroom on the other. A sampling of these apparent differences is presented in Table 1. An example of an academic problem is to identify the factors of the algebraic expression $a^2 - b^2$. Academic problems are well defined and are formulated by others (e.g., a teacher or a textbook author). When teachers give problems to their students, the students may not always be sure of the answers, but they usually will be sure about what the content of the problem is. Furthermore, for most academic problems, additional information is not required. In the present example, if the rules for factoring algebraic expressions have been learned, $a^2 - b^2$ can be solved without any additional information. A single correct answer exists, $(a - b)(a + b)$, and the only method for obtaining it is by correctly applying the relevant factoring rule. Finally, if the rules for factoring algebraic equations are not known, general knowledge gained from everyday experience will not be helpful in

TABLE 1

Characteristics that differentiate academic and practical kinds of problems

Academic Problems	Practical Problems
1. Well defined.	1. Ill defined.
2. Formulated by others.	2. Unformulated.
3. Necessary information provided.	3. Additional information required.
4. One correct answer.	4. Multiple "correct" answers.
5. One method to obtain answer.	5. Multiple methods to obtain answer.
6. Disembedded from everyday experience.	6. Embedded in everyday experience.

SOURCE: Adapted from Neisser (1976) and Wagner & Sternberg (1985).

solving the problem (but may come in handy when students attempt to explain the resultant F to their parents).

An example of a practical problem is that of an employee whose superior appears not to appreciate the employee's work. Unlike the academic problem, the nature of this problem is unclear. Is the problem one of poor performance on the part of the employee, or is the problem one of an erroneous perception of the employee's performance on the part of the superior? Perhaps there isn't a problem at all: The superior may give the impression of not appreciating their work to all employees. Unlike the academic problem that comes with all the necessary information, additional information search appears to be required. The employee might ask other employees to find out if the superior treats them similarly, or the employee might ask the superior directly for a work evaluation. Rarely do practical problems have a single correct answer. Typically, there are multiple "correct" answers, each associated with some liabilities as well as assets. If the superior really does not value the performance of the employee, possible correct answers include (1) improving the level of performance if it is deficient; (2) making the superior aware of the employee's level of performance if it is adequate; or (3) finding a new job if the situation appears to be hopeless.

Based on the distinction between academic and practical problems, a useful working definition of practical intelligence is the ability to solve the ill-defined problems that arise in daily life, for which there may be no clear-cut answers. An advantage of this working definition of practical intelligence is that its considerable breadth makes it unlikely that examples of practical intelligence will be excluded. Its considerable breadth is also a weakness, however, in that little guidance is provided about what exactly practical intelligence is, as opposed to what it is not, and how it might best be studied, measured, and improved.

Practical Know-How. The English language contains a number of expressions that refer to having practical know-how. An individual with considerable practical know-how is said to be "street smart," to have "common sense," or to have "learned the ropes." An individual lacking in such knowledge is said to be "wet behind the ears," an apparent reference to the limited world knowledge possessed by newborns.

Several investigations of practical intelligence have been based upon working definitions that feature practical know-how. For example, Berry and Irvine's (1986) cross-cultural analysis of intelligent behavior is based on the concept of the *bricoleur,* a jack-of-all-trades who accomplishes repairs and odd jobs by employing whatever resources and materials are at hand. The *bricoleur* can be contrasted with a modern service technician who uses a computer printout to determine what system of an automobile is malfunctioning and who then fixes the problem by replacing parts, using specialized tools as necessary. Berry and Irvine's intriguing analysis suggests that examples of practical intelligence are ubiquitous among all of the cultures of the world, including cultures that have been viewed by Western civilization as savage.

A second example of a working definition of practical intelligence based on practical know-how is Richard K. Wagner and Robert J. Sternberg's (Wagner, 1987; Wagner & Sternberg, 1985, 1990) analysis of tacit knowledge, practical know-how that is required to succeed in various career pursuits and that must be acquired informally from experience or from a mentor. One publisher provided the apt description of tacit knowledge as knowing "what goes without saying." In their studies, measures of tacit knowledge distinguished between groups of individuals that varied in amounts of experience and training in fields such as academic psychology and business management. Performance on measures of tacit knowledge was related to criterion measures of performance in the careers examined but was largely unrelated to traditional measures of academic aptitude.

Social Competence. One of the most salient differences between the nature of work assigned to students in school and most other work is whether the work is to be done independently or cooperatively. The majority of schoolwork is to be completed independently. In fact, relying on someone other than the teacher for assistance is known as cheating. In contrast, the majority of nonschoolwork depends heavily on working with and through others.

Several approaches to the study of practical intelligence have relied on working definitions based on social competence. Jane MERCER's (1979) Adaptive Behavior Inventory for Children (ABIC) assesses six kinds of social-role performance in a structured interview with a child's primary caretaker: family roles, community roles, peer roles, nonacademic school roles, earner/consumer roles, and self-maintenance roles. The ABIC and other measures of adaptive behavior (i.e., the ability to meet society's norms in daily functioning) have been used to distinguish children who learn slowly in school but perform adequately outside the school setting from children whose performance is deficient both in and out of school. The motivation behind the measures has been to eliminate what Mercer has referred to as the "6-hour retardate"—children who are considered to be retarded by their teachers but who perform adequately in other contexts. These children are not considered to be truly retarded, but rather are ill prepared for succeeding in school for some other reason.

A second example of a working definition of practical intelligence that is based on social competence is provided by Ford (1986). According to this view, practical intelligence involves transactional goals. Transactional goals involve things outside the body, such as establishing a friendship with a potential playmate, as opposed to things that are thought to remain inside the body, such as mastering a new concept. The relative value of various transactional goals depends upon their importance to an individual and to the individual's social group. Studies described by Ford indicate that many of the important transactional goals are social in nature, including having good relations with friends and family, treating people fairly, and showing concern for the rights of others.

Prototypes of Practical Intelligence. According to Neisser (1976), it is impossible to define practical intelligence as an entity. Rather, what can be done is to rely on a comparative working definition of practical intelligence, namely, the extent to which an individual resembles the "prototypically intelligent person." The prototypically intelligent person is the ideal that emerges when people are asked to describe the most intelligent person that they can imagine. Characteristics of the prototypically intelligent person probably vary across cultures and within cultures over time. For example, before the invention of print, verbatim memory probably would have ranked among the most important characteristics of the prototypically intelligent individual in an oral society, although it probably is not among the most important character-

istics of the prototypically intelligent individual in literate societies (Olson, 1986).

One approach to identifying the characteristics of the prototypically intelligent individual is to examine peoples' implicit conceptions of intelligence. For example, Sternberg et al. (1981) asked laypersons and experts to rate how characteristic 250 descriptions were of an "ideally" (1) intelligent person; (2) academically intelligent person; and (3) everyday intelligent person. The results concerning the everyday intelligent person are of most interest here. The prototypical everyday intelligent person is characterized by practical-problem-solving ability, social competence, character, and interest in learning and culture. Ford (1986) describes using similar methods to examine people's implicit conceptions of social competence. The prototypical socially competent individual is characterized by prosocial skills (i.e., responding to the needs of others), social-instrumental skills (i.e., knowing how to get things done), social ease (i.e., enjoying social activities and involvement), and self-efficacy (i.e., having a good self-concept).

RELATIONS BETWEEN PRACTICAL AND ACADEMIC INTELLIGENCE

One key issue in the study of practical intelligence has been how closely related it is to the academic kind of intelligence that is measured by IQ tests. Two kinds of studies provide evidence about the degree of relation between practical and academic intelligence: studies of the life-span development of academic and practical skills, and correlational studies in which a group of individuals is asked to perform both academic and practical tasks.

Life-Span Development of Academic and Practical Skills. Performance on measures of academic intelligence, especially measures of fluid ability in which examinees are asked to solve abstract-reasoning problems under time pressure, appears to peak in the late teens and then begin a slow decline thereafter. Paradoxically, this peak in academic intelligence coincides roughly with a peak in maladaptive everyday behavior. For example, automobile insurance rates, which are calculated on the basis of accident statistics, are highest for young adults.

For the most part, societal institutions reserve positions of maximum responsibility for individuals who are well beyond their peak levels of academic intelligence. Presidential candidates in the United States must be 35 years of age, and directors and chief executive officers of corporations tend to be in their 50s and early 60s. Empirical studies of the life-span development of academic and practical skills provide some support for these naturally evolved societal norms.

Williams, Denney, and Schadler (1983) interviewed adults over the age of 65 about how they perceived changes in their abilities to think, reason, and solve problems as they aged. Three-fourths of the interviewees believed that their abilities to do these things had increased over the years. When confronted with the fact that performance on IQ tests declines upon completion of formal schooling, the interviewees countered that they were not talking about those kinds of problems but rather the kinds of problems they encountered in their daily lives. Two studies of the actual performance of adults of different ages on academic and practical tasks provide support for these beliefs. Denney and Palmer (1981) gave eighty-four adults between the ages of 20 and 79 an academic reasoning task called the Twenty Questions Task (Mosher & Hornsby, 1966) and a practical reasoning task that asked for responses to situations such as the following: "Now let's assume that you lived in an apartment that didn't have any windows on the same side as the front door. Let's say that at 2 A.M. you heard a loud knock on the door and someone yelled, 'Open up. It's the police!' What would you do?" Performance on the academic reasoning task declined linearly from age 20 on, whereas performance on the practical reasoning task increased to a peak in the 40- and 50-year-old groups, with some decline thereafter. A similar study of 126 adults between the ages of 20 and 78 by Cornelius and Caspi (1987), but using different academic and practical tasks, yielded a comparable pattern of differences between the life-span development of academic and practical competencies.

Correlational Studies of Academic and Practical Intelligence. When individuals are given both academic and practical tasks, investigators can calculate a correlation (a measure of degree of relation that approaches 0 if there is no relation between two things and that approaches plus or minus 1 if there is a perfect relation, positive or negative, between two

things) between performance on the two kinds of tasks. The handful of studies that have been conducted suggest that the correlation between measures of academic and practical intelligence is surprisingly small.

For example, Scribner (1984, 1986) found that "unskilled" milk-processing-plant workers used rather ingenious strategies for combining varied quantities (e.g., pints, quarts, gallons) of varied products (e.g., skim milk, 2% milk, whole milk, buttermilk) when assembling orders to be shipped from the plant. The workers did not rely on the kinds of mathematical algorithms taught in school, but rather they visualized additions or deletions to partially filled cases so as to be able to add and subtract using case units instead of by counting individual items. This enabled them to assemble orders in the fewest possible moves using the least amount of counting of individual items. These assemblers were among the poorest educated in the plant, yet what they were accomplishing was the quite difficult task of calculating quantities expressed in varying base number systems, all in their head. They outperformed better-educated white-collar workers who would substitute when an assembler was absent, and Scribner reported that their skill at assembling orders was unrelated to the workers' levels of previous school performance, arithmetic test scores, or intelligence test scores.

Ceci and Liker's (1986, 1988) study of expert racetrack handicappers tells a similar story. Expert handicappers used a complex algorithm for predicting post-time odds (and thus which horse to bet upon) that included interactions among seven sources of information. A key strategy was to estimate a horse's true speed by obtaining published times for each quarter mile from the horse's previous outing. Track-wise handicappers, however, adjusted these times for factors such as whether the horse was attempting to pass other horses and how fast the overtaken horses were, because these factors determine how long the horse had to run away from the rail. Running away from the rail translates into extra distance and slower times. Use of a complex algorithm would appear to require considerable cognitive complexity, yet the degree to which handicappers used the complex algorithm was unrelated to their IQ.

Lave, Murtaugh, and de la Roche (1984) studied the everyday mathematics used by grocery-store shoppers to determine the best buy when the same product comes in different quantities for different prices. For example, the decision might be between a 12-ounce can of Coke at 59 cents or a 16-ounce bottle at 79 cents. The usual strategy of assuming the largest size is the best buy turned out to be wrong in the grocery stores used in the study about a third of the time. Effective shoppers did not bother attempting to work out the math exactly, but rather used mental shortcuts. For example, the differences between sizes is 4 ounces, which happens to be one-third the amount of the 12-ounce can. When the price of the 12-ounce can, which is almost 60 cents, is divided by 3, the result is that 4 ounces costs about 20 cents. Adding 20 cents to the 12-ounce-can price of 59 cents gives 79 cents, which happens to be the price of the 16-ounce bottle. In this example, the cost per ounce is about the same for the two sizes. Had the price of the 16-ounce bottle been 69 cents, it would have been the better buy; had the price been 89 cents, the smaller size would have been the better buy. Of particular interest in the discussion of relations between academic and practical intelligence, accuracy in picking the best size was unrelated to the shopper's scores on a standard mental arithmetic test.

In a different domain, Wagner and Sternberg (1990) studied business managers who were participating in a leadership development program. The effectiveness of managers' problem-solving abilities was assessed by having them perform in simulated work environments and then having panels of specially trained raters evaluate their performance. The managers also were given an IQ test and a measure of business tacit knowledge or practical know-how. The best predictor of problem-solving performance in the simulated work environments was tacit knowledge, with IQ also being predictive of problem-solving performance, although to a lesser degree. In keeping with results of the studies just described, the correlation between tacit knowledge and IQ did not depart significantly from 0. These results are consistent with previous suggestions that there is little or no relation between academic and practical intelligence in domains such as business management and academic psychology (e.g., Wagner, 1987; Wagner & Sternberg, 1985).

Finally, Mercer, Gomez-Palacio, and Padilla (1986) reported an ambitious study of nearly 2,000 Anglo, Chicano, and Mexican children who were given the Adaptive Behavior Inventory for Children (the measure of social-role performance described above) and the Wechsler Intelligence Scale for Children–Revised (WISC–R), a common IQ test. Virtually no relations were found between scores on the ABIC and the IQ test.

MEASURES OF PRACTICAL INTELLIGENCE

Compared with the psychometric sophistication of traditional IQ tests, measures of practical intelligence are in their infancy. Measures of practical intelligence run the gamut from tests that are very much like IQ tests, except that the content is a bit more practical, to tests that amount to highly realistic simulations of complex problem-solving environments. One generalization that has emerged from attempts to measure practical intelligence concerns the effects of the realism of a test on what it ultimately measures. At one end of a realism continuum are highly realistic assessment devices, such as the in-basket test (Frederiksen, Saunders, & Wand, 1957). Examinees are placed at an executive's desk and are asked to handle items contained in an in-basket. Examinees' performance is evaluated using criteria such as whether the examinee delegated responsibility for completing tasks appropriately. At the other end of the realism continuum are paper-and-pencil tests that are like IQ tests but have somewhat more practical content, such as the Educational Testing Service (ETS) Basic Skills Assessment Test (1977). This test includes tasks such as reading paragraphs and describing the main theme, interpreting written guarantees for products such as calculators, and interpreting maps and charts. In the middle of the realism continuum are paper-and-pencil tests in which the questions describe realistic situations one might encounter in a real-world domain and in which a series of possible responses is evaluated. An example of this approach is the Tacit Knowledge Inventory for Managers (Wagner & Sternberg, 1991), an inventory used for selecting managers.

The generalization about measuring practical intelligence is that whether a measure of practical intelligence assesses something other than academic intelligence may depend on there being at least some realism in the format of the practical intelligence test. The less realistic and more "testlike" the measure of practical intelligence, the greater the correlation between performance on the measure of practical intelligence and IQ (Wagner, 1986). Thus, performance on the ETS test of basic skills is related to performance on IQ tests, whereas performance on more realistic measures such as the Tacit Knowledge Inventory for Managers and the in-basket test does not appear to be as related to IQ (Frederiksen, 1986; Wagner & Sternberg, 1990).

CONCLUSIONS

The phenomenal growth in activity and interest in the topic of practical intelligence represents one of the most exciting and promising developments in the field of intelligence. Despite the practical nature of most conceptions of intelligence, even the conceptions held by the developers of the early IQ tests, much of what we know about intelligence is limited to the subset of intellectual competencies that are of primary importance to performance in the classroom. The developing field of practical intelligence promises to expand our knowledge base to be more consistent with the range of intellectual competencies that characterize the conceptions of intelligence held by laypersons and experts alike.

BIBLIOGRAPHY

BERRY, J. W., & IRVINE, S. H. (1986). Bricolage: Savages do it daily. In R. J. Sternberg & R. K. Wagner (Eds.), *Practical intelligence: Nature and origins of competence in the everyday world* (pp. 271–306). New York: Cambridge University Press.

BINET, A., & SIMON, T. (1916). *The development of intelligence in children* (E. S. Kit, Trans.). Baltimore: Williams & Wilkins.

CECI, S. J. (1990). *On intelligence . . . more or less. A bio-ecological treatise on intellectual development.* Englewood Cliffs, NJ: Prentice Hall.

CECI, S. J., & LIKER, J. (1986). Academic and nonacademic intelligence: An experimental separation. In R. J. Sternberg & R. K. Wagner (Eds.), *Practical intelligence: Nature and origins of competence in the everyday world* (pp. 119–142). New York: Cambridge University Press.

CECI, S. J., & LIKER, J. (1988). Stalking the IQ-expertise relationship: When the critics go fishing. *Journal of Experimental Psychology: General, 117,* 96–100.

CORNELIUS, S. W., & CASPI, A. (1987). Everyday problem solving in adulthood and old age. *Psychology and Aging, 2,* 144–153.

DENNEY, N. W., & PALMER, A. M. (1981). Adult age differences on traditional and practical problem-solving measures. *Journal of Gerontology, 36,* 323–328.

EDUCATIONAL TESTING SERVICE. (1977). *Basic Skills Assessment Test: Reading.* Princeton, NJ: Educational Testing Service.

FORD, M. E. (1986). For all practical purposes: Criteria for defining and evaluating practical intelligence. In R. J. Sternberg & R. K. Wagner (Eds.), *Practical intelligence: Nature and origins of competence in the everyday world* (pp. 183–200). New York: Cambridge University Press.

FREDERIKSEN, N. (1986). Toward a broader conception of human intelligence. In R. J. Sternberg & R. K. Wagner (Eds.), *Practical intelligence: Nature and origins of competence in the everyday world* (pp. 84–116). New York: Cambridge University Press.

FREDERIKSEN, N., SAUNDERS, D. R., & WAND, B. (1957). The in-basket test. *Psychological Monographs, 71*(9, Whole No. 438).

LAVE, J., MURTAUGH, M., & DE LA ROCHE, O. (1984). The dialectic of arithmetic in grocery shopping. In B. Rogoff & J. Lave (Eds.), *Everyday cognition: Is development in social context* (pp. 67–94). Cambridge, MA: Harvard University Press.

MERCER, J. R. (1979). *System of multicultural pluralistic assessment: Technical manual.* New York: The Psychological Corporation.

MERCER, J. R., GOMEZ-PALACIO, M., & PADILLA, E. (1986). The development of practical intelligence in cross-cultural perspective. In R. J. Sternberg & R. K. Wagner (Eds.), *Practical intelligence: Nature and origins of competence in the everyday world* (pp. 307–337). New York: Cambridge University Press.

MOSHER, F. A., & HORNSBY, J. R. (1966). On asking questions. In J. S. Bruner, R. R. Oliver, & P. M. Greenfield (Eds.), *Studies in cognitive growth.* New York: Wiley.

NEISSER, U. (1976). General, academic, and artificial intelligence. In L. Resnick (Ed.), *Human intelligence: Perspectives on its theory and measurement* (pp. 179–189). Norwood, NJ: Ablex.

OLSON, D. R. (1986). Intelligence and literacy: The relationships between intelligence and the technologies of representation and communication. In R. J. Sternberg & R. K. Wagner (Eds.), *Practical intelligence: Nature and origins of competence in the everyday world* (pp. 338–360). New York: Cambridge University Press.

ROGOFF, B., & LAVE, J. (EDS.). (1984). *Everyday cognition: Its developmental and social context.* Cambridge, MA: Harvard University Press.

SATTLER, J. M. (1986). *Assessment of children* (3rd ed.). San Diego, CA: Jerome M. Sattler.

SCRIBNER, S. (1984). Studying working intelligence. In B. Rogoff & J. Lave (Eds.), *Everyday cognition: Its development in social context* (pp. 9–40). Cambridge, MA: Harvard University Press.

SCRIBNER, S. (1986). Thinking in action: Some characteristics of practical thought. In R. J. Sternberg & R. K. Wagner (Eds.), *Practical intelligence: Nature and origins of competence in the everyday world* (pp. 13–30). New York: Cambridge University Press.

SCRIBNER, S., & COLE, M. (1981). *The psychology of literacy.* Cambridge, MA: Harvard University Press.

STERNBERG, R. J. (1985). *Beyond IQ: A triarchic theory of human intelligence.* New York: Cambridge University Press.

STERNBERG, R. J., & BERG, C. A. (1986). Quantitative integration: Definitions of intelligence: A comparison of the 1921 and 1986 symposia. In R. J. Sternberg & D. K. Detterman (Eds.), *What is intelligence? Contemporary viewpoints on its nature and definition* (pp. 155–162). Norwood, NJ: Ablex.

STERNBERG, R. J., CONWAY, B. E., KETRON, J. L., & BERNSTEIN, M. (1981). People's conceptions of intelligence. *Journal of Personality and Social Psychology, 41,* 37–55.

STERNBERG, R. J., & DETTERMAN, D. K. (EDS.). (1986). *What is intelligence? Contemporary viewpoints on its nature and definition.* Norwood, NJ: Ablex.

STERNBERG, R. J., & WAGNER, R. K. (EDS.). (1986). *Practical intelligence: Nature and origins of competence in the everyday world.* New York: Cambridge University Press.

VOSS, J. F., PERKINS, D. N., & SEGAL, J. W. (EDS.). (1991). *Informal reasoning and education.* Hillsdale, NJ: Erlbaum.

WAGNER, R. K. (1987). Tacit knowledge in everyday intelligent behavior. *Journal of Personality and Social Psychology, 52,* 1236–1247.

WAGNER, R. K., & STERNBERG, R. J. (1985). Practical intelligence in real-world pursuits: The role of tacit knowledge. *Journal of Personality and Social Psychology, 48,* 436–458.

WAGNER, R. K., & STERNBERG, R. J. (1990). Street smarts. In K. Clark & M. Clark (Eds.), *Measures of leadership* (pp. 493–504). Greensboro, NC: Center for Creative Leadership.

WAGNER, R. K., & STERNBERG, R. J. (1991). *The Tacit Knowledge Inventory for Managers (TKIM).* San Antonio, TX: The Psychological Corporation.

WECHSLER, D. (1958). *The measurement and appraisal of adult intelligence* (4th ed.). Baltimore: Williams & Wilkins.

WILLIAMS, S. A., DENNEY, N. W., & SCHADLER, M. (1983). Elderly adults' perception of their own cognitive development during the adult years. *International Journal of Aging and Human Development, 16,* 147–158.

RICHARD K. WAGNER

PRACTICE EFFECTS   *Practice effects* refer to gains in scores on cognitive tests that occur when a person is retested on the same instrument, or tested more than once on very similar ones. These gains are due to the experience of having taken the test previously; they occur without the examinee being given specific or general feedback on test items, and they do not reflect growth or other improvement on the skills being assessed. Such practice effects denote an aspect of the test itself, a kind of systematic, built-in error that is associated with the specific skills the test measures. These effects relate to the test's psychometric properties and must therefore be understood well by the test user as a specific aspect of the test's reliability. Retesting occurs fairly commonly in real circumstances for reasons such as mandatory school reevaluations, longitudinal research investigations, unwitting or deliberate duplication by different professionals who are evaluating the same individual, a parent's or teacher's insistence that a child be retested because the test scores imply that the child was not trying, and so forth. A keen understanding of differential practice effects facilitates competent interpretation of test score profiles in those instances in which people are retested on the same or a similar instrument, perhaps several times.

No specific length of time between tests is required to study practice effects; it depends on the generalization sought or needed. If the interval is very short—for example, a few hours, or a couple of days—then examinees are likely to remember many specific items that were administered. They are likely to retain specific picture puzzles, arithmetic problems, or block designs, and recall the strategies that proved most successful; the result is an inflated estimate of the practice effect—that is, relative to an inference about established (learned) effects. In contrast, intervals that are long, perhaps six months or a year or two, are confounded by variables other than the test's psychometric properties and practice as such. Long intervals allow forgetting of the test's content, and therefore reduce the magnitude of the practice effects; at the same time, in lengthy intervals there can be real growth or decline of the abilities measured. When change has occurred, it becomes difficult to separate the test's practice effects, as such, from the person's improvement or decay on the skills. For preschool children, who experience rapid development, even three or four months may be too long an interval for studying a test's practice effects.

The most commonly useful intervals for investigating a test's practice effects are between one week and about two months, with one month or so representing a reasonable midpoint. Intervals of that approximate magnitude are typical of the test–retest reliability investigations reported in the test manuals of popular individually administered intelligence and achievement tests. Table 1 provides data on the practice effects for Wechsler's popular series of intelligence scales. The studies from which the table figures were obtained were based on samples of normal individuals who were retested during the standardization programs of each scale. The data are taken from the test manuals of the 1967 Wechsler Preschool and Primary Scale of Intelligence (WPPSI) for ages 4 to 6.5 years and its 1989 revision (WPPSI–R) for ages 3 to 7 years; the 1974 Wechsler Intelligence Scale for Children–Revised (WISC–R) for ages 6 to 16 years and its 1991 revision (WISC–III), covering the same age range; and the Wechsler Adult Intelligence Scale–Revised (WAIS–R) for ages 16 to 74 years. Intervals averaged about one month, except for the 11-week interval used for the WPPSI; all studies were well designed.

Practice effects are shown in this table for Wechsler's Verbal (V) IQ, Performance (P) IQ, and Full Scale (FS) IQ. The verbal subtests that yield the V-IQ include factual, language-oriented items that require good verbal comprehension and expression for success; most items are reminiscent of the kinds of questions asked in school. In contrast, the performance subtests that contribute to the P-IQ require visual–perceptual–spatial skills and manipulation of concrete

TABLE 1

Practice effect on Wechsler's verbal, performance, and full scale IQs for different age groups

Mean Age	Mean Interval	Wechsler Scale	Gain on Verbal IQ	Gain on Performance IQ	Gain on Full Scale IQ
5	4 wks.	WPPSI–R	+ 2.8	+ 6.3	+ 5.1
5.5	11 wks.	WPPSI	+ 3.0	+ 6.6	+ 3.6
6.5	3 wks.	WISC–III	+ 1.7	+ 11.5	+ 7.6
7	4 wks.	WISC–R	+ 3.9	+ 8.6	+ 6.6
10.5	3 wks.	WISC–III	+ 1.9	+ 13.0	+ 7.7
11	4 wks.	WISC–R	+ 3.4	+ 10.8	+ 7.6
14.5	3 wks.	WISC–III	+ 3.3	+ 12.5	+ 8.4
15	4 wks.	WISC–R	+ 3.2	+ 9.2	+ 6.9
30	4.5 wks.	WAIS–R	+ 3.3	+ 8.9	+ 6.6
50	3.5 wks.	WAIS–R	+ 3.1	+ 7.7	+ 5.7
Median			+ 3.2	+ 9.0	+ 6.8

materials for success, and measure a person's visual–motor coordination and nonverbal reasoning abilities. These tasks are not similar to school-related tests and activities. FS-IQ reflects a combination of the V and P scales; all three IQs are normed to have a mean equal to 100 and standard deviation equal to 15. Sample sizes for the ten groups in the table ranged from 48 to 175, with an overall total of exactly 1,000 individuals.

Practice effects on the FS-IQ averaged about 7 points across instruments and age groups, although an age trend was evident. Increases on the full scale from the first to second testing averaged about 4.5 points for preschool children, 7.5 points for elementary through high school students, and 6 points for adults. Regardless of the age of the sample, practice effects were considerably larger for P-IQ (9 points) than for V-IQ (3 points). The number of points gained on the V-IQ was a fairly constant 3 points for all age groups, but gains on P-IQ averaged 6.5 points for preschoolers, 11 points for elementary and high school students, and 8.5 points for adults.

These results for the Wechsler scales have generally been replicated for other intelligence tests. The overall gains on global IQ (about 7 points) are of the same approximate magnitude as: (a) the 5- to 6-point gains on the KAUFMAN ASSESSMENT BATTERY FOR CHILDREN (K-ABC), MCCARTHY SCALES OF CHILDREN'S ABILITIES, DIFFERENTIAL ABILITY SCALES (DAS), and Kaufman Adolescent and Adult Intelligence Test (KAIT), and (b) the 7- to 7.5-point gains on the Stanford-Binet (Fourth Edition).

As can be seen in Table 1, the gains are substantially larger for Wechsler's P-IQ than for the V-IQ. This finding is seen also on similar scales of other tests, although the differences are not as extreme. In the K-ABC, the Simultaneous Processing Scale resembles the P-Scale, and the Achievement Scale is similar to the V-Scale. Gains on simultaneous processing averaged about 6.5 points, compared with about 2.5-point gains on achievement. In the Binet, the Abstract/Visual Reasoning Scale is similar to P, and the Verbal Reasoning Scale is similar to V. Abstract/visual gains averaged 7.5 to 8 points, whereas verbal gains were 5 points. Gains on the DAS Special Nonverbal Scale (similar to P) averaged 7 points, compared with 4-point verbal ability (similar to V) gains for school-age children; at the preschool level, practice effects were 4 points on

nonverbal ability and 1 to 2 points on verbal ability. In the KAIT, gains on measures of Fluid IQ (similar to P) were generally higher (7 points) than gains on Crystallized IQ (4.5 points), which is similar to V.

A number of factors seem to contribute to the practice effects that have been noted: familiarity with the kinds of tasks that compose an intelligence test, experience solving these tasks, and the development of effective strategies for solving different kinds of problems. Although an occasional specific item may be remembered (e.g., a puzzle of a horse or a car on the WISC–III), the gains in test scores are not due simply to recall of specific facts. Verbal tasks produce the smallest gains because children and adults have had much experience prior to the testing session in answering general information questions, solving arithmetic problems, or defining words. There is still a small practice effect because even school-like verbal tasks have some unique aspects to them, but the pattern of gains on Wechsler's verbal tasks supports an "experience" hypothesis, that experience with erstwhile novel tests produces improvement. On the WISC–III, for example, gains are smallest across the age range, indeed, almost nonexistent, on tests of defining words, solving arithmetic problems, and answering "why" questions (e.g., "Why do cars have seatbelts?"); they are largest (nearly one-third SD) on those verbal tasks that are least like school tests (e.g., telling how two things are alike, repeating digits backward), tests that initially are novel. Very similar results occurred for the WPPSI–R and the WAIS–R.

The magnitude of gains on tests of verbal intelligence, incidentally, is commensurate with the practice effects observed for conventional tests of academic achievement. On the Kaufman Test of Educational Achievement (K-TEA) Brief and Comprehensive Forms, for example, gain scores averaged 3.3 points for mathematics, 2.3 points for reading, and 2.4 points for spelling over a one-week interval.

Experience also helps explain the finding of larger P-IQ than V-IQ practice effects. The P tasks tend to be novel tasks not tried before. As they are administered, they become less novel. Each time they are given, if the interval is not too long, individuals will recall trying to solve the same kinds of problems, and they may recall, too, the strategies that worked best the first time. And even if one is not able to solve many more items correctly on the retest, one is likely to respond more quickly to the items the second time around. On Wechsler's P-Scale, quicker response times translate to higher scores, because several subtests allot bonus points for quick, perfect performance. Indeed, the increase in speed may largely account for the practice effect.

The generally heavy emphasis on visual–motor speed that characterizes P-IQ may also explain the age and test differences seen in Table 1. The largest P-IQ gains were on the WISC–R and WISC–III, followed by the WAIS–R and the preschool scales. Not surprisingly, the WISC–R and WISC–III allot by far the most speed bonus points in the P-Scales. The WAIS–R is next, followed by the WPPSI and WPPSI–R, which place the least emphasis on motor speed. The WAIS–R, for example, does not give bonus points for any items on the Picture Arrangement subtest, whereas the WISC–III allots three bonus points for most items. On the WISC–III, Picture Arrangement (putting pictures in the right order to tell a story) had the largest practice effect of any subtest, a gain of about one standard deviation from test to retest.

The motor speed hypothesis may partially explain why the nonverbal versus verbal distinction was not as pronounced on other intelligence tests as it was on the Wechsler scales. Gains on nonverbal or fluid intelligence scales averaged about 7 to 8 points on the K-ABC, Stanford-Binet IV, DAS, and KAIT, in contrast to gains of about 2.5 to 5 points on these tests' verbal/crystallized scales. The K-ABC, Binet IV, DAS, and KAIT nonverbal/fluid subtests place more emphasis on correct problem solving and less emphasis on motor speed than do Wechsler's P subtests; the outcome may be less exaggerated practice effects for the nonverbal and novel tasks on these "other" tests. Research, however, has not pinpointed the precise explanations for different practice effects. Much of this discussion is therefore speculative.

Catron and Thompson (1979) investigated the role of the test interval on the size of practice effects by retesting five different samples of college students on the WAIS over five intervals: no interval (immediate retest), 1 week, 1 month, 2 months, and 4 months. Gains on V-IQ were 3 to 5 points for the immediate retest and 1-week retest, 2 points after 1 to 2 months, and 1 point after 4 months. Gains on P-IQ averaged 14 points for the immediate retest, and decreased steadily from 11 points after 1 week to 8 points after 4 months. Thus, after a 4-month interval, P-IQ was still elevated 8 points, but V-IQ was elevated only 1 point (i.e., there was virtually no gain).

In a review of 11 test–retest studies of the WAIS, Matarazzo and his colleagues found that, regardless of large differences in samples and some long intervals of time, the results were consistent in indicating about 2 IQ points of gain on the V-Scale and 7 to 8 points on the P-Scale. The intervals ranged from 1 week to 13 years; mean ages ranged from 19 to 70 years; and the samples included groups as diverse as brain-damaged elderly, mentally retarded, chronic epileptics, and college students.

In addition to novelty, motor speed, and interval, at least two other variables seem to relate to different practice effects for different tests: the nature of the task, and subtest reliability. When tests of verbal and visual memory are used in test–retest studies, for example, the pattern of different practice effects observed for cognitive problem-solving tasks no longer holds; in fact, the opposite pattern may emerge. The Wechsler Memory Scale–Revised (WMS–R) includes measures of verbal memory (retelling stories that are read aloud by the examiner, learning eight verbal word pairs) and visual memory (recognizing and recalling abstract designs that are exposed briefly, learning six pairs of visual stimuli). Results indicate that gains on the Verbal Memory Scale for three age groups averaged about 13 points, in contrast to an 8-point gain for the Visual Memory Scale. The visual memory practice effect was commensurate with the P-IQ gain on the WAIS–R, but the verbal memory gain was much larger than V-IQ gains. With verbal memory subtests, adults probably remember specific facts, story lines, and word associations, which greatly facilitate recall when these adults are retested more than a month later. On the KAIT, the largest practice effect for any of its ten subtests over a one-month interval was for Auditory Delayed Recall, which measures a person's ability to remember verbal information (mock news stories) presented by cassette about a half-hour earlier.

The reliability of a subtest, particularly test–retest stability (see RELIABILITY), also relates to the size of its practice effect. Wechsler's P subtests tend to be less reliable than the V subtests. Thus some of the change from one item to another is unreliable change. Vocabulary typically produces the smallest test–retest gain, and it is usually the most reliable Wechsler subtest. Picture Arrangement and Object Assembly tend to produce large practice effects, and these tasks are consistently among the least reliable Wechsler subtests. Block Design, easily the most reliable P subtest on the WISC–III and the WAIS–R, shows the smallest practice effect among P subtests—despite the novel nature of the task and its reliance on bonus points for motor speed. On the KAIT, the least reliable task (Auditory Delayed Recall) had the largest practice effect, and the most reliable (Definitions) had the smallest.

Thus, practice effects do occur, they are different for verbal and nonverbal tasks, and they are of considerable practical importance. Any research study that depends on pre- and posttests should take into account gains due to practice; such gains should not be interpreted as evidence of true growth or change. In the absence of a control group, the average verbal and nonverbal gains known to occur based on routine retesting should be subtracted from any gains demonstrated for experimental groups. Failure to consider such gains or use appropriate control groups has led some researchers to infer, erroneously, gains in IQ following the surgical removal of plaque from the carotid artery in endarterectomy patients; and the inappropriate application of the practice effect data has led to specious conclusions regarding epileptic patients.

Any longitudinal study of changes in intelligence across the life span should take into account the evidence of practice effects. When the same individuals are tested every year or two on a Wechsler battery, the P-Scale, especially, can yield spuriously high IQs as a result of practice effects. Test a person over and over, and the kinds of "novel" tasks that characterize the P-Scale become as familiar as a test of vocabulary or general information. The V-IQ may continue to provide a reasonable estimate of true score over time, but the repeated use of P-IQ will not detect decrements in fluid or visual–spatial intelligence that accompany aging in adulthood. The repeated use of the same instrument in aging studies contributes to "progressive error" in longitudinal research, and has led to a confounding of data interpretation in several studies—including the well-known Duke longitudinal studies, in which the same adults were tested eleven times on the WAIS in the course of twenty-one years. This type of practice effect also makes it difficult to interpret IQs on tests that are administered every two or three years during the mandatory reevaluations of special education students.

Clinicians should understand the average practice effect gains in intelligence scores for children, adolescents, and adults. The expected increase of about 5 to 8 points in global IQ renders any score obtained on a retest as a likely overestimate of the person's true level of functioning—especially if the retest is given within about six months of the original test, or if the person has been administered a Wechsler scale (*any* Wechsler scale) several times in the course of a few years. These inflated IQs, if not interpreted as overestimates resulting from the practice effect, may imply cognitive growth when none has occurred; may suggest that the earlier test yielded an invalidly low score when it was indeed valid; may suggest that a bright individual is gifted or that a retarded person is low-average; and so forth. Even though the average gain is about 5 to 8 points for various tests, the average *range* of gain scores makes it feasible for some individuals to gain as much as 15 IQ points due to practice alone.

And the different practice effects for verbal versus nonverbal tasks can influence the interpretation of profile results. On the WISC–III, for example, the average V-IQ gain is 2.3 points and the average P-IQ gain is 12.3 points, which translates to a net gain of 10 points on P-IQ due to the practice effect. Clinicians commonly use V–P IQ discrepancies as part of a diagnostic process. Other things being equal, V–P discrepancies will shift by an average of 10 points in favor of P-IQ. An initial P > V difference of 12 points will become about 22 points on a retest; a significant V > P difference of 15 points will become a trivial V > P difference of about 5 points. Inappropriate clinical decisions are likely for professionals who do not understand the predictable and substantial practice effects associated with verbal and nonverbal cognitive tests.

(*See also:* WECHSLER SCALES OF INTELLIGENCE.)

BIBLIOGRAPHY

CATRON, D. W., & THOMPSON, C. C. (1979). Test–retest gains in WAIS scores after four retest intervals. *Journal of Clin-*

ical Psychology, 35, 352–357. Evaluates practice effects on WAIS with college students, using four different intervals ranging from 1 week to 4 months; see also Catron's 1978 study of WAIS practice effects on an immediate retest in Psychological Reports, 43, 279–290.

ELLIOTT, C. D. (1990). Differential Ability Scales: Introductory and technical handbook. San Antonio, TX: The Psychological Corporation. Chapter 8 includes studies of practice effects on a diversity of cognitive and achievement tasks for four groups aged 3.5 to 13 years.

KAUFMAN, A. S. (1990). Assessing adolescent and adult intelligence. Boston: Allyn & Bacon. Chapter 4 includes a comprehensive discussion of practice effects on the WAIS and WAIS–R, and their implications for clinical practice and research; chapter 7 relates practice effects to the interpretation of longitudinal data on aging and intelligence; chapter 9 discusses the role of practice effects on the interpretation of Verbal-Performance IQ differences.

KAUFMAN, A. S., & KAUFMAN, N. L. (1983, 1985, 1993). Manuals for the Kaufman Assessment Battery for Children (K-ABC, 1983), Kaufman Test of Educational Achievement (K-TEA, 1985), and Kaufman Adolescent and Adult Intelligence Test (KAIT, 1993). Circle Pines, MN: American Guidance Service. Each test manual includes thorough data on practice effects for the global scores and subtests for each Kaufman battery.

MATARAZZO, J. D., CARMODY, T. P., & JACOBS, L. D. (1980). Test–retest reliability and stability of the WAIS: A literature review with implications for clinical practice. Journal of Clinical Neuropsychology, 2, 89–105. Summarizes and interprets the results of eleven stability studies with the WAIS with a heterogeneous set of samples and widely varied intervals.

MATARAZZO, J. D., & HERMAN, D. O. (1984). Base rate data for the WAIS–R: Test-retest stability and VIQ-PIQ differences. Journal of Clinical Neuropsychology, 6, 351–366. Includes thorough analysis of practice effects on the WAIS–R, and discussion of their clinical and practical implications.

MATARAZZO, R. G., MATARAZZO, J. D., GALLO, A. E., JR., & WIENS, A. N. (1979). IQ and neuropsychological changes following carotid endarterectomy. Journal of Clinical Neuropsychology, 1, 97–116. Reevaluates conclusions about IQ gains following carotid artery surgery based on data on practice effects.

SEIDENBERG, M., O'LEARY, D. S., GIORDANI, B., BERENT, S., & BOLL, T. J. (1981). Test–retest IQ changes of epilepsy patients: Assessing the influence of practice effects. Journal of Clinical Neuropsychology, 3, 237–255. Investigates the relationship between practice effects and functional changes in epileptic patients.

SHATZ, M. W. (1981). WAIS practice effects in clinical neuropsychology. Journal of Clinical Neuropsychology, 3, 171–179. Disputes Matarazzo's claims that practice effects in normal individuals are applicable to neuropsychological patients.

WECHSLER, D. (1981, 1987, 1989, 1991). Manuals for the Wechsler Adult Intelligence Scale–Revised (WAIS–R, 1981), Wechsler Memory Scale–Revised (WMS–R, 1987), Wechsler Preschool and Primary Scale of Intelligence–Revised (WPPSI–R, 1989), and Wechsler Intelligence Scale for Children–Third Edition (WISC–III). San Antonio, TX: The Psychological Corporation. Each test manual includes thorough data on practice effects for the global scores and subtests for the most recent, updated version of each Wechsler battery.

ALAN S. KAUFMAN

PRIMARY MENTAL ABILITIES THEORY

The primary mental abilities theory, proposed by L. L. THURSTONE, posits that intelligence is composed chiefly of seven more or less independent "primary" abilities: verbal comprehension, word fluency, number facility, spatial visualization, reasoning, memory, and perceptual speed.

In the early years of the twentieth century, the most widely accepted view of intelligence, offered by Charles SPEARMAN (1904, 1927), was that it consisted of a single "general factor" (g) in addition to numerous specific abilities of much narrower range, one for each test of a battery. Thurstone (1931) was the most influential of several researchers who questioned this view. By developing mathematical methods for identifying abilities that were more elaborate than those Spearman had used, he was able to test the hypothesis that intelligence is composed of a series of abilities, not necessarily including the general factor that Spearman postulated. Thurstone asked the fundamental question of how many factors of ability were necessary to account for the intercorrelations of various kinds of intelligence or cognitive ability tests. He and his wife and collaborator, Thelma Gwynn Thurstone, developed a large battery of tests that included most of the types of items that are found in paper-and-pencil group tests of intelligence. In 1934, this fifteen-hour battery of fifty-six tests was administered to a group of 240 volunteer subjects, most of whom were students at the University of Chicago. The ages of these subjects ranged from 16 to more than 25; the modal age was 18.

The intercorrelations among fifty-seven scores derived from these tests were computed and subjected to the methods of factor analysis that Thurstone had recently developed. First, the matrix of intercorrelations was analyzed, by a so-called centroid method, into thirteen factors. Second, loadings on these thirteen factors were subjected to graphical rotations of the coordinates to display "simple structure," that is, a structure such that each variable had only one or a small number of large positive values or "loadings" on the factors and a maximum number of values (positive or negative) near zero. Each factor could then be identified and interpreted in terms of what variables had the largest loadings on it, in contrast to the variables that had near-zero loadings on it. For example, one of the factors had large (.40 or greater) positive loadings on thirteen test variables, all of which could be seen to have a common element of being visual or spatial in character, in contrast to nearly all the remaining variables, which did not appear to call for spatial ability in their performance. This factor was therefore named Space and denoted S. Applying this procedure to all thirteen factors initially isolated, Thurstone concluded that seven of them could be given psychologically meaningful interpretations, while two others could be given only tentative interpretations, possibly to be confirmed with further investigation. The remaining four factors were regarded as "residual" factors arising mainly from chance phenomena, and no attempt was made to interpret them.

The results of this large and ambitious investigation were published in a monograph entitled *Primary Mental Abilities* (Thurstone, 1938), which attracted wide attention among psychologists. The seven factors that were given definite psychological interpretations were the following, reproduced here with the designations and descriptions given in Thurstone's monograph:

S: "facility in spatial and visual imagery" (later, usually called Space or Spatial Ability)

P: "facility in finding or in recognizing particular items in a perceptual field" (later, usually called Perceptual Speed)

N: "facility in numerical calculation" (later, usually called Number or Numerical Facility)

V: "verbal relations"—"characterized primarily by its reference to ideas and the meanings of words" (later, usually called Verbal Ability or Verbal Comprehension)

W: "fluency in dealing with words" (later, usually called Word Fluency)

M: "memory" (later, usually called Associative Memory)

I: facility in finding rules or principles in test items (later, usually called Induction)

Thurstone noted in this monograph that he had not found the general factor g of Spearman, but he claimed that his methodology did not preclude finding it. Actually, a late-twentieth-century perspective suggests that his methods were biased against finding a general factor, partly because of the rather highly selective nature of the sample used in his investigation and partly because of the restriction of his factorial methods to the use of orthogonal (rather than oblique) rotations that implied uncorrelated factors. Both Spearman (1939) and H. J. EYSENCK (1939) reanalyzed Thurstone's data, with different methods, and found a general factor, along with "group factors" roughly corresponding to the primary factors that had been identified by Thurstone.

Thurstone and Thurstone (1941) confirmed and expanded the findings reported in the 1938 monograph in a further large factorial investigation. Intercorrelations of sixty tests given to 710 eighth-grade children (in eleven one-hour sessions) were subjected to factor analysis. Ten factors were identified and rotated to a simple-structure framework, but only seven of these were regarded as being amenable to meaningful psychological interpretation. On examination, these seven factors appeared to be precisely the same as the seven factors that had been isolated in the 1938 study and given definite psychological interpretations, even though the sample of subjects was younger and less highly selected, and the tests were generally somewhat easier.

The one interesting difference in the 1941 study was that the primary factors were shown to have some significant intercorrelations. For example, it was found that the number factor N was correlated with the two "verbal" factors V and W, and the space factor S was found to have some association with the verbal comprehension factor V and with the induction factor I. These findings prompted the Thurstones to factor analyze the correlations among the primary factors. This analysis revealed that the correlations could be well accounted for by a single general factor; they called this a "second-order general factor." They implied that such a general factor might be characteristic of populations of children but not necessarily of adults.

The primary mental abilities view of intelligence became popular over several decades (roughly, 1940–1970), partly because of the wide dissemination and availability of batteries of primary mental abilities (PMA) tests that Thurstone and Thurstone (1946–1965) developed for several age/grade levels over the range from kindergarten to grade twelve. These batteries focused attention on separate primary abilities—verbal ability, perceptual speed, number facility, spatial ability, and reasoning—rather than on the general intellective factor that was approximately represented by the total score. Reviewers pointed out, however, that the intercorrelations of the separate abilities could be regarded as at least partly due to the fact that most of the subtests were considerably speeded. The total score indicated not only the overall level of mastery exhibited but also the speed with which subjects performed the items—two elements in test performance that are not necessarily highly correlated.

Until his death in 1955, Thurstone continued work on the identification and interpretation of primary mental abilities, not only the seven that he had isolated in the early studies but also various other factors that might show themselves in more rigorous and refined investigations. For example, in studies of perceptual abilities and mechanical aptitudes, he identified several varieties of perceptual and spatial factors. It is incorrect to claim, as some writers have done, that Thurstone believed that there are only seven primary mental abilities.

The factor analysis of intellectual abilities became a very active field of investigation in the middle and later years of the twentieth century, as is evident in the writings of J. W. French (1951). J. P. Guilford (1967), Raymond Cattell (1971), and John Horn (1985). Many primary mental abilities have been discovered beyond those identified by Thurstone in 1938.

Out of the notion of the second-order factor developed by Thurstone (1944b, 1947), there developed the idea that there could be more than one second-order factor (Horn, 1965; Horn & Bramble, 1967). Cattell (1963), Horn and Cattell (1966), and Cattell and Horn (1978) found evidence for two such second-order factors, which they called fluid intelligence (Gf) and crystallized intelligence (Gc) as well as other factors of the second order. Jan-Eric Gustafsson (1984), Hakstian and Cattell (1974, 1978), and Undheim (1987) replicated this work and extended the theory. John Carroll (1993) summarized the evidence with a series of analyses of most of the data gathered in the twentieth century. The results conform to a three-stratum theory of cognitive abilities, in which primary abilities such as those identified by Thurstone exist at the first or lowest stratum, several second-order factors such as Gf and Gc exist at the second stratum, and Spearman's g exists at the third or highest stratum. Factors at the various strata differ in their degree of generality over cognitive performances.

Although Thurstone's theory of primary mental abilities has now been superseded by more elaborate and adequate theories, it represented an important early step toward the better understanding of the nature of intelligence.

(*See also*: FLUID AND CRYSTALLIZED INTELLIGENCE, THEORY OF; MULTIPLE INTELLIGENCES THEORY; TWO-FACTOR THEORY.)

BIBLIOGRAPHY

CARROLL, J. B. (1993). *Human cognitive abilities: A survey of factor-analytic studies.* New York: Cambridge University Press.

CATTELL, R. B. (1963). Theory of fluid and crystallized intelligence: A critical experiment. *Journal of Educational Psychology, 54,* 1–22.

CATTELL, R. B. (1971). *Abilities: Their structure, growth, and action.* Boston: Houghton Mifflin. Rev. ed. Amsterdam: North-Holland, 1987.

CATTELL, R. B., & HORN, J. L. (1978). A check on the theory of fluid and crystallized intelligence with description of new subtest designs. *Journal of Educational Measurement, 15,* 139–164.

EYSENCK, H. J. (1939). Review of Thurstone's *Primary Mental Abilities,* 1938. *British Journal of Educational Psychology, 9,* 270–275.

FRENCH, J. W. (1951). The description of aptitude and achievement tests in terms of rotated factors. *Psychometric Monographs,* No. 5.

GUILFORD, J. P. (1967). *The nature of human intelligence.* New York: McGraw-Hill.

GUSTAFSSON, J. E. (1984). A unifying model for the structure of intellectual abilities. *Intelligence, 8,* 179–203.

HAKSTIAN, A. R., & CATTELL, R. B. (1974). The checking of primary ability structure on a broader basis of performances. *British Journal of Educational Psychology, 44,* 140–154.

HAKSTIAN, A. R., & CATTELL, R. B. (1978). Higher-stratum ability structures on a basis of twenty primary abilities. *Journal of Educational Psychology, 70,* 657–669.

HORN, J. L. (1968). Organization of abilities and the development of intelligence. *Psychological Review, 75,* 242–259.

HORN, J. L. (1985). Remodeling old models of intelligence. In B. B. Wolman (Ed.), *Handbook of intelligence: Theories, measurements, and applications* (pp. 267–300). New York: Wiley.

HORN, J. L., & BRAMBLE, W. J. (1967). Second order ability structure revealed in right and wrong scores. *Journal of Educational Psychology, 58,* 115–122.

HORN, J. L., & CATTELL, R. B. (1966). Refinement and test of the theory of fluid and crystallized intelligence. *Journal of Educational Psychology, 57,* 253–270.

SPEARMAN, C. (1904). "General intelligence," objectively determined and measured. *American Journal of Psychology, 15,* 201–293.

SPEARMAN, C. (1927). *The abilities of man: Their nature and measurement.* London: Macmillan. Reprint. New York: AMS Publishers, 1981.

SPEARMAN, C. (1939). Thurstone's work reworked. *Journal of Educational Psychology, 30,* 1–16.

THURSTONE, L. L. (1931). Multiple factor analysis. *Psychological Review, 38,* 406–427.

THURSTONE, L. L. (1938). Primary mental abilities. *Psychometric Monographs,* No. 1.

THURSTONE, L. L. (1944a). A factorial study of perception. *Psychometric Monographs,* No. 4.

THURSTONE, L. L. (1944b). Second-order factors. *Psychometrika, 9,* 71–100.

THURSTONE, L. L. (1946). Theories of intelligence. *Scientific Monthly, 62,* 101–112.

THURSTONE, L. L. (1947). *Multiple factor analysis: A development and expansion of* The Vectors of Mind. Chicago: University of Chicago Press.

THURSTONE, L. L., & THURSTONE, T. G. (1941). Factorial studies of intelligence. *Psychometric Monographs,* No. 2.

THURSTONE, L. L., & THURSTONE, T. G. (1946–1965). *Primary Mental Abilities* [*tests*]. Chicago: Science Research Associates.

UNDHEIM, J. O. (1987). The hierarchical organization of cognitive abilities: Restoring general intelligence through the use of linear structural relations (LISREL). *Multivariate Behavioral Research, 22,* 149–171.

JOHN B. CARROLL

PROBLEM FINDING Psychological studies of higher-order intellectual functioning have typically focused on problem-solving strategies. Tests for measuring intelligence, and even creativity, present the subject with a series of questions that have true or false answers or with problems that have agreed-upon solutions. Yet it is not clear that it is the ability to solve well-defined problems that sets apart highly productive, original, and creative thinkers. There is increasing evidence that the higher levels of mental performance involve a process of seeking out as yet undefined problems and that this process is to a certain extent orthogonal to problem solving. If this is true, important implications for curricular changes in education follow. Students are taught to solve problems presented to them by teachers and textbooks; consequently many never learn how to recognize problematic situations and transform these into soluble problems. Thus it is not uncommon to see, for instance, graduate students with brilliant scholastic records who never finish their doctorates because they are unable to formulate a Ph.D. thesis.

Original thinkers have often remarked on the distinction between problem finding and problem solving in their own work. Albert Einstein wrote: "The formulation of a problem is often more essential than its solution, which may be merely a matter of mathematical or experimental skill. To raise new questions, new possibilities, or regard old questions from a new angle, requires creative imagination and marks real advances in science" (Einstein & Infeld, 1938, p. 92). Similarly, Charles Darwin, reflecting on his discoveries, said: "Looking back, I think it was more difficult to see what the problems were than to solve them" (Immergart & Boyd, 1979, p. 2). Francis Upton, one of Thomas Edison's assistants, described the difference between himself and his more creative collaborator as follows: "I can answer questions very easily after they are asked but I find great trouble in framing any to answer" (Hughes, 1983, p. 26). Many would agree with Sir Hans Krebs, the Nobel prize–winning biochemist, who related that the most important thing he learned from his teacher Otto Warburg was "the art of finding problems that can be solved" (Maugh, 1974, p. 184).

But what does the process of problem finding consist of? One of the most compelling descriptions is given by the great British sculptor Henry Moore: "I sometimes begin drawing with no preconceived problem to solve, with only a desire to use pencil on paper and only make lines, tones, and styles without conscious aim. But as my mind takes in what is so produced, a point arrives where some idea becomes conscious and crystallizes, and then control and ordering begin to take place" (Moore, 1955, p. 77). This deceptively simple account contains the main elements of the problem-finding process, namely: (1) it usually originates from an intrinsic desire to use a skill for its own sake, "without conscious aim"; (2) as the skill begins to be used, an interaction arises between the person and the medium (drawing, sculpting, mathematics, music, chemical experimentation, and so on), and this interaction in turn results in unexpected patterns and combinations; and (3) the person, reacting to the results of this interaction, begins to organize and control consciously the emerging pattern, which may or may not suggest new possibilities and new problems.

These elements in turn suggest that problem finding is likely to occur when a person has a skill in a given symbolic domain, when that person is motivated to explore and practice that skill for its own sake, and

when that person is able to recognize in the emergent properties of the interaction a new way of looking at things. Quite often the initial impetus for the problem-finding process is an apparently accidental event, which, however, the person interprets as problematic or potentially meaningful. For instance, when Wilhelm Roentgen found unaccountably fogged photographic plates in his laboratory, he did not discard them as the result of an accident. Instead he asked himself: What physical cause could account for the ruined plates? In answering that question he discovered radiation and the X ray. Similarly, when Alexander Fleming found that some of his colonies of experimental bacteria died out without an apparent cause, he did not dismiss the result as accidental but asked himself: Is there a biological reason for the extinction of some of the bacterial cultures? Having formulated the problem in this way, he discovered that the dishes where the extinguished cultures had been grown had not been cleaned properly and that a mold that had grown in the dishes had apparently killed the bacteria. Having identified the problem, its solution led rather directly to the development of penicillin as a cure for human bacterial infections.

The importance of problem finding for higher-order mental processes has long been recognized. John Dewey, whose definition of what constitutes a problem—"A problem represents a partial transformation of a problematic situation into a determinate situation" (Dewey, 1938, p. 108)—is still unmatched, argued that a well-formulated problem was half-solved. The Gestalt psychologist Max Wertheimer wrote: "The function of thinking is not just solving an actual problem but discovering, envisaging, going into deeper questions. Often in great discoveries the most important thing is that a certain question is found" (Wertheimer, 1945, p. 123). And he was echoed by the philosopher Michael Polanyi: "To see a problem is a definite addition to knowledge.... To recognize a problem which can be solved and is worth solving is in fact a discovery in its own right" (Polanyi, 1958, p. 120). Several psychologists and educators have pointed out the importance of identifying and formulating problems and have decried the exclusive research focus on problem solving (Henle, 1975; Macworth, 1965; Shulman, 1965).

Despite the recognized importance of the topic, no systematic studies of problem finding as such were started until the mid-1960s. There was neither a conceptual framework to support research nor any appropriate methods that could be used for empirical investigation. The development of this field was in part facilitated by the pioneering work of J. P. GUILFORD, whose concept of "divergent" thinking opened up new ways of understanding intellectual functioning (Guilford, 1967). Guilford recognized that standard intelligence tests measured mainly "convergent" thinking, that is, thinking that led to unambiguous results and always gave right answers. But he realized that many important intellectual activities—from landing a disabled plane to painting a picture—required a different type of mental process, one that reconfigured available elements into a unique solution that might be right only in a single situation. Divergent thinking had many obvious resemblances to problem finding, but it was still conceived as a response to a well-defined problem, and the instruments used for measuring it required the subject to respond to externally framed instructions.

The first—and the only—systematic definition of problem finding was the work of Jacob Getzels (1964, 1979, 1982, 1988). In the first of these articles, Getzels sounded the basic theme that was to recur throughout the literature on this topic: Our schools are geared to train problem solvers but fail to provide experience in problem finding; thus students who go through the educational system are unprepared for original thinking. To clarify the difference between problem solving and problem finding, he provided a synthetic review of a broad range of literature bearing on the issue, from Jean PIAGET to Guilford and Sigmund Freud, and related these cognitive perspectives to the emerging research on motivation based on stimulus-seeking rather than stimulus-reducing. As he developed this theme, Getzels set up a model that distinguished ten problem types ranging along a continuum from "presented" to "discovered" and finally "created" problems. At the presented end of this continuum are problems in which the formulation, the method of solution, and the solution itself are known in advance to the person who gives the problem, and only the solution is unknown to the problem solver.

An example of this most trivial of problematic situation would be that of a teacher asking a student to determine the area of a room measuring 3 meters by 5 meters—assuming that the student already knows the relationship between the length of the sides of a rectangle and its area. In such a case the student understands what the problem is and knows how to solve it, and the only missing piece is the actual solution. At the other extreme of the continuum, the "created" end, are problems that nobody in the culture has perceived before, to which no methods of solution exist, and therefore no one can even imagine what a solution would be like. Only the most original scientific and artistic breakthroughs meet all these requirements. Most creative achievements involve fewer degrees of uncertainty and consist in finding either novel solutions, or developing new methods, or discovering new problems, but not all three.

The first test of these ideas in an empirical research context consisted of an extensive series of studies of art students that began in 1962 and continued for twenty years (Csikszentmihalyi & Getzels, 1989; Getzels & Csikszentmihalyi, 1967; Getzels & Csikszentmihalyi, 1975; Getzels & Csikszentmihalyi, 1976; Getzels & Dillon, 1973). The most relevant findings from these studies were that the originality and artistic value of artworks completed in art school, and later success as a practicing artist, were best predicted by the young artists' exploratory behavior, from which may reasonably (if not airtightly) be inferred a *problem-finding approach,* as measured by systematic observations of their behavior as they painted. For example, in an experimental studio situation, a young student who explored the objects available for a still-life arrangement before choosing to paint them was more likely to produce a painting judged to be original by experts, and to be successful as a creative artist eighteen years later, than a student who gave the objects only a perfunctory inspection. Similarly, while time spent actually painting did not differentiate the more original and successful artists from the less successful ones, the former spent substantially more time choosing what to paint. These and similar observational measures were combined in a problem-finding score, and it was this score that showed a robust correlation with the originality rating of the artists' work, and with their creative accomplishments many years later.

This basic research paradigm has been modified and applied to the study of creative thought processes in a variety of situations. For example, it has been used to study differences between professional and amateur artists (Kay, 1991), to study the relationship of problem finding to other higher-order mental functions (Arlin, 1974, 1976), and to study the relationship of problem finding to problem solving (Dillon, 1982, 1988) and to creative insight (Csikszentmihalyi, 1990). Others have explored problem finding in the social realm (Getzels & Smilansky, 1983; Moore, 1990; Schwartz, 1974) or differences in problem-solving and problem-finding abilities within the same task, as in the solution versus the creation of new Raven Matrices problems (Smilansky, 1984). The results generally support the claim that problem-finding activity is an important higher-order mental function, that it is independent of the kind of convergent processes measured by standard intelligence tests, although somewhat related to divergent-thinking abilities (Getzels & Smilansky, 1983).

In the 1980s and early 1990s several investigators made conceptual or empirical contributions to this topic. The consensus appears to be that problem finding offers a very promising alternative to perspectives on creativity that assume it to be nothing but very fast rational mentation. For instance, the way a person identifies problematic situations in the environment appears to fit better than purely rational problem-solving models the late-twentieth century understandings of the emergence and functioning of consciousness (Edelman, 1993). However, it is also clear that the field needs more theoretical development (Hoover, 1990) and a broader empirical base (Moore & Murdock, 1991) before it can establish itself as a successful new paradigm.

One of the directions in which problem-finding research has been urged to move is the study of "real-world problems" (Moore & Murdock, 1991; Okuda, Runco, & Berger, 1990). Some indication of what this might involve is suggested by a study examining the biographies of the 100 most successful entrepreneurs in the United States between 1960 and 1985 (Silver, 1985). These are individuals who with little or no initial capital were able to build up multimillion dollar enterprises—such as William Hewlett and David Packard, who started with 538 dollars and created what was to become the world's largest manufacturer of electronic test instruments, or Leonard Shoen, who

with 5,000 dollars started U-Haul, the first inexpensive and efficient system for moving personal belongings over long distances. Silver concludes: "All successful entrepreneurs have a unique ability to formulate problems" (p. 43), and "Entrepreneurship is not creating a solution to a problem already defined. . . . If the process of entrepreneurial creativity is to be understood fully, the study of what the entrepreneur does cannot be restricted to the visible solution, the finished product. It must include the earlier, crucial step: formulation of the problem to which the solution is a response" (p. 76).

In conclusion, the concept of problem finding is potentially important because it may provide a better model for how the mind works than more linear and determined concepts do and because it highlights an important ingredient of creative thought usually missing from our formal educational processes. For both of these reasons, it opens up an exciting field of investigations for those interested in understanding mental processes.

BIBLIOGRAPHY

ARLIN, P. K. (1974). *Problem finding: The relation between cognitive process variables and problem-finding performance.* Unpublished doctoral dissertation, University of Chicago.

ARLIN, P. K. (1976). A cognitive process model of problem finding. *Educational Horizons, 54,* 99–106.

CSIKSZENTMIHALYI, M. (1990). The domain of creativity. In: R. Albert & M. Runco (EDS.), *Theories of creativity.* Newbury Park, CA: Sage, pp. 190–214.

CSIKSZENTMIHALYI, M., & GETZELS, J. W. (1989). Creativity and problem finding. In: F. H. Farley & R. W. Neperud (Eds.), *The foundation of the aesthetic* (pp. 91–116). New York: Praeger.

DEWEY, J. (1938). *Logic: The theory of inquiry.* New York: Henry Holt.

DILLON, J. T. (1982). Problem finding and solving. *Journal of Creative Behavior, 16,* 97–111.

DILLON, J. T. (1988). Levels of problem finding versus problem solving. *Questioning Exchange, 2*(2), 105–115.

EDELMAN, G. M. (1993). *Bright air, brilliant fire.* New York: Basic Books.

EINSTEIN, A., & INFELD, L. (1938). *The evolution of physics.* New York: Simon & Schuster.

GETZELS, J. W. (1964). Creative thinking, problem-solving, and instruction. In E. Hilgard (Ed.), *Theories of learning and instruction* (pp. 240–267). Chicago: University of Chicago Press.

GETZELS, J. W. (1979). Problem finding: A theoretical note. *Cognitive Science, 3,* 167–172.

GETZELS, J. W. (1982). The problem of the problem. In R. Hogarth (Ed.), *New directions for methodology of social and behavioral science: Question framing and response consistency* (pp. 37–49). San Francisco: Jossey-Bass.

GETZELS, J. W. (1988). Problem finding and creative thought. *Questioning Exchange, 2*(2), 95–103.

GETZELS, J. W., & CSIKSZENTMIHALYI, M. (1967). Scientific creativity. *Science Journal, 3,* 80–84.

GETZELS, J. W., & CSIKSZENTMIHALYI, M. (1975). From problem solving to problem finding. In I. A. Taylor & J. W. Getzels (Eds.), *Perspectives in creativity* (pp. 90–116). Chicago: Aldine.

GETZELS, J. W., & CSIKSZENTMIHALYI, M. (1976). *The creative vision.* New York: Wiley.

GETZELS, J. W., & DILLON, J. T. (1973). Giftedness and the education of the gifted. In R. M. W. Travers (Ed.), *Second handbook of research on teaching* (pp. 689–731). Chicago: Rand McNally.

GETZELS, J. W., & SMILANSKY, J. (1983). Individual differences in pupil perceptions of school problems. *British Journal of Educational Psychology, 53,* 307–316.

GUILFORD, J. P. (1967). *The nature of human intelligence.* New York: McGraw-Hill.

HENLE, M. (1975). Fishing for ideas. *American Psychologist, 30,* 795–799.

HOOVER, S. M. (1990). Problem finding/solving in science: Moving toward theory. *Creativity Research Journal, 3*(4), 330–331.

HUGHES, T. P. (1983). *Networks of power.* Baltimore, MD: Johns Hopkins University Press.

IMMERGART, G. L., & BOYD, D. L. (EDS.). (1979). *Problem finding in educational administration.* Lexington, MA: D. C. Heath.

KAY, S. (1991). The figural problem solving and problem finding of professional and semiprofessional artists and nonartists. *Creativity Research Journal, 4*(3), 233–252.

MACWORTH, N. H. (1965). Originality. *American Psychologist, 20,* 51–66.

MAUGH, T. H. (1974). Creativity: Can it be dissected? Can it be taught? *Science, 184,* 184.

MOORE, H. (1955). Notes on sculpture. In B. Ghiselin (Ed.), *The creative process.* New York: Mentor Books.

MOORE, M. T. (1990). Problem finding and teacher experience. *Journal of Creative Behavior, 24,* 39–58.

MOORE, M. T., & MURDOCK, M. C. (1991). On problems in problem-finding research. *Creativity Research Journal, 4*(3), 290–293.

OKUDA, S. M., RUNCO, M. A., & BERGER, D. A. (1990). Creativity and the finding and solving of real-world problems. *Journal of Psychoeducational Assessment, 9,* 45–53.

POLANYI, M. (1958). *Personal knowledge.* Chicago: University of Chicago Press.

RUNCO, M. A., & OKUDA, S. M. (1988). Problem-discovery, divergent thinking, and the creative process. *Journal of Youth and Adolescence, 17,* 211–220.

SCHWARTZ, D. M. (1974). *A study of interpersonal problem posing.* Unpublished doctoral dissertation, University of Chicago.

SHULMAN, L. S. (1965). Seeking styles and individual differences in patterns of inquiry. *School Review, 73,* 258–266.

SILVER, A. D. (1985). *Entrepreneurial megabucks: The 100 greatest entrepreneurs of the last twenty-five years.* New York: Wiley.

SMILANSKY, J. (1984). Problem solving and the quality of invention: An empirical investigation. *Journal of Educational Psychology, 76*(3), 377–386.

SUBOTNIK, R. F., & MOORE, M. T. (1988). Literature on problem finding. *Questioning Exchange, 2*(2), 87–93.

WAKEFIELD, J. (1988). Problem finding in the arts and sciences. *Questioning Exchange, 2,* 133–140.

WAKEFIELD, J. F. (1985). Towards creativity: Problem finding in a divergent-thinking exercise. *Child Study Journal, 15,* 265–270.

WERTHEIMER, M. (1945). *Productive thinking.* New York: Harper & Row.

MIHALY CSIKSZENTMIHALYI

PROBLEM SOLVING Problem solving is pervasive in intellectual activities—ranging from solving school mathematics problems to making personal decisions—and has long been recognized as an attribute of intelligence. For example, Sternberg (1990) reports that when experts in the field of intelligence were asked to list the attributes of intelligence in 1921, the most common answer was some form of higher level cognition, such as problem solving. Interestingly, the same result was obtained when experts were surveyed in 1986.

Problem solving is high-level cognitive processing directed at transforming a problem situation from its current state into a goal state when a solution is not immediately obvious to the problem solver (Mayer, 1990, 1992). This definition includes the following elements: First, problem solving is *cognitive*—it occurs within the problem solver's information-processing system. Thus, problem solving cannot be directly observed but only can be inferred from changes in the problem solver's behavior. Second, problem solving is *computational*—it involves manipulating (or performing mental operations on) information in the problem solver's memory. Cognitive processing involves changing the contents of the information-processing system, such as constructing, modifying, or rearranging mental representations. Third, problem solving is *directed*—problem solvers engage in problem solving in order to achieve some goal. Thus, undirected thinking such as daydreaming is excluded by this definition. Fourth, problem solving is *personal*—what is a problem for one problem solver may not be a problem for another. Problem solvers may be humans, other animals, or, because of computers, machines.

A *problem* exists when a situation is one state, the problem solver wants it to be in another state, and the problem solver does not know immediately how to transform the situation from the given to the goal state (Mayer, 1990, 1992). Therefore, there are three elements in the definition of a problem—the problem is in the *given state;* the problem solver wants the problem to be in the *goal state;* and transforming the problem from given to goal state is blocked by *obstacles.* Gestalt psychologist Karl Duncker (1945, p. 1) wrote: "A problem arises when a living creature has a goal but

does not know how this goal is to be reached. Whenever one cannot go from the given situation to the desired situation simply by action, then there is recourse to thinking. . . . Such thinking has the task of devising some action which may mediate between the existing and the desired situations."

For example, in the disk problem shown in Figure 1, the problem solver is given three pegs with three disks (a small, medium, and large disk in ascending order) on the first peg and needs to have the three disks on the third peg. The problem solver may move only one disk at a time (i.e., the top disk on one peg may be moved to the top of any other peg) but may never place a larger disk on top of a smaller disk. There is no way to accomplish the goal directly; the major obstacles are the rule that only one disk may be moved at a time, which precludes picking up all three disks and moving them as a group to the third peg, and the rule that a larger disk cannot be placed on top of a smaller disk, which disallows moving the disks sequentially from the first to the third peg.

According to information-processing theories, solving a problem such as the disk problem involves construction of a problem-space and implementation of a search strategy (Newell & Simon, 1972). A problem space is a representation of the given state, goal state, and all intervening states generated by making legal moves; for example, the next possible states after the given state are created by moving the small disk to the second peg or to the third peg, and so on. A search strategy is a procedure for moving from one state to the next in the problem space, including random search, hill climbing, and means–ends analysis. In random search, the problem solver randomly selects a move to one of the possible next states (such as moving any available disk to any available peg). In hill climbing, the problem solver always selects the move

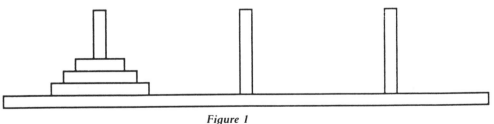

Figure 1
The disk problem

that gets the problem closer to the goal (such as trying to get as many disks as possible on the third peg). Random search is inefficient and hill climbing does not work for problems that require moving away from the goal in order to solve the problem eventually (such as moving a small disk off the third peg in order to make way for the large disk). Means–ends analysis is a more efficient search process that overcomes these problems. In means–ends analysis, the problem solver works on one goal at a time (such as creating the goal state) or, if that is not possible, removing obstacles and selecting operators. In short, the problem solver establishes goals, recognizes obstacles to accomplishing the goal, and selects operators for overcoming the obstacles.

The tumor problem, represented in Figure 2, is another example of a problem: "Given a human being with an inoperable stomach tumor, and rays which destroy organic tissue at sufficient intensity, by what procedure can one free him of the tumor by these rays and at the same time avoid destroying the healthy tissue which surrounds it?" (Duncker, 1945, p. 1). In this problem, the given state is that a person has an inoperable stomach tumor surrounded by healthy tissue, the goal state is that the tumor is not present in the person, and the allowable operators involve using a ray that can destroy tissue at sufficient intensity. According to Gestalt theory (Duncker, 1945; Wertheimer, 1959), the major task of the problem solver is to reorganize the elements in the problem, that is, to see the goals or givens in the problem in a new way. For example, the problem solver may restate the goal so as to avoid contact between the rays and the healthy tissue—a goal that suggests an incorrect solution, such as shooting the rays through the esophagus. Eventually, a problem solver may restate the goal so as to have lower intensity of rays as they pass through the healthy tissue—a goal that suggests an incorrect solution, such as turning up the intensity when the ray reaches the tumor, and the correct solution, such as focusing several weak rays as a lens so they all converge on the tumor. In this case, problem solving involves continually clarifying the problem, a process that can be blocked by one's past experience (Luchins, 1942).

It is useful to make a distinction between well-defined and ill-defined problems, and between routine and nonroutine problems. A well-defined problem has a clearly specified given state, goal state, and set of allowable operators, as in the disk problem. An ill-defined problem lacks a clearly specified given state, goal state, and/or operators. For example, in the tumor problem the allowable operators are not clearly specified, or the problem of how to become a happy person lacks a clear goal state and operators. Information-processing theories provide an account of problem solving with well-defined problems, whereas Gestalt theory attempted to account for how people solve ill-defined problems.

A routine problem is one that the problem solver has learned how to solve previously, so that solving it requires *reproductive thinking* (Wertheimer, 1959), that is, reproducing behaviors that one has already created in the past. A nonroutine problem is a novel problem that is unlike any problem that the problem solver has ever encountered before, so that solving it requires creating an original solution, which Wertheimer (1959) has termed *productive thinking.* The disk problem would be a routine problem for someone who has read a lot about problem solving, but it would be a nonroutine problem for someone who has never studied or solved puzzles before. Similarly, the tumor problem is a nonroutine problem for anyone who has not seen it before.

Problem solving can be analyzed into three major kinds of processes—representation processes, solution

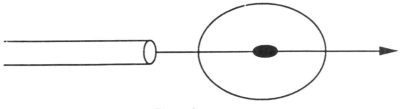

Figure 2
The tumor problem

processes, and control processes. Representing occurs when a problem solver creates an internal mental representation of a problem, including the given state, goal state, and allowable operations. For example, in the disk problem, the problem solver must understand the rules of the game as well as the given and goal configurations. Solving occurs when the problem solver establishes and carries out a plan. For the disk problem, the plan may be to always take the move that results in getting more disks on the third peg. Controlling occurs when a problem solver monitors progress, considers alternative plans, and reviews what has been accomplished. In the disk problem, a problem solver may recognize that the plan has failed when it becomes necessary to move the small disks from the third peg.

INDIVIDUAL DIFFERENCES IN PROBLEM SOLVING

How can we characterize individual differences in problem solving? Three approaches to individual differences are cognitive components, cognitive correlates, and cognitive training. According to the cognitive components approach, a problem-solving activity can be analyzed into its component cognitive and metacognitive processes (Mayer, 1992; Sternberg, 1985). For example, to solve an analogical reasoning problem such as SENTENCE:PARAGRAPH::FINGER:——————— (a. HAND, b. ESSAY, c. PEN, d. KNUCKLE), the problem solver coordinates several component processes including encoding the terms (e.g., the A-term is SENTENCE, the B-term is PARAGRAPH, etc.), inducing the relation between the A-term and the B-term (e.g., part-to-whole), applying the relation from the C-term to potential D-terms (e.g., FINGER is part of HAND), and responding (e.g., producing A as the correct answer). Individual problem solvers may differ on any of these component processes, or on the metacognitive process of coordinating them. For example, Phye (1989) has provided evidence that the inducing process is particularly difficult for some problem solvers, but that they can learn to improve on inducing relations if given appropriate training.

According to the cognitive correlates approach, individual differences in problem solving may be related to differences in the operating characteristics of individuals' information-processing systems (Hunt, Lunneborg, & Lewis, 1975). For example, a person who can hold many words in working memory has a problem-solving advantage in comprehending a written statement of a problem over someone who can hold only a few words at one time (Just & Carpenter, 1987), or a person who can hold many numbers in working memory at one time can use a more sophisticated problem-solving procedure on a mathematical task than someone who can work with only one or two numbers at a time (Case, 1985; Siegler, 1986). One way of overcoming the limitations on working memory is to automate one's problem-solving procedures so that they do not require any cognitive resources.

According to the cognitive-training approach, problem solvers who are deficient in a specific information process or metaprocess need direct instruction in how and when to use the process. For example, mathematical problem solving improves when low-performing students are taught how to represent word problems in diagrammatic form (Lewis, 1989). In this case, a representational process specifically tied to word problems underlies a major individual difference between successful and unsuccessful mathematical problem solvers. In summary, individual differences in problem solving may be specified as differences in problem-solving processes and metaprocesses.

SPECIFIC AND GENERAL ASPECTS OF PROBLEM SOLVING

A major issue for a theory of problem solving is the degree to which problem-solving skills are general or specific. Does problem solving depend mainly on a few weak methods—general strategies that can be applied in many different domains—or on many strong methods—strategies that are specifically tied to limited domains? Are there general principles of problem solving that apply across all problems, or must psychologists be content to build separate theories of problem solving for each domain—such as chess playing, medical decision making, legal reasoning, computer programming, and physics problem solving?

Ongoing research on transfer and on expertise highlights the domain-specificity of problem solving and the role of strong methods. Research on problem-solving transfer shows that problem solvers who know how to solve one kind of problem often fail to solve analogous problems that could be solved by the same methods (Gick & Holyoak, 1980, 1983; Reed, Dempster, & Ettinger, 1985; Reed, Ernst, & Banerji, 1974). For example, in one study, students learned to solve the general problem and later were asked to solve the tumor problem (Gick & Holyoak, 1980, 1983). In the general problem, a general wants to deploy his troops to attack a fortress that has roads radiating outward like spokes on a wheel, but each of the roads leading to the fortress is mined so that a large group of soldiers would detonate the mines. The solution is to deploy small groups along each road so that they all converge on the fortress. This problem is analogous to the tumor problem: The fortress is like the tumor, the mined roads are like the healthy surrounding tissue, attacking groups of troops are like the rays. Most students who learn how to solve the general problem are not able to solve the tumor problem without assistance, even though both can be solved by the convergence idea (Gick & Holyoak, 1980, 1983).

Similarly, research on expertise shows that people who are expert problem solvers in one domain, such as medical reasoning, computer programming, or chess playing, do not show extraordinary problem-solving performance in other domains (Chi, Glaser, & Farr, 1988). Indeed, experts tend to use qualitatively different problem-solving strategies than novices—methods that are specifically tied to a domain and that require a great deal of specific domain knowledge (Chi, Glaser, & Farr, 1988). For example, following the classic work of De Groot (1965), Chase & Simon (1973) found that expert chess players were better able to recall the location of chess pieces on a board than nonexperts when presented with boards from real games but not for randomly created boards. This suggests that experts do not possess better memory overall, but rather have developed chess-specific strategies for how to cluster pieces into meaningful configurations. Similar expert–novice differences have been obtained in programmers' memory for computer programs (McKeithen, Reitman, Rueter, & Hirtle, 1981) and physicians' use of patient case information (Patel & Groen, 1986). Smith (1991, p. i) summarizes this line of research by noting that "recent research in medicine and certain other domains has strongly emphasized the context specificity of the problem-solving process."

In contrast, in their landmark search for a general theory of problem solving, Newell and Simon (1972) emphasized means–end analysis as a problem-solving heuristic that could be applied in a variety of problems. Although computer simulations based on means–ends analysis are successful in solving a wide variety of problems, weak methods such as means–end analysis are more often used by novices than experts (Chi, Glaser, & Farr, 1988; Larkin, McDermott, Simon, & Simon, 1980). Therefore, current research seeks to extract "general characteristics of expert performance across different domains" (Ericsson & Smith, 1991, p. vii) and "consistencies within domain specific problem-solving research" (Smith, 1991, p. ii). In addition, current research focuses on complex problem solving within realistic problem-solving situations (Sternberg & Frensch, 1991).

(*See also:* PROBLEM FINDING.)

BIBLIOGRAPHY

CASE, R. (1985). *Intellectual development: Birth to adulthood.* Orlando: Academic Press.

CHASE, W. G., & SIMON, H. A. (1973). Perception in chess. *Cognitive Psychology, 4,* 55–81.

CHI, M. T., GLASER, R., & FARR, M. J. (1988). (Eds.). *The nature of expertise.* Hillsdale, NJ: Erlbaum.

DE GROOT, A. D. (1965). *Thought and choice in chess.* The Hague: Mouton.

DUNCKER, K. (1945). On problem-solving. *Psychological Monographs, 58*(5, Whole no. 270).

ERICSSON, K. A., & SMITH, J. (1991). (Eds.). *Toward a general theory of expertise: Prospects and limits.* Cambridge: Cambridge University Press.

GICK, M. L., & HOLYOAK, K. J. (1980). Analogical problem solving. *Cognitive Psychology, 12,* 306–355.

GICK, M. L., & HOLYOAK, K. J. (1983). Schema induction and analogical transfer. *Cognitive Psychology, 15,* 1–38.

HUNT, E. G., LUNNEBORG, G., & LEWIS, J. (1975). What does it mean to be high verbal? *Cognitive Psychology, 7,* 194–227.

JUST, M. A., & CARPENTER, P. A. (1987). *The psychology of reading and language comprehension.* Boston: Allyn & Bacon.

LARKIN, J., MCDERMOTT, J., SIMON, D. P., & SIMON, H. A. (1980). Expert and novice performance in solving physics problems. *Science, 208,* 1335–1342.

LEWIS, A. B. (1989). Training students to represent arithmetic word problems. *Journal of Educational Psychology, 81,* 521–531.

LUCHINS, A. S. (1942). Mechanization in problem solving. *Psychological Monographs, 54*(6, Whole no. 248).

MAYER, R. E. (1990). Problem solving. In M. W. Eysenck (Ed.), *The Blackwell dictionary of cognitive psychology* (pp. 284–288). Oxford: Basil Blackwell.

MAYER, R. E. (1992). *Thinking, problem solving, cognition* (2nd ed.). New York: Freeman.

MCKEITHEN, K. B., REITMAN, J. S., RUETER, H. H., & HIRTLE, S. C. (1981). Knowledge organization and skill differences in computer programmers. *Cognitive Psychology, 13,* 307–325.

NEWELL, A., & SIMON, H. A. (1972). *Human problem solving.* Englewood Cliffs, NJ: Prentice-Hall.

PATEL, V., & GROEN, G. J. (1986). Knowledge based solution strategies in medical reasoning. *Cognitive Science, 10,* 91–116.

PHYE, G. D. (1989). Schemata training and transfer of an intellectual skill. *Journal of Educational Psychology, 81,* 347–352.

REED, S. K., DEMPSTER, A., & ETTINGER, M. (1985). Usefulness of analogous solutions for solving algebra word problems. *Journal of Experimental Psychology: Learning, Memory, and Cognition, 11,* 106–125.

REED, S. K., ERNST, G. W., & BANERJI, R. (1974). The role of analogy in transfer between similar problem states. *Cognitive Psychology, 6,* 436–450.

SIEGLER, R. S. (1986). *Children's thinking.* Englewood Cliffs, NJ: Prentice-Hall.

SMITH, U. (1991). (Ed.). *Toward a unified theory of problem solving.* Hillsdale, NJ: Erlbaum.

STERNBERG, R. J. (1985). *Beyond IQ: A triarchic theory of human intelligence.* Cambridge: Cambridge University Press.

STERNBERG, R. J. (1990). *Metaphors of mind: Conceptions of the nature of intelligence.* Cambridge: Cambridge University Press.

STERNBERG, R. J., & FRENSCH, P. A. (1991). (Eds.). *Complex problem solving: Principles and mechanisms.* Hillsdale, NJ: Erlbaum.

WERTHEIMER, M. (1959). *Productive thinking.* New York: Harper & Row.

RICHARD E. MAYER

PRODIGIES The prodigy has been known for millennia but has been hardly understood. In fact, part of the meaning of the word *prodigy* captures some of the mysteriousness of certain events and processes. In its earliest use, *prodigy* referred to any event that seemed to be "out of the usual course of nature" or "inexplicable" or "monstrous" (Gove, 1961). It did not refer necessarily even to human behavior, and it was not originally associated with exceptional mental ability. Over the centuries, there has been a narrowing and focusing of the notion of the prodigy; a 1961 dictionary definition all but removed the distinctiveness of the word by defining a prodigy as a "highly gifted or academically talented child." Were this definition to be accepted, it would mean that a prodigy and a child of high IQ were indistinguishable. In fact, the relationship between the prodigy and psychometric intelligence is not at all straightforward.

A more recent definition is intended to distinguish prodigies from other forms of extreme intellectual capability, as well as to recapture some of the ancient meaning of the term: The prodigy is a child (typically younger than ten years old) who is performing at the level of a highly trained adult in a very demanding field of endeavor. This definition has a number of features: it emphasizes *performance* as a criterion for calling someone a prodigy, as contrasted with psychometric intelligence that tries to measure potential; it labels the prodigy as a *human* phenomenon; it emphasizes the *specific* realms within which prodigious behavior appears, as contrasted with psychometric intelligence, which aims at assessing general intellectual ability; and, it has a *comparative* feature that allows for reasonable measurement of the degree of prodigiousness in relation to the standards of performance within a given field.

Although there is growing consensus that a definition of a prodigy such as the one given above is reasonable, it would be going too far to say that such a consensus exists without controversy. There may be, for example, some wisdom in the view of John Radford (1990), who has argued that there are so many problems with specifying at what age and against what standard a child would have to perform that it is folly to try to be precise in a definition. It is true that each field has its own standards, that these standards change, and that what might be an extremely early age for achievement in one field might be fairly routine in another, making it difficult to classify behavior as prodigious.

Definitions notwithstanding, there is renewed interest in the prodigy as one of the more striking manifestations of human potential, and recognition that prodigies, along with other examples of extreme talent, such as SAVANTS and very high IQ cases, are increasingly seen as worthy of careful study (Morelock & Feldman, 1990). The study of prodigies, therefore, offers an opportunity both to understand better the nature and limitations of the concept of psychometric intelligence, and to offer a perhaps unique avenue into some of the least well-understood aspects of intellectual development.

There have been an amazingly small number of scientific studies of prodigies. In the entire psychological research literature, only three books have reported major studies, and two of these appeared in German some time ago (Baumgarten, 1930; Revesz, 1925). In spite of the many centuries of anecdotes and stories and legends about prodigies, from the young David of the Old Testament to Joan of Arc in medieval times and Yehudi Menuhin in the twentieth century, the scientific knowledge base is remarkably absent. Fewer than twenty cases have been studied in depth.

Prodigies have appeared in many but far from all fields of human endeavor. There is no accurate estimate of the number of prodigies in general, nor are there accurate counts within various fields, but there are some domains in which prodigies are relatively more frequent, others less frequent, still others in which prodigies have not yet been identified.

Music is probably the field in which prodigies appear with greatest frequency, and chess has also had many prodigies in its ranks of strong players. Mozart is often cited as the most extraordinary child prodigy that music composition has produced, and the American chess player Bobby Fischer was a renowned prodigy in the 1960s. Although mathematics is generally believed to be the specialty of prodigies, most known cases have actually been calculators, more akin to savants than to prodigies (Smith, 1983). When original mathematical reasoning is included as a criterion for calling a child a mathematical prodigy, there are actually very few documented cases (Feldman, 1991a; Radford, 1990).

There have been a small number of writing prodigies; the best known is probably the English girl Daisy Ashford, who wrote a popular novel, *The Young Visitors,* not long before the twentieth century. Even fewer prodigies have been found in the visual arts. The only clear case of an artistic prodigy was that of Nadia, a disturbed English girl whose artistic ability diminished as her autism responded to treatment (Selfe, 1977). A mainland Chinese girl, Wang Yani, achieved considerable fame for her exceptionally deft watercolors of monkeys and other subjects that she began producing at three (Ho, 1989). If sports fields are included within the definition of prodigy, then the number of cases increases considerably, particularly in fields like gymnastics and swimming, where an early start seems necessary to achieve the highest levels of performance.

Few if any prodigies have been identified in science, philosophy, the dance, or the plastic arts. Fields like law and business and medicine also seem to require a greater number of years of preparation before the heights are scaled, although there have been a few instances of individuals who have achieved entry level status while still in their teens; a Florida boy named Steven Baccus took the oath to practice law before his eighteenth birthday (Hicks, 1986). Computer programming appears to be a field in which prodigies may appear, although none younger than 10 has come to public attention thus far.

Another feature of the prodigy phenomenon has been that vastly more boys than girls have been identified (Goldsmith, 1987). This seems to be true for at least two reasons: The fields in which prodigies are found have tended to be populated more by males than females (e.g., chess); and, there has been a long history of prejudice against girls participating in and/ or receiving recognition for their work in fields like music or mathematics. If allowed to participate in a field, girls have often been relegated to amateur status or been required to pursue their interests in a field outside of the professional community. In the only published article specifically on girl prodigies, this example is given:

> Sophie Germain began an informal study of mathematics when she was 13, and in six years had mastered the field to such a degree that her work came to the attention of mathematician Joseph Lagrange. Working almost exclusively outside of the established (male) community, Germain nonetheless made a substantial contribution to the field of number theory . . . [Goldsmith, 1987, p. 77].

As social and cultural restrictions on women have been broken down, so have the number of girl prodigies begun to increase. The most striking change has been in the field of music performance, where girls are now found in numbers more or less equal to boys. Girls have also moved toward greater parity in the field of chess; a Hungarian girl named Judit Polgar achieved the rank of grandmaster at age 15 years, 5 months, a month earlier than the great prodigy and eventual world champion Bobby Fischer (McFadden, 1992). It is reasonable to guess that the numbers of girl prodigies will increase during the next few decades as opportunities for participation increase, barriers are lowered, and rewards for high-level achievement are equalized.

RECENT RESEARCH

In the mid-1970s, the first modern study of child prodigies was begun at Tufts University under the direction of David Henry Feldman (Feldman, 1991a). This study followed six boy prodigies over a nearly ten-year period. The boys were between 3 and 10 years old when first observed, and they were involved in fields ranging from writing to chess to music. Two of the children were difficult to classify as pure prodigies, one because his abilities seemed to be so diverse, the other because he was originally identified in mathematics but was in fact more interested in science.

In contrast to earlier studies, which tended to concentrate on the mental abilities of the child subjects as revealed in tests of various kinds, more recent studies have focused on broader processes of development, in-

cluding aspects of the prodigies' family and educational experiences, personal and emotional qualities, and interactions with the various domains in which they are involved (Bamberger, 1982; Feldman, 1991a). The questions of interest to current research have more to do with the processes through which a prodigy achieves such high levels of mastery. Earlier studies focused more on the kinds of logical, spatial, musical, and linguistic abilities the children possessed, although they did establish the distinctive mixture of child and adult qualities that so often marks the prodigy's profile both intellectually and emotionally (Baumgarten, 1930; Revesz, 1925).

DEVELOPMENT IN PRODIGIES

Contrary to what seems to be a common view of the prodigy as an adult who happens to be constrained by a child's body, the evidence suggests that a more accurate description would be that a prodigy is a child who happens to have a powerful talent. Based on observations of the six prodigies in *Nature's Gambit* (Feldman, 1991a), the impression is consistent with earlier accounts that prodigies are indeed remarkably advanced within their specific areas of expertise, but not particularly advanced emotionally or in their social development.

Indeed, to some degree, the kinds of lives that prodigies have been encouraged to lead stand in the way of their normal development in other areas. The focus of resources, both those of the child and those around her or him, can be so intense that there is little emphasis on making sure that the child learns to do things independently. Parents' and teachers' feelings of responsibility for making sure the child's talent is fully developed can lead to their relieving the child of other responsibilities.

On the other hand, prodigies are sometimes given responsibilities far beyond their years, such as responsibilities to earn money to support their families. Particularly in fields such as music and sports and show business, the pressure on children to perform often and in inappropriate settings can lead to precocious adultlike attitudes about professionalism and about money. The Jackson Five, a popular singing group of the 1970s, included the children from a single family, one of whom was five-year-old Michael. This group was earning millions of dollars before its oldest member had reached the age of maturity.

Exploitation of prodigies by parents and other adults has been an unfortunate aspect of the history of the phenomenon. Stories of calculating prodigies being put on display as freaks were not uncommon during the Middle Ages (Smith, 1983). Even the great Mozart at age 8, as well as his sister, were advertised in the newspaper as "Prodigies of Nature" well into the so-called Age of Enlightenment (MacLeish, 1984).

The experience of being a prodigy and the experience of raising a prodigy are unusual. It should not be surprising that there are unusual qualities characteristic of both prodigies and their parents. Prodigies tend to be unusually focused, determined, and highly motivated to reach the highest levels of their fields. They are often marked as well by great confidence in their abilities, along with a naive sense of these abilities in relation to those of others. It is often a surprise to a prodigy that other people have neither the same talents nor the same preoccupations that they do. In this respect, there can be an appearance of overconfidence in the prodigy, as well as a strong sense that doing what she or he does is both natural and comfortable, indeed, that doing anything else would be detrimental to the child's well-being.

Parents of prodigies are often involved in the same or related fields as their offspring (Bloom, 1985). Picasso's father was an artist, Mozart's father a musician, Nijinsky's parents were dancers. Often older when they have their children, parents of prodigies are generally willing to devote major portions of their own time and energy to the development of their children's talents. One or both parents may reduce or give up entirely their own careers, may move long distances to be where their children can receive the best instruction, may sacrifice their own comfort and security so that the very best equipment, technology, competition, and promotion can be provided.

Parents of prodigies are also sometimes driven to extreme behavior because of unresponsiveness or even outright hostility to the needs of their offspring. Prodigies in the United States face substantial difficulties in public (and some private) schools. Schools are often rather inflexible in accommodating the special needs of prodigies, such as allowing time for travel to tour-

naments or competitions or special instructional resources. Parents also find themselves at odds with school authorities over extra resources needed to respond to the exceptional talents of their children. A number of parents of prodigies have found that their children are better served with home instruction. Alternatively, parents find that they must continuously search for appropriate settings for their children, with school changes as frequently as twice a year not unusual.

PRODIGIES AND PSYCHOMETRIC INTELLIGENCE

Research on prodigies has established (or reestablished) that the prodigy is a distinctive form of human intelligence, not reducible to any other form (Feldman, 1991a). This means that prodigies must be understood on their own terms, but it does not mean that the processes that govern expression of potential in the prodigy are fundamentally different from those same processes in all other human beings. Prodigies, as others, are endowed with certain talents and interests, have access to greater or fewer resources, live in families with varying commitments to helping their children achieve their potential, must deal with difficult transitions, must confront changes in their bodies and minds and emotions (Bamberger, 1982), live in cultures where various fields are more or less valued and more or less available; in short, they proceed as best they can with the developmental process.

The question of just what role psychometric intelligence might play in the prodigy's development and expression of potential has not been answered systematically. Possible answers have ranged from the prodigy being nothing more than a very high-IQ child (cf. Cox, 1926; Hollingworth, 1942), to prodigies being nothing more than individuals with a peculiar gift unrelated to more general intellectual functioning—in short, savants (Marshall, 1986). Based on what is now known about prodigies, a more reasonable answer would acknowledge that psychometric intelligence plays a role in the process of prodigy development, but a supporting role rather than a central one.

In the six cases studied in *Nature's Gambit*, for example, IQs were known in two of the cases, SAT college entrance examination scores on two others (highly correlated with IQ), and school achievement scores (also highly correlated with IQ) on the other two. In all six cases, their IQs were above average by at least one standard deviation. That is, these six boys were all well above average in their general ability to succeed in traditional academic pursuits. Their IQ scores could be guessed to fall in the range of a low of about 120 to a high of well above 200.

Although IQ scores are not available on most of the famous prodigies of history, it seems reasonable to guess that most of them were also generally able, if not exceptionally gifted, in the IQ sense (Feldman & Goldsmith, 1989). Mozart, for example, wrote quite well, picked up languages with relative ease, and had a keen ability to judge both musical and nonmusical qualities in other people (Feldman, 1991b). This is not at all to say that Mozart's gifts in verbal areas were equal to his exquisite musical gifts, but rather to suggest that his musical gift was supported and enhanced by his somewhat more modest gifts in verbal (and also interpersonal) intelligence (Gardner, 1983).

There are cases of individuals with striking gifts in highly specific areas that are not supported by more general intellectual abilities. These cases have been studied much more extensively, and are now labeled "savant syndrome." Although it would be overly simplified to say that prodigies and savants differ only with respect to the amount of psychometric intelligence available to them, the difference is clearly a vitally important one.

A savant may be someone who is able to carry out highly complex arithmetic calculations quickly and seemingly effortlessly, or who can play back any piece of music perfectly, holding that piece of music permanently in memory. Savants have been found in many of the same areas as prodigies: mathematics, music, art, and occasionally chess. There are also savants who are able to memorize great volumes of verbal material (e.g., the Manhattan telephone book), or who can provide the correct day of the week for any date in history. Although more is known about savants than prodigies, the knowledge base on which we try to understand savants is similarly scanty.

Comparative studies of various forms of extreme intellectual giftedness should go a long way toward helping answer some of the many questions remaining about prodigies. Are their abilities best conceptualized as isolated and highly specific? Is it necessary for these abilities to be supplemented with more general intellectual capability such as psychometric general intelligence? Why are there prodigies in some fields but not others? Why are there both prodigies and savants in certain fields but not in others? Why are those with very high IQs not likely to sustain themselves as prodigies? Does training in a field like music have different effects on prodigies than on others with more general talents?

These and many other questions can be pursued now that the prodigy has taken a place among the recognized manifestations of extreme human intelligence. We may hope that some of the many questions raised by this most fascinating form of human intelligence will begin to have answers in the future that will shed light on broader questions of human intelligence as well.

BIBLIOGRAPHY

BAMBERGER, J. (1982). Growing up prodigies: The midlife crisis. In D. H. Feldman (Ed.), *Developmental approaches to giftedness and creativity.* San Francisco: Jossey-Bass.

BAUMGARTEN, F. (1930). *Wunderkinder: psychologische Untersuchungen.* Leipzig: Johann Ambrosious Barth.

BLOOM, B. (ED.). (1985) *Developing talent in young people.* New York: Ballantine Books.

COX, C. (1926). *Genetic studies of genius, Vol II: The early mental traits of three hundred geniuses.* Stanford, CA: Stanford University Press.

FELDMAN, D. (1991a). *Nature's gambit: Child prodigies and the development of human potential.* New York: Teachers College Press. (Originally published in 1986.)

FELDMAN, D. (1991b, December). *Mozart and the transformational imperative.* Presented at the Symposium: Mozart and the Perils of Creativity, Smithsonian Institution, Washington, DC.

FELDMAN, D., & GOLDSMITH, L. (1989). Child prodigies: Straddling two worlds. In the *Encyclopedia Britannica Medical and Health Annual* (pp. 32–51). Chicago: Encyclopedia Britannica.

GARDNER, H. (1983). *Frames of mind: The theory of multiple intelligences.* New York: Basic Books.

GOLDSMITH, L. (1987). Girl prodigies: Some evidence and some speculations. *Roeper Review, 10,* 74–82.

HICKS, D. F. (1986, November 15). At 17, prodigy will take his oath as a new lawyer. *Miami Herald.*

HO, W. C. (ED.). (1989). *Wang Yani: The brush of innocence.* New York: Hudson Hills Press.

HOLLINGWORTH, L. (1975). *Children above 180 IQ.* New York: Arno Press. (Originally published in 1942.)

HOWE, M. J. A. (1989). *Fragments of genius.* London: Routledge.

MARSHALL, R. L. (1985). Mozart/Amadeus: Amadeus/Mozart, *Brandeis Review, 5,* 9–16.

McFADDEN, R. D. (1992, February 4). Youngest grandmaster ever is 15, ferocious (and female). *New York Times.*

MACLEISH, R. (1984). The mystery of what makes a prodigy. *Smithsonian, 14,* 12, 70–79.

MORELOCK, M. J., & FELDMAN, D. H. (1990). Extreme precocity. In N. Colangelo & G. Davis (Eds.), *Handbook of gifted education.* Boston: Allyn & Bacon.

RADFORD, J. (1990). *Child prodigies and exceptional early achievers.* New York: Free Press.

REVESZ, G. (1970). *The psychology of a musical prodigy.* Freeport, NY: Books for Libraries Press. (Originally published in 1925.)

SELFE, L. (1977). *Nadia: A case of extraordinary drawing ability in an autistic child.* London: Academic Press.

SMITH, S. B. (1983). *The great mental calculators: The psychology, methods, and lives of calculating prodigies.* New York: Columbia University Press.

DAVID HENRY FELDMAN

PROFILE INTERPRETATION

PROFILE INTERPRETATION Very generally, profile interpretation may be defined as the analysis of intelligence-test results to determine the distinctive cognitive capabilities of the individual. More specifically, profile interpretation is the clinical practice of examining the level, shape, and scatter of a test profile in relation to established interpretive guidelines. The focus of profile interpretation is one of personalization: What do these unique scores tell us about the cognitive functioning of this particular person? The purpose of this brief commentary is to summarize critically the alternative methods for profile interpretation and to discuss limitations of this approach, beginning by describing the nature of intelligence-test profiles.

A profile is a graph or table of scores from the battery of subtests that comprise an intelligence test. Subtest scores are standardized so that they possess identical averages and similar standard deviations, based on the performance of a representative norm group. For example, the average score for each subtest on the Wechsler Intelligence Scale for Children (3rd ed.), or WISC–III, is 10 and the standard deviation is about 3. The subtest scores for an individual examinee are plotted as a profile so that relative strengths and weaknesses can be visually inspected. Consider the WISC–III profile of a 10-year-old boy who was failing the fifth grade (Figure 1). How can we make sense out of this profile?

THE INTERPRETATION OF PROFILE LEVEL

The general level of the profile is the logical starting point for profile interpretation. Fortunately, the profile level corresponds directly to the overall score on the test, so the examiner possesses a handy index for initial profile interpretation. The overall score is variously referred to as an "intelligence quotient (IQ)," "general cognitive index," or "mental processing composite," depending on the instrument in question. This score can be assigned to an intellectual category from a classification system of the examiner's choice (see CLASSIFICATION OF INTELLIGENCE). Although the profile level conveys very little about the specific cognitive capabilities of the examinee, it may provide a great deal of information about general abilities and prospects (Gregory, 1987; Kaufman, 1990). For example, the general level of the profile depicted in Figure 1 is average. These results correspond to an IQ of 100. This proves that low intelligence is not the source of this child's learning difficulties.

PEAKS AND VALLEYS IN THE PROFILE

Peaks and valleys in the profile can be used to identify relative cognitive strengths and weaknesses. An examinee who earns a comparatively high score on one subtest (a peak) is displaying a relative strength in the cognitive skills measured by that subtest. Of course, the converse argument holds for a comparatively low score (a valley) as an indicator of relative weakness in

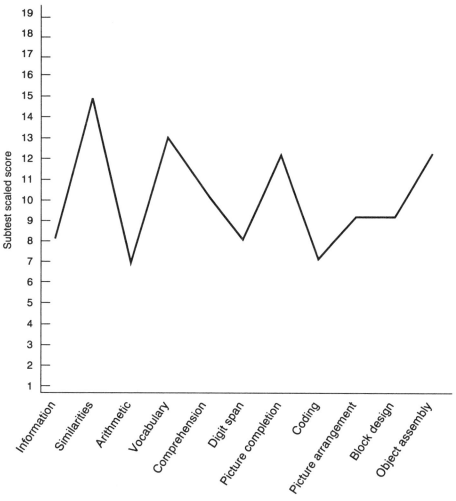

Figure 1
WISC–III profile for a 10-year-old boy

the pertinent cognitive skills. Consider the profile shown in Figure 1. This profile shows a sharp peak on similarities, a subtest that includes questions similar to "In what way are shirts and socks alike?" This peak indicates that the examinee has a cognitive strength in the skills tapped by the similarities subtest, namely, logical and abstractive thinking.

Rather than relying on fallible visual inspection, one should use appropriate statistical procedures for the objective identification of peaks and valleys. In one form of the statistical approach, the examiner first computes the average of all the subtest scores and subtracts each individual subtest score from this value.

Published tables are then consulted to determine the difference that is required to classify each subtest as a relative strength (peak) or comparative weakness (valley). The examiner can select a more stringent criterion for strengths and weaknesses ($p < .01$) or a less stringent one ($p < .05$). Tables 1 and 2 illustrate this approach with the Wechsler Adult Intelligence Scale–Revised (WAIS–R) scores of a young adult. This person shows a cognitive strength in comprehension (a measure of commonsense reasoning) and a weakness in picture completion (a measure of visual recognition and identification). Additional examples of this approach, including some interesting variations, can be

TABLE 1
WAIS–R criteria for subtest strengths and weaknesses

Subtest	Difference Needed Between the Subtest and the Mean of All 11 WAIS–R Subtests	
	$p < .05$	$p < .01$
Information	2.6	3.1
Digit span	3.4	3.9
Vocabulary	1.9	2.2
Arithmetic	3.1	3.7
Comprehension	3.3	3.8
Similarities	3.4	4.0
Picture completion	3.4	4.0
Picture arrangement	3.8	4.4
Block design	2.8	3.2
Object assembly	4.1	4.8
Digit symbol	3.5	4.0

SOURCE: Based on data from Silverstein (1982).

found in R. J. Gregory (1987), A. S. Kaufman (1990), A. S. Kaufman and N. L. Kaufman (1983), and A. B. Silverstein (1991).

THE CONFIGURAL APPROACH

Psychologists have long searched for distinctive subtest profiles associated with schizophrenia, depression, juvenile delinquency, brain damage, and other forms of psychopathology. Although a few broad generalities have emerged from this research, the more notable result is that specific profile shapes and particular psychological syndromes are not reliably interconnected. The few exceptions tend to be quite general. For example, juvenile delinquents typically score higher on performance subtests requiring visual–manipulative skills than on verbal subtests utilizing language skills ($P > V$). Persons with serious depression show the opposite pattern ($V > P$) (Kaufman, 1990). However, these relationships are not sufficiently strong for diagnostic purposes.

TABLE 2
WAIS–R example: Determination of subtest strengths and weaknesses

Subtest	Age-Corrected Scaled Score	Score − Mean	Criterion $p < .01$	
Information	12	3.0	3.1	
Digit span	8	− 1.0	3.9	
Vocabulary	10	1.0	2.2	
Arithmetic	6	− 3.0	3.7	
Comprehension	13	4.0	3.8	S
Picture completion	5	− 4.0	4.0	W
Picture arrangement	13	4.0	4.4	
Block design	12	3.0	3.2	
Object assembly	13	4.0	4.8	
Digit symbol	7	− 2.0	4.0	
Overall mean	9.0			

NOTE: S = strength, W = weakness

One possible exception does exist. Using the Wechsler family of intelligence tests with children and adults, a consensual body of research has identified a subtest profile that is frequently associated with reading and learning disabilities. The profile reflects a pattern of low scores on four subtests, arithmetic, coding, information, and digit span, and is thus called the ACID profile. (Incidentally, "coding" is called "digit symbol" on the WAIS–R.) The test results shown in Figure 1 depict an ACID profile. Based on dozens of research studies, it would be reasonable to suspect from this ACID profile that the 10-year-old student was distractible and reading-disabled (Gregory, 1992; Kaufman, 1979). Of course, further testing would be needed to confirm these hypotheses.

ADDITIONAL APPROACHES

In grouping similar subtests for purposes of profile interpretation, D. Wechsler opted for the simplicity of a two-pronged approach: verbal intelligence versus performance intelligence. For the various Wechsler instruments, five or six subtests are included in each category. Table 3a lists the verbal and performance subtests for the WAIS–R. A prominent feature of the Wechsler family of tests is the comparison of verbal IQ and performance IQ. Although verbal–performance IQ discrepancies are too often overinterpreted, there is no denying that a large spread in either direction (say, 25 IQ points or more) signals a diversity of possible interpretations, as mentioned above (Gregory, 1987; Kaufman, 1990).

In addition to the verbal–performance dichotomy, many other clinically useful ways of shuffling and recombining Wechsler subtests have been proposed. These methods are derived from non-Wechslerian models of intelligence. For example, based on statistical analyses of more than 100 different samples of subjects, J. L. Horn (1985) concluded that the subtests of the WAIS capture not two but four different conceptions of intelligence: crystallized (education-related abilities), fluid (novel problem solving), retrieval (memory-related capacities), and speed (motor speed). The subtests that load most strongly on these four cognitive capacities are listed in Table 3b.

In using this model for profile interpretation of the WAIS or WAIS–R, the clinician can compute the average age-corrected subtest score for each of the four categories. Relative peaks or valleys in one or more categories serve to demarcate areas of cognitive strength or weakness, respectively. Of course, the clinician would have to be well versed in the Horn-Cattell model of intelligence to interpret the practical meaning of strength or weakness (see FLUID AND CRYSTALLIZED INTELLIGENCE, THEORY OF).

Numerous ways of grouping Wechsler subtests have been proposed, but space limitations prohibit a detailed discussion of these alternative strategies for shuffling subtests. Table 3c–e summarizes additional illustrative approaches for the WAIS–R and gives a key reference for each. A. S. Kaufman (1990) provides a detailed treatment of this topic.

SUBTEST SCATTER

A test profile is said to demonstrate "subtest scatter" if the subtest scores are more spread out or dispersed than is the case for normal subjects (Gregory, 1987). Subtest scatter is easy to recognize in extreme cases, as when the test profile is full of extreme peaks and valleys. Nonetheless, scatter is a relative concept, not an absolute one.

Subtest scatter is important because of its increased frequency of occurrence in a wide variety of brain-impairing conditions. Put simply, the presence of subtest scatter raises a suspicion that the examinee may have a learning disability, neurological condition, or psychiatric disorder (Kaufman, 1990). Of course, scatter should not be interpreted in isolation. Rather, it should be interpreted in light of other information, such as work history, academic adjustment, and previous test scores (Matarazzo et al., 1988).

Psychologists have proposed numerous indices of scatter, including the range, the difference between the single highest and single lowest subtest scaled scores; the standard deviation, a statistical index of dispersion based on all scaled scores; significant deviations, the number of subtests whose scaled scores deviate, with statistical significance, from the subject's mean scaled score; and, the range–mean ratio, which is the range divided by the mean of the subject's subtest scores. Kaufman (1990) provided a detailed discussion of these approaches.

Subtest scatter has proved to be an elusive and limited concept, for several reasons. One problem is that test users consistently underestimate the degree of scatter that is normal. For example, the mean difference between the highest and the lowest subtest scaled scores for individual subjects in the WAIS–R standardization sample is almost 7 points. Subtest score differ-

TABLE 3

Summary of alternative approaches to combining WAIS–R subtests

a. Wechsler's Model (Wechsler, 1955, 1981)

Verbal IQ	Performance IQ
Information	Picture completion
Digit span	Picture arrangement
Vocabulary	Block design
Arithmetic	Object assembly
Comprehension	Digit symbol
Similarities	

b. Horn and McArdle Model (McArdle & Horn, 1983)

Fluid	Crystallized	Retrieval	Speed
Similarities	Information	Information	Digit symbol
Digit span	Comprehension	Arithmetic	
Picture completion	Similarities	Digit span	
Block design	Vocabulary		
Picture arrangement			
Object assembly			

c. Factor-Analytic (Three Factor) Model (Kaufman, 1990)

Verbal Comprehension	Perceptual Organization	Freedom from Distractibility
Information	Picture completion	Arithmetic
Vocabulary	Block design	Digit span
Comprehension	Object assembly	
Similarities		

d. Bannatyne Model for WAIS–R Subtests (Bannatyne, 1968)

Verbal Conceptualization Ability	Spatial Ability	Sequential Ability	Acquired Knowledge
Vocabulary	Picture completion	Arithmetic	Information
Comprehension	Block design	Digit span	Vocabulary
Similarities	Object assembly	Digit symbol	Arithmetic

e. Pair-wise Model for Grouping WAIS–R Subtests (Dean, 1983)

Abstract Thought	Remote Memory	Visual Memory	Auditory Memory	Social Comprehension	Visual–Motor Speed
Similarities	Information	Picture completion	Digit span	Comprehension	Object assembly
Block design	Picture completion	Digit symbol	Arithmetic	Picture arrangement	Digit symbol

ences of 8, 9, or even 10 points are not at all unusual (Matarazzo & Prifitera, 1989). A second problem is that the distribution of scatter indices for abnormal groups (e.g., learning disabled, neurologically impaired) overlaps substantially with the distributions for normal subjects. As a consequence, the prediction of normal versus impaired functioning from subtest scatter will be erroneous in a high proportion of cases. Subtest scatter has proved to be of limited diagnostic significance.

ADVANCED APPROACHES TO INTERPRETATION

In addition to scrutinizing test results for peaks, valleys, configurations, and subtest scatter, one can use complex rules to identify characteristic profiles. A case in point is the Fuld profile for Alzheimer's disease (Fuld, 1983, 1984). Alzheimer's disease is a degenerative disease of the brain that mainly affects older persons. The earliest symptoms are subtle and include memory loss. Invariably, Alzheimer's disease proceeds to a serious and generalized debilitation known as senile dementia. In the early stages diagnosis is difficult, and referral for psychological testing is not unusual.

Using age-corrected scores, the Fuld profile is defined by the conditional relationship between seven WAIS or WAIS–R subtests. First, four intermediate scores are derived from the seven subtests as follows:

$A = $ (Information + Vocabulary)/2
$B = $ (Similarities + Digit Span)/2
$C = $ (Digit Symbol + Block Design)/2
$D = $ Object Assembly

If $A > B > C < D$ and $A > D$, then the profile fits the Fuld pattern. The Fuld profile is considered a conditional marker of Alzheimer's disease. The profile is rare among normal elderly but is found in about 38 percent of elderly persons with confirmed Alzheimer's disease (Kaufman, 1990).

LIMITATIONS OF PROFILE INTERPRETATION

Not all psychologists and educators advocate profile interpretation. Some reviewers argue that profile analysis is not justified by the evidence, whereas others note that it is not suited to every test that yields subscores. Both points are briefly reviewed here.

Skeptics assert that, from a practical standpoint, intelligence is not many things but one thing. If this is so, then the only function of the test profile is to help measure the global construct of intelligence. This argument against profile interpretation harks back to Charles SPEARMAN's (1904) view that a general factor of intelligence, g, is a pervasive and dominant component of all intelligence tests. Some reviewers conclude that the g-factor (assuredly captured by the overall score) better predicts real-world outcomes, such as academic achievement, occupational attainment, and environmental adaptation, than do the specific intellectual abilities (perchance captured by the subtest scores). P. A. McDermott, J. W. Fantuzzo, and J. J. Glutting (1990, p. 229) put it this way:

> Based on our current knowledge about the realm of human intelligence, there is little to support the belief that many intelligence constructs are better than one. Until preponderant and convincing evidence shows otherwise, we are compelled to advise that psychologists just say "no" to subtest analysis.

N. Brody (1985) concluded that proposals to replace g with a more differentiated concept of intelligence have failed the crucial test of predictive validity, that is, predictions of performance based on subtest scores do not in general exceed the predictive accuracy obtained from a single global score. In a cluster analysis of the WAIS–R, Silverstein (1985) reached a similar conclusion, namely, that for any practical purpose the WAIS–R measures nothing but g. This would imply that test interpretation should be limited to the full-scale IQ.

The debate about general intelligence versus specific abilities is not likely to be resolved soon. In response to concerns about profile interpretation, R. Zachary (1990) advocates a middle position, whereby practitioners are advised to place the greatest emphasis on the overall score but encouraged to glean the subtest scores for clinical hypotheses that can be checked against other sources of information. Certainly, it is hard to ignore the negative evidence; profile interpretation should be undertaken with caution and conservatism.

Finally, it should be mentioned that not all intelligence tests are suited to profile interpretation. This is especially true for tests derived from stage theories of intelligence. Consider the Ordinal Scales of Psychological Development produced by I. Č. Užgiris and J. McV. Hunt (1989). This instrument is based upon the developmental observations and theories of Jean PIAGET (1952, 1954). The six scales proposed by Užgiris and Hunt (1989) support the existence of a definite, sequential order of intellectual development in early childhood, whereby the achievements of a higher level are intrinsically derived from those at the preceding level. The purpose of this instrument is to bracket a general stage of development in infancy, not to assess areas of relative cognitive strength or weakness. For any test based on stage theories of intelligence, intraindividual comparisons across the subscales are simply irrelevant.

(*See also:* WAIS–R SUBTESTS.)

BIBLIOGRAPHY

BANNATYNE, A. (1968). Diagnosing learning disabilities and writing remedial prescriptions. *Journal of Learning Disabilities, 1,* 242–249.

BRODY, N. (1985). The validity of tests of intelligence. In B. B. Wolman (Ed.), *Handbook of intelligence: Theories, measurements, and applications* (pp. 353–390). New York: Wiley.

CATTELL, R. B. (1963). Theory of fluid and crystallized intelligence: A critical experiment. *Journal of Educational Psychology, 54,* 1–22.

DEAN, R. S. (1983). *Manual: Report of individual evaluation for use with WAIS/WAIS–R.* Orlando, FL: Psychological Assessment Resources.

FULD, P. A. (1983). Psychometric differentiation of the dementias: An overview. In B. Reisberg (Ed.), *Alzheimer's disease: The standard reference* (pp. 201–210). New York: Free Press.

FULD, P. A. (1984). Test profile of cholinergic dysfunction and of Alzheimer's type dementia. *Journal of Clinical Neuropsychology, 6,* 380–392.

GREGORY, R. J. (1987). *Adult intellectual assessment.* Boston: Allyn & Bacon.

GREGORY, R. J. (1992). *Psychological testing: History, principles, and applications.* Boston: Allyn & Bacon.

HORN, J. L. (1985). Remodeling old models of intelligence. In B. B. Wolman (Ed.), *Handbook of intelligence: Theories, measurements, and applications* (pp. 267–300). New York: Wiley.

KAUFMAN, A. S. (1979). *Intelligent testing with the WISC–R.* New York: Wiley.

KAUFMAN, A. S. (1990). *Assessing adolescent and adult intelligence.* Boston: Allyn & Bacon.

KAUFMAN, A. S., & KAUFMAN, N. L. (1983). K-ABC interpretive manual. Circle Pines, MN: American Guidance Service.

MATARAZZO, J. D., DANIEL, M. H., PRIFITERA, A., & HERMAN, D. O. (1988). Inter-subtest scatter in the WAIS–R standardization sample. *Journal of Clinical Psychology, 44*(6), 940–950.

MATARAZZO, J. D., & PRIFITERA, A. (1989). Subtest scatter and premorbid intelligence: Lessons from the WAIS–R standardization sample. *Psychological Assessment: A Journal of Consulting and Clinical Psychology, 1*(3), 186–191.

McARDLE, J. J., & HORN, J. L. (1983). *Validation by systems modeling of WAIS abilities.* Washington, DC: National Institute of Aging.

McDERMOTT, P. A., FANTUZZO, J. W., & GLUTTING, J. J. (1990). Just say no to subtest analysis: A critique on Wechsler theory and practice. *Journal of Psychoeducational Assessment, 8*(3), 290–302.

PIAGET, J. (1952). *The origins of intelligence in children* (M. Cook, Trans.). New York: Basic Books. (Original work published 1936.)

PIAGET, J. (1954). *The construction of reality in the child* (M. Cook, Trans.). New York: Basic Books. (Original work published 1937.)

SILVERSTEIN, A. B. (1982). Pattern analysis as simultaneous statistical inference. *Journal of Consulting and Clinical Psychology, 50*(2), 234–240.

SILVERSTEIN, A. B. (1985). Cluster analysis of the Wechsler Adult Intelligence Scale–Revised. *Journal of Clinical Psychology, 41*(1), 98–99.

SILVERSTEIN, A. B. (1991). Reliability of score differences on Wechsler's intelligence scales. *Journal of Clinical Psychology, 47*(2), 264–265.

SPEARMAN, C. E. (1904). "General intelligence," objectively determined and measured. *American Journal of Psychology, 15,* 201–293.

UŽGIRIS, I. Č., & HUNT, J. McV. (1989). *Assessment in infancy: Ordinal scales of psychological development.* Urbana: University of Illinois Press.

WECHSLER, D. (1955). *Manual for the Wechsler Adult Intelligence Scale (WAIS).* New York: The Psychological Corporation.

WECHSLER, D. (1981). *Manual for the Wechsler Adult Intelligence Scale–Revised (WAIS–R).* San Antonio, TX: The Psychological Corporation.

ZACHARY, R. A. (1990). Wechsler's intelligence scales: Theoretical and practical considerations. *Journal of Psychoeducational Assessment, 8,* 276–289.

ROBERT J. GREGORY

PROJECT INTELLIGENCE   Project Intelligence was a collaborative effort among scientists, educators, and administrators at Harvard University, at Bolt Beranek and Newman; Inc.—a research and development firm in Cambridge, Massachusetts—and at the Venezuelan Ministry of Education. The project was undertaken at the initiative of the Venezuelan Ministry for the Development of Human Intelligence, whence it got its name, and was funded by Petróleos de Venezuela. It was conducted over a period of approximately four years, beginning in December 1979. Descriptions of the project or aspects of it may be found in several publications, including Nickerson, Perkins, and Smith (1985), Chance (1986), and Nickerson (1986). The following account draws mainly from Herrnstein, Nickerson, Sánchez, and Swets (1986).

OBJECTIVES AND PRELIMINARIES

The project sought to develop and evaluate materials and methods for teaching cognitive skills in seventh-grade classrooms in Venezuela. The first several months of the project were devoted to an informal study of the Venezuelan public school system and included many visits to classrooms in session; talks with students, teachers and educational administrators; and perusal of curriculum materials.

A result of this study was the decision to attempt to develop an experimental one-year course, appropriate for seventh-grade students, focused on the teaching of thinking skills, and to test it under reasonably controlled conditions. The intent was to design a course that would engage students in discussion and thought-provoking classroom activities so as to counterbalance what, in many classrooms, appeared to be an overdependence on rote learning.

THE COURSE AND ITS DEVELOPMENT

The course that was developed was structured around a few major themes emphasizing generic capabilities such as observation and classification, critical and careful use of language, deductive and inductive reasoning, problem solving, inventive thinking, and decision making. Each major theme was the focus for a series of from two to five lesson units, each of which was composed of several lessons appropriate for 45-minute class sessions. The course, when completed, contained about 100 lessons.

The individual lessons were designed by members of the Harvard/Bolt Beranek and Newman team working in consultation with several experienced Venezuelan teachers who were to prepare a larger group of Venezuelan teachers to use the materials in a planned year-long evaluation. The evolution of the course was a dynamic process in which materials were discussed by the entire team and tested informally in classroom settings throughout much of the developmental period. Many of the lessons developed during the first year of the project were tested informally in Venezuelan classrooms during the second year; those lessons were modified on the basis of the testing activities, and what was learned affected the ongoing design of additional materials as well.

Although the lessons varied in focus and style, the description of each one adhered to a prescribed format that the team had decided to adopt. This ensured that every description included a rationale for the lesson, a statement of its objective(s), a specification of the materials required, and a "script" illustrating the kinds of activities and dialogues one might expect to occur. Care was taken to emphasize that the scripts were not intended to be followed literally in class, but were included for illustrative purposes only. The reason for including the scripts was to stress continually the importance of student participation in classroom activities and to encourage the use of dialogue.

A teachers' manual containing the full complement of lessons, in several volumes, was the major tangible product that resulted from the project. Following completion of the project, most of this manual was published, with some revisions, in English, under the title *Odyssey: A Curriculum for Thinking,* by Mastery Education Corporation, Watertown, Massachusetts, and made available for use in U.S. classrooms (Adams, 1986).

PREPARATION FOR FORMAL EVALUATION

Concurrently with the development of lesson material, a plan was made for conducting a formal evaluation of the course, and test materials were prepared for that purpose. The formal evaluation was conducted during the project's third year. The evaluation plan included the use of matched experimental and control groups in several public schools in Venezuela, so preparation involved not only selection of appropriate test instruments, but doing the preliminary testing necessary to identify matched groups and establish measures that could be used as performance baselines.

Several standardized tests of mental abilities, selected from a larger number considered, were translated into Spanish, when necessary, and adapted for the Venezuelan context. In addition, about 500 special test items were constructed to assess competence with respect to the specific skills the course was intended to enhance. These test materials were also tried out on an informal basis with small groups of students before they were used in the formal evaluation of the experimental course.

The selection of tests was dictated in part by practical considerations; it was necessary, for example, that the tests used be relatively easy to administer and that the process of scoring be straightforward and unambiguous. The battery chosen was composed of the Otis-Lennon School Ability Test (Otis & Lennon, 1977), the Cattell Culture-Fair Intelligence Test (Cattell & Cattell, 1961), a group of general abilities tests (Manuel, 1962), and the specially designed items, which are referred to as target abilities tests. The total

number of items in the four components of the battery was approximately 700. Tests were always administered by Venezuelan teachers or members of the professional staff of the Ministry of Education.

COURSE IMPLEMENTATION

Twenty-four seventh-grade classes, four from each of six schools in Barquisimeto, a city of approximately 400,000 in the interior of Venezuela, participated in the course evaluation. The student bodies of these schools were primarily children from families of low socioeconomic status and limited parental education. Twelve of the classes, four from each of three of the participating schools, were designated experimental classes, and twelve others, four from each of the remaining schools, were designated controls. Each class had approximately thirty to forty students. Control classes were matched, insofar as was possible, with experimental classes.

Fifty-six of the 100 lessons that had been prepared were taught in the experimental classes (463 students) during the academic year that began partway through the second year of the project. The full complement of 100 lessons proved to be more than could be taught during a single year, given the constraints under which the course was implemented. Generally, the experimental classes met for a 45-minute session four days a week; successive lessons were taught on the first three days, and the fourth day was devoted to review or completion of partially completed lessons.

The course was taught by regular Venezuelan middle-school teachers who had volunteered to participate in the project. The teaching was monitored by the Venezuelan members of the project team, all of whom were teachers themselves. Individual lessons were reviewed and discussed by teachers as a group just prior to their use in class; review sessions were also held at the end of schooldays on which course lessons were taught.

TESTING AND RESULTS

Testing, of both experimental and control students, was done before the course began, after it was over, and several times while it was ongoing. Details of test administration and test results may be found in Herrnstein, Nickerson, Sánchez, and Swets (1986). Both experimental and control groups improved their scores on both the standard general abilities tests and the target abilities tests, as indicated by posttest–pretest differences. Course effectiveness was judged by comparing the magnitudes of the gains realized by the two groups.

Gains on both types of test were significantly greater for the experimental students than for the controls. The magnitude of the differences, expressed in units of standard deviation of control-group gain scores (the measure d often used in the evaluation literature [Light, 1983]), were .11, .35, and .43 for the Cattell, the GAT, and the Olsat, respectively. The same statistic applied to the results with the target abilities tests yielded differences ranging from .46 for problem solving to .77 for decision making. Assuming a normal distribution of such scores, ds of .11, .35, .43, .46, and .77 represent differences between a score at the 50th percentile and scores at the 54th, 64th, 67th, 68th, and 78th percentiles, respectively.

Another way of comparing the test results for the experimental and control groups is to express the gains realized by the former as a percentage of those realized by the latter (100% meaning that the gains of the two groups were equal). The gains realized by the experimental subjects were 121 percent, 146 percent, 168 percent, and 217 percent of those realized by the controls on the Cattell, the Olsat, the GAT, the target abilities battery, respectively. Further analyses showed the magnitude of the gains to have been relatively independent of the initial ability levels of the students as indicated by pretest scores.

In addition to the objective tests described above, several less formal tests were designed and administered on an ad hoc basis in the interest of learning more about effects the experience may have had on participating students' ability to undertake cognitively demanding tasks. These included tests composed of oral and written questions requiring open-ended (as opposed to multiple-choice) answers, a design problem intended to provide an opportunity for students to engage in inventive thinking, and a challenge to prepare and deliver an oral argument justifying the student's answer to an open-ended question. These informal tests were administered to subsets of the students in the experimental and control groups. Students in the experimental group outperformed those in the control group on all of these tests.

CONCLUSIONS

The course, as implemented on a one-time basis, was judged to have had a reliable positive effect of at least modest magnitude, insofar as the consequences of such an experiment could be revealed in objective tests of the type used for evaluation. It should be noted that the evaluation data were obtained during and shortly after completion of the project, so they provide evidence only of a short-term effect. Unfortunately, it was not feasible to obtain data in subsequent years that would have given an indication of whether the gains realized persisted in some measurable way.

Much of what is to be learned from an experiment such as Project Intelligence is not captured by the results of objective tests. Participation in this project left Nickerson (1986) with a number of impressions that are not reflected in the evaluative data that were collected. These include the following.

1. Teacher competence and motivation are major determinants of the degree of success of the utilization of a structured program to teach thinking in the classroom. This is not to deny the usefulness of well-designed material, but only to caution that the potential of any material is likely to be realized only in the hands of a competent and motivated teacher.

2. The supportiveness of the institutional context in which an innovative program is implemented can be an important factor in determining the program's effectiveness. Institutional context here connotes not only the teachers who are participating in the innovation, but those who are not, as well as school administrators and parents.

3. It is important that students not only acquire certain thinking abilities (e.g., the ability to evaluate fairly a formal or informal argument), but that they gain an understanding of those abilities at a conceptual level and of their applicability in different contexts; this addresses the issue of transfer, or how to ensure that what is learned in one context will be used in other contexts for which it is appropriate.

4. Also in the interest of ensuring that what is

learned in a classroom about creative thinking is applied effectively beyond the context in which it is learned, direct and strong connections should be built between the innovation and the regular curriculum. Teachers of traditional courses should be fully informed about the nature and goals of the innovation, and the relevance of the thinking-enhancement activities to those courses should be made clear to the participating students. Ideally, one wants the enhancement of thinking to be an objective of every aspect of a curriculum; a separate course focused on thinking can be seen as a step in that direction.

BIBLIOGRAPHY

ADAMS, M. J. (COORDINATOR). (1986). *Odyssey: A curriculum for thinking.* Watertown, MA: Mastery Education Corporation.

CATTELL, R. B., & CATTELL, A. K. S. (1961). *Culture-fair intelligence test* (Scale 2, Forms A & B). Champaign, IL: Institute for Personality and Ability Testing.

CHANCE, P. (1986). *Thinking in the classroom.* New York: Teachers College Press.

HERRNSTEIN, R. J., NICKERSON, R. S., DE SÁNCHEZ, M., & SWETS, J. A. (1986). Teaching thinking skills. *American Psychologist, 41,* 1279–1289.

LIGHT, R. J. (ED.). (1983). *Evaluation studies: Review annual* (Vol. 8). Beverly Hills, CA: Sage.

MANUEL, H. T. (1962). *Tests of general ability: Inter-American series* (Spanish, Level 4, Forms A & B). San Antonio, TX: Guidance Testing Associates.

NICKERSON, R. S. (1986). Project Intelligence: An account and some reflections. In M. Schwebel & C. A. Maher (Eds.), *Facilitating cognitive development: International perspectives, programs, and practices* (pp. 83–102). New York: Haworth Press.

NICKERSON, R. S., PERKINS, D. N., & SMITH, E. E. (1985). *The teaching of thinking.* Hillsdale, NJ: Erlbaum.

OTIS, A. S., & LENNON, R. T. (1977). *Otis-Lennon school ability test* (Intermediate Level 1, Form R). New York: Harcourt Brace Jovanovich.

RAYMOND S. NICKERSON

PSYCHIATRIC DISORDERS

PSYCHIATRIC DISORDERS Disorders of higher cognitive function are commonly found in patients with severe psychiatric disorders. In some psychiatric disorders, such as schizophrenia, there is often a wide range of cognitive deficits, affecting abstract reasoning, visuospatial skills, memory and attention, language, and perceptual-motor abilities. In other disorders, the cognitive deficits may be restricted to one or more areas (e.g., memory loss and psychomotor slowing in patients with depression). The cause of these deficits has been a matter of considerable debate over the past few decades. Some of the factors that have influenced the debate have been the prevailing theories about the nature and cause of the disorders themselves, and developments in technology and measurement, which have permitted more sophisticated assessments of various patient populations. It has been particularly difficult to determine the extent to which the cognitive deficits are a primary characteristic of the psychiatric disorders or whether they occur indirectly and are related to the patient's inability to attend to or perform the requirements of psychological tests. Recent studies of the relationship between brain metabolism and psychological test performance have begun to clarify the cause of some types of cognitive disturbances in psychiatric disorders. The subsequent sections of this article will discuss the nature of cognitive deficits in the most common and severe psychiatric disorders, and it will review some of the factors that appear to be associated with the presence of those deficits.

SCHIZOPHRENIA

Schizophrenia is a disorder that is characterized by a wide variety of symptoms, which typically include bizarre delusions, hallucinations, decline in cognitive function, inappropriate emotion or behavior, and incoherence. The diagnosis of schizophrenia requires exclusion of other disorders that may have similar symptoms, and there have been several attempts to identify subgroups of patients with common symptom patterns. The onset of schizophrenia is between the ages of 15 and 35 in approximately two-thirds of patients, and it has been estimated that the number of patients with schizophrenia in the United States is between 1.2 and 6 million people. The onset of the characteristic symptoms is often preceded by a period of declining cognitive abilities and social withdrawal. The importance of cognitive decline in this disease is indicated by the fact that the first name given to the condition was *dementia praecox* (premature dementia). Although progressive cognitive decline does not typically occur (and a substantial number of patients improve), decline in higher mental function is a primary feature of schizophrenia.

Since the recognition of schizophrenia as a unique disorder at the end of the nineteenth century, numerous theories have been proposed to explain the disease. These theories have emphasized a broad range of biological and psychological causes including genetics, poor parenting, birth injury, and neurological disease. Because schizophrenia encompasses a variety of symptoms, it is quite possible that this is not a single disease, and, therefore, probably there is no single theory that can account for the diversity of symptoms and course of illness that is seen in schizophrenia. Furthermore, it is possible that the variability in patients with schizophrenia is related to the interaction of several biological, psychological, and sociological factors.

In spite of the complex interactions that are potentially associated with the presence of cognitive deficit in schizophrenia, some progress has been made in identifying those factors that best predict cognitive decline. In general, this progress has been achieved by defining subgroups of patients with similar clinical symptoms. Current diagnostic classifications tend to group patients on the basis of the most prominent clinical symptoms. Most studies of cognitive function have tended to compare patients with and without paranoid symptoms (i.e., pathological suspiciousness), the latter typically a combination of various subtypes: In most cases it has been shown that patients with paranoid symptoms perform better in most areas of cognitive function, and in some cases cannot be distinguished from normal comparison groups. Most studies that have examined the relationship between severity of symptoms and cognitive performance have concluded that the nature, rather than the severity of symptoms, is most predictive of cognitive deficit. More recent studies have defined the subgroups on a classification of symptoms that is broader than the paranoid/nonparanoid distinction.

The most useful of these approaches classifies patients on the basis of "positive" and "negative" symptoms. Positive symptoms are characterized by the presence of a behavior such as hallucinations (e.g., seeing, hearing, or smelling things not there) or delusions (bizarre ideas or other false beliefs), while negative symptoms are characterized by loss or deficit in some area of function such as diminished drive, flattening of emotional expression or social withdrawal. Patients with predominantly negative symptoms are more likely to have a variety of cognitive deficits on formal assessment, and are more likely to have abnormalities demonstrated on brain imaging techniques such as computed axial tomography (CAT scan) or magnetic resonance imaging (MRI). This form of schizophrenia appears to be caused by some type of early damage to parts of the brain that are involved in emotions. Patients with predominantly positive symptoms are more likely to have normal cognitive function, and less likely to have abnormalities on brain imaging studies. The cause of this (positive) form of schizophrenia appears to be an inherited abnormality which affects one of the primary chemical messenger systems in the brain (dopamine).

The nature of cognitive deficit in schizophrenia has been particularly interesting to researchers because of the potential for understanding the parts of the brain that are affected. Because of the behavioral characteristics that schizophrenic patients demonstrate, the most commonly studied aspects of cognitive function include memory, language, planning, and problem solving. The brain regions that are most commonly implicated in schizophrenia include the frontal and temporal lobes because of their association with the cognitive functions of memory, language, planning, and problem solving. A variety of psychological and neuropsychological tests or test batteries have been used to examine cognitive function in schizophrenia. These include the Wechsler Adult Intelligence Scale (WAIS), Halstead Reitan Test Battery (HRB), Luria Nebraska Battery (LNB), and other collections of individual tests that typically have been developed to examine cognitive function in patients with neurological disease. Because of the increased interest in schizophrenia as a brain disease (Nasrallah & Weinberger, 1986) some studies have examined tests of cognitive function as they relate to measures of brain structure; for example, atrophy (or wasting of the brain) or ventricular dilatation (an increase in the width of the communicating cavities in the brain) or metabolism. Although there is agreement that disruption of cognitive function is common in some forms of schizophrenia, there is no evidence that the severity of symptoms is related to the severity of cognitive deficit. Several different theories about the nature and cause of the cognitive deficit have been proposed, based in part on the specific tests that have been used to examine patients. Examinations using large batteries of tests have typically indicated a generalized pattern of deficit that is most prominent on tests that measure problem solving, memory, attention, information processing, and language skills. The finding of generalized cognitive deficits supports studies that used computed tomography or magnetic resonance imaging. Those studies have shown an increase in generalized brain atrophy in schizophrenic patients. In addition, the presence of specific symptoms has generated several theories about the fundamental neuropathological basis of schizophrenia. These theories have focused on a particular brain region or system, and they have examined performance on specific cognitive tests as measures of those systems.

These more narrowly defined theories suggest that the cognitive dysfunction in schizophrenia is related to dysfunction in a particular region or side of the brain. One of the most common theories emphasizes a disturbance of function in the frontal lobe of the brain, whereas another common theory suggests that schizophrenia is related to a dysfunction of the brain's left cerebral hemisphere. Evidence in support of the frontal lobe hypothesis comes from studies that have used neuropsychological tests (such as the Wisconsin Card Sorting Test), which have been shown to be relatively sensitive to dysfunction in the frontal lobes. This theory is further supported by studies of cerebral metabolism, which have demonstrated a lack of frontal lobe activity in patients with schizophrenia while performing this test. Other studies of cerebral metabolism found that the pattern of diminished frontal-lobe activity was related to increased activity in regions in the back of the brain. This evidence of a disruption in frontal-lobe function in schizophrenia is of interest because it may provide a biological explanation for the gross disorganization of higher cognitive functions that are characteristic of many patients. Although there is considerable evidence of abnormal frontal-lobe function in schizophrenia, there is no evidence that this is

the only area of deficit. It is typically the case that schizophrenic patients differ from normal subjects on a broad range of cognitive tasks. Therefore, the deficits on tests of reasoning and other measures of frontal-lobe function should be evaluated in relationship to other cognitive deficits.

Another popular theory of cognitive dysfunction in schizophrenia focuses on the left cerebral hemisphere. In most people (virtually all right-handed people, and probably most left-handed people) the left side of the brain is *specialized* for verbal functions. The interest in abnormal verbal (and left-hemisphere) functions in schizophrenia comes from symptoms exhibited by schizophrenic patients, as well as patterns of performance on tests of a wide range of verbal skills. The peculiar speech and language of schizophrenic patients is, in many respects, similar to that of patients with damage to the brain's left hemisphere from specific neurological diseases such as strokes. In addition, auditory hallucination (usually hearing voices) is one of the most common symptoms in schizophrenia. These symptoms are often accompanied by poor performance on formal measures of language, memory, and standard intelligence measures such as the Wechsler Intelligence Scales. However, as with the previously discussed theory of frontal-lobe dysfunction, the evidence for left-hemisphere disturbance must be viewed in the context of performance on other tasks that are believed to reflect the function of other brain regions. For example, some studies have shown that schizophrenic patients tend to perform as poorly on cognitive tasks (such as eye-hand and other spatial skills) that are more typically associated with functions of the right cerebral hemisphere. Therefore, it is apparent that there is a general pattern of cognitive deficit associated with schizophrenia. It is possible that certain subgroups of patients may show more generalized deficits, but the essential characteristics of those subgroups are currently not known.

Tests of cognitive function have been used for a long time in the evaluation of patients with schizophrenia as well as other psychiatric disorders (Goldstein, 1984, 1986; Steinhauer, Gruzelier, and Zubin, 1991). Although schizophrenic patients perform poorly on a wide range of intellectual functions, there is no single deficit or pattern of abnormalities that is specific to this disorder. Documentation of cognitive deficits is useful additional information, but it cannot be used to make a diagnosis of schizophrenia. Historically, one of the most common uses of cognitive or intelligence tests has been in differentiating between a diagnosis of schizophrenia and organic neurologic disease, because those two disorders have similar symptoms. Neuropsychological tests, which were able to differentiate neurological patients from healthy normals, were, in several studies, unable to differentiate between schizophrenic patients and neurological patients. These studies were initially viewed as evidence that neuropsychological measures were unable to discriminate between biologically based causes and nonbiological causes of disorders. However, recent studies show that a large proportion of chronic schizophrenic patients have abnormalities on structural brain imaging procedures such as MRI scans. It now appears that neuropsychological tests do not reliably discriminate between schizophrenic and neurological patients because, to a large extent, schizophrenic patients have a neurological disorder. Although neuropsychological and intellectual tests are not useful for the diagnosis of schizophrenia, these tests are helpful in understanding the abnormalities in mental function. In spite of the potential value of these tests, it is important to recognize that there are several factors that may influence performance on cognitive ability tests. If the purpose of assessment is to identify the nature and severity of cognitive deficit that is a component of schizophrenia, these factors may jeopardize the validity of these tests in these patients. In general, the goals of psychological assessment are to obtain reliable estimates of cognitive or intellectual function and to minimize the effects of error factors such as fatigue, motivation, or other variables that may interfere with accurate assessment.

The problems in establishing an effective set of requirements for conducting the examination is one of the most important difficulties in the use of cognitive or intelligence tests with schizophrenic patients. Usually these patients are difficult to motivate, may have problems understanding or following test instructions, and may have limited attention span or frustration tolerance. As a result, it is often unclear whether the results of an assessment represent the optimal or even the typical performance of a patient. In some patients it is necessary to perform the assessment over several days because of the patient's inability to pay attention. Although this may yield a more complete assessment, this approach raises problems (particularly for assessments that employ an extensive battery of tests) because of the variability within the individual from day to day. Most such clinical examinations are structured to enhance motivation and thereby show an estimate of optimal level of performance. There is some evidence, however, that schizophrenics may not respond the same as other patients to a positive motivational structure. Therefore, assessments of schizophrenic patients may require a fundamentally different approach.

The effects of psychotropic medications and other drugs with known powerful effects on the brain, or other somatic treatments present numerous problems for the use of cognitive or intelligence tests in schizophrenia. Most patients are maintained on a variety of medications, which may interfere with cognitive function because of their sedating effects. Therefore, some of the problems with attention and mental slowing observed in schizophrenia may be a result of the medications used to treat the disorder. Furthermore, some medications that are used to control the side effects of antipsychotic medications also have potential adverse effects on cognitive function. In fact, some studies of cognitive function in schizophrenia have shown that the differences between schizophrenic patients and normal control groups are greatly diminished when the effects of medication are taken into consideration. In addition to the relatively short term effects of antipsychotic medications, some patients who have received long-term treatment with these medications develop a movement disorder called tardive dyskinesia (involuntary movements, such as hand tremors), which is caused by the chronic alteration of the neurotransmitter systems in the brain. This demonstrates the potent effects of these medications, and indicates why potential medication effects should be considered in the assessment of schizophrenic patients. On the other hand, however, these medications do provide some symptomatic improvement in many patients, and it is possible that this beneficial effect permits patients to perform at a level that more closely approximates their potential level of function. The potential adverse effects of medications are not unique to schizophrenia or to psychiatric disorders in general, but they represent an important issue that should be considered in the cognitive/intellectual assessment of schizophrenic patients.

AFFECTIVE DISORDERS

This group of disorders is characterized by changes in mood and affect (emotional expression), and vary according to the nature and severity of symptoms. Alterations in mood or affect are common in many systemic and neurologic diseases, and it has been estimated that 30 percent of patients with depression have some physical cause, which either partly or completely accounts for their symptoms (Cummings, 1985; Yudofsky & Hales, 1992). Depression is probably the most common psychiatric disorder associated with cognitive or intellectual dysfunction. Among the affective disorders, cognitive/intellectual deficits are most common and have been most carefully studied in patients with unipolar depression (recurrent episodes of severe depression), although there have been some studies of patients with bipolar affective disorder (patients with alternating episodes of depression and mania). In contrast to schizophrenia, the nature of cognitive deficits in patients with depression appears to be more circumscribed; however, to a large extent this is due to the lack of studies that have employed broad-based examinations. The majority of studies have tended to focus on memory, concentration, and psychomotor slowing because these symptoms are prominent in depressed patients. Although cognitive deficits appear to be restricted in most patients with depression, there are some patients with more pervasive deficits. The presence of severe generalized cognitive deficit in the presence of depression has at times been referred to as "pseudo-dementia," but this term has been replaced by "dementia syndrome of depression." The coexistence of depression and dementia represents a significant differential diagnostic question in which the progression of cognitive/intellectual decline is a central issue (see below).

Memory and concentration difficulties are extremely common in all depressed patients regardless of age, and other cognitive impairments are not uncommon. Nevertheless, there have been relatively few studies of memory in nongeriatric depressed patients, and even fewer that have carefully examined other aspects of higher mental function. Deficits in sustained concentration or attention appear to be greatest on those tasks that require "effort." Many depressed patients who respond to test questions with "I don't know" can, with further encouragement by the examiner, provide more appropriate responses. This is interpreted by some as indicating a motivational problem, although it could also be the result of an arousal deficit. Such a deficit would also be likely to interfere with initial stages of learning. Studies of memory processes, in fact, have demonstrated that depressed patients have impairments in initial acquisition, poor use of semantic encoding or processing strategies, and rapid memory decay. These memory deficits are most apparent when the task involves learning unstructured material (e.g., a list of randomly presented recognizable words or a list of made up nonsense words such as Luz, Zic, etc.). In addition, depressed patients appear to have difficulties in retrieving information from memory as indicated by their better performance on a test that requires them to recognize from a list words previously presented orally versus being asked to recall from memory the words on such an orally presented list. Although depressed patients have difficulty acquiring information, the material that is learned appears to be retained reasonably well. In general, the degree of depression is not related to the severity of memory deficit, although there is some relationship with severity of attention and concentration problems. No other aspect of cognitive function in depression has been studied to a comparable degree.

The observation that many depressed patients perform poorly on visuospatial tasks (such as the Performance IQ subtests of the WECHSLER INTELLIGENCE SCALES), as well as some other tasks, has led to the hypothesis that depression and other affective disorders are associated with a disturbance in the right cerebral hemisphere. Most of these studies used a mixed sample of affective disorder patients, and many failed to account for the potential effects of treatments used in depression such as electroconvulsive therapy. However, most comparisons of depressed patients and patients with documented right-hemisphere neurologic disease, using various neuropsychological tests, have shown a clear differentiation of these groups, which argues against the "right-hemisphere" hypothesis. It is possible that the apparent difficulties on visuospatial tasks are related to the fact that these tests tend to be *timed* and require active problem solving. The psychomotor slowing and arousal difficulties, common in depression, may, therefore, explain the visuospatial abnormalities.

As noted above, some patients with depression have severe and generalized cognitive deficits, which are consistent with a diagnosis of dementia. This tends to be more common in elderly depressed patients, and presents a critical differential diagnostic issue. There is a great similarity of symptoms in the dementia syndrome of depression which can occur at any age and other progressive dementing disorders that increase in frequency after the age of 65 (such as Alzheimer's disease). The dementia associated with depression may be partially treatable and is not progressive. Therefore, it is extremely important to differentiate these disorders. This discrimination is complicated by the fact that many patients with Alzheimer's disease are depressed. In addition, patients with the dementia syndrome of depression are often found to have cerebral atrophy on computed tomographic brain scans, although this is common in normal elderly individuals as well. Cognitive and intellectual measures can be extremely helpful in differentiating these disorders. In contrast to depressed patients, Alzheimer's disease patients have an extremely rapid rate of forgetting, do not perform as well on recognition memory tests, and do not improve with prompting or encouragement. In addition, serial examination and reexamination of the same patient will reveal a progressive decline in Alzheimer's disease patients, which is not evident in the dementia syndrome of depression. Depressed patients tend to remain stable, and some may improve.

The use of cognitive/intellectual measures in the examination of patients with depression is limited by the same issues that were reviewed earlier in regard to schizophrenia. Although few depressed patients exhibit hallucinations, many will have problems maintaining their concentration and effort, particularly for extended examinations. As mentioned previously, some patients will need specific encouragement in order to give the optimal response to test items. There is also a potential for medication or other treatments to influence performance on psychological tests. Many

of the medications used in the treatment of depression may result in confusion or sedation, and some medications have been shown to result in memory deficits.

OTHER PSYCHIATRIC DISORDERS

Cognitive or intellectual disorders may be observed in many psychiatric diseases, but with few exceptions have not been subjected to the same degree of examination as have schizophrenia and depression. Recently, however, there have been a number of studies of the cognitive and neurological correlates of obsessive compulsive disorder (OCD). This disorder is characterized by persistent thoughts (obsessions, a recurrent idea or thought such as the same tune recurring in your mind over and over) or compulsions (actions, such as washing your hands 50–100 times a day) that the individual is unable to control. Similar symptoms have been observed in patients following encephalitis, and the symptoms themselves are similar in some respects to the stereotyped and perseverative behavior that is observed in patients with lesions of the frontal lobe. Several studies have indicated that patients with OCD perform normally on many tasks, but they perform poorly on cognitive tasks that are relatively sensitive to the functions controlled by the brain's frontal lobes (e.g., Wisconsin Card Sorting Test). Further support for frontal lobe abnormality in OCD arises from studies of brain metabolism and electrophysiological activity. In contrast to the disorders reviewed previously, the cognitive deficit in these patients appears to be relatively limited.

BIBLIOGRAPHY

CUMMINGS, J. L. (1985). *Clinical neuropsychiatry.* Orlando, FL: Grune & Stratton.

GOLDSTEIN, G. (1984). Neuropsychological assessment of psychiatric patients. In G. Goldstein (Ed.), *Advances in clinical neuropsychology.* New York: Plenum Press.

GOLDSTEIN, G. (1986). Neuropsychology of schizophrenia. In I. Grant & K. Adams (Eds.), *Neuropsychological assessment of neuropsychiatric disorders.* New York: Oxford University Press.

NASRALLAH, H. A., & WEINBERGER, D. R. (1986). *The neurology of schizophrenia.* Amsterdam: Elsevier.

STEINHAUER, S. R., GRUZELIER, J. H., & ZUBIN, J. (1991). Neuropsychology, psychophysiology, and information processing. *Handbook of Schizophrenia* (Vol. 5). Amsterdam: Elsevier.

YUDOFSKY, S. C., & HALES, R. E. (1991). Textbook of neuropsychiatry (2nd ed.). Washington, DC: American Psychiatric Press.

ROBERT A. BORNSTEIN

PSYCHOMETRICS

Psychometrics is the study of the theory, development, and evaluation of measurement procedures in psychology. Measurement procedures may be designed for a variety of psychological characteristics, including cognitive processes and abilities, knowledge, personality features, attitudes, interests, values, and opinions. A central idea in psychometrics is that differences between people on these characteristics can be measured. Measurement is fundamental to all sciences, but measurement in psychology faces unique challenges. Most psychological characteristics cannot be directly measured, but must be inferred from observable behavior or self-report. It is not clear which behaviors should be observed, or which questions should be asked. Behaviors or self-reports are imperfect indicators. Psychometricians address these problems by integrating psychological theory with formal statistical models for measurement.

The most familiar "measuring instrument" used by psychometricians is the written test. It presents examinees with a series of items, each with a standard response format. Increasingly, test items are now administered via computer terminals. Computerized administration facilitates test scoring, and may allow the test content to be tailored to the individual examinee.

Other forms of measurement require the examinee to perform a task. The examinee's score is provided by trained observers. These performance-based tests can elicit behaviors that are not easily accessible to written tests, but the scoring of performance-based tests can be difficult.

HISTORICAL BACKGROUND

Most of the important early developments in psychometrics began in the late nineteenth and early twentieth centuries in England, France, and the United States. Francis GALTON, in England, pioneered the study of individual differences through measurement, developing useful statistical procedures for this purpose. The first modern intelligence test was created by French psychologist Alfred BINET and Théophile Simon. Their measurement approach influences the development of tests of general intelligence even today. Charles SPEARMAN, in England, contributed heavily to the development of formal measurement theory in psychometrics. He was also largely responsible for creating FACTOR ANALYSIS, an important tool for psychometric research. In the United States, E. L. THORNDIKE, James McKeen CATTELL, and L. L. THURSTONE were important early figures in psychometrics. Thurstone created methods for attitude measurement, developed basic theory in ability measurement, and shaped factor analysis into its modern form.

The pace of psychometric research accelerated during the two world wars as the need arose for efficient methods of personnel selection and classification in the military. Since 1945, developments in psychometrics have been influenced by three major trends. First, technological advances in computing have led to greater use of complex statistical models in test design and analysis. Second, the rise of cognitive science has shifted measurement practices in ability and achievement testing toward greater integration of cognitive theory and testing practice. Finally, the civil rights movement has enhanced concern for fairness in testing, and has led to changes in test development and evaluation (see LEGAL ISSUES IN INTELLIGENCE).

TEST DEVELOPMENT

Test development must begin with some understanding of the characteristic to be measured. For example, if someone's "ability" to solve algebra problems is to be measured, the test developer must know something about how people solve such problems, and what types of problems elicit this skill. One important question for psychometricians is the "dimensionality" of the ability: How many separate skills are drawn upon in solving problems that indicate the ability? This question is important because if many separate skills are required, a test of a single skill will not provide a clearly interpretable measure of the ability. Psychometricians assess dimensionality by combining knowledge of the ability gained through psychological research with statistical analyses of test data using techniques such as factor analysis.

Test content varies, depending on the purpose of the test, the intended examinee population, and the characteristic to be measured. Tests that are to be given to many examinees often require formats that are easily scored, such as multiple-choice items. Some characteristics are studied using performance-based response formats. Writing skills, for example, may be assessed by having the examinee write a timed essay on a prescribed topic. In achievement testing and in employment testing, test items are written according to a prepared outline of the domain of knowledge to be tested. In other areas, such as personality assessment, test item creation is guided by psychological theory but does not generally follow any detailed content outline.

Once a preliminary pool of test items is available, the items are given to a large sample of individuals to evaluate how the items perform in practice. The resulting data are used to select items that will produce a test with desired properties. This selection process is known as *item analysis.* Item analysis methods range in complexity from the use of simple descriptive statistics to computer-intensive mathematical modeling. If multiple forms of the test are needed, these forms must be checked for equivalence using the response data. *Test equating methods* are used to transform the scoring scales of different test forms to a common scoring metric.

TEST EVALUATION

Psychometricians evaluate tests on two general criteria: RELIABILITY and VALIDITY.

Reliability. A test is reliable if it gives similar results over repeated administrations to the same individuals. Tests must meet minimum standards for reliability, but the required minimum varies with the purpose of testing. Test reliability is indicated by the *reliability coefficient,* which ranges from 0 to 1 in value, with 1 representing perfect reliability.

Reliability assessment is difficult because most tests cannot be administered repeatedly to the same exam-

inees. For this reason, much of psychometric theory is devoted to the assessment of reliability. Different perspectives on reliability exist within psychometric theory. *Classical test theory* (Lord & Novick, 1968) represents the traditional perspective. This theory partitions observed measurements into "true" and "error" portions, defining reliability as the proportion of the variability in observed scores that is due to variability in true scores. *Generalizability theory* (Cronbach et al., 1972) broadens classical test theory by considering multiple sources of variability in measurement. The relative contributions of these sources are evaluated, replacing classical reliability with the notion of generalizability across sources. Item response theory (Lord, 1980), also called LATENT TRAIT THEORY, introduces the concept of the "information" about an examinee provided by the test. Information is defined within statistical models that link observed scores to examinee characteristics.

Validity. Broadly speaking, a test is valid if it truly supports the conclusions one wishes to draw from the test results. A given test may be valid for one purpose without being valid for others. An achievement test, for example, should support conclusions about the examinee's mastery of the domain of knowledge to be tested, yet it may not be valid for predicting the examinee's future performance in a different domain. Hence different forms of validity are distinguished corresponding to the different purposes for which tests are used. The validity of a test for a given purpose is established through empirical evidence. The nature of the appropriate evidence, and the standards for deciding when sufficient evidence has been presented, are debated topics within psychometrics.

One common purpose for testing is to identify the examinee's status on a psychological characteristic of interest. Any such test is said to be "construct valid" to the extent that the test actually measures the intended characteristic. Public controversies about testing often concern issues of *construct validity.* For example, questions about what tests of intelligence "really" measure are questions about the construct validity of these tests.

Evidence in support of construct validity must come from a variety of sources. Psychological theory about the characteristic to be measured should suggest testable predictions about how test scores are related to other variables. Confirmation of these predictions supports the construct validity of the test. Theory may also suggest plausible alternative interpretations for what is measured by the test. These alternative interpretations must be investigated and eliminated if construct validity is to be established. Methods for testing predictions range from correlational studies to laboratory experiments.

BIBLIOGRAPHY

AMERICAN PSYCHOLOGICAL ASSOCIATION (1985). *Standards for educational and psychological tests.* Washington, DC: Author.

ANASTASI, A. (1988). *Psychological testing* (6th ed.). New York: Macmillan.

BENNETT, R. E., & WARD, W. C. (EDS.). (1993). *Construction versus choice in cognitive measurement.* Hillsdale, NJ: Erlbaum.

BRENNAN, R. L. (1983). *Elements of generalizability theory.* Iowa City, IA: American College Testing Program.

CROCKER, L., & ALGINA, J. (1986). *Introduction to classical and modern test theory.* New York: Holt, Rinehart, & Winston.

CRONBACH, L. J. (1984). *Essentials of psychological testing.* New York: Harper & Row.

CRONBACH, L. J., GLESER, G. C., NANDA, H., & RAJARATNAM, N. (1972). *The dependability of behavioral measurements: Theory of generalizability of scores and profiles.* New York: Wiley.

EMBRETSON, S. E. (ED.). (1985). *Test design: Developments in psychology and psychometrics.* San Diego, CA: Academic Press.

FREDRIKSEN, N., MISLEVY, R. J., & BEJAR, I. (EDS.). (1993). *Test theory for a new generation of tests.* Hillsdale, NJ: Erlbaum.

GHISELLI, E. E., CAMPBELL, J. P., & ZEDECK, S. (1981). *Measurement theory for the behavioral sciences.* San Francisco: W. H. Freeman.

GORSUCH, R. L. (1983). *Factor analysis.* Hillsdale, NJ: Erlbaum.

HAMBLETON, R. K., & SWAMINATHAN, H. (1985). *Item response theory: Principles and applications.* Boston: Kluwer-Nijhoff.

HULIN, C. L., DRASGOW, F., & PARSONS, C. K. (1983). *Item response theory: Application to psychological measurement.* Homewood, IL: Dow Jones–Irwin.

LINN, R. L. (ED.). (1989). *Educational measurement* (3rd ed.). New York: Macmillan.

LORD, F. M. (1980). *Applications of item response theory to practical testing problems.* Hillsdale, NJ: Erlbaum.

LORD, F. M., & NOVICK, M. R. (1968). *Statistical theories of mental test scores.* Reading, MA: Addison-Wesley.

MULAIK, S. A. (1972). *The foundations of factor analysis.* New York: McGraw-Hill.

SHAVELSON, R. J., & WEBB, N. M. (1991). *Generalizability theory: A primer.* Newbury Park, CA: Sage.

WEISS, D. J. (ED.). (1983). *New horizons in testing: Latent trait test theory and computerized adaptive testing.* San Diego, CA: Academic Press.

ROGER E. MILLSAP

PSYCHOMETRIC THEORIES OF INTELLIGENCE

The word *psychometric* is formed from a combination of the words psychology and measurement and in its broadest sense refers to all attempts to measure intellectual abilities. This entry will be based on a narrower definition, namely, the study of individual differences in intellectual abilities.

The difference between narrow and extended meanings of the term psychometric can be illustrated by a brief discussion of Jean PIAGET's theory of intelligence. Piaget's theory is a stage theory of the development of intelligence (see PIAGETIAN THEORY OF DEVELOPMENT). He believed that intellectual development was characterized by an invariant sequence of qualitatively distinct ways of thinking about the world. All normal individuals were assumed to follow the same invariant sequence of developmental stages. He was not particularly interested in age differences in the attainment of different intellectual stages. A psychologist interested in individual differences could study variations in the age at which children attained different intellectual stages of development and use these age differences as a basis for constructing measures of intelligence.

MEASUREMENT

How is intelligence measured? In order to develop measures of intelligence we need to know how to define the class of things that constitute intelligence in order to know what to measure. There is no agreed way of defining the class of measures of intelligence.

There is at least rough common agreement that some abilities or skills are related to the broad domain of intellectual measures. Most people would probably agree that the ability to define words constitutes one kind of intellectual skill or ability. It is possible to measure the size of a person's vocabulary by discovering whether or not a person is able to correctly define a particular word. Performance on this single-item test would not constitute a good measure of a person's vocabulary. A person might have a large vocabulary but be unable to define the particular word selected for a one-item test. It is obvious that a good measure of a person's vocabulary should be based on an aggregate score of responses to many different items, each testing understanding of the definition of a different word. The items that are selected should fulfill the following criterion: Individuals who respond correctly to one item should have a higher probability of correctly responding to a second item than individuals who respond incorrectly to the first item. In other words, responses to each item should be positively related to responses to all other items. This requirement is not difficult to meet in practice. If the requirement is met, then all possible sets of items that are positively related will have aggregate scores that are related to each other. In other words, it does not really matter which items are chosen for inclusion in our test of vocabulary as long as there are enough positively related items in the set.

A score on a test of vocabulary would not constitute a good measure of intelligence. Surely intelligence must encompass more than the ability to define words. Perhaps memory is involved. It would be possible to measure memory abilities by reading a list of digits to a person and then determining whether he or she could repeat them correctly after an initial exposure. Again, many different lists should be chosen in order to develop an aggregate index of memory for digits.

We would now have two different aggregate scores. It is easy to see that this process could be extended and that it is possible to obtain aggregate scores for different kinds of abilities that are commonly thought to be related in some undefined way to intelligence. These several different scores exhibit a surprising property that was first noted by an English psychologist, Charles SPEARMAN, in 1904. The several measures would tend to be positively related—they are said to

form a positive manifold. That is, individuals who receive high scores on the test of vocabulary are likely to receive high scores on the test of memory. Scores on tests of these abilities are likely to be related to scores on other ability measures, such as the ability to solve spatial reasoning problems. The observation that different measures of ability usually tend to be positively related to each other has two useful properties. First, it permits us to solve or at least to circumvent a definitional issue. Something is a measure of intelligence if, and only if, it is positively related to all other measures of intelligence. Since the set of abilities that are positively related is very large, this implies that there are many different kinds of measures of intelligence. Second, if all measures of intelligence tend to be positively related, then any subset of measures when averaged will provide a score that is closely related to a score derived from a different subset of measures. This is actually an extension of the same principle that indicates that selection of items for a measure of vocabulary is not critical as long as there are enough items that are each positively related to each other. So, too, the selection of aggregate measures of abilities for the development of a test of intelligence is not absolutely critical as long as a large enough set of positively related measures is chosen. All possible aggregates will yield somewhat comparable results. This is known as the principle of the indifference of the indicator.

THE STRUCTURE OF INTELLECT

If all possible measures of intelligence are positively related, does this mean that measures of intelligence should result in a single number representing an aggregate index of performance on many different kinds of ability measures? This is certainly a common procedure. The widely used Stanford-Binet and Wechsler tests both provide a single composite index of intelligence, an intelligence quotient (IQ). Although there may be some justification for this procedure, it is possible to argue that it omits much relevant information about an individual's intellectual abilities. Intelligence consists of many different abilities. Measures of intelligence that assess similar abilities tend to be more highly related to each other than measures of intelligence that assess different abilities. For example, scores on tests that are measures of memory will tend to be more related to each other than to scores on tests of spatial reasoning that do not involve memory.

The most comprehensive analysis of the structure of intellectual abilities is contained in a theory developed by John Carroll (1993) called the three-stratum theory of intelligence (see Figure 1). Carroll reanalyzed many different studies of the relationships among different measures of intellectual abilities. Figure 1 presents an overview of his theory of the relationships among different measures of ability. Carroll represents the structure of intelligence as a pyramid with a single common general ability at the top of the pyramid. General ability is related to eight different kinds of abilities at the second stratum. The abilities arrayed from left to right have a decreasing degree of relationship to the single common ability at the third stratum. The ability with the strongest relationship to general intelligence is called fluid ability. Fluid ability is related to a number of narrower abilities at the first stratum, including the ability to reason inductively and to reason quantitatively. Carroll's theory subdivides the domain of intelligence into three different levels of ability, with each level differing in terms of its generality.

It is theoretically possible to subdivide the domain of intellectual abilities into further narrower abilities. For example, the ability at stratum II that has the second highest relationship to general intelligence is

called crystallized ability and it is related to a stratum I ability to comprehend printed language. It would probably be possible to develop measures of the ability to comprehend different kinds of material. Individuals might well differ in their ability to comprehend passages relating to humanistic and scientific topics. It is always possible in principle to subdivide abilities into narrower and more specialized skills that are related to each other. This analysis indicates that intelligence may be conceived as a single general ability or as many specialized and narrow abilities that are related to each other in a hierarchical structure.

Abilities occupying different positions in the hierarchy may differ in a number of ways. The two stratum II abilities with the strongest relationship to general intelligence are fluid and crystallized ability. Not only are these abilities related to different measures at the first stratum of the hierarchy, but they also may be distinguished by an analysis of their theoretical properties. Crystallized abilities tend to be measured by tests of knowledge and skills that are related to formal education. Fluid ability measures tend to be related to abstract reasoning skills that are not formally taught in school but that might be influenced by exposure to formal education. Fluid and crystallized abilities also differ in the way in which they change over a person's lifetime. Individuals tend to exhibit declines in fluid intelligence over the adult life span that are larger than declines in crystallized intelligence. If

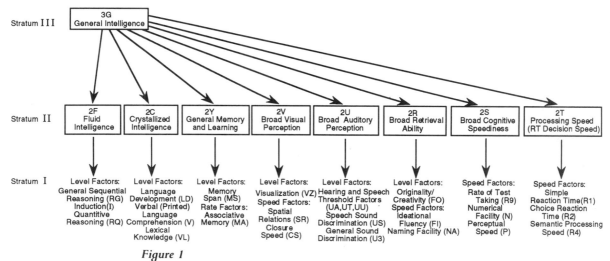

Figure 1

Carroll's three-stratum theory of intelligence (based on Carroll, 1993)

tests of different abilities have different theoretical properties, it is a mistake to think of intelligence as being only a single common thing. It is important to distinguish among different intellectual abilities and to understand their differences as well as to understand what they have in common. (See FLUID AND CRYSTAL-LIZED INTELLIGENCE, THEORY OF.)

There are other ways of representing relationships among different ability measures. Relationships among different measures of abilities may be ordered in two different ways. First, measures differ with respect to the degree to which they are related to all other measures of intelligence. This is called the g loading of a measure. Scores on tests with a high g loading are good predictors of scores on other ability tests. Tests with low g loadings are only weakly related to scores on all other ability measures. Second, abilities differ in terms of their relationship to each other. Spatial ability measures may have relatively low relationships with verbal ability measures. These two principles of ordering relationships may be combined to form a *radex* (Guttman, 1965). A radex represents relationships among

ability measures in a circular space. Tests with high g loadings are placed near the center of the space and tests with low g loadings are located in the periphery of the space. At any given distance from the center of the space, tests may be arrayed in a circle. The location of a test on the circumference of a circle represents its relationship to other tests of ability with comparable g loadings. Tests that are highly related to each other are arrayed at adjacent positions on the circle. Tests that have low relationships to each other are placed at different locations on the circumference of the circle. At the extreme, they are opposite each other (see RADEX THEORY). Figure 2 presents a radex representation of relationships among tests based on a study conducted by Marshalek, Lohman, and Snow (1983).

PROPERTIES OF MEASURES

Why do tests differ in their g loadings? To ask this question is to ask, in effect, for a theory of general intelligence. There is no commonly accepted answer to this question. It is, however, possible to develop

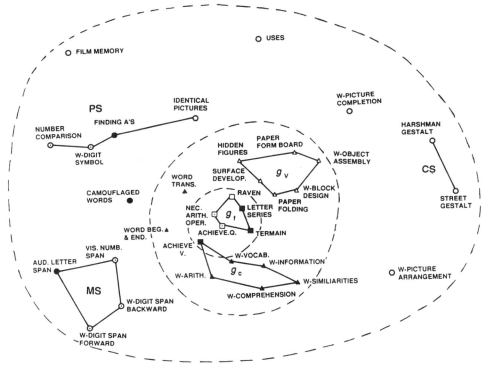

Figure 2

A radex representation of intelligence (based on Marshalek, Lohman, & Snow, 1983)

some notions about the properties of general intelligence that are measured by different tests. In this section several procedures that have been used to measure intelligence will be described and an analysis of the reasons for their relationship to intelligence will be presented.

Simulation of the Ravens. Carpenter, Just, and Schell (1990) developed computer models that differed with respect to their ability to solve problems similar to those on the RAVEN PROGRESSIVE MATRICES —a test of abstract reasoning skills that has a high g loading. Figure 3 presents an example of the kinds of problems that could be solved by the computer pro-

gram once a description of the problem was presented. By examining properties of computer programs that differed in their ability to solve problems, it is possible to develop a theory of how individuals who differ in intelligence differ in their characteristic reasoning abilities. In order to solve difficult problems it was necessary to provide programs that were able to break complex problems into easier and more manageable segments and to provide rules that enabled the program to keep track of the results of the partial problem solutions and to form high-level abstractions. Individuals who excel at solving difficult problems that are good measures of general intelligence may be assumed

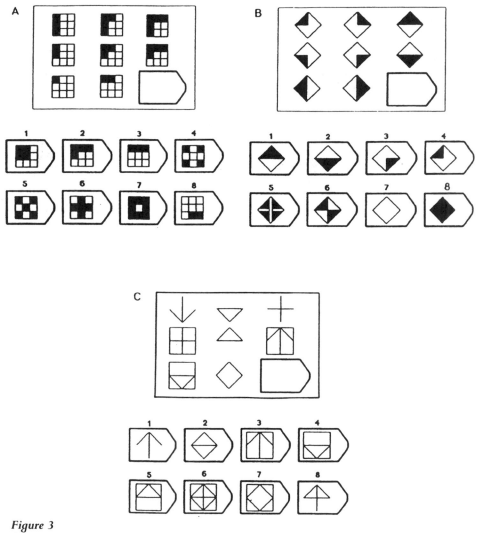

Figure 3

Problems solved in a computer simulation of problems contained in the Raven Progressive Matrices (based on Carpenter, Just, & Schell, 1990)

to have the same skills as computer programs that simulate their performance on these tests.

Vocabulary. Vocabulary tests have high g loadings and are included in many tests of intelligence. Why is size of vocabulary a good measure of general intelligence? Individuals who are exposed to people who use unusual words, who read a lot, and who have good educational opportunities are likely to have more opportunities to acquire a large vocabulary than individuals who do not have these exposures. It is also true that individuals who appear to have had about the same exposure to opportunities to develop their vocabulary may differ in their ability to define words. Most of the words that individuals are able to define have never been formally defined for them. Few individuals systematically look up the meaning of words they do not know. Most of the words we are able to define were learned by inferences about the meaning of words from the contexts in which they were used. In order to test this idea, Sternberg and Powell (1983) presented individuals with a list of unusual words they were not able to define that were used appropriately in sentences. They obtained a measure of each subject's ability to define the unusual words after an exposure to the words that was constant for all of the subjects in their study. Vocabulary scores on this test were predictive of general intelligence test scores. These results suggest that individuals differ in their ability to determine the meaning of words from the context in which they are used. Individuals with high intelligence excel in the ability to determine the meaning of words from the incomplete information that is contained in sentences in which the words are used.

Digit Span. Tests of digit span have been used in many different tests of intelligence. In the standard version of the digit-span test, individuals are asked to repeat back to the examiner in correct order a list of digits they have just heard. The typical adult can repeat without error approximately seven digits. Digit span measures are not highly related to scores on other measures of intelligence. If individuals are required to repeat the digits they have heard in backward order, the relationship between digit span and general intelligence increases. The data in Figure 2 illustrate this relationship. Note that digit span forward is farther from the center of the circular space than digit span backward. The additional transformational complexity

required to reverse the order of the digits in a person's memory increases the relationship between performance on the test and scores on other tests of intelligence.

Infant Habituation. For many years, psychologists attempted to develop measures of intelligence that could be given to children in the first year of life. These efforts were not very successful. Scores on various measures of skills exhibited by infants were not very predictive of intelligence test scores obtained from the same children when they were older. More recently, psychologists have used habituation measures that can be administered to infants in the first several months of life to obtain scores that are related to intelligence test scores obtained from children as old as age 8 (Colombo, 1993). Habituation is the tendency to cease attending to a stimulus that is repeatedly presented. For example, if an infant is presented with a pattern of lights, the infant will initially look at the novel stimulus and will eventually stop attending to it. If the pattern is changed, attention will return. This is called dishabituation. Infants who exhibit rapid habituation and strong dishabituation score higher on tests of intelligence administered to them several years later than infants who do not habituate rapidly and do not exhibit strong dishabituation. Habituation may require an individual to develop a mental representation of the stimulus, which is then used as a basis of comparison with new stimuli. If the new stimulus is similar to the representation of the previously presented stimulus, habituation occurs and individuals do not attend to the new stimulus. If the new stimulus does not match the representation of the original stimulus, dishabituation occurs and attention returns. On this analysis, infant habituation tests measure the speed with which an infant can form an accurate representation of a stimulus and the infant's ability to notice that a novel stimulus is different from stimuli that have previously been presented. Infants who differ in these abilities differ in the rate of intellectual development in early childhood.

Reaction Time. Psychologists have tried to relate scores on tests of intelligence to ability to perform simple tasks rapidly. It is possible to measure reaction time to lights. In a typical reaction time task, individuals are presented with a box that includes one or more lights. The subject is instructed to move his or her finger from a home key to a button located under each light as soon as a particular light is turned on. The time elapsed from the onset of the light to the release of the finger from the home key is called the decision time or reaction time for this task. Individuals who score high on tests of intelligence tend to have shorter reaction times than individuals who score low on tests of intelligence. There are also differences in the variability of reaction times. Individuals who are high in intelligence tend to have reaction times of relatively similar speed that are close to their fastest reaction times. Individuals who score low on tests of intelligence tend to have fast reaction times that are close to the fastest reaction times of individuals scoring high on tests of intelligence, but they have more variable reaction times and are more likely to have slow reaction times. Although reaction time measures are related to scores on tests of intelligence, they tend to have low g loadings—that is, they are not very strongly related to intelligence.

Frearson and Eysenck (1986) developed a variant of the reaction time task called the odd-man-out. In this version of the task, individuals are presented with three lights at a time. The first or last light is always closer to the middle light. If the first light is closer to the middle light, then the last light is the odd-man-out. The subject is required to indicate whether the first or last light is the odd-man-out. The odd-man-out tasks measures speed of reaction time and an additional component that is predictively related to general intelligence (Kranzler & Jensen, 1993). In order to solve this problem, the individual must compare two distances and determine which of the two is larger. A subject's ability to accomplish this task rapidly appears to be related to general intelligence.

Nonacademic Knowledge. Scores on intelligence tests have weak relationships to many different kinds of knowledge, including knowledge about subjects that are usually not taught in school. For example, individuals who score high on tests of intelligence are likely to know more about sports, popular songs, and cars than individuals who score low on tests of intelligence. It is probably the case that individuals with high scores on intelligence would do better in Trivial Pursuit games than individuals with low scores on tests of intelligence. Tests of general information about subjects not usually taught in school are not good measures of intelligence. They are only weakly

related to general intelligence. They have low g loadings and locations at the periphery of the radex. It is also the case that each of these measures has a weak positive relationship to more conventional measures of intelligence. If an aggregate score is formed of knowledge of several different subjects, it will be highly related to scores on general intelligence, since each component of the aggregate is positively related to general intelligence. Such a measure of intelligence would not be practical—it would be necessary to include many items in order to obtain an aggregate index that is highly predictive of general intelligence. Measures of general intelligence may be based on many different kinds of things as long as the components that enter into an aggregate or composite score are each positively related to measures of intelligence.

Heritability. There are many different kinds of measures of intelligence, and they differ in their relationship to general intelligence for many different reasons. Is there a property that may be used to characterize the class of all measures of intelligence that will be related to the extent to which the measure is related to general intelligence? There is at least one such property. Pedersen and colleagues (1992) studied the extent to which scores on each of a battery of tests were influenced by genetic characteristics. They studied identical and fraternal twins who had been reared in the same family or had been reared apart. These data can be used to develop a measure of the influence of genes on each of the tests in their battery. If performance on a test is influenced by genes, identical twins, whether they are reared together or apart, should have similar scores on the test. Fraternal twins should have test scores that are not as similar as those of identical twins. If twins reared apart are less similar on a test than those reared together, and if identical twins are not more alike than fraternal twins, then a person's genes are not likely to influence performance on the test. An estimate of the extent to which genes influence performance on a measure in a particular group is called the heritability of the measure. Pedersen and her colleagues used their data to estimate the heritability of each of the tests in their battery. They then obtained the g loadings of each of the tests. They found that the g loadings of tests were strongly related to the estimated heritability of the tests. Performance on tests that were good measures of general intelligence in the sense that scores on the test could be used to predict scores on many other tests in the battery were more influenced by a person's genes than performance on tests that were not good measures of general intelligence. These data suggest that good measures of general intelligence tend to be more heritable than poor measures of intelligence.

Conclusion. It is obvious that it is not possible to arrive at a single defining set of properties that distinguishes measures of intelligence that differ in the extent to which they are good measures of general intelligence. Nevertheless, the several examples given above do help to narrow our conception of the defining properties of good measures of intelligence. Measures of intelligence appear to be related to the ability to transform and process information rapidly and efficiently.

CONCLUSION

There are many different theoretical characterizations of the class of measures of intelligence and there is no commonly accepted theory that defines the distinguishing properties of tasks that measure intelligence. An examination of the properties of tasks that measure intelligence gives rise to a heterogeneous set of defining features of measures of intelligence. Intelligence on this analysis is related to ability to develop abstractions, to solve problems by learning to divide them into manageable segments, to determine the meaning of words from their use in sentences, to manipulate information in memory, to rapidly compare distance relationships, and to acquire broad knowledge about subjects not included in the curriculum of the schools. Measures of intelligence also differ in the extent to which scores on the measures are influenced by a person's genes.

(See also: MULTIPLE INTELLIGENCES THEORY; STRUCTURE OF INTELLECT MODEL.)

BIBLIOGRAPHY

BRODY, N. (1992). *Intelligence.* San Diego, CA: Academic Press. A review of contemporary research.

CARPENTER, P. A., JUST, M. A., & SCHELL, P. (1990). What one intelligence test measures: A theoretical account of the processing in the Raven Progressive Matrices Test. *Psychological Review, 97,* 404–431.

CARROLL, J. B. (1993). *Human cognitive abilities: A survey of factor-analytic studies.* Cambridge: Cambridge University Press.

COLOMBO, J. (1993). *Infant cognition: Predicting later intellectual functions.* Newbury Park, CA: Sage Publications.

FREARSON, W. M., & EYSENCK, H. J. (1986). Intelligence, reaction-time (RT) and a new "odd-man-out" RT paradigm. *Personality and Individual Differences, 7,* 807–817.

GUTTMAN, L. (1965). The structure of the interrelations among intelligence tests. *Proceedings of the 1964 Invitational Conference on Testing Problems.* Princeton, NJ: Educational Testing Service.

HORN, J. L. (1985). Remodeling old models of intelligence. In B. B. Wolman (Ed.), *Handbook of intelligence: Theories, measurements and applications.* New York: Wiley.

KAIL, R., & PELLEGRINO, J. W. (1985). *Human intelligence: Perspectives and prospects.* New York: W. H. Freeman. A textbook with good coverage of laboratory approaches to the study of intelligence.

KRANZLER, J. H., & JENSEN, A. R. (1993). Psychometric *g* is still not unitary after eliminating supposed "impurities": Further comment on Carroll. *Intelligence, 17,* 11–14.

MARSHALEK, B., LOHMAN, D. F., & SNOW, R. E. (1983). The complexity continuum in the radex and hierarchical models of intelligence. *Intelligence, 7,* 107–127.

PEDERSEN, N. L., PLOMIN, R., NESSELROADE, J. R., & MCLEARN, G. E. (1992). A quantitative genetic analysis of cognitive abilities during the second half of the life span. *Psychological Science, 3,* 346–353.

SPEARMAN, C. (1904). "General Intelligence" objectively determined and measured. *American Journal of Psychology, 15,* 72–101. The original statement of the theory of general intelligence.

STERNBERG, R. J., & POWELL, J. S. (1983). Comprehending verbal comprehension. *American Psychologist, 38,* 878–898.

NATHAN BRODY

PSYCHOPHYSICAL MEASURES OF INTELLIGENCE
At first glance, the idea of using success in identifying briefly flashed geometric designs or equally abrupt tone pips as a measure of intelligence seems somewhat counterintuitive. Nevertheless, the notion of intelligence as an aptitude for problem solv-

ing and the acquisition of knowledge strongly implies the importance of the means by which knowledge is acquired. This idea was first put forth by Sir Francis GALTON (1883), who asserted that "the only information that reaches us concerning outward events appears to pass through the avenue of our senses; and the more perceptive the senses are of the difference, the larger is the field upon which our judgment and intelligence can act" (p. 19). In other words, according to Galton, the quality of sensory information processing in general and the sharpness of sensory discrimination in particular determine the level of intellectual attainment.

Psychophysics, the area of experimental psychology that deals with evaluation of sensory capabilities by observing human response to precisely calibrated stimuli, has lent its name and methods to the area of intelligence research surveyed here. Although in classic psychophysics no clear assumptions were made about the relationship between the brain and the observer's behavior, such a link is presumed when psychophysical methods are applied to the investigation of the mechanisms of intelligence. The senses, which Galton vested with such an important role, serve as intermediaries between the environment and the brain. To integrate multiple autonomous streams of information that originate in a multifaceted environment, the organism ought to translate each into a common language, equally "understandable" by the neurons of such diverse structures as the auditory brainstem nuclei, the olfactory bulb, the primary somatosensory cortex, and the tertiary association areas. The lingua franca of the central nervous system that enables universal interneuronal communication and generation of action orders is the language of discrete electrical events. The implication of the connection between the senses and the brain is that innocuous errors in sensory input, by being transformed and magnified within neuronal ensembles, may foul up the complex workings of the mind at the later stages of processing.

The propagation of the Galtonian view of intelligence depended—as frequently happens in science—on advancement of measurement tools and techniques. Early attempts to relate psychophysical measures to intelligence were hampered by inadequacies of the instrumentation and lack of valid and reliable indices of intelligence. Although Charles SPEARMAN (1904) reported sizable correlations between measures of sensory discrimination and the educational attainment of English schoolboys, previous negative findings from C. Wissler's (1901) methodologically flawed study hampered further progress in the area. After publishing his 1904 results, Spearman dedicated his energy to developing a statistical and psychometric apparatus of intelligence measurement and never returned to psychophysical studies. With the exception of few small-scale attempts, psychophysical exploration of intelligence showed no signs of development for sixty years after Spearman's seminal study. Only the advent of the "information revolution," which helped to recast old metaphors into a more rigorously defined set of constructs, brought about a revival of the "brass-instruments" approach to the mind.

Although the concept of information is not novel, the mathematical theory underlying it dates only to the late 1940s (Shannon & Weaver, 1949). According to the fundamental theorem of the mathematical theory of communication, fidelity of information transmission is determined by four main factors: noise in the information transmission channel, message redundancy, time redundancy, and hardware redundancy. In other words, eliminating competing messages, adding repeated or overlapping features to the message, prolonging the time allotted for information processing and thereby permitting the same message to be recycled several times, and dedicating a greater number of fallible processing elements to the task increase the probability that the message will be transmitted and interpreted without error. All four types of constraints on information processing have been used in designing experimental paradigms for exploration of the foundations of human intelligence. Studies of neurological patients take advantage of unfortunate accidents of nature and measure performance changes under conditions of reduced hardware redundancy and increased noise. Reaction-time (RT) studies feature manipulation of information content of the stimulus message and measurement of the response latency. Finally, in inspection-time (IT) paradigms, the processing time is manipulated and response accuracy is measured.

The body of RT studies aimed at discovering the mechanisms of intelligence is reviewed by D. Detterman (1987). In essence, the results of the RT studies suggest that psychometric indices of intelligence are inversely and modestly correlated with the increase in processing time brought by augmentation of the information load. When a linear function is fitted to the RT data plotted against the information load of the stimuli, subjects who score higher on IQ tests tend to have shallower slopes. This relationship is consistent but not particularly strong: RT slope accounts for about 10 percent of the variance in intelligence (see REACTION TIME).

One of the limitations of the RT methods is their reliance on the speed of the subject's motor response. A psychophysical approach to investigation of information-processing mechanisms of intelligence is free of motor demands. It was introduced by a group of Australian psychologists in the 1970s. Psychophysical methods gauge the resolution of sensory-perceptual systems and establish their ability to detect, discriminate, and identify the incoming stimuli. The IT paradigm designed by D. Vickers (1972) and applied to intelligence research by his colleagues T. Nettelbeck and M. Lally in 1976 differs radically from RT tasks. The most important innovation introduced by the IT tasks was the elimination of speed constraints on subjects' responses. Although there are many procedural variations, in a typical IT task stimuli are presented to a subject for a short time, and the subject is asked to make a decision about some of their physical aspects. In the visual-inspection-time (VIT) paradigm, the target stimuli are two parallel vertical lines of unequal length that are capped with a perpendicular horizontal line, as illustrated in Figure 1. To control for subjects' response bias, a standard two-interval forced choice (2IFC) procedure is used. At each trial of this psychophysical procedure, sketched in Figure 1, a subject

(observer) is presented a sequence of two combinations of a target stimulus and a mask (visual noise).

The mask is used to control the exposure time, called the stimulus onset asynchrony (SOA). The two target–mask pairs are separated by a pause, and each pair of presentations is called "the observation interval." The subject's task is to indicate which of the intervals contained the target stimulus (e.g., the one with left leg shorter than the right). The difference in the length of the lines is large enough to be easily identified when the exposure is relatively long. However, with shortening of the exposure times, the task becomes increasingly difficult. In psychophysics, it is presumed that the relationship between the accuracy of subject's judgment and exposure time is a sigmoid curve, as shown in Figure 2.

The IT is defined as the exposure time (SOA) at which the subject attains a specified threshold value of percentage correct. The stimulus value associated with the probability of success that is exactly halfway between the chance level and the ceiling is called the "threshold." In a 2IFC paradigm, when a guess is equivalent to a coin toss and the ceiling is fixed at 100 percent, the threshold is the value corresponding to the probability of 75 percent. Although IT is defined as the threshold SOA, the latter may be set at a value

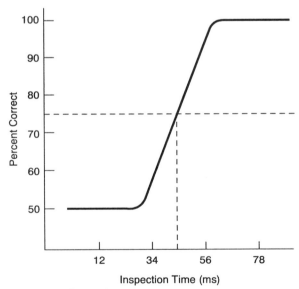

Figure 2

Two-interval forced choice paradigm

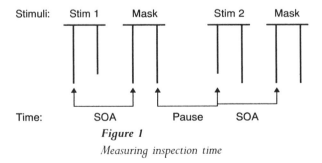

Figure 1

Measuring inspection time

different from the 75 percent correct. Requiring subjects to reach a higher value, such as 97.5 percent correct, as was the case in the work of Nettelbeck and his colleagues, means that a near-ceiling performance is expected.

Although most research on the relationship between IT and intelligence has been confined to the visual modality, auditory analogues of the VIT have been introduced as well. There are several variations of the auditory inspection time (AIT) task. In general, as in the VIT paradigm, stimuli (tones) are presented sequentially in two listening intervals, and the subjects judge some aspect of the tone, such as pitch or duration. The exposure time is controlled by a backward mask, a tone that is presented to the subject after a silent pause following the stimulus. As in the VIT task, the index of performance is the threshold value of the target feature. As a rule, in both paradigms, Pearson product moment correlation is used to assess the strength of association between the sensory threshold and the measure of intelligence.

In the IT studies of the mechanisms of intelligence, a variety of cognitive aptitude measures were correlated with a number of VIT and AIT indices in a broad range of subjects. Some three dozen of these studies have been reviewed by J. H. Kranzler and A. R. Jensen (1989), who combined the results of the original investigations using a statistical technique "meta-analysis." The meta-analysis confirmed the existence of a link between intelligence and the inspection time. This study established that there is a nonzero correlation between the two and that about 25 percent of the variance in IQ may be explained by the ability to make precise sensory discriminations under conditions of low time redundancy.

One of the corollaries of the central theorem of information theory is the trade-off between time and message redundancies. Just as a more efficient system can process highly redundant stimuli under severe time constraints, such as those exemplified by an IT task, it can also excel in making difficult discriminations when the time pressure is minimal.

In a series of experiments, Naftali Raz, L. Willerman, and M. Yama (1987) addressed the question of whether time constraints are necessary to demonstrate the link between intelligence and psychophysical indices. In these experiments, subjects were asked to perform a pitch-discrimination task with short tones presented in a standard 2IFC setup. In contrast to the IT paradigm, the frequency-discrimination task involves no demands on speed, contains no interfering masking tones, and is not known to be amenable to strategic interventions. Although practice effects on the frequency discrimination task are sizable, the learning curve is usually quite steep and flattens after about a hundred trials. The results of the 1987 study have confirmed the essence of Spearman's (1904) findings showing a moderately strong association between intelligence and sensory discrimination. The strength of this relationship was comparable to that between IQ and IT. In a series of studies, I. J. Deary (1992) replicated the findings of Raz and his colleagues as well as his own results previously obtained with the AIT paradigm. Thus, empirical evidence supports the existence of a moderately strong relationship between speed and resolution of the sensory systems, on the one hand, and highly integrative cognitive functions, on the other hand. Nevertheless, there are several caveats to this statement.

It has been suggested that because all psychophysical tasks are peculiar laboratory procedures, they may be linked to intelligence because they capitalize on a response to novelty and an ability to adapt to a strange situation. This argument was put to a test by Raz and colleagues (1989) who presented a signal-detection task to college students drawn from the same population in which the relationship between frequency discrimination and intelligence had been demonstrated. The signal-detection task, in contrast to the frequency-discrimination task, shows very little in the way of individual differences and can be performed without the involvement of the cerebral cortex (Cranford, 1979; Cranford et al., 1982). The results of the study indicate that task novelty per se is not enough to generate covariation between intelligence and the outcome measure: signal-detection thresholds are unrelated to intelligence.

Because no measure is a pure index of a construct it denotes, and psychophysical indices of intelligence are not exempt from this rule, several potential sources of contamination of IT measures exist. It is plausible that subjects' background and pretest experiences may boost their performance on a psychophysical task without any reference to intelligence. It has been surmised that a subject's experience with video games may become a source of such contamination by supplying the subject with strategies unavailable to subjects who have never stepped into a video arcade. Trained musicians may outperform the uninitiated on an AIT task by virtue of their experience with fine tonal discriminations. The response to both of the above-mentioned propositions is a cautious no (Mackenzie & Cumming, 1986; Raz, Willerman, & Yama, 1987), although in all of these studies the measures of video-game experience and musical training were rather crude.

A more serious problem with the VIT paradigm is its proneness to artifacts stemming from subjects' utilization of the "apparent-motion effect," an illusion observed when the mask overwrites the stimulus: As the vertical lines of the mask appear on the display, the shorter line of the stimulus seems to stretch up to the point where it matches the end of the mask. The apparent-motion cues can be used as a strategy to circumvent the mask. The issue of apparent-motion cues was brought up by T. Nettelbeck (1987) and examined experimentally by B. Mackenzie with E. Bingham (1985) and with S. Cumming (1986). The results of these studies indicate that the majority of the observers use apparent-motion cues on the VIT task, and in this group, the relationship between IQ and VIT is rather weak; among those who do not use the cues, this correlation is higher than average. In light of this finding, Kranzler and Jensen's (1989) estimate of the magnitude of association between intelligence and the speed of sensory information processing may be even higher when the use of mask-defeating strategies is taken into account.

What, after all, have we learned about the mechanisms of intelligence by following Galton's path? It is clear that intelligence as expressed in the capacity for symbolic reasoning and organization of sophisticated problem-solving behavior is linked to seemingly simple and elementary psychophysical indices. It is also clear that the era of a psychophysical "culture fair" assessment of intelligence is not coming. A discussion of the plausibility and utility of a notion that it is desirable to predict intelligent behavior in a complex cultural environment using measures devoid of any cultural context is beyond the scope of this essay. It seems, however, that psychophysical measures have very little

use in schools and the work place, for it is unlikely these tasks can outperform conventional IQ tests in educational and vocational assessment or match their record of prediction. As a matter of fact, even in a crude discrimination between college undergraduates and the mentally retarded, IT may prove not to be a match for IQ. The data graphically displayed by N. H. Kirby and T. Nettelbeck (1989) reveal that on the basis of VIT alone, 10 percent of college undergraduates would be placed at a vocational rehabilitation facility, whereas 10 percent of mentally retarded individuals would be classified as college undergraduates. Nevertheless, almost two decades of application of modern psychophysics to the problem of intelligence have yielded important insights into the sources of individual differences in cognition. The notion that success in complex intellectual activity is linked to the seemingly elemental ability to process sensory information has been strengthened. This research effort has opened a window onto the mechanisms underlying information processing, the "mechanics of abilities" (Hunt, 1978). Such a window, no matter how small and opaque, is worth looking through, as long as it is not mistaken for a panoramic view.

BIBLIOGRAPHY

BRAND, C. R. (1984). Intelligence and inspection time: An ontogenetic relationship? In C. J. Turner (Ed.), *The biology of human intelligence.* London: Eugenics Society.

BRAND, C. R., & DEARY, I. J. (1982). Intelligence and "inspection time." In H. J. Eysenck (Ed.), *A model for intelligence* (pp. 133–148). Berlin: Springer-Verlag.

CRANFORD, J. L. (1979). Detection versus discrimination of brief tones by cat with auditory cortex lesions. *Journal of Acoustical Society of America, 65,* 1573–1575.

CRANFORD, J. L.; STREAM, R. W.; RYE, C. V.; & SLADE, T. L. (1982). Detection versus discrimination of brief-duration tones in patients with temporal lobe damage. *Archives of Otolaryngology, 108,* 350–356.

DEARY, I. J. (1992). *Auditory inspection time and intelligence.* Unpublished doctoral dissertation, University of Edinburgh, Scotland.

DETTERMAN, D. (1987). What does reaction time tell us about intelligence? In P. A. Vernon (Ed.), *Speed of information processing and intelligence* (pp. 177–200). Norwood, NJ: Ablex.

GALTON, F. (1883). *Inquiries into human faculty and its development*. London: Macmillan.

HUNT, E. (1978). Mechanics of verbal ability. *Psychological Review, 85*, 109–130.

KIRBY, N. H., & NETTELBECK, T. (1989). Reaction time and inspection time as measures of intellectual ability. *Personality and Individual Differences, 10*, 11–14.

KRANZLER, J. H., & JENSEN, A. R. (1989). Inspection time and intelligence: A meta-analysis. *Intelligence, 13*, 329–347.

MACKENZIE, B., & BINGHAM, E. (1985). IQ, inspection time, and response strategies in a university population. *Australian Journal of Psychology, 27*, 257–268.

MACKENZIE, B., & CUMMING, S. (1986). How fragile is the relationship between inspection time and intelligence: The effects of apparent motion cues and previous experience. *Personality and Individual Differences, 7*, 721–729.

NETTELBECK, T. (1987). Inspection time and intelligence. In P. A. Vernon (Ed.), *Speed of information processing and intelligence*. Norwood, NJ: Ablex.

NETTELBECK, T., & LALLY, M. (1976). Inspection time and measured intelligence. *British Journal of Psychology, 67*, 17–22.

RAZ, N.; WILLERMAN, L.; & YAMA, M. (1987). On sense and senses: Intelligence and auditory information processing. *Personality and Individual Differences, 8*, 201–210.

SHANNON, C. E., & WEAVER, W. (1949). *The mathematical theory of communication*. Urbana: University of Illinois Press.

SPEARMAN, C. (1904). General intelligence, objectively determined and measured. *American Journal of Psychology, 15*, 72–101.

VICKERS, D., NETTELBECK, T., & WILSON, R. J. (1972). Perceptual indices of performance: The measurement of "inspection time" and "noise" in the visual system. *Perception, 1*, 263–295.

WISSLER, C. (1901). The correlation of mental and physical tests. *Psychological Review, Monograph Supplement, 3*(6).

NAFTALI RAZ

PSYCHOPHYSIOLOGICAL MEASURES OF INTELLIGENCE

Psychophysiological research attempts to make inferences about a variety of psychological processes through the measurement of physiological indicators such as heart rate, brain electrical activity, and brain metabolism. This approach is grounded in the view that one of the best windows on psychological processes is the physiological processes that make them possible.

RATIONALE

A person's intelligence is usually inferred through observations of his or her behavior, whether social, verbal, or artistic. Such observations can be made in a controlled testing situation, in a clinical setting, or by informally noting everyday actions. By observing an individual's behavior, and by comparing it to the behaviors of others, researchers can make inferences about the relative power or efficiency of the mental processes that select and guide action.

A central assumption of psychophysiological theories is that these mental processes are executed by the brain. In these theories, the brain may be thought of as a computational device that processes information and solves problems. Since more sophisticated computers can be programmed to solve more complex problems (and solve them more quickly) than less sophisticated computers, we may therefore assess the computational power of a computer by examining the type, organization, and functional properties of its hardware.

Similarly, if the brain is a computer, it should also be possible to assess the "power" of a brain (i.e., its intelligence or intellectual potential) by examining properties of its neural hardware. This can be done by comparing the neurophysiological properties of people thought to be of greater intelligence with those of people thought to be of lesser intelligence (as determined by conventional intelligence tests). Any systematic relationship discovered between scores obtained from conventional intelligence tests and these neurophysiological properties suggests that these properties constitute a psychophysiological measure of intelligence.

Although interest in psychophysiological measures of intelligence dates back to the dawn of intelligence research in the nineteenth century (Fancher, 1985; Gould, 1981), only since the 1970s have we seen the beginnings of real progress, spurred by technological advances. These recent studies have yielded fascinating and tantalizing findings, although the existence of some inconclusive or conflicting experimental results currently preclude any definitive theoretical interpretation.

Psychophysiological measures of intelligence fall into two classes: those involving measurements of anatomical or physical properties and those measuring aspects of the functioning of the nervous system.

ANATOMICAL CORRELATES

Height. Jensen and Sinha (1993) have comprehensively reviewed studies correlating height and scores on intelligence tests. These studies indicate a modest relationship between these variables, although the correlation may be decreasing over time. At present, there is no substantial empirical evidence or plausible theoretical rationale for how a single genetic mechanism might influence both height and intelligence. Instead, Jensen and Sinha argue that environmental or behavioral factors are probably responsible. For instance, quality of nutrition could influence both height and brain development. It is also possible that cross-assortative mating is responsible. For instance, if both intelligence and height are considered desirable characteristics, then people will tend to select mates that exhibit both of these qualities. Such a practice could result in a correlation between two variables that are otherwise genetically independent.

Brain Size. The relationship between brain size and intelligence received considerable study in the nineteenth century. Because much of this early research was methodologically flawed and biased (see Gould, 1981), this area of investigation fell into disrepute, leading to the tacit assumption that these variables are essentially uncorrelated. Several modern studies, however, have overcome many of these problems and have indicated a correlation between brain size and intelligence-test scores. For instance, Willerman, Schultz, Rutledge, and Bigler (1989) measured brain size *in vivo,* using the magnetic resonance imaging (MRI) technique, and found that it correlated with intelligence-test scores. Furthermore, Jensen and Sinha present tentative evidence that this correlation may be mediated by a common genetic mechanism. It should be noted, however, that this approach has been criticized by other theorists. Moreover, its explanatory power is limited; for example, Ankney (1992) showed that (after correcting for body size) men's brains are, on average, about 100 grams heavier than women's brains, even though there is probably no significant difference between men and women in general intelligence. Speculative interpretations of this finding are that women's brains may incorporate a more efficient design, or that different types of intellectual strengths present in men (e.g., greater spatial ability) may require more brain tissue.

Myopia. Myopia (i.e., nearsightedness) occurs when light passing through the lens of the eye focuses on a point before (instead of on) the retina. Jensen and Sinha (1993) review evidence indicating that myopia is correlated with intelligence test scores. Furthermore, myopia is known to be influenced by genetic factors. Unfortunately, the interpretation of the correlation is uncertain, because environmental factors also have a powerful effect on the likelihood of myopia. For example, myopia is quite rare in preliterate societies, suggesting that close visual work, such as reading, can increase the probability of this condition.

NERVOUS SYSTEM FUNCTION

Nerve Conductance Velocity. One view of intelligence originating in the early studies of Sir Francis GALTON in the nineteenth century (Fancher, 1985) is that intelligence somehow reflects the "efficiency" of a person's nervous system. Moreover, this efficiency is hypothesized to be a manifestation of a very simple property of neural functioning, such as greater speed of transmission of impulses along nerves (Vernon, 1990). This view has gained some support from results of recent studies correlating intelligence test scores with speed of conductance along nerves in subjects' arms (Vernon & Mori, 1989, 1992). Since the nerves studied were not in the brain and are therefore not implicated in higher thought processes, substantiation of these findings would suggest that such correlations manifest a simple property of the nervous system and not greater knowledge or superior intellectual strategies in those with higher intelligence-test scores. However, there have been failures to replicate such results (Reed & Jensen, 1991), rendering this hypothesis uncertain.

Electrophysiological Measures (EEG and ERP). Another class of psychophysiological measures involves quantifying the subset of the brain's total electrical activity that can be measured with electrodes attached to a person's scalp. The electroencephalogram (EEG) measures the ongoing electrical activity while a person engages in some task or is at rest. The EEG tends to reflect general brain states such as arousal, sleep, and so forth. There is a large literature on the relationship between EEG and intelligence test scores. Although many studies have found significant and interesting correlations between these two variables, there are others that have yielded negative or contradictory results. The confusion in this area of research is confounded by the lack of standardization among researchers in the types of experimental procedures used. So it is sometimes unclear whether a failure to replicate a particular experimental effect should indicate that the effect is not real, or a change in experimental procedures wiped out a real and interesting (albeit fleeting) phenomenon. Ongoing research should clarify these issues.

Rather than studying the general brain states reflected by EEGs, other researchers have adopted the strategy of investigating the brain's electrical responses to specific stimuli. This involves measuring the EEGs immediately following presentations of a particular class of stimuli (e.g., tones, lights, words). These segments of EEG are then averaged together, thereby filtering out sources of noise and yielding a waveform representing the brain's average response to that class of stimuli. This waveform depicts *event-related potentials (ERPs)*, sometimes called *average evoked potentials (AEPs)*. These ERPs consist of a standard series of peaks and valleys in the waveform known as *components*. The various components have been extensively studied and have been associated with particular neurophysiological or psychological processes (for a review, see Hillyard & Picton, 1987).

From the standpoint of intelligence research, ERPs have some distinct advantages over EEGs. In particular, the fact that individual ERP components seem to reflect specific mental processes should, in principle, enable researchers to determine which mental processes are important to intelligence by correlating properties (e.g., speed, amplitude) of each component with intelligence-test scores. Furthermore, differences in intelligence may clearly manifest themselves only when the brain is actively engaged in performing a task. The fact that ERPs exclusively reflect task-related brain activity rather than general brain states may make them more sensitive to processes of direct relevance to investigations of intelligence.

Unfortunately, the same tendency for researchers to vary experimental and data-analysis procedures makes detailed conclusions difficult. Most of these studies have attempted to test some variant of the neural efficiency hypothesis. For instance, McGarry-Roberts, Stelmack, and Campbell (1992) have shown that greater speed (i.e., shorter latency) of an important ERP component is associated with greater mental ability. Hendrickson (1982) hypothesized that efficient brains would exhibit fewer "transmission errors" in processing a given stimulus. This implies that there would be less trial-by-trial variability in the ERPs to repeated stimuli in higher-intelligence subjects. Hendrickson (1982) presented data to support this hypothesis; his data met with some criticism, but the effect was replicated by Barrett and Eysenck (1992). Hendrickson (1982) also hypothesized that efficient brains will yield more complex ERP waveforms because they presumably transmit more information with fewer errors. This hypothesis received mixed experimental support (Barrett & Eysenck, 1992).

Research examining the relationship between intelligence-test scores and various characteristics of ERPs suggests a number of intriguing hypotheses concerning the electrophysiological bases of intelligence. The published results, however, are in need of systematic replication. Furthermore, such results, even if substantiated, have alternate interpretations. For instance, correlations between the latency, amplitude, variability, and complexity of the components of ERP waveforms and intelligence-test scores could be due to increased or more sustained attention rather than stable differences in the information-processing characteristics of people's brains. Such attentional effects could be caused by motivational differences.

Positron Emission Tomography (PET). This technique involves injecting subjects with glucose attached to a (harmless) radioactive tracer. The brain then utilizes more or less of this glucose as fuel, depending on its need. A gamma-ray detector then ascertains how much of the radioactive tracer is deposited in various areas of the brain as a consequence of the level of glucose metabolism in each location. Different metabolic activity levels in particular brain regions yield a topographic map showing "hot" and "cold" spots.

The preliminary results are consistent with the basic thesis of the neural efficiency model (e.g., Haier et al., 1992); subjects achieving higher scores on tests of intelligence tend to show evidence of *less* glucose metabolism in the brain during task performance than do subjects who receive lower test scores. This could imply that the brains of subjects who are of higher intelligence accomplish more while working less. On the other hand, this could also mean that such people use more efficient cognitive strategies for solving problems; such strategies may be teachable. In either case, these results are based on very small samples of subjects and are in need of extensive replication.

CONCLUSIONS

The use of psychophysiological measures in the assessment and study of intelligence is off to a promising start. In principle, the strategy of looking for biological correlates raises the possibility of new ways of assessing and understanding intelligence. For instance, if a person's level of intelligence is manifested in simple psychophysiological measures that do not require specific knowledge, experience, or even committed participation in a task, then such measures must be considered comparatively culture-free indicators of intelligence. Furthermore, the validation and investigation of psychophysiological measures of intelligence raise the possibility of a truly physiological understanding of the brain mechanisms underlying intelligent thought and behavior. Such an understanding could lead to significant advances in education as well as in the medical and psychological diagnosis and treatment of intellectual deficits.

Nevertheless, even if particular psychophysiological measures of intelligence do receive the necessary experimental replication and clarification, the interpretation of these measures can be problematic. For instance, substantiated differences in brain function between low- and high-intelligence individuals do not necessarily imply a genetic basis, or even that the differences themselves are stable. Environmental variables such as nutrition and education can influence the developing brain. Furthermore, patterns of brain func-

tion hypothetically characteristic of lower intelligence could be the result of inefficient cognitive strategies (or lower motivation), and not be the cause of lower intelligence. According to this scenario, proper education or training could change the observed patterns of brain function.

FURTHER READING

Unfortunately, there are no introductions to the psychophysiology of intelligence written for the interested lay reader. The books by Fancher (1985) and Gould (1981) are accessible accounts of the early history of intelligence research; they discuss some of the relevant views of pioneer researchers. Brody (1992) explains the theoretical and methodological arguments against psychophysiological measures, and Jensen and Sinha (1993) summarize the research on the correlations. Vernon (1993) contains review chapters (written at an advanced level) by a number of the leading figures in the field. The journal *Intelligence* publishes technical articles on this topic as well as on other areas of intelligence research.

BIBLIOGRAPHY

ANKNEY, C. D. (1992). Sex differences in relative brain size: The mismeasure of woman, too? *Intelligence, 16,* 329–336.

BARRETT, P. T., & EYSENCK, H. J. (1992). Brain-evoked potentials and intelligence: The Hendrickson paradigm. *Intelligence, 16,* 361–381.

BRODY, N. (1992). *Intelligence.* San Diego, CA: Academic Press.

FANCHER, R. E. (1985). *The intelligence men: Makers of the IQ controversy.* New York: W. W. Norton.

GOULD, S. J. (1981). *The mismeasure of man.* New York: W. W. Norton.

HAIER, R. J., SIEGEL, B., TANG, C., ABEL, L., & BUCHSBAUM, M. S. (1992). Intelligence and changes in regional cerebral glucose metabolic rate following learning. *Intelligence, 16,* 415–426.

HENDRICKSON, D. E. (1982). The biological basis of intelligence: Part I. Theory. In H. J. Eysenck (Ed.), *A model for intelligence.* Berlin: Springer-Verlag.

HILLYARD, S. A., & PICTON, T. W. (1987). Electrophysiology of cognition. In V. B. Mouncastle (Ed.), *Handbook of phys-*

iology: Sec. 1. The nervous system: Vol. 5. Higher functions of the brain. Bethesda, MD: American Physiological Society.

JENSEN, A. R., & SINHA, S. N. (1993). Physical correlates of human intelligence. In P. A. Vernon (Ed.), *Biological approaches to the study of human intelligence.* Norwood, NJ: Ablex.

McGARRY-ROBERTS, P. A., STELMACK, R. M., & CAMPBELL, K. B. (1992). Intelligence, reaction time, and event-related potential. *Intelligence, 16,* 289–313.

REED, T. E., & JENSEN, A. R. (1991). Arm-nerve conduction velocity (NCV), brain NCV, reaction time, and intelligence. *Intelligence, 15,* 33–47.

VERNON, P. A. (1990). The use of biological measures to estimate behavioral intelligence. *Educational Psychologist, 25,* 293–304.

VERNON, P. A. (ED.). (1993). Biological approaches to the study of human intelligence. Norwood, NJ: Ablex.

VERNON, P. A., & MORI, M. (1989). Intelligence, reaction times, and nerve conduction velocity. *Behavior Genetics* (abstracts), *19,* 779.

VERNON, P. A., & MORI, M. (1992). Intelligence, reaction times, and peripheral nerve conduction velocity. *Intelligence, 16,* 273–288.

WILLERMAN, L., SCHULTZ, R., RUTLEDGE, J. N., & BIGLER, E. D. (1989). Hemisphere size asymmetry predicts relative verbal and nonverbal intelligence differently in the sexes: An MRI study of structure-function relations. *Intelligence, 16,* 315–328.

JOHN KOUNIOS

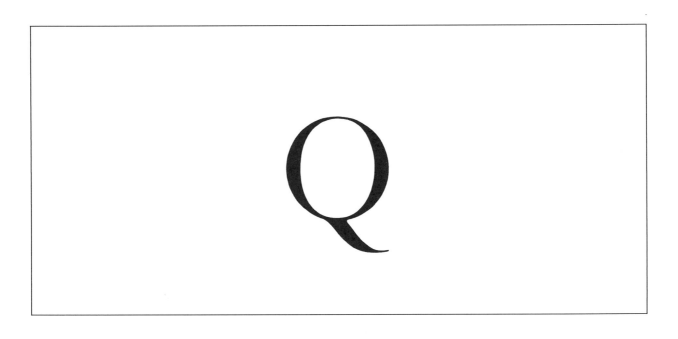

QUICK MEASURES OF INTELLIGENCE

Educators, psychologists, employment officers, and other professionals frequently need to obtain intelligence estimates with minimal investment in testing time. Several options are available to meet such a need, depending on the setting and the use to be made of the test results.

Intelligence tests originated as measures designed for administration to one individual at a time, hence, the use of the descriptive term *individual tests* to describe such measures. With individual tests the development of short versions, or forms, can be observed most directly because of the rather lengthy administration time required—usually 60 to 90 minutes.

Group-administered intelligence tests, the other major class of intelligence measures, originated as a way to capture the benefits of an individual test in a group-administered format (Robertson, 1972). With group tests, administration time per individual is no longer a limiting factor as it is with individual tests; hence, there is little point in developing short versions of group tests. Instead, group tests were by their very nature abbreviated adaptations of individual tests and were influenced more by the conditions embedded within a particular setting or application, such as the length of class periods in schools or the time available for assessing employment applicants. Factors such as these shaped the design of the original test, and multiple versions, or short forms, of a single parent test

did not become a distinguishing characteristic of group tests.

The major focus of this article is on the development of short forms of individual tests, although some group test applications are also considered.

INDIVIDUAL TESTS

Intelligence testing was introduced in the United States in 1916 with the publication of the STANFORD-BINET INTELLIGENCE SCALE. Developed by Stanford University psychologist Lewis TERMAN and his colleagues, the Stanford-Binet was an adaptation of the Binet-Simon tests developed in France to identify retarded school children (Anastasi, 1988, p. 7). The 1937 revision of the Stanford-Binet contained an abbreviated, or short, version that resulted in a savings in administration time of about one-third that required for the complete test. In this instance, the items comprising the short form are a subset of the items in the full test and are said to be "embedded" within the complete test. This section describes the two main types of abbreviated test forms: embedded short forms and free-standing short forms. The latter are short intelligence tests developed from the outset as stand-alone measures; they are in no way part of a longer parent test.

Embedded Short Forms. Two different approaches have been used to develop embedded short forms. One approach attempts to duplicate the content of the longer parent test with fewer items. The 1937 revision of the Stanford-Binet illustrates this way to build a short form. Tests selected for the Stanford-Binet short form were chosen carefully so that they would be representative of the entire scale in terms of their content, level of difficulty, interest to examinees, balance to minimize gender differences, and their statistical relationship (correlation) with total test score. As expected, the resulting short form showed a high relationship to intelligence quotients (IQs) derived from the full scale, although Terman and M. Merrill recommended giving the complete test if at all possible (Terman and Merrill, 1937, pp. 31–32).

A second way to obtain short forms is best illustrated by the WECHSLER SCALES: the Wechsler Preschool and Primary Scale of Intelligence (WPPSI and WPPSI–R); the three editions of the Wechsler Intelligence Scale for Children (WISC, WISC–R, and WISC III); and the original and revised Wechsler Adult Intelligence Scale (WAIS and WAIS–R) in which the content is arranged by eleven subtests grouped into two scales—verbal and performance. A number of short forms of the Wechsler tests have been developed by selecting various combinations of subtests. A. Kaufman (1972, 1976) cites four criteria that proved useful in constructing Wechsler short forms; he recommends selecting four of the eleven subtests—two from the verbal scale and two from the performance scale—that (1) relate highly statistically to (correlate with) results on their own respective scales (Verbal or Performance); (2) measure several mental processes; (3) can be administered and scored quickly; and (4) form an interesting clinical unit (Kaufman, 1990, p. 131). C. Reynolds and colleagues (1983) constructed a four-subtest short form requiring an administration time of about 25 to 30 minutes following Kaufman's guidelines, with apparently excellent results as judged by both test RELIABILITY and VALIDITY data (Kaufman, 1990, pp. 132–133).

Kaufman summarizes the development of WISC–R and WAIS–R short forms using various combinations of two, three, and four subtests as well as "split-half" procedures, which use combinations of odd- or even-numbered items from all WISC–R or WAIS–R subtests (Kaufman, 1979, p. 137; 1990, pp. 127–141). One particular shortcoming mentioned by Kaufman (1990, p. 127) is the dearth of research using the

short-form subtests by themselves. Normative data used to interpret performance on the short forms are based on the various Wechsler standardization samples where the subtests were embedded within the complete test and, hence, were administered in their naturally occurring order in the standardization testing. Short-form norms thus reflect any subtest order effects occurring as a result of their being administered in their naturally occurring order in the complete test; such effects as fatigue, concentration, motivation, and practice may differ when only two, three, or four subtests are extracted for a short form as opposed to their administration in the complete form consisting of eleven subtests. Such effects, in turn, affect the IQ estimates obtained from short forms. Research conducted by Thompson (as summarized in Kaufman, 1990, pp. 130–131) suggests that there is an order bias in short-form IQ estimates because of the factors mentioned previously. Such effects were especially marked with two subtest short-form combinations and resulted in overestimates of IQs (compared with the complete test) when these two-subtest combinations were used; such effects were not present, however, when a four-subtest combination developed by A. Silverstein (1982) was studied.

Results from these studies and others have led Kaufman to advocate the use of short forms primarily in two situations: (1) screening individuals for more thorough evaluations, and (2) in research studies where precise individual intelligence estimates are not required. Jerome Sattler (1988) agrees that the major use of short forms is in screening applications of various types. Kaufman recommends that short forms *not* be used for (1) categorizing the level of individual functioning, for example, retarded or gifted; (2) making inferences from a profile of test scores; and (3) diagnosing cognitive disorders (1990, p. 127).

Stand-Alone Short Forms. Short individual tests that are not part of longer batteries such as those described above have also been developed to provide intelligence estimates. Although these brief tests are, strictly speaking, not short forms of longer parent tests, they are used in place of the longer batteries; hence, this class of measures is another variety of "short form."

Major advantages of such tests are their brief administration time and the fact that their norms, unlike those for the embedded short forms described above, were obtained under the same conditions as those under which the tests are typically used. Although the order effects described previously for embedded short forms are no longer operative for stand-alone short forms, the utility of stand-alone norms does depend on the care with which the individuals comprising the norming sample were selected and may or may not be comparable to the quality of short forms embedded in longer, carefully normed batteries.

Some of the more widely used stand-alone short forms are described briefly in the following section to acquaint readers with the types of measures available. Three measures—the Slosson Intelligence Test (SIT), the Kaufman Brief Intelligence Test (K-BIT), and the Shipley-Hartford Institute for Living Scale (Shipley-Hartford)—provide broad, global estimates of general intelligence. The Test of Nonverbal Intelligence (TONI), the Peabody Picture Vocabulary Test (PPVT), and the RAVENS PROGRESSIVE MATRICES provide estimates of intellectual functioning within narrower ability domains than SIT, K-BIT, or the Shipley-Hartford. Both TONI and the Raven Matrices provide measures of abstract figural reasoning relatively free from the use of language either in presenting the test items or in responding to them; hence, they are termed *nonverbal measures* and are often used in situations where language facility may bias the results from verbal tests. The PPVT, on the other hand, yields an estimate of verbal intelligence that requires only a pointing response and thus renders it useful in certain special assessment applications.

All six tests cited require considerably less administration time than the complete Wechsler scales, Stanford-Binet, KAUFMAN ASSESSMENT BATTERY FOR CHILDREN (KABC), the Kaufman Adolescent and Adult Intelligence Scale (KAIT) and the WOODCOCK-JOHNSON TESTS OF COGNITIVE ABILITY. Caution must be exercised in the use of these stand-alone short forms because there is considerable variability in their technical quality, and their utility must be judged, in part, against their statistical relationship to the standard batteries mentioned above, all of which are tests for which the brief measures are frequently used as substitutes or supplements when conditions warrant the administration of a short form. Brief measures such as those cited here can never entirely replace the use of the longer standard batteries when in-depth assessment of intelligence is needed.

GROUP TESTS

Group administered intelligence tests have not spawned the development of short forms. This difference can be attributed to the evolution of group tests from individual tests and to the fact that the practical requirements of a situation such as the length of a class period or amount of time available for pre-employment screening shaped group tests from the outset. Group intelligence tests for use in schools gave rise, in turn, to shorter tests for use in business and industry.

An early series of group intelligence tests was developed by Arthur S. Otis, a student of Lewis Terman who developed the Stanford-Binet exam. Otis's objective in developing his group test was that of duplicating the Binet insofar as possible in paper-and-pencil format and making it suitable for group administration. Otis was a particularly ingenious developer of test item formats, and he demonstrated the feasibility of group administration with his contributions to the original Army Alpha Test and in 1918 with the publication of the Otis Group Intelligence Scale. The latter made group intelligence testing a reality in schools. Otis developed a shorter, more streamlined version with improvements in administration and scoring for use in employment settings (Otis Employment Test) and, with the publication of the Otis Quick-Scoring Mental Ability Tests in 1937, he developed a primary test (Alpha test) for which he subsequently published a short form in the 1950s.

An earlier instance of group test short form development occurred when the California Short-Form Test of Mental Maturity, a single-class-period edition of the parent test, the California Test of Mental Maturity (CTMM), was released in 1938. The CTMM, like other early group tests such as the Otis test described above, was influenced by the content of the Stanford-Binet. Developed by Elizabeth T. Sullivan, Willis W. Clark, and Ernest W. Tiegs, the CTMM differed from the Otis tests in attempting to break down the Stanford-Binet items into psychological factors of intelligence. The CTMM Short Form met a practical need for a shorter version of the parent test. Both the Otis Alpha

Short Form and the CTMM Short Form required 30 to 40 minutes for administration and are thus longer than the "embedded" and "stand-alone" short forms of individual tests, which typically require 10 to 20 minutes of testing time.

Another setting for the use of group intelligence tests is in business and industry. The assessment of cognitive skills, also referred to as academic intelligence, provides important information useful in predicting success in various kinds of jobs (Anastasi, 1988, p. 458). Short forms of group tests originally developed for use in schools were modified for use in business and industry. The Otis Employment Test was one of the early entrants in this area. The Wonderlic Personnel Test was developed as a revision of one of the early Otis tests (the Otis Self-Administering Tests of Mental Ability) and has achieved widespread use (Anastasi, 1988, p. 459). Other examples of short intelligence tests are the Personnel Tests for Industry and the Wesman Personnel Classification Test. The brief tests discussed here require from 12 to 25 minutes to administer and can be scored easily and quickly, thus making them suitable for use in employment screening where time available for testing is limited. Caution must be exercised to avoid overinterpretation of these brief form test results.

(*See also:* GROUP TESTS; INDIVIDUAL TESTS.)

BIBLIOGRAPHY

ANASTASI, A. (1988). *Psychological testing.* New York: Macmillan.

KAUFMAN, A. S. (1979). *Intelligent testing with the WISC–R.* New York: Wiley.

KAUFMAN, A. S. (1990). *The psychology of adolescent and adult intelligence.* New York: Allyn & Bacon.

REYNOLDS, C. R., WILLSON, V. L., & CLARK, P. L. (1983). *Journal of Clinical Psychology, 5,* 111–116.

ROBERTSON, G. J. (1970). Innovation in the assessment of individual differences: Development of the first group mental ability test. *Test service notebook 30.* San Antonio, TX: The Psychological Corporation.

SATTLER, J. M. (1988). *Assessment of Children* (3rd ed.). San Diego, CA: Jerome M. Sattler.

SILVERSTEIN, A. B. (1982). Two- and four-subtest short forms of the Wechsler Adult Intelligence Scale–Revised. *Journal of Consulting and Clinical Psychology, 50,* 415–418.

SULLIVAN, E. T., CLARK, W. W., & TIEGS, E. W. (1957). *California Short-Form Test of Mental Maturity: Manual, elementary, 1957 S–Form.* Monterey, CA: CTB/McGraw-Hill.

TERMAN, L. M., & MERRILL, M. (1937). *Measuring intelligence.* Boston: Houghton-Mifflin.

GARY J. ROBERTSON

R

RACE   *See* ETHNICITY, RACE, AND MEASURED INTEL-
LIGENCE; RACE AND IQ SCORES.

RACE AND INTELLIGENCE   Studies of the relationship between intelligence and race have focused a great deal of attention on the identification of intellectual differences between African Americans and European Americans, colloquially referred to as blacks and whites. (Since the question of intelligence and race has been studied so often in the context of comparisons between blacks and whites, the discussion here uses these two groups as its focus.) The human variable under question has been that of the ability to adapt, learn, and reason, usually referred to as *intelligence*. The indicators of intelligence most often referred to are test scores generated from intelligence tests. The introduction of the construct of race has reflected the assumption that African Americans (blacks) and European Americans (whites) are biogenetically different groups of human beings. In efforts to explain the genesis of "racial" differences in intelligence, some investigators and propagandists have invoked the construct of heritability (see HERITABILITY).

The constructs of intelligence, race, and heritability have been foundational to the research of the question of "black/white intelligence." These basic constructs and the nature of intelligence testing require clarification. These constructs have been surrounded by am-

biguity and embedded with prior notions of race and associated intellectual superiority or inferiority. As a result, the continuing and controversial research efforts concerning the possible association between intelligence and race have been fraught with conceptual confusion and methodological errors, which have rendered problematic, if not precluded, the scientific discussion of relationships among intelligence, race, and heritability. Furthermore, they have fed the recurrent debates concerning the nature and quality of intelligence in African-American peoples in comparison with the intelligence of European-American peoples.

The question of intelligence and race in the context of comparisons between blacks and whites cannot be properly debated without the resolution of these continuing conceptual ambiguities and resultant methodological inadequacies. However, even if these problems are identified and corrected, the results of continued debate over the relative quality of intelligence in African Americans and the search for causal relationships between intelligence, biological race, and heritability probably would be neither useful nor constructive. If some of these problems are overcome, if problematic constructs are discarded, and if the nature of the questions is changed, it may be possible to discuss diversity in human intellect more productively. Research questions concerned with groups differences in intelligence then may be investigated and debated more appropriately as questions that concern the character, origins, and development of developed adaptive abilities in reliably identified subgroups of human beings.

INTELLIGENCE, RACE, AND HERITABILITY

The Construct of Intelligence. Since the assignment of persons to ethnic and racial groups usually has been based upon inexact social designations, very little is known concerning intelligence in reliably identified biological subgroups. However, there is considerable evidence that higher intellect as measured by traditional intelligence tests favors persons and groups holding higher status in the society (Kamin, 1974; Ogbu, 1983). Some of the most sophisticated analyses of the extant statistical data concern comparisons of test scores in high-status and low-status persons. It is legitimate to ask whether it is the natural intelligence of the group members or the status of the group that contributes to the quality of intelligence measured. Assumptions concerning the gene pool origins (races) of the groups studied are imposed upon these data. Thus, it is assumed that the results of these traditional analyses tend to favor a hypothesis of heritability as the determining factor in the association between the social divisions by which humans are grouped and the quality of developed intellectual function. Quite apart from the validity of some of these assumptions, it is useful to examine some of the issues concerning the construct of intelligence and the character of extant measures of intelligence.

In *Webster's New World Dictionary,* intelligence is defined as the "ability to learn or understand from experiences; the ability to acquire and retain knowledge; [and] mental ability . . . the ability to respond quickly and successfully to a new situation, the use of faculty of reason in solving problems." When Cole and colleagues (1971) concluded that all groups of human beings appear to represent in their developed abilities a wide range of intellectual competencies, they were, no doubt, thinking of intelligence as the capacity to adapt to one's environment, and to use past adaptational experiences in response to similar as well as novel environmental encounters. The origins of the word *intelligence* speak to a narrow, more fixed, idea of intelligence than used by Cole and colleagues. The word *intelligence* can be traced to the Latin *intelligere,*

which means to select, and particularly, to select the good grain from the bad. It follows that researchers and developers of standardized intelligence tests have given preference to the subject's ability to select or distill, a practice that has led to the establishment of a hierarchy for behavioral adaptabilities that gives an advantage to these abilities. It is interesting that the Latin derivation is also reflected in the use of the tests for the selection and prediction of successful individuals. Since the features of human adaptation that have been selected are favored in many advanced technological enterprises, these same features have been reinforced and rarefied, as if they were the sole or most important aspects of intellectual function. Anastasi (1971), Brown and Burton (1975), Gardner (1983), Glaser (1977), Resnick (1976), Sternberg (1986), and others have contributed to much broader conceptions of intelligence. They have also contributed to an awareness of (1) the importance of context for the expression of intelligence, and (2) the restrictive and overly selective nature of extant standardized tests of intelligence.

Attention to possible differences in the potentials of persons and contexts for revealing quality of intellect distinguishes the "splitters'" conceptions of intelligence from the "lumpers'" (Mayr, 1982). Weinberg (1989) refers to Mayr's "lumpers and splitters" and identifies the lumpers with the notion of intelligence as a "general unified capacity for acquiring knowledge, reasoning, and solving problems that is demonstrated in different ways (navigating a course without a compass, memorizing the Koran, or programming a computer)." Even though Weinberg introduces some possible recognition of the diversity in expressions of intelligence in his reference to "different ways," the lumperians' approach to intelligence is basically a narrow one. Not only does intelligence refer to an overall summative ability but this ability is referred to as being manifested in universalist conceptions of intellectual function, that is, those aspects of intellectual function that are privileged in advanced technological cultures and are assumed to apply universally. Abstract reasoning and decontextualized recall are examples. By contrast, the splitters seek to isolate (at least for the purpose of study) different types of intellectual ability. Howard Gardner (1983), for example, has called attention to linguistic, bodily-kinesthetic, and five other specific intelligences, some of which would benefit from different contexts for their optimal expression and assessment. The lumpers' general conception of intelligence privileges communicentric or common indicators of ability, and the splitters' view favors more heterogenous indicators. Thus, the tenuous and protean character of the intelligence construct contributes to some of the confusion concerning the use of the construct of intelligence when it is studied in people whose life experiences differ.

Modern psychological theories of learning and cognition bring us closer to understanding intelligence as a complex phenomenon—a composite of developing aptitudes, abilities, dispositions, and achievements. Intelligence is referred to as a complex phenomenon that results from a combination of factors (Glaser, 1977); that is multi-componential (Sternberg, 1985); that develops in response to stimulation from experiential encounters (Hunt, 1961); and that is modifiable (Bruner, 1966; Sternberg, 1986). These complex developed abilities are expressed through behaviors that are defined socially and culturally, and often are weighted subjectively to reflect the hegemonic culture (see Gordon, 1983).

How intelligent behavior is perceived and specific potentials for adaptation are valued vary from individual to individual and in different contexts. An individual may display intelligence in a way that is congruent with or different from the way that is traditionally honored in his or her culture. When the display is incongruent with the hegemonic culture, it is assumed generally and often faultily that this is indicative of intellectual deficit, since the individual appears not to have learned in the same way as others. Recent work in behavioral individuality indicates that such assumptions may be erroneous in making judgments concerning individuals and groups (Bronfenbrenner, 1979; Shipman & Shipman, 1988; Thomas, 1988). When the same thinking is applied to diverse groups, the error is even more obvious; it is unreasonable to assume that groups whose experiences differ should be expected to have had similar learning opportunities or to have responded in similar ways. Further, it is a mistake to assume that the absence of a specific pattern of developed ability called for by the test reflects an inability to make other adaptations (Gordon & Rubain, 1980). Even in the presence of undeveloped abilities, there is evidence that the quality of intellective behavior can

be altered through the combined force of environmental change and the plasticity of developing human intellect.

Not only is intelligence as a human function quite diverse in its manifestations, the human beings who express this construct are also diverse. While the social divisions into which people are grouped—race, class and gender—may have no primary role in influencing the quality of intelligence, the specific social division to which one belongs may be an important source of human variance in status and function. The specific functional characteristics of behavioral and conditional individuality are highly related to status and cultural experience (Gordon, 1983). It is these characteristics of behavioral and conditional individuality that make for the developmentally relevant dimensions of human diversity, because they influence the ways in which persons express their intellect and often the conditions under which intellect is called into use. Yet it is the fact of conditional and behavioral individuality and diversity that normative and standardized approaches to assessment ignore and, in large measure, are designed to avoid. For example, test items are selected with a view to their capacity to tap stable functions, that is, those functions less likely to be influenced by situational and personal variability. The items must be presented under standard and uniform conditions that are insensitive to differential response tendencies. These processes of engagement, differential response, situational variance, and behavioral individuality are coming to be regarded as important determinants of the character and quality of task engagement, energy deployment, and, ultimately, intellectual performance.

When scientists turn to evaluative judgments concerning the quality of developed abilities in different groups of human beings, these variations in the manner, level, and context of expression must be factored into the equation (Cole et al., 1971) if valid estimates are to result. It does not matter whether investigators focus on practical problem solving, logical reasoning, abstract symbolization, or social reasoning: If their criteria are drawn too narrowly, evaluative judgment with reference to any one or all of these categories of intellectual function is likely to be flawed. This appears to be a common problem in prevailing notions of human intelligence. Traditionally, psychological research on intelligence and on differences in intellectual function has utilized a unitary notion of intelligence and a hegemonic cultural context for assigning value to its expressions, so that these dynamic components and contexts of intellectual function are all but ignored.

The measurement of intelligence through IQ testing is the most prevalent practice by which intellectual ability is assessed. The data from these tests are often interpreted as reflections of basic or innate intelligence. However, the IQ is not a measure of innate intelligence. The IQ is better thought of as an indicator of developed ability (Anastasi, 1971). The level of intellectual function as derived from the test data is actually based upon inference. The judgment of level is an inference based upon the assumption that the abilities of the person being tested have been sampled adequately and that a comparable quality of function would be demonstrated if the universe of the testee's repertoire was available for measurement. Specialists in mental measurement do not have techniques for determining the basic intellective capacities of human beings or for directly measuring what is commonly referred to as innate intelligence. What is measured in tests of intelligence is the product of the organism's response to specific probes presented under specific circumstances and in specific contexts. Typically, this is a small sample of the individual's total potential output, often elicited in contexts that are unlike the individual's preferred conditions for optimal performance. There is no question that many of the probes tap functions that are prerequisite to a large number of successful adaptations in advanced technological societies, but it is not reasonable to assume that these probes appropriately reflect the adaptive abilities of persons living in diverse conditions and contexts (Gordon, 1974). Traditional tests and quantitative scores of mental age and IQ have been useful tools in predicting and planning for academic and some work experience. There is no question but that intelligence testing, and psychological testing in general, are extremely important and significant developments in the sciences of human behavior. However, these tests and their use are not perfect and unbiased. They are certainly not adequate for the wide variety of purposes to which they have been applied.

Standardized tests have not contributed to the definitive description of the intellectual functioning of individuals in part because they have ignored the variety of ways in which the abilities to adapt and learn are manifested, as well as the variety in the nature and complexity of the contexts and situations in which adaptation is expressed. All constellations of human characteristics are not equally adaptive for all environmental circumstances. So when a particular set of environmental conditions is taken as the norm against which the potential for meeting adaptive demands is judged, subjects do arrange themselves hierarchically in relation to such demands; thus the traditional purposes for which these tests were designed are served reasonably well. It follows that standardized IQ test data have been used in much of the debate concerning the intelligence of African Americans. However, the limitations of these tests as adequate and comprehensive measures of human intelligence in all its variation contribute to the confusion rather than to the clearer understanding of the issues concerning intelligence and race.

The Construct of Race. Many scholars have debated definitions of race; however, there has been some consensus as to what the construct refers to. Almost all contemporary definitions of race include some reference to the physical characteristics of the persons referenced. *Webster's New World Dictionary* defines race as "any of the different varieties of mankind distinguished by form of hair, color of skin and eyes, stature, [and] bodily proportions." Most modern anthropologists recognize three primary human groups, the so-called races: Caucasoid, Mongoloid, and Negroid. Within each of these major human divisions, various subdivisions (sometimes incorrectly called races) are recognized. Biologists are inclined to use race to refer to a population that differs from others in the relative frequency of some gene or gene pool patterns. Many scholars, including biologists, disagree not only on the definition of race but also on the existence, meaningfulness, validity, and reliability of the construct and its use. Shuey (1966) and Fried (1968) assert that geographic and typological divisions have been used to categorize humanity into discrete racial groups, but rarely, if ever, has a truly scientific notion of race been made explicit, defined, or employed. Furthermore, scientists have neither isolated gene pool patterns that are specific to specified subpopulations (races, so called) nor determined the factors responsible for race-specific morphological evolutions.

Meaningful classifications of individuals are made even more difficult because of the social and political nature of race designations. According to Fried (1968), individuals are both self- and other-identified and may be assigned to different races by different individuals and in different contexts. Thus self-identification and identification by others may vary from situation to situation and can be in error or simply misrepresented. Some researchers would like to think they have controlled for such factors, but "correct racial typing becomes more and more difficult and demands full-scale attempts to control the genealogical histories of all subjects" (Fried, 1968, p. 128). However, efforts to control genealogical histories are fraught with unresolved problems and have been ill-conceived. For example, in several of the southern states of the United States, effort has been directed at the assignment of race based upon the percent of Negro "blood" or heritage discernible in persons. The criterion has varied from 1/1 to 1/64 "black blood," but the use of this criterion has often been influenced by public records, collective memory, or by inspection of physiognomy. Naturally, effort at detecting proportions of blood attributable to one or the other race was not itself informative. Hence, even when investigators are aware of the problems of classification by race and try to deal with these problems, precise and valid classifications are difficult and seldom if ever achieved.

The problem of achieving reliably identifiable biological subgroups of human beings is intractable. Anthony Appiah (1992, p. 35) reminds us that relatively few physical traits are unique to "racial" groups. As an example, he has called attention to the fact that apart from the visible morphological characteristics by which broad racial assignments have been made, there are "few genetic characteristics to be found in the population of England that are not found in similar proportions in Zaire or China, and few too (though more) that are found in Zaire but not in similar proportions in China and England." Glass and Li (1953), Hiernaux (1975), and Maurant (1983) have called attention to the heterogeneous genetic characteristics of the so-called races. Lewontin (1973) and Rose and Kamin (1984) suggest that the differences within so-

called races are more significant than the differences between such groups. Nonetheless, race designations and membership have been arbitrarily and artificially assigned to individuals based almost solely on a few physical differences such as skin color, hair curl, and eye-fold, which are probably only small morphological adaptations to different physical environments. Individuals are assigned race according to social perceptions and for social purposes. Consequently, the colloquial designation of a group as a race is clearly not a function of significant biological or genetic differences, but is perhaps more importantly a function of society's perception that differences exist and are thought to be important.

A related criticism of the use of the construct of race is its imprecise application in approaches to the classification of humans. Specifically, race is often used as if this social division were synonymous with ethnicity and culture. The constructs of race, ethnicity, and culture are not synonymous, although they cannot be defined using mutually exclusive language. The term *culture* has a variety of definitions; however, the term is most often used to refer to knowledge, belief systems, art, morals, laws, customs, techniques and any other capabilities and habits acquired as a member of a social group. Culture may be said to consist of judgmental, or normative; cognitive; affective; skill, or technique; and technological dimensions. Culture is both the product of human action and the determinant of much of the behavior that is human. Ethnicity is used to refer to one's belonging to and identification with a group that is characterized by shared attributes, such as cultural traditions, belief systems, languages, physical characteristics, and sometimes genetic history. Ethnicity does not reference biological race, but is sometimes used to refer to a group that shares a common gene pool as well as a common culture. Ethnicity may be inherited, assigned, or assumed (Gordon, 1983). The constructs of culture and ethnicity are related to the construct of race, but they are distinct from race as indicators of social division and of group or personal identity.

The frequent use of the race construct instead of culture or ethnicity, when the dimensions being referred to or described might be identified more accurately as ethnicity and culture, is problematic. When race is used in this nonspecific way in behavior-genetic research, it is not used as "a positive analytic tool" (Harrington, 1975, p. 7). This use of the construct of race precludes appropriate analysis by obscuring the fact that it incorrectly refers to traits that are not biological as if they are biological. As we have indicated, race is used as a reference to biological substrata of humanity, while culture and ethnicity are more frequently understood to refer to social substrata, which reflect acquired attitudes, manners, and meanings of behavior. Unlike race, culture and ethnicity are more likely to refer to these differences in behavioral functions, that is, the "hows and whys" of the ways in which persons and groups live their lives. The preoccupation with alleged "racial properties" obscures the differential importance of the status and functional dimensions of culture and ethnicity. "'Subtle differences' of temperament, belief, and intention" are biologized when race is used in ways which assume a correlation between "'gross differences' of morphology" and culture (Appiah, 1992, p. 45). This is indicative of an important distortion, for there is little evidence that cultural differences, which may affect people and their expressions of intelligence most deeply, are biologically determined or morphologically indicated (Appiah, 1992).

The consistent lack of precision in the use of the construct of race, and related misconceptions have been crucial, contributing elements to the continuing debates and distortions concerning the nature and quality of our knowledge of the intelligence of African Americans in particular and "black" peoples in general. Given only knowledge of an individual's assigned race, one cannot make a detailed statement about the individual's genetic makeup, biology, morphology, or for that matter intellectual strengths and weaknesses. Given that assignment practices are not usually made explicit and, moreover, that individuals defy prototypic and clear racial assignments, rigorous methodological control is absent. When rigorous methodological control is absent, there is even less reason to assume that race as assigned from the identification of a few physical traits should indicate innate intellectual capacities. Seligmann (1939, p. 53) cites E. A. Hooten's (1931) assertion that no anthropologist or anatomist believes that there is any relationship between the form of individual features of the face and the character or abilities of the owner. It cannot be assumed that a particular physical trait or set of physical differences is any more indicative of intellectual inheritance than any other. Race as a biological characteristic may have some relationship to intelligence, but there is as yet little knowledge of the mechanisms by which intellect and race are associated. Instead there are many distorted interpretations of the statistical inferences that are usually drawn.

The Heritability of Intelligence. In the prevailing questions around intelligence and race, issues of heritability are colloquially raised as an extension of the nature to nurture debate. Although biological rather than sociocultural characteristics should be referred to when heritability is in question, heritability is often used to refer to phenomena that are probably biosocial in character and origin. In the nature–nurture debate, the nature view is a projective one that centers on the notion that certain characteristics are appropriately thought of as genetically established and bound. The nurture view is a reflectional and interactive view that focuses on the notion that all patterned behaviors are reflections of the interaction between what are the innate "givens" of an organism and its environmental encounters. Environmental interactions, as well as temporal and situational phenomena, are thought of as crucial determinants and shapers of behavior. According to the interactionist view, behavior is not simply released by the environment; rather, it can be influenced and is always mediated by environments. The proponents of racial differences in natural intelligence (among them H. J. EYSENCK and Arthur JENSEN) have suggested that interaction variance contributes minimally to phenotypic variance in intelligence (see RACE AND IQ SCORES).

Heritability implies genetic transfer or the capacity of being genetically transmitted from parent to offspring. Thus a discussion of innate racial intellectual capacity must include a discussion of the nature of heritability and issues related to the genetic transfer of complex behaviors. If characteristics are composed of several traits, we run into the problem of assuming the heritability of organized patterns of behavior, as opposed to single components of a behavior, from parent to child. We also face the problem of identifying the genetic mechanisms by which single inherited traits come to be expressed in complex and protean behaviors such as intelligence. Furthermore, there are issues that relate to the consistency in the expression of complex behaviors in aggregates of people or organisms larger than family lines, if even then (Hirsch, 1968). It is problematic and scientifically questionable to argue, on the basis of differences in some physical traits, for an association between such traits and the existence of inherited and fixed differences in all or overall mental capacities in persons or groups. Many of these questions with respect to heritability may be unanswerable because no one has yet undertaken the definitive study of the nature and modifiability of genetic behavioral processes in human beings. In addition, the definitiveness with which gene pools can be specified does not lend itself to conclusive research on these questions. The technology of scientific research is not yet capable of identifying and isolating the causal genetic variables for race or the genetic mechanisms underlying an association between intelligence and race. Even if this were technically possible, it would remain unlikely that the investigations needed in pursuit of such research would be conducted, in part for reasons of ethics and in part for reasons of absent national will to support the necessary changes in environmental conditions.

If we are ever able to speak definitively about the portion of intellectual functions attributable to heredity, it will only be in reference to specific interactions or conditions. When we talk about intelligence, we are talking about behavioral manifestations of the organism, a phenotype; and phenotype, by definition, is a function of environmental interaction with genotype, which refers to the genetic potential of the organism. When we are able to separate genotype in human behavioral development, its function will be determinable only in relation to or as it is expressed through phenotype and in that relationship its function will be determinable only to the extent that the interaction (between genetic phenomena and environmental encounters) is specified (Gordon, 1969, p. 3).

Those who view the plasticity of human potential in selected populations as limited must also assume that the product of this interaction cannot be modified. This assumption repeatedly has been demonstrated to be false (Birch, 1968; Goldstein, 1969; Manning, 1983). In fact, recent developments in behavior-genetic research suggest that the characteristics of nature (genotype) make it even more important that the influences of nurture (environmental interactions) are understood (Hirsch, 1968; Plomin, 1989). Appropriate intervention and manipulation can make genetic and environmental interactions significant for specific ends despite specific genetic directionality. It is known that genetic influences on behavioral development are often significant and sometimes substantial, but paradoxically, the same evidence also supports the important role of the environment (Plomin, 1989, p. 105). Hirsch (1968) states that "high or low heritability tells us absolutely nothing about how a given individual might have developed under conditions different from those in which he or she actually did develop. Heritability provides no specific information about 'range of reaction'" (p. 20), which refers to the rather wide range of possibilities for the development and expression of a specific gene trait under different environmental conditions. As an example, there is strong support for the heritability of diabetes mellitus, but it is known that insulin is useful in the enablement of diabetic persons to lead normal lives. As another example, phenylketonuria, which is due to an abnormal autosomal recessive gene, seems to be highly related to impaired intellectual development. As many as 85 percent of the children with this disease have IQs under 50; nevertheless, with early diet control, children with this disease can grow up with IQs in the normal range (Goldstein, 1969, p. 9).

Genetic influences on behavior are multifactorial. The complex behaviors (such as intelligence) do not fit the deterministic model of a single-gene effect in which one gene operates independently of other genes or of environmental influences (Plomin, 1989). It is more likely that, for any complex behavior, many genes are involved, each with a small effect. Given this position, rather than seeking to explain the determinants of specific behaviors on the basis of correlational phenomena, and in causal terms, behavior geneticists are now encouraging the investigation of the interaction of specific environments with known genetic factors. They urge intervention in human development to make those interactions significant for specific ends.

By another line of argument, it is inferred that although several statistical analyses report correlations that support the assertion of heredity as an explanatory factor in individual differences in IQ, we cannot be certain of the causal variables when we speak of racial variations in IQ (Plomin, 1989). It is important to remember that behavior-genetic theory and methods address the probable genetic and environmental sources of differences among individuals with little to say about universals of development or about average differences between groups (Plomin, Defries, & Faulkner, 1988).

In conclusion, there is some research evidence and a considerable degree of logic to support the assertion that patterns of intellectual function differ within and across subgroups who share a high proportion of similar experiences, but none of these studies shows patterns to be invariant within subgroups, and none has distinguished patterns that are genetically determined from those that are genetically influenced, or from those that are simply culturally influenced. In addition, this work has not tackled the equally important question of how genetic phenomena or environmental encounters come to be represented in the physiology of the brain, to result in intellectual behaviors or in the ability to learn.

INTELLIGENCE AND RACE: A RECONCEPTUALIZATION OF THE ISSUES

Several problems are crucial to an understanding of questions concerning the relationship between intelligence and race, and to genetic explanations of the variance in IQ scores between blacks and whites, among them: (1) the use of too narrow conceptions of intelligence, resulting in testing for a limited range of intellectual functions; (2) the confusion of biological race with ethnic group labels or social and colloquial conceptions of race; and (3) the use of questionable or problematic assumptions with respect to the nature of heritability.

Despite all of the ambiguities surrounding the constructs of intelligence, race, and heritability, extant research has produced considerable data that reveal some consistent trends suggesting possible relationships between intelligence and groups classified as ra-

cial. These data show that, in the aggregate, people who are classified as African American tend to score about one standard deviation lower on tests of intelligence than do people classified as European American. When black and white groups are matched for education, socioeconomic status (SES), and residence, differences in intelligence test scores are only slightly reduced. Comparisons of the test scores of middle-class blacks with the scores of lower-class whites reveal little difference between the mean scores of these two groups (Eysenck, 1971; Jensen, 1969). It has been asserted that when support for intellectual development, and certain intergenerational factors are controlled for, differences in IQ test scores of blacks and whites are reduced (Mercer, 1973), but the weight of the evidence supports the conclusion that blacks consistently score lower than whites.

Several explanations of the variance in black/white mean scores on tests of intelligence have been offered. Among these are: (1) biological explanations; (2) political-economic explanations; and (3) sociocultural explanations. Explanations that are biological in nature have included heritability, genetic pruning, health and nutritional status, and developmental dysfunction. Explanations of a political economic nature range from the impact of poverty and resource deprivation on the opportunity to learn, to the contributions that such experiences make to learned helplessness and a sense of powerlessness. Social and cultural explanations address such issues as educational and social disadvantagement, cultural differences and dissonance, the character and quality of supports for development, alienation and isolation from the main stream, issues of expectation and perceived opportunity/rewards, incongruity between subgroup and dominant group purposes, and conflicts between the values of human service institutions and the persons served.

Strictly biological explanations of group differences in intelligence must be interpreted with caution since they are based upon our limited ability to identify reliably biological (racial) reference groups and to assign subjects appropriately. This caution should not be interpreted to reflect a lack of respect for the importance of biological phenomena as determinants of the quality of intellective function in individuals or groups. When and if we are able reliably to identify groups of human beings who are known to share identical gene pools, it is entirely possible that those group members, who also share similar environments and social conditions, will show such similarities in intellectual function as to support the heritability hypothesis. Obviously, biological factors and their heritability are important contributors to one's potential intellectual development. Biological factors may even be partial determinants of potential intellectual development in reliably identifiable biological groups (races), but the facts and the mechanisms of such genetic determination have yet to be established scientifically. The best of the work on this issue relies on weak correlations as the basis for the inference that heritable traits are the cause of difference in intelligence in socially identified "racial" groups (Hirsch, 1968).

Research directed at the understanding of possible relationships between biological race and intelligence will continue to be problematic as long as investigators assign race by social inspection. It is common practice for the construct of race to be used to refer to both biological and social phenomena. In addition, the biological and social referents have been used interchangeably, resulting in the imprecise use of the construct. Race, for example, is used to refer both to human social divisions and to human biological subgroups. However, races as biological subgroups have neither been reliably identified nor definitively defined. Furthermore, the existence of races that have sufficiently dissimilar gene pools to qualify as unique biological subgroups has yet to be established. Laypersons' perceptions, assumptions, and biases have been used rather than biological, scientific classifications of humans. Thus, colloquially accepted social divisions (ethnic and racial categories) have been misused routinely to suggest that reliably identifiable biological subgroups have been identified.

The treatment of race as a biological phenomenon that causes or limits certain patterns of intellective behavior necessitates that the existence of biological subgroups of humanity be established and that these groups be significantly dissimilar and reliably identifiable. Additionally, if heritability is to be inferred, the genetic criteria that constitute such groups must be clear. For example, it is a common practice to draw "racial" comparisons between "blacks" and "whites." Those genetic criteria which are thought racially to differentiate members of the Caucasian race (whites)

from the Negro race (blacks) require explicit and valid definition. However, such definitions are not available. As a consequence, sound research on the relationships between intelligence, heritability, and race and the appropriate interpretation of this research have been precluded. No degree of sophistication in research design or eloquence of statistical analysis is sufficient to overcome such problems. Such efforts are prime examples of D. O. HEBB's (1975) admonition against the application of more and more eloquent methodologies and statistical analyses to answer questions that were not worth raising in the first place.

Given that such questions have been raised, to address properly questions of the relationship between intelligence, race, and heritability, more appropriate issues must be investigated, in ways that avoid prior assumptions of racial superiority or inferiority or biological, race-based quality of intellect. Again, however, caution is to be exercised in the search for genetic causation of phenotypic phenomena, since phenotype (the expression of a characteristic) is always the result of environmental interactions with genotype (the actual genetic material). Thus the actual manifestations of intelligence must always be assumed to have been influenced by the interaction between at least these two causal factors.

Problems of this order may require that the issues concerning intelligence and race be reconceptualized. What is essential to the understanding of the relationship between intelligence and race is more and better knowledge concerning the nature and manifestations of adaptive behavior (intelligence) within reliably identified biological subgroups. Call these races if we must, but the research question has to do with the context, nature, and quality of adaptive behavior in persons whose biosocial characteristics differ. Two problems are embedded here. First, scientific criteria must be established for the reliable identification and classification of specific biological subgroup members. Second, serious effort will need to be directed at the comprehensive intragroup analysis of adaptive behaviors in these biological subgroups. Further, if broader and more inclusive conceptions of intelligence are respected, the development of techniques for the more comprehensive and authentic assessment of developed abilities is indicated. If it is necessary to make comparative judgments concerning the quality of developed abilities across biological subgroups, and differences between these subgroups, attention will need to be given to the identification of common and idiosyncratic manifestations of intelligence within and across these biological subgroups. This kind of work will require that attention be given to the contextual analysis of repertories of adaptive responses (see Cole et al., 1971; Gordon, 1971; Haeussermann, 1958). As these more qualitative analyses of the specific components of intellective behavior become available, it may then be possible to associate selected components of intellective behavior with identifiable biological subgroups. In the absence of this kind of conceptual work, efforts at the association of quality of intelligence with specific groups classified by race are likely to be misleading, and to contribute more to political ends than to the production of scientific knowledge.

(*See also:* MULTIPLE INTELLIGENCES THEORY; TRIARCHIC THEORY OF HUMAN INTELLIGENCE.)

BIBLIOGRAPHY

ANASTASI, A. (1971). More on heritability: Addendum to the Hebb and Jensen interchange. *American Psychologist, 26,* 1036–1037.

APPIAH, A. K. (1992). *In my father's house: Africa in the philosophy of culture.* Oxford: Oxford University Press.

BIRCH, H. (1968). Boldness and judgement in behavior genetics. In M. Mead, T. Dobzhansky, E. Tobach, & R. E. Light (Eds.), *Science and the concept of race.* New York: Columbia University Press.

BRONFRENBRENNER, U. (1979). *The ecology of human development.* Cambridge: Harvard University Press.

BROWN, J. S., & BURTON, R. (1975). Multiple representations of knowledge for tutorial reasoning. In D. Bobrow & A. Collins (Eds.), *Representations and understanding studies in cognitive science.* New York: Academic Press.

BRUNER, J. (1966). *Toward a theory of instruction.* Cambridge, MA: Belknap Press of Harvard University.

COLE, M., GAY, J., GLICK, G., & SHARP, D. (1971). *Cultural context of learning and thinking.* New York: Basic Books.

EYSENCK, H. J. (1971). *Race, intelligence, and education.* London: Temple Smith.

FRIED, M. H. (1968). The need to end the pseudoscientific investigation of race. In M. Mead, T. Dobzhansky, E. To-

bach, & R. E. Light (Eds.), *Science and the concept of race.* New York: Columbia University Press.

GARDNER, H. (1983). *Frames of mind: The theory of multiple intelligences.* New York: Basic Books.

GLASER, R. (1977). On intelligence and aptitudes. In A. J. Nitko (Ed.), *Exploring alternatives to current standardized tests: Proceedings of the 1976 National Testing Conference.* Pittsburgh: University of Pittsburgh, School of Education.

GLASS, B., & LI, C. C. (1953). The dynamics of racial intermixture: An analysis based on the American Negro. *American Journal of Human Genetics, 5,* 1–20.

GOLDSTEIN, A. C. (1969, Fall). A flaw in Jensen's use of heritability data. In *Bulletin of the Information Retrieval Center of the Disadvantaged V(4),* 7–9, 20.

GORDON, E. W. (1969, Fall). Education, ethnicity, genetics, and intelligence—Jensenism: Another excuse for failure to educate. In *Bulletin of the Information Retrieval Center for the Disadvantaged V(4)* 1, 10–15.

GORDON, E. W. (1971). Methodological problems and pseudoissues in the nature-nurture controversy. In R. Cancro (Ed.), *Intelligence: Genetic and environmental influences.* New York: Grune and Stratton.

GORDON, E. W. (1974). An affluent society's excuses for inequality: Developmental, economic, and educational. *Journal of Orthopsychiatry 44(1),* 4–18.

GORDON, E. W. (1983). Culture and ethnicity: Implications for development and Intervention. In M. D. Levine, W. B. Carey, A. C. Carey, & R. T. Cross (Eds.), *A textbook of behavioral and developmental pediatrics.* Philadelphia: W. B. Saunders.

GORDON, E. W., & RUBAIN, T. J. (1980). Bias and alternatives in psychological testing. *Journal of Negro Education 49,* 3, 350–360.

HAEUSSERMANN, E. (1958). *Developmental potential of preschool children.* New York: Grune and Stratton.

HARRINGTON, C. (1975, Fall). Ethnicity and schooling. In *Bulletin of the Information Retrieval Center of the Disadvantaged X(4).*

HEBB, D. O. (1975). What is psychology all about? *American Psychologist, 30,* 635–669.

HIERNAUX, J. (1975). *The people of Africa.* New York: Scribner's.

HIRSCH, J. (1968). Behavior genetic analysis and the study of man. In M. Mead, T. Dobzhansky, E. Tobach, & R. E. Light (Eds.), *Science and the concept of race.* New York: Columbia University Press.

HOOTEN, E. A. (1931). *Up from the ape.* New York.

HUNT, J. McV. (1961). *Intelligence and experience.* New York: Ronald Press.

JENSEN, A. R. (1969). How much can we boost IQ and scholastic achievement? *Harvard Educational Review, 29,* 1–23.

JENSEN, A. R. (1980). *Bias in mental testing.* New York: Free Press.

KAMIN, L. (1974). *The science and politics of IQ.* Hillsdale, NJ: Erlbaum.

LEWONTIN, R. C. (1973). The appointment of human diversity. *Evolutionary Biology, 6,* 381–398.

MANNING, K. R. (1983). *Black Apollo of science: The life of Ernest Everett Just.* New York: Oxford University Press.

MAURANT, A. E. (1983). *Blood relations: Blood groups in anthropology.* New York: Oxford University Press.

MAYR, E. (1982). *The growth of biological thought.* Cambridge, MA: Belknap Press.

MERCER, J. R. (1973). *Labelling the mentally retarded: Clinical and social system perspectives on mental retardation.* Berkeley: University of California Press.

OGBU, J. U. (1983). Minority status and schooling in plural societies. *Comparative Educational Review 27*(2), 168–190.

PLOMIN, R. (1989). Environment and genes: Determinants of behavior. *American Psychologist 44*(2), 105–111.

PLOMIN, R., DEFRIES, J. C., & FULKNER, D. W. (1988). *Nature and nurture during infancy and early childhood.* New York: Cambridge University Press.

RESNICK, L. B. (ED.). (1976). *The nature of intelligence.* Hillsdale, NJ: Erlbaum.

ROSE, F., & KAMIN, L. (1984). *Not in our genes: Biology, ideology, and human nature.* New York: Pantheon.

SELIGMANN, H. J. (1939). *Race against man.* New York: G. P. Putnam's.

SHIPMAN, S., & SHIPMAN, V. (1988). Cognitive styles: Some conceptual, methodological and applied issues. In Gordon, E. W. & Associates. *Human diversity and pedagogy.* New Haven, CT: ISPS, Yale University.

SHUEY, A. M. (1966). *The testing of Negro intelligence.* New York: Social Science Press.

STERNBERG, R. J. (1985). *Beyond IQ: A triarchic theory of human intelligence.* Cambridge: Cambridge University Press.

STERNBERG, R. J. (1986). *Intelligence applied: Understanding and increasing your intellectual skills.* J. Kagan (Ed.), San Diego, CA: Harcourt Brace Jovanovich.

THOMAS, A. (1988). Affective response tendency. In Gordon, E. W. (Ed.), *Human diversity and Pedagogy.* Center for research on Education, Culture, and Ethnicity. New Haven, CT: ISPS, Yale University.

WEINBERG, R. A. (1989). Intelligence and IQ: Landmark issues and great debates. *American Psychologist 44*(2), 98–104.

EDMUND W. GORDON
MAITRAYEE BHATTACHARYYA

RACE AND IQ SCORES   Interest in the mental characteristics of Negroid populations (blacks), who originated in sub-Saharan Africa, as compared with European (Caucasoid) populations, has a long history; its literature extends from the ancient Greek philosophers to modern times (Baker, 1974; Eysenck, 1984). Eminent philosophers of the eighteenth and nineteenth centuries, such as Hume, Kant, Rousseau, and Voltaire, discoursed on the subject.

Sir Francis GALTON, whose work directly influenced the development of differential psychology, was the first to attempt to quantify racial differences in general mental ability. In his famous work *Hereditary Genius* (1869), written well before the first intelligence test was invented, Galton assumed that intelligence within each racial population is distributed according to the normal, bell-shaped curve. On the basis of evidence that modern scientists would consider inadequate and inappropriate, he estimated that the intelligence distributions of the black African and the white English populations, although overlapping each other considerably, had a mean difference of "two grades" on his particular scale (equivalent to about 1.3 standard deviations [*SD*] or 20 IQ points on the scale of present-day intelligence tests). Galton, like most other intellectual leaders of the eighteenth and nineteenth centuries, assumed, apparently without investigating, that the average black-white difference in mental ability is hereditary or innate. Today, they are generally forgiven for their expressed belief, since the zeitgeist (the general intellectual, cultural, moral tone) of that era encouraged no awareness that the prevailing "commonsense" view of inherent racial differences in mental and behavioral traits should meet scientific standards of evidence.

It was not until the 1930s that the zeitgeist markedly changed in this respect, less for scientific than for ideological reasons, and largely because of Hitler's aggressive racist politics and overt anti-Semitism. After World War II, in the United States, with the ascendance of cultural anthropology, the growing protest over social, political, and economic injustice for blacks, and the advent of the civil rights movement in the 1950s and 1960s, the zeitgeist favored the doctrine of equality in mental ability and other psychological traits of the races. The formerly prevailing "commonsense" belief that mental differences between blacks and whites are innate had become virtually taboo, especially in intellectual and academic circles. By the late 1960s and early 1970s, the sociopolitical stance had become both the popular and the officially sanctioned "scientific" belief—according to which objectively assessed racial differences in behavior, such as mental test scores and scholastic achievement, were and still are attributed exclusively to cultural and environmental factors. A number of well-recognized anthropologists, geneticists, and psychologists, however, voiced the view that the causal aspect of observed (phenotypic) racial differences in abilities was, from a scientific standpoint, still an open question. This debate over causation has continued, often acrimoniously, clouded by social and political ideology. Some nonideological and empirically oriented treatments of the subject do exist, which express varied but tentative and undogmatic interpretations of the evidence (e.g., Eysenck, 1984; Flynn, 1980; Jensen, 1973; Loehlin, Lindzey, & Spuhler, 1975; Scarr, 1984).

Assuming that race and racial differences are legitimate phenomena for scientific study, it is essential to divide the field clearly into two aspects: (1) the *descriptive,* which is concerned with observable (or measurable), that is, *phenotypic,* characteristics, and (2) the *theoretical,* which is concerned with explaining the nature, causes, or origins of the empirically established phenotypic differences.

The current (early 1990s) state of these two aspects—empirical fact and causal theory—is briefly summarized in this article, which is limited to research based on the black (African-American) and white (Caucasoid of European origin) populations of the United States. To consider research done in Africa, the West Indies, or elsewhere outside the United States would introduce complications beyond the scope of

this review. The relatively few recent (1965 on) black immigrants into the United States are generally not represented in the research literature.

A substantial average difference in IQ scores between blacks and whites in the same locality has been found in every part of the world. The phenomenon is not peculiar to the United States. One generalization, however, is possible: The black population of the United States, on average, scores as least as high (and typically higher) on tests of general mental ability as do black populations in Africa, both in the absolute level of IQ and in comparison with the white population in the same localities.

Scientists recognize that black Americans cannot be considered the same, racially or genetically, as black Africans. Black Americans are a racially hybrid population; about 25 percent of their present gene pool came from Caucasoid ancestors (Chakraborty et al., 1992; Reed, 1969). The percentage of Caucasoid genes in the black population varies in the different U.S. geographical regions, with the smallest (about 10 percent) in the deep South and a positive gradient fanning out toward the North and West (Reed, 1969). This phenomenon is almost entirely the result of selective emigration out of the South, since the black gene pool received the greatest infusion of genes from Caucasoids during the period of slavery (ca. 1650–1863) (Glass & Li, 1953; Gottesman, 1968). Northern and western states and territories ended slavery earlier than did the states of the South.

DESCRIPTIVE STATISTICS

During the twentieth century, hundreds of studies were published comparing samples of blacks and whites on tests of mental abilities. Most of these tests are intended to measure general mental ability, usually scaled as the intelligence quotient (IQ), with a mean of 100 and a standard deviation (*SD*) of 15 in standardization samples that are fairly representative of the general population of the United States. The statistical results of virtually all the U.S. studies done before 1980 are published in two compendiums (Osborne & McGurk, 1982; Shuey, 1966). The number of psychometric studies of black-white differences would probably be fewer, and the differences less enduring as a subject of investigation, if the IQ were not correlated with variables of social, economic, and, especially, educational significance—variables on which U.S. black and white populations differ visibly and markedly. Indeed, this topic cannot be divorced from the distinctive social, economic, and cultural milieu of the comparison groups, which, for the black population, has been thoroughly detailed in Jaynes and Williams (1989). The main conclusions of a purely descriptive nature that can be drawn from this vast literature can be summarized under two headings: magnitude of IQ difference and constancy of IQ difference.

Magnitude of the IQ Difference. There are four main ways to quantify the difference between two groups on a metric trait: (1) the *mean difference* expressed in *SD* units (usually the average *SD* in both groups), which is the mean difference divided by the average *SD;* (2) the *median overlap,* which is the percentage of the lower-scoring group that exceeds the median (the 50th percentile) of the higher-scoring group; (3) the *total percentage overlap,* which is the percentage of persons in one of the groups whose scores are matched by persons in the other group; and (4) the *point-biserial correlation* between the metric variable and group membership (quantitized as 0/1), which ranges between values of 0.00 and 1.00.

The many studies of IQ based on representative samples of the black and white populations show that, on average, blacks are invariably the lower-scoring group. The descriptive statistics are best presented in terms of the range of values most typically reported. The various indices shown here are all derived from the same data. They are mathematically equivalent transformations, based on the assumption of a normal distribution of IQ in both populations and SDs of 13 and 15 IQ points in the black and white populations, respectively. These various statistical indices are simply different ways of viewing the same data.

The mean difference is 1.0 to 1.2 *SD* (equivalent to 15 to 18 IQ points). The median overlap is 8 to 12 percent. The total percentage overlap is 55 to 60 percent. The point-biserial correlation between IQ and group membership (b/w quantitized as 0/1) is +.45 to +.51. These figures are only approximations, being based on the assumption that the distribution of IQ scores conforms to the normal, or Gaussian, curve in

each racial group. In fact, however, the observed distributions often depart slightly from the normal curve. For example, in both racial groups, there are more extreme IQs (both high and low) than would be the case if the distribution were perfectly normal, and the distribution of IQ scores in some black samples is slightly skewed to the right. But these departures from normality would have only a slight effect on the above-mentioned estimates of the average difference in IQ scores between blacks and whites. It is important to note, of course, that the range of individual IQs within each racial group is five to six times greater than the mean difference between the groups. This means that mentally retarded persons and intellectually gifted persons exist in both groups, although their percentages in each group differ markedly as a consequence of the approximately 1-*SD* average difference between the two groups' roughly normal distributions of IQ. The reason for this disparity in percentages can be seen in Figure 1, which shows two normal IQ distributions, each with the same *SD* (15 IQ points) and a mean difference of 1 *SD* (i.e., IQ 85 vs. IQ 100). It is apparent that a cut (horizontal line) made through both curves at any given IQ score results in markedly different percentages of the scores in each distribution that fall below the cut score. For example, the percentages of blacks and whites with scores below IQ 70 are 15.9 and 2.3, respectively, a ratio of nearly 7 to 1. The departures from the normal curve typically observed in the IQ distributions of representative samples of the white and black populations of the United States mainly affect the percentages falling below IQ 70 (relatively more blacks) and above IQ 130 (relatively more whites).

The *variance* (squared *SD*) of IQ in the black population is only about 75 percent of the IQ variance in the white population; this corresponds to a *SD* of 13 for blacks as compared to a *SD* of 15 for whites. When the difference between two groups' means is expressed in terms of the average *SD* within each of the two groups, the size of the mean difference is therefore partly a function of the *SD* within each group. The *SD* of IQ is typically smaller, compared to the *SD* of IQ in the general population, in any groups that have been selected on the basis of intellectual abilities or achievements, such as students in selective colleges. But the

DISTRIBUTION

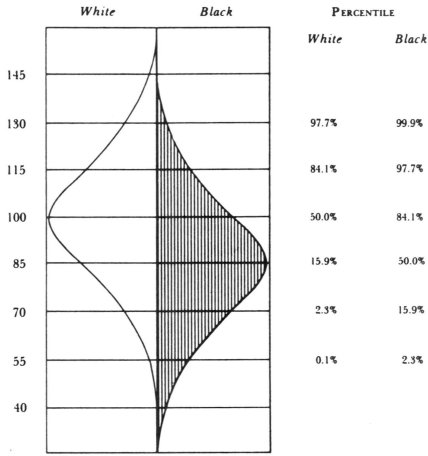

Figure 1

White and black IQ score distributions. The distributions are represented as normal curves with the same standard deviation (SD = 15), showing the percentile ranks of a given IQ in each distribution. (The percentile rank is the percentage of the total distribution that falls below a given IQ score.)

degree of selection is not always the same for blacks and whites. The ratio of the *SD* to the mean (*SD*/mean is technically known as the coefficient of variation) may not be the same within each group. This affects the size of the mean difference between the groups when it is expressed in *SD* units.

For example, black and white high school students who elect to take college admission tests, such as the Scholastic Aptitude Test (SAT) and American College Test (ACT), and college graduates who elect to take the Graduate Record Examination (GRE), Law School Admissions Test (LSAT), and the Medical College Admissions Test (MedCAT) show nationwide average dif-

ferences from one another of about 1.2 to 1.5 *SD* on these tests. Although the self-selected black and white groups are actually more similar to one another in their mean scores on these tests than are randomly selected black and white groups, the amount of variation of scores within the self-selected groups is relatively smaller than in randomly selected groups, hence increasing the self-selected groups' mean difference as expressed in *SD* units. And of course the degree of median overlap (and total overlap) between the black and white groups is related (inversely) to the mean difference expressed in *SD* units. However, when selection or admission is based on the same cut score for blacks and whites, the resultant groups will differ in IQ very much less (typically only 0.1 to 0.3 *SD*) than do blacks and whites in the pool of self-selected applicants.

Constancy of the IQ Difference. The size of the average difference between blacks and whites on IQ tests has remained constant, at between 1.0 and 1.2 *SD,* from the earliest studies (1913) based on fairly representative samples to the present, spanning a period of about eighty years. The average IQ difference between blacks and whites is related to several variables: geographical region, age, sex, and instrument.

Geographical Region. The mean IQ of blacks varies in different parts of the United States, being generally lower in the southeastern states, and increasing on a fan-shaped gradient toward the northern and western states. (There is also a similar south-north gradient of IQ in the white population. For both blacks and whites, the gradient is mainly related to the proportions of urban and rural populations in different regions and to differences in the kinds of employment opportunities associated with this distinction.) Although the percentage of Caucasoid genes in U.S. blacks shows much the same geographical gradient as does IQ (Reed, 1969), this fact neither supports nor contradicts a genetic interpretation of the mean IQ difference between the races, because the emigration of blacks from the South may have been favored by higher mental ability *and* by white social attitudes that favored blacks whose appearance was more Caucasoid than Negroid. In recent years, there has been a trend toward greater geographical homogeneity of the black population with respect to IQ and scholastic performance, with reverse migration of blacks who have comparatively higher levels of education and occupational skills from northern states to developing urban industrialized centers in the South.

Age. Among infants, blacks score higher than do whites on developmental scales that depend mainly on sensory-motor abilities; but scores on these infant scales have near-zero correlations with children's IQs at school age because the IQ predominantly reflects cognitive, not sensory-motor, development. Between ages 3 and 4, before children normally enter school, the mean IQ difference between blacks and whites, of about 1 *SD,* is fully evident; it remains fairly constant thereafter. Therefore, schools do not create the IQ

difference; neither do they seem to increase it or reduce it.

Sex. Beginning with Alfred BINET's test in 1905, most IQ tests were designed to eliminate differences in the overall scores of males and females. Yet even tests that were not expressly designed to satisfy this aim show negligible and inconsistent sex differences in the white population. For reasons not yet known, a larger difference exists between black males and females, with females averaging about 4 to 5 IQ points above males. This difference is also reflected in scholastic achievement, college admissions and graduation, and occupational status, which all favor black females over black males (Jensen, 1971).

Type of Tests. Contrary to popular belief, blacks typically score slightly higher on verbal than on nonverbal and performance tests, even though such verbal and nonverbal tests are all equated in difficulty level in the standardization population. Generally speaking, though, on various mental tests, a considerable amount of true-score variation exists, on average, in the size of the difference between blacks and whites. It was Charles SPEARMAN (1927, p. 379) who first noted that the one aspect of tests that most consistently predicts the size of the mean difference (expressed in *SD* units) between blacks and whites is the test's loading on the psychometric factor *g* inherent in all cognitive tests and other manifestations of mental ability, which Spearman called the general factor (thus *g*) common to virtually all kinds of mental ability tests, however different they may appear superficially (Jensen, 1985, 1987). (See GENERAL ABILITY.)

The mean scoring difference between blacks and whites is essentially a difference in *g* (general ability), rather than in any specific features found in any of the wide variety of psychometric tests. The larger the test's *g* loading, the more poorly blacks score relative to whites. When the standardized mean differences between blacks and whites on a variety of tests are linearly regressed on the tests' *g* loadings, the estimated mean difference on a hypothetical pure measure of *g* is 1.2 *SD*. A test that involves some spatial ability (in addition to *g*) slightly increases the mean difference between blacks and whites, because blacks, on average, score lower than whites on the spatial factor, when blacks and whites are matched on *g* factor scores. A test that involves short-term memory decreases the mean difference, because blacks score higher than whites on the memory factor, when blacks and whites are matched on g factor scores. A test that involves a verbal factor decreases the size of the black–white difference expressed in SD units (i.e. [mean difference]/SD), because blacks and whites, on average, do not differ in verbal ability when blacks and whites are matched on g factor scores, but the total within-group SD on verbal tests (being composed of variance in g + variance in verbal ability) is increased, thereby decreasing the ratio (mean difference)/SD.

These empirical findings are best understood in terms of factor analysis. Factor analyses of a wide variety of tests reveal two other factors besides g, which—independently of g—consistently show relatively small but significant mean differences between whites and blacks. On average, whites exceed blacks on a *spatial reasoning* factor (loaded in tests such as block designs, object assembly, and paper folding); on average, blacks exceed whites on a *short-term memory* factor (loaded in tests such as digit span, coding, and rote learning). It is noteworthy that their difference on the verbal factor (independent of g) is virtually nil. Despite this fact, the size of the average difference between blacks and whites on many verbal tests is still considerable (about 1 SD), because g is a much larger component of variance than the verbal factor per se in certain verbal tests (e.g., vocabulary, similarities, verbal analogies, and reading comprehension).

CAUSAL THEORIES

At present, no scientifically substantiated theory exists that explains the cause of the phenotypic differences in the mental test scores of blacks versus whites; that is, no one interpretation exists for the cause of the undisputed empirical evidence of phenotypic differences. Opinions differ mainly regarding the relative causal importance of genetic and environmental factors. A questionnaire survey (Snyderman & Rothman, 1988) of 661 experts—most of them in the fields of differential psychology, psychometrics, and behavioral genetics—reported the following percentages of responses to the multiple-choice question, "Which of the following best characterizes your *opinion* of the heritability of the black–white difference in IQ?"

15 percent: The difference is entirely due to environmental variation.

1 percent: The difference is entirely due to genetic variation.

45 percent: The difference is a product of both genetic and environmental variation.

24 percent: The data are insufficient to support any reasonable opinion.

14 percent: NQ [does not feel qualified to answer question]. (p. 294).

In science, answers to such questions are not decided by opinion polls, even when the opinions are those of scientists. Answers become recognized scientifically in terms of theory-derived hypotheses, or predictions, that are consistent with a preponderance of the empirical evidence. The present state of the evidence does not allow for a definitive ruling on any of the opinions listed above. The various causal theories and arguments that have been proposed can only be judged in terms of their coherence and plausibility in light of what is already known, with considerable certainty, about the nature of IQ in general.

GENETIC THEORY

The theory that the mean IQ difference between blacks and whites involves genetic factors is inferred from several lines of evidence. The broadest consideration is the theory of evolution by natural selection, which explains the origin of genetic differences between subspecies (in biology, races), that have been geographically separated for hundreds of generations in markedly differing environments; this results in the many physical differences among various races of plants and animals, including humans. It is generally considered implausible that the brain and its behavioral correlates would be wholly exempt from such genetic variation, and it also seems unlikely that genotypes and phenotypes for any characteristic, including general ability (g), would be *negatively* correlated with each other. (Assuming that the influence of genetic factors [technically called the broad heritability] on phenotypic IQ *within* a racial group is .70, the within-group correlation between phenotype and genotype would be $[.70]1/2 = +.84$.)

Significant racial differences exist for human brain size, as measured in terms of either weight or volume, controlled for overall body size. The average difference in the size of the brain in blacks and whites is about 100 cubic centimeters, equivalent to about 0.8 *SD*. This is considered relevant, because studies of the relationship between differences in an individual's brain size and IQ show correlations of about $+.30$ when statistically controlled for general body size (reviewed by Jensen & Sinha, 1992). The interpretation of these facts is problematical, since males and females of the same race differ (about 100 cc) in brain size (with body size controlled), yet no good evidence exists for a sex difference in psychometric *g*.

Additionally, some 50 to 70 percent of the total variance in IQ (within racial groups) is attributable to genetic factors, indicating that genes are the major source of IQ variance *within* races. Although this does not prove that genetic factors are involved in the average IQ difference *between* races, it seems more plausible that genetic factors may be involved than would be the case if IQ had zero heritability. It is important to note, however, that this possibility cannot be tested by the same methodology of quantitative genetics that has been used to establish the heritability of IQ (and other traits) *within* a given racial group, which depends on analyzing the correlations between genetically related persons who differ in their degree of kinship—such as groups of monozygotic (identical) and dizygotic (fraternal) twins—who therefore necessarily share the same racial ancestry. Hence the method cannot apply to the heredity/environment analysis of the mean difference between racial groups.

The results of quasi-genetic studies, based on cross-racially adopted children and children of racially mixed marriages, are so vitiated by uncontrolled and confounded variables as to be virtually uninformative (Flynn, 1980; Jensen, 1973; Nichols, 1987; Scarr, 1984). Since the average difference between blacks and whites on IQ tests is mainly a difference in the *g* factor, and since among a wide variety of other mental tests it is the *g* factor that mainly accounts for their correlations with variables that are entirely outside the realm of psychometrics (such as reaction times and certain physiological variables [e.g., features of the evoked electrical potentials in the brain, the propor-

tion of genetic variance in test scores, and the purely genetic effect known as inbreeding depression]), this increases the plausibility of the hypothesis that the difference in mean IQ scores between whites and blacks involves genetic factors to some degree.

HYPOTHESIZED ENVIRONMENTAL CAUSES

A great many environmental hypotheses have been proposed concerning the lower mean IQ for blacks. Some of these have not yet been empirically tested; some may be inherently untestable; and some can be conclusively rejected by the results of extensive investigations. Researchers have not yet found any environmental factors that account for most or all of the difference. It even remains uncertain what proportion of the difference may be attributed to hypothesized environmental factors. Listed below are the most commonly hypothesized environmental, or nongenetic, factors; they are not mutually exclusive or incompatible with the hypothesis of genetic factors as a partial cause.

Culture-Biased Tests. No longer generally accepted is the assertion that racial/cultural biases in the tests cause the average IQ differences between blacks and whites. Extensive research has shown that the most widely used tests do not behave psychometrically as would be predicted from the culture bias hypothesis. For instance, the average difference is smaller on test items with scholastic and cultural content than on nonverbal tests. By and large, present-day IQ tests have the same reliability, predictive validity, item intercorrelations, factor structure, construct validity, rank order of item difficulty, item-characteristic curves, and heritability coefficients in both racial groups (Jensen, 1980; Osborne, 1980; Reynolds & Brown, 1984).

Educational Inequality. The IQ difference cannot be attributed to inequality in formal education, as the difference between blacks and whites is about 1 *SD* (15 IQ points) even before the age of school entry and remains fairly constant, at about 1 *SD*, from the primary grades through high school.

Socioeconomic Status (SES). It remains debatable to what extent SES is a cause or an effect of

IQ differences. In any case, the mean IQ difference between blacks and whites, after controlling for SES, is about 0.8 *SD,* or 12 IQ points. Also, differences between blacks and whites on various mental ability factors do not show the same pattern as SES differences (within each race). The average difference on spatial-reasoning tests between blacks and whites is larger than on verbal tests, but just the opposite is found in comparing higher and lower socioeconomic groups within either race. This fact is inconsistent with the explanation of the average differences between blacks and whites on mental tests in terms of socioeconomic status.

Teacher Expectations. Research has not supported the idea that teachers' expectations of lower test performances by blacks cause the average IQ difference between blacks and whites. Numerous experimental studies of the effects of "teacher expectancy" on IQ have failed to reject the null hypothesis, although some studies have shown modest but statistically significant effects of teacher expectancy on scholastic achievement.

Biological Environment. Certain environmental factors may have direct biological effects on the brain mechanisms involved in mental development, including the lower rates of prenatal medical care and higher rates of premature birth and low birthweight in the black population. These variables are negatively correlated with IQ. Nutritional differences simply in terms of total caloric intake are not supported by research studies as affecting blacks' IQ (Loehlin et al., 1975). Some experimental evidence does exist to show that deficiencies in certain vitamins and minerals may affect IQ. This research suggests that there are considerable individual differences, even among full siblings, in the daily requirements of certain vitamins and minerals that affect mental functioning. These specific nutritional deficiencies can be detected by means of blood tests; it is claimed that when appropriate dietary supplements are provided to children whose blood tests indicate deficiencies, they show significant gains in IQ (Eysenck & Eysenck, 1991). Although this research is considered controversial at the present stage of investigation, it seems to merit further study, particularly in relation to racial differences.

Style of Childrearing. Research on differences between blacks and whites in childrearing practices has produced conflicting and inconclusive findings. In studies of children reared by their biological parents, parental IQ is completely confounded with differences in the characteristics of the parent-child interactions, ipso facto completely confounding genetics and environment as causal factors in children's mental development (Plomin & Bergeman, 1991). Studies of adopted children show that, within the normal range of environments—families ranging from blue collar to professional—differences in childrearing show little correlation with individual variation in children's IQs. The hypothesis that the average difference in IQ between blacks and whites results from differences in childrearing lacks conviction, because it attributes a large mean difference (1 *SD*) in IQ to weak causes. Research has found that such factors have scarcely any relation to individual variation in IQ (Plomin & Daniels, 1987).

Historical and Social Factors. White racism, a past history of slavery, consciousness of being a disliked and feared racial minority, caste status, social prejudice and discrimination, restricted opportunity that results in lowered levels of aspiration, peer pressure against "acting white," and "the black experience"—all these have been claimed as causes of the differences in average IQ and scholastic achievement between blacks and whites (Ogbu, 1978). This class of variables, however, has not been investigated scientifically, and few specific or empirically testable hypotheses have been proposed. Indeed, many of these hypothesized causes are probably not empirically testable. This is not to argue the reality of these historical conditions per se, but only to question the possibility of ever demonstrating in any scientifically acceptable way that they are causally related to the present mean difference in IQ between blacks and whites. Also, the plausibility of these hypotheses is lessened by the fact that, with the exception of the past history of slavery and its aftermath, many of these conditions have pertained to various other racial and ethnic minorities (particularly Asians and Jews) without any evidence of an enduring adverse effect on their test performance or scholastic achievement.

(*See also:* AFRICAN AMERICANS; ETHNICITY, RACE, AND THE MEASUREMENT OF INTELLIGENCE; RACE AND INTELLIGENCE.)

BIBLIOGRAPHY

BAKER, J. R. (1974). *Race*. New York: Oxford University Press.

CHAKRABORTY, R., KAMOBOH, M. I., NWANKWO, M., & FERRELL, R. E. (1992). Caucasian genes in American blacks: New data. *American Journal of Human Genetics, 50,* 145–155.

EYSENCK, H. J. (1984). The effect of race on human abilities and mental test scores. In C. R. Reynolds & R. T. Brown (Eds.), *Perspectives on bias in mental testing* (pp. 249–291). New York: Plenum.

EYSENCK, H. J., & EYSENCK, S. B. G. (Eds.). (1991). Improvement of I.Q. and behavior as a function of dietary supplementation: A symposium. *Personality and Individual Differences, 12,* 329–365.

FLYNN, J. R. (1980). *Race, IQ, and Jensen*. London: Routledge.

GLASS, B., & LI, C. C. (1953). The dynamics of racial admixture—An analysis based on the American Negro. *American Journal of Human Genetics, 5,* 1–20.

GOTTESMAN, I. I. (1968). Biogenetics of race and class. In M. Deutsch, I. Katz, & A. R. Jensen (Eds.), *Social class, race, and psychological development*. New York: Holt, Rinehart & Winston.

JAYNES, D. G., & WILLIAMS, R. M., JR. (Eds.). (1989). *A common destiny: Blacks and American society*. Washington, DC: National Academy Press.

JENSEN, A. R. (1971). The race × sex × ability interaction. In R. Cancro (Ed.), *Contributions to intelligence*. New York: Grune & Stratton.

JENSEN, A. R. (1973). *Educability and group differences*. London: Methuen.

JENSEN, A. R. (1980). *Bias in mental testing*. New York: Free Press.

JENSEN, A. R. (1985). The nature of the Black-White difference on various psychometric tests: Spearman's hypothesis. *Behavioral and Brain Sciences, 8,* 193–258.

JENSEN, A. R. (1987). Further evidence for Spearman's hypothesis concerning black-white differences on psychometric tests. *Behavioral and Brain Sciences, 10,* 512–519.

JENSEN, A. R., & SINHA, S. N. (1992). Physical correlates of human intelligence. In P. A. Vernon (Ed.), *Biological approaches to research on intelligence* (pp. 135–238). Norwood, NJ: Ablex.

LOEHLIN, J. C., LINDZEY, G., & SPUHLER, J. N. (1975). *Race differences in intelligence*. New York: Freeman.

NICHOLS, R. C. (1987). Racial differences in intelligence. In

S. Modgil & C. Modgil (Eds.), *Arthur Jensen: Consensus and controversy* (pp. 213–220). New York: Falmer Press.

OGBU, J. U. (1978). *Minority education and caste: The American system in cross-cultural perspective*. New York: Academic Press.

OSBORNE, R. T. (1980). *Twins, black and white*. Athens, GA: Foundation for Human Understanding.

OSBORNE, R. T., & MCGURK, F. C. J. (1982). *The testing of Negro intelligence* (Vol. 2). Athens, GA: Foundation for Human Understanding.

PLOMIN, R., & BERGEMAN, C. S. (1991). The nature of nurture: Genetic influence on "environmental" measures. *Behavioral and Brain Sciences, 14,* 373–427.

PLOMIN, R., & DANIELS, D. (1987). Why are children in the same family so different from one another? *Behavioral and Brain Sciences, 10,* 1–16.

REED, T. E. (1969). Caucasian genes in American Negroes. *Science, 165,* 762–768.

REYNOLDS, C. R., & BROWN, R. T. (Eds.). (1984). *Perspectives on bias in mental testing*. New York: Plenum.

SCARR, S. (Ed.) (1984). *Race, social class, and individual differences in IQ*. Hillsdale, NJ: Erlbaum.

SHUEY, A. M. (1966). *The testing of Negro intelligence* (2nd ed.). New York: Social Science Press.

SNYDERMAN, M., & ROTHMAN, S. (1988). *The IQ controversy, the media and public policy*. New Brunswick, NJ: Transaction Books.

SPEARMAN, C. (1927). *The abilities of man*. London: Macmillan.

ARTHUR R. JENSEN

RADEX THEORY   In tests for intellectual abilities, different mental tests generally relate to each other in certain systematic ways. Radex theory is based on Louis GUTTMAN's hypothesis—which has since been verified repeatedly—that ability tests can be classified in at least two ways: differences in kind of content and differences in degree of complexity of the test items. Guttman developed radex theory in the article "A New Approach to *Factor Analysis*" (1954) to provide a theory of the structure of mental abilities as revealed by lawful interrelations between mental tests (see also FACET THEORY).

When dealing with aspects of mental functioning, the researcher often obtains scores on a number of variables for every member of a sample of individuals, such as high school pupils, college students, and job applicants. The scores may be on test items, relating to vocabulary, arithmetic, geometry, foreign language, or other subjects. Because the number of such scores is often large, the experimenter may need to organize the data in a fashion that will summarize the scores in a descriptive way and provide information on relationships among the different variables. Psychometricians have developed methods that attempt to explain how abilities are related; in particular, "factor analysis" has sought a limited number of "common factors" of intelligence (see FACTOR ANALYSIS). In attempting to deal with the problems and limitations posed by common-factor analysis, Guttman was led to develop nonmetric techniques for testing structural hypotheses (Guttman, 1958), in which variables were laid out in geometric configurations leading to the *simplex,* the *circumplex,* and, ultimately, the *radex* structure of mental tests.

A set of variables that have an implicit ordering among themselves from "least complex" to "most complex" is called a *simplex.* A set of variables that contains a circular order among variables representing difference in kind, rather than degree of complexity, is called a *circumplex.* When both kinds of order are present simultaneously, the set is a *radex.*

Radex theory is designed to handle the problem of order among variables such as test items, much as scale theory studies order among people. As compared with previous factor-analytic approaches, radex theory leads to an improvement both in underlying psychological theory and in computing techniques.

DIFFERENCES BETWEEN ABILITY TESTS: LEVEL AND KIND OF COMPLEXITY

Items from a battery of tests limited only to numerical abilities—addition, subtraction, multiplication, division—come from the same "universe of content" (numerical abilities) and differ among themselves largely in their *level of complexity.* In this case, similarities between the tests, as assessed by correlation coefficients or other measures of similarity, entail a simple rank order among the tests from least to most complex.

To study the relationships among variables, such as scores on psychological or ability tests, measures of similarity between the variables—usually correlation coefficients—are computed. The resulting correlations are arranged in an intercorrelation matrix, which contains the correlation coefficients for every possible pair of variables (or items) from the test battery. An example of such an intercorrelation matrix is given in Table 1 for four hypothetical variables. Note that all four variables in this matrix are positively intercorrelated, a phenomenon first observed for mental tests by Charles SPEARMAN (1932) and replicated many times since (Guttman & Levy, 1991).

The matrix can then be analyzed by means of an appropriate nonmetric, multidimensional computer program—such as the Guttman-Lingoes Smallest Space Analysis (SSA) (Lingoes, 1973; Guttman, 1968). This is one of a variety of nonmetric multidimensional data analysis techniques for structural analysis of similarity. SSA represents the tests as points in a Euclidean space such that the higher the correlation is between two variables, the closer the points will be in the space.

The Simplex. With intercorrelations between test items on numerical abilities, Guttman hypothesized (and obtained) a simple unidimensional ordering that he labeled a *simplex,* a "simple order of complexity." In the simplex pattern large correlations exist between tests; the correlations are similar in complexity, and they decrease as the differences in complexity increase. Table 1 represents a simplex with the highest correlations between variables 1 and 2 (.68), a correlation coefficient of .62 between variable 1 and 3, and the lowest between variables 1 and 4 (.52).

The Circumplex. When tests involve different kinds of *abilities* (e.g., mathematics vs. history) that are

TABLE 1

Intercorrelation matrix for four variables showing a simplex configuration

Variable	1	2	3	4
1	—	.68	.62	.52
2	.68	—	.67	.62
3	.62	.67	—	.68
4	.52	.62	.68	—

of the same level of complexity, a circular order for relating different abilities is hypothesized—and often found—in the tables of intercorrelations. Guttman called this structure the *circumplex,* a "circular order of complexity." (Theoretical and mathematic formulations are given in Guttman, 1954, and in Shepard, 1978.) The circumplex correlation matrices exhibit empirical correlations corresponding to a circle of abilities without a beginning or an end. R. N. Shepard (1978) provides two important examples of circumplex configurations for measures of similarity between color hues and for perceptions of musical pitch.

The Radex. The radex combines simplexes and circumplexes simultaneously in a single configuration. The word *radex* was coined by Guttman to indicate a "radial expansion of complexity" (Guttman, 1954). He developed the algebraic basis for radex theory, together with a rationale for its relation to factor analysis. The theory has important implications for the parsimonious prediction of external criteria for test design (see also Van den Wollenberg, 1978). These will be discussed below.

An idealized radex is given in Figure 1. Each element in Figure 1 belongs simultaneously to one cir-

cumplex and one simplex. The concentric circles each represent a circumplex. They are divided into four segments, each segment portraying a simplex with elements (i.e., 9, 10, 11, 12) radiating from the innermost to the outermost circle. Early empirical radexes for mental tests were published by Guttman (1970) and Schlesinger and Guttman (1969).

Figure 2 illustrates one of the first empirical radexes published by Schlesinger and Guttman (1969) of an analysis of the structure of eighteen intelligence tests. Figure 2 is a radex obtained from a smallest-space analysis of the intercorrelation matrix of the eighteen tests. This radex is a two-dimensional structure of three concentric circles subdivided into three wedge-like sectors of verbal, numerical, and figural tests—simplexes—and represented by rays from the origin. This radex structure was predicted by Schlesinger and Guttman on the basis of facet theory (Guttman, 1959; Shye, 1978; Canter, 1985) by defining each test on the basis of two facets: the format of each test item (verbal, numerical, or figural) and the nature of the task imposed on the testee (rule–inference, rule–application, or school performance). A rule–inference test presents examples or only hints at the rule and requires the testee to infer the rule. A rule–applying test presents the rule and requires the testee to apply it. For example, "hen is to chick" as "cat ————," is a rule–inference item, and in "the young of the dog are called ————," a rule must be provided in the question.

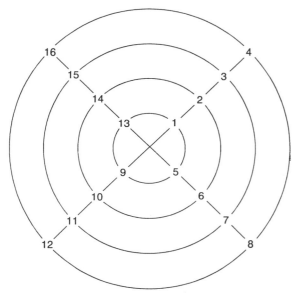

Figure 1

An idealized radex

SOURCE: Lingoes and Borg, 1977, p. 173; see also Canter, 1985, p.37.

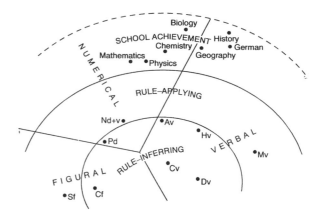

Figure 2

A radex of 18 intelligence tests

SOURCE: Adapted from Schlesinger and Guttman, 1969.

The radex of eighteen intelligence tests as shown in Figure 2 represents a two-dimensional patterning of the space into three angular and three radial regions. Each angular region (sector) corresponds to one of the three elements of the facet "format of communication" divided into verbal, numerical, and figural (or spatial)—with their respective test items. These partition the circular space into wedgelike sections, all emanating from a common origin. The elements are related by circular order and thus differ in kind but not necessarily in complexity. The elements of the second facet, "rule task" (mental operations that are needed), are ordered in concentric rings around an origin, going outward from the innermost task of "rule–inference" to "rule–application" to "achievement." Within these areas are test items of numerical nature, some requiring rule–inference, some rule–application, and so forth. Similarity among items of different content (i.e., different abilities) is greatest among items within the innermost circle of rule inference.

Similarities between test items of the outermost ring (achievement) can be much lower. The original rationale (given by Schlesinger and Guttman, 1969) for the radial order of the rule–task facet was that the application of a rule need not require inferring the rule, whereas rule–inference tasks cannot be solved by application or by learning alone. A more recent approach is that of B. Marshalek and colleagues (1983), who view the hierarchical order of complexity as exhibited by the radex as "the continuum that radiates out from the center of the radex [and] runs from general-complex to simple-specific" (p. 125).

The distinction between rule-applying and rule-inferring tasks and their radex structure has been replicated many times, with additional tests and different subjects. Additional facets can be—and have been—defined and investigated within the framework of the model (Adler and Guttman, 1982; Guttman, et al., 1990; Koop, 1985; Marshalek, Lohman, & Snow, 1983; Shye, 1988; Tziner and Rimmer, 1984). The most re-

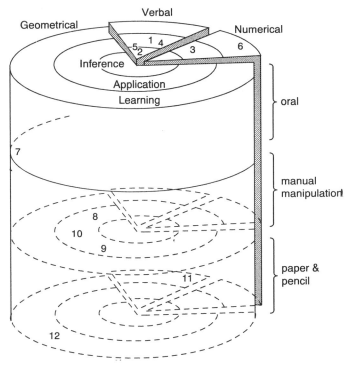

Figure 3

Schematic representation of the cylindrical structure of the Wechsler Intelligence Scale for Children

SOURCE: Guttman and Levy, 1991.

cent contribution is Louis Guttman's posthumous (Guttman and Levy, 1991) three-dimensional model of intelligence tests based on comparative analyses of correlations among subtests of the Wechsler Intelligence Scale for Children (WISC) in a variety of age groups of U.S. and Israeli school children. The three-dimensional cylindrical structure (replicated in each age group in each location) is presented in Figure 3. It consists of three radexes. Each radex has the same facet structure, which is stacked into a cylinder by a third facet. That facet is the "mode of expression" required by the testee. It can be either oral or manual or paper-and-pencil.

PREDICTION AND DESIGN OF TESTS

Radex structure has important implications for prediction issues and for test design. If, for instance, an assessment of success is necessary on a job that requires verbal ability, searches are possible for an appropriate test by relating the criterion to a sequence of verbal ability tests of varied complexity. Ideally, two or three tests that come closest to having the desired complexity will emerge. This will also be helpful in designing new tests that will yield a better prediction. The new tests should fall into a simplex nearer to the complexity that the criterion requires. The same would hold true for tasks requiring numerical ability as a predictor or for tasks requiring a combination of different abilities. Two or three tests of the most appropriate level of complexity or even a limited number of items from each test would be as effective as a large number of tests and items.

From the patterns of correlation (or regression) coefficients, a test will be about as predictable from its immediate two neighbors as from all the tests in the battery. Sampling of test items and design of new items will, according to Guttman, be both more parsimonious and more stringent. Radex theory, using a faceted definition of the universe of observations on specific abilities (see FACET THEORY), thus makes possible the sampling of existing tests and the creation of new tests or new items for existing test batteries. An example of this kind of test design in the domain of spatial abilities has been discussed by R. Guttman and colleagues (1990). It is a spatial test combining elements of the two facets "rule task" and "mental rotation."

The structural theory of the radex is not limited to mental tests. Simplex, circumplex, and radex structures have been found in studies on personality traits and in attitude surveys (Levy, 1985). In the field of perception, R. N. Shepard (1978) gives several excellent examples from data on the perception of color hues and color brightness. New radex examples are continually being added to the psychological and sociological research literature.

BIBLIOGRAPHY

ADLER, N., & GUTTMAN, R. (1982). The radex structure of intelligence: A replication. *Educational and Psychological Measurement, 42,* 739–748.

CANTER, D. (ED.). (1985). *Facet theory: Approaches to social research.* New York: Springer-Verlag.

GUTTMAN, L. (1954). A new approach to factor analysis: The radex. In P. F. Lazarsfeld (Ed.), *Mathematical thinking in the social sciences.* New York: Free Press.

GUTTMAN, L. (1958). What lies ahead for factor analysis? *Educational and Psychological Measurement, 18,* 497–515.

GUTTMAN, L. (1959). Introduction to facet design and analysis. *Proceedings of the 15th International Congress of Psychology* (pp. 130–132). Amsterdam: North Holland Publishing Company.

GUTTMAN, L. (1968). A general nonmetric technique for finding the smallest coordinate space for a configuration of points. *Psychometrika, 33,* 469–506.

GUTTMAN, L. (1970). Integration of test design and analysis. *Proceedings of the 1969 Invitational Conference on Testing Problems.* Princeton, NJ: Educational Testing Service.

GUTTMAN, L. (1980). Integration of test design and analysis: Status in 1979. *New Directions for Testing and Measurement,* Vol. 5. San Francisco: Jossey-Bass.

GUTTMAN, L., & LEVY, S. (1991). Two structural laws for intelligence tests. *Intelligence, 15,* 79–103.

GUTTMAN, R., EPSTEIN, E., AMIR, M., & GUTTMAN, L. (1990). A structural theory of spatial abilities. *Applied Psychological Measurement, 14,* 217–236.

KOOP, T. (1985). Replication of Guttman's structure of intelligence. In D. Canter (Ed.), *Facet theory: Approaches to social research.* New York: Springer-Verlag.

LEVY, S. (1985). Lawful roles of facets in social theories. In D. Canter (Ed.), *Facet theory: Approaches to social research.* New York: Springer-Verlag.

LINGOES, J. C. (1973). *The Guttman-Lingoes nonmetric program series.* Ann Arbor, MI: Mathesis.

LINGOES, J. C., & BORG, I. (1977). Identifying spatial manifolds for interpretation. In J. Lingoes (Ed.), *Geometric representation of relational data.* Ann Arbor, MI: Mathesis.

MARSHALEK, B., LOHMAN, D. F., & SNOW, R. (1983). The complexity continuum in the radex and hierarchical models of intelligence. *Intelligence, 7,* 107–128.

SCHLESINGER, I. M., & GUTTMAN, L. (1969). Smallest space analysis of intelligence and achievement tests. *Psychological Bulletin, 71,* 95–100.

SHEPARD, R. N. (1978). The circumplex and related topological manifolds in the study of perception. In S. Shye (Ed.), *Theory construction and data analysis in the behavioral sciences.* San Francisco: Jossey-Bass.

SHYE, S. (ED.). (1978). *Theory construction and data analysis in the behavioral sciences.* San Francisco: Jossey-Bass.

SHYE, S. (1985). *Multiple scaling.* Amsterdam: North-Holland.

SHYE, S. (1988). Inductive and deductive reasoning: A structural reanalysis of ability tests. *Journal of Applied Psychology, 2,* 308–311.

SPEARMAN, C. (1932). *The abilities of man.* New York: AMS Press.

TZINER, A., & RIMMER, A. (1984). Examination of an extension of Guttman's models of ability tests. *Applied Psychological Measurement, 1,* 59–69.

VAN DEN WOLLENBERG, A. L. (1978). Nonmetric representation of the radex in its factor pattern parameterization. In S. Shye (Ed.), *Theory construction and data analysis in the behavioral sciences.* San Francisco: Jossey-Bass.

RUTH GUTTMAN

RATIONAL THINKING

RATIONAL THINKING Intelligence may be defined as consisting of those general mental abilities that help us achieve our goals, whatever they might be (Baron, 1985). Although many of these abilities are biologically determined and largely out of our control, other abilities have to do with the way in which we conduct our thinking. If rational thinking is the kind of thinking that helps us achieve our goals, then rational thinking is part of intelligence.

THINKING

Thinking starts with some sort of doubt that we try to resolve. The doubt can be about what to do, what to believe, or what to desire (to the extent to which these things are under our control). Thinking may be analyzed into search and inference (Baron, 1988). We search for possibilities, evidence, and goals. Possibilities are possible answers to the question that inspired the thinking. Evidence consists of propositions that can strengthen or weaken the possibilities. Goals are the criteria we use to evaluate possibilities in the light of the evidence. For example, in making a decision about what kind of computer to buy (thinking about what to do), the possibilities are the various kinds of computers; the evidence consists of reported facts about them, such as their price, reliability, and features; and the goals consist of such criteria as low price, large memory, and so on. We search both our own memories and the external world—magazines, friends, and salespeople.

In making inferences, we apply various rules or heuristics to what our search has discovered so far. For example, we can go through our list of goals in some order and eliminate the possibility that is worst on each goal, or we can try to form an overall impression of each possibility, taking all goals and evidence into account.

RATIONAL THINKING

Rational search must be fair and sufficiently thorough. Fair search is not biased toward some particular possibility, such as the one we first noticed. Sufficient thoroughness means that we must search until the benefit of further search is no longer worth the cost in time or effort. Often, this involves very little search. In such a case, we should not hold the kind of confidence in our conclusion that we would hold if it were based on a more thorough search.

People are often highly confident of conclusions based on little thought, however (Kuhn, 1991). They also tend to seek evidence in ways that are biased, looking for evidence that they know will support what they already favor or that will at least be easy to rebut if it does not (Frey, 1986). In judgment experiments, subjects have been asked to think of reasons supporting their favored possibility or reasons opposing it. Typically, asking subjects to think of opposing reasons has an effect on judgment, but asking subjects to think of supporting reasons has no effect (see, e.g., Hoch,

1985). Apparently, subjects think of supporting reasons on their own. This sort of "myside" bias can apparently be corrected by instructing people to try to be fair minded, as has been done in educational experiments (Perkins, 1989).

Rational inference must be based on rules that maximize goal achievement. Some commonly used rules do not seem to do this. For example, people consider sunk costs in making decisions (Arkes & Blumer, 1985)—people who have paid for indoor tennis courts will sometimes play on them despite excellent weather outdoors, so as not to "waste" the money spent. If the outdoor court maximizes goal achievement (the main goal being to have fun), then the money spent should not affect that. Or, people may choose a harmful omission over a less harmful act—some people are reluctant to vaccinate a child to prevent a harmful disease if the vaccine has a risk of causing the same disease, even if the risk is much lower (Ritov & Baron, 1990). Again, the main goal here is reducing the probability of disease, and the distinction between acts and omissions is irrelevant.

These seemingly irrational heuristics may result from overgeneralization of heuristics that are valuable in other cases (Baron, 1990). For example, a rule against waste is a good rule to follow. Sunk costs, however, are already wasted, so they are out of our control. A good counter heuristic is, "Consider the future only." Or, when we judge the behavior of others, harmful acts should be judged more harshly than harmful omissions, because the former are more likely to involve malicious intent. But in the vaccination case, no malice is at issue. A good heuristic here is the Golden Rule.

Harmful heuristics can be corrected through instruction. Larrick, Morgan, and Nisbett (1990) gave subjects a short instructional session on thinking in terms of future costs and benefits rather than sunk costs. The training had immediate effects on questionnaire measures of the sunk-cost effect. There was suggestive evidence that it affected real-life behavior as well: Subjects in the training condition reported being more likely to stop watching a rented videotape before the end. This was something that the control group might have done, too, except for not wanting to "waste" the money spent on the tape. Likewise, Baron (1992) convinced many subjects that the act-

omission distinction did not matter in a vaccination example, by asking the subjects to take the viewpoint of the child.

In these cases and others, many people do not need instruction. They have discovered better heuristics on their own. Some evidence suggests that these people are more successful in life: Specifically, they tend to make more money. One way in which people might discover new heuristics is by reflection on the heuristics themselves. People can think about the effectiveness of different heuristics in achieving goals, just as they can think about what kind of computer to buy (Baron, 1990).

Rational inference, like rational search, must also be fair. Yet people tend to make inferences in ways that favor possibilities that are already strong, especially when they desire that one conclusion be true or best (Kunda, 1990). People commonly interpret evidence as supporting possibilities they already favor. Given totally ambiguous evidence, people will take it as confirmation of what they already favor (Kuhn, 1991).

In one classic study (Lord, Ross, & Lepper, 1979), two groups of subjects were selected, one group favoring capital punishment and another group opposing it. Both groups read two realistic studies, one providing evidence that capital punishment deterred serious crime, the other providing evidence that it did not. We might expect both groups to moderate their views somewhat after reading both studies, but both groups said that their opinion had become stronger. Each group tended to ignore the evidence against their view but to accept the evidence in its favor.

This kind of biased response to evidence may be affected by education: Kuhn (1991) found that philosophy graduate students were less likely to demonstrate it than were other subjects, and people who had not been to college were most likely to demonstrate it. It is also possible that the bias is correlated with other mental abilities that lead people to pursue higher education.

Rational thinking is not the only determinant of good outcomes of decisions. Outcomes are surely affected by specific knowledge, uncontrollable abilities and luck. But thinking may matter. Herek, Janis, and Huth (1987) made independent judgments of outcome quality and the quality of decision makers' thinking—

in much the spirit of the theory outlined here—for major foreign-policy decisions of the U.S. government. Although it is possible that judgments of thinking were contaminated by the judges' knowledge of outcome—despite efforts to minimize this—the correlation was high (.64 for the basic outcome measure).

TESTING OF RATIONAL THINKING

We have no good test for rational thinking as a whole. Tests that purport to measure "critical thinking" (Ennis & Millman, 1985; Watson & Glaser, 1980) seem more designed to measure sensitivity to logical nuances than to measure any of the dispositions described so far (Norris, 1989, 1991). Perhaps the most theoretically relevant measures are those concerned with "integrative complexity" (Schroeder, Driver, and Streufert, 1967; Suedfeld & Tetlock, 1977). Originally applied to paragraph completion tests, these scoring systems can be applied to any verbal production, such as a speech or an essay. They involve a measure of "differentiation" that is essentially equivalent to willingness to consider both sides of an issue. They also involve a measure of "integration" that is more difficult to define in the terms I have used, and in fact appears to be less valid as a measure of individual differences or other effects (Tetlock, 1985). Of course, even the differentiation measure is concerned only with spontaneous recall of arguments, that is, search for evidence. It is not concerned with fairness in inference or with other kinds of search. One study found that the overall measure correlated positively with IQ (Schroeder et al., 1967), although this result is difficult to interpret, given the complexity of the scoring system itself.

A similar but simpler technique involves simply asking people to list arguments on a controversial issue. Perkins, Faraday, and Bushey (1991) did this with a sample of college students; they found that vocabulary (as measured by the Quick Word Test, which was assumed to be a rough indicator of IQ) was significantly correlated with the number of "myside" arguments produced but not with the number of "otherside" arguments produced ($r = .39$ vs. $r = .10$). Avoidance of "myside" bias seems to be somewhat unrelated to other aspects of intelligence.

Another relevant type of measure examines the tradeoff between speed and accuracy in difficult problem-solving tasks such as "matching familiar figures" (Messer, 1976), logic, or difficult arithmetic problems (Baron, Badgio, & Gaskins, 1986). Typically, a negative correlation across subjects is found between time spent and errors made. This means that individual differences in the preferred tradeoff between speed and accuracy are large—larger than common ability components that might be thought to affect time and errors in the same direction. Those who take longer would seem to be engaging in a more thorough search. If most people search too little, then these "reflective" subjects might be better thinkers. Interestingly, they do tend to perform better in a variety of ways (Messer, 1976), and the time taken correlates positively with IQ as measured by the Wechsler Intelligence Scale for Children (Baron et al., 1986).

Still, it is not necessarily the case that taking longer is always better. Each person has an optimum time on a given task. The marginal benefit of spending additional time typically declines as a function of time, but the cost typically remains roughly constant. It is therefore possible to take too much time, and many people do in some tasks (Baron, Badgio, & Ritov, 1991). When children are taught to spend more time thinking, some show reduced error rates—specifically those judged by their teachers to be impulsive—but others do not improve (Baron et al., 1986). Thus despite the fact that taking more time is correlated with good outcomes, we cannot use time taken as a valid measure of appropriate search.

Another type of measure is based on the idea that rational thinking is affected by beliefs about what good thinking is (Baron, 1991; Schommer, 1990)—that is, by naive theories of rationality itself. Some people appear to believe that looking at the other side is not part of good thinking and that it is better to be "loyal" to an initial conclusion. Kuhn (1991) has explored the nature of such belief systems in some detail through interviews. Tests based on such an approach have the advantage of being usable as "final examinations" in courses designed to teach rational thinking. They do not force the student to accept what may be a controversial theory of rationality, only to understand it.

The idea of rational thinking is associated with a more general movement to teach thinking in schools.

Such an approach will require tests of knowledge of particular domains—social studies, math, etc.—that are sensitive to the quality of thinking that is done in the domain. The development of such tests, and the theory behind them, is perhaps a higher priority than the development of overall tests of rational thinking, even if the latter kind of test is possible at all. Perhaps we will find that current essay examinations and papers can be good measures of rational thinking if they are graded with such criteria in mind. At least, by such criteria, students would not get *A*s for defending a conclusion while ignoring available arguments that fly in its face.

BIBLIOGRAPHY

ARKES, H. R., & BLUMER, C. (1985). The psychology of sunk cost. *Organizational Behavior and Human Decision Processes, 35,* 124–140.

BARON, J. (1985). *Rationality and intelligence.* New York: Cambridge University Press.

BARON, J. (1988). *Thinking and deciding.* New York: Cambridge University Press.

BARON, J. (1990). Harmful heuristics and the improvement of thinking. In D. Kuhn (Ed.), *Developmental perspectives on teaching and learning thinking skills* (pp. 28–47). Basel: Karger.

BARON, J. (1991). Beliefs about thinking. In J. F. Voss, D. N. Perkins, & J. W. Segal (Eds.), *Informal reasoning and education* (pp. 169–186). Hillsdale, NJ: Erlbaum.

BARON, J. (1992). The effect of normative beliefs on anticipated emotions. *Journal of Personality and Social Psychology, 63,* 320–330.

BARON, J., BADGIO, P., & GASKINS, I. W. (1986). Cognitive style and its improvement: A normative approach. In R. J. Sternberg (Ed.), *Advances in the psychology of human intelligence* (Vol. 3, pp. 173–220). Hillsdale, NJ: Erlbaum.

BARON, J., BADGIO, P., & RITOV, Y. (1991). Departures from optimal stopping in an anagram task. *Journal of Mathematical Psychology, 35,* 41–63.

ENNIS, R. H., & MILLMAN, J. (1985). *Cornell critical thinking test.* Pacific Grove, CA: Midwest Publications.

FREY, D. (1986). Recent research on selective exposure to information. In L. Berkowitz (Ed.), *Advances in experimental social psychology* (Vol. 19, pp. 41–80). New York: Academic Press.

HEREK, G. M., JANIS, I. L., & HUTH, P. (1987). Decision making during international crises. *Journal of Conflict Resolution, 31,* 203–226.

HOCH, S. J. (1985). Counterfactual reasoning and accuracy in predicting personal events. *Journal of Experimental Psychology: Learning, Memory, and Cognition, 11,* 719–731.

KUHN, D. (1991). *The skills of argument.* New York: Cambridge University Press.

KUNDA, Z. (1990). The case for motivated reasoning. *Psychological Bulletin, 108,* 480–498.

LARRICK, R. P., MORGAN, J. N., & NISBETT, R. E. (1990). Teaching the use of cost-benefit reasoning in everyday life. *Psychological Science, 1,* 362–370.

LORD, C. G., ROSS, L., & LEPPER, M. R. (1979). Biased assimilation and attitude polarization: The effects of prior theories on subsequently considered evidence. *Journal of Personality and Social Psychology, 37,* 2098–2109.

MESSER, S. B. (1976). Reflection-impulsivity: A review. *Psychological Bulletin, 83,* 1026–1052.

NORRIS, S. P. (1989). Can we test validly for critical thinking? *Educational Researcher, 18,* 21–26.

NORRIS, S. P. (1991). Informal reason assessment: Using verbal reports of thinking to improve multiple-choice test validity. In J. F. Voss, D. N. Perkins, & J. W. Segal (Eds.), *Informal reasoning and education* (pp. 451–472). Hillsdale, NJ: Erlbaum.

PERKINS, D. N. (1989). Reasoning as it is and could be: An empirical perspective. In D. Topping, D. Crowell, & V. Kobayashi (Eds.), *Thinking: The third international conference* (pp. 175–194). Hillsdale, NJ: Erlbaum.

PERKINS, D. N., FARADAY, M., & BUSHEY, B. (1991). Everyday reasoning and the roots of intelligence. In J. F. Voss, D. N. Perkins, & J. W. Segal (Eds.), *Informal reasoning and education* (pp. 83–105). Hillsdale, NJ: Erlbaum.

RITOV, I., & BARON, J. (1990). Reluctance to vaccinate: Omission bias and ambiguity *Journal of Behavioral Decision Making, 3,* 263–277.

SCHOMMER, M. (1990). Effects of beliefs about the nature of knowledge on comprehension. *Journal of Educational Psychology, 82,* 498–504.

SCHROEDER, H. M., DRIVER, M. J., & STREUFERT, S. (1967). *Human information processing.* New York: Holt, Rinehart & Winston.

SUEDFELD, P., & TETLOCK, P. E. (1977). Integrative complexity of communications in international crises. *Journal of Conflict Resolution, 21,* 169–184.

TETLOCK, P. E. (1985). A value pluralism model of ideological reasoning. *Journal of Personality and Social Psychology, 50,* 819–827.

WATSON, G., & GLASER, E. M. (1980). *Watson-Glaser critical thinking appraisal.* Cleveland: The Psychological Corporation.

JONATHAN BARON

RAVEN PROGRESSIVE MATRICES

After Charles E. SPEARMAN developed the concept of g as a general factor in mental ability (1927) and subdivided g into eductive and reproductive abilities, John C. Raven worked closely with him at the University of London to generate measures of these two components. This collaboration led to the creation of the Raven Progressive Matrices (RPM), with the standard version of tests to assess eductive ability first appearing in 1938. The RPM has been described as a series of tests of clear thinking ability, or the ability to make meaning out of confusion, rather than as an intelligence test, since the component of reproductive ability needs separate assessment (for which purpose the Mill Hill Vocabulary Scales were constructed later).

The work of Spearman and the work of Raven were complementary. Spearman developed his theoretical model of the nature of intelligence, with his development of factor analysis and the identification of general and specific abilities, which he labeled g and s. Raven applied these principles to the task of identifying the genetic and environmental origins of mental defect, by constructing tests that were based on theory and easy to administer and interpret.

Factor-analytic studies have consistently shown the RPM to have a high loading on g, typically better than 0.8. The RPM is widely considered one of the purest and best measures of g. Nonetheless, Spearman conceptualized g as only one component of intelligent behavior, so that the RPM, while measuring this well, remains only one component in the full assessment of general intelligence. The RPM measures more than problem-solving ability, requiring perceptual ability to deal with gestalts and relationships, as well as a conceptualization of the nature of the problems presented. Successful performance is also heavily influenced by motivational factors.

While the RPM is often represented as being a measure of fluid intelligence, the manual for the tests makes a clear statement identifying the position of Spearman and Raven, that is, that eductive and reproductive mental activities represent two separate components of g, and "Spearman concluded that the nature, origins and consequences of the two abilities were very different. One is *not* a 'crystallized' form of the other, but they *do* interact considerably in that perception and thought are generally dependent on being able to make meaning out of a confused area of discourse."

The factorial relationship between these two components of g and intelligence as commonly assessed with other instruments is such that the RPM typically correlates in the range of 0.6–0.8. The RPM correlates around 0.5–0.6 with the Mill Hill Vocabulary Scales, while it correlates around 0.8–0.95 with tests of intelligence. This suggests that many full-length intelligence tests are primarily measures of reproductive ability.

Increasing support for the view that the RPM measures what Spearman called "mental speed" is coming from the relationship with reaction-time performance (Vernon, 1987). Matrix problems have been at the very heart of debate over the cross-cultural nature of mental ability (e.g., Jensen, 1988) and appear to be more sensitive to cross-national changes in levels of functioning than are tests with a strongly verbal basis. The success of this paradigm of assessment is seen also in the development of the Cattell Culture-Fair Tests (1977) and in J. Naglieri's Matrix Analogies Test (1985).

A significant by-product of the RPM remaining virtually unchanged for more than fifty years has been that not only can generational changes in ability be identified but also more fundamental questions about the heritability of abilities can be explored. The innate, biologically determined nature of g was largely assumed for many years, but the accumulation of data across social groups and ethnic backgrounds is raising significant questions and suggests more-complex factors contributing to the expression of mental ability.

Theoretical questions regarding the relevance of speed in tests of mental efficiency are increasingly amenable to investigation. With the advent of computerized presentations of the RPM and detailed analysis of error rates and types, with reaction and total times, results can be related to other psychometric measures and biological indices. The RPM has so far proved to be well suited to computerized adaptation.

Various sources indicate that the three versions of RPM (Coloured, Standard, and Advanced) are among the most widely used measures of nonverbal ability, but much less so in the United States than elsewhere because of the lack of appropriate norms. New population-based norms and norms based on ethnicity and socioeconomic status have increasingly overcome that difficulty. Because norming studies have shown a particularly striking increase in scores in many countries, the availability of adequate contemporary norms has become even more critical than with most instruments. Manuals are therefore updated frequently and constructed in modular form to enable users to obtain current information. Concurrently, research continues seeking to provide adequate explanations for the secular increases observed, since inheritance and environment are both frequently involved.

BIBLIOGRAPHY

CATTELL, R. B., & CATTELL, A. K. S. (1977). *Culture-Fair Intelligence Tests*. Champaign, IL: Institute for Personality and Ability Testing.

JENSEN, A. R. (1988). Speed of information and population differences. In S. H. Irvine and J. W. Berry (Eds.), *Human abilities in cultural context*. Cambridge: Cambridge University Press.

NAGLIERI, J. (1985). *Matrix Analogies Test*. San Antonio: The Psychological Corporation.

RAVEN, J. C., COURT, J. H., & RAVEN, J. (1992). *Manual for Raven's Progressive Matrices and Mill Hill Vocabulary Scales*. Oxford: Oxford Psychologists Press.

SPEARMAN, C. (1927). *The nature of "intelligence" and the principles of cognition* (2nd ed.). London: Macmillan.

VERNON, P. A. (1987). *Speed of information processing and intelligence*. Norwood, NJ: Ablex.

JOHN H. COURT

REACTION TIME People's reaction times (RTs) to different kinds of stimuli have enjoyed a long but checkered history in studies of intelligence and its correlates. Indeed, RTs were being used as measures of intellectual capacity many years before the first standardized intelligence quotient (IQ) tests were developed in the early twentieth century. Despite a promising beginning, RTs and measures of other simple sensory processes soon fell into disfavor and were largely ignored until the 1960s. Since then, the use of a variety of RT measures of speed of information processing has become quite widespread, with articles describing relationships between these measures and more traditional measures of intelligence appearing frequently in scientific journals such as *Intelligence* and *Personality and Individual Differences*. P. A. Vernon (1987) has described research on this topic.

Sir Francis GALTON, widely considered the founder of psychometrics and differential psychology, viewed RTs as an important component of intellectual ability and administered RT tests to large samples of people in his laboratories in London, England. Despite the generally unpromising results that he obtained, RTs continued to be employed by other researchers of the time who were interested in intelligence, the foremost being Charles SPEARMAN, Sir Cyril BURT, and James M. CATTELL.

Beginning in the 1960s, researchers studying intelligence (e.g., Roth, 1964) began to adopt a cognitive approach to mental abilities, not so much in place of, as in combination with, the psychometric factor-analytic approach that had dominated during the preceding decades. Cognitive psychology attempts to identify the processes or cognitive operations that people are required to execute while performing different tasks. Differential psychologists attempted to explain individual differences in intelligence-test performance in terms of the probability that people could perform the test's requisite underlying cognitive operations successfully. The speed with which persons could execute different cognitive processes was also viewed as important, and in this context, RTs began to regain acceptance.

One of the early contributors to the resurgence of interest in RTs was Arthur JENSEN. In a series of papers (e.g., Jensen, 1979, 1987), Jensen reported correlations between scores on standard IQ tests and RTs measured on what he refers to as the "Hick apparatus" (named after W. E. Hick, who, in 1952, reported that the linear slope of a graph of RTs, as a function of the number of response alternatives people were faced with in different tasks, reflects their information-processing rate). This apparatus, consisting of a central "home" button and eight lights and response buttons arranged in a semicircle around, and equidistant from, the home button, measures subjects' RTs under four levels of complexity, determined by the number of lights (1, 2, 4, or 8) that are exposed and corresponding to 0, 1, 2, and 3 bits (discrete subtasks) of decision-making information processing. On any trial, a subject presses down the home button and waits for one of the lights to turn on. As soon as a light appears, the subject moves his or her hand and presses the response button beneath it. Typically, subjects' RTs increase (become slower) as a linear function of the number of bits involved in the task. The main measures of interest derived from this task are subjects' median RTs at each level and overall; subjects' movement times (MTs, the speed with which they execute a response) at each level and overall; subjects' intraindividual RT standard deviation (RTSD), which indicates how variable their RTs are from trial to trial; and the slope of RTs as a function of bits, which Jensen interprets as a measure of subjects' ability to process information of increasing complexity. Jensen (1987) reported that subjects' overall median RTs on this test correlate about $-.20$ with their scores on IQ tests (the correlation is negative because higher IQ scores are associated with faster, or shorter, RTs).

Besides Jensen, many other researchers in the United States and around the world have investigated IQ/RT correlations using apparatus similar to Jensen's. One interesting variation on the Hick apparatus is the "odd-man-out task," developed by H. J. EYSENCK in England. In this task, a subject presses down the central home button, which triggers three of the eight exposed lights to turn on simultaneously. Two of these three lights are closer to one another than to the third, and the third, more distant light is the odd man out. On each trial, subjects have to identify the odd man out and to press the response button beneath it as quickly as they can. This task is more complex (i.e., it involves more information processing) than any of Jensen's conditions, and correlations between subjects' RTs on the odd-man-out task and their IQ scores are considerably higher—as high as $-.62$ in one study (Frearson and Eysenck, 1986).

Not all researchers have found significant correlations between IQs and RT measures derived from the Hick apparatus, nor have Jensen's studies gone unchallenged or without criticism. D. K. Detterman (1987), for example, reported IQ/RT correlations ranging between $-.29$ and $-.33$ in different samples, but found no correlation between IQs and slope of RTs. Detterman also found no evidence of IQ/RT correlations increasing as a function of complexity. Unlike Jensen, Detterman argued that RTs in this task do not reflect a simple cognitive process. Rather, Detterman describes RTs as comprising a complex set of processes, only some of which may be related to intelligence, a position also held by D. B. Marr and R. J. Sternberg (1987). Detterman also noted that too little attention had been paid to factors such as motivation, attention, memory, and sensory acuity, any or all of which might be expected to influence subjects' RT performance. In this regard, J. S. Carlson and K. F. Widaman (1987) examined the role of attention and arousal factors in Hick RT performance and the possible contribution of these factors to IQ/RT correlations.

L. E. Longstreth (1984) criticized Jensen's studies on several methodological grounds and concluded that there was little support for an IQ/slope correlation or for IQ/RT correlations increasing with increasing complexity. More recently, A. C. Neubauer (1991) designed a modified Hick apparatus that avoided the methodological problems described by Longstreth. Subjects' RTs on this apparatus were moderately highly correlated with their IQs (between $-.26$ and $-.45$), and a significant slope/IQ correlation of $-.38$ was found. Support was also found for increasing IQ/RT correlations as a function of increasing complexity. In sum, when appropriate steps are taken to avoid a number of possible confounds and artifacts, it appears that correlations of approximately $-.20$ to $-.30$ may be found between IQ and a number of RT parameters derived from the Hick apparatus. Debate continues as to the meaning of these correlations and the nature of the specific cognitive processes underlying the IQ/Hick RT correlation (e.g., Matthews and Dorn, 1989).

In a 1979 paper, J. W. Pellegrino and R. Glaser distinguished between two information-processing approaches to the study of intelligence: the cognitive correlates approach, which "seeks to specify the information processing abilities that are differentially related to high and low levels of aptitude," and the cognitive components approach, which "is task analytic and attempts to directly identify the information processing components of performance on tasks that have been generally used to assess mental abilities" (p. 188). Researchers who have adopted each approach have often employed RTs in their studies.

Earl Hunt and his colleagues provide a good example of the cognitive correlates approach, employing a RT paradigm originally developed by M. Posner (Posner et al., 1969; Posner and Mitchell, 1967) to study cognitive processes that may underlie, and contribute to, individual differences in verbal abilities. In this task, subjects are presented with pairs of letters that have the same name and appear in the same case (e.g., A,A), that have the same name but appear in different cases (e.g., A,a), that have different names but appear in the same case (e.g., A,B), or that differ both in name and case (e.g., A,b). For any pair of letters, the time it takes subjects to make a same or different judgment based on name identity (NI) or physical identity (PI) is recorded.

One measure of particular interest is the difference between subjects' RTs to "same" pairs in the NI (e.g., A,a) and the PI (e.g., A,A) conditions. This difference, which averages about 70 milliseconds in random samples of college students (Posner et al., 1969), is interpreted as the extra time it takes subjects to access the name of the letter in long-term memory, information that is required for a correct "same" decision in the NI but not in the PI condition. E. Hunt, C. Lunneborg, and J. Lewis (1975) divided college students into high and low groups on the basis of their verbal ability and then found that high verbals showed a smaller NI-PI difference (about 64 ms) than low verbals (89 ms). In a later report, Hunt (1978) showed an even larger NI-PI difference (310 ms) among mildly mentally retarded children and, among adults, reported a correlation of about −.30 between NI-PI RT differences and verbal ability as measured by a college entrance exam.

The conclusion to be drawn from these and related studies (e.g., Hunt, Davidson, & Lansman, 1981) is that individuals with higher verbal ability can access and retrieve relevant semantic information from long-term memory more quickly than can individuals of lower verbal ability. Faster memory access is thus identified as a basic information-processing correlate of verbal ability.

A similar cognitive correlates approach has been taken to identify information processes underlying performance on psychometric measures of spatial ability (e.g., Egan, 1979). R. N. Shepard and J. Metzler (1971) developed a "mental rotation" RT task that required subjects to make same–different judgments about pairs of three-dimensional objects that either were the same shape or were mirror images of one another and that also differed in their orientations. In order to make a correct judgment, subjects had to rotate mentally one of the objects until it matched the orientation of the other.

Subjects' RTs in this task were found to increase as a linear function of the difference in orientation of the two objects. The slope of this function is interpreted as an estimate of the rate at which subjects could perform the necessary mental rotation. The intercept of the function estimates the time required for all other processes involved in the task, such as encoding the objects, comparing them after the rotation has been accomplished, and selecting and executing a response. L. A. Cooper and R. N. Shepard (1973a,b) showed that the time it took subjects to rotate mentally letters of the alphabet from nonstandard orientations also increased as a function of the difference between the letters' orientations and their standard upright positions.

Contrary to what might have been expected, D. E. Egan (1979) reported only low correlations between slopes in a mental-rotations RT task and spatial ability. That is, the speed with which subjects could perform mental transformations or rotations was not related to their performance on spatial measures, despite the fact that the spatial tests were taken under timed conditions. At the same time, Egan found a significant correlation of −.30 between spatial ability and the intercept of the rotation function, suggesting that the speed with which subjects can execute encoding and/or responding processes is a cognitive correlate of spatial ability.

In a multivariate study adopting the cognitive correlates approach, M. Lansman, G. Donaldson, E. Hunt, and S. Yantis (1982) administered university students a battery of paper-and-pencil tests selected to define four ability factors: fluid intelligence, crystallized intelligence, spatial visualization, and clerical perceptual speed. The subjects were also given paper-and-pencil and computerized versions of three information-processing tests, including mental rotations, letter matching, and a sentence-verification task. Correlations between the information-processing variables and the ability factors were quite specific, indicating that different cognitive processes underlie different abilities. For example, mental rotations correlated strongly (.78) with spatial visualization but not at all with crystallized and fluid intelligence. Letter matching was correlated with perceptual speed (.69) but not with any of the other three factors. Sentence verification correlated only moderately with perceptual speed (.38) and crystallized intelligence (.28) and showed no correlation with the other two factors. Interestingly, fluid intelligence did not correlate with any of the information-processing variables.

A study such as this illustrates one of the potential benefits of the cognitive correlates approach, the identification of particular cognitive processes specific to one or another ability; this is not possible with the more general speed-of-processing approach taken by Jensen. At the same time, the approach has not always been successful; D. P. Keating, J. A. List, and W. E. Merriman (1985), for example, reported that correlations between letter-matching and mental-rotation information-processing tasks, on the one hand, and ability measures, on the other hand, "failed substantially to conform to the theoretically predicted convergent/discriminant pattern" (p. 149). More critically, Keating and D. J. MacLean (1987) argued that "There seems to be an emerging pattern within the literature that the more carefully specified and rigorously validated the processing parameters become, the *less* cognitive ability variance they account for" (p. 266).

A good example of the cognitive components approach is provided by the work of Robert Sternberg. Sternberg (1977) employed a componential approach in an attempt to specify the particular cognitive processes that subjects have to perform when solving analogical reasoning problems of the form "A is to B as C is to what?" The component processes that Sternberg identified included "encoding" the terms in the

analogy, "inferring" the relationship between the first two terms (i.e., A and B), "mapping" the relationship between the first and third terms (A and C), "applying" the information gained from the inference and mapping stages to the third term and generating an ideal solution that can be used to evaluate and to select among the alternative provided answers, and "responding" with the chosen answer.

By presenting subjects with varying numbers of terms, Sternberg was able to estimate the amount of time subjects devoted to each of these component processes. These RTs were subsequently correlated with their scores on a standardized general reasoning test. Multiple correlations between reasoning scores and RTs for all of the components were high. Not all RTs correlated negatively with reasoning, that is, subjects with high reasoning scores performed some component processes more slowly than subjects of lower reasoning ability. In this regard, E. Hunt (1982) noted that several studies have shown that subjects who obtain high scores on a variety of problem-solving tasks tend to devote a lot of time to early stages of a problem before proceeding to the solutions, whereas lower-scoring subjects tend to devote less time to the initial information and to move quickly to examine the alternative provided solutions. He went on to suggest that with the appropriate use of RTs "it should be possible to design tests that tell us how, as well as how well, people respond to the problems now presented on intelligence tests" (p. 235).

Another RT paradigm that has been used quite extensively in intelligence research is based on a probe-recognition test developed by Saul Sternberg (1966), which measures the speed with which subjects can scan or process information that they are storing in short-term or working memory. In this test, subjects are first shown a string of digits (or letters or other symbols, such as geometric shapes) on the screen of a computer monitor. Typically, anywhere from one to seven digits will be presented and subjects are instructed to read these and to try to remember them. After a short period of time, perhaps 2 seconds, the string of digits will disappear and be replaced by a single "probe" digit. The subjects' task is to indicate as quickly as they can whether or not the probe digit was a member of the previous string.

Early studies using the Sternberg test reported that

mentally retarded subjects responded significantly more slowly than did subjects of average intelligence (e.g., Dugas and Kellas, 1974). D. P. Keating and B. L. Bobbitt (1978) administered the Sternberg test to sixty children, twenty each from the third, seventh, and eleventh grades, in addition to giving them a simple and choice RT test, a card-sorting task that was a modification of the letter-sorting task involving name identity versus physical identity, described above, and the RAVEN PROGRESSIVE MATRICES as a measure of general intelligence. Adopting the cognitive correlates approach, Keating and Bobbitt derived measures from the information-processing tasks to estimate decision-making efficiency, long-term memory retrieval speed, and short-term memory scanning speed. After controlling for age differences, these cognitive measures accounted for 15 percent of the variance in Raven scores, which the authors interpreted as showing that a significant proportion of the variance in intelligence can be accounted for by basic cognitive-processing efficiency. When the Sternberg test performance of children of different ages and levels of ability was examined, an interesting relationship between age and ability approached statistical significance. The authors interpreted this result as suggesting that ability differences in basic cognitive-processing efficiency may become less pronounced with increasing age, as more general processing strategies are acquired.

In a number of studies, P. A. Vernon (e.g., 1983, 1989a; Vernon and Kantor, 1986) administered a battery of RT tests to different groups of subjects, including university and high school students and samples of identical and fraternal twins, in addition to obtaining intelligence test scores. The RT tests included measures of short-term memory scanning speed, long-term memory retrieval speed, and estimates of the efficiency with which subjects could process one kind of information in working memory while simultaneously storing other information. Multiple correlations between IQ scores and RTs on the several tests range from .37 to .74 across the different samples, again indicating that the speed with which subjects can execute different cognitive processes is quite highly related to their performance on standard tests of intelligence. Vernon interpreted the results as showing that individuals with higher intelligence employ faster information-processing speed as a means to overcome

or to compensate for such limitations of the working memory as its limited storage capacity and the rapid loss of information that occurs in the absence of rehearsal.

From the twin samples, Vernon (1989b) estimated the heritabilities of eleven RT measures. These ranged from .23 to .92, indicating that a moderate to a substantial amount of the between-subject variance in RTs is attributable to genetic factors. Moreover, there was a positive correlation (.60) between the heritabilities of the RT tests and the degree to which each one correlated with IQ. L. A. Baker, P. A. Vernon, and H-Z. Ho (1991) extended these findings and reported a substantial genetic correlation between measures of RTs and intelligence, suggesting a common biological basis for both. In this regard, a number of physiological measures, such as averaged evoked potentials and nerve-conduction velocity have been reported to correlate moderately highly both with IQ scores and with RTs (Vernon & Mori, 1990, 1992).

In conclusion, researchers have developed numerous RT tests that vary in complexity and tap a number of different cognitive operations. Correlations between these tests and standard tests of intelligence range between approximately −.20 and −.50; multiple correlations as high as .70 have been reported. Researchers have employed RTs in a variety of ways, most of which can be classified as examples of either the cognitive correlates approach or the cognitive components approach. Despite the potential value of RT studies, they have been the subject of a number of methodological and theoretical criticisms. Notwithstanding such criticism, RTs continue to play a role in many different types of investigations into the nature of human intelligence.

BIBLIOGRAPHY

BAKER, L. A., VERNON, P. A., & HO, H-Z. (1991). The genetic correlation between intelligence and speed of information-processing. *Behavior Genetics, 21,* 351–367.

CARLSON, J. S., & WIDAMAN, K. F. (1987). Elementary cognitive correlates of *g*: Progress and prospects. In P. A. Vernon (Ed.), *Speed of information-processing and intelligence.* Norwood, NJ: Ablex.

COOPER, L. A., & SHEPARD, R. N. (1973a). Chronometric studies of the rotation of mental images. In W. C. Chase

(Ed.), *Visual information processing*. New York: Academic Press.

COOPER, L. A., & SHEPARD, R. N. (1973b). The time required to prepare for a rotated stimulus. *Memory and Cognition, 1,* 246–250.

DETTERMAN, D. K. (1987). What does reaction time tell us about intelligence? In P. A. Vernon (Ed.), *Speed of information-processing and intelligence.* Norwood, NJ: Albex.

DUGAS, J. L., & KELLAS, G. (1974). Encoding and retrieval processes in normal children and retarded adolescents. *Journal of Experimental Child Psychology, 17,* 177–185.

EGAN, D. E. (1979). *An analysis of spatial orientation test performance.* Paper presented to the American Educational Research Association, San Francisco.

FREARSON, W. M., & EYSENCK, H. J. (1986). Intelligence, reaction time (RT) and a new "odd-man-out" RT paradigm. *Personality and Individual Differences, 7,* 807–817.

HICK, W. E. (1952). On the rate of gain of information. *Quarterly Journal of Experimental Psychology, 4,* 11–26.

HUNT, E. (1978). Mechanics of verbal ability. *Psychological Review, 85,* 109–130.

HUNT, E. (1982). Towards new ways of assessing intelligence. *Intelligence, 6,* 231–240.

HUNT, E., DAVIDSON, J., & LANSMAN, M. (1981). Individual differences in long-term memory access. *Memory and Cognition, 9,* 599–608.

HUNT, E., FROST, N., & LUNNEBORG, C. (1973). Individual differences in cognition: A new approach to intelligence. In G. Bower (Ed.), *The psychology of learning and motivation* (Vol. 7). New York: Academic Press.

HUNT, E., LUNNEBORG, C., & LEWIS, J. (1975). What does it mean to be high verbal? *Cognitive Psychology, 7,* 194–227.

JENSEN, A. R. (1979). g: Outmoded theory or unconquered frontier? *Creative Science and Technology, 2,* 16–29.

JENSEN, A. R. (1987). Individual differences in the Hick paradigm. In P. A. Vernon (Ed.), *Speed of information-processing and intelligence.* Norwood, NJ: Albex.

KEATING, D. P., & BOBBITT, B. L. (1978). Individual and developmental differences in cognitive-processing components of mental ability. *Child Development, 49,* 155–167.

KEATING, D. P., LIST, J. A., & MERRIMAN, W. E. (1985). Cognitive processing and cognitive ability: A multivariate validity investigation. *Intelligence, 9,* 149–170.

KEATING, D. P., & MACLEAN, D. J. (1987). Cognitive processing, cognitive ability, and development: A reconsideration. In P. A. Vernon (Ed.), *Speed of information-processing and intelligence.* Norwood, NJ: Albex.

LANSMAN, M., DONALDSON, G., HUNT, E., & YANTIS, S. (1982). Ability factors and cognitive processes. *Intelligence, 6,* 347–386.

LONGSTRETH, L. E. (1984). Jensen's reaction-time investigations of intelligence: A critique. *Intelligence, 8,* 139–160.

MARR, D. B., & STERNBERG, R. J. (1987). The role of mental speed in intelligence: A triarchic perspective. In P. A. Vernon (Ed.), *Speed of information-processing and intelligence.* Norwood, NJ: Albex.

MATTHEWS, G., & DORN, L. (1989). IQ and choice reaction time: An information processing analysis. *Intelligence, 13,* 299–317.

NEUBAUER, A. C. (1991). Intelligence and RT: A modified Hick paradigm and a new RT paradigm. *Intelligence, 15,* 175–192.

PELLEGRINO, J. W., & GLASER, R. (1979). Cognitive correlates and components in the analysis of individual differences. *Intelligence, 3,* 187–214.

POSNER, M., BOIES, S., EICHELMAN, W., & TAYLOR, R. (1969). Retention of visual and name codes of single letters. *Journal of Experimental Psychology Monographs, 79*(1, Pt. 2).

POSNER, M., & MITCHELL, R. (1967). Chronometric analysis of classification. *Psychological Review, 74,* 392–409.

ROTH, E. (1964). Die Geschwindigkeit der Verarbeitung von Information und ihr Zusammenhang mit Intelligenz [The speed of information processing and its relationship with intelligence]. *Zeitschrift für experimentelle und angewandte Psychologie, 11,* 616–622.

SHEPARD, R. N., & METZLER, J. (1971). Mental rotation of three-dimensional objects. *Science, 171,* 701–703.

STERNBERG, R. J. (1977). *Intelligence, information processing, and analogical reasoning: The componential analysis of human abilities.* Hillsdale, NJ: Erlbaum.

STERNBERG, R. J. (1980). Sketch of a componential subtheory of human intelligence. *Behavioral and Brain Sciences, 3,* 573–584.

STERNBERG, R. J. (1985). *Beyond IQ: A triarchic theory of human intelligence.* New York: Cambridge University Press.

STERNBERG, S. (1966). High-speed scanning in human memory. *Science, 153,* 652–654.

VERNON, P. A. (ED.). (1987). *Speed of information-processing and intelligence.* Norwood, NJ: Albex.

VERNON, P. A. (1989a). The generality of g. *Personality and Individual Differences, 10,* 803–804.

VERNON, P. A. (1989b). The heritability of measures of speed of information-processing. *Personality and Individual Differences, 10,* 573–576.

VERNON, P. A., & KANTOR, L. (1986). Reaction time correlations with intelligence test scores obtained under either timed or untimed conditions. *Intelligence, 10,* 315–330.

VERNON, P. A., & MORI, M. (1990). Physiological approaches to the assessment of intelligence. In C. R. Reynolds & R. W. Kamphaus (Eds.), *Handbook of psychological and educational assessment of children: Intelligence and achievement.* New York: Guilford Press.

VERNON, P. A., & MORI, M. (1992). Intelligence, reaction times, and peripheral nerve conduction velocity. *Intelligence, 16,* 273–288.

PHILIP ANTHONY VERNON

READING   Two kinds of reading-ability differences among individuals have been identified and studied. The first, contrasting those who succeed at learning to read and those who do not, entails a consideration of *developmental dyslexia,* the failure to learn to read at a level expected on the basis of the student's intelligence and opportunity to learn. The second shows the individual variation among those who appear to be competent in reading. One of the earliest discussions of such variation appears in the landmark treatise on reading by Edmund Burke Huey (1908–1968). Noting the wide differences in reading rate observed among college students, Huey cited a study by Abell (1894) at Wellesley College that found rate differences of 600 percent between the fastest and slowest readers, an individual difference estimate that remains compatible with more recent ones.

Reading can be defined broadly or narrowly. On the narrow definition, reading is translating information encoded in a writing system into language; its key process is recognition of printed words, or decoding. On the broader view, reading is understanding printed language; here there is no single key process because all the processes that allow language comprehension are relevant. These two definitions have different implications for the analysis of individual differences. The narrow definition focuses attention on processes that superficially appear peculiar to reading, that is, the elements of the decoding process. The broad definition entails attention to all the processes used in language comprehension. Ironically, it is the narrow definition that has been most fruitful in uncovering links between language processes and reading. This is because it allows discovery of the linguistic factors embedded in the task of learning to read. It also simplifies the picture of what learning and failing to learn to read are about (see Gough & Tunmer, 1986).

LEARNING TO READ

The central requirement for the acquisition of reading competence is learning a writing system. This requires the learner to figure out implicitly an answer to this question: How does the writing system encode my language? Whatever additionally is involved in becoming a skilled reader, the learner must learn to decode the writing system. (For theoretical accounts of this learning, see Gough & Juel, 1991; Ehri, 1991; and Perfetti, 1991.)

The universal acquisition of language stands in contrast with the variable acquisition of reading skill. Although the design principles of language may be biologically given (Pinker, 1984), writing systems are substantially the result of human invention. They vary, accordingly, in how they work: Alphabetic systems (e.g., English, Italian, and Korean) map graphic units (letters, such as *b*) onto speech segments (*phonemes,* such as the sound "bee"). Syllabary systems (e.g., Japanese Kana) keep the mapping between written units and speech, but at the level of the syllable instead of the phoneme. Still other systems (e.g., Arabic, Hebrew, and Persian) are primarily alphabetic, but represent only consonants in the writing system. Logographic systems (e.g., Chinese), however, map graphic units not to speech, but to meaning (morphemes). Each system presents its own set of problems to the learner.

Learning to Read a Language with a Phonetic Alphabet.   The Phoenician-Greek invention of the alphabet was a unique achievement, following far behind the adaptation of visual forms as symbols for meanings. This invention—a writing system in which a written unit represents a meaningless spoken unit (phoneme)—required the discovery that speech has such units. Because phonemes are abstractions over highly variable acoustic events and because they are meaningless, children have a difficult time in replicating the discovery of this principle.

This is the problem of *phonemic awareness,* an explicit demonstration of the segmental structure of speech, e.g., to say "cat" without the /t/. Before they have had reading instruction, many children cannot make such a demonstration. Research in a number of languages has further shown that phonemic awareness predicts reading success and that gains in reading can follow gains in phonemic awareness. Moreover, there is evidence that the relationship between learning to read and phonemic awareness is reciprocal, with learning-to-read measures predicting gains in phonemic-awareness measures, as well as vice versa. Adult illiterates develop little phonemic awareness.

Learning to read in nonalphabetic systems provides a contrast. In Chinese, students must learn hundreds of individual characters. (Leong [1973] estimates 3,500 characters during the six years of elementary school.) Since this is largely form-meaning associative learning, the opportunity to acquire phonemic awareness is reduced. Indeed, Chinese adults who have learned only the traditional character system show little phonemic awareness, in contrast to those who have also learned pinyin, an alphabetic complement to the character system (Read et al., 1986).

Thus phonemic awareness appears not to develop spontaneously outside of appropriate literacy contexts, but the ability to acquire it as part of learning to read is a critical factor in learning to read an alphabetic writing system.

Dyslexia and Difficulties in Learning to Read—Overview. Children are considered dyslexic if their reading achievement is sufficiently low relative to some standard (usually two grades below their grade level), and if the deficit cannot be accounted for by low IQ or lack of an opportunity to learn. (See Stanovich [1988] for a good discussion of these complex definition issues.) It is not clear, however, whether the causes of reading failure are different for a carefully defined subgroup than for a more broadly defined category of "garden variety" poor readers. The designation *less skilled* serves to represent readers who are below norm in reading achievement, without necessarily fitting a narrower category of dyslexia.

Children with reading problems show deficits in phonological processing, including phonemic awareness. There is a distinction between awareness, exhib-

ited in an explicit form, and phonological processing, demonstrated implicitly in ordinary speech perception and production. The high correlations among various phonological tasks, however, may point to a unitary phonological ability (Stanovich, Cunningham, & Cramer, 1984).

Working Memory. One pervasive difference is in working memory. Less skilled readers, defined by performance on comprehension tests, are less able to remember words that they have just read than are skilled readers (Goldman et al., 1980). Furthermore, this same memory difference is observed for spoken language (Perfetti & Goldman, 1976). The implication is that less skilled readers have reduced working memory capacities, a deficit that can show itself in a number of processes engaged during language processing. Word identification, meaning processes, syntactic analysis of sentences (parsing), and text integration co-occur in a limited-capacity working memory system. Among these, word identification is singled out for its potential to be relatively automatic, or free of resource limitations (Perfetti, 1985).

There is some evidence that this working memory deficit is phonological and restricted to linguistic inputs (Katz, Shankweiler, & Liberman, 1981). A phonological deficit is also implicated in the finding that less skilled readers, unlike skilled readers, sometimes fail to show phonological confusions in memory when presented with phonemically similar words and sentences (Mann, Liberman, & Shankweiler, 1980). Less clear is whether less skilled readers have deficits in basic speech perception, as well as in speech-based memory. There is evidence both for such deficits (Brady, Shankweiler, & Mann, 1983) and against them (Snowling, Stackhouse, & Rack, 1986; Pennington et al., 1990).

Dyslexia and Lexical Processes. The central defining characteristic of reading disability is a problem of reading words, and the phonological system is heavily implicated in this problem. A particularly indicative diagnostic is the child's inability to read aloud *pseudowords,* pronounceable letter strings that conform to spelling conventions, e.g., *brait.* Pseudoword reading reflects the reader's knowledge of the writing system and the way it encodes phonology, and is something typically beyond the reach of a disabled reader. Furthermore, differences in pseudoword naming between skilled and less skilled readers are typically greater than their differences in reading actual words (Hogaboam & Perfetti, 1978). Real words can be recognized on the basis of word-specific memories, whereas knowledge of the code—decoding—is necessary for pseudoword reading. Thus pseudoword reading is especially sensitive to the decoding failures that are the marker of dyslexia.

How to understand the decoding problem in detail is not completely clear. It may be a particular manifestation of a general phonological deficit. Or it may be a mapping problem, specific to acquiring letterphoneme mappings. A plausible alternative goes as follows: Phonological representations are unreliable for disabled readers. Decoding adds stress to an unreliable phonological system because it requires structural analysis of spelling patterns plus phonological "translation." (See Perfetti, 1985, for further discussion; see Stanovich, 1988, for a discussion of the phonological deficit hypothesis.)

A Genetic Basis for Dyslexia. Reading disabilities occur much more frequently among relatives of people with such disabilities than among nonrelatives (DeFries & Decker, 1982). More direct evidence that this familial pattern reflects genetic differences rather than environmental ones comes from a longitudinal study of identical and same-sex fraternal twins (Olson et al., 1990). The key result is the heritability estimates, based on the correlations between general word recognition and each of two component tasks, one measuring orthographic (spelling) knowledge, and the other measuring phonological processing through a pseudoword decoding test. The correlation between pseudoword naming and word recognition was significantly heritable (.93), whereas the correlation between orthographic coding and word recognition was not heritable (or had zero heritability). To put it another way, for identical twins one can predict the word recognition of the second twin by knowing the pseudoword reading of the disabled twin; but knowing the orthographic score of the disabled twin does not allow prediction of the word recognition of the second twin. In terms of word knowledge, knowing that *rain* (but not *rane*) is a word is a matter of learning, of environment rather than heredity; but knowing how to pronounce *framble* (a pseudoword) is a phonological coding ability with a genetic component. Olson et al.

(1990) suggest this ability is not directly heritable, but is a reflection of a heritable segmentation ability (phonemic awareness).

Methodological Issues. Individual difference research has significant methodological problems. Much of the research comparing readers of different skill uses an age-match design by which two groups of the same age, one average in reading and one below average, are compared. Differences found between the two groups on some task that taps a component of reading are difficult to interpret, because the more highly skilled group is likely to have had more experience in reading. Observed differences in, say, pseudoword reading may merely reflect different exposures to letter strings in the course of reading. Because of this, many researchers have advocated reading-match designs, in which an older, less skilled reading group is compared with a younger, more skilled reading group (Bryant & Bradley, 1985). Because the age difference is assumed to reverse the experience advantage, any differences in a component task favoring the younger, more skilled group cannot be attributed to experience. There are arguments in favor of the agematch design as well (Shankweiler et al., 1992).

A related methodological issue is the definition of reading disability, particularly the degree of exclusivity. The definition of dyslexia excludes general low intellectual functioning, thus honoring the assumption that there is a disability specific to reading (or at least to language). The fact that intellectual abilities, including reading, are inconveniently intercorrelated creates problems for researchers in subject selection, and not all studies are successful in isolating "pure" cases of specific reading disability. Because of its correlation with reading ability, controlling for IQ creates its own problems, e.g., regression toward the mean (Stanovich, 1986, 1988). It remains to be seen whether the conclusions about processing problems are different for differently defined subgroups.

READING COMPETENCE— WORD IDENTIFICATION

Individual differences among older children and adults appear both in higher-level processes of comprehension and in word identification. Even among college readers, word identification differences continue to be found (Cunningham, Stanovich, & Wilson, 1990).

Phonology and Word Identification. Individual differences in phonological processes may extend to adults. The role of phonology in skilled word identification, however, has been a matter of some dispute. The dominant theory of word recognition has been dual route theory (Coltheart, 1978; Besner, 1990). Readers access printed words in parallel along two routes: a direct route based on the word's specific visual form, that is, its letters and its appearance; and a mediated second route, based on converting spellings to phonemic sequences, which, in turn, produce lexical access. Words that are high in frequency tend to be recognized along the direct route, whereas words that are low in frequency but high in regularity—words whose phonemic segments are well predicted by their letter constituents—are recognized along the mediated phonological route. For skilled readers, the direct route is used whenever possible. Considerable evidence is consistent with the predictions of dual route theory (Paap & Noel, 1991), and it lends itself to an interesting hypothesis concerning individual differences. Some readers may use mainly the direct route, whereas other readers may use primarily the phonological route.

This preference for one route over another was proposed as an individual difference for skilled adult readers by Baron and Strawson (1976), who referred to readers who use the direct route as "Chinese" and readers who use the phonological group as "Phoenicians."

There is evidence for distinct orthographic and phonological processing abilities in word recognition (Stanovich & West, 1989). The orthographic skill arises from experience with specific words and is reflected in tasks that require word knowledge, especially spelling. The phonological skill, reflected in pseudoword decoding, is based on basic linguistic and decoding abilities. These twin abilities can be viewed as contributing jointly to word reading, rather than as all-or-nothing strategies for word recognition. In effect, they describe not qualitative differences but simply what readers know that allows them to read words.

Alternatives to dual route theories come from generalized activation models with a single mechanism by which perceived letter strings activate word candidates (McClelland & Rumelhart, 1981; see also connectionist models of Seidenberg & McClelland, 1990, and Van Orden, Pennington & Stone, 1990). Such a model can be modified to allow phonemes to be routinely activated as part of word identification, making phonology nonoptional in word identification (Perfetti & Mc-Cutchen, 1982). Individual differences in generalized activation models imply a quantitative description of any "preferences" for phonological or graphemic "routes" to word recognition. Whether phonological activation is always part of word recognition or an optional path remains an active focus of research.

Word Identification in Context. A second word identification issue is how words are identified in ordinary text reading. The research consensus is that some part of the process of identifying a word is facilitated by context. Skilled readers, however, do *not* make greater use of context than less skilled readers. The hallmark of a skilled reader is context-free word identification. Skilled readers' use of context is limited by their basic fluent abilities in identifying words. It is less skilled readers who use contexts to identify words, simply because their context-free word identification skills are not up to the task of reading.

Of the many studies addressing skill and age differences in discourse and sentence context effects on word identification, none reports a greater context facilitation effect for skilled readers, and most report greater facilitation for less skilled readers. The conclusion, however, is not that skilled readers do not use context. The same skilled readers whose time to name words is relatively unaffected by context are much better than less skilled readers in predicting the word that would appear next in a discourse (Perfetti & Roth, 1981). The skill reflected in this difference is one that aids comprehension processes, those that select the appropriate meaning of a word and integrate it into a message representation. For discussions of the substantial research on this issue, see Perfetti (1985) and Stanovich (1980).

READING COMPETENCE— TEXT LEVEL PROCESSES

Beyond word identification are the processes of comprehension, understanding sentences, integrating sentence meanings, and making inferences. Individual differences presumably exist in any of the components of reading comprehension. And they clearly exist in the outcome of these processes, that is, the comprehension of written texts.

Although a detailed account of comprehension depends on specific models, a descriptively coherent view helpful for considering individual differences goes as follows: Readers access words (lexical access), select the meanings of words required by context (meaning selection), build syntactic structures from strings of words (parsing), interpret the meanings of these word strings (proposition encoding), integrate these meanings (proposition integration) and, by using other sources of knowledge and making inferences, construct mental models of what these meanings are about (constructing a situation model). Some of these processes, especially lexical access and parsing, appear to operate very rapidly and with only limited influence from higher level knowledge sources. Global differences in reading comprehension skill have been related to all of these processes, from lexical access (Perfetti, 1985) through inference making (Oakhill & Garnham, 1988).

Working Memory. What must be added to the account of these various processes is the assumption that many of them demand mental resources, that is, working memory. Individual differences can then be attributed to individual differences in working memory capacity. This conclusion has been an important part of the individual difference research for some time (Perfetti & Lesgold, 1977; Just & Carpenter, 1992). The appeal of this account is that it can provide a single mechanism for a wide range of individual differences in text comprehension, including differences in remembering the gist of a story, drawing necessary inferences, and making incorrect syntactic analyses. It has two other generalities: It applies to children and adults, and it applies to differences among skilled adults and between skilled readers and dyslexics.

Lexical Processes. Although it might be possible to reduce all observed differences to working memory factors, individual differences in lexical processes are less naturally explained by memory capacity difference. Adult college students who differ in comprehension scores also differ in lexical processing (Cunningham, Stanovich, & Wilson, 1990) and in letter-level processing (Jackson & McClelland, 1979).

Furthermore, a body of research on individual differences in verbal ability is relevant. In this work, variability among college students in verbal components of college admission tests is associated with low-level symbol manipulation speed (Hunt, Lunneborg, & Lewis, 1975). Although such differences might be traced to differences in verbal experience, they might also reflect basic processing factors, such as symbol manipulation and memory access. Such processes can be united with working memory factors if one focuses not on the capacity of memory but on its function in accessing and manipulating information.

Individual differences go beyond lexical access to the selection of word meaning. In text reading, more than one meaning of an ambiguous word is activated initially. This very brief activation stage is followed by the selection of the meaning that is appropriate for the context. Thus, a reader who encounters the ambiguous word *spade* in the sentence "He dug with the spade" appears to have both the digging instrument and the playing-card sense of *spade* activated for a few milliseconds before he or she selects the required interpretation. Gernsbacher (1990) summarizes studies finding that skilled adult readers follow the process just described, but less skilled adult readers do not. Instead, they show evidence that the inappropriate meaning of the word remains activated for nearly a second. Skilled readers have a mechanism that suppresses irrelevant meanings, but this suppression mechanism is not effective for less skilled readers.

General Language Differences. Reading ability differences are largely general language processing differences. Indeed, among adults, for whom decoding abilities have reached asymptotic levels, very high correlations are observed between spoken and written comprehension. Gernsbacher, Varner, and Faust (1990), for example, report correlations of .92 between written and spoken comprehension among their sample of college students. And the best predictor of adult *effective reading speed*—the product of reading speed and comprehension—appears to be listening comprehension (Jackson & McClelland, 1979). These results point to a compelling conclusion: Once a reader has learned how the writing system encodes the language, then reading comprehension is largely a matter of language comprehension. Factors distinctive to written texts do exist, but they are not significant sources of ability differences compared to general language and cognitive factors.

Reading Rate. Differences in reading rate are controlled by individual response to text demands. However, within broad limits, rates are relatively stable for individuals (Carver, 1983). The rate of individual reading seems to reflect the efficiency with which basic processes are executed, and this rate is usually positively associated with comprehension. Faster readers are better comprehenders, in general. Furthermore, differences between more skilled and less skilled readers are increased when faster reading is required. Nevertheless, there appears to be a component to reading speed that is a style factor independent of comprehension. Although there is a general positive correlation between rate and comprehension, many relatively slow readers are good at comprehension, as Huey noted in citing Abell's study (Palmer et al., 1985).

THEORIES OF
INDIVIDUAL DIFFERENCES

Theories of individual differences tend to emphasize particular component processes that produce skill differences. For example, the interactive-compensatory model (Stanovich, 1980) emphasizes the weak word-processing abilities of less skilled readers and their compensating use of context in word identification. Verbal efficiency theory (Perfetti & Lesgold, 1979; Perfetti, 1985) explains differences in reading comprehension skill by variability in the efficiency of lower-level processes, especially word identification, that occur in a limited-capacity working memory system. A related model, developed in considerably more detail, is the capacity model of Just and Carpenter (1992), which explains a wide range of specific comprehension differences by individual differences in working memory, as measured by a memory span task.

Two models emphasize phonological processes as central to reading problems in children. The phonological capacity model follows the assumption of verbal efficiency theory that working memory is a bottleneck to the flow of information in comprehension, adding explicitly the assumption that phonological processing is the specific source of the memory problem (Crain & Shankweiler, 1988). The phonological-core-variable difference model (Stanovich, 1988) is a descriptive statistical model that integrates data on dyslexia and garden variety low-skilled readers. The basic claim is that reading skill is distributed as a continuum, rather than as a nonnormal distribution with a "bump" at the lower end of the distribution representing dyslexic readers (Rutter & Yule, 1975). According to this model, the central processing deficit is phonological for both those readers whose IQs are high relative to their reading and for those with lower IQs. The garden variety poor reader, however, has a less severe phonological deficit accompanied by a variety of cognitive deficits.

The structure building framework of Gernsbacher (1990) integrates individual difference research with adult readers into a general theory of comprehension. This theory targets the mechanisms that serve structure building, the incremental construction of meanings from a text, in both reading and spoken language comprehension. It focuses on two problems: Less skilled comprehenders shift too often from a current structure to a new structure, a mechanism that explains their poorer memory for just-read information; and less skilled comprehenders have ineffective suppression mechanisms, explaining poor comprehenders' slowness at deactivating the irrelevant meaning of unambiguous words.

(*See also:* DYSLEXIA.)

BIBLIOGRAPHY

ABELL, A. M. (1894). Rapid reading. *Educational Review, 8,* 283.

BARON, J., & STRAWSON, C. (1976). Use of orthographic and word specific knowledge in reading words aloud. *Journal of Experimental Psychology: Human Perception and Performance, 2,* 386–393.

BESNER, D. (1990). Does the reading system need a lexicon? In D. Balota, G. B. Flores d'Arcais, & K. Rayner (Eds.), *Comprehension processes in reading* (pp. 73–99). Hillsdale, NJ: Erlbaum.

BRADY, S., SHANKWEILER, D., & MANN, V. (1983). Speech perception and memory coding in relation to reading ability. *Journal of Experimental Child Psychology, 35,* 345–367.

BRYANT, P. E., & BRADLEY, L. (1985). *Children's reading problems.* Oxford, England: Blackwell.

CARVER, R. P. (1983). Is reading rate constant or flexible? *Reading Research Quarterly, 18,* 190–215.

COLTHEART, M. (1978). Lexical access in simple reading tasks. In G. Underwood (Ed.), *Strategies of information processing* (pp. 151–216). New York: Academic Press.

CRAIN, S., & SHANKWEILER, D. (1988). Syntactic complexity and reading acquisition. In A. Davison & G. M. Green (Eds.), *Linguistic complexity and text comprehension: Readability issues reconsidered* (pp. 167–192). Hillsdale, NJ: Erlbaum.

CUNNINGHAM, A. E., STANOVICH, K. E., & WILSON, M. R. (1990). Cognitive variation in adult students differing in reading ability. In T. H. Carr & B. A. Levy (Eds.), *Reading and its development: Component skills approaches* (pp. 129–159). New York: Academic Press.

DEFRIES, J. C., & DECKER, S. N. (1982). Genetic aspects of reading disability: A family study. In R. N. Malatesha & P. G. Arron (Eds.), *Reading disorders: Varieties and treatments* (pp. 255–279). New York: Academic Press.

EHRI, L. C. (1991). Learning to read and spell words. In L. Rieben & C. A. Perfetti (Eds.), *Learning to read: Basic research and its implications* (pp. 57–73). Hillsdale, NJ: Erlbaum.

GERNSBACHER, M. A. (1990). *Language comprehension as structure building.* Hillsdale, NJ: Erlbaum.

GERNSBACHER, M. A., VARNER, K. R., & FAUST, M. E. (1990). Investigating differences in general comprehension skill. *Journal of Experimental Psychology: Learning, Memory, and Cognition, 16,* 430–445.

GOLDMAN, S. R., HOGABOAM, T. W., BELL, L. C., & PERFETTI, C. A. (1980). Short-term retention of discourse during reading. *Journal of Educational Psychology, 72,* 647–655.

GOUGH, P. B., & JUEL, C. (1991). The first stages of word recognition. In L. Rieben & C. A. Perfetti (Eds.), *Learning to read: Basic research and its implications* (pp. 47–56). Hillsdale, NJ: Erlbaum.

GOUGH, P. B., & TUNMER, W. E. (1986). Decoding, reading, and reading disability. *Remedial and Special Education, 7,* 6–10.

HOGABOAM, T. W., & PERFETTI, C. A. (1978). Reading skill and the role of verbal experience in decoding. *Journal of Educational Psychology, 70,* 717–729.

HUEY, E. B. (1968). *The psychology and pedagogy of reading; with a review of the history of reading and writing and of methods, texts, and hygiene in reading.* Cambridge, MA: MIT Press.

HUNT, E., LUNNEBORG, C., & LEWIS, J. (1975). What does it mean to be high verbal? *Cognitive Psychology, 7,* 194–227.

JACKSON, M. D., & MCCLELLAND, J. L. (1979). Processing determinants of reading speed. *Journal of Experimental Psychology: General, 108,* 151–181.

JUST, M. A., & CARPENTER, P. A. (1992). A capacity theory of comprehension: Individual differences in working memory. *Psychological Review, 99,* 122–149.

KATZ, R. B., SHANKWEILER, D., & LIBERMAN, I. Y. (1981). Memory for item order and phonetic recoding in the beginning reader. *Journal of Experimental Child Psychology, 32,* 474–484.

LEONG, C. K. (1973). Reading in Chinese with reference to reading practices in Hong Kong. In J. Downing (Ed.), *Comparative reading: Cross-national studies of behavior and processes in reading and writing.* New York: Macmillan.

MANN, V. A., LIBERMAN, I. Y., & SHANKWEILER, D. (1980). Children's memory for sentences and word strings in relation to reading ability. *Memory & Cognition, 8,* 329–335.

MCCLELLAND, J. L., & RUMELHART, D. E. (1981). An interactive activation model of context effects in letter perception: 1. An account of basic findings. *Psychological Review, 88,* 357–407.

OAKHILL, J., & GARNHAM, A. (1988). *Becoming a skilled reader.* New York: Basil Blackwell.

OLSON, R., WISE, B., CONNERS, F., & RACK, J. (1990). Organization, heritability, and remediation of component word recognition skills in disabled readers. In T. H. Carr & B. A. Levy (Eds.), *Reading and its development: Component skills approaches* (pp. 261–322). New York: Academic Press.

PAAP, K. R., & NOEL, R. W. (1991). Dual-route models of print and sound: Still a good horse race. *Psychological Research, 53,* 13–24.

PALMER, J., MACLEOD, C. M., HUNT, E., & DAVIDSON, J. E. (1985). Information processing correlates of reading. *Journal of Memory and Language, 24,* 59–88.

PENNINGTON, B. F., VAN ORDEN, G. C., SMITH, S. D., GREEN, P. A., & HAITH, M. M. (1990). Phonological processing skills and deficits in adult dyslexics. *Child Development, 61,* 1753–1778.

PERFETTI, C. A. (1985). *Reading Ability.* New York: Oxford University Press.

PERFETTI, C. A. (1991). Representations and awareness in the acquisition of reading competence. In L. Rieben & C. A. Perfetti (Eds.), *Learning to read: Basic research and its implications* (pp. 33–44). Hillsdale, NJ: Erlbaum.

PERFETTI, C. A., & GOLDMAN, S. R. (1976). Discourse memory and reading comprehension skill. *Journal of Verbal Learning and Verbal Behavior, 14,* 33–42.

PERFETTI, C. A., & LESGOLD, A. M. (1977). Discourse comprehension and sources of individual differences. In P. A. Carpenter & M. A. Just (Eds.), *Cognitive processes in comprehension* (pp. 141–183). Hillsdale, NJ: Erlbaum.

PERFETTI, C. A., & LESGOLD, A. M. (1979). Coding and comprehension in skilled reading and implications for reading instruction. In L. B. Resnick & P. A. Weaver (Eds.), *Theory and practice in early reading* (Vol. 1, pp. 57–84). Hillsdale, NJ: Erlbaum.

PERFETTI, C. A., & McCUTCHEN, D. (1982). Speech processes in reading. In N. Lass (Ed.), *Speech and language: Advances in basic research and practice* (pp. 237–269). New York: Academic Press.

PERFETTI, C. A., & ROTH, S. F. (1981). Some of the interactive processes in reading and their role in reading skill. In A. M. Lesgold & C. A. Perfetti (Eds.), *Interactive processes in reading* (pp. 269–297). Hillsdale, NJ: Erlbaum.

PINKER, S. (1984). *Language learnability and language development.* Cambridge, MA: Harvard University Press.

RAYNER, K., & POLLATSEK, A. (1989). *The psychology of reading.* Englewood Cliffs, NJ: Prentice-Hall.

READ, C., ZHANG, Y., NIE, H., & DING, B. (1986). The ability to manipulate speech sounds depends on knowing alphabetic reading. *Cognition, 24,* 31–44.

RUTTER, M., & YULE, W. (1975). The concept of specific reading retardation. *Journal of Child Psychology and Psychiatry, 16,* 181–197.

SEIDENBERG, M. S., & McCLELLAND, J. L. (1990). More words but still no lexicon: Reply to Besner et al. (1990). *Psychological Review, 97*(3), 447–452.

SHANKWEILER, D., CRAIN, S., BRADY, S., & MACARUSO, P. (1992). Identifying the causes of reading disability. In P. B. Gough, L. C. Ehri, & R. Treiman (Eds.), *Reading acquisition* (pp. 275–305). Hillsdale, NJ: Erlbaum.

SNOWLING, J., STACKHOUSE, J., & RACK, J. (1986). Phonological dyslexia and dysgraphia—a developmental analysis. *Cognitive Neuropsychology, 3,* 309–339.

STANOVICH, K. E. (1980). Toward an interactive-compensatory model of individual differences in the development of reading fluency. *Reading Research Quarterly, 16,* 32–71.

STANOVICH, K. E. (1986). Matthew effects in reading: Some consequences of individual differences in the acquisition of literacy. *Reading Research Quarterly, 21,* 360–407.

STANOVICH, K. E. (1988). Explaining the differences between the dyslexic and the garden-variety poor reader: The phonological-core variable-difference model. *Journal of Learning Disabilities, 21,* 590–604.

STANOVICH, K. E., CUNNINGHAM, A. E., & CRAMER, B. (1984). Assessing phonological awareness in kindergarten children: Issues of task comparability. *Journal of Experimental Child Psychology, 38,* 175–190.

STANOVICH, K. E., & WEST, R. F. (1989). Exposure to print and orthographic processing. *Reading Research Quarterly, 24,* 402–433.

VAN ORDEN, G. C., PENNINGTON, B., & STONE, G. (1990). Word identification in reading and the promise of subsymbolic psycholinguistics. *Psychological Review, 97,* 488–522.

CHARLES A. PERFETTI

REASONING, DEDUCTIVE Some people seem to be good at thinking in a clear manner—they are able to consider all the relevant alternative possibilities in a situation, they can evaluate each one critically but dispassionately, and on this basis, they can reach a decision about which alternative to pursue. We often consider such people to be "logical" or "rational" thinkers. How do people manage to engage in this kind of thinking? The answer lies in the human ability to make *deductive inferences.*

Deductive reasoning is the process of reaching a *valid* conclusion, that is, a conclusion that *must* be true if the premises on which it is based are true. Suppose you know the following general fact about a friend of yours:

If Ali is thirsty, then she drinks milk.

Now suppose you also hear the following information:

Ali drank milk this afternoon.

You might be tempted to conclude:

Ali was thirsty.

Is this conclusion valid? Is it possible for the premises to be true and the conclusion false? The premises do not rule out the possibility that Ali drinks milk under other circumstances, for example, whenever she has lunch or when she visits her grandmother. So the conclusion is not valid: It may be true or it may be false. People who are good at deductive reasoning seem to be able to think through the alternative possibilities and reach conclusions that *must* be true, not just conclusions that *may* be true.

Human rationality rests on the ability to engage in reasoned thought. Thinking in general, and deductive reasoning in particular, lie at the heart of human cognition. What is it in the human mind that enables people to make deductive inferences? Ever since Aristotle constructed a logic to distinguish valid arguments from invalid ones over 2000 years ago, humans have attempted to understand the principles that underlie deduction. The quest has attracted scholars from the cognitive sciences, such as philosophers, linguists, artificial intelligence workers, and psychologists. Cognitive scientists have aimed to provide an account of the "machinery in the mind" that enables people to make inferences.

Cognitive scientists have attempted to explain the psychological phenomena observed in over eighty years of experimentation on deduction with human participants. Psychological experiments have established that certain kinds of deductions are easy and others are difficult, people tend to make certain sorts of errors, and the accuracy of their inferences is influenced by the content of the argument. Consider the information about Ali again:

If Ali is thirsty then she drinks milk.

Suppose the following information is also true:

Ali was thirsty this morning.

You might find it easy to infer:

Therefore, she drank milk.

In this case, you would be right: The conclusion is valid—whenever the premises are true, the conclusion is bound to be true. Now suppose you know the following information:

Ali did not drink milk this morning.

You might, along with most participants in psychological experiments, find it more difficult to make the valid inference:

Therefore, she was not thirsty.

Many people make the mistake of saying that nothing follows from the premises. Why is the first inference easy and the second inference more difficult? Reflection on the subjective experience of making these inferences is fascinating, but it rarely provides reliable insights. When you make the inference you may be consciously aware of the input (the premises) and the output (the conclusion), but you are unlikely to be aware of the unconscious cognitive processes that intervened between the two (see Eysenck & Keane, 1990). Cognitive scientists have constructed alternative theories about what goes on in people's minds when they make an inference. To gain reliable information on the mechanism of reasoning, they have carried out experiments to test these alternative theories. They have also written computer programs to simulate the theories, so that the computer program makes the same inferences that people do, and relies on the same kinds of processes that people do, according to the theory. Three main kinds of theories of reasoning have emerged from this endeavor. One theory is based on *formal rules of inference,* a second theory is based on *content-sensitive rules of inference,* and the third theory is based on *mental models.* The following sections illustrate each of these kinds of theories with reference to the difference in difficulty between the easy valid inference and the hard valid inference we encountered earlier (for a review, see Evans, Newstead, & Byrne, 1993).

THEORIES BASED ON FORMAL INFERENCE RULES

One of the first theories of reasoning to emerge was based on the idea that the mind is equipped with a "mental logic" that contains *inference rules.* Inference rules are general rules that cover many situations regardless of the content of the situation. Consider the following rule, familiar to many students of logic:

If p then q

p

Therefore q

The *p*s and *q*s can stand for any situation; for example, *p* can stand for "Ali is thirsty" and *q* can stand for "she drinks milk." The rule specifies what can be concluded on the basis of the *form* of the argument. It specifies that whenever the second premise asserts that the first part of the *if . . . then* premise is true, the second part of the *if . . . then* premise can be concluded.

Some psychologists have proposed that the mind contains such formal rules of inference (e.g., Braine & O'Brien, 1991; Rips, 1983). According to this view, reasoning requires three stages. First, you recover the logical form or underlying skeleton of the premises: You remove the content of the premises to enable the application of an abstract set of rules. Second, you gain access to the mental repertoire of inference rules. Individual rules are matched to the premises if they share a similar form. You apply the rules to the premises in a series of steps, similar to the proofs constructed by logicians, until a conclusion is proven. Finally, you translate the logical skeleton of the conclusion back into a meaningful sentence. Each of these steps is carried out beneath conscious awareness by the mental machinery responsible for reasoning.

Let us look at this theory in operation. Consider the premises:

If Mark works late then he eats in a restaurant.

Mark works late.

They can be matched to the simple rule we encountered earlier:

If p then q

p

Therefore q

where p stands for "Mark works late" and q stands for "he eats in a restaurant." The rule specifies that the conclusion corresponds to q, that is, to "he eats in a restaurant." The theory explains why this inference is an easy inference: It requires just a single step in its proof, and there is an inference rule that matches the premises directly. The situation is different for the more difficult inference:

If Mark works late then he eats in a restaurant.

Mark does not eat in a restaurant.

The form of the premises is:

If p then q

not q

The inference is difficult because you do not have a rule that corresponds directly to it, according to the inference-rule theory. Because there is no corresponding inference rule, some people conclude erroneously that nothing follows. Other people appreciate that they can reach a conclusion by making a series of inferences in an indirect fashion. They find the inference more difficult because it requires a series of inferential steps in its proof.

The theory proposes that the more steps in the proof of an inference, the more difficult the inference will be. This proposal has been successful in explaining the difference in difficulty between many inferences. The theory can also explain the nature of the errors that people make, for example, people erroneously conclude that nothing follows from the premises of an inference when they cannot construct a proof of a conclusion. Different versions of the theory have been specified in sufficient detail to be simulated in computer programs (e.g., Rips, 1983).

The theory has been criticized by opponents who claim that it cannot account for a variety of phenomena of human reasoning (see e.g., Johnson-Laird & Byrne, 1991). The major chink in its armor is its account of the effects of content on reasoning. Arguments of the same form, but with different sorts of content, lead people to make dramatically different patterns of inferences, as we will see in the next section. A second theory proposes that the mechanism of reasoning depends on rules that are not based on the form of the premises but instead are sensitive to content.

THEORIES BASED ON CONTENT-SENSITIVE INFERENCE RULES

People are affected by the content of an argument in a variety of ways. Suppose you know the general rule:

If there is a vowel on one side of the card then there is an even number on the other side.

Suppose you are presented with four cards, and on the front of each is a letter or number:

| A | 4 | B | 7 |

This task, devised by Peter Wason and known as Wason's selection task, requires you to turn over those cards that can test whether the rule is true or false (see, e.g., Wason & Johnson-Laird, 1972). Which cards do you think you should turn over to test the rule? The logically correct answer is the "A" card and the "7" card. Perhaps you found it easy to decide that you had to turn over the "A" card. It seems obvious that if it has an even number on its other side, the rule is true; but if it has an odd number on its other side, the rule is false. But, you might, along with most participants in experiments, think it is not important to choose the "7" card. In fact, if the "7" card contains a vowel on the other side, then the rule is false, so this card is just as important as the "A" card in testing the rule.

When the task contains more realistic content, it is much easier. Consider the following regulation:

If a person drinks beer then the person must be over 18.
Suppose you are presented with four cards, and on the front of each is an indication of what a person is drinking, or what the person's age is:

Beer	Over 18	Coke	Under 18

The correct answer is to turn over the "beer" card and the "under 18" card. This version of the task is identical to the previous one except for the content: The "A" card corresponds to the "beer" card, and the "7" card corresponds to the "under 18" card. But, along with most participants in experiments, you probably found this version of the task much easier. You know it is important to choose the "beer" card—if there is "over 18" on the other side then the rule has been observed, but if there is "under 18" on the other side, then it has been violated. Likewise, you appreciate that it is important to check the "under 18" card—if there is "coke" on the other side then the rule has been observed, but if there is "beer" on the other side, then it has been violated. The content of an inference can help people to make more accurate inferences, but equally, the content can sometimes lead them to make more *inaccurate* inferences. It is difficult to account for such content effects if people rely on content-free rules of inference that apply by virtue of their form. Hence, psychologists have proposed that rules of inference are sensitive to content.

One content-sensitive inference-rule theory proposes that the mind contains *pragmatic reasoning schemas* that are sensitive to domains such as permissions or obligations (Cheng & Holyoak, 1985). For example, a permission schema contains a set of rules that specify the relations between actions and their preconditions, such as "If the action is to be taken, then the precondition must be met." This schema can apply to a range of permission situations. The theory explains the difference in difficulty between the abstract and the realistic versions of the selection task. The realistic version is easier because it cues a schema that you can use to help you make your selections of cards. The rules of the schema in this case happen to coincide with those prescribed by formal logic, and so you choose the correct selections. The abstract version is difficult because it does not cue a schema that can be used to guide the selections. In other domains, such as causality, the schemas rules may not coincide with formal logic, and reasoners will make logical errors. A reasoner need not be familiar with the specific information in the premises for it to affect his or her inferences: Familiar and less familiar contents can cue a schema such as the permission schema. The theory can account for content effects, but it does not explain how people make inferences with abstract or unfamiliar materials. The final theory attempts to explain both abstract reasoning and content effects: It does not rely on rules of inference, but on rules to construct mental models.

THEORIES BASED ON MENTAL MODELS

The third alternative proposes that reasoners have the competence to be rational, but they make errors in practice. It proposes that people make inferences by relying on a mental logic that does not consist of rules of inference, either formal or content-sensitive. Instead, they are equipped with mental processes that construct *models* (see, e.g., Johnson-Laird, 1983; Johnson-Laird & Byrne, 1991). A mental model is a representation that corresponds to the *structure of the world* rather than to the structure of the *language* used to describe the world, as in the previous two theories. It corresponds to the states of affairs that would be true if the premises were true. Consider the premise:

If Mark works late then he eats in a restaurant.
You understand this premise by constructing a model of it. The tokens in models may turn out to be images, or some other symbol. The content may be enriched with information about who Mark is, what sort of work he does, and what sort of restaurants he likes to eat in, depending on the background knowledge of the reasoner. The premise can be true in the world in several alternative situations. It is certainly true in the

situation where Mark works late and eats in a restaurant. We can use the following diagram to symbolize this situation:

$$w \qquad r$$

where w stands for "Mark works late" and r stands for "he eats in a restaurant." But, the premise is also true in other situations: It is true when Mark does not work late, and in that case, he may eat in a restaurant or he may not. The premise is consistent with three alternative models, and it rules out only one possibility: It would be false in the situation where Mark works late and does not eat in a restaurant. You might not have thought through these alternative situations systematically when you understood the meaning of the premise, but you were probably aware that some alternatives existed. The following diagram attempts to capture this general awareness of alternatives:

$$w \qquad r$$
$$\ldots$$

where the three dots symbolize that there are alternatives to the first model, and where we represent separate models on separate lines. The second model—the three dots—contains implicit information: It indicates that there are alternative models to the first one, but they have not been "fleshed out" yet. To reason clearly from the premise requires that the alternatives are kept in mind. Because people have limited working memories and cannot keep many alternatives in mind, the theory proposes that they construct an initial set of models that maintains as much information as possible *implicitly* (see Johnson-Laird, Byrne, & Schaeken, 1992, for details).

Consider once again the premises of the following easy inference:

If Mark works late then he eats in a restaurant.
Mark works late.

The conclusion that Mark eats in a restaurant can be reached by relying on the initial models: The models do not have to be made more explicit. You can understand the first premise by constructing an initial set of models, as in the diagram above. The second premise fits in directly with the first model, where Mark finishes work late and eats in a restaurant. The inference is easy because the initial set of models do not need to be fleshed out to make the inference, and you do not need to keep multiple models in mind. The situation is different for the more difficult inference:

If Mark works late then he eats in a restaurant.
Mark does not eat in a restaurant.

The second premise does not fit in with the initial models—the models must be "fleshed out." The inference is more difficult because you have to think through the alternatives with which the first premise is consistent. The first premise is true in the following three situations:

$$w \qquad r$$
$$not\text{-}w \qquad r$$
$$not\text{-}w \qquad not\text{-}r$$

where *not-w* means Mark does not work late, and *not-r* means Mark does not eat in a restaurant. The second premise fits in with just one of these situations:

$$not\text{-}w \qquad not\text{-}r$$

In this model, Mark does not work late and he does not eat in a restaurant. You can conclude that Mark does not work late. The inference is difficult because you must keep several alternative models in mind.

The theory proposes that the more models an inference requires the more difficult it will be. This proposal has been successful in explaining the difference in difficulty between many inferences. The theory can also account for the nature of the errors that people make: Their errors are consistent with keeping just a subset of the models in mind. The theory also explains the effects of content on reasoning: Content affects the ability to flesh out a set of models appropriately. The theory has been specified in sufficient detail to be simulated in a computer program (Johnson-Laird & Byrne, 1991).

CONCLUSIONS

Three alternative theories of the unconscious cognitive processes underlying deductive reasoning have been proposed by cognitive scientists to account for the many established empirical phenomena of human reasoning. One phenomenon from the area of conditional reasoning was chosen in this article to illustrate how each theory differs in its explanation of the reasoning mechanism. Theories of deductive reasoning also attempt to account for inferences based on the meaning of other logical connectives, such as "and," "or," and "not"; inferences based on the meaning of quantifiers, such as "all," "none," and "some"; and inferences based on the meaning of relational terms, such as "bigger than" or "in front of." Each of the three sorts of theory has been extensively tested in experiments and modeled in computer programs. The debate continues to flourish between them as to which one more closely approximates human deductive reasoning.

BIBLIOGRAPHY

BRAINE, M. D. S., & O'BRIEN, D. P. (1991). A theory of *if*: A lexical entry, reasoning program, and pragmatic principles. *Psychological Review, 98,* 182–203.

CHENG, P., & HOLYOAK, K. J. (1985). Pragmatic reasoning schemas. *Cognitive Psychology, 17,* 391–416.

EYSENCK, M. W., & KEANE, M. T. (1990). *Cognitive psychology: A student's handbook.* Hillsdale, NJ: Erlbaum.

EVANS, J. ST. B. T. (1982). *The psychology of deductive reasoning.* London: Routledge.

EVANS, J. ST. B. T., NEWSTEAD, S. E., & BYRNE, R. M. J. (1993). *Human reasoning: The psychology of deduction.* Hillsdale, NJ: Erlbaum.

JOHNSON-LAIRD, P. N. (1983). *Mental models.* Cambridge: Cambridge University Press.

JOHNSON-LAIRD, P. N., & BYRNE, R. M. J. (1991). *Deduction.* Hillsdale, NJ: Erlbaum.

JOHNSON-LAIRD, P. N., BYRNE, R. M. J., & SCHAEKEN, W. (1992). Propositional reasoning by model. *Psychological Review, 99,* 418–439.

RIPS, L. J. (1983). Cognitive processes in propositional reasoning. *Psychological Review, 90,* 38–71.

WASON, P. C., & JOHNSON-LAIRD, P. N. (1972). *Reasoning: Structure and content.* London: Batsford.

RUTH M. J. BYRNE

REASONING, INDUCTIVE   Inductive reasoning occurs when a person *induces* a general rule, hypothesis, or pattern from a series of instances, examples, or events and *applies* the induction to predict a new case. For example, after learning that the plural of *dog* is *dogs* and the plural of *cat* is *cats,* a child may induce the rule "add *s* to make a noun plural" and conclude that the plural of *house* is *houses.* J. G. Pellegrino (1985, p. 195) defined induction as "the development of general rules, ideas, or concepts from sets of specific instances or examples." Accordingly, "we extract the general characteristics of objects, events,

and situations" from our specific experiences, and "we apply these generalizations to new experiences" (p. 195). Similarly, Ekstrom, French, and Harman (1976, p. 79) described induction as "forming and trying out a hypothesis that will fit a set of data."

Inductive reasoning has long been recognized as a basic component in human intelligence. L. L. THURSTONE (1938) classified inductive reasoning as one of seven primary mental abilities, and Ekstrom, French, and Harman (1976) listed induction as one of twenty-three basic cognitive factors. John B. Carroll's extensive analysis of cognitive tests identified induction, deduction, and quantitative reasoning as three distinct types of reasoning. As a fundamental form of human reasoning, inductive reasoning ability is "at or near the core of what is ordinarily meant by intelligence" (Carroll, 1993, p. 196).

Although inductive and deductive reasoning are recognized as different types of reasoning, they may be intertwined in many human reasoning tasks. Carroll notes that "inductive tasks always involve at least one deductive step in arriving at a conclusion, classification, or other required response" (1993, p. 211). For example, deductive reasoning requires the problem solver to apply the rule to a new case (such as determining that the plural of *house* is *houses*).

Inductive reasoning can be studied with a psychometric or a cognitive approach. In the psychometric approach, researchers seek to identify basic cognitive factors by examining the relations among scores on mental tests. For example, upon finding that scores on classification, series completion, and analogy tests tend to be related, psychometricians propose that these kinds of tasks tap the same cognitive factor, namely, inductive reasoning.

In the cognitive approach to inductive reasoning, researchers seek to determine the cognitive processes that reasoners use in solving inductive reasoning problems. For example, solving an inductive reasoning problem requires the processes of encoding the presented problem, inducing a rule based on the presented instances, applying the rule to a new case, and responding by selecting or producing an answer. In addition, a reasoner must coordinate and monitor these processes by using strategies that Sternberg (1985) calls *metacomponents.* In summary, although psychometric research and theory have identified the types of problems that tap the mental factor called inductive reasoning, cognitive research and theory have provided a description of the component processes and metaprocesses involved in solving them.

Examples of classic inductive reasoning tasks often found on tests of intellectual ability include classification, series completion, and analogy. More recently, the study of inductive reasoning has been broadened to include induction in real-world contexts such as scientific reasoning.

CLASSIFICATION PROBLEMS

In a classification problem, the reasoner's job is to find a common rule or characteristic in two or more items. For example, concept-learning tasks represent a highly studied example of classification problems. In a concept-learning task, the reasoner receives or selects a series of items in verbal, pictorial, or literal form. For each item the reasoner must predict whether or not it is a member of the target category; the reasoner is then given feedback. Category membership is determined by a rule. For example, if the items are cards that present various numbers of objects (one, two, or three), of various shapes (circles, squares, or crosses), and of various colors (red, green, or black), then the rule might be "all red items."

According to cognitive theories of concept learning, reasoners generate and test hypotheses corresponding to the cognitive processes of inducing and applying rules, respectively. One hypothesis-testing strategy is "win-stay–lose-switch," in which a reasoner keeps a hypothesis as long as it predicts the correct answer and selects a new hypothesis if it predicts an incorrect answer. A reasoner using this strategy learns by making errors because a hypothesis is changed only when it fails.

Another example of a classification task is Wason's (1960) *2-4-6 task*. A reasoner is told that the triplet 2-4-6 is a member of a category; then the reasoner is asked to generate a triplet, and the experimenter tells whether or not it is a member of the category. This process is repeated until the reasoner can correctly state the rule. In addition to encoding and responding, this task requires inducing a hypothesis, such as "all triplets that increase by twos," and applying the hypothesis to generate tests, such as expecting that

4-6-8 will also be a member of the category. Students tend to test their hypotheses by generating examples that conform to it, a strategy that Wason (1960) termed *confirmation bias*. This strategy can lead to the formation of incorrect rules; for example, the correct rule could be "any three numbers in ascending order." Klayman and Ha (1989, p. 601) show that the tendency to confirm one's hypothesis in the 2-4-6 task makes it "easier for a tester to see ways of restricting a current hypothesis than ways of expanding it." Individual differences in concept learning or rule learning are related to differences in strategies that reasoners use for selecting hypotheses and in the ability of reasoners to discern relevant dimensions of the stimuli.

For purposes of mental testing, shorter versions of classification tasks, such as oddity problems or similarity problems, are often used. In an oddity problem, a reasoner must choose which item does not belong in a collection; for example, given the collection KK LL MM KL, a reasoner must induce the rule (identical letters in each pair) and determine that KL conflicts with it. In a similarity problem, a reasoner is given some items and must determine which other items belong with them; for example, given "dog cat parakeet," the reasoner must determine which of the following belongs: "hamster," "elephant," or "dinosaur." In this example, the reasoner must induce the rule (house pets) and apply it to find that only "hamster" belongs.

ANALOGY PROBLEMS

In an analogy problem, the reasoner is presented with a problem in the form "A is to B as C is to ___" and must select or generate a D term that has the same relation to the C term that the B term has to the A term. The terms may be verbal, pictorial, or numerical. For example, in the verbal analogy page : book :: room : (a. door, b. window, c. house, d. kitchen), the correct answer is "c." According to cognitive analyses of analogical reasoning, solving analogies involves the coordination of several component processes, including *encoding* the terms (page, book, room, etc.), *inducing* the relation between the A and B terms (part-to-whole), *applying* the relation from the C term to each potential D term (room is a part of house), and *responding* (marking "c" as the answer). Sternberg and Gardner (1983) found that individual differences on inducing and applying rules were related to individual differences in overall performance as well as to psychometric measures of intelligence. Individual differences in knowledge of the kinds of possible relations between terms (such as part-to-whole, subordination, coordination, and cause/effect) are related to differences in ability to induce relations and therefore to differences in overall performance on analogy problems (Robins & Mayer, 1993).

SERIES COMPLETION PROBLEMS

In a series completion problem, the reasoner is presented with a series of items, such as letters, numbers, words, or pictorials, and must select or generate the next item. For example, a number series completion problem is 11122233344_____. In addition to encoding and responding, solving a series completion task requires inducing the pattern for each cycle (e.g., for each cycle of three digits, each digit in a cycle is one more than the corresponding digit in the previous cycle) and *applying* the rule to the missing item in the problem (e.g., "add 1" to the digit "3"). In a study of letter completion tasks, Simon and Kotovsky (1963; Kotovsky & Simon, 1973) used the term "extrapolation" to refer to applying, and they separated inducing into three subprocesses: discovery of periodicity (e.g., there are three digits per cycle), detection of interitem relations (e.g., the major rule is "add 1"), and completion of pattern description (e.g., each digit in a cycle is one more than the corresponding digit in the previous cycle). Individual differences in knowledge of interitem relations and strategies for discovering periodicity are related to differences in rule induction and hence to differences in overall performance on series completion problems (Holtzman, Glaser, & Pellegrino, 1976).

SCIENTIFIC REASONING PROBLEMS

Although not commonly found on traditional psychometric tests of intelligence, scientific reasoning tasks are used to evaluate level of cognitive development (Inhelder & Piaget, 1958) and in performance tests of reasoning (Baxter et al., 1992). In a scientific reasoning task, the reasoner's job is to generate and test hypotheses concerning the relations between two or more variables. For example, in the oscillation problem the reasoner must conduct experiments to determine whether the rate of oscillation of a pendulum depends on the length of the string, the weight of the ball, the height of the released object, or the force used to release the object; and in the circuit problem, the reasoner must determine what is inside a box by connecting it to objects such as wires, lights, and batteries (Baxter et al., 1992).

Analyses of the processes involved in scientific reasoning focus on the role of generating and testing hypotheses (Holland et al., 1986; Klahr, Dunbar, & Fay, 1990; Langley et al., 1987). Individual differences in the rate and accuracy of scientific reasoning depend on the strategies that reasoners use for generating and testing hypotheses. For example, successful reasoners tend to consider several alternative hypotheses of different types and design experiments to examine surprising results, whereas unsuccessful reasoners focus on one hypothesis and seek to confirm rather than disconfirm their hypothesis (Klahr, Dunbar, & Fay, 1990).

BIBLIOGRAPHY

BAXTER, G. P., SHAVELSON, R. J., GOLDMAN, S. R., & PINE, J. (1992). Evaluation of procedure-based scoring for hands-on science assessment. *Journal of Educational Measurement, 29*, 1–17.

BRUNER, J. S., GOODNOW, J. J., & AUSTIN, G. A. (1956). *A study of thinking.* New York: Wiley.

CARROLL, J. B. (1993). *Human cognitive abilities: A survey of factor-analytic studies.* Cambridge: Cambridge University Press.

EKSTROM, R. B., FRENCH, J. W., & HARMAN, H. H. (1976). *Manual for kit of factor-referenced cognitive tests.* Princeton, NJ: Educational Testing Service.

HOLTZMAN, T. G., GLASER, R., & PELLEGRINO, J. W. (1976). Process training derived from a computer simulation theory. *Memory and Cognition, 4*, 349–356.

HOLLAND, J. H., HOLYOAK, K. J., NISBETT, R. E., & THAGARD, P. R. (1986). *Induction: Processes of inference, learning, and discovery.* Cambridge, MA: MIT Press.

HULL, C. L. (1920). Quantitative aspects of the evolution of concepts. *Psychological Monographs, 28* (whole No. 123).

INHELDER, B., & PIAGET, J. (1958). *The growth of logical thinking from childhood to adolescence.* New York: Basic Books.

KLAHR, D., DUNBAR, K., & FAY, A. (1990). Designing good experiments to test bad hypotheses. In J. Shrager & Langley, P. (Eds.), *Computational models of scientific discovery and theory formation.* Los Altos, CA: Kaufmann.

KLAYMAN, J., & HA, Y. W. (1989). Hypothesis testing in rule discovery: Strategy, structure, and content. *Journal of Experimental Psychology: Learning, Memory, and Cognition, 15,* 596–604.

KOTOVSKY, K., & SIMON, H. A. (1973). Empirical tests of a theory of human acquisition of concepts for sequential patterns. *Cognitive Psychology, 4,* 399–424.

LANGLEY, P., SIMON, H. A., BRADSHAW, G. L., & ZYTKOW, J. M. (1987). *Scientific discovery: Computational explorations of the creative processes.* Cambridge, MA: MIT Press.

LEVINE, M. (1975). *A cognitive theory of learning: Research on hypothesis testing.* Hillsdale, NJ: Erlbaum.

MAYER, R. E. (1992). *Thinking, problem solving, cognition.* New York: Freeman.

PELLEGRINO, J. G. (1985). Inductive reasoning ability. In R. J. Sternberg (Ed.), *Human abilities: An information-processing approach* (pp. 195–226). New York: Freeman.

PELLEGRINO, J. G., & GLASER, R. (1982). Analyzing aptitudes for learning: Inductive reasoning. In R. Glaser (Ed.), *Advances in instructional psychology* (Vol. 2, pp. 269–345). Hillsdale, NJ: Erlbaum.

ROBINS, S., & MAYER, R. E. (1993). Schema training in analogical reasoning. *Journal of Educational Psychology, 85,* 529–538.

SIMON, H. A., & KOTOVSKY, K. (1963). Human acquisition of concepts for sequential patterns. *Psychological Review, 70,* 534–546.

STERNBERG, R. J. (ED.). (1982). *Handbook of human intelligence.* Cambridge: Cambridge University Press.

STERNBERG, R. J. (1985). *Beyond IQ: A triarchic theory of human intelligence.* Cambridge: Cambridge University Press.

STERNBERG, R. J., & GARDNER, M. K. (1983). Unities in inductive reasoning. *Journal of Experimental Psychology: General, 112,* 80–116.

THURSTONE, L. L. (1938). *Primary mental abilities.* Chicago: University of Chicago Press.

TRABASSO, T., & BOWER, G. H. (1968). *Attention in learning: Theory and research.* New York: Wiley.

WASON, P. C. (1960). On the failure to eliminate hypotheses in a conceptual task. *Quarterly Journal of Experimental Psychology, 12,* 129–140.

RICHARD E. MAYER

REASONING, MORAL

Morality refers to concerns with what is good or right in people's relationships with each other. A key to understanding morality is to be specific about definitions of good (or bad) and right (or wrong), since these terms can be used in several different ways. When we say, for example, that there is a "right" way to teach arithmetic or a "good" way to bake a cake, neither term is being used in its moral sense. Also, it does not suffice to say that morality refers to good or right in interpersonal or social situations. Social relationships can be judged by standards such as efficiency or prudence. Social systems and institutions have customs, conventions, and some laws that do not necessarily pertain to moral issues. Morality—as distinguished from nonmoral concerns with good or right—refers to judgments about welfare, justice or fairness, and rights.

Moral issues are intensely felt, heatedly debated, and very important in most people's lives. Recently, in the United States, debates have occurred, to list a few, over war and peace, civil rights, affirmative action, abortion, and the distribution of wealth. Worldwide, morality pervades politics, religion, business, medicine, and education. Young children begin to confront moral issues and conflicts in school, in the family, and in their dealings with peers. The development of moral judgments and their sources in children's social relationships were first studied in the 1920s by the great Swiss psychologist Jean PIAGET. Piaget viewed morality as related to human intelligence in that it involved reasoning, solving social problems, and resolving social conflicts. He also believed that social reasoning is informed by other aspects of intelligence, including logic. Studies in the Piagetian tradition were revived in the 1960s, most notably by Lawrence Kohlberg (1969), and they have continued to the present time. In the early research, moral development was studied without much attention to how children's moral judgments differed from their judgments about nonmoral social considerations. Increasingly it has been recognized that children's concepts of welfare, justice, and rights differ from their concepts of societal conventions and personal prerogatives. Controversies exist, however, among researchers. Major controversies, discussed below, pertain to possible differences in moral reasoning between males and females, as well as among people living in different cultures.

EARLY FORMULATIONS OF MORAL DEVELOPMENT

Piaget (1932) recognized, as had some prominent philosophers before him, that thinking about social problems and conflicts is central to the way people make moral decisions; children do not simply acquire a set of values or habitual ways of behaving from what adults transmit to them. Piaget, therefore, attempted to explain how children make sense of social experiences and to portray age-related changes in moral judgments. Piaget's research included observations of children playing games, as well as study of their judgments about the application and violation of the game rules (marble games for boys and a game of hide-and-seek for girls). He also studied children's judgments about sharing (distributive justice), punishment for wrong doing (retributive justice), and the role of people's intentions and the consequences of their actions in assessing responsibility for transgressions. In Piaget's formulation, the moral judgments of young children (aged approximately 4 to 7 years) are characterized by an absolutistic conception of the good or right as necessitating strict adherence to existing social rules and unvarying obedience to the commands of adults (Piaget referred to this level as "heteronomy"). For example, young children think that the participants in a game should not and cannot decide to alter its rules. Children also think adults are all-knowing and that their commands must be followed to the letter. Moreover, since young children are concrete in their intelligence, they are better able to understand material consequences than more abstract motives or intentions (e.g., they believe that it is worse to cause greater damage to material goods unintentionally than to cause lesser damage intentionally).

Piaget proposed that children's thinking shifts from heteronomy to autonomy through social relationships allowing them to experience equality and mutuality. Very young children are dependent upon adults and attuned to the adult's status, size, and power. Older children's relationships with each other are more likely to be mutual and based on cooperation, because the perceived equality allows greater give-and-take. Children thus begin to construct understandings of equality among persons, as well as fairness, justice, and cooperative relationships. Since older children's intelligence includes a greater ability to think abstractly, rules are no longer seen as fixed and unalterable; they can be changed by agreement to serve the goals of achieving greater fairness and fostering cooperation.

Piaget's ideas were later extended by Kohlberg (1969), who focused on thinking about moral conflicts. Kohlberg characterized the development of moral judgments beyond early adolescence and encompassed judgments about social institutions, the legal system, and people's roles in society. An often cited example used in Kohlberg's research is a hypothetical story of a man who must decide whether to steal a drug in order possibly to save his wife's life; the husband is faced with that decision because he cannot raise enough money to pay an exorbitant price charged by the druggist who discovered the drug. The moral dilemma of theft versus saving a life can be resolved in either direction, but the moral reasoning changes with development. Other stories pose conflicts between parents and children. One situation depicts a father who first promises his son that he can go to summer camp if the son earns the needed money; after the son has earned the money, the father wants it for himself in order to go on a fishing trip with friends. The son is faced with the dilemma of obeying his father or refusing to adhere to a command he does not consider fair. Participants in the research were asked several questions about each story, including ones pertaining to the decision (should the husband steal the drug, should the son give his father the money), to the rights of the actors (wife, druggist, father, son), and whether laws and rules should be obeyed in these circumstances.

Kohlberg formulated a sequence of stages and levels of the development of moral reasoning that differed somewhat from the levels previously proposed by Piaget. Briefly stated, the initial moral judgments of children (at approximately ages 4 to 10 years) are determined by sanctions, material consequences, and achieving individuals' needs and desires (these stages are labeled a *preconventional* level). In late childhood and early adolescence, there is a shift to thinking about morality primarily in terms of social expectations (fulfilling one's roles in society and gaining approval for being a good person) and strictly maintaining the social order by upholding laws, respecting authority, and fulfilling duties (the "conventional" level). Subsequently, there is a shift (the earliest it occurs is late adolescence) to understanding moral concepts that underlie society's system of laws, authority, and norms. Particular social institutions and norms are regarded to be subordinate to the broader goals of ensuring justice and fair treatment, serving the general good, respecting the dignity of persons, and ensuring individual rights (the *postconventional* level).

Kohlberg and his colleagues thought that development through stages of moral reasoning was dependent upon the development of more basic forms of intelligence. Specifically, they proposed that children must develop "concrete" ways of thinking about logic, mathematics, and the physical world before they can form the types of moral judgments characteristic of the conventional level, and that, in turn, abstract or formal thinking about these realms develops before the development of moral reasoning characteristic of the postconventional level. Most of the research conducted to see if these proposed relationships hold involved administering, to the same children and adolescents, measures of moral reasoning and of reasoning in the logical, mathematical, and physical realms. The results of these studies have not provided support for these propositions. In many studies, the correlations between the two types of measures were low; in a few studies it was even found that the development of moral reasoning outpaced development in the other realms. The most plausible conclusion is that morality entails intelligence in the sense that it constitutes a domain of reasoning and that it takes a form of intelligence that differs from the intelligences involved in the nonsocial realms (Turiel, 1983). Moreover, there are features of moral reasoning that differ from reasoning in other social realms.

DISTINCTIONS BETWEEN MORAL AND SOCIAL CONCEPTS

Piaget and Kohlberg demonstrated that philosophical moral ideas are also central to children's moral thinking and decision-making processes. They did much to overturn the view that the psychology of moral development is nonrational and determined by the emotionally laden values and behaviors transmitted to children in their culture. Children's social experiences are contexts in which they deal with, as examples, the perspectives of others, the need to resolve conflicting needs and goals, and ways that people can affect each other that are undesirable (e.g., inflicting harm) and desirable (e.g., helping others in need).

The early research, however, did not sufficiently attend to the ways children's concepts of morality, in the form of their understandings of welfare, justice, and rights, differ from their nonmoral social concepts. One reason is that the methods of study did not adequately separate different types of social issues (e.g., game rules from rules prohibiting inflicting physical harm on others). Explaining distinctions between moral and social judgments is important not only because it more precisely describes children's thinking, but also because it helps explain the factors involved in moral decision-making.

Systematic inquiries of children's thinking about various facets of rules show children place game rules into a category different from rules pertaining to issues like harm, theft, and trust (Turiel, 1983a). Young children recognize that game rules legitimately can be changed by agreement among the participants and that a particular game can be played with different rules in different social contexts (e.g., in different countries). By contrast, other types of rules are not judged to be legitimately alterable solely by general agreement, or contingent on existing rules, or dependent on what authorities dictate, or relative to the social and cultural context. As an example, we can consider children's judgments about a school rule prohibiting people from hitting each other. Children judge that the rule should be upheld, that people in a particular school cannot legitimately decide to abolish the rule and allow hitting (the rule is not alterable by consensus), and that even if there were no rule, hitting would still be wrong (the evaluation of the act is not contingent on a rule). Children also maintain that a teacher or the principal should not abolish the rule, and if they did so, it would still be wrong (not contingent on authority dictates). Furthermore, the act is judged to be wrong even in another country that allows it (the evaluation of the act is generalized across settings or contexts). Children's reasons for these types of judgments are that welfare of persons should be maintained. This constellation of judgments and reasons applies to acts within the moral domain.

Many philosophers, going back to Aristotle, have contrasted the moral domain with other types of social judgments in ways consistent with the kinds of judgments found to be used by children, adolescents, and adults. The moral domain contrasts with social conventions. Most societies and religious systems have norms or expected behaviors that serve to coordinate people's interactions within the social system. These are uniformities in behavior of a "conventional" nature; they are customary and allow greater efficiency in that people know what to expect of each other. Conventional modes of behavior and associated rules (e.g., uniformities and school rules pertaining to modes of greeting, forms of address, dress codes) are recognized by children to be alterable by consensus, contingent on common use, rules, or authority expectations, and relative to social contexts. Accordingly, children judge violations of conventions to be wrong only insofar as there is a rule about it, or it is dictated by an authority with the appropriate jurisdiction. It is judged, for instance, that a conventional rule in a school can be changed or eliminated by a principal. Similarly, conventions are not generalized across contexts in that it is judged that other cultures legitimately can have an alternative set of customary behaviors. Whereas it is reasoned that certain actions (e.g., hitting another person) are wrong because of harmful consequences, injustice, or the violation of rights, other actions (e.g., referring to a teacher by his or her first name) are judged unacceptable because they violate customs or traditions within a community.

Many studies of behaviors and judgments encompassing the range from toddlerhood to early adulthood have examined moral and conventional concepts. One set of studies provides strong confirmation of the differences in thinking about the moral and conventional domains (Nucci & Turiel, 1993). The participants in

these studies were children and adolescents from Orthodox Jewish and Amish–Mennonite communities. Orthodox Jews adhere to religious rules and prescriptions in a strict fashion. The Amish–Mennonites form a community that is isolated from contemporary society and rejects modern technology. For instance, they adhere to a prohibition against radio or television in the home. The children in the study attend a fundamentalist school overseen by congregational religious authorities.

The Jewish and Amish–Mennonite children and adolescents judged the strictly binding religious prohibitions and prescriptions (issues such as days of worship, work on the Sabbath, head coverings, circumcision, and interfaith marriage) differently from moral prescriptions (pertaining to stealing, hitting, and slander). Three types of judgments were elicited regarding moral and religious prescriptions. First, the children thought that religious authorities, such as rabbis, ministers, or members of the congregation, could not legitimately change or eliminate the moral or religious rules. However, they thought that the religious rules, and not the moral ones, were relative to their particular social context. That is, acts like hitting or stealing would be wrong even if other people's religions did not have rules prohibiting them. Other religions could legitimately allow the religious acts prohibited by their own religion. In these children's thinking, the ultimate authority for the nonmoral religious prescriptions is the word of God; they would judge those acts acceptable if they were not prohibited in the Bible. The moral acts would be wrong even in the absence of a biblical prohibition. Thus, moral issues are evaluated neither by group norms nor by a particular source of authority. Rather, they are judged in accordance with other criteria, such as welfare or justice, that children maintain as important.

Across childhood, adolescence, and adulthood, people think about social conventions differently from the way they think about morality. This research has shown that children form concepts of welfare and justice earlier than is suggested in the original studies by Piaget and Kohlberg. However, there are changes, with age, in types of thinking in each domain. In the conventional domain, there are shifts to more abstract understandings of social institutions and society. In the moral domain young children are mainly concerned with preventing harm and promoting welfare, whereas older children include in their moral concepts both welfare and concepts of fairness and reciprocity between persons' rights.

MORAL REASONING AND MORAL BEHAVIOR

People's moral concepts and principles do not directly or in a simple way translate into the decisions or actions in morally relevant situations. Of course, in some cases people just fail to act upon their espoused moral convictions. At a deeper level of analysis, however, people's moral concepts do not directly translate into decisions because several aspects of thought are brought to bear in particular situations. Moral and conventional concepts, along with personal choices considered legitimate, are all part of the thinking that goes into people's decisions. Additionally, the accepted facts or information bearing upon the goals of a moral decision have been shown to contribute significantly to the decision-making process.

The ways informational assumptions, entailing beliefs regarding reality, are part of the decision-making process can be illustrated through two examples from recent research. One study (Wainryb, 1991) examined how children, adolescents, and young adults make decisions regarding whether it is right or wrong to inflict harm (as well as other moral issues). Consider the possibility that a parent hits a child. Do people judge that as wrong, or is it all right to do so? As might be anticipated, the answer depends on the circumstances surrounding the act. In the study, people were posed with two different circumstances in which a parent hits a child. In one, a father spanks a child solely out of fatigue and frustration. All participants in the study judged the act as wrong because of the pain it causes. A second situation depicted a father spanking his son after the child's misbehavior. In that case, people were divided in their evaluations. Most who judged that instance of spanking as acceptable also held the point of view (an informational assumption) that children learn through spanking. Those who judged the spanking as wrong maintained that children do not learn that way. In other words, one's assumptions about the psychological reality of how punishment affects learning contributes to the decision of right and wrong. Furthermore, most would judge the act as acceptable if it were conclusively known that spanking is an effective teaching method; they would judge the act as wrong if it were known to be ineffective.

A relationship between informational assumptions and decisions regarding the morality of abortion has also been demonstrated (Smetana, 1982). The central "fact about reality" is whether the fetus is a life (i.e., the question of when life begins). As is well known, in the United States (and many other places), people disagree in their evaluations of abortion. Evaluations of abortion as acceptable or not are closely associated with differing assumptions about the start of life. People who assume that the fetus is a life judge abortion to be wrong and those assuming the fetus is not a life judge abortion as acceptable. Evaluations of abortion are closely related to the behavioral choices of women (Smetana, 1982). Therefore, to understand how moral judgments relate to behaviors, it is necessary to account for features like informational assumptions, as well. People who hold different informational assumptions about the fetus do agree in evaluating killing as wrong in contexts outside the abortion decision. This means that solely knowing a person's moral judgments regarding the value of life and killing would not provide a basis for predicting that persons's actions with regard to abortion.

It has been documented that measures of people's moral judgments, by themselves, only partially correlate with their behaviors (Blasi, 1980). People do not simply apply their moral concepts to situations in which they take action. Rather, several types of judgments are brought to bear in most situations (Turiel & Smetana, 1984). In addition to informational assumptions, these include judgments about conventional features (e.g., rules, authority expectations) and judgments about personal goals. Given the multiple factors that contribute to moral decision making, accurate predictions are difficult to make without a good deal of information about varying aspects of social reasoning.

GENDER, CULTURE, AND SOCIAL DEVELOPMENT

Through the ages, debates have been waged over explanations of morality. In recent times, psychologists have been concerned with the question of whether the moral orientation of females differs from that of males. Carol Gilligan (1982) and others have proposed that girls and women develop a morality based on a concern with care in networks of relationships, which is distinct from a morality of justice characteristic of males. For women, caring and helping others is of more importance than a morality based on rules, individual rights, and equal treatment. According to this view, females do not apply abstract rules or principles across situations. Instead, they are oriented to specific circumstances and people's connections with each other. It is responsibilities for the well-being of those in relationships that motivates a morality of care.

These propositions regarding possible differences in moral orientations are controversial for two reasons. First, the research findings do not clearly show that females and males actually do reason differently. Second, it is not accepted by everyone that justice is distinct from care. For many, a morality of justice includes concerns with care and empathy (Okin, 1989).

A different debate that is not of recent origin pertains to cultural differences and similarities in morality. Some have argued that morality is relative. Relativists argue that values are derived from the culture, that cultures differ in their moral codes, and that the moral codes of different cultures are not comparable. Others have argued that people's moral reasoning does not solely mirror ready-made cultural codes transmitted to them in childhood. Moral judgments stem from efforts at understanding how people should act toward each other and that certain key moral prescriptions apply to human relationships in general.

Controversies over morality, culture, and relativism will not be readily resolved. However, three general conclusions drawn from analyses of the psychology of moral and social reasoning are informative as to how to think about culture and morality. First, as already noted, the research described so far shows that moral decisions are not solely nonrational applications of learned cultural codes or ideologies. People think about moral issues and thus are able to reflect upon cultural ideologies. Furthermore, a rational approach to social matters is not restricted to Western cultures. Several studies conducted in non-Western settings (Indonesia, Nigeria, Korea, Zambia, and India) have shown that people make judgments about welfare, jus-

tice, and rights which differ from their judgments about customs and conventions.

The second issue pertains to the distinction between moral concepts and informational assumptions. Cultural differences in social practice often are due to varying informational assumptions in the context of similar moral concepts. Differences exist among cultures in nonmoral assumptions regarding, for instance, the existence of an afterlife and the sources and cures of disease. An illustrative example is the practice in some societies of children putting their elderly parents to death (parricide). Researchers have pointed out that where the practice occurs, people believe they are better off in the afterlife if they enter it while still in good health. Thus a concern with the well-being of one's parents leads to the practice in some societies. In other societies, where that assumption about afterlife is not accepted, the similar concern with parents' welfare leads to the opposite conclusion. Indeed, anthropologists have cautioned that drawing a distinction between moral concepts and informational assumptions is necessary to understand similarities and differences between societies (Hatch, 1983).

Finally, one of the premises upon which cultural relativism rests is highly questionable. Relativism often is based on the idea, in the words of the well-known anthropologist Ruth Benedict (1934), that cultures form "integrated patterns" dictating their moral codes. In keeping with Benedict's notion, some psychologists and anthropologists propose that cultures are patterned on either the dimension of individualism or collectivism. Western cultures in particular are said to be oriented to autonomous individuals detached from others. This translates into a morality emphasizing freedoms and rights. By contrast, in traditional and collectivistic cultures the individual is subordinated to the group; morality is structured by people's place in the social hierarchy and fulfilling fixed moral duties.

It is questionable that cultures can be characterized with these categories because in any culture people are concerned with diverse social problems, including those bearing on individuals and the social system. Even in the United States, which is supposedly highly individualistic, many surveys of attitudes toward civil liberties have shown that people believe freedoms and rights should be restricted in many situations (McClosky & Brill, 1983). In some situations, people do uphold rights and liberties, but they also believe that freedoms (e.g., of speech, press, religion), rights (e.g., to assembly), and life-styles should be greatly curtailed when they conflict with the welfare of the group or even the traditional norms of society. That there would be diversity of social and moral judgments in any culture is not surprising if one takes into account that individuals reflectively address the variety of social and moral problems that are part of the human experience.

BIBLIOGRAPHY

BENEDICT, R. (1934). *Patterns of culture.* Boston: Houghton Mifflin.

BLASI, A. (1980). Bridging moral cognition and moral action: A critical review of the literature. *Psychological Bulletin, 88,* 1–45.

DAMON, W. (1977). *The social world of the child.* San Francisco: Jossey-Bass.

GILLIGAN, C. (1982). *In a different voice: Psychological theory and women's development.* Cambridge, MA: Harvard University Press.

HATCH, E. (1983). *Culture and morality: The relativity of values in anthropology.* New York: Columbia University Press.

KAGAN J., & LAMB, S. (EDS.). (1987). *The emergence of morality in young children.* Chicago: University of Chicago Press.

KOHLBERG, L. (1969). Stage and sequence: The cognitive-developmental approach to socialization. In D. Goslin (Ed.), *Handbook of socialization theory and research* (pp. 347–480). Chicago: Rand McNally.

KOHLBERG, L. (1984). *Essays on moral development: Vol. 2. The psychology of moral development.* New York: Harper & Row.

KURTINES, W. M., & GEWIRTZ, J. L. (EDS.). (1984). *Morality, moral behavior, and moral development: Basic issues in theory and research.* New York: Wiley.

KURTINES, W. M., & GEWIRTZ, J. L. (EDS.). (1991). *Handbook of moral behavior and development. Vol. 1: Theory; Vol. 2: Research; Vol. 3: Applications.* Hillsdale, NJ: Erlbaum.

MCCLOSKY, M., & BRILL, A. (1983). *Dimensions of tolerance: What Americans believe about civil liberties.* New York: Russell Sage Foundation.

NUCCI, L., & TURIEL, E. (1993). God's word, religious rules, and their relation to Christian and Jewish children's concepts of morality. *Child Development, 64,* 1475–1491.

OKIN, S. M. (1989). *Justice, gender, and the family.* New York: Basic Books.

PIAGET, J. (1932). *The moral judgment of the child.* London: Routledge.

SMETANA, J. G. (1982). *Concepts of self and morality: Women's reasoning about abortion.* New York: Praeger.

TURIEL, E. (1983). Domains and categories in social-cognitive development. In W. F. Overton (Ed.), *The relationship between social and cognitive development* (pp. 53–90). Hillsdale, NJ: Erlbaum.

TURIEL, E. (1983a). *The development of social knowledge: Morality and convention.* Cambridge: Cambridge University Press.

TURIEL, E., & SMETANA, J. G. (1984). Social knowledge and action: The coordination of domains. In W. M. Kurtines & J. L. Gewirtz (Eds.), *Morality, moral behavior, and moral development: Basic issues in theory and research* (pp. 261–282). New York: Wiley.

WAINRYB, C. (1991). Understanding differences in moral judgments: The role of informational assumptions. *Child Development, 62,* 840–851.

ELLIOT TURIEL

REGIONAL DIFFERENCES IN INTELLIGENCE

The quantification of an elusive construct called *intelligence* through the use of IQ tests has led to much controversy. This has been especially true when these tests demonstrate mean-score differences across individuals who are grouped by nominal categories such as gender, ethnicity, socioeconomic status, or geographic region of residence. When such differences are revealed, some theorists reason that they are artifacts of test development (i.e., they represent cultural bias); others suggest that they reflect biological differences (e.g., Jensen, 1980), and still others attribute them to more subtle sociocultural influences (e.g., Reynolds & Brown, 1984). Confounding influences certainly exist, such as migration, economic patterns, and regional differences in schooling, but causality can seldom be proved to the satisfaction of the scientist.

When intelligence tests are standardized, the subsamples of different categories (ethnic groups, genders, etc.) are drawn proportional to the category proportions in the population. For example, if 10 percent of the population (of the United States) lives in towns of less than 50,000 people, the standardization sample is required to have 10 percent of the total from towns of less than 50,000 people. Also, the samples are stratified, which means that the proportions in each stratum are the same in the sample and in the population. In the stratum of gender, for example, the standardization sample matches the population in the proportions of males and females living in towns of less than 50,000 people. Typically, the stratification and proportional sampling are along the factors of age, gender, race, socioeconomic status, occupation, education level, urban/suburban residence, and geographic region of residence. This procedure is known as *population proportionate sampling*. Test performance is often analyzed by these demographic factors to provide information about group differences in the data. When such data have been made available, score differences among the four U.S. Bureau of the Census–defined geographic regions have been noted. States clustered into these four regions are noted in Table 1.

Individually administered intelligence tests are considered to be the best indicators of intellectual functioning. Of the many available, the Wechsler series has emerged as the most widely used scales. The Wechsler scales provide a Verbal (V) IQ, a Performance (P) IQ (which relies heavily upon nonverbal reasoning and perceptual motor skills), and a summary score, the Full Scale (FS) IQ, all of which are scaled to a mean of 100 and a standard deviation (SD) of 15.

Small but consistent regional IQ differences appear on the various Wechsler scales and are relatively consistent across age from 4 years to 74 years and across time, at least since about 1965. Data for earlier versions of the Wechsler scales are not available. Overall, regional differences in IQ range from 3.6 to 7.8 IQ points across age and time on the Wechsler scales.

For the Wechsler Preschool and Primary Scale of Intelligence (WPPSI; see Wechsler, 1967), which was standardized using population proportionate sampling techniques for ages 4 years to 6 ½ years, A. S. Kaufman (1973) reported the means and standard deviations shown in Table 2 for children from different regions of the country.

As seen in the top portion of Table 2, the mean Verbal, Performance, and Full Scale IQs by region ranged from 98.0 in the South to 104.9 in the West. By statistical analysis of variance (ANOVA), Kaufman found that "there was a significant relationship between geographic region and each of the WPPSI IQs ($p < .01$)" (Kaufman, 1973, p. 356). When each region was pair-compared to the others using univariate statistical t-tests, results showed that children from the West had significantly higher V, P, and FS IQs than children from the other three regions; the mean IQs of children from the Northeast, North Central, and

TABLE 1

Grouping of states by geographic region by U.S. Bureau of Census

Northeast	North Central	South	West
Connecticut	Illinois	Alabama	Alaska
Maine	Indiana	Arkansas	Arizona
Massachusetts	Iowa	Delaware	California
New Hampshire	Kansas	Florida	Colorado
New Jersey	Michigan	Georgia	Hawaii
New York	Minnesota	Kentucky	Idaho
Pennsylvania	Missouri	Louisiana	Montana
Rhode Island	Nebraska	Maryland	Nevada
Vermont	North Dakota	Mississippi	New Mexico
	Ohio	North Carolina	Oregon
	South Dakota	Oklahoma	Utah
	Wisconsin	South Carolina	Washington
		Tennessee	Wyoming
		Texas	
		Virginia	
		West Virginia	

945

TABLE 2

Regional differences in intellectual performance on the Wechsler scales

Wechsler Scale Specific IQ	Northeast		North Central		South		West	
	Mean	SD	Mean	SD	Mean	SD	Mean	SD
WPPSI[1] (age 4–6 ½ yrs.)								
Verbal IQ	101.4	14.8	101.0	15.4	98.3	15.2	104.7	12.7
Performance IQ	102.2	13.8	99.6	15.2	98.1	15.6	104.1	12.9
Full Scale IQ	101.9	14.0	100.4	15.6	98.0	15.2	104.9	12.6
WISC–R[2] (ages 6–16 ½ yrs.)								
Verbal IQ	102.8	14.6	100.0	14.0	96.9	15.7	101.8	14.3
Performance IQ	101.3	14.4	101.0	14.6	96.7	15.9	103.1	13.6
Full Scale IQ	102.3	14.6	100.5	14.2	96.6	15.9	102.6	13.8
WISC–III[3] (ages 6–16 ½ yrs.)								
Verbal IQ	105.45	14.25	100.41	14.59	97.65	15.30	100.09	14.71
Performance IQ	102.37	14.98	100.32	14.85	98.01	15.35	101.96	13.97
Full Scale IQ	104.21	14.29	100.28	14.54	97.49	13.30	100.92	14.09
WAIS–R[4] (ages 16–74 ½ yrs.)								
Verbal IQ	101.6	14.8	98.6	14.3	98.6	15.7	101.0	14.3
Performance IQ	101.4	14.9	100.0	14.4	97.0	16.1	102.0	14.1
Full Scale IQ	101.6	15.0	99.0	14.2	98.0	16.3	101.5	14.3

[1]Wechsler Preschool and Primary Scale of Intelligence (Wechsler, 1967); data from Kaufman, 1973.

[2]Wechsler Intelligence Scale for Children–Revised (Wechsler, 1974); data from Kaufman & Doppelt, 1976.

[3]Wechsler Intelligence Scale for Children–III (Wechsler, 1991); data reprinted courtesy of The Psychological Corporation.

[4]Wechsler Adult Intelligence Scale–Revised (Wechsler, 1981); data from Reynolds, Chastain, Kaufman, & McLean, 1987.

NOTE: IQs are scaled to a mean of 100 and SD of 15 within their respective standardization samples.

South were not significantly different in these comparisons (p. 357). Kaufman cautioned that the mean IQs from the northeastern, north central, and southern regions were all 100 ± 2 points, and the mean for the western children was less than 5 points (one-third of a standard deviation) different from the test mean of 100, indicating that although statistically significant, regional differences may not be as important as other demographic differences in populations. When sample sizes are large, even very small differences in averages show up as not simply chance (i.e., they are "significant"), but this does not mean that we know what the nonchance effects are or that they are important.

Similar results occurred for the Wechsler Intelligence Scale for Children–Revised (WISC–R; see Wechsler, 1974), an intelligence test for children ages 6 to 16 ½ years (as can be seen in the middle portion

of Table 2). Kaufman and Doppelt (1976) reported mean WISC–R IQs for the South, Northeast, North Central, and West. Similarities are noted between this study and Kaufman's WPPSI analysis in that the mean IQs for children from the West were generally higher than for children from other regions. The mean IQs for the total group ranged from 96.6 to 103.1. The mean IQs were lowest in the South and highest in the West. Kaufman and Doppelt did not complete statistical analyses with these scores, but they noted the similarity of the averages to those for the WPPSI scores: Scores in the north-central states were 100 ± 1 point; scores in the northern states were 100 ± 2.8 points; and scores in the western states were 100 ± 3.1 points, indicating that regional area may not be as important a factor in these states as other demographic differences. The scores from the South were much lower than the scores Kaufman reported in the WPPSI study: All were 3.1–3.4 points below 100, which is still less than one-fourth of a standard deviation below the mean.

The recent revision of the WISC–R, published as the WISC–III in 1991, affords another opportunity to view regional differences in IQ. Regional data for the WISC–III are summarized in the lower-middle section of Table 2. Mean scores range from 97.49 to 105.45, a difference of 7.96 points. Again the lowest mean scores are for the South. The highest mean scores are for the Northeast (not the West). Scores in the Northeast were 100 ± 5.45, scores for North Central were 100 ± .41 point, scores in the South were 100 ± 2.35 points, and scores in the West were 100 ± 1.96 points. The northeastern mean IQs are between 4.88 and 7.96 points higher than the mean IQs of the other regions. This is a larger difference than was previously seen for this region. The pattern of lower southern scores seen in other IQ measures is apparent in these data, but the mean difference of nearly one-half of a standard deviation is larger on the WISC–III than on the other Wechsler scales.

Adults show a similar pattern of regional differences in IQ. These are indicated in the lower part of Table 2. The Wechsler Adult Intelligence Scale–Revised (WAIS–R; Wechsler, 1981), the revision of the 1955 WAIS, is normed for ages 16 to 74 years. Reynolds and colleagues (1987) report a complete analysis of the WAIS–R standardization sample as a function of the stratification variables. As part of this study, IQs from the four regions were evaluated. As noted in Table 2, scores ranged from 97.05 to 101.93; the lowest scores were from the north-central and southern regions (97.05–99.99), and the highest scores came from the western and northeastern regions (101.2–101.93). Results of ANOVA statistical tests indicated that the effect on IQ due to region was nonsignificant ($p >$ .05). The mean differences between the North Central/South scores and the West/Northeast scores were seen as "trivial and insignificant, and of no consequence for test interpretation" (p. 331). Similarities to Kaufman's studies of the WPPSI and WISC–R are apparent: All scores are within 2.95 points of the test mean of 100, less than one-fifth of a standard deviation.

Based on the findings of these studies, it appears that, though scores in the southern states tend to be lower than for other regions, regional area as a separate demographic variable does not appear to have an effect that is large enough to be of practical value even if statistically significant, although it may be of interest to determine why the difference arises. The robust nature of the differences indicates that such discrepancies across region are not due to chance. A variety of speculative theories have been offered to explain such differences. The theories point to migration patterns, socioeconomic status, number of years of education, quality of education, and employment patterns as possible determinants. Socioeconomic status has a positive correlation with IQ, just as one might suspect, and the South traditionally has had the lowest overall socioeconomic status among the four Bureau of the Census–defined regions of the United States. Other regions, particularly the Northeast and North Central, have been more heavily industrialized with jobs that demanded greater technical skill and training. More jobs have been available in these regions as well, and thus not only has more and better education been demanded, but skilled workers often migrated from the South. Urban and rural populations also differ in mean level of performance on intelligence tests, with urban groups scoring higher. The South is a predominantly rural culture, and, under population-proportionate sampling, a higher percentage of southern subjects will be drawn from rural areas than from urban ones, thus lowering the mean IQ level of the region. The South has had the highest rate of school dropouts of the four regions of the United States as well, adding to the complexity of determining how and why these regions differ in mean IQ level. Yet despite all of the variables discussed above that may be related to the causes of IQ differences by region, when all are considered simultaneously, region of residence continues to make a unique, though quite small, contribution to mean level of intelligence (see Barona, Reynolds, & Chastain, 1984). This holds true even if one adds gender, age, and race or ethnicity to the equation; regional differences continue to appear in the face of all such controlling variables (Barona, Reynolds, & Chastain, 1984).

Clearly there are also IQ differences *within* region due to differences in urban, suburban, and rural demographic variables. Within-region differences are greater than between-region differences. This is due in part to the "smoothing over" effect that occurs when one pools data from many smaller areas into numbers representative of one large region. Unless the within-region differences are several points greater than the between-region differences discussed above, their importance in interpreting IQ will remain minor.

So many interactive variables influence the development of intelligence that singling out one for study in an effort to determine a causal relationship, as we have done with region, is at best an exercise in wishful thinking. The development of intelligence depends on the interaction of many biological, environmental, social, and educational factors whose effects are difficult to separate.

RACE AND REGION

Although region is not listed among the most frequently cited sources of potential bias in IQ tests (Reynolds & Brown, 1984), when IQs have been separated into racial as well as regional groups, there have been some reported regional effects. Anastasi (1958) reported that Army-Alpha test scores from World War I and Army General Classification test scores from World War II showed that "mean scores tended to be lower for southern states than for northern states, the difference persisting even when men in the same occupations were compared across states. Similar state differences were found in both white and Negro populations" (p. 528). She goes on to say, "The superior test performance of northern Negroes [over southern Negroes] has been repeatedly demonstrated with varied samples, including draftees in both World Wars, college students, and schoolchildren. Such regional differences persist when comparisons are made between groups matched in occupational level" (p. 584). Also in 1958, A. M. Shuey determined that black children living in the North had an average IQ of 86, which was three points higher than the average for black children living in the South (83); the average for children living in the "border cities" of Oklahoma City and Kansas City was three points above the average for the other regions of the country, but there were only very small differences in scores.

Willerman (1979) reported the general finding that children in the South, regardless of race, have lower

IQs than children in the North. This finding has been reported throughout the literature. Mean test scores within racial groups differ by region, but do not "approach the difference of one standard deviation" typically found across race (Jensen, 1980; Osborne & McGurk, 1982).

BIBLIOGRAPHY

ANASTASI, A. (1958). *Differential psychology: Individual and group differences in behavior* (3rd ed.). New York: Macmillan.

BARONA, A., REYNOLDS, C. R., & CHASTAIN, R. (1984). A demographically based index of premorbid intelligence for the WAIS–R. *Journal of Consulting and Clinical Psychology, 52,* 885–887.

JENSEN, A. R. (1980). *Bias in mental testing.* New York: Free Press.

KAUFMAN, A. S. (1973). The relationship of WPPSI IQ to SES and other background variables. *Journal of Clinical Psychology, 29,* 354–307.

KAUFMAN, A. S., & DOPPELT, J. E. (1976). Analysis of WISC–R standardization data in terms of the stratification of variables. *Child Development, 47,* 165–171.

OSBORNE, R. T., & MCGURK, F. C. J. (1982). *The testing of Negro intelligence* (Vol. 2). Athens, GA: The Foundation for Human Understanding.

REYNOLDS, C. R., & BROWN, R. T. (EDS.). (1984). *Perspectives in bias in mental testing.* New York: Plenum.

REYNOLDS, C. R., CHASTAIN, R. L., KAUFMAN, A. S., & MCLEAN, J. E. (1987). Demographic characteristics and IQ among adults: Analysis of the WAIS–R standardization sample as a function of stratification variables. *Journal of School Psychology, 25,* 323–342.

SHUEY, A. M. (1958). *The testing of Negro intelligence.* Lynchburg, VA: J. P. Bell.

WECHSLER, D. (1974). *Wechsler Preschool and Primary Scale of Intelligence.* San Antonio, TX: The Psychological Corporation.

WECHSLER, D. (1974). *Wechsler Intelligence Scale for Children–Revised.* San Antonio, TX: The Psychological Corporation.

WECHSLER, D. (1981). *Wechsler Adult Intelligence Scale–Revised.* New York: The Psychological Corporation.

WECHSLER, D. (1991). *Wechsler Intelligence Scale for Children–III.* San Antonio, TX: The Psychological Corporation.

WILLERMAN, L. (1979). *The psychology of individual and group differences.* San Francisco: W. H. Freeman.

CECIL R. REYNOLDS
ELIZABETH MURDOCH JAMES

RELIABILITY Most dictionaries define reliability in terms of dependability, trustworthiness, or the degree to which one can have confidence in something. Reliability of educational and psychological tests of ability is concerned with many of these same factors, but it also extends to concepts such as stability and consistency, all of which are surely related. Broadly conceived, *test reliability* refers then to the relative precision or accuracy of a test as a measuring device. In thinking about reliability, one must address such questions as what the probability is of a person obtaining the same score if tested at a different time. Many sources of error come to mind that may inhibit a person's performance at any given time, such as not feeling well, a lack of sleep the night before testing, anxiety about the test, and recent trauma of a physical or psychological nature. Many different intelligence tests are available to psychologists and educators, no two of which are alike, yet each draws questions from an infinite domain of questions believed to reflect intellectual function. What is the probability that a person would obtain the same score if asked a different set of questions sampled from the domain of "intelligence questions"?

The first question noted above refers to errors of time sampling and is evaluated by calculating a type of reliability coefficient known as a test–retest reliability coefficient, which is often symbolized as $r_{1,2}$ to reflect the correlation (r) between scores obtained from testing on one occasion (the subscript 1) with scores obtained on a second occasion (the subscript 2). The second question deals with the accuracy of domain sampling, that is, how well a particular set of items represents the intended domain. To the extent that test items are highly correlated with one another, the test is believed to be measuring a single attribute (i.e., it is unidimensional) and would be said to have a high degree of internal consistency. This form of reliability is assessed by calculating what is known as an internal

reliability coefficient, which is most often symbolized as r_{xx} to denote simply that it is the correlation (r) of items within a test (x) with themselves. *Correlation* is a term indicating the degree of co-relationships between variables, that is, how much change in one variable can be predicted from knowing the amount of change in another, correlated variable.

Classically, the test score obtained by an individual can be seen to be composed of two components, the true score (the score that would be obtained if there were no error involved in measurement) and the error component. The error component is calculated by means of a complex formula based on the statistical notion of variance; the reliability coefficient is then derived from the error component by means of another formula. Mathematically speaking, the reliability coefficient is the summary mathematical representation of the proportion of a test score due to true score variance (variance due to real differences among those persons taking the test) and error variance (random or chance fluctuations in scores that have little or no meaning for measurement of the trait in question) and is thus a type of correlation coefficient. Reliability coefficients are always estimates because the actual true score cannot be known; it can only be estimated.

METHODS OF ESTIMATION OF RELIABILITY

Many methods are used to estimate reliability, some of which deal with different purposes. The most prominent methods of estimation are reviewed here.

Internal-Consistency Estimates. Reliability determined from internal-consistency estimates is most directly related to errors of domain sampling, though it will also encompass random error due to administrative and scoring mistakes. Domain sampling error is estimated by several means, most determined from how well the items relate to one another, that is, the degree to which they are consistent with one another.

Split-Half Reliability Estimates. Split-half reliability estimates are so called because they are derived from correlating each person's total score on one-half of the test items with the person's score on the other half. Many possible splits are conceivable. One might cor-

949

relate scores on the first half of the test with scores on the second half. This is not usually a good idea, as it may introduce some extraneous factors, such as speed of response, and it assumes that the order of difficulty of the test items is random, which it definitely is not on individually administered tests of intelligence. It is best to derive a split-half reliability estimate from the Pearson product moment correlation between scores on the odd-numbered items and scores on the even-numbered items. This approach is so prevalent that such estimates are frequently referred to as "odd–even reliability estimates or coefficients." Typically this coefficient will be symbolized by r_{oe}, where the subscript designates that the correlation is between odd and even halves of the same test.

Before one can settle on this correlation coefficient as an estimate of reliability, one more task must be performed. Since one correlates two halves of a test, the reliability coefficient does not properly take into account the reliability of the test when the two halves are combined. It only considers half of the total number of items. If there are twice as many test items, then the test can potentially sample the domain of test questions more accurately; and the better the sample of the domain, the higher the reliability of the measure and the lower the error due to domain sampling.

To put the two halves of the test back together with regard to a reliability estimate, a correction formula is used that has become known as the Spearman-Brown prophecy formula. Often the term *prophecy* is dropped, but it is an appropriate descriptor because the formula will predict, or prophesy, the reliability of any test when its length is to be increased.

Item Homogeneity and Consistency. A more complex but more fruitful approach to evaluating the internal consistency reliability of tests is to evaluate the co-relationships among the items at the item level. Rather than correlate scores on two halves of a test, one looks, at least conceptually, at how the test items all correlate with one another and with the true scores of the individuals tested. One infers that reliability estimates based in such procedures indicate how well or to what extent the items in the test are all measuring the same thing. The more closely they are measuring something that is common to all of the items, the more likely the items chosen have sampled the item domain well.

If all test items are scored dichotomously—that is,

simply right or wrong, 0 or 1, with no other values assigned to a response—the task is somewhat simplified, and one can apply one of the Kuder-Richardson formulas (Kuder & Richardson, 1937). The most frequently used formula in this regard is known as Kuder-Richardson formula 20, or just KR_{20}.

A more general form of KR_{20} is available to deal with tests when items may take multiple values (e.g., 0, 1, or 2), as is common on most individually administered intelligence tests or on rating scales, and is known as Cronbach's alpha (Cronbach, 1951) or simply as alpha. Alpha will deal effectively with dichotomous items as well, but the computation is more extensive than that involved with KR_{20}. Alpha has many practical uses and is most helpful in evaluating the psychometric properties of standardized tests.

Alpha is superior to split-half reliability estimates, which may be influenced by unknown chance factors or by the particular way in which the test is divided into two halves. Alpha may be considered the average of all possible split-half correlations, thus expunging any sampling error due to the method of dividing the test for the purpose of calculating a correlation between each half.

Alternate-Form Reliability Estimates. Another means of evaluating error due to domain sampling is to create two tests, preferably of equivalent length, from two independent samplings of the item or content domain. This is typically not a very practical approach to individually administered tests of intelligence and is used almost exclusively with group tests, where one will frequently see multiple forms of standardized tests. In such cases, one should look for alternate-form reliability estimates, as they determine the equivalency of the two measures. Alternative forms of a test are sometimes referred to as "parallel forms."

Once one has created two tests of the same length, the tests must be administered in very close temporal proximity to the same group of individuals. Often, two groups are given the tests in opposite order so that the reliability can be computed for each other, as order of administration may also affect scoring. The Pearson correlation between the two sets of scores reveals how well each test has sampled the item domain, or at least how well the worst of the two forms samples the domain. The alternate-form reliability estimate thus obtained is usually symbolized by r_{ab} (*a* and *b* referring to alternate forms of any given test). This method assumes one of two things: that taking the first form of the test has no effect on taking the second, alternate form or that any effect of taking the first test on taking the second test is exactly equal for all persons who take the tests. All in all, if both forms of the test are well conceived and well executed according to a detailed table of specifications and if the trait is unlikely to be much affected by the test taking or to change over short periods of time, the correlation between alternate forms of a test is a worthwhile approach to evaluating test reliability. Alpha remains the choice for estimating reliability, nevertheless. It is difficult to create a true alternate form, and alpha can be interpreted as an estimate of the correlation (r_{ab}) between hypothetical but true alternate forms of a test.

Clerical-Error Effects. Administrative and scoring errors will reduce internal-consistency reliability estimates (as well as measures of stability). Even the best psychologists make occasional errors in the administration and scoring of such complicated tests as the 1991 Wechsler Intelligence Scale for Children–Third Edition. These clerical errors lower the interitem correlations for a test, thus contributing to error variance of items. The larger the item variance relative to the total score variance, the lower the reliability. Scoring and administrative errors detract from the common core of measurement among the items. If an item is scored correct when it should have been scored incorrect, it will not be as consistent with the individual's performance on other items. This is readily apparent in the case of alternate-form reliability estimates, where, if an individual answers an item measuring the same objective in the same way on both forms but one is scored as correct and the other as incorrect, the correlation between the measures will be lowered. Errors of scoring and administration are internal to the test and, as such, come under the purview of the domain sampling model (Nunally, 1978). Clerical errors lower the average correlation of all the items with one another. The average interitem correlation is at the crux of the calculation of alpha and KR_{20} and, as such, will reflect measurement error due to random effects of scoring, administrative, and similar clerical errors.

Stability of Test Scores. The stability of a test, the degree to which a person obtains the same score when tested on repeated occasions, long has been considered a major characteristic of a test's reliability. In fact, one will frequently see *reliability* defined as the degree to which persons would obtain the same score if testing again under ideal conditions. This would seem to be a reasonable state of affairs, but it requires too many assumptions. It is unreasonable to expect persons to be unaffected by repeated measurements; simply put, repeated measurements will change the persons being assessed, affecting them in different ways, thus confounding measurement error with true changes in a trait from one time to the next.

Stability of scores is another matter of interest. It is beneficial to know just how much one can expect scores to change over time, and in some cases, this may be a test of the validity of the measure used. For traits that are deemed relatively stable over short periods, such as chronic trait anxiety and intelligence, measures of stability can tell one something about the reliability of a test, but only with the appropriate caveats of interpretation delineated above. To establish the degree of stability, one must administer the same test twice to the same set of individuals with the passage of some predetermined interval between the two testings. The Pearson correlation between the two testings, typically symbolized as $r_{1,2}$ (1 for the first testing and 2 for the second testing), is taken as the stability coefficient of the test. When interpreting this coefficient, it is necessary to know the length of time between the two testings and the rationale for this particular amount of time. As stated, for traits thought to change relatively slowly, such as intelligence, a stability coefficient taken over a week or two may offer information about test reliability, but a test–retest correlation with a year interval between testings is likely to tell one more about the reliability of the trait.

CAUTIONS IN EVALUATING RELIABILITY COEFFICIENTS

Reliability coefficients, whether they be r_{xx}, r_{12}, r_{ab}, or other variations, have a range from 0 to $+1.00$, the closer to 1.00 being better, except under special circumstances. Note that it is certainly possible for the correlation between two supposedly alternate forms of a test or one test administered twice to be negative. This would, of course, be highly unusual and would signal an absence of any kind of reliability or stability and, except for chance fluctuations around 0, is not something one will ordinarily encounter.

Several unfortunate mistakes in the estimation of reliability are all too common in commercially published tests. Usually, the errors are in such a direction as to overestimate the reliability coefficient of a test, but sometimes the effect is just the opposite.

Reliability estimates may become artificially inflated if the total test score variance increases relative to the item variance. There are several ways for this to happen. The first is the expansion of the range of scores by testing children across a wide age range. If, as is true on virtually all cognitive tests, raw scores (i.e., the number of correct answers) increase with age, then it is possible to increase the total test score variance with relatively little effect on the variance of individual items. This occurs as a function of using raw scores based on children of widely disparate ages. Probably about a one-year interval is the maximum for calculating internal-consistency reliability estimates and alternate-form estimates if raw scores are used. With the method of alternate forms, it is best to use age-corrected standard scores, a set of scores that have been mathematically manipulated to have the same amount of variability at each age level (i.e., the standard deviation of the scores is made constant across age). Nevertheless, one should view internal-consistency estimates of reliability with great suspicion if based on multiple age levels collapsed into a single group. For test–retest or stability estimates, using a broad range and age-correlated raw scores can produce an even greater exaggeration of true reliability. Here again, age-corrected standard scores should be used.

Artificially increased reliability estimates also result from a nonnormal distribution that is more heavily weighted at the two ends than it should be. For example, if one wants to compute alpha for an intelligence test at age 7, one should obtain a random sample of this age group. Yet, suppose one comes to the conclusion that each IQ level should be equally represented; one would not sample subjects in the same way. Table 1 contrasts these two distributions collapsed into 10-point intervals of IQ. As can be deduced from the table, the total test score variance

TABLE 1

Comparison of number of children in each IQ interval for 1,000 children under two methods of sampling

IQ Interval	Approximate Number of Children per Interval	
	Random Sampling	Equal Sampling of Each Interval
Below 60	4	100
60–69	16	100
70–79	60	100
80–89	150	100
90–99	240	100
100–109	260	100
110–119	170	100
120–129	80	100
130–139	16	100
140 and above	4	100

increases substantially in the "stratified," or equal-interval, sampling condition, whereas the item variance is affected very little and likely not at all in the case of dichotomous items. Reliability coefficients calculated from such nonrandom, nonnormal distributions are not accurate indications of the test's relative degree of precision.

Following the opposite logic could inordinately lower the value of a reliability coefficient. Suppose in the above example, the entire sample comes from the IQ range 90–109. The item variances do not change, yet the total test score variance will decrease dramatically. One must be watchful, then, of factors that improperly influence reliability estimates.

STANDARD ERROR OF MEASUREMENT

While a reliability coefficient is a useful way of representing the precision of a test, the standard error of measurement (SEM) is a more practical statistic for use with any given test. Reliability coefficients are useful for comparisons across tests, but the SEM is usually specific to the test in question, unless a number of other conditions are met. The primary benefit to be gained from the SEM is knowledge of how much the obtained score, X_i (X being the score for the one individual, i, of interest) departs from the true score, T_i.

The SEM is the expected standard deviation of the distribution of scores that would be obtained by one person, were the person to be tested on an infinite number of true alternate forms of a test made up of equal numbers of items randomly and independently sampled from the same item domain. If one were to create an infinite number of alternate forms of a test and had the same person take them all, even though taking the test had no effect on each subsequent test, this person would not earn the same score every time. Although each sample of items might represent the item domain about equally well, by chance some will be more familiar to the person than will others and some items will be far more difficult. One will not get an equal number of such items in each sample; rather, some error will be involved in each of the item samples (the test). All of these tests produce a set of scores, and a distribution of scores results. The mean of this hypothetical distribution of scores is the true score, the score that would result if there were no error, and the standard deviation of this distribution is the SEM. The SEM is the standard deviation of error. Since errors cause the observed score to depart from the true score, a measure of the degree of departure is the standard deviation of errors, or SEM. Obviously, the conditions for determining the true score and its accompanying SEM never actually exist. One must estimate both of these values, and each is dependent to a large extent on the reliability of the test.

Estimating the True Score. The obtained score of any individual is considered to be a biased estimate of the true score. If it is biased, it contains error that must be corrected. This error operates in such a way as to cause the obtained score to move away from the true score. To estimate the true score, one starts with the obtained score and regresses it toward the mean as a function of the reliability coefficient.

The errors of measurement are assumed to be normally distributed around the actual true score. Since the true score cannot be calculated but only estimated, it is necessary to set a band of confidence around this estimated true score. If one recalls that the SEM is conceptualized as the standard deviation of the distribution of which the true score is the mean and that the errors around this score are normally distributed, one can use the knowledge of the normal curve to establish a confidence interval around the true score. In a normal distribution of scores, 68 percent (or about 2 out of 3) of the scores will fall within 1 standard deviation (SD) of the mean: $\bar{X} \pm 1$ SD. About 95 percent of all scores will fall within 2 SDs of the mean. If one bands T_i with 1 SEM, then one can expect that 68 percent of the intervals constructed this way will contain the true score. Of course, for one interval the true score is either in the interval or it is not.

Estimating the Standard Error of Measurement. The SEM is a function of the reliability (r_{xx}) of a test and the SD. As the reliability of a test goes down, the SEM will increase, as it will if the SD of the scores increases.

A Good Reliability Coefficient. What constitutes a good reliability coefficient is at best a difficult question, one whose answer is laden with qualifications, nuances of interpretation, and sufficient caveats to cause nearly anyone to stumble, yet it must be addressed in some way. What constitutes a good reliability coefficient depends on, at a minimum, what trait or attribute is being measured, the amount of time available for testing, and the use to be made of the scores.

The Trait. Some variables are more difficult to measure than others because the item domain is relatively more difficult to sample accurately. As a general rule, personality variables are more difficult to measure than academic knowledge. What might be an acceptable level of reliability for a measure of dependency might be uniformly heralded as unacceptable for a standardized test of reading comprehension or of, for example, U.S. history prior to the Civil War. In evaluating the acceptability of a reliability estimate then, one must consider the variable under investigation and just how difficult it may be to measure. Knowledge of reliability estimates will assist one in determining the best measure of dependency or other variable.

The Time. If the amount of time for testing is restricted, then fewer items can be administered, and the sampling of the item domain is subsequently open to greater error. This could easily happen in a research project wherein the superintendent of schools permits one to conduct a research study in the district but allows one only 30 minutes to measure the three dependent variables of the study. As another example, a districtwide screening for reading problems may be conducted, but the budget allows only 15 minutes of testing time per child. In contrast, a psychologist may have an hour or more to devote to individual children in the assessment of their intellectual functioning. It would be not only unreasonable but unrealistic to expect the same level of reliability from each measure. The reliability coefficients of the measures available to meet one's time demands again can help to choose the best instrument nonetheless.

The Purpose. The purpose of the testing will also be a major consideration in evaluating reliability. Diagnostic tests that form the basis for major decisions about individuals should typically be held to a higher standard than research or screening measures. Even this apparently agreeable statement may provoke some uneasiness. It could prove very difficult to develop a reliable test of the probability of success in air force pilot training, where failure is defined as crashing and destroying a $10 million aircraft and death in 50 percent of the cases. A test with better than chance reliability, if it were the best one could do, would be very attractive and save many lives and much money, even though the level of error might be great. Tests for screening and research purposes typically are not expected to be as reliable as individual diagnostic scales, though high reliability remains desirable.

Empirical Guides. In spite of these caveats, one can make some general but arbitrary statements about preferred levels of reliability, knowing that these levels should be adjusted according to the factors discussed above. To be useful in research, reliability estimates of at least .60 should be required. Otherwise, the samples

under study should be increased in size to stabilize the effect under study. Errors of measurement interact with sampling errors in a research design to increase the total error in a research project. Ideally, tests with reliability estimates comparable to longer standardized tests are desired.

For diagnostic and screening tests, one will be very uncomfortable with reliability estimates below .80 and much prefer reliabilities to be .90 or higher (a level easily attained by most current measures of intellectual skill). Most ability tests that are in use today have a summary score with an internal-consistency reliability estimate of .95 or better.

Reliability is secondary only to VALIDITY in terms of evaluating tests and understanding test scores. Reliability coefficients of several types are routinely reported in test manuals and should guide users in test selection and interpretation. Readers wishing a more detailed and broader discussion of reliability and its mathematics are referred to L. S. Feldt and R. L. Brennan (1989) and J. Nunally (1978).

BIBLIOGRAPHY

CRONBACH, L. (1951). Coefficient alpha and the internal structure of tests. *Psychometrika, 16,* 297–334.

FELDT, L. S., & BRENNAN, R. L. (1989). Reliability. In R. Linn (Ed.), *Educational measurement* (3rd ed., pp. 105–146). New York: Macmillan.

GULLIKSEN, H. (1950). *Theory of mental tests.* New York: Wiley.

KUDER, F., & RICHARDSON, M. (1937). The theory of estimation of test reliability. *Psychometrika, 2,* 151–160.

NUNALLY, J. (1978). *Psychometric theory.* New York: McGraw-Hill.

CECIL R. REYNOLDS

S

SAVANTS Savants are people who are mentally handicapped but nevertheless display striking levels of ability in one or more areas of competence. As descriptive terms, *idiot savant, retarded savant,* and simply *savant* have been used more or less interchangeably. Until the 1970s *idiot savant* was the term most commonly encountered in case histories and the research literature, but more recent investigators have tended to drop the word *idiot* because of its pejorative implications. Even when *idiot* had a precise definition, which is now largely obsolete, referring to individuals with an IQ below 25, its appearance in the term *idiot savant* was misleading. Savants' IQs are usually considerably above 25, and typically in the region of 40 to 70 (Howe, 1989).

Savants are often withdrawn and solitary individuals who appear to lack social skills and interests. A large proportion, perhaps the majority, have some autistic tendencies, and a substantial minority are clearly autistic. Savants are fairly rare. One authority (Treffert, 1989) estimates their incidence as 1 per 2,000 in the population of institutionalized developmentally disabled individuals. Among people with early infantile autism (which itself occurs in roughly 7 cases per 100,000 children), as many as about 10 percent of individuals may also be savants. These individuals are sometimes described as autistic savants, but the absence of that adjective cannot be taken to imply that the individual being identified is not autistic.

SAVANT FEATS

The feats exhibited by savants take a number of different forms, although in most cases exceptional memory provides a crucial component. Another attribute that is shared by virtually all savants is an ability to concentrate on a single topic for long periods of time. In this particular respect, savants display behavior that is relatively uncommon in mentally handicapped individuals and more to be expected in people of above-average intelligence.

The actual levels of expertise displayed by savants within their islands of ability vary. First, in some savants, there exist abilities that appear striking and discordant against the individual's background of restricted functioning in most areas of mental expertise but would seem relatively unexceptional if observed in a person of normal intelligence. Second, it is relatively common for savants to perform feats that are virtually never seen in people of normal ability, but that ordinary people would be capable of achieving in some circumstances. For example, one of the better-known feats exhibited by savants takes the form of calendar calculating. A calendar calculator, if given a specified calendar date either in the past or in the future, is able to specify, usually within several seconds, the day of the week on which that date occurs. Some individuals can also rapidly solve a variety of other calendar problems, such as specifying the months in a particular year that began on a Tuesday, or the years in which the 9th of October fell on a Friday. In the case of calendar calculating feats like these, it is likely that the reason that people of normal ability so rarely perform them is not that they are incapable of learning to do so but that the time-consuming regime of learning that is necessary in order to achieve a high degree of mastery is simply too boring and insufficiently rewarding to engage and maintain the attention of ordinary people. Most normally intelligent individuals would find the idea of devoting long periods of time and effort to the acquisition of calendar skills distinctly unattractive. The very few intelligent people who have been willing to study calendars for lengthy periods of time have made at least as much progress as the majority of savant calculators.

A third level of expertise, however, is seen in a small number of savants, most if not all of whom are also autistic. This level is striking not only by the standards of performance expected in mentally handicapped people and exhibited in people of normal ability, but it is clearly beyond the capacity of the vast majority of ordinary people, even if those people were sufficiently motivated to devote a long-term commitment to the sphere of interest. These especially remarkable levels of ability are seen in two areas, music and artistic visual representation. For example, one four-year-old retarded autistic child with profound deficits in language ability (described by Selfe, 1977) produced drawings of animals and objects that involved representational skills never seen in a normal child at the same age. It would appear that in this child much of the mental-processing activity that is normally directed toward meaningfully analyzing perceived objects may have been exclusively engaged in processing information concerning structural, nonmeaningful attributes of perceived objects. Another autistic savant, who was also blind and had very little language development, showed prodigious musical abilities by the age of five. This child, who had perfect pitch perception, could transform tunes to different keys, could improvise extensively, and showed a much better sensitivity to the rules reflecting the structure inherent in musical composition than is normally found in children of his age (Miller, 1989).

The majority of other abilities seen in savants are largely or exclusively ones of memory. A savant may have an impressive knowledge of timetable information, or population statistics, or dates, for example. Savants who perform calendar calculations usually depend upon retaining substantial amounts of information about specific calendars and dates. Although there exist methods for performing some kinds of calendar calculations that make relatively small demands upon memory and depend more upon the introduction of rules and algorithms, such methods are rarely if ever drawn upon by savant calculators.

In savants one encounters impressive isolated abilities that exist despite an individual's low intelligence and against a background of mental incapacity. This demonstrates that at least in some circumstances it is possible for individual mental skills to be surprisingly autonomous and independent, and not to any substantial extent limited or controlled by the individual's general level of intelligence. Although it is possible that savants are unusual in this respect, it is conceivable that a similar degree of autonomy of specific skills can exist in people of normal intelligence. Compared with intelligent people, savants suffer from an inability to adapt or extend their skills to new tasks and different situations. It is unusual for savants to apply their skills in ways that contribute to the practical tasks encountered in everyday life.

(*See also:* MEMORY, EXCEPTIONAL.)

BIBLIOGRAPHY

HOWE, M. J. A. (1989). *Fragments of genius: The strange feats of idiots savants.* London: Routledge.

MILLER, L. K. (1989). *Musical savants: Exceptional skill in the mentally retarded.* Hillsdale, NJ: Erlbaum.

SELFE, L. (1977). *Nadia: A case of extraordinary drawing ability in an autistic child.* London: Academic Press.

TREFFERT, D. A. (1989). *Extraordinary people.* London: Bantam Press.

MICHAEL J. A. HOWE

SCHOLASTIC ASSESSMENT TESTS (SAT)

Formerly the Scholastic Aptitude Tests, the Scholastic Assessment Tests are a set of tests designed to measure verbal and quantitative reasoning skills, developed over many years of education, that are related to academic performance in college. The SATs are a source of information useful in assessing the readiness of students for college work. Other sources include high school grades, other tests, study and work habits, and degree of motivation. Usually taken during a student's senior year, the tests are used by colleges for admission, placement, and guidance; and by students, their parents, and high school counselors for help in educational planning and guidance. The Preliminary Scholastic Aptitude Test/National Merit Scholarship Qualifying Test (PSAT/NMSQT) is a shorter version, taken for guidance and scholarship selection early in the junior year. More than 1.1 million college-bound seniors and about an equal number of juniors participated in the SAT and PSAT programs in the school year 1992–1993.

The COLLEGE BOARD (formerly the College Entrance Examination Board) was organized in 1899 by the Association of Colleges and Preparatory Schools of the Middle States and Maryland to deal with a lack of agreement between schools about subject matter preparation and standards. It is now a national association with over 2,900 member schools, colleges, and school systems. The board developed a common set of essay examinations in nine subject areas which were first administered to prospective college entrants in 1901 and continued annually.

In 1925, the College Board adopted an approach to test development growing from the work of the World War I committee for classification of army personnel. The result was the Scholastic Aptitude Test, a largely multiple-choice test comprising nine subtests: definitions, arithmetical problems, classification, artificial language, antonyms, number series, analogies, logical inference, and paragraph reading. The test was first administered to 8,040 students in 1926 (Donlon, 1984). Since verbal and mathematics aptitude scores were first reported in 1929, the SAT has undergone continual development and refinement. The verbal section format of reading comprehension, analogies, antonyms, and sentence completion questions was established in 1952, but antonyms were discontinued in 1994. During the 1950s, verbal items came to be drawn from social, political, and scientific areas, in addition to literary, artistic, and philosophical ones. In 1959, data sufficiency test questions, which reduced computation and stressed insight, were added to the mathematics section. In 1974, the data sufficiency questions were replaced by the quantitative comparison type, which require similar skills. The respondent is asked to compare two mathematical expressions and indicate whether they are equal, unequal (along with the direction of their inequality), or whether insufficient information is provided to make this decision.

Several approaches to assessing writing skills have been employed. The Test of Standard Written English (TSWE) was used from 1977 to 1994 to assess ability to handle conventions of standard written English, but this task is now part of the SAT-II writing test.

The SAT-I: Reasoning Test and SAT-II: Subject Tests currently constitute the Scholastic Assessment Tests, renamed to emphasize changes in content and format that provide greater emphasis on mastery of high school subject matter but continue to tap developed reasoning skills. For the SAT-I: Verbal Reasoning Test, the changes are reflected in longer text passages with emphasis on critical reading and reasoning, vocabulary in context, and paired passages of text chosen to reflect different points of view. On the SAT-I: Math Reasoning, the changes mean greater emphasis on the application of mathematical concepts, the interpretation of data, and the use of questions requiring the actual construction of a response, rather than the more typical multiple-choice format. Calculator use is now recommended but not required.

Scores for SAT-I and SAT-II are reported on 200 to 800–point scales. The SAT-II Subject Tests include English composition; mathematics, levels I and II; American history and social studies; world history; biology, chemistry, physics; literature; Spanish, French, Chinese, Italian, Japanese, German, Latin, and modern Hebrew. In the school year 1992–1993, nearly 200,000 graduating seniors took one or more SAT Achievement Tests.

TEST DEVELOPMENT

The College Board contracts with the Educational Testing Service for developing and administering the SAT, and conducting an extensive program of research. The tests are constructed using contemporary principles of assessment construction and measurement theory to relate them broadly to school-based educational experiences in the case of the SAT-I, and more narrowly to specific high school course content in the SAT-II. The scale currently being developed represents a slight repositioning of the scale originally constructed for the 1941 norming of the SAT. The two scales are isomorphic, but the rescaling allows for more reliable measurement in upper and lower score ranges by broadening the distribution of item difficulty level, but leaving the mean difficulty unchanged. Adopted for research and for operational planning in 1994, the rescaling will be applied to students graduating from high school in 1996.

VALIDITY

The VALIDITY of the SAT has been documented extensively by researchers, yet it has been the basis of criticism by detractors. Since the SAT is used to assess the current readiness of students for college, the major element of construct validity evidence is short-term prediction, usually first-year college grades. In particular, the improvement in prediction when adding the SAT to high school rank is reported. The College Board Validity Study Service has helped colleges perform validity studies without charge since 1964. Donlon (1984) summarized these studies through 1981, which included 685 colleges that had examined freshman grade point average (GPA) and its relation to SAT-verbal, SAT-mathematical, and high school record (HSR). Among these studies, the HSR was the best predictor, having an average correlation with GPA of .48 across these 605 studies. The two SAT scores had a .42 average correlation with GPA over the same studies, and when they were combined with HSR, the mean correlation rose to .55 (Donlon, 1984). These same data have been a basis for criticism of SAT validity because half the schools studied had lower correlations with GPA. The fact that there is considerable range in first-year prediction across colleges should be noted, and that half of the schools had correlations with GPA *higher* than these median coefficients. Also, the relatively narrow range of scores at many institutions due to admission selection or self-selection reduces validity estimates. Recent validity research has examined prediction of specific course grades rather than GPA, and has employed corrections for restriction of range and criterion (course grade or GPA) unreliability. This resulted in higher prediction coeffi-

cients (from .40 to above .60) and a stronger weight for the SAT in prediction over the HSR. These findings should be interpreted in the context of the nature of SAT use by schools and the range of scores among applicants, recognizing that the size of the validity coefficient is not the only consideration in appraising the usefulness of the tests. If a school uses SAT score information fully by adopting a policy of maximizing resources to motivate, develop, and improve performance of students entering college with relatively lower scores, and still continues to interest, motivate, and demand excellence from higher scoring students, performance gaps are likely to be reduced and predictive validity coefficients may be smaller, because the relationship between test score at entry and first-year performance will be reduced. In such a case, valuable and appropriate use has been made of test data that is not reflected in the prediction equation. Thus, validity statistics need interpretation in the context of programmatic information from colleges. If adequate grades are earned by lower-scoring students, relatively lower validity coefficients for the SAT might actually yield information on positive test use.

TEST–RETEST STABILITY AND COACHING

The mean score gain for the SAT verbal and mathematics scores is about + 12 points for the seven-month period from April to November, with about 35 to 40 percent of repeaters showing a decrease (Donlon, 1984). There is considerable variability, however, and the change is likely due to growth, practice, selection, and statistical error. All of these factors result in lower-scoring students showing the greatest improvement (Donlon, 1984), with average increases in verbal and math scores from 10 to 20 points. Students who choose to repeat the SAT have, on the average, scored lower than nonrepeaters. They may have scored lower than other achievement indicators suggest they would have. They also may be more motivated and think they are likely to do better. Repeaters are often studying essential preparatory material in their school class between testings, are often taking special preparation or coaching classes, and may recognize personal factors that interfered with their first testing. Thus it is not surprising that among students who choose to retest, students with lower scores tend to gain more on re-test.

There is an important positive factor here, as well as a caution. A student may effectively combine motivated, self-directed study, academic resources, and self-appraisal and then use the results to better prepare for college, consider alternate college choices, and make a test-retaking decision. This process helps to improve the validity of the college admission process as well as that of the SAT. However, if elements of this process, such as the encouragement of others who have attended college and the availability of test preparation help, are more accessible to students from higher income backgrounds, then this process has the potential to increase the relationship between income and test scores.

These data also relate to coaching findings and claims. Student motivation and the quality and extent of regular academic instruction are important factors in appraising coaching effects. Messick (1980) noted that most studies of coaching failed to control for motivational effects. Given the motivation to seek coaching, several studies have reported large mean increases on combined verbal and math scores (45 to 110 points) (Johnson et al., 1985; Zuman, 1987). Largest gains are found for lower-scoring students with weaker academic backgrounds when rigorous, well-structured coaching instructional programs were buttressed by parental involvement. Smyth (1990) found lower gains (9 points for verbal, 24 points for math) in a study of coaching effects among 700 students in independent schools who had been enrolled in a college preparatory curriculum prior to the first testing.

THE SAT AND THE AMERICAN COLLEGE TEST (ACT)

The ACT Assessment, begun in 1960 as an extension of the high school–level Iowa Tests of Educational Development, is also designed for examining readiness for college work. It reports subtest scores in English, mathematics, social studies, natural science, and a composite on 1 to 36 point scales. Concordance tables are established periodically between the ACT and the SAT for estimating equivalency of the two instruments. Though its total national volume is smaller, the ACT is more widely used in some midwestern and southern states than the SAT (see AMERICAN COLLEGE TEST).

USES AND MISUSES

The strong reputation of the SAT results in national attention to the annual report on college-bound seniors, which summarizes score results and demographic characteristics of the more than 1.1 million senior test takers. While these are useful national indicators, the average scores for individual states are not, due to great differences in the proportion of high school seniors taking the SAT across states. In three or four states, as few as 5 percent of the senior class takes the SAT, while in other states nearly all college-bound seniors take it.

The acceptance of one student and the rejection of another with a higher test score is a complaint heard regarding the SAT and other tests used in the admissions process. Such a criticism reflects the belief that the measure serves as the perfect yardstick for admission. Neither SAT scores nor any other indicator should be used alone for selection. The scores, high school records, local validity information, and other data describing motivation, interest, leadership qualities, resources of the high school attended, and other factors are all considered by an institution when selecting a freshman class. In fact, the College Board specifically advises against the use of an arbitrary cutting score for admission.

BIAS AND FAIRNESS

SAT items are extensively reviewed for sensitivity and potential bias, through procedures that involve subject matter experts, teachers, and test developers. Statistical procedures are applied after testing to examine and correct for differences in the functioning of test items across racial or gender groups. Much of the theoretical work as well as applied research in bias in assessment has been done by present or former ETS researchers, and it has been broadly adopted for assessment improvement throughout the industry. The most serious charges of bias against the SAT are in the systematic and long-term differences in average SAT scores across parental income level, by gender, and by racial/ethnic group, even though the scores of all categories in these groups cover the full spectrum of scores. The primary response has been that educational resources and quality of schooling are distributed inequitably, often in ways that are likely to produce racial/ethnic and income group differences, and that parents with greater resources provide enriching educational and travel experiences for children that extend and enrich classroom learning. It would be surprising if these differences in educational experiences did not result to some extent in effects on test scores. This rationale may even apply for gender differences, for the average reported parental income level for female SAT takers is lower than that for males (College Board, 1993; Johnson, 1990), although this may be an artifact of students' perceptions of their family situations. While studies have documented gender differences in SAT scores among students achieving equal success in college courses (Wainer & Steinberg, 1992), they have not adequately controlled for school and family resource effects. Yet these studies and others do suggest more unexplained variance in performance among high-achieving female and minority students than among nonminorities.

The College Board has developed Equity 2000, a program to serve as a national model in making high quality educational experiences available to all students in large diverse school districts, rather than to only a select few. The program has been effective in greatly increasing the number and proportion of high school students enrolled in a standard precollege mathematics program involving algebra and geometry in ninth and tenth grades across participating districts. Such programs, if extensively implemented, offer promise of distributing educational opportunities more equitably, and making college choice and academic success available to all students.

BIBLIOGRAPHY

ANASTASI, A. (1988). *Psychological testing* (6th ed.). New York: Macmillan.

COFFMAN, W. E. (1963). *The Scholastic Aptitude Test: 1926–1962* (Test Development Report No. 63-2). Princeton, NJ: Educational Testing Service.

COLLEGE BOARD (1993). *College-bound seniors: 1993 profile of SAT and Achievement Test takers.* New York: Author.

DONLON, T. F. (1984). The *College Board technical handbook for the Scholastic Aptitude Test and Achievement Tests.* New York: The College Board.

JOHNSON, S. T. (1990, April). *Gender bias and the SAT.* Paper presented at the annual meeting of the National Council on Measurement in Education, Chicago.

JOHNSON, S. T., WALLACE, M. B., ASBURY, C. A., THOMPSON, S., & VAUGHN, J. (1985). *Effects of a program to improve SAT scores among low-income students in three cities.* Paper presented at the annual meeting of the American Educational Research Association and the National Council on Measurement in Education, New Orleans.

MARCO, G. L., ABDEL-FATTAH, A. A., & BARON, P. S. (1992). *Methods used to establish score comparability on the enhanced ACT Assessment and the SAT* (College Board Report No. 92-3). New York: The College Board.

MESSICK, S. (1980). *The Effectiveness of coaching for the SAT: Review and reanalysis of research from the fifties to the FTC.* Princeton, NJ: Educational Testing Service.

SMYTH, F. L. (1990, Fall). SAT coaching: What really happens to scores and how we are led to expect more. *Journal of National Association of College Admission Counselors,* 7–16.

WAINER, H., & STEINBERG, L. (1992). Sex differences in performance on the mathematics section of the SAT: A bidirectional validity study. *Harvard Educational Review, 62,* 323–336.

WILLINGHAM, W. W., LEWIS, C., MORGAN, R., & RAMIST, L. (1990). *Predicting college grades: An analysis of institutional trends over two decades.* Princeton, NJ: Educational Testing Service.

ZUMAN, J. P. (1987). The effectiveness of special preparation for the SAT: An evaluation of a commercial coaching school. *Dissertation Abstracts International, 48,* 1749. (University Microfilms No. ADG 87-22714.880.1)

SYLVIA T. JOHNSON

SCHOOLING Throughout the history of psychometric testing, many influential proponents of intelligent quotient (IQ) testing argued that such tests measured the inborn, inherited capacity to behave in an intelligent manner—something that neither schooling nor training was thought to affect. For instance, Cyril BURT, in a 1933 interview on BBC radio, asserted that "by intelligence the psychologist understands inborn, all-around intellectual ability . . . inherited, not due to teaching or training . . . uninfluenced by industry or zeal."

Hence, intelligence, as measured by the most popular mental ability tests, was claimed to be unaffected by schooling. Attending school was alleged to have no substantial impact on mental ability scores, and therefore the low scores of those who were unschooled could not be attributed to their failure to attend school.

The best known and most thoroughly validated measure of mental ability was, then as now, in the late twentieth century, the IQ test. It seems hard to believe that anyone would assert that IQ scores were not related to school attendance because so much of the knowledge required to do well on such tests is directly or indirectly taught in school. Today, many who do research in the field of intelligence argue against this older view, claiming that schooling *does* influence intelligence, if by the latter one means IQ scores. The theme of this article is that, notwithstanding past claims, there is an inextricable relationship between schooling and IQ test performance. Simply put, the less that a group of children attends school, the more their IQ scores will decline.

The strongest type of support for the above statement would be a fully randomized block design in which two groups of children were matched on IQ scores at the start of school, but one group dropped out and the other finished school. We would expect that the former's IQ scores would plummet vis-à-vis the group who remained in school. Such evidence is, in practice, impossible to collect, and researchers of the link between schooling and IQ have had to look to other forms of evidence to support their claim. The five types of evidence that are summarized below support the view that schooling is very important for the maintenance of IQ scores. Greater details of this evidence appear in Ceci (1991). That earlier paper reviews eight classes of evidence for the link between attending school and IQ scores and argues that alternative explanations for changes in IQ scores fail to account for the full corpus of findings. Only one explanation fits the totality of the evidence, namely, each lost opportunity for schooling conveys a drop in potential IQ.

THE FIVE TYPES OF EVIDENCE

The Deleterious Effects of Dropping Out of High School. The easiest accomplishment to document is the correlation between years of schooling completed and IQ scores. For each year of missed or abbreviated schooling, there is a corresponding decrease in IQ. If two boys at age 13 have identical IQs and grades, and they are retested at age 18, after one of the boys has completed high school (or gymnasium, since these studies were done in the Scandinavian countries) but the other boy had dropped out in ninth grade, the latter boy will, on average, have lost around 1.8 IQ points for every year of missed school, thus differing from his former classmate by approximately a half standard deviation (7.5 IQ points) by the age of 18. This is a very big difference for two boys who at age 13 had identical IQs. In three independent studies a similar finding has emerged. The moral seems to be that dropping out of high school has very negative consequences for one's IQ.

Starting School Late/Frequent Absences. It is informative to examine geographic regions where some children are permitted to enter school at age 6 while those in a neighboring township are not, because of the unavailability of a teacher. In such cases, the two groups of children grow up possessing significantly different IQ scores, favoring those who started school on time. In some of these studies the two groups of children come from the same genetic stock, so it does not appear that the differences in IQs can be due to one group being biologically superior.

The most famous case of this type that has been studied is known as the "Hollows Children." M. Sherman and C. B. Key (1932) studied children reared in remote regions of the Blue Ridge Mountains. Some of the hollows, however, were more remote than others. Colvin, the most remotely situated of the hollows, had a single school, but it was in session infrequently, only a total of sixteen months between 1918 and 1930. Only three of Colvin's adults were literate, and physical contact with the outside world appears to have been nonexistent. The other three hollows were progressively more modern. Sherman and Key (1932) observed that the IQ scores of the hollows children fluctuated systematically with the level of schooling available in their hollow, the differences being quite substantial. Advantages of 10 to 30 points were found for the children who received the most schooling.

In another investigation, which was carried out in South Africa, a study was done of the mental development of children of Indian ancestry whose schooling was delayed for up to four years because of the unavailability of teachers in their village. Compared to children from nearby villages inhabited by Indian settlers of similar genetic stock who had teachers, children whose schooling was delayed experienced a decrement of 5 IQ points for every year that their schooling was delayed. Other studies also have documented deficits in IQ scores that accompany delayed entrance into school. For example, in the Netherlands during World War II, many schools were closed as a consequence of the Nazi occupation, and many children entered school several years late. Their IQs dropped approximately 7 points, probably as a result of their delayed entry into school, though other factors cannot be ruled out (e.g., malnutrition).

Intergenerational Changes in School and IQ. Systematic changes in IQ scores have been associated with increases or decreases in formal schooling across different generations. This can be seen by comparing various members of a family who differ in their years of schooling. For every year of school completed by a younger member of a family, there is a corresponding increase in IQ over an older sibling who attended school less.

In families where children attended school intermittently, there is a high negative correlation between chronological age and IQ, implying that as these children got older, their IQ scores dropped commensurate with the number of their absences from school. For instance, children of Gypsies and canal boat pilots began school in England at the start of the twentieth century with IQs in the low average range, which was presumably the same IQ level that their older brothers and sisters possessed when they had started school some years earlier. By the time their older siblings had reached adolescence, however, their IQs had plummeted to the retarded range, $r = -.75$ between age and IQ. In other words, there was every reason to expect that the IQ scores of these younger children would have shown a large drop if they had been tested as adolescents—which they were not, unfortunately. In the Sherman and Key (1932) study of the hollows children mentioned above, there was a similar age-related decrement in IQ: The older the child, the lower was the IQ. The IQs of 6-year-olds were not much below the national average, but by age 14 the children's IQs had plummeted into the retarded range. A later study by another researcher reached a similar conclusion for children born in a mountainous area of Tennessee where, on average, their IQ scores were 11 points higher in 1940 than the IQs of their older siblings in 1930.

Summer Vacations. There are even small drops in IQ for those whose summer vacations are less academically oriented than others. Middle-class youngsters, whose summers are more likely to be filled with organized events and academic activities (computer camp, nature camp), exhibit a significantly smaller decline in IQ over the summer vacation than do poor children whose summers are less organized and less academic. Even achievement levels decline over the summer months, so that by the beginning of the new school year they are lower than they were at the end of the previous school year.

Being the Oldest or Youngest in Class. An interesting methodology for studying the relationship between schooling and IQ is to identify those children who are the oldest members of their class and compare their IQs to the youngest members of the next higher class. In most school districts there are strict cut-off dates for school entrance; children's birth dates must fall on a certain date or else they must wait to start school an entire year later. Thus, in some neighborhoods there are playmates who differ in age by only a month or so, but only the older child will be allowed to enter school that year. Hence, it is easy to locate a third-grade child who is 10 years and 2 months old and compare this child's IQ to a child in fourth grade who is 10 years and 3 months old. Whenever this has been done, it has been found that the child who is slightly older has a higher mental ability score. The only difference between the two children is that one of them started school a year earlier and therefore at the time of testing has an extra year of schooling. If schooling were not the basis for the older child's higher IQ, then what is? Surely being 30 days older could not explain it. The most likely explanation is that the child who is 30 days older had the benefit of an extra year of schooling.

The most parsimonious explanation of the full corpus of data and findings (Ceci, 1991) is that schooling helps prop up IQ because much of what is tapped by IQ tests is either (a) directly taught in school (e.g., information questions on popular IQ tests—such as "Who wrote Hamlet?" and "What are hieroglyphics?"—are taught in school or confronted in school-related activities such as plays and class trips, as are vocabulary items such as "What is espionage?") or (b) indirectly taught by schools (e.g., modes of cognizing that emphasize one form of conceptual organization over another). In addition, schooling fosters disembedded ways of construing the world in terms of hypotheticals and inculcates attitudes toward testing that may be favored by test manufacturers, such as sitting still for prolonged periods, trying hard, and making certain assumptions about the purposes of testing.

"Modes of cognizing" refers, for example, to the following. When students reach the age of about 7 or 8, most schools begin to encourage taxonomic sorting, not as an end in itself but as a means of classifying materials in history, social studies, and geography (e.g., "these are the grain states, these are the dairy states, these are the manufacturing states, etc."). It is not a coincidence that the developers of IQ tests reward children of this age for using precisely these same taxonomic organizations when they answer IQ questions such as "How are an apple and an orange alike?" (e.g., a taxonomic answer such as "they are both fruit" is awarded bonus points) instead of a perceptually based answer (e.g., "they are all round") or a functionally based answer (e.g., "they both can be eaten"). That children who do not attend school perform worse on such subtests of IQ items ought not surprise anyone, in view of the content of most IQ tests. Unschooled adults also have a tendency to employ the same nontaxonomic (i.e., perceptual and functional) organizations as younger children. But nontaxonomic modes of cognizing are not inherently less abstract or complex than taxonomic modes, and examples of perceptual/functional organizations can be found that are more complex than taxonomic ones. But there is no ignoring the fact that schooling conveys an advantage as far as

IQ performance is concerned because it encourages the type of taxonomic organization that is rewarded on the IQ test.

CAVEAT LECTOR

It is important to make a disclaimer: Although schooling helps prop up IQ scores, this is not equivalent to claiming that it props up *intelligence*. The latter entails more than the acquisition of certain modes of cognizing that are valued by a test manufacturer or the acquisition of cultural artifacts—no matter how important some may regard such shared knowledge. While intelligence has as many definitions as there are knowledgeable respondents, most researchers agree that it includes some element of novel problem solving. If intelligence is defined as the ability to solve novel problems, then nothing in the literature indicates that schooling actually increases intelligence. Individuals who have never set foot in a school are often capable of engaging in high levels of cognitively complex problem solving, while many who graduate with advanced degrees often cannot. Schooling may make it more likely that one will engage in complex thought processes, but the relationship is imperfect at best. So, while schooling seems to prop up IQ test performance, it does not seem as obvious that it increases intellectual development, particularly if the latter is conceptualized in terms of novel problem solving as opposed to IQ scores.

WHY DOES SCHOOLING ASSIST IQs BUT NOT SATs?

If it is true that staying in school is the best way to prevent a decline in IQ, then why is it that staying in school is not associated with a similar benefit for scores on the Scholastic Aptitude Test (SAT)? The technical answer is that it *is* associated with such a benefit. To see this one needs only to do the following experiment: Administer the SAT to pairs of youngsters who scored similarly on the SAT at age 13 but who differed in their subsequent level of schooling. It will readily become apparent that being out of school hurts SAT performance, too. The confusion comes when it is reported that SAT scores have been declining even as the mean level of schooling has been increasing. The sample taking the SAT always consists of high school seniors, however; thus, there is no difference in the level of schooling of today's SAT takers from those of an earlier generation. The decline in SATs may therefore reflect a comparative failure among today's high school seniors to go as far beyond the basics as did earlier high school seniors. Since the number of years of completed schooling is constant among SAT takers, it cannot be blamed or credited with SAT fluctuations. (It should be noted that today's cohort of SAT takers is more economically and culturally diverse than earlier cohorts taking the SAT; this factor accounts for approximately 25 percent of the drop in scores over the past thirty years.) Therefore, while the level of schooling among IQ test takers is related to changes in their scores, the level of schooling among SAT takers is not because there is no variation in *quantity* of schooling completed by SAT takers. Of course, there may be large variation in the *quality* of schooling, but data pertaining to the quality of schooling are not as clear. Most large-scale studies find little, if any, relationship between the level of economic resources invested in schools (e.g., the amount of money spent per pupil, teacher credentials, class size) and various achievement outcomes, including IQ.

BIBLIOGRAPHY

CECI, S. J. (1991). How much does schooling influence intellectual development and its cognitive components? A reassessment of the evidence. *Developmental Psychology, 27,* 703–722.

SHERMAN, M., & KEY, C. B. (1932). The Intelligence of Isolated Mountain Children. *Child Development, 3,* 279–290.

STEPHEN J. CECI

SERIAL AND PARALLEL PROCESSING

The use of the terms *serial processing* and *parallel processing* has changed since the early 1980s. Currently, the contrasted words are used for computing processes (see ARTIFICIAL INTELLIGENCE), whereas before they were used synonymously with dichotomies such as *synchronic–sequential* and *global–analytical.* Serial processing is the processing of information in consecutive steps; parallel processing is the execution of several different operations simultaneously (Sutherland, 1989).

For the purpose of this article, the terms *successive* and *simultaneous* are used synonymously with *serial* and *parallel.* There is no opposition between an orientation represented by successive and simultaneous processing, arising, as it does, from cognitive neuropsychology, on the one hand, and the computer modeling of serial and parallel processes, on the other. In fact, H. A. Simon (1992, pp. 153–154) suggested "that at the network of neurons, modeling will have to be largely parallel . . . [while] at the symbolic level—the level of events taking place in hundreds of milliseconds or more—modeling will continue to be largely serial."

The neuropsychological view of simultaneous and successive processing has been taken from A. R. LURIA's (1966a, b) clinical observations and developed further in order to describe and explain normal cognitive processes (Das, Kirby, & Jarman, 1979). Discussing the two processes, Luria (1966a, p. 74) wrote, "Analysis shows that there is strong evidence for distinguishing two basic forms of integrative activity of the cerebral cortex by which different aspects of the outside world may be reflected. . . . The first of these forms is the integration of the individual stimuli arriving in the brain into *simultaneous, and primarily spatial groups,* and the second is the integration of individual stimuli arriving consecutively in the brain *into temporally organized, successive series."* Simultaneous-processing deficits can be detected in copying a figure, such as a cube, and detecting differences between terms such as *father's brother* and *brother's father.* Similarly, successive-processing deficits are detected in the rapid repetition of word strings (e.g., *egg, bus, leaf*) and the imitation of hand movements (palm, fist, fist, palm).

Early evidence of the existence of two processes in nonclinical populations was provided by a wide variety of studies conducted with different samples. Age, culture, socioeconomic status, intelligence quotient (IQ), and selection of tests were varied; yet two factors representing the two processes have usually emerged (Kirby & Das, 1990).

Neuropsychology is the branch of knowledge that relates brain to behavior, and simultaneous–successive, or parallel–serial, processes can be broadly localized in specific parts of the brain. Simultaneous processing is associated with the occipital and parietal lobes in the back of the brain, and successive processing with the temporal region and the frontal region of the brain (over the temples) adjacent to it. These regions overlap, and it is in the overlapping regions that the higher information coding occurs. For example, consider reading an unfamiliar multisyllabic word, *taciturn*. The single letters are to be recognized, and that involves simultaneous coding. The reader matches the visual shape of the letter with a mental dictionary and comes up with a name for it. The letter sequences, then, have to be formed (successive coding) and blended together as a syllable (simultaneous). Then the string of syllables has to be made into a word (successive), the word is recognized (simultaneous), and a pronunciation program is then assembled (successive), leading to oral reading (successive and simultaneous). Of course, this is a simplified view of what may be occurring when a reader is confronted with a word. But one will not be able to read if there is damage to the overlapping region of the brain (Das, Kirby, & Jarman, 1979). Reading involves sentences and paragraphs, too. A sentence has a syntax, a grammatical structure, and the logical relationship of the structure has to be understood for understanding the sentence. "Dog bites man" has the same syntax as "Man bites dog" and yet has a different meaning. Relatively speaking, syntax involves successive processing, whereas the meaning or semantics requires simultaneous processing. Consider answering yes or no to the sentence as soon as you can. My father's grandfather is my grandfather's father. Does it not require mainly simultaneous processing? Paragraph comprehension must involve both processes; not only syntax and semantics have to be understood, but the idea units have to be organized as well.

Tasks that do not require reading or that do not play upon language also need simultaneous coding. In young children around the age of 6 or 7, some tasks devised by Jean PIAGET, the Swiss child psychologist, directly involve simultaneous processing. One such task is conservation: You show a child a tall and a short glass; fill the short one with water, and then pour it into the tall one. The child is then asked, Does the glass now have the same amount of water as the other one had? Those who answer such conservation questions correctly are found to prefer simultaneous processing (see CHILDREN'S CONSERVATION CONCEPTS).

Tests that measure simultaneous and successive processing can be constructed from tasks such as those discussed above. Two systematic attempts at making

such tests are the KAUFMAN ASSESSMENT BATTERY FOR CHILDREN, or K-ABC (Kaufman & Kaufman, 1983), and the Das-Naglieri Cognitive Assessment System (Das & Naglieri, 1983).

The K-ABC uses seven tests for measuring simultaneous processing and three tests for sequential processing; the two together yield a composite score that is equivalent to an IQ. Additionally, the K-ABC has a school-achievement battery. Its theoretical core is not clearly defined and it is not sufficiently different from existing intelligence tests, such as the WECHSLER SCALES OF INTELLIGENCE (Keith & Novak, 1987).

The Das-Naglieri battery (Das & Naglieri, 1993) attempts to provide comprehensive and representative measures of the two processes, comprising in the simultaneous measures verbal as well as nonverbal tasks. Included among its successive tasks are those that involve rapid articulation: "Say *key, wall, hot* as fast as you can 10 times." Other tasks require working memory and comprehension of sequential relations: "The blue purpled the white that greened the yellow." Who was purpled? The battery also measures two other cognitive processes, planning and attention (Das, Naglieri, & Kirby, 1994).

Thus, the concepts of simultaneous and successive processes have a theoretical base in both cognitive and neuropsychology. The concepts have been operationalized for measurement by tests and have been useful in understanding intellectual performance related to children's cognitive development and reading acquisition.

BIBLIOGRAPHY

DAS, J. P., KIRBY, J. R., & JARMAN, R. F. (1979). *Simultaneous and successive cognitive processes.* New York: Academic Press.

DAS, J. P., & NAGLIERI, J. A. (1993). *Cognitive assessment system: Standardization version.* Chicago: Riverside.

DAS, J. P., NAGLIERI, J. A., & KIRBY, J. R. (1994). *Assessment of cognitive processes.* Needham Heights, MA: Allyn & Bacon.

KAUFMAN, A. S., & KAUFMAN, N. L. (1983). *Kaufman Assessment Battery for Children.* Circle Pines, MN: American Guidance.

KEITH, T. M., & NOVAK, C. G. (1987). Joint factor structure of the WISC–R and K-ABC for referred school children. *Journal of Psychoeducational Assessment, 4,* 370–386.

KIRBY, J. R., & DAS, J. P. (1990). A cognitive approach to intelligence: Attention, coding, and planning. *Canadian Psychology, 31,* 320–333.

LURIA, A. R. (1966a). *Human brain and psychological processes.* New York: Harper & Row.

LURIA, A. R. (1966b). *Higher cortical functions in man.* New York: Basic Books.

MWAMWENDA, T., DASH, U. N., & DAS, J. P. (1984). A relationship between simultaneous–successive synthesis and concrete operational thought. *International Journal of Psychology, 19,* 547–563.

SIMON, H. A. (1992). What is an "explanation" of behavior? *Psychological Science, 3,* 150–161.

SUTHERLAND, S. (1989). *The international dictionary of psychology.* New York: Continuum.

J. P. DAS

SEX CHROMOSOMAL ABNORMALITIES

Humans have forty-six chromosomes, consisting of twenty-three pairs. One pair, the sex chromosomes, consists of two X chromosomes in women and one X and one Y chromosome in men. All the other pairs, the autosomes, consist of two matched chromosomes. It was not possible to identify any one of the forty-six human chromosomes until 1949, when Barr and Bertram discovered the sex chromatin spot, or Barr body, to be present on only one of each pair of X chromosomes. In 1956 researchers were able to identify all forty-six chromosomes (Tjio & Levan, 1956) and to magnify and photograph them. Subsequently, with special staining techniques, it became possible to identify bands on chromosomes, some of which correlated with genetically transmitted syndromes. Gene mapping and sequencing will eventually permit identification of specific gene sequences that may be related to intellectual function and malfunction. In the meantime, the state of the art does not allow intellectual dysfunction to be related to genetics at the molecular level of specific genes on chromosomes, but only at the global level of a whole chromosome or a large part of one missing, added, or malformed.

The most widely known and frequently occurring example of a chromosomally induced lowering of intelligence is DOWN SYNDROME, which is caused by an extra 21st chromosome. This is called trisomy-21. The

incidence of trisomy-21 worldwide is 1 in every 700 live births. (All incidence figures are taken from Mange & Mange, 1980.)

Psychologists interested in the genetics of sex differences in intellectual and cognitive functioning have been interested also in chromosomal errors that involve the pair of sex chromosomes. These conditions include

Turner's syndrome (45,X). (In this genetics notation and the similar ones that follow, the number indicates the total number of chromosomes and the letter(s) shows the sex chromosomes—e.g., a "45,X" patient has a total of forty-five chromosomes, with one X chromosome, and a "47,XXY" patient has a total of forty-seven chromosomes, with two X chromosomes and one Y chromosome.);

Klinefelter's syndrome (47,XXY);

supernumery-Y syndrome (47,XYY);

triple-X syndrome (47,XXX); and

fragile-X syndrome, usually abbreviated as Fra(X).

TURNER'S SYNDROME

Turner's syndrome is characterized by a missing sex chromosome. It afflicts only women (45,X instead of the normal 46,XX) because a male embryo that is 45,Y instead of the normal 46,XY is not viable. According to one estimate, about 98 percent of all 45,X embryos also are not viable.

The missing chromosome may be present in one cell line, but not another. The result is then a mix, or mosaic, of cells: either 45,X/46XY or 45,X/46,XX, or some other mosaic combination, such as 45,X/46,XX/47,XXY.

Screening of newborns for Turner's syndrome has yielded widely disparate incidence figures. These range from 1 in every 240 to 1 in every 4,900 live female births.

The neurocognitive impairment that may affect intelligence and learning in Turner's syndrome is evident throughout childhood and beyond. Although it must represent an error of brain differentiation, if there are regional or hemispheric localizations, they have not yet been demonstrated.

For twenty-five years after Turner first described the syndrome, impairment of intellect and learning, if present, was mislabeled as mental retardation. The correct label, a highly specific cognitive deficit, was discovered in the course of psychohormonal testing (Shaffer, 1962) and has since been confirmed in many studies. It is widely agreed that although the deficit does not affect verbal intelligence, it may severely affect nonverbal intelligence. On tests of intelligence, such as the Wechsler scales, the disparity between Verbal and nonverbal (Performance) IQs may be as great as 30 points. The verbal IQ may be as high as 130.

By pooling and comparing the data drawn from various studies based either on standardized psychological tests or on special tests, it may be construed that the basic deficiency pertains to the mental processing and sequencing of rotational transformations of shapes in the spatial dimensions of left–right, up–down, and back–front. The latter is also the push–pull rotation that rotates the self-image, as in a mirror. In the activities of everyday life, the rotational transformation deficit translates into a handicap that interferes with map reading, following travel directions, drawing a floor plan of a familiar room, deciphering sounds stereophonically, and recognizing changes in facial expression.

In psychological testing, rotational transformation wreaks havoc on what the individual is able to produce on a test requiring the drawing of a person. This test necessitates rotational transformation of the self-image onto a flat page on which the left and right of the figure being drawn and thus depicted before one's very eyes is a mirror rotation of one's own left and right.

The mirror rotational effect in Turner's syndrome also interferes with the ability to copy either a human figure or a geometric shape (Alexander, Ehrhardt, & Money, 1966). The rotation of angles and points has the effect of turning the shape defined inside out (e.g., the points of a triangle become pouches) and creates more distortion than does the rotation of curves.

The link between rotational disability and shapes apparently extends from geometry to calculation in general. Mathematics is a great academic stumbling block for girls with Turner's syndrome. It frequently necessitates intervention from the physician, to obtain from the school a special dispensation so that a verbally superior student with Turner's syndrome will not be penalized for a genetically based specific nonverbal disability.

Vocationally as well as academically, rotational transformation disability is a handicap in all assignments that involve arrangements and rotations of designs and configurations. With accumulated experience, the degree of handicap in a girl with Turner's syndrome may be lessened by the device of transliterating from shapes and directions into silently spoken language.

Rotational transformation disability is not a handicap in learning to read. It may even be an advantage, insofar as the shapes of letters and words retain their meanings by remaining stable and not being rotated. Those with rotational disability do not transform *b* into *d*, or *p* into *q*. The psychological law of object constancy dictates that the meaning of a shape or object perceived remains constant, even if it is turned around or upside down, added to or subtracted from, or broken (Alexander & Money, 1967; Money, 1967). The ordinary child has to resist the law of object constancy in learning to read. Girls with Turner's syndrome are spared this resistance.

KLINEFELTER'S SYNDROME

In Klinefelter's syndrome, there is always at least one Y chromosome and one extra X chromosome (47,XXY); thus it afflicts only males. Very rarely, there may be two Ys and three or four Xs.

The reported prevalence of 47,XXY males varies with the type of population screened:

general population—1 in 900;
tall males—1 in 260;
tall males in penal or psychiatric institutions—1 in 100;
males in infertility clinics—1 in 20.

The majority of noninstitutionalized 47,XXY males are of average and sometimes superior IQ. Even though average, however, the IQ might have been several points higher without the supernumerary X chromosome—and this does appear to be the case when 47,XXY males as a group are compared with, say, their 46,XY siblings, or a matched 46,XY control group (Theilgaard et al., 1971).

It became evident, from the early 1970s onward, that the missing IQ points are more often missing from the Verbal IQ than from the Performance (nonverbal)

IQ (in contrast to Turner's syndrome, in which Verbal IQ is usually higher than Performance IQ). Specific linguistic disability is more pronounced in some 47,XXY males than in others. In some 47,XXY boys, the disability is manifested early in infancy as a developmental delay in the use of speech. It may be severe enough to require speech therapy. Later in childhood it may be manifested as a learning disability specific for reading (dyslexia) and spelling. On the basis of a broad spectrum of tests, it was concluded that linguistic disability in 47,XXY boys is characterized by deficits in processing the rate and order of auditory stimuli, and in word finding, narrative sequencing, and arranging meanings syntactically.

The hypothesis that linguistic disability might exist only in one hemisphere of the brain was experimentally investigated. It was found that the ratio of left–right lateralization deviated from the norm, which could be interpreted to indicate an inadequate degree of linguistic lateralization in the left versus the right hemisphere of the brain.

The foregoing data are compatible with those from an earlier sentence-verification experiment (Netley & Rovet, 1982) in which 47,XXY boys (and also 47, XXX girls) matched sentences and pictures for agreement on meaning (e.g., *The boy is kicking the girl; The girl is kicking the boy; The boy is not kicking the girl; The girl is not kicking the boy*). The children with the extra X chromosome did not do as well as the chromosomally normal controls.

The data suggest that the basic deficiency in Klinefelter's syndrome pertains to the mental processing of sequence and synchrony in time. Language is a temporal sequence: It takes time to speak a sentence, or to read it, just as it takes time to tell or read a story. By contrast, it does not take time to perceive a landscape, a picture, or a vehicle—only to inspect it, or to watch its rotational transformation in space.

Whereas 47,XXY males in general do not have difficulty with rotational transformation, they do have difficulty with temporal sequencing. It is possible that one extension may be to the sequencing and synchrony of logical meaning. For example, some 47,XXY boys and adolescents confabulate tall stories and tell them as if they were historically and logically correct. Such fantastic logic is known as *pseudologia fantastica*.

The relationship of anomalies of sequencing and synchrony to anomalies of hemispheric lateralization in the brain is conjectural only, and will undoubtedly remain so until technological advances allow data to be obtained directly from the brain itself. In the meantime, ascertainment of such anomalies in those 47,XXY boys and men who have them is by means of behavioral and psychological tests.

TRIPLE-X SYNDROME

The prevalence of three X chromosomes (47,XXX) or more in newborn girls was 1 in every 950 in one study, and 1 in every 470 in another. More than one extra X chromosome, with or without mosaicism (e.g., 46,XX/48,XXXX), is very rare. In institutions for the severely mentally retarded and psychotic, the reported prevalence of the syndrome was as high as 1 in 215 and 1 in 425, respectively. Absence of both mental and bodily symptoms allow some women to live without being identified as 47,XXX. Analyses of specific cognitive strengths and weaknesses, if any, have not yet been undertaken.

SUPERNUMERARY-Y SYNDROME

Reports of the prevalence of the supernumerary-Y (47,XYY) syndrome are as follows:

general population—1 in 1,000;
tall males—1 in 325;
tall males in penal or psychiatric institutions—1 in 29.

The IQs of supernumerary-Y boys and men range from high to low. Item-by-item analysis of pass-and-fail responses on an intelligence test indicates a disproportionate ratio between failures on easy items and passes on difficult ones. The failures result from excessive distractibility, which hinders the growth of intelligence measured as IQ. Catch-up growth and concomitant elevation of IQ may, however, proceed with remarkable speed under changed conditions, as for example, living in a prison cell and studying. Distractibility and impulsivity (including impulsive suicide) are frequent concomitants of the syndrome. Impulsivity manifested as antisocial or lawbreaking behavior accounts for the prevalence of institutionalization.

FRAGILE-X SYNDROME

The prevalence and incidence of Fra(X) syndrome in the general population are not known. Developmental deficits and anomalies of cognitive and intellectual function are variable in degree and may pass unnoticed. There are no regularly occurring diagnostic signs from which to suspect the chromosomal defect. Thus, the diagnosis is based on the cytogenetic finding of a fragile locus on the long arm of the X chromosome. The fragility of the chromosome at this locus has been attributed to extra genetic material containing genes that code for brain proteins. Fra(X) syndrome may be transmitted from one generation to the next. Since females have two X chromosomes, the negative sequelae of having one Fra(X) may be canceled by having a second, nonfragile X. About two-thirds of females known to have one Fra(X) do not have a below-average IQ. By contrast, in boys, the single Y chromosome does not protect against the negative sequelae of the only X chromosome if it is Fra(X), and the IQ is severely impaired both globally and with respect to specific disabilities of cognitive functioning as well (Freund, Abrams, & Reiss, 1991).

(*See also:* CHROMOSOMAL ABNORMALITIES.)

BIBLIOGRAPHY

ALEXANDER, D., EHRHARDT, A. A., & MONEY, J. (1966). Defective figure drawing, geometric and human, in Turner's syndrome. *Journal of Nervous and Mental Disease, 142,* 161–167.

ALEXANDER, D., & MONEY, J. (1967). Reading disability and the problem of direction sense. *The Reading Teacher, 20,* 404–409.

FREUND, L. S., ABRAMS, M. T., & REISS, A. L. (1991). Brain and behavior correlates of the fragile X syndrome. *Current Opinion in Psychiatry, 4,* 667–673.

MANGE, A. P., & MANGE, E. J. (1980). *Genetics: Human aspects.* Philadelphia: Saunders College.

MONEY, J. (1967). Learning disability and the principles of reading. *The Slow Learning Child: The Australian Journal on the Education of Backward Children, 14,* 69–87.

NETLEY, C., & ROVET, J. (1982). Verbal deficits in children with 47,XXY and 47,XXX karyotypes: A descriptive and experimental study. *Brain and Language, 17,* 58–72.

SHAFFER, J. W. (1962). A specific cognitive defect observed in gonadal aplasia (Turner's syndrome). *Journal of Clinical Psychology, 18,* 403–406.

THEILGAARD, A., NIELSEN, J., SORENSEN, A., FROLAND, A., & JOHNSEN, S. G. (1971). A psychological-psychiatric study of patients with Klinefelter's syndrome, 47,XXY. Copenhagen: Ejnar Munksgaard.

TJIO, J. H., & LEVAN, A. (1956). The chromosome number of man. *Hereditas, 42,* 1–6.

JOHN MONEY

SIBLINGS, NUMBER AND SPACING OF

See BIRTH ORDER, SPACING, AND FAMILY SIZE.

SIMILARITIES   *See* WAIS–R SUBTESTS.

SIMON, HERBERT A. (1916–   )   Herbert Alexander Simon was born in Milwaukee, Wisconsin, on June 15, 1916. He obtained his undergraduate education at the University of Chicago (1933–1936), where he earned a bachelor's degree with a major in political science at the age of 20. Among the Chicago faculty who influenced his intellectual development were the mathematical biophysicist Nicholas Rashevsky, who taught him about model construction; the economist Henry Schultz, who demonstrated the use of mathematics in economics; the psychologist L. L. THURSTONE, who taught him about factor analysis; and the philosopher Rudolf Carnap, who instructed him in logic and the philosophy of science.

After graduation, Simon took a staff position with the International City Managers' Association developing measures of governmental effectiveness. The Association's director was Clarence Ridley, a political scientist working in the area of public policy whose specialty was the evaluation of municipal governmental services. Ridley, who was to become Simon's dissertation adviser, was coauthor of his first publication, "Measuring Municipal Activities," which appeared in *Public Management* (1937). Simon then went to the University of California at Berkeley to become the director of the administrative measurement studies program (1938–1942). One outcome of the studies of administrative effectiveness and decision making was the completion of his doctoral dissertation, later published as *Administrative Behavior* (1947). The book revolutionized the study of administrative and organizational behavior and started Simon on his lifelong quest to understand capacity-constrained thinking ("bounded rationality") and decision making.

For that early work and its subsequent extensions, Simon received the Nobel Memorial Award in Economics in 1978. His work formed a powerful alternative to neoclassical economics, which assumes perfect rationality in human decision makers. His more behavioral approach to human decision making recognized the limitations of human information-processing mechanisms, and the effects of these limitations on behavior, economic and otherwise. His pursuit of the implications of this basic view of capacity-constrained thinking and decision making motivated his subsequent explorations of many basic processes and mechanisms of thought. His success in exploring these cognitive mechanisms was accomplished by his developing a methodology for obtaining information about people's thinking during problem solving (the collection of verbal protocols), and a way of implementing and testing theories based on the behavioral data obtained from the protocol studies (computer modeling of thinking processes).

Simon moved to Carnegie Mellon University (then Carnegie Institute of Technology) as associate dean of the Graduate School of Industrial Administration in 1949 to help start a new business school based on the scientific study of administration, decision making, and economics, and the use of mathematical and (eventually) computational tools in management. The approaches developed there played a major role in reshaping graduate training in management. Very early on he was exposed to the first electronic computers, and as his interest in their use in decision making developed, he and his close colleagues Allen Newell and J. C. Shaw came to realize that computers were much more than numerical machines, and could be viewed as machines that can process many kinds of symbols, that is, that the patterns of electromagnetic signals, or binary bits, could stand for anything. This insight was crucial to the development of the Logic Theorist, the

first artificial intelligence program, and to the importation of computers into psychology as vehicles for constructing psychological theory in the form of computer simulations that can provide precise accounts of the cognitive processes ("information processing mechanisms") involved in many types of thinking. This development, along with the development of information theory, cybernetics, the recognition of brain–computer relations, and analytic work on visual information processing and on modern linguistics, ushered in the cognitive revolution in psychology.

Simon's work on the processing limitations inherent in human cognition, limitations that affect human performance in a wide variety of situations ranging from economic decision making to memory for chess positions, has been one of the cornerstones of modern psychological work on the function of mind. His work has given rise to a rich understanding of the basis of expertise and how it is acquired.

Simon extended his view of human bounded-rationality, so central to his economic theory, to a lifelong work of uncovering the thought processes involved in problem solving, learning, the acquisition of expertise, and scientific discovery. In all of these areas, he has made major defining contributions, and has done it not as a set of disparate phenomena but as the outcome of his discovery of some basic properties of human information-processing mechanisms.

The breadth and impact of Simon's work on basic cognitive mechanisms is indicated by the awards he has received to date. In addition to the Alfred Nobel Memorial Prize in Economics (1978), they include: National Medal of Science (1986); Distinguished Scientific Contribution Award, American Psychological Association (1969); Frederick Mosher Award, American Society of Public Administration (1974); A. M. Turing Award, Association for Computing Machinery (1975); Proctor Prize, Sigma Xi (1980); James Madison Award, American Political Science Association (1984); Gold Medal Award for Life Achievement in Psychological Science, American Psychological Foundation (1988); John Von Neumann Theory Prize, Operations Research Society of America (1988); and the Distinguished Fellow Award from the American Economic Association (1976). He has played a major role in national scholarly and scientific organizations. He has been a member or fellow of numerous scholarly societies, a member and council member of the National Academy of Sciences, a member of the U.S. President's Science Advisory Committee, a chair of the National Research Council Committee on Behavioral Sciences in the National Science Foundation, and a chair of the Social Science Research Council. He is author of 33 books and over 800 scholarly articles, and the recipient of honorary doctorates or professorships from 24 universities, and has had volumes published honoring his work in the fields of artificial intelligence, psychology, and economics.

Herbert Simon represents something of a paradox. His monumental achievements across such an astonishing range of disciplines suggest an intellect that can only be described as unbounded. Yet his Nobel prize and the core ideas that define his work stem from his insistence on the boundedness of rationality.

BIBLIOGRAPHY

ERICSSON, K. A., & SIMON, H. A. (1993). *Protocol analysis* (rev. ed.). Cambridge, MA: MIT Press.

NEWELL, A., & SIMON, H. A. (1972). *Human problem solving.* Englewood Cliffs, NJ: Prentice-Hall.

SIMON, H. A. (1976). *Administrative behavior* (3rd ed.). New York: Free Press.

SIMON, H. A. (1979). *Models of thought.* New Haven, CT: Yale University Press.

SIMON, H. A. (1982). *Models of bounded rationality* (Vols. 1 and 2). Cambridge, MA: MIT Press.

SIMON, H. A. (1982). *The sciences of the artificial* (rev. ed.) Cambridge, MA: MIT Press.

SIMON, H. A. (1989). *Models of thought* (Vol. II). New Haven, CT: Yale University Press.

SIMON, H. A. (1991). *Models of my life.* New York: Basic Books.

SIMON, H. A., LANGLEY, P., BRADSHAW, G., & ZYTKOW, J. M. (1987). *Scientific discovery: Computational explorations of the creative processes.* Cambridge, MA: MIT Press.

KENNETH KOTOVSKY

SITUATED COGNITION
Situated cognition, or *situated action,* is the belief that an adequate description of cognitive or intellectual activity must include details of how such activity is situated in its physical, social, cultural, and historical environment. This view stresses the dominant role of these kinds of contextual factors and, as such, contrasts with the more traditional absolutist views of cognition that stress the role of universal principles of internal mental functioning. Situated cognition as an intellectual tradition has its origins in anthropological and sociological studies of cognitive functioning in real-world situations (e.g., Lave, 1988; Suchman, 1987; Winograd & Flores, 1986). It has led to sharp critiques of modern theories of cognitive psychology and artificial intelligence (Bobrow, 1991; Brooks, 1991).

The collection of theories that might be classified as instances of situated cognition is quite diverse. All have emerged partly in reaction to the mainstream accounts of intellectual activity that have dominated modern cognitive psychology since the mid-twentieth century. These cognitive theories have all attempted to explicate the internal mental representations and processes that underlie cognitive activity. The major research issues for mainstream theorists have centered on the characteristics of these internal structures. Dominant questions have included the nature of internal representations (e.g., verbal versus imaginal, procedural versus declarative), the organization of internal processing stages (e.g., serial versus parallel, automatic versus controlled, implicit versus explicit), and the general architecture of the internal cognitive system (e.g., Anderson, 1993; Newell, 1990). The goal has been to characterize the universal, context-independent characteristics of the mind.

The advocates of situated cognition argue that this focus has resulted in the study of what D. A. Norman (1993a) called "disembodied intelligence." For them, human behavior is only mildly influenced by the universal characteristics of the mind and largely shaped by the specifics of a person's situation, including the physical environment, the person's interactions with other persons who are present, and the larger cultural and historical framework. Situationist theorists stress that the relationship of a person and the situation is bidirectional, with each influencing the other. This interdependence means that one cannot study the person isolated from the situation or, for that matter, the situation isolated from the persons who act in it. This represents a more holistic approach to the analysis of cognitive activity than the traditional view.

Situated cognition contrasts with modern cognitive theories in at least three interrelated ways. First, as pointed out, they differ in focus or goals. Cognitive theories have had as their goal the explication of the processes and representations of the mind, whereas situated cognition explores the nature of human activity in its material, social, and historical settings. The two approaches present a contrast between an inward focus on the mind and an outward focus on activity in relation to its setting.

Second, they differ in their intellectual heritage. Modern cognitive theory arose partly in reaction to the behaviorist psychology of the early twentieth century and rejected the behaviorists' exclusive concern with functional relations among observable stimuli and responses. (It is perhaps not surprising that some cognitive theorists have characterized situated cognition as a return to behaviorism.) Cognitive psychology has been heavily influenced by the metaphors of modern information processing, and research in computer simulations of thought and artificial intelligence has had a great impact. Cognitive psychology has also had strong ties with the universalist goals of Chomskyan linguistics and most modern philosophy of mind. In contrast, situated cognition has its origins principally in anthropology and sociology, drawing on such traditions as ethnography, ethnomethodology, activity theory, conversational analysis, and critical theory. The ecological psychologists who have followed in Gibson's footsteps, who have represented an isolated line of work within modern psychology, have influenced many situationist theorists. Finally, some emerging work in philosophy and linguistics on situation semantics (e.g., Barwise & Perry, 1983) has influenced some varieties of situated cognition.

Third, they differ in their principal methods. Modern cognitive psychology has been based mostly on data collected in the experimental laboratory, using simplified tasks in order to focus on single variables and statistical techniques to capture trends across large numbers of observations. It is assumed that one can isolate various factors for study through experimental control. Some of the work is highly mathematical or has involved computer simulations. Even modern

studies of intelligence represent a blend of these traditional methods with the older psychometric traditions (e.g., Sternberg, 1985). In contrast, the study of situated cognition is based mostly on field research and looks at cognitive activity in a variety of natural world settings, including cross-cultural studies. It has relied primarily on rich case studies, using descriptive observational methods and qualitative analyses. Researchers in this tradition argue against the factoring of human cognitive activity into isolated components and for a more holistic, interactionist approach.

Several other developments are not strictly situated cognition, but are so closely related that they deserve brief mention. The first is coming to be called "distributed cognition," which asserts that it is often useful to look at cognitive activity at a level of social aggregation larger than that of the individual. This is not a new idea. J. G. March and H. A. Simon (1958) talked about organizations as information-processing systems, an approach that has continued to be important in organizational studies. Similarly, sociology has a tradition that talks about such broader cognitive phenomena as "collective representations" (Durkheim, 1898), meaning ideas that are disbursed throughout a society in a fashion that may not exist in any individual's head. E. Hutchins (1990) has given eloquent analyses of the cognitive activity of teams carrying out intellectual functions, such as navigating a navy ship. In this view, individual minds are components of a larger cognitive system, and it is the analysis of the cognitive activity of the system that is especially useful.

Another closely related topic is that of "cognitive artifacts." Here the focus is on what Norman (1993b) calls "the things that make us smart." Analyses of cognitive activity, even of individuals, have tended to neglect the role of artifacts and notations humans have developed that play a key role in how they carry out various routine tasks. For instance, almost anyone who does a simple calculation does it via paper and pencil or a calculator. Hutchins (1990) showed how a variety of instruments were used to make calculations in a rapid and error-resistant fashion. Writing systems, number systems, mathematical and logical notations, charts and graphs, instruments, clocks, calculators, computers, and a host of other things are all examples of cognitive technologies that qualitatively change how humans perform tasks. Many artifacts transform tasks from highly symbolic, computationally intensive activities that are difficult to do in one's head into easy perceptual, recognition-based tasks that exploit the richness of human pattern recognition abilities. M. Donald (1991) incorporated the role of such cognitive technologies into an evolutionary theory of cognition. He argued that the development of such technologies is of as much significance for the distinctiveness of human cognition as the earlier developments of the brain.

Situated cognition, in all diverse manifestations, and the several closely related views just mentioned are quite recent developments. Considerable debate still surrounds the relationship between situated cognition and more-traditional approaches. The character of this debate can be seen in one issue of the journal *Cognitive Science*. In the lead article, A. H. Vera and H. A. Simon (1993) criticized the notion of situated cognition, arguing that its principle tenets are not in the end inconsistent with traditional symbolic views of cognition. They acknowledge that though traditional accounts have not given a lot of attention to the contextual aspects of intellectual functioning, no inherent reasons exist for why they could not. Thus, they argue, situated cognition offers nothing new. P. E. Agre (1993) and L. A. Suchman (1993) argue in response that situated cognition is a qualitatively different approach and cannot be subsumed in traditional accounts. J. G. Greeno and J. L. Moore (1993) and W. J. Clancey (1993) offer a compromise view, namely, that the two approaches can be combined in a way that yields a superior approach to cognition than either offers on its own. The eventual status of situated cognition cannot be predicted, but the widespread attention it has received is sure to have some impact on the study of cognitive activity.

BIBLIOGRAPHY

AGRE, P. E. (1993). The symbolic worldview: Reply to Vera and Simon. *Cognitive Science, 17,* 61–69.

ANDERSON, J. R. (1993). *Rules of the mind.* Hillsdale, NJ: Erlbaum.

BARWISE, J., & PERRY, J. (1983). *Situations and attitudes.* Cambridge, MA: MIT Press.

BOBROW, D. G. (1991). Dimensions of interaction: A shift in perspective in artificial intelligence. *AI Magazine, 12,* 64–80.

BROOKS, R. (1991). Intelligence without representations. *Artificial Intelligence, 47,* 139–159.

CLANCEY, W. J. (1993). Situated action: A neurophysiological interpretation response to Vera and Simon. *Cognitive Science, 17,* 87–116.

DONALD, M. (1991). *Origins of the modern mind: Three stages in the evolution of culture and cognition.* Cambridge, MA: Harvard University Press.

DURKHEIM, E. (1898). Représentations individuelles et représentations collectives. *Revue de Métaphysique et de Morale, 6,* 273–302.

GREENO, J. G., & MOORE, J. L. (1993). Situativity and symbols: Response to Vera and Simon. *Cognitive Science, 17,* 49–59.

HUTCHINS, E. (1990). The technology of team navigation. In J. Galegher, R. E. Kraut, & C. Egido (Eds.), *Intellectual teamwork: Social and technological foundations of cooperative work.* Hillsdale, NJ: Erlbaum.

LAVE, J. (1988). *Cognition in practice: Mind, mathematics, and culture in everyday life.* New York: Cambridge University Press.

MARCH, J. G., & SIMON, H. A. (1958). *Organizations.* New York: Wiley.

NEWELL, A. (1990). *Unified theories of cognition.* Cambridge, MA: Harvard University Press.

NORMAN, D. A. (1993a). Cognition in the head and in the world: An introduction to the special issue on situated action. *Cognitive Science, 17,* 1–6.

NORMAN, D. A. (1993b). *Things that make us smart.* Reading, MA: Addison-Wesley.

STERNBERG, R. J. (1985). *Beyond IQ: A triarchic theory of human intelligence.* New York: Cambridge University Press.

SUCHMAN, L. A. (1987). *Plans and situated action: The problem of human-machine communication.* New York: Cambridge University Press.

SUCHMAN, L. A. (1993). Response to Vera and Simon's situated action: A symbolic interpretation. *Cognitive Science, 17,* 71–75.

VERA, A. H., & SIMON, H. A. (1993). Situated action: A symbolic interpretation. *Cognitive Science, 17,* 7–48.

WINOGRAD, T., & FLORES, F. (1986). *Understanding computers and cognition: A new foundation for design.* Norwood, NJ: Ablex.

GARY M. OLSON

SOCIAL INTELLIGENCE The concept of social intelligence has a long but relatively undistinguished history. Much of the work in this area has treated social intelligence as if it were little more than "academic" intelligence applied to social situations. Early assessments of social intelligence, although focused on interpersonal problems and stimuli, were very similar in form to traditional psychometric tests of general intelligence and tended to correlate more highly with these kinds of tests than with assessments of social functioning. Consequently, the literature spanning the first sixty years of research on this topic (from the 1920s through the 1970s) is notable primarily for its inability to demonstrate in a convincing manner either the discriminant validity or practical utility of a purely cognitive conception of social intelligence (see, e.g., Keating, 1978; Thorndike & Stein, 1937; Walker & Foley, 1973).

A NEW CONCEPTUALIZATION OF SOCIAL INTELLIGENCE

The ascendance of contextual and cross-cultural views of intelligence during the 1970s and 1980s (see, e.g., Berry, 1974; Cantor & Kihlstrom, 1987; M. Ford, 1986; Sternberg, 1985) set the stage for a renewal of interest in social intelligence. This emerging perspective suggested a new way of conceptualizing social intelligence—one that focused not on social insight or reasoning ability, but more broadly on *people's effectiveness in accomplishing valued social goals within a particular context or cultural setting.* This definition of social intelligence has proven to be more defensible not only on empirical grounds (Brown & Anthony, 1990; Lowman & Leeman, 1988; Marlowe, 1986; Riggio, Messamer, & Throckmorton, 1991), but also with respect to its utility for clinical and educational intervention efforts (Cantor & Kihlstrom, 1987; Marlowe, 1986). Moreover, it is a better fit with people's everyday conceptions of social intelligence (Sternberg et al., 1981).

From this exciting new perspective, social intelligence is conceptualized not as an attribute of the person but as a quality of person-environment interactions that can be assessed only in relation to a set of social goals and boundary conditions (e.g., norms, values, and laws) that define the nature and meaning of socially effective behavior patterns in a particular set of contexts. This, of course, implies that *social intelligence is not a unitary or fixed trait.* The same behavior pattern may be judged as intelligent or unintelligent depending on whether the person's social context defines that behavior pattern as valued and appropriate on relevant evaluative dimensions. Moreover, to the extent that the person is capable of adaptive social learning (and the context affords the opportunities for such learning), it should be possible for individuals to increase their social intelligence with respect to the social goals and contexts anchoring a particular evaluation. Finally, one would generally expect people to be more socially intelligent with respect to some goals and contexts (e.g., those in which they have a high degree of personal investment and experience) than others. Social intelligence is thus conceptualized in this perspective from an interactionist, developmental orientation. Personal skills and abilities are still central, but only in relation to the social contexts in which they are applied, and only to the extent that they are considered in conjunction with motivational, educational, and socialization processes that may contribute to a person's learning of and commitment to valued patterns of social behavior. This contemporary view is much more complex than a simple trait conception of social intelligence because it encompasses the full range of psychological processes and a diversity of social goals, contexts, and behavior patterns.

SOCIAL GOALS THAT MAY SERVE AS CRITERIA FOR DEFINING AND ASSESSING SOCIAL INTELLIGENCE

At a context-specific level, the range of social patterns and outcomes that might be used to define and evaluate social intelligence for a particular assessment purpose is virtually limitless. Much of this social content can be summarized using a limited number of goal "themes," however. These broad goal categories are outlined in Table 1.

Integrative Social Relationship Goals. A focus on this set of values and concerns is appropriate when one wishes to define social intelligence in terms of how well a person is able to maintain or promote the well-being of other individuals or social groups.

TABLE 1

Social goals that serve as criteria for defining and assessing social intelligence

Goal Categories	Goal Content Within Each Category
Integrative social relationship goals	
Belongingness	Building or maintaining attachments, friendships, intimacy, or a sense of community; avoiding feelings of social isolation or separateness
Social responsibility	Keeping interpersonal commitments, meeting social role obligations, and conforming to social and moral rules
Equity	Promoting fairness, justice, reciprocity, or equality; avoiding unfair or unjust actions
Resource provision	Giving approval, support, assistance, advice, or validation to others; avoiding selfish or uncaring behavior.
Self-assertive social relationship goals	
Individuality	Feeling unique, special, or different; avoiding similarity or conformity with others
Self-determination	Experiencing a sense of freedom to act or make choices; avoiding the feeling of being pressured, constrained, or coerced
Superiority	Comparing favorably to others in terms of winning, status, or success; avoiding unfavorable comparisons with others
Resource acquisition	Obtaining approval, support, assistance, advice, or validation from others; avoiding social disapproval or rejection
Social self-evaluative goals	
Positive self-evaluations	Maintaining a sense of self-confidence, pride, or self-worth in social situations; avoiding feelings of social failure, guilt, or incompetence
Social "task" goals	
Management	Maintaining order, organization, or productivity in everyday social situations; avoiding interpersonal hassles, inefficiency, or disorganization
Safety	Being unharmed, physically secure, and free from risk at the hands of others; avoiding threatening, depriving, or harmful social circumstances

SOURCE: M. Ford, 1992.

Belongingness reflects success in creating, preserving, or enhancing the integrity of valued social units, such as friendships, family ties, and intimate relationships. *Social responsibility* represents a pattern of functioning in which social and ethical transgressions are avoided and rules, commitments, and obligations—both interpersonal and societal—are taken seriously. It is associated with such concepts as character and integrity. *Equity* is an achievement reflecting the maintenance or promotion of fair, unbiased action toward other people, such as those who have been victimized by an inequitable distribution of resources, a lack of attention or concern from powerful societal institutions, or some other form of social injustice. Finally, *resource provision* is associated with caring and helping behavior. Success on this dimension is measured by how much one's actions are effective in facilitating the development or well-being of a cared-for individual or social group.

Self-Assertive Social Relationship Goals. An emphasis on this set of values and concerns is appropriate when one wishes to define social intelligence not in terms of other-enhancing accomplishments but in terms of self-enhancing achievements that occur in the context of interpersonal relationships and events. *Individuality* is the successful maintenance or strengthening of personal belief systems or distinctive behavior patterns in the face of a social context characterized by uniformity or conformity. It is associated with a strong sense of identity and, in some circumstances, courage. *Self-determination* also reflects an effective countering of social constraints, although in this case it is one's freedom to act and choose that is at stake. *Superiority* is the successful attainment of an elevated status compared to one's peers on some relevant evaluative dimension. Such dimensions might include academic or occupational achievement, income or material possessions, territorial coverage, athletic performance, popularity, beauty, moral virtue, and so forth. Finally, *resource acquisition* is the effective pursuit of valued emotional, informational, and material resources from parents, friends, teachers, counselors, government agencies, and the like.

Three other kinds of social goals are sometimes implicated in efforts to define and assess social intelligence. Although not strictly social in content, the maintenance of *positive self-evaluations* with respect to social situations and relationships is widely regarded not only as an important prerequisite for effective action, but also as a desirable outcome in its own right. The effective *management* of people and complex social circumstances is another criterion that is often applied to judgements about social intelligence. Finally, *safety* with respect to social situations involving health risks or physical hazards (e.g., sexual encounters, parenting episodes) is another potentially relevant criterion for defining and assessing social intelligence.

PSYCHOLOGICAL PROCESSES ASSOCIATED WITH SOCIAL INTELLIGENCE

Humans are complexly organized living systems characterized by the unitary functioning of a diversity of psychological, biological, transactional, and environmental processes (D. Ford, 1987). Social intelligence reflects the effective functioning of this entire unit in relation to a relevant set of goals and contexts (M. Ford, 1986, 1992). Consistent with the emphasis on cognition and action in conceptions of general intelligence, however, the concept of social intelligence is associated primarily with the psychological and transactional components of effective behavior patterns rather than the biological or environmental components. Thus, efforts to understand the processes underlying social intelligence have focused primarily on the motivational processes directing and regulating effective social behavior patterns and the skill-related cognitive and transactional processes involved in executing those patterns. A description of the most commonly studied processes within these two categories follows.

Goal Importance. Although the links between social goals and intelligent behavior patterns are complex (M. Ford, 1986, 1992), it seems clear that people who have greater interest in or concern about a relevant social goal (e.g., social responsibility or resource provision) are more likely to be successful in attaining those goals than people who do not. This is presumably because highly prioritized goals are more likely to direct attention and effort in productive ways and to activate the cognitive and emotional processes responsible for controlling and regulating behavior (Locke & Latham, 1984).

Personal Agency Beliefs. People who believe that they have the personal capabilities needed to be successful—*capability beliefs*—as well as the opportunity and support needed from the context to be successful—*context beliefs*—are much more likely to continue to pursue (and ultimately to achieve) relevant social goals than those who lack the fundamental conviction that success is possible (Bandura, 1986; M. Ford, 1992). Robust or tenacious personal agency beliefs (M. Ford, 1992) enable people to make the most of their capabilities and opportunities and to maintain motivation when they encounter obstacles or need to change their existing patterns.

Emotional Responsiveness. The tendency for people to respond to actual or anticipated social successes and failures with strong, situationally appropriate emotions appears to be an important factor in energizing and regulating efforts to be socially intelligent. For example, people who tend to feel guilt when they commit social transgressions, or empathic concern when they encounter distress in others, are much more likely to behave intelligently with respect to integrative goals than are those who do not experience such emotions. Emotional *over*arousal can, of course, lead to decrements in social functioning; nevertheless, emotions are normally of great adaptive value in facilitating effective behavior (D. Ford, 1987; M. Ford, 1992). The emphasis in the literature on the problematic consequences of acute or chronic emotional distress does not do justice to this important principle of human motivation.

Behavioral Repertoire. A well-learned and well-rehearsed repertoire of appropriate social skills and knowledge is a prerequisite for socially intelligent functioning (Bandura, 1986). With such a repertoire, one can handle familiar social situations with efficiency and ease, as well as adapt to new or changing circumstances with "generative flexibility" (D. Ford, 1987; M. Ford, 1992).

Social Encoding/Decoding Skills. Although it does not appear that sophisticated social reasoning and inferencing skills are needed to function effectively in most social situations (M. Ford, 1986; Sternberg & Smith, 1985), social intelligence does appear to be associated with a person's capabilities for accurately interpreting social cues, especially in novel or ambiguous circumstances (Barnes & Sternberg, 1989). Socially unintelligent people are notorious for interpreting such situations in nonnormative ways (see, e.g., Dodge, Murphy, & Buchsbaum, 1984).

Social Planning and Problem-Solving Capabilities. Many social situations involve a significant degree of novelty or unpredictability. Because previously learned patterns are likely to be inadequate in such situations, social intelligence can be sustained only if one is able to create flexible plans and strategies

and accurately anticipate their consequences. That is why practical problem-solving skills, such as means–ends thinking (constructing step-by-step solutions to complex interpersonal problems) and consequential thinking (anticipating the likely outcomes of a course of action), are among the best predictors of effective social behavior in such circumstances (M. Ford, 1982).

CONCLUSION

The theoretical foundation for research and intervention efforts focusing on the nature and development of social intelligence is strong, growing, and closely linked with a broader stream of work in the field of human intelligence. The empirical base for such efforts is still relatively weak, partly because some of the notions are fairly new and partly because of the complexity of the phenomena involved in defining, assessing, and understanding socially intelligent behavior patterns. The topic is therefore particularly ripe for continued exploration and study.

BIBLIOGRAPHY

Bandura, A. (1986). *Social foundations of thought and action: A social cognitive theory.* Englewood Cliffs, NJ: Prentice-Hall.

Barnes, M. L., & Sternberg, R. J. (1989). Social intelligence and decoding of nonverbal cues. *Intelligence, 13,* 263–287.

Berry, J. W. (1974). Radical cultural relativism and the concept of intelligence. In J. W. Berry & P. R. Dasen (Eds.), *Culture and cognition: Readings in cross-cultural psychology* (pp. 225–229). London: Methuen.

Brown, L. T., & Anthony, R. G. (1990). Continuing the search for social intelligence. *Personality and Individual Differences, 11,* 463–470.

Cantor, N., & Kihlstrom, J. F. (1987). *Personality and social intelligence.* Englewood Cliffs, NJ: Prentice-Hall.

Dodge, K. A., Murphy, R. M., & Buchsbaum, K. (1984). The assessment of intention-cue detection skills in children: Implications for developmental psychopathology. *Child Development, 55,* 163–173.

Ford, D. H. (1987). *Humans as self-constructing living systems: A developmental perspective on behavior and personality.* Hillsdale, NJ: Erlbaum.

Ford, M. E. (1982). Social cognition and social competence in adolescence. *Developmental Psychology, 18,* 323–340.

FORD, M. E. (1986). A living systems conceptualization of social intelligence: Processes, outcomes, and developmental change. In R. J. Sternberg (Ed.), *Advances in the psychology of human intelligence* (Vol. 3, pp. 119–171). Hillsdale, NJ: Erlbaum.

FORD, M. E. (1992). *Human motivation: Goals, emotions, and personal agency beliefs.* Newbury Park, CA: Sage.

KEATING, D. P. (1978). A search for social intelligence. *Journal of Educational Psychology, 70,* 218–223.

LOCKE, E. A., & LATHAM, G. P. (1984). *Goal setting: A motivational technique that works.* Englewood Cliffs, NJ: Prentice-Hall.

LOWMAN, R. L., & LEEMAN, G. E. (1988). The dimensionality of social intelligence: Social abilities, interests, and needs. *Journal of Psychology, 122,* 279–290.

MARLOWE, H. A. (1986). Social intelligence: Evidence for multidimensionality and construct independence. *Journal of Educational Psychology, 78,* 52–58.

MARLOWE, H. A., & BEDELL, J. R. (1982). Social intelligence: Evidence for independence of the construct. *Psychological Reports, 51,* 461–462.

RIGGIO, R. E., MESSAMER, J., & THROCKMORTON, B. (1991). Social and academic intelligence: Conceptually distinct but overlapping constructs. *Personality and Individual Differences, 12,* 695–702.

STERNBERG, R. J. (1985). *Beyond IQ: A triarchic theory of human intelligence.* New York: Cambridge University Press.

STERNBERG, R. J., CONWAY, B. E., KETRON, J. L., & BERNSTEIN, M. (1981). People's conceptions of intelligence. *Journal of Personality and Social Psychology, 41,* 37–55.

STERNBERG, R. J., & SMITH, C. (1985). Social intelligence and decoding skills in nonverbal communication. *Social Cognition, 3,* 168–192.

THORNDIKE, R. L., & STEIN, S. (1937). An evaluation of the attempts to measure social intelligence. *Psychological Bulletin, 34,* 275–285.

WALKER, R. E., & FOLEY, J. M. (1973). Social intelligence: Its history and measurement. *Psychological Reports, 33,* 839–864.

MARTIN E. FORD

SOCIALIZATION OF INTELLIGENCE

The degree of influence that social factors have on intellectual development has been hotly debated by behavioral scientists for many years. In the last decade, several major theorists of intelligence (e.g., Ceci, 1990; Rogoff, 1990; Sternberg, 1985) have proposed theories that address the role of contextual factors on intellectual development. This article focuses on factors within the child's immediate context and reviews evidence supporting the claim that the child's home, school, and community contexts help direct the child's intellectual development. Factors in the child's immediate context influence intellectual development by providing and constraining the child's opportunities both to practice and develop specific intellectual skills and to gain familiarity with and develop expertise in specific knowledge domains.

INTELLECTUAL DEVELOPMENT WITHIN THE HOME

Research on the relation between home environment and children's intelligence have included (1) studies in which global assessments of the quality of the home environment have been conducted and subsequently related to children's school achievement or intelligence quotient (IQ) scores, and (2) studies that have examined specific aspects of parenting behaviors and looked at children's performance on cognitive tasks thought to be related to those particular parenting behaviors. Both types of studies have obtained evidence indicating that what happens in the home environment does influence children's intellectual development.

Among possible influences within the home environment, researchers have primarily focused on parents' potential contribution to their children's intellectual development. Parents may influence children's intellectual development through direct interaction with the child (e.g., the parent's verbal responsiveness to the child) as well as through indirect behaviors (e.g., parent's organization of the physical environment and of the family's daily schedule). A typical example of research on the quality of the home environment is found in the longitudinal research conducted by Bradley and Caldwell (1984), in which the primary measures of the home environment have been age-specific (i.e., infant, preschool, childhood) versions of the Home Observation for Measurement of the Environment (HOME Inventory) (Caldwell & Bradley, 1984). The HOME Inventory attempts to capture both direct and indirect parenting behavior in subscales that include: (1) maternal responsivity, (2) maternal acceptance of child, (3) organization of the environment, (4) provision of appropriate play materials, (5) maternal involvement with child, (6) variety of stimulation in the home, (7) language stimulation, and (8) encouragement of social maturity. Using the infant and preschool HOME Inventories to assess children's home environment at 12, 24, and 36 months, Bradley and Caldwell (1984) found that several HOME subscales at 12 months were significantly related to first-grade achievement-test scores. For example, the type of play materials that the mother gives a 12-month-old was significantly related to the child's first-grade reading, language, and math achievement scores (r's ranging from .44 to .58). Even when children's early intellectual development had been controlled for using the Bayley Mental Development score at 12 months and the Stanford-Binet score at 3 years, the subscale assessing provision of appropriate toys was still significantly related to first-grade reading scores (r = .36).

Is the home environment during infancy related to school achievement in later childhood? In a subsequent study, Bradley, Caldwell, and Rock (1988) examined the relations between early home environment and school achievement when the children were 10 years old. They reported finding little relation between home environment at 6 months and school achievement; however, home environment at 6 months was significantly related to classroom behavior (r's ranging from .29 to .38). The HOME scores taken when the children were 24 months old showed several significant correlations to school achievement test scores and to classroom behavior at age 10. When HOME scores at age 10 were controlled for, several of the HOME scores taken at 24 months were still significant, thus, providing some support for the importance of early home environment on children's cognitive development.

Theoretically, parents may contribute to their children's development both through the environment they provide and through a genetic component. Consequently, it is difficult to tell if the relations between HOME scores and children's intelligence is a function of socialization processes or genetic factors or both. Studies in which the variation in children's intelligence scores attributable to maternal intelligence has been statistically accounted for have yielded mixed results concerning the relation between home environment and children's intelligence. To explain the mixed results, Luster and Dubow (1992) hypothesized that when multiple aspects of the home environment are evaluated (as is done in the HOME Inventories) and when children are assessed at younger rather than older ages, then home environment accounts for significant amounts of the variance in children's intelligence scores, even when maternal intelligence is also considered. In their analyses of the mother-child merged data set from the National Longitudinal Survey of Youth, they found a statistically significant relation between home environment, as measured by shortened versions of the HOME Inventory, and verbal intelligence scores of children from 3 to 8 years old. The influence of the home environment on children's intelligence was stronger for younger children in the sample (3–5 years old) than for older children (6–8 years old).

Another source of evidence supporting the hypothesis that home environment affects intellectual development is garnered from adoption studies. For example, Scarr and Weinberg (1976) found that both the quality of preadoptive placements and social characteristics of the adoptive placement contributed to IQ scores of children socially defined as black who had been adopted by white families.

Several researchers have examined the relation between specific dimensions of parenting behavior and children's intelligence. For example, Baumrind (1973) found that preschool children's cognitive and social development were related to parenting style (a global analysis of parenting behavior including discipline, responsiveness to child, structure, lack of anger at child, and warmth with child). Dornbusch and his colleagues (1987) found that adolescents' perceptions of their parents' parenting style were associated with their school achievement. Similarly, over a series of studies, Schaefer and Edgerton (1985) consistently found that traditional authoritarian beliefs (e.g., children are passive learners; all children should be treated in the same way) were negatively correlated with children's ability test scores and with teacher ratings of children's creativity and curiosity. In contrast, progressive democratic beliefs (e.g., children are active learners; the primary goal of education is to teach children how to learn) were positively related to children's cognitive performance. Microanalytic studies of parenting behavior have indicated that authoritative parents (those who are more democratic, more responsive to child cues, but not permissive) seem to use more effective teaching strategies when working one-on-one with their children than do authoritarian, permissive, or uninvolved parents (Pratt, Kerig, Cowan, & Cowan, 1988).

The research that has been discussed thus far has been the results of studies in which only one child within each family was studied. These studies indicate that aspects of the home environment do facilitate intellectual development. In particular, opportunities within the home for children to watch parents' problem-solving strategies, to engage in learning and problem-solving activities with parental guidance, and to be exposed to a variety of activities promote children's ability on intelligence tests and other school-related tasks. To better understand the degree of influence home environments have on children's intelligence, it is also important to consider within-family variance on intelligence tests.

Biological siblings raised in the same home share both genetic and environmental input from their parents. Correlations among siblings' IQ scores range from .35 to .50 with absolute differences in scores of 12–13 IQ points (Scarr & Grajek, 1982). What contributes to the differences in siblings' IQ scores? On average, siblings share about 50 percent of their genes, hence genetic differences account for some of the variation among sibling IQ scores. According to Rowe and Plomin (1981), genetic differences cannot account for all the variation among siblings' IQ scores. They have estimated that 25 percent of the variation in IQ scores may be accounted for by within-family environmental differences, such as differences in parent-child interactions across siblings, differences in interaction among the siblings themselves, and differences in nonfamily influences directly related to individual siblings (e.g., teachers). McCall (1983) has also estimated nonshared within-family environmental variation to contribute to 15 percent to 25 percent of all IQ variance based on his analyses of sibling IQ data from the Berkeley Growth Study and the Fels Longitudinal Study.

Finally, microanalytic studies of parenting behavior have been used to identify specific parenting behaviors that are associated with children's performance on various cognitive tasks. Following Lev VYGOTSKY's (1962) proposal that growth in children's cognitive skills comes by exercising partially mastered skills with adults providing the necessary support or "scaffolding" to enable the children to successfully execute those skills, Rogoff and Gardner (1984) have described behaviors mothers used to help their children attempt new problems and, thereby, develop their intellectual skills. Mothers use a variety of supportive strategies, such as making a new problem relate to a more familiar context, providing task-relevant information, explaining why particular strategies are helpful, directing children's attention to specific details in the problem context, and giving children opportunities to execute steps in the process before attempting entire tasks by themselves. Sigel and his colleagues (Sigel, 1982; McGillicuddy-De Lisi, 1985) have found that the strategies parents use to engage and instruct children during problem-solving and storytelling tasks are related to children's performance on cognitive tasks.

Although any single study is not strong enough by itself to demonstrate that the home environment has an effect on children's intellectual development, taken together, the research just discussed provides a solid basis for concluding that contextual factors within the home do influence children's intelligence.

INTELLECTUAL DEVELOPMENT WITHIN THE SCHOOL ENVIRONMENT

Several studies have documented that if a group of adults are given an IQ test, their IQ scores will be correlated with years of schooling (e.g., monozygotic twins, Bouchard, 1984; racetrack gamblers, Ceci & Liker, 1986). These studies do not, however, provide strong evidence for the hypothesis that schooling influences intellectual development. For a more direct test of whether schooling affects intelligence, researchers need to examine children who attend school versus those who do not. Arranging an experiment of this nature is virtually impossible or it requires comparisons of communities that differ on a multitude of other social, cultural, and economic dimensions. However, some scientists have cleverly utilized some natural experiments to look at the relation between schooling and intellectual development.

Swedish psychologists have taken advantage of the IQ testing of entire classes of grade-school children and the later testing of young men when they are inducted into military service. For example, the entire 1938 third-grade class in the Swedish city of Malmö had been given a school-administered intelligence test, and ten years later, the males in the class were given IQ tests as part of their induction into military service. Husén (1951) was able to compare the IQ scores of men who differed in how much schooling they subsequently obtained while controlling for their third-grade IQ scores. There was a 3-point advantage for men who had completed tenth grade and an 11-point advantage for men who had graduated from secondary school. Similar findings were obtained in Härnqvist's study (1968) of the changes in IQ scores in a group of boys who were tested at ages 13 and 18. As in Husén's study, the amount of schooling the men had obtained after the first testing varied, and those who remained in school longer had higher scores at age 18 when compared to boys who were comparable on IQ, SES, and school grades at age 13.

Summer vacations are a time when many children are not in school. Researchers have found that, particularly for children in lower income groups, there is a small decrease in IQ scores after summer when compared to scores taken before summer vacation (e.g., Jencks et al., 1972).

Both Klineberg (1935) and Lee (1951) obtained evidence that when African-American families migrated to northern cities children's IQ scores improved relative to their southern counterparts. In particular, Lee demonstrated that southern-born children's scores improved as time in Philadelphia schools increased. In both studies, improvement in IQ scores was attributed to differences in quality of schooling.

Finally, at least three studies (a German study by Baltes & Reinhert, 1969; an Israeli study by Cahan & Cohen, 1989; a Canadian study by Morrison, 1987, as cited by Ceci, 1990) have capitalized on school birthdate cutoff criteria for first-grade admission to compare same-age children with different amounts of schooling. At any given chronological age, children born just prior to the cutoff date have had one year additional schooling relative to children born just after the cutoff date. In each study, children with the additional year of schooling outperformed their counterparts whose school entrance had been delayed. For example, Cahan and Cohen (1989) compared the youngest children in grades 5 and 6 with the oldest children in grades 4 and 5, respectively. One year of schooling had its largest effect on verbal abilities, and its least effect on nonverbal abilities. In Morrison's Canadian study, both groups of children were given IQ tests and memory tasks at age six (prior to school admission) and were found to be equivalent on all measures. One year later, the group that had gone to first grade did better than the delayed-entrance group. Moreover, Morrison retested children two years later on the memory tasks that allowed him to compare the scores of both groups of children at the end of their respective first-grade years. Even though the delayed-entrance children were almost a full year older than the early-entrance children at the end of their respective first-grade years, the scores of the early-entrance children were higher than those of the delayed-entrance group.

The foregoing data provide support for the hypothesis that schooling positively affects intelligence as measured by IQ tests. A more thorough critique of the existing research is provided by Ceci (1990).

Finally, numerous studies have compared schooled and nonschooled populations on specific cognitive tasks, such as categorization, conservation, syllogistic reasoning, picture perception, and memory tasks. Data from these studies are not easily interpreted for several reasons. First, for the most part, they have not controlled for other factors that might distinguish the schooled and nonschooled populations. For example, in many of the countries in which these studies have been conducted, children from urban areas who go to school are compared with children from rural areas who do not have access to schools. Much about these children's lives differ in other ways besides whether they go to school. Hence, it is not clear that formal education is the only difference between these groups of children that might result in differences in performance on cognitive tasks. Second, the kinds of problems that researchers have typically used and the testing situation itself are generally more familiar to school populations than to those who have not been in school. Familiarity with the task and with the social constraints of the testing situation may affect children's performance. Third, the results are often conflicting. On some tasks (e.g., memory tasks), school children generally perform better than their nonschooled counterparts, and on other tasks (e.g., perceptual tasks using visual illusions) there is no difference or nonschooled groups may do better than schooled populations. Fourth, inconsistent research findings may also result from the "school experience" varying greatly across schools both in quality and in specific aspects that comprise the overall experience.

Excellent reviews of this research have been done by Nerlove and Snipper (1981) and by Rogoff (1981). In her review, Rogoff (1981) concluded that schooling provides children with the opportunities to learn strategies for solving selected types of problems. For example, children learn specific rules for deciphering depth cues in two-dimensional drawings, strategies for memorizing unrelated pieces of information, organization strategies that use taxonomic rules rather than functional rules, and verbalization of one's problem-solving strategies. Simply put, children learn the rules that guide problem solving for specific types of problems. The question many researchers are currently addressing concerns the transferability of skills learned in one context (e.g., school) to problems arising in other contexts (e.g., work). It is not enough to know that children who go to school are able to solve school-related problems better than children who do not go to school. Attention is now focused on determining the conditions under which children are most likely to develop skills that they will be able to apply to new problems and to use in new situations.

INTELLECTUAL DEVELOPMENT WITHIN THE COMMUNITY ENVIRONMENT

Specific community practices can provide and constrain children's opportunities to practice and develop specific intellectual skills and to work with different stimuli. For example, in an agricultural community in which grains and seeds were very important to community survival, Indian children were able to provide precise descriptions of the grains and seeds and to interpret a given description accurately. However, Lantz (1979) found that the children provided less specific descriptions when asked to do the same task with an array of colors. The strategies for classifying grains versus strategies for classifying colors that the children had developed in the context of their community's use of grains versus its use of color categories were different. Similarly, studies have shown that adults are better able to discriminate and flexibly categorize items that are regularly used in their daily lives versus items with which they are relatively unfamiliar (e.g., Irwin & McLaughlin, 1970; Irwin, Schafer, & Feiden, 1974).

Two Piagetian studies of children's performance on conservation tasks also illustrate the effect of communities providing the opportunities to develop specific strategies. In the first study (Price-Williams, Gordon, & Ramirez, 1969), children from two Mexican villages were asked to do a task requiring conservation of matter. In both villages, adults made pottery using a process in which balls of clay are pressed into molds. When a mistake occurred, the clay was taken out of the mold, rolled back into balls, and then pressed back into the mold. Thus, the process of reforming balls of clay models conservation of matter— the shape of the clay changes, while the amount of the clay remains constant. In one village, children had the opportunity to be active participants in making pottery. These children did better on the conservation of matter task than children from the other village who did not routinely work with clay.

In the second study (Steinberg & Dunn, 1976), children of potters in another Mexican village who also actively participated in making pottery did not do better on conservation of matter tasks than children with no pottery-making experience. In this study the pottery-making process was different. For these pottery-making children, long coils of clay were placed one on top of the other to form a pot. Hence, although they used clay, the process did not require them to notice that a given amount of clay could be formed and reformed into different shapes.

For other research on the cognitive consequences of varying opportunities across communities, research on cultural influences on intelligence may be explored.

CONCLUSIONS

In general, do factors in the child's immediate context affect intellectual development? The research described above suggests that they do. The boundaries of the child's home, school, and community contexts determine to some degree the child's opportunities to practice specific intellectual skills and to develop familiarity with particular content domains. Consequently, the child's intellectual abilities may be shaped directly, as an adult teaches the child specific problem-solving strategies or rules to follow in certain situations, and indirectly, by being exposed to or not being exposed to different skills and knowledge domains.

(*See also:* FAMILY ENVIRONMENTS; NATURE, NURTURE, AND DEVELOPMENT; PARENTING AND INTELLIGENCE.)

BIBLIOGRAPHY

BALTES, P. & REINHERT, G. (1969). Cohort effects in cognitive development in children as revealed by cross-sectional sequences. *Developmental Psychology, 1,* 169–177.

BAUMRIND, D. (1973). The development of instrumental competence through socialization. In A. D. Pick (Ed.), *Minnesota symposium on child psychology* (Vol. 7, pp. 3–46). Minneapolis: University of Minnesota Press.

BOUCHARD, T. J. (1984). Twins reared together: What they tell us about human diversity. In S. W. Fox (Ed.), *Individuality and determinism* (pp. 147–178). New York: Plenum.

BRADLEY, R. H., & CALDWELL, B. M. (1984). The relation of infants' home environments to achievement test performance in first grade: A follow-up study. *Child Development, 52,* 708–710.

BRADLEY, R. H., CALDWELL, B. M., & ROCK, S. L. (1988). Home environment and school performance: A ten-year follow-up and examination of three models of environmental action. *Child Development, 59,* 852–867.

CAHAN, S., & COHEN, N. (1989). Age versus schooling effects on intelligence development. *Child Development, 60,* 1239–1249.

CALDWELL, B. M., & BRADLEY, R. H. (1984). *Home observation for measurement of the environment.* Little Rock, AK: University of Arkansas.

CECI, S. J. (1990). *On intelligence . . . more or less: A bio-ecological treatise on intellectual development.* Englewood Cliffs, NJ: Prentice-Hall.

CECI, S. J., & LIKER, J. (1986). A day at the races: A study of IQ, expertise, and cognitive complexity. *Journal of Experimental Psychology: General, 115,* 255–266.

DORNBUSCH, S. M., RITTER, P. L., LEIDERMAN, P. H., ROBERTS, D. F., & FRALEIGH, M. J. (1987). The relation of parenting style to adolescent school performance. *Child Development, 58* (5), 1244–1257.

HUSÉN, T. (1951). The influence of schooling upon IQ. *Theoria, 17,* 61–88.

IRWIN, H. M., & MCLAUGHLIN, D. H. (1970). Ability and preference in category sorting by Mano school children to adults. *Journal of Social Psychology, 82,* 15–24.

IRWIN, H. M., SCHAFER, G. N., & FEIDEN, C. P. (1974). Emic and unfamiliar category sorting of Mano farmers and U.S. undergraduates. *Journal of Cross-Cultural Psychology, 5,* 407–423.

JENCKS, C., SMITH, M., ACLAND, H., BANE, M. J., COHEN, D., GINTIS, H., HEYNS, B., & MITCHELSON, S. (1972). *Inequality: A reassessment of the effects of family and schooling in America.* New York: Basic Books.

KLINEBERG, O. (1935). *Negro intelligence and selective migration.* New York: Columbia University Press.

LANTZ, D. (1979). A cross-cultural comparison of communication abilities: Some effects of age, schooling and culture. *International Journal of Psychology, 14,* 171–183.

LEE, E. S. (1951). Negro intelligence and selective migration: A Philadelphia test of the Klineberg hypothesis. *American Sociological Review, 16,* 227–232.

LUSTER, T., & DUBOW, E. (1992). Home environment and maternal intelligence as predictors of verbal intelligence: A comparison of preschool and school age children. *Merrill-Palmer Quarterly, 38*(2), 151–175.

MCCALL, R. B. (1983). Environmental effects on intelligence: The forgotten realm of discontinuous nonshared within-family factors. *Child Development, 54,* 408–415.

MCGILLICUDDY-DE LISI, A. V. (1985). The relationship between parental beliefs and children's cognitive level. In I. E. Sigel (Ed.), *Parental belief systems: The psychological consequences for children* (pp. 7–24). Hillsdale, NJ: Erlbaum.

MORRISON, F. (1987, November). *The 5 to 7 shift revisited: A natural experiment.* Paper presented at the Annual Meeting of the Psychonomic Society, Seattle, WA.

NERLOVE, S. G., & SNIPPER, A. S. (1981). Cognitive consequences of cultural opportunity. In R. H. Munroe, R. L. Munroe, & B. B. Whiting (Eds.), *Handbook of cross-cultural human development* (pp. 423–474). New York: Garland STM Press.

PRATT, M., KERIG, P., COWAN, P., & COWAN, C. P. (1988). Mothers and fathers teaching 3-year-olds: Authoritative parenting and scaffolding of young children's learning. *Developmental Psychology, 24,* 832–839.

PRICE-WILLIAMS, D., GORDON, W., & RAMIREZ, M. (1969). Skill and conservation: A study of pottery-making children. *Developmental Psychology, 1,* 769.

ROGOFF, B. (1981). Schooling and the development of cognitive skills. In H. C. Triandis & A. Heron (Eds.), *Handbook of cross-cultural psychology: Developmental psychology* (Vol. 4, pp. 233–294). Boston: Allyn & Bacon.

ROGOFF, B. (1990). *Apprenticeship in thinking: Cognitive development in social context.* New York: Oxford University Press.

ROGOFF, B., & GARDNER, W. (1984). Adult guidance of cognitive development. In B. Rogoff & J. Lave (Eds.), *Everyday cognition: Its development in social context* (pp. 95–116). Cambridge, MA: Harvard University Press.

ROWE, D. C., & PLOMIN, R. (1981). The importance of non-shared (E_1) environmental influences in behavioral development. *Developmental Psychology, 17* (5), 517–531.

SCARR, S., & GRAJEK, S. (1982). Similarities and differences among siblings. In M. E. Lamb & B. Sutton-Smith (Eds.), *Sibling relationships: Their nature and significance across the lifespan* (pp. 357–382). Hillsdale, NJ: Erlbaum.

SCARR, S., & WEINBERG, R. A. (1976). IQ test performance of Black children adopted by White families. *American Psychologist, 31,* 726–739.

SCHAEFER, E. S., & EDGERTON, M. (1985). Parent and child correlates of parental modernity. In I. E. Sigel (Ed.), *Parental belief systems: The psychological consequences for children* (pp. 287–318). Hillsdale, NJ: Erlbaum.

SIGEL, I. E. (1982). The relationship between parental distancing strategies and the child's cognitive behavior. In L. M. Laosa & I. E. Sigel (Eds.), *Families as learning environments for children* (pp. 47–86). New York: Plenum.

STEINBERG, B. M., & DUNN, L. A. (1976). Conservation competence and performance in Chiapas. *Human Development, 19,* 14–25.

STERNBERG, R. J. (1985). *Beyond IQ: A triarchic theory of human intelligence.* New York: Cambridge University Press.

VYGOTSKY, L. S. (1962). *Thought and language.* New York: Wiley.

LYNN OKAGAKI

SOCIAL POLICY, INTELLIGENCE, AND TESTING

Few topics in the social sciences arouse as much passionate public interest and as much controversy as intelligence. This situation is perhaps not surprising because we rely heavily on the concept of intelligence to distinguish ourselves from other species: Other animals may be faster and stronger, but we like to think we are smarter. It is no wonder that attempts to measure intelligence and to rate people in terms of having more or less of it cut quickly to existential nerve endings.

As vital as intelligence is to our self-definition, however, the concept itself eludes definition. Herein lies a paradox: Our ability to recognize intelligent behavior and inquire about its more general meaning is surely evidence of its existence, and our failure to construct a comprehensive definition is just as surely evidence of its inherent bounds. Just as the Supreme Court found it easier to recognize pornography than to define it, most of us can more readily recognize intelligent behavior than articulate a definition that is generally applicable.

The intelligence quotient (IQ), a measure of general problem-solving and verbal ability that derived from the pioneering work of Alfred BINET, has for nearly a century filled the definitional breach. Although intended as a tool for estimating some important cognitive functions, the IQ has widely and mistakenly been adopted as a surrogate *definition* of intelligence, to the chagrin of many scientists and laypersons familiar with the limitations of using any single metric to capture the intricacies of human thought and action. Binet himself, who generally viewed intelligence in terms of practical *judgment,* preferred to keep the concept vague; but even he conceded—under pressure to provide an all-inclusive definition—that "intelligence is what my tests measure!" (Schneider, 1992).

To this day, the application of IQ to social policy decisions is fraught with suspicion and conflict largely because modest research findings are often used to support decisions of potentially monumental importance to individuals and society. For decades psychological researchers have been studying the degree to which differences in measured intelligence can explain differences in academic achievement, workplace productivity, and economic well-being. The results have been complex, in part because of challenges to the validity of using IQ as a proxy for intelligence, in part because of challenges to the reliability of the data used in the studies, and in part because of the methodological barriers to isolating innate abilities from their environmental influences. Nonetheless, the IQ construct continues to be used with equal force by those seeking to change and those wishing to legitimize the existing social order. The debate often comes down to whether score differences reflect unequal status of different population groups or whether unequal status is a natural (if unfortunate) result of differences in ability that are reflected in test score differences.

Indeed, the debate becomes most heated when differences in measured intelligence are cast in genetic terms. From the earliest days of the "mental testing" movement, there has been a fascination with the hereditary basis of intelligence, especially among those researchers following in the footsteps of Francis GALTON, James CATTELL, and Charles SPEARMAN. Since then, uncertainty over exactly what intelligence is or how it can affect people's life chances has not prevented researchers from inquiring about who has more of it and where they got it. This line of research typically attempts to disentangle the effects of nature (genes) and nurture (the environment or context in which peoplelive) on measured abilities; estimates of the heritability of IQ range from near zero (Kamin, 1974) to 70 percent or higher (Jensen, 1981). Because these studies inevitably involve differences in average IQ among various racial and ethnic groups, the science of mental measurement has always been a political powder keg.

Closely related to the heritability problem is the question of malleability. Those who define intelligence as a fixed, unitary trait determined largely at birth, are generally not optimistic about the effects of schooling or other human capital investments, at least as these are intended to raise intelligence. Arthur JENSEN, for example, raised a stir when he published the article

"How much can we boost IQ and scholastic achievement?" (1969). His answer was, essentially, not very much, and he seemed to be recommending a policy of providing different forms of education to black and white Americans. On the other hand, those persons who define intelligence as more context dependent, encompassing a wide range of skills and behaviors not necessarily captured by standard intelligence tests and only partially genetically influenced, are usually more optimistic about our ability to learn how to be smarter (Sternberg, 1988; Gardner, 1983). Robert Linn (1986) notes that "whatever the actual role of heredity, Americans place great stock in the role of education and hard work." Linn finds that the large increase in general ability of soldiers between the two world wars and the narrowing of the gap between achievement scores for blacks and whites (Linn & Dunbar, 1990) are grounds for optimism about the return to investments in education.

Measurement of intelligence may well be "the most important single contribution of psychology to the practical guidance of human affairs," (Cronbach, 1975) and "psychology's most telling accomplishment to date" (Herrnstein, 1971). Confusion still reigns, however, over what intelligence is, where it really matters (or should matter), how we get it, and whether it can be improved. With this background established, a discussion is necessary of two areas of social policy—schooling and employment—most directly affected by theories of intelligence and applications of intelligence tests.

INTELLIGENCE IN THE SCHOOLS

Two basic questions about intelligence have been central in education policy: How does schooling affect the development of intelligence? How does intelligence testing affect schooling? Historically, the latter question came first, as American public schools developed increasing reliance on various standardized intelligence and achievement tests to classify, sort, and teach pupils of varying academic abilities. The first question has arisen in the context of broader resource allocation debates, such as over the relative merits of investing public monies in early childhood or other compensatory education programs.

Management and Governance of Schooling.

It is a common fallacy to blame aptitude tests and their achievement test cousins for the ability grouping (or tracking) that has long been a fixture in American public education. Sorting and classifying of students predates the modern intelligence test by over half a century. Horace Mann and other mid-nineteenth-century reformers were determined to make schooling available to the masses and latched onto written testing because it appeared to offer a fair and efficient instrument of educational management (Tyack, 1974). Testing of IQ began on a large scale after World War I and signified an important technological leap: It supposedly measured individual mental development; test administration and scoring had substantially more standardization than earlier written examinations, and the test included norms that ranked individual performance in comparison with the rest of the population (Chapman, 1988). With the advent of electromechanical scoring, the administration of the tests to mass numbers of individuals became economically efficient.

From the onset, some people argued that the norms produced standards with a bias against the lower classes, immigrants, and blacks. Other persons were concerned with the influence of heredity on test performance, and still others found the test too closely aligned with scholastic performance rather than with innate ability. Objections arose as to using the IQ test as a basis for important decisions about the fate of school children because of uncertainties over its validity and reliability.

The contemporary debate over intelligence or aptitude testing in the schools revolves around similar issues. Elementary and secondary schools in the United States today are at least as demographically diverse as in the nineteenth century, and ability grouping is still a common practice. However, both the practice itself and the uses of intelligence or aptitude tests as criteria for the grouping have been challenged. On one side of the debate is the "bureaucratic perspective," which focuses on managerial efficiencies to be obtained from sorting students by individual differences in their academic backgrounds and strengths; on the other side is the "communitarian perspective," which emphasizes the role of school in fostering a common experience for all students and rejects rigid classification and sorting (Lee, Bryk, & Smith, 1993).

There is mixed evidence on the pervasiveness of testing as the main criterion for tracking. One study in 1970 found that 82 percent of school districts surveyed used achievement and/or IQ tests as a basis for sorting students (Findley & Bryan, 1975). According to the National Academy of Sciences (Wigdor & Garner, 1982), though, tracking does not seem to depend in any absolute way on test results, as only a small percentage of the schools that practice tracking rely on test scores *alone*. Where testing does play a more prominent role is in selection for compensatory education (i.e., special programs for educationally or economically disadvantaged students) and for so-called gifted and talented or special enrichment classes. Test scores have also played a central role in the placement of disabled students in special education programs outside the regular course of instruction (Sherman & Robinson, 1982).

Intelligence and achievement testing has been used not only *within* schools for ability grouping or placement but more overtly for admissions *into* schools. Attempts to introduce paper-and-pencil "readiness" tests have raised an outcry from both scientific and lay communities. The state of Georgia, for example, passed a law in 1985 mandating that all 6-year-olds must pass a written achievement test to enter first grade. Concerns arose over the age-appropriateness of the tests: Many children have not yet acquired the developmental skills needed for written work, a fact with obvious implications for the validity of the test score in predicting success in school. For this and other reasons the Georgia Department of Education initiated a project to redesign the assessment system, hoping to incorporate broader and more authentic concepts of readiness, including social, emotional, and physical development. Nevertheless, these improvements did not erase the opposition among many educators to the *principle* of using tests—of any kind—to deny children the right to enter school. Meanwhile, other states have abandoned the use of tests in the early grades (Office of Technology Assessment, 1992).

A more prevalent form of intelligence testing related to schooling is in college admissions. Some 1.5 million applicants to American colleges and universities take the SCHOLASTIC ASSESSMENT TESTS (SAT), and about 800,000 persons take the admissions tests of the AMERICAN COLLEGE TEST. The SAT was originally intended as a test of general abilities thought to be required for success in college-level work and as a tool to enable colleges to acquire standardized information on the abilities of students from diverse educational and economic backgrounds. The word *aptitude* in the original name of the test hinted to some that the SAT measured innate abilities, which was a source of persistent controversy and confusion. Over time the notion of "developed abilities" emerged, suggesting that the test covered some combination of innate intellectual skills and knowledge acquired in school or elsewhere. The test was (and still is) perceived by many to reflect the desire to *widen* access to higher education to broader segments of the population by filtering out irrelevant criteria from admissions policies, minimizing highly subjective decisions, and recognizing the wide variation in the quality of high schools from which students graduate and seek postsecondary education. Linn (1982) has argued that objective admissions tests "provide students with an alternative means of demonstrating academic ability" and "provide a measure that is comparable across schools and across time."

With their narrow reliance on one type of task—answering multiple-choice questions—tests such as the SAT have often engendered bitter controversy. Some persons have argued that these tests are biased in favor of students from relatively high socioeconomic backgrounds and against members of certain population groups (especially women and minorities). Others have questioned the utility of the test, citing evidence of its marginal value in aiding admissions officers. Still others fear that the test wrongly conveys to high school students the signal that they should concentrate on learning and memorizing abstract bits of information, such as vocabulary lists (Crouse & Trusheim, 1988). Finally, some persons have raised questions about test coaching and outright cheating. Similar arguments are heard about all standardized multiple-choice tests, whether designed to assess general aptitude or more specific mastery of curricula or used for student selection, diagnosis of learning problems, or monitoring of school systems.

Although the debate often reaches a strident pitch, there is fairly widespread agreement that neither the SAT nor any other single measure should ever be used in high-stakes selection and placement decisions. Recent revisions to the SAT, adding some non–multiple-choice items that call for performance on more complex written and analytical tasks, reflect changing attitudes toward the utility of traditional aptitude measures. New approaches to test validation are also influencing test design, use, and interpretation. Nevertheless, policymakers concerned with college admissions testing still must tread a narrow and slippery path: Proponents contend that large and statistically significant differences in test scores among various population groups faithfully mirror the unequal distribution of educational resources in society (Stewart, 1989) and that the tests supply the empirical evidence needed to remedy the underlying inequalities. On the other hand, critics claim that standardized tests do not merely reflect the impact of social inequalities but compound them (Neill & Medina, 1989) because the results are used to sort the population into fundamentally unequal educational and economic strata.

Effects of Schooling on Intelligence. Quantity of schooling has a positive and significant impact on an individual's future economic opportunities and income. In the language of human capital theory, there are positive economic returns to investments in education generally and schooling specifically (Becker, 1975). From a psychological or cognitive perspective, though, the relationship between school activities and the intelligences required for successful performance in everyday life is unclear. Many reform efforts in the United States are predicated on the assumption that most schools do not provide sufficient training in the higher-order thinking skills necessary for productive work and citizenship. This assumption is debatable, of course, because evidence on the overall quality of American schooling, using a variety of outcome measures, is mixed (National Commission on Excellence in Education, 1983; Cremin, 1990; Berliner, 1993), and the empirical basis for predictions of future workforce skill requirements is limited (Levy & Murnane, 1992). There are substantial differences of opinion, too, regarding the purposes of school, the extent to which it should emphasize academic ability over other skills, and the degree to which it is reasonable to expect schools to impart the skills necessary for effective functioning in a wide range of occupations. In the highly decentralized American system, as many definitions of the purposes of schooling abound as there are definitions of intelligence.

Amid this chronic ambiguity over the purposes and effects of schooling, IQ has at times become a convenient focal point, reflecting the powerful intuition that schooling ought somehow to be related to intelligence and that intelligence is somehow related to IQ. Stephen Ceci (1990), for example, though himself opposed to the idea of defining intelligence solely in terms of IQ, builds a persuasive case for considering the effects of schooling on IQ. He notes that people often know their IQ score, that surrogates such as the SAT and various employment tests play important gatekeeping functions, that other social outcomes such as criminality and occupational trainability can be correlated to IQ, and that many people define their own intelligence in terms of IQ. Pertinent to this list are additional considerations: Important public policy decisions, such as the continuation of investment in Head Start or other early childhood interventions, often hinge on a demonstration that these programs have positive and lasting effects on IQ—even if the architects of the programs have other objectives in mind (see INTERVENTION, INFANT AND PRESCHOOL). Finally, attention to the origins and variability of IQ is important because various ethnic and racial groups in America have been stigmatized by their low scores, by claims that the scores reflect innate abilities determinative of economic opportunity, and by the myth that inherited traits are immutable (Sarasson & Doris, 1979; Jencks, 1992). Clarifying the effects of schooling on IQ could therefore have important consequences for education specifically and social policy more generally.

Not surprisingly, the evidence is mixed and complex. From a review of over thirty separate studies of the influence of schooling on IQ, Ceci (1990) distills the following:

1. There is a high correlation between number of years of school completed and IQ, controlling for age, socioeconomic status, and other variables.
2. Starting school at later than the normal age is associated with significant decrements in IQ; continued deprivation (in terms of schooling) builds a cumulative deficit in IQ; and early termination of schooling correlates with lower IQ.
3. Correlations between IQ test performance and achievement test scores suggest that IQ tests reflect skills that schools teach.

4. Increased educational opportunity leads to intergenerational improvements in IQ.
5. The very high correlation between IQ and schooling cannot be accounted for on the basis of genetic selection, motivational differences, or parental socioeconomic status.

In a word, Ceci finds a causal link between quantity of schooling and IQ. His review of the data leads to a more ambiguous result concerning the effects of *qualitative* differences among schools on variance in IQ scores.

Other social scientists interpret the evidence quite differently. Arthur JENSEN (1969), for example, interprets intelligence as a distinct unitary entity, presumably determined by a specific set of neurological functions, largely genetically determined. For him, arguments about the plastic (rather than fixed) nature of intelligence represent an "ostrich-like denial of biological factors in individual differences and [a] slighting of the role of genetics in the study of intelligence." Most important, Jensen has concluded that IQ heritability is in the range from .7 to .9. This finding led him to speculate that compensatory education programs had failed largely because they could not offset the enormously important genetic causes of low intelligence among poor people.

The genetic or hereditary bases of intelligence have been emphasized in the work of other prominent psychologists as well, such as Richard Herrnstein (1971), and M. Snyderman and S. Rothman (1988). The search for a biological explanation of observed differences in human intelligence continues full-steam. Robert Plomin and coworkers, for example, are trying to link IQ to specific sets of genes. C. Jencks (1992) provides a lucid, brief, and compelling analysis of the basic hereditarian argument as well as the public policy myths that it has spawned.

INTELLIGENCE AND THE WORKPLACE

A survey by Walter Haney and his colleagues (1993) of the testing marketplace in America reveals the importance of various kinds of intelligence or aptitude tests in decisions regarding selection and placement of personnel in the workplace. Although precise numbers are unavailable, demand for various types of employment tests (intelligence as well as other personality tests) is clearly growing. As with many public policy questions, using aptitude tests for job placement and advancement is viewed by many in terms of a tradeoff between expected efficiency gains and expected equity setbacks. Proponents of intelligence testing point to the validity of test scores in predicting performance, and critics emphasize the discrepant distribution of scores between minority and white candidates and the resultant imbalance in workplace opportunities that would ensue. Balancing these claims has proven to be a complicated, if not intractable, public policy issue.

Although testing for personnel selection has a long history (Guion, 1991), recent developments in test validity research have had particularly important implications for public policy. Through the late 1970s and 1980s, Frank Schmidt and John Hunter analyzed many studies of the relationship between scores on certain tests and performance in various job settings and began to challenge the theory that test validity was situationally specific. They advanced the theory that test validity could be generalized to new situations and that general ability (g) was the underlying trait of importance to virtually all jobs. Impressed with the Hunter and Schmidt "validity generalization" (VG) analysis, the U.S. Department of Labor modified its nationwide job referral system based on the GENERAL APTITUDE TEST BATTERY (GATB). With estimates that the United States could save literally tens of billions of dollars from the improved matching of individuals and jobs, VG–GATB was hailed as a major breakthrough in the application of psychometrics to policy. By the end of 1986, some 38 states had experimented with the new system, and out of 1,800 local Job Service offices nationwide some 400 introduced VG–GATB referral (Schmidt & Hunter, 1977; Hartigan & Wigdor, 1989).

The down side of this program lay in the large differences in average scores between minority and white test takers. Because of both this discrepancy and the differences in typical IQ levels in jobs by job level, Gottfredson (1986) argued that different endowments of IQ limit the pool of eligible candidates for high-level work (executives, physicians, other professionals) to about 25 percent of whites but to only 1 percent of blacks. Awareness of the severe adverse impact that would otherwise ensue from strict top–down referral of GATB test takers led the Labor Department to institute a within-group scoring adjustment system: Applicants were ranked with reference to their own racial or ethnic group, effectively erasing the effects of group differences in test scores. Several years later, the U.S. Department of Justice challenged the within-group scoring system on the grounds of reverse discrimination. Higher scoring individuals claimed that they were being penalized on the grounds of their group membership rather than on their test performance, leading to a confrontation between the Departments of Labor and Justice over the technical and policy implications of test-based referrals. The matter was referred to the National Academy of Sciences for a thorough analysis.

The National Academy study concluded that the GATB had predictive validity, although less than believed, and that within-group scoring was scientifically justified because it could compensate for the different passing rates of majority and minority candidates that were attributable to *statistical or measurement error* rather than underlying differences in *true ability*. The scientific basis of this latter finding could not outweigh the politically charged nature of any program that on the surface seemed to legalize race-based preferential treatment, and in the 1991 Civil Rights Act within-group scoring as a basis for job referrals was outlawed.

It is important to note that the policy debate over GATB and other employment testing programs is not limited to equity issues. For example, the National Academy raised the question of whether reliance on the GATB was in the nation's best long-term *economic* interests. Similarly, Henry Levin (1988) has argued that the advocates of test-based referrals ignore many important determinants of economic productivity and rely too heavily on what he considers to be a weak correlation between tested ability and workplace performance. Levin emphasizes the influential role of workplace organization and management in worker productivity and cites the research of Sylvia Scribner (1987) and others, which shows that workers are often able to perform tasks that would not have been predicted by test scores. Linn (1986) has neatly linked the equity and economic aspects of the problem, noting that estimates of the potential economic returns to increased reliance on ability measures for job sorting are exaggerated—largely because they ignore the high social costs of increasing inequality.

CONCLUSIONS: THE CURRENT POLICY SCENE

This article has concentrated on schooling and employment, two arenas in which the battle over the meanings, origins, effects, and malleability of intelligence have been most bitterly fought. Others who have considered social policy and intelligence have focused on preschool programs (Zigler & Seitz, 1982), crime (Wilson & Herrnstein, 1985), and the more general effects of testing on culture and society (Nelkin & Tancredi, 1989; Hanson, 1993).

Decades of research on how people learn and apply their knowledge at school and at work, coupled with growing disaffection with paper-and-pencil tests that appear to rely heavily on a single method for assessing broad cognitive abilities, have created an opportunity for fundamental change in the measurement of intelligence and its applications to public policy. Howard Gardner (1983) has discussed the implications of MULTIPLE INTELLIGENCES for teaching and learning in the primary and secondary grades. Robert Sternberg (1988) has suggested whole new ways of approaching competence and learning at work and in everyday life. Stephen Ceci (1990) has bridged the biological and environmental determinants of intelligence.

These research efforts benefit greatly from their policy environment. The widespread sense of urgency about improving our education and human resource systems has created a climate of reform perhaps unparalleled since the industrial revolution of the late nineteenth century. A powerful tenet of current policy is that all students can learn, a belief with profound implications for the design and use of cognitive ability measures.

Ironically, though, this atmosphere of change, which stimulates interest in and support for research on new theories of cognition and mental measurement, simultaneously poses a great threat to the research and to its potentially extraordinary applications. Simply put, the press for political and social reform can obscure from view the rudimentary and fragile status of new assessment methods and press them into action both prematurely and in unintended ways.

If an overarching lesson for social policy exists, then, it is that the science and technology of intelligence are inseparable from their moral, political, and historical contexts. Policymakers must therefore tread lightly and cautiously, clarifying the intended purposes, capacities, and fragilities of their measurement tools.

BIBLIOGRAPHY

ANASTASI, A. (1988). *Psychological testing* (6th ed.). New York: Macmillan.

BECKER, G. S. (1975). *Human capital: A theoretical and empirical analysis, with special reference to education* (2nd ed.). New York: Columbia University Press.

BERLINER, D. C. (1993). Mythology and the American system of education. *Phi Delta Kappan, 74*(8), 632–640.

BLACKBURN, M., BLOOM, D., & FREEMAN, R. (1990). The declining position of less skilled American men. In G. Burtless (Ed.), *A future of lousy jobs.* Washington, DC: Brookings Institution.

CECI, S. J. (1990). *On intelligence . . . more or less.* Englewood Cliffs, NJ: Prentice Hall.

CHAPMAN, P. D. (1988). *Schools as sorters.* New York: New York University Press.

CONGRESSIONAL BUDGET OFFICE. (1986). *Trends in educational achievement.* Washington, DC: U.S. Government Printing Office.

CREMIN, L. (1989). *Popular education and its discontents.* New York: Harper & Row.

CRONBACH, L. (1975). Five decades of public controversy over mental testing. *American Psychologist, 30,* 1–14.

CROUSE, J., & TRUSHEIM, D. (1988). *The case against the SAT.* Chicago: University of Chicago Press.

FANCHER, R. E. (1985). *The intelligence men: Makers of the IQ controversy.* New York: W. W. Norton.

FINDLAY, W. G., & BRYAN, M. M. (1975). *The pros and cons of ability grouping.* Bloomington, IL: Phi Delta Kappa Press.

FREDERIKSEN, N. (1984). The real test bias: Influences of testing on teaching and learning. *American Psychologist, 39,* 193–202.

FULLER, B. (1987). Defining school quality. In J. Hannaway & M. Lockhead (Eds.), *The contribution of the social sciences to educational policy and practice: 1965–1985.* Berkeley, CA: McCutchan.

GARDNER, H. (1983). *Frames of mind: The theory of multiple intelligences.* New York: Basic Books.

GLAZER, S. (1993). Intelligence testing. *The CQ Researcher, 3*(28), 649–672.

GOLDBERGER, A. S. (1976). Mysteries of the meritocracy. In

N. Block & G. Dworkin (Eds.), *The IQ controversy.* New York: Random House.

GOTTFREDSON, L. (1986). Societal consequences of the *g* factor in employment. *Journal of Vocational Behavior, 29*(3), 379–410.

GOULD, S. J. (1981). *The mismeasure of man.* New York: W. W. Norton.

GUION, R. (1965). *Personnel testing.* New York: McGraw-Hill.

GUION, R. (1991). Personnel assessment, selection, and placement. In M. D. Dunnette & L. M. Hough (Eds.), *Handbook of industrial and organization psychology* (2nd ed.). Vol. 2, pp. 327–397. Palo Alto, CA: Consulting Psychologists Press.

HANEY, W., MADAUS, G., & LYONS, R. (1993). *The fractured marketplace for standardized testing.* Boston: Kluwer.

HANSON, F. A. (1993). *Testing testing: Social consequences of the examined life.* Berkeley and Los Angeles: University of California Press.

HARTIGAN, J., & WIGDOR, A. (EDS.). (1989). *Fairness in employment testing.* Washington, DC: National Academy Press.

HERRNSTEIN, R. (1971). IQ. *Atlantic Monthly, 228,* 43–64.

JENCKS, C. (1992). *Rethinking social policy.* Cambridge, MA: Harvard University Press.

JENSEN, A. (1969). How much can we boost IQ and scholastic achievement? *Harvard Educational Review, 39*(5), 1–123.

JENSEN, A. (1980). *Bias in mental testing.* New York: Free Press.

KAMIN, L. J. (1974). *The science and politics of IQ.* Hillsdale, NJ: Erlbaum.

KARIER, C. (1976). Testing for order and control in the liberal corporate state. In N. Block & G. Dworkin (Eds.), *The IQ controversy.* New York: Random House.

LEE, V., BRYK, A., & SMITH, J. (1993). The organization of effective secondary schools. In L. Darling-Hammond (Ed.), *Review of Research in Education 19.* Washington, DC: American Educational Research Association.

LEVIN, H. (1988). Issues of agreement and contention in employment testing. *Journal of Vocational Behavior, 33*(3), 398–403.

LEVY, F., & MURNANE, R. J. (1992). U.S. earnings levels and earnings inequality: A review of recent trends and proposed explanations. *Journal of Economic Literature, 30*(3), 1333–1381.

LINN, R. L. (1982). Admissions testing on trial. *American Psychologist, 37,* 279–291.

LINN, R. L. (1986). Comments on the *g*-factor in employment testing. *Journal of Vocational Behavior, 29*(3), 438–444.

LINN, R. L., & DUNBAR, S. (1990). The nation's report card goes home: Good news and bad about trends in achievement. *Phi Delta Kappan, 72*(2), 127–133.

MADAUS, G. (1990, December 6). Testing as a social technology. The inaugural annual Boisi Lecture in Education and Public Policy, Boston College.

MESSICK, S. (1989). Validity. In R. Linn (Ed.), *Educational measurement* (3rd ed.). New York: American Council on Education & Macmillan.

NATIONAL COMMISSION ON EXCELLENCE IN EDUCATION (1983). *A nation at risk.* Washington, DC: U.S. Government Printing Office.

NEILL, M., & MEDINA, N. (1989). Standardized testing: Harmful to educational health. *Phi Delta Kappan, 70*(9), 691.

NELKIN, D., & TANCREDI, L. (1989). *Dangerous diagnostics.* New York: Basic Books.

OAKES, J. (1985). *Keeping track: How schools structure inequality.* New Haven, CT: Yale University Press.

OFFICE OF TECHNOLOGY ASSESSMENT, U.S. CONGRESS. (1992). *Testing in American schools: Asking the right questions.* Washington, DC: U.S. Government Printing Office.

OWEN, D. (1985). *None of the above: Behind the myth of scholastic aptitude.* Boston: Houghton-Mifflin.

SARASON, S., & DORIS, J. (1979). *Educational handicap, public policy, and social history.* New York: Free Press.

SCHMIDT, F., & HUNTER, J. (1977). Development of a general solution to the problem of validity generalization. *Journal of Applied Psychology 62,* 529–540.

SCHNEIDER, W. H. (1992). After Binet: French intelligence testing, 1900–1950. *Journal of the History of the Behavioral Sciences, 28,* 111–132.

SCRIBNER, S. (1987). Thinking in action: Some characterizations of practical thought. In R. J. Sternberg & R. K. Wagner (Eds.), *Practical intelligence: Nature and origins of competence in the everyday world.* New York: Cambridge University Press.

SHEPARD, L. (1993). Evaluating test validity. In L. Darling-Hammond (Ed.), *Review of research in education 19.* Washington, DC: American Educational Research Association.

SHERMAN, S., & ROBINSON, N. (EDS.). (1982). *Ability testing of handicapped people.* Washington, DC: National Academy Press.

SNYDERMAN, M., & ROTHMAN, S. (1988). *The IQ controversy:*

Media and public policy. New Brunswick, NJ: Transaction Books.

STAUDENMAIER, J. M. (1985). *Technology's storytellers: Reweaving the human fabric.* Cambridge, MA: MIT Press.

STERNBERG, R. J. (1988). *The triarchic mind.* New York: Penguin.

STEWART, D. (1989, February). Thinking the unthinkable: Standardized testing and the future of American education. Speech before the Columbus Metropolitan Club, Columbus, OH.

TYACK, D. (1974). *The one best system.* Cambridge, MA: Harvard University Press.

WAINER, H., & BRAUN, H. (1988). *Test validity.* Hillsdale, NJ: Erlbaum.

WEINBERG, R. (1989). Intelligence and IQ. *American Psychologist, 44*(2), 98–104.

WHITE, S. (1977). Social implications of IQ. In P. Houts (Ed.), *The myth of measurability.* New York: Hart.

WIGDOR, A., & GARNER, W. (EDS.). (1982). *Ability testing.* Washington, DC: National Academy Press.

WILSON, J. Q., & HERRNSTEIN, R. (1985). *Crime and human nature.* New York: Simon & Schuster.

ZIGLER, E., & SEITZ, V. (1982). Social policy and intelligence. In R. Sternberg (Ed.), *Handbook of human intelligence.* Cambridge: Cambridge University Press.

MICHAEL J. FEUER

SOCIOECONOMIC STATUS AND INTELLIGENCE

Intelligence and socioeconomic status (SES) are correlated. Why they are correlated is a matter of considerable disagreement and complexity. The question is crucial to many of the most heated controversies in the field of intelligence: the validity of psychometric intelligence quotient (IQ), the nature–nurture question, and the origins of phenotypic differences between social and ethnic groups.

Why are some people more successful in life than others are? One reason is that some people are born with greater social advantages. In a society with a rigid caste system, it is almost impossible to deviate from the social circumstances into which one is born: The advantaged remain advantaged no matter how lazy or foolish they are, and the poor remain poor, despite talent and hard work. Although modern Western society is more fluid, the SES to which one is born is still important: People inherit money directly from their parents, and the wealthy are provided with superior education, health care, and many other social advantages.

Nevertheless, in modern society it is possible to improve or worsen one's social standing. Most people would agree that social mobility is a good thing, but it poses a potential dilemma. If the ability to move up in the world were simply a matter of hard work and good character, there would be no problem. But if some of the ingredients of social success are inherited genetically, then the class system that was once perpetuated by custom might instead be perpetuated by genes.

This possibility was the focus of a controversial article by R. J. Herrnstein in the *Atlantic Monthly* (1971), which was later expanded into a book (Herrnstein, 1973). Herrnstein stated his hypothesis in the form of a syllogism:

1. If differences in mental abilities are inherited, and
2. If success requires those abilities, and
3. If earnings and prestige depend on success,
4. Then social standing (which reflects earnings and prestige) will be based to some extent on inherited differences among people [Herrnstein, 1973, pp. 197–198].

Herrnstein referred to a society in which SES was transmitted genetically via intelligence as a "meritocracy."

Not surprisingly, Herrnstein's article was met with an outpouring of opposition, some of it directed at him personally. Critics argued that the first two items in Herrnstein's syllogism were incorrect: Differences in mental abilities are not inherited, and social success does not depend on intelligence. Instead, said the critics, the educational, medical and social advantages available to the affluent cause their children to have higher intelligence quotient (IQ) scores. In fact, the sociological and population-genetic considerations involved in the dynamics of intergenerational mobility and stability are extremely complex, depending on the heritability of intelligence, the magnitude of the relationship between intelligence and SES, and the strength of cultural transmission of class, among many other factors (Gottesman, 1968). This article will consider the controversy of whether or not intelligence and SES have causal effects on each other (but see also HEREDITY, HERITABILITY).

Two basic hypotheses for explaining the relationship between social class and intelligence were originally described by S. Scarr-Salapatek (1971). The "environmental disadvantage hypothesis" asserts that biological and cultural factors associated with low SES cause deficits in intelligence. The "genetic differences hypothesis" holds that differences in intelligence are genetically transmitted and that lower intelligence causes individuals to achieve lower levels of socioeconomic status. To one degree or another, both hypotheses are almost certainly true. As is often the case in the study of intelligence, empirical analysis of these hypotheses is complicated by the fact that it is not possible to discriminate between them using cross-sectional studies of subjects raised by their biological parents. Moreover, for ethical reasons, it is impossible to design experimental studies in which genotypes and rearing environments are randomly paired. Studies of reciprocal causal relationships between intelligence and SES must therefore rely on quasi-experimental research designs that permit a limited degree of discrimination between the two basic hypotheses.

Of the many possible research designs, two will be described in detail. "Social-mobility designs" are the most important test of the causal effect of intelligence on social class. Social mobility studies examine intergenerational change in SES as a function of the intelligence of the younger generation. "Adoption designs" offer the clearest methods for studying the causal effect of social class on intelligence. Adoption studies examine the intellectual development of children who have been adopted away from their biological parents and reared in a different environment.

DEFINITION AND MEASUREMENT OF SOCIAL CLASS

Like intelligence, social class is a difficult variable to define precisely or measure reliably. The term *social class* has connotations of a traditional caste system in which people are born into classes and rarely move out of their class. This usage also implies some independence between social class and economic success, in that aristocratic families are not necessarily wealthier than families from relatively lower classes. In most modern empirical studies, SES is measured rather than social class per se. SES is a continuous variable that measures overall degree of social success, usually by some combination of occupational status, income, and education. No system for measuring SES has achieved universal acceptance. Two of the most widely used are the Hollingshead Index (Hollingshead & Redlich, 1958), which combines education, neighborhood of residence, and occupation, and the system of N. C. Myrianthopoulos and K. S. French (1968), which was derived by factor analysis and combines education, occupation, and income.

MAGNITUDE OF THE RELATIONSHIP

The numerical value of the correlation between SES and IQ depends to a large extent on how SES is measured and on the sample on which the study is based. Table 1 is a summary of results from the National Collaborative Perinatal Project, a large-scale study of mothers and their children in the United States that was conducted in the 1960s and 1970s. It is clear that Stanford-Binet IQ scores at 4 years of age are moderately related to SES among both whites ($r = .38$) and blacks ($r = .24$). J. C. Loehlin, G. Lindzey, and J. N. Spuhler (1975) summarized a large number of studies and concluded that the correlation is close to 0.3 among blacks and whites. C. Jencks (1972) estimated that the correlation between children's IQ scores and the economic status of their parents is about .35.

VALIDITY OF INTELLIGENCE ACROSS LEVELS OF SES

An important preliminary question is whether the construct validity of intelligence is invariant across different socioeconomic groups; there is substantial evidence to indicate that it is. Factor analyses of the WISC–R using the standardization sample (Carlson,

TABLE 1
Mean IQ by social class

	Low	Middle	High
Whites	95.6	101.2	110.9
	($n = 1266$)	($n = 5775$)	($n = 4870$)
Blacks	88.0	92.0	98.1
	($n = 4612$)	($n = 8095$)	($n = 1476$)

SOURCE: Broman, Nichols, & Kennedy, 1975.

Reynolds, & Gutkin, 1983) and independently collected samples (Hale, 1983) show essentially no differences in factorial structure as a function of SES. Studies of concurrent and predictive validity also demonstrate invariance across SES groups when IQ scores are used to predict achievement test scores (Guterman, 1979) or WRAT scores and teacher ratings of achievement (Hale, Raymond, & Gajar, 1982; Svanum & Bringle, 1982).

SOCIAL MOBILITY STUDIES

One way to separate the reciprocal causal effects of intelligence and SES is to study change in SES between two generations. SES is correlated between parents and children, but substantially less than perfectly correlated. Therefore, whereas SES has some degree of stability between generations because of the cultural perpetuation of privilege, children's SES levels also tend to regress toward the population mean. In order to preserve the distribution of SES from generation to generation, there must be a certain amount of mobility in SES between generations (Anderson, Brown, & Bowman, 1952). Social-mobility studies ask whether such mobility is partially a function of children's intelligence.

Causal relations in studies such as these are complex: Parental SES and parental intelligence are correlated with each other, and both may have causal effects on children's IQ and eventual social class, through genetic and environmental mechanisms. The most commonly used statistical method for separating these effects has been the use of difference scores: Differences in SES between parent and child generations are correlated with corresponding differences in intelligence. Significant positive correlations suggest that intelligence is a determinant of social class after the cultural stability of SES between generations has been controlled.

The first analysis of this problem was undertaken by C. A. Anderson, J. C. Brown, and M. J. Bowman (1952). They obtained occupational ratings and group IQ scores for 1,000 father–son pairs. Using now-dated distributional statistics, they proceeded as follows: Fathers' and sons' occupation scores were divided into quintiles and placed in a joint frequency distribution, that is, the distribution of sons' occupation was com-

puted for each level of fathers' occupation. They then computed the total discrepancy between this distribution and an "ideal" distribution in which sons' occupational levels were perfectly related to fathers' occupations. The total discrepancy was then partitioned into three independent factors: maldistribution of fathers, referring to the fact that the relationship between fathers' occupation and fathers' IQ was substantially less than perfect (68% of total discrepancy); changes in the distribution of occupation between the father and son generations (9%); and the regression of sons' occupation on sons' intelligence (23%). The last figure is an estimate of the influence of intelligence on SES after parental SES has been controlled.

The best-known demonstration of social mobility as a function of intelligence was published by J. H. Waller (1982). Waller obtained SES ratings and IQ scores for 131 fathers and 173 sons (Hollingshead's system for SES; Otis and Kuhlman tests from school records; mean age at testing was 15.9 years for fathers and 13.4 years for sons). He then computed correlations between father–son differences in IQ and father–son differences in SES. When sons born into the highest or lowest SES brackets are excluded (because they can move in only one direction), $r = .368$. Figure 1 is a

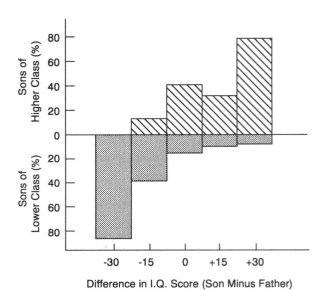

Figure 1

Percentage of sons moving up or down from their fathers' social class by differences in IQ score
SOURCE: Waller, 1982. Reprinted by permission of the publisher.

histogram of the mean difference in SES as a function of mean difference in intelligence.

A somewhat different approach was taken by J. B. Gibson and C. G. N. Mascie-Taylor (1973). They obtained Wechsler IQs and SES ratings for 75 university scientists and their fathers. The sons were selected to be in the highest SES; because the fathers' intelligence scores were related to their own SES, there was a correlation between the difference in intelligence between fathers and sons and the difference in SES. Scientists born into the highest SES were not significantly different from their fathers in intelligence, whereas those born into SES II were about 6 IQ points higher than their fathers, and those born into SES III were about 7 points higher. Results were roughly similar for verbal and performance IQ. Mascie-Taylor and Gibson (1978) obtained an SES measure and Wechsler IQ scores for 79 fathers and 85 sons. They classified the sons as upwardly mobile ($n = 35$), downwardly mobile ($n = 17$), or nonmobile ($n = 33$) in SES and computed difference scores between father and son IQ in each group. The upwardly mobile group had full-scale IQ scores 7.5 points higher than their fathers, the nonmobile group was 2.2 points lower, and the downwardly mobile group was 8.4 points lower than their fathers in IQ. The effect was somewhat larger for performance IQ than for verbal IQ.

ADOPTION STUDIES

Although adoption studies have usually been conducted in an attempt to separate genetic and environmental factors determining intelligence and other individual differences, they are also studies of the causal effects of SES on intelligence. In adoption studies, the intelligence of adopted children is analyzed as a function of the characteristics of their biological parents and adoptive parents. Similarity between adoptees and their biological parents is an indication of pre-adoption, primarily prenatal (if the children are adopted in infancy), and presumably genetic influence. Similarity between adoptees and their adoptive parents is an indication of environmental effects, SES included.

Similarity between adoptees and their biological or adoptive parents can take two forms. Because children are often adopted from lower-class families into homes that are at least middle class, adoptees are usually raised in a higher SES environment than they would have been had they not been adopted. One can therefore examine the mean IQ of a sample of adoptees to see if it is more similar to the mean expected on the basis of the SES of their biological or adoptive parents. The other kind of similarity is correlational: Individual differences in the IQs of adoptees can be related to differences in the biological and adoptive parents, with correlations between adoptees and biological parents being an indication of genetic influence and correlations with adoptive parents being an indication of environmental influence.

Because the IQ scores of any sample of adoptees is composed of both a mean and individual differences around the mean, all adoption studies have the potential to provide both kinds of data, although traditionally only one kind of analysis has been undertaken in any particular study (Turkheimer, 1991). One reason the analyses are usually not conducted together is that they often appear to lead to opposite conclusions: Mean difference analyses appear to confirm the causal effect of SES, but correlational analyses appear to disconfirm it.

Skodak and Skeels's Iowa Study. The classic, if not the ideal, study of the effect of adoption on the mean IQ of adoptees was conducted in Iowa by M. Skodak and H. M. Skeels (Skeels, 1936, 1938; Skodak, 1938, 1950; Skodak & Skeels, 1945, 1949). Subjects were tested with the Kuhlman-Binet or Stanford-Binet, administered at a mean age of 2 years; subsequent testing took place at 4, 7, and 13 years, by which time attrition had reduced the sample to 100. The biological parents of these children were below average. The mean IQ of 63 tested mothers from the final sample of 100 was 85.7; the average educational level of 92 biological mothers was 9.8 grades; the average occupational level of 73 of the biological fathers was in the range of slightly skilled laborers. The adoptive parents were not tested for IQ but were substantially better educated than the biological parents. The adoptees' mean IQ was 116.8 at 2 years and then slowly declined to about 108 by age 13. This increase in adoptee IQ relative to the biological mothers produced a wave of enthusiasm for the potency of the environment, followed by several strong critiques of the study's methodology (McNemar, 1940; Munsinger, 1975a). The study also produced correlational results, which will be discussed in the following section.

Scarr and Weinberg's Interracial Study. Another well-known analysis of the effects of adoption on the mean SES of adoptees is the study of interracial adoptees conducted in Minnesota by S. Scarr and R. A. Weinberg (1976, 1983). Scarr and Weinberg studied 176 children adopted by white families; 130 were socially classified as black (most had one black and one white biological parent), and 111 of these were adopted before age 12 months. The latter group had a mean IQ of 110, substantially higher than would be expected for a sample of black children selected from the population. The mean has dropped somewhat as the children have completed adolescence (Scarr & Weinberg, 1983), although the decrease is difficult to interpret because of a change in IQ standardization between the two testings.

The French Adoption Studies. A team of French investigators has conducted an important study of the effects of SES on intelligence in a sample of adoptees and their nonadopted siblings (Schiff et al., 1978, 1982; Schiff & Lewontin, 1986). The adoptees and their siblings were selected for very large differences between the SES of their biological and rearing environments. The study was designed to provide an answer to A. R. Jensen's (1969) notorious question about how much we can boost IQ and scholastic achievement.

French adoption records were searched, and cases were included if the adoptees had been "abandoned" at birth and the adoption took place before the age of 6 months, the biological mother's and the putative father's occupations were in the lowest classification, and the occupation of the head of the adoptive family was in the highest classification. Thirty-two adoptees (including three pairs of twins who were included as single subjects) met these qualifications and were included in the study. Twenty of the adoptees had a total of thirty-nine half-siblings who had not been adopted and had been reared by their biological mothers. School records and intelligence test scores (individual tests, mostly WISC, and a group test obtained from school records; intelligence scores were analyzed in twenty nonadopted children, one from each mother who contributed nonadopted siblings) were compared in the adopted and nonadopted half-siblings.

The differences between the adopted and non-adopted children are striking. Thirteen percent of adopted children had repeated a grade in school, compared to 62 percent of the nonadopted siblings. The mean IQ score of the adoptees was 106.8 on the group test and 110.6 on the Wechsler, whereas the non-adopted siblings had a mean of 94.2 on the group test and 94.6 on the Wechsler. The scores of the adoptees were at or above national norms. Schiff and his associates (1982) interpreted these findings as strong support for the potency of SES as a determinant of psychometric intelligence and success in school, which they certainly are. Several qualifications of the results should nevertheless be considered. The adopted children were selected expressly for the purpose of maximizing the effect of SES, so the observed effects must be interpreted in that context. Most biological parents are not as low in SES as those in this study, and most adoptive parents are not as well-off; the effect is therefore an estimate of the maximum, not the typical, effect of SES on intellectual and educational development (Turkheimer, 1991). Furthermore, the data contain within-group as well as between-group relationships: The intelligence-test scores of the adoptees can be correlated with the SES of their biological and adoptive parents, just as in any other adoption study. Doing so suggests that genetic relationships (i.e., those with the biological parent) are about as large as the environmental effects.

In a separate adoption study, C. Capron and M. Duyme (1989) conducted an adoption study of IQ-test scores in France approximating the powerful cross-fostering design of animal genetics. Adopted children and their biological and adoptive parents were selected so as to place them in one of four groups comprised by a two-by-two analysis of variance (ANOVA) design. Children were selected for either high or low socioeconomic and educational background of their biological parents and high or low socioeconomic and educational background of their adoptive parents. An analysis of variance was then performed on the IQ scores of the children, revealing significant and approximately additive (i.e., no significant interaction) effects of biological and adoptive parents. The results are summarized briefly in Table 2.

Once again, the authors of this study interpreted the results as a strong demonstration of the potency

TABLE 2

Mean and SD of IQ in four groups of adoptees

		Adoptive Parents' SES	
		High	Low
Biological Parents' SES	High	119.6 (12.3) n = 10	107.5 (11.9) n = 8
	Low	103.6 (12.7) n = 10	92.4 (15.4) n = 10

SOURCE: Capron & Duyme (1991).

of rearing environment for the determination of intelligence. The cautions discussed above still apply, however. In particular, the IQ differences between the adoptees raised in high- and low-SES homes are the result of very large differences in rearing environment. In addition, this study also found a substantial effect of the biological parents' SES. The authors argue that the effect of biological parents could result either from genetic differences between the low- and high-SES parents or from nongenetic prenatal differences.

Individual Differences in SES and Adoptee IQ. The results of correlational studies of the relationship between SES of an adoptive home and adoptee intelligence are very consistent across a great many studies conducted over fifty years. Early studies by B. S. Burks (1928) and A. M. Leahy (1931) found correlations between 0 and 0.3 between adoptee IQ and various aspects of the adoptive environment, including IQ and education of adoptive parent, and several more specific measures of the home environment. Skodak and Skeels (1949), in sharp contrast to their findings regarding the mean of adoptee IQ, reported that the correlation of adoptee IQ with the adoptive parents' education was not significantly different from zero.

Other adoption studies have produced very similar results. H. Munsinger (1975b) reported that the adoptive parents' SES was uncorrelated with adoptee IQ in two samples (but see Kamin, 1977). The Texas Adoption Project (Horn, Loehlin, & Willerman, 1982) found correlations of .21 and .14 between adoptee IQ and adoptive father's and mother's intelligence, respectively.

In the interracial study, Scarr and Weinberg report a correlation of .26 between the IQs of adoptive parents and adoptees, and a surprising correlation of .49 between unrelated children adopted into the same home. In a separate adoption study of adolescent adoptees (Scarr & Weinberg, 1978), neither of these correlations was significantly different from zero, and another study of the interracial adoptees, now adolescents themselves, showed the correlations to be substantially reduced.

Teasdale and Owen published a series of studies of the intelligence, education, and SES of a large ($n = 14,427$) sample of adult adoptees drawn from the Copenhagen adoption register. These studies are noteworthy in this context because adoptee SES, rather than adoptee IQ, was the major outcome variable in several analyses. An initial study (Teasdale, 1979) showed modest but significant positive correlations between the SES of adoptees and the SES of their biological ($r = .152, n = 1633$) and adoptive ($r = .197, n = 1948$) fathers. Both of these relationships appear to be mediated by education, that is, the primary influence of the biological and adoptive parents' SES is on the education of the adoptee, which in turn influences the adoptee's SES (Teasdale & Sorenson, 1983).

In a subsample of biological full- and half-sibling sets who were adopted into separate homes and unrelated adoptees who were adopted into a single home, only biological full siblings showed positive intraclass correlations for adult social class ($r = .22, n = 99$ pairs; $r = .39, n = 29$ early adopted pairs), suggesting that some inborn characteristic is an important determinant of adult SES (Teasdale & Owen, 1981). Another study analyzed a sample of separated siblings, pairs in which one sibling was adopted and another reared by the biological parents (Teasdale & Owen, 1984a). Once again, full-sibling pairs showed moderate intraclass correlations for SES ($r = .24, n = 88$ pairs); in contrast to the study of separated adoptees, half-sibling pairs ($r = .14, n = 457$ pairs) and unrelated adoptees reared together ($r = .18$, NS, $n = 69$ pairs) also showed positive correlations.

SES was the focus of a separate study of 290 male adoptees born in Copenhagen between 1944 and 1947 (Teasdale & Owen, 1984b). Occupational levels were obtained for the adoptees and their biological and adoptive fathers. Once again, there were significant but modest positive correlations between the SES of biological and adoptive fathers and the adoptees.

The Colorado Adoption Project includes much more comprehensive assessment of adoptive rearing environment, obtaining very similar results (Coon et al., 1990; Rice et al., 1988). The relationship between an index of the quality of the rearing environment (the HOME Scales of Elardo, Bradley, and Caldwell, 1975) was significant at age 1 and 2, but not thereafter.

THE NATURE OF THE RELATIONSHIP BETWEEN SES AND IQ

The results of social mobility studies suggest that intelligence is a determinant of SES, independent of the effects of paternal SES. The extent to which SES is a determinant of intelligence is somewhat less clear. Although Skodak and Skeels's Iowa studies and the French studies make it apparent that large changes in SES are associated with increases in intelligence scores, adoption studies of relationships between the SES of adoptive homes and adoptee intelligence have produced results ranging from small to zero.

The most likely explanation for these apparently contradictory findings is that the causal effect of SES on intelligence is nonlinear (Locurto, 1991; Turkheimer & Gottesman, 1991). The improvement in mean IQ experienced by children adopted from disadvantaged circumstances into middle- and high-SES homes is a reflection of the causal effect of SES in a range between very poor families and chaotic environments (unwed mothers, unemployed parents) and middle-class families that are selected for provision of a stable environment (because it is unlikely that a very poor or otherwise troubled family will be permitted to adopt a child). In contrast, correlations between rearing environment and intelligence in adoptees is a measure of the causal effect of SES only in the range of the adopted families.

Independent evidence indicates that the greatest effects of SES are those resulting from differences between very poor and middle-class families. Scarr-Salapatek (1971) classified black and white twin pairs into relatively advantaged and relatively disadvantaged groups, and estimated variance components attributable to between-family and within-family genetic and environmental differences on the Iowa Test of Basic

Skills (a group test given in schools) in each of the four combinations of social class and race. Between-family environmental differences (which include differences in SES) accounted for more variance in the low-SES families than in the high-SES families in both black and white twins.

BIBLIOGRAPHY

ANDERSON, C. A., BROWN, J. C., & BOWMAN, M. J. (1952). Intelligence and occupational mobility. *Journal of Political Economy, 60,* 218–239.

BROMAN, S. H., NICHOLS, P. L., & KENNEDY, W. A. (1975). *Preschool IQ: Prenatal & Early Development Correlates.* Hillsdale, NJ: Erlbaum.

BURKS, B. S. (1928). The relative influence of nature and nurture upon mental development. *27th Yearbook of the National Society for Studies in Education,* 219–236.

CAPRON, C., & DUYME, M. (1989). Assessment of effects of socio-economic status on IQ in a full cross-fostering study. *Nature, 340,* 552–553.

CAPRON, C., & DUYME, M. (1991). Children's IQs and SES of biological and adoptive parents in a balanced cross-fostering study. *Cahiers de Psychologie Cognitive, 11,* 323–348.

CARLSON, L., REYNOLDS, C. R., & GUTKIN, T. B. (1983). Consistency of the factorial validity of the WISC–R for upper and lower SES groups. *Journal of School Psychology, 21,* 319–326.

COON, H., FULKER, D. W., DeFRIES, J. C., & PLOMIN, R. (1990). Home environment and cognitive ability of 7-year-old children in the Colorado Adoption Project: Genetic and environmental etiologies. *Developmental Psychology, 26,* 459–468.

ELARDO, R., BRADLEY, R., & CALDWELL, B. M. (1975). The relation of infants' home environments to mental test performance from six to thirty-six months: A longitudinal analysis. *Child Development, 46,* 71–76.

GIBSON, J. B., & MASCIE-TAYLOR, C. G. N. (1973). Biological aspects of a high socioeconomic group: II. IQ components and social mobility. *Journal of Biosocial Science, 5,* 17–30.

GOTTESMAN, I. I. (1968). Biogenetics of race and class. In M. Deutsch, I. Katz, and A. R. Jensen (Eds.), *Social class, race, and psychological development.* New York: Holt, Rinehart & Winston.

GUTERMAN, S. S. (1979). IQ tests in research on social stratification: The cross-class validity of the tests as measures of scholastic aptitude. *Sociology of Education, 52,* 163–173.

HALE, R. L. (1983). An examination for construct bias in the WISC–R across socioeconomic status. *Journal of School Psychology, 21,* 153–156.

HALE, R. L., RAYMOND, M. R., & GAJAR, A. H. (1982). Evaluating socioeconomic status bias in the WISC–R. *Journal of School Psychology, 20,* 145–149.

HERRNSTEIN, R. J. (1971, September). I.Q. *Atlantic Monthly,* pp. 43–64.

HERRNSTEIN, R. J. (1973). *I.Q. in the meritocracy.* Boston: Little, Brown.

HOLLINGSHEAD, A. B., & REDLICH, F. C. (1958). *Social class and mental illness.* New York: Wiley.

HORN, J. L., LOEHLIN, J. C., & WILLERMAN, L. (1982). Aspects of the inheritance of intellectual abilities. *Behavior Genetics, 12,* 479–516.

JENCKS, C. (1972). *Inequality: A reassessment of the effect of family and schooling in America.* New York: Basic Books.

JENSEN, A. R. (1969). How much can we boost IQ and scholastic achievement? *Harvard Educational Review, 39,* 1–123.

KAMIN, L. J. (1977). Comment on Munsinger's adoption study. *Behavior Genetics, 7,* 403–409.

LEAHY, A. M. (1931). A study of certain selective factors influencing prediction of the mental status of adopted children. *Journal of Genetic Psychology,* 294–326.

LOCURTO, C. M. (1991). *Sense and nonsense about IQ: The case for uniqueness.* New York: Praeger.

LOEHLIN, J. C., LINDZEY, G., & SPUHLER, J. N. (1975). *Race differences in intelligence.* San Francisco: W. H. Freeman.

MASCIE-TAYLOR, C. G. N., & GIBSON, J. B. (1978). Social mobility and IQ components. *Journal of Biosocial Science, 10,* 263–276.

MCNEMAR, Q. (1940). A critical examination of the University of Iowa studies of environmental influence on the IQ. *Psychological Bulletin, 37,* 63–92.

MUNSINGER, H. (1975a). The adopted child's IQ: A critical review. *Psychological Bulletin, 82,* 623–659.

MUNSINGER, H. (1975b). Children's resemblance to their adopted parents in two ethnic groups. *Behavior Genetics, 5,* 239–254.

MYRIANTHOPOULOS, N. C., & FRENCH, K. S. (1968). An application of the U.S. Bureau of the Census socioeconomic index to a large, diversified, patient population. *Social Science and Medicine, 2,* 283–299.

RICE, T., FULKER, D. W., DEFRIES, J. C., & PLOMIN, R. (1988). Path analysis of IQ during infancy and early childhood

and an index of the home environment in the Colorado Adoption Project. *Intelligence, 12,* 27–45.

SCARR-SALAPATEK, S. (1971). Race, social class, and IQ. *Science, 174,* 1285–1295.

SCARR-SALAPATEK, S., & WEINBERG, R. A. (1976). IQ test performance of black children adopted by white families. *American Psychologist, 31,* 726–739.

SCARR-SALAPATEK, S., & WEINBERG, R. A. (1978). The influence of "family background" on intellectual attainment. *American Sociological Review, 43,* 674–692.

SCARR-SALAPATEK, S., & WEINBERG, R. A. (1983). The Minnesota adoption studies: Genetic differences and malleability. *Child Development, 54,* 260–267.

SCHIFF, M., DUYME, M., DUMARET, A., STEWART, J., TOMKIEWICZ, S., & FEINGOLD, J. (1978). Intellectual status of working-class children adopted early into upper-middle-class families. *Science, 200,* 1503–1504.

SCHIFF, M., DUYME, M., DUMARET, A., & TOMKIEWICZ, S. (1982). How much could we boost scholastic achievement and IQ scores: A direct answer from a French adoption study. *Cognition, 12,* 165–196.

SCHIFF, M., & LEWONTIN, R. (1986). Education and class: The irrelevance of IQ genetic studies. Oxford: Clarendon Press.

SKEELS, H. M. (1936). Mental development of children in foster homes. *Journal of Genetic Psychology, 49,* 91–106.

SKEELS, H. (1938). Mental development of children in foster homes. *Journal of Consulting Psychology, 2,* 33–42.

SKODAK, M. (1938). The mental development of adopted children whose true mothers are feebleminded. *Child Development, 9,* 303–308.

SKODAK, M. (1950). Mental growth of adopted children in the same family. *Journal of Genetic Psychology, 77,* 3–9.

SKODAK, M., & SKEELS, H. M. (1945). A follow-up study of children in adoptive homes. *Journal of Genetic Psychology, 66,* 21–58.

SKODAK, M., & SKEELS, H. M. (1949). A final follow-up study of one hundred adopted children. *Journal of Genetic Psychology, 75,* 85–125.

SVANUM, S., & BRINGLE, R. G. (1982). Race, social class, and predictive bias: An evaluation using the WISC, WRAT, and teacher ratings. *Intelligence, 6,* 275–286.

TEASDALE, T. W. (1979). Social class correlations among adoptees and their biological and adoptive parents. *Behavior Genetics, 9,* 103–114.

TEASDALE, T. W., & OWEN, D. R. (1981). Social class correlations among separately adopted siblings and unrelated individuals adopted together. *Behavior Genetics, 11,* 577–588.

TEASDALE, T. W., & OWEN, D. R. (1984a). Heredity and familial environment in intelligence and educational level: A sibling study. *Nature, 309,* 620–622.

TEASDALE, T. W., & OWEN, D. R. (1984b). Social class and mobility in male adoptees and non-adoptees. *Journal of Biosocial Science, 16,* 521–530.

TEASDALE, T. W., & SORENSON, T. I. A. (1983). Educational attainment and social class in adoptees: Genetic and environmental contributions. *Journal of Biosocial Science, 15,* 509–518.

TURKHEIMER, E. (1991). Individual and group differences in adoption studies of IQ. *Psychological Bulletin, 110,* 392–405.

TURKHEIMER, E., & GOTTESMAN, I. I. (1991). Individual differences and the canalization of human behavior. *Developmental Psychology, 27,* 18–22.

WALLER, J. H. (1982). Achievement and social mobility: Relationships among IQ score, education, and occupation in two generations. *Social Biology, 29,* 255–263.

ERIC TURKHEIMER

SOMPA *See* SYSTEM OF MULTICULTURAL PLURALISTIC ASSESSMENT.

SPATIAL ABILITY Spatial ability may be defined as the ability to generate, retain, retrieve, and transform well-structured visual images. It is not a single ability. There are, in fact, several spatial abilities, each emphasizing different aspects of the process of image generation, storage, retrieval, and transformation. One way to appreciate the diversity of spatial abilities and their impact on individuals and society is to survey some of the abilities and occupations that require (and develop) spatial abilities. High levels of spatial abilities are common among architects, engineers, draftpersons, and designers of all sorts, cabinetmakers and mechanics, quilt makers, airplane pilots, and air traffic controllers, to name a few occupations (McGee, 1979). Many artists also show good spatial abilities. Indeed, paintings, drawings, and sculpture provide rich histories of the visual-spatial skills of individuals (Gardner, 1980; Goodnow, 1977), but one

that is heavily influenced by culture and craft (Freeman, 1980). This is probably why high levels of artistic ability are much less common among preadolescents than are giftedness in other domains, such as music or mathematics (Goodenough, 1926; Selfe, 1977).

SPATIAL ABILITIES AND CREATIVITY

High levels of spatial ability have frequently been linked to creativity, not only in the arts but in science and mathematics as well (Shepard, 1978; West, 1991). For example, on several occasions Albert Einstein reported that verbal processes seemed not to play a role in his creative thought. Rather, he claimed that he achieved insights by means of thought experiments on visualized systems of waves and physical bodies in states of relative motion. Other physicists (such as James Clerk Maxwell, Michael Faraday, and Herman Von Helmholtz), inventors (such as Nikola Tesla and James Watt), and generalists (such as Benjamin Franklin, John Herschel, Francis GALTON, and James Watson) also displayed high levels of spatial abilities and reported that such abilities played an important role in their most creative accomplishments.

DEVELOPMENT OF SPATIAL GIFTEDNESS

Individuals who show high levels of visual-spatial creativity as adults often showed similar childhood characteristics. R. N. Shepard (1978) identified four such factors in his review of the literature. First, many showed delayed language development. Some degree of dyslexia was also common. Second, many were kept home from school during early school years and were often isolated from age mates as well. Third, most displayed a fascination for physical objects, mechanical models, and geometric puzzles. Fourth, many suffered from hallucinations and mental breakdowns.

The fact that individuals who exhibit high levels of spatial abilities sometimes experience one or more of a variety of specific language disabilities has been noted by several authors (e.g., West, 1991). Problems in verbal fluency and spelling are most common, although dyslexia is also observed with some frequency. Individuals with high levels of spatial abilities frequently report difficulty in translating their thoughts into words, especially when required to speak extemporaneously. However, they may exhibit high levels of verbal knowledge, verbal comprehension, and written expression. Thus, the difficulty lies in fluency and phonological encoding, not in a more general verbal ability.

Several theorists have suggested that many young children possess unusually vivid (or eidetic) imagery abilities that they lose as their language abilities increase (see Palvio, 1971). However, the infrequency of such children and the absence of longitudinal studies on them make inference difficult. Kosslyn (1983) argues that individuals of all ages rely on visual imagery to answer unfamiliar questions, but with practice tend to rely instead on verbal knowledge. By this account, children rely more on imagery because their verbal knowledge is less extensive.

BRAIN INJURY
AND SPATIAL ABILITIES

Studies of brain-injured individuals complete the picture by showing the consequences of a severe lack of spatial abilities (see Bradshaw, 1983; Ellis & Young, 1988). Such individuals often exhibit some form of agnosia, which is a general term used to describe those conditions in which percepts are stripped of their meaning. Individuals who exhibit apperceptive agnosia appear to have difficulty in constructing stable representations of visual forms. They have difficulty identifying complete pictures, recognizing unusual views, and separating overlapping figures. These agnosias are typically associated with damage to the right hemisphere of the brain. Those with associative agnosia have difficulty accessing semantic knowledge about objects. Sometimes the loss is restricted to certain categories such as faces (even one's own face) and other potentially ambiguous stimuli (such as cars, clothes, birds). Damage to either the right or left hemisphere can lead to these difficulties. Indeed, both hemispheres of the brain appear to play a role in the construction of images of multipart objects (Kosslyn, 1988).

The right hemisphere appears to be the location of coordinate-stored memory traces that maintain information about proportions and configuration, at least in most right-handed individuals. Damage to the right

hemisphere often affects the ability to manipulate images (such as on tests of mental rotation) or to infer their missing parts, to use maps without reference to one's own progression through space, and even to neglect information in the left visual field. Drawings made by such individuals often are haphazard, with inappropriate combinations of correctly discriminated features, faulty overall configuration, proportions, and spatial relationships.

The left hemisphere appears to store categorical information (such as which part goes next to or above another part) that is required to organize parts into a coherent image. Damage to the left hemisphere results in drawings that are oversimplified, that show poor detail or discrimination among elements, but that generally preserve overall configuration. Individuals with left-hemisphere lesions often show difficulties in route-finding tasks (suggesting that large-scale spatial tasks may rely on different abilities than small-scale tasks), and on figure disembedding tasks (see Bradshaw, 1983).

PSYCHOMETRIC STUDIES
OF SPATIAL ABILITY

Predictive Validity of Spatial Tests. Tests of spatial abilities are the best predictors of successful completion of training for machine workers and bench workers (Ghiselli, 1973) and of success in the training of air crews (Guilford & Lacey, 1947). They are moderately good predictors of grades in engineering and trade schools, particularly in courses such as engineering drawing. The United States Employment Service (1957) lists eighty-four job categories that require high levels of spatial abilities. The job categories of engineer, scientist, draftsman, and designer account for 85 percent of these job categories (McGee, 1979). Furthermore, the predictive validities of spatial tests also vary across groups, being in general somewhat higher for younger and female samples (Vernon, 1950).

Although spatial tests are correlated with success in traditional school subjects, they add little to the prediction of grades in these courses—even geometry—beyond that made by tests of GENERAL INTELLIGENCE. In fact, Charles SPEARMAN (see Spearman & Wynn-Jones, 1950) long considered spatial and performance tests as merely unreliable measures of g (general intelligence). However, the converse is also possible: measures of *g* or *Gf* (fluid intelligence) may measure or simply be highly correlated with the ability to reason with spatial mental models. Alternatively, both *g* and spatial abilities may be heavily influenced by a third variable, such as individual differences in working-memory capacity (see FLUID AND CRYSTALLIZED INTELLIGENCE, THEORY OF).

Individuals who score higher on tests of spatial abilities than on tests of verbal abilities are often called visualizers, whereas their counterparts who show the opposite score pattern are called verbalizers. The hypothesis that verbalizers and visualizers would profit from different methods of instruction stretches from Francis GALTON (1883) to the present. It has been one of the most popular, yet one of the most elusive aptitude by treatment interaction (ATI) hypotheses. However, interactions between a verbalizer-visualizer score and instructional treatments are few, usually small, and inconsistent, for reasons statistical and psychological.

Measuring Spatial Abilities. Spatial abilities have been measured using four different types of tests: performance tests, paper-and-pencil tests, verbal tests, and film or dynamic computer-based tests. Performance tests were the earliest. Form board, block manipulation, and paper-folding tasks were among the items Alfred BINET and Théodore Simon (1916) used to measure the intelligence of children. Others created entire tests of a particular item type, such as form boards or blocks. Many of these tasks are used in contemporary intelligence tests as measures of performance or nonverbal intelligence (e.g., Wechsler, 1955). Another type of performance test seeks to estimate the ability to function in large-scale space. However, measures of the ability to orient oneself, to find efficient routes between locations, for instance, show at best moderate correlations with other measures of spatial abilities (Allen, 1982; Lorenz & Neisser, 1986), perhaps in part because such tasks may be solved in ways that do not demand analog processing.

Many paper-and-pencil tests of spatial abilities have been devised over the years. Eliot and Smith (1983) give directions and example items for 392 spatial tests, most of which were used in factorial investigations of abilities. Early factor analyses sought to demonstrate the existence of one or more spatial factors (Kelley, 1928; El Koussy, 1935). Some researchers, particularly

those in Britain, were satisfied when they showed that a single spatial factor could be identified in the correlations among mental tests once the general factor had been removed. These researchers tended to construct tests of spatial abilities that contained several different types of items and to study young, age-heterogenous samples. American researchers used different methods of factor analysis, more homogeneous tests, and older, more homogeneous subject samples, and, therefore, identified many different spatial factors. French (1951) made an early attempt to catalog these factors. Others (e.g., Guilford, 1967) proposed rational models that classified existing factors and suggested how others might be identified. Recent efforts to understand the dimensions of spatial abilities have moved away from these rational schemes. Instead, they have attempted to reanalyze old data sets using modern factor analytic methods and a hierarchical factor model in which factors of spatial abilities are organized according to breadth, from broad group factors, to narrow group factors, to specifics (Carroll, 1993; Lohman, 1979). Table 1 lists the five major spatial factors identified in these reviews, a brief definition of each, and the name of a test that commonly evaluates the factor. However, the specific variance in such tests is large, and so attempts to measure these abilities should always employ multiple tests for each factor.

Verbal tests of spatial abilities have received much less attention, despite the fact that they often show high correlations with other spatial tests and various criterion measures (Guilford & Lacey, 1947). In this type of test, examinees must listen to a problem, presumably one that requires construction of a mental image, and then answer one or more questions. For example, "imagine that you walk north for a while, then take a right turn, then walk further and take another right turn. In what direction are you facing?" Such tests require subjects to use spatial abilities in a way that is probably more representative of the manner in which such abilities are used in every day life than do the items on most paper-and-pencil tests. Many cognitive tasks often require—or at least benefit from—the ability to construct a mental image that can be coordinated with linguistic inputs.

Although spatial tests may require subjects to transform objects (such as by rotating or transposing them mentally), they typically present static objects. Some

TABLE 1
Major spatial factors, definitions, and a representative test for each

Factor	Definition[a]	Example Test[b]
Visualization	Ability in manipulating visual patterns, as indicated by level of difficulty and complexity in visual stimulus material that can be handled successfully, without regard to the speed of task solution.	Paper folding
Speeded Rotation	Speed in manipulating relatively simple visual patterns, by whatever means (mental rotation, transformation, or otherwise).	Cards
Closure Speed	Speed in apprehending and identifying a visual pattern, without knowing in advance what the pattern is, when the pattern is disguised or obscured in some way.	Street Gestalt
Closure Flexibility	Speed in finding, apprehending, and identifying a visual pattern, knowing in advance what is to be apprehended, when the pattern is disguised or obscured in some way.	Concealed Figures
Perceptual Speed	Speed in finding a known visual pattern, or in accurately comparing one or more patterns, in a visual field such that the patterns are not disguised or obscured.	Identical Pictures

[a]From Carroll, 1993, pp. 362–363.
[b]See Ekstrom, French, Harman, & Dirmen (1976).

have hypothesized that the perception of dynamic (moving) spatial relationships involves somewhat different abilities. Gibson (1947) and later Seibert and Snow (1965) developed a variety of motion-picture tests that were designed to measure these dynamic spatial abilities. However, individual differences on most dynamic spatial tasks appear to be well accounted for by performance on paper-and-pencil tests. One exception is a task called "serial integration" that appeared in several studies. Tests defining this ability required subjects to identify a common object from a series of incomplete pictures presented successively.

Pellegrino and Hunt (1989) have devised several computer-administered tests of dynamic spatial abilities. Results to date show that individual differences in the ability to predict object trajectories and arrival times can be reliably measured and evaluate different abilities than paper-and-pencil tests.

Response Mode and Speededness. Spatial tests differ in the type of response required (such as the selection of an alternative, construction of a response, or a verbal statement), in addition to differences in presentation format (e.g., performance, paper-and-pencil, verbal, dynamic). For paper-and-pencil tests, there is some evidence that constructed-response tests are somewhat better measures of spatial ability (Lohman, 1988). For this reason they have long been preferred by British psychometricians (Eliot & Smith, 1983). Smith (1964) argues that spatial ability is best measured when subjects are required to maintain an image in its correct proportions. This is often done by presenting well-structured but fairly simple geometric designs that subjects must remember and then reproduce. However, constructed-response tests are more difficult to score than are multiple-choice tests. On the other hand, much additional information about subjects' abilities and test strategies can be obtained by carefully analyzing the type of errors they make in drawing or constructing their answers (e.g., Kyllonen, 1984).

Another important aspect of spatial tests is the relative emphasis placed on speed versus degree of difficulty. Tests administered under time-limited conditions tend to measure more specific aspects of spatial ability than do tests administered under relatively untimed conditions. Altering the complexity of test items generally results in a change in the ability that a test estimates. Simple items must be administered under time-limited conditions in order to generate individual differences. Therefore, a change in task complexity usually means a change in time limitation of a test as well. Computer-based tests offer the opportunity to gather both error and latency scores, which can then be combined to predict criterion performances with greater precision than from either measure considered separately (Ackerman & Lohman, 1990). However, performance on such tests is influenced more by the speed or accuracy emphasis that subjects adopt than is performance on time-limited tests.

Practice and Training Effects. Spatial tests often show substantial practice effects. Gains in score after retest range from .2 to 1.2 standard deviations, effects being somewhat larger for simpler tests, shorter retest intervals, and subjects who are given feedback. Effects of this magnitude can seriously compromise interpretations of test scores if examinees are differentially familiar with test problems. However, transfer to nonpracticed tests that evaluate the same spatial ability is typically much smaller, often nonexistent. Several studies now suggest that the key variable in predicting transfer to nonpracticed tests is similarity of procedures employed rather than of the particular figures or stimuli used, at least when subjects are young adults and the problems are regular polygons (Lohman, 1993).

Spatial abilities can be improved with practice and training, even though particular courses of instruction (such as engineering drawing) have inconsistent effects. This may reflect in part the fact that treatments

designed to improve performance on spatial tasks often are disruptive for high-verbal–ability subjects. One possibility is that these treatments impose or induce regulation of performance by someone other than the subject. Such external regulation may compensate for the inadequate self-regulation activities of low verbal subjects, but it interferes with the self-regulation activities of high-verbal subjects.

Although short-term studies often produce small or conflicting findings, Balke-Aurell's (1982) study of the effects of tracking in the Swedish-secondary–school system suggest that the cumulative effects of differential educational and work experiences can be quite large. Students educated in a verbally-oriented curriculum showed greater growth in verbal abilities whereas those educated in a technical curricula showed greater growth in spatial abilities.

Personality Correlates. Several investigators have noted that individuals who show relatively high spatial abilities but low oral-fluency abilities tend to obtain high scores on measures of introversion and masculinity. Smith (1964) concludes that individuals with high spatial abilities also show traits of self-sufficiency, perseverance, and emotional stability. However, correlatives of spatial ability may differ by sex (e.g., Ozer, 1987), and so generalizations are difficult. Here, as with sex differences, the contrast between spatial and verbal fluency or phonological sequencing abilities is probably more important than the level of either ability considered by itself. For example, Riding and Cheema (1991) claim that the habit of making imagistic instead of semantic elaboration is highly correlated with introversion, at least in children.

CONTRIBUTIONS OF COGNITIVE RESEARCH

Spatial Cognition. Cognitive psychology has contributed importantly to our understanding of how subjects encode, remember, and transform visual images, and, thus, to our understanding of what spatial abilities might be. The seminal research here was that of Roger Shepard and his students. Shepard (1978) poses an interesting challenge to cognitive scientists:

Suppose that we do not start by asking what kinds of thought processes are most accessible to empirical study, are most conveniently externalized in the form of discrete symbols, words, or sentences, or are most readily described by existing models imported into cognitive psychology from linguistics or computer science. Suppose, instead, that we first ask what sorts of thought processes underlie human creative acts of the highest and most original order. Perhaps we shall come to be less than fully satisfied with research that is exclusively motivated by current theories of linear sequential processing of discrete symbolic or propositional structures. [p. 134]

The challenge to propositional theories of cognition was made most forcefully in an early series of experiments on mental rotation (see Shepard & Cooper, 1982, for a summary). The basic finding was that the time required to determine whether two figures could be rotated into congruence was a function of the amount of rotation required. On the basis of this and other evidence, Shepard claimed that mental rotation was an analog process that showed a one-to-one correspondence with physical rotation. The second claim was that this rotation process was performed on a mental representation that somehow preserved information about structure at all points during the rotation transformation.

Others have been more explicit about the nature of this representation. Most agree that spatial knowledge can be represented in more than one way. One representation (sometimes called an image code) is thought to be more literal (Kosslyn, 1980) or at least more structure- or configuration-preserving (Anderson, 1983). Another representation is more abstract and is more meaning—or interpretation—preserving (Kosslyn, 1980; Anderson, 1983; Palmer, 1977) and is usually modeled by the same propositional structures used to represent meaningful verbal knowledge. Much of the confusion in understanding spatial abilities can be traced to whether spatial abilities are restricted to image-coded memories and the analog processes that operate on them or whether proposition-coded memories and the general procedural knowledge that operate on them are also considered part of the term. In other words, much of the confusion lies in whether abilities are defined by performance on a certain class of tasks or by skill in executing certain types of mental processes.

Individual Differences in Spatial Cognition. Although research and theory in cognitive psychology and artificial intelligence suggest much about the nature of spatial knowledge and processes, they do not explicitly address the source of individual differences in spatial processing. Research on this question has followed four hypotheses: Spatial abilities may be explained by individual differences in (1) speed of performing analog transformations; (2) skill in generating and retaining mental representations that preserve configural information; (3) the amount of visual-spatial information that can be maintained in an active state; or (4) the sophistication and flexibility of strategies available for solving such tasks.

Males outperform females on most spatial tasks, although the magnitude of the male advantage varies across tasks. For adolescents and adults, it is generally largest on three-dimensional rotation tests, being approximately .8–1.0 SD (Linn & Petersen, 1985). Differences are small for two-dimensional rotation tasks and for complex spatial tasks (such as paper-folding and form-board tasks) that involve or may be solved by reasoning (Halpern, 1992). The difference can be reliably measured as early as fourth grade (Johnson & Meade, 1987), although prior to adolescence, sex differences are larger on somewhat easier tests such as Hands and Block Counting than on the more difficult three-dimensional rotation or figure-disembedding tasks.

There is considerable controversy about the origin of this difference. Some (e.g., Nyborg, 1983) emphasize biological factors, particularly hormones, whereas others (e.g., Newcombe & Dubas, 1992) emphasize experiential factors, particularly involvement in sex-typed activities. The experiential argument is bolstered by findings that performance on spatial tasks improves markedly with training (e.g., Lohman & Nichols, 1990), but challenged by the finding that males and females show comparable improvements.

(*See also:* ARTISTIC ABILITY: CHILDREN'S DRAWINGS.)

BIBLIOGRAPHY

ACEDOLO, L. P. (1981). Small- and large-scale spatial concepts in infancy and childhood. In L. S. Liben, A. H. Patterson, & N. Newcombe (Eds.), *Spatial representation* and behavior across the life span (pp. 63–81). New York: Academic Press.

ACKERMAN, P. L., & LOHMAN, D. F. (1990). An investigation of the effect of practice on the validity of spatial tests. Final Report (NPRDC Contract N66001-88C-0291). Minneapolis, MN: Personnel Decisions Research Institute.

ALLEN, G. L. (1982). Assessment of visuospatial abilities using complex cognitive tasks. Norfolk, VA: Department of Psychology, Old Dominion University.

ANDERSON, J. R. (1983). The architecture of cognition. Cambridge, MA: Harvard University Press.

BADDELEY, A. (1986). Working memory. Oxford, UK: Clarendon Press.

BALKE-AURELL, G. (1982). Changes in ability as related to educational and occupational experience. Goteborg, Sweden: Acta Universitatis Gothoburgensis.

BINET, A., & SIMON, T. (1916). The development of intelligence in children (E. S. Kite, Trans.). Baltimore: Williams & Wilkens.

BRADSHAW, J. L. (1983). Human cerebral asymmetry. Englewood Cliffs, NJ: Prentice-Hall.

CARROLL, J. B. (1993). Human cognitive abilities: A survey of factor-analytic studies. New York: Cambridge University Press.

CRONBACH, L. J., & SNOW, R. E. (1977). Aptitudes and instructional methods: A handbook for research on interactions. New York: Irvington.

ELIOT, J. (1987). Models of psychological space. New York: Springer-Verlag.

ELIOT J. C., & SMITH, I. M. (1983). An international directory of spatial tests. Windsor, England: NFER-Nelson.

ELLIS, A. W., & YOUNG, A. W. (1988). Human cognitive neuropsychology. Hillsdale, NJ: Erlbaum.

FREEMAN, N. H. (1980). Strategies of representation in young children: Analysis of spatial skills and drawing processes. London: Academic Press.

FRENCH, J. W. (1951). The description of aptitude and achievement tests in terms of rotated factors. Psychometric Monographs, No. 5.

GALTON, F. (1883). Inquiries into human faculty and its development. London: Macmillan.

GARDNER, H. (1980). Artful scribbles: The significance of children's drawings. New York: Basic Books.

GHISELLI, E. E. (1973). The validity of aptitude tests in personnel selection. Personnel Psychology, 26, 461–477.

GIBSON, J. J. (ED.). (1947). Motion picture testing and research. Army air forces aviation psychology programs (Report No. 7). Washington, DC: Government Printing Office.

GOODENOUGH, F. L. (1926). Measurement of intelligence by drawings. New York: Harcourt, Brace, & World.

GOODNOW, J. (1977). Children's drawing. Cambridge, MA: Harvard University Press.

GUILFORD, J. P. (1967). The nature of human intelligence. New York: McGraw-Hill.

GUILFORD, J. P., & LACEY, J. I. (EDS.). (1947). Printed classification tests. AAF aviation psychology research program reports (No. 5). Washington, DC: Government Printing Office.

GUSTAFSSON, J. E. (1976). Verbal and figural aptitudes in relation to instructional methods: Studies in aptitude-treatment interaction. Gotenborg Studies in Education Sciences, No. 17, Gotenborg, Sweden.

GUSTAFSSON, J. E. (1989). Broad and narrow abilities in research on learning and instruction. In R. Kanfer, P. L. Ackerman, & R. Cudeck (Eds.), Abilities, motivation, and methodology: The Minnesota Symposium on learning and individual differences (pp. 203–237). Hillsdale, NJ: Erlbaum.

HABER, R. N., & HABER, R. B. (1964). Eidetic imagery: I. Frequency. Perceptual and Motor Skills, 19, 131–138.

HALPERN D. F. (1992). Sex differences in cognitive abilities (2nd ed.). Hillsdale, NJ: Erlbaum.

JOHNSON, E. S., & MEADE, A. C. (1987). Developmental patterns of spatial ability: An early sex difference. Child Development, 58, 725–740.

JOHNSON-LAIRD, P. N. (1983). Mental models: Towards a cognitive science of language, inference, and consciousness. Cambridge, MA: Harvard University Press.

KELLY, T. L. (1928). Crossroads in the mind of man. Stanford, CA: Stanford University Press.

KINTSCH, W. (1986). Learning from text. Cognition and Instruction, 3, 87–108.

KOHS, S. C. (1923). Intelligence measurement: A psychological and statistical study based upon the block designs test. New York: Macmillan.

KOSSLYN, S. M. (1980). Image and mind. Cambridge, MA: Harvard University Press.

KOSSLYN, S. M. (1983). Ghosts in the mind's machine. New York: Norton.

KOSSLYN, S. M. (1988). Aspects of a cognitive neuroscience of mental imagery. Science, 240, 1621–1626.

KOUSSY, A. A. H. EL (1935). The visual perception of space. British Journal of Psychology, 20 (Monograph supplement).

KYLLONEN, P. C. (1984). Information processing analysis of spatial ability. (Doctoral dissertation, Stanford University) *Dissertation Abstracts International, 45,* 819A.

LINN, M. C., & PETERSEN, A. C. (1985). Emergence and characterization of sex differences in spatial ability: A meta-analysis. *Child Development, 56,* 1479–1498.

LOHMAN, D. F. (1979). *Spatial ability: A review and reanalysis of the correlational literature* (Tech. Rep. No. 8). Stanford, CA: Stanford University, Aptitude Research project, School of Education. (NTIS NO. AD-A075 972).

LOHMAN, D. F. (1986). Predicting mathemathanic effects in the teaching of higher-order thinking skills. *Educational Psychologist, 21,* 191–208.

LOHMAN, D. F. (1988). Spatial abilities as traits, processes, and knowledge. In R. J. Sternberg (Ed.), *Advances in the psychology of human intelligence* (Vol. 40, pp. 181–248). Hillsdale, NJ: Erlbaum.

LOHMAN, D. F. (1993). *Effects of practice and training on the acquisition and transfer of spatial skills: Two speed-accuracy studies.* (Final Report Grant AFOSR-91-0367). Iowa City, IA: Lindquist Center for Measurement.

LOHMAN, D. F., & NICHOLS, P. D. (1990). Training spatial abilities: Effects of practice on rotation and synthesis tasks. *Learning and Individual Differences, 2,* 69–95.

LORENZ, C. A., & NEISSER, U. (1986). Ecological and psychometric dimensions of spatial ability. Atlanta, GA: Department of Psychology, Emory University, Report #10.

McGEE, M. (1979). *Human spatial abilities: Sources of sex differences.* New York: Praeger.

NEWCOMBE, N., & DUBAS, J. S. (1992). A longitudinal study of predictors of spatial ability in adolescent females. *Child Development, 63,* 37–46.

NYBORG, H. (1983). Spatial ability in men and women: Review and new theory. *Advances in Behavior Research and Therapy, 5,* 89–140.

OZER, D. J. (1987). Personality, intelligence, and spatial visualization: Correlates of mental rotation's test performance. *Journal of Personality and Social Psychology, 53,* 129–134.

PALMER, S. E. (1977). Hierarchical structure in perceptual representation. *Cognitive Psychology, 9,* 441–474.

PALVIO, A. (1971). *Imagery and verbal processes.* New York: Holt, Rinehart, & Winston.

PATERSON, D. G., ELLIOT, R. M., ANDERSON, L. D., TOOPS, H. A., & HEIDBREDER, E. (1930). *Minnesota mechanical ability tests.* Minneapolis: University of Minnesota Press.

RIDING, T., & CHEEMA, I. (1991). Cognitive styles: An overview and integration. *Educational Psychology, 11,* 193–215.

SALTHOUSE, T. A. (1991). *Theoretical perspectives on cognitive aging.* Hillsdale, NJ: Erlbaum.

SEIBERT, W. F., & SNOW, R. E. (1965). *Studies in cine-psychometry I: Preliminary factor analysis of visual cognition and memory.* Lafayette, IN: Audio Visual Center, Purdue University.

SELFE, L. (1977). *Nadia.* New York: Academic Press.

SHEPARD, R. N. (1978). Externalization of mental images and the act of creation. In B. S. Randhawa & W. E. Coffman (Eds.), *Visual learning, thinking, and communication* (pp. 133–190). New York: Academic Press.

SHEPARD, R. N. (1990). *Mind sights.* New York: W. H. Freeman.

SHEPARD, R. N., & COOPER, L. A. (1982). *Mental images and their transformations.* Cambridge, MA: MIT Press.

SMITH, I. M. (1964). *Spatial ability.* San Diego, CA: Knapp.

SPEARMAN, C., & WYNN JONES, L. L. (1950). *Human ability.* London: Macmillan.

UNITED STATES EMPLOYMENT SERVICE. (1957). *Estimates of worker trait requirements for 4,000 jobs.* Washington, DC: Government Printing Office.

VERNON, P. E. (1950). *The structure of human abilities.* London: Methuen.

WECHSLER, D. (1955). *Wechsler adult intelligence scale.* New York: Psychological Corporation.

WEST, T. G. (1991). *In the mind's eye.* Buffalo, NY: Prometheus Books.

DAVID F. LOHMAN

SPEARMAN, CHARLES EDWARD (1863–1945)

Arguably the most distinguished figure in the history of British psychology, Charles Spearman, although he died in 1945, is one of the notably few psychologists of his period whose pioneering contributions remain widely known in the late twentieth century and are still frequently cited by modern psychologists. Indeed, it would be hard to exaggerate his significance for contemporary psychology. His theories spawned some of the controversies still holding center stage in differential psychology, and his major works, after almost three-quarters of a century, are still a wellspring of problems for contemporary researchers.

Spearman was the first systematic psychometrician and the father of what is known today as classical test theory. He also wrote the first book to deal with a subject matter now recognized as cognitive psychology, thereby crediting him also as a pioneer in that field.

Spearman has perhaps become best known for his methodological contributions, particularly FACTOR ANALYSIS, a widely used mathematical method for analyzing the correlational structure among a number of different variables. On that point of history, however, his claim to priority as the inventor of factor analysis is a bit complicated and calls for a more detailed explication, to be given later on in this article. There seems to be no question, though, that Spearman was the first really important theorist in the study of human mental ability and that he discovered g, the general factor in the correlations among all complex mental tests.

Born in London, Spearman also died in London, committing suicide at age 82. Although Spearman's reserved and modest autobiography (1930) is totally silent about his family background and personal life, according to his most famous student, Raymond B. CATTELL (1968), Spearman came from "an English family of established status and some eminence" (p. 110). It is also on record that he was educated entirely in the most upper-class English schools. As a boy he was unusually questioning and reflective; he confesses that in his teens he felt "an excessive but secret devotion to philosophy." He also evinced an aptitude for mathematics and science, and in college he studied engineering. He never sought a career in that field, however, as philosophy remained his chief interest. Having become engrossed in the philosophy of India and desiring to go there to study, he decided he might best accomplish this purpose by joining the British military service, which had stations in India. He imagined that a military career would allow more leisure and freedom for pursuit of his self-directed scholarly interests than any other remunerative occupation, so he applied and received commission in the Royal Engineers of the British Army. Instead of being sent to India, however, he was sent to Burma. There he won a medal for distinguished service in the Burmese War of 1886. He rapidly attained the rank of major, but as his study and interest gradually turned from philoso-

phy to psychology, he began longing for a full-time career in that field. He believed that philosophy could be advanced only through the development of psychology as a natural science, and he was then eager to try his hand at furthering this objective. Later he wrote that joining the army was the mistake of his life, and that "for these wasted years I have since mourned as bitterly as ever Tiberius did for his lost legions" (1930, p. 300). Thus he was a latecomer to a career in psychology. At age 34, he resigned his commission as an army engineer and went to Leipzig University to study psychology under Wilhelm Wundt, who was the founder of experimental psychology and the pioneer of a new scientific psychology as a distinct discipline in its own right, separate from philosophy. After two years' work in Wundt's laboratory, Spearman's studies were interrupted by his call to army service during the Boer War (1899–1902), after which, then newly married, he returned to Leipzig. In 1906 he finally submitted his doctoral thesis ("Normal Illusions in Spatial Perception") to Wundt and received the doctor of philosophy degree in psychology. Spearman always regarded Wundt with great admiration and personal affection and declared that Wundt and Francis GALTON (whom Spearman knew only through reading) were the most important influences in his life. He remained in Germany for one more year to study with the noted experimental psychologists Oswald Kulpe at Wurzburg and Georg E. Muller at Göttingen.

Returning to England in 1907 at age 43, Spearman was hired as reader in experimental psychology in University College, London, in the department headed by the famous British psychologist William McDougal, who soon was impressed by Spearman's originality and productivity as a researcher. Hence, in 1911, when McDougal was offered a chair at Oxford, he recommended Spearman as his successor at University College, and Spearman was appointed Grote Professor of Mind and Logic, a position that was renamed professor of psychology in 1928. He held this position, with a leave for service on the general staff of the British army during World War I (1914–1917), until his retirement in 1932, when he was succeeded by Cyril BURT. During this most productive period of his career, Spearman received many honors in England and abroad, including election as a fellow of the Royal Society and, in the United States, membership in the National Academy of Sciences.

PSYCHOMETRIC THEORY, FACTOR ANALYSIS, AND THE DISCOVERY OF g

Early in his studies in Leipzig, Spearman decided that his aim as a researcher would be, in his words, "to connect the psychics of the laboratory with those of real life (Spearman, 1930)." While still a student in Wundt's lab, Spearman published in 1904 a lengthy and strikingly non-Wundtian article in the *American Journal of Psychology* entitled "'General Intelligence' Objectively Determined and Measured." It became one of the landmarks in the history of psychology. Spearman and his own students further explored and theoretically elaborated its main themes in a great many subsequent articles and books (see also GENERAL INTELLIGENCE).

To begin with, Spearman was attracted to Galton's concept of a *general* mental ability with biological underpinnings as a product of the evolutionary process. The notion of a general ability seemed more compelling to Spearman than the then prevailing doctrine that there are a great number of separate faculties of the mind, such as span of attention, recognition, comprehension, recall, perception, memory, and imagination—the list was virtually unlimited.

Spearman was also attracted by Galton's hypothesis that discrimination and reaction time were fundamentally related to general mental ability and hence could be used to measure it objectively. Spearman knew, however, that the use of these "brass instrument" techniques in Galton's laboratory and especially in later studies (done in 1901) in the same vein by Galton's American disciple James McKeen CATTELL (who coined the term *mental test*) and his student Clark Wissler at Columbia University failed to reveal any substantial correlations among the various Galtonian tests of discrimination and reaction time. This finding flatly contradicted Galton's idea of a general ability that should be reflected in substantial positive correlations among all of the tests. Moreover, these laboratory tests showed no appreciable correlation with the intelligence levels of Columbia College students, which had to be surmised from their course grades, as there were

no intelligence tests at that time. These two main findings, issuing from a prestigious psychological laboratory, generally cast a pall over Galton's ideas about the nature and measurement of mental ability. Spearman, however, took an especially critical look at these studies. He himself tested a number of schoolchildren with some of the Galtonian tests and found moderate correlations among the tests and between the tests and teachers' estimates of the pupils' intelligence based on their scholastic performance. This discrepancy between the correlations found in his own study and those found in previous studies demanded an explanation. Spearman's discovery of the explanation led to virtually everything else for which he is now most famous, particularly the invention of factor analysis. Up until this point, the concept of attenuation of correlations had not been recognized. The obtained correlations between any real variables are always based on fallible measures, and the errors of measurement cause attenuation (i.e., underestimation) of the magnitude of the true correlation between the variables. We see here the fundamental formulation of classical test theory, namely, that an obtained measurement, X, is analyzable into two additive components, a true score (t) and random error (e), hence $X = t + e$. It follows that the total variance of X consists of the true-score variance plus the error variance. The e of a given variable, being random, therefore cannot be correlated with the random e of another variable. Only the t components of the two variables can possibly be correlated. Spearman realized that, in evaluating the obtained correlation between variables, one must take into account the proportion of the total variance of each variable that consists of true-score variance. This proportion became known as the reliability coefficient.

Working with this formulation, Spearman invented the correction for attenuation of a correlation coefficient, which yields an estimate of the correlation between the true-score components of the correlated variables. If the obtained correlation between variables x and y is r_{xy}, it is corrected for attenuation by dividing it by the geometric mean of the reliability coefficients of x and y, that is,

$$r_{xy}/(r_{xx} \, r_{yy})^{\frac{1}{2}}.$$

It is also a fact that when there is a restriction of the range of talent in the sample of persons on whom measurements were obtained, compared with the range of talent in the general population, both the reliability and the true-score correlations between variables are diminished accordingly. The correlations obtained in Wissler's sample of Columbia College students, for example, were drastically diminished by the exceedingly low reliability coefficients of the intercorrelated measurements and by the severe restriction of the range of mental ability in the sample. When Spearman corrected the correlations for these attenuating effects, he found such substantial positive correlations among all of the variables as to lead him to suspect that Galton's notion of general ability was really correct after all. After correction for attenuation, not only were the sensory and reaction time tests themselves substantially intercorrelated, but they were substantially correlated with independent estimates of the subjects' levels of intelligence.

Spearman still needed a mathematically rigorous method for testing the hypothesis that a single general factor accounted for all of the correlations among the diverse mental tests. The method he invented was actually just an extension of his formula for the correction for attenuation. By means of this extended formula, he was able to show the correlation between a given test and whatever it had in common with two or more other tests. He termed this common source of variance the general factor and labeled it g. For example, if we know the correlations among three variables, x, y, and z, the correlation of, say, x with the general factor, g, common to the three variables is

$$r_{xg} = [(r_{xy} \, r_{xz}/r_{yz})]^{\frac{1}{2}}.$$

Similarly,

$$r_{yg} = [(r_{xy} \, r_{yz})/r_{xz}]^{\frac{1}{2}}.$$

Spearman generalized the applicability of this simple formula to the intercorrelations among any number of variables, thus:

$$r_{ag} = [(r_{ab} \, r_{ac} + r_{ab} \, r_{ad} + \ldots + r_{ax} \, r_{ay})/(r_{bc}$$
$$+ \, r_{bd} + \ldots + r_{xy})]^{\frac{1}{2}}.$$

The correlation of a variable with a factor, for example, r_{xg}, is called a factor loading. If only one factor, g, accounts for the correlations among all of the variables, then the correlation between any pair of variables, say x and y, can be expressed as the product of their factor loadings, that is, $r_{xy} = r_{xg} \, r_{yg}$.

But how could Spearman definitely prove that g is the only common factor underlying the correlations among all of the tests? Spearman invented the needed proof, which involves three features of the correlation matrix, the first two of which are inevitable if the third is met within the limits of sampling error: (1) showing all positive correlation coefficients among the tests; (2) showing that the square matrix of correlations among the tests can be arranged in a hierarchical order; and (3) showing that all the tetrad differences are zero. In a hierarchical matrix the correlation coefficients can be ordered from larger to smaller in both directions, from left to right and top to bottom of the square matrix. For example, the following is a perfectly hierarchical matrix of correlations among four different tests, labeled A to D:

Test	A	B	C	D
A	—	.56	.48	.40
B	.56	—	.42	.35
C	.48	.42	—	.30
D	.40	.35	.30	—

A tetrad is any set of four correlations in the hierarchical matrix between which two equal-length crossing diagonals can be drawn. In the above matrix, for example, there are only three possible distinct tetrads, that is,

$$\begin{array}{ccccc} .48 & .40 & .56 & .40 & .56 & .48 \\ .42 & .35 & .42 & .30 & .35 & .30 \end{array}$$

The number of distinct tetrads (N_T) in a matrix increases rapidly as the number of variables (n) increases:

$$N_T = {}_4C_n = 3n!/4!(n - 4)! \text{ [Recall that } 0! = 1.]$$

Spearman's famous tetrad difference criterion is the difference between the products of each of the cross-diagonal correlations, that is, for the first tetrad in our example, $(.48 \times .35) - (.42 \times .40) = 0$. If all of the possible tetrad differences are 0 (as in this example), it necessarily follows mathematically that the correlation matrix contains only one factor, and ipso facto, all of the correlations can be regenerated from the loadings of each of the variables on this single factor. Applying Spearman's formula for determining the g factor in each of the tests in the above matrix, we find their g loadings are A = .8, B = .7, C = .6, and D = .5. The correlation between any pair of tests, then, is simply the product of their g loadings, e.g., $r_{AB} = .8 \times .7 = .56$, $r_{AC} = .8 \times .6 = .48$, and so forth.

This all looks extremely neat and simple, but that is because this is an artificial matrix intended for didactic purposes. In reality, the tetrad differences are not all equal to 0 but at best are only distributed symmetrically around 0. This would be expected, however, because of the sampling error in correlations obtained from real data. Spearman worked out a formula for the probable error of the mean tetrad differences that could be calculated quite reliably, as the total number of distinct tetrads even in a relatively small matrix is very large. (With 10 tests there are 630 tetrads.) He obtained the frequency distributions of the tetrad differences for many correlation matrices of diverse mental tests and showed that the distributions, in relation to their probable errors, deviated from 0 no more than would be statistically expected by chance, given the sampling error of the correlations in a given matrix. Hence Spearman argued that all of the correlations between different tests was due to one general factor (g) common to all of the tests. The proportion of g variance in a given test is simply the square of its g loading. The square root of the difference between the test's reliability and its squared g loading Spearman termed the test's specificity, or s. The s^2 of a given test is the proportion of its total variance that is specific to that particular test. A test's s, in other words, is what it does not have in common (besides measurement error) with any other test that was entered into the factor-analyzed correlation matrix. Thus, according to Spearman's original theory, the true score (X_t) on each and every distinct test of cognitive ability represents a composite of a general factor (g) common to all tests and a specific factor (s) that is unique to the particular test, $X_t = g + s$. This formulation is Spearman's famous TWO-FACTOR THEORY.

The two-factor theory, however, was destined to be short-lived. Other investigators soon came up with larger collections of tests whose intercorrelations, even though all positive, could not all be arranged hierarchically and hence could not conform to the so-called vanishing tetrads criterion for a single common factor. Spearman at first argued that certain groups of tests that were responsible for breaking the hierarchy were too similar to one another (e.g., vocabulary, similarities, and verbal analogies) to be regarded as truly distinctive tests, and they therefore had "overlapping" (i.e., intercorrelated) specificities. (Of course, by the definition of specificity, to speak of correlated or "overlapping" specificities is self-contradicting.) To restore the hierarchical matrix, Spearman could either eliminate all but one of the similar tests or combine their scores as if they were a single test. Then his "vanishing tetrads" rule again showed there was only a single factor, g. As argumentation based on evidence mounted against Spearman's overly simple two-factor theory, however, he finally admitted the existence of other factors besides g, factors common to only certain groups of tests that are relatively similar in the type of knowledge or skill they call for—categories of tests such as verbal, spatial, and numerical. These factors that are common to only certain groups of rather similar tests Spearman therefore called group factors. Regardless of whatever groups factors could be found in any correlation matrix, however, the g and s remained ubiquitous in all batteries of cognitive tests.

Spearman's theory of mental ability thus evolved finally to include various group factors in addition to g and s. This concession momentarily posed quite a problem, though, because the method Spearman had invented for extracting the g factor from a correlation matrix would work only on a hierarchical matrix that would meet the vanishing tetrad criterion (within the limits of sampling error). It was powerless, mathematically, for dealing with a matrix containing other factors in addition to g and s. (This point is well explicated by Thurstone, 1947, pp. 279–281.) To apply his method of factor analysis, Spearman was forced to make his matrix hierarchical, either by combining any similar tests that, if treated individually, would create a group factor, or by eliminating any tests that broke the hierarchy. This was a most unsatisfactory state of affairs, and some new method was needed for dealing with multiple-factor matrices. The outcome of this situation has fueled disputes over Spearman's priority as the inventor of factor analysis.

Completely unknown to Spearman at the time, and three years prior to the publication of his classic 1904 paper that first described his two-factor theory based on his relatively simple factor-analytic formulas, the eminent mathematician and statistician Karl Pearson had published an obscure paper entitled "On lines and planes of closest fit to systems of points in space." What he had invented here was, in fact, what we know today as principal components analysis, for which Harold Hotelling, in 1933, provided a practicable computational algorithm. It turned out to be the preferred method that has since been used in many different scientific fields for extracting orthogonal components (i.e., uncorrelated "factors") from a correlation matrix of multiple "factors." The first principal component extracted by the computational procedure is necessarily the largest component, in terms of the proportion of total variance accounted for, and is considered the general factor in the particular matrix. But unlike Spearman's method, the number of orthogonal components that can be extracted from a correlation matrix by the method of principal components is limited only by the number of experimentally independent variables. As early as 1909, however, Cyril BURT had proposed a simplified but inexact method called "simple summation" for approximating the results obtained by Pearson's mathematically exact but much more complex formulation. In 1931 Louis L. THURSTONE put forth the same approximate formulation as Burt's, naming it the "centroid" method, which was used extensively by Thurstone and by many other researchers in the empirical development of the multiple-factor theory of mental ability. The upshot is that these methods, as well as principal components analysis and the various modern forms of factor analysis (see Harman, 1976), completely superseded Spearman's much more limited method. All of the modern methods of factor analysis are essentially mathematical derivatives and variations, not of Spearman's formulation of 1904, but of Pearson's formulation of 1901. Spearman's formulation is merely a special case of Pearson's more general formulation. Hence there is some ambiguity regarding Spearman's priority as the inventor of factor analysis, especially if we consider only the methods of exploratory factor analysis in use

in the late twentieth century. There is no argument, however, that Spearman was the first to introduce the essential idea of factor analysis to the study of ability, and later to personality. Also, Spearman's momentous discovery of g in all cognitive tests that involve any kind of information processing has been firmly established by innumerable studies in the half-century since he died. Spearman's conception of the nature of g, however, is another story and involves his noegenetic laws of cognition.

Before getting to that, however, mention should be made of two other quantitative methods invented by Spearman that are well known to modern psychometricians and statisticians: (1) the Spearman-Brown prophecy formula, which shows the mathematical relation between the length (e.g., number of items) of a test and the test's reliability coefficient, and (2) the Spearman rank-order correlation coefficient, r_s, which is the most widely used nonparametric alternative to r, the parametric Pearsonian correlation. These formulations can be found in most textbooks of psychological measurement and of statistics.

NOEGENETIC LAWS OF COGNITION AND THE NATURE OF INTELLIGENCE

Spearman's judgment that future historians of psychology would consider his noegenetic laws his most important contribution seems to have been wrong. These "laws" have been largely forgotten compared to his other main achievements.

In Spearman's (1923) theory of mental ability, the g factor is most clearly manifested in tests to the extent that successful performance represents an example of noegenesis. By noegenesis Spearman means the generation, or creation, of new relationships, concepts, or mental content, as contrasted with conditioning, rote learning, and memory, or the reproduction (rather than production) of mental contents. Noegenesis, he held, involves three self-evident processes of cognition, which he termed the noegenetic laws (or principles). The three qualitative principles are as follows: (1) *The apprehension of experience:* "Any lived experience tends to evoke immediately a knowing of its characters and experiencer." (Spearman points out that "immediately" in this context has no temporal connotation but only means the absence of any mediating process.) (2) *The eduction of relations:* "The mentally presenting of any two or more characters (simple or complex) tends to evoke immediately a knowing of relation between them." (3) *The eduction of correlates:* "The presenting of any character together with any relation tends to evoke immediately a knowing of the correlative character." The best tests of *g* should be those that best elicit the eduction of relations and *correlates,* or, in other words, that involve some form of inductive or deductive reasoning.

In addition to these qualitative principles, there are five quantitative principles, which determine individual differences in the manifestations of the three qualitative principles: (1) *Mental energy,* which is the basis of individual differences in *g.* This "energy" (or "power"), whatever its physiological basis (about which Spearman remained agnostic), serves in common the whole cortex or even the whole nervous system. Group factors and specificity reflect the action of particular groups of neurons (analogized as "engines") that partake of the common supply of "neural energy." Any mental task therefore reflects both the potential "energy" and the efficiency of the particular "engine" involved in the performance of the given task. The existence of individual differences in "potential energy" and in the efficiency of specific "engines" is reflected in the factor structure of a battery of diverse mental tests as consisting of a general factor, two or more group factors, and as many specific factors as the number of tests in the battery. (2) *Retentivity:* "The occurrence of any cognitive event produces a tendency for it to occur afterwards." (3) *Fatigue:* "The occurrence of any cognitive event produces a tendency opposed to its occurring afterwards." (4) *Conative control:* "The intensity of cognition can be controlled by conation" (i.e., drive, motivation, will). (5) *Primordial potencies:* "Every manifestation of the preceding four quantitative principles is superposed upon, as its ultimate basis, certain primordial but variable individual potencies." It should be emphasized that a book-length discussion (Spearman, 1923) of these principles reveals them to be much more profound intellectually than is suggested by this very brief summary.

Regarded today as perhaps the most important principle enunciated by Spearman, but not included with his noegenetic laws because it is a strictly psychometric principle, is the principle of *the indifference of the indicator.* This refers to the fact that variation in the particular form or content of the items that enter into a test of intelligence is totally irrelevant so long as there is a large number and a wide diversity of items, provided all of them are to some extent *g* loaded. In other words, the total scores derived from *any* sizable collection of diverse test items that to some degree involve the noegenetic principles will all measure one and the same *g.* Hence an almost unlimited variety of so-called intelligence tests will all rank individuals in much the same order. (Spearman rather reluctantly and tentatively equated *g* with "intelligence," a word he seldom used, and even then he usually put it in quotes.) However, Spearman noted one crucial proviso for the validity of his principle of the indifference of the indicator of *g,* namely, that for a test item to be appropriate, its fundaments must be readily familiar to the subjects being tested. He defined fundaments simply as the things between which relations are to be educed. (E.g., *table* and *chair* are fundaments; an educed relation is *furniture.*) Analogy problems exemplify the eduction of relations and correlates, for example, "boy:man::girl:_____.

In Spearman's greatest work, *The Abilities of Man* (1927), he makes clear the important distinction between objectively identifying *g,* which he had accomplished, and explaining the nature, or cause of *g,* which he had not accomplished. He wrote,

> That which this magnitude [*g*] measures has not been defined by declaring what it is like, but only by pointing out where it can be found. It consists in just that constituent—whatever it may be—which is common to all the abilities inter-connected by the tetrad equation. This way of indicating what *g* means is just as definite as when one indicates a card by staking on the back of it without looking at its face. Such a defining of *g* by site rather than by nature is just what was meant originally when its determination was said to be only "objective." [1927, pp. 75–76]

Spearman's factor analysis of more than 100 extremely diverse kinds of tests (Spearman & Jones, 1950) confirmed his conclusion that the "site" of the largest *g* loadings is in those tests that most completely involve the eduction of relations and correlates and that also have the quality of "abstractness," that is, tests of abstract reasoning. All kinds of diverse tests, however, showed positive, albeit often modest, g loadings, such as pitch discrimination, perceptual speed, and reaction time. Spearman's conclusions in this regard have been amply confirmed by modern research (Jensen, 1987). Although Spearman proposed a number of hypotheses concerning the possible physiological basis of g, he did no empirical research on that aspect of the problem. He hoped, however, that the nature of g would eventually be explained in terms of brain physiology—an eventuality, he wrote, "whereby physiology will achieve the greatest of all its triumphs" (1927, p. 407).

BIBLIOGRAPHY

BURT, C. (1909). Experimental tests of general intelligence. *British Journal of Psychology, 3*, 94–177.

BURT, C. (1940). *The factors of the mind.* London: University of London Press.

CATTELL, R. B. (1968). C. E. Spearman. In D. L. Sills (Ed.), *International Encyclopedia of the Social Sciences* (Vol. 15, pp. 108–111). New York: Macmillan.

HARMAN, H. H. (1976). *Modern factor analysis.* (3rd ed., rev.). Chicago: University of Chicago Press.

JENSEN, A. R. (1987). The *g* beyond factor analysis. In J. C. Conoley, J. A. Glover, & R. R. Ronning (Eds.), *The influence of cognitive psychology on testing and measurement.* Hillsdale, NJ: Erlbaum.

PEARSON, K. (1901). On lines and planes of closest fit to systems of points in space. *Philosophical Magazine, 6*, 559–572.

SPEARMAN, C. E. (1904). 'General intelligence' objectively determined and measured. *American Journal of Psychology, 15*, 201–293.

SPEARMAN, C. E. (1923). *The nature of 'intelligence' and the principles of cognition.* (2nd ed.). London: Macmillan. (1923 edition reprinted in 1973 by Arno Press, New York).

SPEARMAN, C. (1927). *The abilities of man.* London: Macmillan (1932 edition reprinted in 1970 by AMS Press, New York).

SPEARMAN, C. (1930). Autobiography. In C. Murchison (Ed.), *A history of psychology in autobiography* (Vol. 1, pp. 299–333). Worcester, MA: Clark University Press. (Reprinted 1961 by Russell & Russell, New York.)

SPEARMAN, C., & JONES, L. W. (1950). *Human ability.* London: Macmillan.

THURSTONE, L. L. (1931). Multiple factor analysis. *Psychological Review, 38*, 406–427.

THURSTONE, L. L. (1947). *Multiple-factor analysis.* Chicago: University of Chicago Press.

ARTHUR R. JENSEN

SPEEDINESS   A relationship between intelligence and mental quickness is reflected in our culture and language. Early theories about the structure of intelligence by Edward THORNDIKE and by Louis THURSTONE included speed as an independent dimension, and most abilities tests reward faster performance. Speed in a wide variety of performances is positively related to a wide variety of cognitive abilities, to age changes, and to physiological correlates (Birren, Woods, & Williams, 1980). Two perspectives have emerged about how mental speed relates to intelligence. *Speediness* has been identified as a common factor in test performance and defined as quickness in undemanding or overlearned tasks (Horn, 1968). Conceptualized by John Horn and Raymond Cattell as more cognitive than sensory, speediness is separable from the major intellectual dimensions responsible for perception, reasoning, problem solving, and memory. A different view is that speed of information processing is fundamental to intelligence (Eysenck, 1967). This approach focuses on correlations between "chronometric" procedures like reaction time and intelligence quotient (IQ). Mike Anderson (1992) has extended Hans EYSENCK's position, integrating GENERAL INTELLIGENCE and specific abilities within a speed of processing mechanism, to distinguish these from noncognitive modules—and thereby arguing that speed provides a sufficient explanation for intelligence.

PSYCHOMETRIC SPEEDINESS

Horn and Cattell have defined speediness as a second-order factor, reliant on but broader than primary perceptual speed. Also termed "general cognitive speed" (Cattell, 1971) or "general perceptual speed" (Hakstian & Cattell, 1978), speediness is identified within the Horn-Cattell theory as Gs. At least before old age, it is relatively independent from fluid intelligence (Gf) and crystallized intelligence (Gc) and from the other intelligences identified in terms of perceptual and memory performance. However, *Gs* has not been as reliably identified as these other abilities.

John Horn and Gary Donaldson (1980) questioned whether speed functions besides *Gs* are required to describe speediness in all situations. For example, different processes may be involved in "speed" tests (situations so easy that only speed differentiates individuals) than in "power" tests, for which accuracy is critical. Speediness in easy situations may be more a question of motivation and temperament (in the sense of being characteristically alert) than of thinking quickly. When accuracy is required, however, a different kind of speediness reflecting more complex decisions about strategies to apply or when to abandon a course of action may be involved. Constructs such as "decision speed" and "quit decision speed" are conceptualized as metacognitive organizations, such as the general, higher order "intellectual speed" (Furneaux, 1960), included by Cattell (1971) as a contributor to *Gf.* Thus, Horn and Cattell view mental speed as multifaceted, with primary forms defined by different test situations and with "speediness" referring to quick responding where probability of error is extremely low. They concede, however, that executive mental speed may contribute to intelligent performance.

SPEED OF INFORMATION PROCESSING

Eysenck (1967) proposed a two-part variable (speed and power) reflecting biological efficiency and distinguishable from personality variables as the major determinant of intellectual differences. Eysenck (1987) distinguished a power–speed relationship; power equals capacity to process information reliably, resulting in quicker transmission time. His theory is consistent with evidence that those who produce correct test solutions more quickly do tend to get more items correct than do slower performers, irrespective of time constraints; but this theory is contradicted by other findings. Thus, speed and accuracy can be relatively independent (Egan, 1979) and higher IQ individuals have not always been found to be quicker than those less able (Horn, Donaldson, & Engstrom, 1981).

Following Donald O. HEBB's distinction between Intelligence A and Intelligence B, Eysenck (1987) distin-

guished the biological basis to intelligence from the common-sense conception formulated from everyday observations. The latter focuses more on the complex end-products of problem solving and reasoning than on underlying brain functions, which Eysenck argues should be the focus of research. Although Cattell and Horn also distinguish physiological and acculturated forms of intelligence, they give speed a different emphasis, stemming from a different conceptualization about the biological substrate underpinning intelligent behavior. Horn (1968) described different *Anlage* functions (i.e., fundamental, central neural capacities for perception and memory) from which intelligence develops, with primary speed functions located in more peripheral neural organizations.

Reaction Times. Despite failed attempts based on Francis GALTON's conjecture about speed of reaction reflecting intelligence, interest in this possibility remains active (Jensen, 1982; Vernon, 1987). Thus far no widespread agreement has been secured about the nature of REACTION TIME, although a range of tasks of varying complexity has been devised to estimate the latency of processes like attention, apprehension, perceptual encoding, short-term memory scanning, lexical access, and response execution. Individual differences in these tasks have then been related to measures of cognitive abilities. Although reaction times are frequently considered as "elementary cognitive tasks" (Carroll, 1983), there is debate about the validity of this label (Jensen, 1985, pp. 219–258). Most researchers agree that simple reaction time tasks have low, if not negligible, knowledge requirements. Choice reaction time measures, however—in which one must consider a number of alternatives and choose just one—generally have been found to be positively related to measures of abilities that are regarded as indicative of intelligence. It is this characteristic that proponents of this "cognitive-correlates" approach see as most promising. That choice reaction time could explain performance on RAVEN PROGRESSIVE MATRICES, given the different knowledge bases to these two situations, is widely regarded as counterintuitive.

Robert Sternberg (1977), however, has criticized the cognitive-correlates approach as insufficiently theoretically focused, instead proposing an analysis of reaction time to infer elementary cognitive "components" underpinning solutions in analogical reasoning test items. Reservations about the generalizability of this method notwithstanding (Kline, 1991), Sternberg found that higher IQ subjects were slower than less able subjects to encode but quicker to complete the remaining three component processes involved in reasoning to a correct solution. This has been supported by demonstrations that executive strategies determining attention, transformation, storage, and retrieval can influence latency of responding (Marr & Sternberg, 1987), thereby shifting the focus of explanation away from speed to higher cognitive functions.

The cognitive-correlates perspective is that the correlation between reaction time and accuracy in analogical reasoning simply reflects the widely observed speed–power correlation in complex situations. Arthur Jensen (1982, 1987) has therefore focused on correlations between choice reaction time and IQ. His theory is that, because at any time the brain has a limited capacity for processing information, the quality of mental functioning is determined by the speed of operation. He has adapted reaction time tasks assumed to measure speed of various psychological processes, the most used apparatus separating choice responding time into two components: (1) reaction time between stimulus onset and the subject's releasing of a "home" key on the mechanism used in the experiment, and (2) movement time between the subject releasing the home key and pressing another key adjacent to the stimulus. The basic finding is that as the amount of information that must be processed (in order to respond) increases, the relationship to intelligence increases. (Information increases logarithmically as number of choices increases linearly, i.e., "Hick's Law"). Substantial correlations have been found between reaction time–movement time variables and IQ (Jensen, 1985; Smith & Stanley, 1987).

Although more successful than previous cognitive-correlates research, Jensen's results have proved difficult to interpret. Doubts have been expressed about individual conformity to Hick's Law (Barrett, Eysenck, & Lucking, 1986), practice and order effects, and attentional artifacts (Longstreth, 1984). Furthermore, there is doubt that these procedures can delineate specific underlying processes, because multiple regression has defined different optimal sets of chronometric pre-

dictors of IQ across studies and some results have been antithetical (e.g., significant movement time–IQ correlations). Finally, compared with the more common reaction time method (separate fingers on separate response keys specified by the stimulus array), Jensen's home-key procedure is not well suited to analysis of "speed-accuracy trade-off" (Pachella, 1974), and this constitutes a major limitation to interpretation.

Speed–Accuracy Trade-Off. Reaction time is always influenced to some degree by experiential and motivational factors, reflecting more than just the speed of processing. Subjects learn increasingly effective strategies (Salthouse & Somberg, 1982), continuing to improve even after sustained practice. Subjects do voluntarily monitor and control criterial factors, such as attention, compliance with instructions, and caution, increasing speed at a cost of increasing errors, or preserving accuracy by slowing responding (Rabbitt, 1981). These changes occur within a speed band close to optimum—defined as the point on the speed–accuracy operating function where minimum reaction time is balanced by perfect accuracy (Pachella, 1974). Within this band, relatively large changes in speed are accompanied by barely discernible changes in accuracy.

The speed–accuracy trade-off in reaction time is similar to the distinction that Horn (1968) has drawn between speediness and "carefulness," although analysis of correct and incorrect test scores suggests that these are not necessarily poles in a single dimension. In speed tests, number of correct responses correlates positively with number of incorrect, consistent with a speed–accuracy trade-off, because quicker responding improves performance despite the cost of increased errors. In power tests (in which all persons answer all questions), correct and incorrect responses are negatively correlated, higher correct scores being accompanied by fewer incorrect responses. On this basis Horn argued that speediness reflects temperament or strategy more than intellectual capability as such; similarly, carefulness reflects an executive strategy to avoid errors. However, reaction time reflects both speed and power. Speed and accuracy tend to be negatively correlated within subjects, as suggested by the term "trade-off," but positively between-subjects across a wide band of IQ scores, consistent with the usual association between speed and power. Because both negative and positive correlations may exist simultaneously, it will readily be appreciated how an overall zero correlation can be found.

Returning to Jensen's results, reaction time research attempts to minimize confounding from experiential and motivational variables by aiming for small, constant levels of error (e.g., 2–3 percent), thereby confirming that subjects are responding very near to optimum speed. Unless errors are made, an experimenter cannot be confident that subjects have complied with instructions to respond as quickly as possible. The home-key procedure is problematic in this regard, producing near-zero error rates, perhaps because responses initially planned incorrectly can be corrected during movement from the home key. Slower reaction times and movement times may also reflect overcaution or different standards about the relevance of quick actions, so that group differences in reaction time may reflect noncognitive factors rather than IQ differences (see Jensen, 1985).

Inspection Time. Inspection time measures threshold discrimination in an easy task using a backward masking procedure. Typically, the exposure durations of a target figure consisting of two vertical lines of markedly different lengths are controlled by using a masking pattern of two equal-length lines. These follow after the target and overlie it, thereby obliterating it. The subject reports whether the shorter line is located to the left or to the right. Inspection time is effectively defined as the minimum duration required for reliably high accuracy (Nettelbeck, 1987). Although conceived as estimating perceptual encoding speed, debate continues about the processes tapped by inspection time but, because the method stresses accuracy without speed, it does reduce the impact of criterial aspects of performance (e.g., caution) under the subject's control.

Inspection time correlates around −.5 with IQ (Kranzler & Jensen, 1989) but it is not clear what aspects of intellectual functioning account for this. Among children, attentional control is an important determinant of the inspection time–IQ correlation but this has not been found for adults, where more general perceptual-spatial capacities seem involved. Ted Nettelbeck and Patrick Rabbitt (1992) found that among

elderly persons inspection time (and reaction time and coding substitution) parsimoniously accounted for several age-related differences in Gf tasks, although this did not hold for learning and recall. These results provided limited support for the proposition that decline in fluid cognition during old age is the consequence of slowed information processing (Salthouse, 1985), although this may reflect executive capacities controlling concentration and attention rather than speediness (Horn, 1987).

CONCLUSIONS

At least among the elderly, reaction time, inspection time, and coding substitution share a significant common speed component (Nettelbeck & Rabbitt, 1992), but the nature of this is unknown. Reaction time may additionally reflect executive control more than the others, these seeming closer to Horn's concept of speediness. Conceivably, speediness could represent an Anlage function, some neuronal capacity common to all levels of mental activity, functioning as a threshold variable necessary to the development of viable intellectual qualities. However, speediness does not necessarily represent the same structures across the life-span; for example, marked slowing in old age could result from deterioration of neural connectivity, whereas improving speed during childhood might depend more on changing neural activation thresholds.

Chronometric research reinforces the view that, although speed differences contribute to variance in intelligence, they do not provide a sufficient explanation for IQ differences. There are four reasons for this. First, high-IQ individuals can be slower than those who are less able, where this strategy results in improved overall effectiveness. Second, even during old age, when processing speed assumes more importance, some aspects of cognitive aging are speed-independent. Third, average childhood reaction time and inspection time does not improve beyond early adolescence, whereas intelligent behavior clearly does. Fourth, instances of below-average persons exhibiting short inspection times contradict speed as a sufficient explanation (Wilson et al., 1992).

BIBLIOGRAPHY

ANDERSON, M. (1992). *Intelligence and development: A cognitive theory.* Oxford: Basil Blackwell.

BARRETT, P., EYSENCK, H. J., & LUCKING, S. (1986). Reaction time and intelligence: A replicated study. *Intelligence, 10,* 9–40.

BIRREN, J. E., WOODS, A., & WILLIAMS, M. V. (1980). Behavioral slowing with age. In L. W. Poon (Ed.), *Aging in the 1980's* (pp. 293–308). Washington, DC: American Psychological Association.

CARROLL, J. B. (1983). Individual differences in cognitive abilities. In S. H. Irvine & J. W. Berry (Eds.), *Human assessment and cultural factors* (pp. 213–235). New York: Plenum.

CATTELL, R. B. (1971). *Abilities: Their structure, growth, and action.* Boston: Houghton-Mifflin.

EGAN, D. E. (1979). Testing based on understanding: Implications for studies of spatial ability. *Intelligence, 3,* 1–15.

EYSENCK, H. J. (1967). Intelligence assessment: A theoretical and experimental approach. *British Journal of Educational Psychology, 37,* 81–98.

EYSENCK, H. J. (1987). Speed of information processing, reaction time, and the theory of intelligence. In P. A. Vernon (Ed.), *Speed of information-processing and intelligence* (pp. 21–67). Norwood, NJ: Ablex.

FURNEAUX, W. D. (1960). Intellectual abilities and problem solving behaviour. In H. J. Eysenck (Ed.), *Handbook of abnormal psychology* (pp. 167–192). London: Pitman.

HAKSTIAN, A. R., & CATTELL, R. B. (1978). Higher stratum ability structures on a basis of twenty primary abilities. *Journal of Educational Psychology, 70,* 657–669.

HORN, J. L. (1968). Organization of abilities and the development of intelligence. *Psychological Review, 75,* 242–259.

HORN, J. L. (1987). A context for understanding information processing studies of human abilities. In P. A. Vernon (Ed.), *Speed of information-processing and intelligence* (pp. 201–238). Norwood, NJ: Ablex.

HORN, J. L., & DONALDSON, G. (1980). Cognitive development in adulthood. In O. G. Brim & J. Kagan (Eds.), *Constancy and change in human development* (pp. 445–529). Cambridge, MA: Harvard University Press.

HORN, J. L., DONALDSON, G., & ENGSTROM, R. (1981). Apprehension, memory, and fluid intelligence decline in adulthood. *Research on Aging, 3,* 33–84.

JENSEN, A. R. (1982). Reaction time and psychometric *g.* In H. J. Eysenck (Ed.), *A model for intelligence* (pp. 93–132). New York: Springer-Verlag.

JENSEN, A. R. (1985). The nature of the black–white difference on various psychometric tests: Spearman's hypothesis. *Behavioral and Brain Sciences, 8,* 193–263.

JENSEN, A. R. (1987). Individual differences in the Hick paradigm. In P. A. Vernon (Ed.), *Speed of information-processing and intelligence* (pp. 101–175). Norwood, NJ: Ablex.

KLINE, P. (1991). *Intelligence: The psychometric view.* London: Routledge.

KRANZLER, J. H., & JENSEN, A. R. (1989). Inspection time and intelligence: A meta-analysis. *Intelligence, 13,* 329–347.

LONGSTRETH, L. E. (1984). Jensen's reaction-time investigations of intelligence: A critique. *Intelligence, 8,* 139–160.

MARR, D. B., & STERNBERG, R. J. (1987). The role of mental speed in intelligence: A triarchic perspective. In P. A. Vernon (Ed.), *Speed of information-processing and intelligence* (pp. 271–294). Norwood, NJ: Ablex.

NETTELBECK, T. (1987). Inspection time and intelligence. In P. A. Vernon (Ed.), *Speed of information-processing and intelligence* (pp. 295–346). Norwood, NJ: Ablex.

NETTELBECK, T., & RABBITT, P. M. A. (1992). Aging, cognitive performance, and mental speed. *Intelligence, 16,* 189–205.

PACHELLA, R. G. (1974). The interpretation of reaction time in information-processing research. In B. Kantowitz (Ed.), *Human information processing: Tutorials in performance and cognition* (pp. 41–82). Hillsdale, NJ: Erlbaum.

RABBITT, P. M. A. (1981). Sequential reactions. In D. H. Holding (Ed.), *Human skills* (pp. 153–175). London: Wiley.

SALTHOUSE, T. A. (1985). *A theory of cognitive aging.* Amsterdam: North-Holland.

SALTHOUSE, T. A., & SOMBERG, B. L. (1982). Skilled performance: Effects of adult age and experience on elementary processes. *Journal of Experimental Psychology: General, 111,* 176–207.

SMITH, G. A., & STANLEY, G. (1987). Comparing subtest profiles of *g* loadings and correlations with RT measures. *Intelligence, 11,* 291–298.

STERNBERG, R. J. (1977). *Intelligence, information processing, and analogical reasoning: The componential analysis of human abilities.* Hillsdale, NJ: Erlbaum.

VERNON, P. A. (1987). *Speed of information-processing and intelligence.* Norwood, NJ: Ablex.

WILSON, C., NETTELBECK, T., TURNBULL, C., & YOUNG, R.

(1992). IT, IQ and age: A comparison of developmental functions. *British Journal of Developmental Psychology, 10,* 179–188.

TED NETTELBECK

STABILITY OF INTELLIGENCE The question of the stability of intelligence is important for several reasons. Intelligence tests may be used to predict later educational or vocational success or to examine the relative contributions of heredity versus environment. Moreover, intellectual functioning is a core parameter by which to ascertain intraindividual change as well as the impact of cognitive interventions in younger or older persons.

Psychologists and educators have placed a great deal of emphasis on reliability as a prerequisite for validity, but the stability of intelligence is difficult to study for several reasons. First, the nature of intelligence may itself change over time because of maturational reasons or the interaction of the individual with a changing environmental context. This contrasts with the notion that intelligence is a fixed quality that people carry with them over their lives. If different measures are required to assess qualitatively distinct types of intelligence, then the stability of these measures is likely to vary. Second, as the time interval between assessments is increased, test–retest correlations generally decrease for both infants and young children, with increases noted after age 2. Last, the notion of stability itself is varied. How stability is defined in part dictates whether one sees intelligence as changing or not across the life span. Several types of stability have been identified (Caspi & Bem, 1990; Humphreys, 1989): (1) *Absolute stability* is defined as constancy in the quantity (level) of an attribute or behavior over time and is typically examined in longitudinal comparisons of group averages over time. (2) *Differential stability* is the consistency of individual differences over time. (3) *Ipsative stability* is consistency across time in a particular individual for a given attribute or behavior. (4) *Coherence* is defined as consistency over time of an underlying intellectual construct or attribute, despite changes in observable behaviors. Changes (or lack of them) over time in the complexity of intelligence (i.e.,

in its factor structure) are referred to as forming a developmental simplex. In research on intelligence, most studies deal with absolute stability, differential stability, and coherence.

INFANCY THROUGH ADOLESCENCE

In early infancy, test–retest correlations, indexing the stability of individual differences, have been generally fairly low, ranging from −.24 to .44, but for older infants and young children, they are in the range of .60 to .85 or higher (Hynd & Semrud-Clikeman, 1993). Findings from longitudinal studies such as the Berkeley Growth Study suggest that the correlation between intelligence quotient (IQ) at early school ages and in late adolescence is about .80 (Jones & Bayley, 1941). Yet, a great deal of ipsative instability (± 10 IQ points) was observed for nearly half the sample. In the Fels Longitudinal Study, the correlation between IQs taken at ages 3 and 4 was .83, but dropped to .46 between ages 3 and 12. In this case as well, considerable ipsative instability (± 40 IQ points) was observed for some persons between the ages of 2 and 17 (McCall, Appelbaum, & Hogarty, 1973; Sontag, Baker, & Nelson, 1958). It may be that the essential sensorimotor nature of intelligence in infancy versus its more verbal-memorial nature later in life, the unreliability of global measures of intelligence (IQ) as an estimate of a complex construct, or the extent to which intelligence is genetic (Brody, 1992) are each responsible for such instability.

Other factors mediating such instability, as well as estimates of absolute stability (which are generally positive with age, based on the longitudinal findings cited above), are the presence of family stress, such as divorce or serious illness; developmental shifts in the child's motivation or personality attributes; or variations in parental style, such as permissive versus authoritarian (Honzik, Macfarlane, & Allen, 1948).

Such instability undermines the predictive validity of IQ scores, particularly with respect to scores derived from scales administered to infants. Measures of habituation (response to novelty over time), attentional capacity, and task persistence may be better predictors of later intellectual development to the extent that they influence the ability to encode and process information. With the exception of later educational achievement and job performance, the predictive validity of most measures of IQ is relatively poor.

CROSS-SECTIONAL STUDIES OF ADULT INTELLIGENCE

Available data quite clearly indicate that in adulthood intelligence is best considered as multidimensional. Consequently, IQ is not an adequate or accurate estimate of adult intelligence.

Among the earliest studies of the effects across age on intellectual functioning that targeted absolute stability are those cross-sectional studies by C. C. Miles and W. R. Miles (1932) and H. E. Jones and H. S. Conrad (1933), where noticeable declines in IQ with increasing age (10 and older) were obtained. J. Botwinick (1967, 1984) noted the pervasiveness of this assumed decline with age in his discussion of the "age credit" built in as a correction to the definition of IQ. Later cross-sectional studies (Droppelt & Wallace, 1955) also found overall Wechsler Adult Intelligence Scale (WAIS) performance with increased age (relative to the reference group of those 20–34 years old as a standard) to peak between ages 20 and 34 and to decline slowly until about age 60, with more severe declines afterward.

Botwinick (1984) noted that individual differences in intelligence may outweigh such age-related differences, particularly for older persons, accounting for the relatively low correlations between age and intelligence. Such variability affects estimates of differential stability, but such estimates are curiously underemphasized in the aging literature, which has tended to focus on absolute stability and coherence.

On the basis of WAIS and Wechsler-Bellevue cross-sectional standardization data (Matarazzo, 1972), a "classic aging pattern" of intelligence is found: Both verbal and performance subtests decline with age (after about age 16), but the decrement for performance is a great deal more severe. This finding, as noted by Botwinick (1984), has been replicated in at least nine other major studies. With the Stanford-Binet, the cross-sectional standardization data obtained by Lewis TERMAN have yielded similar results (Kausler, 1991).

Likewise, using a cross-sectional design, D. Papalia and her associates (Hooper, Fitzgerald, & Papalia,

1971; Papalia, 1972; Papalia & Bielby, 1974) and J. N. Hornblum and W. F. Overton (1976) all reported decrements in Piagetian conservation tasks with increasing chronological age, arguing that the decline in conservation performance in old age is paralleled by the observed decrement in fluid abilities (Horn & Cattell, 1966, 1967), each being relatively unaffected by formal schooling, culture, or specific life experiences. In contrast, it may be that older adults' thinking is of a quality different from that of younger adults, causing the former to redefine the Piagetian tasks put to them. Consequently, the hypothesis of a new stage of intellectual development termed "postformal reasoning" has emerged. This stage has a relative quality to it, being highly dependent on the immediate context (Rybash, Hoyer, & Roadin, 1986).

K. W. Schaie (1977–1978, 1979) advanced a stage theory of adult intellectual development, wherein intelligence in childhood and adolescence is best seen in terms of acquisition, as skills and abilities are being acquired. During young adulthood, in the stage of achieving, these skills are directed to the creative application to, and solution of, real-life problems. In middle age occurs the responsible stage, wherein skills are applied to the management of "increasingly complex environmental demands" (Schaie, 1979, p. 109) varying with individual and historical change. Coinciding with the responsible stage is, Schaie suggests, an executive stage, which more specifically targets the use of skills to deal with "systems transcending the nuclear family or self-confined job responsibility." The last stage, the reintegrative, is a highly personal, pragmatic one that in many respects bears little resemblance to the previous stages. In earlier stages, issues such as school- or job-related achievement, occupational responsibilities, or active raising of one's family were important. In the reintegrative stage, one's intellect may instead be applied to the solution of more personally meaningful intellectual tasks (Schaie, 1978; Scheidt, 1981).

LONGITUDINAL STUDIES OF ADULT INTELLIGENCE

In the case of longitudinal research, most studies have failed to support an age-related decrement in intellectual performance, generally finding increases up to a point, followed by a leveling-off thereafter (Dearborn & Rothney, 1963). W. A. Owens (1966) found gains in Army Alpha total scores with age, up to approximately age 40 or 50. Schaie's 28-year longitudinal data suggest that there is a gain in intellectual abilities through one's 40s, followed by relative stability for most skills through one's 50s and early 60s; average losses become significant for most abilities after age 60. Such declines are greater for persons with significant health difficulties (e.g., cardiovascular illness), where performance is speeded, for those who are poorly educated, and for those who live in intellectually depriving environments (Schaie, 1979, 1990). Moreover, there are vast individual differences in the extent of decline in abilities after the age of 60, and global loss of all types of abilities is rare, based on Schaie's 28-year longitudinal analyses (Schaie, 1990). Less than one-third experience decrement until age 74, and only 30–40 percent experience significant losses in intellectual skills by age 81 (Schaie, 1990). Though many individuals "selectively optimize" (Baltes, 1987) certain skills in familiar, supportive situations after age 80, the reduction in intellectual abilities becomes most apparent into one's 80s and 90s (Schaie, 1990).

Other longitudinal investigations (e.g., Cunningham & Owens, 1983; Palmore et al., 1985; Shock et al., 1984) yield similarly positive data on adult developmental change in intelligence. In contrast, Brody (1992) argued that when controls for independent versus dependent samples are made, longitudinal findings suggest progressive intellectual decline with age during the adult years.

In most cases, depending on the interaction of the sociocultural environment (whether it is stimulating or supportive) and aging, the age decrement in intelligence may be reduced or intensified. Moreover, the nature of this interaction between historical change and aging seems to vary with cohort membership (Schaie, 1990).

CRYSTALLIZED AND FLUID ABILITIES

The distinction between the second-order factors of crystallized (Gc) and fluid (Gf) abilities is especially suited to adult development, in that both intelligences are defined in such a way that predictions about developmental change are possible (see FLUID AND CRYSTALLIZED INTELLIGENCE, THEORY OF). Because of different sets of underlying causal factors (decreased neurophysiological functioning with age for Gf, cumulative intensive acculturation/education for Gc), cross-sectional data suggest that Gf increases and then declines over the adult life span, whereas Gc generally increases and/or remains stable over most of the adult years. J. L. Horn (1978, 1985) suggested, however, that the distinction between Gf and Gc is in some cases not as clear-cut as it would appear, as when the task could require the exercise of either general ability.

Because considerable variation in the level of Gf and Gc functioning can be observed both within and across individuals, one must be cautious in interpreting the curves of respective growth and decline for Gc and Gf (or any other measures of intelligence) in adulthood too rigidly. For example, some individuals make more effort to sharpen their skills than others do. Moreover, some individuals are more prone to depression, fatigue, anxiety, or attentional lapses than others are.

Brody (1992) argued that when adjustments are made for practice and selective dropout, declines in Gf and Gc are observed in longitudinal studies. If Gf is seen as an estimate of G, then declines in general intelligence with age are the rule. Declines in Gf with age have also been attributed to changes in the speed of information processing (Hertzog, 1989), the rapidity with which similar cognitive operations can be repeatedly performed (Salthouse, 1988), and deficits in attention and short-term memory (Stankov, 1988).

METHODOLOGICAL CONCERNS

Many researchers have highlighted the inadequacies of the traditional cross-sectional and longitudinal designs for assessing developmental change, and so, the effects of cohort (generational) differences, time-of-measurement effects, and regression effects need to be given serious consideration (Baltes, 1968; Schaie, 1965, 1990). These factors, as well as practice and attrition, do have an impact on the confidence one can have in available cross-sectional and longitudinal data, though the latter are clearly preferable in that they are more likely to reflect age changes; practice especially seems to affect WAIS performance findings (Kaufman, 1990).

COHORT EFFECTS ON INTELLIGENCE

One of the most important findings in adult intelligence is the recognition of cohort effects in intellectual functioning, independently of age (Kaufman, 1990; Schaie, 1990). Schaie's data clearly suggest that cohort effects are at least as important as maturation as an influence on intelligence in adulthood, in that they affect the baseline reference point from which age-related changes in intelligence can be understood. For some abilities, cohort differences are positive (younger cohorts perform more adequately), as in the case of Primary Mental Abilities (PMA) of verbal meaning, spatial orientation, and inductive reasoning (Schaie, 1990), largely because of higher levels of education and better health for such persons. For other skills, cohort effects are negative (younger cohorts perform less adequately), as in the case of PMA number skill or word fluency. Indeed, when controls for level of education are made, age differences in WAIS verbal scores are affected more strongly than are WAIS performance scores, supporting education as a major factor influencing intelligence that is cohort-specific (Kaufman, 1990).

Schaie (1979) and Baltes, Reese, and Nesselroade (1988) believed cross-sectional differences in Gc reflect differing amounts of acquired "information accumulation" gained by generations. This difference reflects a disparity of information available to that generation compared with another generation. Longitudinal measures of Gc simply reflect "environmental treatment impact" at differing times of measurement. Age differences in Gf will be overestimated by cross-sectional studies if there are positive generational differences and underestimated if there exist negative cohort differences in fluid ability (Schaie, 1970). Longitudinal studies should yield the proper age gradients of fluid scores. Schaie (1970), using measures of primary mental abilities (Thurstone & Thurstone, 1962), found positive time-of-measurement effects for $Gc;$ those obtained for Gf were negative, utilizing a time-sequential method of analysis (separating age and time of measurement; Schaie, 1965). The data were then reorganized into a cross-sequential matrix (separating cohort and time of measurement) to obtain longitudinal difference scores for each cohort. When corrected for time-of-measurement effects and environmental treatment effects, the cohort-specific changes in Gc were almost nil; the fluid decrements with age were more severe. Cohort differences at age 23 yielded improvements in both components. Average cohort differences were greatest for Gc and less so for Gf. Thus, time-of-measurement and information-input differences between successive cohorts, according to Schaie, account for the net increment in Gc and the net decrement in Gf as obtained through a cross-sequential analysis (Schaie, 1983, 1990).

Schaie's early work suggests that inferences pertaining to age changes in intelligence obtained from cross-sectional studies are valid only if the effects of cohort change are taken into account. Available data do suggest that cohort-specific patterns do differ for diverse ability variables, and, as such, genuine maturational changes cannot be inferred when different cohorts are measured at different points in their individual ontogenies. Likewise, results of longitudinal studies, being cohort-specific, may vary as a function of the lack of generation generalizability. It is only when these gradients yield similar ontogenetic (age-related) trends that the results can be ascribed to the influence of maturational factors alone.

Schaie (1979) also noted that data obtained from independent samples will overestimate loss for abilities where losses in fact occur (given that these persons do not have the benefit of practice). Dependent (repeated-measurement) samples data will accurately estimate age changes for those in better health and in more-stimulating environments, while underestimating loss for those in poorer health and/or living in more-impoverished situations. Yet, even when corrections for time-of-measurement, attrition, and cohort effects are made, declines with age in PMA verbal meaning, spatial orientation, and reasoning are seen (Schaie, 1983).

The conditions under which adults' intelligence are tested will also influence conclusions about intellectual functioning in adulthood. Specifically, factors that are considered noncognitive (performance-related) may undermine the accurate assessment of intelligence in many adults (Hayslip & Kennelly, 1985), just as practice, selective attrition, or cohort-related educational background may prove advantageous. Examples of noncognitive influences are fatigue, sensory loss, anxiety, speededness, attentional deficits, and depression

(Kausler, 1991). Sensory deficits in hearing and vision may put many adults at a disadvantage (Sands & Meredith, 1989), and persons who are in poor physical and mental health have lower fluid abilities (Perlmutter & Nyquist, 1990). C. Hertzog, K. W. Schaie, and N. Gribbin (1978) found that persons suffering from hypertension perform more poorly over time, while for those who are treated for hypertension, declines in intelligence are minimal (Schultz et al., 1986, 1989).

An important factor found to influence intelligence in adulthood is education. On the average, those who are more highly educated tend to maintain their crystallized skills better than their fluid skills, which are less dependent on formal education (Kaufman, 1990). Those who are initially more able appear to decline more rapidly, while those who are less able appear to gain somewhat (Alder, Adam, & Arenberg, 1990). Others have found that those who are initially more able decline less (Birren & Morrison, 1961; Eisdorfer & Wilkie, 1973).

There may also be a relationship between personality factors and intellectual performance, but the reasons for this relationship remain unclear. It may be that persons who have adaptive personalities age better intellectually or that intelligence may permit more flexibility in adulthood. B. Hayslip (1988) found that older persons who were more anxious about their intellectual skills had higher Gc scores. Higher-functioning individuals may therefore utilize defense mechanisms that serve to "insulate the older individual from feelings of self-worthlessness and failure and/or a loss of control over external forces via the development of intellectual skills" (Hayslip, 1988, p. 79). M. E. Lachman and L. Leff reported that control beliefs did not predict changes in intellectual (Gf/Gc) functioning among aged adults, but changes in intellectual control beliefs were predicted by fluid intelligence.

C. Schooler (1987) emphasized the impact that the complexity of the everyday (e.g., work) environment may have on cognitive performance. Complexity is related to numbers of stimuli, decisions, contingencies associated with the environment, and the amount of structure in the environment. Individuals in optimally complex environments who are reinforced for using existing skills or developing new skills may develop higher cognitive abilities that generalize to other situations and may be better in problem solving.

In contrast to studies of absolute stability, findings for coherence generally suggest stability of factor structure across age, using cross-sectional comparison of PMA measures (Schaie et al., 1989), and stability across cohorts for Gf and Gc, using a time-lagged comparison of two samples of older adults (Hayslip & Brookshire, 1985).

Newer ideas about adult intelligence have emerged that impact on the interpretation of available data. P. B. Baltes, F. Dittmann-Kohli, and R. Dixon (1984) and Baltes (1987) suggest a dual-process concept of intellectual development, emphasizing a distinction between the mechanics of intelligence, which are the basic cognitive skills, such as speeded performance (Gf), and the pragmatics of intelligence, which reflect more-organized systems of knowledge, such as social intelligence and wisdom (Gc). The mechanics of intelligence are more structural and involve basic skills, such as logic, information processing, and problem solving. The pragmatic aspect of intelligence is more applied or adaptive and thus reflects intelligent behavior in a specific context or situation. Mechanics are the prerequisites for pragmatics.

N. W. Denny (1982) maintained that both "unexercised" and "optimally exercised" abilities will decline with increased age during adulthood. Furthermore, because of such factors as poor health and isolation from others, the differences between the levels of unexercised and optimally exercised abilities will be least for a given person during childhood and old age versus during adolescence and adulthood.

Robert J. Sternberg (1985, 1988, 1991) developed a TRIARCHIC THEORY OF INTELLIGENCE. Sternberg's approach understands intelligence in terms of (1) the internal world of the individual, or the mental processes that underlie intelligent behavior (componential); (2) experience, or the degree of novelty or lack of novelty involved in the application of one's information-processing skills (experiential); and (3) the external world of the individual, where the above mental processes are used to adapt to the environment (contextual). The most important mechanisms are "metacomponents" (executive processes) of intelligence, which plan what one is going to do, monitor it while one is doing it, and evaluate it after it is done. More specific to the task are "performance components," which are the actual mental operations themselves (e.g., encoding, making inferences, making comparisons) people use to solve specific problems. The last dimension of intelligence is the set of "knowledge-acquisition components," which help one gain new knowledge.

C. A. Berg and Sternberg (1985) found younger adults to be superior in most metacomponents of intelligence and in the performance components. Older adults have more difficulty in defining problems to be solved, in managing their attention to solve problems, and in monitoring solutions effectively, but these skills may improve with practice. Likewise, making inferences and combining and comparing information are impaired in older persons. It may be that the knowledge-acquisition components that are based on experience do not decline with age, especially if they are critical in helping people to cope with new situations (Cunningham & Tomer, 1991).

A complex picture emerges from research in the area of intellectual functioning. Growth seems to characterize the early years of life, but the perception of irreversible declines in intelligence with age is clearly inaccurate. Indeed, when and under what conditions intelligence is stable is individual-specific. Such factors clearly influence estimates of intraindividual stability and are affected by them (Baltes, Reese, & Nesselroade, 1988). For some dimensions of intelligence, stability or growth with age better represents the pattern of age changes, while for others, moderate (though not irreversible) declines are more typical.

(*See also:* AGING AND INTELLIGENCE.)

BIBLIOGRAPHY

ALDER, A. G., ADAM, J., & ARENBERG, D. (1990). Individual differences assessment of the relationship between change and initial level of adult cognitive functioning. *Psychology and Aging, 5,* 560–568.

BALTES, P. B. (1968). Longitudinal and cross-sectional sequence in the study of age and generation effects. *Human Development, 11,* 145–171.

BALTES, P. B. (1987). Theoretical propositions of life-span development psychology: On the dynamics between growth and decline. *Development Psychology, 23,* 611–626.

BALTES, P. B., DITTMANN-KOHLI, F., & DIXON, R. (1984). New perspectives on the development of intelligence in adulthood: Toward a dual process conception and model of selective optimization with compensation. In P. B. Baltes & O. Brim (Eds.), *Life-span development and behavior* (Vol. 6, pp. 33–76). New York: Academic Press.

BALTES, P. B., REESE, H. W., & NESSELROADE, J. R. (1988). *Life-span developmental psychology: Introduction to research methods.* Hillsdale, NJ: Erlbaum.

BERG, C. A., & STERNBERG, R. J. (1985). A triarchic theory of intellectual development during adulthood. *Developmental Review, 5,* 353–389.

BIRREN, J. E., & MORRISON, D. F. (1961). Analysis of WAIS subtests in relation to age and education. *Journal of Gerontology, 16,* 363–369.

BOTWINICK, J. (1967). *Cognitive processes in maturity and old age.* New York: Springer-Verlag.

BOTWINICK, J. (1984). *Age and behavior.* New York: Springer-Verlag.

BRODY, N. (1992). *Intelligence.* New York: Academic Press.

BUKATO, D., & DAEHLER, M. W. (1992). *Child development: A topical approach.* Boston: Houghton-Mifflin.

CASPI, A., & BEM, D. J. (1990). Personality change and continuity across the life course. In L. A. Pervin (Ed.), *Handbook of personality: Theory and research* (pp. 549–575). New York: Guilford Press.

CUNNINGHAM, W., & OWENS, W. (1983). The Iowa State Study of the adult development of intellectual abilities. In K. W. Schaie (Ed.), *Longitudinal studies of adult psychological development* (pp. 20–39). New York: Guilford Press.

CUNNINGHAM, W. A., & TOMER, A. (1991). Intellectual abilities and age: Concepts, theories, and analysis. In E. Lovelace (Ed.), *Aging and cognition: Mental processes, self-awareness, and interventions* (pp. 141–169). Amsterdam: North-Holland.

DEARBORN, W. F., & ROTHNEY, J. W. (1963). *Predicting the child's development.* Cambridge, MA: Sci-Art.

DENNY, N. W. (1982). Aging and cognitive changes. In B. B. Wolman (Ed.), *Handbook of developmental psychology* (pp. 807–827). Englewood Cliffs, NJ: Prentice-Hall.

DROPPELT, J. E., & WALLACE, W. L. (1955). Standardization of the Wechsler Adult Intelligence Scale for older persons. *Journal of Abnormal and Social Psychology, 51,* 312–330.

EISDORFER, C., & WILKIE, F. (1973). Intellectual changes with advancing age. In L. F. Jarvik, C. Eisdorfer, & J. Blum (Eds.), *Intellectual functioning in adults* (pp. 102–111). New York: Springer-Verlag.

HAYSLIP, B. (1988). Personality–ability relationships in aged adults. *Journal of Gerontology: Psychological Sciences, 43,* 74–84.

HAYSLIP, B. (1989). Alternative mechanisms for improvements in fluid ability performance among aged adults. *Psychology and Aging, 4,* 122–124.

HAYSLIP, B., & BROOKSHIRE, R. (1985). Relationships among abilities in elderly adults: A time-lagged analysis. *Journal of Gerontology, 40,* 748–750.

HAYSLIP, B., & KENNELLY, K. J. (1985). Cognitive and non-cognitive factors affecting learning among older adults. In D. B. Lumsden (Ed.), *The older adult as learner* (pp. 73–98). New York: Hemisphere.

HAYSLIP, B., KENNELLY, K. J., & MALOY, R. (1990). Fatigue, depression, and cognitive performance among aged persons. *Experimental Aging Research, 16,* 111–115.

HAYSLIP, B., & STERNS, H. L. (1979). Age differences in relationships between crystallized and fluid intelligences and problem solving. *Journal of Gerontology, 34,* 404–414.

HERTZOG, C. (1989). The influence of cognitive slowing on age differences in intelligence. *Developmental Psychology, 25,* 636–651.

HERTZOG, C., SCHAIE, K. W., & GRIBBIN, N. (1978). Cardiovascular disease and changes in intellectual function from middle to old age. *Journal of Gerontology, 33,* 872–883.

HONZIK, M. P., MACFARLANE, J. W., & ALLEN, L. (1948). The stability of mental test performance between two and eighteen years. *Journal of Experimental Education, 17,* 309–329.

HOOPER, F., FITZGERALD, J., & PAPALIA, D. (1971). Piagetian theory and the aging process: Extensions and speculations. *Aging and Human Development, 2,* 3–20.

HORN, J. L. (1978). Human ability systems. In P. B. Baltes (Ed.), *Life-span development and behavior* (Vol. 1, pp. 221–256). New York: Academic Press.

HORN, J. L. (1985). Remodeling old models of intelligence. In B. B. Wolman (Ed.), *Handbook of intelligence* (pp. 267–300). New York: Wiley.

HORN, J. L., & CATTELL, R. B. (1966). Refinement and test of the theory of fluid and crystallized intelligence. *Journal of Educational Psychology, 57,* 253–270.

HORN, J. L., & CATTELL, R. B. (1967). Age differences in fluid and crystallized intelligence. *Acta Psychologica, 26,* 107–129.

HORNBLUM, J. N., & OVERTON, W. F. (1976). Area and volume conservation among the elderly: Assessment and training. *Developmental Psychology, 12,* 68–74.

HUMPHREYS, L. G. (1989). Intelligence: Three kinds of instability and their consequences for policy. In R. L. Linn (Ed.), *Intelligence: Measurement, theory, and public policy* (pp. 193–216). Urbana: University of Illinois Press.

HYND, G. W., & SEMRUD-CLIKEMAN, M. (1993). Developmental considerations in cognitive assessment of young children. In J. L. Culbertson & D. J. Willis (Eds.), *Testing young children* (pp. 11–28). Austin, TX: Pro-Ed.

JONES, H. E., & BAYLEY, N. (1941). The Berkeley Growth Study. *Child Development, 12,* 167–173.

JONES, H. E., & CONRAD, H. S. (1933). The growth and decline of intelligence: A study of a homogenous group between the ages of ten and sixty. *Genetic Psychology Monographs, 13,* 223–298.

KAUFMAN, A. S. (1990). Age and IQ across the adult lifespan. In A. S. Kaufman (Ed.), *Assessing adolescent and adult intelligence* (pp. 181–232). Boston: Allyn & Bacon.

KAUSLER, D. H. (1991). *Experimental psychology, cognition and human aging* (2nd ed.). New York: Springer-Verlag.

LACHMAN, M. E., & LEFF, L. (1989). Perceived control and intellectual functioning: A five-year longitudinal study. *Developmental Psychology, 25,* 722–728.

McCALL, R. B., APPLEBAUM, M. I., & HOGARTY, P. S. (1973). Developmental changes in mental performance. *Monograph of the Society for Research in Child Development, 38* (3, Serial No. 150).

MATARAZZO, J. D. (1971). *Measurement and appraisal of adult intelligence.* Baltimore, MD: Williams & Wilkins.

MILES, C. C., & MILES, W. R. (1932). The correlation of intelligence scores and chronological age from early to later maturity. *American Journal of Psychology, 44,* 44–78.

OWENS, W. A. (1966). Age and mental abilities: A second adult follow-up. *Journal of Educational Psychology, 57,* 311–325.

PALMORE, E., BUSSE, E., MADDOX, G., NOWLIN, J., & SIEGLER, I. (1985). *Normal aging III.* Durham, NC: Duke University Press.

PAPALIA, D. (1972). The status of several conservation abilities across the lifespan. *Human development, 15,* 229–243.

PAPALIA, D., & BIELBY, D. D. (1974). Cognitive functioning in middle-aged and elderly adults: A review of research based on Piaget's theory. *Human Development, 17,* 424–443.

PERLMUTTER, M., & NYQUIST, L. (1990). Relationships between self-reported physical and mental health and intellectual performance across adulthood. *Journal of Gerontology: Psychological Sciences, 45,* 145–155.

RYBASH, J. M., HOYER, W. J., & ROADIN, P. A. (1986). *Adult cognition and aging.* New York: Pergamon Press.

SALTHOUSE, T. A. (1988). Resource-reduction interpretations of cognitive aging. *Developmental Research, 8,* 238–272.

SANDS, L. P., & MEREDITH, W. (1989). Effects of sensory and motor functioning on adult intellectual performance. *Journal of Gerontology: Psychological Sciences, 44,* 56–58.

SCHAIE, K. W. (1965). A general model for the study of development problems. *Psychological Bulletin, 64,* 92–107.

SCHAIE, K. W. (1970). A reinterpretation of age-related changes in cognitive structure and functioning. In L. R. Goulet & P. B. Baltes (Eds.), *Life-span developmental psychology: Theory and research* (pp. 486–508). New York: Academic Press.

SCHAIE, K. W. (1977–1978). Toward a stage theory of adult intellectual development. *International Journal of Aging and Human Development, 8,* 120–138.

SCHAIE, K. W. (1978). External validity in the assessment of intellectual development in adulthood. *Journal of Gerontology, 33,* 696–701.

SCHAIE, K. W. (1979). The primary mental abilities in adulthood: An exploration in the development of psychometric intelligence. In P. B. Baltes & O. Brim (Eds.), *Life-span development and behavior* (Vol. 2, pp. 68–115). New York: Academic Press.

SCHAIE, K. W. (1983). The Seattle Longitudinal Study: A 21-year exploration of psychometric intelligence in adulthood. In K. W. Schaie (Ed.), *Longitudinal studies of adult psychological development* (pp. 102–139). New York: Guilford Press.

SCHAIE, K. W. (1990). Adult intellectual development. In J. E. Birren & K. W. Schaie (Eds.), *Handbook of the psychology of aging* (3rd ed., pp. 292–309). New York: Academic Press.

SCHAIE, K. W., WILLIS, S. L., JAY, G., & CHIPUER, H. (1989). Structural invariance of cognitive abilities across the adult life span: A cross-sectional study. *Developmental Psychology, 25,* 652–662.

SCHEIDT, R. (1981). Ecologically valid inquiry: Fait accompli? *Human Development, 23,* 225–228.

SCHOOLER, C. (1987). Cognitive effects of complex environments during the life span: A review and theory. In C. Schooler & K. W. Schaie (Eds.), *Cognitive functioning and social structure over the life course* (pp. 24–49). Norwood, NJ: Ablex.

SCHULTZ, N., ELIAS, M. F., ROBBINS, M. A., STREETON, D. H., & BLAKEMAN, N. (1986). A longitudinal comparison of hypertensive and normotensive subjects on the WAIS: Initial findings. *Journal of Gerontology, 41,* 169–175.

SCHULTZ, N., ELIAS, M. F., ROBBINS, M. A., STREETON, D. H., & BLAKEMAN, N. (1989). A longitudinal study of hypertensive and hypotensive subjects on the WAIS. *Psychology and Aging, 4,* 496–503.

SHOCK, N., GREULICH, R., ANDRES, R., ARENBERG, D., COSTA, P., LUKATTA, E., & TOBIN, J. (1984). *Normal human aging: The Baltimore longitudinal study of aging.* Washington, DC: Government Printing Office.

SONTAG, L. W., BAKER, C. T., & NELSON, V. L. (1958). Mental growth and personality development: A longitudinal study. *Monographs of the Society for Research in Child Development, 23* (2, Serial No. 68).

STANKOV, L. (1988). Aging, attention, and intelligence. *Psychology and Aging, 3,* 59–74.

STERNBERG, R. J. (1985). Cognitive approaches to intelligence. In B. B. Wolman (Ed.), *Handbook of human intelligence* (pp. 59–118). New York: Wiley.

STERNBERG, R. J. (1988). *The triarchic mind.* New York: Viking.

STERNBERG, R. J. (1991). Theory-based testing of intellectual abilities: Rationale for the triarchic abilities test. In H. Rowe (Ed.), *Intelligence: Reconceptualization and measurement* (pp. 183–202). Hillsdale, NJ: Erlbaum.

THURSTONE, L. L., & THURSTONE, T. G. (1962). *SRA Primary mental abilities.* Chicago: Science Research Associates.

BERT HAYSLIP, JR.

STAGES OF COGNITIVE DEVELOPMENT

Anyone who has had occasion to inspect child psychology textbooks, whether as a student or as a teacher, knows that there are two traditional approaches to psychological development: the *content approach* and the *stage approach*. The content approach looks at development by type of behavior rather than by time of life. Well-researched categories of human behavior (e.g., memory, perception, personality, reasoning) are examined sequentially, with development from birth to maturity being separately described. In the stage approach, presentation is by time of life rather than type of behavior. The life span is sliced into segments (usually infancy, early childhood, middle childhood, adolescence, adulthood), with the varieties of behavioral change within each segment being described before moving on to the next segment.

These approaches, as they are used by teachers and textbook authors, are merely pedagogical devices. Developmental researchers have long speculated about whether stages have some deeper significance. Are there real stages of psychological development, periods in which pretty much all behavioral change revolves around a few common themes? If the answer is yes, the deep complexities of psychological development can be potentially pared down to a few distinct, chronologically ordered behavioral states. This is a happy prospect to be sure.

As a result of the enormous influence of Jean PIAGET's work on stages (e.g., Piaget & Inhelder, 1969), the stage question has been most extensively studied in connection with intelligence and closely related behaviors, such as moral reasoning and social judgment, at least in recent decades. This work will occupy us here; the presentation is organized into three historical periods—an early period spanning the first six decades of this century, a middle period spanning the next two decades, and a recent period spanning the years since then.

EARLY PERIOD: 1900–1960

Throughout the first half of the twentieth century, theories about stages were much more prevalent than they are today. As a rule, they were proposed with little regard for the experimental procedures needed to verify their existence. Indeed, such theories were rarely accompanied by data of any sort and, when they were, the evidence did not go far beyond anecdotes, case studies, and make-shift illustrations. Sigmund Freud's stages of psychosexual development and Erik Erikson's stages of psychosocial development are perhaps the quintessential examples of such work.

Kessen (1962) provided what is widely viewed as the definitive historical analysis of early stage theories. He noted that the stage approach is rooted in certain Darwinian ideas—especially the notion that ontogeny recapitulates phylogeny—that were influential in the early days of developmental psychology. These ideas

encouraged the use of animal models to interpret human development; consequently, child psychology textbooks published early in this century were filled with allusions to the "chimpanzee stage," the "fish stage," and the like. For our purposes, however, the key feature of Kessen's analysis was a classification scheme for then-extant stage theories, a scheme that set forth five general ways in which the stage framework had been used in theories of psychological development:

1. *Literary-evocative.* Here, the stage framework was simply a metaphorical device that was designed to evoke an image or an orientation, not to suggest anything precise or researchable. This usage was the most common early in the twentieth century. Theories that identified human behavior during certain age ranges with the behavior of animal species (e.g., the "chimpanzee stage") are classic examples of the literary-evocative usage of *stage.* Such theories were prescientific, in that they appealed to the power of poetic suggestion rather than to scientific data.

2. *Age paraphrase.* This is the basic way in which the stage construct is used by parents, teachers, and textbook authors, namely, as a synonym for chronological age. The child is characterized as being in the "infancy stage," the "preschool stage," the "adolescent stage," and so on, because these are convenient and widely understood shorthands for certain age ranges. This usage of *stage* is also common among developmental researchers with close ties to learning theory (e.g., Bijou & Baer, 1961).

3. *Description of the environment.* This use of *stage* does not refer to children's behavior but to characteristics of the environments in which children develop. Most cultures treat children in prototypical ways at specific times of life. During the first two years of life children are encouraged to be strongly dependent on adults, who protect them from the dangers of their physical immaturity. During the preschool years, however, children are encouraged to become less dependent. Consequently, it is not uncommon to refer to the former interval as a "dependence stage" and to the latter interval as an "independence stage."

4. *Description of parameters of variation.* This use of *stage,* as well as that in the next section (5), is much more theoretical than the preceding ones. Here, in

Kessen's words, "stages are taken as variations of a fundamental set of theoretical statements." As a matter of course, a general theory of development will contain certain assumptions about mechanisms that regulate psychological change throughout the life span, e.g., the process of cognitive assimilation and accommodation in Piaget's theory. Stages then implement more detailed assumptions about differences in the ways that these mechanisms express themselves during different age ranges, that is, a stage refers to a time of life in which the regulatory mechanisms are operating in a specified manner.

5. *Description of different rule systems.* The last use of *stage* was rare at the time Kessen described it, but it has subsequently become commonplace through the increased use of computer simulation. In computer simulation, a stage is synonymous with the operation of a well-defined set of rules (usually represented in a computer program) that govern behavior in many domains. Different rule systems operate during different developmental epochs, and each such system defines a distinct stage. In the language of computer simulation, a stage denotes an interval in which a certain behavioral program is "running."

MIDDLE PERIOD: 1960–1980

Whether judged by the quality of new ideas or by sheer effort, the middle period was by far the most productive of the three. It was a time of intense concern with a particular stage model: Piaget's theory—the conceptualization of cognitive development as a sequence of four global stages (sensorimotor, preoperational, concrete operational, and formal operational). Looking back on those years, three major events define the period. First an explosion of interest in Piaget's theory took place in the early and middle 1960s. Second, three landmark papers by Flavell (1970, 1972; Flavell & Wohlwill, 1969) were published at about the time the Piagetian movement crested. Third, a multiauthor analysis of the limitations of the stage construct (Brainerd, 1978, 1979) was published as the middle period came to a close.

Regarding the first of these events, numerous factors spurred interest in Piaget. One was a group of conferences and symposia on his theory. The 1960 conference at which Kessen's (1962) paper was pre-

sented was entitled, "Thought in the Young Child: A Conference on Intellective Development with Particular Attention to the Work of Jean Piaget." In 1962, a similar conference, entitled "Piaget Rediscovered," was held at Cornell University. Another factor was renewed interest in the study of cognitive development after many years of concentration on social and personality development. For researchers, Piaget's theory was a welcome source of new hypotheses. Surely the most important factor, however, was Flavell's (1963) marvelous exposition of the theory. Anyone who has read Piaget in the original knows that the theory is complex and that its complexities are exacerbated by Piaget's writing style, which is often difficult to understand. Moreover, at the time, most of his works were available only in French. Flavell's book made the theory accessible to English-speaking audiences, and it did so in prose that somehow managed to combine profound scholarship with great clarity. Perhaps most important of all, however, the book whetted researchers' appetites by reviewing many of the unique findings generated by the theory.

Turning to the second event, Flavell's three papers codified some of the criteria of stages of cognitive development and examined data that bore upon their validity. In the first paper, Flavell and Wohlwill (1969) listed two properties, *qualitative change* and *abruptness,* with the list being expanded to four when *concurrence* and *structures* were added in the second paper. Flavell's (1970) definitions of these notions appear in Table 1. The phenomenon of sequence in cognitive development formed a second, related theme of Flavell and Wohlwill's paper. Piaget had placed a great emphasis on the claim that his stages followed a culturally universal sequence—sensorimotor intelligence came first, then preoperational intelligence, then concrete-operational intelligence, and finally formal-operational intelligence. This meant that the cognitive skills that were associated with any later stage should always develop after, never before, the cognitive skills that were associated with any earlier stage. Flavell and Wohlwill, however, isolated multiple varieties of sequence—which denied the universality claimed by Piaget. They listed four variations: *none, substitution, implicative mediation,* and *nonimplicative mediation.* Flavell (1972) later produced a modified list, which appears in Table 2.

TABLE 1
Flavell's criterial properties of stages of cognitive development

Property	Definition
Qualitative change	"Stage-to-stage development entails qualitative rather than quantitative changes in thinking" (p. 423).
Abruptness	"The development of individual stage-specific items is characteristically abrupt rather than gradual; that is, there is a zero-order transition period between the initial appearance of each item and its stage of functional maturity" (p. 425).
Concurrence	"The various items that define a given stage develop concurrently, i.e., in synchrony with one another" (p. 435).
Structures	"Stage-specific items become organized and interrelated to form cognitive structures" (p. 443).

SOURCE: Flavell, 1970.

Flavell's papers prompted a good deal of research by others, much of it highly critical of the stage framework; this work comprises the last major event in the middle period. Flavell had begun the job of critical analysis; his papers did more than formalize the properties of stages, they also considered the match between those properties and the facts of cognitive development as they were then understood. The match was not very good in some cases. This was especially true for abruptness, which Flavell (1970, p. 428) concluded "can immediately be ruled out of contention." He added that "it is the usual case that a stage-

TABLE 2
Flavell's five types of sequentiality

Type of Sequence	Definition
Addition	"Item X_1 begins its development at some point in childhood, and item X_2 begins its development at some later point . . . once X_2 has been acquired, X_1 continues to be fully and permanently available" (p. 287).
Substitution	"X_1 becomes thoroughly extinguished as a response form upon emergence of X_2, X_2 then becomes routinely evoked in all the situations that had once elicited X_1" (p. 291).
Modification	"X_1 and X_2 give more the impression of being merely different forms or varieties of 'the same thing.' That is, X_2 strikes one rather as being some sort of transform, derivative, or variate of X_1" (p. 298).
Inclusion	"X_1 becomes 'included' in X_2, in the same sense that a subroutine is 'included in,' or forms a part of, a computer program" (p. 305).
Mediation	"Once a certain level of maturity [of item X_1] has been achieved, it becomes capable of serving as one of the developmental bridges to (or 'mediators' of) the attainment of item X_2" (p. 311).

SOURCE: Flavell, 1972.

TABLE 3
Piaget's five criteria for his stages of cognitive development

Criterion	Definition
Major criteria	
Invariant sequence	"Suppose that we have some set of stages $S_1, S_2, \ldots, S_n$ and procedures for measuring illustrative behaviors from each stage. . . . If we administer tests for the behaviors to our subjects and scale that data, we should find that they appear in the order specified by the stages . . . this sequence should be culturally universal" (Brainerd, 1978, p. 175).
Structure	"The structure criterion . . . specifies that the members of a set of stages shall each be characterized by a unique complement of cognitive structures" (Brainerd, 1978, p. 177).
Minor criteria	
Integration	"This criterion asserts that each stage presupposes the immediately preceding one . . . the cognitive structures of any given stage 'integrate' those of earlier stages" (Brainerd, 1978, p. 179).
Consolidation	"According to the consolidation criterion, each stage is simultaneously an achievement phase for its own behaviors and a preparation phase for those of the next stage" (Brainerd, 1978, p. 179).
Equilibration	"Piaget views cognitive development as consisting of the attainment of successive states of equilibrium, each more stable than the last. Each state is temporary and eventually dissolves into disequilibrium by a combination of internal and external forces" (Brainerd, 1978, pp. 179–180).

specific item continues to develop towards whatever eventually constitutes its functional maturity after one or more subsequent stages are in process" (p. 431).

Critical analysis of the stage framework continued and intensified in subsequent writings by others. The principal lines of criticism were eventually drawn together in a series of commentaries that appeared in *The Behavioral and Brain Sciences* (Brainerd, 1978, 1979). Piaget had proposed five criteria to verify the existence of his stages. These five criteria were subdivided into a pair of major ones (*invariant sequence* and *structure*) and a trio of minor ones (*integration, consolidation,* and *equilibration*). (See Table 3 for definitions.) These criteria proved to be subject to many limitations, limitations so serious that they made the Piagetian stage model seem dubious. For instance, it was argued that the cul-

turally universal stage sequences that Piaget had postulated were not falsifiable because they involved *measurement sequences* that could not turn out any other way. Measurement sequences are situations in which (1) some behavior, B_1, develops during some stage, S_i; (2) some behavior, B_2, develops during some later stage, S_j; and (3) the two are linked by an inclusion relationship such that B_2 consists of B_1 "plus some other things." To illustrate, suppose that B_1 is the ability to count up to 5 and B_2 is the ability to count up to 20. This is a measurement sequence because it is impossible to count up to 20 without counting up to 5 on the way. Thus it is a truism, not an empirical hypothesis, that all children will exhibit B_1 before they exhibit B_2. Surprisingly, Piaget's culturally universal stage sequences were found to be replete with truisms of this sort, although abilities other than counting were naturally involved.

Equally serious objections were raised to the remaining four criteria. Concerning the second major criterion, *cognitive structures,* Piaget (e.g., 1949) had postulated distinct structural models for his stages. However, it was discovered that these models were formalizations of the structures of reasoning problems that had been administered to children rather than the structures of the reasoning behaviors that the problems had elicited. In other words, Piaget's models were descriptions of *task* structure, not cognitive structure. Concerning the three minor criteria, it was found that Piaget had never spelled out their empirical implications and that, therefore, it was impossible to decide whether cognitive development did or did not satisfy these criteria.

RECENT PERIOD: 1980–PRESENT

The legacy of the middle period is a formidable literature on the stage framework, much of it highly critical, together with associated programs of experimentation. Therefore, would-be stage theorists of today must digest a vast literature, and they must do so with the knowledge that, in the end, they may be unable to overcome the main objections to the stage approach. This has reduced enthusiasm for stage theorizing in the Piagetian mold.

Generally speaking, researchers have responded in one of two ways to the criticisms that were raised at the end of the middle period. The first response, the modal one, has been to ignore stages entirely and to adopt a pure content orientation. This response is characteristic of the literatures on memory and perceptual development, for example. The other response, characteristic of some literatures on the development of complex reasoning and social-cognitive development, has been to retain the stage framework but to greatly restrict its scope. In particular, grand stages that cut across many behavioral domains are not offered, but microstage theories are permitted that describe development in some narrow domain distinguished by a well-defined set of tasks. Feldman's (1980) stages in the development of specific map-drawing skills and Thomas and Turner's (1991) stages in the development of the understanding of how grav-

ity affects the position of water surfaces illustrate this domain-specific response.

Although the stock of stage theories has fallen in recent years, there are signs that the situation may be turning around. For researchers, the basic implication of the stage metaphor has always been that development is a process of fits and starts—periods of abrupt change interspersed with periods of stability. As mentioned above, this abruptness property is generally thought to have been disproved many times over at the level of individual cognitive skills. Some researchers have suggested, however, that the data on which this conclusion rests are off-point and that new modeling techniques may be required to decide the issue. Some techniques of this sort have now been developed (e.g., Brainerd, 1987; Thomas & Turner, 1991). To date, they have been applied to age changes in performance on certain reasoning tasks associated with Piaget's concrete-operational stage. Remarkably, the results have consistently favored the conclusion that age changes *are* very abrupt, typically consisting of two or three discrete performance levels with all-or-none transitions between levels. It remains to be seen, however, whether such findings will inspire a new generation of stage theories of cognitive development.

(*See also:* AGING AND INTELLIGENCE; DEVELOPMENT, COGNITIVE; PIAGETIAN THEORY OF DEVELOPMENT.)

BIBLIOGRAPHY

BIJOU, S. W., & BAER, D. E. (1961). *Child development* (Vol. 1). New York: Appleton Century Crofts.

BRAINERD, C. J. (1978). The stage question in cognitive-developmental theory. *The Behavioral and Brain Sciences, 2,* 173–213.

BRAINERD, C. J. (1979). Further reflections and replies on invariant sequences, explanation and other stage criteria. *The Behavioral and Brain Sciences, 3,* 149–154.

BRAINERD, C. J. (1987). Structural measurement theory and cognitive development. In J. Bisanz, C. J. Brainerd, & R. V. Kail (Eds.), *Formal models in developmental psychology.* New York: Springer-Verlag.

FELDMAN, H. D. (1980). *Beyond universals in cognitive development.* Norwood, NJ: Ablex.

FLAVELL, J. H. (1963). *The developmental psychology of Jean Piaget.* Princeton, NJ: Van Nostrand.

FLAVELL, J. H. (1970). Stage-related properties of cognitive development. *Cognitive Psychology, 2,* 421–453.

FLAVELL, J. H. (1972). An analysis of cognitive-developmental sequences. *Genetic Psychology Monographs, 86,* 279–350.

FLAVELL, J. H., & WOHLWILL, J. F. (1969). Formal and functional aspects of cognitive development. In D. Elkind & J. H. Flavell (Eds.), *Studies in cognitive development: Essays in honor of Jean Piaget.* New York: Oxford University Press.

KESSEN, W. (1962). "Stage" and "structure" in the study of children. In W. Kessen & C. Kuhlman (Eds.), *Thought in the young child. Monographs of the Society for Research in Child Development, 28,* 2 (Whole No. 83).

PIAGET, J. (1949). *Traite de logique.* Paris: Colin.

PIAGET, J., & INHELDER, B. (1969). *The psychology of the child.* New York: Basic Books.

THOMAS, H., & TURNER, G. F. W. (1991). Individual differences and development in water-level task performance. *Journal of Experimental Child Psychology, 51,* 171–194.

CHARLES J. BRAINERD

STANDARDIZATION

One distinction between a test and a causal observation is the standardization of the situation from specification of the taxonomy to the interpretation of the scores (see NORMS). The goal of standardization is to give a uniform meaning to scores.

All tests begin with a taxonomy of the trait to be measured. This taxonomy is a description of the behaviors or concepts that represent what is to be measured. The taxonomy is standardized so that everyone involved with developing, producing, distributing, administering, scoring, and interpreting the test has a common understanding of the nature of the instrument. The taxonomy also provides guidance for the (frequently multiple) item writers who must all write items with the same goal. Further, when new or replacement forms of the test are produced, following the taxonomy ensures that the same trait will be measured in new versions.

The instructions of the test must be standardized. A set of instructions that can be used in all testing situations is produced and refined through small group tryout studies. This can be especially important if the testing situation is new or novel, as in the case of an unfamiliar answer sheet, computer, computer response keypad, or joystick. If instructions were not the same across situations there would be no assurance that the test responses would mean the same thing for each examinee.

Another step in standardization is in the presentation of the stimulus. Many individual IQ tests use both ordinary verbal questions and performance tasks such as arranging blocks to form specific patterns. It is necessary to make the stimulus presentation identical for each examinee. One way to achieve standardization is to use a verbatim script for asking test questions. Individual intelligence tests often use such scripts. A second way is to print the questions on paper and let each examinee read them. Another way is to let a computer administer the test. Each of these standardization methods has its problems; for example, the ability of the test administrator to gain examinee rapport can lead to differences in the scores. Different printing fonts can lead to different reading speeds and affect test scores, and different computer character generators can change the score distributions. Further, moving tests from one computer to another with a different processor speed, keyboard condition, or action can affect scores, especially in response time collection or in speed tests. All these and other sources of differences need to be considered when one is designing or using tests.

Standardization must also exist in the method of collecting examinee responses. When individual intelligence tests require specific verbal responses or the precise arrangement of objects (pictures, blocks, etc.), the acceptable answers are clearly defined. This extends to which words are acceptable answers and which completed object is scored as correct. In paper-and-pencil tests, answer sheets must be identical from one testing situation to the next. Ree and Wegner (1990) have shown that the type of answer sheet can cause large differences in score distributions. The use of differing computer keyboards, keypads, control sticks, mice, or track balls may also change scores.

A second mode of standardization of tests is in timing the administration or time to respond to individual questions. There are several ways to time tests. The most accurate is with a computer. Some tests require stopwatches or use count-down timers. Finally, in power tests with generous time limits, a wall clock or wristwatch may be adequate. Experience shows that highly speeded tests are very susceptible to errors caused by careless timing. Poor timing may change the constructs measured by the test.

Scoring the response also requires standardization. This is usually not a problem in intelligence test items that have only one correct answer. Items should be written to include only common usage of words and avoid words that have regional or other special meanings. It is necessary that no item have more than one arguably correct answer. To achieve this, large item tryout samples are administered candidate items.

Many tests have mechanical answer-key templates, which are placed on top of answer sheets so that marked and unmarked answers are visible. These must be standardized with regard to location of the holes in the template. Also, the mechanical answer key must be kept in proper alignment, which may be especially difficult when the test grader moves from column to column. Optical scanning helps standardize scoring, but caution must be exercised in the handling of answer sheets. Unpublished studies indicate that the number of errors made by optical scanners is very low. However, wrinkling or bending answer sheets prior to scanning increases the number of errors. Computers can score responses accurately, but care must be taken that keyboards, joysticks, mice, and track balls stay in calibration. Prior to any optical scanning or computer scoring, systems checks should be accomplished.

A final step in the standardization of tests is in reporting and interpreting the score or scores. Reporting of scores should be consistent across situations. Many score report forms use graphic displays to provide simple and direct preliminary interpretation. The nature of the score report should reflect the needs of the user, whether examinee, counselor, or psychologist. Although score reports may differ by user, a standardized format for each is essential to foster proper test use.

A specific standard must be applied to each individual score. Scores may be referred to a normative distribution that is appropriate to the age or sex of the examinee, for example. The norm used and the relative position of the examinee must be reported. If profile interpretation is employed, a uniform method of interpretation must be applied. Additionally, the score report should show the error bands associated with true differences and indicate which differences between scores are attributable to random fluctuation.

Standardization begins with the blueprint of the test and continues through the interpretation of the scores to the user. Failure to standardize a test dooms its usefulness even before it is administered. Proper standardization allows the test and the user to achieve their goals.

BIBLIOGRAPHY

ANASTASI, A. (1988). *Psychological testing* (6th ed.). New York: Macmillan. A text used by several generations of students.

REE, M. J., & WEGNER, T. G. (1990). Correcting differences in answer sheets for the 1980 Armed Services Vocational Aptitude Battery reference population. *Military Psychology, 2,* 157–169.

SAKLOFSKE, D. H., & SCHWEAN KOWALCHUK, V. L. (1992). Influence on testing and testing results in M. Zeidner & R. Most (Eds.), *Psychological testing: An inside view.* Palo Alto, CA: Consulting Psychologists Press. A good source for understanding what affects test scores.

WAINER, H. (1990). *Computerized adaptive testing: A primer.* Hillsdale, NJ: Erlbaum. The single best compendium on practical aspects of computerized adaptive testing.

WAINER, H., WADKINS, J. R. J., & RODGERS, A. (1984). Was there one distractor too many? *Journal of Educational Statistics, 9,* 5–24. What happens when a major testing organization finds a poor test item.

MALCOLM REE

STANFORD-BINET INTELLIGENCE SCALE, FOURTH EDITION

The Stanford-Binet Intelligence Scale, Fourth Edition (SB IV) (Thorndike, Hagen, & Sattler, 1986), is the latest version of the Stanford-Binet Intelligence Scale. The SB IV is a battery of fifteen subtests that covers the age range 2–23. Not all subtests are administered at every age; each subtest has a range of ages for which it is appropriate, and only six of the fifteen subtests cover the entire age range of the scale.

The history of the Stanford-Binet Scale dates back to 1905, when the first practical intelligence test, the Binet-Simon Scale, was developed in Paris by Alfred BINET and Théophile Simon. Lewis TERMAN and his associates at Stanford University modified and extended the Binet-Simon Scale, publishing their version of the scale—the Stanford-Binet Intelligence Scale—in 1916. This version utilized William Stern's concept of intelligence quotient (IQ): the ratio of mental age to chronological age multiplied by 100 (MA/CA $\times$ 100 $=$ IQ). The Stanford-Binet Scale underwent its first revision in 1937, in which two new forms, Form L and Form M, were created. The 1937 revision represented a significant improvement over the 1916 scale in that it was better standardized, offered two forms, and provided more performance tests at earlier age levels.

In 1960 a new revision appeared, in which the best items from Form L and Form M were combined to create a single new form, Form L-M. An important development in the 1960 revision was the replacement of the 1937 scale's conventional ratio IQ tables with Deviation IQs for ages 2–18. The Deviation IQ is a normalized standard score with a mean of 100 and a standard deviation of 16. Thus, the Deviation IQ indicates the same relative ability, regardless of the age of the examinee. Revised norms for the 1960 Form L-M were published in 1972. Except for two minor item changes, the tests in the scale and the directions for scoring and administration remained the same. The most recent revision, the SB IV, while maintaining some continuity with earlier versions, represents a significant departure from the earlier versions.

THEORETICAL BASIS

One of the most important differences between the SBIV and earlier versions of the scale is the shift from an age scale format to a point scale format. In an age scale format, items that most children of a certain chronological age pass are assigned to that age level. A person's score is thus based on what the majority of people his or her age are able to do. In a point scale format, points are given according to the quality and correctness of a person's responses. In an age scale, tests are selected on the assumption that important forms of behavior appear at various points in development, whereas in a point scale, tests are selected to measure specific functions. Age scales contain heterogeneous collections of tests (or items), with different tests (or items) included for different age groups. Point

scales are designed to measure the same aspects of behavior at every age covered by the test.

A three-level hierarchical model was used to guide the construction of the SB IV. The model postulates g (a general intelligence factor) at the highest level; crystallized intelligence, fluid intelligence, and short-term memory factors at the second level; and verbal reasoning, quantitative reasoning, and abstract/visual reasoning at the third level. The three specific factors at the third level, plus the short-term memory factor from the second level, form four area scores in the SB IV. Each of the fifteen subtests are assigned to one of the area scores: four each to Verbal Reasoning, Abstract/Visual Reasoning, and Short-Term Memory, and three to Quantitative Reasoning. The Composite Score (similar to the IQ) reflects the highest level of the theoretical model, and is considered the best estimate of g in the scale. It has a mean equal to 100 and a standard deviation of 16. The subtest scores have a mean equal to 50 and a standard deviation of 8.

PSYCHOMETRIC PROPERTIES

Standardization. The standardization sample consisted of 5,013 individuals between the ages of 2 and 23 years. There were seventeen age groups sampled, with the number of individuals in each age group ranging from 194 in the 18- to 24-year-old group to 460 in the 5- to 6-year-old group. The sample was selected to represent the U.S. population according to 1980 census data. Stratification variables included geographic region, community size, ethnic group, age, gender, and socioeconomic status (SES). Because the final sample included too many individuals from high-SES backgrounds, weighting procedures were used to make the sample conform to the census data.

Reliability. The internal consistency reliability of the SBIV Composite Score is strong. All of the subtests also have adequate internal consistency reliability. Test–retest reliability is adequate for the Composite Score, but not for several individual subtests. This indicates that the Composite Score, but not subtest scores, can be relied on to provide stable measures of ability.

Validity. A considerable amount of research has been conducted on the VALIDITY of the SB IV. Studies investigating the scale's concurrent validity have compared the SB IV with the Stanford-Binet Form L-M, several Wechsler tests, and the KAUFMAN ASSESSMENT BATTERY FOR CHILDREN (K-ABC). Overall, there is good support for the concurrent validity of the SB IV (Thorndike, Hagen, & Sattler, 1986). Research suggests that for populations within the average intellectual range, the SB IV is likely to yield Composite Scores similar to those provided by the above-mentioned tests. With gifted and mentally retarded populations, however, the SB IV may yield significantly lower scores than those obtained with Form L-M and the WAIS–R.

Construct validity of the SB IV has been established in several ways. First, raw scores on the test increase as a function of age. Second, factor analyses indicate adequate to high g loadings of the subtests and the presence of specific factors at various age levels of the scale. Third, all of the subtests correlate moderately to highly positively with the Composite Score.

Relationship of Test Scores to Demographic Characteristics of Norm Group. The relationship between Composite Scores and the demographic characteristics of the standardization sample indicates that gender does not differentially affect Composite Scores. Differences were found, however, between ethnic groups, parental occupation groups, and level of parental education. Overall, white American examinees scored higher than did African American examinees, and examinees whose parents were college graduates and managerial and professional workers scored higher than did those whose parents had lower levels of education and lower-ranked occupations, respectively.

ADMINISTRATION AND SCORING

In the SB IV, items in each subtest are arranged in order of increasing difficulty, with two items of approximately equal difficulty placed at each level. Levels are designated by letters, and are used to determine starting and stopping points. The technical manual provides detailed guidelines for administration and for querying verbal responses when they are not clear. Examiners must be familiar with these guidelines to administer the test.

Adaptive Testing. The SB IV uses an adaptive testing design, a unique feature retained from previous editions of the scale. The Vocabulary subtest is administered first. The score on the Vocabulary subtest is then used to "route" the examinee to items of appropriate difficulty on subsequent subtests. Thus, the vocabulary score serves as an initial estimate of the examinee's ability. The Vocabulary subtest is highly correlated with the other subtests in the battery, making it an appropriate routing test. Although this procedure may reduce testing time, its efficiency depends upon its ability to direct the examiner to appropriate starting points. Therefore, for subtests with which Vocabulary shares lower correlations, or for mentally retarded children, the routing procedure may be less accurate.

Basal and Ceiling Levels. The two consecutive levels at which all items are passed (four items total) are termed the *basal level*. The two consecutive levels at which at least three of the four items are failed are termed the *ceiling level*. The ceiling level is the point at which a subtest is discontinued.

Recommended Subtest Battery. Of the fifteen subtests in the SB IV, only six are given at all ages: Vocabulary, Comprehension, Pattern Analysis, Quantitative, Bead Memory, and Memory for Sentences. Sattler (1992) recommends a specific battery of subtests for various ages, using twelve of the fifteen subtests: Absurdities, Copying, Memory for Digits, Memory for Objects, Matrices, and Verbal Relations in addition to the six mentioned above. He recommends that the three other subtests—Paper Folding and Cutting, Number Series, and Equation Building—be used for special diagnostic purposes.

Scoring. Correct responses receive a score of 1 and incorrect responses receive a score of 0 on all items. After testing has been completed, the examiner computes a raw score and standard age scores for each subtest. Area scores are then computed, followed by computation of the Composite Score.

SB IV SUBTESTS

Vocabulary. The Vocabulary subtest contains forty-six items, divided into a picture vocabulary section and an oral vocabulary section. For the picture items, the child names each picture or gives the most pertinent detail of the picture. For the oral vocabulary section, the child explains the meaning of each word. This subtest taps language abilities. Performance may be influenced by home and school environment or by language-based handicapping conditions.

Vocabulary is a reliable subtest. It correlates highly with the Composite Score and contributes substantially to the Verbal Comprehension factor. Vocabulary is administered at all ages.

Comprehension. The Comprehension subtest contains forty-two items, six of which require a pointing response and thirty-six of which require a verbal response. The first six items measure knowledge of body parts, and the remaining items tap the child's understanding of survival skills, social skills, and political and economic processes. Performance on this subtest may be influenced by oral expression skills and understanding of social and cultural norms.

Comprehension is a reliable subtest. It correlates moderately with the Composite Score and contributes substantially to the Verbal Comprehension factor. Comprehension is administered at all ages.

Absurdities. The Absurdities subtest contains thirty-two picture items. Items 1–4 are in multiple-choice format and require the child to point to the inaccurate picture. Items 5–32 require the child to state the essential incongruity in each picture. Performance depends upon perception of detail, alertness, concentration, and social understanding. Furthermore, the tasks are largely conceptual and involve some understanding of the notion of correctness/incorrectness.

Absurdities is a reliable subtest. It correlates moderately with the Composite Score and contributes moderately to the Verbal Comprehension factor and Nonverbal Reasoning/Visualization factor. Absurdities is administered to examinees aged 2–14.

Verbal Relations. The Verbal Relations subtest contains eighteen items, each consisting of four words. The examinee has to state what the first three words have in common that the fourth does not. This subtest assesses verbal concept formation and reasoning, and requires the examinee to distinguish among subtle differences in meaning.

Verbal Relations is a reliable subtest. It correlates moderately with the Composite Score and contributes

substantially to the Verbal Comprehension factor. The subtest is administered to examinees aged 12 and older.

Pattern Analysis. The Pattern Analysis subtest contains forty-two items. The first six items require the examinee to place puzzle pieces into a form board. For the remaining items, the examinee reproduces two-dimensional, black-and-white patterns with blocks. Items 7–42 are timed. This subtest assesses visual and perceptual organization, and it is largely affected by speed of performance.

Pattern Analysis is a reliable subtest. It correlates moderately with the Composite Score and contributes substantially to the Nonverbal Reasoning/Visualization factor. The subtest is administered at all ages.

Copying. The Copying subtest contains twenty-eight items, divided into two sections. For the first twelve items, the examinee must reproduce models with single-color blocks. For the remaining items, the examinee copies printed line drawings of various geometric designs. This subtest involves visual–motor ability and hand–eye coordination. Successful performance requires appropriate fine motor development and perceptual discrimination ability.

Copying is a reliable subtest. It correlates moderately with the Composite Score and contributes moderately to the Nonverbal Reasoning/Visualization factor. The subtest is administered to examinees aged 2–13.

Matrices. The Matrices subtest contains twenty-six items. The examinee is presented with figural matrices in which one portion of the matrix is missing and asked to select the best alternative to complete the matrix. Perceptual reasoning ability, attention to detail, and concentration are required for successful performance.

Matrices is a reliable subtest. It correlates moderately with the Composite Score and contributes moderately to the Nonverbal Reasoning/Visualization factor. The subtest is administered to examinees aged 7–23.

Paper Folding and Cutting. The Paper Folding and Cutting subtest contains eighteen items. The examinee first looks at a sequence of drawings showing a piece of paper being folded and cut, and then must select the diagram that shows how the folded and cut paper would look unfolded. This subtest involves visualization, spatial ability, and attention to visual clues.

Paper Folding and Cutting is a reliable subtest. It correlates moderately with the Composite Score and contributes substantially to the Nonverbal Reasoning/Visualization factor. The subtest is administered to examinees aged 12 and older.

Quantitative. The Quantitative subtest consists of forty problems that cover a range of mathematical concepts. The test uses visual and oral stimuli, and the examinee is allowed to use scratch paper and pencil for solving the problems. Scores are likely to be influenced by the examinee's knowledge of mathematics, which in turn may be determined by interest in and quality of schooling.

The Quantitative subtest is a reliable subtest. It correlates highly with the Composite Score and contributes moderately to the Nonverbal Reasoning/Visualization factor and modestly to the Verbal Comprehension factor. The subtest is administered at all ages.

Number Series. The Number Series subtest contains twenty-six items in which five to seven numbers are arranged in a logical sequence. The examinee must indicate (either orally or in writing) which two numbers would come next in the series. This subtest involves logical reasoning and concentration, and examinees must be able to discover the rationale underlying the series. Scores may be affected by academic achievement in mathematics and related factors, such as achievement motivation and academic self-concept.

Number Series is a reliable subtest. It correlates highly with the Composite Score and contributes substantially to the Nonverbal Reasoning/Visualization factor. The subtest is administered to examinees aged 7 and older.

Equation Building. Equation Building has eighteen items. The examinee must take numerals and mathematical signs and resequence them to produce a correct equation. Paper and pencil can be used, and the responses may be given either orally or in writing. This subtest involves working with relationships among numbers. Performance is aided by logical, flexible, and trial-and-error strategies.

Equation Building is a reliable subtest. It correlates moderately with the Composite Score and contributes

moderately to the Nonverbal Reasoning/Visualization factor. The subtest is administered to examinees aged 12 and older.

Bead Memory. The Bead Memory subtest contains forty-two items. For the first ten items, the examinee must recall which of one or two beads was briefly exposed by the examiner. For the remaining items, the examinee is shown a picture of a line of beads; the picture is then removed from sight, and the examinee is asked to place beads on a stick in the same sequence as was shown in the picture. The subtest uses four bead shapes in three colors. It involves short-term memory for visual stimuli, form perception and discrimination, spatial relations, and alertness to detail.

Bead Memory is a reliable subtest. It correlates moderately with the Composite Score and contributes moderately to the Nonverbal Reasoning/Visualization factor and the Memory factor. The subtest is administered at all ages.

Memory for Sentences. The Memory for Sentences subtest contains forty-two items. The examinee is asked to repeat a sentence exactly as stated by the examiner. The sentences range from simple two-word phrases to complex statements of twenty-two words. This subtest measures immediate recall and attention. Because success may depend on verbal facility, failure may not reflect poor memory. Children with medical or neurodevelopmental problems or whose first language is not English may have difficulty with this subtest.

Memory for Sentences is a reliable subtest. It correlates moderately with the Composite Score and contributes moderately to both the Verbal Comprehension factor and Memory factor. The subtest is administered at all ages.

Memory for Digits. The Memory for Digits subtest comprises two parts: Digits Forward and Digits Reversed. For Digits Forward, the examinee must repeat a series of digits exactly as they were stated by the examiner. For Digits Reversed, the examinee must repeat the series in reverse order. Memory for Digits measures short-term auditory memory and attention.

Memory for Digits is a reliable subtest. It correlates moderately with the Composite Score and contributes substantially to the Memory factor. The subtest is administered to examinees aged 7 and older.

Memory for Objects. The Memory for Objects subtest contains fourteen items. For each item, the examiner presents a series of objects on illustrated cards one at a time, after which the examinee must identify the objects from a larger array. To receive credit, the examinee must point to the objects in the exact order in which they were shown. Performance may be enhanced by familiarity with the objects or by verbal labeling to help encode stimuli.

Memory for Objects is a moderately reliable subtest. It correlates moderately with the Composite Score and contributes moderately to the Memory factor. It is administered to examinees aged 7 and older.

EVALUATION OF THE SB IV

Strengths. The SB IV is a well-standardized test, with strong reliability and validity. In addition, the large age range and standard score range make the SB IV useful for several applications. The administration procedures are flexible, and the guidelines for administration and scoring are good. In particular, the relatively straightforward scoring system makes the scoring of verbal responses easier than on the Wechsler tests. The SB IV is useful for classifying children as mentally retarded or gifted, and some subtests in the scale may be especially sensitive to brain damage. The memory subtests are valuable in the assessment of learning-disabled children as well as those with brain injury.

Limitations. Because the SB IV uses different combinations of subtests at different ages, scores obtained by children of different ages are based on different combinations of subtests. This lack of continuity makes it difficult to monitor changes in performance over time and to perform longitudinal studies. Furthermore, there are different ranges of possible Composite, factor, and subtest scores at different age levels, which complicates profile analysis and limits comparisons between students for individual cases. Other weaknesses of the SB IV are the limited factor analytic support for the four area scores and the relatively long administration time.

CONCLUDING COMMENT

The SB IV is a potentially powerful tool for assessing the cognitive ability of young children, adolescents, and young adults. It has good validity, high reliabilities, excellent standardization, good administrative procedures, and helpful scoring criteria. It also has some shortcomings, as noted. Overall, the SB IV is an impressive collection of measures useful for the assessment of cognitive ability.

BIBLIOGRAPHY

DELANEY, E. A., & HOPKINS, T. F. (1987). *The Stanford-Binet Intelligence Scale, fourth edition: Examiner's handbook*. Chicago: Riverside.

SATTLER, J. M. (1992). *Assessment of children* (rev. and updated 3d ed.). San Diego: Author.

THORNDIKE, R. L., HAGEN, E. P., & SATTLER, J. M. (1986). *Technical manual for the Stanford-Binet Intelligence Scale: Fourth edition*. Chicago: Riverside.

NAOMI G. SINGER
JEROME M. SATTLER

STATISTICAL CONCEPTS The use of statistical tools in the study of intelligence has been productive. Although this partnership has benefited both statistics and ability measurement, it is no exaggeration to assert that the understanding of intelligence and all its practical manifestations could not exist without the superstructure provided by statistics. The contributions have not been simply a matter of statistics furnishing tools for the analysis and summarization of data, although this has been invaluable. At key periods in the history of the measurement of intelligence, statistical ideas caught the imagination of the research community so powerfully that the utility of a single equation quite directly fueled the development of new ideas in ability measurement. Fechner and Ebbinghaus, for example, made extensive use of probability as a fundamental component in psychophysics and the theory of memory, and Francis GALTON was captivated by the normal distribution.

I know of scarcely anything so apt to impress the imagination as the wonderful form of cosmic order expressed by the "Law of Frequency of Error" [the normal distribution]. The law would have been personified by the Greeks and deified, if they had known of it. It reigns with serenity and with complete self-effacement amidst the wildest confusion. The huger the mob and the greater the apparent anarchy, the more perfect is its sway. It is the supreme law of Unreason. Whenever a large sample of chaotic elements are taken in hand and marshaled in the order of their magnitude, an unsuspected and most beautiful form of regularity proves to have been latent all along [Galton, 1889, p. 86].

E. G. Boring (1920, p. 8), in another glowing review of the influence of the bell-shaped curve, characterized its appeal this way: "There is a bit of magic in the formula. The law came to play the part of a first principle of nature, of an ideal, given *a priori,* to which nature seeks to conform. The mathematicians wrought slowly, but they wrought a god." For many years at the beginning of the twentieth century, if a sample of ability measurements appeared to be consistent with certain statistical laws, this empirical fact alone was taken as evidence of the validity of the measurements. Conversely, if a collection of measurements did not correspond to these statistical ideals, they were viewed as unsatisfactory or inadequate (Stigler, 1986).

The inexhaustible utility of mathematics in the sciences is a fact that scientists take for granted, but it can be unexpected, even surprising, to a layperson. A host of theoretical and practical matters are involved in the measurement of ability. The use of statistics here, as in other scientific domains, has been of critical importance, and any overview of the field would be incomplete without a background in statistical theory. The purpose of this article is neither to review the history of statistics in ability measurement nor to summarize general features of mathematical models as they pertain to the study of intelligence. Some of these ideas are the topics of other articles. The immediate goal is to define and survey some basic statistical tools that, although not uniquely associated with ability assessment, have been fruitfully used in the measurement of intellectual performance. This article then illustrates how the tools are applied in a simple mathematical model that describes certain features of an achievement test.

SOME PROBABILITY CONCEPTS

In Table 1 the scores of seventy students on an examination in a statistics class are summarized in a "frequency distribution." The ordered values of the test scores are listed in the left column, and the number of

TABLE 1

Frequency distribution of statistics exam scores

Scores	F.	Rel. F.	Cumulative F.	Cumulative Rel. F.
18	1	.014	70	1.000
17	2	.029	69	.986
16	8	.114	67	.957
15	7	.100	59	.843
14	9	.129	52	.743
13	12	.171	43	.614
12	6	.086	31	.443
11	9	.129	25	.357
10	6	.086	16	.229
9	2	.029	10	.143
8	3	.043	8	.114
7	2	.029	5	.071
6	2	.029	3	.043
5	1	.014	1	.014
	70			

NOTE: F. denotes the frequency of individuals who received a score; Rel. F. is the relative frequency; Cumulative F. is the cumulative frequency; Cumulative Rel. F. is cumulative relative frequency.

students who received a particular score (the frequency of occurrence, F.) in the next column. The third column shows the relative frequencies or proportions (*Rel. F.*). For example, 9 of the 70 students received a score of 11 on the test. The relative frequency of 11 is .129 = 9/70, approximately 13 percent of the class. The cumulative frequencies, a running sum of the original numeric frequencies, are in the fourth column. Cumulative relative frequencies in the last column are the running sum of the proportions in the third column. For example, 25 students received a score of 11 or less on this exam; this translates to a cumulative relative frequency of 0.357 = 25/70 for the value of 11. The figure (Figure 1) drawn from a table (Table 1) is called a "histogram" for these data. The height of the bar over each score in the figure reflects the relative frequency.

The cornerstone of statistics is "probability." Probability is often closely tied to observed relative frequencies, such as the entries in the third column. Unlike empirical relative frequencies, probability con-

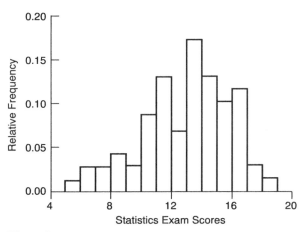

Figure 1

Histogram of statistics exam scores

veys an aspect of uncertainty. The relative frequency describes the proportion of times a score has actually occurred in a sample, but probability is a measure that quantifies how often values of a variable *may* occur. Suppose all the students' scores from this examination were written on separate pieces of paper, placed into a box, and thoroughly mixed; one score is then withdrawn. The outcome of this operation is initially uncertain, yet the relative frequencies in the distribution provide information about what might be expected when a draw is made from the box. Since 11 is written on 9 of the 70 pieces of paper, it seems intuitive that the probability of choosing a score of 11 at random from the box should be 0.129. A working definition of *probability* is that it is the relative frequency of a score that is expected to be observed in an infinite number of repetitions of a chance experiment, such as the one above.

Concepts of probability are established as general rules that apply to many different situations. The rules are used with many different kinds of data, particularly for the measurement of intelligence. It is traditional to distinguish between two classes of variables. A "discrete variable" is one in which the number of possible values the variable may take is countable. Multiple-choice examination questions scored correct or incorrect are an example. The eighteen different test scores in Table 1 are another. Actual measurements of ability of most kinds are discrete. A "continuous variable" is one in which the number of possible values within a

permissible range is infinite. Examples are the reaction time in a perception experiment and the judged length of a physical stimulus, since these variables can be thought of conceptually as existing at infinitely fine gradations. Intelligence as an unobserved psychological construct is usually viewed as continuous, although particular measurements are almost always discrete.

A "probability distribution" is a rule that assigns probabilities to values of a variable. For discrete variables, probability distributions specify a probability for each particular value, with the requirement that the sum of the probabilities over the collection of scores is scaled to unity. For example, range of talent on an intelligence quotient (IQ) test can be grouped into four broad classes. In the general population, the probability distribution for these classes is as follows:

	Inferior	Normal	Superior	Gifted
IQ range	≤89	90–110	111–139	≥140
Probability	.266	.468	.260	.006

The sum of the probabilities is 1. The likelihood of a randomly selected individual having IQ in the normal range is written thus: Prob (normal) = 0.468. The likelihood of an individual with normal or superior IQ is written thus: Prob (normal or superior) = 0.468 + 0.260 = 0.728.

A continuous variable assumes infinitely many different values. Perhaps surprisingly, the probability of any distinct score of a continuous variable is zero. Instead, probability is associated with ranges of values. To illustrate, the upper section of Figure 2 shows the distribution of time to solution of a simple task in which the measurements are made in seconds. As required in a probability distribution, the total area represented by the figure is unity. The probability marked by the shaded area represents the expected proportion of subjects who solve the task in 3–5 seconds. More precisely, it represents the expected proportion who solve the problem between exactly 3 but less than 4 seconds and exactly 4 but less than 5 seconds. In the middle part of Figure 2, measurements are taken to the nearest 0.20 second. The shaded area is a more finely grained distinction of the same information as is in the upper figure. The intervals cover the range of 3.0 to less than 3.2 seconds (3.0–<3.2), then (3.2–<3.4), and so on to the interval (4.8–<5.0). In the

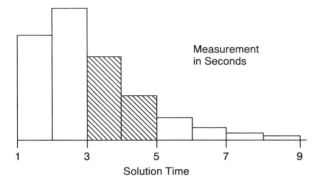

Measurement
in Seconds

Solution Time

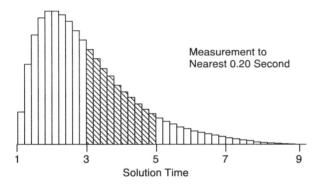

Measurement to
Nearest 0.20 Second

Solution Time

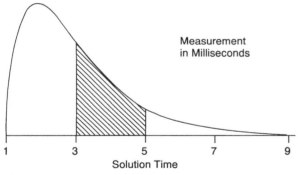

Measurement
in Milliseconds

Solution Time

Figure 2
Probability density of time to solution, by refining a histogram

lowest part of Figure 2, the solution time is recorded in milliseconds. As more precise measurements are taken, the histogram becomes increasingly smooth, until eventually it is described by a curve. The figure is still constructed so that the total area under the curve is unity. Probabilities are available for any arbitrary range of the variable. As this example shows, probability distributions for continuous variables are somewhat different from those for discrete variables.

The curve for the former is called a "probability density."

A "cumulative probability distribution" describes the probability that a variable equals a particular value or less. For a discrete variable, this is the sum of the probability for any specific value and all others that are less. For a continuous variable, the cumulative probability is the proportion of the area under the density to the left of the value.

The "arithmetic mean" of an empirical distribution, such as in Table 1, is the sum of the scores divided by the number of observations. The mean of scores in Table 1 is 12.44. An equivalent operation for finding the arithmetic mean is to multiply each score by its relative frequency and accumulate a running total. With the same data, the operation is

$$18 \cdot (.014) + 17 \cdot (.029) + \ldots \tag{1}$$
$$+ 6 \cdot (.029) + 5 \cdot (.014) = 12.44.$$

This operation carries over directly when computing the mean for discrete probability distributions, except that probabilities for the scores are used in place of relative frequencies. When computed in this way, the mean of a discrete variable is called the "expected value" of the distribution.

The expected value is also defined for continuous distributions, but instead of a summing of the products of values of the variable with the associated probabilities, calculus is needed to compute the analogous quantity over the density of the distribution. To give an idea of the process, one can think of approximating the expected value of the continuous variable in the lowest section of Figure 2 by computing the expected value of the discrete variable in the uppermost distribution. A better approximation would be to use the expected value from the distribution in the middle part of Figure 2, which has many narrower bars. The expected value of the lowermost distribution is the mean that results from using increasingly finer-grained versions of the variable.

PROBABILITY DISTRIBUTIONS

It is meaningful to discuss probability distributions for a particular variable in a particular population, such as IQ in high school students. Another approach to the use of probability is to consider general distributions apart from specific empirical variables. The utility of general probability distributions is that they are not limited to just one case, but instead can be applied to many different situations. For example, questions on an ability test that are scored correct–incorrect can be treated by the same statistical principles that are used to study voter behavior in an election between two candidates.

Consider the case of a "born test taker." Although no better prepared than her classmates, a student nonetheless manages consistently to perform well on multiple-choice examinations. Someone who guesses randomly at test questions may respond almost as if they pick answers by tossing a fair coin: About half of true–false items might be picked correctly. The person in question does better. She was not prepared for a 4-item test, yet answers all 4 items correctly. How can this unusual situation be represented? Table 2 shows the possible scores on four items. It also lists the number of different ways a score can be achieved, and the associated probability assuming each answer pattern is equally likely. If chance alone is operating, a perfect score should occur about 1 time in 16. It has a probability of 0.063. This is a precise way of quantifying the unexpectedly successful way a born test taker performs on a test.

The likelihood of a test score computed from several true–false items is an example of a particular kind of probability distribution called the "binomial." In a binomial distribution, there are n items, each of which is scored correct–incorrect. The response to an item is assumed to be unaffected by responses to any other item. The probability of answering an item correctly by chance alone is the same for all items. This proba-

bility is denoted as p. Permissible scores, k, are integers between zero and n. The probabilities are available from the formula

Prob (k correct out of n items)

$$= \frac{n!}{k!(n-k)!} \cdot p^k \cdot (1-p)^{n-k}, \quad (2)$$

where the operator $k!$ is the product $k \cdot (k-1) \cdot (k-2) \cdot \ldots \cdot 2 \cdot 1$. For a test with n items, the probability of obtaining a score of k varies according to the probability of chance success on the items. In the above example, the probability of 4 correct out of 4 items was 0.063, assuming $p = 0.5$. One could characterize a born test taker as someone who performs as if they bring a larger value of p to the items. If we take $p = 0.6$, then Prob (4 correct out of 4 items) = 0.13, while if $p = 0.7$, the probability is 0.24. In Figure 3, distributions are shown for a 15-item test with three different values of p: 0.2, 0.5, and 0.8. (To avoid the clutter of three histograms in one figure, only the outlines of the histograms are shown. The top of each bar is marked with dot, and the dots are connected. This kind of graph is called a "frequency polygon.") A score of 12 correct is rather likely when $p = 0.8$; it is rare when $p = 0.5$ and extremely unusual when $p = 0.2$.

Figure 4 gives three binomial distributions based on $p = 0.2$. For 5 items, scores of 0, 1, or 2 are most likely, while scores of 3 or more are rare. With 15 items, the largest probabilities are associated with total scores between 1 and 5. Compared to the distribution for $n = 5$, the distribution of the 15-item test is more nearly symmetrical. For a 50-item test, the shape of the distribution is quite regular. This latter distribution

TABLE 2
Illustration of the binomial probability distribution for a four-item test

Possible Answer Patterns					Number of Patterns	Test Scores	Probability
				1111	1	4	.063
	1110	1101	1011	0111	4	3	.250
1100	1010	1001	0110	0101	0011	6	2	.375
	1000	0100	0010	0001	4	1	.250
				0000	1	0	.063
					Total 16		

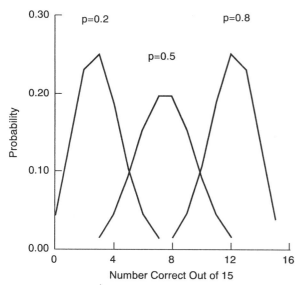

Figure 3

Binomial distributions for 15-item tests

is centered at a score of 10. Scores of 12 or 16 (2 and 6 units above 10) are about as likely as scores of 8 or 4 (an equivalent number of items below 10).

The bell-shaped curve toward which the binomial distribution approaches as *n* increases is called the "normal distribution." Although it was here introduced as a distribution based on a discrete variable, the normal curve is actually the best-known of the

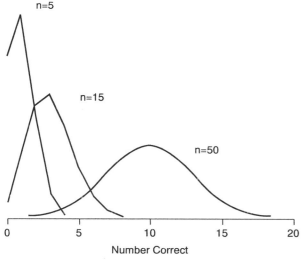

Figure 4

Binomial distributions for tests of differing lengths (probability of correct response on individual items is p = 0.2*)*

continuous distributions. Its probability density has been studied extensively. Statistics texts contain tables that list the probability that a randomly selected score from a normally distributed variable falls between particular points of the distribution. For example, a table was presented earlier showing the probability that IQ in the general population falls between particular scores; these probabilities were found by referring to a standard table.

A MEASUREMENT MODEL

When the domain of ability assessment is viewed as a general area of research, the number of ways that statistical methods can be applied is very large. The investigation of intelligence generates a wealth of empirical data that can be summarized by a host of techniques from applied statistics. A different but equally valuable use of statistical theory involves the direct application of probability concepts to mathematical models of behavior. The process to be studied can be as different as the development of a specific ability through childhood or patterns of learning in a particular laboratory task. One attempts to translate essential characteristics of the behavior into a system of equations. The relationships thought to exist among aspects of the process in the organism are specified as algebraic relations in the model. Then, the variables and equations are studied in their own right as prototypes for the process they are designed to represent. This method of investigation is extremely valuable as a scientific tool. The advantages are a gain in control over the analogue of the process, the ability to replicate easily, the ease and precision in communication, and deductive power (e.g., Coombs, Dawes, & Tversky, 1970).

An interesting example of a statistical model is based directly on the binomial probability rule (Lord, 1965; Allen & Yen, 1979 also review the model). The binomial law specifies a particular relationship between a probability, *p*, and the number of dichotomous test items answered correctly. In the binomial test model, *p* represents a person's "true score" on the test. *True score*, contrary to the meaning it might be expected to have on the face of it, is not the same as a person's true ability in a domain; rather, it refers to the value a variable would have if it was averaged over many administrations. Suppose a woman has an actual height of 5 feet, 5 inches. Consider an imprecise scale of height, one that gives values that are consistently too small. The average of many measurements on the inaccurate device might be 5 feet, 2 inches, 3 inches less than her actual height. Nonetheless, the measurement 5 feet, 2 inches is her true score for this scale. (Allen & Yen, 1979, explain the idea carefully.)

Denote the jth person's true score as p_j. If all p_j's were equal (i.e., all examinees had the same true score), the value of p in the binomial equation above (2) would remain constant and the distribution of total test scores, k, would be directly described by the binomial model, but in general, p is assumed to vary from one individual to another. As a result, the characteristics of the binomial test model will also vary, and Figure 3 can now be reevaluated within the context of different degrees of latent ability.

As illustrated in Figure 3, the shape of an individual's probability distribution (i.e., the probability of an observed score, given p_j) will vary according to true score. A true score of 0.5 will tend to yield a symmetric distribution, provided the number of test items is sufficiently large. Ability levels lower and higher than this will define asymmetric distributions that are positively and negatively skewed, respectively. As the general binomial model establishes, the probability of a low test score is relatively large when a true score value is low, and the converse is also true.

As the above implies (and Figure 3 depicts), the location of an individual's probability distribution along the measurement scale also varies with true score. That higher ability clearly leads to higher mean performance again follows directly from the definition of the general binomial model where the expected value of a distribution with parameters n and p is given as $n \cdot p$. Therefore, the expected values on the 15-item test for individuals with true scores 0.2, 0.5, and 0.8 are 3, 7.5, and 12, respectively. More generally, if the assumptions of the model are met, the expected number of correct items on a test of length n for individual j is $n \cdot p_j$.

An individual's probability distribution can be characterized by its variance, in addition to expected value. Within the context of this model, the variance is defined as $n \cdot p_j \cdot (1 - p_j)$ (Lord & Novick, 1968). It is clear

that this term—which can be interpreted as an index of measurement error—also depends on true score. Specifically, error variance is largest when p_j equals 0.5 and decreases sharply when the true score is near 0 or 1. The implication of this is that the observed score of a person with average ability will be measured with the least precision. The specification of this concept of measurement error is an extremely valuable feature of the model.

This model is called a "strong true-score theory" because it makes specific predictions about the way true scores of individuals are translated into the probability of correct item responses. These probabilities, assumed to vary across individuals, are further used to describe the distribution of total test scores. Finally, if the model performs adequately in large samples, estimates of the true scores can be obtained. Elaborations are reviewed at a technical level in F. M. Lord and M. R. Novick (1968). J. B. Carlin and D. B. Rubin (1991) discuss other extensions.

CONCLUSION

After more than a century of research, measurement of intelligence remains an incomplete puzzle. "Statistics is the art of making numerical conjectures about puzzling questions" (Freedman et al., 1991, p. xiii), and the concrete role of statistics in addressing these questions has assumed various forms. At times, statistical tools have been instrumental in offering solutions. At other times, statistical ideas have driven progress by providing a framework for conceptualizing the study of human ability. Today, the prospect of statistics as a component of mathematical models of intelligence appears to be especially promising. The gain in precision that this method of investigation provides, coupled with more traditional applications of statistics in data analysis, will ensure that the partnership between statistical tools and the study of intelligence continues to flourish.

A final note is offered about further reading. Statistics as a domain of study is certainly no less formidable than the study of human ability. Some patience and expenditure of time is required before one can expect a return on investment. There are scores of excellent textbooks available to aid the process. These give extensive coverage of topics only touched on here. A sizable percentage of the topics they address are relevant to the study of intelligence in some manner, although a goodly portion are concerned with traditional issues of descriptive and inferential statistics. At the college level for behavior science students, J. Devore and R. Peck (1990) is excellent. For statistical theory that emphasizes probability throughout, W. Mendenhall, R. L. Scheaffer, and D. D. Wackerly (1986) review the essential topics. An introductory knowledge of calculus is needed.

BIBLIOGRAPHY

ALLEN, M. J., & YEN, W. M. (1979). *Introduction to measurement theory.* Monterey, CA: Brooks/Cole.

BORING, E. G. (1920). The logic of the normal law of error in mental measurement. *American Journal of Psychology, 31,* 1–33.

CARLIN, J. B., & RUBIN, D. B. (1991). Summarizing multiple-choice tests using three informative statistics. *Psychological Bulletin, 110,* 338–349.

COOMBS, C. H., DAWES, R. M., & TVERSKY, A. (1970). *Mathematical psychology: An elementary introduction.* Englewood Cliffs, NJ: Prentice-Hall.

DEVORE, J., & PECK, R. (1990). *Introductory statistics.* St. Paul, MN: West.

FREEDMAN, D., PISANI, R., PURVES, R., & ADHIKARI, A. (1991). *Statistics* (2nd ed.). New York: W. W. Norton.

GALTON, F. (1889). *Natural inheritance.* London: Macmillan.

LORD, F. M. (1965). A strong true-score theory, with applications. *Psychometrika, 30,* 239–270.

LORD, F. M., & NOVICK, M. R. (1968). *Statistical theories of mental test scores.* Reading, MA: Addison-Wesley.

MENDENHALL, W., SCHEAFFER, R. L., & WACKERLY, D. D. (1986). *Mathematical statistics with applications* (3rd ed.). Boston: Duxbury.

STIGLER, S. M. (1986). *The history of statistics: The measurement of uncertainty before 1900.* Cambridge, MA: Harvard University Press.

ROBERT CUDECK
LISA L. O'DELL

STREET INTELLIGENCE Definitions of intelligence vary across theories and researchers and also for "just plain folks." However, most definitions have some things in common. Intelligence is valued positively (Goodnow, 1986; Mugny & Carrugati, 1989), is an adaptive process (Piaget, 1956; Sternberg, 1986), and involves solving problems in novel ways rather than by rote memory (Laboratory of Comparative Human Cognition, 1982; Sternberg, 1986; Thorndike, 1926).

On the other hand, aspects of the definition of intelligence that formerly seemed uncontroversial are currently subject to questioning. Among these, the issue of consistency across situations stands out. Despite variations in the criteria for defining intelligence, it seemed always clear that intelligence was a characteristic of people rather than of situations. Admittedly, even in the initial stages of research, there were controversies about whether there was a single "intelligence" or several types of intelligence—verbal, spatial, and so on (Thurstone, 1938)—but in both global and specific conceptions of intelligence, within-subject consistency across situations was taken for granted.

Since the early 1970s, however, a considerable amount of evidence on within-subject variation across situations has accumulated. The significance of these findings lies in the fact that within-subject variation is not a matter of different aspects of intelligence but has been observed with respect to the same ability (see, e.g., Lave, 1988; Carraher, Carraher, & Schliemann, 1985). These findings have led to the conception of intelligence as not fixed within the individual but as culturally constituted and emerging in social encounters (Light, 1986). Below are a brief outline of this approach and a description of some of the findings that support it.

THE CULTURAL CONSTRUCTION OF INTELLIGENCE

The conception of intelligence as culturally constructed was developed by A. R. LURIA (1976) and Lev VYGOTSKY (1962) in Russia, S. Scribner and M. Cole (1981) in the United States, and D. Olson (1986) in Canada. They all argued that complex intellectual activity is necessarily mediated by culturally developed systems of signs. A discontinuity between nonmediated and culturally mediated abilities is proposed, and only the latter represent complex intellectual functions. For example, simple knowledge of numbers—such as perceiving differences in quantities—is possible without the mediation of cultural systems. However, complex reasoning about numbers depends on culturally developed systems of signs, such as numeration systems or algebraic representation. According to this view, symbolic systems do not merely express reasoning that subjects carry out in some other fashion: They are an essential part of the reasoning process itself. Counting, for example, cannot be carried out without a numeration system. In order to count properly, as R. Gelman and C. R. Gallistel (1978) pointed out, one must (1) have a set of distinctive counting labels in one-to-one correspondence with the objects counted, and (2) keep the labels in a fixed order. Thus, in order to count one thousand objects, one must produce one thousand labels in a fixed order. Remembering such long ordered lists is beyond the limits of human memory. Numeration systems are cultural solutions to this memory limitation. When we master the numeration systems in our culture, they become an essential part of our ability to count and calculate.

STREET INTELLIGENCE AND SCHOOL INTELLIGENCE

In a culture there are often several systems of signs that can support a single intellectual function. For example, many cultures use both an oral numeration system and a written one. The situation in which an intellectual function is carried out influences the choice of symbolic system used. Counting objects by writing numbers, for example, would be awkward and slow. Thus counting is most often done orally.

The choice of symbolic system is influenced not only by practical considerations but also by social conventions. For example, although children may answer questions in either oral or written form, school practices require children to perform in the written mode most of the time. This social demand is not without consequences. If the symbolic system is an integral part of the intellectual process, the shift from oral to written representation, for example, requires that subjects adopt a different cultural practice, which they might not master as well.

Within-subject differences cannot always be accounted for by changes in type of representation and cultural practices. For example, Ceci, Bronfenbrenner, and Baker (1988) compared children's ability to learn to predict where an image would end up on a screen. Children learned to make predictions either by viewing geometric figures moving on the screen or by playing a video game in which the moving images were butterflies to be captured. In both cases, the images moved according to fixed additive algorithms. Children's accuracy in predicting the location of geometric figures was only 22 percent, even after 750 feedback trials, while their performance in the video game after the same number of trials was near ceiling. These differences are very clear but still poorly understood. Thus far there is no specific hypothesis about the processes involved in children's solutions to this task and the role of cultural practices in producing such differences.

Following is a review of differences in cultural practices that have been related to within-subject differences in two types of abilities: mathematical and logical reasoning. In some of the studies, a within-subject design was used; that is, the same subjects solved comparable tasks in different types of situations. In other studies, a between-subjects design was used; subjects sampled from the same population were randomly distributed to the different situations. Despite the fact that different subjects participate in the experimental conditions in between-subjects studies, the design is expected to guarantee that similar results will be obtained within subjects.

Mathematics in the Streets and in School. Carraher, Carraher, and Schliemann (1985) investigated the ability of five young street vendors in Brazil to solve arithmetic problems either in the course of their vending activity or in school tasks. The youngsters performed significantly better in the course of vending, correctly solving 98 percent of the problems. In contrast, their performance dropped significantly in the school tasks: Only 74 percent of the word problems and 37 percent of the computation exercises were solved correctly.

To set aside the possibility that these within-subject differences were due to differences in motivation, Carraher, Carraher, and Schliemann (1987) saw a second group of children who solved arithmetic problems in three situations: a simulated shop, word problems, and computation exercises. Although the children in this study did not perform as well in the simulated shop as did the vendors in the street, they performed significantly better in the simulated shop than they did in the computation exercises. These results were explained by the youngsters' relying predominantly on oral representation in the simulated shop and on written symbols in the computation exercises. When type of symbolic system was statistically controlled for, differences across situation were no longer significant. Errors observed in oral calculation were significantly smaller than those resulting from written calculation (Nunes, Schliemann, & Carraher, 1993).

Nunes (1993) later examined the extension of these findings to the domain of directed numbers. Negative numbers are marked in written representation by the sign " − ," the same sign that indicates subtraction. In oral representation, the distinction between negative numbers and positive numbers is supported by descriptions used in situations, such as "debt" or "profit." The subjects in this study solved directed-number problems in either the oral or the written mode. Subjects in the oral condition performed significantly better than did those in the written condition. Qualitative analyses of protocols indicated that subjects' errors in the written condition often resulted from difficulties with the representational system itself. Subjects often corrected themselves by figuring out the response orally. They were able to handle the cancellation of debts and profits when thinking about the problem in the oral mode, but made mistakes when they tried to solve the problem in writing.

In summary, different arithmetic practices support reasoning in diverse ways. Clearly, the question of expertise with each particular cultural practice must be taken into account in studies of mathematical reasoning. Evaluations of mathematical abilities restricted to school practices will be characterized by a number of "false negatives"—that is, identifying as "unable" people who are capable of solving the same problems in street mathematics.

Reasoning: Everyday Thinking and Formal Logic. Reasoning skills have been evaluated in several ways in psychology. This discussion will concentrate on conditional reasoning, a well-explored form of logical reasoning analyzed in many studies through the Wason Selection Task (Wason, 1966). The advantage of a single paradigm across studies is that comparability is more easily achieved.

The Wason Selection Task involves announcing a rule (e.g., "If a card has a vowel on one side, then it has an even number on the other side") and asking subjects to test whether the rule is true. Since Wason designed this task within a particular cultural practice, namely, formal logic, the "correct response" is to search for examples that could falsify the rule. For example, the subject sees four cards, showing E, M, 2, and 5. The correct response is to check only those two cards (E and 5) which could falsify the conditional rule. Within this framework, if there were only three cards, M, 2, and 5, the "correct response" would be to check only the card showing 5. In this case, the rule may not be falsified—but it may not apply at all, if the card showing 2 does not have a vowel on the other side. The cultural practice of testing the truth of a rule by "falsification" in formal logic ignores the need for "verification," which is so important both in empirical sciences and in everyday life.

Wason (1966) and Wason and Johnson-Laird (1972) observed that British college students did not perform well on this task. Their errors were mostly due to their turning over the card showing 2–an attempt at verification rather than falsification.

In a later study, Johnson-Laird, Legrenzi, and Legrenzi (1972) analyzed subjects' ability to solve the selection task in another context. Subjects were asked to imagine that they were postal workers sorting the mail, and that they had to verify whether the rule "If a letter is sealed, then it has a 50-lire stamp on it" had been respected in a set of letters. In this context, almost 90 percent of the subjects selected only those cards that would falsify the rule. Johnson-Laird, Legrenzi, and Legrenzi explained this success as the activation of a falsification strategy in a realistic context. It is more likely, however, that subjects worked with an extra bit of implicit but clearly understood information: Overpayment does not matter to the postal service, but underpayment is not acceptable. Thus, only cases of possible underpayment need checking—that is, closed letters and those with cheaper stamps.

Further studies showed that social practices related to the "if–then" statements significantly influence children's and adults' performance in reasoning tasks even if the particular rules are arbitrary and unfamiliar. "If–then" statements that involve permission (e.g., "If one drives over 100 km/h, then one must have a fluorescent car") and prohibition (e.g., "If you drive a truck, you must not go through the town center") typically result in higher rates of correct responses than the "vowel–even number" rule. These contexts supplement the basic rule with information known about permissions or prohibitions that does not have to be made explicit. For example, "If you drive a truck, you must not go through the center of town" is complemented by knowledge about prohibitions, such as "If you drive a car, this rule does not apply." "Logically valid" tests, in this case, are obtained because they coincide with other cultural ways of thinking.

In contrast, "if–then" statements embedded in the context of conditional promises and threats result in *logically invalid* conclusions that make perfect sense in the cultural context of promises and threats. For example, considering the premise "If you mow the lawn, then I'll give you five dollars," most adults conclude that "If you don't mow the lawn, then I will not give you five dollars"—an inferential error in formal logic.

In short, when people interpret a verbal statement, they do so in the context of cultural practices that allow for a meaningful representation of the situation. In the context of a logical analysis, it may be appropriate to test the truth of a statement simply by showing that it is not false. It may also be all right to give five dollars to someone who was supposed to, but did not, mow your lawn. In other contexts, rules are valid if they actually apply, not if you cannot prove them to be false, and you get the money if and only if you mow the lawn. Reasoning about things that matter, as J. J. Goodnow (1986) pointed out, is reasoning about things that one "needs to know" in life. To accomplish this, both logical coherence and understanding of cultural practices are needed. In the evaluation of reasoning skills, as in the evaluation of mathematical abilities, sampling only from one type of cultural practice, formal logic, is likely to produce many false negatives.

CONCLUSIONS

Briefly, this analysis indicates that thinking and problem solving in the streets are embedded in cultural practices that differ from those practices prevailing in academic settings. Reasoning, whether in the streets or in academic institutions, is valid only within the realm in which it makes sense from the social and cultural perspective.

BIBLIOGRAPHY

CARRAHER, T. N., CARRAHER, D. W., & SCHLIEMMAN, A. D. (1985). Mathematics in the streets and in schools. *British Journal of Developmental Psychology, 3,* 21–29.

CARRAHER, T. N., CARRAHER, D. W., & SCHLIEMANN, A. D. (1987). Written and oral mathematics. *Journal for Research in Mathematics Education, 16,* 37–44.

CECI, S. J., BRONFENBRENNER, U., & BAKER, J. G. (1988). Prospective remembering, temporal calibration, and context. In M. M. Gruneberg, P. Morris, U. R. Sykes (Eds.), *Practical Aspects of Memory: Current Research and Issues.* New York: Wiley.

CHENG, P. W., & HOLYOAK, K. J. (1985). Pragmatic reasoning schemas. *Cognitive Psychology, 17,* 391–416.

CHENG, P. W., HOLYOAK, K. J., NISBETT, R. E., & OLIVER, L. M. (1986). Pragmatic versus syntectic approaches to training deductive reasoning. *Cognitive Psychology, 18,* 293–328.

FILLENBAUM, S. (1975). IF: Some uses. *Psychological Research, 37,* 245–260.

FILLENBAUM, S. (1976). Inducements: On the phrasing and logic of conditional promises, threats, and warnings. *Psychological Research, 38,* 231–250.

FILLENBAUM, S. (1977). A condition of plausible inducements. *Language and Speech, 20,* 136–141.

GEIS, M. L., & ZWICKY, A. M. (1971). On invited inferences. *Linguistic Inquiry, 2,* 561–566.

GELMAN, R., & GALLISTEL, C. R. (1978). *The child's understanding of number.* Cambridge, MA: Harvard University Press.

GIROTTO, V., GILLY, M., BLAYE, A., & LIGHT, P. H. (1989). Children's performance in the selection task. *British Journal of Psychology, 80,* 79–95.

GIROTTO, V., LIGHT, P. H., & COLBOURN, C. J. (1988). Pragmatic schemas and conditional reasoning in children. *Quarterly Journal of Experimental Psychology, 40,* 469–482.

GOODNOW, J. J. (1986). Some lifelong everyday forms of intelligent behavior: Organizing and reorganizing. In R. J. Sternberg, & R. K. Wagner (Eds.), *Practical intelligence: Nature and origins of competence in the everyday world.* Cambridge: Cambridge University Press, 143–182.

JOHNSON-LAIRD, P. N., LEGRENZI, P., & LEGRENZI, M. (1972). Reasoning and sense of reality. *British Journal of Psychology, 63,* 395–400.

LABORATORY OF COMPARATIVE HUMAN COGNITION. (1982). Culture and intelligence. In R. Sternberg (Ed.), *Handbook of human intelligence*. Cambridge, England: Cambridge University Press, 642–719.

LAVE, J. (1988). *Cognition in practice: Mind, mathematics and culture in everyday life*. New York: Cambridge University Press.

LIGHT, P. (1986). Context, conservation, and conversation. In P. Light, & M. Richards (Eds.), *Children of social worlds: Development in a social context*. Oxford: Polity Press.

LURIA, A. (1976). *Cognitive development: Its cultural and social foundations*. Cambridge, MA: Harvard University Press.

MUGNY, G., & CARRUGATI, F. (1989). *Social representations of intelligence*. Cambridge: Cambridge University Press.

NUNES, T. (1993). Learning mathematics: Perspectives from everyday life. In R. B. Davis & C. A. Maher (Eds.), *Schools, mathematics, and the world of reality*. Needham, MA: Allyn & Bacon, 61–78.

NUNES, T., SCHLIEMANN, A. D., & CARRAHER, D. W. (1993). *Street mathematics and school mathematics*. New York: Cambridge University Press.

OLSON, D. (1986). Intelligence and literacy: The relationships between intelligence and the technologies of representation and communication. In R. J. Sternberg & R. K. Wagner (Eds.), *Practical intelligence: Nature and origins of competence in the everyday world*. Cambridge: Cambridge University Press.

PIAGET, J. (1956). *La Psychologie de l'intelligence*. Paris: Armand Colin.

SCRIBNER, S., & COLE, M. (1981). *The psychology of literacy*. Cambridge, MA: Harvard University Press.

STERNBERG, R. J. (1986). The evolution of theories of intelligence. *Intelligence, 5*, 209–230.

STERNBERG, R. J., CONWAY, B. E., KETRON, J. L., & BERNSTEIN, M. (1981). People's conceptions of intelligence. *Journal of Personality and Social Psychology, 41*, 37–55.

STERNBERG, R. J. (1986). A triarchic theory of intellectual giftedness. In R. Sternberg, J. Davidson (Eds.), *Conceptions of giftedness*. Cambridge: Cambridge University Press.

THORNDIKE, E. L. (1926). *Measurement of intelligence*. New York: Teachers College Press.

THURSTONE, L. L. (1938). *Primary mental abilities*. Chicago: University of Chicago Press.

VYGOTSKY, L. S. (1962). *Thought and language*. Cambridge, MA: MIT Press.

WASON, P. C. (1966). Reasoning. In B. Foss (Ed.), *New horizons in psychology*. Harmondsworth, England: Penguin.

WASON, P. C., & JOHNSON-LAIRD, P. N. (1972). *Psychology of reasoning: Structure and content*. Cambridge, MA: Harvard University Press.

TEREZINHA NUNES

STRUCTURE-OF-INTELLECT MODEL

J. P. GUILFORD's "structure-of-intellect" (1967, 1982; Guilford & Hoepfner, 1971) is a factor-analytic model of intelligence. Like other factor-analytic models, it posits that the observed differences between people's performance on psychometric tests can be traced to underlying mental abilities, or factors of intelligence.

Originally, Guilford (1967) proposed that the structure of the intellect was composed of 120 different intellectual abilities. These abilities are organized along three dimensions. The dimensions include mental operations (5 category types), contents, or areas of information in which operations are performed (4 category types), and products resulting from applying specific operations in particular contents (6 category types). Thus, there are $5 \times 4 \times 6 = 120$ intellectual abilities, or factors. Each ability is represented by a triad of a particular operation in a particular content area resulting in a specific product.

The operation dimension contains general intellectual processes. They are cognition, memory, divergent production, convergent production, and evaluation. *Cognition* comprises discovery, awareness, comprehension, and understanding. *Memory* is the ability to recall information. *Divergent production* is the process of generating multiple solutions to a problem. *Convergent production* is the process of deducing a single solution to a problem. Finally, *evaluation* is deciding whether an answer is accurate, consistent, or valid; it is similar to the process of judgment (Sternberg, 1990).

The content dimension encompasses the broad areas of information in which operations are applied. It is divided into the figural, symbolic, semantic, and behavioral categories. Guilford's introduction of symbolic and behavioral category types goes beyond a simple semantic (verbal thinking and communication) versus figural (nonverbal/pictorial) distinction (Kail &

Pellegrino, 1985). The symbolic category comprises information organized as symbols or signs that have no meaning in and of themselves, such as numbers and letters of the alphabet. The behavioral category includes behavioral-psychological acts of people.

The product dimension contains results of applying particular operations in specific contents. It includes units, classes, relations, systems, transformations, and implications. A *unit* is a single item of information. A *class* is a set of items that share some attributes, such as a class of domestic animals or pieces of furniture (Guilford & Hoepfner, 1971). A *relation* involves connections between items or variables, such as recognizing that two is less than three, and four is twice as much as two. A *system* is an organization of items, or networks with interacting parts. A *transformation* is a change in an item's attributes; an example is reversing the order of letters in a word, such as *otatop* instead of *potato*. Lastly, an *implication* is an expectation or prediction, such as the Gestalt "laws of organization," which specify how groupings of small parts construct wholes; examples include the "law of good continuation" (points that form straight or curved lines are grouped together, and lines are perceived as following the smoothest path) and the "law of similarity" (similar features tend to be grouped together).

RELATION TO OTHER FACTOR-ANALYTIC MODELS

The structure-of-intellect model departs from the majority of factor-analytic models in two ways. First, most factor-analytic models (see Cattell, 1963, 1971; Vernon, 1965) are hierarchical. Usually, they suggest that at the top of the intellectual abilities hierarchy there is a single general factor of intelligence (*g*). Below *g* are lower-order factors representing more specific mental abilities. At the bottom of the hierarchy are the most specific abilities, which cannot be broken down into factors any further. Inherent in a hierarchical model is the idea that some mental abilities are related and thus converge on a higher-level ability. For example, P. E. VERNON (1965) suggested that mathematical abilities and scientific and technical abilities load on a single spatial-abilities factor. It, in turn, loads on the spatial-practical-mechanical ability, which itself loads on *g*. J. L. Horn and R. B. CATTELL (1967) pro-

posed five second-order factors of intelligence. The ones they emphasized in particular were *Gf* (fluid ability) and *Gc* (crystallized ability); *Gf* refers to the ability to infer and apply relations and is considered to be biological in nature, and *Gc* refers to verbal comprehension ability and is believed to be affected by culture and environment. The fact that *Gf* and *Gc* tend to be correlated lends support to the existence of a single higher-order factor *g* (Kail & Pellegrino, 1985). In contrast, Guilford (1967) continued with L. L. THURSTONE's (1938) kind of theory, which does not include a single general factor of intelligence; instead, it is posited that the intellect is composed of primary mental abilities. Thurstone suggested that nine such primary mental abilities exist, but Guilford proposed an ambitious 120 different ones (later increased to 150). Guilford initially claimed that the mental abilities were independent of one another. Later, for reasons discussed below, Guilford (1982) succumbed to the notion that some of the factors converged onto higher-level ones. Nonetheless, he maintained a persistent disbelief in a single general higher-order factor such as *g*.

Second, while other factor-analytic models focus mainly on the factorial structure of intelligence, Guilford's model also emphasizes cognitive processes and products of cognition. For example, it includes such mental operations as generating multiple solutions to a problem (divergent thinking) and recalling information from memory.

GUILFORD'S TESTS OF MENTAL ABILITIES

Guilford (1962; Guilford & Hoepfner, 1971) originally made the assumptions that each mental ability had a corresponding unique location on each of the three dimensions and that the abilities were independent of each other. He thus attempted to devise tests that purported to map uniquely onto the 120 different mental abilities. For example, the tests of cognition of symbolic transformations (CST) assess whether a person can detect particular changes in a stimulus, such as in finding letter transformations (FLT), wherein a person is given a word that is spelled both correctly and incorrectly and is asked to detect the changes that occurred between one spelling and the other, including omissions or substitutions of letters. Another CST task includes reading backward (RB). In this test, subjects are asked to read sentences with words that are printed in reverse order. An example of such a sentence is "nezod a ni selppa ynam woH" (Guilford & Hoepfner, 1971).

Other examples are the tests of cognition of symbolic units (CSU). They include alterations, disemvoweled words, four-letter words, and omelet tests (examples of each test are taken from Guilford & Hoepfner, 1971). On alterations tests, people are asked to decide whether alternative words can be constructed by reversing the order of adjacent letters (e.g., *sue, brake, time, lion*). Disemvoweled tests ask people to recognize words in which the vowels are left out (e.g., m__g__c, d__ct__r, s__rpr__s__). The four-letter-word test requires people to discern words within lines of consecutive letters (e.g., *amgewindyetkcqrockwzluremv*). Finally, omelet tests ask people to rearrange four letters in order to construct a known word (e.g., *panl*).

RESEARCH APPLICATIONS

Guilford's structure-of-intellect model has been applied in programs aiming to enhance thinking skills. One of the notable examples of such a program is SOI (structure of intellect), designed by M. Meeker (1969). Meeker claims that by using the method of factor analysis, she was able to demonstrate the empirical validity of 96 of Guilford's 120 factors. R. J. Sternberg and K. Bhana (1986) show that most children who receive training on the SOI program usually perform better on the post- than on the pretest. However, they also make the point that SOI is designed explicitly to teach to the posttest. Thus, in order to accept the gain as an increase in thinking skills, rather than in performing on SOI-like test items, one needs to believe that the structure of intellect is an accurate model of intelligence.

The structure-of-intellect model also had a major effect on research on creativity. In 1950, Guilford delivered his parting address as president of the American Psychological Association (APA). As part of his speech, he noted that only 186 out of 121,000 entries in *Psychological Abstracts* were about creativity. As F. Barron and D. M. Harrington (1981) point out, the

numbers since then have grown almost exponentially. Guilford primarily relied on divergent-thinking tests for assessing creative thinking. Divergent thinking, remember, is the ability to produce multiple solutions to a single problem. For example, word fluency requires people to produce as many words as possible from a particular letter of the alphabet (Christensen & Guilford, 1958). Many researchers have been greatly influenced by Guilford's work on divergent thinking and creativity (McCrae, Arenberg, & Costa, 1987; Runco, 1992; Torrance, 1974). A growing number of others argue that divergent-thinking tests have limited criterion validity (for more details, see Eysenck, 1979; Wallach, 1986); in other words, such tests may not be adequate for assessing real-world creativity.

CRITICISMS OF STRUCTURE OF INTELLECT

Guilford's model has come under attack from a statistical point of view. In order to produce the factors in the structure-of-intellect model, Guilford used a form of factor-analytic rotation called targeted, or procrustean, rotation. When a researcher uses procrustean rotation technique, he or she specifies a priori the kind of best-fitting model he or she desires to achieve. The outcome is thus forced to match the hypothesized model as much as possible. In fact, when J. L. Horn and J. R. Knapp (1973) used procrustean rotation to test random models of intelligence using Guilford's own data, they found significant support for these random models as well. As R. Kail and J. W. Pellegrino (1985) pointed out, this evidence is not a direct disconfirmation of Guilford's model, but it shows that using procrustean rotations for devising a factor-analytic model of intelligence may be methodologically problematical.

Statistical criticisms were also directed at the evidence of correlations between mental tests designed to assess different abilities. It was noted above that Guilford attempted to devise tests that would uniquely map onto every single factor in his model. In order to show that a particular test maps uniquely onto a particular mental ability, one has to show not only that the test measures the mental ability of interest but, just as important, that the test does not measure any other mental ability. Thus, the correlation between mental tests designed to assess different mental abilities should be equal to, or very close to, zero. Guilford (1982) found that tests for certain mental abilities did indeed correlate significantly. He was thereby forced to conclude that there exist interrelations among the mental abilities.

LATER CHANGES TO THE STRUCTURE-OF-INTELLECT MODEL

In subsequent years, Guilford (1977, 1982) modified the structure-of-intellect model. First, he replaced the figural category within the content dimension with auditory and visual content categories. Since the content dimension was changed to 5 categories, the overall number of intellectual abilities increased to $5 \times 6 \times 5 = 150$. Second, Guilford acknowledged the fact that specific mental abilities or factors could be intercorrelated. The revised model thereby allows for the notion that there exist underlying higher-order factors, or mental abilities. The lowest, or first-order, factors are the 150 cells of the model. The cells are represented by triads of operation-content-product abilities. For example, cognition of semantic classes and evaluation of symbolic relations are first-order relations. The second-order factors consist of the pairwise combinations of cells, which result in 85 factors. Each pair is a combination of two dimensions (e.g., content and operation) collapsed over the third dimension (e.g., product). Examples of second-order relations are memory for symbolic content and convergent production of relations. The factors add up thus:

$$
\begin{array}{rcl}
5 \text{ (operation)} \times 6 \text{ (product)} & = & 30 \\
5 \text{ (operation)} \times 5 \text{ (content)} & = & 25 \\
6 \text{ (content)} \times 5 \text{ (product)} & = & 30 \\
\text{Total} & & 85
\end{array}
$$

The third-order factors are the sixteen category types $(5 + 5 + 6)$. Thus, cognition, implication, and behavioral content are all examples of third-order components. As Kail and Pellegrino (1985) noted, Guilford's revisions to his model move it closer to being a hierarchical model that allows for the intercorrelation of its specific factors. However, Guilford still maintains that a single general factor of intelligence, g, does not exist at the top of the hierarchy.

(*See also:* FACTOR ANALYSIS.)

BIBLIOGRAPHY

BARRON, F., & HARRINGTON, D. M. (1981). Creativity, intelligence, and personality. *Annual Review of Psychology, 32,* 439–476.

CATTELL, R. B. (1963). Theory of fluid and crystallized intelligence: A critical experiment. *Journal of Educational Psychology, 54,* 1–22.

CATTELL, R. B. (1971). *Abilities: Their structure, growth, and action.* Boston: Houghton-Mifflin.

CHRISTENSEN, P. R., & GUILFORD, J. P. (1958). *Word Fluency, Form A.* Beverly Hills, CA: Sheridian Supply.

EYSENCK, H. J. (1979). *The structure and measurement of intelligence.* Berlin: Springer-Verlag.

GUILFORD, J. P. (1967). *The nature of human intelligence.* New York: McGraw-Hill.

GUILFORD, J. P. (1977). *Way beyond the IQ: Guide to improving intelligence and creativity.* Buffalo, NY: Creative Education Foundation.

GUILFORD, J. P. (1982). Cognitive psychology's ambiguities: Some suggested remedies. *Psychological Review, 89,* 48–59.

GUILFORD, J. P., & HOEPFNER, R. (1971). *The analysis of intelligence.* New York: McGraw-Hill.

HORN, J. L., & CATTELL, R. B. (1967). Refinement and test of the theory of fluid and crystallized ability intelligences. *Journal of Educational Psychology, 57,* 253–270.

HORN, J. L., & KNAPP, J. R. (1973). On the subjective character of the empirical base of Guilford's structure of intellect model. *Psychological Bulletin, 80,* 33–43.

KAIL, R., & PELLEGRINO, J. W. (1985). *Human intelligence: Perspectives and prospects.* New York: W. H. Freeman.

MCCRAE, R. R., ARENBERG, D., & COSTA, P. T. (1987). Declines in divergent thinking with age: Cross-sectional, longitudinal, and cross-sequential analyses. *Psychology and Aging, 2,* 130–137.

MEEKER, M. (1969). *The structure of intellect: Its interpretation and uses.* Columbus, Ohio: Merrill.

RUNCO, M. A. (1992). Children's divergent thinking and creative ideation. *Developmental Review, 12,* 223–264.

SPEARMAN, C. (1904). "General intelligence" objectively determined and measured. *American Journal of Psychology, 15,* 201–293.

STERNBERG, R. J. (1990). *Metaphors of mind: Conceptions of the nature of intelligence.* New York: Cambridge University Press.

STERNBERG, R. J., & BHANA, K. (1986). Synthesis of research on the effectiveness of intellectual skills programs:

Snake-oil remedies or miracle cures? *Educational Leadership, 44,* 60–67.

THURSTONE, L. L. (1938). *Primary mental abilities.* Chicago: University of Chicago Press.

TORRANCE, E. P. (1974). *Torrance tests of creative thinking.* Lexington MA: Personnel Press.

VERNON, P. E. (1965). Ability factors and environmental influences. *American Psychologist, 20,* 723–733.

WALLACH, M. A. (1986). Creativity testing and giftedness. In F. D. Horowitz & M. O'Brien (Eds.), *The gifted and talented: Developmental perspectives.* Washington, DC: American Psychological Association.

TALIA BEN-ZEEV

SYSTEM OF MULTICULTURAL PLURALISTIC ASSESSMENT (SOMPA)

The System of Multicultural Pluralistic Assessment (SOMPA) (Mercer, 1979a; Mercer & Lewis, 1977, 1978) is a battery of measures designed to yield racially and culturally nondiscriminatory assessments of children from Hispanic, African-American, and working-class white backgrounds who are being evaluated for placement in special education classes. SOMPA is needed because a disproportionately large percentage of children from cultural, linguistic, and racial minorities are identified as mentally subnormal when English-language IQ tests standardized on the general population are used to make inferences about "intelligence" (Mercer, 1973, 1979b).

Overrepresentation of minorities occurs because IQ tests cannot directly measure a biological substrate; they measure only what a person has learned. Because learning depends upon opportunity and motivation as well as intelligence, a low IQ score may be the result of few opportunities to learn, low motivation to learn, low intelligence, or some combination of these factors. Children from minority groups have less opportunity and less motivation to learn the materials in IQ tests and, consequently, earn scores that average 10 to 15 points below the average for the general population. When psychologists interpret their IQ scores as direct measures of intelligence and ignore the cultural factors influencing test performance, many children from minority groups are misdiagnosed as mentally subnormal.

Often, their lower scores are the result of limited exposure to the linguistic and cultural materials in the test (Mercer, 1988, 1989).

NATURE AND ORGANIZATION OF SOMPA

Premises About Assessment. SOMPA is based on three premises. First, a good assessment screens children to determine whether their difficulties may have a medical or organic basis. Second, a good assessment is multidimensional, examining children's performance in multiple settings with multiple measures. Third, a good assessment takes into account the cultural loading in IQ tests before making inferences about a child's intelligence.

Standardization of SOMPA. The English-language version of the SOMPA was standardized on a probability sample of 690 Hispanic, 627 African-American, and 699 white students aged 6–11 attending California public schools (Mercer, 1979a). The Spanish-language version was standardized on 1,100 public school students aged 6–16 in Mexico City (Palacio, 1982a, b; Palacio, Hinojosa, & Padilla, 1982; Palacio, Padilla, & Roll, 1984).

Three Assessment Models in SOMPA. (1) The *medical model* includes six measures of the child's biological status: a health and medical history based on information from the mother; a hearing test; a vision test; a measure of body stature; a test of visual–motor coordination; and a set of physical dexterity measures. Scores are evaluated to determine whether the child's difficulties in school can be related to medical or health problems. Significantly, there were no differences among racial, ethnic, or socioeconomic groups in the number or kinds of biological problems identified in children.

(2) The *social system model* measures how well children are adapting to the demands of their social environments. The assessment is based on information about the child's social behavior reported by the mother in response to questions in the Adaptive Behavior Inventory for Children (ABIC). During the interview, the mother is asked age-appropriate questions about the child's social behaviors in family roles, community roles, peer group roles, nonacademic school

roles, earner/consumer roles, and self-maintenance roles. Many children who have difficulty in school, especially minority group children, are socially competent outside of school. This competence indicates that they are probably not mentally retarded, regardless of their score on an IQ test. No differences were found in the average adaptive behavior of children from different racial, ethnic, or socioeconomic groups, indicating that the ABIC is not racially and culturally discriminatory.

(3) The *pluralistic model* yields an estimate of the child's intelligence by controlling, statistically, for the cultural loading in IQ tests. It uses the Wechsler Intelligence Scale for Children–Revised (WISC-R) to measure children's accumulated knowledge and current functioning level in English. This test has five subtests that measure verbal skills—Vocabulary, Information, Comprehension, Arithmetic, and Similarities—and five subtests that measure the speed and accuracy of other types of performance, such as putting puzzles together, making a design with blocks, repeating numbers forward and backward, and coding nonsense symbols. When children's raw scores on the WISC-R are compared with the published norms for the test, the score is *not* interpreted as a measure of intelligence, but is interpreted as a measure of "achievement," defined as the child's *current functioning level* relative to the general population in the skills and knowledge covered in the test.

To make inferences about children's intelligence using the WISC-R, SOMPA assumes that it is necessary to take into account the fact that children of different ages and different cultural backgrounds have not had the same opportunities to learn the materials in the test. Younger children have had less opportunity than older children; therefore WISC-R scores have traditionally been standardized by age. Children from minority backgrounds have had less opportunity than children reared in the U.S. core culture; therefore, in SOMPA, WISC-R scores are standardized by sociocultural background.

To measure sociocultural background, each mother provides information about the family: language spoken in the home, community participation, family size, family structure, socioeconomic status, education of the parents, country and region of origin of the par-

ent, and the mother's sense of efficacy. Multiple regression equations were created for each group (Hispanic, African-American, and white) by predicting children's IQ scores on the WISC-R from the sociocultural background information provided by the mother. To interpret children's individual scores as a measure of intelligence, the scores are compared with the average IQ score (the norm) of other children from the same ethnic group and the same sociocultural background, producing a racially and culturally nondiscriminatory basis for making inferences about intelligence. SOMPA contains simple tables that enable the psychologist to make unbiased inferences about a child's *estimated learning potential* (i.e., intelligence) by using appropriate sociocultural norms.

A complete SOMPA profile consists of all the measures described above. When they are used in making assessments, the overrepresentation of racial and ethnic minorities in special education classes and their underrepresentation in classes for the gifted disappear (Mercer, 1979a).

CRITICISMS OF SOMPA

Criticisms of SOMPA have focused primarily on the pluralistic model, which makes inferences about the child's intelligence using sociocultural norms. Criticisms can be grouped into four major categories.

Criticisms from a Traditional Psychomedical Perspective. The traditional psychomedical model of assessment assumes that psychological reality is external, objective, and measurable, consisting of entities, such as a concrete intelligence, that exist in individual persons. It further assumes that individuals have different amounts of the intelligence entity and that these differences can be measured by IQ tests (Cleary et al., 1975; Jensen, 1980). Because traditionalists conceptualize intelligence as an objective, measurable entity, they compare IQ tests to thermometers and to tuberculin tests (Clarizio, 1979) and to measures of height and weight (Gordon, 1977) that have a single set of norms for everyone. They reject sociocultural norms.

SOMPA argues that such critics are reifying intelligence. They forget that intelligence is "something that is inferred from the way (a person) thinks, talks, moves" (Wechsler, 1974, pp. 3–7) and is not a physical attribute of the organism.

Other critics of SOMPA recognize that IQ tests measure that which has been learned, and that intelligence is inferred rather than measured directly. They argue that sociocultural norms are not necessary, however, because U.S. society is homogenous and that "practically all our present standardized tests, culture reduced or not, span as wide or wider a range of cultural distance as is found among any native-born, English-speaking racial and socioeconomic groups within the United States today" (Jensen, 1980, p. 642). SOMPA disagrees with this assertion. It assumes U.S. society is culturally heterogenous.

Finally, traditionalists argue that IQ tests are valid and do not require sociocultural norms because they have comparable predictive validity for majority and minority groups. When scores on IQ tests are correlated with "socially relevant criteria," such as scores on the Scholastic Aptitude Test, high school and college grades, and academic achievement tests, they are able to predict with equal accuracy which majority and minority students are most likely to succeed or fail (Cleary et al., 1975; Jensen, 1980). Of course, IQ tests will predict more failures for persons from minority groups because minorities, on average, score 10 to 15 points below the majority on IQ tests. This latter fact is not interpreted as an indication of cultural loading or bias in IQ tests but as an indication that minorities have less intelligence than the majority group.

SOMPA disagrees with both positions. It argues that equal predictive validity does not mean IQ tests are an equally valid basis for inferring the intelligence of all sociocultural groups. Scores on IQ tests, scholastic aptitude tests, school grades, and achievement tests are highly correlated for all groups because they are all measuring the same thing—student knowledge of U.S. mainstream culture and standard English. Furthermore, SOMPA interprets the 10- to 15-point difference between the average scores of majority and minority groups as a clear indication that the tests are culturally loaded and favor the majority group. Such large differences are both statistically and substantively significant and cannot be ignored. Separate sociocultural norms are needed for statistically distinct populations.

Holistic and Humanistic Criticisms. Humanists criticize both SOMPA and the traditional psychomedical model for their objectivist view of intelligence. Humanists assume that psychological realities are socially constructed, and that intelligence is an abstract concept, not an objective, measurable entity. Individuals in a particular society reach a consensus on the types of behavior they will classify as intellectual. IQ tests simply reflect what psychologists have agreed to call intelligence. From the holistic/constructivist viewpoint, it is nonsense to reify a social construction, to act as if it were a substantive entity, to standardize, measure, and quantify that abstraction, and then to create descriptions of children segmented into hypothetical traits.

Humanists criticize SOMPA because, like the traditional psychomedical model, it assumes that intelligence can be inferred if the inference is based on the appropriate sociocultural norm. They argue that each individual is a unique whole person and cannot be partitioned into the hypothetical traits and processes presumably measured by standardized tests—that children cannot be decomposed into a set of scores (Heshusius, 1982; Poplin, 1984, 1988).

Criticisms from a Social Conflict Perspective. SOMPA has also been criticized by those who see intelligence testing as a procedure devised by the majority to systematically devalue and oppress minority groups in U.S. society (Kamin, 1974). Such critics regard sociocultural norms as another device to perpetuate the pernicious practice of intelligence testing. In *Larry P. v. Riles* (495 F. Supp. 926 [N.D. Cal. 1979]), African-American plaintiffs successfully argued not for sociocultural norms but for the abolition of all tests that purport to measure the intelligence of African-American children. In a similar vein, others contend that U.S. society is now so linguistically and culturally diverse that it is simply impossible to create sociocultural norms for every linguistic and cultural group (Goodman, 1979).

Pragmatic Criticisms. Psychological assessments are already being criticized as expensive, lengthy, complicated, and educationally irrelevant. Critics of traditional assessment contend that (1) psychologists cannot reliably distinguish disabled from nondisabled children or differentiate one type of handicapping condition from another (Ysseldyke et al., 1983); (2) tests have low reliability and validity (Kavale & Forness, 1987); and (3) psychometric information is essentially useless in planning educational interventions (Arter & Jenkins, 1979). Because SOMPA is a pluralistic version of the traditional psychomedical model, it, too, is vulnerable to all these criticisms. In addition, it increases the amount of time spent in assessment.

CONCLUSION

SOMPA was developed during the 1970s to challenge some of the assumptions of the traditional psychomedical model and to counteract abuses in the evaluation of sociocultural minorities. It served that purpose. Today, the psychomedical model no longer completely dominates assessment. It is being replaced by more humanistic, cognitive approaches to assessment that do not purport to measure intelligence but, instead, focus on the child's current performance and on providing appropriate learning experiences.

(*See also:* MERCER, JANE R.)

BIBLIOGRAPHY

ARTER, J. A., & JENKINS, J. R. (1979). Examining the benefits and prevalence of modality considerations in special education. *Journal of Special Education, 11,* 281–298.

CLARIZIO, H. F. (1979). In defense of the IQ test. *School Psychology Digest, 8,* 79–88.

CLEARY, T. A., HUMPHREYS, L. G., KENDRICK, S. A., & WESMAN, A. G. (1975). Educational uses of tests with disadvantaged students. *American Psychologist, 30,* 15–41.

GOODMAN, J. F. (1979). Is tissue the issue? A critique of SOMPA's models and tests. *The School Psychology Digest, 8*(1), 47–62.

GORDON, R. (1977). Examining labelling theory: The case of mental retardation. In Walter R. Gove (Ed.), *The labelling of deviance: Evaluating a perspective.* New York: Halstead.

HESHUSIUS, L. (1982). At the heart of the advocacy dilemma: A mechanistic world view. *Exceptional Children, 49,* 6–13.

JENSEN, A. R. (1980). *Bias in mental testing.* New York: The Free Press.

KAMIN, L. J. (1974). *The science and politics of I.Q.* New York: Wiley.

KAVALE, K. A., & FORNESS, S. (1987). Substance over style: Assessing the efficacy of modality testing and teaching. *Exceptional Children, 54*(3), 228–239.

MERCER, J. R. (1973). *Labeling the mentally retarded.* Berkeley: University of California Press.

MERCER, J. R. (1979a). *SOMPA: Technical and conceptual manual.* New York: The Psychological Corporation.

MERCER, J. R. (1979b). In defense of racially and culturally nondiscriminatory assessment. *The School Psychology Digest, 8*(1), 89–115.

MERCER, J. R. (1988). Ethnic differences in IQ scores: What do they mean? (A response to Lloyd Dunn). *Hispanic Journal of Behavioral Sciences, 10* (3), 199–218.

MERCER, J. R. (1989). Alternative paradigms for assessment in a pluralistic society. In James A. Banks & Cherry A. McGee Banks (Eds.), *Multicultural education: Issues and perspectives* (pp. 289–304). Boston: Allyn & Bacon.

MERCER, J. R., & LEWIS, J. F. (1977). *SOMPA: Parent interview manual.* New York: The Psychological Corporation.

MERCER, J. R., & LEWIS, J. F. (1978a). *SOMPA: Student assessment manual.* New York: The Psychological Corporation.

MERCER, J. R., & LEWIS, J. F. (1978b). The system of multicultural pluralistic assessment: SOMPA. In W. Alan Coulter & Henry W. Morrow (Eds.), *Adaptive Behavior: Concepts and Measurements.* New York: Grune & Stratton.

PALACIO, M. G. (1982a). *SOMPA: Sistema de evaluación multicultural y pluralístico: Manual de aplicación.* Mexico City: Department of Special Education

PALACIO, M. G. (1982b). *SOMPA: Sistema de evaluación multicultural y pluralistico. Manual de calificación.* Mexico City: Department of Special Education

PALACIO, M. G., HINOJOSA, E. R., & PADILLA, E. (1982). *Estandarización de la batería de pruebas SOMPA en México D. F.: Informe sobre teoría y resultados.* Mexico City: Department of Special Education.

PALACIO, M., PADILLA, E. R., & ROLL, S. (1984). *Wechsler Intelligence Scale for Children–Revised: Mexicano (WISC–RM).* Mexico City: El Manual Moderno, S.A.

POPLIN, M. (1984). Toward an holistic view of persons with learning disabilities. *Learning Disability Quarterly, 7,* 290–294.

POPLIN, M. (1988). Holistic/constructivist principles of the teaching/learning process: Implications for the field of learning disabilities. *Journal of Learning Disabilities, 21*(7), 401–416.

WECHSLER, D. (1974). *Manual for the Wechsler Intelligence Scale for Children–Revised.* New York: The Psychological Corporation.

YSSELDYKE, J. E., THURLOW, M. L., GRADEN, J. L., WESSON, C., DENO, S. L., & ALGOZZINE, B. (1983). Generalizations from five years of research on assessment and decision making. *Exceptional Education Quarterly, 4,* 75–93.

JANE R. MERCER

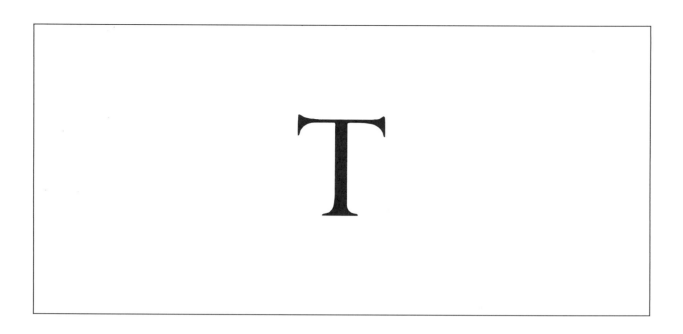

T

TERMAN, LEWIS M. (1877–1956) The conception of mental ability certainly derives from the pioneering work of Francis GALTON (1869) and Alfred BINET (1902) in Europe; it owes much of its conceptual permeation in psychology and education throughout the world to the scientific empiricism of Lewis M. Terman. Terman developed, researched, and promulgated the systematic measurement of mental ability with carefully constructed tests. Galton's major concern with the heritability of genius and eugenic manipulation had its impact on Terman, as it did on a large number of psychologists in the early twentieth century, but Terman remained the empiricist ever open to scientific evidence. He was chiefly concerned with the nature of human ability and with the impact of experience and education on the development of intelligence.

It was Binet, of course, whose work on the development of tests to measure mental ability most directly influenced Terman. With a doctorate in science completed in 1894, Binet set to work studying individual differences in intelligence by constructing psychological tests to measure judgment, memory, and imagination. Two years later, Binet and Henri (1896) reported their work (unsuccessful to that date) on developing tests to measure attention, comprehension, imagery, aesthetic appreciation, moral judgment, and visual space appreciation. Much of Binet's still unsuccessful continuing work during this period was later reported in *The Experimental Study of Intelligence* (1902). Binet is most well remembered for his 1905 work with Simon on the specific tasks of developing tests in Paris to screen "mentally defective" children for special educational programs. Refined scales developed for this project were reported by Binet and Simon in 1908. A short time later, Wilhelm Stern (1914) introduced the intelligence quotient as the ratio of the mental age score to the chronological age; the ground work had then been laid for the measurement of intelligence on a larger and more refined basis.

Lewis M. Terman was born and grew up on a farm near the small town of Needham, in southern Indiana, a short distance from Indianapolis. He attended a one-room rural school in Needham and was grade advanced twice, so that he completed eighth grade by age 12. His education was augmented by active reading in the Terman's family library, which included the *Encyclopedia Britannica,* travel books, atlases, the Bible, and a variety of classic novels.

At 15 he was enrolled at Central Normal College at Danville, Indiana, near Indianapolis, to study for the field of teaching. The teachers at the college were stimulating scholars who evoked high-level intellectual motivation in Terman. The grade book of Central Normal College, dated January 14, 1893, recently found in the attic of an old building that was once a part of this now-defunct college, shows Terman sharing the top grade honors with another student. At 17 he graduated and began teaching in a one-room rural school. He returned to the college for two additional periods, so that by 1898 he had earned three degrees: bachelor of science, bachelor of pedagogy, and bachelor of arts.

Terman's lifelong struggles with illness began at 19, with typhoid fever, and a short time later at 21, with tuberculosis. This chronic affliction led to his decision, later, to move to a better climate and to take a number of prolonged rest periods, during which he had abundant time to read.

By 1901, his health being quite restored, Terman entered Indiana University at Bloomington as a junior to pursue B.A. and M.A. degrees. In two years he completed nearly four years of college study in psychology, education, philosophy, two languages, and other subjects; however, it was psychology that became his passion. Professor E. H. Lindley became Terman's mentor and introduced him to the writings of the major German and French psychologists of the time, including Alfred Binet, Jean-Martin Charcot, Francis Galton, Edward B. Titchener, Wilhelm Wundt, and Hermann Ebbinghaus.

Terman had married Anna Minton in 1899 and their first child, Fred, was born in 1900. When Terman gradated from Indiana University in 1903, the family moved to Worcester, Massachusetts, where he began studies toward a Ph.D. in psychology at Clark University. There, Terman came under the influence of the then great patriarch of psychology, G. Stanley Hall. Hall expressed great expectations for Terman because of communications from Terman's mentors at Indiana University. Terman attended Hall's seminars on Monday evenings and reported that he always found them intellectually "intoxicating." However, his major mentor at Clark was E. C. Sanford, who inspired Terman to read voraciously. Terman also found his fellow students powerfully stimulating, particularly his close friend Arnold Gesell. An attack of Terman's tuberculosis condition struck near the end of the first year and caused great concern about his potential to carry on with his graduate studies. Nevertheless, after several months of rest, his health returned; by spring of 1904 he was planning his doctoral dissertation research. During the spring of 1905, Terman administered a series of tests to two groups of subjects, twelve boys selected from Worcester public school as "bright" and twelve selected as "stupid." The tests, all developed by

Terman, included measures of (1) inventiveness and imagination, (2) logical thinking, (3) mathematical skills, (4) language, (5) interpretation of fables, (6) skill in learning to play chess, (7) memory, and (8) motor skills. The "bright" boys outscored the "stupid" boys on all tasks except the motor measures.

Terman's degree was completed in 1905 and he accepted a position as principal of a school in San Bernardino, California. In 1907, he was appointed to a professorship at Los Angeles Normal School and, in 1910, to a professorial position at Stanford University. During this five-year period Terman had undoubtedly read widely in the emerging literature on intelligence testing and especially Binet's publications. Thus, in part as an outgrowth of his Ph.D. dissertation research and as a result of his increasing interest in the Binet scales, Terman began experimental work with the Binet scales almost immediately after arriving at Stanford. This activity culminated in his publication, in 1916, of the Stanford-Binet Scales (his American adaptation of Binet's mental ability testing), and the book *The Measurement of Intelligence* in which he defined intelligence as ability to conceptualize and think abstractly.

National and international recognition came to Terman as a result of the widespread use of the Stanford-Binet Scales for intelligence testing. Terman's next contribution to the field of intelligence testing came with World War I and a newly recognized problem—the army's need for a means of mass assessment of the abilities of the U.S. Army recruits for training and placement in jobs commensurate with their abilities and potentials. A committee led by Robert YERKES was organized and charged to develop and administer intelligence tests to all recruits. The resulting Army Alpha Test became the benchmark for later group-administered, pencil-and-paper tests of intelligence. Terman's role in this project was substantial, but it should be noted that the committee included a number of psychologists who would become pioneers in the field, and especially the field of psychological testing, like Arthur Otis, Edward L. THORNDIKE, and Truman Kelly.

In the 1920s, Terman undertook two major lines of research and development activity, one being the development of a measure of school learning to include all basic subject matters. The result of this effort, *The*

Stanford Achievement Test, published in 1923, was a model for standardized achievement tests (which could be administered to a whole class of students) that prevails to this day. *The Stanford Achievement Test,* after many revisions and updatings, stands as a model of objective, reliable, and valid measurement of children's learning in school.

The second major project of the 1920s was the initiation of Terman's subsequent lifelong longitudinal research on the development of gifted youth, a sample of children he followed from age 12 through adulthood and into old age. It is perhaps to Terman more than to any other person, that we attribute the recognition in the United States (and eventually throughout the world) of the special nature of gifted children—of their educational needs and their potential role as a resource of talent for society.

That longitudinal study, which continues to this day, now led by Lee J. Cronbach, was initiated in 1921 with a grant from the Commonwealth Fund. From 1921 to 1956, when Terman died, grants for this project totaled approximately $200,000. The population studied in 1921 was the top 1 percent in mental ability of 12- to 13-year-olds, as assessed with the Stanford-Binet scales. The purpose of the research was to draw an accurate picture of these youth, as opposed to the popular mythology of the time that often characterized them in negative stereotypes. The working definition for selection of subjects was an IQ of 140; the final sample was 1,528 children with IQs ranging from 140 to 200.

The first results of the research were reported in 1925 in the volume *Genetic Studies of Genius,* Volume 1, *Mental and Physical Traits of a Thousand Gifted Children.* Terman was listed as the first and only author but he presented a list of fourteen assistants, many of whom would become leaders in the field of psychology, including James DeVoss, Florence L. Goodenough, G. M. Ruch, and Truman L. Kelley.

The research results showed that gifted students performed at superior levels in school, were highly motivated, and were quite normal socially and emotionally. In curricular achievements and in personal and moral character development, the children were generally functioning two to four years ahead of their chronological age. Nevertheless, in spite of this generally favorable picture of the status of the gifted, Ter-man was greatly concerned about society's general neglect of them in school and urged that both curriculum and teaching methods be adapted to their unique needs. He especially advocated that they be accelerated in school to grade levels commensurate with their abilities to sustain the momentum of their intellectual growth and to provide the motivational challenges they need and thrive on.

Subsequent reports during Terman's lifetime, resulting from follow-up studies of the sample as those in the initial sample moved into higher education, careers, young adulthood, and midlife were reported in Volumes 3, 4, and 5 of the *Genetic Studies of Genius.* In Volume 5 (published after Terman's death in 1956), Terman and his coauthor Melita H. Oden (1959) concluded that the gifted group generally maintained their superiority in mental activities throughout their lives and that they actually continued to grow in intelligence over the life span. They also noted the importance of motivational factors that had first been observed in the sample in childhood:

> Since the less successful subjects do not differ to any extent in intelligence as measured by tests, it is clear that notable achievement calls for more than a high order of intelligence. After the 1940 follow-up a detailed analysis was made of the life histories of the 150 most successful and 150 least successful men among the gifted subjects in an attempt to identify some of the nonintellectual factors that affect life success. The results of this study indicated that personality factors are extremely important determiners of achievement. The correlation between success and such variables as mental health, emotional stability, and social adjustment is consistently positive rather than negative. In this report the data run directly counter to the conclusions reached by Lange-Eichbaum in his study of historical geniuses. A number of interesting differences between the two sub-groups were brought out but the four traits on which they differed most widely were "persistence in the accomplishments of ends," "integration toward goals," "self-confidence," and "freedom from inferiority feelings." In the total picture the greatest contrast between the two groups was in all-round emotional and social adjustment, and in drive to achieve (pp. 148–149).

In a biography, *Terman and The Gifted,* Seagoe (1975) summarized Terman's points of view regarding gifted youth. They are the top 1 percent in intelligence. They should be identified as early as possible in childhood, accelerated through school whenever feasible, have a special or differentiated curriculum and instruction, have specially trained teachers, and be viewed as a national resource for the betterment of society as a whole. At the same time, Terman felt strongly that "the gifted should be permitted to develop in whatever directions their talents and interests dictated, and not forced into a narrow mold set by society" (p. 102).

While Terman carried out considerable research and published extensively on other aspects of personality and mental hygiene, his major influence was certainly in the realms of intelligence testing and gifted youth. In a more recent biography, *Lewis M. Terman, Pioneer in Psychological Testing,* Minton (1988) concludes that "his seminal contributions to the development of psychological testing and the study of the intellectually gifted ensure his position as one of the pioneers of American psychology" (p. 263). At the same time, Minton indicts Terman for the unintended "dehumanizing effects" testing has had on the less-favored groups in our society, for what Minton sees as the use of science to control the "social order and organizational efficiency" in society, and for his often dogmatic defense of his beliefs. Nevertheless, Minton acknowledges the general politically liberal stance Terman took in his time and his devotion to the development of a better society:

What he wanted to accomplish with his psychological tests and identification of the intellectually gifted was a more socially just and democratic society. His faith was that science could serve the purposes of humanistic social evolution so that a more democratic, tolerant, and just society could be created (p. 264).

Other critics of Terman's work such as Stephen Jay Gould (1981) and P. C. Chapman (1988) have certainly joined in the more general and widespread questioning, if not denunciation, of intelligence testing in schools and other social institutions. Perhaps most controversial of all is the underlying belief held by Galton, Terman, and modern-day psychological researchers such as Bouchard (1984) and Burt (1941, 1975) that intelligence is genetically determined or inherited. Our American faith is that all are created equal, with-

out limits on potential for development. During the past twenty-five years, systemic attacks on intelligence and aptitude testing have been so pervasive and effective that, as Snyderman and Rothman (1990) conclude:

The literate and informal public today is persuaded that the majority of experts in the field believe it is impossible to adequately define intelligence, that intelligence tests do not measure anything that is relevant to life performance, and that they are biased against minorities, primarily Blacks and Hispanics, as well as against the poor (p. 250).

The empirical evidence from an extensive survey of 661 psychologists and researchers from related areas, including a large portion who were fellows of the American Psychological Association, shows quite a different reality. Their views, as summarized by Snyderman and Rothman, paints quite a different picture:

Expert views have not undergone the fundamental change characteristic of the attitudes of the informed public, despite the expansion of environmentalism within the expert community. On the whole, scholars with any expertise in the area of intelligence and intelligence testing (defined very broadly) share a common view of the most important components of intelligence, and are convinced that it can be measured with some degree of accuracy. An overwhelming majority also believe that individual genetic inheritance contributes to variations in IQ within the white community, and a smaller majority express the same view about the black-white and SES [socioeconomic status] differences in IQ (p. 250).

Lewis M. Terman died on December 21, 1956, shortly before his 80th birthday, leaving behind to his credit a fine department of psychology—due in no small part to his scholarly and administrative leadership. Terman was instrumental in establishing both empiricism and the scholarly freedom to explore as hallmarks of American scholarship. His own research was directed toward a wide variety of topics in psychology and education. Above all, he was a devoted and insightful scholar who paved the way toward two major areas of research in American education and psychology—human intelligence, as represented, for example, in the work of Robert Sternberg and Howard

Gardner, and gifted and talented children, as represented in the work of Julian Stanley and Joseph Renzulli.

In the following bibliography, Terman's listed publications are but a few of the hundreds available; these are offered as representative of his lifelong work.

BIBLIOGRAPHY

BINET, A. (1902). *The experimental study of intelligence.* Paris: Schleicher.

BINET, A., & HENRI, V. (1986). Individual psychology, *L'Année Psychologie, 2,* 411–463.

BINET, A., & SIMON, T. (1908). The development of intelligence in children. *L'Année Psychologie, 14,* 1–90.

BOUCHARD, T. J. (1984). Twins reared together and apart: What they tell us about human diversity. In S. W. Fox (Ed.), *Individuality and determinism* (pp. 147–184). New York: Plenum.

BURT, C. L. (1941). *The factors of mind.* New York: Macmillan.

BURT, C. L. (1975). *The gifted child.* New York: Wiley.

CHAPMAN, P. C. (1988). *Schools as sorters, Lewis M. Terman, applied psychology, and the intelligence testing movement.* New York: New York University Press.

GALTON, F. (1869). *Hereditary genius.* London: Julian Friedman.

GOULD, S. J. (1981). *The mismeasure of man.* New York: Norton.

JENSEN, A. R. (1980). *Bias in mental testing.* New York: Free Press.

MINTON, H. L. (1988). *Lewis M. Terman, pioneer in psychological testing.* New York: New York University Press.

SEAGOE, M. V. (1975). *Terman and the gifted.* Los Altos, CA: William Kaufman.

SNYDERMAN, M., & ROTHMAN, S. (1990). *The IQ controversy, the media and public policy.* New Brunswick, NJ: Transaction.

STERN, W. (1914). *The psychological methods of testing intelligence.* Baltimore: Warwick & York.

TERMAN, L. M. (1916). *The measurement of intelligence.* Boston: Houghton Mifflin.

TERMAN, L. M. (1921). Mental growth and the IQ. *Journal of Educational Psychology, 12,* 325–341, 401–407.

TERMAN, L. M. (1925). *Genetic studies of genius: Vol. 1. The mental and physical traits of a thousand gifted children.* Stanford: Stanford University Press.

TERMAN, L. M. (1938). *Psychological factors in marital happiness.* New York: McGraw-Hill.

TERMAN, L. M. (1943). Education and the democratic ideal. *Educational Forum, 7,* 5–8.

TERMAN, L. M. (1954). The discovery and encouragement of exceptional talent. *American Psychologist, 9,* 221–230.

TERMAN, L. M., & ODEN, M. H. (1959). *Genetic studies of genius: Vol. 5. The gifted group at mid-life.* Stanford: Stanford University Press.

TERMAN, L. M., & ODEN, M. H. (Eds.). (1947). *Genetic studies of genius: Vol. 4. The gifted child grows up.* Stanford: Stanford University Press.

JOHN F. FELDHUSEN

TERMAN'S GIFTEDNESS STUDY

Lewis TERMAN began his study of gifted children at Stanford University in 1921. Named the Stanford Studies of Genius, his work was intended to provide empirical data about gifted children and to disprove common misperceptions, such as the stereotype of gifted children as socially and physically inferior. It was later revised by Robert Sears to focus on how gifted individuals adapted to aging and adulthood. It was the first comprehensive, longitudinal study of intellectually gifted individuals.

SAMPLE SELECTION AND SURVEY

Terman's study included 1,528 subjects, 672 females and 856 males. The original group ranged in age from 3 to 19 years, but the majority of subjects were 8 to 12 years old. Most of the children came from Oakland, San Francisco, and Los Angeles, California.

The first cut at identification and selection of study participants was based on teacher nomination. Nominated students were asked to complete a group intelligence test. The top 10 percent of this group then completed a portion of the Stanford-Binet Intelligence Test. The complete Stanford-Binet was administered to any student with an intelligence quotient (IQ) of 130 or above. Students with an IQ of 135 or above were included in the study.

The participants were surveyed and interviewed in 1922 and again in 1928. Data collection focused on family life and school experience. Many parents and teachers were interviewed as well. The 1936, 1940, and 1945 waves of questionnaires focused on education, work, and marriage. Marriage, family, and career accomplishments shaped the 1950, 1955, and 1960 waves. Follow-up surveys reflected the life cycle of participants and investigators, focusing on aging, retirement, family, and reflection in 1972, 1977, 1982, and 1986. A questionnaire was sent out in late 1991; the returns were still coming into Stanford as of 1993.

FINDINGS

The findings of the study were reported in five volumes titled the *Genetic Studies of Genius* (Terman, 1925–1959). The study proved that gifted children were neither physically nor socially inferior and demonstrated that gifted children surpassed their peers in many areas, including career accomplishments. In addition, the study documented their physical growth.

Lewis Terman and Melita Oden compared the most and the least successful subjects in terms of career, happiness, and overall satisfaction in the study in 1940 and again in 1960 in an attempt to explain the wide variation in achievement. They found that the most successful participants were physically and mentally healthier than the least successful participants. In addition, they found that family background, vocational interests, academic scores, and years of education accounted for much of the difference between the groups. They also identified one of the most powerful differences between the two groups: the drive to succeed.

One hundred of the most successful men were labeled group A, and the least successful 100 men were labeled group C. A third group of men were classified as average work-life achievers. The successful group was primarily composed of professionals, including 24 professors, 11 lawyers, 8 scientists, and 5 physicians. The remainder were business executives, entrepreneurs, and owners of successful businesses. Group C was primarily composed of individuals in technician-level occupations, including clerks and salesman, as well as a few professionals. To place this relative rank-ing in perspective, the so-called unsuccessful C group *exceeded* the national average in income and related indices.

The study made numerous comparisons, ranging from state of health to level of education. The health of participants in groups A and C were roughly equivalent throughout most of the study. At age 40, A's were more physically active than C group members, however, and significantly less likely to have problems with alcohol abuse. (Self-reports indicated that 3 percent of the A's and 15 percent of the C's had problems with alcohol.) By 1960, the mortality rate for group C was higher than for group A.

Group A subjects came from educated families that fostered initiative, independence, learning, and ambition more frequently than did the families of group C participants. Group A homes were stabler and had larger family libraries than did group C families. Twice as many group A participants came from Jewish families as did C participants. (Jewish families traditionally have a strong commitment to education and achievement.)

Based on a comparison of a subsample of the groups in 1960, 80 from group A and 77 from group C, group A members had a wider range of vocational interests than group C members. The Strong Vocational Interest Test was used to make the comparisons.

Group A members were more goal-oriented and self-confident than C's, according to parents, spouses, and self-ratings. Group A members selected careers, whereas C's typically entered occupations in a more haphazard manner. In addition, A's selected their careers much earlier than did members of the C group.

The A group maintained many of its early advantages, and the difference between the two groups grew as the subjects aged. For example, A's skipped more grades than C's and received more graduate education. The growing difference between A and C scores on the Concept Mastery Test (which includes esoteric analogies such as "Aristotle is to Socrates as Sophocles is to . . . ?") as the subjects aged was evident in the 1940 and 1950 follow-up studies. Group A members made more money than C's and were more satisfied with their careers. All A's married; 80 percent of C's married. In addition, A's stayed married longer than C's. Almost 50 percent of all C's were divorced; only 16 percent of A's were divorced.

In 1972, the focus of the Terman study was on satisfaction in life. Sources of satisfaction included occupation, family, friends, cultural experience, service, and overall pleasure. (Subjects' desires in youth were compared with their satisfaction in adulthood.) Robert Sears, former director of the Terman study, using the Marital Aptitude Test and the Marital Happiness Test, found that young men ranked a happy family life high and as adults reported deriving their greatest pleasure from family life. Work was ranked second in youth and third in adulthood. Overall joy in life was not ranked as significant in youth, but it ranked second in adulthood. (The final study ranked work satisfaction higher than overall joy because greater weight was given to categories prized in youth and ranked highly in adulthood.)

According to the work of Pauline Sears and Ann Barbee (1978), women found the same level of satisfaction as men in family, service, and overall joy in life. They found more satisfaction in friends and cultural activities, and overall they ranked work lower as a source of satisfaction. However, when this later finding concerning work is corrected for sample comparability (working women compared with working men), the satisfaction level is the same. Single women without children who worked had the highest work-satisfaction level. Married women without children who did not have jobs or careers had the lowest work-satisfaction rate. This pattern foreshadowed later social and cultural developments in the United States concerning women in the work force.

RELATED STUDIES AND REPORTS

Carole Holahan studied Terman participants' attitudes toward marriage from young adulthood to old age in 1981, using some of the questions from the 1940 survey. She also created a comparison group consisting of a random sample of 1968–1972 Stanford University graduates. The comparison group was used primarily to control for historical context and developmental change.

Holahan found an increase in egalitarian attitudes toward marital matters on the part of both men and women. Subjects (both men and women) reported that women should be more financially independent,

should earn or otherwise have their own money, and should not be financially dependent on their spouse. At age 70, Terman men stated that they believed in verbal expressions of their love, in contrast to their statements at age 30. Terman women reported more strongly than in their youth that men and women should be held to the same standards of morality and that men need not be the single authority figure in the household.

Holahan (1992) also surveyed 814 Terman participants between 60 and 70 years of age to explore their psychological adjustment to aging. She found that goal-oriented behavior and a sense of purpose helped subjects adjust to aging. Terman participants refocused their goal-oriented behavior from work or achievement goals to self-protective autonomous goals (taking care of oneself) as well as to goals associated with involvement with others (participating in social groups and hobbies). Her work has implications for other aging populations that must adjust to the latter phase of the life cycle.

G. E. Vaillant and C. O. Vaillant (1990) reinterviewed forty Terman women in 1987 to study determinants and consequences of creativity. They defined creativity as "putting something in the world that was not there before," with a focus on literary, artistic, and musical manifestations of creativity, as well as on the creation of new organizations. They found Terman women to be academically precocious and mentally and physically healthier than their chronological peers. Their mortality at age 80 was half that of the norm. Of the Terman women interviewed, 67 percent had attended college and 24 percent had attended graduate school. Almost half maintained dual careers—at work and at home. The overwhelming majority appear to have preferred this life-style over a single-career life-style.

The Vaillants documented a link between creativity and creating new organizations. One-fourth of the twenty women identified as creative had published or given a musical recital or created a social organization. These women were committed to pursuing an active life outside the home from an early age. They also made creative use of leisure time. There is some evidence that creative women continue to contribute late in life and enjoy life longer. All creative women in this study used altruism, humor, and/or sublimation as an ego mechanism of defense. (These mechanisms are not correlated with mental health.)

There were no differences in mental health and marital happiness between creative and less creative subjects. In addition, the Binet and the Concept Mastery scores did not distinguish between creative and less creative women. Parental education or support, social class, and literature in the home did not correlate with creativity.

Overall, the pattern of creativity, in fields ranging from the literary to the dramatic arts, is clear at an early age. However, various cultural norms and historical events (including World War II and the Depression) minimized the productive expression of creativity. Creative contributions late in life suggest that the creative impulse was derailed, inhibited, or put on hold rather than extinguished.

The work of Elder, Pavalko, and Hastings (1991) focused on the impact of historical events on the career achievements of Terman men born between 1904 and 1917. They found that career advancement for the older cohort of Terman men was severely hindered by the Depression. National economic stagnation limited the career-related life trajectories of the older cohort of Terman men, who entered the work force during the Depression. Similarly, World War II further disrupted their careers and separated them from their families for long periods to time. However, Terman men who found a match between their talents and the requirements of the armed forces were likely to have careers of distinction. The key to success for many of these individuals appears to be adaptation: establishing a functional link between occupational skills and the new context.

David Sears, Robert and Pauline Sears's son, used the Terman files to study the political attitudes of the gifted. Sears and Funk (1990) found a high level of attitude stability and a high level of consistency between party identification and ideology. In addition, they found that attitude crystallization rose with age. Sears, Zucker, and Funk (1992) focused on gender and ideological change in the 1960s and 1970s. They found a substantial gender gap in party identification and ideology during this period.

Cronbach (1992) studied acceleration among Terman men. In general, he found that Terman participants who completed high school at age 16½ or

earlier continued to achieve in many areas later in life. They were more likely than controls to progress through the educational system. However, there was little difference between Terman men and controls in numbers completing graduate school. Terman midlife incomes were higher than those of controls. Individuals without any graduate degree earned the highest incomes. Terman men identified as accelerates also appeared to have moderately greater marital stability, mental health, and work- and social-satisfaction levels.

CRITICISMS AND LIMITATIONS

There have been a number of criticisms of the original Terman study. Some critics point to limitations of the study, the state of the art at the time, and the historical time period in which the study was conducted.

An important criticism is that the sample was not representative. The majority of the participants were drawn from Northern California. In terms of their numbers in the overall population, Jewish children were disproportionately represented, and black, Hispanic, and American Indian children were disproportionately underrepresented. Moreover, there were no Chinese subjects in the sample (they were generally not attending public school at that time). In addition, the sample was skewed toward professional families; unskilled laborers were not represented. These sample problems limit the generalizability of the findings.

Another criticism focused on sample identification. Teacher nomination is a logical approach, and there was virtually no literature on identification at the time the study began. Unfortunately, later research shows that teachers demonstrate an inconsistent ability to identify gifted children. The study was thus limited by the methodological state of the art at the time.

A third criticism focuses on the haphazard and unsystematic quality of some sample selection. Terman added to the initial sample younger siblings of subjects, children who scored close to the cutoff, and a small number of children who demonstrated special abilities in art and music but who did not otherwise qualify for the study. This and other methodological problems—including a failure to control tightly for length of career when making career achievement ratings—may have amplified or obscured differences between group A and group C.

In addition, the study was shaped by a unique period in history. The Depression and World War II created specific obstacles and opportunities for that generation of gifted children. Every study is a product of its time, but because researchers cannot control for that variable, the historical period should be used as a lens through which to interpret study findings. A valid criticism in this area is that the follow-up surveys did not explore the role of World War II on Terman men to determine how it affected their lives.

A concern exists that the study findings were affected by observer bias. When participants were asked to take part in follow-up studies, they were informed that they were subjects in the Terman study, and they learned that this was a study of gifted and talented people. Thus, they were identified and labeled as gifted and were reminded of it during each wave of questionnaires. This could have produced a Hawthorne effect, that is, the effect that occurs when people who are getting attention by being members of a group under study try to shape their behavior to provide the results they believe are being sought in the study participants, providing them with continual positive reinforcement. Some evidence suggests that the study also had a potentially negative effect on group C subjects, who may have been continually reminded of their relative lack of success. In addition, some participants may have demonstrated a John Henry effect, that is, an attempt to live up to a particular standard. This could be particularly true for some of the lower group A and higher group C participants, who may have felt the need to overcompensate to match their potential.

The physical development component of the study has also come under attack. Much work since that time has demonstrated that there is little correlation between anthropometric characteristics or physical characteristics and intelligence. Here again the effort must be viewed in its historical context and with the intended purpose of the study in mind. Its goal was to disprove stereotypic images about the gifted, such as assumptions about their physical inferiority. The emphasis on physical characteristics is more understandable given this purpose. Nevertheless, any extended use of the data and causal inferences concerning intelligence and physical development are clearly inappropriate.

ANONYMITY AND ACCESSIBILITY OF THE DATA

The Terman study files have been conscientiously maintained at Stanford University for decades. Confidentiality of study data and participant anonymity has been meticulously preserved. Successful security measures, however, have limited the availability of the data for review and secondary analysis.

Although the quality and confidentiality of the study data are still diligently maintained, two events marked a shift in the ease of access to subjects and the data for secondary analysis: the holding of a gifted and talented conference at Stanford and the appointment of a new curator of the files.

A handful of the study participants—including a Stanford University dean, a prominent professor, an actress, and a successful attorney and Stanford Board of Trustees member—broke with tradition and revealed their identities at a 1988 conference on gifted and talented education at Stanford University to discuss their role in the study. Their purpose was to establish a bond with the current generation of gifted and talented children and to provide personal insights into their participation in the study (see Fetterman, 1988).

In addition, during this period Albert Hastorf assumed the role of curator of the Terman study files. Files on each participant continue to be housed at Stanford, and coded data are also available at the Inter-University Consortium for Political and Social Research. To supplement this source, Hastorf has made a concerted effort to ensure the accessibility of the Terman study files. The files have thus become accessible to a wider range of scholars than at any time before. In addition to inviting scholars to use the files, Hastorf has reproduced a significant amount of the data on microfiche. These data are available in the archives at the Murray Research Center at Radcliffe College. Data will continue to be collected throughout the lifetime of the study participants.

BIBLIOGRAPHY

CRONBACH, L. J. (1992). *Acceleration among the Terman males: Correlates in midlife and after.* Paper presented at the Symposium in Honor of Julian Stanley, San Francisco.

ELDER, G. H., PAVALKO, E. K., & HASTINGS, T. J. (1991).

Talent, history, and the fulfillment of promise. *Psychiatry, 54,* 251–267.

FETTERMAN, D. M. (1988). *Excellence and equality: A qualitatively different perspective on gifted and talented education.* Albany, NY: SUNY Press.

HOLAHAN, C. K. (1992). Psychology of aging. *Discovery: Research and Scholarship at the University of Texas at Austin, 12*(2), 13–16.

ODEN, M. H. (1968). The fulfillment of promise: Forty-year follow-up of the Terman gifted group. *Genetic Psychology Monographs, 77,* 3–93.

SEARS, D., & FUNK, C. L. (1990, August). *The persistence and crystallization of political attitudes over the life-span: The Terman gifted children panel.* Paper presented at the annual meeting of the American Sociological Association, Washington, DC.

SEARS, D., ZUCKER, G. S., & FUNK, C. L. (1992, September). *Gender and ideological change in the 1960's and 1970's: A longitudinal study.* Paper presented at the annual meeting of the American Political Science Association.

SEARS, R. R. (1977). Sources of life satisfaction of the Terman gifted men. *American Psychologist, 32,* 119–128.

SEARS, R. R. (1984). The Terman gifted children study. In S. A. Mednick, M. Harway, & K. M. Finello (Eds.), *Handbook of longitudinal research* (Vol. 1). New York: Praeger.

SEARS, P. S., & BARBEE, A. H. (1978). Career and life satisfaction among Terman's gifted women. In *The gifted and the creative: Fifty-year perspective.* Baltimore: Johns Hopkins University Press.

TERMAN, L. M. (1925–1959). *Genetic studies of genius* (Vols. 1–5). Stanford, CA: Stanford University Press.

TERMAN, L. M., & ODEN, M. (1959). *Genetic studies of genius: Vol. 5. The gifted group at mid-life.* Stanford, CA: Stanford University Press.

VAILLANT, G. E., & VAILLANT, C. O. (1990). Determinants and consequences of creativity in a cohort of gifted women. *Psychology of Women Quarterly, 14,* 607–616.

DAVID M. FETTERMAN

TESTING IN GOVERNMENT AND INDUSTRY

From the time of the Army's success with the Alpha test during World War I, employers have been eager to capitalize on employment testing in the hiring process. For almost fifty years, tests were believed and shown to be valid predictors of job performance; the notion of *test fairness* was seldom raised as an issue. Since the passage of Title VII of the Civil Rights Act of 1964, however, employers have become extremely cautious in using the tests because they have feared charges of unfairness and resulting adverse impact on employment programs.

Employees selected by *valid tests* produce more than those selected by other methods. Brogden's landmark equation developed in 1949 for estimating costs and benefits of a selection program has been an important means of demonstrating that testing can save money. How much is saved depends on the predictive efficiency of the selection device, the proportion of applicants hired, and two additional variables recently recognized as important—dollar-valued performance and testing costs.

IMPROVED HUMAN RESOURCE UTILIZATION THROUGH PERSONNEL TESTING

A job description states what an individual is expected to do and the degree of proficiency needed to do it. Individuals also can be described in terms of skills and abilities. It follows that effective utilization of employees hinges on *matching the job and the individual,* but there is a hitch. Do we have the ability to measure a person's appropriate skills and abilities, assuming we have evaluated a job properly? If so, can we measure the correct characteristics and determine how validly or accurately we measure them?

The measure of ability may be useless if it is irrelevant to job success. Suppose, for example, that we want to measure an individual's ability as a salesperson. We might accurately describe his or her verbal, spatial, and numerical reasoning abilities. But none of these may be closely related to successful sales work. The first requirement in measurement, then, is to identify and describe the critical job skills. The second requirement is to determine ways of measuring the desired skills. Even if we were to select the correct job characteristics, they would be of little value if measurements representing them were expressed crudely or inaccurately. The need for a consistently applicable scale in comparing individual differences is indicated.

Role of Selection Tests. All of us know individuals who have proved themselves such good judges of human abilities in given situations that we would rate their evaluative abilities very high on any kind of scale. Why, then, use any other means of evaluation? Why use a test?

Admittedly, if there were enough good judges, and if they had time to make judgments, and if their judgments could be passed along without misunderstanding or distortion, there would be no need for tests. But all evidence indicates that not many judges can evaluate people consistently. Judges have their own personal standards based on their own experiences. Consciously or unconsciously, they tend to evaluate according to their own standards, leading to inaccuracies and disparities in their judgments. Further, the practicality of using judges becomes even more limited when they are permitted only brief observation of the applicant (in typical circumstances). Thus, judgments by individuals can be relied upon as neither practical nor economic assessments of future performance.

The purpose of every psychological test is to measure differences among individuals. Such measures can serve a number of functions: prediction, diagnosis, or research. A personnel selection test's primary purpose is to predict potential job performance. The fact that two individuals perform differently on tests is of little real value, unless such differences can be shown to relate to some future activity of interest to the organization. A test's predictive value depends on how well it can serve as an indicator of a significant aspect of job performance. A close relationship must be demonstrated between applicants' scores on a selection test and their performance on the job. If there is a close correspondence, that is, if high scorers on the test turn out to be good performers on the job, the test is serving its purpose. Such a test is valid because it can be used to make accurate hiring decisions. Large-scale, carefully developed validation studies have confirmed the power of employment tests for predicting performance and thus for increasing the productivity of the workforce.

Types of Selection Tests. There are many ways of classifying tests. One way is to group them according to the behaviors they measure. For example, tests can be divided into those that describe what people *can* do and those that describe what they *will* do. Tests in the first group may be called ability measures; tests in the second group, personality measures.

Ability measures can be subdivided into measures of potential or capacity, called aptitude tests, and into measures of present knowledge, called achievement tests. The difference between aptitude and achievement tests is not very clear; whether a test is one or the other depends on the use the employer will make of it. For example, an achievement (or trade proficiency) test can be used as an aptitude test when it is used to predict future performance. Individuals may be given an automotive information test before they have any automotive training to help determine their potential for this kind of work.

Personality tests, providing descriptions of what people *will* do, constitute a rather broad category of measures. Objective personality tests focus on what individuals do or how they respond to a given situation; these tests do not attempt to measure feelings or aspirations, since these qualities are not directly observable. The answers to personality test questions can be scored objectively and used to predict typical behavior of the individual.

Other tests that may be used in selection programs include interest tests measuring preferences for certain kinds of activities; attitude tests measuring how favorably an individual feels toward institutions, individuals, groups, and a wide range of objects and concepts; temperament tests measuring such attributes as energy level, sociability, and aggressiveness; and adjustment tests measuring behavioral patterns to determine if individuals are reasonably comfortable with themselves and with their social settings.

TEST USAGE

Testing in Business and Industry. In 1988 the Bureau of National Affairs (BNA) surveyed recruiting and selection practices of 245 organizations representing a wide variety of businesses. They found that nine out of ten give preemployment tests or examinations to applicants in at least one of five job categories. About 67 percent of responding firms give skill performance tests or work samples—most often to potential office/clerical workers and production/service workers.

Mental ability tests are administered by 31 percent of firms, mainly to clerical and production applicants. Ability tests include measures of verbal, mathematical, and perceptual skills. Job-knowledge tests (paper-and-pencil tests for jobs requiring specific knowledge) are administered by 27 percent of firms to clerical, production, or technical job applicants.

About 18 percent of firms administer personality tests to sales and managerial job applicants. Twelve percent of firms use *assessment-center measures* (evaluations in a simulated work environment) in the selection of managerial personnel. Also included in exams or tests administered to job applicants are medical, drug, physical ability, polygraph, and written tests assessing honesty of applicants.

The BNA survey indicated that about 50 percent of the firms validated their mental ability and knowledge tests in accordance with the *Uniform Guidelines on Selection Procedures,* established by the federal government in 1978 to ensure that selection procedures do not violate antidiscrimination laws.

Testing in the Public Sector. The most comprehensive and systematic testing for selection and classification is accomplished in the military, in the federal civil service, and in the U.S. Employment Service (USES) for making job referrals by state employment service offices. At the state and local levels, testing is often an integral part of merit selection procedures and is also used in promotion, licensing, and certification programs under the auspices of public or private entities or both.

Military Testing. In the military context, decision makers see that a significant way of improving performance is to improve the selection and matching of recruits to jobs. During the 1980s, the military selected approximately 300,000 new applicants each year after testing that helped determine entry qualifications and decide the job specialty for which each recruit should be trained and assigned. Since most recruits have little or no civilian work experience, the services rely heavily on educational background and aptitude test information.

The ARMED SERVICE VOCATIONAL APTITUDE BATTERY (ASVAB), administered to about 1 million candidates each year, is the principal means of selecting and classifying applicants. The ASVAB is comprised of ten aptitude tests, four of which yield the Armed Forces Qualification Test (AFQT) score, a measure of general cognitive ability and trainability. The AFQT score and educational attainment information are used to determine enlistment eligibility.

While the AFQT is the single psychometric measure used by all services for determining acceptance into the military, aptitude composites or combinations of ASVAB tests unique to each service are used for classifying recruits for various types of technical training and subsequent assignment to jobs. In the army, for example, the tests of ASVAB are combined into nine aptitude composites, such as clerical and administrative, combat, electronic, and general maintenance. Aptitude area composites are used in matching soldiers to specific army jobs or military occupational specialties (MOS) from among the 260 or so entry-level MOS that are clustered or grouped into job families or career-management fields.

In simple selection situations—typical in many employment settings—only a single job is involved and selection can be accomplished with one or more predictors. The decision to accept or reject an applicant is determined by an individual's position along a single predicted performance continuum. Selection capitalizes on differences *among* people. In the military, the AFQT is used for selection as the first of a two-stage process. Classification decisions provide the basis for assigning a single pool of selected individuals to more than one job. The aptitude composites are used in the second stage for assignment to jobs. *Classification* capitalizes on differences *within* an individual and requires multiple predictors measuring more than one ability in both predicting and assessing ultimate job performance.

Federal Civil Service Testing. The Office of Personnel Management (OPM) uses a testing program for college graduates, the Administrative Careers with America (ACWA), to fill entry-level positions in more than one hundred administrative and professional occupations. A predecessor test, the Professional and Administrative Career Examination (PACE), a generalized aptitude battery, was administered in the past to as many as 200,000 applicants per year. The OPM also administered written tests to about 500,000 applicants per year, mostly for clerical positions (National Academy of Sciences, 1982).

Job Referral Testing. Since World War II the USES has administered, through state-administered employment offices, the General Aptitude Test Battery (GATB) to potential applicants who seek assistance in finding private- or public-sector jobs. The GATB consists of twelve tests that are grouped into three general ability factors: cognitive ability, perceptual ability, and psychomotor coordination. According to a 1989 National Academy of Science report, 19 million people passed through the system annually in search of jobs and perhaps about 1 million were given the GATB. However, in the late 1980s the USES started to promote the use of GATB for referral to all jobs. According to the U. S. Labor Department, about thirty states rely on the GATB to evaluate roughly 600,000 job applicants a year.

DEVELOPMENTS IN PERSONNEL SELECTION

The decades since 1960 have seen much social controversy surrounding testing. Critics have directed questions on the fairness of tests and their adverse impact on minorities, their limited predictive powers for long-term job performance, and the often narrow range of skills covered by them. Such challenges to testing stimulated a growth in theoretical and practical studies on employment testing. Generally, studies show that employment tests are essentially unbiased—they are equally effective in predicting the job performance of minorities and women as they are for the majority (Schmidt & Hunter, 1981).

Validity Generalization.   A long-dormant interest in using previously validated tests in new but similar job situations was stimulated by research on validity generalization. The prevailing view has been that employment test validations are situation specific and that empirical data are needed for each new test-usage situation. Findings correcting for various sources of statistical variability support the utility of validity generalization and thus make it possible to develop general principles for linking ability tests to families of jobs.

Criterion Issues.   In the past tests were usually validated against available criterion measures, with little effort made to evaluate the criterion measure itself. Scientists gradually turned their attention to the difficult, time-consuming, and expensive task of measuring job performance through a combination of objective

hands-on measures of performance, job-knowledge measures, and behaviorally anchored rating scales. When selection batteries are validated against carefully defined and measured job criteria, highly useful predictions of job performance are generally obtained.

Computerized Adaptive Testing.   The everyday application of computer adaptive testing (CAT) became possible with recent advances in microcomputer technology and refinements in item-response theory. CAT permits automated testing using a display screen and a light pen and other devices for responding. Successive test questions are tailored by the response to the previous question and are computer scored after each response. Practical CAT advantages include improved precision of estimating ability, improved test security, simplicity of test revision and scoring, improved accuracy, and more efficient use of time. Another significant potential of CAT is that it provides the capability for using entirely new types of tests via computer displays and input–output devices.

Cognitive Assessment.   Many cognitive psychologists look for a deeper understanding of individual differences in information processing ability through the use of an experimental rather than a correlational approach. In the cognitive approach, response to stimulus variations within an individual is closely examined, rather than variations among individuals for a given stimulus. Research is now under way to see to what extent the two approaches can form a common, improved basis of testing.

Utility.   Historically, to assess and communicate the practical impact of testing, experts have resorted to using difficult-to-understand statistical concepts or behavioral terms. But starting with the development of the first utility (cost-benefit) models, a new language began to emerge. Based on clear empirical findings, it became possible in the 1980s to make economically meaningful bottom-line statements on personnel intervention programs designed to improve job performance. Today, productivity gains attributable to selection can be expressed in dollar-valued terms comparable to other financial investments made by organizations.

(*See also:* ARMY ALPHA AND BETA TESTS OF INTELLIGENCE; JOB PERFORMANCE; OCCUPATIONS.)

BIBLIOGRAPHY

ANASTASI, A. (1984). Aptitude and achievement tests: The curious case of the indestructible strawperson. In B. S. Plake (Ed.), *Social and technical issues in testing: Implications for test construction and usage* (pp. 129–140). Hillsdale, NJ: Erlbaum.

ANASTASI, A. (1988). *Psychological testing.* (6th ed.). New York: Macmillan.

ARVEY, R. D., & FALEY, R. H. (1988). *Fairness in selecting employees* (2nd ed.). New York: Addison-Wesley.

BOUDREAU, J. W. (1991). Utility analysis for decisions in human resource management. In M. D. Dunnette & L. M. Hough (Eds.), *Handbook of industrial and organizational psychology* (2nd ed., Vol. 2., pp. 621–745). Palo Alto, CA: Consulting Psychologist Press.

BROGDEN, H. E. (1949). When testing pays off. *Personnel Psychology, 2,* 171–183.

BROGDEN, H. E. (1959). Efficiency of classification as a function of number of jobs, percent rejected, and the validity and intercorrelation of job performance estimates. *Educational and Psychological Measurement, 19,* 181–190.

BROGDEN, H. E., & TAYLOR, E. K. (1950). The dollar criterion—applying the cost accounting concept to criterion construction. *Personnel Psychology, 3,* 133–154.

Bureau of National Affairs. (1988). *Recruiting and selection procedures.* PPF Survey No. 146. Washington, DC: Bureau of National Affairs.

CASCIO, W. F. (1987). *Costing human resources: The financial impact of behavior in organizations* (2nd ed.). Boston: PWS-Kent.

CASCIO, W. F. (1991a). *Applied psychology in personnel management* (4th ed.). Englewood Cliffs, NJ: Prentice-Hall.

CASCIO, W. F. (1991b). *Costing human resources: The financial impact of behavior in organizations* (2nd ed.). Boston: Kent.

COHEN, R. J., SWERDLIK, M. E., & SMITH, D. K. (1992). *Psychological testing and assessment: An introduction to tests and measurement* (2nd ed.). Mountain View, CA: Mayfield.

Equal Employment Opportunity Commission. (1979). *Affirmative action guidelines.* 44 FR 4421–4424.

GATEWOOD, R. D., & FIELD, H. S. (1990). *Human resource selection* (2nd ed.). Chicago: Dryden.

GHISELLI, E. E. (1973). The validity of aptitude tests in personnel selection. *Personnel Psychology, 26,* 461–477.

GOTTFREDSON, L. S. (GUEST ED.). (1986). The *g* factor in employment. *Journal of Vocational Behavior, 29,* 293–461.

GOTTFREDSON, L. S., & SHARF, J. C. (GUEST EDS.). (1988). Fairness in employment testing. *Journal of Vocational Behavior, 33,* 225–477.

GUION, R. M. (1991). Personnel assessment selection and placement. In M. D. Dunnette & L. M. Hough (Eds.), *Handbook of industrial and organizational psychology* (2nd ed., Vol. 2, pp. 327–397). Palo Alto, CA: Consulting Psychology Press.

HANEY, W. (1981). Validity, vaudeville and values. A short history of social concerns over standardized testing. *American Psychologist, 36,* 1021–1034.

HARTIGAN, J. A., & WIGDOR, A. K. (EDS.). (1989). *Fairness in employment testing: Validity generalization, minority issues, and the general aptitude battery.* Washington, DC: National Academy Press.

HUNTER, J. E., & HUNTER, R. F. (1984). Validity and utility of alternative predictors of job performance. *Psychological Bulletin, 96,* 72–98.

HUNTER, J. E., & SCHMIDT, F. L. (1982). Fitting people to jobs: The impact of personnel selection on national productivity. In M. D. Dunnette, & E. A. Fleishman (Eds.), *Human performance and productivity. Human capability assessment* (Vol. 1, pp. 233–284). Hillsdale, NJ: Erlbaum.

JOHNSON, C. D., & ZEIDNER, J. (1991). *The economic benefits of predicting job performance: Vol. 2. Classification efficiency.* New York: Praeger.

LANDY, F. J., & FARR, J. L. (1980). Performance rating. *Psychological Bulletin, 87,* 72–107.

LANDY, F. J., FARR, J. L., & JACOBS, R. R. (1982). Utility concepts in performance measurement. *Organizational Behavior and Human Performance, 30,* 15–40.

LEDVINKA, J., & SCARPELLO, V. G. (1990). *Federal regulation of personnel and human resource management* (2nd ed.). Boston: PWS-Kent.

LINN, R. L. (1978). Single-group validity, differential validity, and differential prediction. *Journal of Applied Psychology, 63,* 507–512.

MURPHY, K. R., & DAVIDSHOFER, C. O. (1991). *Psychological testing, principles and applications* (2nd ed.). Englewood Cliffs, NJ: Prentice-Hall.

National Academy of Sciences. (1982). A. K. Wigdor, & W. E. Garner (Eds.), *Ability testing: Uses, consequences and controversies: Part I. Report of the Committee.* Washington, DC: National Academy Press.

National Academy of Sciences. (1986). A. K. Wigdor, & B. F. Green (Eds.), *Assessing the performance of enlisted personnel.* Report of the Committee Evaluation of a Joint-

Service Research Project. Washington, DC: National Academy Press.

National Academy of Sciences. (1988). J. A. Hartigan, & A. K. Wigdor (Eds.), *Fairness in employment testing. Validity generalization, minority issues, and the general aptitude test battery.* Washington, DC: National Academy Press.

NORD, R., & SCHMITZ, E. (1991). Estimating performance and utility effects of alternative selection and classification policies. In J. Zeidner, & C. D. Johnson, (Eds.), *The economic benefits of predicting job performance. The gains of alternative policies* (Vol. 3, pp. 73–137). New York: Praeger.

PEARLMAN, K. (1980). Job families: A review and discussion of their implications for personnel selection. *Psychological Bulletin, 87, 1–28.*

Project A. (1990). Project A: The U. S. Army Selection and Classification Project. *Personnel Psychology, 43,* Special Issue, 231–378.

PULAKOS, E. D., BORMAN, W. C., & HOUGH, L. M. (1988). Test validation for scientific understanding: Two demonstrations of an approach to studying predictor-criterion linkages. *Personnel Psychology, 41,* 703–716.

SCHMIDT, F. L., & HUNTER, J. E. (1977). Development of a general solution to the problem of validity generalization. *Journal of Applied Psychology, 62,* 529–540.

SCHMIDT, F. L., & HUNTER J. E. (1981). Employment testing: Old theories and new research findings. *American Psychologist, 36,* 1128–1137.

Society for Industrial and Organizational Psychology. (1987). Principles for the validation and use of personnel selection procedures (3rd ed.). College Park, MD: Author.

ZEIDNER, J., & JOHNSON, C. D. (1991). *The economic benefits of predicting job performance: Vol. 1. Selection Utility.* New York: Praeger.

JOSEPH ZEIDNER

TESTS OF INTELLIGENCE *See* AMERICAN COLLEGE TEST; APTITUDE TESTS; ARMED SERVICES VOCATIONAL APTITUDE BATTERY; ARMY ALPHA AND BETA TESTS OF INTELLIGENCE; CULTURE-FAIR AND CULTURE-FREE TESTS; DRAW-A-FIGURE TEST; GROUP TESTS; INDIVIDUAL TESTS; INFANT TESTS AS MEASURES OF EARLY COMPETENCE; KAUFMAN ASSESSMENT BATTERY FOR CHILDREN; MCCARTHY SCALES OF CHILDREN'S ABILITIES; SCHOLASTIC ASSESSMENT TESTS; STANFORD-BINET INTELLIGENCE SCALE, FOURTH EDITION; WAIS–R SUBTESTS; WECHSLER SCALES OF INTELLIGENCE; WOODCOCK-JOHNSON TESTS OF COGNITIVE ABILITY–REVISED

TEST-TAKING STRATEGIES To what extent is performance on measures of intelligence affected by the test-taking strategy of the examinee, over and above the ability presumed to be measured by the test? Is it possible for one or two examinees who are *of equal ability with respect to the object of measurement* to obtain a higher score than his or her counterpart because of special techniques or knowledge about guessing strategies, test format, or other test characteristics? The research literature on this topic is large and diverse. For standardized multiple-choice tests of scholastic aptitude, especially the Scholastic Aptitude Test, extensive reviews are now available. The literature on other group tests of cognitive ability and individually administered tests (i.e., traditional IQ tests) has been reviewed and summarized by Philip E. VERNON (1950, 1954, 1969), the recognized authority on the subject, and by Arthur JENSEN (1980).

In discussing the effects of "test-wiseness" and "test sophistication" on measures of cognitive ability, the traditional distinction between timed multiple-choice tests and individually administered measures of IQ is a useful one to retain. In the former, examinees have available to them for each test item the actual correct response, along with a set of incorrect alternatives; in the latter, examinees must generate the correct response on their own. This difference in test format has important implications for what constitutes test-wiseness and test sophistication.

TEST-TAKING STRATEGY, TEST-WISENESS, AND TEST SOPHISTICATION

Millman, Bishop, and Ebel (1965) define test-wiseness as "the subject's capacity to utilize the characteristics and formats of the test and the test-taking situation to receive a high score" (p. 707). The terms *test-taking strategy, test-wiseness,* and *test sophistication* will be used interchangeably here to denote knowledge about the format and structure of tests (especially timed multiple-choice tests) and a class of test-taking techniques that, if possessed in sufficient measure, would presumably lead to higher performance on cognitive ability tests than would otherwise be the case. Included are such things as being familiar with separate answer sheets, carefully reading instructions before beginning, considering *all* alternatives before picking one, not spending too much time on difficult, doubtful, or puzzling items, knowing when to guess and when not to, being alert to cues in the set of alternatives or other flaws in the item that suggest the correct response, and checking over completed items when time permits.

Levels of test-wiseness have not been experimentally manipulated in any study the authors could find, so the extent to which individuals differ in these skills and the degree to which "test-wise" examinees are advantaged over "test-naive" examinees is not known with certainty. Investigators have estimated the effects of test-wiseness by comparing subjects who have received coaching and/or practice on cognitive ability measures with those who have not, the assumption being that such subjects are more test-wise than their uncoached counterparts.

Vernon (1950) distinguishes between *intrinsic* and *extrinsic* determinants of performance on cognitive ability measures, a distinction that it will be useful to keep in mind. Bond (1989) makes a similar distinction in his use of the terms *alpha* (intrinsic) abilities and *beta* (extrinsic) abilities. Intrinsic determinants of performance on measures of cognitive ability refer to influences which can be modified only by education and training over a long period of time and which are designed to develop the underlying ability. Extrinsic determinants are all those influences that can more or less readily be reduced or eliminated through changes in the instructions or administration of the test, through minor changes in the form or content of the test items, or through a limited amount of practice by which the examinee becomes familiar with characteristics of the test. The reader will note that extrinsic factors are in fact synonymous with the list of abilities we have subsumed under the general rubric of test-wiseness.

Ideally, test scores should reflect only individual differences in intrinsic determinants. It would not exaggerate matters to suggest that an implicit assumption in the measurement of human intelligence is that in-

dividual examinees are indistinguishable with respect to extrinsic determinants, and that the observed variation in scores is solely a function of intrinsic determinants (along with, of course, the inevitable, presumably random, errors of measurement).

THE NATURE OF SPECIAL INSTRUCTION AND COACHING

Instruction in test-taking strategies can be divided into three broad categories: (1) instruction on techniques for responding correctly that do *not* depend upon the underlying ability the test purports to measure (e.g., optimal guessing strategies and time management); (2) instruction that is test-specific in that it involves instruction, with immediate feedback, on a sample of items like those found on the actual test; and (3) instruction that is relatively content-free and attempts to teach broad intellectual reasoning skills that are applicable to a wide range of cognitive ability measures. Coaching for multiple-choice tests has typically involved some combination of all three types of instruction, with emphasis on instruction that is test-specific on a sample of items like those found on the test. Coaching for individually administered IQ tests such as the Stanford-Binet and the Wechsler scales has typically combined familiarization and practice on samples of tasks like those found on such tests with practice taking alternate forms of the actual tests.

THE EFFECTS OF COACHING AND PRACTICE ON SCHOLASTIC ABILITY MEASURES

By far the most frequently studied effects of practice and coaching have been of attempts to improve performance on the Scholastic Aptitude Test (SAT), a multiple-choice measure of quantitative and verbal reasoning widely used by American colleges and universities in student admissions. This test is distinguished by the fairly modest demands it makes upon one's declarative knowledge base in mathematics (basic arithmetic, a year of algebra, and an introductory semester of geometry are all that are necessary) and the substantial demands it makes upon conceptual understanding and "insight."

What is known about effective test-taking strategies and the effects of practice and coaching for the SAT and similar tests can be summarized as follows:

1. Where there is no penalty for guessing, the obvious optimal strategy is to guess randomly when one does not know the answer to a question. (Surprisingly, even under these circumstances, some examinees decline to answer some questions.)

2. When random guessing is penalized (as it is on the SAT), it is to one's advantage to guess if at least one of the incorrect alternatives can be eliminated.

3. For quantitative-reasoning tests, short, intensive drill and review (e.g., for less than thirty hours) of relevant mathematical topics may significantly increase performance for those who are already firmly grounded, but perhaps rusty, in these areas. For examinees whose preparation in the relevant mathematical topics is weak, a short course involving drill and practice on test-taking strategies or on retired SAT items has little or no effect on performance. For verbal tests, short drill and practice are relatively ineffective.

4. Coaching and practice on tests of quantitative reasoning typically result in higher gains in performance than coaching and practice on measures of verbal reasoning.

5. The most effective method of special preparation for specific tests appears to involve instruction and practice on the tasks and task formats similar to those found on the actual test, rather than more general instruction (Whether this kind of instruction increases "general" verbal and mathematical abilities, rather than abilities measured specifically by a given test, is open to debate.)

6. The law of diminishing returns appears to apply to the effects of coaching and practice; beyond thirty hours of instruction, more and more instructional time and effort is required for smaller and smaller gains in test performance.

7. Predictably, coaching and practice devoted exclusively to extrinsic determinants (optimal guessing strategies, searching for clues in items that suggest the right answer, etc.) are not as effective in raising performance as instruction in the underlying ability measured by the test.

The research studies on coaching for multiple-choice measures of scholastic aptitude noted above unfortunately differ widely in their delineations of the duration and amount of instruction provided, and contain inadequate descriptions of the actual content of the instruction and grossly inadequate descriptions of the level of knowledge of those being coached. They also differ in design quality, with many studies having no control groups, others having matched groups of coached and uncoached students, and a few involving random assignment of students to control and experimental treatments. Small wonder, then, that the reported increases range from no effect at all to over 100 points on the 200–800 SAT-score scale.

Based upon a large number of investigations, Bond (1989) concludes that regardless of a student's initial status, one can expect an approximately 15-to-20–point increase in SAT-Quantitative scores over 6-month intervals during the high school years. This increase results from practice and typical high school growth alone (i.e., no coaching per se). The effects of practice and growth on the verbal reasoning skills measured by the SAT-Verbal, however, appear to depend upon the initial abilities of the students involved. For students in the 450-point range, the gains from practice and growth average around 15 points; for individuals with initial scores between 500 and 600, the gains from practice and growth average approximately 25 points. Becker (1990) reports similar figures.

THE EFFECTS OF COACHING AND PRACTICE ON TRADITIONAL IQ TESTS

Because they are open-ended examinations that require the examinee to produce, rather than select, correct responses, individually administered assessments of intelligence (IQ tests) do not lend themselves as readily to coaching and to typical test-taking strategies. To be sure, if examinees have had grossly unequal exposure to the actual symbols, artifacts, and manipulatives of the test such as would be the case with persons from non-Western or isolated cultures, one would expect that familiarity and practice with such artifacts would result, at least initially, in increased performance. Vernon (1950, 1969) has in general found such to be the case.

Research on the effects of practice on various tasks typically found on group-administered paper-and-pencil measures of intelligence and individually administered tests goes back at least to the 1920s. The general conclusions regarding coaching and PRACTICE EFFECTS on such tests are as follows (gains have all been converted to a scale with a standard deviation of 15):

1. Practice effects are largest for "naive" subjects (subjects with no test-taking experience), and such effects are greatest on group paper-and-pencil tests, as distinct from individually administered tests, and on heterogeneous, as distinct from homogenous tests.

2. More able subjects (as measured by a pretest) tend to benefit more from practice than do less able subjects.

3. The curve of gains from unassisted practice is negatively accelerated, with initial gains being substantially greater than gains from extended practice.

4. Practice effects are greater for speeded than for untimed tests.

5. Practice effects tend to be greater for nonverbal and performance tests than for verbal tests such as vocabulary and verbal reasoning tests.

6. The transfer of training from practice gains tends, in general, to be relatively small. Largest gains logically result from retaking the identical test after practice, with gains falling off increasingly for parallel tests, similar or comparable tests, different tests in the same general domain, and completely different tests.

7. Practice effects are not ephemeral; rather, they are enduring, with fully half of the gain remaining after one year.

8. The coaching effect without concomitant practice (over and above the gains due solely to practice from taking a similar test once or twice previously) is about 4 or 5 points.

9. The typical *combined* coaching-and-practice gain is approximately 9 IQ points, so the initial coaching and practice effects are about equal.

10. As with practice effects, IQ score increases resulting from instruction alone are greater for nonverbal, performance, and numerical-reasoning tests than for verbal tests.

11. Again, as with practice effects, coaching-without-practice gains are greatest for naive subjects, and greater still for the more able naive subjects.

12. The coaching effects for IQ tests appear to be specific, with as yet little demonstrated transfer to other types of tasks.

Just as there is no universal agreement on precisely what human intelligence is, there is a similar lack of clarity on which cognitive elements are being affected by coaching and practice for standardized measures of human intelligence. To some, the notion of studying for an intelligence test (as distinct from an "achievement" test) is itself illogical. Intelligence cannot be "taught." It turns out, however, that whatever theoretical distinctions exist between "intelligence" and "achievement," they have not been realized in the actual instruments that have been developed to measure these related constructs. Even experienced measurement specialists cannot reliably distinguish among items from a test labeled an "achievement test" and one labeled a "mental ability test" (Cooley & Lohnes, 1976).

It has been said that one of the most efficient and informative ways to understand a phenomenon is to try to change it. Coaching and special instruction have, unfortunately, not appreciably advanced our understanding of intelligence and mental ability. This, however, may change if future carefully controlled studies of coaching and test-wiseness take advantage of recent cognitive approaches to understanding mental ability.

BIBLIOGRAPHY

BECKER, J. B. (1990). Coaching for the Scholastic Aptitude Test: Further synthesis and appraisal. *Review of Educational Research, 60*(3), 373–417.

BOND, L. (1989). The effects of special preparation on measures of scholastic ability. In R. L. Linn (Ed.), *Educational Measurement* (3rd ed., pp. 429–444). New York: American Council on Education/Macmillan.

COLE, N. (1982). The implications of coaching for ability testing. In A. K. Wigdor & W. R. Garner (Eds.), *Ability Testing: Uses, consequences, and controversies* (pp. 389–414). Washington, DC: National Academy Press.

COOLEY, W., & LOHNES, P. (1976). *Evaluation research in education.* New York: Wiley.

DERSIMONIAN, R., & LAIRD, N. M. (1983). Evaluating the effect of coaching on SAT scores: A meta-analysis. *Harvard Educational Review, 53,* 1–15.

JENSEN, A. R. (1980). *Bias in mental testing.* New York: The Free Press.

MESSICK, S., & JUNGEBLUT, A. (1981). Time and method is coaching for the SAT. *Psychological Bulletin, 89,* 191–216.

MILLMAN, J., BISHOP, H., & EBEL, R. (1965). An analysis of test-wiseness. *Educational and Psychological Measurement, 25,* 707–726.

NICKERSON, R. S., PERKINS, N. O., & SMITH, E. E. (1985). *The teaching of thinking.* Hillsdale, NJ: Erlbaum.

PIKE, L. W. (1978). *Short-term instruction, test-wiseness, and the Scholastic Aptitude Test: A literature with recommendations.* New York: College Entrance Examination Board.

STERNBERG, R., & DETTERMAN, D. K. (EDS.). (1987). *What is intelligence?* Norwood, NJ: Ablex.

VERNON, P. E. (1950). The structure of human abilities. London: Methuen.

VERNON, P. E. (1954). Symposium on the effects of coaching and practice on intelligence tests: V. Conclusions. *British Journal of Educational Psychology, 24,* 57–63.

VERNON, P. E. (1969). Intelligence and cultural environment. London: Methuen.

LLOYD BOND
ANN E. HARMAN

THEORIES OF INTELLIGENCE See BIOECOLOGICAL THEORY OF INTELLIGENCE; BOND SAMPLING THEORY OF HUMAN ABILITIES; CONTEXTUALIST THEORIES OF INTELLIGENCE; FLUID AND CRYSTALLIZED INTELLIGENCE, THEORY OF; HEBB'S THEORY OF INTELLIGENCE; HIERARCHICAL THEORIES OF INTELLIGENCE; MULTIPLE INTELLIGENCES THEORY; PIAGETIAN THEORY OF DEVELOPMENT; PSYCHOMETRIC THEORIES OF INTELLIGENCE; TRIADIC THEORY OF ABILITY STRUCTURE; TRIARCHIC THEORY OF HUMAN INTELLIGENCE; VYGOTSKIAN THEORIES OF INTELLIGENCE

THOMSON, GODFREY HILTON (1881–1955) Born on March 27, 1881, in Carlisle, England, Godfrey Hilton Thomson was the son of Charles and Jane Hilton Thomson. The family had limited financial means, but Thomson won a scholarship at age 13 to a secondary school in a neighboring town. He described the school as "one of the early precursors of the presentday 'free places' in England" and attributed the direction in his professional career to "a practical desire to improve the selection of children for higher education" stemming from his own educational history (Thomson, 1939, pp. xiii–xv).

Thomson's higher education started at Rutherford College, Newcastle, and continued at the University of Durham, where he held a Pemberton Fellowship from 1903 to 1906. From Durham, Thomson received a bachelor of science degree with distinction in mathematics and physics, a master of science degree in 1906, and a doctorate in science for psychology in 1913. Also, he worked on a Ph.D. from Strasbourg early in his career.

After the award of the M.S., Thomson became a lecturer in education at Armstrong College, Durham, a position that he held from 1906 to 1920. He married Jane Hutchinson in 1912; they had one child, a son named Godfrey. In 1920, Thomson received a professorship, which he held until 1925, when he moved to Edinburgh. There he was professor of education and director of studies at the Training Center until his retirement in 1951. Thomson died in 1955.

During his career, Thomson published many journal articles, too numerous and varied to describe. The titles of his books, however, reveal the breadth of his interests: *Essentials of Mental Measurement* (written with William Brown), *A Modern Philosophy of Education, Factorial Analysis of Human Ability, Instinct, Intelligence, and Character: An Educational Psychology,* and *Geometry of Mental Measurement.* He also published two widely used tests: *Northumberland* (1921–1922) and the better known *Moray House* (1932), which was used in the survey of the intelligence of Scottish children between 1932 and 1947. The Scottish Mental Survey Committee, of which Thomson was a member, conducted the survey. The study determined a gain in intelligence of children in spite of the disruptive effects of World War II. A number of psychologists who defined intelligence in the Spearmanian tradition had expected a decline on dysgenic grounds, but a gain was fully acceptable in Thomson's point of view.

Thomson spend nineteen years in the Volunteer and Territorial Forces at Durham, including the years of World War I, and served as the acting adjutant from 1915 to 1919 and as commander from 1921 to 1923.

During World War II he was a member of the War Office Committee for Selection.

Thomson's achievements were widely recognized both at home and abroad. He was a member of the British Psychological Society and its president from 1945 to 1946. He belonged to the American Statistical Association and the Institute of Mathematical Statistics. He held elective membership in the Royal Society of Edinburgh and honorary foreign memberships in the American Academy of Arts and Sciences and in the National Academy of Science of the United States. Thomson was also the honorary secretary of the 12th International Congress of Psychology, held in Edinburgh in 1948. He was knighted in 1949.

Thomson brought to psychology a breadth and depth of understanding of mathematics not matched by any of his contemporaries. Thomson's background led him almost inevitably to testing, test theory, and factor analysis. Although the numerous editions of his book on FACTOR ANALYSIS were highly sophisticated, they did not overpower readers with unfamiliar mathematics. In this important work, Thomson's long-standing interest in the psychological interpretation of factors is much in evidence; it is as sophisticated as his methodology.

Thomson summarized his approach to education and social science in the final sentence of the preface to the first edition: "But much mathematical study and many calculations have to precede every improvement in engineering, and it will not be otherwise in the future with the social as well as with the physical sciences." Although Thomson's goal is admirable, its realization will be more distant than Thomson presumably hoped.

BIBLIOGRAPHY

THOMSON, G. H. (1939). *The factorial analysis of human ability.* Boston: Houghton-Mifflin.

THOMSON, G. H. (1951). *The factorial analysis of human ability* (5th ed.). London: University of London Press.

LLOYD G. HUMPHREYS

THOMSON'S RANDOM OVERLAP THEORY

G. H. THOMSON's first articles outlining an alternative to Charles SPEARMAN's explanation of the general factor of intelligence (see TWO-FACTOR THEORY) as a unitary power of the organism appeared relatively early in his career (Thomson, 1916, 1919). Neither in these articles nor in the ones that followed did Thomson cast doubt on the reality of generality in intelligent behavior. His position was that psychologists need not reify their empirical observations. Postulating an entity within the organism has been very common in both biology and psychology, and this common tendency has frequently had undesirable consequences.

The failure to do the analytical research required to understand the phenomenon is a frequent consequence. The entity is accepted as sufficient explanation. Thomson (1939) suggests that this is a primitive human tendency (p. 284), and there is much in the history of science to support his characterization.

Probability had a central role in Thomson's articles from early on. His first example of creating Spearman's hierarchical order of correlations involved casting dice to simulate 10 variates determined by randomly overlapping group factors in a sample of 36 hypothetical persons (Thomson, 1916). Highly acceptable fits to the hierarchical order supposedly required for the existence of a unitary general factor were obtained. Note, however, that Thomson's group factors were not defined, as they were later by Cyril BURT and L. L. THURSTONE (see FACTOR ANALYSIS). Thomson's group factors could affect any number of variates other than all of them, and the variates affected were selected at random. A formula for the correlation coefficient attributed to Brown (1911) was used to compute correlations among the randomly determined variates. The number of group factors in common for any two variates was divided by the product of the roots of the total number of factors, both group and specific, entering the separate variances.

Thomson's next paper (1919) was invited by a member of the Royal Society. The initial example in this paper involved a well-shuffled deck of cards. Intercorrelations of 13 variates based on 13 overlapping, randomly selected group factors were obtained. There was the expected variation from sample to sample in the goodness of fit of the criterion of hierarchical order, but even the poorest fits approximated the expected order.

In a second example, Thomson drew, with replacement, black objects and white objects from a container in the classic probability paradigm. One of the two types of objects represented specific factors, the other the overlapping common factors. Because he fixed the probability of a common factor, variability among the correlations of the variates was reduced. In spite of this, hierarchical order was still apparent.

In the discussion of the second model in 1919, Thomson introduced *elements* as a more general way of describing his common factors. *Bonds* came later, and were credited to Edward THORNDIKE. Whether overlapping group factors, elements, or bonds, it seems clear that Thomson used these terms in a generic sense. His random explanation did not rest on a particular view of the central nervous system or on how behavioral elements were acquired, stored, retrieved, and used.

Thomson also recognized subpools of elements that would lead to group factors in the Burt-Thurstone sense. The subpools can be determined genetically, environmentally, or both. Spearman had characterized his general factor as reflecting a high degree of organization of the mind. "Mental energy" could be turned to the solution of any human problem. However, Thomson had demonstrated that a general factor could be a consequence of the operation of the laws of chance operating in organisms that had successfully adapted to their environments during their evolutionary history. In contrast, group factors did constitute evidence for organization in cognitive abilities.

An available and thorough summary of Thomson's views can be found in the first edition of his book on factor analysis (1939). Here he described the expected values of tetrad differences in contrasts of unitary and random explanations of the general factor. The expected value of the mean tetrad difference is zero under both hypotheses, but the expected value of the standard deviation is larger under the random overlap explanation. A statistical test, however, requires that there be an adequate number of variates that fit the criteria for a single factor in the population R-matrix. The latter assumption is contrary to empirical expectation because test data are too noisy.

If each hypothesis is plausible, but they cannot be distinguished one from the other in any set of behavioral data, there is still a basis for choice. Intelligence as a capacity or power of the organism uses an entity as an explanatory device. This is deceiving, however, unless the postulated entity leads to testable hypotheses. By definition, a testable hypothesis must be subject to the possibility of disconfirmation.

As an entity is typically used, it leads to misinterpretation and misuse of scores on intelligence tests as judged against dependable empirical correlates of the test. This misuse occurs among both those who accept the entity as real and critics who reject both the entity and the test. Thomson's alternative explanation places less within the organism and focuses attention on the correlates.

Thomson also discussed the frequently occurring criticism that the elements or bonds sampled by a standard test of intelligence did not include the highest levels of human intellectual functioning in technology, science, humanities, and the learned professions. The test that samples elements also samples elements in patterns. Given adequate combinations of genetic and environmental bases for more complex patterns of elements, scores on a standard intelligence test can and do indicate the possibility of the highest levels of functioning.

BIBLIOGRAPHY

BROWN, W. (1911). *The essentials of mental measurement.* Cambridge: Cambridge University Press.

THOMSON, G. H. (1916). A hierarchy without a general factor. *British Journal of Psychology, 8,* 271–281.

THOMSON, G. H. (1919). On the cause of hierarchical order among correlation coefficients. *Proceedings of the Royal Society, A, 95,* 400–408.

THOMSON, G. H. (1939). *The factorial analysis of human ability.* New York: Houghton-Mifflin.

LLOYD G. HUMPHREYS

THORNDIKE, EDWARD L. (1874–1949)

Edward Lee Thorndike, one of the most productive American psychologists during the first half of the twentieth century, made major contributions to both psychology and education, but he always considered himself a psychologist. His primary interest was in applying scientific method to the study of social and behavioral phenomena, particularly discovering how human learning takes place and how it can be made most efficient. Although he is most often remembered for his studies of problem solving in cats, this work represents an early and relatively minor part of his contribution to psychology. During his fifty-year career, he published about 500 books and articles on subjects as diverse as learning in fish, methods of statistical analysis, and the elements of aesthetic quality in urban life. However, he did more research and published more articles on intelligence and individual differences in mental ability than on any other subject. A list of 507 of his publications can be found in the *Teachers College Record* for May 1940 and October 1949.

LIFE AND CAREER

Thorndike was born in Williamsburg, Massachusetts, on August 31, 1874, to Edward R. and Abbie (Ladd) Thorndike. His father was a Methodist minister who served churches in Maine and Massachusetts, where he eventually became the presiding elder of the Lynn District. Edward Lee, the second of four children, was thus raised in a devout Christian home environment. Probably partly as a reaction to his mother's fundamentalist beliefs, he later adopted a strictly empirical view of the world and rejected religious practices. He graduated from Wesleyan University in 1895 with an outstanding academic record and went to Harvard University for graduate study. After two years of work with William James, he was attracted to Columbia University by James McKeen CAT-TELL, who was greatly interested in studying individual differences in intelligence. Thorndike's famous cat studies were completed for his doctoral dissertation under Cattell in 1898.

Thorndike married Elizabeth Moulton of Lynn, Massachusetts, on August 29, 1900; they had four children who survived infancy, all of whom earned doctorates in science or mathematics. The second son, Robert Ladd Thorndike, would follow so closely in his father's footsteps that he would eventually occupy the same office that his father used at Teachers College.

Upon completing his graduate study, Thorndike took a position as an assistant professor of pedagogy at Case Western Reserve University. This appointment lasted only one year, because James E. Russell, who was establishing a new Teachers College in affiliation with Columbia University, brought Thorndike back to New York to serve as one of the institution's founding faculty members. The remainder of Thorndike's career was spent at Teachers College, and by 1924 both of his brothers were also on the faculty of Columbia, one in English, the other in history.

By 1921, Thorndike was considered by his peers to be among the foremost American psychologists. He had been elected president of the American Psychological Association in 1912 and was a member of the National Academy of Sciences. His work and the program that he developed at Teachers College were known worldwide, and his students were prominent members of schools of education throughout the United States. Later, he was a founding member and the second president of the Psychometric Society and president of the American Association for the Advancement of Science. His retirement in 1940 capped a career of international renown. He died of a stroke at his home in Montrose, New York, on August 9, 1949.

CONTRIBUTIONS TO INTELLIGENCE

Thorndike's first paper on human intelligence was published in 1901, and he made frequent reference to "intellect" (his preferred term) in his writings on education. Although Alfred BINET is generally credited with producing the first scale to measure intelligence in 1905, Thorndike and his students were using objective measures of academic ability to study factors influencing educational achievement as early as 1903. By the time the United States entered World War I, Thorndike had developed methods for measuring a wide variety of abilities and achievements, ranging from school subjects to aesthetic judgments. During the 1920s he developed a test of intelligence that consisted of completion, arithmetic, vocabulary, and directions tests, known simply as the CAVD. This instrument, which never gained wide popularity, was designed to measure intellectual level on an absolute scale. The method was somewhat crude, but the logic underlying the test predicted elements of test design that would eventually become the foundation of intelligence tests sixty years later.

Shortly after the war, Thorndike (1920) drew an important distinction among what he saw as three broad classes of intellectual functioning. Standard intelligence tests, such as the Binet scales and the Army Alpha tests, measured what he called "abstract intelligence." These tests emphasized abilities related to academic success. Also important, but fundamentally different, were mechanical intelligence, the ability to visualize relationships among objects and understand how the physical world worked, and social intelligence, the ability to function successfully in interpersonal situations. Thorndike called upon psychologists to develop measures of these other types of intellect.

Thorndike's psychology was called CONNECTIONISM, a term derived from his early work on learning. He believed that through experience neural bonds or connections were formed between perceived stimuli and emitted responses. His view was that intellect facilitated the formation of the neural bonds. People of higher intellect could form more bonds and form them more easily than people of lower ability. The ability to form bonds was rooted in genetic potential through the genes' influence on the structure of the brain, but the content of intellect was a function of experience. Thorndike rejected the idea that a measure of intelligence independent of cultural background was possible.

In his definitive statement on intellect in 1926, Thorndike proposed that there were four general dimensions of abstract intelligence: altitude, width, area, and speed. *Altitude* refers to the complexity or difficulty of tasks one can perform; *width* signifies the variety of tasks of a given difficulty; *area* is a function of width and altitude; and *speed* refers to the number of tasks one can complete in a given time. Thorndike considered the altitude of a person's intellect to be most important, and he believed this dimension was controlled by genetic endowment.

From his earliest statements on the subject, Thorndike saw intelligence as consisting of many dimensions. An alternative view, that there was a single general factor of intelligence, was proposed by Charles SPEARMAN in 1904. For twenty-five years Thorndike and Spearman carried on a widely publicized debate over the fundamental nature of intelligence, one dimension or many. In the 1930s, L. L. THURSTONE and other factor analysts took over Thorndike's position. The debate still rages, although at a level of much greater subtlety and complexity.

BIBLIOGRAPHY

JONCICH, G. (1968). *The sane positivist: A biography of Edward L. Thorndike.* Middletown, CT: Wesleyan University Press.

LORGE, I. (1949, October). Thorndike's publications from 1940 to 1949: A bibliography. *Teachers College Record,* pp. 42–45.

Teachers College Record (1940, May), pp. 699–725.

THOMSON, G. H. (1940, May). The nature and measurement of intellect. *Teachers College Record,* pp. 726–750.

THORNDIKE, E. L. (1903). *Educational psychology.* New York: Science Press.

THORNDIKE, E. L. (1920, January). Intelligence and its uses. *Harper's Magazine,* pp. 227–235.

THORNDIKE, E. L., BREGMAN, E. O., COBB, M. V., & WOODYARD, E. (1926). *The measurement of intelligence.* New York: Teachers College Bureau of Publications.

THORNDIKE, R. M. (1990). *A century of ability testing.* Chicago: Riverside.

ROBERT M. THORNDIKE

THURSTONE, L. L. (1887–1955)

Psychologist Louis Leon Thurstone was a major contributor to a diverse range of areas in psychology during a career that spanned more than forty years. His early influence on theory and research in human intelligence, test development and methodology, learning, and attitude scaling in psychophysics is still evident in contemporary approaches to these issues. This article will describe Thurstone's major contributions to each of these areas of study, although the focus will be on his work in intelligence, and particularly his theory of primary mental abilities and his writings on the nature of intelligence.

Although his professional career was in psychology, Thurstone received his undergraduate degree in electrical engineering from Cornell University. Thurstone later noted that even as a student of engineering he was intrigued by the psychological aspects of machine design (Still, 1987). In 1914, Thurstone became a graduate student in psychology at the University of Chicago, where he attended G. H. Mead's lectures on social psychology. Thurstone later stated that Mead's lectures were perhaps the greatest influence on his intellectual development in psychology (Thurstone, 1952). Mead's influence was apparent in a series of Thurstone's early papers, beginning with "The anticipatory aspect of consciousness" (Thurstone, 1919) and culminating with *The Nature of Intelligence* (Still, 1987; Thurstone, 1924). One of Thurstone's primary interests as a graduate student was the study of learning. For his Ph.D. dissertation in psychology, Thurstone attempted to devise a statistical method for treating the telegraphy learning data of a number of subjects (Gulliksen, 1968; Thurstone, 1919). The problems of learning and intelligence continued to occupy Thurstone for much of his professional career.

CONTRIBUTIONS TO INTELLIGENCE THEORY AND RESEARCH

Thurstone began his postgraduate career in 1916 at the Division of Applied Psychology at the Carnegie Institute of Technology. There he published his first major work on intelligence, *The Nature of Intelligence* (1924). In this work, Thurstone rejected the stimulus-oriented psychology that was popular at the time in favor of a person-centered approach. Thurstone distinguished between the focus of experimental or "normal" psychology and abnormal or psychoanalytic psychology. He referred to the former as the "old" psychology and to the latter as the "new" psychology. He noted that what differentiates them is the emphasis they place on the actor versus the environment. The primary interests of experimental psychology, according to Thurstone, are environmental stimuli, which are viewed as eliciting responses and are treated as the starting point in cause-and-effect explanations of behavior. In contrast, explanations in abnormal psychology start with the person and with the behavior that the person manifests to satisfy his or her needs. Thurstone believed that experimental psychology treated the normal person as little more than a responding machine. He advocated turning the focus of psychology from stimuli to the "satisfactions" the normal person is trying to attain and the ways he or she attempts to attain them.

Consistent with the new psychology, Thurstone believed that an understanding and analysis of intelligence must begin with people and their attempts to reach their goals. He argued that the biological function of intelligence is to protect individuals by allowing them to satisfy their needs with the least possible chance of failure by deflecting impulses that are headed toward failure. According to Thurstone, instinctual responses and lower levels of intelligence are characterized by the tendency to act on impulses without reflection. With increasing intelligence comes the capacity for abstraction. Also associated with greater intelligence is the ability to make impulses focal at an earlier unfinished stage and to reflect on alternatives before acting, thereby reducing the possibility of failure. Higher levels of intelligence provide greater protection and increase the likelihood that individuals will eventually reach their goals by deflecting less than optimal impulses at earlier stages in the process of attempting to reach a goal. Simply put, Thurstone saw intelligence as an inhibitory process: the ability to inhibit instinctive responses while those responses are still in a loosely organized form and to use abstraction to redefine the instinctive behavior in light of imagined consequences.

The Theory of Primary Mental Abilities. In 1924, Thurstone returned to the University of Chicago and remained there until he moved to the University of North Carolina in 1952. While at Chicago, Thurstone turned his attention to issues of testing and to developing a theory of intelligence based on the measurement of many intellectual skills (Gulliksen, 1968). In a booklet he wrote on testing, Thurstone (1931) stressed the effects of both subject group composition and range of ability on test reliability, noting that restricted range lowers test reliability.

During this same period, Thurstone developed the theory for which he is best known, the PRIMARY MENTAL ABILITIES THEORY. It is based, in large part, on the results of two large-scale studies (Thurstone, 1938; Thurstone & Thurstone, 1941). The earlier of these two investigations laid the groundwork for the theory. It involved 56 tests, chosen to represent a wide range of mental tasks, given to 240 subjects (Sternberg, 1990; Thurstone, 1938). According to the theory of primary mental abilities, intelligence does not consist of a single general factor. Rather, the theory posits that intelligence is composed of seven primary abilities or factors (Thurstone, 1938; Thurstone & Thurstone, 1941).

Word Fluency. According to Thurstone, this ability is involved whenever a subject is asked to think of isolated words at a rapid rate, as with anagrams, or in producing words with a given initial letter, suffix, or prefix.

Verbal Comprehension. This ability is required in the understanding of words, and tests for this require subjects to comprehend the meaning of given words but not to supply the words. Vocabulary tests, in which the subject checks the response word that has the same meaning as a stimulus word, are used to measure this ability.

Space. This factor is involved in any task in which the subject mentally manipulates an object in two or three dimensions. Tests for this spatial visualization ability require the mental rotation of pictures or figures.

Number. Numerical ability is involved in performing simple arithmetic computation tasks. This ability can be expected in any test in which the subject performs simple arithmetic work, but, Thurstone notes, it is not involved in a task simply because the task contains numbers.

Memory. This factor is present in any test requiring a subject to memorize material, using rote memory and in recall of pictures and words.

Induction. The induction factor is involved in tasks that require the subject to determine a principle or rule covering the test material. Frequently used tasks to measure this ability include word- or number-series tasks and analogies.

Perceptual Speed. This ability is measured by tests that require the subject to recognize small differences in pictures or to identify all the instances of a particular letter in a series of letters.

Thurstone considered these seven factors to be distinct abilities. This notion is in contrast to Charles SPEARMAN's emphasis on a general factor. A major contributor to the literature on FACTOR ANALYSIS, Thurstone believed that Spearman obtained a general factor because he did not rotate the axes in his factor analysis after obtaining the initial solution (Sternberg, 1990). Thurstone advocated a form of rotation, termed "simple structure," that involved rotating factor axes so that given tests display either high or low loadings on each of the factors. Sternberg (1990) notes that either solution, rotated or unrotated factor axes, is mathe-

matically correct, and that the choice ultimately is a matter of preference. British theorists have historically preferred unrotated axes, and American theorists, rotated axes. Furthermore, although Thurstone believed that rotation to simple structure was psychologically more valid, this, too, Sternberg notes, is arguably a matter of preference.

Thurstone's initial research was obtained from a group of college undergraduates, a relatively homogeneous and intellectually select group of subjects differentiated by specific abilities rather than level of intelligence. A set of primary abilities provided a better accounting for the data than did a general factor. The latter was essentially unnecessary to explain the results. However, an eventual resolution of the debate between Thurstone and Spearman was not a matter of preference. First, difficulties arose with Thurstone's original notion of *independent* abilities when the test battery was administered to a second group of subjects, a more intellectually heterogeneous group of public school children (Thurstone & Thurstone, 1941). The results were quite different. Here the primary abilities were themselves correlated, raising the possibility of a general factor (Kail & Pellegrino, 1985). Because of the difference in the data, Thurstone was forced to give up a factor solution involving independent or uncorrelated axes and instead to develop a solution involving oblique or correlated axes. The outcome was a solution that included both a general factor and specific abilities loading differentially on the general factor.

The result is a partial agreement between Thurstone's theory of primary mental abilities and Spearman's theory. The difference between the two theories is primarily one of emphasis, with either the general factor or the specific abilities considered less important in explaining intelligence. Historically, the resolution contributed to the development of subsequent HIERARCHICAL THEORIES OF INTELLIGENCE, which include both a general factor and various levels of specific abilities (see, e.g., Burt, 1940; Vernon, 1971).

ADDITIONAL CONTRIBUTIONS

Although Thurstone is best known for his contributions to research and theories of intelligence, he made considerable contributions to other areas of psychology, primarily psychophysics, and attitude scaling and learning theory.

During the 1920s and early 1930s, Thurstone and his students produced a range of work on attitude scaling and psychophysics (see, e.g., Thurstone, 1927). Of particular interest and importance was the development of procedures that allowed psychophysical methods to be used in measuring subjective characteristics that have no corresponding physical dimensions.

It was also during the 1930s that Thurstone returned to the study of learning. During this period he devised a model of learning based on the urn model, basically the probability of drawing black and white balls from an urn, that was to become a fixture in mathematical learning theory (Still, 1987).

CONCLUSIONS

Thurstone was a major contributor to a variety of areas of psychology, and in each case he brought a unique and person-oriented approach to his research. Still (1987) has commented that Thurstone is a "strangely neglected" psychologist, given the breadth and depth of his contributions to the field of psychology. He proposes that Thurstone's greatest skill was his ability to mediate between data and theory through the flexible application of mathematics. Gulliksen (1968) states that Thurstone emphasized both accurate experimentation and accurate analysis in multivariate situations, particularly through his use of large numbers of variables in an effort to more fully understand complex problems. Sternberg (1990) notes that Thurstone was among the first to propose and demonstrate that there are numerous ways in which a person can be intelligent. This recognition of the range of types of intelligence is reflected in Sternberg's TRIARCHIC THEORY OF INTELLIGENCE (1985) and Gardner's MULTIPLE INTELLIGENCES THEORY (1983). In addition, modern hierarchical theories of intelligence owe much to the resolution of the debate between Thurstone and Spearman.

But what is most evident in any survey of Thurstone's work is that his contributions continue to influence psychology as it is practiced today, and those contributions have been instrumental in the development of both theory and research methodology.

BIBLIOGRAPHY

BURT, C. (1940). *The factors of the mind.* London: University of London Press.

GARDNER, H. (1983). *Frames of mind: The theory of multiple intelligences.* New York: Basic Books.

GULLIKSEN, H. (1968). Louis Leon Thurstone, experimental and mathematical psychologist. *American Psychologist, 23,* 786–802.

KAIL, R., & PELLEGRINO, J. W. (1985). *Human intelligence: Perspectives and prospects.* New York: W. H. Freeman.

STERNBERG, R. J. (1985). *Beyond IQ: A triarchic theory of human intelligence.* New York: Cambridge University Press.

STERNBERG, R. J. (1990). *Metaphors of mind.* New York: Cambridge University Press.

STILL, A. (1987). L. L. Thurstone: A new assessment. *British Journal of Mathematical and Statistical Psychology, 40,* 101–108.

THURSTONE, L. L. (1919). The anticipatory aspect of consciousness. *Journal of Philosophy, Psychology, and Scientific Method, 16,* 561–568.

THURSTONE, L. L. (1924). *The nature of intelligence.* London: Routledge.

THURSTONE, L. L. (1927). The law of comparative judgment. *Psychological Review, 34,* 273–286.

THURSTONE, L. L. (1931). *The reliability and validity of tests.* Ann Arbor, MI: Edwards Publishing Co.

THURSTONE, L. L. (1938). *Primary mental abilities.* Chicago: University of Chicago Press.

THURSTONE, L. L. (1952). Autobiography. In E. G. Boring, H. S. Langfeld, H. Werner, & R. M. Yerkes (Eds.), *A history of psychology in autobiography* (Vol. 4). Worcester, MA: Clark University Press.

THURSTONE, L. L., & THURSTONE, T. G. (1941). *Factorial studies of intelligence.* Chicago: University of Chicago Press.

VERNON, P. E. (1971). *The structure of human abilities.* London: Methuen.

PATRICIA RUZGIS

TRIADIC THEORY OF ABILITY STRUCTURE
The first and most important enterprise in studying intelligence is to get a firm grip on its structure. Such an attempt took most of the twentieth century, but the field of abilities (along with behaviorism) now stands as one of the most secure in the whole area of psychological endeavor.

From the beginning, in 1905, the development of tests of intelligence has followed two quite distinct streams. From that year, when Alfred BINET and Théodore Simon invented the Binet test, a straggling troop of inventive psychologists have added new tests which they believe, on commonsense grounds, must be tests of intelligence. This stream has never had any precise theory about the nature of intelligence. Binet, it is true, had several partial theories, but they were, like those that followed, subjective hunches, with no feasible experimental test of them.

Charles SPEARMAN, in his 1904 article, "'General Intelligence' Objectively Determined and Measured," had both a new research method—FACTOR ANALYSIS—and a theory of a single relation-perceiving power. Few psychologists mastered the method, and Spearman's excellent intelligence test was scarcely known in the rush of new tests that had begun in America. Raymond CATTELL followed with the Cattell Intelligence Tests, Scales 1, 2, and 3 (Cattell, 1932), based on Spearman's theory. One of Cattell's tests is still used in the United States as the basis of entry to the Mensa Society. W. Line's modest advance in 1931 introduced culture-fair measures that J. Raven and Cattell had devised earlier. Spearman's g theory of intelligence was the focus of these measures (see FLUID AND CRYSTALLIZED INTELLIGENCE, THEORY OF).

By 1940 Spearman's g theory had a mixed reception among psychologists. In that year Cattell and Donald HEBB gave papers at the convention of the American Psychological Association claiming that *two,* not one, general factors existed. Cattell's designation of fluid intelligence, $Gf,$ and crystallized intelligence, $Gc,$ derived from improvements in the art of factor analysis, whereas Hebb based his conclusions on neurological leads.

Research in the following twenty years discovered real other differences in these first factor-analytical "split-offs" from Spearman's g theory of intelligence, as follows (Cattell, 1978):

1. A quite different life course separates Gf from $Gc.$ Whereas Gc goes on growing slowly through a person's middle age, Gf declines after about age 22, along with various measures of vitality such as hearing acuteness, oxygen consumption, and strength of hand grip.

2. Culture-fair perceptions of geometrical and other relations measure Gf validly, whereas Gc resides in learned complexities of everyday life. Consequently, as a practical resource, Gf tests are used internationally. They show no difference of mean, for example, between Americans and Chinese. No Gc test, such as the Wechsler Adult Intelligence Scales (WAIS) can do this, even in translations.

3. The work of Hebb and others suggests that injury to the brain can produce purely local effects in Gc performance, for example, in verbal ability, whereas Gf declines in proportion to the weight of the disabled area anywhere in the cortex.

4. The investment theory supposes that Gc is built up by investment of Gf in everyday complex learning experiences. Cattell (1978) has presented a formula that correctly tracks the life course of Gc on this assumption. Throughout life, Gc receives positive contributions, from a diminishing $Gf.$ The result is a .5 correlation, normally, between Gf and $Gc.$

5. Genetics research shows that the heritability correlation (across families) of Gf is around .80 whereas for Gc it is only about .40. This finding (Cattell, 1987) explains the debates about the value when obtained from confused instances of Gf and Gc in such tests as the WAIS.

It would appear that Gc is less constant in pattern, at later ages, than $Gf.$ The constancy of its pattern arises partly from the underlying pattern of Gf and partly from the impact of a pattern in the environment—the school curriculum. Consequently, when children grow up and become doctors, truck drivers, and lawyers, Gc not surprisingly takes on different coloring in different groups. Unless the tests stick to the material at the end of high school, results from such tests as the Wechsler Intelligence Scales for Children (WISC), WAIS, and STANFORD-BINET INTELLIGENCE SCALE give very erratic results when applied to 40- and 60-year-olds (Cattell & Johnson, 1986).

The ends of the two streams of intelligence test construction described above are very different. One ends in an intellectual desert. When asked the theoretical question, "What is intelligence?," the constructors of the WISC and WAIS tests have no answer but "Intelligence is what intelligence tests measure."

In g theory, g depends on the data base from which one starts, though Gf and Gc are set abilities. Actually, the correct basis for seeking second factors or "general capacities" is the whole collection of primary abilities.

In 1937 L. L. THURSTONE and T. G. Thurstone, using a new and improved method of multifactor factoring, exposed six primary factors, among them verbal ability, spatial ability, and perceptual ability. The social effect was amusing. All those who disliked the intelligence quotient (IQ), either because of its personal reference or, as sociologists, because it demonstrated human genetic inequalities, clamored for substituting primary ability measurements for the new visual, general ability, g. The fashion was premature and brief, however, for both the Thurstones and Spearman found g again as a clear second-order factor among the primaries. The primaries were all positively correlated; factoring them yielded a general factor with substantial loading (investment) in each primary. It remained next to discover the extent of the primaries. This finding came about from a wide range of performances by Ralph Hakstian and Cattell in 1978. They discovered no fewer than twenty primaries but recognized that further exploration would almost certainly turn up more. Joy GUILFORD's analysis, although restricted to orthogonal factors, agreed, as did some others on fewer performances.

Cattell's view in the 1970s was that the primary abilities arose from investment of Gf in life-learning experiences and called them "aids" because individuals acquired them as means to social ends. This opinion may be true, but investigation shows that some abilities have higher inheritance than could derive from the loading in Gf.

Two ranks of unitary abilities seemed to exist: capacities such as Gf, Gc, Gm and Gr; and aids, such as verbal, spatial, reasoning, perceptual speed, ideational fluency, word fluency, and spelling ability. The Thurstones had also found a very high heritability of spelling ability.

Doubts arose, however, about this two-rank theory from neurological considerations. Evidence indicated that around the brain area specifically devoted to receiving sensation from a specific sense there was an association area. Finally, a factor of auditory ability was isolated by John Horn and Stankov. Visual ability, previously put among the capacities, soon became more a local *provincial ability* as researchers began to call the category. Kinesthesia, known for some time, probably belongs to this group.

TABLE 1

The basic types of ability components in the triadic theory

Powers		Agencies		
1 Capacities	*2* Provincials	*3* Agencies		Contributors beyond abilities
[Unity of action over the whole cognitive field]	[Unity of organization of neural sensory or motor zone in brain]	Aids [unity of learned transfer]	Effector proficiencies [unity of dynamic learning]	Dynamic and personality noncognitive contributors outside triadic components
Examples: g_f, g_s, g_r, etc. g_x,	Examples: p_v, p_a, p_m, etc.	Examples: a_g, a_n, a_m, etc.		

Variables: actual performances

v_1, v_2, v_3, v_4, v_5, v_6, v_7, v_8, . . ., v_n

All this has led to the present triadic theory (Cattell, 1986), as represented in Table 1.

The position of provincials, *ps*, which complete this triadic picture cannot be assigned with confidence. Obviously they fall somewhere between the capacities and the aids (agencies). Do they mediate the action of capacities, being steps on their way to agencies, or are they parallel and independent in their contribution to aids? We do not know, and a combination of factorial methods with neurological advances is probably necessary to clarify the uncertainty.

BIBLIOGRAPHY

BOYLE, G. A. (1989). Review of the factor structure of the 16PF and the clinical analysis questionnaire. *Psychological Test Bulletin.*

CATTELL, R. B. (1932). *The Cattell intelligence tests: Scales 1, 2, and 3.* Windsor: Educational Testing Publisher.

CATTELL, R. B. (1937). *The fight for our national intelligence.* London: P. S. King & Son.

CATTELL, R. B. (1950). *Culture-fair intelligence scales 1, 2, and 3.* Champaign, IL: Institute for Personality and Ability Testing.

CATTELL, R. B. (1970). *The culture-fair intelligence scales.* Champaign, IL: Institute for Personality and Ability Testing.

CATTELL, R. B. (1984). *Intelligence, its structure, growth, and action.* Amsterdam: North-Holland.

CATTELL, R. B., & JOHNSON, R. (1986). *Functional psychological testing.* New York: Brunner/Mazel.

GUILFORD, J. P. (1967). *The nature of human intelligence.* New York: McGraw-Hill.

HAKSTIAN, A. R., & CATTELL, R. B. (1978). Higher-stratum ability structures on a basis of twenty primary abilities. *Journal of Educational Psychology, 70,* 657–669.

HEBB, D. O. (1939). Intelligence in man after large removals of cerebral tissue: Report of four left frontal lobe cases. *Journal of General Psychology, 21,* 73–88.

LASHLEY, K. S. (1963). *Brain mechanisms and intelligence: A quantitative study of injuries to the brain.* New York: Dover.

RAVEN, J. C. (1947). *Progressive matrices: Sets A, B, C, D, and E, 1938.* London: H. K. Lewis.

SPEARMAN, C. E. (1904). "General intelligence," objectively determined and measured. *American Journal of Psychology, 15,* 201–293.

SPEARMAN, C. E. (1923). *The nature of "intelligence" and the principles of cognition.* London: Macmillan.

THURSTONE, L. L., & THURSTONE, T. G. (1947). *SRA general primary abilities test.* Chicago: Science Research Associates.

VINING, C. (1982). On the possibility of the reemergence of a dysgenic trend with respect to intelligence in American fertility differentials. *Intelligence, 6,* 241–264.

RAYMOND B. CATTELL

TRIARCHIC THEORY OF HUMAN INTELLIGENCE

The triarchic theory of human intelligence (Sternberg, 1985, 1988) seeks to explain in an integrative way the relationship between (1) intelligence and the internal world of the individual, or the mental mechanisms that underlie intelligent behavior; (2) intelligence and the external world of the individual, or the use of these mental mechanisms in everyday life in order to attain an intelligent fit to the environment; and (3) intelligence and experience, or the mediating role of one's passage through life between the internal and external worlds of the individual. Consider some of the basic tenets of the theory.

INTELLIGENCE AND THE INTERNAL WORLD OF THE INDIVIDUAL

It is important to understand the processes that underlie intelligent thought. In the triarchic theory, this understanding is sought through the identification and understanding of three basic kinds of information processes, referred to as *metacomponents, performance components,* and *knowledge-acquisition components.* A component, in each case, refers to a mental process.

Metacomponents. Metacomponents are higher-order executive processes used to plan what one is going to do, to monitor it while one is doing it, and to evaluate it after it is done. These metacomponents include (1) recognizing the existence of a problem; (2) deciding upon the nature of the problem; (3) selecting a set of lower-order processes to solve the problem; (4) selecting a strategy into which to combine these components; (5) selecting a mental representation upon which the components and strategy can act; (6) allocating one's mental resources; (7) monitoring one's problem solving as it is happening; and

(8) evaluating one's problem solving after it is done. For example, in solving a mathematical problem you need to know you have the problem, figure out what the problem asks, decide what steps to use in solving the problem, and so on.

Performance Components. Performance components are lower-order processes that execute the instructions of the metacomponents. These lower-order components solve the problems according to the plans laid out by the metacomponents. Whereas the number of metacomponents used in the performance of various tasks is relatively limited, the number of performance components is probably quite large. Many of these performance components are relatively specific to narrow ranges of tasks (Sternberg, 1979, 1983, 1985).

Consider, for example, the main performance components of inductive reasoning: encoding, inference, mapping, application, comparison, justification, and response. They can be illustrated with reference to an analogy problem, such as LAWYER : CLIENT :: DOCTOR: (a) PATIENT, (b) MEDICINE. In encoding, the subject retrieves from memory semantic attributes that are potentially relevant for analogy solution. In inference, the subject discovers the relation between the first two terms of the analogy, here, LAWYER and CLIENT. In mapping, the subject discovers the higher-order relation that links the first half of the analogy, headed by LAWYER, to the second half of the analogy, headed by DOCTOR. In application, the subject carries over the relation inferred from the first half of the analogy to the second half of the analogy, generating a possible completion for the analogy. In comparison, the subject compares each of the answer options to the mentally generated completion, deciding which, if any, is correct. In justification, used optionally if none of the answer options matches the mentally generated solution, the subject decides which, if any, of the options is close enough to constitute an acceptable solution. In response, the subject indicates an option, by means of pressing a button, making a mark on a piece of paper, or something similar.

Knowledge-Acquisition Components. Knowledge-acquisition components are used *to learn how to do* what the metacomponents and performance components eventually do. Three knowledge-acquisition components appear to be central in intellectual functioning: (1) *selective encoding;* (2) *selective combination;* and (3) *selective comparison.*

Selective encoding involves sifting out relevant information from irrelevant information. When new information is presented in natural contexts, relevant information for one's given purpose is embedded in the midst of large amounts of purpose-irrelevant information. A critical task for the learner is that of sifting "the wheat from the chaff," recognizing just what among all pieces of information is relevant for one's purposes (see Schank, 1980).

Selective combination involves combining selectively encoded information in such a way as to form an integrated, plausible whole. Simply sifting out the relevant from the irrelevant is not enough to generate a new knowledge structure. One must know how to combine the pieces of information into an internally connected whole (see Mayer & Greeno, 1972).

Selective comparison is involved in seeing analogies to past experience, and, generally, in bringing old information to bear on new problems.

To summarize, then, the components of intelligence are an important part of the intelligence of the individual. The various kinds of components work together. Metacomponents activate performance and knowledge-acquisition components. These latter components in turn provide feedback to the metacomponents. Although one can isolate various kinds of information-processing components from task performance using experimental means, in practice, the components function together in highly interactive ways that are not easy to isolate. Thus, diagnoses as well as instructional interventions need to consider all three types of components in interaction, rather than any one kind of component in isolation. But understanding the nature of the components of intelligence is not in itself sufficient for understanding the nature of intelligence, because there is more to intelligence than a set of information-processing components. One could scarcely understand all of what it is that makes one person more intelligent than another by understanding the components of processing on, say, an intelligence test. The other aspects of the triarchic theory address some of the other aspects of intelligence that contribute to individual differences in observed performance, outside of testing situations as well as within them.

INTELLIGENCE AND EXPERIENCE

Components of information processing are always applied to tasks and situations with which one has some level of prior experience. According to the experiential subtheory, the components are not equally good measures of intelligence at all levels of experience. Assessing intelligence requires one to consider not only components but also the levels of experience at which they are applied.

According to the experiential subtheory, intelligence is best measured at those regions of the experiential continuum that involve tasks or situations that are either relatively novel, on the one hand, or in the process of becoming automatized, on the other. As Raaheim (1974) pointed out, totally novel tasks and situations proved to be poor measures of intelligence: One would not want to administer, say, trigonometry problems to a first-grader. But one might wish to administer problems that are just at the limits of the child's understanding in order to test how far this understanding extends. Related is Lev VYGOTSKY's concept of the zone of proximal development (1978), in which one examines a child's ability to profit from instruction to facilitate his or her solution of novel problems. In order to measure automatization skill, one might wish to present a series of problems—mathematical or otherwise—to see how long it takes for solution of them to become automatic, and to see how automatized performance becomes. Thus, both slope and asymptote (if any) of automatization are of interest. The ability to deal with novelty and the ability to automatize information processing are interrelated. If one is well able to automatize, one has more resources left over for dealing with novelty. Similarly, if one is well able to deal with novelty, one has more resources left over for automatization. Thus, performance at the various levels of the experiential continuum are related to one another.

These abilities should not be viewed in a vacuum with respect to the componential subtheory. The components of intelligence are applied to tasks and situations at various levels of experience: The ability to deal with novelty can be understood in part in terms of the metacomponents, performance components, and knowledge-acquisition components involved in it. Automatization refers to the way these components are executed. Hence, the two subtheories considered so far are closely intertwined. We need now to consider the application of these subtheories to everyday tasks, in addition to their application in the laboratory.

INTELLIGENCE AND THE EXTERNAL WORLD OF THE INDIVIDUAL

According to the contextual subtheory, intelligent thought is directed toward one or more of three behavioral goals: *adaptation to an environment, shaping of an environment,* and *selection of an environment.* These three goals may be viewed as the functions toward which intelligence is directed: Intelligence is not aimless or random mental activity that happens to involve certain components of information processing at certain levels of experience. Rather, it is activity purposefully directed toward the pursuit of these global goals, all of which have more specific and concrete instantiations in people's lives.

Adaptation. Most intelligent thought is directed toward the attempt to adapt to one's environment. The requirements for adaptation can differ radically from one environment to another—whether environments are defined in terms of families, jobs, subcultures, cultures, or some other context. Hence, although the components of intelligence required in these various contexts may be the same or quite similar, and although all of them may involve, at one time or another, dealing with novelty and automatization of information processing, the concrete instantiations that these processes and levels of experience take may differ substantially across contexts, but the particular instantiations of these processes, facets, and functions can differ radically. Thus the content of intelligent thought and its manifestations in behavior will bear no necessary resemblance across contexts. As a result, although the mental elements that an intelligence test should measure do not differ across contexts, the vehicle for measurement may have to differ. A test that measures a set of processes, experiential facts, or intelligent functions in one context may not provide equally adequate measurement in another context. To the contrary, what is intelligent in one culture may be viewed as unintelligent in another.

Different contextual milieus may result in the development of different mental abilities. For example, Kearins (1981) found that aboriginal children probably develop their visuospatial memories to a greater degree than do Anglo-Australian children, who are more likely to apply verbal strategies to spatial memory tasks than are the aborigines, who employ spatial strategies. In contrast, participants in Western societies probably develop their abilities for thinking abstractly to a greater degree than do societies in which concepts are rarely dealt with outside their concrete manifestations in the objects of the everyday environment.

Shaping.　Shaping of the environment is often used as a backup strategy when adaptation fails. If one is unable to change oneself to fit the environment, one may attempt to change the environment. For example, repeated attempts to adjust to the demands of one's romantic partner may eventually lead to attempts to get the partner to adjust to oneself. But shaping is not always used in lieu of adaptation. In some cases, shaping may be used before adaptation is ever tried, as in the case of an individual who attempts to shape a romantic partner with little or no effort to shape himself or herself to better suit the partner's wants or needs.

In some respects, shaping may be seen as the quintessence of intelligent thought and behavior. One essentially makes over the environment rather than allowing the environment to make over oneself. Perhaps it is this skill that has enabled humankind to reach its current level of scientific, technological, and cultural advancement (for better or for worse). In science, the greatest scientists are those who set the paradigms (shaping) rather than those who merely follow them (adaptation). Similarly, in art and in literature, the individuals who achieve greatest distinction are often those who create new modes and styles of expression rather than those who merely follow existing ones. It is not their use of shaping alone that distinguishes them intellectually but rather a combination of their willingness to do it and their skill in doing it.

Selection.　Selection involves renunciation of one environment in favor of another. In terms of the rough hierarchy established so far, selection is sometimes used when both adaptation and shaping fail. After at-

tempting both to adapt and to shape a marriage, one may decide to deal with one's failure in these activities by "deselecting" the marriage and choosing the environment of the newly single. Failure to adjust to the demands of a work environment, or to change the demands placed upon one so as to make them a reasonable fit to one's interests, values, expectations, or abilities, may result in the decision to seek another job altogether. But selection is not always used as a last resort. Sometimes one attempts to shape an environment only after attempts to leave it have failed. At other times, one may decide almost instantly that an environment is simply wrong for oneself and feel that one need not or should not even try to fit into it or to change it. For example, every now and then, a new graduate student realizes almost immediately that he or she chose graduate school for the wrong reason, or finds that graduate school is nothing at all like the continuation of undergraduate school he or she expected. In such cases, the intelligent thing to do may be to leave the environment as soon as possible, in order to pursue activities more in line with one's goal in life.

To conclude, adaptation, shaping, and selection are functions of intelligent thought as it operates in context. They may, although they need not, be employed hierarchically, with one path followed when another one fails. It is through adaptation, shaping, and selection that the components of intelligence, as employed at various levels of experience, become actualized in the real world. In this section, it has become clear that the modes of actualization can differ widely across individuals and groups, so that intelligence cannot be understood independently of the ways in which it is manifested.

COMPARISON WITH OTHER THEORIES OF INTELLIGENCE

Underlying theories of intelligence are various "metaphors of mind." For example, some theories—in particular, the test-based ones—tend to view the mind as a map. Theorists viewing the mind as a map try to chart the regions of the mind that harbor various abilities. Some theorists have argued that, in contrast, the mind is best viewed in terms of the software of a computer: People process information much in the way that computers run programs. Still other theorists have viewed intelligence biologically, or in terms of culture. (See Sternberg, 1990, for a review of these various theories.)

The triarchic theory views intelligence as a system with interrelated parts. The processes of intelligence work together in order to produce the behavior we observe in the everyday world and label as "intelligent." The processes constituting the system are viewed as universal. For example, people in all cultures need to recognize when they have problems, design strategies to solve these problems, monitor how well the strategies are working, and so on. But the perceived "intelligence" of the particular plans—the contents of intelligence—are seen as variable across cultures. What is considered to be intelligent in one culture—for example, answering questions rapidly—may be perceived as not very intelligent in another culture. It is for this reason that a distinction is made in the theory between the processes (components) of intelligence and the context in which these processes operate.

Although there has been success in measuring the various aspects of the triarchic theory and in teaching them as well, the theory is obviously in no way perfect. For example, it specifies processes of intelligence (e.g., inference) without specifying in detail how these processes are executed. As another example, although many parts of the theory have been tested, the theory has not been tested in its entirety nor is it clear whether there is any master experiment that would adequately test all aspects of the theory. Hence, the theory may not be fully disconfirmable, although parts of it certainly are. Ideally, the theory will continue to generate research and educational applications, and eventually lead either to refined versions or to newer theories. This theory, like others, is a step toward a better theory of intelligence, not the last word in such theories.

BIBLIOGRAPHY

KEARINS, J. M. (1981). Visual spatial memory in Australian aboriginal children of desert regions. *Cognitive Psychology, 13,* 434–460.

MAYER, R. E., & GREENO, J. G. (1972). Structural differences between learning outcomes produced by different instructional methods. *Journal of Educational Psychology, 63,* 165–173.

RAAHEIM, K. (1974). *Problem solving and intelligence.* Oslo: Universitetsforlaget.

SCHANK, R. C. (1980). How much intelligence is there in artificial intelligence? *Intelligence, 4,* 1–14.

STERNBERG, R. J. (1979). The nature of mental abilities. *American Psychologist, 34,* 214–230.

STERNBERG, R. J. (1983). Components of human intelligence. *Cognition, 15,* 1–48.

STERNBERG, R. J. (1985). *Beyond IQ: A triarchic theory of human intelligence.* New York: Cambridge University Press.

STERNBERG, R. J. (1988). *The triarchic mind: A new theory of human intelligence.* New York: Viking.

STERNBERG, R. J. (1990). *Metaphors of mind.* New York: Cambridge University Press.

VYGOTSKY, L. S. (1978). *Mind in society: The development of higher psychological processes.* Cambridge, MA: Harvard University Press.

ROBERT J. STERNBERG

TWIN STUDIES OF INTELLIGENCE Twin studies employ a number of different analytic methods that capitalize on the fact that twins are an experiment of nature (Bouchard & Propping, 1993). Every human being is genetically unique, except for identical twins (called monozygotic, or MZ, twins because they arise from a single fertilized egg, or zygote), who share all their genes in common. Fraternal twins (called dizygotic, or DZ, twins because they arise from two fertilized eggs, or zygotes) share many genes by virtue of the fact that they are human beings, but in addition, they share half their genes in common by descent; that is, both their mother and father contributed their genes equally to each twin. As a consequence, with respect to those genes on which human beings differ (e.g., blood types), DZ twins on average have 50 percent similarity.

THE ORDINARY TWIN METHOD

The most widely used twin-study method makes use of these elementary genetic facts in the following manner. If we assume that MZ and DZ twins are treated pretty much alike by their parents and measure the similarity of the twins on a phenotype (measurable characteristic of an organism), such as an intelligence-test score, the difference in similarity between the two types of twins will reflect one-half the influence of heredity. Similarity is measured using the intraclass correlation coefficient. This measure varies from zero to +1.00. A value of zero indicates no more similarity between pairs of twins than one would expect if the individuals had been paired at random rather than as twins. A value of 1.00 would indicate that the members of each twin pair are absolutely the same. Real values always fall somewhere between these extremes. MZ twins may be alike with respect to their intelligence-test scores for two reasons: First, they share all their genes; second, they share many common environmental influences (same parents, same school, same home, etc.). Either or both of these factors may or may not influence their scores. MZ twins also undergo many unique environmental influences (not all of them are necessarily social environmental; they may be biological, i.e., unique prenatal insults). Let us symbolize the influence of genetic factors as G, the influence of common environmental factors as CE. The similarity between MZ twins is thus due to $G + CE$. Any differences between MZ twins, who by definition are genetically identical, must be environmental, and we call this component unique environmental (UE, this component also contains errors of measurement). The similarity between DZ twins would be $1/2\,G + CE$ (recall that we assume that CE is the same for MZ and DZ twins—the equal-environment assumption). Notice that the difference between DZ twins is made up of two parts, $1/2\,G$ and UE. DZ twins differ because of both heredity and environment. We can now write the equations in the left-hand column of Table 1. Note

that r_{mzt} means the correlation of MZ twins reared together, r_{dzt} means the correlation of DZ twins reared together.

In words, the difference between the similarity of MZ and DZ twins reflect one-half the genetic influence. To estimate the full influence of heredity, we simply multiply the difference by 2. An estimate of the influence of genetic factors on a trait is called a "heritability estimate," symbolized h^2. When it is based on twin data, it is called "the Falconer heritability estimate," after the quantitative geneticist who proposed it (Falconer, 1990). The symbol h^2 does not mean that the value should be squared; it is simply a symbol. Heritability estimates are not fixed values. They vary as a function of a number of factors, such as age of the sample, the population sampled, the conditions under which the population grew up, and the type of test used. The influence of all these factors needs to be investigated with respect to every trait of interest. The numbers in Table 1 illustrate this issue nicely. The large body of twin data (Bouchard & McGue, 1981) was updated and partitioned into two groups, children 4–12 years of age and adults over 20 years of age. The heritability for children is lower than the heritability for adults. It appears that heritability increases with age. These studies, however, sample different generations, and some would argue that perhaps it was the conditions of rearing that caused the difference in heritability. Before we turn to this problem, a few other assumptions of the ordinary twin method must be discussed. One assumption of the ordinary twin method is that with regard to the trait in question—in this case IQ—there is no assortative mating. We know that this assumption is violated, as the correlation between spouses for IQ is .38 (Bouchard & McGue,

TABLE 1
Equations showing the components of IQ similarity for MZ and DZ twins, the heritability, and real data examples of correlation from children and adults (N = pairs of twins)

Symbolic Equation	Real Data: Children 4–12 years of age	Real Data: Adults 20 years of age and over
$r_{mzt} = G + CE$	.79 ($N = 1688$)	.84 ($N = 1144$)
$r_{dzt} = 1/2\,G + CE$	.56 ($N = 2708$)	.55 ($N = 1698$)
$h^2 = 2(r_{mzt} - r_{dzt})$	.46	.58
or G		

1981). Assortative mating on a trait enhances the similarity between first-degree relatives in proportion to the importance of genetic factors. The IQ correlation for DZ twins is thus somewhat enhanced, leading us to underestimate the influence of heredity when it is subtracted from the MZ correlation. The second assumption is that the influence of heredity is largely polygenic additive; that is, the influence is due to many small genes whose independent effects simply add up. An alternative to this type of influence is that genes act configurally (in a nonadditive fashion). In such a case, the MZ twins would have all their genes in exactly the same configuration, and thus, their similarity would reflect such effects, if they exist. DZ twins share half their genes by descent, but they do not share the same configurations of genes. Consequently, if a genetic influence is configural, the DZ twin correlation would be less than half the MZ correlation (Lykken et

al., 1992). Clearly, the influences of assortative mating and configural effects work against each other. We will return to these issues shortly.

STUDYING TWINS OVER TIME

The hypothesis that the conditions of rearing caused the different heritabilities for children and adults can be tested by examining data from studies of the same twins over time (longitudinal studies). Figure 1 shows the similarity in mental development of MZ twins, DZ twins, twin–sibling sets, midparent–offspring sets, and each child with itself age to age from 3 months to 15 years (Wilson, 1983). Twins (MZ and DZ) at 3 months of age are very much alike and quite different from sib–twin pairs. MZ and DZ twins begin to diverge after 6 months of age, but strong divergence does not occur until after age 4. DZ twin similarity

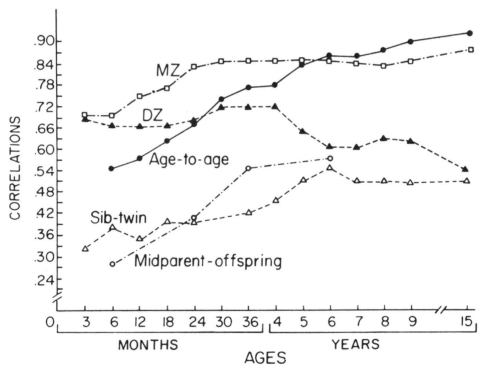

Figure 1

Mental development correlations for MZ twins, DZ twins, twin–sibling sets, parent–offspring sets; and for each child with itself, age to age

SOURCE: Wilson, 1983. Reproduced by permission.

converges with sib–twin similarity at about age 15 (both kinds of pairs share 50% of their genes by descent, as they are first-degree relatives). This evidence suggests that there are powerful environmental forces (*CE*) causing twins to be alike in childhood, but these forces dissipate with age. An alternative hypothesis asserts that while environmental forces toward similarity may dissipate with age for DZ twins, for MZ twins powerful environmental forces are at work making them more alike; that is, because of the twins' morphological similarity, their mothers, friends, teachers, and others treat them so much alike that they become alike. The equal-environment assumption is thus asserted to be false. How might we test this idea?

THE MZ TWIN DIFFERENCE METHOD

One way to test this hypothesis is to examine the data to see if indeed twins who are treated similarly are more alike than twins who are not treated similarly. This method works best with MZ twins. As we have shown, the differences between such twins must be entirely environmental in origin. J. C. Loehlin and R. C. Nichols (1976) explored this question and were unable to explain twin differences on the basis of how parents reportedly treated the twins. Although MZ twins were clearly treated much more alike than DZ twins, none of the differences in personality or ability related to differences in treatment. Indeed, the correlations were very modest and much the same for both MZ and DZ twins, about +.05 to +.06. These surprising findings have stood the test of time (Plomin & Daniels, 1987). The question of whether twins are alike because they are treated alike or are treated alike because they are alike has also been examined in observational studies, which tend to support the latter conclusion.

GENETIC INFLUENCE ON MENTAL DEVELOPMENT

Like other human beings, MZ twins undergo dramatic morphological change as they grow up. With regard to height, they, like ordinary children, sometimes grow rapidly, so rapidly that they outgrow their clothes. At other times, they appear to stop growing, and their parents become concerned. These spurts and lags in stature clearly reflect genetic influences. Genes

appear to turn growth hormones on and off in spurts (Lampl, Veldhuis, & Johnson, 1992). Interestingly, observations of mental development in twins tell us the same story: MZ twins show remarkable similarity in their spurts and lags in mental development, and DZ twins show only partial similarity (Wilson, 1983).

STUDYING TWINS REARED APART

The equal-environment assumption of the ordinary twin method is a great stumbling block to the acceptance of the findings from ordinary twin studies, because in spite of overwhelming evidence in support of the assumption, it seems so obviously false. This assumption can fortunately be avoided by using twins reared apart. If MZ twins are separated very early in life and reared in separate homes with little or no contact, the only component making them similar would be *G*. Similarly DZ twins reared apart would be alike only for genetic reasons. Such twins are called MZA and DZA twins, and twins reared together are called MZT and DZT twins, to denote the conditions of rearing. Note that if MZA twins were very much alike and DZA twins showed a level of similarity less than half the MZA twins, this would be evidence for configural genetic influence. Consistent with the equations in Table 1, $r_{mza} = G$.

The data from one study of adult (average age about 65) MZT, MZA, DZT, and DZA twins (Pedersen et al., 1992) is shown in Table 2. The evidence from this study is consistent with the adult twin data shown in Table 1. (This data was not included in the data base used to create Table 1.) There is a very strong genetic influence on variation in measured adult intelligence—about 78 percent. In addition, this study also supports the hypothesis that nonadditive genetic influence plays a role in this trait, r_{dza} is much less than half r_{mza}, and *CE* is very small—the difference between r_{mza} and r_{mzt} being very small and r_{dzt} being less than r_{dza}. The MZA

TABLE 2

Intraclass correlations for intelligence by zygosity and rearing group for intelligence

MZA	MZT	DZA	DZT
.78	.80	.32	.22

findings from this study are very consistent with the evidence from previous studies of (mostly adult) MZA twins. Previous studies have reported correlations of .71, .69, .75, and .75 (Bouchard et al., 1990).

When all the findings are taken together, they make a convincing argument in favor of genetic influence on intelligence. Nevertheless, additional lines of evidence using different methods should be brought to bear on this question, as no single method is infallible. One of the most interesting lines of independent evidence is from an experiment with unrelated individuals reared together (ut) in the same family (adoptees). Such individuals do not share any genes. The only reason they should be alike is because they share a common environment while growing up. In line with the equations in Table 1, $r_{ut} = CE$. Three studies of intelligence in adult adoptees reared together yield a correlation of about zero. Studies of intelligence in adoptees reared together whose IQs were measured when they were children yield a correlation near .30. These studies consequently confirm the conclusion drawn from ordinary twin studies that common family-environmental influences in intelligence are important in childhood, but dissipate with time and tend to disappear in adulthood.

Twin studies have shed a great deal of light on the nature and nurture of intelligence; they are however, even more informative when combined with appropriate samples of nontwins (Neale & Cardon, 1992).

BIBLIOGRAPHY

BOUCHARD, T. J. J., LYKKEN, D. T., McGUE, M., SEGAL, N. L., & TELLEGEN, A. (1990). Sources of human psychological differences: The Minnesota Study of Twins Reared Apart. *Science, 250,* 223–228.

BOUCHARD, T. J. J., & McGUE, M. (1981). Familial studies of intelligence: A review. *Science, 212,* 1055–1059.

BOUCHARD, T. J. J., & PROPPING, P. (1993). *What are the mechanisms mediating the genetic and environmental determinants of behavior?: Twins as a tool of behavior genetics.* Chichester: Wiley.

FALCONER, D. S. (1990). *Introduction to quantitative genetics* (3rd ed.). New York: Longman.

LAMPL, M., VELDHUIS, J. D., & JOHNSON, M. L. (1992). Saltation and stasis: A model of human growth. *Science, 258,* 801–803.

LOEHLIN, J. C., & NICHOLS, R. C. (1976). *Heredity, environment, and personality: A study of 850 sets of twins.* Austin: University of Texas Press.

LYKKEN, D. T., McGUE, M., TELLEGEN, A., & BOUCHARD, T. J. J. (1992). Emergenesis: Genetic traits that may not run in families. *American Psychologist, 47,* 1565–1577.

LYTTON, H. (1977). Do parents create, or respond to, differences in twins? *Developmental Psychology, 13,* 456–459.

NEALE, M. C., & CARDON, L. R. (EDS.). (1992). *Methodology for genetic studies of twins and families.* Dordrecht: Kluwer.

PEDERSEN, N. L., PLOMIN, R., NESSELROADE, J. R., & MCCLEARN, G. E. (1992). A quantitative genetic analysis of cognitive abilities during the second half of the life span. *Psychological Science, 3,* 346–353.

PLOMIN, R., & DANIELS, D. (1987). Why are children in the same family so different from one another? *Behavior and Brain Sciences, 10,* 1–60.

WILSON, R. S. (1983). The Louisville Twin Study: Developmental synchronies in behavior. *Child Development, 54,* 298–316.

THOMAS J. BOUCHARD, JR.

TWO-FACTOR THEORY

In a 1904 article in the *American Journal of Psychology,* Charles SPEARMAN, at the time a doctoral student in Wilhelm Wundt's laboratory in Leipzig, first presented his theory of GENERAL INTELLIGENCE. In subsequent articles and books—notably *The Nature of "Intelligence" and the Principles of Cognition* (1923) and *The Abilities of Man: Their Nature and Measurement* (1927)—Spearman developed his ideas into what has become known as his two-factor theory of intelligence.

Spearman's article drew heavily on Sir Francis GALTON's notion of a general intellectual ability, individual differences in which were hypothesized to influence performance on all measures of mental ability. Spearman also shared with Galton the belief that this general mental ability was related to simple sensory discrimination and REACTION TIME. In a series of studies, Spearman (1904) reported moderate correlations between estimates of intelligence and measures of sensory discrimination; he then applied a formula that he had developed for correcting correlations for attenuation due to unreliability that had the effect of markedly boosting the correlations, thereby supporting his hypothesis.

To correct an observed correlation between two variables (r_{12}) for unreliability, the correlation is divided by the square root of the product of each variable's reliability (r_{11} and r_{22}). The corrected correlation (r'_{12}) is thus given by

$$r'_{12} = r_{12} / \sqrt{(r_{11}r_{22})}. \qquad (1)$$

Spearman argued that the average correlation among a number of measures of intelligence could be taken as an estimate of their reliability. Similarly, the average correlation among sensory discrimination measures estimated their reliability. These estimates of reliability could then be used to correct the average correlation among the several intelligence and discrimination measures for attenuation.

From a sample of village schoolchildren, Spearman (1904) computed the average correlation among different measures of intelligence to be .55, the average correlation among a number of sensory discrimination measures to be .25, and the average correlation between the intelligence and the discrimination measures to be .38. Applying the above formula, the corrected correlation between intelligence and sensory discrimination was computed to be

$$.38/\sqrt{(.55)(.25)} = 1.02. \qquad (2)$$

Spearman was well aware that a correlation could not exceed 1.0, but by applying somewhat different formulas to different combinations of tests he computed corrected correlations between intelligence and sensory discrimination of 1.04 and 0.96. The average of the three corrected correlations was 1.0, leading Spearman to conclude that "We arrive at the remarkable result that the common and essential element in the Intelligences wholly coincides with the common and essential element in the Sensory Functions" (p. 269).

From examples such as this, Spearman concluded that all measures of mental ability were related to a common general intelligence factor (designated g). Different measures might not all be equally highly related to the general factor, but all measures would share at least something in common with one another. Moreover, the degree to which two different measures would correlate with one another would depend entirely on the extent to which each was itself correlated with general intelligence: the more "g-loaded" two measures were, the more highly correlated they would be.

Because different tests of mental ability rarely correlated perfectly with one another (even after correction for unreliability), it was clear that each test must measure something other than g alone. That part of a test that was "left over" after taking g into account, Spearman referred to as the tests's specificity (designated s). By definition, the specifics of two or more tests could never correlate with one another, because any correlation between the tests was entirely attributed to g. Rather, each test was now seen as a composite of the g (or general intelligence) factor and the s (or specific) factor. This identification of two distinct factors composing every test was Spearman's two-factor theory.

Because the correlation (r_{12}) between any two measures of mental ability was entirely attributable to each one's correlation with g (or its g loading), it followed that if the measures' g saturation were removed, the correlation (called a partial correlation and written $r_{12.g}$) would drop to zero: With g removed, the measures would no longer have anything in common and thus would not correlate with one another.

That is,

$$r_{12.g} = 0. \qquad (3)$$

If this was true, then the entire formula for a partial correlation would also equal zero.

That is,

$$r_{12.g} = r_{12} - r_{1g}r_{2g} / \sqrt{(1 - r_{1g}^2)} \sqrt{(1 - r_{2g}^2)} = 0. \qquad (4)$$

From this it follows that

$$r_{12} - r_{1g}r_{2g} = 0. \sqrt{(1 - r_{1g}^2)}. \sqrt{(1 - r_{2g}^2)}. \qquad (5)$$

Therefore,

$$r_{12} - r_{1g}r_{2g} = 0. \qquad (6)$$

And

$$r_{12} = r_{1g}r_{2g}. \qquad (7)$$

In this manner, Spearman (1927) demonstrated that the correlation between any two measures is equal to the product of each one's correlation with g (or the product of each measure's g-loading).

That is,

$$r_{13} = r_{1g}r_{3g}. \tag{8}$$

And

$$r_{23} = r_{2g}r_{3g}. \tag{9}$$

Continuing from this, Spearman developed what he referred to as the *tetrad difference criterion*, a criterion that could be used to prove (mathematically) whether any given correlation matrix indeed contains only a single, general factor. Consider the ratio of two correlations:

$$r_{12}/r_{13}. \tag{10}$$

From the above, each of these correlations is equal to the product of each variable's correlation with g.

That is,

$$r_{12}/r_{13} = r_{1g}r_{2g}/r_{1g}r_{3g} = r_{2g}/r_{3g}. \tag{11}$$

Similarly, any other correlations involving variables 2 and 3 will yield the same outcome.

That is,

$$r_{24}/r_{34} = r_{2g}r_{4g}/r_{3g}r_{4g} = r_{2g}/r_{3g}. \tag{12}$$

Since r_{12}/r_{13} and r_{24}/r_{34} both equal r_{2g}/r_{3g}, they must be equal to each other.

That is,

$$r_{12}/r_{13} = r_{24}/r_{34}. \tag{13}$$

Or

$$r_{12}r_{34} = r_{13}r_{24}. \tag{14}$$

Or

$$r_{12}r_{34} - r_{13}r_{24} = 0. \tag{15}$$

This last equation is an example of the tetrad difference criterion: The difference between the products of cross-diagonal correlations in a correlation matrix should all equal (or average to) zero. The number of such tetrads (or sets of four cross-diagonal correlations) in a matrix is a function of the number of variables, n (specifically, there are $3n!/4!(n-4)!$ tetrads; a matrix with six variables has forty-five tetrads). Because the tetrad difference equation follows from the premise that the correlation between any two tests is entirely attributable to a single factor (g) that each test

has in common, different matrices could be tested for the presence of a single factor by demonstrating that the average of all possible tetrad differences did not deviate significantly from zero.

Continuing further, Spearman (1927) derived a simple means of determining any test's correlation with g. Consider the following:

$$r_{12}r_{13}/r_{23}. \tag{16}$$

If only one factor (g) is responsible for each of these correlations, then,

$$r_{12}r_{13}/r_{23} = r_{1g}r_{2g} \cdot r_{1g}r_{3g}/r_{2g}r_{3g} = r_{1g}^2. \tag{17}$$

Therefore, the correlation between variable 1 and g is given by

$$r_{1g} = \sqrt{(r_{12}r_{13}/r_{23})}. \tag{18}$$

Similarly,

$$r_{1g} = \sqrt{(r_{14}r_{15}/r_{45})}, \tag{19}$$

or any other like combination of correlations.

In this manner, any test's g loading could be computed from the test's correlations with any number of other tests. The use of different combinations of correlations should yield approximately the same value for the test's g loading, differences being attributable to sampling error.

John Raven, working with Spearman, developed his well-known series of RAVEN PROGRESSIVE MATRICES tests from the principle of the eduction of relations and correlates. These tests consistently show high g loadings when they are factor analyzed with other intelligence tests and may be among the best measures of g that are available. In terms of the two-factor theory, this means that they have a high g to s ratio.

Spearman (1927) also characterized g in terms of "mental energy" and hypothesized that the physiological basis or bases of g would one day be identified. In this regard, R. J. Haier and colleagues (1988) reported significant negative correlations between Raven Matrices scores and cerebral glucose metabolic rates (an index of energy consumption). That is, individuals who obtained high Raven scores consumed *less* energy as they worked on the test, a finding in keeping with Spearman's notion of "mental energy." The neurophysiological nature of g, however, has been and continues to be a subject of much debate among intelligence theorists.

One topic that is no longer under debate in the late twentieth century is whether Spearman's two-factor theory provides a viable theory to explain all the phenomena indicating intelligence. The theory quickly came under criticism, notably from Alfred BINET, Cyril BURT, Godfrey THOMSON, and L. L. THURSTONE, and even Spearman himself eventually acknowledged that factors other than g and s were required to explain correlations between different tests accepted as indicating intelligence. This acknowledgment came after it was found that most correlation matrices, particularly those based on a large number of ability measures, did not satisfy the tetrad difference criterion and thus must contain more than one common factor. Rather than having only g in common, groups of tests might also be correlated with one or more additional factors. For example, a vocabulary test and a verbal analogies test might load on a verbal factor in addition to g (and also each have a specific factor unique to themselves). Thus, Spearman's two-factor theory as originally conceived was in fact quite short-lived, though this does not diminish the immense contributions that Spear-

man made to the development of theories of intelligence.

BIBLIOGRAPHY

BURT, C. (1940). *The factors of the mind.* London: University of London Press.

HAIER, R. J., SIEGEL, B. V., NUECHTERLEIN, K. H., HAZLETT, E., WU, J. C., PAEK, J., BROWNING, H. L., & BUCHSBAUM, M. S. (1988). Cortical glucose metabolic rate correlates of abstract reasoning and attention studied with positron emission tomography. *Intelligence, 12,* 199–217.

SPEARMAN, C. E. (1904). "General Intelligence," objectively determined and measured. *American Journal of Psychology, 15,* 201–293.

SPEARMAN, C. E. (1923). *The nature of "intelligence" and the principles of cognition.* London: Macmillan.

SPEARMAN, C. E. (1927). *The abilities of man: Their nature and measurement.* New York: Macmillan.

SPEARMAN, C. E. (1930). Autobiography. In C. Murchison (Ed.), *A history of psychology in autobiography* (Vol. 1). Worcester, MA: Clark University Press.

SPEARMAN, C. E., & JONES, L. W. (1950). *Human ability.* London: Macmillan.

PHILIP ANTHONY VERNON

U

UNDERACHIEVEMENT Discrepancies between expected and actual achievements are called *underachievement* when expectations exceed performance. Expectations are often based on other assessments of "potential" achievement, such as intelligence quotients (IQ) or scores on other ability tests that are used in schools to predict future levels of achievement. If present achievements fall below levels predicted by ability or intelligence tests, the person may be labeled an underachiever.

Three major definitions of underachievement present conflicting ideas and findings. One definition is related to the competence/performance distinction. If a measure of competence shows that the person has the required skills to solve a problem or perform a task, but the person fails to solve the problem or do the task when asked to do so, the underachievement problem may lie in poor motivation to perform or in task requirements that hinder performance. For example, young preschool children may show they understand counting routines with small numbers, but they may fail to count larger numbers accurately because they cannot keep track of the task.

A second definition of underachievement is statistical: in every bivariate plot of achievement measures (e.g., school grades) with IQ or ability, measures will result in scatter of people above and below the regression line—that is, people whose abilities predict lower achievement scores than they actually had and people whose abilities predict higher achievements than they actually had (underachievers). It might seem sensible to call the former group *overachievers,* because their actual performance exceeds their abilities, but the non-sensical nature of this claim (that one performed better than one could) calls the statistical definition of *underachievement* into question as well. In any event, the scatter occurs because ability and achievement measures are not perfectly correlated. Some psychologists over-interpret statistical underachievement as a property of the person, when it is in fact a statistical artifact.

A third definition is more substantial than the other two. Robert McCall (in press) has shown that a group of "true" underachievers can be identified by multiple assessments of intelligence, personality, and school achievements. Chronic underachievers are a distinctive group of poorly adjusted youngsters who do not catch up with their peers and do not achieve at levels predicted by their intellectual abilities alone.

(*See also:* COMPETENCE/PERFORMANCE DISTINCTION.)

BIBLIOGRAPHY

MCCALL, R. (in press). Underachievers. *Current Directions in Psychological Science.*

SANDRA SCARR

V

VALIDITY   In the context of educational and psychological measurement, the term *validity* refers to the evaluation of any description or action resulting from the use of a test or other assessment procedure. Although there is universal agreement among measurement professionals on the unique importance of validity, there are subtle and not so subtle differences in the way validity is characterized. These differences can influence the way validity research is carried out and the kinds of tests that are likely to find favor.

The 1985 *Standards for Educational and Psychological Testing,* which is jointly prepared by the American Educational Research Association (AERA), the American Psychological Association (APA), and the National Council on Measurement in Education (NCME), provides an authoritative description of validity. It is, however, under revision. Moreover, the description of validity in the 1985 *Standards* was, in a sense, out of date when it was published. A review of the theoretical literature on validity available prior to 1985 evinces an evolving consensus among measurement theorists that is not articulated in the 1985 *Standards.* The most widely cited, comprehensive description of validity is S. Messick's chapter for the 1989 edition of *Educational Measurement.* Although Messick's formulation accurately reflects the emerging consensus in the field (a consensus for which his contributions were seminal), his analysis is subtle, complex, and, in places, controversial.

In light of these complexities, the aims of this article are (1) to characterize validity as it is presented in the existing 1985 *Standards* and to summarize the most frequently articulated criticisms of this presentation; (2) to characterize the emerging consensus on validity among measurement theorists, which is not reflected in the 1985 *Standards* but may be reflected in the revised version; and (3) to indicate areas where consensus does not exist among members of the measurement community.

VALIDITY IN THE 1985 STANDARDS

The 1985 *Standards for Educational and Psychological Testing* represent the fourth in a series of authoritative documents on test development and use published once per decade since the 1950s. Since the second edition (1966), the *Standards* have been prepared by a joint committee representing the AERA, APA, and NCME. The committee solicits commentary and critique from many groups who develop, use, or are affected by tests. As such, it represents the most authoritative guidelines for professional practice in test development and evaluation.

Validity, as presented in the 1985 *Standards,* is "the most important consideration in test evaluation" (AERA, APA, & NCME, 1985, p. 9). The 1985 *Standards* define validity as referring to "the appropriateness, meaningfulness, and usefulness of the specific inferences made from test scores. Test validation is the process of accumulating evidence to support such inferences" (p. 9). Given this definition, to speak of the validity of a test is inappropriate; rather *validity* refers to a particular inference (interpretation or description of a person or group) or action based upon a test score. Tests may be used and interpreted in a variety of ways—evidence must be collected to support each interpretation and use. Consider, for instance, some of the many ways in which standardized achievement tests have been used from kindergarten to grade 12: to certify individual students for graduation, to help teachers plan classroom instruction, or to provide the public with accountability information about schools and districts. Each of these purposes implies a different interpretation and use of test scores, which must be validated by accumulating appropriate evidence.

The *Standards* go on to describe categories or sources of validity evidence that should be considered in the process of validation. These include content-, criterion-, and construct-related evidence of validity. This framework has been used since the second edition of the *Standards* (APA, 1966) and continues in most major measurement texts. The first edition of the Standards (APA, 1954) was different in that it used categories labeled "predictive" and "concurrent" instead of "criterion."

Content-related evidence of validity "demonstrates the degree to which the sample of items, tasks, or questions on a test are representative of some defined universe or domain of content." (AERA, APA, & NCME, 1985, p. 10). The universe or domain of content may refer, for instance, to an academic curriculum, a description of the behaviors required to perform a job, and a description of the psychological or educational characteristic (e.g., analytical reasoning) being assessed. The evidence typically involves professional judgments of the fit between the test items and the domain description.

Criterion-related evidence of validity "demonstrates that test scores are systematically related to one or more outcome criteria" (AERA, APA, & NCME, 1985, p. 11). The criterion refers to the behavior or performance of primary interest. For instance, in the case of college admissions tests, a typical criterion is success in college as measured by first-year grade-point average. The relationship between the criterion

and the test refers to the extent to which the two measures are ranking examinees in the same way—the extent to which higher scores on the test accompany higher scores on the criterion and lower scores on the test accompany lower scores on the criterion.

Construct-related evidence of validity is more complex to describe because it can encompass a variety of types of evidence, including content and criterion related evidence. As the *Standards* describe it, construct-related evidence "focuses on the test score as a measure of the psychological characteristic of interest" (AERA, APA, & NCME, 1985, p. 9). Examples of constructs offered in the *Standards* include reasoning ability, reading comprehension, sociability, and endurance. The process of construct validation is characterized as follows:

> The construct of interest for a particular test should be embedded in a conceptual framework, no matter how imperfect that framework may be. The conceptual framework specifies the meaning of the construct, distinguishes it from other constructs, and indicates how measures of the construct should relate to other variables.
>
> The process of compiling construct-related evidence for test validity starts with test development and continues until the pattern of empirical relationships between test scores and other variables clearly indicates the meaning of the test score [AERA, APA, & NCME, 1985, pp. 9–10].

The *Standards* go on to cite examples of the many different kinds of evidence that can support construct validation, including relationships among responses to test items, relationship of test scores to other measures of the same and different constructs and to other nontest variables, questioning test takers about the strategies they used in responding, questioning judges of constructed responses about their reasons for their ratings, and collecting content- and criterion-related evidence. In each case, the evidence is evaluated in terms of its consistency with the proposed interpretation. For example, one would expect to see substantial relationships among measures of the same construct and weaker relationships between test scores and measures of different constructs.

Although still widely used, this framework has been criticized by many measurement theorists. As a careful reading of the above description will demonstrate, the content-criterion-construct categories are not logically distinct nor are they of equal importance. Construct-related evidence is the larger category, which subsumes criterion- and content-related evidence and much more. Moreover, because of the way these categories had been described in earlier editions of the *Standards,* critics have raised concerns that readers will treat them as alternatives or options rather than as aspects of a unified view of validity, which integrates evidence from across categories as the authors of the 1985 *Standards* intended. Further, the framework and definition of validity contained in the 1985 version has also been criticized for failing to include explicit consideration of the social consequences of testing in its description of validity.

THE EMERGING CONSENSUS ON VALIDITY

Because views of validity in educational measurement have evolved beyond what is described in the 1985 *Standards for Educational and Psychological Testing,* it is important to become familiar with those developments that are likely to be reflected in the revised *Standards.* Consequently, this section summarizes the emerging consensus in the field—not reflected in the 1985 *Standards*—about the centrality of construct validity to the evaluation of any test use and about the importance of expanding the concept of validity to include explicit consideration of the consequences of test use. Here the work of several validity theorists— A. ANASTASI, L. J. CRONBACH, and S. MESSICK—is seminal to the evolving understanding of validity. The emerging consensus is reflected in the work of many other measurement theorists (see Moss, 1992, and Shepard, 1993, for reviews).

In 1975, Messick (p. 962) suggested that two questions needed to be asked *whenever* a decision about test use is made:

First, is the test any good as a measure of the characteristic it is interpreted to assess? Second, should the test be used for the proposed purpose?

These questions anticipated much of the current development in validity theory. The first question, as Messick notes, is a technical one referring primarily to

construct validity; the second is an ethical one, referring to the potential consequences of testing and the values implied therein. In subsequent work, Messick described these questions as the "evidential" and "consequential" bases of test interpretation and use (Messick, 1989a, 1989b). Taking into account both of these bases, he defined validity as "an integrated evaluative judgment of the degree to which empirical evidence and theoretical rationales support the adequacy and appropriateness of inferences and actions based on test scores or other modes of assessment" (p. 13). Cronbach (1988) suggested that readers think of validation as an *argument* that "must link concepts, evidence, social and personal consequences, and values" (p. 4). In fact, a growing number of researchers are likening the concept of validation to the process of building an argument (Kane, 1992; Shepard, 1993).

The Evidential Basis of Validity. Consistent with the criticisms of the content-criterion-construct framework outlined above, most theorists now argue that all validity research should be conducted within a construct-validity framework. This means that validity research requires an explicit conceptual framework, testable hypotheses deduced from it, and multiple lines of relevant evidence to test the hypotheses.

The description of construct-related evidence presented in the 1985 *Standards* is consistent with this emerging consensus. Presentations in the work of Anastasi, Cronbach, Messick, and others offer a more elaborated view, however, albeit with some difference in the use of the term *construct validity.* Messick (1989a, 1989b), who distinguishes test interpretation from test use, applies the term to evidence about a test interpretation (e.g., "intelligence" as conceptualized by the developers of the test in question). He also uses the terms *construct validity plus relevance/utility* to refer to evidence about the use of a test (e.g., for placement in special education). Together, these concepts form the "evidential basis" of validity. Others (e.g., Shepard, 1993) disagree with the (partial) distinction Messick draws between interpretation and use and employ the label *construct validity* to cover all of what Messick means by the evidential basis of validity. L.A. Shepard (1993) argues that validity research should begin with the question, "What does the testing practice claim to do?" (p. 429) and should then build an evidence-based argument in response to that question. The presentation below assumes a conception of construct validity that covers both interpretation and use.

Here, the distinction between RELIABILITY and construct validity is important. In the 1985 *Standards,* reliability is discussed in a separate chapter from validity. As it is described there, and in most major measurement texts, reliability is viewed as a necessary but insufficient condition for validity. Typically, reliability is assessed by examining consistency, quantitatively defined, among measures that are intended as *interchangeable*—for instance, consistency among evaluations of a test response, consistency among responses to tasks or items, and consistency across different forms of a test administered on different days. Inadequate consistency is viewed as measurement error. With tests that encourage complex performances by examinees, distinctions between reliability and construct validity blur, as it becomes harder to distinguish "interchangeable" measures from different measures of the same construct (Moss, 1994; Wiley & Haertel, 1992).

Construct validity begins with descriptions of the purpose for which the assessment is being developed and one or more constructs appropriate to the purpose. The construct is the proposed interpretation or meaning for the test score (e.g., reading comprehension) and the purpose is the use to which it will be put, such as certification for high school graduation. The construct description should locate the construct in a conceptual framework, no matter how informal, that defines the construct and distinguishes it from other constructs. The description of the purpose should specify the desired outcomes of test use, the population of persons for whom the test is intended, and the situations in which the test will be used. Hypotheses to be tested in subsequent studies concern the fit between the descriptions of construct and purpose and the evidence collected. Construct validation rarely results in a summative decision about whether or not a given interpretation is justified. More typically, the outcomes of a given study or line of research result in the modification of the test, the construct, the conceptual framework surrounding the construct, or all three. Thus, construct validity is as much an aspect of test development as it is of test evaluation.

In designing such studies, both "convergent" and "discriminant" evidence should be considered. *Conver-*

gent evidence indicates that test scores are related to other measures of the same construct and to other variables that they should relate to as predicted by the conceptual framework; *discriminant* evidence indicates that test scores are not unduly related to measures of other, distinct constructs. For instance, within some conceptual frameworks, scores on a multiple-choice test of reading comprehension may be expected to relate more closely (convergent evidence) to other measures of reading comprehension, perhaps using other reading passages or other response formats (e.g., essay or oral responses); conversely, test scores may be expected to relate less closely (discriminant evidence) to measures of the specific subject matter knowledge reflected in the reading passages on the test.

Construct validation is most efficiently guided by the testing of "rival hypotheses," which suggest alternative explanations or meanings for the test score. Rival hypotheses suggest what may be wrong with the proposed interpretation. Prominent rival hypotheses or threats to construct validity include "construct underrepresentation" and "irrelevant test variance" (Messick, 1989a). *Construct underrepresentation* refers to a test that is too narrow in that it fails to capture important aspects of the construct. *Irrelevant test variance* refers to a test that is too broad in that it requires capabilities irrelevant or extraneous to the proposed construct. Continuing with the above example, a potential rival hypothesis to the claim that a test measures reading comprehension is that it depends unduly on specific subject matter knowledge, thus reflecting "test irrelevant variance." Another rival hypothesis may be that the test "underrepresents" the construct by focusing on literal recall to the exclusion of interpretation. These rival hypotheses suggest studies that may be conducted as part of the construct validation effort. For instance, a researcher may ask experts to examine the items on the test to determine whether any of them emphasize interpretation or require specific subject matter knowledge. The researcher may also ask test takers to think aloud to assess what knowledge and skills they draw on in responding to test items. Additionally, the researcher may examine the relationship between test scores and measures of relevant subject matter knowledge or of interpretive reading, predicting weaker relationships in the first case and stronger relationships in the second.

Descriptions of construct validation typically include lists of sources of evidence for testing hypotheses similar to the list suggested by authors of the Standards. In fact, Anastasi (1986) suggested that "almost any information gathered in the process of developing or using a test is relevant to its validity" (p. 3). Cronbach (1989), however, cautions validity researchers to avoid presenting readers with a "do-it-yourself" kit of empirical results. A "strong" program of construct validation requires that the validator integrate the evidence collected into an overall argument describing the current degree of support for the desired interpretation and use of a test.

The Consequential Basis of Validity. According to most current validity theorists, a strong program of validation also involves consideration of the intended and unintended consequences of testing along with an ethical justification of why the test should be used for the proposed purpose and whether that purpose should be served. Consensus on this expansion of the concept of validity is widespread but not universal. A few writers have raised concerns about overburdening the concept of validity to the point where it ceases to provide useful guidance (Wiley, 1991).

In the context of educational achievement and accountability, attention to consequences has become increasingly prominent. There is a growing body of evidence about the impact of high-stakes testing, such as for certification to graduate or public accountability, on what teachers teach and what students learn. Concerns about the extent to which multiple-choice tests are narrowing the curriculum to focus on the form and content of these tests have led educators to develop alternative forms of assessment that address a broader range of learning goals.

In the context of intelligence testing for placement or intervention, S. Scarr (1988) notes that differing theories of intelligence have different implications for intervention and that they should be evaluated in terms of their usefulness. Similarly, Shepard (1993) notes that when intelligence tests are used to place students in special education, the success of the placement must play a central role in evaluating the validity of the test use. Shepard (1993) provides descriptions of three extended cases of validity research spanning both construct and consequential validity. These cases

and the references that accompany them should provide readers with a good sense of how others have built and evaluated arguments for the validity of a test interpretation and use.

Messick (1989a) and Cronbach (1988, 1989) offer general advice for evaluating the intended and unintended consequences of a test interpretation and use. Messick suggests pitting the proposed test against alternative assessment techniques and alternative means of serving the same purpose, including the general alternative of no assessment. Messick also suggests contrasting different value perspectives and considering the consequences. As an example, he cites varied value perspectives that may underlie systems of selecting individuals for societal rewards such as college admission or employment. Consider the differential consequences of a system that selects individuals according to their abilities versus their efforts or accomplishments or needs. These contrasts, whether empirical or speculative, provide opportunity for well-informed debate and suggest needed areas for study. Cronbach (1988, 1989) articulates distinctions among functional, political, and economic consequences of testing and uses stakeholders' interests as a starting point. He suggests canvassing all types of stakeholders for possible validity questions and then investigating those questions most likely to influence their judgments. "Democracy is functioning well when every party learns how a pending decision would affect his or her interests, and feels that the decision process is being suitably sensitive to them" (Cronbach, 1988, p. 7).

UNRESOLVED ISSUES

Clearly, the task of following the evolving conception of validity in measurement is a complex one. Although the emerging consensus on validity described here may be reflected in the revised Standards, how the concept will be analyzed into categories of evidence that guide validity research is not clear. Moss (1992), has reviewed the category schemes used by Messick, Cronbach, and other validity theorists to organize their discussions of validity. The categories that appear to be most widely cited—evidential and consequential—represent a vast oversimplification of the scheme proposed by Messick. These labels are too broad to provide useful guidance to validity researchers and Messick's entire scheme, not described here, remains controversial (see Shepard, 1993, for a critique). Another line of criticism suggests that we should expand our conception of validity, which currently draws on quantitative research traditions, to include principles from interpretive and critical research traditions (Cherryholmes, 1988; Johnston, 1989; Moss, 1992, 1994). The principles of validity reflected in both the traditional and emerging views of validity privilege standardized forms of assessment. This situation, in turn, constrains possibilities for alternative assessments that might address goals like encouraging students to develop and explore their own purposes in reading and writing.

Although the issues underlying the different characterizations of validity summarized here seem academic to some, these differences can have a profound influence on the way validity research is conducted, on the kinds of assessments that are likely to find favor, and, most important, on the opportunities available to those who are tested.

BIBLIOGRAPHY

AERA, APA, & NCME (1985). *Standards for educational and psychological testing.* Washington, DC: Authors.

ANASTASI, A. (1986). Evolving concepts of test validation. *Annual Review of Psychology, 37,* 1–15.

ANASTASI, A. (1990). Ability testing in the 1980's and beyond: Some major trends. *Public Personnel Management, 18*(4), 471–485.

CHERRYHOLMES, C. H. (1988). Construct validity and discourses of research. *American Journal of Education, 96*(3), 421–457.

CRONBACH, L. J. (1980). Validity on parole: How can we go straight? *New directions for testing and measurement: Measuring achievement, progress over a decade,* no. 5 (pp. 99–108). San Francisco: Jossey-Bass.

CRONBACH, L. J. (1988). Five perspectives on validity argument. In H. Wainer (Ed.), *Test validity.* Hillsdale, NJ: Erlbaum.

CRONBACH, L. J. (1989). Construct validation after thirty years. In R. E. Linn (Ed.), *Intelligence: Measurement, theory and public policy* (pp. 147–171). Urbana: University of Illinois Press.

JOHNSTON, P. (1989). Constructive evaluation and the improvement of teaching and learning. *Teachers College Record, 90*(4), 509–528.

KANE, M. T. (1992). An argument-based approach to validity. *Psychological Bulletin, 112,* 527–535.

MESSICK, S. (1975). The standard problem: Meaning and values in measurement and evaluation. *American Psychologist, 30,* 955–966.

MESSICK, S. (1989a). Validity. In R. E. Linn (Ed.), *Educational measurement* (3rd ed.). New York: Macmillan.

MESSICK, S. (1989b). Meaning and values in test validation: The science and ethics of assessment. *Educational Researcher, 18*(2), 5–11.

MOSS, P. A. (1992). Shifting conceptions of validity in educational measurement: Implications for performance assessment. *Review of Educational Research, 62*(3), 229–258.

MOSS, P. A. (1994). Can there be validity without reliability? *Educational Researcher, 23* (2), p. 5–12.

NATIONAL COMMISSION ON TESTING AND PUBLIC POLICY. (1990). *From gatekeeper to gateway: Transforming testing in America.* Boston: National Commission on Testing and Public Policy, Boston College.

SCARR, S. (1989). Protecting general intelligence: Constructs and consequences for interventions. In R. E. Linn (Ed.), *Intelligence: Measurement, theory and public policy* (pp. 74–118). Urbana: University of Illinois Press.

SHEPARD, L. A. (1993). Evaluating test validity. *Review of Research in Education, 19,* 405–450.

WILEY, D. E. (1991). Test validity and invalidity reconsidered. In R. E. Snow & D. E. Wiley (Eds.), *Improving inquiry in the social sciences: A volume in honor of Lee J. Cronbach.* Hillsdale, NJ: Erlbaum.

WILEY, D. E., & HAERTEL, E. H. (in press). *Extended assessment tasks: Purposes, definitions, scoring, and accuracy.* In R. Mitchell and M. Kane (Eds.), *Implementing performance: Promises, problems, and challenges.* Washington, DC: Pelavin Associates.

PAMELA A. MOSS

VERBAL ABILITY Reliable standardized tests exist to differentiate people along some dimension called verbal ability, and scores on these tests are often used to predict performance on a wide variety of tasks, as well as school achievement and job success (see, e.g., Hunt, 1978). Nevertheless, a great deal is not yet known about what those tests demonstrate or what causes individual differences in performance.

As described in this article, *verbal ability* is a technical term used by cognitive and educational psychologists to refer to (1) the amount and structure of one's verbal knowledge, often called vocabulary knowledge, and (2) the ability to reason by using this verbal knowledge. People who possess large vocabularies, who have developed intricate maps of the semantic connections among various verbal concepts, and who are able to use inference to comprehend complex passages are said to be higher in verbal ability than people who have smaller, more concrete vocabularies, who have sketchy semantic maps, and who are limited in their ability to use inference to see connections between parts of a passage and to fill in missing information. Thus, verbal ability has two broad facets: a knowledge facet and a cognitive-processing facet. Research on verbal ability has tended to approach the topic from one viewpoint or the other, resulting in an unintegrated picture of what verbal ability is.

THE PLACE OF VERBAL ABILITY IN IMPLICIT AND EXPLICIT THEORIES OF INTELLIGENCE

Both laypeople and experts agree that verbal ability is an important part of overall intellectual ability. Verbal ability, represented by such behaviors as "displays a good vocabulary," "reads with high comprehension," "is verbally fluent," and "converses easily on a variety of subjects," was found by Sternberg et al. (1981) to be the first of three major factors defining intelligence for both experts in the field of intelligence and laypeople. Verbal ability is seen as important for individuals from age 2 and up (Siegler & Richards, 1982).

Verbal ability also has a well-recognized place in discussions of explicit theories of intelligence. It is highly predictive of intelligence quotient (IQ) (Horn, 1989; Matarazzo, 1972), and of other measures believed to reflect Charles SPEARMAN's (1923) concept of *g* (a general intellectual ability factor) (Jensen, 1980). Verbal comprehension ability is one of the seven primary mental abilities proposed by Lewis Thurstone (1938); another is verbal fluency ability. Although later factor analyses have discovered additional, replicable,

primary mental abilities (Horn, 1989), verbal ability reliably emerges as a unique type of cognitive ability.

Verbal ability is also an excellent measure of crystallized intelligence (*Gc*) in the fluid intelligence (*Gf*)–crystallized intelligence theory proposed by Horn and Cattell (Cattell, 1963, 1971; Horn, 1968; Horn & Cattell, 1966). In this theory, intelligence is seen as hierarchical in nature, with a GENERAL INTELLIGENCE (*g*) factor at the top of the hierarchy. The next level proposes several broad categories of intellectual reasoning, including fluid and crystallized intelligence factors (see, e.g., Horn, 1989; Horn & Hofer, 1992). Crystallized intelligence is the knowledge aspect of intelligence, described by Horn as "measured in tasks indicating breadth and depth of the knowledge of the dominant culture" (Horn & Hofer, 1992, p. 56). Fluid intelligence refers to reasoning ability, independent of the prior knowledge possessed, and is usually measured by inductive and deductive reasoning tasks. Traditionally, the crystallized, or knowledge, aspects of verbal ability have been stressed in factor analytic studies of verbal ability. Fluid intelligence, however, has also been found to be implicated in complex verbal tasks, such as verbal analogy tests, if the vocabulary in the items is either equally familiar or equally unfamiliar for the individual taking the test (Horn, 1989). Thus, although verbal ability is often equated with crystallized intelligence, the two are not synonymous (see FLUID AND CRYSTALLIZED INTELLIGENCE, THEORY OF).

TESTING AND VERBAL ABILITY

Vocabulary tests are the most commonly used measure of verbal ability, and, because of their high theoretical (Jensen, 1980) and empirical (Matarazzo, 1972) correlation with general intelligence, vocabulary tests are often used as a stand-in for intelligence overall. Correlations obtained between vocabulary tests and a variety of IQ and achievement tests range from .71 to .98 (Anderson & Freebody, 1981). Most vocabulary tests ask the individual to select the correct meaning of a target word presented in isolation or in a short phrase; others may ask the individual to produce a word's definition. Vocabulary tests for younger children often require the child to select a picture that matches a word spoken by the tester.

Other measures of verbal ability stress the reasoning aspects by including verbal analogies, antonyms, sentence completions, or reading comprehension items that ask the test taker to read a short passage and then answer multiple-choice questions about stated or implied information in the passage. A list of some of the most commonly used tests, including those that may be readily available in school files, is presented in Table 1.

Factor analyses of these verbal tests tend to produce a general verbal factor that is well represented by vocabulary test scores, but there are many other skills and abilities that seem to flesh out the verbal component of most of these tests, and a closer look at the sorts of items included reveals that "verbal ability" is not consistently defined from test to test. For example, the verbal IQ score for the WAIS-R, the WISC-R, and the WPPSI-R actually combines performance on vocabulary and comprehension subtests with that on such other subtests as digit span, arithmetic, information, and similarities. In other verbal ability tests, the knowledge and the reasoning/reading aspects of verbal

TABLE 1
Frequently used measures of verbal ability

Verbal subtests of the following general aptitude tests:
    Stanford-Binet Intelligence Scale
    Wechsler Adult Intelligence Test, Revised (WAIS-R)
    Wechsler Intelligence Scale for Children, Revised (WISC-R)
    Wechsler Preschool and Primary Scale of Intelligence, Revised (WPPSI-R)
    Scholastic Aptitude Test (SAT-V)
    Graduate Record Exam (GRE-V)
    Differential Aptitude Tests (DAT)
Reading and vocabulary subtests of the following broad achievement batteries:
    California Achievement Tests
    Comprehensive Tests of Basic Skills
    Iowa Tests of Basic Skills
    Metropolitan Achievement Tests
    Stanford Achievement Tests
Specific tests of reading ability:
    Nelson-Denny Reading Test
    Gates-MacGinitie Reading Tests
Appropriate subtests of the following laboratory battery used in research on primary ability factors:
    French Kit of Reference Abilities

ability are divided into separate vocabulary and comprehension subscores, which tend to be highly correlated with each other. Even within tests that claim to measure the same thing, there are often distinct differences in subtest inclusions and item types, and one must look closely at the particular test in question to identify the particulars of its specific manifestation of verbal ability. The user of a particular measure is advised to consult the respective test manuals and the test descriptions and reviews in the most recent *Mental Measurements Yearbook* (e.g., Conoley & Kramer, 1989) for more specific information as to how each test defines verbal ability and which type of population the test is designed to measure.

VERBAL ABILITY AS A MEASURE OF VERBAL KNOWLEDGE

Why are vocabulary tests so important as measures of verbal ability and intelligence? In a provocative paper, Anderson and Freebody (1981) proposed three hypotheses to explain their prominence, particularly in predicting verbal comprehension. The *instrumentalist* hypothesis proposes that vocabulary knowledge is necessary (instrumental) for reading comprehension. The *general aptitude* hypothesis downplays those aspects of verbal ability that are unique to the primary ability, and claims that the relationship between vocabulary and comprehension lies in their mutual connection to g. The *general knowledge* hypothesis also posits a third source of mutual influence on vocabulary and comprehension, a general knowledge store; these theorists argue that vocabulary knowledge is correlated with general knowledge, which predicts reading comprehension ability. Sternberg and Powell (1983) have proposed a fourth, *learning-from-context* hypothesis. In this view, vocabulary tests are so prominent because they serve as a bridge between crystallized and fluid aspects of intelligence; one's vocabulary store is the crystallized result of the past functioning of fluid intelligence, in the form of one's ability to derive meaning from context. The question of which hypothesis is correct is still unresolved (see, e.g., Daneman, 1988; Stahl, 1991; Sternberg, 1985) and probably will remain so until the development of models of real-time solutions to more complex tasks than are usually tested in laboratory paradigms.

Verbal ability involves the number of words a person knows, but what does it mean to "know" a word, and how can one tell whether someone "knows" a word? To thoroughly know a word's meaning is to know both how to relate it to other words/concepts and how to use it. Complete word knowledge would include, among other factors, awareness of the word's dictionary definition, including all of its alternate meanings; the word's synonyms, antonyms, and hyponyms (words for the general category to which the thing denoted by a particular word belongs); the word's etymological relationships to other words; the semantic contexts in which the word is likely to be used; the situational contexts in which the word is likely to be used; the syntax of the word's use; and the emotional connotations of the word.

Early in the acquisition of a vocabulary item, whether that acquisition is based on studying a word's definition (McKeown, 1991; Miller & Gildea, 1987) or presentation of a word in one or more brief contexts (Daalen-Kapteijns & Elshout-Mohr, 1981; Elshout-Mohr & Daalen-Kapteijns, 1987; McKeown, 1985; Sternberg & Powell, 1983; Werner & Kaplan, 1952), individuals are prone to letting a fragment of the word's meaning represent the whole (see also Scott & Nagy, 1989, 1990). Thus, many of the elements of the word's meaning are likely to be absent from a given individual's definition of the word, inaccurate elements are likely to be present, and connections between elements are likely to be sketchy.

Differences in quality of word knowledge have been ignored in most vocabulary studies, although as early as 1912, researchers were noting that it might be important (Feifel & Lorge, 1950). Those studies that have addressed the issue of depth of word knowledge find that knowledge of a word's meaning is not an all-or-none affair. Curtis (1987) classified four stages of knowing a word:

Stage 1. "I never saw it before."
Stage 2. "I've heard of it, but I don't know what it means."
Stage 3. "I recognize it in context—it has something to do with _____."
Stage 4. "I know it."

Curtis asked fifth-grade students to rate their knowledge of each item in a list of words that she later presented to the students in a standardized vocabulary test. She found that an imprecise knowledge (Stage 3) of a word's meaning is sufficient for most reading vocabulary tests. Consequently, individuals who get high verbal ability scores on these tests are distinguished from those who get low scores by their possession of *some* versus *no* knowledge of a word, not by the precision of their knowledge of the word's meaning. Marshalek (1981) found that young adults have a large number of words in partially learned states (see Table 2), and he speculates that this is a natural part of the vocabulary acquisition process.

In an in-depth study of trait and process aspects of vocabulary knowledge and verbal ability, Marshalek (1981) asked high school seniors to complete a faceted vocabulary test through which he could investigate sources of difficulty on vocabulary tests and correlate performance on the various types of items with performance on standardized reference ability measures of general mental ability, verbal ability, spatial ability, memory span, and perceptual speed. He found that vocabulary item difficulty increased with word abstractness, with word infrequency, when item format required more precise word knowledge, and when items required the individual to produce a definition for the word rather than just recognize the definition from a list of multiple-choice alternates.

In the same study, Marshalek also found that correlations of various vocabulary measures with composite measures of reasoning ability (fluid intelligence), memory span, and spatial ability depended on the type of vocabulary item tested. For example, reasoning ability mattered more for the more complex (precise definition) measures of vocabulary knowledge than it did for the less complex ones. Furthermore, vocabulary tests tended to pose difficulties for people who were low in reasoning ability, whereas those who were of medium and high reasoning ability tended to perform similarly on most of the vocabulary measures. Spatial ability was more strongly implicated in the definition of concrete words than in the definition of abstract words; memory span was a more important predictor of performance on abstract words than on concrete words. These findings certainly support Snow and Swanson's (1992) warning that different vocabulary items may measure different abilities for different people. To truly understand individual differences in ver-

TABLE 2

Percentage of tested vocabulary in unlearned, partial knowledge, learned, and anomalous states in high school seniors, by verbal ability level

	Low Verbal Ability	Medium Verbal Ability	High Verbal Ability	Mean
Unlearned state: cannot choose correct definition from unrelated semantic alternatives and cannot produce any information as to word's definition	24	10	3	12
Partial knowledge states:				
Can choose correct definition from unrelated semantic alternatives but cannot produce even a partial definition	23	16	8	16
Can choose correct definition from unrelated semantic alternatives and can produce a partial definition	13	12	11	12
Learned state: can choose correct definition from unrelated semantic alternatives and can produce an accurate definition	36	59	76	57
Anomalous state: cannot choose correct definition from unrelated semantic alternatives but can produce a partial or accurate definition	4	3	2	3

SOURCE: Marshalek, 1981.

bal ability, it is important to look more closely at how individuals are processing the specific items used. Even vocabulary tests are not the simple measures of verbal ability they may at first appear to be.

VERBAL ABILITY AS A MEASURE OF COGNITIVE PROCESSES

In 1975, Earl Hunt and his associates published a paper, asking the crucial question, "What does it mean to be high verbal?" (Hunt, Lunneborg, & Lewis, 1975), which spearheaded the cognitive correlates approach to defining verbal ability in information-processing terms. This approach attempts to identify simple, information-processing tasks that account for significant variance in complex verbal performance (see Hunt, 1985, for an excellent primer). Hunt was one of the first to note the surprisingly strong connection between very low-level, mechanistic information-processing tasks and verbal ability—which we usually think of as a complex, knowledge-based process. Initially, Hunt and his colleagues used the Posner letter-matching task to investigate whether the ability to access overlearned codes in memory is a cognitive correlate of complex measures of verbal ability. The Posner task is a timed test, in which subjects are given two letters and asked to determine whether they are the "same" or "different" according to one of two assigned criteria: being physically identical or being identical in name. For example, if a subject were asked to respond "same" or "different" on the physical identity criterion, she or he would respond "same" to "AA" or "bb," but "different" to "Aa" or "Ba." The same subject responding on the name identity criterion would respond "same" to "bb," "Bb," or "AA," but "different" to "BA," "Ab," or "ba." Decisions based on physical similarity can be made on perceptual features alone, without the subject's accessing any information about the letter's name. Decisions based on name similarity require the subject to mentally "look up" the name of the letter, which requires access to lexical memory. Hunt and his colleagues asked subjects to perform both sets of identifications. They found that the *difference* in the mean time it took a subject to make a name identification and the mean time it took the subject to make a physical identification (sometimes called the NI–PI difference) was negatively correlated ($r = -.30$) with the verbal score on the Washington Pre-College Test, a complex measure of verbal ability similar to the SCHOLASTIC ASSESSMENT TEST.

Hunt and others in the cognitive correlates tradition have identified a variety of information-processing tasks that consistently account for a small but significant percentage of the variance in standardized measures of verbal ability. Overall, the deeper the amount of semantic access in the task, the higher the correlation with complex verbal performance. For example, Goldberg, Schwartz, and Stewart (1977) found that reaction times to match *word* stimuli at the physical identity, homophonic identity, and taxonomic category identity levels, respectively, predicted 10, 40, and 46 percent of the variance in verbal ability scores. Hunt (1987) summarizes many of these studies, and Table 3 presents a list of some of the primary cognitive correlates of verbal ability identified to date.

Of the cognitive correlates Hunt (1987) discusses, one in particular has received a great deal of recent research attention: memory. Obviously, memory would be implicated in knowledge-based aspects of verbal ability, such as the breadth and depth of one's vocabulary or the amount of prior knowledge one brings to bear on verbal comprehension. Such processes rely heavily on long-term memory. But another aspect of memory—working memory—is being increasingly implicated in verbal ability. Working mem-

TABLE 3
Correlates of verbal ability

Speed of sublexical access

    ability to recognize and temporally order sounds versus nonspeech sounds in dichotic listening task (measured by rapid, successive presentation of stimuli to left and right ears)

    speed with which one can extract letter information from a nonword stimulus

    speed with which one can access letter name information (measured by comparing the speed of a name-matching task to that of a visual matching task)

Speed of lexical access

    ability to perform lexical decision tasks (decide whether a stimulus is a word or a nonword)

    ability to perform stimulus matching at increasingly deeper semantic levels, from physical judgments to homophonic judgments to taxonomic judgments

Rapid consolidation of information into long-term memory

    working-memory span while reading

    comprehension of garden path (syntactically ambiguous) sentences

    comprehension of anaphoric references in passages

Possession of general knowledge of situations (scripts), and knowledge of how to process discourse in general

    ability to derive word meaning from contexts

    ability to draw appropriate inferences to connect a text's macropropositions

SOURCE: Hunt, 1987.

ory refers to the part of memory responsible for the temporary storage and processing of information necessary to perform cognitive tasks (Baddeley, 1986). Such information may enter working memory from long-term memory or from perceptual processes, such as reading or listening. The processing and storage functions of working memory are assumed to compete for the same mental resources, defined as working-memory capacity. If much of working-memory capacity is consumed with processing a task, then little is left for the temporary storage of information—one is able to work with only a small amount of material at a time. If, however, the mental-processing aspects of the task are fairly automatized, then one is able to consider a larger amount of information at one time. Working memory is theorized to be especially important for verbal comprehension, which requires the individual to mentally "hold" semantic information while it is being processed and integrated to create sense out of text.

To measure this working-memory capacity, Daneman and Carpenter (1980) developed a reading-span test, which measures both the storage and the processing aspects of working memory. In this test, subjects are given increasingly longer sets of sentences to read aloud. At the end of each set of sentences, subjects are asked to recall the last word of each of the sentences in the set. For example, a subject might see:

> When at last his eyes opened, there was no gleam of triumph, no shade of anger.
> The taxi turned up Michigan Avenue where they had a clear view of the lake. (p. 453)

The subject would read these sentences aloud, and then recall the end words, "anger" and "lake." Reading span is defined as the maximum number of sentences the subject can read aloud while maintaining perfect recall of the final words. Note that this task—which taxes ability to remember while simultaneously performing verbal processing—differs significantly from traditional, short-term memory tasks, such as the digit span or the word span tests, which measure only the storage aspects of short-term memory and which show less relationship with verbal comprehension. Daneman and her colleagues have found that the reading-span measure of working memory correlates significantly with a variety of tasks involving verbal comprehension, including the ability to integrate information within and across sentences to determine the theme of a passage, the ability to process syntactically or semantically ambiguous sentences, and the ability to infer the meaning of an unfamiliar word from its context; other investigators have also found correlations ranging from .59 to .90 between reading span and these various aspects of verbal ability (Daneman & Carpenter, 1980, 1983; Daneman & Green, 1986; MacDonald, Just, & Carpenter, 1992). Differences in working-memory capacity may also be behind the sizable amount of research supporting the significance of the use of holistic versus analytic processing in accounting for differences in deriving word meaning from context (Daalen-Kapteijns & Elshout-Mohr, 1981; McKeown, 1985;

Sternberg & Powell, 1983; Werner & Kaplan, 1952), although strategy differences are likely to be important sources of individual differences here, as well.

Research into the nature of verbal abilities varies in the extent to which it emphasizes knowledge or processes, and whether it focuses on the micro or macro level of information processing. Often the studies do not so much contradict one another as "talk past" one another. For example, process-oriented researchers, such as Hunt, may begin with mechanistic processes, hoping to understand verbal ability from the bottom up, or they may begin by looking at complex comprehension processes, especially inference ability, hoping to understand verbal ability from the top down. Others may look at the role that specific knowledge structures play in verbal tasks. Identifying whether a given study approaches verbal ability from a knowledge-based, a bottom-up, or a top-down perspective will help the reader coordinate the plethora of studies being conducted in the area of verbal ability (see, e.g., Sternberg, 1985, 1987; Sternberg & Powell, 1983). In addition, it is important to keep in mind that research on individual differences, particularly the cognitive correlates approach, focuses on those aspects of verbal ability in which there are substantial differences among individuals in performance (Hunt, 1985). Process and knowledge aspects that are common across individuals, and thus of little interest to many of these information-processing researchers, may also be important to defining basic verbal ability.

HEREDITY, ENVIRONMENT, GENDER, AND VERBAL ABILITY

A great deal is known about verbal ability. It can be measured reliably by standardized tests, and scores on these tests can be used to predict performance on a wide variety of tasks. Twin studies have indicated that verbal ability has a strong heritability component, although significant variance is accounted for by experiential and environmental influences (Plomin, 1988). In discussions of the stability of verbal ability across the life-span, verbal ability is usually seen as a relatively invulnerable ability, meaning that it does not significantly decline with age; this invulnerability is hypothesized to be primarily attributable to the strong crystallized knowledge aspects of the factor. As Horn

(1989) has noted, however, the question of whether different aspects of verbal ability follow different developmental progressions has not been addressed.

Contrary to public perceptions and to many introductory psychology textbooks, females no longer tend to be higher in verbal ability than males (Hyde & Linn, 1988). Earlier studies (Maccoby & Jacklin, 1974) did document an ability difference favoring girls, but more recently, Hyde and Linn (1988) performed a meta-analysis of 165 studies and concluded that "the magnitude of the gender difference in verbal ability is currently so small that it can effectively be considered to be zero" (p. 64). Hyde and Linn found little or no evidence of female verbal superiority, regardless of which types of measures of verbal ability were used or which types of verbal cognitive processes were involved. This finding is in line with the recent trend of males and females' generally becoming less differentiated in their performance on various cognitive tasks (Feingold, 1988; Jacklin, 1989).

CONCLUSION

Although it is possible to identify a broad concept of verbal ability, the experience is a little like grasping a wet fish: One can feel a definite solid entity in one's hands, but the concept is slippery, and its scales reflect different colors depending on how the light catches it. A great deal has been learned about verbal ability in the last ten to fifteen years. It is now considered a complex, multifaceted concept. As more is found out about the various processes involved in verbal ability, we are likely to find that verbal ability actually defines a slightly different set of weighted processes for different tasks and for different people. In the decade to come, research is likely to dig deeper into its multifacets and attempt to come up with an integrated model of verbal ability that exhibits knowledge, processing, and subject facets in a single gem (see Just & Carpenter, 1987; Schwanenflugel, 1991; and Sternberg, 1985, 1987, for a move in this direction).

BIBLIOGRAPHY

ANDERSON, R. C., & FREEBODY, P. (1981). Vocabulary knowledge. In J. T. Guthrie (Ed.), *Comprehension and teaching:* *Research reviews* (pp. 77–117). Newark, DE: International Reading Association.

BADDELEY, A. D. (1986). *Working memory.* New York: Oxford University Press.

CATTELL, R. B. (1963). Theory of fluid and crystallized intelligence: An initial experiment. *Journal of Educational Psychology, 54,* 105–111.

CATTELL, R. B. (1971). *Abilities: Their structure, growth and action.* Boston: Houghton-Mifflin.

CONOLEY, J. C., & KRAMER, J. J. (EDS.). (1989). *The tenth mental measurements yearbook.* Lincoln: Buros Institute of Mental Measurements, University of Nebraska.

CURTIS, M. E. (1987). Vocabulary testing and vocabulary instruction. In M. G. McKeown & M. E. Curtis (Eds.), *The nature of vocabulary acquisition* (pp. 37–51). Hillsdale, NJ: Erlbaum.

DAALEN-KAPTEIJNS, M. M. VAN, & ELSHOUT-MOHR, M. (1981). The acquisition of word meanings as a cognitive learning process. *Journal of Verbal Learning and Verbal Behavior, 20,* 386–399.

DANEMAN, M. (1988). Word knowledge and reading skill. In M. Daneman, G. E. MacKinnon, & T. G. Waller (Eds.), *Reading research: Advances in theory and practice* (Vol. 6, pp. 145–175). New York: Academic Press.

DANEMAN, M., & CARPENTER, P. A. (1980). Individual differences in working memory and reading. *Journal of Verbal Learning and Verbal Behavior, 19,* 450–466.

DANEMAN, M., & CARPENTER, P. A. (1983). Individual differences in integrating information between and within sentences. *Journal of Experimental Psychology: Learning, Memory, and Cognition, 9,* 561–584.

DANEMAN, M., & GREEN, I. (1986). Individual differences in comprehending and producing words in context. *Journal of Memory and Language, 25,* 1–18.

ELSHOUT-MOHR, M., & DAALEN-KAPTEIJNS, M. M. VAN (1987). Cognitive processes in learning word meanings. In M. G. McKeown & M. E. Curtis (Eds.), *The nature of vocabulary acquisition* (pp. 53–71). Hillsdale, NJ: Erlbaum.

FEIFEL, H., & LORGE, I. (1950). Qualitative differences in the vocabulary responses of children. *Journal of Educational Psychology, 41,* 1–18.

FEINGOLD, A. (1988). Cognitive gender differences are disappearing. *American Psychologist, 43,* 95–103.

GOLDBERG, R. A., SCHWARTZ, S., & STEWART, M. (1977). Individual differences in cognitive processes. *Journal of Educational Psychology, 69,* 9–14.

HORN, J. L. (1968). Organization of abilities and the development of intelligence. *Psychological Review, 75,* 242–259.

HORN, J. L. (1989). Cognitive diversity: A framework for learning. In P. L. Ackerman, R. J. Sternberg, & R. Glaser (Eds.), *Learning and individual differences: Advances in theory and research* (pp. 61–116). New York: Freeman.

HORN, J. L., & CATTELL, R. B. (1966). Refinement and test of the theory of fluid and crystallized intelligence. *Journal of Educational Psychology, 57,* 253–270.

HORN, J. L., & HOFER, S. M. (1992). Major abilities and development in the adult period. In R. J. Sternberg & C. A. Berg (Eds.), *Intellectual development* (pp. 44–99). New York: Cambridge University Press.

HUNT, E. B. (1978). Mechanics of verbal ability. *Psychological Review, 85,* 109–130.

HUNT, E. B. (1985). The correlates of intelligence. In D. K. Detterman (Ed.), *Current topics in human intelligence: Vol. 1. Research methodology* (pp. 157–178). Norwood, NJ: Ablex.

HUNT, E. B. (1987). The next word on verbal ability. In P. A. Vernon (Ed.), *Speed of information-processing and intelligence* (pp. 347–392). Norwood, NJ: Ablex.

HUNT, E. B., LUNNEBORG, C., & LEWIS, J. (1975). What does it mean to be high verbal? *Cognitive Psychology, 7,* 194–227.

HYDE, J. S., & LINN, M. C. (1988). Are there sex differences in verbal abilities? A meta-analysis. *Psychological Bulletin, 104,* 53–69.

JACKLIN, C. N. (1989). Female and male: Issues of gender. *American Psychologist, 44,* 127–133.

JENSEN, A. R. (1980). *Bias in mental testing.* New York: Free Press.

JUST, M. A., & CARPENTER, P. A. (1987). *The psychology of reading and language comprehension.* Boston: Allyn & Bacon.

MACCOBY, E. E., & JACKLIN, C. N. (1974). *The psychology of sex differences.* Stanford: Stanford University Press.

MACDONALD, M. C., JUST, M. A., & CARPENTER, P. A. (1992). Working memory constraints on the processing of syntactic ambiguity. *Cognitive Psychology, 24,* 56–98.

MARSHALEK, B. (1981). *Trait and process aspects of vocabulary knowledge and verbal ability* (Tech. Rep. No. 15). Stanford: Stanford University, Aptitude Research Project, School of Education. (NTIS No. AD-A102 757).

MATARAZZO, J. D. (1972). *Wechsler's measurement and appraisal of adult intelligence* (5th ed.). New York: Oxford University Press.

MCKEOWN, M. G. (1985). The acquisition of word meaning from context by children of high and low ability. *Reading Research Quarterly, 20,* 482–496.

MCKEOWN, M. G. (1991). Learning word meanings from definitions: Problems and potential. In P. J. Schwanenflugel (Ed.), *The psychology of word meanings* (pp. 137–156). Hillsdale, NJ: Erlbaum.

MCKEOWN, M. G., & CURTIS, M. E. (Eds.). (1987). *The nature of vocabulary acquisition.* Hillsdale, NJ: Erlbaum.

MILLER, G., & GILDEA, P. (1987). How children learn words. *Scientific American, 257*(3), 94–99.

PLOMIN, R. (1988). The nature and nurture of cognitive abilities. In R. J. Sternberg (Ed.), *Advances in the psychology of human intelligence* (Vol. 4, pp. 1–33). Hillsdale, NJ: Erlbaum.

SCHWANENFLUGEL, P. J. (ED.). (1991). *The psychology of word meanings.* Hillsdale, NJ: Erlbaum.

SCOTT, J. A., & NAGY, W. (1989, November). *Fourth graders' knowledge of definitions and how they work.* Presented at the Annual Meeting of the National Reading Conference, Austin, TX.

SCOTT, J. A., & NAGY, W. (1990, April). *Definitions: Understanding students' misunderstandings.* Presented at the Annual Meeting of the American Educational Research Association, Boston, MA.

SIEGLER, R. S., & RICHARDS, D. D. (1982). The development of intelligence. In R. J. Sternberg (Ed.), *Handbook of human intelligence* (pp. 897–971). New York: Cambridge University Press.

SNOW, R. E., & SWANSON, J. (1992). Instructional psychology: Aptitude, adaptation, and assessment. *Annual Review of Psychology, 43,* 583–626.

SPEARMAN, C. (1923). *The nature of "intelligence" and the principles of cognition.* London: Macmillan.

STAHL, S. A. (1991). Beyond the instrumentalist hypothesis: Some relationships between word meanings and comprehension. In P. J. Schwanenflugel (Ed.), *The psychology of word meanings* (pp. 157–186). Hillsdale, NJ: Erlbaum.

STERNBERG, R. J. (1985). *Beyond IQ: A triarchic theory of human intelligence.* New York: Cambridge University Press.

STERNBERG, R. J. (1987). The psychology of verbal comprehension. In R. Glaser (Ed.), *Advances in instructional psychology* (Vol. 3, pp. 97–151). Hillsdale, NJ: Erlbaum.

STERNBERG, R. J., CONWAY, B. E., KETRON, J. L., & BERNSTEIN, M. (1981). People's conceptions of intelligence. *Journal of Personality and Social Psychology: Attitudes and Social Cognition, 41,* 37–55.

STERNBERG, R. J., & POWELL, J. S. (1983). Comprehending verbal comprehension. *American Psychologist, 38,* 878–893.

THURSTONE, L. L. (1938). *Primary mental abilities.* Chicago: University of Chicago Press.

WERNER, H., & KAPLAN, E. (1952). *The acquisition of word meanings: A developmental study.* Monographs of the Society for Research in Child Development, No. 51.

JAN STARR CAMPITO

VERNON, PHILIP EWART (1905–1987)

Philip Ewart Vernon was born in Oxford, England, on June 6, 1905 and died in Calgary, Canada, on July 28, 1987. During a career that lasted over sixty years he became recognized as one of the world's leading educational psychologists and was also highly regarded for his many contributions to the fields of intelligence, personality, and psychometrics.

Vernon was the only son of H. M. Vernon, a lecturer in physiology at Oxford University, who later wrote several books in the then new field of industrial psychology. It was he and Philip's older sister, Magdalen, who would become Chair of Psychology at Reading University, who encouraged Vernon to study psychology.

Vernon received private schooling at the Dragon school in Oxford, and then at Oundle, after which he went to Cambridge University. Here he earned First Class Honours in the Natural Science Tripos, Part I (physics, chemistry, and physiology) and in the Moral Science Tripos, Part II (psychology) in 1926–1927, and obtained his M.A. degree at St. John's College. He then studied psychology in F. C. Bartlett's department and was introduced to statistics by Udny Yule and to mental testing by Lucy Fildes. He earned his Ph.D. in 1927; the topic of his dissertation was the psychology of music. He also earned a D.Sc. degree and was awarded an honorary Doctor of Laws degree.

Upon graduation, Vernon was awarded the Laura Spelman Rockefeller Fellowship, which allowed him to study in the United States: first working on personality testing with Mark May at Yale, then working with Gordon Allport at Harvard on expressive movement. This latter collaboration resulted in *Studies in Expressive Movement* (1932) and the Allport-Vernon *Study of Values* (1931), an instrument still widely used and referenced some sixty years after its development.

After returning to Britain in 1931, Vernon held a number of positions. He started as a research and teaching Fellow at St. John's College, Cambridge; then he moved to London, where he served as a psychologist in the London County Council at the Maudsley Hospital's Child Guidance Clinic. He was later appointed head of the psychology department at Jordanhill Training Centre in Glasgow, and he became head of the department of psychology at the University of Glasgow in 1938. During World War II, he held the position of Psychological Research Adviser to the Admiralty and War Office. Following this service, he was appointed professor of educational psychology at the Institute of Education in the University of London and, in 1964, professor of psychology at the same university. In 1968 he moved to Calgary, Alberta, where he was professor of educational psychology at the University of Calgary.

Throughout this period, Vernon wrote fourteen books and some two hundred journal articles. His books include *The Assessment of Psychological Qualities by Verbal Methods* (1938); *The Measurement of Abilities* (1940); *Personnel Selection in the British Forces* (1949); *The Structure of Human Abilities* (1950); *Personality Tests and Assessments* (1960); *Personality Assessment: A Critical Survey* (1964); *Intelligence and Cultural Environment* (1969); *The Psychology and Education of Gifted Children* (1977); *Intelligence: Heredity and Environment* (1979); and *The Abilities and Achievements of Orientals in North America* (1982).

Vernon's earlier work in the area of intelligence (e.g., *The Structure of Human Abilities*) typified the factor-analytic approach to the field that was favored by such members of the so-called London school of differential psychology as Charles SPEARMAN and Cyril BURT. Vernon's major contribution of this period was his hierarchical group-factor theory of the structure of intellectual abilities. This model retaining Spearman's *g* (GENERAL INTELLIGENCE) factor as the largest source of variance, also contained major group factors (*v:ed*—verbal-numerical-educational; and *k:m*—practical-mechanical-spatial-physical), minor group factors, and specific factors. Its hierarchical organization served to reconcile the seemingly contrary two-factor theory of Spearman, which did not allow for the existence of group factors, and the multiple-factor model of Thurstone, which did not allow a *g* factor. A recent review of different approaches to the structure of abilities concluded that a hierarchical model such as Vernon's has received strong empirical support in the time since it was developed (Gustafsson, 1988).

Beginning with *Intelligence and Cultural Environment* (1969), Vernon became increasingly involved in studying the contributions of environmental and genetic factors to intellectual development. In this book, Vernon summarized and integrated the results of a wide variety of cross-cultural research, including his own studies of 11-year-old boys in England, Scotland, Jamaica, Uganda, and Canada (where he tested Canadian Indians and Inuit). In these researches, which involved the administration of sixteen tests of mental abilities to groups of fifty boys in each country, Vernon was accompanied and assisted by his wife, Dorothy Vernon, herself a school psychologist and coauthor (with P. Vernon and G. Adamson) of *The Psychology and Education of Gifted Children* (1977). Besides describing the influence of cultural factors on the development of mental abilities, Vernon's 1969 book also noted Hebb's important distinction between two kinds of intelligence: Intelligence A, which refers to a person's genotype for intelligence and which cannot be directly observed or measured, and Intelligence B, which is the phenotype that can be observed. To these Vernon added Intelligence C, which is that (limited) part of Intelligence B that is measured by intelligence (or IQ) tests.

In *Intelligence: Hereditary and Environment* (1979), the book that he personally regarded as the culmination of the more than fifty years he had spent in the field of mental measurement, Vernon continued to analyze the effects of genes and the environment on both individual and group differences in intelligence. This book carefully and painstakingly reviews the arguments and evidence on both sides of these still-contentious topics. From the wealth of material that he reviewed (the book contains some thirty-six pages of references), Vernon concluded that individual differences in intelligence are approximately 60 percent attributable to genetic factors, and that there is some evidence implicating genes in racial group differences in average levels of mental ability. A similar conclusion, with respect to ability differences between North Americans of Asian and European descent was drawn in *The Abilities and Achievements of Orientals in North America* (1982), Vernon's last book. Despite his acknowledgement of

the role of genetic factors in individual and group differences, it would be an error to refer to Vernon as an hereditarian. Perhaps more than anyone working in this area, he recognized the importance of both genetic *and* environmental factors, and went to great lengths to clarify that the nature-nurture debate should more properly (and profitably) consider the interaction between the two.

One measure of the influence that Vernon's books had was that they contributed to his being invited to lecture or study in at least twenty-eight countries on six continents. Other honors included his being named president of the psychology section of the British Association for the Advancement of Science (1952); President of the British Psychological Society (1945–1955) and Honorary Life Member of this society; president of the industrial, educational, and Scottish sections of the British Psychological Society, and chairman of the society's Committee on Secondary School Selection; vice-president of the Eugenics Society (1961); honorary fellow of the International Association for Cross-Cultural Psychology; fellow of the American Psychological Association; life fellow of the Canadian Psychological Association; fellow of the United States National Academy of Education (1968); fellow of the Center for Advanced Study in the Behavioral Sciences (1961 and 1975); fellow of the Scottish Council for Research in Education; first recipient of the Distinguished Lecturer Award of the Faculty of Education at the University of Calgary; and emeritus professor of educational psychology at the universities of London and Calgary.

In addition to his research and writing, Vernon had a lifelong passion for music. While attending college he won a scholarship in sacred music and was an accomplished pianist and organist. He also played the French horn and the oboe and composed several pieces of music. After moving to Calgary, he served as a member of the Board of Directors of the Calgary Philharmonic Orchestra and was keenly involved in the activities and music of the choir of the Calgary Cathedral Church of the Redeemer. He once compared the intricate structure of a Bach fugue with the mathematical elegance of a factor analysis, the latter of which he preferred to perform by hand, using a slide rule, even long after computers became available.

Although he officially retired from the University of Calgary in 1975, Vernon continued to supervise graduate students and to publish books and articles until he died of cancer in 1987. His last publication, which appeared after his death, was a chapter on scientific creativity. Beyond his contributions to theory and research in intelligence, perhaps Vernon's greatest gift was his ability to integrate vast amounts of material and to present the results of his reviews in a clear and impartial manner. His obituary in the *London Times* stated, "Vernon was probably the most critical member of the (London) school, and the least partisan; his integrity, honesty and impartiality were universally recognized. . . . Always critical but always fair, he seemed the embodiment of the ideal scientist."

BIBLIOGRAPHY

ALLPORT, G. W., & VERNON, P. E. (1931). *Study of values: A scale for measuring the dominant interests in personality.* Boston: Houghton Mifflin.

ALLPORT, G. W., & VERNON, P. E. (1932). *Studies in expressive movement.* New York: Macmillan.

GUSTAFSSON, J. E. (1988). Hierarchical models of individual differences in cognitive abilities. In R. J. Sternberg (Ed.), *Advances in the psychology of human intelligence,* Vol. 4. Hillsdale, NJ: Erlbaum.

VERNON, P. E. (1938). *The standardization of a graded word reading test.* London: University of London Press.

VERNON, P. E. (1938). *The assessment of psychological qualities by verbal methods.* Industrial Health Research Board Report, No. 83. London: Her Majesty's Stationery Office.

VERNON, P. E. (1940). *The measurement of abilities.* London: University of London Press.

VERNON, P. E. (1950). *The structure of human abilities.* London: Methuen.

VERNON, P. E. (1953). *Personality tests and assessments.* London: Methuen.

VERNON, P. E. (Ed.). (1957). *Secondary school selection.* London: Methuen.

VERNON, P. E. (1958). *Educational testing and test-form factors.* Princeton, NJ: Educational Testing Service, RB-58-3.

VERNON, P. E. (1960). *Intelligence and attainment tests.* London: University of London Press.

VERNON, P. E. (1964). *Personality assessment: A critical survey.* London: Methuen.

VERNON, P. E. (1969). *Intelligence and cultural environment.* London: Methuen.

VERNON, P. E. (Ed.). (1970). *Creativity: Selected readings.* Harmondsworth: Penguin.

VERNON, P. E. (1970). *Methodological problems in cross-cultural research.* St. John's: Institute for Resarch in Human Abilities, Memorial University of Newfoundland.

VERNON, P. E. (1979). *Intelligence: Heredity and environment.* San Francisco: W. H. Freeman.

VERNON, P. E. (1982). *The abilities and achievements of Orientals in North America.* New York: Academic Press.

VERNON, P. E., ADAMSON, G., & VERNON, D. F. (1977). *The psychology and education of gifted children.* London: Methuen.

VERNON, P. E., & PARRY, J. B. (1949). *Personnel selection in the British forces.* London: University of London Press.

PHILIP ANTHONY VERNON

VOCABULARY   *See* WAIS–R SUBTESTS.

VOCATIONAL ABILITIES   The term *human abilities* refers to special talents or skills that an individual has developed. More specifically, *vocational abilities* refers to those human abilities that are relevant to the world of work—they include cognitive, physical, perceptual, and creative abilities. Abilities are measured by tests, which ask individuals to perform their best, which assess an individual's level of current performance, and which reflect an individual's previous experience and learning (Dunnette, 1976; Cronbach, 1984; Reschly, 1990).

Historically, abilities have been considered distinct from aptitudes (e.g., Cronbach, 1984; Dunnette, 1976), but the distinctions are subtle. Abilities are specific patterns of skills or talents, while aptitudes encompass more general patterns of performance. Furthermore, although ability and aptitude tests are very similar, aptitude tests are used to predict future success in training or educational programs and in occupations. This article focuses primarily on vocational abilities, but the concepts of ability and aptitude will be used in this chapter according to the aforementioned distinctions.

HISTORICAL OVERVIEW

During the first part of the twentieth century, theoretical and applied psychologists added greatly to the research and literature on human abilities. Theoretical descriptions of abilities; statistical procedures used to identify ability factors, such as factor analysis; and aptitude testing all subsequently contributed to the burgeoning field of vocational abilities.

Theoretical Contributions. Numerous theories have been proposed to identify and categorize mental abilities. Charles SPEARMAN (1904, 1927) suggested that all mental tests shared, to a greater or lesser extent, a common factor called the general, or g, factor of ability. The g factor represented the power of reasoning, or the ability of a person to perform mental operations across a variety of tasks, such as vocabulary or numerical tests. Mental tests also measured a specific, or s, factor of ability. The s factor represented the unique ability measured by each test.

Generally, theories or parts of theories that are most useful for guiding the development of vocational ability tests are those that identify fairly independent factors. For example, Lewis THURSTONE identified seven primary mental abilities—verbal comprehension, word fluency, number, space, associative memory, perceptual speed, and induction—that frequently are measured in multiple aptitude tests (Thurstone, 1938; Thurstone & Thurstone, 1941). J. P. GUILFORD (1967) proposed an even more elaborate model of the structure of intellect that resulted in 120 possible factors or abilities.

The general, or g, factor of ability has been shown to be extremely important for predicting occupational success; however, the importance of the g factor versus the relevance of other special abilities in making employment and career decisions has been widely debated. Tyler (1986) suggested that the assessment of special talents, in addition to general ability, was important to help an individual choose a career. She argued that although the importance of g has been demonstrated, for the individual a measure of g alone is not enough to facilitate a choice about which abilities are the best ones to develop.

Applied Contributions. Around the time of World War I, psychologists began to recognize the need for tests of special abilities in addition to tests of general intelligence. The U.S. Army needed a method to classify the large number of new personnel into appropriate military jobs, and a group of psychologists led the way in constructing tests useful for personnel selection and classification. At the same time, psychologists recognized the usefulness of such testing for the civilian population. By the 1930s, tests of mechanical abilities were developed and began to be widely used (Paterson et al., 1930). Tests of clerical abilities came next (Andrew, Paterson, & Longstaff, 1933), followed by a battery of tests of musical abilities and attempts to measure artistic talent (Seashore, 1939).

During World War II, the military's need for tests of special abilities once again increased, and additional test construction and research took place. Following World War II, psychologists transferred the use of ability testing from military purposes to the civilian population (Anastasi, 1988; Super, 1983).

To meet the needs of the civilian population, psychologists using ability tests split into two related areas of the discipline: personnel psychology and vocational psychology (Super, 1983). Personnel psychology focused on (1) the industrial and military processes of selection and classification of personnel and (2) job performance and occupational success. Vocational psychology focused on an individual's process of (1) career exploration, (2) preparation for and entry into occupations, and (3) career changes. Thus, personnel psychology was concerned with institutional decisions, and vocational psychology was concerned with individual decisions (Anastasi, 1988).

VOCATIONAL ABILITIES IN PERSONNEL SELECTION

Personnel psychology focuses on an organization's selection and classification of employees. Both employers and employees benefit when individuals are assigned to jobs that match their abilities. Therefore, selection tests, also known as tests of specific abilities, are developed to measure abilities that are required for successful job performance. Employees then are selected for jobs if they possess the abilities required for successful job performance.

According to Cascio (1987), the traditional model of the process of personnel selection consists of several steps.

Step 1. An analysis is conducted to determine important job characteristics including the tasks required by the job and the individual behaviors and abilities required to perform the job.

Step 2. Two sets of tests are chosen or developed based on the job analysis. One set measures variables important for job performance, such as tests of cognitive ability or mechanical ability. The other set of tests measures an individual's success or failure on the job.

Step 3. The ability tests are given to the individual before she or he starts the job.

Step 4. The measures of job performance are given to the individual after she or he has been on the job for a period of time.

Step 5. The relationship between the two sets of tests is examined.

Step 6. If the relationship between the ability test and the performance measure is strong, in other words if the test predicts job performance, then the test may be accepted as a selection test.

A variety of vocational ability tests are used in personnel selection. For example, tests of general cognitive aptitude or tests of scholastic aptitude frequently are administered for a range of occupations. Tests of special abilities also are used in personnel selection including measures of mechanical, clerical, musical, visual, and auditory abilities (Anastasi, 1988). Finally, tests of physical abilities may be important for particular occupations (Hogan, 1991a).

VOCATIONAL ABILITIES IN CAREER DECISIONS

Vocational psychology focuses on helping an individual make career choices. Individuals possess numerous career-related characteristics including abilities, interests, values, and personality. Through the process of career counseling, an individual's characteristics are assessed and matched with jobs that have requirements compatible with the strengths of the person (Parsons, 1909). The matching process in vocational psychology is similar to personnel psychology in that both approaches require knowledge of the individual's abilities, knowledge of the world of work, and an understanding of the relationship between the two.

The matching process often is called the Person × Environment Fit Approach. Several classification systems have been developed to describe the abilities required for satisfactory performance of occupations and to compare an individual's assessed abilities with those occupations (see Dawis, Dohm, Lofquist, Chartrand, & Due, 1987; U.S. Department of Labor, 1979).

For example, finger dexterity and motor coordination are essential abilities for dentists and surgeons; spatial ability, the ability to visualize and manipulate objects in space, is important for architects and civil engineers; and clerical abilities, especially perceptual speed and accuracy, are relevant for typists and proofreaders.

ASSESSING VOCATIONAL ABILITIES

A variety of methods exist for measuring abilities. In personnel selection, ability assessment may involve situational tests (a situation in which an individual performs work-related tasks). In career decisions and career counseling, ability assessment may involve an individual's self-assessment using worksheets or computer guidance programs. Most frequently, however, abilities are assessed through psychological testing. Table 1 describes several ability tests that range from multiple aptitude test batteries to tests of individual special abilities.

A multiple aptitude test battery consists of a set of ability tests that measure a range of abilities such as numerical ability, verbal reasoning, and other abilities. An individual's scores suggest her or his strengths and weaknesses across the various ability subtests. Special ability tests consist of a single test that measures an ability such as manual dexterity or spatial ability. An individual's score suggests his or her strength in that particular area.

CONCLUSION

Vocational abilities, then, are important in two domains of psychology: personnel psychology and vocational psychology. Personnel psychology focuses on institutional decisions, and, therefore, uses vocational abilities in personnel selection and classification. Vocational psychology focuses on individual decisions,

TABLE 1
Selected tests of vocational abilities

Test Name and Publisher	Description
Multiple aptitude test batteries	
General Aptitude Test Battery (GATB) (U.S. Government Printing Office, 1970)	The GATB was developed by the U.S. Employment Services for use by employment counselors. It consists of twelve tests that combine to yield scores on nine factors. The nine factors include general learning ability, verbal aptitude, numerical aptitude, spatial aptitude, form perception, clerical perception, motor coordination, finger dexterity, and manual dexterity.
Armed Services Vocational Aptitude Battery (ASVAB) (U.S. Military Enlistment Processing Command, 1976)	The ASVAB was developed through a project conducted by the Department of Defense. It is used for the selection and classification of enlistees into military service. The ASVAB consists of the following ten subtests: Arithmetic Reasoning, Numerical Operations, Paragraph Comprehension, Word Knowledge, Coding Speed, General Science, Mathematics Knowledge, Electronics Information, Mechanical Comprehension, and Automotive and Shop Information.
Special ability tests	
Torrance Tests of Creative Thinking (Scholastic Testing Service, 1966)	The Torrance Tests of Creative Thinking was designed to measure creative thinking abilities. The test consists of two parts. The verbal test includes seven subtests: Asking, Guessing Causes, Guessing Consequences, Product Improvement, Unusual Uses, Unusual Questions, and Just Suppose. The figural test includes three subtests: Picture Construction, Picture Completion, and Parallel Lines.
Crawford Small Parts Dexterity Test (The Psychological Corporation, 1981)	The Crawford Small Parts Dexterity Test was designed to measure manual dexterity. The test consists of two parts, which both require simple manipulative skills. Part I has the test-taker use tweezers to insert pins in close-fitting holes, and then place a small collar over each pin. Part II has the test-taker place small screws in threaded holes, and then screw them down with a screwdriver.
Revised Minnesota Paper Form Board Test (The Psychological Corporation, 1970)	The Revised Minnesota Paper Form Board Test was designed to measure spatial ability, specifically, the ability to visualize and manipulate objects in space. Each test item consists of a figure cut into two or more parts. The test-taker must determine what figure would result if the pieces were put together, and then choose the correct option listed.
Minnesota Clerical Test (The Psychological Corporation, 1979)	The Minnesota Clerical Test was designed to assess clerical ability; specifically, it measures perceptual speed and accuracy necessary to perform clerical activities. The test consists of two timed subtests. The Number Comparison subtest has the test-taker compare 200 pairs of numbers, indicating whether or not the two numbers in each pair are identical. The Name Comparison subtest is similar, except that proper names are used instead of numbers.
Computer Aptitude, Literacy, and Interest Profile (PRO-ED, 1984)	The Computer Aptitude, Literacy, and Interest Profile was developed to assess computer-related aptitudes; it is used for both personnel selection and classification and career counseling. The test consists of six subtests. Four aptitude subtests include estimation, graphic patterns, logical structures, and series. Individual subtest and total scores are given for aptitude. The two remaining subtests include interest and literacy.

Test Name and Publisher	Description
Wonderlic Personnel Test (E. F. Wonderlic and Associates, 1981)	The Wonderlic Personnel Test was developed as a test of general cognitive ability for use in personnel selection. The test consists of fifty items, covering a wide range of problem types (e.g., definitions, analogies, analysis of geometric figures), which become increasingly difficult.

and, therefore, uses vocational abilities in career counseling and career decision-making. Vocational abilities are measured primarily through psychological testing, using either multiple aptitude test batteries or special ability tests.

BIBLIOGRAPHY

ANASTASI, A. (1988). *Psychological testing.* New York: Macmillan.

ANDREW, D. M., PATERSON, D. G., & LONGSTAFF, H. P. (1933). *Minnesota Clerical Test.* San Antonio, TX: The Psychological Corporation.

ANDREW, D. M., PATERSON, D. G., & LONGSTAFF, H. P. (1979). *Minnesota Clerical Test* (revised). San Antonio, TX: The Psychological Corporation.

CASCIO, W. F. (1987). *Applied psychology in personnel management* (3rd ed.). Englewood Cliffs, NJ: Prentice-Hall, Inc.

CHARTRAND, J. M. (1991). The evolution of trait-and-factor career counseling: A person × environment fit approach. *Journal of Counseling and Development, 69* (6), 518–524.

CRAWFORD, J. E., & CRAWFORD, D. M. (1981). *Crawford Small Parts Dexterity Test.* San Antonio, TX: The Psychological Corporation.

CRONBACH, L. J. (1984). *Essentials of psychological testing* (4th ed.). New York: Harper & Row.

DAWIS, R. V., DOHM, T. E., LOFQUIST, L. H., CHARTRAND, J. M., & DUE, A. M. (1987). *Minnesota Occupational Classification System III: A psychological taxonomy of work.* Minneapolis, MN: Vocational Psychology Research, Department of Psychology, University of Minnesota.

DUNNETTE, M. D. (1976). Aptitudes, abilities, and skills. In M. D. Dunnette (Ed.), *Handbook of industrial and organizational psychology* (pp. 473–520). Chicago: Rand McNally.

GHISELLI, E. E. (1966). *The validity of occupational aptitude tests.* New York: Wiley.

GHISELLI, E. E. (1973). The validity of aptitude tests in personnel selection. *Personnel Psychology, 26,* 461–477.

GOTTFREDSON, L. S. (1986). Societal consequences of the g factor. *Journal of Vocational Behavior, 29,* 379–410.

GUILFORD, J. P. (1967). *The nature of human intelligence.* New York: McGraw-Hill.

HOGAN, J. (1991a). Structure of physical performance in occupational tasks. *Journal of Applied Psychology, 76,* 495–507.

HOGAN, J. (1991b). Physical abilities. In M. D. Dunnette & L. M. Hough (Eds.). *Handbook of industrial-organizational psychology* (2nd ed. pp. 753–831). Palo Alto, CA: Consulting Psychologists Press.

HUNTER, J. E. (1986). Cognitive ability, cognitive aptitudes, job knowledge, and job performance. *Journal of Vocational Behavior, 29,* 340–362.

LIKERT, R., & QUASHA, W. H. (1970). *Revised Minnesota Paper Form Board Test.* San Antonio, TX: The Psychological Corporation.

LORD, F. M., & NOVICK, M. R. (1968). *Statistical theories of mental test scores.* Reading, MA: Addison-Wesley.

MITCHELL, J. B. (1985). *The ninth mental measurement yearbook.* Lincoln, NE: Buros Institute of Mental Measurements of the University of Nebraska.

PARSONS, F. (1909). *Choosing a vocation.* Boston: Houghton-Mifflin.

PATERSON, D. G., ELLIOTT, R. M., ANDERSON, L. D., TOOPS, H. A., & HEIDBREDER, E. (1930). *Minnesota Mechanical Ability Tests.* Minneapolis, MN: University of Minnesota Press.

POPLIN, M. S., DREW, D. E., AND GABLE, R. S. (1984). *Computer Aptitude, Literacy, and Interest Profile.* Austin, TX: PRO-ED.

RESCHLY, D. J. (1990). Aptitude tests in educational classification and placement. In G. Goldstein & M. Hersen (Eds.), *Handbook of psychological assessment* (2nd ed.) (pp. 148–172). New York: Pergamon Press.

SEASHORE, C. E. (1939). *Psychology of music.* New York: McGraw-Hill.

SPEARMAN, C. (1904). "General Intelligence" objectively determined and measured. *American Journal of Psychology, 15,* 201–293.

SPEARMAN, C. (1927). *The abilities of man.* London: Macmillan.

SUPER, D. E. (1983). The history and development of vocational psychology: A personal perspective. In B. Walsh & S. Osipow (Eds.), *Handbook of vocational psychology, Vol. I* (pp. 5–37).

THORNDIKE, R. L. (1986). The role of general ability in prediction. *Journal of Vocational Behavior, 29,* 332–339.

THURSTONE, L. L. (1938). Primary mental abilities. *Psychometric Monographs,* No. 1.

THURSTONE, L. L., & THURSTONE, T. G. (1941). Factorial studies of intelligence. *Psychometric Monographs,* No. 2.

TORRANCE, E. P. (1966). *Torrance tests of creative thinking.* Bensenville, IL: Scholastic Testing Service.

TYLER, L. (1986). Back to Spearman? *Journal of Vocational Behavior, 29,* 445–450.

U. S. DEPARTMENT OF LABOR, EMPLOYMENT AND TRAINING ADMINISTRATION (1979). *Manual for the USES General Aptitude Test Battery. Section II-A: Development of the Occupational Pattern Structure.* Washington, DC: U. S. Government Printing Office.

U. S. DEPARTMENT OF LABOR, EMPLOYMENT AND TRAINING ADMINISTRATION (1970). *Manual for the USES General Aptitude Test Battery. Section III: Development.* Washington, DC: U. S. Government Printing Office.

U. S. MILITARY ENLISTMENT PROCESSING COMMAND (1976). *Armed Services Vocational Aptitude Battery.* Fort Sheridan, IL: U. S. Military Enlistment Processing Command.

WONDERLIC, E. F. (1981). *Wonderlic Personnel Test.* Northfield, IL: E. F. Wonderlic & Associates.

JO-IDA C. HANSEN
DEBORAH G. BETSWORTH

VYGOTSKIAN THEORIES OF INTELLIGENCE

It is difficult to imagine the atmosphere in the period immediately following the 1917 revolution to the Soviet Union. Political, social, and economic chaos led to civil war, but also to intellectual ferment and the enthusiasm of young scholars to pursue new ideas. At least at the beginning, the government and the Communist party were willing to explore and exploit the practical implications of those ideas. It was in this context that Lev VYGOTSKY appeared on the scene of academic psychology.

At that time there were a number of competing viewpoints within the psychological establishment. The old-guard psychologists, such as Chelpanov, had been trained in the traditional Wundtian perspective of structuralist psychology. For them, of course, analysis of the conscious content of the mind revealed by introspection was the primary approach. A contrary, more behaviorist view was also being promulgated by the physiologist Ivan Pavlov and the psychologist Vladimir Bekhterev. Both of them emphasized nonconscious reflexes as the basic units for understanding behavior. Such a behaviorist view was appealing to those favoring a Marxist materialist orientation. However, a third viewpoint was held by those psychologists (e.g., Kornilov, the director of the Institute of Psychology in Moscow) who, while wanting to put psychology on a materialistic basis, felt that the unique contribution of psychology was to understand conscious experience. They attempted an integration of approaches that emphasized behavior, on the one hand, and conscious experience, on the other. For Kornilov, the form of this integration was a crude analogy with the Hegelian-Marxist dialectic, in which the objective behavior and the subjective conscious experience served as the thesis and antithesis of a new synthesis, the reaction. In fact, the approach was called "reactology."

It was not surprising that Vygotsky, who was invited to work at the Institute of Psychology by Kornilov, was particularly concerned with developing an approach to psychology that accounted for conscious experience. In doing this, Vygotsky distinguished between elementary (or natural) mental functions, characteristic of animals and young children, and higher (or cultural) mental functions, more characteristic of older children and adults. The natural mental functions include basic processes of sensation, perception, memory, attention, and the like and do not involve any conscious awareness of the mental processes themselves. In contrast, the higher mental functions are uniquely human and are characterized by conscious awareness and volition. They include such consciously modulated mental processes as intentional memory, strategically directed perceiving, and problem solving. Vygotsky exemplifies the natural mental functions with the anecdote of a boy being asked if he knows his name; the boy responds by stating his name rather than reflecting on the process of knowing his name.

The adjective of *cultural* applied to the higher mental functions captures a very important feature of Vygotsky's approach. Higher mental functions develop in children as they are socialized into their culture. A central aspect of this acculturation is what Vygotsky termed "mediation." An essential difference between natural and higher mental functions is that the latter are mediated (described below). Natural mental functions are characterized by immediate registration or reaction to stimuli, but higher mental functions involve some kind of mediating processes between the stimuli and reaction. This mediation may be as simple as tying a string around one's finger to help one remember something, but it may be as complex as an entire linguistic or symbolic system, such as that of mathematics, to help in problem solving.

Vygotsky and his students conducted a number of experiments investigating the development of the use of mediating stimuli by children. In one such study, children were asked to play a question-answering game in which they were not to say particular color name words at all and were also not to use any other color name more than once. Colored cards were provided for the children to use as aids in remembering the forbidden names and the color names that they had already used. Observation of the behavior of the children indicated that preschool children were not capable of using the colored cards at all to help them; in fact, in some cases, the cards interfered with their performance by distracting them. Older children were able to use the cards, but it sometimes required practice to be able to do so most effectively. Adults internalized the requirements of the game and the process of monitoring which names had been used, and were able to perform the task without external mediators.

While this is an example of the development of use of external mediators, Vygotsky more generally considered three sources of mediation (Kozulin, 1990): material tools, symbol systems, and the behavior of other persons. Indeed, he sometimes referred to symbols as psychological tools. He suggested that material tools mediate human action directed at objects and symbolic tools mediate one's own psychological processes. Although he did not want to overdo this comparison, he did note that children's use of tools in their preverbal period is like that of apes. However, as soon as speech or signs are involved in action, the action is transformed completely and is organized along entirely new lines. Initially, speech, like tools, is used to master one's surroundings and then to master one's own behavior.

Words and language constitute the prototype of mediators, and social context is, of course, essential for their acquisition. In Vygotsky's view, children learn and first use words in social settings; they first respond to words of others, and then they use words in an interpersonal way to attract the attention or guide the behavior of others. Subsequently, they use words and language overtly to guide their own behavior. This egocentric language can often be observed when a child is trying to solve a difficult problem. Finally, children regulate their own behavior with implicit internal language. This internalization of originally external interpersonal language with an intermediate stage of egocentric language contrasts sharply with Jean PIAGET's almost opposite interpretation of egocentric language. Piaget considered the symbolic function of language to arise at the end of the sensory-motor period out of nonverbal representational capacities such as images and implicit motor actions revealed in deferred imitation.

It is difficult to overestimate the importance for Vygotsky of both the developmental theme and the social theme encapsulated in this idea of internalization. Vygotsky thought that the main methodological approach in psychology was a developmental one. His idea of a developmental approach was very broadranging. It included phylogenetic development, which reflected an interest in comparison of animal and human mental processes; historical-cultural development, captured empirically by anthropological investigations of cognitive processes of Siberian ethnic groups being integrated into the Soviet Union; ontogenetic development, on which he did most of his empirical work; and microgenetic development, involving understanding the often rapid changes in psychological processes as they occur across short intervals of time when people are engaged in cognitive tasks. For Vygotsky, understanding a psychological process meant understanding its development.

The social theme is implicated in all these forms of development. As J. V. Wertsch (1985a, 1985b) pointed out, there are two levels of the social setting of psychological importance. One is the level of social institutions, which is the level of analysis at which Marx operated, and the other is the level of social interaction of individuals and small groups of people. Vygotsky's analysis is concentrated at the level of interaction of individuals. Of particular interest is how the social context permeates ontogenetic development. Not only is language acquired in a social setting, as noted above, but all manner of behavior and psychological processes occur first in social situations and are guided by adults or more sophisticated peers. This emphasis by Vygotsky has had considerable influence in Western developmental psychology, as exemplified by Jerome Bruner's (1985) use of the term *scaffolding* to describe the social interaction of a supportive adult with a child learning a new task. *Scaffolding* refers to the idea, stimulated by Vygotsky, of the exquisite fit between a sensitive tutor and a naive child learner. The tutor adjusts the level of help provided to the learner to fit the learner's current level of competence. As the learner becomes more skilled, the support is decreased commensurately. This helps the learner to become independent but keeps motivation high. Other researchers with an anthropological bent have made similar observations and interpreted them in a similar way (Greenfield, 1984; Lave, 1977; Rogoff, 1990).

Although much of Vygotsky's empirical work is concentrated at the level of interaction of individuals, his interest in historical-cultural aspects of development suggests a way in which social institutions impact on individuals (see also Cole, 1985; Wertsch, 1985a). This possibility can be illustrated by using an example of complex mediation of symbol systems from Vygotsky's comparison of written and oral speech (Rieber & Carton, 1987).

Vygotsky observed that the acquisition of written speech occurs much later than oral speech and very slowly, in spite of the fact that the child has mastered the grammar of the language and possesses a very large vocabulary. "Written speech is more than the translation of oral speech into the written sign" (Rieber & Carton, 1987, p. 202). He pointed out that the context of written speech is completely different from that of oral speech. The child must abstract thoughts from the sounds, from the sensory aspects of speech. Written speech occurs in a context without a conversation partner, without intonation or expression. The child must abstract from the social situation to the conditions of putting one's thoughts on paper for a nonpresent reader. The motivation for written speech is completely different from, and much less immediate than, that for oral speech. And so on.

Written speech provides an excellent example of how the social-cultural context may guide the development of individual cognitive processes. Writing is a cultural invention that involves not only mastery of an abstracted sound to grapheme coding system but also the mastery of technological implements for writing (pencils, pens, keyboards and computers) and the use of appropriate surfaces to write upon, an understanding of what is to be written about, and acquisition of styles of writing that in many ways guide and constrain the way the writer thinks or, at the very least, expresses thoughts. Learning to write involves a lot more than mastering a particular low-level motor skill; it involves engaging in culturally determined ways of thinking and aspects of educational and economic systems that are very subtly pervasive. It is a human activity that captures current notions of natural cognition, situated cognition, and so on.

Vygotsky used his observations of the individual level of social interaction in ontogenetic development to elaborate a perspective both on instruction and on intellectual assessment with his concept of the "zone of proximal development." He, like many Soviet psychologists, was bemused by American psychology's strong attraction to mental tests. Vygotsky noted that an important feature of traditional mental tests was their emphasis on isolated individual performance at a given moment in time. He argued that any such evaluation was deficient precisely because it focused on the momentary state of the individual rather than on the possibility of learning and development. He suggested the zone of proximal development, the difference between the individual's unaided performance and optimal performance with structured help from a more-knowledgeable person, as a much more sensible evaluation. Vygotsky illustrated this with the example of a gardener who assesses the state of his orchard by evaluating only the matured or harvested fruits rather than the state of the maturing trees (Rieber & Carton, 1987, p. 208).

The concept is very relevant for instruction, since, as Vygotsky pointed out, it is not the case that a person can perform any task with appropriate structured help. If a person knows arithmetic and runs into difficulty with a problem, a demonstration by a knowledgeable person can lead immediately to the mastery of the problem, but if a person does not know higher mathematics, a demonstration of how to solve differential equations will not lead anywhere. In the context of such examples, Vygotsky analyzed the relation between development and instruction. When instruction is adjusted to the level of a learning child, it will move the child from one developmental level to a more-advanced level. What previously could only be accomplished with the aid of a more-knowledgeable person becomes possible independently and defines a new developmental level. The idea that instruction will work with a child at a particular level of development is reminiscent of biological sensitive periods. And Vygotsky recognized this but argued that such sensitive periods are intimately connected with the social processes of instruction and collaboration.

The idea of a zone of proximal development is quite clear in principle and almost obvious to the thoughtful person decades after Vygotsky formulated it. The concept has attracted considerable interest in Western psychology among scholars who shared the Soviet dissatisfaction with traditional techniques of assessment (Rogoff & Wertsch, 1984). However, rigorous research based on the concept is hard work. Nevertheless, the concept can be used most fruitfully, as A. L. Brown and her colleagues (Brown & French, 1979; Brown & Ferrara, 1985) have demonstrated. Their approach involved initial assessment of the level of independent functioning of the child on a particular type of task. Then, the optimal level of performance of which the child is capable with help was determined by providing the child with a series of standardized prompts for solving the particular types of problems involved. Fi-

nally, the level of independent functioning achieved was assessed by transfer problems that ranged from ones very similar to the training problems to rather different and more-complex transfer problems. Brown and R. A. Ferrara conducted their research using series-completion problems and problems like those of the Raven Progressive Matrices. This procedure yielded three major different indices of performance: initial level, ease of learning with help as specified by number of standardized prompts needed, and final level of independent functioning as indicated by performance on the transfer tests. Results on these measures were correlated with standard static intelligence quotient (IQ) performance. As might be expected, more average children than high-IQ children showed narrow transfer, and more high-IQ children showed wide transfer. Still, the indices derived from Vygotsky's concept of zone of proximal development yielded a far richer diagnostic pattern. For example, there were high-IQ children who showed fast learning but narrow transfer (context-bound) and average-IQ children who were slow learners but showed wide transfer (reflective).

A. S. Palincsar and A. L. Brown (1984) also interpreted some of their instructional research in terms of Vygotsky's zone of proximal development. The idea was to organize instruction in a very socially interactive mode and to direct it beyond the current level of performance. They worked with seventh-grade students who were having reading difficulties. The students were competent in letter-to-sound decoding but were very poor in comprehension. The instructional program involved training the children to be group leaders in discussing passages that they had read by trying to identify and paraphrase the main idea, raising questions about points of ambiguity, predicting questions that might be asked about the passage, and hypothesizing how the passage might continue. Initially, an adult leader had to model this leadership behavior, but gradually the children learned to take on this role themselves. Their reading comprehension improved not only in their reading classes but also in other subject matter, and the improvement was long-lasting.

This final result illustrates another important point in Vygotsky's ideas, that of functional system. Vygotsky believed that the important aspects of mental functioning were not domain-specific but of a much more general nature that is realized in conscious awareness of the cognitive processes and the ability to modulate them voluntarily. This is exactly what the procedures of Palincsar and Brown achieved. Vygotsky's ideas about functional systems were subsequently elaborated in the neuropsychological domain by one of his most-famous students and colleagues, A. R. LURIA.

BIBLIOGRAPHY

BROWN, A. L., & FERRARA, R. A. (1985). Diagnosing zones of proximal development. In J. V. Wertsch (Ed.), *Culture, communication, and cognition: Vygotskian perspectives.* Cambridge: Cambridge University Press.

BROWN, A. L., & FRENCH, L. A. (1979). The zone of potential development: Implications for intelligence testing in the year 2000. *Intelligence, 3,* 255–277.

BRUNER, J. (1985). Vygotsky: A historical and conceptual perspective. In J. V. Wertsch (Ed.), *Culture, communication, and cognition: Vygotskian perspectives.* Cambridge: Cambridge University Press.

COLE, M. (1985). The zone of proximal development where culture and cognition create each other. In J. V. Wertsch (Ed.), *Culture, communication, and cognition: Vygotskian perspectives.* Cambridge: Cambridge University Press.

GREENFIELD, P. M. (1984). A theory of the teacher in the learning activities of everyday life. In B. Rogoff & J. Lave (Eds.), *Everyday cognition: Its development in social context.* Cambridge, MA: Harvard University Press.

KOZULIN, A. (1990). *Vygotsky's psychology: A biography of ideas.* Cambridge, MA: Harvard University Press.

LAVE, J. (1977). Tailor-made experiments and evaluating the intellectual consequences of apprenticeship. *Quarterly Newsletter of the Institute for Comparative Human Development, 1,* 1–3.

PALINCSAR, A. S., & BROWN, A. L. (1984). Reciprocal teaching of comprehension and monitoring activities. In U. Neisser (Ed.), *Cognition and instruction.* Hillsdale, NJ: Erlbaum.

RIEBER, R. W., & CARTON, A. S. (EDS.). (1987). *The collected works of L. S. Vygotsky: Vol. 1. Problems of general psychology.* New York: Plenum.

ROGOFF, B. (1990). *Apprenticeship in thinking: Cognitive development in social context.* New York: Oxford University Press.

ROGOFF, B., & WERTSCH, J. V. (EDS.). (1984). *Children's learning in the "zone of proximal development,"* no. 23. New Directions for Child Development. San Francisco: Jossey-Bass.

VALSINER, J. (1988). *Developmental psychology in the Soviet Union.* Bloomington, IN: Indiana University Press.

VYGOTSKY, L. S. (1962). *Thought and language.* Cambridge, MA: MIT Press.

VYGOTSKY, L. S. (1978). *Mind in society: The development of higher psychological processes.* Cambridge, MA: Harvard University Press.

VYGOTSKY, L. S. (1982–1984). *Sobranie sochenenn* [Collected works] (Vols. 1–6). Moscow: Pedogigica.

WERTSCH, J. V. (1985a). *Vygotsky and the social formation of mind.* Cambridge, MA: Harvard University Press.

WERTSCH, J. V. (ED.). (1985b). *Culture, communication, and cognition: Vygotskian perspectives.* Cambridge: Cambridge University Press.

HERBERT L. PICK, JR.
JULIA B. GIPPENREITER

VYGOTSKY, LEV (1896–1934) Lev Semenovich Vygotsky, a brilliant scholar and scientist, introduced between 1925 and 1934 a view of intelligence that emphasized the social and cultural origins of intellectual behavior and its development. The profound implications of this perspective are only now being fully realized.

Born in Orsha, Belorussia, Vygotsky was the second of eight children in a middle-class Jewish family. He grew up in Gomel, another Belorussian town.

EDUCATION

Vygotsky completed his secondary schooling at a Jewish Gymnasium in Gomel, graduating in 1913. He was admitted to Moscow University and matriculated with the intention of studying medicine, one of the few professions open to Jews. He soon transferred to the study of law, however, and completed his law degree at Moscow in 1917. While in Moscow, Vygotsky also attended courses in history, philosophy, psychology, and the humanities at Shanyavskii's People's University, an unofficial university formed in 1911 after many students and faculty had been dismissed from

Moscow University for anticzarist activities. After graduating from Moscow University, Vygotsky returned to Gomel where he taught literature in a gymnasium, aesthetics and history of art in a conservatory, and psychology at Gomel Teacher's College.

CAREER

Although Vygotsky was not trained formally as a psychologist, by the time of his early death at the age of 37 he had established the basis of a unique Soviet approach to understanding psychology, one that his colleagues and students in the Soviet Union continued to elaborate over the next sixty years and one that has become very influential in Western psychology.

In 1924 Vygotsky presented such an impressive paper at a psychoneurological congress in Leningrad that he was invited to join the staff of the Institute of Psychology in Moscow. There his ideas were so exciting and his personality so engaging that he attracted two talented younger colleagues, A. R. LURIA and A. N. Leontiev, to work with him. Vygotsky's ideas quickly evolved and matured in the minds and writings of this "troika" (and other scholars who joined them) in an approach which essentially dominated Soviet psychology for the next fifty years.

Vygotsky completed his dissertation on the psychology of art in 1925 and continued to work at the Institute of Psychology with his increasing number of collaborators. He became more and more interested in problems of psychopathology and actively pursued studies in medicine. In addition, he developed a strong interest in abnormal development and by 1929 had established an institute for the study of "defectology." He wrote, conducted experiments, and supervised research at a furious pace in spite of a number of bouts of hospitalization with tuberculosis to which he succumbed in 1934.

THEORY OF INTELLIGENCE

Vygotsky was minimally interested in intelligence as a thing in itself but was centrally concerned with intellectual functioning. His approach emphasizes process rather than state, in contrast to studies focusing on the measurement of intelligence. Furthermore, Vygotsky's analysis focused on the emergence of the pro-

cesses themselves. In these respects his orientation was very dynamic. The most important features of his theory are as follows:

Genetic or Developmental Perspective. The distinction Vygotsky made between lower (or natural) and higher (or social) mental functions is a point of departure for understanding his approach. In lower psychological functioning are the processes that humans share with animals, such as sensation, involuntary memory and attention. Higher mental functions, on the other hand, include all forms of voluntary mental activity, such as voluntary attention and memory, voluntary movement, and logical thinking. Relating this distinction to differences between humans and animals brings to the fore the focus on the emergence of intellectual functions, that is, Vygotsky's genetic perspective, which has four aspects—phylogenetic, cultural-historical, ontogenetic, and microgenetic. Relevant to the phylogenetic aspect is the change that occurred in the evolution from animal to human in the relation between the individual and the environment. Animals adjusted to their environment by means of evolution. Humans adjusted to their environment by acting on it and changing it. (A strong Marxist perspective is evident here. Karl Marx and Friedrich Engels stressed the importance of acting upon and interacting with the environment in the acquisition of knowledge.) In the transition from animal to human there is an emergent property in relation to psychological functioning. Humans learn to reflect on and control their own mental processes, yielding so-called higher mental functions that are absent in animals. Intimately involved in this control of one's own mental processes is the emergence of psychological tools and the mediation of mental functioning by means of them.

Mediation by Psychological Tools. One type of psychological tool particularly emphasized by Vygotsky is that of signs and symbols. These range from the very simplest mnemonic devices to the most complex of symbol systems used in logical analysis. For illustrative purposes Vygotsky took a graphic example of the former from a fable by the Russian writer Arseniev, who once visited a forest-dwelling people in the Far East. They complained of mistreatment by Tau Ku, their Chinese leader, and asked Arseniev to report their difficulties to the officials in Vladivostok. When he agreed to do this, an old wise man approached him from out of the crowd and gave him a nail from a lynx's claw. The old man said, "Put the nail in your pocket, and when you arrive in Vladivostok, let it remind you to tell the officials of our severe mistreatment." The mediation of the process of remembering by using this simple psychological tool is an example of higher intellectual functioning that animals never exhibit. Vygotsky made his greatest contribution in trying to understand how children come to achieve these forms of mediation through psychological tools and their consequent higher levels of intellectual functioning.

Internalization. Vygotsky's observations and research with children led him to conclude that children's acquisition of higher intellectual functioning occurs in, and is completely dependent on, a social context. He suggested a number of implications of that perspective. One concerned the child's acquisition of speech. In terms of his analysis, an adult first uses words to guide a child to do something. Then the child begins to imitate this style of using communication and may use words to command an adult. Finally, the child uses words for self-direction or guidance. This sequence is an example of the very important process of internalization. It suggests not only a mechanism for the child's acquisition of speech—in Vygotsky's terms one of the most important psychological tools—but also how internal speech would function for the development of voluntary control. Vygotsky suggested that this process was an explanation of the commonly observed egocentric speech of three-to-five-year-old children, who often talk to themselves while performing some task or other. He saw egocentric speech as an intermediate stage between use of speech to guide other people (interpsychological) and implicit speech to guide oneself (intrapsychological). Vygotsky observed that such vocalization occurred most frequently at times of difficulty in tasks. (This interpretation of egocentric speech was diametrically opposed to that of Jean PIAGET, who regarded egocentric speech as a transition in the opposite direction, from the more autistic state of mind of the young child to a more socialized state of mind.)

Zone of Proximal Development. Another implication of the importance of social context in the development of higher mental functioning drawn by Vygotsky is his concept of *zone of proximal development.* This concept evolved from his dynamic functional perspective to replace the more traditional assessment of static intelligence. The zone of proximal development refers to the gap between the developmental level measured by independent problem solving and the potential developmental level measured by problem solving under the guidance of an adult or in collaboration with more capable peers. In relation to assessment, such a concept focuses attention immediately and obviously on the positive potential of an individual rather than on his or her current state of independent performance, a fact that Soviet psychologists enjoyed pointing out to Western visitors. In applying this idea to instruction for mentally retarded children, Vygotsky observed that traditional assessment techniques suggested that retarded children tended to think concretely. Such assessment led to the formulation of instructional programs for the mentally retarded that featured concrete processes, which were largely unsuccessful. Instead, Vygotsky argued, what was needed was the kind of programs that stressed the abstract processes that retarded children would not develop spontaneously.

In relation to acquisition of knowledge and conceptual thinking, the concept of zone of proximal development focuses attention more generally on the social context of intellectual performance and learning. This idea in particular has captured the imagination of a number of researchers interested in cognitive behavior and development, if not specifically in intelligence. The term *scaffolding* refers to the means by which experts (such as parents, older siblings, or more skilled peers) may adjust their help for novices (such as young children) so that they can perform a task that they were incapable of doing independently. Gradually the support would be reduced as the novices' independent skills developed (Wood, Bruner, & Ross, 1976; Greenfield, 1984; Rogoff, 1990). Others have stressed the social context of cognitive activities themselves in most natural settings. This is captured in the terms *situated cognition* or *situated learning,* which refer to the often complex cognitive behavior that goes on in practically all cultures in everyday life, even in mundane activities such as grocery shopping or organizing the items in a delivery truck. The social context of most of our everyday tasks—ranging from children preparing something from a recipe to scientists engaged with teams on research projects—is obvious (e.g., Cole & Traupmann, 1981). There is typically a division of labor with different people taking responsibility for different parts of the task. Moreover, in many cases a task structure is suggested or imposed by the social or cultural environment, for example, by the provision of some resources and not others or by the organization of the resources that reduce memory loads. The very definition of what is intelligent behavior as a consequence becomes somewhat vague and takes on a social and cultural aspect which was obvious to Vygotsky sixty years ago.

(*See also:* VYGOTSKIAN THEORIES OF INTELLIGENCE.)

BIBLIOGRAPHY

COLE, M., & TRAUPMANN, K. (1981). Comparative cognitive research: Learning from a learning disabled child. In W. A. Collins (Ed.), *Minnesota symposium on child psychology,* Vol. 14: *Aspects of the development of competence.* Hillsdale, NJ: Erlbaum.

GREENFIELD, P. M. (1984). A theory of the teacher in the learning activities of everyday life. In B. Rogoff and J. Lave (Eds.), *Everyday cognition: Its development in social context.* Cambridge, MA: Harvard University Press.

KOZULIN, A. (1990). *Vygotsky's psychology: A biography of ideas.* Cambridge, MA: Harvard University Press.

LEVITIN, K. (1983). *One is not born a personality.* Moscow: Progress.

ROGOFF, B. (1990). *Apprenticeship in thinking: Cognitive development in social context.* New York: Oxford University Press.

VALSINER, J. (1988). *Developmental psychology in the Soviet Union.* Bloomington, IN: Indiana University Press.

VARI-SZILAGYI, I. (1991). G. H. Mead and L. S. Vygotsky on action. *Studies in Soviet Thought, 42,* 93–121.

VYGOTSKY, L. S. (1956). *Izbrannye psikhologicheskie issledovaniya (Selected psychological investigations).* Moscow: Akademiya Pedagogicheskikh Nauk RSFSR.

VYGOTSKY, L. S. (1962). *Thought and language.* Cambridge, MA: MIT Press.

VYGOTSKY, L. S. (1968). *Psikhologiya iskusstva (Psychology of art).* Moscow: Isskustva.

VYGOTSKY, L. S. (1978). *Mind in society: The development of higher psychological processes.* Cambridge, MA: Harvard University Press.

VYGOTSKY, L. S. (1982–1984). *Sobranie sochenenii (Collected works)* Volumes 1–6. Moscow: Pedigogika.

WERTSCH, J. V. (ED.). (1985). *Culture, communication, and cognition: Vygotskian perspectives.* Cambridge: Cambridge University Press.

WERTSCH, J. V. (1985). *Vygotsky and the social formation of mind.* Cambridge, MA: Harvard University Press.

WOOD, D. J., BRUNER, K. S., & ROSS, G. (1976). The role of tutoring in problem solving. *Journal of Child Psychiatry and Psychology, 17,* 89–100.

HERBERT L. PICK, JR.
JULIA B. GIPPENREITER

W

WAIS–R SUBTESTS The Wechsler Adult Intelligence Scale-Revised (WAIS-R) subtests comprise eleven tests first selected in 1939 by David WECHSLER for his original intelligence scale. Believing that intelligence was expressed in both verbal and nonverbal human abilities, Wechsler grouped the eleven into six verbal subtests (Information, Digit Span, Vocabulary, Arithmetic, Comprehension, and Similarities) and five performance subtests (Picture Completion, Picture Arrangement, Block Design, Object Assembly, and Digit Symbol). These choices have survived extensive analysis and revision.

In the field of intelligence testing, FACTOR ANALYSIS is a statistical procedure by which the scores from seemingly different intelligence tests (or subtests) are analyzed to determine how much of one or more common (or core) elements (factors) of intelligence are measured by each test. For example, when the eleven subtests of a Wechsler scale are factor analyzed, such a statistical analysis typically reveals that the eleven subtests are principally measures of two basic components of intelligence. These are the verbal component, which is individually mirrored in an individual's score on each of the six verbal subtests, and the performance component, which similarly is reflected or mirrored in each of the five performance subtests.

Alternatively, use of a different statistical type of factor analysis of the eleven subtests elicits a three-factor solution instead of the two-factor solution just

described. The names of these three factors, which emerge from the second type of factor analytic approach, with the subtests mirroring each, are shown in Table 1. As can be seen in Table 1, this grouping excludes the Picture Arrangement and Digit Symbol subtests.

Current theorists who work in the field of intelligence are employing approaches to and tests of intelligence that are very different from the eleven subtests employed by David Wechsler in his scale, and, therefore, factor analyses of these newer types of tests yield core factors of intelligence that are quite different from the two types just described.

There are other useful methods of grouping the WAIS-R subtests. For example, John Horn built upon R. B. CATTELL's (1971) description of FLUID AND CRYSTALLIZED INTELLIGENCE, and later Horn and McArdle (Horn, 1985) expanded the schema to include the categories of retrieval of information and speed as a model for grouping Wechsler's subtests.

VERBAL SUBTESTS

1. *Information.* This subtest includes twenty-nine questions that sample general knowledge, including practical, historical, scientific, and literary information. It is related to breadth of knowledge, intellectual alertness, motivation, retention of information, and retrieval of information. Scores on this subtest may be

TABLE 1
WAIS-R subtest grouping for three-factor model

Verbal Comprehension	Perceptual Organization	Freedom from Distractibility
Information	Picture Completion	Arithmetic
Vocabulary	Block Design	Digit Span
Comprehension	Object Assembly	
Similarities		

influenced by the educational opportunities to which the subject has been exposed, as well as by intellectual curiosity.

Scores on the information subtest correlate 76 percent with the WAIS-R full scale IQ score, 79 percent with verbal IQ, and 62 percent with performance IQ. The subtest is a relatively good measure of general intelligence (g), with a factor loading of 81 percent. Following Horn and McArdle's model, it is considered to be a measure of crystallized intelligence and ability to retrieve information.

2. *Digit Span.* This subtest contains sequences of digits of increasing length that are read aloud by the examiner. These sequences, up to nine digits in length, are then repeated back to the examiner by the examinee. Other sequences up to eight digits in length are read by the examiner and the examinee is asked to repeat them in reverse order (digits backward). The test is a measure of immediate rote auditory recall, as well as attention span, freedom from distractibility and sequencing ability. Scores may be affected by anxiety or by an injury to the brain or other neuropsychological impairment.

Digit Span correlates 58 percent with the WAIS-R full scale IQ score, 57 percent with verbal IQ, and 50 percent with performance IQ. Although included by Wechsler among the verbal subtests, in a three-factor grouping it is most closely related to freedom from distractibility. It is a relatively poor measure of general intelligence (g) with a factor loading of 62 percent. Following Horn and McArdle's model, it is considered to be a measure of fluid intelligence and ability to retrieve information.

3. *Vocabulary.* This subtest includes thirty-five words presented in order of increasing difficulty. The words are read to the examinee, who may also read

them from a card. The examinee is asked to tell the meaning of each word. It is a measure of word knowledge, fund of information, and long-term memory. Scores on this subtest may be influenced by the educational and cultural opportunities to which the examinee has been exposed.

Scores on the Vocabulary subtest correlate 81 percent with the WAIS-R full scale IQ score, 85 percent with verbal IQ, and 65 percent with performance IQ. Among the WAIS-R subtests it is the best single measure of general intelligence (g), with a factor loading of 86 percent. Following Horn and McArdle's model it is considered to be a measure of crystallized intelligence.

4. *Arithmetic.* This subtest includes fourteen timed items arranged in order of difficulty. Item one involves counting blocks, and the remaining thirteen are story problems that are orally administered. They measure numerical reasoning, verbal comprehension, concentration, and freedom from distractibility. Scores may be influenced by educational background or emotional blocking that interferes with concentration.

Scores on the Arithmetic subtest correlate 72 percent with the WAIS-R full scale IQ score, 70 percent with verbal IQ, and 62 percent with performance IQ. Although included by Wechsler among the verbal subtests, in a three-factor grouping it is most closely related to freedom from distractibility. On general intelligence (g) it has a factor loading of 75 percent. Following Horn and McArdle's model it is considered to measure ability to retrieve information.

5. *Comprehension.* This subtest includes sixteen questions about practical aspects of everyday living, including social, legal, and health matters. It is sometimes called a test of common sense. Three of the questions require interpretation of proverbs. It requires application of judgment and reasoning to practical situations, a knowledge of conventional social standards, and an ability to verbalize. It may be influenced by cultural deprivation or social nonconformity.

Scores on the Comprehension subtest correlate 74 percent with the WAIS-R full scale IQ score, 76 percent with verbal IQ, and 61 percent with performance IQ. On general intelligence (g) it has a factor loading of 78 percent. Following Horn and McArdle's model it is considered to be a measure of crystallized intelligence.

6. *Similarities.* This subtest consists of fourteen pairs of words such as *horse-cow.* The examinee is asked to explain what is alike or similar about the two words in each pair. It is a test of verbal reasoning and verbal concept formation. The examinee must understand the meaning of each word and bring the meanings together into a concept. It may be influenced by overly concretistic thinking.

Scores on the Similarities subtest correlate 75 percent with the WAIS-R full scale IQ, 74 percent with verbal IQ, and 64 percent with performance IQ. It is a relatively good measure of general intelligence (g), with a factor loading of 79 percent. It is considered by Horn and McArdle to reflect both crystallized and fluid intelligence.

PERFORMANCE SUBTESTS

1. *Picture Completion.* This subtest includes twenty drawings of common objects, from which some essential feature is missing (e.g., one of the numbers on the face of a clock). The examinee is given twenty seconds in which to identify the missing part. It requires visual recognition and the ability to distinguish essential from nonessential characteristics. It may be influenced by lack of alertness and indecisiveness in the face of uncertainty.

Scores on the Picture Completion subtest correlate 67 percent with the WAIS-R full scale IQ score, 65 percent with performance IQ, and 61 percent with verbal IQ. On GENERAL INTELLIGENCE (g) it has a factor loading of 70 percent. Following Horn and McArdle's model it is considered to be a measure of fluid intelligence.

2. *Picture Arrangement.* This subtest consists of ten sets of small drawings that the examinee is required to place in a sequence which tells a story. Each set is similar to a cartoon strip in which the drawings are presented in a mixed-up order. It involves the ability to comprehend and interpret a total situation. It requires social perception, visual organization, and sequencing. It may be influenced by a lack of social or cultural opportunities.

Scores on the Picture Arrangement subtest correlate 61 percent with the WAIS-R full scale IQ score, 56 percent with performance IQ, and 57 percent with verbal IQ. On general intelligence (g) it has a factor

loading of 63 percent. Following Horn and McArdle's model it is considered to be a measure of fluid intelligence.

3. *Block Design.* The subtest includes a photo of each of nine geometric designs of increasing levels of complexity and, thus, difficulty, which can be reproduced by assembling blocks that are red on two sides, white on two sides, and diagonally half red and half white on the remaining two sides. The first five designs are to be completed using only four blocks, and the last four designs using nine blocks. There are time limits with bonus points for speed of completion. The subtest measures the ability to analyze whole into component parts and then to synthesize them. It involves visual perception, visual concept formation, visual-motor coordination, and speed of execution.

Scores on the Block Designs subtest correlate 68 percent with the WAIS-R full scale IQ score, 70 percent with performance IQ, and 60 percent with verbal IQ. It is the best measure of general intelligence (g) among the Performance subtests, with a factor loading of 72 percent. Following Horn and McArdle's model it is considered to be a measure of fluid intelligence.

4. *Object Assembly.* This subtest consists of four sets of large jigsaw puzzle pieces, each of which is to be assembled to form a common object: a manikin; a profile; a hand; or an elephant. It measures visual analysis and ability to synthesize parts into wholes. It is timed, and, thus, it is partially a measure of visual-motor speed. It may be influenced by experience with puzzles, and by persistence.

Scores on the Object Assembly subtest correlate 57 percent with the WAIS-R full scale IQ score, 62 percent with performance IQ, and 49 percent with verbal IQ. It is a relatively poor measure of general intelligence (g), with a factor loading of 61 percent. Following Horn and McArdle's model it is considered to be a measure of fluid intelligence.

5. *Digit Symbol.* This subtest includes four rows of slots containing a drawing of each of nine symbols, each of which is to be paired below itself with a number from one through nine. The symbol to be written in the slot below each number is presented in a code at the top of the sheet. The examinee is then presented with ninety-three pairs of boxes. One box in each pair contains a number from one to nine, presented in random order, while the other box below it is empty. The examinee must draw, in the empty box, the symbol that is paired with each number. Time for the task is limited to ninety seconds. It is a measure of speed and accuracy, visual motor coordination, and concentration. It may be influenced by anxiety and distractability.

Scores on the Digit Symbol subtest correlate 57 percent with the WAIS-R full scale IQ score, 52 percent with performance IQ, and 54 percent with verbal IQ. Among the subtests it is the poorest measure of general intelligence (g), with a factor loading of 59 percent. Following Horn and McArdle's model it is considered to be a measure of scanning speed.

BIBLIOGRAPHY

CATTELL, R. B. (1971). *Abilities: Their structure, growth and action.* Boston: Houghton-Mifflin.

HORN, J. L. (1985). Remodeling old models of intelligence. In B. B. Wolman (Ed.), *Handbook of intelligence: Theories, measures and applications* (pp. 267–300). New York: Wiley.

KAUFMAN, A. S. (1990). *Assessing adolescent and adult intelligence.* Boston: Allyn & Bacon.

LINDEMANN, J. E., & MATARAZZO, J. D. (1990). Assessment of adult intelligence. In G. Goldstein & M. Hersen (Eds.) *Handbook of psychological assessment* (pp. 79–101). New York: Pergamon Press.

MATARAZZO, J. D. (1972). *Wechsler's measurement and appraisal of adult intelligence* Baltimore, MD: Williams & Wilkins.

SATTLER, J. M. (1990). *Assessment of children.* San Diego, CA: Jerome M. Sattler.

JAMES E. LINDEMANN

WECHSLER, DAVID (1896–1981)

Born in Romania to Moses and Leah (Pascal) Wechsler, David was the last of seven children. His scholar father brought the family to New York City in 1902, where David was educated in the public schools and at the College of the City of New York, before going on to Columbia University for his graduate work. There, in 1917, he received his M.A. and, in 1925, his Ph.D. in experimental psychology.

Wechsler's involvement with the testing movement began during World War I, with his entrance into the U.S. Army, in 1917. Assigned as a psychologist to Camp Logan, Texas, he participated in the administration and interpretation of the few then available mental examinations that had been developed for use in assigning army recruits to military jobs best suited to their abilities. The intelligence tests available for such placement decisions included the Army Alpha Test, the 1916 Revision of the Stanford-Binet Scale, the Yerkes Point Scale, and the Army Individual Performance Scales (see ARMY ALPHA AND BETA TESTS OF INTELLIGENCE. Wechsler noted that there was some discrepancy between the intellectual competencies an individual had presumably shown in civilian life and performance on the mental tests Wechsler was using to judge soldiers. This suggested to him that the then commonly accepted definitions of intelligence that had been used to develop tests were partially inadequate and possibly misleading. As a result, he decided that an adequate definition must be broader than the popular ones of the day, and that then current measures, based solely on intellectual abilities as a total assessment of the ability of an individual, were both limiting and lacking in validity. This rationale was reinforced by subsequent experience and strongly influenced the subsequent development of his own intelligence scales.

In 1918, Wechsler was sent by the army to the University of London, where he worked with Charles SPEARMAN and Karl Pearson. His contact with these two influenced his notions of the nature of intelligence, particularly Spearman's concept of g (GENERAL INTELLIGENCE). Later, Wechsler decided that the TWO-FACTOR THEORY of g and many s's (specific abilities), which was implicit in Spearman's work and was later elaborated by Louis THURSTONE, was simplistic. Eventually, Wechsler concluded that intelligence is an effect, not a cause. Thus, intelligence must be conceived as a part of personality, the totality of each individual's persona.

After his discharge from the army in 1919, Wechsler attended the University of Paris on a scholarship, studying with H. Pieron and L. Lapique. There, under Lapique, he began a study of the psychogalvanic reflex (the data subsequently forming the basis of his 1925 doctoral dissertation at Columbia University). In 1922, he returned to the United States.

PROFESSIONAL CAREER

Wechsler became a clinical psychologist with the Bureau of Child Guidance, in New York City, during the 1920s. He prepared for his new responsibilities by working with H. L. Wells at the Psychopathic Hospital in Boston and attending the conference of W. Healy and A. F. Bronner. The director of the bureau was Bernard Glueck, a psychiatrist who advocated and used a team approach in evaluation and diagnosis. These professionals played a major part in Wechsler's practice of psychology—and on his views about decision making and clinical inference—for the remainder of his life. After receiving his doctorate, Wechsler entered private practice in 1925, as a clinical psychologist, continuing in that role until 1932. In 1930, he published an article entitled "The Range of Human Capacities" in the *Scientific Monthly* (Vol. 31, pp. 35–39). This led to the publication in 1935 of the work Wechsler considered his most significant effort—*The Range of Human Capacities.* His assessment of that book's importance seems reasonable considering that (1) its content was comprehensive rather than focusing on specific traits; (2) it anticipated research that was to follow and substantiate his findings; (3) it used group data for analysis rather than individual interpretation of the clinical setting; and (4) it provided the basis for controlled experimentation for interpretation of the roles that humans play in our society.

After leaving his own practice, Wechsler joined the staff of New York City's Bellevue Psychiatric Hospital, as chief psychologist in 1932, and he remained there until his retirement in 1967. By the 1940s, he was recognized internationally as the role model for the clinical psychologist working in institutional settings.

CONTRIBUTIONS TO THE TESTING MOVEMENT

In 1939, Wechsler published his book, *The Measurement of Adult Intelligence,* to accompany his newly developed test, the Wechsler-Bellevue Scale of Intelligence. This volume (and its subsequent revisions) included a section on "The Nature and Classification of Intelligence"—on standardization and norming procedures for his Bellevue Scale, plus the manual for its administration and scoring. Wechsler's intent was to fill a void with a test designed for and developed with adults.

Earlier, Wechsler had offered his definition of intelligence, namely, that it is the aggregate, or global,

capacity to act purposefully, think rationally, and deal effectively with the environment. This formulation, which remained unchanged during the rest of his life, was the basis from which he developed his scales of intelligence—that is, those for preschool age and older children (and their revisions), as well as his revisions of the adult scale. He had decided that the point scale was the preferred format because it provided a structure of subtests, each of which contained items of similar content ranked from easy to difficult. Each subtest reflected an ability that allowed expression of general intelligence. The alternative, the mental age scale used by others, Wechsler felt to be inappropriate for adults, while the point scale was appropriate for any age. As a corollary, that decision also led to the use of the deviation intelligence quotient (in contrast to the prevailing mental age quotient) as the expression of the derived intelligence quotient (the IQ) score.

The rationale underlying the content, administration, and scoring of the 1939 Bellevue and all subsequent scales assumes that test content is a medium (a language) with which an individual can express abilities. Some people are better with verbal symbols, others with concrete symbols that require manipulation and assembly. Wechsler believed that general intelligence (g) is multifaceted, as is the brain. Subsequent revisions of his 1939 adult test, and its extensions for children, also included the idea that intelligence is an aspect of the total personality, rather than an isolated entity. This idea introduced the possibility of the role of nonintellective factors in intellectual ability and thus on test performance, although no specific quantitative measure of such nonintellective factors is included in the test scores.

OTHER CONTRIBUTIONS

During his lifetime, Wechsler published more than seventy major papers and monographs. In addition, he made numerous presentations at professional and scholarly meetings, to laypersons as well as professionals and academics. His interests extended from experimental psychology to test theory and applications, with a particular emphasis on clinical decision making and training. He was challenged by unique problems in a society and world showing rapid and confusing change. He felt there was a need to extend the concept of intelligence from the individual to "collective" instances. Thus, persons in groups may not only contribute their idiosyncratic competencies but be a part of a summative process that exceeds the combination of their individual abilities. This issue was a major focus for him in the last decade of his life.

Wechsler had felt for some years that discussions and analyses of sex differences in IQ and related aspects of intelligence were more politicized than real and thereby neglected major issues that needed definition and research. For example, Wechsler believed that study was needed on such issues as the potential role of sex hormones on differential brain functioning. Memory storage and its function, dating from an earlier interest in changes in subtest performance as adults aged, remained a challenge he wished to pursue with greater intensity. This was extended to the nature of abilities in old age, with the possibility (unrealized at his death) of developing a scale to be called the Wechsler Intelligence Scale for the Elderly (WISE).

In summary, Wechsler's contributions have been both practical (as shown in the various tests he constructed) and theoretical (as demonstrated by his concept of nonintellective influences on test performance). Edwards (1971) pointed out that the scales constructed by Wechsler had received wide acceptance and use, both clinically and educationally. Though other contributions by Wechsler have been relatively overlooked because of his dedication to the testing devices, it is possible that his scales may be less significant than some of his theoretical interests: The emphasis ascribed to nonintellective factors in test scores, their role in determining scores of intellectual abilities, and their independence from intelligence offer possibilities, for example, not previously proposed. Distinguishing intellectual abilities from intelligence is a significant theoretical contribution as well. That assessment of Wechsler's contributions is as valid today as it was in his time.

Any judgment of David Wechsler must include recognition of the complexity of the mind that produced the test that is most widely accepted and significant in measuring adult intelligence yet emphasizes a humane focus in the application and interpretation of test results. The wide-ranging interests with which he involved himself mark him as the major figure in the

testing movement during the second half of the twentieth century.

(*See also:* WAIS–R SUBTESTS; WECHSLER SCALES OF INTELLIGENCE.)

BIBLIOGRAPHY

EDWARDS, A. J. (1971). *Individual mental testing: Part I: History and theories.* Scranton, PA: Intext Educational Publishers.
WECHSLER, D. (1944). *The measurement of adult intelligence* (3rd ed.). Baltimore: Williams & Wilkins.
WECHSLER, D. (1935; 1969). *The range of human capacities.* New York: Hafner.
WECHSLER, D. (1974). *Selected papers of David Wechsler.* New York: Academic Press. (This is the single most comprehensive compilation of the published works of Wechsler. Readers interested in learning more about his life, career, and contributions will find this book an excellent resource.)

ALLEN JACK EDWARDS

WECHSLER ADULT INTELLIGENCE SCALE–REVISED   *See* WAIS–R SUBTESTS.

WECHSLER SCALES OF INTELLIGENCE
The current versions of the Wechsler scales of intelligence include three scales, the Wechsler Adult Intelligence Scale–Revised (WAIS–R, Wechsler, 1981), the Wechsler Intelligence Scale for Children–Third Edition (WISC–III, 1991), and the Wechsler Preschool and Primary Scale of Intelligence–Revised (WPPSI–R, 1989).

The first of the Wechsler scales was called the Wechsler-Bellevue Intelligence Scale and it was published in 1939 by David WECHSLER, then working at Bellevue Psychiatric Hospital in New York City as chief psychologist. Wechsler published two versions of the Wechsler-Bellevue: Form I in 1939 and Form II in 1946. Form I was developed for use by the U. S. military during World War II; the rights were returned to the author, and it was published in 1946. Form I was revised and named the Wechsler Adult Intelligence Scale (WAIS, 1955). Form II was adapted for younger children, ages 6–16, and was subsequently called the Wechsler Intelligence Scale for Children (WISC, 1949). The Wechsler Preschool and Primary Scale of Intelligence (WPPSI) was published in 1967 to meet the needs for assessing intelligence in preschool children. The WPPSI was revised in 1989 as the WPPSI–R.

Currently, the Wechsler scales are the most frequently used instruments for the assessment of intelligence. In addition, the WAIS–R is the most frequently used test in neuropsychological assessments. Among school psychologists, the WISC–R is used with much greater frequency than the next most frequently used measure of intelligence, the Stanford-Binet–Fourth Edition. Use of the Wechsler scales is international; the scales have been translated into numerous languages, including Spanish, French, German, Dutch, Swedish, Chinese, Portuguese, Hebrew, and Italian.

All the Wechsler scales are individually administered tests. Testing is done one-on-one, which requires an examiner with special training in individual testing. The test is performed in a private, comfortable room without distractions. Individual testing affords several advantages over group testing. For example, the individualized testing situation allows for monitoring of the examinee's level of motivation. The rapport between examiner and examinee as well as the monitoring of behaviors allows the examiner to encourage the individual to work to his or her highest level. In addition, since all instructions and items are verbally administered, other factors not related to performance on the test, such as reading difficulties or failing to comprehend written instructions (which affect scores on group-administered tests), are eliminated.

The most recent versions of the WPPSI and WISC—The WPPSI–R and WISC–III—were developed after Wechsler's death (1981) by in-house staff at The Psychological Corporation, the publisher of all the Wechsler tests. While Wechsler had no involvement with the development of these two tests, they are clearly molded in the Wechsler tradition, in terms of content and structure. For example, the WISC–III (1991) contains a 73 percent item overlap with the WISC–R (1974). Some of the more noticeable changes in the WISC–III, compared to the WISC–R, include the introduction of color artwork, which makes the test more appealing to children; the calculation of factor scores in addition to the intelligence quotient (IQ) scores; and a presentation of test items balanced to include minorities and females. In addition, the most recent versions of the WPPSI and WISC scales include representative samples of minority children, and bias analysis of items were conducted prior to publication, to ensure the fairness of the tests.

WECHSLER'S CONCEPT OF INTELLIGENCE

Wechsler was primarily a clinical practitioner, who developed his tests out of a practical need to understand his patients, rather than from the perspective of a theoretician. He was also an astute statistician and psychometrician, having studied with several of the founders of twentieth-century psychometrics and statistics, including Charles SPEARMAN and Karl Pearson.

The Wechsler scales of intelligence are based on Wechsler's definition of intelligence, which views intelligence as an aggregate or global ability of the individual "to act purposefully, to think rationally, and to deal effectively with his environment" (Wechsler, 1944). Wechsler believed that because intelligence is multidetermined, it can be expressed in a variety of ways. Therefore, he developed numerous subtests that seek to probe intellectual functioning in a variety of ways. Table 1 presents the subtests included in the WISC–III and WAIS–R with a description of the subtests. Table 2 describes the WPPSI–R subtests.

Wechsler divided his tests into two major domains of intellectual functioning—verbal and performance. In addition to a total, or full scale IQ score, the Wechsler scales yield verbal and performance IQ scores that provide a measure of an individual's intellectual functioning in these two domains. The verbal subtests assess verbal reasoning, verbal concept formation and verbal comprehension. The performance subtests tap abstract nonverbal reasoning, perceptual organizational abilities, and visual–motor abilities.

According to Wechsler (1950), the IQ score is not meant to be equated with intelligence, because of several other factors that comprise intelligence behaviors. Wechsler maintained that intelligent behavior is impacted by intellective aspects (the intellectual ability

TABLE 1

Descriptions of the WISC–III and WAIS–R subtests

Verbal Subtest	Description
Information	A series of orally presented questions that tap the individual's knowledge about common events, objects, places, and people.
Comprehension	A series of orally presented questions that require the solving of everyday problems or understanding of social rules and concepts. In addition, the WAIS–R contains a few questions that require the examinee to explain the meanings of proverbs.
Similarities	A series of orally presented pairs of words for which the individual explains the similarity of the common objects or concepts they represent.
Arithmetic	A series of arithmetic problems that the child solves mentally and responds to orally.
Vocabulary	A series of orally presented words that the individual orally defines.
Digit Span	A series of orally presented number sequences that the child repeats verbatim for Digits Forward and in reverse order for Digits Backwards.
Picture Completion[a]	A set of colorful pictures of common objects and scenes, each of which is missing an important part, which the child must identify.
Coding[b]	A series of simple shapes (Coding A) or numbers (coding B), each paired with a simple symbol. The individual draws the symbol in its corresponding shape (Coding A) or under its corresponding number (Coding B), according to a key.
Picture Arrangement[a]	A set of colorful pictures, presented in mixed-up order, which the child rearranges into a logical story sequence.
Block Design	A set of modeled or printed two-dimensional geometric designs that the individual replicates using two-color cubes.
Symbol Search[c]	A series of paired groups of symbols, each pair consisting of a target group and a search group. The individual indicates whether or not the target shape is contained in the search group.
Mazes[c]	A set of increasingly difficult mazes that the individual solves by tracing the path out of the maze with a pencil.

[a]Pictures are in black and white on previous editions of the WISC and on the WAIS and WAIS–R.

[b]This subtest is called Digit Symbol on WAIS–R and is similar to the Coding B.

[c]This subtest is not included in the WAIS–R or WAIS.

SOURCE: The Psychological Corporation (1992). Reprinted by permission of the publisher.

measured by IQ tests) and nonintellective aspects (which include such things as drive, motivation, persistence, and other personality factors). In addition, as Matarazzo points out (1972, 1990), environmental factors and other factors, such as social and medical history, must be taken into account in assessing intelligence. As such, the assessment of intelligence goes beyond obtaining a test score; it requires clinical skills and judgment that weigh a variety of factors—all of which affect intelligent behavior.

TEST SCORES

One of the major innovations of the Wechsler scales was the introduction of the deviation IQ score with the publication of the WISC in 1949. All the

TABLE 2
Descriptions of the WPPSI–R subtests

Verbal Subtests	
Information	The Information subtest requires the child to demonstrate knowledge about events or objects in the environment. Several questions require less advanced verbal skills. On these items the child needs only to point to a picture to answer the question. The remaining items are brief oral questions about commonplace objects and events to which the child responds orally.
Comprehension	This subtest requires the child to express in words his or her understanding of the reasons for actions and the consequences of events.
Arithmetic	This subtest requires the child to demonstrate understanding of basic quantitative concepts. The subtest begins with picture items, progresses through simple counting tasks, and ends with more difficult words.
Vocabulary	This is a two-part test. The first part contains picture-identification items. For the remaining items, the child is asked to provide verbal definitions for orally presented words.
Similarities	The Similarities subtest requires the child to demonstrate an understanding of the concept of similarity in three ways. The initial items constitute a task on which the child chooses which of several pictured objects is the most similar to a group of pictured objects that share a common feature. No spoken response is required; the child responds simply by pointing. On the second set of items, the child completes a verbally presented sentence that reflects a similarity or analogy between two things. The final section of the subtest requires the child to explain how two verbally presented objects or events are alike.
Sentences	The examiner reads a sentence aloud, and the child is asked to repeat it verbatim.
Performance Subtest	
Object Assembly	The child is presented with the pieces of a puzzle arranged in a standardized configuration. The child is required to fit the pieces together to form a meaningful whole within a specified time limit.
Geometric Design	This subtest includes two distinct types of tasks. The first section is a visual recognition task. The child looks at a simple design and, with the stimulus still in view, points to one exactly like it from an array of four designs. On the remaining items the child draws a geometric figure from a printed model.
Block Design	This subtest requires the child to analyze and reproduce, within a specified time limit, patterns made from flat, two-colored blocks.
Mazes	This subtest requires the child, under time constraints, to solve paper-and-pencil mazes of increasing difficulty.
Picture Completion	This subtest requires the child to identify what is missing from pictures of common objects or events.
Animal Pegs	This subtest requires the child to place pegs of the correct colors in holes below a series of pictured animals. Both the child's accuracy and speed of performance contribute to the score on this subtest.

SOURCE: The Psychological Corporation. Reprinted by permission of the publisher.

Wechsler scales yield IQ scores that have a mean (or average score) of 100 and a standard deviation of 15. The use of a deviation IQ score means that individuals are compared to other individuals their own age when computing the IQ score. Therefore, it is a measure of relative ability (relative to others of similar age) rather than an absolute ability. Prior to the development of the deviation IQ score method by Wechsler, use of mental age was popular for calculating IQ scores. In this method, IQ score equals mental age divided by chronological age. The use of mental age caused a variety of problems because an IQ of 120, for example, would mean different things as a function of the person's age or the age at which scores on the test no longer increased with age on a particular ability. The problems with the use of mental age are discussed in detail by Wechsler (1974).

TECHNICAL PROPERTIES OF THE SCALES

The Wechsler scales are considered to be outstanding examples of individually administered intelligence tests because of their standardization sampling and psychometric properties. As part of the development of these scales, a standardization sample is taken, which is representative of the U.S. population with respect to important demographic variables such as age, race and ethnicity, socioeconomic level, gender, and region of the country. Matching the standardization sample to the U.S. population ensures that scores on the test for any individual examinee will be meaningful by having a well-defined reference group. Therefore, a child who scores 100 (an average score at the 50th percentile) on the WISC–III can be said to be average compared to his or her same-aged peers in the United States.

During the standardization phase, the tests are administered to the representative sample in a manner that ensures consistency of test administration for all examiners. Consistent administration of the test is important in order to obtain reliable and valid results, because variations in test administration procedures can cause significant variation in scores. With consistent, standard procedures, two examiners administrating the same test to the same individual should obtain comparable results.

In addition to the outstanding standardization sampling that is characteristic of the Wechsler scales, the scales also have outstanding reliabilities. RELIABILITY refers to the precision and accuracy of measurement. The higher the reliability coefficient, the more precise and certain is the measurement. The Wechsler IQ scores all have reliabilities (test–retest repeatability) in the mid- to upper .90s (1.0 would be a perfect correlation).

VALIDITY

The Wechsler scales have been used for a wide range of different applications. The WISC series is frequently used in the schools for psychoeducational purposes, such as placement in special education services (e.g., gifted programs, programs for the mentally retarded, or learning disability programs).

Parts of the legal or administrative definition of certain handicapping conditions use the IQ score as partial criteria for diagnosing the conditions. Although the Wechsler scales have been used in the diagnosis of these handicapping conditions, no one profile of Wechsler test scores is diagnostic of a specific condition (Kaufman, 1979; 1990; Sattler, 1988). For example, a common pattern found among children with a learning disability (LD) is the ACID profile in which four subtests, Arithmetic, Coding, Information, and Digit Span (ACID), are the four lowest subtest scores in the child's profile. Not all LD children will exhibit this profile, although it is more common among LD children as compared to normal children.

The Wechsler IQ Scales are also frequently used in conjunction with achievement tests in psychoeducational assessments, especially for diagnosing learning disabilities (The Psychological Corporation, 1992). Similarly, other patterns of Wechsler scores such as the Bannatyne profile (Bannatyne, 1974) are characteristic of children with learning disabilities. Again, however, not all children with learning disabilities will show a particular subtest profile.

The Wechsler scales have been found to be useful in assessing other childhood disorders as well, such as ATTENTION-DEFICIT HYPERACTIVITY DISORDER and behavior disorders. The verbal/performance IQ dichotomy has been found useful in the intellectual assessment of hearing-impaired children (Braden,

1990). Matarazzo (1972) discusses in detail the validity of the Wechsler IQ score, that is, the correlation of IQ with a variety of factors such as occupation, academic achievement, socioeconomic status, nutrition, and various physiological and environmental factors.

Another use of subtest score patterns using the Wechsler scales has been in neuropsychological evaluations (Boll, 1981; Lezak, 1983; Kaufman, 1990). A frequently researched pattern is the comparison of verbal and performance IQ scores. Large discrepancies between the two scales are sometimes suggestive of brain dysfunction. Furthermore, in some individuals with unilateral brain damage, left-hemisphere damage is associated with lower verbal IQ scores compared to performance IQ scores, and right-hemisphere damage is sometimes associated with lower performance IQ scores compared to verbal IQ scores (Bornstein, 1983; Matarazzo, 1972), although such findings have not been consistent. R. M. Reitan (Reitan & Wolfson, 1985) was one of the first to point out this relationship, and the WAIS and WAIS–R are parts of the currently much administered Halstead-Reitan battery for neuropsychological evaluation. Again, profiles of test scores on the Wechsler scales are useful for diagnosis but profiles made up from the subtest score are not necessarily unique to a specific condition. As Wechsler argued, and Matarazzo (1972, 1990) and others have echoed, accurate assessment is dependent upon the clinician's ability to integrate several sources of information in addition to the IQ score.

METHODOLOGICAL ISSUES

Although the Wechsler scales are widely used and considered to be the standards in the field of intelligence testing, use of the test has recently been criticized. The first area of criticism, coming primarily from the school psychology profession, concerns the limited evidence for the treatment validity of the Wechsler scales. Treatment validity refers to the utility of the test for specifying effective intervention strategies. Some critics (e.g., Witt and Gresham, 1985) have pointed out that the Wechsler scales do not readily lend themselves to developing intervention strategies, which limits the tests' treatment validity.

A second criticism is related to the use of profile analysis by the Wechsler scales. Critics of this ap-

proach (e.g., McDermott, Fantuzzo, & Glutting, 1990) argue that the use of profile analysis by the Wechsler subtests is limited because the subtests may not measure specific-enough abilities to warrant interpretation of profiles.

THEORETICAL ISSUES

A third major area of criticism (e.g., Sternberg, 1993) maintains that the Wechsler scales are based on old technologies and theories of intelligence and should be abandoned in favor of newer approaches of assessing intelligence. However, Sternberg notes that tests of intelligence based on more contemporary theory are not readily available and have limited reliability and validity evidence, which is why conventional tests of intelligence, such as the Wechsler tests, remain popular. He advocates using newer tests in conjunction with more conventional tests, such as the Wechsler scales, in the transition period while newer tests are being developed.

Despite Sternberg's criticisms, he does note that the Wechsler scales do contain useful information and are "as good as one gets with conventional intelligence tests" (Sternberg, 1993, p. 164). Sternberg also notes that parts of the WISC–III are reasonably good measures of constructs based on more recent theories of intelligence. The Wechsler scales are typically considered to be the best standardized measures in the field (Kaufman, 1993), they are easy to use, and their psychometric properties and interpretation approaches are well known and taught in most graduate programs in psychology. The hundreds of articles, book chapters, and books written on the Wechsler scales add to their practical utility. In addition, despite the criticisms of profile analysis, psychologists find the variety of subtests included in the scales useful for diagnosis. Also, with some modifications, the scales have been demonstrated to be clinically rich instruments providing information consistent with modern approaches to neuropsychology that have implications for treatment planning (Kaplan et al., 1991).

TEST BIAS ISSUES

One of the most frequent criticisms of intelligence tests is that they are biased against members of minority groups. During the development of the most recent versions of the Wechsler scales, a great deal of effort was placed on investigating potential *bias* in the test. It is now standard procedure during test development to review test items for bias through content reviews and statistical procedures. For example, during the development of the WISC–III (Wechsler, 1991), items were reviewed by the developers, the research literature was reviewed for issues of item bias, and experts familiar with minority issues reviewed the test items for bias. Questionable items were discarded or modified. In addition, statistical tests of bias were used to identify potentially biased items. Statistical tests of item bias identify an item as biased if a person of equal ability from one group (e.g., male) is more or less likely to answer that item correctly than is a person from another group (e.g., female). Very few of the WISC–R and WISC–III items were found to be biased against minority group members. Items that were found to be biased and retained were not all biased in favor of the majority group; approximately an equal number were found to be biased in favor of minority groups.

This approach as well as other approaches used for assessing test bias have found the Wechsler scales to be relatively free of bias (Reynolds & Kaiser, 1990). Researchers have also found that the WISC–R and WISC–III predict school achievement equally well for whites, African Americans, and Hispanics. Studies have found that minority groups obtain lower IQ scores than whites on the Wechsler scales (e.g., Kaufman & Doppelt, 1976; Kaufman, 1990), as has been the case on other major scales of intelligence. Certain groups (e.g., Hispanics and Native Americans) have been found to have higher performance than verbal IQs. Gender bias has also been studied on the Wechsler scales, and the results have generally shown minimal differences between males and females (Kaufman, 1990; Matarazzo, 1972).

(*See also:* WAIS–R SUBTESTS.)

BIBLIOGRAPHY

ACKERMAN, P. T., DYKMAN, R. A., & PETERS, J. E. (1977). Learning-disabled boys as adolescents: Cognitive factors and achievement. *Journal of the American Academy of Child Psychiatry, 16,* 296–313.

BANNATYNE, A. (1974). Diagnosis: A note on recategorization of the WISC scaled scores. *Journal of Learning Disabilities, 7,* 272–274.

BARKLEY, R. A., DuPAUL, G. J., & McMURRAY, M. B. (1990). Comprehensive evaluation of attention deficit disorder with and without hyperactivity as defined by research criteria. *Journal of Consulting and Clinical Psychology, 58,* 775–789.

BOLL, T. J. (1981). The Halstead-Reitan Neuropsychological Battery. In S. B. Filskov, & T. J. Boll (Eds.), *Handbook of clinical neuropsychology* (pp. 577–607). New York: Wiley.

BORNSTEIN, R. A. (1983). VIQ-PIQ discrepancies on the WAIS-R in patients with unilateral or bilateral cerebral dysfunction. *Journal of Consulting and Clinical Psychology, 51,* 779–780.

BRADEN, J. P. (1990). Do deaf persons have a characteristic psychometric profile on the Wechsler Performance Scales? *Journal of Psychoeducational Assessment, 8,* 518–526.

CHATTIN, S. H., & BRACKEN, B. A. (1989). School psychologists' evaluation of the K-ABC, McCarthy Scales, Stanford-Binet IV, and WISC-R. *Journal of Psychoeducational Assessment, 7,* 122–130.

JOSCHKO, M., & ROURKE, B. P. (1985). Neuropsychological subtypes of learning-disabled children who exhibit the ACID pattern on the WISC. In B. P. Rourke (Ed.), *Neuropsychology of learning disabilities: Essentials of subtype analysis* (pp. 65–88). New York: Guilford Press.

KAPLAN, E., FEIN, D., MORRIS, R., & DELIS, D. (1991). *The WAIS–R as a neuropsychological instrument.* San Antonio, TX: The Psychological Corporation.

KAUFMAN, A. S. (1979). *Intelligent testing with the WISC–R.* New York: Wiley.

KAUFMAN, A. S. (1990). *Assessing adolescent and adult intelligence.* Boston: Allyn & Bacon.

KAUFMAN, A. S. (1993). King WISC the Third assumes the throne. *Journal of School Psychology, 31,* 345–354.

KAUFMAN, A. S., & DOPPELT, J. E. (1976). Analysis of the WISC–R standardization data in terms of the stratification variables. *Child Development, 47,* 165–171.

LEZAK, M. D. (1983). *Neuropsychological assessment* (2nd ed.). New York: Oxford University Press.

LONGMAN, R. S., INGLIS, J., & LAWSON, J. S. (1991). WISC-R patterns of cognitive abilities in behavior disordered and learning disabled children. *Psychological Assessment: A Journal of Consulting and Clinical Psychology, 3,* 239–246.

LUBIN, B., LARSEN, R. M., MATARAZZO, J. D., & DEEVER, M.

(1987). Psychological test usage patterns in five professional settings. *American Psychologist, 40,* 857–861.

MATARAZZO, J. D. (1972). *Wechsler's measurement and appraisal of adult intelligence* (5th ed.). Baltimore, MD: Williams & Wilkins.

MATARAZZO, J. D. (1990). Psychological assessment versus psychological testing. *American Psychologist, 45,* 999–1017.

MCDERMOTT, P. A., FANTUZZO, J. W., & GLUTTING, J. J. (1990). Just say no to subtest analysis: A critique of Wechsler theory and practice. *Journal of Psychoeducational Assessment, 8,* 290–302.

PIOTROWSKI, C., & KELLER, J. W. (1989). Psychological testing in outpatient mental health facilities: A national study. *Professional Psychology: Research and Practice, 20,* 423–425.

PRIFITERA, A., & DERSH, J. (1993). Base rates of WISC-III diagnostic subtest patterns among normal, learning disabled, and ADHD samples. *Journal of Psychoeducational Assessment.* WISC–III Monograph.

REITAN, R. M., & WOLFSON, D. (1985). *The Halstead-Reitan Neuropsychological Test Battery: Theory and clinical interpretation.* Tucson, AZ: Neuropsychology Press.

REYNOLDS, C. R., & KAISER, S. M. (1990). Bias in assessment of aptitude. In C. R. Reynolds & R. W. Kamphaus (Eds.), *Handbook of psychological and educational assessment of children: Intelligence and achievement* (pp. 611–653). New York: Guilford Press.

SANDOVAL, J. (1984, April). *Verifying the WISC-R ACID profile.* Paper presented at the 1984 meeting of the National Association of School Psychologists, Philadelphia.

SATTLER, J. M. (1988). *Assessment of children* (3rd ed.). San Diego, CA: Jerome M. Sattler.

SLICK, D. J., & CRAIG, P. L. (1991). Neuropsychological assessment in public psychiatric hospitals: The changing state of practice 1979–1989. *Archives of Clinical Neuropsychology, 6,* 73–80.

STERNBERG, R. J. (1993). Rocky's back again: A review of the WISC-III. *Journal of Psychoeducational Assessment,* WISC–III Monograph.

THE PSYCHOLOGICAL CORPORATION (1992). *Manual for the Wechsler Individual Achievement Test.* San Antonio, TX: The Psychological Corporation.

WECHSLER, D. (1944). *The measurement of adult intelligence* (3rd. ed.). Baltimore, MD: Williams & Wilkins.

WECHSLER, D. (1949). *Manual for the Wechsler Intelligence Scale for Children.* New York: The Psychological Corporation.

WECHSLER, D. (1950). Cognitive, conative, and non-intellective intelligence. *American Psychologist, 5,* 78–83.

WECHSLER, D. (1955). *Manual for the Wechsler Adult Intelligence Scale.* New York: The Psychological Corporation.

WECHSLER, D. (1981). *Manual for the Wechsler Adult Intelligence Scale–Revised.* San Antonio, TX: The Psychological Corporation.

WECHSLER, D. (1974). *Manual for the Wechsler Intelligence Scale for Children–Revised.* San Antonio, TX: The Psychological Corporation.

WECHSLER, D. (1989). *Manual for the Wechsler Preschool and Primary Scale of Intelligence–Revised.* San Antonio, TX: The Psychological Corporation.

WECHSLER, D. (1991). *Manual for the Wechsler Intelligence Scale for Children–Third Edition.* San Antonio, TX: The Psychological Corporation.

WEISS, L. G., PRIFITERA, A., & ROID, G. (1993). The WISC–III and the fairness of predicting achievement across ethnic and gender groups. *Journal of Psychoeducational Assessment.* WISC–III Monograph.

WITT, J., & GRESHAM, F. M. (1985). [Review of the Wechsler Intelligence Scale for Children–Revised (pp. 1351–1353)]. In J. Mitchell (Ed.), *Mental measurements yearbook* (9th ed.). Lincoln: University of Nebraska Press.

AURELIO PRIFITERA

WISDOM, PSYCHOLOGY OF

For millennia, wisdom and related constructs have been considered the ideal of knowledge and personal functioning. Indeed, the idea of wisdom as one of the highest forms of knowledge and skill is evident in the very definition of the historical grand master of all scholarship, philosophy (*philosophia*): "the love or pursuit of wisdom." Historically, wisdom was defined in terms of a state of idealized being (such as Lady Wisdom), as a process of perfect knowing and judgment as in King Solomon's judgments, or as an oral or written product such as wisdom-related proverbs and the so-called wisdom literature.

The identification of wisdom with individuals (such as wise persons), the predominant approach in psychology, is but one of the ways by which wisdom is instantiated. In fact, in the general historical literature on wisdom, the identification of wisdom with the mind and character of individuals is not the preferred mode of analysis. Wisdom is considered an ideal that is difficult for individuals to attain fully.

Over history, the interest in the topic of wisdom has waxed and waned. In general, two main lines of argument have been central to the historical evolution of the concept of wisdom. The first is the distinction between philosophical and practical wisdom often attributed to Aristotle's differentiation between *theoria* and *phronesis*. The second is the question of whether wisdom is divine or human.

In the Western world, these two issues (philosophical versus practical; divine versus human) were the subject of heated discourse during the Renaissance, and many important works were written on these wisdom topics during the fifteenth through seventeenth centuries (Rice, 1958). This discourse initially concluded during the later phases of the Enlightenment. Wisdom was still critical, for instance, to the thinking of Immanuel Kant and Georg Friedrich Wilhelm Hegel. Both understood wisdom as based on the coordination of the world of science and the practical world of humankind. The eighteenth-century French encyclopedia of Denis Diderot, however, despite its more than fifty volumes, barely mentioned the topic, nor did other works of the time. During the Enlightenment and the process of secularization, wisdom lost its salience as one of the fundamental categories guiding human thought and conduct.

Nevertheless, from time to time, scholars in such fields as philosophy, political science, theology, and cultural anthropology have addressed the subject of wisdom, although rather than build a cumulative theory of wisdom, they have tended to rejuvenate and revisit its meaning, historical roots, and implications for raising human awareness about the complexities and uncertainties of life. During the 1980s and early 1990s, for example, some philosophers struggled with the definition of wisdom, including the polarization of practical and philosophical wisdom, the integration of different forms of knowledge into one overarching whole, and the search for orientation in life (Kekes, 1983; Nozick, 1989; Oelmueller, 1989). In Germany, the latter issue has gained special importance in relation to the advent of postmodernity (e.g., Marquart, 1989).

Finally, there is archaeological-cultural work dealing with the origins of religious and secular bodies of wisdom-related texts in China, India, Egypt, Old Mesopotamia, and the like (Assmann, 1991; Rudolph, 1987). The cultural-historical scholarship is important to the understanding of the cultural evolution and foundation of wisdom-related thought. Proverbs (Mieder & Dundes, 1981), maxims, and fairy tales (Chinen, 1987) constitute a great part of the materials underlying such efforts. Wisdom-related proverbs and tales evince a high degree of cultural and historical invariance. This relative invariance gives rise to the assumption that concepts such as wisdom and its related body of knowledge and skills have been culturally selected because of their adaptive value for humankind (Csikszentmihalyi & Rathunde, 1990).

DEFINITION OF WISDOM

A useful first approach to the definition of wisdom is a review of its treatment in encyclopedias and dictionaries. The major German historical dictionary (Grimm & Grimm, 1854/1984), for instance, defined wisdom as "insight and knowledge about oneself and the world . . . and sound judgment in the case of difficult life problems." Similarly, the Oxford dictionary (Fowler & Fowler, 1964) includes in its definition of wisdom "good judgement and advice in difficult and uncertain matters of life."

When psychologists approach the definition of wisdom (Sternberg, 1990), they, like philosophers, are confronted with the need to specify further the content and formal properties of wisdom-related thought, judgment, and advice in terms of psychological categories and also to describe the characteristics of persons who have approached a state of wisdom and are capable of transmitting wisdom to others. These initial efforts by psychologists were for the most part theoretical and speculative. In his pioneering piece on senescence, G. Stanley Hall (1922), for example, associated wisdom with the emergence of a meditative attitude, philosophic calmness, impartiality, and the desire to draw moral lessons that emerge in later adulthood. Other writers emphasized that wisdom involves the search for the moderate course between extremes, a dynamic between knowledge and doubt, a sufficient detachment from the problem at hand, and a well-balanced coordination of emotion, motivation, and thought. In line with dictionary definitions, such writings typically included varied statements that wisdom is knowledge about the human condition at its frontier, knowledge about the most difficult questions of the meaning and conduct of life, and knowledge about the uncertainties of life—about what cannot be known and how to deal with that limited knowledge.

IMPLICIT (SUBJECTIVE) THEORIES ABOUT WISDOM

As of the early 1990s, most empirical research on wisdom in psychology had focused on further elaboration of the definition of wisdom. Moving beyond the dictionary definitions of wisdom, research explored the nature of everyday beliefs, folk conceptions, or implicit (subjective) theories of wisdom. The pursuit of an answer to questions such as What is wisdom?, How is wisdom different from other forms of intelligence?, Which situations require wisdom?, and What are the characteristics of wise people? was at the center of psychological wisdom research during the 1980s.

These studies, in principle, built on research initiated by V. P. Clayton (1976). In her work, three dimensions were found to be typical of wise people: (1) affective characteristics such as empathy and compassion; (2) reflective processes such as intuition and introspection; and (3) cognitive capacities such as experience and intelligence (see also Table 1).

The focus of a study by Robert J. Sternberg (1986) investigating implicit theories was the location of wisdom in the semantic space marked by other constructs such as creativity and intelligence. Within that frame of reference, Sternberg found wisdom described by six dimensions: (1) reasoning ability; (2) sagacity; (3) learning from ideas and environment; (4) judgment; (5) expeditious use of information; and (6) perspicacity. When asking people about their views on wisdom, the greatest overlap was found between intelligence and wisdom. The sagacity dimension, however, was

TABLE 1
Implicit theories of wisdom: A comparison of findings from three studies with sample items

Clayton (1976)	Sternberg (1986)	Holliday & Chandler (1986)
• affective (1) 　empathy 　compassion	• sagacity (2) 　concern for others 　considers advice • perspicacity (6) 　intuition 　offers right and true solutions	• interpersonal skills (4) 　sensitive 　sociable • judgment and communication skills (2) 　is a good source of advice 　understands life
• reflective (2) 　intuition 　introspection	• judgment (4) 　acts within own limitations 　is sensible • learning from ideas and environment (3) 　perceptive 　learns from mistakes	• social unobtrusiveness (5) 　discrete 　non-judgmental • exceptional understanding of ordinary experience (1) 　has learned from experience 　sees things in a larger context
• cognitive (3) 　experience 　intelligence	• reasoning ability (1) 　good problem-solving ability 　logical mind • expeditious use of information (5) 　experienced 　seeks out information	• general competence (3) 　intelligent 　educated

NOTE: Sequence of factors or dimensions obtained in original research is given in parentheses. Studies are based on different methodologies (e.g., factor analysis, multidimensional scaling).

specific to wisdom. Sagacity seems to build on Clayton's affective dimension and includes such behavioral expressions as displaying concern for others or considering advice. In later theoretical work, Sternberg (1990) used these results and others to specify six characteristics relating to six domains that lead people to label a person as wise: (1) understanding of presuppositions, meaning, and limits (knowledge); (2) resisting automization of own thought but seeking to understand it in others (process); (3) judicial (primary intellectual style); (4) understanding of ambiguity and obstacles (personality); (5) interest in understanding what is known and what it means (motivation); and (6) depth of understanding needs to find appreciation in context (environmental context).

Another major study on subjective theories of wisdom was conducted by S. G. Holliday and M. J. Chandler (1986). Their work included an analysis of the words people use to describe wisdom and wise persons and the attributes judged to be the most typical indicators of these concepts. A summary of their outcomes and also the results of Clayton (1976) and Sternberg (1986) is presented in Table 1.

A factor analysis of the attributes judged to be "most prototypical" of a wise person and wise behavior revealed two factors. Holliday and Chandler labeled one dimension "exceptional understanding of ordinary experience." This dimension combines qualities of the mind with the practical virtues of leading a good life. The second factor they labeled "judgment and communication skills." This factor referred to qualities like comprehending, weighing consequences, and giving good advice. Combining such results with notions from Jurgen Habermas (1970) led Chandler and Holliday (1990) to emphasize the importance of a multidimensional account of wisdom comprising technical, practical, and emancipatory knowledge.

Two studies in the tradition of implicit-theory research involved asking subjects to nominate wise people and subsequently characterize nominees (Orwoll & Perlmutter, 1990; Sowarka, 1989). D. Sowarka (1989) reported two findings of special importance. First, it seemed that the characterization of wisdom and wise persons was a task readily performed by elderly research participants. Second, subjects emphasized the notion that the persons they had nominated as wise displayed "excellent character." Using a similar procedure, L. Orwoll and M. Perlmutter (1990) found that high-wisdom nominees tended to be middle-aged to old, male rather than female, and more highly educated. None of these studied employed heterogeneous, representative samples, however. Therefore, it may very well be that as such research is systematically applied to nominators from various cultural subgroups, new constellations of personal characteristics including different gender and age distributions would emerge.

From this research on implicit theories of wisdom and wise persons, it is evident that people in Western samples hold fairly clear-cut images of the nature of wisdom. Four findings are especially noteworthy. First, in the minds of people, wisdom seems to be closely related to wise persons as "carriers" of wisdom. Second, wise people are expected to combine features of mind and character. Third, wisdom carries a very strong interpersonal and social aspect with regard to both its application (advice) and the consensual recognition of its occurrence. Fourth, wisdom exhibits overlap with other related concepts such as intelligence, but in aspects like sagacity, prudence, and the integration of cognition, emotion, and motivation, it also carries unique variance.

EXPLICIT THEORIES OF WISDOM AND BEHAVIORAL ASSESSMENT

Another line of empirical psychological inquiry on wisdom addresses the question of how to measure behavioral expressions of wisdom. Within this tradition, three lines of work can be identified: (1) assessment of wisdom as a personality characteristic; (2) assessment of wisdom in the Piagetian tradition of postformal thought (see PIAGET, JEAN); and (3) assessment of wisdom as an individual's problem-solving performance with regard to difficult problems involving the interpretation, conduct, and management of life. This article will concentrate on the assessment of wisdom as a personality characteristic and as a performance on difficult life problems.

Within personality theories, wisdom is usually conceptualized as an advanced if not the final stage of personality development. Wisdom, in this context, is comparable to "optimal maturity." A wise person is characterized, for instance, as integrating rather than ignoring or repressing self-related information, by having coordinated opposites, and by having transcended personal agendas and turned to collective or universal issues. Ryff (Ryff & Heincke, 1983) and S. K. Whitbourne (e.g., Walaskay, Whitbourne & Nehrke, 1983–1984), for example, developed self-report questionnaires based on Eriksonian notions of personality development, especially integrity or wisdom. In a similar vein, Orwoll (1988) investigated people who had been nominated as wise according to subjective beliefs about wisdom. She found that wise nominees were indeed characterized by high scores on Eriksonian measures of ego integrity and showed a greater concern for the world state or humanity as a whole than the comparison group. Utilizing her sentence-completion technique, J. Loevinger developed a measure of her theoretically postulated stages of ego development (e.g., Loevinger & Wessler, 1978). Loevinger's last stage, labeled "ego integrity," has been found to be related to other personality dimensions, such as Competence from the CPI Inventory (Helson & Wink, 1987) or Openness to Experience from the NEO-PI (McCrae & Costa, 1980).

Besides these measures of wisdom as a personality characteristic, there is also work that attempts to assess wisdom-related performance in tasks dealing with the interpretation, conduct, and management of life. The conceptual approach taken by the Berlin Max Planck Institute group is based on life-span theory, the developmental study of the aging mind and aging personality, research on expert systems, and cultural-historical definitions of wisdom. By integrating these perspectives, wisdom is defined as "an expert knowledge system in the fundamental pragmatics of life permitting exceptional insight, judgment, and advice involving complex and uncertain matters of the human condition."

The body of knowledge and skills associated with wisdom as an expertise in the fundamental pragmatics of life entails insights into the quintessential aspects of the human condition, including its biological finitude and cultural conditioning. Central to this approach are questions concerning the conduct, interpretation, and meaning of life. Furthermore, wisdom involves a fine-tuned coordination of cognition, motivation, and emotion. More specifically, wisdom-related knowledge and skills can be characterized by a family of five criteria shown in Table 2.

To elicit and measure wisdom-related knowledge and skills, the Berlin group of wisdom researchers presented subjects with difficult life dilemmas such as the following: "Imagine, a good friend of yours calls you up and tells you that she can't go on anymore and has decided to commit suicide. What would you be thinking about, how would you deal with this situation?" Participants are then asked to "think aloud" about such dilemmas. The five wisdom-related criteria introduced in Table 2 are used to evaluate these protocols. The obtained scores are reliable and provide an approximation of the quantity and quality of the wisdom-related knowledge and skills of a given person. When using this wisdom paradigm to study people who were nominated as wise according to nominators' subjective beliefs about wisdom, wisdom nominees received higher wisdom scores than comparable control samples of various ages and professional backgrounds.

Researchers of wisdom are usually quite aware that it is a courageous undertaking to try, empirically, to study wisdom, a complex and content-rich phenomenon, which, as many scholars have claimed, defies attempts at scientific identification (Baltes & Smith, 1990). Nevertheless, research on explicit theories of wisdom has shown that it is possible to measure wisdom in terms of personality characteristics (standardized or open-ended) as well as performance (judgment, advice) on difficult life tasks.

DEVELOPMENT OF WISDOM

The least developed domain of work in the field is research and theory on the development of wisdom across the life span. Historically and theoretically, of course, works by Erik Erikson and also Carl Jung (1971) are critical.

Erikson, in his epigenetic theory of personality development, identified the achievement of integrity and wisdom as the last and highest form of personality functioning. Achieving this last stage requires, on the one hand, successful mastery of the previous life tasks and, on the other hand, accelerative and supportive conditions associated with the social environment. Wisdom, in the Eriksonian sense, necessitates the full expression of mature identity including the transcendence of personal interests, mastery of one's own finitude, and attention to collective and universal issues.

TABLE 2
A family of five criteria characterizing wisdom and wisdom-related products

Basic Criteria	
Factual Knowledge	To what extent does this product show general (*conditio humana*) and specific (e.g., life events, institutions) knowledge about life matters and the human condition as well as demonstrate scope and depth in the coverage of issues?
Procedural Knowledge	To what extent does this product consider decision strategies, how to define goals and to identify the appropriate means, whom to consult with and about strategies of advice giving?
Meta-level Criteria	
Life-Span Contextualism	To what extent does this product consider the past, current, and possible future contexts of life and the many circumstances in which a life is embedded?
Value Relativism	To what extent does this product consider variations in values and life priorities and the importance of viewing individuals within their own framework despite a small set of universal values?
Awareness and Management of Uncertainty	To what extent does this product consider the inherent uncertainty of life (in terms of interpreting the past and predicting the future) and effective strategies for dealing with uncertainty?

NOTE: For further detail, see Baltes & Smith, 1990, or Baltes & Staudinger, 1993.

Empirical research on these Eriksonian notions in the narrow sense is scarce. However, as alluded to above, a few studies derived from theories of the life-span development of personality, based largely on Eriksonian ideas, appeared in the literature in the 1980s and early 1990s. Ryff and Heincke (1983) compared people of different ages on self-report measures based on the Eriksonian notions of personality development. They found that, as expected, the oldest group (average age: 70 years) reported higher levels of integrity than the middle-aged and young participants. In a longitudinal study with a sample of young and middle-aged adults, Whitbourne, Zuschlag, Elliot, and Waterman (1992)

also found indications of integrity à la Erikson. At the same time, however, there was a historical trend toward declining levels of integrity in the population. The authors related this finding to the increasing materialism and individualism in Western societies that in their view was characteristic of the 1980s.

A general framework has been established outlining the conditions for the development of wisdom as it is instantiated in persons. The model (see Figure 1) presents a set of factors and processes that need to "cooperate" for wisdom to develop. It postulates cognitive and emotional-motivational processes as well as certain experiential factors associated with the inter-

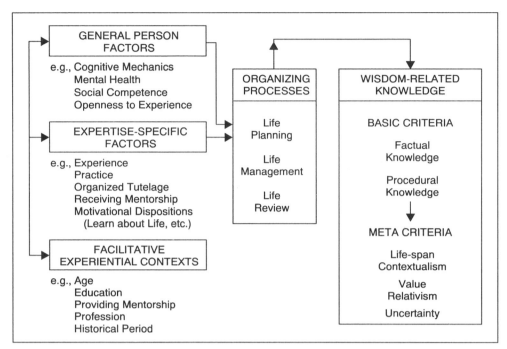

Figure 1

A research framework describing factors and mediating processes for the acquisition and maintenance of wisdom-related knowledge and skills across the life span

pretation, conduct, and management of life to be important antecedents of wisdom.

First, as shown on the left-hand side of Figure 1, there are general individual characteristics related to adaptive human functioning such as intelligence and personality. Second, the model presumes that the development of wisdom is advanced by certain expertise-specific factors, such as practice and being guided by a mentor. Third, the model implies the operation of macro-level facilitative experiential contexts. For instance, certain professional and historical periods are more facilitative than others. In the center of Figure 1, some of the organizing processes (life planning, life management, and life review) that may be critical for the development of wisdom-related knowledge are identified. Certain theoretical assumptions about where the five criteria fall in the course of the development of wisdom are depicted on the right-hand side. Applying general models of expertise development (e.g., Anderson, 1987), individuals first may reach good performance levels on the two basic criteria, factual and subsequently procedural knowledge

about life. Good performance on the three meta-criteria of life-span contextualism, value relativism, and awareness and management of uncertainty, are expected to emerge in later phases of the acquisition process.

The empirical work based on this ontogenetic model and the measurement paradigm presented above produced outcomes consistent with expectations. For instance, contrary to work on the fluid mechanics of cognitive aging, older adults performed as well as young adults (Smith & Baltes, 1990; Staudinger, 1989). Furthermore, when age was combined with wisdom-related experiential contexts, such as professional specializations specifically involving training and experience in matters of life (e.g., clinical psychology), even higher levels of performance were observed (Staudinger, Smith, & Baltes, 1992). Initial explorations into the role of personality characteristics suggested—as McCrae and Costa (1980) had found for Loevinger's ego integrity—that Openness to Experience was an important correlate of wisdom (Baltes & Staudinger, 1993).

SUMMARY AND FUTURE DIRECTIONS

The concept of wisdom is a fruitful topic for psychological research in various respects: (1) it represents an opportunity for the study of lifelong cognition in the context of the interpretation, conduct, and management of life; (2) it emphasizes the search for continued optimization and evolution of the human condition; and finally (3) in a prototypical fashion, it allows for the study of collaboration among cognitive, emotional, and motivational processes. Future research on wisdom will expand in at least four directions: (1) the use of social-interactive or communicative paradigms to make more explicit the social nature of wisdom; (2) the further identification of social and personality factors and life processes relevant for the ontogeny of wisdom; (3) the delineation of communalities and differences in wisdom-related processes within the larger framework of research on intelligence and personality; and (4) the comparison of psychological conceptions of wisdom with counterpart approaches in the humanities and cultural anthropology.

BIBLIOGRAPHY

ANDERSON, J. R. (1987). Skill acquisition: Compilation of weak-method problem solutions. *Psychological Review, 94,* 192–210.

ARLIN, P. K. (1990). Wisdom: The art of problem finding. In R. J. Sternberg (Ed.), *Wisdom: Its nature, origins, and development* (pp. 230–243). New York: Cambridge University Press.

ASSMANN, A. (ED.). (1991). Weisheit. Archäologie der Kommunikation [Wisdom. Archaeology of communication]. Munich: Fink Verlag.

BALTES, P. B., & SMITH, J. (1990). Toward a psychology of wisdom and its ontogenesis. In R. J. Sternberg (Ed.), *Wisdom: Its nature, origins, and development* (pp. 87–120). New York: Cambridge University Press.

BALTES, P. B., SMITH, J., & STAUDINGER, U. M. (1992). Wisdom and successful aging. *Nebraska Symposium on Motivation, 39,* 123–167.

BALTES, P. B., & STAUDINGER, U. M. (1993). The search for a psychology of wisdom. *Current Directions in Psychological Science, 2,* 1–6.

BIRREN, J. E., & FISHER, L. M. (1990). The elements of wisdom: Overview and integration. In R. J. Sternberg (Ed.), *Wisdom: Its nature, origins, and development* (pp. 317–332). New York: Cambridge University Press.

BRYCE, G. E. (1979). *A legacy of wisdom: The Egyptian contribution to the wisdom of Israel.* Lewisburg, PA: Bucknell University Press.

CHANDLER, M. J., & HOLLIDAY, S. (1990). Wisdom in a postapocalyptic age. In R. J. Sternberg (Ed.), *Wisdom: Its nature, origins, and development* (pp. 121–141). New York: Cambridge University Press.

CHINEN, A. B. (1987). Fairy tales and psychological development in late life: A cross-cultural hermeneutic study. *The Gerontologist, 27,* 340–346.

CLAYTON, V. P. (1976). *A multidimensional scaling analysis of the concept of wisdom.* Unpublished doctoral dissertation, University of Southern California.

CLAYTON, V. P., & BIRREN, J. E. (1980). The development of wisdom across the life-span: A reexamination of an ancient topic. In P. B. Baltes & O. G. Brim (Eds.), *Life-span development and behavior* (Vol. 3, pp. 103–135). New York: Academic Press.

CRENSHAW, J. L. (1987). Wisdom literature. In M. Eliade (Ed.), *Encyclopedia of Religion: Wisdom* (Vol. 15, pp. 401–408). New York: Macmillan.

CSIKSZENTMIHALYI, M., & RATHUNDE, K. (1990). The psychology of wisdom: An evolutionary interpretation. In R. J. Sternberg (Ed.), *Wisdom: Its nature, origins, and development* (pp. 25–51). New York: Cambridge University Press.

DITTMANN-KOHLI, F., & BALTES, P. B. (1990). Toward a neofunctionalist conception of adult intellectual development: Wisdom as a prototypical case of intellectual growth. In C. Alexander & E. Langer (Eds.), *Higher stages of human development* (pp. 54–78). New York: Oxford University Press.

ERIKSON, E. H. (1959). *Identity and the life cycle.* New York: International University Press.

ERIKSON, E. H., ERIKSON, J. M., & KIVNICK, H. (1986). *Vital involvement in old age: The experience of old age in our time.* London: W. W. Norton.

FOWLER, H. W., & FOWLER, F. G. (1964). *The concise Oxford dictionary of current English.* Oxford: Clarendon Press.

GRIMM, J., & GRIMM, W. (1854). *Deutsches Wörterbuch.* Munich: Deutscher Taschenbuch-Verlag (1984).

HABERMAS, J. (1970). *Knowledge and human interests.* Boston: Beacon Press.

HALL, G. S. (1922). *Senescence: The last half of life.* New York: Appleton.

HARTSHORNE, C. (1987). *Wisdom as moderation: A philosophy of the middle way*. Albany: State University of New York Press.

HELSON, R., & WINK, P. (1987). Two conceptions of maturity examined in the findings of a longitudinal study. *Journal of Personality and Social Psychology, 53,* 531–541.

HOLLIDAY, S. G., & CHANDLER, M. J. (1986). *Wisdom: Explorations in adult competence*. Basel: Karger.

JUNG, C. G. (1971). *The stages of life*. In J. Campbell (Ed.), *The portable Jung*. New York: Viking.

KEKES, J. (1983). Wisdom. *American Philosophical Quarterly, 20,* 277–286.

KITCHENER, K. S., & BRENNER, H. G. (1990). Wisdom and reflective judgment: Knowing in the face of uncertainty. In R. J. Sternberg (Ed.), *Wisdom: Its nature, origins, and development* (pp. 212–229). New York: Cambridge University Press.

KRAMER, D. A. (1990). Conceptualizing wisdom: The primacy of affect-cognition relations. In R. J. Sternberg (Ed.), *Wisdom: Its nature, origins, and development* (pp. 279–313). New York: Cambridge University Press.

LABOUVIE-VIEF, G. (1990). Wisdom as integrated thought: Historical and developmental perspectives. In R. J. Sternberg (Ed.), *Wisdom: Its nature, origins, and development* (pp. 52–83). New York: Cambridge University Press.

LABOUVIE-VIEF, G. (1992). A neo-Piagetian perspective on adult cognitive development. In R. J. Sternberg & C. A. Berg (Eds.), *Intellectual development* (pp. 197–228). Cambridge: Cambridge University Press.

LOEVINGER, J. (1976). *Ego development. Conceptions and theories*. San Francisco: Jossey-Bass.

LOEVINGER, J., & WESSLER, R. (1978). *Measuring ego development I: Construction and use of a sentence completion test*. San Francisco: Jossey-Bass.

MARQUART, O. (1989). Drei Betrachtungen zum Thema "Philosophie und Weisheit" [Three observations concerning "philosophy and wisdom"]. In W. Oelmueller (Ed.), *Philosophie und Weisheit* [Philosophy and wisdom] (pp. 275–308). Paderborn: Schoeningh.

MCCRAE, R. R., & COSTA, P. T. (1980). Openness to experience and ego level in Loevinger's sentence completion test: Dispositional contributions to developmental models of personality. *Journal of Personality and Social Psychology, 39,* 1179–1190.

MEACHAM, J. A. (1990). The loss of wisdom. In R. J. Sternberg (Ed.), *Wisdom: Its nature, origins, and development* (pp. 181–211). New York: Cambridge University Press.

MIEDER, W., & DUNDES, A. (EDS.). (1981). *The wisdom of many: Essays on the proverb*. New York: Garland.

NOZICK, R. (1989). *The examined life: Philosophical meditations*. New York: Simon & Schuster.

OELMUELLER, W. (ED.). (1989). *Philosophie und Weisheit* [Philosophy and wisdom]. Paderborn: Schoeningh.

ORWOLL, L. (1988). *Wisdom in late adulthood: Personality and life history correlates*. Unpublished doctoral dissertation, Boston University.

ORWOLL, L., & PERLMUTTER, M. (1990). The study of wise persons: Integrating a personality perspective. In R. J. Sternberg (Ed.), *Wisdom: Its nature, origins, and development* (pp. 160–177). New York: Cambridge University Press.

PASCUAL-LEONE, J. (1990). An essay on wisdom: Toward organismic processes that make it possible. In R. J. Sternberg (Ed.), *Wisdom: Its nature, origins, and development* (pp. 244–278). New York: Cambridge University Press.

RICE, E. F. (1958). *The renaissance idea of wisdom*. Cambridge, MA: Harvard University Press.

ROBINSON, D. N. (1990). Wisdom through the ages. In R. J. Sternberg (Ed.), *Wisdom: Its nature, origins, and development* (pp. 13–24). New York: Cambridge University Press.

RUDOLPH, K. (1987). Wisdom. In M. Eliade (Ed.), *Encyclopedia of Religion: Wisdom* (Vol. 15, pp. 393–401). New York: Macmillan.

RYFF, C. (1982). Self-perceived personality change in adulthood and aging. *Journal of Personality and Social Psychology, 42,* 108–115.

RYFF, C. D., & HEINCKE, S. G. (1983). The subjective organization of personality in adulthood and aging. *Journal of Personality and Social Psychology, 44,* 807–816.

SMITH, J., & BALTES, P. B. (1990). A study of wisdom-related knowledge: Age/cohort differences in responses to life planning problems. *Developmental Psychology, 26,* 494–505.

SOWARKA, D. (1989). Weisheit und weise Personen: Common-Sense-Konzepte älterer Menschen [Wisdom and wise persons: Common-sense views from elderly people]. *Zeitschrift für Entwicklungspsychologie und Pädagogische Psychologie, 21,* 87–109.

STAUDINGER, U. M. (1989). *The study of life review: An approach to the investigation of intellectual development across the life span*. Berlin: Edition Sigma.

STAUDINGER, U. M., SMITH, J., & BALTES, P. B. (1992). Wisdom-related knowledge in a life review task: Age differences and the role of professional specialization. *Psychology and Aging, 7,* 271–281.

STERNBERG, R. J. (1986). Implicit theories of intelligence, creativity, and wisdom. *Journal of Personality and Social Psychology, 49,* 607–627.

STERNBERG, R. J. (ED.). (1990). *Wisdom: Its nature, origins, and development.* New York: Cambridge University Press.

WALASKAY, M., WHITBOURNE, S. K., & NEHRKE, M. F. (1983–1984). Construction and validation of an ego-integrity status interview. *International Journal of Aging and Human Development, 18,* 61–72.

WHITBOURNE, S. K., ET AL. (1992). Psychological development in adulthood. A 22-year sequential study. *Journal of Personality and Social Psychology, 63,* 260–271.

URSULA M. STAUDINGER

PAUL B. BALTES

WOODCOCK-JOHNSON TESTS OF COGNITIVE ABILITY–REVISED

The Woodcock-Johnson Tests of Cognitive Ability–Revised, or WJTCA–R (Woodcock & Johnson, 1989), are an expanded revision of the Woodcock-Johnson Tests of Cognitive Ability, or WJTCA (Woodcock & Johnson, 1977). The original WJTCA consisted of twelve individual tests designed to assess intellectual abilities from the basic to the complex. The twelve tests could be organized into different combinations of two to twelve tests to measure nine aspects of intellectual functioning. The major interpretive features included four measures of specialized cognitive abilities (reasoning, verbal ability, memory, and perceptual speed), four aptitude measures for making statements about a person's predicted achievement (reading, mathematics, written language, and knowledge aptitude), and two brief and one comprehensive measure of overall cognitive ability.

The WJTCA was designed according to a pragmatic decision-making model. The complete battery was called the Woodcock-Johnson Psycho-Educational Battery, or WJ (Woodcock & Johnson, 1977). When used together with the WJ achievement battery, the WJTCA provided the major types of information (comparisons between predicted and actual achievement, strength and weakness comparisons within a person's cognitive and achievement abilities) needed by assessment professionals to make important clinical and educational decisions.

The WJTCA was the first individually administered intelligence battery to be normed together with a battery of achievement and interest tests. When combined with the related achievement tests, this feature provided the ability to compare a person's expected and actual achievement directly with discrepancy norms. The WJTCA was also unique in that it included three controlled learning tasks (Kaufman, 1985). Additional information regarding the history, development, use, and interpretation of the WJTCA can be found in G. L. Hessler (1982), K. S. McGrew (1986), and R. W. Woodcock (1978).

In 1989 the WJ battery was revised, expanded, and renormed. The Woodcock-Johnson Psycho-Educational Battery–Revised, or WJ–R (Woodcock & Johnson, 1989) again included separate cognitive and achievement sections standardized on the same sample. The battery of interest tests were not included in the revised battery. The WJ–R retained the pragmatic decision-making model, but also embedded the model within a comprehensive theoretical model of intelligence.

The Horn-Cattell model of the *Gf–Gc* theory of intelligence guided the revision of the WJTCA–R. The Horn-Cattell *Gf–Gc* model is based on reviews of the existing factor-analytic research that has identified eight to ten major factors of intelligence (Carroll, 1993). The Horn-Cattell *Gf–Gc* model has identified nine broad abilities of FLUID AND CRYSTALLIZED INTELLIGENCE: visual and auditory processing, long-term storage and retrieval, short-term memory, quantitative abilities, and cognitive processing and correct decision speed. By including tests of eight of the Horn-Cattell *Gf–Gc* factors, the WJTCA–R became a more comprehensive measure of intelligence than other individually administered intelligence batteries.

The WJTCA–R consists of twenty-one individual tests that provide for the measurement of general cognitive ability, specific cognitive abilities, and specialized aptitudes for predicting academic achievement. A number of interpretive features, including the seven-test standard and fourteen-test extended battery options, allow examiners to administer only those specific tests required to obtain the necessary information. The tests in the WJTCA–R are normed on individuals as young as 24 months and as old as 95 years of age.

ORGANIZATION OF THE WJTCA–R

The twenty-one WJTCA–R tests are briefly described in Table 1. The tests are organized into separate standard and supplemental batteries that are each contained in separate easel test books that include the test items and administration and scoring instructions. Some of the WJTCA–R materials differ from other individually administered intelligence batteries by not requiring the use of concrete materials that must be manipulated by the examinee. The intellectual abilities typically measured by manipulable materials (i.e., visual–spatial ability) are measured by visual stimuli presented in the test easels. The WJTCA–R also includes prerecorded audiotapes that ensure accurate administration of two standard and five supplemental tests. When combined with the achievement battery, the WJTCA–R comprises one portion of the assessment structure presented in Figure 1.

The four major interpretive components of the WJTCA–R, as well as the subcomponents presented in Figure 1, are based on combinations of two or more individual tests. Each component listed under the rubrics Broad Cognitive Abilities, Cognitive Factors, and Differential Aptitudes in Figure 1 is referred to as a "cluster," the intended level of interpretation. The clusters are based on various combinations of the WJTCA–R tests and thus minimize the danger of overgeneralizing from a single, narrow sample of behavior (i.e., individual test) to a broad ability. In addition to providing information regarding a person's relative standing in a group (i.e., percentile ranks and standard scores) on the tests and clusters, the WJTCA–R provides information regarding a person's quality of performance (i.e., relative mastery, instructional ranges) and level of development (i.e., age and grade equivalent) for individual tests and clusters.

Broad Cognitive Abilities. The WJTCA–R includes three Broad Cognitive Ability cluster options for measuring a person's general level of intellectual functioning. The Broad Cognitive Ability–Extended cluster is the broadest measure of an individual's general intellectual ability and is based on fourteen cognitive tests (two tests from each of the seven Horn-Cattell Gf–Gc abilities measured by the WJTCA–R). The Broad Cognitive Ability–Standard cluster consists of one test of each of the seven Horn-Cattell Gf–Gc abilities measured by the WJTCA–R. The Broad Cognitive Ability–Early Development cluster consists of five cognitive tests and is intended for use with preschool children, although it can also be used with low-functioning individuals of any age.

Cognitive Factors. The WJTCA–R Cognitive Factor clusters are designed to measure seven of the abilities described in the Horn-Cattell model of the Gf–Gc theory of intelligence. (An eighth Gf–Gc cluster, Quantitative Abilities, is available in the achievement section of the WJ–R battery.) A brief description of the WJTCA–R's operational measures of seven Horn-Cattell Gf–Gc abilities is presented in Table 2. Each of the Gf–Gc factor clusters consists of two tests of each ability as determined through factor-analytic studies (see FACTOR ANALYSIS). Performance on the seven Gf–Gc cognitive clusters can be used to develop hypotheses about a person's pattern of intellectual strengths and weaknesses. In addition, a special five-test Oral Language cluster is provided.

Differential Aptitudes. The Differential Aptitude component distinguishes the WJTCA–R from all other individually administered batteries of intelligence. Each of these five clusters is based on the statistically derived combination of four cognitive tests that best predicted reading, mathematics, written language, knowledge, and oral language skills across the age range assessed by the WJTCA–R. The differential aptitude clusters are specialized intelligence measures for predicting a person's achievement in reading, mathematics, written language, knowledge, and oral language. When combined with the appropriate WJ–R achievement clusters (see Figure 1), these clusters help to determine the extent to which a person is achieving in relation to the expectations based on their measured aptitude. The WJTCA–R is the only individually administered intelligence battery that recognizes that individuals have different levels of aptitude for achieving in oral language, reading, writing, mathematics, and the acquisition of general knowledge.

Psychoeducational Discrepancies. Two types of psychoeducational discrepancy information can be derived from the WJTCA–R (Figure 1). Comparisons can be made between predicted achievement (based on broad cognitive ability or differential aptitudes) and

TABLE 1
Description of the individual WJTCA–R tests

WJTCA–R Test	Description
Standard Battery (Tests 1–7)	
Memory for Names (*Glr*)	Measures the ability to learn associations between unfamiliar auditory and visual stimuli through a controlled learning task.
Memory for Sentences (*Gsm*)	Measures the ability to remember and repeat simple words, phrases, and sentences presented auditorially.
Visual Matching (*Gs*)	Measures the ability to locate rapidly (timed test) and circle 2 identical numbers from a row of numbers.
Incomplete Words (*Ga*)	Measures the ability to name a complete word after hearing a recording of the word with one or more missing phonemes.
Visual Closure (*Gv*)	Measures the ability to name a picture or drawing of an object that is altered or distorted in one of several ways.
Picture Vocabulary (*Gc*)	Measures the ability to name pictured objects.
Analysis-Synthesis (*Gf*)	Measures the ability to analyze the parts of an incomplete logic puzzle and name the missing part during a controlled learning task.
Supplemental Battery (Tests 8–14)	
Visual–Auditory Learning (*Glr*)	Measures the ability to learn associations between new visual symbols and familiar words and to translate them into verbal sentences during a controlled task.
Memory for Words (*Gsm*)	Measures the ability to repeat lists of unrelated words in sequence that are presented auditorially.
Cross Out (*Gs*)	Measures the ability to scan rapidly (timed test) and compare visual figures by marking 5 identical figures in a row of 20.
Sound Blending (*Ga*)	Measures the ability to integrate and speak whole words that are presented auditorially in parts.
Picture Recognition (*Gv*)	Measures the ability to recognize a subset of previously presented figures within a larger set of figures.
Oral Vocabulary (*Gc*)	Measures knowledge of word meanings through antonyms and synonyms.
Concept Formation (*Gf*)	Measures categorical reasoning based on principles of logic during a controlled learning task.
Supplemental Battery (Tests 15–21)	
Delayed Recall—Memory for Names (*Glr*)	Measures the ability to recall, after 1–8 days, the visual–auditory associations learned during Memory for Names.
Delayed Recall—Visual–Auditory Learning (*Glr*)	Measures the ability to recall, after 1–8 days, the visual–auditory associations learned during Visual–Auditory Learning.

WJTCA–R Test	*Description*
Numbers Reversed (*Gsm/Gf*)	Measures the ability to repeat in reverse order a series of random numbers presented auditorially.
Sound Patterns (*Ga/Gf*)	Measures the ability to discriminate between complex sound patterns.
Spatial Relations (*Gv/Gf*)	Measures the ability to match shapes visually.
Listening Comprehension (*Gc*)	Measures the ability to listen to a short passage and then provide the single word missing at the end of the passage.
Verbal Analogies (*Gc/Gf*)	Measures the ability to complete phrases with words that indicate appropriate analogies.

NOTE: Abbreviations indicate the classification of the individual tests according to the Horn-Cattell model of the *Gf–Gc* theory of intelligence.

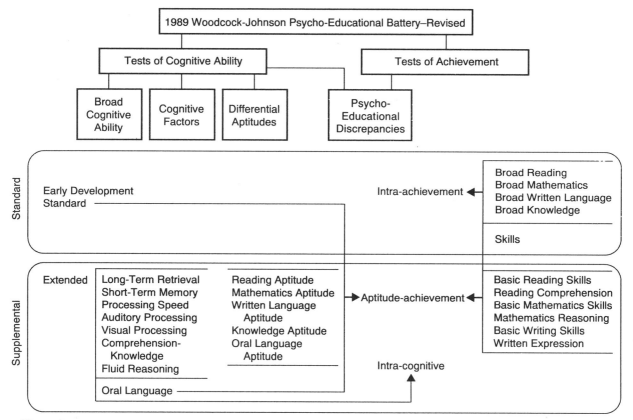

Figure 1

Assessment structure of the Woodcock-Johnson Psycho-Educational Battery–Revised

SOURCE: McGrew, K. S. (1994). *Clinical Interpretation of the Woodcock-Johnson Tests of Cognitive Ability–Revised.* Boston: Allyn & Bacon. Reprinted by permission.

TABLE 2
Description of the WJTCA–R clusters

WJTCA–R Cluster Name	Gf-Gc Symbol	Cluster Description
Fluid Reasoning	Gf	A combination of the Analysis–Synthesis and Concept Formation tests that measures the ability to reason, form concepts, and solve problems, often with unfamiliar information or procedures.
Comprehension–Knowledge	Gc	A combination of the Picture and Oral Vocabulary tests that measures a person's breadth and depth of verbal knowledge.
Visual Processing	Gv	A combination of the Visual Closure and Picture Recognition tests that measures the ability to analyze and synthesize nonlinguistic visual stimuli.
Auditory Processing	Ga	A combination of the Incomplete Words and Sound Blending tests that measures the ability to analyze and synthesize auditory–linguistic stimuli.
Processing Speed	Gs	A combination of the Visual Matching and Cross Out tests that measures the ability to perform automatic cognitive tasks rapidly, especially when under pressure to maintain concentration.
Short-Term Memory	Gsm	A combination of the Memory for Sentences and Memory for Words tests that measures the ability to store verbal information temporarily and then use it within a few seconds.
Long-Term Retrieval	Glr	A combination of the Memory for Names and Visual–Auditory Learning tests that measures the ability to store information and retrieve it later through association.

NOTE: The *Gf–Gc* symbols correspond to abilities included in the Horn-Cattell model of the *Gf–Gc* theory of intelligence.

actual achievement as measured by the WJ–R achievement clusters. This comparison provides information regarding an individual's aptitude–achievement discrepancies that can be compared against provided discrepancy norms. Intracognitive discrepancy norms are provided to quantify the degree of strengths and/or weaknesses present in an individual's intelligence-test profile.

DEVELOPMENT AND TECHNICAL CHARACTERISTICS

The development of the WJTCA–R followed a thorough process that addressed the major criteria established for the development of educational and psychological tests (American Psychological Association, 1985; McGrew, Werder, & Woodcock, 1991). The concepts of LATENT TRAIT THEORY were used exten-

sively during the development and analysis of the test's items.

Norm Sample. An individual's performance on the WJTCA–R can be compared against others of the same age (age norms) or grade (grade norms) based on the 6,359 individuals who were tested during the test's STANDARDIZATION. The norming subjects were selected to be representative of the population of the United States by gathering data in more than 100 communities, based on the 1980 U.S. Census. Representativeness of the norming sample was achieved by controlling for five characteristics of individuals (i.e., sex, race, Hispanic origin, occupation, and education of adults) and fifteen characteristics of the communities (i.e., location, size, and thirteen community socioeconomic variables). The preschool sample consisted of 705 subjects, the kindergarten-to-twelfth-grade sample consisted of 3,245 subjects, the college and university sample consisted of 916 subjects, and the adult nonschool sample consisted of 1,493 subjects. The standardization sample is large and technically sound.

Reliability. The extent to which the WJTCA–R scores are free of errors of measurement (RELIABILITY) varies according to the breadth of the measures. The average reliability coefficients for the individual tests range from .72 to .94, with most being in the .80–.90 range. These levels of reliability correspond favorably to those for the individual tests of other individually administered intelligence batteries. The average reliability coefficients for the seven *Gf–Gc* cognitive clusters range from .82 to .95. The average reliability for the eight clusters typically used for making critical clinical or educational decisions (i.e., three Broad Cognitive Ability and five Scholastic Aptitude clusters) are all in the mid .90s. The average reliabilities for the Broad Cognitive Ability and Scholastic Aptitude clusters meet or exceed the minimal levels typically recommended for measures used for making important decisions about individuals.

Validity. Extensive data regarding the usefulness of specific inferences that can be made from the WJTCA–R scores (i.e., VALIDITY) has been reported by K. S. McGrew, J. K. Werder, and R. W. Woodcock (1991) and Woodcock (1990). Correlations between the WJTCA–R Standard and Extended Broad Cognitive Ability clusters and full scale scores from the KAUFMAN ASSESSMENT BATTERY FOR CHILDREN, MCCARTHY SCALES OF CHILDREN'S ABILITIES, STANFORD-BINET INTELLIGENCE SCALE–FOURTH EDITION, Wechsler Adult Intelligence Scale–revised, and Wechsler Intelligence Scale for Children–Revised (see WECHSLER SCALES OF INTELLIGENCE) have been reported. The correlations are similar to those typically reported between individually administered intelligence tests (ranging from the .60s to .70s).

The WJTCA–R Scholastic Aptitude clusters demonstrate average correlations in the .60s and .70s with measures of academic achievement. The correlations between the WJTCA–R Scholastic Aptitude clusters and a variety of reading, mathematics, writing, and knowledge achievement tests find the Scholastic Aptitude clusters to be stronger predictors of academic achievement than the WJTCA–R Broad Cognitive Ability clusters and the full scale scores from other

individually administered intelligence batteries (McGrew, Werder, and Woodcock, 1991).

The validity of the seven Horn-Cattell *Gf–Gc* cognitive clusters has been established through a network of research (McGrew, Werder, and Woodcock, 1991; Woodcock, 1990). Different rates of change for the seven WJTCA–R *Gf–Gc* cluster scores as a function of age (i.e., growth curves) and different relationships between the cognitive clusters and different aspects of academic achievement support the WJTCA–R cognitive clusters as measures of distinct abilities. Validity evidence has also been reported in the form of significant correlations with measures of specialized abilities and the differential performance of individuals with different exceptionalities (e.g., mental retardation, learning disabilities, giftedness) on the WJTCA–R clusters.

Extensive analyses of the patterns of relationships (factor analysis) among the WJTCA–R tests by themselves and in combination with tests from the Kaufman Assessment Battery for Children, Stanford-Binet Intelligence Scale–Fourth Edition, Wechsler Adult Intelligence Scale–Revised, and Wechsler Intelligence Scale for Children–Revised support the *Gf–Gc* interpretation of the WJTCA–R tests and clusters. The WJTCA–R tests that measure the Horn-Cattell *Gf–Gc* abilities of visual processing, processing speed, short-term memory, and fluid and crystallized intelligence were found to correlate, or load on, the same factors with measures of the same abilities in the other intelligence batteries. The joint analyses with other intelligence tests indicate that the WJTCA–R is the only individually administered intelligence battery to provide measures of the Horn-Cattell *Gf–Gc* factors of auditory processing and long-term storage and retrieval.

CONCLUSION

The WJTCA–R is a collection of twenty-one individual tests embedded within a larger assessment battery that includes measures of academic achievement. The WJTCA–R is a psychometrically sound battery of tests that was standardized on a large nationally representative sample of individuals from early childhood to late adulthood. Individuals who use the WJTCA–R or the complete WJ–R battery "can feel confident that the norms, reliability, and validity characteristics are comparable to, or better than, those of other measures of intellectual and academic ability" (McGhee & Buckhalt, 1993, p. 149). The WJTCA–R is unique among intelligence batteries in that it can be organized and interpreted from a theoretical model of intelligence as well as from a pragmatic decision-making perspective.

BIBLIOGRAPHY

AMERICAN PSYCHOLOGICAL ASSOCIATION (1985). *Standards for educational and psychological testing.* Washington, DC: Author.

CARROLL, J. B. (1993). *Human cognitive abilities: A survey of factor-analytic studies.* New York: Cambridge University Press.

HESSLER, G. L. (1982). *Use and interpretation of the Woodcock-Johnson Psycho-Educational Battery.* Chicago: Riverside.

KAUFMAN, A. S. (1985). Review of the Woodcock-Johnson Psycho-educational Battery. In J. F. Mitchell (Ed.), *The ninth mental measurements yearbook* (pp. 1762–1765). Lincoln: University of Nebraska Press.

KAUFMAN, A. S. (1990). *Assessing adolescent and adult intelligence.* Boston: Allyn & Bacon.

MCGHEE, R. L., & BUCKHALT, J. A. (1993). Test review: Woodcock-Johnson Psycho-Educational Battery–Revised. *Journal of Psychoeducational Assessment: Advances in Psychoeducational Assessment Monograph Series.*

MCGREW, K. S. (1986). *Clinical interpretation of the Woodcock-Johnson tests of cognitive ability.* Boston: Allyn & Bacon.

MCGREW, K. S., WERDER, J. K., & WOODCOCK, R. W. (1991). *WJ–R technical manual.* Chicago: Riverside.

RESCHLY, D. J. (1990). Found: Our intelligences: What do they mean? *Journal of Psychoeducational Assessment, 8,* 259–267.

WOODCOCK, R. W. (1978). *Development and standardization of the Woodcock-Johnson Psycho-Educational Battery.* Chicago: Riverside.

WOODCOCK, R. W. (1990). Theoretical foundations of the WJ–R measures of cognitive ability. *Journal of Psychoeducational Assessment, 8,* 231–258.

WOODCOCK, R. W., & JOHNSON, M. B. (1977). *Woodcock-Johnson Psycho-Educational Battery.* Chicago: Riverside.

WOODCOCK, R. W., & JOHNSON, M. B. (1989). *Woodcock-Johnson Psycho-Educational Battery–Revised.* Chicago: Riverside.

YSSELDYKE, J. E. (1990). Goodness of fit of the Woodcock-Johnson Psycho-Educational Battery–Revised to the Horn-Cattell *gf–gc* theory. *Journal of Psychological Assessment, 8,* 268–275.

KEVIN S. MCGREW

WORK FORCE, INTELLIGENCE IN THE

Most adults have taken multiple psychometric tests over their lifetimes, and their performance altered the probability of their having access to a variety of opportunities. Among the most common psychometric tests are those designed to measure mental ability or scholastic aptitude. For years, psychometric ability tests were administered routinely to all children for the purpose of grouping them on the basis of their ability, although this practice has declined in recent years. Currently, ability tests are widely used to qualify children with learning problems for special-education services and to identify gifted children for enrichment programs. They are used in deciding whom to admit to selective colleges (e.g., SCHOLASTIC ASSESSMENT TESTS) and to advanced degree and professional programs (such as the Graduate Record Exams, Medical College Admission Test, and the General Management Aptitude Test) and in steering young adults into career paths they are likely to be successful in.

Ability tests also have a long history of use in the workplace, particularly in selecting whom to hire. The use of psychometric testing for hiring decisions has been, and remains, a controversial endeavor. Proponents argue that such testing results in substantial economic benefits to society by enabling organizations to select the most able workers at a time when global competitiveness is becoming increasingly essential to the survival of industries. Opponents counter that such testing is unfair to minority-group members at a time when the proportion of minority-group members in the workplace and job-applicant pool is rising steadily in industrialized countries such as the United States. The controversy over psychometric testing for hiring decisions is unlikely to be settled in the foreseeable future. Nevertheless, a great deal is now known about the likely benefits and limitations. This knowledge will be reviewed here by first considering the question of how valid psychometric tests are when used as predictors of workplace performance. Then, the proposed advantages and disadvantages of using psychometric ability tests for selecting whom to hire will be considered, and some political and social policy ramifications of this issue will be mentioned.

PSYCHOMETRIC TESTS AS PREDICTORS OF PERFORMANCE

Perhaps the most important question that can be asked about a test is its validity for a particular use, such as selecting salespersons to work at a local car dealership. A valid test for selecting car salespersons measures what it purports to, and what it measures is related to, and predictive of, sales performance. Views about how valid psychometric tests are as predictors of workplace performance range from quite optimistic (Hunter & Schmidt, 1983) to quite pessimistic (Mc-Clelland, 1973).

One way to examine the question of how valid psychometric tests are for predicting JOB PERFORMANCE is to consider how accurately workplace performance can be predicted by knowing psychometric-test scores. If psychometric tests were completely valid predictors of workplace performance, one could predict with perfect accuracy how well job applicants would perform in the workplace by knowing their psychometric ability scores. In this case, 100 percent of the variability in job performance across workers could be explained or accounted for by knowledge of their psychometric ability scores. Alternatively, if psychometric tests were completely invalid predictors of workplace performance, then knowing the psychometric ability scores of job applicants would be useless information, because their test scores would be unrelated to their job performance. In this case, zero percent of the variability in job performance across workers could be explained or accounted for by knowledge of their psychometric ability scores.

In studies of how well psychometric-test scores predict workplace performance, the key statistic reported is called a "validity coefficient," just a fancy name for the correlation coefficient between test performance and job performance. The square of a validity coefficient indicates the percentage of variability in job performance that can be accounted for or explained by variability in test scores. Across a large number of studies, the average validity coefficient between psychometric ability-test scores and job perfor-

mance is about .2 (Wigdor & Garner, 1982). The square of this value indicates that only about 4 percent of the variability in job performance can be attributed to variability in psychometric ability-test scores. Obviously, although 4 percent is better than nothing, it is far from the ideal of accounting for a full 100 percent of the variability in job performance. How, then, does this result square with the view that psychometric ability tests have substantial validity for all jobs?

The average validity coefficient of .2 underestimates the true VALIDITY of psychometric ability-test scores for predicting job performance for two reasons. First, studies of relations between test scores and job performance necessarily rely on employees as subjects rather than job applicants, even though it is the validity of the test when used with job applicants that is of interest. This is because measures of job performance are available for employees but not for job applicants. But if only high-scoring job applicants are hired and if test scores predict job performance, then a sample of employees will show less variability in test scores and in job performance than would a sample of job applicants if they were hired without regard to their test scores. This situation is referred to as "restriction of range," and the size of validity coefficients is reduced by restricted variability in test scores and job performance. Second, few studies measure actual job performance, but rather must rely on such indirect measures as supervisor ratings. Supervisor ratings are not perfectly reliable or accurate, and this also serves to reduce the size of obtained validity coefficients. Validity coefficients appear to be higher for work samples than for ratings of performance (Nathan & Alexander, 1988).

When statistical adjustments are made to estimate the validity of psychometric ability tests for predicting job performance that would obtain if there were no restriction of range and if supervisor ratings were perfectly accurate, the average estimated validity coefficient falls in the range 0.3–0.5, which means that roughly 10–25 percent of job performance can be explained or accounted for by psychometric ability-test scores. These adjusted validity coefficients probably overestimate the actual validity of psychometric ability tests for predicting job performance. For example, validity coefficients, whether adjusted or unadjusted, ignore the existence of other, correlated predictors of job performance (Hartigan & Wigdor, 1989). Consequently, the validity coefficients overestimate the amount of predictive validity that is uniquely attributable to psychometric ability-test scores, as opposed to some other related variable. For a second example, D. C. McClelland (1973) suggested that supervisor ratings may be biased in a way that inflates validity coefficients. He argued that supervisors, who, on average, tend to be white, male, and relatively high in socioeconomic status, are likely to give higher performance ratings to workers who share their socioeconomic status and lower ratings to workers who do not. Lower socioeconomic status is associated with lower performance on psychometric ability tests, and so, if McClelland is correct, validity coefficients between psychometric ability-test scores and job performance ratings will be inflated because of their joint association with socioeconomic status. It is difficult to address this question empirically, because many jobs (for example, business manager) have no more-direct measures of job performance to be used to check out the accuracy of supervisor ratings. For jobs in which direct measures of job performance are available, such as gross monthly sales for salespersons, decisions often are based on the direct measures of job performance, which obviates the need for obtaining supervisor ratings.

Evidence used to support the belief that psychometric ability-test scores are valid for all jobs, as opposed to only some jobs, comes from quantitative reviews of large numbers of studies (meta-analysis). These results suggest that the observed variability in validity coefficients from one study to the next is no greater than that expected on the basis of chance alone (Schmidt & Hunter, 1981). A closer examination of the methods used to make this determination indicated that the method is very insensitive and unlikely to detect variability in validity coefficients if it existed (Drasgow, 1982).

In all likelihood, the true validity of psychometric ability-test scores for predicting job performance is at a level at which more than 4 percent but less than 25 percent of the variability in job performance is explained or accounted for by variability in test scores. Whether such test scores are more valid for some jobs and less so or even invalid for others remains an open question until such time as more sensitive methods can be applied to this question.

USING PSYCHOMETRIC ABILITY TESTING FOR HIRING

Procedures for selecting whom to hire ideally ought to be mutually and substantially beneficial to potential employees and employers alike. Failure to thrive in a job as a result of an inability or unwillingness to do what is required is costly to both parties in time, money, and the psychological pain that inevitably accompanies poor performance. How closely do existing practices that employ psychometric ability tests approach this ideal?

Advantages of Testing for Hiring. An advantage to potential employees of using psychometric ability testing for hiring is opening up access to jobs for able applicants that might have been closed otherwise. At one time, getting into an Ivy League college depended largely on family background, connections, and wealth, which barred the majority of Americans who lacked these credentials from access. Admission criteria evolved over the years as rising endowments and federal assistance made it economically feasible to admit students almost entirely on an assessment of their ability to succeed, without regard to their economic circumstances. Because applicants outnumber available seats, the majority of Americans still do not have access to Ivy League schools, but at least now it is possible for a very bright high school senior whose family has little wealth and no prior connections to be admitted.

The same argument applies to hiring decisions. For example, government jobs often compare quite favorably to similar private-sector jobs in terms of salary, benefits, and job security. Getting a job as a U.S. Postal Service employee in Peoria or as a fireman in Miami depends largely on scores on civil service exams and previous employment record, rather than on an applicant's ties to the political power structures in these cities. Although far from perfect, the hiring decisions made on the basis of objective criteria such as test scores improve access to jobs by potential employees, relative to the alternatives of patronage or nepotism. In small, privately held businesses it is not unusual for jobs to be doled out to members of the owner's immediate or extended family.

How advantageous it is for employers to use psychometric ability testing for hiring decisions depends not only on the test's validity but also on other aspects of the hiring situation, such as selectivity in hiring. For some jobs, nearly everyone possesses enough mental ability to do the job, and a large proportion of applicants will be hired. Under these conditions, psychometric ability scores will be of little use. Other personal characteristics, such as dependability and integrity, and job history may prove much more important. For other jobs, the demands on mental ability are much greater, and only a relatively small percentage of the general population can do the job. Under these conditions, only a small fraction of applicants will be hired, and psychometric ability scores will be of greater use.

An important potential advantage to employers of using psychometric ability testing for hiring is savings in personnel costs (Hunter & Schmidt, 1983; Ree & Earles, 1992). If test performance is related to job performance, then selecting high-scoring employees ought to result in higher-performing employees than would be the case if a test were not used. If higher-performing employees can accomplish the same amount of work as a larger number of average employees, then fewer employees can accomplish the same amount of work, which results in savings in personnel costs. (This assumes, of course, that a high-performing worker who might accomplish the work of two average workers will not be given double their salary.)

A formula provided by H. E. Brogden (1946) can be used to estimate the potential savings in dollar amounts. Estimates of such savings have been as high as $376 million over ten years if the federal government would use an IQ test to select computer programmers (Schmidt et al., 1979) to $80 billion per year for the economy as a whole if the General Aptitude Test Battery (GATB) were administered to all applicants for jobs with employers using the U.S. Employment Service (Hunter & Schmidt, 1982). (The GATB is a psychometric ability test that was developed by the U.S. Department of Labor to be used by the U.S. Employment Service, an agency that screens nearly 20 million individuals per year for public- and private-

sector jobs.) Such estimates appear to be inflated and unlikely to be realized in practice (Hartigan & Wigdor, 1989). Some reasons for this assessment are that the savings estimates are compared to a baseline of random selection, even though random selection is rarely, if ever, practiced (Hunter & Schmidt, 1983); the estimates ignore that within communities and the country as a whole hiring is a zero-sum game in that if one company corners the market on promising rocket scientists, the promising candidates will not be available to other companies and, as a result, gains for some companies are offset by losses for others (Hartigan & Wigdor, 1989); and the estimates ignore the economic and social costs of adverse impact, a disadvantage of using psychometric ability testing for hiring.

Using the identical formula to estimate personnel savings that J. E. Hunter and F. L. Schmidt used to obtain their estimate of $80 billion in savings, but with figures it considered to be more realistic, the National Research Council reported personnel-savings estimates in the range $1.5 billion to $10 billion (Hartigan & Wigdor, 1989). Although much less than the previous estimate of $80 billion, this still represented a considerable amount of money. The National Research Council cautioned that it is unreasonable to believe that the economy as a whole would save this amount or that the gross national product would rise by this amount. The reason for pessimism about total savings is the previously mentioned problem of gains for one company necessarily being offset by losses for another. In the present example, use of the GATB will not improve the competence of the labor force as a whole. If the GATB is used routinely by the Employment Service, employers who get their workers through the Employment Service indeed get more competent workers, but employers not using the Employment Service necessarily will have to choose from the remaining, less competent workers. One might think that the way to get around this is for all employers to get their workers through the Employment Service. But here again, there can be no overall savings for all employers, because use of the GATB will not increase the competence of the labor force as a whole.

Disadvantages of Testing for Hiring. A primary disadvantage of using psychometric ability testing for hiring is the potential for adverse impact, which for present purposes is defined as using a selection procedure that unfairly affects a group of individuals. Fairness and bias in testing are complicated topics for which many controversial issues remain to be resolved. In general, psychometrists have adopted the classical criterion that a test is fair if a given test score predicts the same level of job performance for majority- and minority-group members. Thus, selection bias is described in the *Standards for Educational and Psychological Testing* (American Educational Research Association et al., 1985, p. 12) as follows: "There is differential prediction, and there may be selection bias, if different algorithms (e.g., regression lines) are derived for different groups and if the predictions lean to decisions regarding people from the individual groups that are systematically different from those decisions obtained from the algorithm based on the pooled groups."

In general, the research literature suggests that differences in prediction across groups are small, although they can occur. For example, the National Research Council (Hartigan & Wigdor, 1989) examined seventy-two studies of relations between scores on the GATB and supervisor ratings of job performance in which there were at least fifty minority-group employees and fifty majority-group employees. The correlation for majority-group employees was .19, which fits nicely with the average validity coefficient of .20 reported previously. For African-American employees, the correlation was just .12. An examination of the results of using GATB scores to predict supervisor ratings indicated a small but reliable difference in favor of scores being more predictive of majority-group performance than of minority-group performance.

Regardless of whether differences in accuracy of prediction exist for majority- and minority-group members, adverse impact can occur under typical circumstances when psychometric ability tests are used for hiring. Assume that a test is fair by virtue of the fact that for any given test score, the predicted level of job performance is the same for majority- and minority-group members. Assume further that test performance favors majority-group members by one standard deviation (a measure of variability that corresponds to 15 points on an IQ test), which it typically

does, and that the correlation between test performance and job performance is .25. Finally, assume that a cutoff score is used that would select the top half (that is, those scoring above average) of majority-group members. Under these realistic conditions, only 16 percent of minority-group members would be hired, yet fully 40 percent are expected to perform above the majority-group mean in job performance itself (Hunter & Hunter, 1984; Thorndike, 1971).

This discrepancy is caused by the fact that the majority and minority groups differ more on test performance than on predicted job performance, which will occur under realistic assumptions as long as the correlation between test scores and job performance is less than 1. The size of the discrepancy is determined primarily by the size of the correlation between test scores and job performance. If test scores perfectly predict job performance (that is, if the correlation is 1) and test performance still favors the majority group by one standard deviation, then only 16 percent of minority-group members will be hired but only 16 percent of minority-group members will perform above the majority-group members' average in job performance, reducing the discrepancy to 0. If job performance is unrelated to test scores (that is, if the correlation is 0), then only 16 percent of minority-group members will be selected, even though fully 50 percent will perform above the majority-group members' average in job performance. Unfortunately, as noted previously, typical correlations between test scores and job performance are nearer to 0 than to 1. The resultant discrepancy between the percentage of minority-group members who meet the test cutoff score and the percentage who would meet the intended level of job performance if hired is adverse impact.

The troublesome dilemma about using psychometric ability tests for hiring is that widespread usage maximizes both the positive outcome of savings in personnel costs associated with hiring the most productive workers and the negative outcome of adverse impact for minority-group members, relatively few of whom will be hired. What is required are strategies for maximizing the economic benefits and minimizing the social costs. Two such strategies will be mentioned.

The first strategy is to use test scores to order job candidates within Caucasian, African-American, and

Hispanic groups, and then to hire from the top down in each group in numbers that are comparable to the make up of the job-applicant pool (Schmidt, Ones, & Hunter, 1992). This strategy maintains most of the economic benefits and eliminates the kind of adverse impact discussed here. Yet, the strategy effectively is a quota system, and quota systems have been successfully challenged in the United States and some other countries on the grounds of reverse discrimination. The cutoff score for majority-group members typically will be higher than that for minority-group members, and it will be the case that some majority-group members will not be hired who would have performed better than some minority-group members who are hired. Unfortunately, given imperfect tests, there is no possible way to be completely fair to both minority- and majority-group applicants.

In view of this dilemma, a second strategy for maximizing economic benefits and minimizing adverse impact is to improve the accuracy of prediction: "If we could find predictors . . . other than ability to add to the prediction supplied by ability tests, then we could simultaneously increase validity and decrease adverse impact" (Hunter & Hunter, 1984, p. 74). Recall that with perfect accuracy of prediction, adverse impact is eliminated and the economic benefits associated with hiring the best applicants are maximized. Examples of predictors other than psychometric ability tests that are currently being examined include measures of practical intelligence or common sense (Wagner & Sternberg, 1991), various personality measures, biographical data, and structured interviews (Schmidt, Ones, & Hunter, 1992). Surprisingly few studies have looked at multiple predictors of job performance, but the few that have support the feasibility of this strategy. The large-scale U.S. Army selection and classification project (Project A) indicated that the service could improve its prediction of job performance by combining noncognitive and cognitive predictors (McHenry et al., 1990), and a study of business managers carried out at the Center for Creative Leadership indicated that performance in a realistic problem-solving simulation was best predicted by a combination of a measure of practical intelligence, a measure of verbal ability, and selected personality scales (Wagner & Sternberg, 1990).

CONCLUSION

Psychometric ability-test scores appear to account uniquely for more than 4 percent but less than 25 percent of variability in job performance. Whether the validity of test scores varies for different jobs remains an open question until more-sensitive studies can be carried out. How useful psychometric ability-test scores are for hiring decisions depends not only on the test's validity but also on characteristics of the hiring situation, such as the percentage of applicants who will be hired.

Advantages of using psychometric ability-test scores for hiring include greater access to jobs for able applicants that might otherwise have been closed and savings in personnel costs, although the amount of such potential savings is open to disagreement. A primary disadvantage of using psychometric ability-test scores for hiring is adverse impact for minority-group members, which is likely to occur even for tests that are considered to be fair predictors of performance.

By ranking applicants on the basis of psychometric ability-test scores and hiring from the top down within racial or ethnic groups in proportions that compare to their representation in the applicant population, adverse impact is eliminated for minority-group members, with little cost in the overall utility of the test. This strategy is likely to result in adverse impact for majority-group members in that some majority-group applicants who are not hired would have performed better than some minority-group applicants who were hired. Given the imperfect validities of current psychometric ability tests for predicting job performance, this dilemma is inescapable.

The best long-range solution appears to be to supplement psychometric ability-test scores with other predictors that combine to predict job performance more accurately. As accuracy of prediction improves, adverse impact is reduced for everyone and the usefulness of the selection battery for hiring increases.

(*See also:* INDIVIDUAL TESTS.)

BIBLIOGRAPHY

BROGDEN, H. E. (1946). On the interpretation of the correlation coefficient as a measure of predictive efficiency. *Journal of Educational Psychology, 2,* 171–183.

DRASGOW, F. (1982). Biased test items and differential validity. *Psychological Bulletin, 92,* 526–531.

HARTIGAN, J. A., & WIGDOR, A. K. (EDS.). (1989). *Fairness in employment testing: Validity generalization, minority issues, and the General Aptitude Test Battery.* Washington, DC: National Academy Press.

HUNTER, J. E., & HUNTER, R. F. (1984). Validity and utility of alternative predictors of job performance. *Psychological Bulletin, 96,* 72–98.

HUNTER, J. E., & SCHMIDT, F. L. (1982). The economic benefits of personnel selection using psychological ability tests. *Industrial Relations, 21,* 293–308.

HUNTER, J. E., & SCHMIDT, F. L. (1983). Quantifying the effects of psychological interventions on employee job performance and work-force productivity. *American Psychologist, 38,* 473–478.

MCCLELLAND, D. C. (1973). Testing for competence rather than for "intelligence." *American Psychologist, 28,* 1–14.

MCHENRY, J. J., HOUGH, L. M., TOQUAM, J. L., HANSON, M. A., & ASHWORTH, S. (1990). Project A validity results: The relationship between predictor and criterion domains. *Personnel Psychology, 43,* 335–353.

NATHAN, B. R., & ALEXANDER, R. A. (1988). A comparison of criteria for test validation: A meta-analytic investigation. *Personnel Psychology, 41,* 517–535.

REE, M. J., & EARLES, J. A. (1992). Intelligence is the best predictor of job performance. *Current Directions, 1,* 86–89.

SCHMIDT, F. L., & HUNTER, J. E. (1981). Employment testing: Old theories and new research findings. *American Psychologist, 36,* 1128–1137.

SCHMIDT, F. L., HUNTER, J. E., MCKENZIE, R. C., & MULDROW, T. (1979). The impact of valid selection procedures on work force productivity. *Journal of Applied Psychology, 64,* 609–626.

SCHMIDT, F. L., ONES, D. S., & HUNTER, J. E. (1992). Personnel selection. *Annual Review of Psychology, 43,* 627–670.

THORNDIKE, R. L. (1971). Concepts of culture-fairness. *Journal of Educational Measurement, 8,* 63–70.

WAGNER, R. K., & STERNBERG, R. J. (1990). Street smarts. In K. Clark & M. Clark (Eds.), *Measures of leadership* (pp. 493–504). Greensboro, NC: Center for Creative Leadership.

WAGNER, R. K., & STERNBERG, R. J. (1991). *The Tacit Knowledge Inventory for Managers (TKIM).* San Antonio, TX: The Psychological Corporation.

WIGDOR, A. K., & GARNER, W. R. (1982). *Ability testing: Uses, consequences, and controversies: Pt. 1. Report of the committee.* Washington, DC: National Academy Press.

RICHARD K. WAGNER
ZACK LOUKIDES

Y-Z

YERKES, ROBERT M. (1876–1956) Robert Mearns Yerkes was a comparative psychologist who influenced human intelligence testing more through his leadership in introducing group mental testing into the U.S. Army—as president of the American Psychological Association (APA) during World War I—than through his scientific investigations into animal and human intelligence. Appreciation of his wartime leadership, which was much more reluctant and contentious than the postwar success of group testing (or his own historical accounts) would suggest, requires an understanding of Yerkes's unconventional conception and methods of evaluating intelligence. This entry reviews Yerkes's career to recover some of the forgotten origins of "group intelligence" and multiple-choice testing, and to recall the ferment of diverse opinions that agitated the early years of modern mental testing. Although the kind of intelligence Yerkes wanted to test proved untestable, which made his wartime leadership as much a personal failure as it was a professional achievement, the story of his failure can be helpful in comprehending the kind of intelligence and style of testing that succeeded.

EARLY CAREER

Like many of his contemporaries in early professional intelligence testing, Yerkes grew up on a farm, departed it in adolescence, and joined the new, cosmopolitan society of academic professionals. Yerkes was born in Bucks County, Pennsylvania, the son of Silas Marshall Yerkes, a farmer of old but diminishing wealth, and Susanna Carrell. Yerkes's autobiography (1930) describes an ornery youngster who resembles the "somewhat dictatorial and headstrong" personality others witnessed in the adult (Angell, 1917). The boy was close to his religious mother, who hoped her son would enter the ministry, and rebellious against his practical, business-minded father: This was one source of the high-minded and uncompromising spirit Yerkes displayed in his later evangelism for secular science. Childhood experience with farm animals was the origin of Yerkes's later zoological interests, while friendship with the family's doctor (an uncle) initiated his lifelong interest in—and association with, though never a practice of—medicine.

Yerkes's formal education proceeded from an ungraded country schoolhouse to the State Normal School at West Chester, Pennsylvania, to Ursinus College (B.A., 1897), and to Harvard University (B.A., 1898; M.A., 1899; Ph.D., 1902). He discovered the excitement of laboratory work at Ursinus and decided not to attend medical school when a benefactor offered to pay tuition at Harvard. There Yerkes enrolled in the zoology courses of E. L. Mark, W. E. Castle, and Charles B. Davenport. The latter directed Yerkes's first published study, "Reaction of Entomostraca to Stimulation by Light," which described the "preferences"

(1899, p. 171) of small crustaceans for varying intensities of light. Despite Yerkes's preference for zoology, his first academic adviser was a philosopher, Josiah Royce, the leader of U.S. idealism. Royce persuaded Yerkes to take his Ph.D. in Harvard's philosophy department, which contained a psychology laboratory. Hugo Münsterberg, who lately had become more idealist in his own philosophy, supervised the laboratory and Yerkes's research of animal intelligence.

Animal Intelligence was the dissertation title of a recent Harvard graduate student, E. L. THORNDIKE, who had left Harvard for more supportive supervision of animal research at Columbia University. As an adherent to the conventional Anglo-American psychology of associationism, Thorndike believed animal and human intelligence originated in trial-and-error experience. He developed puzzle-box tests to demonstrate that cats were "stupid" automata and thus disprove the sympathetic anecdotes of preexperimental naturalists. Instructing Yerkes at the Woods Hole, Massachusetts, Marine Biological Laboratory during the summer of 1899, Thorndike greatly influenced Yerkes's ideas and methods of testing intelligence, not least by encouraging opposition to the conclusion of animal stupidity.

A paper originating from this summer, "The Formation of Habits in the Turtle," shows Yerkes's (1901) attempt to consider intelligence differently from Thorndike and as something preceding mere habit formation. It also shows the beginning of a lifelong inclination to anthropomorphize animal mental ability (Elder, 1977). Yerkes believed that the transition Thorndike had effected, from naturalist observations "in the field" to experimental examinations of animals in controlled laboratory settings, neutralized the effect of the researcher's subjective feelings. Therefore, Yerkes created a test that "baffled" the turtle and started it "meditating," if not making "inferences from judgments" (1901, pp. 523–524). Although he concluded this paper by toeing the associationist line, most of the article is concerned with the organism's inner "tendency" or capacity to "form habits," not with the influences of environment or habits per se. Yerkes suggested that new kinds of tests were necessary to meet the particular physiological conditions of various species before they could demonstrate reasoning. For example, while Thorndike's puzzle test had used animal hunger to motivate learning (as means to

the end of food), Yerkes developed a labyrinth test to provide the incentive turtles desired more often than food, namely, a dark warm nest.

After writing a dissertation on the sensory reaction of jellyfish, Yerkes became a Harvard instructor in 1902 and, upon publishing *The Dancing Mouse* in 1907, assistant professor. The monograph contained an innovative test of brightness discrimination, which encouraged mice to choose a white door over a black one (movable color cards prevented mere habituation to location). The test offered electric shocks as punishment to be averted, instead of food or shelter as rewards. Yerkes believed the discrimination test was more suitable for the whirling rodent and its "motor equipment" (1973a, p. 200) and produced more quantifiable results than the puzzle and labyrinth methods.

The Dancing Mouse is also notable for demonstrating change in Yerkes's definition of intelligence. Yerkes earlier (1905) equated intelligent consciousness with "docility," "modifiability," and Jacques Loeb's "ability to learn," which terms imply a passive or reactive kind of learning; Yerkes used "rational" to describe "initiative," or an active capacity for "sudden, apparently spontaneous, adaptation to the demands of situations" (pp. 143–146). Royce was responsible for the category names of docility and initiative, to which Yerkes assigned the more scientific terms of modifiability and variableness. In the mouse book, however, Yerkes defined intelligence as "insight" (1973a, p. 234), or an ability to discern and understand, but not with modifiability, which received separate discussion. Making matters ambiguous, however, he also equated intelligence with initiative, which resulted from individual differences. Yerkes created the brightness discrimination test to discover whether the dancing mice showed insight. They did not show insight; some showed initiative, but some also showed initiative on tests that measured mere ability to learn (e.g., a ladder-climbing test), which Yerkes no longer called intelligent.

Yerkes equated modifiability with "educability," and proposed that knowledge of mouse educability would help improve the teaching of humans. Although he did not elaborate the connection, its inclusion reflects Yerkes's recent educability in the academic environment. The Harvard administrations of C. W. Eliot and, after 1909, A. L. Lowell pressured Yerkes to humanize his research (O'Donnell, 1985), hoping that he would switch from animal to educational psychology as Thorndike had at Columbia. Although Yerkes showed willingness to accommodate his employers, he continued to see himself as an animal psychologist. Yerkes (1909) believed he had replaced Thorndike as the leader of experimental animal psychology and published a stern critique of Thorndike's methodology in the popular *Century Magazine*.

SHIFT TO HUMAN PSYCHOLOGY

Although Yerkes was not indifferent to the needs of human education and shared Thorndike's reformist hope for progress through eugenics (Davenport appointed them to the American Breeders Association's Committee on the Inheritance of Mental Traits in 1909), they held opposite views regarding whether intelligence was unitary or multifold. Thorndike (Thorndike, Lay, & Dean, 1909) rejected Charles SPEARMAN's (1904) theory of GENERAL INTELLIGENCE, also known as *g*, partly because he had left animal research to apply psychology to pedagogy and found the theory of *g* impracticable for assisting teachers in their evaluation of various student abilities. Yerkes's desire to demonstrate evolutionary progress, as if up a ladder of animal kingdom progress—from crustaceans to earthworms, to turtles, to mice, and so on—led him to assume intelligence was "general." While Thorndike's view of intelligence reflected the demands of the vocational environment for a schoolchild's accommodation, Yerkes's view increasingly emphasized the individual's capacity for ideas, which would allow control over environment.

More surprising than his association with the associationist Thorndike was Yerkes's collaboration with the archenvironmentalist John B. Watson, who developed Thorndike's puzzle tests and "laws of learning" into the movement known as behaviorism. Yerkes and Watson edited the *Journal of Animal Behavior* from 1911 to 1917 and *The Behavior Monographs* from 1913 to 1919. Of further irony, given Yerkes's preference for endogenous factors and his later "protest against . . . the cult of behaviorism" (Yerkes, 1973b, p. 381) was his priority in translating (Yerkes & Morgulis, 1909) and reporting Ivan Pavlov's reflex research with dogs.

Yerkes went further against the grain of Anglo-American associationism when he published his *Intro-duction to Psychology* (1911). The textbook advanced Wilhelm Wundt's notion of "psychic causation," which surprised even E. B. Titchener (1911), Wundt's main disciple in the United States. Leaving out the obligatory early chapters on physiology, Yerkes substituted advocacy of introspectionism. The extreme metaphysical position of "psychic causation" (at least in the United States) showed the effects of Royce and Münsterberg's idealism and the latter's repeated reminders to publish "human psychology" for the sake of further promotion. What went against the grain of conventional American psychology also worked to accommodate Yerkes's superiors, thus allowing the Harvard son to rebel and remain loyal at the same time.

Yerkes also humanized his psychology by counseling outpatients at the new Boston Psychopathic Hospital in 1912, while continuing to teach half-time. One of his courses was very humanistic, for which he (with Daniel La Rue, 1913) wrote *Outline of a Study of the Self*. This manual encouraged a crude form of introspection (as mere self-awareness) as it solicited pedigree information from Harvard undergraduates for Davenport's Eugenics Record Office. During the next two years, Yerkes created the *Point Scale for Measuring Mental Ability* (Yerkes, Bridges, & Hardwick, 1915) and quickly became a leader in the new field of mental testing.

The Point Scale differed from the prevailing style of intelligence diagnosis, the "mental age" scale of Alfred BINET's American followers, in format and purpose. The Point Scale required a trained observer to monitor a subject's performance on twenty tests and assign a maximum score of 100 points. The abstract quality of the score freed the instrument from bias, in Yerkes's opinion. Its purpose was implicit, however, in the assumption that all (English-speaking) humans could be measured on a unilinear scale from 0 to 100. Yerkes promised that the collection of norms for different racial, class, and gender groups would allow better understanding of an individual's intelligence, as the Point Scale allowed his or her score to be compared to the intelligence percentile range that could be expected of—or presumed for—the group or cross-section of groups to which the individual belonged. The Binet method, which Henry H. Goddard had translated in 1908, also required a trained observer to monitor performance on a series of tests, but its purpose was more evident in the method's scoring, which yielded (what purported to be) the subject's "mental age." This concept, a little more concrete than so many points on an abstract scale, derived from comparison of the subject's raw test score with the average scored by all others (who previously had taken the test) in his or her chronological age group. Yerkes (1917a) saw mental age as an artificial category testers had constructed for the needs of efficient school administration. Instead of having separate tests for each age group, Yerkes (Yerkes & Anderson, 1915) designed one test that could be given to all social classes, races, and genders under age 13, to demonstrate differential evolution by group according to (what he considered) natural categories.

When Lewis TERMAN produced the Stanford Revision of the Binet Scale in 1916, which offered the convenient IQ ratio and forms to measure intelligence through age 16, Yerkes revised the Point Scale to include ages 13–16 (Yerkes & Rossy, 1916). He and Terman competed for Rockefeller Foundation support of a national testing project, although neither agreed to unify their efforts, as the foundation suggested (while rejecting their separate requests). The rivalry led Yerkes to call for professional consensus on intelligence testing, and to presume that his Point Scale—not Terman's IQ test—would become the national standard ("Mentality Tests," 1916).

Simultaneously, Yerkes was developing the first so-called multiple-choice test, using psychopathic humans, crows, rats, and pigs as his first subjects. This was not the beginning of what became conventional paper-and-pencil multiple-choice testing for human consumption, although the human version may have borrowed its name from Yerkes's (Samelson, 1987). His multiple choice, following on his brightness discrimination test, required the test taker's discernment of a pattern chosen by the test giver. It tested for "ideational and allied types of behavior" (Yerkes, 1916a, p. 93). Using a set of twelve doors for animals—twelve keys for the more portable human model—the device allowed the experimenter to choose a directional template, for example, "leftmost" (as opposed to "middle" and "rightmost") before presenting various series of doors (such as every other door for the first series, every third door for the next presentation,

etc.) for the subject's choice. The subject demonstrated insight, Yerkes believed, after inferring the experimenter's template. Just as Yerkes intended the Point Scale to test every human, so did he expect the multiple-choice test to become the standard for comparing the human with several animal species.

An opportunity to test an orangutan, Julius, and a few monkeys on a millionaire's estate in Santa Barbara, California, allowed Yerkes to polish the test further. His supposed discovery of insight in Julius corroborated Wolfgang Köhler's findings on ape mentality. Even one of the monkeys, Skirrl, showed "the ability . . . to try a method out and then to abandon it suddenly," which, Yerkes thought, "is characteristic of animals high in intelligence" (1979, p. 127). The idea of creating a primate research station now became Yerkes's main career ambition, although just at this moment he was becoming the most influential person in human psychology.

During the 1916 meetings of the National Education Association, Yerkes called upon teachers to elevate scientific research as the most important mental skill. Sounding like a eugenist version of John Dewey, Yerkes asked teachers to help adjust students to life by awakening them to their racial responsibilities. The APA elected Yerkes president in December 1916, not long before the University of Minnesota offered him the directorship of its psychology department and, more significantly, the United States entered the terrible war that was raging overseas.

YERKES'S WARTIME LEADERSHIP

Even before Congress declared war, on April 6, 1917, Yerkes had begun mobilizing his profession. In the month after the declaration, he lobbied and received permission from the new National Research Council (NRC) to create a Committee on Psychology and forge closer contacts with the military. Yerkes contacted William Gorgas, the U.S. Army surgeon general, about establishing a Division of Psychology—and gaining officer commissions for himself and colleagues—in the Medical Corps. In late April, Yerkes submitted a "Plan for the Psychological Examining of Recruits to Eliminate the Mentally Unfit," and again applied for Rockefeller funds for large-scale administration and refinement of the Point Scale. The military received the plan suspiciously, however, believing it would encourage malingering as it helped an idealistic professor exploit the national emergency to collect research data.

Also in the first month of war, Yerkes directed the formation of several APA committees to assist the U.S. military, including one he chaired on the Psychological Examining of Recruits. He planned to call an extraordinary meeting of testers in Boston or Washington, once the Rockefeller funds materialized. He intended to invite Terman, but not Goddard or other Binet testers, some of whom Yerkes criticized harshly at this time. The invitation list changed after the Rockefeller application failed. Army psychiatrists quashed it, sensing that Yerkes's Point Scale was an encroachment on their diagnostic turf.

Financial assistance for a national meeting came instead from Joseph Byers, a trustee of the Vineland, New Jersey, Training School for Feeble-minded Boys and Girls, whose research director was Goddard. The school agreed to host Yerkes's Psychological Examining Committee, which now included Goddard, Terman, G. M. Whipple, and W. V. Bingham among other test developers. On the first day of meetings, Yerkes found himself arguing an unpopular position, as he opposed the plans of Bingham and Terman that the committee develop a test that could be given to large numbers of recruits simultaneously. Their plan was to help the military select the "upper zone" of intelligence for positions of officer leadership or skill expertise. That a *group* test—as a classificatory and not a diagnostic instrument—would placate the military's psychiatrists was another argument in favor of innovation. Yerkes (and Terman, until that time) believed that a mass test would be unscientific; it would weaken experimental control, allowing extraneous qualities such as attention to be tested. After a day of debate, Yerkes acquiesced to the majority, which allowed creation of the first group intelligence test, known by 1918 as "Army Alpha." This was the most important testing achievement of the Vineland meeting and the entire war.

Meanwhile, other mental testers, much more practical-minded than even the Binet testers, gained military recognition for a device Yerkes considered to be much further beyond the scientific pale than the IQ. This instrument, which had originated with Francis Galton and become developed by Thorndike, was the Rating Scale of mental abilities, which attempted to objectify, on a scale from 1 to 10, the subjective evaluations of laypersons. As his neighbor became assistant to the secretary of war, Thorndike was able to gain quick access for the Rating Scale for Selecting Captains. The United States's foremost "applied psychologist," Walter D. Scott, created this variation on Thorndike's model, which organized the evaluations of personal (leadership) as well as mental qualities.

By the end of July 1917, the War Department became so intrigued by Scott's Scale that Thorndike suggested the abandonment of the yet untested group test and the other activities Yerkes planned in the surgeon general's office. The new purpose of mental testing became installed in the name of the organization Thorndike and Scott would now lead in the adjutant general's office; Yerkes's colleague at Vineland, Bingham, jumped Yerkes's ship to join and name the Committee on the *Classification* of Personnel in the Army. But as Yerkes could claim that a major's commission was pending for him in the Sanitary Corps (army psychiatrists refused to allow the psychologists to serve in the Medical Corps) and as he wanted autonomy for the individualized Point Scale testing he intended to continue, he kept the group testing project alive. Yerkes's desire for military rank, based partly on conceit and partly on a concern to ensure authority for a science that most soldiers had never heard of, saved the wartime creation of the group intelligence test. The day Yerkes became a major, August 15, 1917, was also the day that Thorndike reassured the military that the new group test correlated with officer estimations of intelligence, by way of Scott's Scale, at + .5. Although Yerkes disdained the Rating Scale and alienated Scott early in the war, the less-than-scientific device saved his commission and provided one of the first instances of modern psychological validation through use of an external criterion (von Mayrhauser, 1992).

After the autumn tryout of the group test received favorable estimations from a few line officers and Scott—especially after Yerkes attempted to unload the group test on the more practical-minded personnel committee—the War Department established the Division of Psychology under Yerkes's direction in the surgeon general's office in December 1917. The secretary of war promised funding or allocations for psychology buildings, but the promise was rescinded as a result of Scott's efforts. Scott had the intelligence test score removed from each recruit's personnel identification card in April 1918, returning it only after Yerkes agreed to allow correlation of the group test with military occupations and the new Trade Tests (forerunners of the 1923 Achievement Tests). Although these obstacles and two military investigations prevented effective use of the new test until the very end of the war, 1.7 million recruits took Army Alpha and Beta (for illiterates and non-English-speaking testees) by the middle of 1919.

During the postwar era, Yerkes began publishing the intelligence test results of average recruits. The utilitarian perspective that Yerkes adopted in 1918 continued after the war, when U.S. businesses became interested in the new technology. The main practical objective of *Army Mental Tests* (Yoakum & Yerkes, 1920) was to relate recruit scores to military and occupational categories. They made passing reference to low African-American and immigrant scores, but their main concern was commercial, not racial. The prospective market for psychology was in claiming to predict employee performance, not in reinforcing the racism of the Jim Crow era. After Yerkes (1921) published the 890-page National Academy of Sciences *Memoir,* which ostensibly demonstrated the reliability and accuracy of the group tests, the educated public became shocked by the low intelligence (test scores) of so many of their fellow voting citizens.

While editing and writing the first four chapters of the mammoth report, Yerkes assisted Terman, Thorndike, and others in developing a National Intelligence Test for schoolchildren in grades three to eight. Although invited to participate in the important 1921 *Journal of Educational Psychology* symposium on the definition and testing of intelligence, which paralleled the symposium he had inspired five years before, Yerkes did not respond. Instead of finally taking the professorship at Minnesota, Yerkes resigned it and remained in Washington as chair of the NRC Research Information Service. He soon became chair of two notable

NRC committees: Research in Problems of Sex, which years later helped fund the groundbreaking studies of Alfred Kinsey (as well as the research of Yerkes and others); and Scientific Problems of Human Migrations, which was a short-lived response to the current American wave of nativism. Although the report of low Alpha scores by immigrants from southern and eastern Europe did not cause the nativist push for immigration restriction laws between 1921 and 1924, they did incite the brief but heated intellectual debate in *The New Republic* and other opinion journals over the sources of intelligence. Yerkes (1923) entered the nature–nurture debate less readily than Terman, and attempted to moderate the extreme hereditarian position offered by Albert Wiggam, a popularizer. Tiring of scientific administration, demands for accommodation, and the controversies of human intelligence testing, Yerkes left human psychology for good in 1924.

DEVELOPING PRIMATE RESEARCH LABORATORIES

Yerkes returned to animal research, as a professor in Yale University's new Institute of Psychology. After visiting a millionaire's chimpanzee collection in Cuba, he wrote *Almost Human,* and, with B. W. Learned, *Chimpanzee Intelligence and Its Vocal Expressions,* both in 1925. The Laura Spelman Rockefeller Foundation helped Yerkes create a research laboratory for chimpanzees in New Haven the same year. Also that year, another millionaire allowed Yerkes to study his gorilla Congo at his estate near Jacksonville, Florida. After having researched all the anthropoid primates except gibbons, Yerkes and his wife Ada published the landmark comparative study *The Great Apes* in 1929. Congo's performance on tests led them to conclude that the gorilla was more intelligent than the chimpanzee in certain ways, such as in reflecting on a problem, although less intelligent in other ways, such as imitation. Yerkes now defined intelligence as "adaptivity involving ideation . . . evidenced by (Congo's) general adjustment to the conditions of experimentation and her sudden solution of certain novel problems" (Yerkes, 1973b, p. 168).

Also in 1929, Yale acquired land in Orange Park, Florida, which became the university's second Laboratory of Comparative Psychobiology. Yerkes directed it and the New Haven laboratory until his retirement in 1941, when Yale renamed them the Yerkes Laboratories of Primate Biology. Yerkes requested and received a new academic affiliation and designation from Yale in 1929; from then until 1944 he was professor of comparative psychobiology in the physiology department of the Yale School of Medicine. After 1930, the Florida research station received numerous chimpanzees from the Cuban estate Yerkes had visited. The opportunity to research so many allowed Yerkes to conclude—in his last book, *Chimpanzees: A Laboratory Colony* (1943)—that this species (and not gorillas, whose slowness he now interpreted as dullness) was closest in intelligence to human beings.

During World War II, Yerkes was active on the NRC Emergency Committee on Psychology, and chaired the subcommittee on Survey and Planning. Although contributing relatively little to his younger colleagues' psychological service to the military, the retired Yerkes led a successful movement to combine the older APA with the new American Association of Applied Psychologists and some smaller organizations. Yerkes delivered the opening address at the Intersociety Constitutional convention of May–June 1943, which created the modern confederation structure of the APA. During the last decade of his life, Yerkes served as chair and member of the Advisory Board of the Fels Research Institute in Yellow Springs, Ohio. (Its founder, Samuel S. Fels, formerly a trustee of the Vineland Training School, long had been interested in the inherited, physiological sources of intelligence.) Robert Yerkes died on February 3, 1956.

TESTING THE UNTESTABLE: INTELLIGENCE AS VOLUNTARY IDEATION

Yerkes's keynote call for "disinterestedness" at the 1943 Intersociety Convention, which effectively legitimated the transfer of professional dominance from basic experimentalism to applied engineering, was very symbolic. During his career, his advocacy of "pure" science remained as consistent as the opportunities for "applied" service expanded irresistibly—to use Yerkes's dualistic terms ("The Scientific Way," p. 133).

Even when he humanized his psychology for the benefit of Harvard or army superiors, Yerkes persisted in his search for intelligence as the essence of all evolution. To most of the assembled delegates in 1943, Yerkes was the hero of the previous world war, the most famous hero of applied psychology. That he was addressing them instead of participating in World War II, however, was due to the more accurate memories that the military and Bingham, now the army's chief psychologist, had of Yerkes's earlier leadership (Capshew, 1986). In 1917–1918, Yerkes had been a leader with very few followers, until he finally agreed to cooperate.

Throughout much of World War I, Yerkes was indifferent to the development and use of Army Alpha. As a group test, and as a test given under wretched physical and emotional conditions, Alpha was, at least for Yerkes, painfully unscientific. Moreover, it tested for quickness and obedience, not for insight or reflectiveness. Yerkes was more interested in developing his individualized Point Scale examination and collecting test scores from recruits already suspected of deficient intelligence. Although Yerkes was hardly disinterested, he believed he was helping the military much more by offering only to diagnose mental deficiency; he saw the desire to predict normal or superior recruit performance as outrunning the available technology by far.

In his published autobiography, Yerkes (1930, pp. 397–399) claimed that he had exercised the (most) "initiative and leadership" of the psychologists who participated in World War I, that these had been "the most trying years of [his] life," and that his previous work at the Boston Psychopathic Hospital "prepared" him well for service. Although others initiated and led during the military psychological experience, Yerkes deserves great credit for promoting the cause of intelligence testing as a whole. The "most trying years" claim is even more true, primarily because the preparation claim was far from true. Yerkes had entered human psychology belatedly, if not grudgingly. His purpose and method of intelligence testing suited the kind of intelligence he wanted to test and the needs of experimental science; practical social needs were an afterthought to this cantankerous idealist.

Yerkes failed to develop a test of human intelligence—the Point Scale received no further attention after 1923—and he returned to animal psychology be-cause he wanted to test a kind of intelligence that is untestable given the scientific criterion of experimen-tal replicability. This kind of intelligence was voluntary ideation, which Royce had encouraged. In 1905 Yerkes used Royce's threefold division of discrimination, do-cility, and initiative to begin distinguishing his interest in intelligence—as ideational initiative—from Loeb's and Thorndike's view of intelligence as modifiability. While Thorndike had disparaged the ability of cats to learn, Yerkes looked for animal rationality. Yerkes was optimistic about discovering voluntary ideation in lower ranks of the animal kingdom until around 1913, when he began testing humans and Watson delivered his famous behaviorism lectures. After that time, Yerkes decided that fewer and fewer animals—by 1943, only chimpanzees and humans—were capable of sudden flashes of insight.

Yerkes developed the brightness-discrimination and multiple-choice tests to allow animals to demonstrate judgment. Both tests (and the individualized Point Scale) required the presence of a monitor to witness abrupt behavioral changes that appeared to be abrupt changes in thinking. On the multiple-choice test, the subject's rational discernment of the observer's prese-lected template required a one-on-one relationship be-tween the administrator and subject, thus obviating a group test format. Yerkes opposed the kind of intelli-gence that he believed Thorndike, Terman, and the military wanted to test, namely, practical, vocational, goal-oriented mentality. While they wanted to dis-cover how well a subject could learn in an environ-ment—whether in a puzzle box, a classroom, or on drill parade—Yerkes wanted to show the individual's endogenous ability to adapt by active thinking, not by passive reaction. Yerkes saw himself improving on Thorndike's exposé of anthropomorphism in most nat-uralists' observations of animals. Just as experimental control of animals' mental performance had produced more scientific results, he hoped human mental testing would continue on the same experimental path. When psychologists adapted their tests to the practical needs of clients, however, they were, in Yerkes's opinion, op-erating like naturalists making uncontrolled observa-tions in the field.

The other kind of intelligence—the "ability to profit by experience," or "ability to learn," or the modern sense of "aptitude" (defined as ability to learn by Thorndike's student Truman L. Kelley in 1917)—represented the majority of American middle-class views on learning. It is this kind of practical-minded intelligence that connects means to ends ("What do I need to learn in this class to get an A?"). Yerkes was trying to preserve the older leisure-class notion, often denoted by "intellect" or "intellectual," that learning was an intrinsic value ("Learning is good in itself and of lifelong use"). Just as it is impossible to demonstrate the material benefit of an intrinsic value, however, so is it impossible to demonstrate repeatedly and for pub-lic observation a subject's insight, that, like miracles or free-will, are one-of-a-kind events. In this way, Yerkes's project can be seen as an extension of Royce's voluntarist idealism, of William James's (1987) call in 1907 for "intellectual" (college-educated) "class con-sciousness" and of Royce and James's efforts to make room for free-will in a world of scientific law.

The price Yerkes paid to lead his profession in World War I was to oversee the movement of intelli-gence testing in directions he did not want. The easily graded multiple-choice format of Alpha did not en-courage demonstration of intellectual insight, but in-stead encouraged the possession or mere acquisition of information, not its use. The military called the test one of "mental alertness," which Scott had certainly demonstrated in deferring to the needs of the military environment, and which Yerkes later found in the very imitative chimpanzee. The kind of intelligence Yerkes preferred, which he hoped his multiple-choice test would test, which he demonstrated in World War I, and which he saw in the gorilla was steady, if some-times impractically slow or recalcitrant, reflectiveness. Before the war, Yerkes had equated intelligence with evolutionary advance. Afterward, Yerkes (1973b, pp. 183–184) was not so sure, asking "(If . . . the gorilla is intellectually more highly developed than the orangu-tan or chimpanzee, how can we account for the fact that it has lost relatively in the struggle for existence? We incline to believe that intelligence is a condition of success and survival." Yerkes's research and personal experience caused him to see that superior intelligence was not the key to evolution he had once believed: "I am not convinced that superiority of intelligence assures human survival, but on the contrary I am prepared to believe that an intellectually superior type of man may from time to time have been swamped by inferior hordes."

Like the turtle Yerkes believed was motivated by the need for a warm secure nest, Yerkes retreated from human psychology to his cherished primate research station. He needed an environment he could control, to demonstrate the "intelligence" he valued. In the outside world of democratic America, the forces of the environment on the individual, and environmentalism in psychology, were too powerful.

FURTHER READING

Yerkes wrote two autobiographies: An essay, "Robert Mearns Yerkes: Psychobiologist," is in Carl Murchison, ed., A History of Psychology in Autobiography, vol. 2 (Worcester, Mass., 1930), pp. 381–407; the other, a large, unpublished manuscript, "The Scientific Way" (no date, c. 1950), is located in the voluminous Robert M. Yerkes Papers, Yale University Library, New Haven. Besides this collection, the Central File of the National Academy of Sciences, Washington, D.C., contains papers on the activities of Yerkes's various National Research Council committees.

Although Yerkes's life never has become the subject of a book, excellent biographical essays have appeared over the last thirty years. Ernest R. Hilgard, "Robert Mearns Yerkes, May 26, 1876–February 3, 1956," National Academy of Sciences Biographical Memoirs, vol. 38 (New York, 1965), pp. 384–425, contains a bibliography of Yerkes's most important publications. Other standard references include John C. Burnham, "Yerkes, Robert Mearns," in Charles C. Gillispie, ed., Dictionary of Scientific Biography, vol. 14 (New York, 1976), pp. 549–551, Hamilton Cravens, "Yerkes, Robert Mearns," in John A. Garraty, ed., Dictionary of American Biography, suppl. 6 (New York, 1980), pp. 717–719, and James Reed, "Robert M. Yerkes and the Mental Testing Movement," in Michael M. Sokal, ed., Psychological Testing and American Society: 1890–1930 (New Brunswick, N.J., 1987), pp. 75–94.

Secondary accounts of Yerkes's activities in World War I are numerous and can be found in the endnotes following Reed's essay. Further consideration of

Yerkes's conception of intelligence and his view of test validation can be found in Richard T. von Mayrhauser's, "The Practical Language of American Intellect," History of the Human Sciences, 4 (1991): 371–393 and "The Mental Testing Community and Validity: A Prehistory," American Psychologist, 47 (1992): 244–253. A discussion of Yerkes's concern for medical prestige can be found in JoAnne Brown, The Definition of a Profession: The Authority of Metaphor in the History of Intelligence Testing, 1890–1930 (Princeton, 1992). A number of essays, mostly reminiscences, on Yerkes's chimpanzee studies are in Geoffrey H. Bourne, ed., Progress in Ape Research (New York, 1977). Jill Morawski, "Impossible Experiments and Practical Constructions: The Social Bases of Psychologists' Work," in Jill Morawski, ed., The Rise of Experimentation in American Psychology (New York, 1988), pp. 72–93, and Donna Haraway, Primate Visions: Gender, Race, and Nature in the World of Modern Science (New York, 1989) discuss Yerkes's use of primatology to address human social questions.

(See also: ANIMAL INTELLIGENCE: PRIMATES; ARMY ALPHA AND BETA TESTS OF INTELLIGENCE.)

BIBLIOGRAPHY

ANGELL, J. R. (1917, May). Letter to G. E. Hale. Washington, DC: Central File, National Academy of Sciences.

CAPSHEW, J. H. (1986). Psychology on the march: American psychologists and World War II. Unpublished doctoral dissertation, University of Pennsylvania.

ELDER, J. H. (1977). Robert M. Yerkes and memories of early days in the laboratories. In G. H. Bourne (Ed.), Progress in ape research (pp. 29–38). New York: Academic Press.

HALE, M. (1980). Human science and social order: Hugo Münsterberg and the origins of applied psychology. Philadelphia: Temple University Press.

JAMES, W. (1987). The social value of the college bred. In William James: Writings, 1902–1910 (pp. 1242–1249). New York: Library of America. (Original work published 1907.)

Mentality tests. (1916). Journal of Educational Psychology, 7, 163–166, 229–240, 278–286, 348–360, 427–433.

Nation's Educators Open Great Meeting. (1916, July). *New York Times.* Sec. I, p. 7.

O'DONNELL, J. M. (1985). *The origins of behaviorism: American psychology, 1870–1920.* New York: New York University Press.

REED, J. (1987). Robert M. Yerkes and the mental testing movement. In M. M. Sokal (Ed.), *Psychological testing and American society: 1890–1930* (pp. 75–94). New Brunswick, NJ: Rutgers University Press.

SAMELSON, F. (1979). Putting psychology on the map: Ideology and intelligence testing. In A. R. Buss (Ed.), *Psychology in social context* (pp. 103–168). New York: Irvington.

SAMELSON, F. (1987). Was early mental testing: (a) racist inspired, (b) objective science, (c) a technology for democracy, (d) the origin of the multiple-choice exams, (e) none of the above? (mark the RIGHT answer). In M. M. Sokal (Ed.), *Psychological testing and American society: 1890–1930* (pp. 113–127). New Brunswick, NJ: Rutgers University Press.

SCOTT, W. D. *A history of the committee on the classification of personnel in the army.* Unpublished manuscript in the W. V. Bingham Papers, Hunt Library, Carnegie-Mellon University, Pittsburgh.

SPEARMAN, C. (1904). "General intelligence": Objectively determined and measured. *American Journal of Psychology, 15,* 201–293.

THORNDIKE, E. L., LAY, W., & DEAN, P. R. (1909). The relation of accuracy in sensory discrimination to general intelligence. *American Journal of Psychology, 20,* 364–369.

TITCHENER, E. B. (1911, November). *Letter to K. Dunlap.* Knight Dunlap Papers. Archives of the History of American Psychology. Akron, OH: University of Akron.

VON MAYRHAUSER, R. T. (1992). The mental testing community and validity: A prehistory. *American Psychologist, 47,* 244–253.

YERKES, R. M. (1899). Reaction of entomostraca to stimulation by light. *American Journal of Physiology, 3,* 157–182.

YERKES, R. M. (1901). The formation of habits in the turtle. *Popular Science Monthly, 58,* 519–525.

YERKES, R. M. (1905). Animal psychology and criteria of the psychic. *The Journal of Philosophy, Psychology and Scientific Methods, 2,* 141–149.

YERKES, R. M. (1909). Imitation among animals: Do animals imitate one another voluntarily? *The Century Magazine, 78,* 395–403.

YERKES, R. M. (1911). *Introduction to psychology.* New York: Henry Holt.

YERKES, R. M. (1914). The study of human behavior. *Science, 39,* 625–633.

YERKES, R. M. (1916a). Methods of studying ideational behavior in man and other animals. *Psychological Bulletin, 13,* 93–94.

YERKES, R. M. (1916b). Provision for the study of monkeys and apes. *Science, 53,* 231–234.

YERKES, R. M. (1917a). The Binet versus the point scale method of measuring intelligence. *Journal of Applied Psychology, 1,* 111–122.

YERKES, R. M. (1917b, May). *Letter to R. M. Embree.* Washington, DC: Central File, National Academy of Sciences.

YERKES, R. M. (1917c, May). *Letter to B. Baldwin.* Washington, DC: Central File, National Academy of Sciences.

YERKES, R. M. (1918). Educational and psychological aspects of racial well-being. Washington, DC: National Education Association.

YERKES, R. M. (ED.). (1921). *Memoirs of the National Academy of Sciences: Vol. 15. Psychological examining in the United States Army.* Washington, DC: U.S. Government Printing Office.

YERKES, R. M. (1923). Testing the human mind. *Atlantic Monthly, 131,* 358–370.

YERKES, R. M. (1930). Robert Mearns Yerkes: Psychobiologist. In *A history of psychology in autobiography* (Vol. 2, pp. 381–407). Worcester, MA: Clark University Press.

YERKES, R. M. (1943). *Chimpanzees: A laboratory colony.* New Haven, CT: Yale University Press.

YERKES, R. M. (1973a). *The dancing mouse: A study in animal behavior.* New York: Arno. (Original work published 1907.)

YERKES, R. M. (1973b). *The mind of a gorilla.* New York: Arno. (Original work published 1927.)

YERKES, R. M. (1979). *The mental life of monkeys and apes.* Delmar, NY: Scholars' Facsimiles & Reprints. (Original work published 1916.)

YERKES, R. M. (n.d.). *The scientific way.* Unpublished manuscript. New Haven, CT: R. M. Yerkes Papers, Yale University Library.

YERKES, R. M., & ANDERSON, H. M. (1915). The importance of social status as indicated by the results of the point-scale method of measuring mental capacity. *Journal of Educational Psychology, 6,* 137–150.

YERKES, R. M., BRIDGES, J. W., & HARDWICK, R. S. (1915).

A point scale for measuring mental ability. Baltimore, MD: Warwick & York.

YERKES, R. M., & LA RUE, D. W. (1913). *Outline of a study of the self.* Cambridge, MA: Harvard University Press.

YERKES, R. M., & MORGULIS, S. (1909). The method of Pawlow in animal psychology. *The Psychological Bulletin, 6,* 257–273.

YERKES, R. M., & ROSSY, C. (1916). Diagnostic mental measurement: A point scale for adolescents and adults. *Psychological Bulletin, 13,* 93.

YERKES, R. M., & YERKES, A. W. (1970). *The great apes: A study of anthropoid life.* New York: Johnson Reprint Corp. (Original work published 1929.)

YOAKUM, C S., & YERKES, R. M. (EDS.). (1920). *Army mental tests.* New York: Henry Holt.

RICHARD T. VON MAYRHAUSER

ZONE OF PROXIMAL DEVELOPMENT *See* VYGOTSKIAN THEORIES OF INTELLIGENCE.

Index

Page numbers in **boldface** indicate article titles. Page numbers in *italics* indicate tables or charts.

Belgrade school of developmental
	psychology, 594
Belief systems. *See* Reasoning, moral; Social
	intelligence
Bellevue Psychiatric Hospital (N.Y.C.),
	1135, 1136
Bell-shaped curve, 1039, 1043
Belmont, L., 206–207
Benedict, Ruth, 943
Bennett Mechanical Comprehension Test
	(BMCT), 115, 698
Bentley, Madison, 550
Benton, Arthur L., **173–175**
Benzodiazepines, 365–366, 522
Bereiter, C., 599
Berg, C. A., 1024
Berger, Hans, 391
Bergson, Henri, 809
Berkeley, George, 345
Berkeley Growth Study, 1019
Berlin Max Planck Institute, 60, 1147
Berry, J. W., 823
Bersoff, D., 177
Beta Test. *See* Army Alpha and Beta tests of
	intelligence
Bhana, K., 1051
Bias in Medical Testing (Jensen), 630
Bias in testing, **175–178**, 324–325, *326*
	culture loading vs., 324, 325, 403, 405,
		544
	definition, 175–176, 403
	General Aptitude Test, 468
	language issues, 179–181, 319, 543–544
	as minority-group issue, 176–177, 324,
		403, 541, 671, 685, 711, 713–714,
		724–725, 905, 986, 989
	misunderstanding of, 325
	personnel tests, 1158–1159, 1162–1163
	Scholastic Assessment Tests, 277, 959–
		960
	sources in norms, 773–774, 775
	Terman's giftedness study, 1067
	Wechsler scales, 671, 1137, 1141–1142
	see also Culture-fair and culture-free tests
Big families. *See* Birth order, spacing, and
	family size
Bilingualism, **178–181**
	affecting IQ test performance, 404, 405,
		540, 543–544
	balanced, 179
	Carroll studies, 235
	compound vs. coordinate, 180
	and literacy skills, 558
	Mercer studies, 725
	psycholinguisitic definitions, 180–181

second-language acquisition, 179–180
sociolinguistic definition, 180–181
System of Multicultural Pluralistic
	Assessment, 1053
test translation problems, 543–544
Bill of Rights for Children (1967), 550
Binet, Alfred, **182–189**, 231, 431, 810
	case-study analyses of mental adaptation,
		594
	conception of intelligence, 183, 184,
		355, 357, 473, 822, 984, 1085
	criticism of two-factor theory, 1098
	digits matrix memorization test, *706*,
		709
	discovery of mental age concept, 183,
		184, 347, 711
	influence on Terman, 1059, 1060
	personality assessment theories, 795–796
	on special-education placement, 686
	testing approach, 473, 508, 866
	testing of mental calculator, 705–706
	see also Binet-Simon Scale; Stanford-
		Binet Intelligence Scale
Binet, Alice (daughter), 182, 183
Binet, Madeleine (daughter), 182, 183
Binet-Simon Scale (1905)
	academic content, 822
	background, 79, 183–188, 347, 469–470,
		498, 591–592, 683, 711, 795–796,
		885, 1059, 1167–1168
	as basis for other tests, 231, 261, 347,
		1033–1034
	Doll's warnings on misuse of, 355
	examination conditions, 187–188
	exclusion of sensory/biological functions,
		193
	Goddard translation, 355, 504, 505
	as group test, 508
	inclusion of mathematical problems, 688
	mental age vs. chronological age, 711,
		796
	questions, 186–187
	revisions, 187–188, 469–470, 797, 1060
		(*see also* Stanford-Binet Intelligence
		Scale)
	subtests, 796
	uses, 188
Bingham, Walter V., 125, 1169, 1171
Binomial distribution, 1042–1043
Bioecological theory of intellectual
	development, **189–193**, 741, 990
	adaptive behavior, 20–21, 592–594,
		1089–1090
	African-American IQ differences and,
		906, 989

age-related changes, 55, 56, 58–60
aim of, 193
contextual factors, 192, 193, 293–294,
	295, 640, 1089
contrasted with other views of
	intelligence, 191–192
cultural perspective, 332–333
Galton and, 458, 460
gender differences, 466
genetic factors, 434–435
health effects, 523–524
interactionist perspective, 191, 192, 193,
	295, 592–594
Japanese IQ differences and, 627
motivation's importance in, 191, 193
Native-American IQ differences, 750–
	751
nutrition, 775–778
Pearson and, 460
Piaget's, 811–813, 814, 819–820
situated cognition, 972
social factors, 986–990 (*see also* Family
	environments; Schooling)
three tenets, 189, 190–191
triarchic theory, 1089–1090
universalist approach to intelligence,
	318–319, 641–642
see also Nature, nurture, and
	development
*Biographies of Child Development: The Mental
	Growth Careers of Eighty-four Infants and
	Children* (Gesell and others), 490
Biological intelligence, theory of, 101, 519–
	520
Biological measures of intelligence, **193–
	199**
	brain damage (*see* Brain, pathologies of)
	brain functions and, 212, 213–214, 768–
		769
	brain-size theories and, 90, 96–97, 198–
		199, 213, 407–408, 410, 881, 905
	cross-cultural correlates, 318, 326–327
	EEG evoked potentials, 391–394
	exercise and, 146
	Eysenck studies, 196, 318, 326–327,
		418, 874, 918, 1014, 1015
	Galton studies, 213, 416, 459–460, 461–
		462, 876, 881
	g and, 1097–1098
	as generational IQ comparison, 620
	Halstead studies, 519–520, 767–769
	indices, 194
	as information-processing measures, 582,
		640
	and Intelligence A and C, 417

Development quotient (DQ), 489–490,
491, 576, 577, 578
Devereux Schools (Devon, Pa.), 355
Deviation concepts (d-model), 320, 750–
751
Deviation quotient (DQ), **347**, 592, 771–
772, 1034, 1135, 1138, 1140
DeVoss, James, 1061
Dewey, John, 837
Dexedrine, 156
Diabetes, 201
*Diagnostic and Statistical Manual of Mental
Disorders*
attention deficit hyperactivity disorder,
152–153, 554
hyperactivity, 552
learning disability complications, 650
Dialectical thinking, **347–349**, 594
Diamond, M. C., 526
Diderot, Denis, 1144
Diencephalon, 677
Dietary supplements. *See* Nutrition
Difference model, 320
Differential Ability Scales (DAS), **350–354**,
569
retesting gains, 80, 831
theoretical basis, 351–352
Differential Aptitude Tests (DAT), 114–
115
Differential psychology
Burt's work, 231–233
Cattell's (R. B.) work, 241–242
cognitive psychology vs., 917
Eysenck's work, 416–418
Galton's work, 457, 458–459, 917
Jensen's work, 629–630
Spearman's work, 1007–1014
Vernon's work, 1115–1117
Differential Psychology (Anastasi), 80
Differentiation, in cognitive complexity,
287–289, *288*, 290
Digit span tests
anxiety/poor performance link, 102, 103,
104
exceptional performance, 705–706, 708,
709, 710
factor analysis, 431–432, 433
for individual memory differences, 701,
703, *706*
performance relationship with general
intelligence, *872*, 873
Stanford-Binet, 1037
Wechsler scales subtests, 46, *402*, 564,
565, 566, 853, 1132, *1138*, *1139*,
1140

Digit symbol subtest
Army Beta, 127
development of, 796
mathematical deficiency diagnosis, 375
WAIS-R, 431, 432, 433, 564, 853,
1133–1134
Dilantin, 366
Dioula (people), 334
Direct Instruction Reading (DISTAR)
program, 384
Disabilities. *See* Birth defects; Learning
disability; Mental retardation *headings*;
specific conditions
Disadvantaged children. *See* Ethnicity, race,
and measured intelligence;
Socioeconomic status and intelligence
Disadvantage/deprivation model. *See*
Deviation concepts
Discriminant evidence, in validity
assessment, 172
Discrimination (characteristic), intelligence
and, 1009, 1166, 1172
Discrimination (socioeconomic). *See* Legal
issues in intelligence
Discrimination learning paradigm, 98–99
Discrimination transfer, 244
Disease. *See* Health and intelligence; *specific
conditions*
Dishabituation. *See* Habituation
Disintegrative psychosis. *See* Childhood
disintegrative disorder
Disk problem, 841–842, 843
Disparate impact analysis, 672
Disruption. *See* Interference
DISTAR. *See* Direct Instruction Reading
(DISTAR) program
Distractibility. *See* Attention; Interference
Divergent thinking, 47, *481*, 838, 1051
Divided attention. *See* Multitask
performance
d-models. *See* Deviation concepts
DMT (n,n-dimethyltryptamine), 363, 367
DNA variation, 762
Docility, intelligence and, 1166, 1172
Doll, Edgar A., 78, 80, **354–356**
Doll, E. E. (son), 357
Dolphin studies, 92–94
Domain sampling error, 949
Donald, M., 973
Donaldson, G., 919–920, 1015
Dopamine, 524
Down, Langdon, 256
Down syndrome, **357–360**
chromosomal abnormality, 254, 255–
256, 357–358, *359*, 721, 966

factors, 200, 201, 202, 255–256
health effects, 523
mental retardation, 712, *718*, 721
occurrence risk, 721
physical characteristics, 256, 357, *358*
prenatal test for, 720
DQ. *See* Development quotient; Deviation
quotient
Draw-a-figure test, 139, **361–362**, 569
Draw-A-Person: A Quantitative Scoring
System, 361
Drawings. *See* Artistic ability: children's
drawings; Draw-a-figure test
Dressing apraxia, 676
Drive-free behavior, 733–734
Drugs and intelligence, **362–367**, 522
abstract-thinking loss, 11
for attention deficit hyperactivity
disorder, 155, 156
creativity-enhancing, 366–367
effects on elderly people, 524
effects on mental functions, 522, 524,
863–864
fetal risks, 201, 202, 203, *718*, 722
intelligence-improving, 366
see also Alcohol and alcohol abuse; *specific
drugs and drug types*
DS. *See* Down syndrome
*DSM. See Diagnostic and Statistical Manual of
Mental Disorders*
Dualisms, 8, 347–349
Duke longitudinal studies, 832
Duncker, Karl, 841
Duns Scotus, John, 803
Duyme, M., 996
Dweck, Carol, 735–736
Dynamic aphasia. *See* Transcortical motor
aphasia
Dynamic assessment of mental abilities,
368–371
as culture-fair test, 327
defined, 368
models of, 369–371, 660–665
see also Learning Potential Assessment
Device
Dyscalculia, **372–375**
Dysergic acid diethylamide. *See* LSD
Dyslexia, **376–386**, 923
adult outcomes, 385–386
brain pathology, 226, 677, 680, 792
causes/characteristics, *377*, 378, 381–
383, 648–649, 792, 924–925, 928
coping techniques, 384–385
definition problems, 376, 377, 924, 925
dyscalculia linked with, 373, 375, 650

Infancy (*cont.*)
> competence/performance distinction, 284
> conceptual/perception skills, 345
> conservation concepts, 248–253, 284, 345, 815
> correlation of early tests with later IQ development, 4, 169, 571, 573, 579, 1019–1020
> developmental stages studies, 488, 489–490, 812, 814–815, 818
> genetic influences, 574
> home environment/later school achievement correlate, 978–979
> individual differences, 150, 572–574
> information processing, 571–574
> IQ/DQ identification in, 490
> learning style, 244
> life-span height predictor, 170
> low birth-weight, 201–202, 203, 601
> malnutrition effects, 723
> mental retardation prevention, 719–720
> motor skills, 738, 739, 812, 814–815
> object constancy (*see subhead* conservation concepts *above*)
> parenting effects on cognition, 737, 788
> short-term apprehension and retrieval, 448, 815
> traumatic brain injury effects, 723
> *see also* Child and adolescent intelligence; Intervention, infant and preschool
Infancy and Human Growth (Gesell), 489
Infant Development (Gesell), 489, 490
Infantile autism. *See* Autism
Infant Mullen Scales of Early Learning, 578
Infant tests as measures of early competence, **575–580**, 599–605, 696
> Bayley Scales, 169, 170, 568–569, 570, 578
> black/white performance differences, 903
> Cattell Scale, 577
> common features, 576, 577
> description of, 577–578
> Gesell Scales, 490–491, 576, 577
> Griffiths Scale, 577–578
> habituation technique, 150, 571–574, 873, 1019–1020
> HOME Inventory, 978–979
> lack of predictive validity, 571
> Mullen Scales, 578
> reliability, 571, 572, 578
> validity, 571, 572–574, 578–579
> *see also* Intervention, infant and preschool

Inferences
> age-impaired, 1024
> deductive, 930–935
> performance component, 1088
> transitive, 245–247
Influence of Nature upon Native Differences, The (Kelley), 228
Information. *See* Knowledge
Information processing, **580–587**
> age and IQ test content, 48–49
> aging-associated changes, 52, 59–60, 62, 63
> alcohol effects on, 73–76
> animal studies, 92–94
> from artificial intelligence perspective, 131–135
> attention and, 146–151
> autistic, 165–166
> brain energy and, 198
> as child/adolescent intelligence development metaphor, 246–247
> cognitive complexity and, 286–290
> cognitive-components method, 583–584, 585–586, 919, 920–921
> cognitive-correlates method, 581–583, 918–920, 1015, 1016
> cognitive functioning and, 145–146
> cognitive styles and, 266–270
> cognitive task analysis method, 585
> competence/performance distinction, 283–286
> component learning, 244
> component-training method, 584–585
> connectionist model, 291–292
> context as crucial to speed in, 192, 640–641
> critique of approach, 585–586
> cultural adjustments/preferences, 332–333, 400
> decision making and judgment, 339–343
> development theories and, 345–346
> dyslexic sequencing problems, 382
> executive control strategies, 609, 640, 1016, 1087–1088
> in fluid/crystallized intelligence hierarchy, *444, 455*
> gender differences, 465–467
> heritability, 761
> in Hunt's view of intelligence, 550, 551
> inductive reasoning in, 935–936
> infant, 571–574
> Japanese preference for simultaneous, 626, 627
> language studies, 640

> mathematical communication theory, 876
> metacomponents, 604, 640, 1016, 1087–1088
> motivation and, 734–735
> in multiple intelligences theory, 741
> perceptual factors in, 792–794
> personal experience and, 1089–1090
> problem solving in, 841, 842, 843
> psychiatric disorder effects, 860–865
> as reaction to behaviorist theory, 581
> reaction time, 318, 640, 876–877, 917–921
> Simon studies, 970
> situated cognition theory, 971–973
> speed/intelligence correlation, 99–100, 192, 640–641, 793, 921, 1014, 1015–1017 (*see also subhead* reaction time *above*)
> theories described, 581, 640
> traditional approaches vs., 580–581
> triarchic theory of, 1087–1091
> types of, 666
> verbal ability and, 1107, 1110–1112
> visual perceptual differences, 792–794
> Wonderlic Personnel Test, 1121
> *see also* Learning and intelligence
Inhelder, Bärbel, 810, 811, 813, 817
Inherited abilities. *See* Genetics, behavior; Heritability
Inhibitory processes. *See* Interference
Initiative, intelligence equated with, 1166, 1172
Innate abilities. *See* Abilities and aptitudes
Inouye, A. R., 400
Inquiries into Human Faculty and Its Development (Galton), 459, 461, 462
Insecticides, 524
Insight, **588–591**
> in creative process, 302, 616
> definitions, 588, 613
> intelligence relationship, 590–591, 1166, 1172
> intuition vs., 613, 615
> in Piagetian second stage of development, 818
> in problem solving, 615–616
> processes of, 590
> visual-spatial ability, 1000
> *see also* Creativity
Inspection-time (IT) paradigms, 876, 877–879, 1017
Institute for Advanced Medical Studies (Moscow), 679